BLACK AMERICANS INFORMATION DIRECTORY

ISSN 1045-8050

BLACK AMERICANS INFORMATION DIRECTORY

1992-93

Second Edition

A Guide to Approximately 4,800 Organizations, Agencies, Institutions, Programs, and Publications Concerned with Black American Life and Culture, Including Associations, Awards, Honors, and Prizes, Colleges and Universities, Cultural Organizations, Government Agencies and Programs, Industrial and Service Companies, Libraries, Museums, Newsletters, Directories, Newspapers and Periodicals, Publishers, Radio and Television Stations, Religious Organizations, Research Centers, Studies Programs, and Videos.

Julia C. Furtaw, Editor

Amy Lucas, *Senior Editor*
Julia C. Furtaw, *Editor*
Kimberly A. Burton, *Assistant Editor*

Aided by: Elizabeth Hildreth, Gary P. Iott, and Catherine A. Lada

Victoria B. Cariappa, *Research Manager*
Jack Radike, *Research Supervisor*
Joseph R. Schroeder, *Editorial Associate*
Giavanna M. Palazzolo, Dolores S. Perelli,
and Pamela Taylor, *Editorial Assistants*

Mary Beth Trimper, *Production Manager*
Mary Winterhalter, *Production Assistant*

Benita Spight, *Data Entry Supervisor*
Tara McKissack, *Data Entry Associate*

Arthur Chartow, *Art Director*
Bernadette M. Gornie, *Graphic Designer*
C.J. Jonik, *Keyliner*

Theresa Rocklin, *Systems and Programming Supervisor*
Timothy Richardson, *Computer Programmer*

The paper used in this publication meets the minimum requirements of American National Standard for Information Sciences—Permanence Paper for Printed Library Materials, ANSI Z39.48-1984. ∞™

835 Penobscot Bldg.
Detroit, MI 48226-4094

ISSN 1045-8050
ISBN 0-8103-7535-4

Printed in the United States of America

Published simultaneously in the United Kingdom
by Gale Research International Limited
(An affiliated company of Gale Research Inc.)

Contents

HIGHLIGHTS

The *Black Americans Information Directory (BAID)* is a comprehensive guide to resources for and about Black Americans. *BAID* provides, in a convenient one-volume format, descriptive and contact information on a wide range of resources, including:

- Nonprofit Organizations
- Awards, Honors, & Prizes
- Colleges & Universities
- Cultural Organizations
- Directories
- Government Agencies & Programs
- Industrial & Service Companies
- Libraries
- Newsletters
- Newspapers
- Periodicals
- Publishers
- Radio & Television Stations
- Religious Organizations
- Research Centers
- Studies Programs
- Videos

New in This Edition

The second edition of *BAID* features:

- More than 4,800 entries. Listings have been completely updated, with thousands of changes to addresses, phone numbers, personnel and other important details

- Additional contact points, including toll-free and FAX numbers and contact names

- Enhanced indexing through inclusion of former and alternate names and titles in the **Master Name and Keyword Index**

Content and Arrangement

BAID is published in one easy-to-use volume consisting of **descriptive listings** arranged within 17 chapters by type of resource, and the **Master Name and Keyword Index**, which offers an alphabetical listing of all listed organizations and publications, as well as significant keywords in names and titles.

Other Format

The information in *BAID* is available in customized mailing list arrangements.

INTRODUCTION

Blacks and other minorities represent a growing and increasingly important segment of the American population. As the largest minority group in the United States, Black Americans numbered 29.3 million in 1988. According to the latest statistical information from the U.S. Bureau of the Census, this number is expected to reach 33.0 million by 1995, or 12.7% of the total population. As this segment of the population continues to grow, so does the need for information on all aspects of the Black experience in the United States. It was out of this need that *Black Americans Information Directory (BAID)* was born.

BAID, now in its second edition, meets the needs of libraries, schools, businesses, civic groups, and others interested in some aspect of the Black experience. *BAID* is a comprehensive guide to more than 4,800 information resources for and about Black Americans. It provides contact and descriptive information on a wide variety of print and "live" resources, including:

- Nonprofit Associations
- Religious and Cultural Organizations
- Library Collections
- Colleges, Universities, and Black Studies Programs
- Research Centers
- Federal, State, and Local Government Agencies and Programs
- Industrial and Service Companies
- Publishers and Publications
- Broadcast Media
- Videos

Features of this Edition

In addition to more than 4,800 entries and an easy-to-use entry format, the second edition of *BAID* ushers in several enhancements to better meet user needs:

- Identifying organizations and publications is easier due to the inclusion of former and alternate names in the **Master Name and Keyword Index**.

- Additional contact data—including fax and toll-free numbers and the names of key individuals—simplifies contacting an organization and speaking with the "right" person at that organization.

Arrangement, Content, and Indexing

BAID consists of the main body of **descriptive listings** and the **Master Name and Keyword Index**.

The **descriptive listings** are arranged within 17 chapters based on type of information resource, as outlined on the "Contents" page. Entries typically contain complete contact data as well as descriptive information.

The **Master Name and Keyword Index** provides one-stop access to all organizations, agencies, programs, publications, and other significant details mentioned within the descriptive listings. It also provides inversions on significant keywords in organization and publication titles.

For more information on the content, arrangement, and indexing of *BAID*, consult the "User's Guide."

Method of Compilation

BAID is compiled from a variety of sources. Information was carefully selected from other Gale Research Inc. directories, government publications, and lists and directories supplied by numerous national and local organizations. Telephone research was used in conjunction with secondary source information to verify contact information.

Specific source information on individual *BAID* chapters is provided in the "User's Guide" following this introduction.

BAID Offered in Alternate Format

The information in *BAID* is available in customized mailing list arrangements. Call 800-877-GALE for details.

Acknowledgments

The editor thanks *Black Enterprise* magazine (Copyright June 1991, Earl G. Graves Publishing Co., Inc., 130 Fifth Ave., New York, NY 10011. All rights reserved.) for granting permission to use their June issue in compiling the chapter on the top 100 Black industrial/service companies. Thanks also to Camille A. Killens and Cynthia Grayson and to the editors and staffs of other Gale directories that have contributed to the usefulness of *BAID*.

Comments Welcome

We encourage users to bring new or unlisted organizations to our attention. Every effort will be made to provide information about them in subsequent editions of the directory. Comments and suggestions for improving the directory are also welcome. Please contact:

Black Americans Information Directory
Gale Research Inc.
835 Penobscot Bldg.
Detroit, MI 48226-4094
Telephone: (313)961-2242
Toll-Free: 800-347-GALE
FAX: (313)961-6815
Telex: 810-221-7086

Julia C. Furtaw

USER'S GUIDE

BAID consists of:

- Descriptive entries, numbered sequentially and arranged in 17 chapters by type of information resource
- Master Name and Keyword Index

The content, arrangement, and indexing of each chapter is detailed below.

1. National Organizations

- **Scope:** Over 470 primarily nonprofit membership organizations, including social, philanthropic, professional, and business groups concerned with Black Americans or minorities.
- **Entries include:** Organization name, address, telephone number, name of contact, and a brief description of the organization's purpose and activities.
- **Arrangement:** Alphabetical by organization name.
- **Source:** *Encyclopedia of Associations, Volume 1, National Organizations of the U.S.*, 25th Edition (published by Gale Research Inc.)
- **Indexed by:** Organization name and significant keywords.

2. Regional, State, and Local Organizations

- **Scope:** More than 1,200 regional, state, and local organizations and chapters of selected national organizations including social, philanthropic, professional, and business groups concerned with Black Americans and minorities. (For further information on local chapters of national organizations contact the national office listed in Chapter 1.)
- **Entries include:** Organization name, address, telephone number, and name of contact.
- **Arrangement:** Geographical by state with organizations listed alphabetically within states.
- **Source:** *Encyclopedia of Associations: Regional, State, and Local Organizations*, 2nd Edition (published by Gale Research Inc.), lists provided by national organizations, and original research conducted by the *BAID* editorial staff.
- **Indexed by:** Organization name and significant keywords, including geographic location when included in the name.

3. Religious Organizations

- **Scope:** Covers 124 religious organizations, primarily founded by and for Black Americans.
- **Entries include:** A general description of the group's development, beliefs, and leaders; addresses, educational facilities, membership, and publications are included when available.
- **Arrangement:** Alphabetical by organization name.
- **Source:** *Encyclopedia of American Religions*, 3rd Edition (published by Gale Research Inc.) and original research by the *BAID* editorial staff.
- **Indexed by:** Organization name and significant keywords.

4. Library Collections

- **Scope:** Approximately 230 libraries with special collections of interest to Black Americans, including historical, literary, and cultural archives.
- **Entries include:** Library name, address, telephone number, name of contact, and a general description of special collections, holdings, services, and other details.

- **Arrangement:** Alphabetical by institution name.
- **Source:** *Directory of Special Libraries and Information Centers*, 14th Edition (published by Gale Research Inc.)
- **Indexed by:** Institution and library name and significant keywords.

5. Museums and Other Cultural Organizations

- **Scope:** Approximately 200 museums, galleries, and other organizations featuring African American culture and artists..
- **Entries include:** Organization name, address, and telephone number. Some entries also include a brief description.
- **Arrangement:** Geographical by state with organization names listed alphabetically within states.
- **Source:** Lists of minority arts organizations provided by the National Endowment of the Arts and original research by the *BAID* editorial staff.
- **Indexed by:** Organization name and significant keywords.

6. Historically Black Colleges and Universities

- **Scope:** 107 currently operational colleges and universities founded for the education of Black Americans at a time when many existing institutions were racially exclusive.
- **Entries include:** Institution name, address, telephone number, president, founding year, number of students, cost (includes room and board if appropriate), application deadlines, required tests, and name of admissions director.
- **Arrangement:** Alphabetical by institution name.
- **Source:** Original research by the *BAID* editorial staff.
- **Indexed by:** College or university name.

7. Black Studies Programs

- **Scope:** Nearly 200 colleges and universities that offer Black studies programs. Universities or colleges that offer one or more courses, but that lack a formal studies program were not included.
- **Entries include:** Institution name, address, telephone number, sponsoring department, and name of contact.
- **Arrangement:** Alphabetical by institution name within three categories: 1) Two Year Colleges, 2) Four-Year Colleges and Universities, and 3) Graduate Programs.
- **Source:** College catalogs and directories and original research conducted by the *BAID* editorial staff.
- **Indexed by:** Institution or program name.

8. Research Centers

- **Scope:** Over 140 university-related and other nonprofit organization research centers covering topics of concern to Blacks such as sickle cell anemia, and African American life, history, and culture.
- **Entries include:** Sponsoring institution, research center name, address, telephone number, name of contact, and a short description of activities, facilities, and services.
- **Arrangement:** Alphabetical by institution and/or research center name.
- **Source:** *Research Centers Directory*, 15th Edition (published by Gale Research Inc.)
- **Indexed by:** Institution and research center name and significant keywords.

9. Awards, Honors, and Prizes

- **Scope:** Over 100 awards and other distinctions bestowed by 80 government, civic, professional, and business groups for meritorious service to the Black community at large.

- **Entries include:** Sponsoring organization, address, telephone number, name of the award, and a brief description its nature.
- **Arrangement:** Alphabetical by sponsoring organization.
- **Source:** *Awards, Honors, and Prizes*, 9th Edition (published by Gale Research Inc.)
- **Indexed by:** Sponsoring organization and award name.

10. Federal Government Agencies

- **Scope:** Covers 170 units of the federal government concerned with civil rights, affirmative action, equal employment opportunity, and other areas of interest to the Black community.
- **Entries include:** Sponsoring agency and sub-units, address, telephone number and contact person.
- **Arrangement:** Alphabetical by agency name.
- **Source:** *United States Government Manual* and original research by the *BAID* editorial staff.
- **Indexed by:** Sponsoring agency and unit names and significant keywords.

11. Federal Domestic Assistance Programs

- **Scope:** Approximately 47 federally funded programs offering a wide variety of benefits and services to the Black community in areas such as minority business assistance, civil rights, and education.
- **Entries include:** Parent agency or organization, intermediate office or agency, address, telephone number, name of contact person, program name, and a brief description of services. *Catalog of Federal Domestic Assistance* numbers are also included for easy cross-reference.
- **Arrangement:** Alphabetical by agency or organization name.
- **Source:** *Catalog of Federal Domestic Assistance*.
- **Indexed by:** Parent agency, program name, and significant keywords.

12. State and Local Government Agencies

- **Scope:** 240 state and local government agencies offering programs covering equal employment, fair housing, minority business development, and other areas.
- **Entries include:** Parent and intermediate agency name, address, telephone number, and name of contact.
- **Arrangement:** Geographical by state with agencies and programs listed alphabetically.
- **Source:** Original research by the *BAID* editorial staff.
- **Indexed by:** Parent agency and sub-unit names, state designations, and significant keywords.

13. Businesses (Top 100 Companies)

- **Scope:** The top 100 Black industrial/service companies in the United States as listed in the June 1991 *Black Enterprise* magazine. To be eligible for the Industrial/Service 100, a company must have been fully operational in the previous calendar year and be at least 51% Black-owned. It must manufacture or own the product it sells or provide industrial or consumer services. Brokerages, real estate firms, and firms that provide professional services (accountants, lawyers, etc.) are not eligible.
- **Entries include:** Company name, address, telephone numbers, name of chief executive, year founded, number of employees, type of business, 1990 sales, and current and former rankings.
- **Arrangement:** By descending rank.
- **Source:** Reprinted with permission from *Black Enterprise* magazine, Copyright June, 1991 (published by Earl G. Graves Publishing Co., Inc., 130 Fifth Ave., New York, NY 10011. All rights reserved.)
- **Indexed by:** Company name.

14. Publications

- **Scope:** Almost 600 newspapers, periodicals, newsletters, and directories with a significant focus towards Black Americans or minorities, covering a wide variety of topics, including business, lifestyle, family, health, and education.
- **Entries include:** Publication and publisher name, address, telephone number, and a brief description, including publication scope, editor, frequency, and other details.
- **Arrangement:** Alphabetical by publication title within four subcategories: 1) Newspapers, 2) Periodicals, 3) Newsletters, and 4) Directories.
- **Source:** *Gale Directory of Publications and Broadcast Media*, 123rd Edition (formerly *Ayer Directory of Publications*), *Newsletters in Print*. 5th Edition, *Directories in Print*, 8th Edition, *City and State Directories in Print*, 1st Edition (all published by Gale Research Inc.), and original research conducted by the *BAID* editorial staff.
- **Indexed by:** Publication title and significant keywords.

15. Publishers

- **Scope:** 81 large and small firms that publish books by and about Black Americans.
- **Entries include:** Publisher name, address, telephone number, and a short description of representative titles or areas of publishing activity.
- **Arrangement:** Alphabetical by publisher name.
- **Source:** *Publishers Directory*, 11th Edition (published by Gale Research Inc.)
- **Indexed by:** Publisher name.

16. Broadcast Media

- **Scope:** Over 400 radio and television stations and networks with music, information, and entertainment programming aimed at the Black community. (Some may offer programming segments targeted at other audiences as well.)
- **Entries include:** Station call letters or network name, address, and telephone number. Entries for stations also include a brief description covering frequency, programming hours, contacts, year founded, and network affiliations.
- **Arrangement:** Divided into three subsections: 1) Networks, 2) Radio Stations, and 3) Television Stations. Networks are arranged alphabetically, broadcast stations are arranged alphabetically by call letters within states.
- **Source:** *Directory of Publications and Broadcast Media*, 123rd Edition (Formerly *Ayer Directory of Publications*, published by Gale Research Inc.) and original research by the *BAID* editorial staff.
- **Indexed by:** Network name or station call letters.

17. Videos

- **Scope:** Approximately 450 educational and general interest videos focusing on the Black community, including those covering the historic role of Blacks in American society to selected contemporary films.
- **Entries include:** Video title, distributor name, address, telephone number, program description, release date, run time, format, and acquisition availability.
- **Arrangement:** Alphabetical by video title.
- **Source:** The *Video Source Book*, 12th Edition (published by Gale Research Inc.)
- **Indexed by:** Video title and significant keywords.

Master Name and Keyword Index

The alphabetical **Master Name and Keyword Index** provides access to all entries included in *BAID* as well as former or alternate names which appear within its text. The index also provides access to entries via inversions on all significant keywords appearing in an entry name. The term "Black" has not been used as a subject keyword in the index, since, as a general category, it covers all the entries in the book. More specific terms, however, such as "Afro-American" and "African-American" have been used as subject keywords since they appear less frequently and may help direct the user to specific index citations.

Index references are to book entry numbers rather than page numbers. Entry numbers appear in the index in **boldface** type if the reference is to the unit for which information is provided in *BAID* and in lightface if the reference is to a program or former or alternate name included within the text.

If several entries have the same parent organization, as is the case with many of the government groups listed in *BAID*, related units are indexed individually by name and as a group under the name of the parent organization. The names of all federal government organizations are indexed under "U.S."

BLACK AMERICANS INFORMATION DIRECTORY

(1) NATIONAL ORGANIZATIONS

Entries in this chapter are arranged alphabetically by association name. See the User's Guide at the front of this directory for additional information.

★1★

A Better Chance (ABC)
419 Boylston St.
Boston, MA 02116 — Phone: (617)421-0950
Judith B. Griffin, Pres.

Description: Identifies, recruits, and places academically talented and motivated minority students into leading independent secondary schools and selected public schools. Students receive need-based financial assistance from member schools. Prepares students to attend selective colleges and universities and encourages their aspirations to assume positions of responsibility and leadership in American society. Conducts research and provides technical assistance on expanded educational opportunities for minority group students in secondary and higher education. Maintains statistical files. **Founded:** 1963. **Budget:** $1,636,500. Member Schools: 152. **Telecommunications Services:** Fax, (617)421-0965. **Publications:** Abecedarian, 2/year. Newsletter. Annual Report. Letters to Member Schools, annual. Also publishes brochure. **Formerly:** Independent Schools Talent Search Program.

★2★

A. Philip Randolph Educational Fund (APREF)
260 Park Ave., S., 6th Fl.
New York, NY 10010 — Phone: (212)533-8000
Norman Hill, Pres.

Description: Seeks to: eliminate prejudice and discrimination from all areas of life; educate individuals and groups on their rights and responsibilities; defend human and civil rights; assist in the employment and education of the underprivileged; combat community deterioration, delinquency, and crime. **Founded:** 1964.

★3★

A. Philip Randolph Institute (APRI)
260 Park Ave., S., 6th Fl.
New York, NY 10010 — Phone: (212)533-8000
Norman Hill, Pres.

Description: Promotes cooperation between the labor force and the Black community. Primary interest is political action through the organization of affiliate groups and the building of coalitions for social change. Major areas of activity include voter registration, labor education, and trade union leadership training. Founded by and named after A. Philip Randolph (1889-1979), founder of the Brotherhood of Sleeping Car Porters (which was absorbed by the Brotherhood of Railway, Airline and Steamship Clerks, Freight Handlers, Express and Station Employees). Presents the A. Philip Randolph/Bayard Rustin Freedom Award, the Bayard Rustin Humanitarian Award, the A. Philip Randolph Achievement Award, and the Rosina Tucker Award. Conducts research and specialized education programs. Maintains speakers' bureau and library. **Founded:** 1964. **State Groups:** 13. **Local Groups:** 200. **Publications:** Annual Report. News and Notes, bimonthly. Working Paper, annual. Also publishes the Norman Hill column.

★4★

Ad Hoc Monitoring Group on Southern Africa (AHMGSA)
2232 Rayburn House Office Bldg.
Washington, DC 20515 — Phone: (202)225-3335
Rep. Thomas J. Downey, Co-Chair

Description: Bipartisan group of Senate and House members that monitors human rights conditions in southern Africa. Seeks congressional support for pertinent legislation. Serves as information clearinghouse on human rights violations in southern Africa. Maintains Political Prisoner Project, through which members adopt individual political prisoners, write letters to congressmen, and make statements on prisoners' behalf for inclusion in the Congressional Record. Sponsors educational seminars; presents information briefs. **Founded:** 1978. **Members:** 48. **Also known as:** Congressional Monitoring Group on Southern Africa.

★5★

Africa Faith and Justice Network (AFJN)
PO Box 29378
Washington, DC 20017 — Phone: (202)832-3412
Rev. Thomas Hayden Ph.D., Exec.Dir.

Description: Religious groups with personnel working in Africa; individuals concerned with justice issues as they relate to Africa. Purpose is to examine the role the network believes Europe, America, and other northern countries play in causing injustices in Africa. Challenges national policies found to be detrimental to the interest of African peoples. Gathers information on issues and policies that adversely affect Africa, analyzes the data, and makes recommendations for advocacy or action. Consults with churches of Africa, field missionaries, and other African individuals and groups. **Founded:** 1983. **Members:** 53. **Telecommunications Services:** Fax, (202)832-9051. **Publications:** AFJN Newsletter, bimonthly.

★6★

The Africa Fund (AF)
198 Broadway
New York, NY 10038 — Phone: (212)962-1210
Jennifer Davis, Exec.Sec.

Description: Established by the American Committee on Africa (see separate entry). Works to: defend human and civil rights of needy Africans by providing or financing legal assistance; provide medical relief to Africans, particularly refugees; render aid to indigent Africans in the U.S., Africa, or elsewhere who are suffering economic, legal, or social injustices; provide educational aid or grants to Africans, particularly refugees; inform the American public about the needs of Africans; engage in study, research, and analysis of questions relating to Africa. Encourages divestment by U.S. corporations in South Africa; seeks to increase public support for U.S. economic sanctions against South Africa; has supported legislation which prevents U.S. corporations operating in South Africa from claiming U.S. tax credits for taxes paid to the South African government. Operates Unlock Apartheid's Jails Project, which seeks to inform the U.S. public about the plight of political prisoners in South Africa; disseminates information on the activities of South African puppet forces, including those in other areas of southern Africa. Provides information on southern Africa to interested individuals, organizations, and media in the U.S. Maintains Africa Fund Research Center, library, and files. **Founded:** 1966. **Members:** 5000. **Computerized Services:** Mailing list. **Telecommunications Services:** Cable, AMCOMMAF. **Publications:** Annual Report. Southern Africa Literature List, semiannual. Southern Africa Perspectives Series, periodic. Unified List of United States Companies Doing Business in South Africa and Namibia, annual. Also publishes U.S. Policy and Southern Africa and Namibia, North American Investment and South African Occupation (pamphlets), reprints, and fact sheets. **Formerly:** (1969) Africa Legal Defense and Aid Fund.

★7★
Africa Network (AN)
PO Box 5366
Evanston, IL 60204 Phone: (708)328-9305
Y. B. Holly, Sec.

Description: Professors, students, writers, and individuals working to defend just law, freedom, and human rights. Opposes "the crime of racist, apartheid law." Provides resource materials and information on South Africa; offers educational outreach program. Sponsors programs commemorating important historical events of South Africa, including Sharpeville Memorial Day and Soweto Anniversary Commemoration. Bestows annual Kwanzaa Awards for Literature, Film, and Video. (Group was originally named for Dennis Brutus, former political prisoner, South African poet, scholar, and anti-apartheid activist. Brutus was granted political asylum in the U.S. in 1983.) **Founded:** 1981. **Budget:** Less than $25,000. **Publications:** Africa Network Directory of Resources, periodic. Newsletter, periodic. Also issues newsbriefs. **Formerly:** (1988) African National Network.

★8★
African-American Family History Association (AAFHA)
PO Box 115268
Atlanta, GA 30310 Phone: (404)730-1942
Herman Mason, Pres.

Description: Persons interested in African-American family history and genealogy. Conducts research programs and tours; sponsors seminars, lectures, and workshops. **Founded:** 1977. **Members:** 200. **Computerized Services:** Surname databank. **Telecommunications Services:** Fax, (404)730-1992. **Publications:** AAFHA Newsletter, quarterly. Reports on research inquiries and information on new titles.

★9★
African-American Institute (AAI)
833 United Nations Plaza
New York, NY 10017 Phone: (212)949-5666
Vivian Lowery Derryck, Pres.

Description: Works to further development in Africa, improve African-American understanding, and inform Americans about Africa. Engages in training, development assistance, and informational activities. Sponsors African-American conferences, media and congressional workshops, and regional seminars. Maintains training and visitor program offices in Washington, DC and representatives in 21 African countries. **Founded:** 1953. **Budget:** $15,000,000. **Telecommunications Services:** Fax, (212)682-6174; telex, 666565. **Publications:** Africa Report, bimonthly. Magazine focusing on the political and economic development of Africa. Includes book reviews and annual subject index. AALC Reporter, bimonthly. Newsletter reporting on AFL-CIO and center projects in Africa.

★10★
African-American Labor Center (AALC)
1400 K St. NW, Ste. 700
Washington, DC 20005 Phone: (202)789-1020
Patrick J. O'Farrell, Exec.Dir.

Description: AFL-CIO. Assists, strengthens, and encourages free and democratic trade unions in Africa. Has undertaken projects in 43 countries in partnership with African trade unions. Programs are developed upon request and advice of African unions with knowledge of host government. Projects are geared to eventual assumption of complete managerial and financial responsibility by African labor movements. Objective is to help build sound national labor organizations that will be of lasting value to workers and the community, institutions that contribute to the economic and social development of their countries and to Africa's total political and economic independence. Major areas of activity are workers' education and leadership training, vocational training, cooperatives and credit unions, union medical and social service programs, administrative support for unions, and communication and information. Sponsors study tours and visitor programs to permit African and American trade unionists to become familiar with each other's politics, economies, and trade union movements; Africans are exposed to technical training not available in their homeland. Conducts basic trade union seminars and assists in establishment of labor institutes. Policy is set by board of directors, which is composed of the president and secretary-treasurer of the AFL-CIO and the presidents of 14 major American unions. **Founded:** 1964. **Also known as:** Centre Afro-Americain du Travail.

★11★
African American Museums Association (AAMA)
PO Box 50061
Washington, DC 20004 Phone: (202)783-7744

Description: Museums, museum professionals, and scholars concerned with preserving, restoring, collecting, and exhibiting African-American history and culture. Provides technical information to African-American museums. Conducts professional training workshops, surveys, evaluations, and consultant and referral services. Compiles statistics; bestows awards. **Founded:** 1978. **Members:** 430. **Budget:** $180,000. **Regional Groups:** 6. **State Groups:** 28. **Computerized Services:** Mailing list. **Publications:** Black Museums Calendar, monthly. Blacks in Museums, biennial. Directory. Scrip, quarterly. Newsletter. Also publishes Profile of Black Museums (statistical survey) and brochures.

★12★
African American Publishers, Booksellers, and Writers Association (AAPBWA)
American Booksellers Association
137 W. 25th St.
New York, NY 10001 Phone: (212)463-8450
Haki Madhubuti, Chair

Description: Designed for Black American members of the publishing industry. Conducts annual book fairs and holds annual meetings. Plans to create a networking organization.

★13★
African Heritage Federation of the Americas (AHF)
PO Box 2964
Pittsburgh, PA 15230 Phone: (412)361-8425
A. Ndubisi Ezekoye, Pres.

Description: Individuals of African ancestry working to promote knowledge and understanding of African heritage. Conducts educational programs; sponsors charitable programs; maintains speakers' bureau; compiles statistics. **Founded:** 1983. **Members:** 36. **Budget:** Less than $25,000. **Publications:** African Heritage Coloring Book (in seven volumes).

★14★
African Heritage Studies Association (AHSA)
c/o Africana Studies and Research Inst.
Queens Coll.
Flushing, NY 11367 Phone: (718)997-5478
Dr. W. Ofuatey-Kodjoe, Pres.

Description: Persons of African descent engaged in the research and teaching of African history. Purposes are: to reconstruct and present African history and cultural studies in a manner that is relevant to African people; to encourage intellectual union and cooperation among Black scholars; to act as a clearinghouse for information in the structuring of a more factual African program; to present papers at conferences, seminars, and symposia; to relate, interpret, and disseminate African materials for Black education. Conducts seminars and curriculum development workshops; maintains speakers' bureau. Bestows awards. **Founded:** 1969. **Budget:** Less than $25,000. **Publications:** International Journal of Africana Studies, semiannual. Newsletter, 3/year.

★15★
African Literature Association (ALA)
Cornell University
Africana Studies and Research
310 Triphammer Rd.
Ithaca, NY 14850-2599 Phone: (607)255-0539

Description: Scholars, teachers, students, and writers of African literature. Objectives are: to assemble African literature scholars and teachers from all levels of instruction and from all parts of the world; to promote the teaching of African literature; to disseminate information about African literature. Supports freedom and dignity for all people in Africa. Maintains archives of papers and historical records. **Founded:** 1974. **Members:** 800. **Computerized Services:** Data base. **Telecommunications Services:** Fax, (403)492-0692. **Publications:** Bulletin, quarterly. Conference Papers, annual. Directory, annual. Journal: Research in African Literatures, quarterly.

★16★
African National People's Empire Re-Established (AFANPERA)
c/o William Bert Johnson
18900 Schoolcraft
Detroit, MI 48223 Phone: (313)837-0627
William Bert Johnson, Pres.

Description: Americans of African heritage; natives of the African continent. Promotes the health, education, and welfare of African people. Conducts specialized education program. **Founded:** 1951. **Members:** 351,642. **State Groups:** 48. **Publications:** AFANPERA Bulletin, bimonthly. AFANPERA Newsletter, quarterly.

★17★
African Studies Association (ASA)
c/o Dr. Edna Bay
Emory University
Credit Union Bldg.
Atlanta, GA 30322 Phone: (404)329-6410
Dr. Edna Bay, Exec.Sec.

Description: Persons specializing in teaching, writing, or research on Africa including political scientists, historians, geographers, anthropologists, economists, librarians, linguists, and government officials; persons who are studying African subjects; institutional members are universities, libraries, government agencies, and others interested in receiving information about Africa. To foster communication and to stimulate research among scholars on Africa. Sponsors placement service; conducts panels and discussion groups; presents exhibits and films. Bestows annual Herskovits Award. **Founded:** 1957. **Members:** 2200. **Budget:** $250,000. **Computerized Services:** Mailing list (available by rental). **Publications:** African Studies Review, 3/year. Directory of African and Afro-American Studies in the U.S., periodic. History in Africa, annual. Issue: A Journal of Opinion, semiannual. News, quarterly. Also publishes scholarly and bibliographical material.

★18★
Afro-American Cultural Foundation (AACF)
c/o Westchester Community College
Student Affairs
75 Grasslands Rd.
Valhalla, NY 10595 Phone: (914)285-6600
John Harmon, Exec.Dir.

Description: Purposes are: to improve the self-esteem of African Americans; to improve the attitude of white people toward African Americans and their talents; to raise the level of awareness of the potentials and problems of African Americans; to help create a new self-image. Sponsors lectures and seminars. Conducts annual workshop, known as the Institute of Racism. Acts as consultant on African and African American history and economics. Conducts historical and economic research programs. Maintains speakers' bureau and biographical archives. Sponsors Students Essay Oratorical Contest. Bestows awards to recognize outstanding citizens. Operates library of 500 volumes on history, literature, and sociology. Maintains a museum of African American history in honor of businesswoman Madam C. J. Walker (1867-1919) and a mobile exhibit on the African American history of Westchester County, New York. Operates Committee on Higher Education for Minorities in Westchester County, NY and Community Coalition on Education in Greenburgh, NY. **Founded:** 1969. **Members:** 500. **Publications:** Black Survival Seminar, periodic. Guide to Black Westchester, biennial. Guide Book to Black Organizations in Westchester County, periodic. New Black Image, quarterly. Also publishes Afro-American book lists.

★19★
Afro-American Historical and Genealogical Society (AAHGS)
PO Box 73086
Washington, DC 20056 Phone: (301)381-1292
Sylvia Cooke Martin, Pres.

Description: Individuals, libraries, and archives. Encourages scholarly research in Afro-American history and genealogy as it relates to American history and culture. Collects, maintains, and preserves relevant material, which the society makes available for research and publication. Conducts seminars and workshops; plans to maintain a library on Afro-American family and church history, now in acquisition. Holds competitions and awards 60-day internship in archive or library. **Founded:** 1977. **Members:** 800. **Budget:** Less than $25,000. **Publications:** Journal, quarterly. Newsletter, periodic.

★20★
Afro-American Police League (AAPL)
PO Box 49122
Chicago, IL 60649 Phone: (312)568-7329
Edgar Gosa, Exec. Officer

Description: Police officers of Afro-American descent. Seeks to: improve the relationship between citizens of the Black community and police departments; improve the relationship between Black policemen and White policemen; educate the public about police departments; aid police departments in planning successful law enforcement programs in the Black community. Maintains speakers' bureau. Conducts professional training seminars; presents National Law and Social Justice Leadership Award to the individual in public service who has done most to improve the relationship between the community and police department. Has initiated referral program for matters of police brutality and legal services. Conducts research on subjects such as police malfeasance and law and order legislation. Maintains 200 volume library on police science, law enforcement, and statistics. **Founded:** 1968.

Members: 2500. **Publications:** Bulletin on Special Events, quarterly. Grapevine, quarterly. **Formerly:** (1979) Afro-American Patrolmen's League.

★21★
Afro-Asian Center (AAC)
PO Box 337
Saugerties, NY 12477 Phone: (914)246-7828
Robert Carroll, Dir.

Description: Social studies teachers throughout the U.S., Africa, and Asia. Promotes international friendship and cultural understanding between students in Africa, Asia, and the U.S. through correspondence. Operates solely through cooperating teachers worldwide; provides teachers with outreach organizations in Africa, Latin America, the Middle East, and Asia. Promotes student contests; makes available grant applications for teachers to study and travel in Africa and Asia; offers commercial advertisements on topics dealing with Africa and Asia; sponsors seminars and discussions. Maintains speakers' bureau; bestows awards; provides children's services. **Founded:** 1972. **Budget:** Less than $25,000.

★22★
Afro-Hispanic Institute (AHI)
3306 Ross Pl. NW
Washington, DC 20008 Phone: (202)966-7783
Dr. Stanley A. Cyrus, Pres.

Description: Promotes the study of Afro-Hispanic literature and culture. **Founded:** 1981. **Publications:** Short Stories by Cubena and When the Guyacans Were in Bloom (books).

★23★
All-African People's Revolutionary Party (A-APRP)
1738 A St. SE
Washington, DC 20003
M. Shabaka, Admin.

Description: Africans and persons of African descent who support Pan-Africanism, "the total liberation and unification of Africa under an all-African socialist government." Conducts seminars, conferences, and symposia; compiles statistics. Maintains speakers bureau and library on African history and politics, politics of the Western Left, and revolutionary forces. **Founded:** 1971. **Members:** 783. **Regional Groups:** 5. **State Groups:** 34. **Publications:** Political and educational brochures.

★24★
Alliance of Minority Women for Business and Political Development
c/o Brenda Alford
Brasman Research
814 Thayer Ave., Ste. 202A
Silver Spring, MD 20910 Phone: (301)565-0258
Brenda Alford, Pres.

Description: Minority women who own businesses in industries including manufacturing, construction, service, finance, insurance, real estate, retail trade, wholesale trade, transportation, and public utilities. Objectives are to unite minority women entrepreneurs and to encourage joint ventures and information exchange for political influence. **Founded:** 1982. **Members:** 650. **Budget:** $100,000. **Formerly:** (1982) Task Force on Black Women Business Owners.

★25★
Alpha Kappa Alpha Sorority (AKA)
5656 S. Stony Island Ave.
Chicago, IL 60637 Phone: (312)684-1282
Alison A. Harris, Exec.Dir.

Description: Social service sorority. Provides community services; presents awards; compiles statistics. Operates Cleveland Job Corps. **Founded:** 1908. **Members:** 110,000. **Budget:** $8,000,000. **Regional Groups:** 10. Active Chapters: 750. Alumnae Chapters: 420. Undergraduate Chapters: 410. **Publications:** Along the Ivy Line, 2-3/year. Ivy Leaf Quarterly. Magazine. Contains feature stories, membership section, and obituaries.

★26★
Alpha Phi Alpha Fraternity
4432 Martin Luther King Dr.
Chicago, IL 60653 Phone: (312)373-1819
James B. Blanton III, Exec.Dir.

Description: Service fraternity. **Founded:** 1906. **Members:** 100,000 (since founding). **Budget:** $1,800,000. **Regional Groups:** 5. Active Chapters: 564. Alumni Chapters: 274. College Chapters: 290. **Publications:** Alpha News Letter, monthly. Directory, annual. The Sphinx, quarterly.

★27★
Alpha Pi Chi Sorority
PO Box 255
Kensington, MD 20895
Magoline Carney, Pres.

Description: Service sorority - business and professional women. Conducts fundraising activities for civil rights organizations and Black charities. Sponsors Talent a Rama, a charity showcase of young amateurs. Local chapters "adopt" senior citizens' homes. Awards scholarships. **Founded:** 1963. **Members:** 1300. **Publications:** The President Speaks, quarterly. Newsletter.

★28★
American Academy of Medical Directors (AAMD)
1 Urban Centre, Ste. 648
Tampa, FL 33609 Phone: (813)287-2000
Michael B. Guthrie M.D., Pres.

Description: Physicians with full- or part-time administrative, management, or leadership responsibilities. Acts as an educational forum exclusively for physicians to aid them in preparing for positions of organizational leadership. Offers scholarship program for physicians practicing management in minority fields. **Founded:** 1975. **Members:** 3500. **Budget:** $2,000,000. **Telecommunications Services:** Internet, network for physician managers; PIM Network and Medical Management Information Center, abstract-literature search services; direct mail membership surveying; specialized consultations. **Publications:** American Academy of Medical Directors–Academy Digest, bimonthly. Membership activities newsletter. Includes calendar of events and lists new members, member promotions, and employment opportunities.

★29★
American-African Affairs Association (AAAA)
1001 Connecticut Ave., NW, Ste. 1135
Washington, DC 20036 Phone: (202)223-5110
Lt.Gen. Max Gallimore, Chm.

Description: Individuals, foundations, and business corporations who contribute funds to carry on the program. Educational organization designed to circulate information about African countries to the people of the U.S., especially with respect to "the cause of freedom in its struggle against world Communism and the best interests of the United States of America." Distributes literature to opinion molders, political leaders, university personnel, and business leaders, both here and in other countries. Exchanges publications and information. Sponsors conferences, seminars, and meetings. **Founded:** 1965. **Publications:** Spotlight on Africa, bimonthly. Newsletter on American-African affairs. Covers such issues as foreign involvement in Africa, famine relief, and African economic issues.

★30★
American Association for Affirmative Action (AAAA)
11 E. Hubbard St., Ste. 200
Chicago, IL 60611 Phone: (312)329-2512
Judith Burnison, Exec.Dir.

Description: Equal Opportunity/Affirmative Action officers at educational institutions and industrial firms; public administration and representatives from national, state, and local EO/AA related agencies. Purposes are: to foster the implementation of affirmative action and equal opportunity in employment and in education nationwide; to provide formal liaison with federal, state, and local agencies involved with equal opportunity compliance in employment and education. Is developing speakers' bureau and training program. **Founded:** 1974. **Members:** 1000. **Budget:** $160,000. **Regional Groups:** 10. **State Groups:** 32. **Telecommunications Services:** Fax, (312)329-9131. **Publications:** American Association for Affirmative Action–Membership Directory, annual. American Association for Affirmative Action–Newsletter, quarterly. Includes employment listings.

★31★
American Association of Blacks in Energy (AABE)
801 Pennsylvania Ave., SE, Ste. 250
Washington, DC 20003 Phone: (202)547-9378
Mary L. Boyd-Foy, Chm.

Description: Blacks in energy-related professions, including engineers, scientists, consultants, academicians, and entrepreneurs; government officials and public policymakers; interested students. Represents Blacks and other minorities in matters involving energy use and research, the formulation of energy policy, the ownership of energy resources, and the development of energy technologies. Seeks to increase the knowledge, understanding, and awareness of the minority community in energy issues by serving as an energy information source for policymakers, recommending Blacks and other minorities to appropriate energy officials and executives, encouraging students to pursue professional careers in the energy industry, and advocating the participation of Blacks and other minorities in energy programs and policymaking activities. Updates members on key legislation and regulations being developed by the Department of Energy, the Department of Interior, the Department of Commerce, the Small Business Administration, and other federal and state agencies. Provides a scholarship program for higher education students; offers information on current job openings; maintains speakers' bureau; holds seminars for minority energy professionals. Operates archive; bestows awards. **Founded:** 1977. **Members:** 500. **Budget:** $170,000. **Regional Groups:** 6. **State Groups:** 20. Chapters: 13. **Computerized Services:** Membership data base. **Publications:** Energy News, quarterly. Also publishes educational and research materials.

★32★
American Baptist Black Caucus (ABBC)
c/o Dr. Jacob L. Chatman
St. John Missionary Baptist Church
34 W. Pleasant St.
Springfield, OH 45506 Phone: (513)323-4401
~~Dr. Jacob L. Chatman, Chm.~~

Description: Black congregations of the American Baptist Churches, U.S.A.; represents approximately 484,200 individuals. Concerned with reforming the American Baptist Convention in terms of bridging the gap between Whites and minority members. Seeks to develop convention support for: scholarship aid for disadvantaged students; resources for business and religious projects in the inner city; adequate representation of minorities in the convention structure; support for Black colleges and universities; open hiring policies on local, state, and national levels. Is developing a placement service in cooperation with the convention. Operates speakers' bureau. **Founded:** 1968. **Members:** 13,000. **Regional Groups:** 5. **Computerized Services:** Information services. **Publications:** ABC TAB, monthly. Black Caucus Newsletter, semiannual. The Caucus Voice, biennial. **Formerly:** (1981) Black American Baptist Churchmen.

★33★
American Black Book Writers Association (ABBWA)
PO Box 10548
Marina Del Rey, CA 90295 Phone: (213)822-5195
Will Gibson, Pres.

Description: Writers, illustrators, publishers, booksellers, literary agents, librarians, and others who promote books that are either written by Black authors or have particular relevance to the U.S. Black community. Represents Blacks in the U.S. publishing industry. Encourages development of Black authors; works to preserve and advance Black literature. Promotes and gives market support to members' works; holds mutual promotions and tours; sponsors cooperative advertising in Black-oriented media. Conducts research on problems affecting Black authors and their works in the U.S. Compiles statistics. **Founded:** 1980. **Members:** 4000. **Publications:** ABBWA Journal, quarterly. Trade magazine reporting on trends in the industry and featuring profiles of Blacks in the field, nonpublishing news relevant to the industry, book release listings, and annual Black book guide.

★34★
American Black Chiropractors Association (ABCA)
1918 E. Grand Blvd.
St. Louis, MO 63107 Phone: (314)531-0615
Dr. Bobby Westbrooks, Dir.

Description: Persons who have earned a recognized doctorate degree in chiropractic and students enrolled in a chiropractic college; associate members are institutions, organizations, and interested individuals. Objectives are to: educate the public, health care institutions, and health care providers about chiropractic and promote Black chiropractic in the community; develop career orientation programs for high school and college students and sponsor scholarship funds; study history of chiropractic; sponsor publicity programs, public forums, counseling services, research, and establishment of free chiropractic clinics; provide for exchange of information, techniques, and reports of researchers and clinicians. Conducts research surveys and prepares educational programs and articles on the history of Blacks in chiropractic concerning aspects such as early Jim Crow chiropractic schools, discrimination in licensing and practice, and notable achievements of Blacks in the profession. **Founded:** 1980. **Budget:** Less than $25,000. **Publications:** Plans to issue newsletter, conference materials, and membership directory. **Formerly:** (1981) Association of Black Chiropractors.

★35★
American Bridge Association (ABA)
c/o Gloria Christler
2798 Lakewood Ave., SW
Atlanta, GA 30315 Phone: (404)768-5517
Gloria Christler, Exec.Sec.

Description: Individuals, primarily Blacks, interested in the game of bridge. Encourages the playing of duplicate bridge. Sponsors annual tournaments as benefits for charitable organizations. **Founded:** 1932. **Members:** 6000. **Regional Groups:** 7. **Local Groups:** 215. **Publications:** Bulletin, bimonthly.

★36★
American Civil Liberties Union (ACLU)
132 W. 43rd St.
New York, NY 10036 Phone: (212)944-9800
Ira Glasser, Exec.Dir.

Description: Champions the rights set forth in the Bill of Rights of the U.S. Constitution: freedom of speech, press, assembly, and religion; due process of law and fair trial; equality before the law regardless of race, color, sexual orientation, national origin, political opinion, or religious belief. Activities include litigation, advocacy, and public education. Maintains library of more than 3000 volumes. Sponsors litigation projects on topics such as women's rights, gay and lesbian rights, and children's rights. **Founded:** 1920. **Members:** 375,000. **State Groups:** 50. **Local Groups:** 200. **Telecommunications Services:** Fax, (212)354-5290. **Publications:** Civil Liberties, quarterly. Civil Liberties Alert, monthly. Also publishes policy statements, handbooks, reprints, and pamphlets.

★37★
American Civil Liberties Union Foundation (ACLUF)
132 W. 43rd St.
New York, NY 10036 Phone: (212)944-9800
Ira Glasser, Exec.Dir.

Description: Established as the tax-exempt arm of the American Civil Liberties Union (see separate entry). Purposes are legal defense, research, and public education on behalf of civil liberties including freedom of speech, press, and other First Amendment rights. Sponsors projects on topics such as children's rights, capital punishment, censorship, women's rights, immigration, prisoners' rights, national security, voting rights, and equal employment opportunity. Conducts research and public education projects to enable citizens to know and assert their rights. Seeks funds to protect liberty guaranteed by the Bill of Rights and the Constitution. **Founded:** 1966. **Regional Groups:** 2. **Publications:** Annual Report. Civil Liberties, quarterly. Newsletter covering the legal defense, research, and public education projects of the foundation. Includes legislative news. **Formerly:** (1969) Roger Baldwin Foundation of ACLU.

★38★
American Colonization Society - Charity and Social Welfare Organization (ACS)
PO Box 8340
New Fairfield, CT 06812
A. McAllister, Pres.

Description: Provides assistance in relocation, repatriation, and resettling of people of African-American descent to Africa. Conducts social activities; compiles statistics. **Founded:** 1817. **Publications:** none.

★39★
American Committee on Africa (ACOA)
198 Broadway
New York, NY 10038 Phone: (212)962-1210
Jennifer Davis, Exec.Dir.

Description: Devoted to supporting African people in their struggle for freedom and independence. Focuses on southern Africa and the Western Sahara and support for African liberation movements. Works with legislators, churches, trade unions, and interested students to help stop what the group feels is U.S. collaboration with racism in South Africa and Namibia. Arranges speaking tours for African leaders; publicizes conditions and developments in Africa; sponsors research, rallies, and demonstrations. Serves as a coordinating and collection agency for information and materials on southern Africa. Maintains speakers' bureau. **Founded:** 1953. **Members:** 15,000. **Computerized Services:** Mailing list. **Publications:** ACOA Action News, semiannual. Committee activities newsletter.

★40★
American Constitutional and Civil Rights Union (ACCRU)
18055 SW Jay St.
Aloha, OR 97006 Phone: (503)649-9310
Earhl R. Schooff, Exec. Officer

Description: Provides consulting services to trustees of established trusts who believe their constitutional and/or civil rights are being violated. **Founded:** 1979.

★41★
American Coordinating Committee for Equality in Sport and Society (ACCESS)
Northeastern University - 244 HN
Center for Study of Sport
360 Huntington Ave.
Boston, MA 02115 Phone: (617)437-5815
Dr. Richard E. Lapchick, Chair

Description: Coalition of 30 national civil rights, religious, political, and sports organizations. Works for equality in sports as a reflection of society; focuses on South Africa. Has worked to end all sports contacts with South Africa until its apartheid system has been eradicated. Holds seminars; maintains speakers' bureau. Compiles statistics and conducts research programs. **Founded:** 1976. **Telecommunications Services:** Fax, (617)437-5830.

★42★
American Foundation for Negro Affairs (AFNA)
117 S. 17th St., Ste. 1200
Philadelphia, PA 19103 Phone: (215)854-1470
Samuel L. Evans, Pres.

Description: Has developed a model for educational programs preparing minority students for professional careers. The model, New Access Routes to Professional Careers, which has been used to implement programs for medicine and law in Philadelphia, PA and New Orleans, LA, consists of four interlocking educational phases designed to enable students to meet the academic standards of professional schools through one-to-one preceptorships, tutorials, advanced study, and counseling, beginning at the 8th grade and continuing through the completion of professional school. Among the aims of the program are solidification of the student's career identification and self-image and improvement of basic communications and abstract reasoning skills. Bestows awards; compiles statistics. Sponsors African American Hall of Fame. Maintains small library and biographical archives. Programs carried out by American Foundation for Negro Affairs National Education and Research Fund. **Founded:** 1968. **Publications:** AFNA Projections to the Year 2000 and Beyond, biennial. Monograph.

★43★
American Health and Beauty Aids Institute (AHBAI)
111 E. Wacker Dr., Ste. 600
Chicago, IL 60601 Phone: (312)644-6610
Geri Duncan Jones, Exec.Dir.

Description: Minority-owned companies engaged in manufacturing and marketing health and beauty aids for the Black consumer. Represents the interests of members and the industry before local, state, and federal governmental agencies. Assists with business development and economic progress within the minority community by providing informational and educational resources. Maintains speakers' bureau. Conducts annual Proud Lady Beauty Show. **Founded:** 1981. **Publications:** American Health and Beauty Aids Institute–Membership Directory, annual.

★44★
American Institute for Economic Development (AIED)
715 8th St. SE
Washington, DC 20003 Phone: (202)547-8094
Freddie John Martin Ph.D., Contact

Description: Participants include federal government funding sources, corporations, and individuals interested in the economic well-being of minority communities in the U.S. Promotes economic prosperity of minority communities. Seeks to shape educational policies in order to emphasize business education for minority students and to influence public policy and judicial opinion as they affect minority economics. Develops resources within minority communities to make them self-sufficient and economically-viable. **Founded:** 1983.

★45★
American League of Financial Institutions (ALFI)
1709 New York Ave. NW, Ste. 801
Washington, DC 20006 Phone: (202)628-5624
John W. Harshaw, Pres.

Description: Federal and state chartered minority savings and loan associations in 25 states and the District of Columbia. Undertakes programs to increase the income of and savings flow into the associations including a direct solicitation effort; provides counseling and technical assistance for member associations through a series of regional conferences and seminars; offers consultant services to assist individual associations and groups wishing to organize new associations or acquire existing associations with development potential; collects, organizes, and distributes materials that will aid member associations. Conducts research to improve investment capability, resolve common management problems, and evaluate statistical data on an industry-wide basis to develop and institute training programs for management personnel. Conducts research programs; maintains placement service. **Founded:** 1948. **Members:** 71. **Telecommunications Services:** Fax, (202)637-8983. **Publications:** Directory of Members and Associate Members, periodic. ALFI Focus Magazine. **Formerly:** (1983) American Savings and Loan League.

★46★
American Newspaper Publishers Association Foundation (ANPAF)
The Newspaper Center
Box 17407
Dulles Airport
Washington, DC 20041 Phone: (703)648-1000
Rosalind G. Stark, V.Pres & Dir.

Description: Educational arm of the American Newspaper Publishers Association. Seeks to: develop an informed readership; combat illiteracy; educate the public regarding their rights under the First Amendment; increase opportunities for minorities in the industry; foster professionalism in the press. Aids local newspapers with the creation of programs that promote the foundation's objectives and meet the needs of the newspaper and the needs of the community it serves. These programs include: the Newspaper in Education Program, which supplies primary and secondary school systems with curriculum materials and encourages the use of newspapers in the classroom as an educational tool; the Minority Opportunity Program; the Literacy Program. Works with the Accrediting Council on Education in Journalism and Mass Communications. Sponsors projects related to the U.S. Constitution and the Bill of Rights; cosponsors annual Newspaper in Education Week, International Newspaper Literacy Day, and National Read Aloud Day. Bestows awards and fellowships for minority newspaper professionals. Conducts workshops and seminars; provides speakers. **Founded:** 1961. **Telecommunications Services:** Fax, (703)620-1265. **Publications:** Annual Report. Minority Task Force Newsletter, quarterly. Update, 8/year. Press to Read, quarterly. Newsletter. Also publishes Bibliography: NIE Publications, Newspaper: What's In It for Me? (career booklet), and Family Focus: Reading and Learning Together.

★47★
American Psychological Association
Division of the Psychology of Women
Section on the Psychology of Black Women
c/o Dr. Janice L. Nickelson
Howard University
Academic Computer Services
PO Box 722
Washington, DC 20059 Phone: (202)806-6374
Dr. Janice L. Nickelson, Chm.

Description: A section of the American Psychological Association. Purpose is to present to the APA scientific and applied research and theoretical findings related to the psychology of Black women. **Founded:** 1984. **Members:** 200. **Formerly:** (1984) Committee on Black Women's Concerns.

★48★
Amnesty International of the U.S.A. (AIUSA)
322 8th Ave.
New York, NY 10001 Phone: (212)807-8400
John G. Healey, Exec.Dir.

Description: Works impartially for the release of men and women detained anywhere for their conscientiously held beliefs, color, ethnic origin, sex, religion, or language, provided they have neither used nor advocated violence. Opposes torture and the death penalty without reservation and advocates fair and prompt trials for all political prisoners. Has consultative status with the United Nations and the Council of Europe, has cooperative relations with the Inter-American Commission on Human Rights (see separate entry), and has observer status with the Organization of African Unity. Was the recipient of the 1977 Nobel Prize for Peace. Local groups and volunteers participate in 7 networks: Educators; Freedom Writers; Health Professionals; Labor; Legal Professionals; Religion; Urgent Action. **Founded:** 1966. **Members:** 400,000. **Regional Groups:** 5. **Local Groups:** 1500. **Publications:** Amnesty Action, bimonthly. Newsletter.

★49★
Anti-Repression Resource Team (ARRT)
PO Box 122
Jackson, MS 39205 Phone: (601)969-2269
Ken Lawrence, Dir.

Description: Combats all forms of political repression including: police violence and misconduct; Ku Klux Klan and Nazi terrorism; spying and covert action by secret police and intelligence agencies. Focuses on research, writing, lecturing, organizing, and publishing. Conducts training workshops for church, labor, and community organizations. Maintains library of materials on spying, repression, covert action, terrorism, and civil liberties. Maintains speakers' bureau. **Founded:** 1979. **Budget:** Less than $25,000.

★50★
Artists and Athletes Against Apartheid (AAAA)
545 8th St. SE, Ste. 200
Washington, DC 20003 Phone: (202)547-2550
Arthur Ashe, Co-Chm.

Description: Celebrities in the arts and sports who vow not to perform in South Africa because of its apartheid policy of racial segregation. Objective is to implement an international sports and cultural boycott of South Africa until apartheid is no longer imposed. Seeks to educate others in sports and the performing arts about apartheid and to dissuade them from performing. Members make television and public appearances to denounce apartheid. Operates speakers' bureau. Monitors the decline in the number of art and sports celebrities working in and traveling to South Africa; organizes symposia; compiles statistics. **Founded:** 1983. **Members:** 500. **Budget:** Less than $25,000.

Telecommunications Services: Fax, (202)547-7687. **Publications:** Brochures.

★51★
Artists United Against Apartheid (AUAA)
c/o The Africa Fund
198 Broadway
New York, NY 10038 Phone: (212)962-1210

Description: Coalition of popular musicians who seek to make the public aware of the lack of freedoms for Blacks under the apartheid system in South Africa through their music. Members performed on the "Sun City" record album and single and music video, the profits of which are donated to the Africa Fund (see separate entry). Seeks to educate performers and the public regarding conditions in South Africa. Appeals to entertainers to forego performing at the Sun City resort complex in South Africa. (The group believes that by performing there, entertainers show tacit support for apartheid.) **Members:** 54. **Publications:** Press releases.

★52★
Assault on Illiteracy Program (AOIP)
410 Central Park W., PH-C
New York, NY 10025 Phone: (212)967-4008
Benjamin Wright, Exec.Dir.

Description: Coalition of Black community development organizations. Works to compliment and supplement the role of teachers and tutors in overcoming illiteracy. **Founded:** 1980. **Members:** 94. **Telecommunications Services:** Faxes, (212)971-4682 and (212)222-3556. **Publications:** The Advancer, weekly. Black Monitor, periodic. Magazine. Newsletter to Board Members, semimonthly. Also publishes Who Am I? Guide To Learning.

★53★
Association for Multicultural Counseling and Development (AMCD)
c/o American Association for Counseling and Development
5999 Stevenson Ave.
Alexandria, VA 22304 Phone: (703)823-9800
Dr. Theodore P. Remley Jr., Exec.Dir.

Description: A division of the American Association for Counseling and Development. Professionals involved in personnel and guidance careers in educational settings, social services, and community agencies; interested individuals; students. Seeks to: develop programs aimed at improving ethnic and racial empathy and understanding; foster personal growth and improve educational opportunities for all minorities in the U.S.; defend human and civil rights; provide in-service and pre-service training for members and others in the profession. Works to enhance members' ability to serve as behavioral change agents. Bestows awards; offers placement service. **Founded:** 1972. **Members:** 2891. **Telecommunications Services:** Fax, (703)823-0252; toll-free number, (800)545-AACD. **Publications:** Journal of Multicultural Counseling and Development, quarterly. **Formerly:** (1986) Association for Non-White Concerns in Personnel and Guidance.

★54★
Association for the Preservation and Presentation of the Arts (APPA)
2011 Benning Rd. NE
Washington, DC 20002 Phone: (202)529-3244
Bernice Hammond, Pres.

Description: Individuals representing the visual and performing arts; interested others. Serves as a vehicle for the promotion of Blacks in the arts. Seeks to increase public awareness and appreciation of the arts and its representation of African American culture. Works on the development of musical and dance productions. Produces children's shows; sponsors lectures. Offers scholarships to children and young people interested in the arts. Bestows awards. **Founded:** 1964. **Members:** 500. **Publications:** Cultural Magnet, semiannual. Newsletter. Also publishes pamphlets and information on artists.

★55★
Association for the Study of Afro-American Life and History (ASALH)
1407 14th St. NW
Washington, DC 20005 Phone: (202)667-2822
Karen Robinson, Exec.Dir.

Description: Historians, scholars, and students interested in the research and study of Black people as a contributing factor in civilization. To promote historical research and writings, collect historical manuscripts and materials relating to Black people throughout the world, and bring about harmony among the races by interpreting one to the other. Encourages the study of Black history and training in the social sciences, history, and other disciplines. Cooperates with governmental agencies, foundations, and peoples and nations in projects designed to advance the study of ethnic history, with emphasis on Black heritage and programs for the future. Maintains Carter G. Woodson home in Washington, DC. Sponsors essay contest for undergraduate and graduate students and Afro-American History Month. **Founded:** 1915. **Members:** 2200. **Budget:** $200,000. **State Groups:** 30. **Local Groups:** 5. **Publications:** Journal of Negro History, quarterly. **Formerly:** (1973) Association for Study of Negro Life and History.

★56★
Association of African American People's Legal Council (AAPLC)
c/o William Bert Johnson
13902 Robson St.
Detroit, MI 48227 Phone: (313)837-0627
William Bert Johnson, Pres.

Description: African-American attorneys. Seeks to achieve equal justice under the law for African-Americans and to provide free legal counsel to people of African-American descent. Compiles statistics and reports on cases of international inequality. Obtains research from public systems on education and its effect on discrimination. **Founded:** 1959. **Members:** 1100. **State Groups:** 50. **Telecommunications Services:** Records of the District and Circuit Courts of Appeals. **Publications:** Membership Roster, annual.

★57★
Association of African-American Women Business Owners (BWE)
c/o Brenda Alford
Brasman Research
814 Thayer Ave., Ste. 202A
Silver Spring, MD 20910 Phone: (301)565-0258
Brenda Alford, Pres.

Description: Small business owners in all industries, particularly business services. Seeks to assist in developing a greater number of successful self-employed Black women through business and personal development programs, networking, and legislative action. Is conducting a 2-year project identifying Black women business owners as role models and historical figures; plans to establish an archive. **Founded:** 1983. **Members:** 1200. **Local Groups:** 10. **Publications:** Black Business Women's News, quarterly. Journal of Minority Business, annual. **Formerly:** (1990) American Association of Black Women Entrepreneurs.

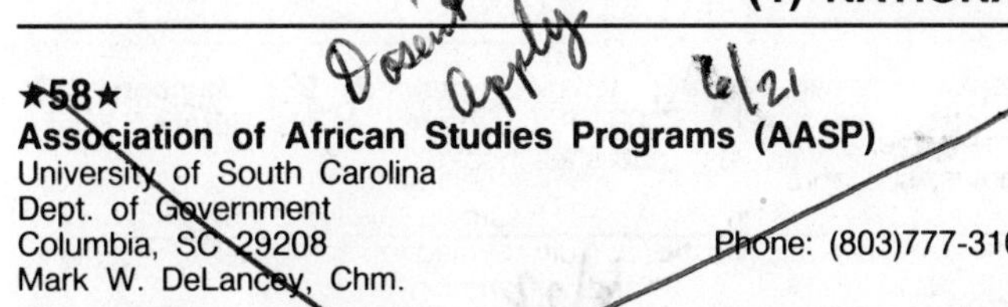

★58★

Association of African Studies Programs (AASP)
University of South Carolina
Dept. of Government
Columbia, SC 29208 Phone: (803)777-3108
Mark W. DeLancey, Chm.

Description: African studies programs, departments, and committees at universities and colleges. Works to promote, develop, and further African studies in the U.S. and Africa. Represents the interests of African studies programs before funding agencies, universities, and state and federal authorities. **Founded:** 1972. **Members:** 41. **Publications:** AASP Newsletter, semiannual.

★59★

Association of Black Admissions and Financial Aid Officers of the Ivy League and Sister Schools (ABAFAOILSS)
c/o Lloyd Peterson
Admissions Office
149 Elm St.
Yale University
New Haven, CT 06520 Phone: (203)432-1916
Lloyd Peterson, Co-Chwm.

Description: Present and former minority admissions and financial aid officers employed at Ivy League or sister schools. These schools include: Brown, Columbia, Cornell, Dartmouth, Harvard/Radcliffe, Massachusetts Institute of Technology, University of Pennsylvania, Princeton, Yale, Barnard, Bryn Mawr, Mount Holyoke, Smith, and Wellesley. Aids minority students who wish to pursue a college education. Seeks to improve methods of recruitment, admittance, and financial services that support the growth and maintenance of the minority student population at these institutions. Encourages Ivy League and sister schools to respond to the needs of minority students and admissions and financial aid officers. **Founded:** 1970. **Members:** 77. **Publications:** Unequalled Opportunities (guide to Ivy League and sister schools).

★60★

Association of Black Cardiologists (ABC)
2300 Garrison Blvd., Ste. 150
Baltimore, MD 21216 Phone: (301)945-2525
B. Waine Kong Ph.D., Exec.Dir.

Description: Physicians and other health professionals interested in lowering mortality and morbidity resulting from cardiovascular diseases. Seeks to improve prevention and treatment of cardiovascular diseases. Conducts educational and research programs; bestows awards; maintains speakers' bureau. **Founded:** 1974. **Members:** 350. **Budget:** $300,000. **Telecommunications Services:** Fax, (717)848-4486.

★61★

Association of Black Foundation Executives (ABFE)
1828 L St., NW
Washington, DC 20036 Phone: (202)466-6512
Jacqui Burton, Prog. Dir.

Description: Board and staff members of corporate and foundation grantmaking organizations. Encourages increased recognition of economic, educational, and social issues facing Blacks in the grantmaking field. Promotes support of Blacks and their status as grantmaking professionals. Seeks an increase in the number of Blacks entering the grantmaking field; helps members improve their job effectiveness. Though involved with grantmaking organizations, the ABFE itself does not award grants. **Founded:** 1971.

★62★

Association of Black Nursing Faculty in Higher Education (ABNF)
5823 Queens Cove
Lisle, IL 60532 Phone: (708)969-3809
Sallie Tucker-Allen Ph.D., Pres.

Description: Black nursing faculty teaching in baccalaureate and higher degree programs accredited by the National League for Nursing. Works to promote health-related issues and educational concerns of interest to the Black community and ABNF. Serves as a forum for communication and the exchange of information among members; develops strategies for expressing concerns to other individuals, institutions, and communities. Assists members in professional development; develops and sponsors continuing education activities; fosters networking and guidance in employment and recruitment activities. Promotes health-related issues of legislation, government programs, and community activities. Supports Black consumer advocacy issues. Encourages research. Maintains speakers' bureau, hall of fame, and biographical archives. Offers charitable program and placement services. Sponsors competitions; compiles statistics. Bestows Dissertation Awards, Lifetime Achievement in Education and Research Award, Young Publisher Award, and Young Researcher Award. Is establishing a computer-assisted job bank; plans to develop bibliographies related to research groups. **Founded:** 1987. **Members:** 127. **Budget:** Less than $25,000. **State Groups:** 25. **Publications:** ABNF Journal, semiannual. Includes research reports and scholarly papers.

★63★

Association of Black Psychologists (ABPsi)
PO Box 55999
Washington, DC 20040-5999 Phone: (202)722-0808
G. Evelyn LeSure, Sec.

Description: Professional psychologists and others in associated disciplines. Aims to: enhance the psychological well-being of Black people in America; define mental health in consonance with newly established psychological concepts and standards; develop policies for local, state, and national decision-making which have impact on the mental health of the Black community; support established Black sister organizations and aid in the development of new, independent Black institutions to enhance the psychological, educational, cultural, and economic situation. Offers training and information on AIDS. Conducts seminars, workshops, and research. Bestows awards. **Founded:** 1968. **Members:** 1250. **Budget:** $350,000. **Regional Groups:** 4. **State Groups:** 29. **Local Groups:** 31. **Telecommunications Services:** Fax, (202)722-5941. **Publications:** Association of Black Psychologists–Newsletter, quarterly. Includes calendar of events and research updates.

★64★

Association of Black Sociologists (ABS)
University Missouri
5100 Rockhill Rd., SSB 215
Kansas City, MO 64110 Phone: (409)845-4944
Sandra V. Walker, Pres.

Description: Purposes are to: promote the professional interests of Black sociologists; promote an increase in the number of professionally trained sociologists; help stimulate and improve the quality of research and the teaching of sociology; provide perspectives regarding Black experiences as well as expertise for understanding and dealing with problems confronting Black people; protect professional rights and safeguard the civil rights stemming from executing the above objectives. Presents annual award to Black graduate student for excellence in scholarly work; conducts research programs. **Founded:** 1968. **Members:** 400. **Budget:** Less than $25,000. **Publications:** ABS Newsletter, monthly. Includes profesional and career in development information, announcements, and updates. **Formerly:** (1976) Caucus of Black Sociologists.

★65★
Association of Black Storytellers (ABS)
PO Box 27456
Philadelphia, PA 19118 Phone: (215)898-5118
Linda Goss, Pres.

Description: Black storytellers and enthusiasts. Seeks to establish a forum to promote the Black oral tradition and to attract an audience. Works for the reissue of out-of-print story collections. Bestows Zora Neale Hurston Award to pioneers in Black storytelling. **Founded:** 1984. **Members:** 175. **Publications:** ABS Newsletter, 3/year.

★66★
Association of Black Women in Higher Education (ABWHE)
c/o Lenore R. Bell
Fashion Institute of Technology
Office of V.Pres. of Academic Affairs
227 W. 27th St. C-913
New York, NY 10001 Phone: (212)760-7911
Lenore R. Gall, Pres.

Description: Faculty members, education administrators, students, retirees, consultants, managers, and affirmative action officers. Objectives are to nurture the role of Black women in higher education, and to provide support for the professional development goals of Black women. Conducts workshops and seminars. **Founded:** 1979. **Members:** 350. **Computerized Services:** Mailing list. **Publications:** ABWHE Newsletter, quarterly.

★67★
Association of Caribbean Studies (ACS)
PO Box 22202
Lexington, KY 40522 Phone: (606)257-6966
Dr. O. R. Dathorne, Exec.Dir.

Description: Scholars and researchers concerned with the interdisciplinary nature of Caribbean studies. Objectives are to: develop knowledge and understanding of Caribbean studies through study, research, and travel; promote academic studies and disseminate information to the public; encourage research on Caribbean politics, history, linguistics, trade, psychology, music, anthropology, sociology, folk culture, religion, art, literature, and economics; promote the Caribbean as a cultural whole and use of its languages, which include English, French, Spanish, Portuguese, Dutch, and related Creoles. Maintains speakers' bureau; compiles statistics; bestows awards. Conducts periodic seminar. **Founded:** 1978. **Members:** 1200. **Budget:** Less than $25,000. **Computerized Services:** Data base; mailing list. **Telecommunications Services:** Fax, (606)257-4000. **Publications:** Abstracts From Annual Conference. Journal of Caribbean Studies, 3/year. Newsletter, 3/year. Also publishes Hot Ice, Songs from a New World, and monographs; produces audiocassettes and audiovisual materials.

★68★
Association of Concerned African Scholars (ACAS)
Oregon State University
Dept. of History
Bldg. Milam, Rm. 306
Corvallis, OR 97331 Phone: (503)737-1261
Ed Ferguson, Exec.Sec.

Description: Individuals and institutions. Goals are to: aid in the articulation of scholarly analysis of U.S. policy toward Africa; suggest alternatives to U.S.-African policies; develop a communication and action network among African scholars; coordinate activities with other national and local organizations. Mobilizes support on current issues; provides local sponsors for public education programs; stimulates research on policy-oriented issues and disseminates findings; informs and updates members on international policy developments. Operates speakers' bureau; compiles statistics. **Founded:** 1977. **Members:** 175. **Budget:** Less than $25,000. **Publications:** ACAS Bulletin, 3/year. Newsletter, 3/year. Also publishes books.

★69★
Association of Haitian Physicians Abroad (AMHE)
608 Ogden Ave.
Teaneck, NJ 07666 Phone: (201)836-2199
Serge Bontemps M.D., Pres.

Description: Haitian doctors. Purpose is to unite Haitian doctors abroad and to organize professional activities among them. Provides charitable assistance to the Haitian community. Sponsors educational programs. **Founded:** 1972. **Members:** 900. **Budget:** $35,000. **State Groups:** 8. **Publications:** Directory of Haitian Physicians in N.Y., biennial. Journal des Medecins Haitien a l'Etranger, 6/year. Also publishes educational materials. **Formerly:** (1986) Haitian Medical Association Abroad.

★70★
Association of Minority Health Professions Schools (AMHPS)
711 2nd St. NE, Ste. 200
Washington, DC 20002 Phone: (202)544-7499
Dale P. Dirks, Exec. Officer

Description: Predominantly Black health professions schools. Seeks to: increase the number of minorities in health professions; improve the health of Blacks in the U.S.; increase the federal resources available to minority schools and students. Provides information to the U.S. Congress; conducts educational programs. **Founded:** 1978. **Members:** 8. **Telecommunications Services:** Fax, (202)546-7105. **Publications:** Study of the Health Status of Minorities in the U.S., periodic.

★71★
Audience Development Committee (AUDELCO)
PO Box 30, Manhattanville Sta.
New York, NY 10027 Phone: (212)289-5900
Vivian Robinson, Exec.Dir.

Description: Individuals interested in or pursuing a career in Black theatre. Purposes are to develop a greater appreciation of theatrical productions among Blacks and to build an audience for Black theatrical and dance companies. Operates Black theatre archives; maintains speakers' bureau. Bestows awards for excellence in Black theatre. Offers a low-cost ticket program for senior citizens, children, and those who are unable to afford tickets at box office prices. **Founded:** 1973. **Members:** 1000. **Publications:** Black Theatre Directory, periodic. Intermission, monthly. Newsletter. Overture, semiannual. Magazine.

★72★
Auxiliary to the National Medical Association (ANMA)
1012 10th St. NW
Washington, DC 20001 Phone: (202)371-1674
Mrs. Ruby H. Franks, Adm.Sec.

Description: Spouses of active members of the National Medical Association (see separate entry); widows and widowers of former members. Purposes are to: create a greater interest in the NMA; assist and encourage the medical profession in its efforts to educate and serve the public in matters of sanitation and health; develop and promote a national program on health and education with subcategories in community needs, legislation, and human relations. Conducts workshops on teenage pregnancy, breast self-examinations, high blood pressure screening, and sickle cell anemia screening. Plans and implements an annual youth forum under the auspices of the March of Dimes Birth Defects Foundation (see separate entry). Provides youth with professional guidance and the opportunity for peer exchange in the areas of mental and physical health; deals with the health of newborns, health services, nutrition, and teenage pregnancy. Also conducts programs for youth on parenting, socially transmitted diseases, nutrition, birth defects, and continued education after pregnancy. Bestows annual Alma Wells Givens Scholarships to medical students and the Omega Mason Memorial Scholarship Awards to outstanding student nurses. Maintains archive. **Founded:** 1935. **Regional Groups:** 6. **State Groups:** 14. **Local Groups:** 40. **Publications:** Membership Directory, periodic. **Formerly:** (1975) Women's Auxiliary to the National Medical Association.

★73★
Beatrice M. Murphy Foundation (BMMF)
2737 Devonshire Pl. NW, Apt. 222
Washington, DC 20008 Phone: (202)387-6053
Beatrice M. Murphy, Exec.Dir.

Description: Encourages the reading, appreciation, and further production of Black literature. Promotes and encourages the study of such literature by: awarding scholarships to the disadvantaged, the blind, and the physically handicapped; sponsoring contests, presentations, and displays; providing assistance to authors. Disseminates descriptive indexes, annotated bibliographies, and other information on Black literature. Conducts research; maintains biographical archives. Sponsors seminars and contests; offers services to children. Encourages individuals to donate reference materials pertaining to Black literature to libraries for public use. **Founded:** 1977. **Members:** 50. **Budget:** Less than $25,000.

★74★
Bessie Smith Society (BSS)
c/o Prof. Michael Roth
Franklin & Marshall College
Lancaster, PA 17604 Phone: (717)291-3915
Prof. Michael Roth, Adviser

Description: Admirers of blues singer Bessie Smith, who attained her greatest success in the 1920s and 30s.

★75★
Big Eight Council on Black Student Government (BECBSG)
Minority Student Services
Hester Hall, Rm. 213
731 Elm Ave.
University of Oklahoma
Norman, OK 73019 Phone: (405)325-3163
Norris Williams, Dir.

Description: Black student unions and other groups at Big Eight Athletic Conference universities. Seeks to represent the concerns of Black collegians at universities where the majority of students are White. Encourages the genesis of all Black student organizations and lends support to them. Seeks to effect changes in curricula and to help legitimize and develop Black studies departments as accredited degree programs. Functions as a communications medium among member schools and assists in efforts to reduce the attrition rate of Black students. Promotes the placement of students and the hiring of Black faculty and staff. Presents group and individual awards. Member schools conduct seminars and workshops including Internships, Working for Corporate America, Coping with Stress and Pressure, Young Entrepreneurships, and Leadership. Presently inactive. **Founded:** 1978. **Members:** 5000. **Budget:** $35,000. **Publications:** Big Eight Update, annual. Directory. Harambee, semiannual. New Renaissance, semiannual.

★76★
Black Affairs Center for Training and Organizational Development (BACTOD)
c/o Margaret V. Wright
10918 Jarboe Ct.
Silver Spring, MD 20901 Phone: (301)681-9822
Margaret V. Wright, Pres.

Description: Multidisciplinary management research organization which promotes social change, educational improvement, organization renewal and goal achievement, systematic problem solving and multicultural skills development through custom-designed training programs and consultation services. Individuals, groups, educational systems, and governmental and community agencies use programs such as Equal Employment Opportunity Training; Employee Motivation, Productivity and Improvement Training; Career Education and Development Training. Programs are continually being developed in areas including women's concerns, single parents, youth and sex, drugs and alcoholism, the aging, daycare, sexual harassment, and stress management. **Founded:** 1970. **Publications:** Brochure. **Formerly:** (1976) Black Affairs Division, National Training Laboratories; (1989) Black Affairs Center.

★77★
Black American Cinema Society (BACS)
3617 Monclair St.
Los Angeles, CA 90018 Phone: (213)737-3292
Mayme Agnew Clayton Ph.D., Founder & Dir.

Description: Faculty members, students, senior citizens, and film and jazz enthusiasts. Works to bring about an awareness of the contributions made by Blacks to the motion picture industry in silent films, early talkies, and short and feature films. Feels that by viewing these films Black children can see the sacrifice and humiliation endured by Black actors and actresses, directors, film writers, and producers while making films. Maintains collection of early Black films owned by the Western States Black Research Center. Conducts research projects, film shows, and Black History Month seminars. Provides financial support to independent Black filmmakers. Maintains 30,000 volume library on Black history, literature, records, films, and art that includes museum pieces and documents. Compiles statistics; maintains biographical archives, speakers' bureau, and charitable program; sponsors competitions; bestows awards. Sponsors traveling film festival. **Founded:** 1975. **Members:** 1350. **Budget:** $32,000. **Publications:** Black Talkies Souvenir Book, annual.

★78★
Black American Response to the African Community (BARAC)
127 N. Madison Ave., Ste. 400
Pasadena, CA 91101 Phone: (818)584-0303
Frank E. Wilson, Exec.Dir.

Description: A grass roots organization of entertainers, journalists, clergy, and business, health, and community leaders working to assist the victims of drought and famine in Africa. Focuses on emergency efforts involving medical needs, water irrigation, housing, and food supplies. Provides relief for orphans through its Family Network Program. Disseminates current information on drought-stricken areas in Africa; assists in the development of regeneration projects in affected areas. Maintains the National Education Task Force to educate Americans on the African crisis; sponsors media updates. Raises funds through television documentaries, benefit movie premieres, art exhibits, and collection boxes. Is donating proceeds and royalties from the song Love Returns to aid the African hunger crisis. **Founded:** 1984. **Publications:** Action Update Newsletter, semiannual.

★79★
Black Awareness in Television (BAIT)
13217 Livernois
Detroit, MI 48238 Phone: (313)931-3427
David Rambeau, Dir.

Description: Produces Black media programs for television, video, radio, film, and theatre. Trains individuals in the media and conducts research projects including surveys. Produces public affairs, soap opera, and exercise programs; sponsors theatre companies. Seeks television exposure for Black-produced products; promotes September is Black Reading Month program. **Founded:** 1970. **Members:** 100. **Local Groups:** 5. **Publications:** Thedamu Arts Magazine, monthly. **Also known as:** Project BAIT.

★80★
Black Business Alliance (BBA)
PO Box 26443
Baltimore, MD 21207 Phone: (301)467-2225
Willie H. Scott, CEO

Description: Act as a national and international support system for Black businesses, providing assistance in organizational management and resource development. Provides children's services; sponsors fundraising events; offers placement services. Bestows awards. Conducts monthly seminar. **Founded:** 1979. **Members:** 250. **Regional Groups:** 3. **State Groups:** 6. **Local Groups:** 14. **Telecommunications Services:** Fax, (301)467-2226. **Publications:** Alliance Speaks, monthly. At Your Service, annual. Directory. **Formerly:** (1986) National Black People's Assembly.

★81★
Black Caucus of the American Library Association (BCALA)
c/o Dr. John Tyson
Virginia State Library and Archives
11th St. & Capitol Sq.
Richmond, VA 23219 Phone: (804)786-2332
Dr. John Tyson, Pres.

Description: Black librarians; Blacks interested in library services. To promote librarianship; to encourage active participation of Blacks in library associations and boards and all levels of the profession. Monitors activities of the American Library Association with regard to its policies and programs and how they affect Black librarians and library users. Reviews, analyzes, evaluates, and recommends to the ALA actions that influence the recruitment, development, advancement, and general working conditions of Black librarians. Facilitates library services that meet the informational needs of Black people including increased availability of materials related to social and economic concerns. Encourages development of authoritative information resources concerning Black people and dissemination of this information to the public. Bestows annual Distinguished Service Awards. **Founded:** 1970. **Members:** 600. **Telecommunications Services:** Fax, (804)289-8757. **Publications:** Black Caucus Newsletter, bimonthly. Reports news of interest about Black librarians. Recurring features include notices of professional opportunities and activities of individuals within the caucus and the ALA.

★82★
Black Citizens for a Fair Media (BCFM)
156-20 Riverside Dr., No. 13L
New York, NY 10032 Phone: (212)568-3168
Emma L. Bowen, Pres.

Description: Community organizations concerned with employment practices in the television industry, images of Black people projected by television, and how those images affect viewers. Works to improve programming, employment proctices, and training of Blacks; evaluates compliance with the Federal Communication Commission's equal opportunity rules for the electronic media. Believes that the airways belong to the people and seeks to prevent any change in that ownership. Has established advisory boards with New York City television stations which meet quarterly to discuss programming and employment. **Founded:** 1971. **Members:** 250. **Publications:** Brochure.

★83★
Black Data Processing Associates (BDPA)
PO Box 7466
Philadelphia, PA 19101 Phone: 800-727-BPDA
Vivian Wilson, Pres.

Description: Persons employed in the information processing industry, including electronic data processing, electronic word processing, and data communications; others interested in information processing. Seeks to accumulate and share information processing knowledge and business expertise in order to increase the career and business potential of minorities in the information processing field. Conducts professional seminars, workshops, tutoring services, and community introductions to data processing. Bestows honorary memberships and awards to distinguished data processing professionals; offers scholarships to qualified high school graduates and makes annual donation to the United Negro College Fund (see separate entry). **Founded:** 1975. **Members:** 1500. **Local Groups:** 39. **Publications:** Data News, quarterly. National Journal, quarterly.

★84★
Black Entertainment and Sports Lawyers Association (BESLA)
111 Broadway, 7th Fl.
New York, NY 10006 Phone: (212)587-0300
Kendall Minter, Exec.Dir.

Description: Black attorneys specializing in entertainment and sports law. Purpose is to provide more efficient and effective legal representation to African-American entertainers and athletes. Offers referral system for legal representation and a resource bank for providing information to students, groups, and nonprofit and civic organizations involved in the entertainment industry; and serves as an industry watchdog in protecting the rights of Blacks within the entertainment community. Maintains speakers' bureau; conducts research programs. **Founded:** 1979. **Members:** 400. **Regional Groups:** 2. **Telecommunications Services:** Faxes, (212)732-1522 and (708)383-7414. **Formerly:** (1986) Black Entertainment Lawyers Association.

★85★
Black Filmmaker Foundation (BFF)
375 Greenwich St., Ste. 600
New York, NY 10013 Phone: (212)941-3944
Monica Breckenridge, Exec.Dir.

Description: Serves as media arts center and distributor of Black independent film and video productions. Fosters audience development by programming local, national, and international film festivals. Produces weekly television interview show on Black filmmakers. Maintains video library. Conducts seminars, scenes workshop, and monthly film screening. Operates skills bank for job referrals. **Founded:** 1978. **Members:** 750. **Publications:** Annual Report. BFF News, monthly. Newsletter.

★86★
Black Filmmakers Hall of Fame, Inc. (BFHFI)
405 14th St., Ste. 515
Oakland, CA 94612 Phone: (415)465-0804
Mary Perry Smith, Pres.

Description: Seeks to study, teach, and preserve the contributions of Black filmmakers to American cinema. Fosters cultural awareness through educational, research, and public service programs in the film arts. Holds film-lecture series, Black Filmworks Festival, and annual International Film Competition; presents annual awards. Maintains biographical archives and speakers' bureau. **Founded:** 1973. **Members:** 500. **Budget:** $200,000. **Telecommunications Services:** Fax, (415)839-9858. **Publications:** Black Filmworks, annual. Also publishes catalog.

★87★
Black Military History Institute of America (BMHIA)
c/o Col. William A. De Shields
404 Golf Course Ct.
Arnold, MD 21012 Phone: (301)757-4250
Col. William A. De Shields, Exec. Officer

Description: Individuals interested in promoting the military achievements of Black Americans and publicizing other aspects of Black history. Seeks to: provide archival facilities to collect, preserve, and exhibit materials pertaining to military history; motivate and support underprivileged youths by using military role models as a source of inspiration; foster a spirit of camaraderie and goodwill among all persons sharing an interest in community involvement programs for the underprivileged. Sponsors slide lectures and photographic exhibit. Maintains speakers' bureau. **Founded:** 1987. **Members:** 60. **Budget:** $50,000. **Regional Groups:** 1. Chapters: 1. **Publications:** Newsletter, quarterly.

★88★
Black PAC
PO Drawer 6865
McLean, VA 22106 Phone: (703)442-7510
William Keyes, Exec. Officer

Description: Represents political interests of working-class and middle-class African-Americans. Does not lobby, but assists in the election of favorable candidates to Congress. Supports economic growth, traditional family values, and a strong national defense. **Founded:** 1984.

★89★
Black Psychiatrists of America (BPA)
c/o Dr. Thelissa Harris
664 Prospect Ave.
Hartford, CT 06105 Phone: (203)236-2320
Dr. Thelissa Harris, Pres.

Description: Black psychiatrists, either in practice or training, united to promote Black behavioral science and foster high quality psychiatric care for Blacks and minority group members. Sponsors public information service. Bestows awards; maintains speakers' bureau and biographical archives; compiles statistics; conducts educational programs. **Founded:** 1968. **Members:** 550. **Regional Groups:** 10. **Publications:** BPA Quarterly, journal; Directory of Black Women in Psychology, periodic. Also has compiled and edited Bibliographic Guide to Materials on Black Women in the Social Sciences and Mental Health.

★90★
Black Resources Information Coordinating Services (BRICS)
614 Howard Ave.
Tallahassee, FL 32304 Phone: (904)576-7522
Emily A. Copeland, Pres.

Description: Designed to solidify the various sources of information and research by and about minority groups in America and convert them into a coordinated information system by using bibliographic control, storage, retrieval, transfer, and dissemination. Focuses on information by and about Afro-Americans, but also includes other minorities. Acts as referral and consulting service; aids in genealogical research and archival management and organization. Offers bibliographic services and lecture demonstrations on Afro-American culture. Sponsors seminars, workshops, and institutes. Conducts national exhibit program, which serves as a source of exposure for new books, publications, and other media forms. Maintains library of over 8000 items, including cassettes, slides, microfiche, and microfilms. Provides abstracting, indexing, and advisory services to Black studies programs and collections. **Founded:** 1972. **Members:** 670. **Publications:** Brics Bracs, quarterly. Journal. Media Showcase, annual. Minority Information Trade Annual. Newsletter, bimonthly. Also publishes Guide to Afro-American Resources.

★91★
Black Revolutionary War Patriots Foundation (BRWPF)
1612 K St. NW, Ste. 1104
Washington, DC 20006 Phone: (202)452-1776
Maurice A. Barboza, Pres.

Description: Raises private funds for the establishment of a memorial, in Washington, DC, to Black patriots of the American Revolutionary War. **Founded:** 1985. **Budget:** Less than $25,000. **State Groups:** 2. **Local Groups:** 1. **Also known as:** The Patriots Foundation.

★92★
Black Rock Coalition (BRC)
PO Box 1054, Cooper Station
New York, NY 10276
Donald C. Eversley, Exec. Officer

Description: Artists, musicians, writers, and supporters of alternative/Black music. (Alternative/Black music refers to popular musical styles, such as rock, that are usually not performed or recorded by Black artists and musicians.) Works to foster change in the conventional operation and classification of Black music and musicians within the entertainment industry. Seeks to counteract competition among musicians through networking programs and the sharing of resources. Opposes what the group terms the American "apartheid-oriented" rock circuit, which BRC feels perpetuates racism, commerical restrictions, and double standards within the music industry that may deter Black artists from receiving the same musical freedom of expression and marketing privileges afforded White artists. Promotes, produces, and distributes alternative/Black music and provides information, technical expertise, and performance and recording opportunities for "musically and politically progressive musicians." Also works to increase the visibility of Black rock artists in music media and on college radio stations. Conducts seminars on all aspects of music, musical technology, and the entertainment industry. Offers concert promotion services. Plans to develop videotape recording opportunities for the archival documentation of cultural events. **Founded:** 1985. **Members:** 50. **Budget:** Less than $25,000. **Publications:** Ravers, 4-6/year.

★93★
Black Silent Majority Committee of the U.S.A. (BSMC)
2714 West Ave.
Box 5519
San Antonio, TX 78201 Phone: (512)340-2424
Clay Claiborne, Dir.

Description: Seeks to show the people of America and the world that there is a Black majority in the U.S. which is patriotic and believes in saluting the flag, going to church, and paying taxes. Organizes Americans who do not want to be identified with Black "radicals" and emphasizes the positive gains that Blacks have made. Works throughout the U.S. and the world for better race relations. Opposes forced busing and supports prayer in public schools. **Founded:** 1970. **Members:** 70,000. **Publications:** The Crusader, quarterly. Newspaper. Newsletter, bimonthly. Also publishes booklets and brochures. **Formerly:** National Black Silent Majority Committee.

★94★
Black Stuntmen's Association (BSA)
8949 W. 24th St.
Los Angeles, CA 90034 Phone: (213)870-9020
Eddie Smith, Pres.

Description: Men and women (ages 18 to 50) who are members of the Screen Actors Guild and the American Federation of Television and Radio Artists. Serves as an agency for stuntpeople in motion pictures and television. Conducts stunt performances at various local schools. Maintains library of television and motion picture films. Plans to operate school for Black stuntpeople. Offers placement service. **Founded:** 1966. **Members:** 34.

★95★
Black Tennis and Sports Foundation
1893 Amsterdam Ave.
New York, NY 10032 Phone: (212)926-5991
Kenneth R. Harris, Pres.

Description: Participants include members of the business community involved in sports who are dedicated to helping Black and minority inner-city children and teenagers and developing athletes interested in tennis or other individual sports such as skating and gymnastics. Acts as a source of support and resources for Black and minority young people. Organizes tennis teams and sponsors these teams and their coaches on trips and games overseas. Sponsors the Annual Arthur Ashe/Althea Gibson Tennis Classic in New York city. Conducts educational and charitable programs. Compiles statistics. Awards scholarships and grants. **Founded:** 1977. **Affiliated with:** International Tennis Federation; United States Tennis Foundation. **Formerly:** (1984) Black Tennis Foundation.

★96★
Black Veterans (BV)
686 Fulton St.
Brooklyn, NY 11217 Phone: (718)935-1116
Job Mashariki, Pres.

Description: Black veterans of the military services. To aid Black veterans in obtaining information concerning their rights, ways to upgrade a less-than-honorable discharge, and Veterans Administration benefits due them and their families. Seeks to prohibit discrimination against Black veterans. Provides educational programs; facilitates veterans' sharing of skills acquired while in service. Services include counseling and community workshops on veteran issues and a program to provide services to veterans in local prisons. Assists veterans who have suffered from the effects of Agent Orange, an herbicide containing dioxin, used as a defoliant in Vietnam until 1969. **Founded:** 1979.

★97★
Black Women in Church and Society (BWCS)
c/o Interdenominational Theological Center
671 Beckwith St. SW
Atlanta, GA 30314 Phone: (404)527-7740
Jacquelyn Grant Ph.D., Dir.

Description: Women in ministry, both ordained and laity. Seeks to provide: structured activities and support systems for Black women whose goals include participating in leadership roles in church and society; a platform for communication between laywomen and clergywomen. Conducts research into questions and issues pivotal to Black women in church and society. Sponsors charitable programs and semiannual seminar; compiles statistics. Maintains a research/resource center and a library with subject matter pertaining to liberation and Black theology, feminism, and womanist movements. **Founded:** 1982. **Computerized Services:** Mailing list. **Publications:** Black Women in Ministry, quadrennial. Directory.

★98★
Black Women in Publishing (BWIP)
PO Box 6275, F.D.R. Sta.
New York, NY 10150 Phone: (212)772-5951
Dolores Gordon, Pres.

Description: Designers, editors, financial analysts, freelancers, personnel directors, photographers, production managers, and publicists within the print industry. A networking and support group whose purpose is to encourage minorities interested in all sectors of book, newspaper, and magazine publishing. Promotes the image of minorities working in all phases of the book, newspaper, and magazine industries; recognizes achievements of minorities in the media. Works for a free and responsible press. Facilitates the exchange of ideas and information among members, especially regarding career planning and job security. Keeps members informed about the publishing industry and their impact on it. Encourages and works to maintain high professional standards in publishing. Collaborates with other organizations in striving to improve the status of women and minorities. Sponsors lectures, panel discussions, seminars, workshops, and other programs on topics such as computers in publishing, freelance journalism, images of minority women in literature, interviewing techniques, networking, magazine publishing, money management, office politics, trends in children's literature for minority children, and women and stress. Organizes social events. Maintains biographical archives, placement service, and a resume bank in collaboration with major corporations. **Founded:** 1979. **Publications:** Interface, bimonthly.

★99★
Black Women's Educational Alliance (BWEA)
6625 Greene St.
Philadelphia, PA 19119
Deidre Farmbey, Pres.

Description: Active and retired women in the field of education. Seeks a strong union among members in order to foster their intellectual and professional growth. Conducts public awareness programs to improve educational standards and delivery of educational services; works for equal opportunities for women. Bestows student scholarships and education and service awards; maintains speakers' bureau. Conducts instructional seminars and workshops. **Founded:** 1976. **Members:** 300. **Local Groups:** 2. **Publications:** BWEA Bulletin, periodic. BWEA Newsletter, semiannual.

★100★
Black Women's Network (BWN)
PO Box 12072
Milwaukee, WI 53212 Phone: (414)562-4500
Joan Prince, Pres.

Description: Black professional women organized to improve the political, economic, and educational conditions of minority women. Offers support services and networking opportunities to address issues affecting African-American women. **Founded:** 1979. **Members:** 56. **Publications:** Cross Roads, quarterly. Newsletter.

★101★
Black Women's Roundtable on Voter Participation (BWRVP)
1101 14th St. NW, Ste. 925
Washington, DC 20005 Phone: (202)898-2220
Sonia R. Jarvis, Exec.Dir.

Description: A program of the National Coalition on Black Voter Participation (see separate entry). Black women's organizations committed to social justice and economic equity through increased participation in the political process. Organizes voter registration, education, and empowerment programs in the Black community; emphasizes the importance of the women's vote. Seeks to: develop women's leadership skills through nonpartisan political participation; encourage Black women's involvement in discussions concerning the influence of the women's vote in elections. Supports volunteer coalitions that work on voter registration, voter education, and get-out-the vote efforts. Conducts series of forums. **Founded:** 1983. **Members:** 17. **Budget:** $50,000.

★102★
Black World Foundation (BWF)
PO Box 2869
Oakland, CA 94609 Phone: (415)547-6633
Robert Chrisman, Pres.

Description: Black persons united to develop and distribute Black educational materials and to develop Black cultural and political thought. Maintains Prisoner Fund to supply free copies of foundation publications to prisoners. Offers books in the areas of Black literature, history, fiction, essays, political anaylsis, social science, poetry, and art. Maintains library. **Founded:** 1969. Subscribers: 10,000. **Publications:** The Black Scholar, bimonthly. Listing of Black Books in Print, annual. Also publishes books of poetry and on Black sociology.

★103★
Blacks Against Nukes (BAN)
3728 New Hampshire Ave. NW, Ste. 202
Washington, DC 20010 Phone: (202)882-7155
Brenda and Gregory Johnson, Co-Founders

Description: Black, Third World, or low-income individuals concerned with the threat of nuclear war and the effects of radiation. Seeks to educate Black, low-income, and Third World communities on the dangers of nuclear war, nuclear energy, and radiation already present in the environment, on the premise that there has been a "failure by anyone to address the Black community on the nuclear issue." Supports the use of nonnuclear energy sources; encourages Blacks to apply for government funds allotted for purchase of solar energy products. Strives to make Black youths aware of issues affecting their communities; encourages Black parents to boycott war toys. Offers seminars and workshops to community groups; provides speakers on nuclear weapons and the nuclear energy industry. Maintains library of news clippings concerning nuclear issues. Bestows annual scholarship to high school senior for writing the best essay opposing use of nuclear energy. **Founded:** 1981. **Publications:** Blacks Against Nukes–Newsletter, bimonthly.

★104★
Blacks in Government (BIG)
1820 11th St. NW
Washington, DC 20001 Phone: (202)667-3280
Marion Bowden, Pres.

Description: Federal, state, or local government employees or retirees concerned with the present and future status of Blacks in government. Develops training and other programs to enhance the liberty and sense of well-being of Blacks in government. Offers seminars and workshops for professional and nonprofessional government employees. **Founded:** 1975. **Members:** 6000. **Local Groups:** 100. **Publications:** Blacks in Government–News, quarterly. Newsletter.

★105★
Blacks in Law Enforcement (BLE)
256 E. McLemore Ave.
Memphis, TN 38106 Phone: (901)774-1118
Clyde R. Venson, Dir.

Description: Blacks employed by law enforcement agencies in the U.S.; others interested in the history of Blacks in U.S. law enforcement. Seeks to educate the public concerning the contributions made by Blacks in the field of law enforcement. Documents the lives and achievements of the first Blacks to participate in law enforcement in the U.S. Develops programs to improve the public image of law enforcement officers; has established a short-term training program for law enforcement officers. Provides children's services, including the operation of an animal farm. Operates library and hall of fame. Sponsors competitions; bestows scholarships and awards. Compiles statistics; maintains speakers' bureau. **Founded:** 1986. **Members:** 500. **Budget:** $45,000. **Telecommunications Services:** Toll-free number, (800)533-4649. **Publications:** Blacks in Law Enforcement, semiannual. Newsletter. Black Law Enforcement Directory, periodic. Top Blacks in Law Enforcement, annual. **Formerly:** (1988) Top Blacks in Law Enforcement.

★106★
Booker T. Washington Foundation (BTWF)
4324 Georgia Ave. NW
Washington, DC 20011
Charles E. Tate, Pres.

Description: Funded by federal agencies, foundations, and private corporations to provide policy research, technical assistance, and development and management expertise to minority entrepreneurs who are involved in business development. Maintains library in the areas of communications technology, media, community economic development, minority ownership, and business development. Presently inactive. **Founded:** 1967.

★107★
Campaign for Political Rights (CPR)
201 Massachusetts Ave., NE, Rm. 316
Washington, DC 20002 Phone: (202)547-4705
Sue Sullivan, Exec.Dir.

Description: Serves as national network of committed people and religious, civil liberties, environmental, academic, foreign policy, disarmament, press, women's, Native American, Black, and Latino organizations. Objectives are to end intelligence agency abuse at home and abroad; and to promote government accountability and access to information about government policies and actions. Provides educational materials and films, organizing assistance, press and publicity advice, and referral services for organizations. **Founded:** 1977. Board Members: 11. **Publications:** ALERT (news service), monthly. Organizing Notes (newsletter), 8/year. Also publishes Former Secrets (book on Freedom of Infomation Act), special reports, and guides. **Formerly:** Campaign to Stop Government Spying. Presently inactive.

★108★
Caribbean Action Lobby (CAL)
c/o Oswald B. Silvera
391 Eastern Pkwy.
Brooklyn, NY 11216 Phone: (718)756-1416
Oswald B. Silvera, Treas.

Description: Caribbeans, American-Caribbeans, and others interested in Caribbean issues. Seeks to educate Caribbean immigrants on subjects such as U.S. immigration laws, the U.S. government, and effective voting. Works to sensitize elected American officials to the needs of and issues affecting Caribbean immigrants. Activities include issue education, workshops, and seminars. **Founded:** 1980. **Members:** 4000. **Telecommunications Services:** Fax, (718)756-8519. **Publications:** Newsletter, monthly.

★109★
Caribbean American Intercultural Organization (CAIO)
PO Box 27099
Washington, DC 20038 Phone: (202)829-7468
Helen Madison Kinard, Pres.

Description: Citizens of the Caribbean-American community in the Washington, DC metropolitan area. Purpose is to promote, encourage, and maintain intercultural relations between the various peoples of the Caribbean and the people of the U.S. Sponsors exhibitions, forums, and audiovisual educational programs. Conducts charitable programs. Presents awards to outstanding individuals of Caribbean ancestry who have made significant contributions to the development of the U.S., Caribbean, or Third World. Maintains speakers' bureau. **Founded:** 1958. **Members:** 170. **Telecommunications Services:** Fax, (202)842-0215. **Publications:** Newsletter, quarterly.

★110★
Caribbean Studies Association (CSA)
c/o Department of Social Sciences
Interamerican University of Puerto Rico
Call Box 5100
San German, PR 00753 Phone: (809)892-1095
Gilberto Arroyo, Sec.-Treas.

Description: Scholars and other professionals interested in Caribbean studies. Encourages, supports, and conducts professional, interdisciplinary research on the Caribbean; disseminates information about developments in the Caribbean. Presents the Annual Caribbean Review Award, in collaboration with Caribbean Review, to an individual who has made an outstanding contribution to Caribbean studies. Maintains biographical archives. **Founded:** 1974. **Members:** 700. **Budget:** $30,000. **Publications:** Caribbean Studies Newsletter, quarterly. Includes occasional Spanish texts, book notes, congress and conference news, research notes, commentaries on Caribbean current events, member news, and annual conference program.

★111★
Catholic Interracial Council of New York (CIC)
899 10th Ave.
New York, NY 10019 Phone: (212)237-8255
Hubert Johnson, Exec.Asst.

Description: Promotes interracial justice. Works in cooperation with local parishes and governmental and voluntary groups to combat bigotry and discrimination and to promote social justice for all racial, religious, and ethnic groups. Sponsors research, educational forums, workshops, and community action programs. Presents annual John LaFarge Memorial Award for Interracial Justice to community leaders and annual Hoey Award to community leaders who have worked to promote objectives of the council. Presents scholarship awards. Maintains speakers' bureau and library of 500 volumes. **Founded:** 1934. **Members:** 1600. **Budget:** $150,000. **Publications:** Interracial Review, quarterly. News, quarterly. Also publishes transcripts of forums, symposia, conferences, and workshops.

★112★
Catholic Negro-American Mission Board (CNAMB)
2021 H St. NW
Washington, DC 20006 Phone: (202)331-8542
Rev.Msgr. Paul A. Lenz, Exec.Dir.

Description: Supports Catholic sisters' teaching program among Blacks. **Founded:** 1907. **Members:** 14,000. **Budget:** $310,000. **Telecommunications Services:** Fax, (202)331-8542. **Publications:** Educating in Faith, quarterly. **Formerly:** (1970) Catholic Board for Mission Work Among the Colored People.

★113★
Center for Constitutional Rights (CCR)
666 Broadway, 7th Fl.
New York, NY 10012 Phone: (212)614-6464
[illegible]r, Exec.Dir.

Description: "To halt and reverse the steady erosion of civil liberties in the U.S." Works in areas such as abuse of the grand jury process, women's rights, civil rights, freedom of the press, racism, electronic surveillance, criminal trials, and affirmative action. Conducts the Ella Baker Student Program, the Movement Support Network, and in Mississippi, The Voting Rights Project. sponsors training for law student interns. Maintains speakers' bureau. Distributes legal briefs. **Founded:** 1966. **Budget:** $1,800,000. **Telecommunications Services:** Cable, Centerites NY; fax, (212)614-6499. **Publications:** Annual Report. Listing of litigation and educational programs of the center. **Formerly:** (1967) Civil Rights Legal Defense Fund; (1970) Law Center for Constitutional Rights.

★114★
Center for Democratic Renewal (CDR)
PO Box 50469
Atlanta, GA 30302 Phone: (404)221-0025
Daniel Levitas, Exec.Dir.

Description: Advocates federal prosecution of the Ku Klux Klan and any groups or individuals involved in racist violence. Seeks to build public opposition to racist groups and their activities, and assist victims of bigoted violence. Works with trade unions, public officials, and religious, women's, civil rights, and grass roots organizations. Programs include education, research, victims' assistance, community organizing, leadership training, and public advocacy. Acts as a national clearinghouse for community-based response to hate group activities. Maintains network of lawyers and archive on far-right activities, individuals, and organizations; conducts seminars, specialized education programs, and research on trends in the far right; compiles data; maintains speakers' bureau. Constituencies: African Americans; Educators; Labor; Legal; Media; Minorities; Religious; Women; Youth. **Founded:** 1979. **Publications:** The Monitor, bimonthly. Reports on White supremacist efforts and activities. **Formerly:** (1985) National Anti-Klan Network.

★115★
Center for Sickle Cell Disease (CSCD)
2121 Georgia Ave., NW
Howard University
Washington, DC 20059 Phone: (202)636-7930
Roland B. Scott M.D., Dir.

Description: Seeks to foster education and research in sickle cell disease and to improve patient care. Holds scientific seminars and sickle cell "grand rounds." Conducts experimental research on antisickling agents and preservation through freezing of sickled blood cells.

Operates the Mid-Atlantic Regional Counseling Program, in collaboration with 3 other clinics, to provide screening and counseling for couples "at risk" of having children with sickle cell disease and other hemoglobinopathies. Maintains speakers' bureau and 380 volume library. Provides children's services. Compiles statistics and bestows awards. **Founded:** 1972. **Budget:** Less than $25,000. **Publications:** Bibliography, periodic. Center for Sickle Cell Disease-Annual Report. **Formerly:** Center for Sickle Cell Anemia.

★116★
Center for the Study of Human Rights (CSHR)
1108 International Affairs Bldg.
Columbia University
New York, NY 10027 Phone: (212)854-2479
Dr. J. Paul Martin, Exec.Dir.

Description: Academic advisers (23) and directors (11). Promotes teaching and scholarship in the field of human rights. Sponsors interdisciplinary human rights research. Offers advice, fellowships, and other assistance in conducting and financing such research; provides assistance in teaching and curriculum development. Operates library; offers consultation service, which provides information on human rights research, resources, and programs at other institutions. **Founded:** 1977. **Members:** 29. **Publications:** Annual Report. Center for the Study of Human Rights-Newsletter, quarterly. Includes bibliographies, calendar of events, course listings, and information on funding opportunities.

★117★
Center for Third World Organizing (CTWO)
3861 Martin Luther King Jr. Way
Oakland, CA 94609 Phone: (415)654-9601
Gary Delgado, Dir.

Description: Provides training, issue analyses, and research to low-income minority organizations including welfare, immigrant, and Native American rights groups. Monitors and reports on incidents of discrimination against people of color. Sponsors Minority Activist Apprenticeship Program, which works to develop minority organizers and leaders for minority communities. Sponsors seminars on issues affecting minorities. Maintains speakers' bureau; operates placement service. Compiles statistics. **Founded:** 1980. **Budget:** $1,000,000. **Local Groups:** 200. **Publications:** Directory of Church Funding Sources, periodic. Issue Pac, quarterly. Minority Trendsetter, quarterly. Also publishes Surviving America: What You're Entitled to and How to Get It, Images of Color: A Guide to Media from and for Asian, Black, Latino and Native American Communities, occasional papers series, guides, and manuals.

★118★
Center for Urban Black Studies (CUBS)
Graduate Theological Union
2465 LeConte Ave.
Berkeley, CA 94709 Phone: (415)841-8401
Dorsey O. Blake, Dir.

Description: Theological students and laypersons studying for the ministry; members of community groups. Provides seminarians and laypersons with resources "to respond to life in the urban community and to represent its oppressed minority people." Develops and offers courses, seminars, and other training programs dealing with issues of race, social justice, urban life, and the Black religious experience. Initiates new ministries; develops and implements community service programs; counsels and assists Black seminarians in placement and in obtaining and developing employment. Sponsors Martin Luther King, Jr. lectures, emphasizing Black cultural creativity. Conducts workshops and seminars addressing racial justice, church and race, and urban ministry. **Founded:** 1969.

★119★
Center on Budget and Policy Priorities (CBPP)
777 N. Capitol St. NE, Ste. 705
Washington, DC 20002 Phone: (202)408-1080
Robert Greenstein, Dir.

Description: Promotes better public understanding of the impact of federal and state governmental spending policies and programs primarily affecting low and moderate income families and individuals; acts as resource center and information clearinghouse for the media, national and local organizations (including major church denominations), and individuals. Areas of research include national poverty trends, tax policy, housing affordability, effectiveness and funding for social programs, hunger and nutrition issues, unemployment, and minimum wage. Maintains library; compiles statistics. Conducts special studies on minorities and poverty. Organizes educational campaign concerning the Earned Income Tax Credit. **Founded:** 1981. **Budget:** $1,300,000. **Telecommunications Services:** Fax, (202)543-1915. **Publications:** Women, Infants, and Children Newsletter, monthly. Also publishes fact sheets, articles, and reports, including: A Place to Call Home: The Crisis in Housing for the Poor, Poverty in Rural America: A National Overview, Making Work Pay: A New Agenda for Poverty Policies, Shortchanged: Recent Developments in Hispanic Poverty, Income, and Unemployment, Still Far From the Dream: Recent Developments in Black Poverty, Income, and Unemployment, Saving to Serve More: Ways to Reduce WIC Infant Formula Costs, and Holes in the Safety Net: Poverty Programs and Policies in the States.

★120★
Chi Delta Mu Fraternity
c/o Henry Wineglass, R.Ph.
1012 10th St. NW
Washington, DC 20001 Phone: (202)529-4345
Henry Wineglass R.Ph., Sec.

Description: To improve relationships among physicians, dentists, and pharmacists so that they may better serve their respective communities. Maintains revolving loan funds; bestows awards. **Founded:** 1913. **Members:** 650. **Budget:** Less than $25,000. **Publications:** Dragon, annual. Newsletter, quarterly. Proceedings, annual.

★121★
Chi Eta Phi Sorority
3029 13th St. NW
Washington, DC 20009 Phone: (202)232-3858
Jewell Gaither R.N., Exec.Sec.

Description: Professional sorority - registered and student nurses. Objectives are to: encourage continuing education; stimulate friendship among members; develop working relationships with other professional groups for the improvement and delivery of health care services. Sponsors leadership training seminars every two years and holds additional seminars at the local, regional, and national levels. Offers educational programs for entrance into nursing and allied health fields. Presents scholarships and other financial awards to assist students. Maintains health screening and consumer health education programs; volunteers assistance to senior citizens; sponsors recruitment and retention programs for minority students in nursing. **Founded:** 1932. **Members:** 5000. **Publications:** Chi Line, semiannual. Newsletter. The Directory, triennial. Glowing Lamp, annual. Also publishes History of Chi Eta Phi Sorority, Inc and annotated bibliography of members' publications; has also published Mary Eliza Mahoney, America's First Black Professional Nurse.

★122★
Cities in Schools (CIS)
1023 15th St. NW, Ste. 600
Washington, DC 20005 Phone: (202)861-0230
William E. Milliken, Pres.

Description: To promote an increase in attendance and grade improvement among underprivileged school children and thus enhance their opportunities for employment. Works to help cities and communities develop leadership cooperation among public and private sector institutions (including the school system, business community, and public and private social service agencies) in order to assist in the training and education of young people. Provides training and technical assistance through national and regional centers. Since initiated in Atlanta, GA, the CIS program has been duplicated in numerous cities throughout the U.S.. **Founded:** 1974. **Budget:** $2,700,000. **Regional Groups:** 5. **Telecommunications Services:** Fax, (202)289-6642. **Publications:** Annual Report. Newsletter, quarterly. Also publishes technical manuals and brochure.

★123★
Citizens' Commission on Civil Rights (CCCR)
2000 M St. NW, Ste. 400
Washington, DC 20036 Phone: (202)659-5565
Dr. Arthur Flemming, Chm.

Description: Bipartisan former federal cabinet officials concerned with achieving the goal of equality of opportunity. Objectives are to: monitor the federal government's enforcement of laws barring discrimination on the basis of race, sex, religion, ethnic background, age, or handicap; foster public understanding of civil rights issues; formulate constructive policy recommendations. **Founded:** 1982. **Members:** 16. **Telecommunications Services:** Fax, (202)293-2672. **Publications:** One Nation Indivisible: The Civil Rights Challenge For the 1990s, Barriers to Registration and Voting: An Agenda for Reform, and reports on fair housing, busing and the Brown Decision, and affirmative action; provides press releases.

★124★
Citizens for a Better America (CBA)
PO Box 356
Halifax, VA 24558 Phone: (804)476-7757
Cora Tucker, Pres.

Description: Churches and individuals united to create a better America by strengthening individual rights in the U.S. Serves as a public advocacy organization that lobbies for civil rights and environmental legislation. Conducts legal research in civil rights cases; provides research services to communities investigating issues such as fair housing and toxic waste disposal. Maintains placement and children's services; operates charitable program; bestows awards; compiles statistics. Sponsors annual Citizenship Day of Prayer. **Founded:** 1975. **Members:** 500. **Local Groups:** 5. **Publications:** Newsletter, monthly. Yearly Report. Also publishes special issue bulletins; has also published 10-Year Report.

★125★
City Kids Foundation (CKF)
57 Leonard St.
New York, NY 10013 Phone: (212)925-3320
Laurie Elizabeth Meadoff, Pres.

Description: Designs and organizes youth initiative programs including: City Kids Coalition, which works with multiracial teenagers from schools and youth groups to organize projects and events; City Kids Speak, an annual event which provides a platform for young people to express themselves on youth issues; Developing the Manhattan Empire, a youth social and cultural center in Manhattan. Collaborates with professionals to provide social services and job training. Conducts workshops. Primary programs are currently conducted in the New York City area, but plans to expand activities internationally. **Founded:** 1984. **Budget:** $1,000,000. **Telecommunications Services:** Fax, (212)925-0128. **Publications:** Monthly Letter. **Formerly:** (1989) Network International.

★126★
Co-Ette Club
2020 W. Chicago Blvd.
Detroit, MI 48206 Phone: (313)867-0880
Mary-Agnes Miller Davis, Founder & Chm.

Description: Teenage high school girls "outstanding in one or all of the following categories - Academic Scholarship, School and Community, Extra-Curriculars, Community Volunteer Service, and Leadership"; membership consists primarily of Black girls, but is open to any girl; number of members limited to 35 per chapter. Helps members channel interests and become leaders in educational, cultural, and artistic activities on local and national levels; maintains speakers' bureau and museum. Offers placement services. Raises funds for United Negro College Fund (see separate entry) and contributes to local charity and social service groups in each community. Assisted in establishing the metropolitan Detroit Teen Conference Coalition. Offers John Fitzgerald Kennedy Memorial Award annually for distinguished humanitarian service or concern. **Founded:** 1941. **Local Groups:** 35. **Publications:** Co-Ette Manual, annual. Co-Ette Souvenir Magazine, annual. Membership Directory, periodic. Newsletter, periodic.

★127★
Coalition of Black Trade Unionists (CBTU)
PO Box 73120
Washington, DC 20056-3120 Phone: (202)429-1203
William Lucy, Pres.

Description: Members of 76 labor unions united to maximize the strength and influence of Black and minority workers in organized labor. Activities include voter registration and education, improvement of economic development, and employment opportunities for minority and poor workers. Sponsors regional seminars. **Founded:** 1972. **Local Groups:** 27. **Publications:** Bulletin, quarterly.

★128★
Coalition on Southern Africa (CSA)
c/o Bishop Richard L. Fisher
Episcopal District Office, Ste. 701
607 N. Grand Ave.
St. Louis, MO 63103 Phone: (314)531-1112
Bishop Richard L. Fisher, Exec. Officer

★129★
College Language Association (CLA)
c/o Lucy C. Grigsby
Clark Atlanta University
James P. Brawley Dr. at Fare St.
Atlanta, GA 30314 Phone: (404)880-8000
Lucy C. Grigsby, Sec.

Description: Teachers of English and modern foreign languages, primarily in Black colleges and universities. Presents CLA Award for scholarly publication; also sponsors creative writing award to students in member colleges. Maintains placement service. **Founded:** 1937. **Members:** 350. **Publications:** CLA Journal, quarterly. Covers English language and literature. **Formerly:** (1949) Association of Modern Language Teachers in Negro Colleges.

★130★
Commission for Catholic Missions Among the Colored People and the Indians (CCMACPI)
2021 H St. NW
Washington, DC 20006 Phone: (202)331-8542
Rev.Msgr. Paul A. Lenz, Exec.Dir.

N/A

Description: Coordinates the distribution of funds from the annual Black and Indian Mission Collection in Catholic churches across the U.S.; these funds go to support priests, nuns, and other religious workers at Black and Indian missions and schools. Compiles statistics. **Founded:** 1884. **Telecommunications Services:** Fax, (202)331-8544. **Publications:** Posters and other promotional materials.

★131★
Commission for Racial Justice (CRJ)
475 Riverside Dr., Rm. 1948
New York, NY 10115 Phone: (212)870-2077
ev.Dr. Benjamin F. Chavis Jr., Exec.Dir.

N/A

Description: A racial justice agency representing the 1.7 million members of the United Church of Christ. Promotes human rights programs and strategies to foster racial justice in Black, Third World, and other minority communities. **Founded:** 1963. **Budget:** $1,200,000. **Publications:** Civil Rights Journal, weekly. Commission News, 3/year. Also publishes The Black Family: An Afro-Centric Perspective and Like A Ripple On A Pond: Crisis, Challenge, Change (a resource book on the plight of displaced homemakers).

★132★
Commission on U.S. African Relations (CUSAR)
c/o International Center for Development Policy
731 8th St. SE
Washington, DC 20003 Phone: (202)547-3800
Nenzi Plaatjies, Exec. Officer

N/A

Description: Businessmen, church officials, former government officials, scholars, and others. Primarily a research and educational commission of the International Center for Development Policy. Provides resources and information to the president, congressional representatives, and other officials on U.S.-African issues. Members, referred to as Commissioners, pool their knowledge and expertise in the preparation of reports for Congress, the media, and other interested parties. Encourages greater participation of Americans in African issues. Maintains library consisting of current publications, congressional reports, government documents, and reports from other institutions concerning African affairs. **Founded:** 1983. **Members:** 105. **Budget:** $50,000. **Telecommunications Services:** Fax, (202)546-4784; telex, 5106017738. **Publications:** Briefings and Reports, periodic.

★133★
Committee of Black Gay Men (CBGM)
PO Box 7209
Chicago, IL 60680 Phone: (312)248-5188
Larry Baker, Exec.Sec.

7/7

Description: Purposes are to disseminate information concerning problems that affect Black members of the gay community and to provide services through outreach programs and networking with similar organizations. Attempts to gain recognition and understanding within the church in the Black community; plans to establish an alcoholism and substance abuse program; cooperates with food pantries in the Chicago, IL area. Plans a program to disseminate information on AIDS to the Black homosexual community. Offers services, including: blood pressure screening; individual and group counseling; access to hot lines and other crisis intervention and prevention services; arrangements for legal defense and legal advice; religious educational counseling; information on lobbying techniques for city, state, and national legislation; protection and support for homosexual teachers and students; support and promotion of persons in art fields. Conducts seminars and workshops. Maintains speakers' bureau; compiles statistics. **Founded:** 1978. **Members:** 1500. **Budget:** $70,000. **Regional Groups:** 4. **Computerized Services:** Data bases. **Telecommunications Services:** Telephone referral services. **Publications:** Newsletter, monthly.

★134★
Committee of Concerned Africans (CCA)
PO Box 1892
Trenton, NJ 08608 Phone: (609)771-1666
Kassahun Checole, Coord.

Description: Scholars, students, and other interested volunteers. Monitors violations of human rights in Africa. Publicizes issues and developments regarding such violations; petitions states and organizations regarding the conditions of peoples or individuals whose human rights are being violated; conducts seminars and teach-ins. **Founded:** 1980. **Members:** 100. **Publications:** Working Papers, monthly.

★135★
Conference of Minority Public Administrators (COMPA)
1120 G St. NW, Ste. 500
Washington, DC 20005 Phone: (202)393-7878
~~Shirley H. Wester~~, Exec.Dir. JOHN THOMAS

7/13

Description: A section within the American Society for Public Administration. Members of ASPA who belong to a minority group or are interested in the promotion of minorities within public administration. Seeks to affect the betterment of government and advance excellence in public service. **Founded:** 1971. **Members:** 700. **Publications:** COMPA Spectrum, quarterly.

★136★
Conference of Prince Hall Grand Masters (CPHGM)
4311 Portland Ave., S.
Minneapolis, MN 55407 Phone: (612)825-2474
Morris Miller, Steering Comm.Chm.

Description: Black fraternal order united to coordinate efforts of member groups in providing leadership in and formulating goals for the Black community. Sponsors seminars and workshops to train progressive leaders. Operates charitable program; maintains biographical archives; sponsors competitions and bestows awards. **Founded:** 1919. **Members:** 300,000. **State Groups:** 44. **Telecommunications Services:** Fax, (612)758-5000. **Publications:** The Conservators, quarterly. Prince Hall Masonic Directory, biennial. Local lodges publish newsletters and proceedings.

★137★
Congress of National Black Churches (CNBC)
600 New Hampshire Ave. NW, Ste. 650
Washington, DC 20037 Phone: (202)333-3060
H. Michael Lemmons, Exec.Dir.

Disc

Description: Major Black denominations in the U.S. and Africa. Seeks to find answers to problems that confront Blacks in the U.S. and Africa, including economic development, family and social support, housing, unemployment, education, and foreign relations. Focus is on religious education and evangelism. Conducts theological education programs and an educational program for nondegreed ministers; also conducts banking, insurance, and purchasing programs for church administrations. Compiles statistics. Plans to sponsor research programs. **Founded:** 1978. **Members:** 6. **Publications:** Newsletter, quarterly.

★138★
Congress of Racial Equality (CORE)
1457 Flatbush Ave.
Brooklyn, NY 11210 Phone: (718)434-3580
Roy Innis, Chm.

Description: Persons of African ancestry. Black nationalist organization whose philosophy is based on the tenets of Marcus Garvey (1887-1940), Jamaican-born Black nationalist leader, and his progenitors. Looks to Africa, the fatherland, for inspiration; seeks the right of Black people to govern themselves in those areas which are demographically and geographically defined as theirs. Compiles statistics; engages in research. Maintains placement service, charitable program, and speakers' bureau; bestows awards. Sponsors CORE Community School, a private alternative school for grades one through eight in the Bronx, NY and Memphis, TN. **Founded:** 1942. **Budget:** $750,000. **Regional Groups:** 5. **State Groups:** 39. **Local Groups:** 116. **Publications:** CORE Magazine, quarterly. The Correspondent, monthly. Newsletter. Equal Opportunity Employment Journal, monthly. Also publishes Population Studies and Profiles in Black.

★139★
Congressional Black Associates (CBA)
L'Enfant Plaza Sta. SW
PO Bos 23793
Washington, DC 20026 Phone: (202)225-4288
Michael Wallace, Pres.

Description: Black congressional staff members. Provides information on the operations of the federal government to members and the Black community; fosters contacts among members and the community. Works to enhance the social, political, and economic status of all people, but concentrates on the Black experience in America. Organizes political education seminars; maintains placement service. **Founded:** 1979. **Publications:** CBA Newsnotes, periodic. News from Congressional Black Associates, quarterly. **Formerly:** Pendulum.

★140★
Cooperative Assistance Fund (CAF)
2100 M St., NW, Ste. 306
Washington, DC 20037 Phone: (202)833-8543
David C. Rice, Exec.V.Pres.

Description: Foundations and charitable organizations. Purpose is to use private investment capital to support the economic development of minority and low-income communities. Goal is to reduce poverty and dependence by stimulating economic development. Provides the opportunity for organizations to work together to address the unfulfilled needs of these communities. Pools funds from foundations and other investors to obtain resources for equity-type program related investments (PRI). Provides PRI services such as evaluating proposals, structuring financing, and monitoring results. Conducts research on developing means of channeling capital into low-income areas. **Founded:** 1968. **Members:** 12. **Budget:** $469,000. **Telecommunications Services:** Fax, (202)833-1432. **Publications:** Annual Report. Also publishes 20 Years: A Report from the Cooperative Assistance Fund.

★141★
Council for a Black Economic Agenda (CBEA)
1367 Connecticut Ave. NW
Washington, DC 20036 Phone: (202)331-1103
Robert L. Woodson Sr., Exec. Officer

Description: Dedicated to advancing the economic self-sufficiency of Black Americans. Works to reverse the dependence of many Blacks on government programs; advocates strategies based on a spirit of free enterprise and individual initiative. Encourages full use of the Black community's own resources for selfhelp and development. Goals include: financial incentives for development of areas with vacant or underused property; legislation allowing tax write-offs for investments in small businesses that are in distressed areas; a program of underwriting rehabilitation, ownership, and management of public housing by residents' organizations; authorization for Black churches and other neighborhood institutions to arrange adoptions of those children presently within the government's foster care system; expanded educational choice for low-income persons; an increase in work incentives for poor families. The latter goal, in the council's view, would be achieved by: providing affordable day-care for children of working parents; boosting the earned income tax credit and the income tax exemption for dependents; allowing unemployment compensation and other government payments to be used for education, job training, or self-employment. **Founded:** 1984.

★142★
Council for Alternatives to Stereotyping in Entertainment (CASE)
139 Corson Ave.
Staten Island, NY 10301 Phone: (718)720-5378
Michael Johnson, Sec.

Description: Individuals in the arts and entertainment industry. Seeks to educate the public on the widespread, undesirable effects inflicted upon the entertainment industry by stereotyping. Disseminates information on self-image, reality perception, and receptivity to accurate performance feedback. Maintains speakers' bureau and 1000 volume library. **Founded:** 1982. **Members:** 25. **Publications:** Case Cares, quarterly.

★143★
Council of 1890 College Presidents (CCP)
Langston University
Langston, OK 73050 Phone: (405)466-2231
Ernest L. Holloway, Sec.-Treas.

Description: Presidents and chancellors of land-grant institutions attended predominantly by Blacks. (Land-grant institutions were established by an act of Congress in 1890.) **Founded:** 1913. **Members:** 18. **Formerly:** (1955) Conference of Presidents of Negro Land Grant Colleges; (1979) Council on Cooperative College Projects.

★144★
Council of Independent Black Institutions (CIBI)
PO Box 40519
Pasadena, CA 91104 Phone: (818)798-5406
Kofi Lomotey, Sec.

Description: Independent Black educational institutions and learning centers. Dedicated to the development of educational programs in historically Black institutions that promote a positive self-concept and encourage academic achievement. Conducts training workshops for teachers of independent Black institutions. Sponsors contests and trips; organizes camps. **Founded:** 1976. **Members:** 15. **Publications:** Fundisha, semiannual. Newsletter.

★145★
Council of the Great City Schools (CGCS)
1413 K St. NW, Ste. 400
Washington, DC 20005 Phone: (202)371-0163
Samuel B. Husk, Exec.Dir.

Description: Large city school districts. Conducts studies of problems shared by urban schools; coordinates projects designed to provide solutions to these problems; uses the findings and recommendations of studies for the improvement of education in the great cities. Provides informational support for legislative activities. Conducts seminars, workshops, and special projects to provide forum for members to share successful projects and to learn of new programs. Has studied: the educational needs of urban children exposed to the effects of discrimination; school financing; teacher preparation for urban schools; more functional approaches to out-moded urban schools; current status and needs in the areas of testing and technology. **Founded:** 1961. **Members:** 45. **Publications:** Council Directory, annual. Roster of Board of Directors, periodic. Teaching and Leading in the Great City Schools, periodic. Urban Education Review, weekly. Newsletter. Also publishes special reports and film reports; produces sound/slide presentation. **Formerly:** Research Council of the Great Cities Program for School Improvement.

7/13

★146★
Council on Career Development for Minorities (CCDM)
1341 W. Mockingbird Ln., Ste. 412-E
Dallas, TX 75247 Phone: (214)631-3677
Verna G. Bennett, Chm.

Description: Works to heighten the awareness and employability of minority college students and to improve career counseling and referral services offered to them. Provides programs to help minority students improve test-taking and learning skills. Promotes the inclusion of career education into college curricula and the establishment of career counseling and placement services. Conducts consultative visits by teams of specialists who evaluate the needs of a given institution and make recommendations for the creation or improvement of counseling and placement services. Serves as a consultant to colleges involving government grants. Sponsors training activities such as annual institute for new personnel, semiannual career services institute, and secretarial development workshops. Also provides professional development programs that offer training in techniques and theory of career development and current labor market and employment trends. Conducts Corporate Orientation Program which provides sophomore-level minority students with the opportunity to study actual business activities and the factors that affect their employability and chances for promotion in the corporate business world. Offers workshops for college presidents from historically Black colleges to improve awareness of the role and importance of career counseling and placement on the college campus. Also offers consultations to advise employers on policies, practices, and strategies involving the recruitment of college-trained minorities; provides training for recruiting personnel on minority interviewing techniques. Sends association representatives to meetings of similar organizations. Maintains Julius A. Thomas Fellowship Program to grant minority students the opportunity for graduate studies; awards one or two fellowship grants annually. **Founded:** 1964. **Budget:** $350,000. **Computerized Services:** Data base on historically Black colleges and universities and other educational institutions with large concentrations of minority students. **Publications:** CCDM Minority Student Recruitment Guide, biennial. Lists minority fraternities, sororities, honor societies, and professional organizations. Includes enrollment statistics. **Formerly:** (1984) College Placement Services.

★147★
Council on Interracial Books for Children (CIBC)
1841 Broadway, Rm. 608
New York, NY 10023 Phone: (212)757-5339
Melba Johnson Kgositsile, Exec.Dir.

Description: Promotes children's books and other learning materials that are free of bias based on race, sex, age, or physical disability. Reviews new children's books, television programs, and films; conducts studies and seminars. Develops criteria enabling teachers to identify and counteract racism and sexism in classroom materials. Administers the Racism and Sexism Resource Center for Educators, which develops and disseminates antiracist, antisexist teaching materials, books, pamphlets, lesson plans, fact sheets, and audiovisual materials. **Founded:** 1965. Sponsors: 26. Directors: 13. **Computerized Services:** Mailing list. **Publications:** Interracial Books for Children Bulletin, 8/year. Newsletter; includes book reviews, calendar of events, and research updates.

★148★
Council on Legal Education Opportunity (CLEO)
1800 M St. NW, Ste. 290
N. Lobby
Washington, DC 20036 Phone: (202)785-4840
Denise W. Purdie, Dir.

Description: Federally funded program that assists economically and educationally disadvantaged students gain entrance to American Bar Association approved law schools. Sponsors six-week summer institutes for selected college graduates and provides a $2200 annual living stipend to those certified summer institute graduates who continue in law school. **Founded:** 1968. **Budget:** $1,950,000.

★149★
Council on Southern Africa (CSA)
Box 22484
Denver, CO 80222 Phone: (303)758-8536
Ms. Don McAlvany, Contact

Description: Investors, academics, conservatives, and professionals united to objectively assess and educate Americans on the geopolitical events in southern Africa and the rest of the continent, and its strategic and economic significance to the West. Maintains library of 2000 volumes on history, the military, gold mining, politics, warfare, and international affairs. Conducts educational tours to southern Africa; sponsors seminars. **Founded:** 1974. **Members:** 5000. **Formerly:** (1984) Americans Concerned about Southern Africa.

★150★
Delta Sigma Theta Sorority
1707 New Hampshire Ave. NW
Washington, DC 20009 Phone: (202)483-5460
Rose McKinney, Exec.Dir.

Description: Public service sorority of Black women. Maintains Delta Research and Educational Foundation. **Founded:** 1913. **Members:** 175,000. **Budget:** $2,000,000. **Regional Groups:** 7. Active Chapters: 760. **Telecommunications Services:** Fax, (202)223-3929. **Publications:** The Delta, semiannual. Journal.

★151★ CB 7/7
Democratic Council on Ethnic Americans (DCEA)
430 S. Capitol St., SE
Washington, DC 20003 Phone: (202)863-8027
Seth Levin, Exec.Dir.

Description: Works to enhance the political participation and visibility of all ethnic Americans in the processes, projects, and decisions of the Democratic party. Promotes the full participation of ethnic American Democrats in Democratic party activities. Develops, articulates, and advocates issues that concern many ethnic American communities. Coordinates a national network of ethnic American Democrats which is neighborhood-based, that utilizes multilingual press, and other local media. Supports the election and appointment of candidates for national, state, and local offices who have demonstrated commitment to the goals of the council. **Founded:** 1983. **Publications:** Democratic Ethnic Calendar, annual. Ethnic Council Update, quarterly.

★152★ 7/13
Department of Civil Rights, AFL-CIO
815 16th St. NW
Washington, DC 20006 Phone: (202)637-5270
Richard Womack, Dir.

Description: Staff arm of the AFL-CIO (see separate entry) Civil Rights Committee. Serves as official liaison with women's and civil rights organizations and government agencies working in the field of equal opportunity; helps to implement state and federal laws and AFL-CIO civil rights policies; aids affiliates in the development of affirmative programs to expand opportunities for minorities and women; prepares and disseminates special materials on civil rights; speaks at union and civil rights institutes, conferences, and conventions; helps affiliates resolve complaints involving unions under Title VII of the 1964 Civil Rights Act and Executive Order 11246. **Founded:** 1955. **Publications:** AFL-CIO and Civil Rights, biennial.

★153★
Detroit Jazz Center (DJC)
2628 Webb
Detroit, MI 48206
Sam Sanders, Exec.Dir.

Description: Jazz artists, composers, educators, historians, critics, broadcasters, and supporters united to create a multipurpose clearinghouse for jazz. Components include: Professional Artists Program, which will provide management consulting services to the jazz musician; Jazz Studies Program, which consolidates existing jazz instruction and educational programs; Detroit Jazz Archive, which will provide an institutional approach to the archival, historical, research, and exhibition needs of the jazz and African-American music community; Creative and Administrative Services Program, which will provide concert production, recording, videotaping, and community arts consulting services; Community Services Program, which will include services such as the Jazz Art Gallery, Jazz Hot Line, and other support services. Maintains archives of 500 original tape recordings and 200 volumes. **Founded:** 1973. **Members:** 185. **Publications:** Detroit Jazz Center Calendar, annual. World Stage, monthly. Newsletter. Also publishes Jazz Space Detroit: Photographs of Black Music, Jazz and Dance. **Formerly:** (1980) Detroit Jazz Center/Jazz Research Institute.

★154★
Earl Warren Legal Training Program (EWLTP)
99 Hudson St., Ste. 1600
New York, NY 10013 Phone: (212)219-1900
Butler T. Henderson, Exec.Dir.

Description: Special project of the NAACP Legal Defense and Educational Fund (see separate entry). Primary goal is to increase the number of practicing Black lawyers in the U.S. Provides law scholarship aid (limited by available funds) to academically qualified entering students in need for the full three years of law school. Conducts one or more Lawyers Training Institutes each year, which are attended by both experienced and young minority lawyers. Seeks to retain a close personal and professional relationship with program graduates. Offers program on public interest law. Bestows awards. **Founded:** 1972. **Telecommunications Services:** Fax, (212)226-7592.

★155★
EDGES Group (EDGES)
Amerada Hess Corp.
1 Hess Plaza
Woodbridge, NJ 07095 Phone: (201)750-6408
Walter Vertreace, Pres.

Description: Entrepreneurs and management personnel. Membership and activities are concentrated in New York, New Jersey, and Connecticut, but the group plans to expand nationally. Facilitates the entry of Blacks into the private sector, government, and industry in management positions, and introduces Black vendors and suppliers of goods and services into the mainstream of American business. Focuses on issues of affirmative action and urban and community affairs. Bestows awards; offers scholarships. **Founded:** 1969. **Members:** 115. **Computerized Services:** Job Skills Bank, a system that matches resumes with job orders. **Publications:** Voice of EDGES, quarterly. Newsletter.

★156★
Episcopal Churchpeople for a Free Southern Africa (ECFSA)
339 Lafayette St.
New York, NY 10012 Phone: (212)477-0066
William Johnston, Pres.

Description: Episcopalian group united to help strengthen those who witness for freedom and equality. "Seeks to support and succor those who suffer from racist totalitarianism in South Africa and Namibia; to inform Americans of the violent and repressive nature of the regimes of those countries; and to help prepare and guide Americans as southern Africa moves toward drastic changes which threaten to draw the United States into standing on the wrong side of history." **Founded:** 1956. **Publications:** Newsletter, periodic. **Formerly:** (1985) Episcopal Churchmen for South Africa.

★157★
Episcopal Commission for Black Ministries (ECBM)
c/o Episcopal Church
815 2nd Ave.
New York, NY 10017 Phone: (212)867-8400
Rev. Canon Harold Lewis, Chm.

Description: Black members of the Episcopal church representing geographically diverse dioceses, including one diocese outside of the U.S. Works to strengthen the witness of Black Episcopalians in the church through programs that include parish and clergy development, scholarships and grants, and international relations. Provides financial assistance and consultations to parishes and church organizations. Compiles statistics; holds workshops. A commission of the Episcopal church. **Founded:** 1973. **Members:** 15. **Telecommunications Services:** Fax, (212)949-6781; toll-free number, (800)334-7626. **Publications:** Directory of Black Clergy in the Epicopal Church, annual. Linkage, 3/year. Newsletter. Has produced Black Ministries in the Episcopal Church (film).

★158★
Equal Employment Advisory Council (EEAC)
1015 15th St. NW
Washington, DC 20005 Phone: (202)789-8650
Jeffrey A. Norris, Pres.

Description: Principal attorneys and personnel officers representing companies and trade associations. Promotes and presents the mutual interests of employers and the public regarding affirmative action and equal employment opportunity practices. Sponsors equal employment training courses and seminars. **Founded:** 1976.

★159★
Equal Rights Congress (ERC)
4167 S. Normandy Ave.
Los Angeles, CA 90037 Phone: (213)291-1092
Nacho Gonzalez, Exec.Dir.

Description: National minority organizations united to struggle for equality of all people who have been discriminated against because of nationality, color, religion, sex, or economic status. Conducts educational program and seminars; provides training and technical assistance for organizing; maintains speakers' bureau and biographical archives; compiles statistics; sponsors competitions. **Founded:** 1976. **Budget:** Less than $25,000. **Regional Groups:** 2. **Local Groups:** 35. **Publications:** Equal Rights Advocate, bimonthly. Southern Advocate, bimonthly. Also publishes a series of pamphlets.

★160★
Eta Phi Beta Sorority
c/o Elizabeth Anderson
1724 Mohawk Blvd.
Tulsa, OK 74110 Phone: (918)425-7717
Elizabeth Anderson, Pres.

Description: Professional sorority - business. Conducts national projects concerning retarded citizens and retarded children. Presents scholarships and grants. Conducts leadership and career programs and seminars; sponsors competitions. Operates speakers' bureau; provides children's services; maintains charitable program; bestows awards. **Founded:** 1942. **Members:** 8000. **Budget:** Less than $25,000. **Regional Groups:** 6. Active Chapters: 85. **Publications:** Beeline, semiannual. Membership Directory, biennial. News, quarterly.

★161★
Ethiopian Community Mutual Assistance Association (ECMAA)
c/o Fetene Hailu
327 Union Sq., W.
New York, NY 10003 Phone: (212)627-8358
Fetene Hailu, Pres.

Description: Individuals of Ethiopian descent; members reside primarily in New York City metropolitan area. To advance the economic and social welfare of Ethiopians living in the U.S. Identifies the needs of the Ethiopian community, particularly regarding immigration and civil rights, and provides appropriate assistance. Works to strengthen communication among Ethiopians; aims to preserve Ethiopian culture as a source of historical identity; promotes understanding between Ethiopians and non-Ethiopians. Operates refugee assistance project that provides newly-arrived Ethiopians refugees or migrants with access to various educational, health, and other facilities; also offers overall orientation, guidance, and job placement assistance. Conducts a community-wide educational/information program with a view to hastening the acculturation and social adjustment efforts of members. Maintains museum. Plans to establish: cultural/educational center; emergency aid fund; job data bank; referral system. **Founded:** 1981. **Members:** 500.

★162★
Ethnic Cultural Preservation Council (ECPC)
6500 S. Pulaski Rd.
Chicago, IL 60629 Phone: (312)582-5143
Stanley Balzekas Jr., Dir.

Description: Membership includes North American ethnic museums, other museums, historical societies, libraries, archives, fraternal organizations, universities, university libraries, and cultural centers. Functions as vehicle for other ethnic and nonethnic groups to become viable art and education centers in their communities; aids in the exchange of ideas and helps to facilitate development of arts and humanities programs in other institutions. Provides information on grants; conducts cultural/artistic workshops; disseminates information on ethnic activities to other individuals and institutions. Offers referrals to information on artists, ethnic groups, and institutions. Sponsors seminars and exhibits. Operates on a national level, with primary concentration in Illinois, Indiana, Wisconsin, and Michigan. **Founded:** 1977. **Members:** 100. **Also known as:** Association of North American Museums, Libraries, Archives, Cultural Centers, and Fraternal Organizations.

★163★
Ethnic Employees of the Library of Congress (EELC)
6100 Eastview St.
Bethesda, MD 20817 Phone: (301)229-6366
George E. Perry, Pres.

Description: Ethnic and racial minority employees and majority employees of the Library of Congress. Objectives are to promote and strengthen brotherhood among ethnic employees and ethnic members of society, and to ensure equal employment opportunities in the Library of Congress and elsewhere. Monitors the Library of Congress with regard to its policies and practices affecting minority and majority employees through the American Black and Ethnic Helsinki Monitoring Group made up of leadership from EELC and Black Employees of the Library of Congress. Testifies annually before Congress; compiles statistics; provides statistical background material for court litigation; assists attorneys defending employees in racial, ethnic, and sex discrimination cases. Maintains library containing congressional correspondence, drafts, testimony, and labor management materials. Conducts research program on Library of Congress budget. **Founded:** 1973. **Publications:** Aletheia (in conjunction with the ABEHMG and BELC), periodic.

★164★
Ethnic Materials and Information Exchange RoundTable (EMIERT)
c/o American Library Association
Office for Library Outreach Services
50 E. Huron
Chicago, IL 60611 Phone: (312)944-6780
Mario Gonzales, Chm.

Description: Former members of the Social Responsibilities Round Table of the American Library Association (see separate entry). To exchange information about minority materials and library services for minority groups in the U.S. Conducts educational programs. Maintains library at Queens College of 2000 volumes of ethnic materials including directories, trade books, and filmstrips. **Founded:** 1971. **Members:** 530. **Budget:** Less than $25,000. **Publications:** Bulletin, quarterly. Directory of Ethnic Studies Librarians, periodic. Directory of Minority/Third World Publishers and Dealers, periodic. Also has published Multi-Ethnic Media: Selected Bibliographies; plans to publish a journal. **Formerly:** (1983) Ethnic Materials Information Exchange Task Force; (1987) Ethnic Materials Information Exchange RoundTable.

★165★
Federation of Masons of the World (FMW)
1017 E. 11th St.
Austin, TX 78702 Phone: (512)477-5380
M. J. Anderson Sr., Bd.Chm.

Description: Masonic jurisdictions in 22 countries. Researches and authenticates Masonic documents held by various jurisdictions. Organizes competitions; bestows awards; maintains library of 1005 volumes; compiles statistics. **Founded:** 1958. **Members:** 300,000. **Budget:** $105,000. **Regional Groups:** 38.

★166★
Federation of Southern Cooperatives and Land Assistance Fund (FSC/LAF)
100 Edgewood Ave., NE, Ste. 1228
Atlanta, GA 30303 Phone: (404)524-6882
Ralph Page, Exec.Dir.

Description: Cooperative associations chartered or doing business in the 17 southern states or the District of Columbia. Objectives are to assist people in building community-owned enterprises so they can control their own livelihood and to create housing, health care, and educational programs to complement economic development. Aids in the retention, acquisition, and development of Black land holdings.

Sponsors training programs in membership education, board responsibilities, management, and bookkeeping. Makes available to members full-time marketing specialists in both agricultural and handicraft production; also offers technical assistance in areas of accounting, establishing credit unions, consumer education, research in co-op expansion, market and product development, and improvement of production techniques. Provides legal, technical, and limited financial assistance to Black farmers and landowners throughout the Southeast. Operates the FSC Rural Training and Research Center in Sumter County, AL. Has established the "Forty Acres and a Mule" endowment fund for educational and social programs that have the potential to be self-supporting. Provides educational materials to member cooperatives. **Founded:** 1985. **Members:** 30,000. **Budget:** $850,000. **State Groups:** 9. **Publications:** Newsletter, quarterly.

★167★
Florence Ballard Fan Club (FBFC)
PO Box 36A02
Los Angeles, CA 90036 Phone: (213)658-5260
Alan K. White, Pres.

Description: Music fans and collectors. Purpose is to serve as a living memorial to Florence Ballard (1943-76). Ballard was a member of the original pop/soul trio the Supremes, which also included Diana Ross (1944-) and Mary Wilson (1944-), and who recorded a string of hits in the 1960s and early '70s. Ballard was replaced by Cindy Birdsong (1939-) in 1967 and then pursued a solo recording career. Seeks to: keep Ballard's memory alive in a positive light; honor Ballard's musical contributions and achievements; conduct research and disseminate information concerning Ballard's life and career; collect memorabilia related to Ballard and the original Supremes. Awards the Florence Ballard Scholarship annually to needy college students pursuing degrees in performing arts in accredited 4-year colleges and universities. **Founded:** 1985. **Members:** 275. **Publications:** Florence Ballard, quarterly. Newsletter; contains photographs, clippings, essays, and book and music reviews pertaining to Ballard.

★168★
Foundation for Ethnic Dance (FED)
1521 N. Hudson
Oklahoma City, OK 73103
Judith V. Hankins Brown, Pres.

Description: Answers inquiries on ethnic dance; provides advisory, consulting, reference, and literature searching services; conducts seminars and workshops; evaluates and analyzes data; makes referrals to other sources of information on ethnic dance. Services of the foundation are by appointment only and may be subject to a fee. Maintains biographical archives and library (in the process of being recataloged) of approximately 250 volumes, and several thousand recordings of ethnic (multiracial) dance. Offers specialized education programs; compiles statistics. **Founded:** 1967.

★169★
Foundation for Research in the Afro-American Creative Arts (FRACA)
PO Drawer I
Cambria Heights, NY 11411
Eileen Southern, Sec.

Description: Promotes research into the Afro-American creative arts including music, theatre, and dance. Maintains small library on Black music and history, including 15 taped oral histories of Black musicians. **Founded:** 1971. **Members:** 1000. **Budget:** $45,000. **Publications:** The Black Perspective in Music, annual. Journal.

★170★
Frederick Douglass Memorial and Historical Association (FDMHA)
c/o Mary E.C. Gregory
10594 Twin Rivers Rd., Apt. No. E-1
Columbia, MD 21044 Phone: (301)854-2938
Mary E.C. Gregory, Pres. Emeritus

Description: Chartered by Congress and administered by the National Park Service, U. S. Department of the Interior. Gives daily guided tours of the Frederick Douglass Memorial Home to inform visitors of how Douglass (1817-95) lived and of his contributions to the struggle for liberty, brotherhood, and citizenship. Maintains Douglass's personal library. Sponsors competitions; bestows awards; operates speakers' bureau. **Founded:** 1900. **Budget:** Less than $25,000. **Publications:** Brochure.

★171★
Free South Africa Movement (FSAM)
c/o TransAfrica
545 8th St. SE, Ste. 200
Washington, DC 20003 Phone: (202)547-2550
Randall Robinson, Exec.Dir.

Description: A project of TransAfrica (see separate entry) supported nationally by Black leadership and created to organize protests at South African consulates, American banks providing loans to South Africa, and corporations doing business in South Africa. Supporters, whose involvement in demonstrations was solicited by FSAM, have submitted to arrest in order to call attention to demands that the apartheid system in South Africa be abolished immediately. Seeks to bring about what the group sees as a more sensitive U.S. policy toward South Africa, in accordance with the goals of the South African majority supporting democratic rule. Encourages adoption and passage of divestment legislation at all government levels. **Founded:** 1984. **Telecommunications Services:** Fax, (202)547-7687.

★172★
Freedom Information Service (FIS)
PO Box 3568
Jackson, MS 39207 Phone: (601)352-3398
Jan Hillegas, Treas.

Description: Researches activities of workers, Blacks, and grass roots organizations through the FIS Deep South People's History Project. Maintains extensive Mississippi-centered library and archives. Distributes press releases on current southern news; reprints items on women's liberation and political education. **Founded:** 1965. **Budget:** Less than $25,000. **Publications:** FIS Mississippi Newsletter, periodic. Has also issued political and economic publications relevant to the civil rights movement and Black candidates. **Formerly:** (1965) Freedom Information Center.

★173★
Friends of Haiti (FOH)
1398 Flatbush Ave.
Brooklyn, NY 11210 Phone: (718)434-8100
Jill Ives, Coord.

Description: Volunteers interested in generating political and material support in the U.S. for the Haitian national liberation struggle, particularly the Mouvement Haitien de Liberation, an anti-imperialist, national liberation movement based in Haiti. To disseminate information on the Haitian social structure and the liberation process, with an emphasis on U.S. economic, political, and military involvement. Activities include conducting research and fundraising. Maintains data center on Haiti and the Caribbean and library of 3000 volumes. **Founded:** 1971. **Publications:** Produces slide show and film programs; contributes articles to publications.

★174★
Friends of Johnny Mathis (FJM)
2700 Jasper St. SE, No. 248
Washington, DC 20020 Phone: (202)678-6731
Alice T. Williams, Pres.

Description: Admirers of Johnny Mathis (1935-), singer of love ballads, including Misty and Chances Are. Promotes interest in Mathis' career and attendance at his concerts. **Founded:** 1983. **Members:** 30. **Budget:** Less than $25,000. **Publications:** Newsletter, quarterly. Includes news and reviews. **Formerly:** Mathis Magic Fan Club.

★175★
Fund for an Open Society (OPEN)
311 S. Juniper St., Ste. 400
Philadelphia, PA 19107 Phone: (215)735-6915
D. Richard Wenner, Exec.Dir.

Description: Mortgage fund established to provide an economic incentive in the form of financially advantageous loans to persons making housing moves that decrease segregation, that is, moves by a minority family to a White neighborhood or by a White family to a predominantly minority or well-integrated neighborhood. Purposes are to: help neighborhoods become interracial; help existing interracial neighborhoods maintain stability; help prevent displacement in gentrifying neighborhoods; strengthen neighborhoods by facilitating the purchase and rehabilitation of abandoned homes; help solve the problem of segregated schools by breaking down walls of residential segregation. Actively seeks the support of local institutions, businesses, and community groups. Provides mortgages below the prevailing rates. **Founded:** 1975. **Members:** 10,000. **Budget:** $549,000. **Publications:** Newsletter, periodic. Also publishes pamphlets.

★176★
Funders Committee for Voter Registration and Education (FCVRE)
c/o New World Foundation
100 E. 85th St.
New York, NY 10028 Phone: (212)249-1023
Colin Greer, Pres.

Description: Individuals representing 25 community, corporate, and private foundations. Purpose is to broaden the base of support for nonpartisan voter education and registration, particularly among underrepresented groups such as Blacks, Hispanics, women, and young people. Encourages funding organizations to support programs encouraging full political participation. Collects and disseminates information. Sponsors briefings and consultations on issues related to citizen participation in the U.S. Compiles statistics. **Founded:** 1983. **Members:** 35. **Publications:** Take Note, bimonthly. Newsletter. Year End Report. Also publishes Funders Guide to Voter Registration and Education (booklet) and fact sheets. **Formerly:** (1985) Ad Hoc Funders Committee for Voter Registration and Education.

★177★
Girl Friends (GF)
c/o Rachel Norcom Smith
2228 Lansing Ave.
Portsmouth, VA 23704 Phone: (804)397-1339
Rachel Norcom Smith, Exec. Officer

Description: Black women "who have been friends over the years." Primary aim is to "keep the fires of friendship burning." Conducts charitable projects and contributes annually to a selected charity. Bestows awards. **Founded:** 1927. **Members:** 1200. **Budget:** $120,000. **Local Groups:** 40. **Publications:** The Chatterbox, annual. Chatterletter, biennial. Directory, quinquennial. President's News and Friendship Letter, annual.

★178★
Global Women of African Heritage (GWAH)
PO Box 1033, Cooper Sta.
New York, NY 10003 Phone: (212)929-6449
Thelma Dailey-Stout, Founder & Pres.

Description: Women of African heritage worldwide. Purpose is to bring together women of African heritage to share common experiences and knowledge. Also seeks to share this knowledge with women who are not of African heritage. **Founded:** 1982.

★179★
Gospel Music Association (GMA)
PO Box 23201
Nashville, TN 37202 Phone: (615)242-0303
Donald W. Butler Sr., Exec.Dir.

Description: Music industry personnel and fans united to promote gospel music worldwide. Presents annual Dove Award for excellence in gospel music. Maintains speakers' bureau, museum, archive, library, and hall of fame; conducts educational and research programs; compiles statistics. **Founded:** 1964. **Members:** 2500. **Telecommunications Services:** Fax, (615)254-9755. **Publications:** Gospel Music Resource Guide, periodic. Newsletter, quarterly.

★180★
Gospel Music Workshop of America (GMWA)
3908 W. Warren St.
Detroit, MI 48234 Phone: (313)898-2340
Edward Smith, Exec.Sec.

Description: Individuals interested in gospel music. Promotes the enjoyment and performance of gospel and spiritual music. Offers musical instruction in performance and composition. **Founded:** 1966. **Members:** 18,000. **Publications:** Bulletin, annual.

★181★
Grand United Order of Odd Fellows (GUOOF)
262 S. 12th St.
Philadelphia, PA 19107 Phone: (215)735-8774
Joseph Boulware, Grand Sec.

Description: Individuals united for social and charitable purposes. Conducts seminars and professional training. Maintains library. **Founded:** 1843. **Members:** 108,000. **Regional Groups:** 7. **Publications:** Bulletin, quarterly. National Directory, biennial.

★182★
Haitian and Co-Arts Association
165 Park Row, Ste. 8-D
New York, NY 10038 Phone: (212)732-9735
Andre Letellier, Pres. & Exec.Dir.

Description: Professionals, business executives, clergy, artists, and others both in the U.S. and Haiti. Serves as a charitable educational assistance program "to voluntarily contribute to the elimination of hunger, eradication of disease, and promotion of literacy of deprived children of the peasants in rural areas of Haiti." Establishes rural and mobile free clinics to provide community-wide vaccination against polio, diphtheria, whooping cough, tuberculosis, yaws, malaria, and tetanus to needy children in remote villages. Provides villagers with advice on common tropical diseases, prenatal care, hygiene, and birth control. Promotes the self-sufficiency of small peasant farmers by encouraging cooperative rural agroforestry and aquaculture programs and new irrigation and farming techniques. Promotes literacy, with primary emphasis on modern industrial technology and advanced vocational trade schools. Provides medical and dental care, food, and shelter to needy schoolchildren enrolled in the five geographic departments of Haiti's rural areas. U.S. corporations and individuals donate funds, medical and dental supplies, drugs, seeds, and educational materials for distribution by the association. Also attempts to develop public interest in Haiti by sponsoring cultural endeavors in such fields as folklore, dance, music, history, literature, art, theater, photography, and wood sculpture; sponsors sports events and trade exhibits. **Founded:** 1956. **Members:** 582. **Formerly:** (1973) Haiti Voluntary Central Committee.

★183★
Haitian Coalition on AIDS (HCA)
50 Court St., Ste. 605
Brooklyn, NY 11201 Phone: (718)855-0972
Yvon Rosemond, Exec.Dir.

Description: Community centers; professional groups of doctors, journalists, lawyers, nurses, social workers, and civil rights and media representatives. Purpose is to educate the public concerning what the coalition feels is the discriminatory classification of Haitians as an ethnonational group that runs a high risk of contracting AIDS. Seeks to heighten AIDS awareness within the Haitian community. Offers social services and placement for victims of AIDS; provides counseling to their families. Sponsors conferences and seminars at churches and universities. Compiles statistics; maintains data base and speakers' bureau. Bestows awards; operates library. **Founded:** 1983. **Members:** 70. **Budget:** $300,000. **Regional Groups:** 8. **State Groups:** 7. **Local Groups:** 6.

★184★
Haitian Patriotic Union (UPH)
3900 Yuma St. NW
Washington, DC 20016 Phone: (202)362-4743
Paul Louis Casagnol, Pres.

Description: Exiled Haitians united to fight oppression and to promote social and economic programs that will aid in restoring the Haitian governmental structure to normalcy. Seeks to: organize a Haitian democratic opposition front and elect a democratic and constitutional government. Strongly opposes countries that support Haitian oppression and which condone the enslavement of the Haitian workers in the Dominican sugar fields. Works to restore human rights to Haiti. Promotes an integrated agricultural, industrial, and social development plan. Testifies before congressional committees and other government groups. Supports Amnesty International, Inter-American Commission on Human Rights, the United Nations, and the Human Rights Office of the State Department which have condemned the violations of human rights in Haiti. **Founded:** 1977. **Members:** 49. **Publications:** Bulletin, periodic. Haiti Patriote, monthly. Has also published Foreign Aid: Its Promises, Its Deceptions. **Also known as:** Union Patriotique Haitienne.

★185★
Haitian Refugee Center (HRC)
32 NE 54th St.
Miami, FL 33137 Phone: (305)757-8538
Rolande Dorancy, Exec.Dir.

Description: Provides free legal support and social services to indigent Haitian aliens in their political asylum proceedings and in federal court litigation designed to protect and establish the basic constitutional and international legal rights of asylum seekers. Works to impede deportations and to publicize the plight of Haitian refugees. Documents U.S. Immigration and Naturalization Service abuses. Represents Haitian refugees in class action lawsuits resulting from violations involving political asylum. During the rule of the Duvalier family more than 1.5 million people have fled Haiti, according to the center. **Founded:** 1974. Directors: 21. **Publications:** Press releases, legal documents, and briefs.

★186★
Hola Kumba Ya!
PO Box 50173
Philadelphia, PA 19132 Phone: (215)848-5118
Imani Lumumba, Exec.Dir.

Description: Participants are folk artists including storytellers, craftsmen and women, ethnic dancers, and musicians. Works to preserve, promote, and perpetuate the work of traditional folk artists. Seeks to demonstrate how traditional arts can be used as a positive educational tool. Provides resource information to schools, museums, festivals,and communities. Sponsors folk art programs in conjunction with the Artist Network Program. Conducts workshops, showcases, storytelling performances, charitable programs, and annual Unknown Ancestors program. Maintains library, museum, and speakers' bureau. **Founded:** 1986. **Budget:** $50,000. **Publications:** Newsletter, quarterly.

★187★
Horace Mann Bond Center for Equal Education (HMBCEE)
University of Massachusetts
Library Tower
Amherst, MA 01003 Phone: (413)545-0327
Meyer Weinberg, Dir.

Description: School boards, lawyers, and teachers. To perpetuate the memory and contributions of Dr. Horace Mann Bond (1904-73), distinguished Black educator and scholar. Serves as national clearinghouse of research and information on racism, desegregation, anti-Semitism, and other social issues, aimed at contributing to the achievement of a superior education for all children. Collects clippings, articles, books, dissertations, government publications, and other documents. Maintains extensive library including papers, reports, and court decisions. **Founded:** 1963. **Formerly:** (1965) Teachers for Integrated Schools.

★188★
Improved Benevolent Protective Order of Elks of the World (IBPOEW)
PO Box 159
Winton, NC 27986 Phone: (919)358-7661
Donald P. Wilson, Grand Exalted Ruler

Description: International fraternal organization of primarily Black membership. Concerned with civil liberties and equal opportunity. Provides scholarships for youth of all races. **Founded:** 1898. **Members:** 450,000. **Publications:** Elks News, bimonthly.

★189★
Inroads
1221 Locust St., Ste. 800
St. Louis, MO 63103 Phone: (314)241-7488
Reginald D. Dickson, CEO & Pres.

Description: Participants are U.S. corporations that sponsor internships for minority students and pledge to develop career opportunities for the interns. Prepares Black, Hispanic, and Native American high school and college students for leadership positions within major American business corporations in their own communities. Screens and places over 4000 individuals for internships with more than 1000 American business corporations per year. Offers professional training seminars on time management, business presentation skills, team building, and decision making. Provides personal and professional guidance to pre-college and college interns. **Founded:** 1970. **Regional Groups:** 5. **Local Groups:** 37. **Computerized Services:** Data base. **Telecommunications Services:** Fax, (314)241-9325. **Publications:** Annual Report. INROADS Newsletter, quarterly.

★190★
Institute for the Advanced Study of Black Family Life and Culture (IASBFLC)
155 Filbert St., Ste. 202
Oakland, CA 94607 Phone: (415)836-3245
Wade Nobles Ph.D., Exec.Dir.

Description: Seeks to reunify African American families and to revitalize the Black community. Advocates the reclamation of what the group considers traditional African American culture. Conducts research on issues impacting the Black community such as teenage pregnancy, child-rearing practices, mental health support systems, and the effects of alcohol and drugs. Maintains HAWK Federation, also known as the High Achievement, Wisdom, and Knowledge Federation, a training program employed in school systems to aid in the character development of young Black males. Sponsors in-service training for agencies, school systems, and the juvenile justice system. Develops training curricula for teen parents. Maintains speakers' bureau. **Publications:** African American Families - Issues, Insights, and Direction and African Psychology (books).

★191★
Inter-American Travel Agents Society (ITAS)
c/o Almeda Travel
1020 Holcombe Blvd., Ste. 1306
Houston, TX 77030 Phone: (713)799-1001
Jackye Alton, Pres.

Description: Black-owned and -operated travel agencies; other travel related businesses and interested individuals. Works to unify Black travel agents and increase members' market share and business contacts. Offers travel opportunities geared toward Black travelers. Assists members in developing new businesses; maintains standard of ethics among member agencies. **Founded:** 1955. **Members:** 300. **Publications:** Inter-American Travel Agents Society Newsletter, quarterly. Membership List, periodic. Includes updates. Also publishes brochure.

★192★
International Association of African and American Black Business People (IAAABBP)
13902 Robson St.
Detroit, MI 48227 Phone: (313)837-0627
William Bert Johnson, Pres.

Description: African and African-American businesspersons. Establishes, operates, and fosters business education and related activities among African-American and African members of the business community worldwide. Conducts seminars; bestows awards; compiles statistics. **Founded:** 1965. **Members:** 84,000. **Regional Groups:** 170. **Publications:** Bulletin, bimonthly. Journal, quarterly.

★193★
International Association of Black Business Educators (IABBE)
3810 Palmira Ln.
Silver Spring, MD 20906
Paul A. Young, Project Dir.

Description: Institutions of higher education (55) and individuals (100) interested in promoting development of business related academic programs and educational activities designed to enhance participation of minorities in business. Purposes are to: develop channels of communication and opportunities for interfacing with constituencies; generate constructive relationships between the U.S. and other nations concerning development of business education and related fields; study and propose minority business programs; promote cooperation within and between institutions and individuals in the business community; identify and evaluate business opportunities; promote the IABBE's involvement in academic affairs. Operates Strategic Business Development Network, which designs and produces a business development educational video series. **Founded:** 1978. **Members:** 155. **Publications:** IABBE Newsletter, quarterly. Also produces videotape series on how to start, own, and operate a business.

★194★
International Association of Black Professional Fire Fighters (IABPFF)
1025 Connecticut Ave. NW, Ste. 610
Washington, DC 20036 Phone: (202)296-0157
Romeo O. Spaulding, Pres.

Description: Fire fighters, dispatchers, and individuals in related professions. Strives to: promote interracial communication and understanding; recruit Blacks for the fire services; improve working conditions for Blacks in the fire services; assist Blacks in career advancement; promote professionalism; represent Black fire fighters before the community. **Founded:** 1970. **Members:** 8000. **Budget:** $160,000. **Computerized Services:** Mailing list. **Telecommunications Services:** Fax, (202)296-0158. **Publications:** Smoke, biennial. Newsletter.

★195★
International Association of Official Human Rights Agencies (IAOHRA)
444 N. Capitol St., Ste. 240
Washington, DC 20001 Phone: (202)624-5410

Description: Governmental human rights agencies with legal enforcement powers. Objectives are to foster better human relations and to enhance human rights procedures under the law. Conducts training services that include: administration and management training; technical assistance in civil rights compliance and curriculum development for colleges and universities, business, industry, and other organizations; training for administrators and commissioners to promote awareness and capability in current literature, theory, and philosophy relative to equal opportunity. Maintains ongoing liaison with federal agencies involved with civil rights enforcement in order to coordinate development of state legislation. Has developed and conducted training and technical assistance workshops for regional planning units and state planning agencies. Plans to establish a human rights training institute. Sponsors workshops; bestows awards; compiles statistics. **Founded:** 1949. **Members:** 187. **Budget:** $100,000. **Regional Groups:** 5. **Telecommunications Services:** Fax, (202)624-8588. **Publications:** IAOHRA Newsletter, quarterly.

★196★
International Black Women's Congress (IBWC)
1081 Bergen St.
Newark, NJ 07112 Phone: (201)926-0570
Dr. La Francis Rodgers-Rose, Pres.

Description: Women of African descent; interested individuals. Objective is to unite members for mutual support and socioeconomic development through: annual networking tours to Africa; establishing support groups; assisting women in starting their own businesses; assisting members in developing resumes and other educational needs; offering to answer or discuss individual questions and concerns. Conducts workshops and charitable program; compiles statistics. Bestows Oni Award annually to the person identified as "someone who protects, defends and enhances the general well being of African people." Operates speakers' bureau. Maintains 100 volume library. **Founded:** 1983. **Members:** 5800. **Budget:** $65,000. **State Groups:** 35. Undergraduate Chapters: 3. **Telecommunications Services:** Fax, (201)761-1878. **Publications:** International Black Women's Directory, periodic. Oni Newsletter, quarterly.

★197★
International Black Writers (IBW)
PO Box 1030
Chicago, IL 60690 Phone: (312)995-5195
Mable J. Terrell, Exec.Dir. & Pres.

Description: To discover and support new Black writers. Conducts research and monthly seminars in poetry, fiction, nonfiction, music, and jazz. Operates library of 500 volumes on Black history. Sponsors monthly workshop and panel discussion. Provides writing services and children's services. Presents Alice Browning Award for Excellence in Writing and bestows awards in journalism and poetry. Maintains library and speakers' bureau. Sponsors competitions; offers referral service. Plans to establish hall of fame, biographical archives, and museum. **Founded:** 1970. **Members:** 500. **Budget:** $40,000. **Regional Groups:** 5. **State Groups:** 4. **Local Groups:** 1. **Publications:** The Black Writer, quarterly. Magazine. Bulletin, periodic. Directory of Afro-American Writers, periodic. In Touch Newsletter, monthly. Poetry Contest, annual. Urban Voices Poetry, annual. **Formerly:** (1982) International Black Writers Conference.

★198★
International Black Writers and Artists (IBWA)
PO Box 43576
Los Angeles, CA 90043 Phone: (415)532-6179
Linda A. Hughes, Exec. Officer

Description: Black writers and artists in the United States and West Indies. Provides encouragement and support to members. Conducts workshops annually and sponsors social gatherings. Plans to publish anthology. **Founded:** 1974. **Members:** 500.

★199★
International Committee Against Racism (INCAR)
PO Box 904
Brooklyn, NY 11202 Phone: (212)629-0003
Carol Deak, Exec.Dir.

Description: Is dedicated to fighting all forms of racism and to building a multi-racial society. Opposes racism in all its economic, social, institutional, and cultural forms. Believes racism destroys not only those minorities that are its victims, but all people. Sponsors on-the-job, community, college, and high school workshops. **Founded:** 1973. **Members:** 2800. **Regional Groups:** 4. **State Groups:** 30. **Local Groups:** 28. **Publications:** Arrow (in English and Spanish), bimonthly. Newsletter reporting on racist incidents in the United States. Includes calendar of events, committee news, and member profiles.

★200★
International Defense and Aid Fund for Southern Africa, U.S. Committee (IDAF)
PO Box 17
Cambridge, MA 02138 Phone: (617)491-8343
Kenneth N. Carstens, Exec.Dir.

Description: Purposes are to aid, defend, rehabilitate, and provide for the legal defense of the "victims of unjust laws and arbitrary procedures in South Africa and Namibia;" to support their families and dependents; "to keep the conscience of the world alive to the issues at stake" through the dissemination of information on apartheid and political prisoners in South Africa and Namibia. Programs and activities have developed according to changing situations in the countries of southern Africa; primary emphasis is on political prisoners and their families. Rents slide shows. Operates speakers' bureau. **Founded:** 1972. **Budget:** $160,000. **Publications:** Focus on Political Repression in Southern Africa, bimonthly. Newsletter on political repression in South Africa and Namibia.

★201★
International League for Human Rights (ILHR)
432 Park Ave., S., Rm. 1103
New York, NY 10016 Phone: (212)684-1221
Felice Gaer, Exec.Dir.

Description: Individuals and national affiliates promoting human rights, including political and civil rights, racial and religious freedom, and the implementation of the Universal Declaration of Human Rights. Serves as nongovernmental agency accredited by the United Nations, International Labor Organization, United Nations Educational, Scientific and Cultural Organization, and Council of Europe (see separate entries). Participates in studies and programs on human rights. Advocates effective procedures to protect human rights, including protection of minorities; deals with issues of torture, political imprisonment, due process of law, racial discrimination, genocide, apartheid, treatment of prisoners, status of women, and religious freedom; promotes ability of local human rights groups to exist and work unimpeded by government. Intervenes directly with governments concerning violations of human rights. Sends special investigators to areas where human rights violations exist and sends observers to political trials. Bestows annual Human Rights Award. **Founded:** 1942. **Publications:** Annual Review. Human Rights Bulletin, periodic. Also publishes books, booklets, pamphlets, and special reports on worldwide human rights conditions, including Human Rights Conditions in Poland, Report of a Medical Fact-Finding Mission to El Salvador, Petitions Before the U.N. Trusteeship Council, and Guinea's Human Rights Record. **Formerly:** (1976) International League for the Rights of Man.

★202★
International Rhythm and Blues Association (IRBA)
PO Box 288571
Chicago, IL 60628 Phone: (312)326-5270
William C. Tyson, Pres.

Description: Musicians, record companies, songwriters, and individuals in 3 countries interested in preserving and promoting rhythm and blues music. Gathers information on rhythm and blues; maintains library. Is currently raising funds for scholarships for students pursuing careers in rhythm and blues music. **Founded:** 1966. **Members:** 500.

★203★
Interracial Council for Business Opportunity (ICBO)
51 Madison Ave., Ste. 2212
New York, NY 10010
William A. Young, Pres.

Description: Assists minority businessmen and women in developing, owning, and managing business ventures with substantial employment and economic impact. Services include business feasibility studies, financing, market development, and other technical assistance to start or expand minority-owned companies. Offers free management training courses. **Founded:** 1963. **Telecommunications Services:** Fax, (212)779-4365; toll-free number (800)252-4226. **Publications:** Annual Report. Newsletter, monthly.

★204★
Interracial Family Alliance (IFA)
PO Box 16248
Houston, TX 77222 Phone: (713)454-5018
Ron Radcliffe, Pres.

Description: Families that are interracial through marriage, adoption across racial lines, or biracial birth. Purposes are to: strengthen and support the interracial family unit; promote acceptance of interracial families by the public; focus on solutions to problems unique to interracial families such as developing self-esteem in biracial children. Maintains resource library of books, articles, videotapes, and other materials. Conducts social activities involving biracial children. Has compiled a bibliography on interracial family experience and transracial adoption. **Founded:** 1983. **Members:** 200. **Computerized Services:** national network of interracial family organizations. **Publications:** Interracial Family Alliance–Communique, quarterly. Newsletter.

★205★
Interracial-Intercultural Pride (I-PRIDE)
1060 Tennessee St.
San Francisco, CA 94107 Phone: (415)399-9111
Carlos A. Fernandez, Pres.

Description: Members of interracial and intercultural families; concerned individuals. Supports and encourages the well-being and development of children and adults who are of more than one ethnic or cultural heritage. Maintains library and speakers' bureau. Membership is currently concentrated in the San Francisco, CA area. **Founded:** 1979. **Members:** 75. **Budget:** Less than $25,000. **Publications:** I-Pride Newsletter, bimonthly.

★206★
Iota Phi Lambda Sorority
503 Patterson St.
Tuskegee, AL 36088 Phone: (205)727-5201
Mrs. Billie O. Glover, Exec.Dir.

Description: Social sorority - business and professional civic. Seeks to: develop leadership expertise among business and professional women; promote increased interest in business education among high school and college girls through planned programs and scholarships; encourage the development of personalities for all areas of leadership through provision of educational opportunities; establish and promote civic and social service activities for youth and adults. Conducts children's services and tutoring sessions. Maintains small library. Bestows Lola M. Parker Achievement Award and Mahala S. Evans Award. Provides educational, tutorial, senior citizen, and health programs. **Founded:** 1929. **Members:** 5000. **Regional Groups:** 5. Chapters: 100. **Publications:** Annual Convention Proceedings. Journal, annual. Let's Chat, semiannual. Membership Directory, biennial.

★207★
Jack and Jill of America Foundation (JJAF)
c/o Violet D. Greer
PO Drawer 3689
Chattanooga, TN 37404 Phone: (615)622-4476
Violet D. Greer, Exec.Sec.

Description: Officers of Jack and Jill of America, community leaders, parents, youth representatives, and others. Seeks to improve educational, cultural, and civic opportunities for minority youth. Monitors legislative changes affecting the development of youth. Awards grants to exemplary educational community projects throughout the country. Supports college-level achievement motivation projects, preschool programs, and college preparatory programs for high school students. Maintains library of films about foundation projects. Bestows awards. Sponsors training symposia. **Founded:** 1968. **Members:** 29. **Budget:** $200,000. **Publications:** Jack and Jill of America Foundation–Intercom, semiannual. Newsletter containing grant information and foundation news.

★208★
Jackie Robinson Foundation (JRF)
80 8th Ave.
New York, NY 10011 Phone: (212)675-1511
Betty Adams, Pres.

Description: Seeks to develop the leadership and achievement potential of minority and urban youth. Founded by the friends and family of Jackie Robinson (1919-72), the first Black athlete to play major league baseball. Trains minority and poor youths for sports management careers. Provides counseling, support, and placement services. Awards full college scholarships to promising minority students. Maintains library and collection of Jackie Robinson memorabilia; has produced a national touring exhibit of archival materials pertaining to Robinson. Bestows Robie Award for Humanitarianism and Robie Award for Achievement in Industry annually. **Founded:** 1973. **Budget:** $800,000. **Regional Groups:** 6. **Computerized Services:** Mailing list. Programs: Education and Scholarship; JRF Alumni Association; Sports Management. **Publications:** Jackie Robinson Foundation Awards Dinner, annual. Journal describing foundation programs and services; includes profiles of award recipients and scholarship sponsors.

★209★
Jazz for Life Project (JLP)
400 City Center Bldg.
Ann Arbor, MI 48104 Phone: (216)987-4249
Max Dehn, Exec.Dir.

Description: Works to raise money, through benefit jazz concerts, to improve the lives of children six years of age and under living in low-income situations. Strives to increase public awareness of the plight of poverty-stricken children. Distributes funds to nonprofit agencies that provide nutritional, educational, and health care services to children. Sponsors cultural programs for children. **Founded:** 1985. **Local Groups:** 2. **Publications:** Newsletter, periodic.

★210★
Joint Center for Political and Economic Studies (JCPES)

1301 Pennsylvania Ave. NW, Ste. 400
Washington, DC 20004 Phone: (202)626-3500
Eddie N. Williams, Pres.

Description: Funded in part by the Ford Foundation. Organized to provide, on a nonpartisan basis, research, public policy analysis, and information programs for Black and other minority elected and appointed public officials. Collects and analyzes data on all aspects of Black political participation. Monitors elections throughout the U.S. at all levels of government; collects and disseminates statistical and interpretive data on Black voting patterns and political participation. Conducts analyses of public policy issues that affect Black and disadvantaged Americans and pinpoints resources that can be used by socially and economically disadvantaged communities. Provides public policy forums, which bring together experts from a variety of disciplines to focus on issues and examine alternatives. Maintains library of 3000 volumes on Black politics. **Founded:** 1970. **Budget:** $3,000,000. **Telecommunications Services:** Fax, (202)626-8774. **Publications:** Annual Report. CPRJ News, periodic. Newsletter. Focus, monthly. Magazine. National Roster of Black Elected Officials, annual. NPI News, periodic. Newsletter. Quarterly Alert. Newsletter. Also publishes analyses of public policy issues, statistical studies, and monographs. **Formerly:** (1990) Joint Center for Political Studies.

★211★
Kappa Alpha Psi Fraternity
2320 N. Broad St.
Philadelphia, PA 19132 Phone: (215)228-7184
W. Ted Smith Ph.D., Exec.Sec.

Description: Social fraternity. Sponsors competitions and bestows awards; maintains placement service; compiles statistics. **Founded:** 1911. **Members:** 80,000. Active Chapters: 323. Alumni Chapters: 308. **Telecommunications Services:** Fax, (215)228-7181. **Publications:** Confidential Bulletin, quarterly. Journal, quarterly. Also publishes The Story of Kappa Alpha Psi.

★212★
Klanwatch
PO Box 548
Montgomery, AL 36195 Phone: (205)264-0286
Danny Welch, Contact

Description: Purpose is to gather and disseminate information about the Ku Klux Klan and to create a body of law to protect the rights of those the Klan is attacking. Collects information from 13,000 U.S. publications and other sources concerning the Klan. Conducts educational programs and distributes films for schoolchildren. Compiles statistics. **Founded:** 1980. **Budget:** $230,000. **Telecommunications Services:** Fax, (205)264-0629. **Publications:** Klanwatch Intelligence Report, bimonthly. Contains updates on White supremacy activities throughout the United States.

★213★
Lawyers' Committee for Civil Rights Under Law (LCCRUL)
1400 I St. NW, Ste. 400
Washington, DC 20005 Phone: (202)371-1212
Barbara R. Arnwine, Dir.

Description: Operates through local committees of private lawyers in eight major cities to provide legal assistance to poor and minority groups living in urban centers. National office undertakes reform efforts in such fields as employment, voting rights, and housing discrimination. Maintains library. **Founded:** 1963. **Members:** 165. **Budget:** $2,000,000. **Local Groups:** 7. **Telecommunications Services:** Cable, LAWCIV. **Publications:** Annual Report. Committee Report, quarterly.

★214★
Leadership Conference on Civil Rights (LCCR)
2027 Massachusetts Ave., NW
Washington, DC 20036 Phone: (202)667-1780
Ralph G. Neas, Exec.Dir.

Description: Coalition of national organizations working to promote passage of civil rights, social and economic legislation, and enforcement of laws already on the books. Has released studies examining former President Ronald Reagan's tax and budget programs in areas including housing, elementary and secondary education, social welfare, and Indian affairs, and tax cuts. Has evaluated the enforcement of activities in civil rights by the U.S. Department of Justice; has also reviewed civil rights activities of the U.S. Department of Education. Bestows Hubert H. Humphrey Award. **Founded:** 1950. **Members:** 185. **Publications:** LCCR Memo. **Formerly:** Civil Rights Mobilization.

★215★
Lincoln Institute for Research and Education (LIRE)
1001 Connecticut Ave. NW, Ste. 1135
Washington, DC 20036 Phone: (202)223-5112
J. A. Parker, Pres.

Description: Studies public policy issues affecting middle-class Black Americans and disseminates research findings to elected officials and the public. Re-evaluates theories and programs that it feels are harmful to the long-range interests of Blacks. Transmits pro-private enterprise views to public policymakers at local, state, and federal levels. Emphasizes the common national destiny of Black and White Americans; supports a strong, steadily growing economy and a strong national defense. Sponsors and cosponsors conferences, seminars, and symposia on current issues. Maintains a comprehensive research and education program. **Founded:** 1978. **Publications:** Lincoln Review, quarterly. Journal containing public policy articles, essays, and reviews on issues affecting middle-class Black Americans.

★216★
Links
1200 Massachusetts Ave. NW
Washington, DC 20005 Phone: (202)842-8686
Mary P. Douglass, Dir.

Description: Organization of women committed to the community through educational, cultural, and civic activities. Provides enrichment experiences for those who are educationally disadvantaged and culturally deprived, and support for talented individuals. Sponsors charitable activities and a National Grant-In-Aid program. **Founded:** 1946. **Members:** 8000. **Budget:** $300,000. **Regional Groups:** 4. **State Groups:** 40. **Local Groups:** 240. **Publications:** Journal, semiannual. Link to Link, quarterly. Newsletter. Links Directory, quadrennial. Also publishes brochure.

★217★
Majestic Eagles (ME)
2029 Rhode Island Ave. NE
Washington, DC 20018 Phone: (202)635-0154
John Raye, Pres.

Description: Business owners. Offers outreach and support services to small and minority (especially African-American) owned businesses, and provides a clearer understanding of business operations and management of resources to individuals interested in establishing a business. Seeks to: emphasize individual development to help members become financially secure; increase business volume among the membership and the public; encourage business ownership. Sponsors Youth Entrepreneurship Program and Real Estate Development Club; also operates a credit union. **Founded:** 1983. **Publications:** Brochures and fact sheet.

★218★
Martin Luther King, Jr. Center for Nonviolent Social Change, Inc. (MLKCNSC)
449 Auburn Ave., NE
Atlanta, GA 30312 Phone: (404)524-1956
Coretta Scott King, Pres.

Description: Seeks to build a permanent and living memorial to Dr. Martin Luther King, Jr. (1929-68), American clergyman, civil rights leader, and Nobel Peace Prize winner (1964); and continue the work he began through study, education, training, research, and constructive action. Committed to providing a place where men and women of goodwill, regardless of origin or background, may seek nonviolent solutions to world problems such as poverty, racism, and violence. The U.S. Congress has established the 23.5 acres that accommodate the physical facilities of the center as a Martin Luther King, Jr. National Historic Site. Facilities house the staff and programs of the center, including its Ten Program Institutes and Freedom Hall, an international conference and cultural center, Dr. King's entombment area, reflection pool and park, a city-operated Martin Luther King, Jr. Community Center, and the home of Dr. King's birth. Freedom Hall Complex includes a theater, screening room where films of Dr. King's life and work are shown, and major exhibits. Ten Program Institutes focus on nonviolence, international affairs, government affairs, cultural affairs, economic development, community development, youth, labor, King theology and philosophy, and research policy analysis and dissemination. Center's library and archives contain the largest collection of manuscripts on the U.S. civil rights movement and Dr. King's personal papers. Also operates Early Learning Center for children and Basic Skills Academy for youth and adults. **Founded:** **Telecommunications Services:** Fax, (404)522-6932. **Formerly:** (1980) Martin Luther King, Jr. Center for Social Change.

★219★
MCAP Group (MCAP)
89-50 164th St., Ste. 2B
Jamaica, NY 11432 Phone: (718)657-6444
Sherman L. Brown, Pres.

Description: Provides bonding, financial, technical, and management assistance to minority and small construction contractors in cities for the purpose of assisting the contractors to compete for a more equitable share of the construction industry. Services include: surety bonding program; financial and construction management; financial analysis; construction project management, including estimating, engineering, joint venture, and consortia arrangements; procurement referrals for several federally funded building programs. Sponsors conferences and workshops on matters of particular interest to minority contractors, such as bonding and nonprofit housing. Operates MCAP Bonding and Insurance Agency, a for-profit subsidiary. **Founded:** 1970. **Telecommunications Services:** Fax, (718)523-2063. **Formerly:** (1989) Minority Contractors Assistance Project.

★220★
Meiklejohn Civil Liberties Institute (MCLI)
PO Box 673
Berkeley, CA 94701 Phone: (415)848-0599
Ann Fagan Ginger, Pres.

Description: Established to collect attorney workpapers and unreported rulings filed in courts in cases involving civil rights, due process, and civil liberties, in order to assist attorneys and legal workers confronted with similar issues. Concentrates effort on a peace law and education project, with a brief bank of legal case files and in-depth findings and reports relating to current issues about U.S. military policies and conventional and nuclear war. Maintains extensive library of over 8000 case files. Houses archives of National Lawyers Guild as well as other primary source materials documenting the Cold War Period, the Civil Rights Movement, the Free Speech Movement, and the Vietnam War era. Operates speakers' bureau. **Founded:** 1965. **Budget:** $110,000. **Computerized Services:** PeaceNet. **Publications:** Human Rights Organizations and Periodicals Directory, biennial. News from MCLI, semiannual. Peace Law Docket, biennial. Has also published Human Rights Docket, The Ford Hunger March, Alexander Meiklejohn: Teacher of Freedom, The Cold War Against Labor, materials for the public, and specialized materials for attorneys and social scientists.

★221★
Metropolitan Travel Agents (MTA)
c/o Ethan C. Smythe
Calendar Travel
227 Utica Ave.
Brooklyn, NY 11213 Phone: (718)771-8400
Ethan C. Smythe, Pres.

Description: Travel agents employed by Black-owned travel agencies united to promote travel among Blacks. **Founded:** 1969. **Members:** 35. **Budget:** $75,000. **Publications:** none. Presently inactive.

★222★
Minorities in Media (MIM)
c/o Barbara Noble
Parkway School District
455 N. Woods Mill Rd.
Chesterfield, MO 63017 Phone: (314)469-8538
Barbara Noble Sr., Pres.

Description: Minority media professionals including librarians, media specialists, and media vendors. Facilitates communication among members; conveys members' programs and ideas to the Association for Educational Communications and Technology. Maintains collection of members' publications. Plans to make available scholarships. **Founded:** 1975. **Members:** 85. **Publications:** Newsletter, semiannual.

★223★ N/S 7/13
Minority Business Enterprise Legal Defense and Education Fund (MBELDEF)
300 I St. NE, Ste. 200
Washington, DC 20002 Phone: (202)543-0040
Anthony W. Robinson, Pres.

Description: Minority businesspersons united to defend, enhance, and expand minority business. Acts as advocate and legal representative for the minority business community, offering legal representation in matters of national or regional importance. **Founded:** 1980. **Members:** 2000. **Publications:** MBE Vanguard, quarterly. Newsletter.

★224★
Minority Business Information Institute (MBII)
130 5th Ave., 10th Fl.
New York, NY 10011 Phone: (212)242-8000
Earl G. Graves, Exec.Dir.

Description: Purpose is to expand information on minority economic development. Maintains 2200 volume library of books, periodicals, and reports focusing on minority businesses. **Founded:** 1970. **Telecommunications Services:** Fax, (212)989-8410. **Publications:** Index to Black Enterprise, periodic. Magazine.

★225★
Minority Caucus of Family Service America (MCFSA)
341/2 Beacon St.
Boston, MA 02108 Phone: (617)523-6400
Howard E. Prunty, Pres.

Description: Any member of a minority group who is involved with a family service agency in any capacity. Works to combat racism in FSA and to make FSA more relevant to the needs of minority families. Conducts negotiations with and participates in policymaking groups. Maintains Minority Resource Council and Task Force to Eradicate Institutional Racism. Presents Grady B. Murdock Award for outstanding service to minorities. **Founded:** 1969. **Telecommunications Services:** Fax, (617)523-3034. **Publications:** Newsletter, annual. **Formerly:** (1973) Black Caucus of Family Service Association of America; (1986) Minorities Caucus of Family Service Association of America.

N/S 7/13
★226★
Minority Rights Group U.S.A. (MRG)
c/o Sue Roff
35 Claremont Ave., Box 4S
New York, NY 10027 Phone: (212)864-7986
Sue Roff, Convener

Description: A branch of Minority Rights Group. Aims are to: secure justice for minority or majority groups suffering discrimination by investigating their situation and publicizing the facts internationally; help prevent violations of human rights by using publicity and to prevent such problems from developing into dangerous and destructive conflicts; foster, by its research findings, international understanding of the factors that create prejudiced treatment and group tensions; promote the growth of a world conscience regarding human rights. Sponsors seminars on minority issues; commissions multidisciplinary research into the causes of minority problems and their solutions. Granted consultative status by the United Nations (see separate entry). Maintains library. **Founded:** 1968. **Publications:** Newsletter, bimonthly. Also publishes reports.

★227★
Mobility Haiti (MH)
PO Box 56538
Washington, DC 20011 Phone: (301)589-1810
Ken Hughes, Dir.

Description: Seeks to enhance the mobility and efficiency of Haitian development and health workers through the donation of bicycles and spare parts. Solicits bicycle donations; sponsors art shows featuring Haitian artists to help defray costs of shipping the bicycles to Haiti. Participates in forums addressing Haitian concerns. Maintains speakers' bureau. Seeks to influence policymakers through slide shows highlighting the mobility problem in Haiti and presenting the bicycle as a viable solution to this problem. **Founded:** 1982. **Telecommunications Services:** Electronic mail, PEACENET, MOBILITY; telex, 155217437 MOBILITY. **Publications:** Information sheet. **Formerly:** (1989) Haitian Development Fund.

★228★
Modern Free and Accepted Masons of the World (MFAMW)
PO Box 1072
Columbus, GA 31902 Phone: (404)322-3326
Soammes Williams, Asst.Dir.

Description: Fellowship organization dedicated to educating members so that they may become better leaders and citizens. Holds seminars and workshops on topics such as leadership and business skills. Conducts Sunday school classes for children. **Founded:** 1917. **Members:** 18,000. **Budget:** $50,000. **Publications:** Searchlight, monthly. Newspaper.

★229★
Most Worshipful National Grand Lodge Free and Accepted Ancient York Masons
26070 Tryon Rd.
Oakwood Village, OH 44146 Phone: (216)232-9495
Hon. Jefferson D. Tufts Sr., National Grand Master

Description: Organizes and installs grand and subordinate lodges for the purpose of "mutual uplifting and moral improvement." Conducts annual seminars; sponsors scholarship programs; maintains state archives. **Founded:** 1847. **Members:** 50,000. **Budget:** $50,000. **State Groups:** 38. **Local Groups:** 96. **Publications:** York Rite Bulletin, quarterly. **Also known as:** Most Worshipful National Grand Lodge Free and Accepted Ancient York Masons Prince Hall Origin National Compact U.S.A.

★230★
Multicultural Network of the American Society for Training and Development (MNASTD)
c/o Ms. Shakura A. Sabur
1620 NE 99th St.
Kansas City, MO 64155 Phone: (816)734-4640
Ms. Shakura A. Sabur, Dir.

Description: A member service of the American Society for Training and Development. Provides training and information resources to human resource development practitioners of culturally diverse backgrounds or in the business of training and development of multicultural populations. Seeks to develop products and services that address the needs of the multicultural human resource development work force. **Members:** 1000. **Telecommunications Services:** Fax, (816)421-5538; toll-free number, (800)821-6180. **Publications:** Multicultural Network News, 3/year. Newsletter. Also publishes Valuing Differences in the Workplace (monograph) and makes available The Making of a Multicultural Network (videotape).

★231★
Museum of African American History (MAAH)
301 Frederick Douglass St.
Detroit, MI 48202 Phone: (313)833-9800
Marian J. Moore, Exec.Dir.

Description: Persons interested in developing the national, public-sponsored Black Historical Museum. The museum is dedicated to preserving, documenting, interpreting, and exhibiting the cultural heritage of African-Americans and their ancestors. Serves as a learning and resource center; collects and documents contributions of Black people. Offers permanent and traveling exhibits. Conducts workshops, seminars, and lecture series. Bestows Paul Robeson Scholarship. Sponsors competitions; bestows awards; maintains children's services; offers specialized education program. Maintains reference library containing books, films, and audiotapes of African world history, art, and culture. Plans to interview and tape stories of elderly Blacks. **Founded:** 1965. **Members:** 5000. **Budget:** $350,000. **Publications:** The Gallery, quarterly. Newsletter. **Formerly:** (1969) International Afro-American Museum Committee; (1978) International Afro-American Museum; (1983) Afro-American Museum of Detroit.

★232★
Music Educators National Conference (NBMC)
National Black Music Caucus
c/o Dr. Willis Patterson
University of Michigan
Ann Arbor, MI 48109 Phone: (313)764-0586
Dr. Willis Patterson, Exec.Sec.

Description: Purpose is to foster the creation, study, and promotion of Black-derived music in education. Seeks to heighten public awareness of the problems faced by Black music educators and students and to increase public understanding of those problems. Provides a forum for the discussion of concerns. Coordinates and disseminates materials concerning Black-derived music in order to assist music teachers in teaching Black music and students. Encourages Blacks to aspire to leadership positions and to demand inclusion in the development and presentation of Music Educators National Conference activities, including participation in MENC's regional conferences. Sponsors collegiate and high school gospel choir competitions. Bestows annual national achievement awards to educators successful in demonstrating values inherent in music education. Compiles list of music, books, and related music materials by Blacks. **Founded:** 1972. **Computerized Services:** Data base of Black musicians and educators capable of functioning as clinicians in all areas of music. **Publications:** Con Brio, quarterly. Newsletter; reports on regional conferences, collegiate and high school gospel choir competitions, and activities of members.

★233★
Mutual Musicians Foundation (MMF)
1823 Highland
Kansas City, MO 64108 Phone: (816)421-9297
Al Peterson, Exec. Officer

Description: Musicians and other interested persons. Seeks to promote, preserve, and perpetuate the Kansas City jazz heritage. Performs for youth and senior citizens' organizations. Maintains Musicians Foundation Building, which was designated as a national historic landmark. The foundation's building served as headquarters for the city's Black musicians' union, and NMA hopes it will serve as the symbol of Kansas City's place in the history of jazz. Sponsors educational and charitable programs. Plans to open a museum, studio, classrooms, lounge, and entertainment hall and to offer scholarships. **Founded:** 1917. **Members:** 125. **Publications:** Plans to publish newsletter. **Formerly:** (1917) Negro Musicians Association; (1930) Black Musicians Union of the American Federation of Music.

★234★
Nation of Ishmael (NI)
2696 Ben Hill Rd.
East Point, GA 30344 Phone: (404)349-1153
Jacob Smith, Founder

Description: Individuals and corporations. Nondenominational religious organization working to improve the economic, educational, spiritual, and social potential of Black communities in the U.S. Provides administrative assistance to and facilitates procurement of loans by minority-owned small businesses. Conducts programs for youth and senior citizens. Holds quarterly seminar for business owners. **Founded:** 1975. **Members:** 300. **Publications:** Brochures.

★235★
National Action Council for Minorities in Engineering (NACME)
3 W. 35th St.
New York, NY 10001 Phone: (212)279-2626
~~George Campbell Jr., Pres.~~

Description: Seeks to increase the number of African American, Hispanic, and Native American students enrolled in and graduating from engineering schools. Offers incentive grants to engineering schools to recruit and provide financial assistance to increasing numbers of minority students. Works with local, regional, and national support organizations to motivate and encourage precollege students to engage in engineering careers. Conducts educational and research programs; operates project to assist engineering schools in improving the retention and graduation rates of minority students. Maintains speakers' bureau; bestows awards; compiles statistics. **Founded:** 1980. **Budget:** $4,000,000. **Telecommunications Services:** Fax, (212)629-5178. **Publications:** Annual Report. Directory of Pre-College and University Minority Engineering Programs, periodic. Financial Aid Unscrambled: A Guide for Minority Engineering Students, biennial. NACME News, 3/year. Newsletter for educators, counselors, and program directors who participate in minority engineering education.

★236★
National Alliance Against Racist and Political Repression (NAARPR)
11 John St., Rm. 702
New York, NY 10038 Phone: (212)406-3330
Charlene Mitchell, Exec.Dir.

Description: Coalition of political, labor, church, civic, student, and community organizations; individuals dedicated to protecting people's right to organize. Seeks to mobilize millions of people to unite in word and action against many forms of repression of human rights in the U.S. including: persecution and jailing of political activists; attempts to suppress prisoners' rights movements and use of behavior control against prisoners and the poor; assaults on labor's right to organize, strike, and act effectively; police crimes against the people, especially nonWhites; legislation and court decisions repressing basic rights; the death penalty. Opposes: use of grand juries and the FBI, CIA, and government spying programs to persecute those working for social change; suppression of movements for democracy and against racism in the military; failure to grant full amnesty to war resisters; attacks on lawyers who fight militantly for oppressed people; attacks on educators and students who struggle against racism and for democratic rights; harassment and deportation of the foreign-born, especially "undocumented" workers who come to the U.S. as "economic victims of U.S.-dominated countries." Conducts speaking tours, sponsors petition campaigns, and organizes demonstrations. Combines legal action with mass action. Establishes task forces. **Founded:** 1973. **Members:** 5000. **Telecommunications Services:** Fax, (212)406-3542. **Publications:** The Organizer, quarterly. Newsletter. Also publishes pamphlets and produces slide shows and films.

★237★
National Alliance of Black Organizations (NABO)
3724 Airport Blvd.
Austin, TX 78722 Phone: (512)478-9802
M. J. Anderson Sr., Pres.

Description: Presidents of Black organizations and associations. Coordinates and encourages voter registration efforts among member organizations. Serves as a forum for the exchange of ideas and experiences. Assists charitable organizations. **Founded:** 1976. **Budget:** Less than $25,000.

★238★
National Alliance of Black School Educators (NABSE)
2816 Georgia Ave. NW
Washington, DC 20001 Phone: (202)483-1549
~~William J. Saunders~~, Exec.Dir.

Description: Black educators from all levels; others indirectly involved in the education of Black youth. Purpose is to promote awareness, professional expertise, and commitment among Black educators. Goals are to: eliminate and rectify the results of racism in education; work with state, local, and national leaders to raise the academic achievement level of all Black students; increase members' involvement in legislative activities; facilitate the introduction of a curriculum that more completely embraces Black America; improve the ability of Black educators to promote problem resolution; create a meaningful and effective network of strength, talent, and professional support. Sponsors workshops, commission meetings, and special projects. Encourges research, especially as it relates to Blacks, and the presentation of papers during national conferences. Plans to establish a National Black Educators Data Bank and offer placement service. **Founded:** 1970. **Members:** 4000. **Budget:** $500,000. **Local Groups:** 42. **Telecommunications Services:** Fax, (202)483-8323. **Publications:** Membership Roster, annual. News Briefs, periodic. **Formerly:** (1973) National Alliance of Black School Superintendents.

★239★
National Alliance of Postal and Federal Employees (NAPFE)
1628 11th St. NW
Washington, DC 20001 Phone: (202)939-6325
Shirley E. Davis, Sec.

Description: Independent. Works to eliminate employment discrimination. Bestows scholarship awards to dependent children of members. **Founded:** 1913. **Members:** 70,000. **Budget:** $2,000,000. **Regional Groups:** 10. Locals: 137. **Publications:** National Alliance, monthly. Labor union newsletter covering the postal and other branches of the federal service. **Formerly:** (1968) National Alliance of Postal Employees.

★240★
National Alliance of Third World Journalists (NATWJ)
1419 V St. NW
Washington, DC 20009 Phone: (202)462-8197
Leila McDowell, Co-Coord.

Description: Journalists, journalism students, and persons in related communications fields. Proposes to increase the quality and quantity of media coverage of the Third World. Acts as an informational bridge between minorities in the U.S. and the Third World. Provides the opportunity for minority journalists to travel to the Third World to gain first-hand knowledge of the situation in the respective countries. Provides speakers on Third World related issues and topics, including official representatives of national liberation movements, and on media coverage of the Third World. Schedules forums and seminars. **Founded:** 1981. **Members:** 330. **Budget:** $100,000. **Regional Groups:** 4. **Local Groups:** 5. **Publications:** Alliance Report, quarterly. Newsletter providing an alternative view of national and international issues, including news analyses, fact-finding reports, and critiques of popular culture. Includes book and film reviews.

★241★

National Alumni Council of the United Negro College Fund (NAC)

c/o United Negro Coll. Fund
500 E. 62nd St.
New York, NY 10021 Phone: (212)326-1193
Judith Walburg, Dir.

Description: Inter-alumni councils, national alumni associations, and students. Purposes are to: stimulate the interest of Black college alumni; acquaint the public with the value of Black colleges and Black higher education; inform students and the public about contributions of Black college alumni to civic betterment and community progress; recruit students for member colleges; raise funds for United Negro College Fund (see separate entry); encourage and provide a structure for cooperation among Black college alumni groups and friends of Black higher education. Bestows awards; compiles statistics. **Founded:** 1946. **Members:** 3000. **Publications:** Conference Journal, annual. Newsletter, periodic.

★242★

National Association for Black Veterans (NABV)

3929 N. Humboldt
PO Box 11432
Milwaukee, WI 53211-0432 Phone: (414)332-3931
Thomas H. Wynn Sr., Exec. Officer

Description: Black and other minority veterans, primarily those who fought in Vietnam. Represents the interests of minority veterans before the Veterans Administration. Operates Metropolitan Veterans Service to obtain honorable discharges for minority and low-income veterans who in the organization's opinion unjustly received a less than honorable discharge. Defends incarcerated veterans through its Readjustment Counseling Program; operates job creation program; offers services to geriatric and homeless veterans. Conducts workshops to acquaint lawyers and clinicians with problems associated with Post Traumatic Stress Disorder. Sponsors geriatric seminar and training program. Operates library of military regulations; compiles statistics; bestows awards; maintains speakers' bureau. **Founded:** 1970. **Members:** 25,000. **Budget:** $350,000. **Local Groups:** 13. **Computerized Services:** Data bases; mailing list. **Telecommunications Services:** Fax, (414)332-4627; toll-free number, (800)842-4597. **Publications:** Eclipse, monthly. Newspaper. **Formerly:** (1970) Interested Veterans of the Central City.

★243★

National Association for Equal Educational Opportunities (NAEEO)

2181 Brigden Rd.
Pasadena, CA 91104 Phone: (714)625-6607
Juan Francisco Lara, Pres.

Description: College and university personnel concerned with the development and operation of secondary school and collegiate programs to serve the needs of low-income and disadvantaged students. Provides speakers on issues confronting students who are the first generations in their families to go on to higher education. Conducts seminars on the relation between postsecondary and secondary education for teachers, faculty, and administrators. Compiles statistics. **Founded:** 1975. **Members:** 60. **Budget:** Less than $25,000. **Telecommunications Services:** Fax, (714)621-8390.

★244★

National Association for Equal Opportunity in Higher Education (NAFEO)

Lovejoy Bldg.
400 12th St. NE, 2nd Fl.
Washington, DC 20002 Phone: (202)543-9111
Dr. Samuel L. Myers, Pres.

Description: Provides a unified framework representing historically and predominantly Black universities and colleges and similarly situated institutions in their attempt to continue as viable forces in American society. Seeks to build a case for securing increased support from federal agencies, philanthropic foundations, and other sources, and to increase Black leadership of educational organizations and membership on federal boards and commissions relating to education. Offers placement service. Bestows Distinguished Alumni Citation of the Year, Research Achievement, and Leadership awards. Maintains biographical data on member colleges/universities and presidents/chancellors. **Founded:** 1969. **Members:** 117. **Budget:** $750,000. **Computerized Services:** Data base on programs sponsored by the U.S. Agency for International Development . **Telecommunications Services:** Fax, (202)543-9113. **Publications:** Distinguished Alumni of the Historical and Predominantly Black Colleges and Universities, annual. Institutional and Presidential Profiles of the Historical Black Colleges and Universities, annual. NAFEO/AID Update, quarterly. Newsletter. NAFEO Brochure, annual. National Alumni Association Calendar, annual. Directory. National Association for Equal Opportunity in Higher Education–Inroads, monthly. Newsletter; includes profiles

★245★

National Association for Ethnic Studies (NAES)

Arizona State University
Department of English
Tempe, AZ 85287 Phone: (602)965-3168
Gretchen Bataille, Treas.

Description: Individuals, libraries, and institutions. Promotes research, study, and curriculum design in the field of ethnic studies. Annually bestows Ernest M. Pon Award. **Founded:** 1975. **Members:** 300. **Budget:** Less than $25,000. **Computerized Services:** Mailing list. **Telecommunications Services:** Fax, (602)965-2012. **Publications:** The Ethnic Reporter, semiannual. Newsletter. Monitors developments in the field, discusses educational issues; and reports on activities of the association. **Formerly:** (1976) National Association of Interdisciplinary Studies for Native American, Black, Chicano, Puerto Rican, Asian Americans; (1985) National Association of Interdisciplinary Ethnic Studies.

★246★

National Association for Sickle Cell Disease (NASCD)

3345 Wilshire Blvd., Ste. 1106
Los Angeles, CA 90010-1880 Phone: (213)736-5455
Dorothye H. Boswell, Exec.Dir.

Description: Community groups involved in sickle cell anemia programs throughout the U.S. (Sickle cell anemia is an inherited blood disease that primarily affects Black people and is a major health problem within the Black community.) Purposes are to: provide leadership on a national level in order to create awareness in all circles of the negative impact of sickle cell anemia on the health and economic, social, and educational well-being of the individual and his/her family and to create awareness of the requirements for resolution; prepare and distribute substantive educational materials; develop and promote implementation of service program standards that will be in the best interest of the affected population; provide ongoing technical assistance to interested groups; encourage adequate support for research. Resources include: counselor training; workshops and seminars; blood banks; screening and testing; tutorial services; camps for children with sickle cell disease; vocational rehabilitation. Bestows awards for outstanding service. **Founded:** 1971. **Budget:** $970,000. **Local Groups:** 86. **Telecommunications Services:** Toll-free number, (800)421-8453. **Publications:** HELP, A Guide to Sickle Cell Disease Programs and

Services, periodic. National Association for Sickle Cell Disease–Newsletter, quarterly.

★247★

National Association for the Advancement of Black Americans in Vocational Education (NAABAVE)
c/o Dr. Ethel O. Washington
5057 Woodward, Rm. 976
Detroit, MI 48202 Phone: (313)494-1660
Dr. Ethel O. Washington, Pres.

Description: Educational institutions, teachers, administrators, students, and government employees committed to the greater involvement of Black Americans in all areas of vocational/technical education. Goal is to generate national leadership and increase the impact of Blacks in the field of vocational/technical education by: assuring opportunities and promoting recruitment and the retention of Black Americans in all areas and levels; utilizing research discoveries as a basis for influencing key funding sources at the national, state, and local levels; providing a career information exchange system. Develops training models for marketable skills; links Black talent with vocational/technical employment opportunities in the public and private sectors at the federal, state, and local levels; identifies, assesses, and evaluates critical issues that affect the extent of participation of Blacks and offers recommendations for improvement. Conducts regional workshops. Maintains placement service for Blacks and other minorities. Sponsors competitions. Operates speakers' bureau; compiles statistics. **Founded:** 1977. **Members:** 900. **Budget:** Less than $25,000. **State Groups:** 6. **Publications:** Conference Proceedings, annual. National Association for the Advancement of Black Americans in Vocational Education–Newsletter, quarterly. Contains discussions of equity issues and successful programs in vocational education. Includes chapter news and employment listings.

★248★

National Association for the Advancement of Colored People (NAACP)
4805 Mt. Hope Dr.
Baltimore, MD 21215 Phone: (212)481-4100
Benjamin L. Hooks, Exec.Dir.

Description: Persons "of all races and religions" who believe in the objectives and methods of the NAACP. To achieve equal rights through the democratic process and eliminate racial prejudice by removing racial discrimination in housing, employment, voting, schools, the courts, transportation, recreation, prisons, and business enterprises. Offers referral services, tutorials, job referrals, and day care. Sponsors seminars; maintains law library. Awards Spingarn Medal annually to a Black American for distinguished achievement. Sponsors the NAACP National Housing Corporation to assist in the development of low and moderate income housing for families. Compiles statistics. **Founded:** 1909. **Members:** 400,000. **Local Groups:** 1802. **Publications:** Crisis, 10/year. Report, annual.

★249★

National Association for the Advancement of Colored People (LDF)
NAACP Legal Defense and Educational Fund
99 Hudson St., 16th Fl.
New York, NY 10013 Phone: (212)219-1900
Julius LeVonne Chambers, Dir.-Counsel

Description: Legal arm of the civil rights movement, functioning independently of the National Association for the Advancement of Colored People (see separate entry) since the mid-1950s. Works to provide and support litigation in behalf of Blacks, other racial minorities, and women defending their legal and constitutional rights against discrimination in employment, education, housing, and other areas. Represents civil rights groups as well as individual citizens who have bona fide civil rights claims. Contributed funds are used to finance court actions for equality in schools, jobs, voting, housing, municipal services, land use, and delivery of health care services. Has organized litigation campaign for prison reform and the abolition of capital punishment. Hosts annual institute to develop public awareness of new problems being faced by minorities. Maintains Herbert Lehman Education Fund, through which scholarships are awarded to Black students attending state universities; sponsors Earl Warren Legal Training Program (see separate entry), which provides scholarships to Black law students. Compiles statistics on capital punishment. Maintains library of 15,000 volumes on law. Committee of 100, a voluntary cooperative group of individuals, has sponsored the appeal of the fund since 1943. **Founded:** 1939. **Budget:** $8,900,000. **Publications:** Annual Report. Equal Justice, quarterly. Newsletter. Also publishes legal materials, brochures, press releases, and occasional watchdog reports.

★250★

National Association for the Southern Poor (NASP)
749B Delaware Ave., SW
Washington, DC 20024 Phone: (202)554-3265
Donald Anderson, Exec.Dir.

Description: Black, low-income individuals in Virginia, North Carolina, South Carolina, and Georgia. Seeks to create local organizations, known as Assemblies, through which low-income people can become involved in local decision-making regarding community services and opportunities. Concentrates on organizing Southern Blacks in an effort toward raising levels of health, education, and income. Compiles statistics; bestows awards. Assemblies hold monthly meeting. **Founded:** 1968. **Members:** 240,000. **Publications:** The Epistle Newsletter, monthly. **Formerly:** (1976) Virginia Community Development Organization.

★251★

National Association of African American Students of Law (NAAASL)
PO Box 20053
Ferndale, MI 48220 Phone: (313)837-0627
William Bert Johnson, Pres.

Description: Law school instructors, professors, and African-American law students; attorneys who have practiced law between one and five years. Promotes friendship between students and faculties of law schools and universities; works to aid students in advancing their education, employment, and extracurricular activities. Seeks to eliminate discrimination. Bestows awards; operates charitable program; compiles statistics. **Founded:** 1973. **Members:** 4300. **State Groups:** 43. **Publications:** Bulletin, monthly. Newsletter, bimonthly.

★252★

National Association of Bench and Bar Spouses (NABBS)
3055 Ludlow Rd.
Shaker Heights, OH 70808 Phone: (216)752-4986
Dee Ann Character, Pres.

Description: Spouses of attorneys united to conduct civic, cultural, and social activities in order "to enhance the prestige of the legal profession" and to encourage fellowship among attorneys' spouses. Sponsors conferences on the family and child advocacy programs; maintains Dorothy Atkinson Legal Scholarship Fund for worthy law students and college students interested in careers in law. **Founded:** 1951. **Members:** 400. **Budget:** Less than $25,000. **Regional Groups:** 4. Chapters: 28. **Publications:** Membership Directory, annual. Newsletter, semiannual. Also publishes historical brochure and program aids. **Formerly:** (1987) National Barristers' Wives.

★253★
National Association of Black Accountants (NABA)
900 2nd St. NE, Ste. 205
Washington, DC 20002 Phone: (202)682-0222
Beverly E. Jones, Exec.Dir.

Description: CPAs, accountants, and accounting students. To unite accountants and accounting students who have similar interests and ideals, who are committed to professional and academic excellence, who possess a sense of professional and civic responsibility, and who are concerned with enhancing opportunities for minorities in the accounting profession. Programs include: free income tax preparation; student scholarships; high school and university career seminars; regional student conferences; technical seminars and lectures. Maintains speakers' bureau and placement service. Bestows awards. **Founded:** 1969. **Members:** 3000. **Budget:** $244,000. **Local Groups:** 100. **Telecommunications Services:** Fax, (202)682-3322. **Publications:** News Plus, bimonthly. Newsletter. Spectrum, semiannual. Technical and educational journal addressing current and future accounting issues.

★254★
National Association of Black and White Men Together: A Gay Multiracial Organization for All People (NABWMT)
584 Castro St., Ste. 140
San Francisco, CA 94114 Phone: (415)431-1976
John Teamer, Co-Chair

Description: Gay men, lesbians, and other individuals. Promotes and fosters interracial fellowship and the formation of coalitions among gays and other minorities. Opposes racism within the gay community and homophobia within ethnic communities. Sponsors seminars and litigation. Compiles literature on the Black and interracial gay experience. Conducts research on resisting racism. Maintains speakers' bureau; bestows awards. Offers charitable program and discussion groups. **Founded:** 1980. **Members:** 1200. **Budget:** $870,000. **Regional Groups:** 3. **Local Groups:** 28. **Computerized Services:** Mailing list. **Publications:** Annual Convention Program. Monthly Board Memos. NABWMT Journal, annual. Collection of members' writings. Newsletter, quarterly. Provides announcements, fundraising information, and obituaries. Also publishes Resisting Racism and Reflections: Five Years of Collected Writings of Black and White Men (books), and brochures. **Formerly:** (1984) International Association of Black and White Men Together.

★255★
National Association of Black Catholic Administrators (NABCA)
c/o Ministry for Black Catholics
50 N. Park Ave.
Rockville Centre, NY 11570 Phone: (516)678-5800
Barbara Horsham-Brathwaite, Exec. Officer

Description: Black administrators and representatives of archdiocesan and diocesan offices concerned with the development of Black leadership within the Catholic church. Assists the church in its role of evangelization and in defining its mission to the Black community. Seeks to provide an inner resource for the social and spiritual needs and concerns of Catholics of African ancestry. Addresses world issues of civil and human rights in the local, national, and international communities. **Founded:** 1976. **Budget:** Less than $25,000. **Regional Groups:** 7. **Local Groups:** 50.

★256★
National Association of Black Consulting Engineers (NABCE)
6406 Georgia Ave. NW
Washington, DC 20012 Phone: (202)291-3550
John W. Levermore, Pres.

Description: Engineering consulting firms and related businesses. Purpose is to gain recognition and increase professional opportunities for Black consulting engineers. Lobbies the federal government. Gives presentations to high schools on career day to promote the engineering consulting field to Black students. **Founded:** 1975. **Members:** 100. **Publications:** Plans to issue newsletter. **Formerly:** (1978) National Council of Minority Consulting Engineers.

★257★
National Association of Black Geologists and Geophysicists (NABGG)
PO Box 720157
Houston, TX 77272
Michael Carrol, Pres.

Description: Black geologists and geophysicists. Assists minority geologists and geophysicists in establishing professional and business relationships. Informs minority students of career opportunities in geology and geophysics. Seeks to motivate minority students to utilize existing programs, grants, and loans. Provides scholarships and oversees the educational careers of scholarship recipients. Assists minority students in their pursuit for summer employment and members interested in obtaining employees for summer positions. **Founded:** 1981. **Members:** 120. **Computerized Services:** Data base. **Publications:** Platform Network, quarterly.

★258★
National Association of Black Hospitality Professionals (NABHP)
PO Box 5443
Plainfield, NJ 07060 Phone: (201)354-5117
Mikoel Turner, Pres.

Description: Individuals involved in the hospitality profession on a managerial or supervisory level, and those interested in careers in the food service, hotel, and restaurant field. Provides a forum for the sharing of ideas, experiences, and job opportunity information; seeks to improve the image of Blacks in the hospitality industry; provides support to educational institutions. Conducts educational and research programs; operates placement service. Plans to: bestow awards to members for outstanding accomplishments; offer scholarships to high school and college students interested in careers in hospitality management; sponsor high school educational programs on the industry in conjunction with the National Urban League (see separate entry). Compiles statistics on Blacks in hospitality management. **Founded:** 1985. **Members:** 100. **Computerized Services:** Data base. **Publications:** Bulletin, monthly. Insights, quarterly. Newsletter.

★259★
National Association of Black Journalists (NABJ)
PO Box 17212
Washington, DC 20041 Phone: (703)648-1270
Carl E. Morris Sr., Exec.Dir.

Description: Persons employed in the production, dissemination, and distribution of news by newspapers, magazines, and radio and television stations. Aims are to: strengthen the ties between Blacks in the Black media and Blacks in the White media; sensitize the White media to the "institutional racism in its coverage"; expand the White media's coverage and "balanced reporting" of the Black community; become an exemplary group of professionals that honors excellence and outstanding achievement among Black journalists. Works with high schools to identify potential journalists; awards scholarships to journalism programs that especially support minorities. Acts as a national clearinghouse for job information. Maintains biographical archives . Sponsors competitions. **Founded:** 1975. **Members:** 2000. **Budget:** $450,000. **Regional Groups:** 10. **Local Groups:** 36. **Telecommunications Services:** Fax, (703)476-6245. **Publications:** NABJ Journal, 10/year. Tabloid newsletter concerned with Black issues and association news.

★260★
National Association of Black Owned Broadcasters (NABOB)
1730 M St. NW, Rm. 412
Washington, DC 20036 Phone: (202)463-8970
James L. Winston, Exec.Dir.

Description: Black broadcast station owners; Black formatted stations not currently owned or controlled by Blacks; organizations having an interest in the Black consumer market or Black broadcast industry; individuals interested in becoming owners; and communications schools, departments, and professional groups and associations. Represents the interests of existing and potential Black radio and television stations. Is currently working with the Office of Federal Procurement Policy to determine which government contracting major advertisers and advertising agencies are complying with government initiatives to increase the amount of advertising dollars received by minority-owned firms. Conducts lobbying activities; provides legal representation for the protection of minority ownership policies. Participates in the reorganization of the Advisory Committee on Radio Broadcasting. Sponsors annual Communications Awards Dinner each March. Conducts workshops; compiles statistics. **Founded:** 1976. **Members:** 150. **Regional Groups:** 5. **Computerized Services:** Mailing list of Black-owned broadcast facilities. **Publications:** Black-Owned Station Directory, quarterly. NABOB News, monthly. Newsletter. **Also known as:** National Black Owned Broadcasters Association.

★261★
National Association of Black Professors (NABP)
Dept. of Chemistry
430 S. Michigan Ave.
Roosevelt University
Chicago, IL 60605 Phone: (312)341-3817

Description: College professors of African descent. Goals are to: provide a forum for the exchange of information among college professors; enhance education for Black people and enrich the educational process in general; support and promote intellectual interests of Black students. Disseminates professional improvement information. Conducts monthly seminar and monthly workshop; sponsors one public lecture each academic year. Compiles statistics; bestows awards and scholarship; maintains placement service and speakers' bureau. **Founded:** 1974. **Members:** 135. **Budget:** Less than $25,000.

★262★
National Association of Black Real Estate Professionals (NABREP)
PO Box 21421
Alexandria, VA 22320 Phone: (703)684-9052
Sherman L. Ragland II, Pres.

Description: Black professionals in real estate, including the areas of design, development, law, engineering, management, and investment. Provides a forum for the discussion of information related to the industry. Offers career development and networking opportunities. Provides placement and consulting services; maintains speakers' bureau. **Founded:** 1984. **Regional Groups:** 5.

★263★
National Association of Black Social Workers (NABSW)
PO Box 92698
Atlanta, GA 30314 Phone: (404)584-7967
Mrs. E. Hill DeLoney, Exec.Dir.

Description: Social workers and other concerned individuals. Seeks to support, develop, and sponsor community welfare projects and programs which will serve the interest of the Black community and aid it in controlling its social institutions. Assists with adoption referrals. Bestows education awards; maintains library. **Founded:** 1968. **Members:** 10,000. **Publications:** Black Caucus, annual. Proceedings, annual. Also publishes Preserving Black Families: Research and Action Beyond the Rhetoric.

★264★
National Association of Black Women Attorneys (NABWA)
3711 Macomb St., NW, 2nd Fl.
Washington, DC 20016 Phone: (202)966-9693
Mabel D. Haden, Pres.

Description: Black women who are members of the bar of any U.S. state or territory; associate members include law school graduates, paralegals, and law students. Seeks to: advance jurisprudence and the administration of justice by increasing the opportunities of Black and non-Black women at all levels; aid in protecting the civil and human rights of all citizens and residents of the U.S.; expand opportunities for women lawyers through education; promote fellowship among women lawyers. Provides pre-law and student counseling; serves as job placement resource for firms, companies, and others interested in the field. Holds regional seminars; sponsors scholarship awards competition and brief-writing contest. Maintains hall of fame; offers charitable program. **Founded:** 1972. **Members:** 500. **Budget:** $30,000. **Regional Groups:** 8. **State Groups:** 10. **Local Groups:** 2. **Computerized Services:** Data base; mailing list. **Telecommunications Services:** Fax, (202)244-6648; telephone referral service. **Publications:** Convention Bulletin, annual. NABWA News, quarterly. Also publishes job announcements.

★265★
National Association of Black Women Entrepreneurs (NABWE)
PO Box 1375
Detroit, MI 48231 Phone: (313)341-7400
Marilyn French-Hubbard, Founder

Description: Black women who own and operate their own businesses; Black women interested in starting businesses; organizations and companies desiring mailing lists. Acts as a national support system for Black businesswomen in the U.S. and focuses on the unique problems they face. Objective is to enhance business, professional, and technical development of both present and future Black businesswomen. Maintains speakers' bureau and national networking program. Offers symposia, workshops, and forums aimed at increasing the business awareness of Black women. Shares resources, lobbies, and provides placement service. Bestows annual Black Woman Entrepreneur of the Year Award. **Founded:** 1979. **Members:** 3000. **Budget:** $230,000. **Regional Groups:** 4. **State Groups:** 28. **Publications:** Making Success Happen Newsletter, bimonthly. Membership Directory, annual.

★266★
National Association of Blacks in Criminal Justice (NABCJ)
PO Box 66271
Washington, DC 20035 Phone: (215)686-2961
Levan Gordon, Chm.

Description: Criminal justice professionals concerned with the impact of criminal justice policies and practices on the minority community.

Advocates with local, state, and federal criminal justice agencies for the improvement of minority recruitment practices and for the advancement of minority career mobility within those agencies. Sponsors regional conferences, career development seminars, and annual training institutes; maintains speakers' bureau. Provides financial and in-kind services to community groups. Bestows annual awards; compiles statistics on minority involvement in the criminal justice field. **Founded:** 1972. **Members:** 5000. **Budget:** $50,000. **State Groups:** 27. **Publications:** Local Criminal Justice Issues Newsletter, bimonthly. NABCJ Annual Report. NABCJ Minority Criminal Justice Personnel Directory, annual. NABCJ Newsletter, quarterly. Proceedings of Annual Conference..

★267★

National Association of Blacks Within Government (NABG)
1820 11th St., NW
Washington, DC 20001 Phone: (202)667-3280
Marion A. Bowden, Pres.

Description: Purpose is to enhance and increase the employability of Black officials within government and to prepare Black youths for government and private sector careers. Sponsors yearly seminar to help young people develop management, learning, interpersonal, and specialized skills. Bestows annual Black Humanitarian Award; compiles statistics. **Founded:** 1982. **Regional Groups:** 1. **Publications:** Newsletter, semiannual.

★268★

National Association of College Deans, Registrars, and Admissions Officers (NACDRAO)
917 Dorsett Ave.
Albany, GA 31701 Phone: (912)435-4945
Helen Mayes, Exec.Sec.

Description: Deans, registrars, and admissions officers of collegiate institutions with predominantly Black student bodies. **Founded:** 1925. **Members:** 325. **Budget:** Less than $25,000. **Publications:** NACDRAO Directory, annual. Newsletter, quarterly. Proceedings, annual. **Formerly:** (1949) National Association of Collegiate Deans and Registrars in Negro Schools; (1970) National Association of College Deans and Registrars.

★269★

National Association of Colored Women's Clubs (NACWC)
5808 16th St. NW
Washington, DC 20011 Phone: (202)726-2044
Carole A. Early, Hdqtrs.Sec.

Description: Federation of Black women's clubs. Carries on program of civic service, education, social service, and philanthropy. Sponsors National Association of Girls Clubs (see separate entry). **Founded:** 1896. **Members:** 45,000. **State Groups:** 38. **Local Groups:** 1000. **Publications:** National Notes, quarterly.

★270★

National Association of Educational Office Personnel (NAEOP)
7223 Lee Hwy., Ste. 301
Falls Church, VA 22046
Rebecca W. Grim, Exec.Sec.

Description: Secretaries, stenographers, administrative assistants, bookkeepers, receptionists, and other office workers employed by schools, colleges and universities, educational associations, and county and state departments of education. Conducts professional standards program to measure the services of office personnel in education and awards certificates for achievements on five levels of education, experience, and professional activity. Sponsors competitions; maintains speakers' bureau; annually bestows National Educational Administrator of the Year and National Educational Office Employee of the Year awards. Also annually bestows scholarships. **Founded:** 1934. **Members:** 6000. **Publications:** Beam, quarterly. Newsletter for retirees. **Formerly:** (1952) National Association of School Secretaries; (1980) National Association of Educational Secretaries.

★271★

National Association of Extension Home Economists (NAEHE)
1801 Robert Fulton Dr., Ste. 400
Reston, VA 22091 Phone: (703)758-3547
Kathy Huggins, Admin.

Description: Conducts out-of-school educational programs. Helps individuals and families find solutions to problems concerning family life such as child care and development, nutrition, energy conservation, budgeting, and family recreation. Sponsors conferences and trains volunteer leaders to work with individuals and groups. Conducts public policy forum; bestows awards. **Founded:** 1931. **Members:** 4000. **Budget:** $500,000. **State Groups:** 54. **Publications:** The Communique, semiannual. The Reporter, quarterly. **Formerly:** National Association of Negro Home Demonstration Agents; National Home Demonstration Agents' Association.

★272★

National Association of Fashion and Accessory Designers (NAFAD)
2180 E. 93rd St.
Cleveland, OH 44106 Phone: (216)231-0375
Beatrice Spencer, Pres.

Description: Persons engaged in the field of fashion design or other allied fields. Fosters the development of the Black fashion designer; encourages integration of members in all phases of the fashion industry through the extension of educational and economic opportunities. Disseminates information; awards local and national scholarships. Holds workshops and fashion seminars; maintains library and Black Historical Museum of Fashion Dolls (see separate entry). Presented biographical archives to the Mary McLeod Bethune Historical Development Project. **Founded:** 1949. **Members:** 240. **Budget:** Less than $25,000. **Regional Groups:** 2. **State Groups:** 2. **Local Groups:** 12. **Publications:** Membership Roster, annual. Newsletter, semiannual.

★273★

National Association of Girls Clubs (NAGC)
5808 16th St. NW
Washington, DC 20011 Phone: (202)726-2044
Carole A. Early, Hdqtrs.Sec.

Description: Sponsored by National Association of Colored Women's Clubs (see separate entry). Black girls, ages 6-18. Promotes the moral, mental, and material development of members; fosters positive attitudes toward health, beauty, love, home, and service among members. **Founded:** 1930. **Formerly:** (1976) National Association of Colored Girls Clubs.

★274★

National Association of Health Services Executives (NAHSE)
1400 Spring St., Ste. 300
Silver Spring, MD 20910 Phone: (301)608-0024
William L. Jackson, Pres.

Description: Black health care executive managers, planners, educators, advocates, providers, organizers, researchers, and consumers participating in academic ventures, educational forums, seminars, workshops, systems design, legislation, and other activities. Conducts National Work-Study Program and sponsors educational programs. Bestows annual Humanitarian Award for outstanding service in the field of human services. **Founded:** 1968. **Members:** 500. **Budget:** $35,000. **Local Groups:** 8. **Publications:** Notes, bimonthly. Newsletter.

★275★
National Association of Human Rights Workers (NAHRW)
c/o Ronald McElreath
Florida Commission on Human Relations
Bldg. F., Ste. 240
325 John Knox Rd.
Tallahassee, FL 32303 Phone: (904)488-7082
Ronald McElreath, Pres.

Description: Professional association of governmental or private organization employees working in the areas of civil rights, civil liberties, interracial and interethnic relations, and religious understanding. Maintains speakers' bureau; conducts research programs; compiles statistics. Bestows awards. **Founded:** 1947. **Members:** 350. **Budget:** Less than $25,000. **Regional Groups:** 4. **Local Groups:** 16. **Publications:** Journal of Intergroup Relations, quarterly. NAHRW Newsletter, bimonthly. **Formerly:** National Association of Intergroup Relations Officials.

★276★
National Association of Investment Companies (NAIC)
1111 14th St. NW, Ste. 700
Washington, DC 20005 Phone: (202)289-4336
JoAnn H. Price, Pres.

Description: Aims to: represent the minority small business investment company industry in the public sector; provide industry education; develop research material on the activities of the industry; promote the growth of minority-owned small businesses by informing the public of their contribution to the vitality of the nation's economy; collect and disseminate relevant business and trade information to members; facilitate the exchange of new ideas and financing strategies; assist organizing groups attempting to form or acquire minority enterprise small business investment companies; provide management and technical assistance to members; monitor regulatory agency actions. Conducts three professional seminars; sponsors research; compiles statistics. **Founded:** 1971. **Members:** 150. **Publications:** NAIC Membership Directory, annual. **Formerly:** (1987) American Association of Minority Enterprise Small Business Investment Companies.

★277★
National Association of Management Consultants (NAMC)
3101 Euclid Office Plaza, Ste. 701
Cleveland, OH 44115 Phone: (216)431-0101
Hosiah Huggins, Pres.

Description: Minority management consultants. Seeks to increase minority participation in the industry. Provides for the sharing of information, collaboration on projects, and improvement of professionalism in the field. **Founded:** 1985. **Members:** 50. **Publications:** Newsletter, annual.

★278★
National Association of Market Developers (NAMD)
1422 W. Peachtree NW, Ste. 500
Atlanta, GA 30309 Phone: (404)892-0244
Bunnie Jackson Ransom, Exec.Dir.

Description: Professionals engaged in marketing, sales, sales promotion, advertising, or public relations who are concerned with the delivery of goods and services to the minority consumer market. Maintains placement service; conducts research programs; sponsors speakers' bureau. Presents awards to majority- and minority-owned corportions; cites a Communicator of the Year. **Founded:** 1953. **Members:** 700. **Local Groups:** 18. **Telecommunications Services:** Fax, (404)874-7100. **Publications:** Briefcase, bimonthly. Contains articles about the social position of African-Americans, convention reports, and job opportunity listings. EMPHASIS, annual. Magazine; includes chapter news, convention reports, and articles about minority markets in the U.S. President's Report, bimonthly.

★279★
National Association of Minority Automobile Dealers (NAMAD)
11000 W. McNichols
Detroit, MI 48221 Phone: (313)863-3655
Jesse J. Jones, Pres.

Description: Automobile dealers. Acts as liaison between membership, the government, the community, and industry representatives; seeks to better the business conditions of its members on an ongoing basis. Acts as confidential spokesperson for dealers. Offers business analysis, financial counseling, and short- and long-term management planning. Conducts research programs; compiles statistics. **Founded:** 1980. **Members:** 350. **Telecommunications Services:** Fax, (313)863-3211. **Publications:** Newsletter, quarterly.

★280★
National Association of Minority Contractors (NAMC)
1333 F St. NW, Ste. 500
Washington, DC 20004 Phone: (202)347-8259
Ralph C. Thomas, Exec.Dir.

Description: Minority construction contractors and corporations wishing to do business with minority contractors. Identifies procurement opportunities; provides specialized training; acts as national advocate for minority construction contractors. Holds workshops and seminars; compiles statistics; bestows awards. **Founded:** 1969. **Members:** 3500. **Local Groups:** 50. **Telecommunications Services:** Fax, (202)628-1876; telex, 202-628-1876. **Publications:** Building Concerns, bimonthly. Newsletter. Legislative Bulletin, periodic. Procurement Bulletin, periodic.

★281★
National Association of Minority Women in Business (NAMWIB)
906 Grand Ave., Ste. 200
Kansas City, MO 64106 Phone: (816)421-3335
Inez Kaiser, Pres.

Description: Minority women in business ownership and management positions; college students. Serves as a network for the exchange of ideas and information on business opportunities for minority women in the public and private sectors. Conducts workshops, conferences, seminars, and luncheons. Maintains speakers' bureau, hall of fame, and placement service; compiles statistics; bestows awards to women who have made significant contributions to the field. **Founded:** 1972. **Members:** 5000. **Telecommunications Services:** Fax, (816)421-3336. **Publications:** Today, bimonthly. Newsletter.

★282★
National Association of Negro Business and Professional Women's Clubs (NANBPWC)
1806 New Hampshire Ave., NW
Washington, DC 20009 Phone: (202)483-4206
Ellen A. Graves, Exec. Officer

Description: Women actively engaged in a business or a profession who are committed to rendering service through club programs and activities. Seeks to direct the interest of business and professional women toward united action for improved social and civic conditions, and to provide enriching and ennobling experiences that will encourage freedom, dignity, self-respect, and self-reliance. Offers information and help regarding education, employment, health, housing, legislation, and problems of the aged and the disabled. Presents honors and awards for national and community service. Sponsors educational assistance program, which includes local and national scholarships. Conducts consumer education and prison reform programs. Maintains youth department clubs. Provides placement services; operates speakers' bureau; compiles statistics. **Founded:** 1935. **Members:** 10,000. **Budget:** $500,000 **Regional Groups:** 6. **Local Groups:** 350. **Telecommunications Services:** Fax, (202)462-7253. **Publications:** Convention Proceedings, annual. Directory, annual. President's Newsletter, monthly. Program Idea Exchange, bimonthly. Responsibility, quarterly. Also publishes handbooks and manuals.

★283★
National Association of Negro Musicians (NANM)
PO Box S-011
237 E. 115th St.
Chicago, IL 60628 Phone: (312)779-1325
Ona B. Campbell, Exec.Sec.

Description: Amateur, professional, and retired musicians; interested individuals. Promotes the advancement of all types of music, especially among young Black musicians. Sponsors annual competitions in which regional winners compete for scholarships; also sponsors concerts by recognized musicians. **Founded:** 1919. **Members:** 2500. **Budget:** $150,000. **Regional Groups:** 5. **Local Groups:** 34. **Publications:** NANM Newsletter, quarterly. Post-Convention Newsletter, annual.

★284★
National Association of Securities Professionals (NASP)
10 E. 87th St.
New York, NY 10128 Phone: (212)427-8100

Description: Seeks to represent the interests of minority securities professionals. Has drafted a list of equal-employment principles to be sent to firms throughout the industry. **Members:** 300. **Telecommunications Services:** Fax, (212)876-6278.

7/16

★285★
National Association of University Women (NAUW)
1553 Pine Forest Dr.
Tallahassee, FL 32301 Phone: (904)878-4660
Ruth R. Corbin, Pres.

Description: Women college or university graduates. Works to promote constructive work in education, civic activities, and human relations; studies educational conditions with emphasis on problems affecting women; encourages high educational standards and stimulate intellectual attainment among women generally. Theme is New Visions, New Insights, New Directions. Offers tutoring and sponsors After High School-What? program. Maintains placement service. Awards annual national fellowship; two sectional groups also award scholarships annually. **Founded:** 1923. **Members:** 4000. **Regional Groups:** 5. **Local Groups:** 92. **Publications:** Bulletin, biennial. Directory of Branch Presidents and Members, annual. Journal of the National Association of University Women, biennial. **Formerly:** (1974) National Association of College Women.

★286★
National Association of Urban Bankers (NAUB)
122 C St. NW, Ste. 580
Washington, DC 20001 Phone: (202)783-4743
Lethia A. Kelly, Exec.Dir.

Description: Minority professionals in the financial services industry; financial services institutions and banks. Supports minority professionals in the banking services industry. Communicates information and sponsors programs to further careers for minority bankers. Utilizes member resources to solve problems of minority entrepreneurs. Awards scholarship to a minority banking student. **Founded:** 1975. **Members:** 1500. **Budget:** $150,000. **Regional Groups:** 4. **Publications:** Membership Directory, periodic. President's Bulletin, periodic. Urban Banker, quarterly. Newsletter. Also publishes brochure.

★287★
National Athletic Steering Committee (NASC)
PO Box 982
Florida State University
Tallahassee, FL 32307 Phone: (904)599-3868
Walter Reed, Pres.

Description: Objective is to study problems of segregation and discrimination in intercollegiate athletics on a national level. Provides recommendations for action to conference and nonconference schools whose programs are involved in "undemocratic practices." **Founded:** 1951. **Budget:** Less than $25,000. **Telecommunications Services:** Fax, (904)599-3206.

★288★ 7/18
National Bankers Association (NBA)
122 C St. NW, Ste. 580
Washington, DC 20001 Phone: (202)783-3200
John P. Kelly Jr., Pres.

Description: Minority banking institutions; minority individuals employed by majority banks and institutions. To serve as an advocate for the minority banking industry. Organizes banking services, government relations, marketing, scholarship, and technical assistance programs. Sponsors conferences; offers placement services; compiles statistics; bestows awards. **Founded:** 1927. **Members:** 160. **Budget:** $360,000. **Regional Groups:** 5. **Computerized Services:** Data base. **Publications:** NBA Today, semiannual. Magazine. **Formerly:** (1951) National Negro Bankers Association.

★289★
National Bar Association (NBA)
1225 11th St. NW
Washington, DC 20001 Phone: (202)842-3900
John Crump, Exec.Dir.

Description: Minority (predominantly Black) attorneys, members of the judiciary, law students, and law faculty. Programs and involvements represent the interests of members and the communities they serve. Offers specialized education and research programs. Presents annual C. Francis Stradford Award and Equal Justice Award. **Founded:** 1925. **Members:** 12,500. **Budget:** $1,000,000. **Regional Groups:** 12. **Local Groups:** 60. **Publications:** NBA Bulletin, quarterly. NBA Journal, biennial. NBA Magazine, monthly. Legal information for minority legal professionals. Includes legal briefs and industry outlook.

★290★
National Bar Association
Women Lawyers Division
c/o Brenda Girton
1211 Connecticut Ave. NW, Ste. 702
Washington, DC 20036 Phone: (202)291-1979
Brenda Girton, Pres.

Description: Women lawyers, law students, and other individuals. Purposes are to: provide a forum to discuss and address issues unique to women in the legal profession; promote professional growth and honor achievements of minority attorneys; promote admission to practice at all levels of the judicial system; foster interactions between minority and other bar associations; encourage participation in community service. Awards scholarhsips; holds seminars. **Founded:** 1972. **Members:** 300. **Telecommunications Services:** Fax, (202)347-7127. **Publications:** Newsletter, periodic.

★291★
National Beauty Culturists' League (NBCL)
25 Logan Circle NW
Washington, DC 20005 Phone: (202)332-2695
Cleolif Richardson, Pres.

Description: Beauticians, cosmetologists, and beauty products manufacturers. Encourages standardized, scientific, and approved methods of hair, scalp, and skin treatments. Offers scholarships and plans to establish a research center. Sponsors: National Institute of Cosmetology, a training course in operating and designing and business techniques; National Beauty Week. Maintains hall of fame; conducts research programs; compiles statistics. **Founded:** 1919. **Members:** 10,000. **State Groups:** 39. **Local Groups:** 250. **Formerly:** (1920) National Hair System Culture League.

★292★
National Black Alcoholism Council (NBAC)
1629 K St. NW, Ste. 802
Washington, DC 20006 Phone: (202)296-2696
Maxine Womble, Exec.Dir.

Description: Individuals concerned about alcoholism among Black Americans. Works to support and initiate activities that will improve alcoholism treatment services and lead to the prevention of alcoholism in the Black community. Provides training on how to treat Black alcoholics from a cultural perspective. Bestows political and service awards. Maintains biographical archives. Compiles statistics concerning alcoholism among Blacks. **Founded:** 1978. **Members:** 1050. **Budget:** $85,000. Chapters: 20. **Telecommunications Services:** Fax, (202)296-2707. **Publications:** National News and Views, semiannual. Also publishes Treatment of Black Alcoholics (book) and Model for Working With Children of Alcoholic and Drug Addicted Parents, (booklet).

★293★ 7/18
National Black Alliance for Graduate Level Education (NBAGLE)
c/o Dr. John W. Wilson
University College
Spicer Hall
University of Akron
Akron, OH 44325 Phone: (216)972-7066
Dr. John W. Wilson, Pres.

Description: Black educators, administrators, students, and individuals interested in the recruitment, financial assistance, retention, and placement of Black graduate students. Advocates on behalf of Black students, faculty, and administrators. Provides the opportunity to discuss and resolve problems and issues affecting Blacks in graduate and professional schools. Seeks to increase educational opportunities for Black students. **Founded:** 1970. **Publications:** Newsletter, periodic.

★294★
National Black Catholic Clergy Caucus (NBCCC)
343 W. Walnut St.
PO Box 1088
Opelousus, LA 70571
Bro. Roy Smith, Contact

Description: Black priests, brothers, seminarians, and deacons. Purpose is to support the spiritual, theological, educational, and ministerial growth of the Black Catholic community within the church. Serves as a vehicle to bring contributions of the Black community to the church. Advances the fight against racism within the Catholic church and society. Offers computerized service. **Founded:** 1968. **Members:** 650. **Regional Groups:** 4. **Publications:** Directory, annual. Newsletter, 6-8/year.

★295★
National Black Catholic Seminarians Association (NBCSA)
780 Porter St.
Beaumont, TX 77701
Freddy Washington, Pres.

Description: Black Catholic seminarians united for the growth and development of each member as a person, Christian, and potential priest or religious brother. "Attempts to reflect both the heritage of the church and Black people in terms of the richness of their spirituality." Stresses the importance of individual contribution and total involvement of each Black seminarian to the organization. Maintains speakers' bureau and charitable programs; bestows awards; compiles statistics. **Founded:** 1969. **Members:** 330. **Budget:** Less than $25,000. **Regional Groups:** 10. **Publications:** National Black Catholic Seminarians Association–Newsletter, quarterly. Includes articles on the history, theology, and education of Black seminaries in the Catholic church.

★296★
National Black Caucus of Local Elected Officials (NBC/LEO)
1301 Pennsylvania Ave. NW, Ste. 400
Washington, DC 20004 Phone: (202)626-3597
Russell Owens, Exec.Dir.

Description: Elected Black municipal and county officials united to recognize and deal with problems of members. Attempts to provide the organizational structure required to better present and respond to issues affecting constituents. Seeks to influence the National League of Cities (see separate entry) in the development of policies affecting Black Americans; promotes legislative and economic development initiatives directed toward the needs of the Black community. Presents annual Liberty Award. **Founded:** 1970.

★297★
National Black Caucus of State Legislators (NBCSL)
Hall of States
444 N. Capitol St. NW, Ste. 206
Washington, DC 20001 Phone: (202)624-5457
Rep. David P. Richardson Jr., Pres.

Description: Black state legislators. Organized to provide more political networking to Black legislators from the federal and state levels. Goals are to: provide a network through which state legislators can exchange information and ideas on state and national legislation; provide a unified front or platform; serve as a focal point for involvement of Black legislators in the "new federalism." Activities include arranging meetings between all governmental groups representing Black elected officials and analyzing and forming a position on the "new federalism." Conducts seminars. Maintains speakers' bureau and biographical archives; compiles statistics. Bestows awards. **Founded:** 1977. **Members:** 415. **Regional Groups:** 12. **State Groups:** 42. **Telecommunications Services:** Fax, (202)737-1069. **Publications:** Directory of Black State Legislators, biennial. Newsletter, quarterly. Also publishes Issues in State.

★298★
National Black Chamber of Commerce (NBCC)
5741 Telegraph Ave.
Oakland, CA 94609 Phone: (415)601-5741
Oscar J. Coffey Jr., CEO & Pres.

Description: Black and minority chambers of commerce organized to create a strategy for members of local chambers to share in the collective buying power of Black and minority communities. Primary focus is on the tourism industry, because, according to the association, minorities spend approximately $25 billion in the tourism market each year, but minority-owned businesses net very little from this industry. Conducts training sessions to acquaint Black and minority businesspeople with the tourism market and marketing strategies. Manages Advocacy Program which researches and analyzes issues given priority by local chambers. **Founded:** 1983. **Members:** 10,451. **Budget:** $300,000. **State Groups:** 72. **Telecommunications Services:** Fax, (415)601-6911. **Publications:** Black Business News, quarterly. National Minority Chamber Directory, annual. **Formerly:** (1990) National Association of Black and Minority Chambers of Commerce.

★299★
National Black Child Development Institute (NBCDI)
1463 Rhode Island Ave. NW
Washington, DC 20005 Phone: (202)387-1281
Evelyn K. Moore, Exec.Dir.

Description: Individuals dedicated to improving the quality of life for Black children and youth. Conducts direct services and advocacy campaigns aimed at both national and local public policies focusing on issues of health, child welfare, education, and child care. Organizes and trains network of members in a volunteer grassroots affiliate system to voice concerns regarding policies that affect Black children and their families. Stimulates communication between Black community groups, through conferences and seminars, to discuss and make recommendations that will be advantageous to the development of Black children. Analyzes selected policy decisions and legislative and administrative regulations to determine their impact on Black children and youth. Informs national policymakers of issues critical to Black children. **Founded:** 1970. **Members:** 3250. **Regional Groups:** 38. **Telecommunications Services:** Fax, (202)234-1738. **Publications:** Black Child Advocate, quarterly. Newsletter providing public policy and legislative updates and information on local service programs. **Formerly:** (1979) Black Child Development Institute.

★300★
National Black Coalition of Federal Aviation Employees (NBCFAE)
PO Box 44392
Washington, DC 20026-4392 Phone: (202)267-9938
Alfredia Brooks, Pres.

★301★
National Black Evangelical Association (NBEA)
5736 N. Albina Ave.
Portland, OR 97217 Phone: (503)289-5754
Aaron M. Hamlin, Exec.Dir.

Description: Individuals of all backgrounds, churches, and religions. Conducts seminars; sponsors educational programs on drug abuse, church education, evangelism, Black theology mission, and social action. Provides children's services and placement service. Bestows awards; compiles statistics. **Founded:** 1963. **Members:** 600. **Regional Groups:** 3. **Local Groups:** 13. **Publications:** Journal, annual. Outreach, quarterly. Also publishes history of NBEA. **Formerly:** National Negro Evangelical Association.

★302★
National Black Law Student Association (NBLSA)
1225 11th St. NW
Washington, DC 20001 Phone: (202)583-1281
Juliette Williams, Chair

Description: Black law students united to meet the needs of Black people within the legal profession and to work for the benefit of the Black community. Objectives are to: articulate and promote professional competence, needs, and goals of Black law students; focus on the relationship between Black students and attorneys and the American legal system; instill in Black law students and attorneys a greater commitment to the Black community; encourage the legal community to bring about change to meet the needs of the Black community. Supports Black law students at Harvard University who recently called for a boycott of a course on racial discrimination to protest the law school's faculty-hiring practices. Sponsors the Frederick Douglass Moot Court Competition; bestows awards; sponsors scholarship program; offers placement service. **Founded:** 1967. **Members:** 8000. **Regional Groups:** 6. **Local Groups:** 200. **Publications:** Reports, quarterly. **Formerly:** (1983) Black American Law Student Association.

★303★
National Black Leadership Roundtable (NBLR)
2135 Rayburn House Bldg.
Washington, DC 20515 Phone: (202)331-2030
Rep. Walter E. Fauntroy, Pres.

Description: Chief executive officers of national Black organizations. Goals are to: provide a forum for leaders of national Black organizations to discuss and exchange ideas on issues critical to Black Americans; aid in the development of political, economic, and networking strategies that are advantageous to the needs of the Black community; ensure that elected and appointed officials represent and are accountable to the Black community. Bestows annual Youth Award to an individual who has demonstrated excellence in the fields of art, entertainment, education, and science. **Founded:** 1983. **Members:** 300. **Publications:** Roundtable Record, quarterly. Newsletter.

★304★
National Black MBA Association (NBMBAA)
180 N. Michigan Ave., Ste. 1820
Chicago, IL 60601 Phone: (312)236-2622
Derryl L. Reed, Pres.

Description: Business professionals, lawyers, accountants, and engineers concerned with the role of Blacks who hold Master of Business Administration degrees. Encourages Blacks to pursue continuing business education; assists students preparing to enter the business world. Provides programs for minority youths, students, and professionals, including workshops, panel discussions, and Destination MBA seminar. Sponsors student mini-conference and job fair; holds competitions. Works with graduate schools; grants scholarships to graduate business students. Presents Outstanding Educator Award, MBA of the Year Award, Silver Touch Award, H. Naylor Fitzhugh Award, and Outstanding Educational Institution Award. **Founded:** 1971. **Members:** 2000. **State Groups:** 23. **Telecommunications Services:** Fax, (312)236-4131. **Publications:** National Black MBA Association–Newsletter, quarterly. Covers membership activities; includes business news and chapter profiles.

★305★
National Black McDonald's Operators Association (NBMOA)
c/o Mrs. Fran Jones
6290 Sunset Blvd., Ste. 1026
Hollywood, CA 90028 Phone: (213)962-2806
Mrs. Fran Jones, Pres.

Description: Black owners of McDonald's restaurants. Provides a forum for the exchange of ideas on the improvement of community relations and on the operation and management of restaurants. Seeks to build and improve the McDonald's restaurant image throughout the community. Sponsors training seminars on marketing, better sales practices, labor relations, and profit sharing. Bestows awards; conducts charitable programs. **Founded:** 1972. **Members:** 169. **Regional Groups:** 5. **Local Groups:** 1. **Publications:** Newsletter, quarterly. Also publishes Historical Highlights (book).

★306★
National Black Media Coalition (NBMC)
38 New York Ave. NE
Washington, DC 20002 Phone: (202)387-8155
Carmen Marshall, Exec.Dir.

Description: Black media advocacy group seeking to maximize media access for Blacks and other minorities in the communications industry through employment, ownership, and programming. Has been recognized by the FCC, Congress, and trade organizations concerned with Blacks and other minorities in the media. Past activities include participating in FCC rulemaking proceedings, speaking before university and professional audiences, conducting classes, and negotiating affirmative action plans with large media corporations. Maintains resource center; offers job referral service; compiles statistics. **Founded:** 1973. **Members:** 500. **Budget:** $100,000. **Regional Groups:** 80. **Publications:** Action Bulletin, periodic. For the Record, semiannual. Media Line, monthly. Newsletter; includes information on employment opportunities.

★307★
National Black Nurses Association (NBNA)
PO Box 1823
Washington, DC 20013 Phone: (202)393-6870
Sadako S. Holmes, Exec. Officer

Description: Registered nurses, licensed practical nurses, licensed vocational nurses, and student nurses. Functions as a professional support group and as an advocacy group for the Black community and their health care. Recruits and assists Blacks interested in pursuing nursing as a career. Presents scholarships to student nurses, including the Dr. Lauranne Sams Scholarship and the Ambi Scholarship. Compiles statistics; maintains biographical archives and charitable program. **Founded:** 1971. **Members:** 5000. **Publications:** Annual Report. Journal of Black Nurses Association, semiannual.

★308★
National Black on Black Love Campaign (BOBL)
111 E. Wacker Dr., Ste. 600
Chicago, IL 60601 Phone: (312)644-6610
Geri Duncan Jones, Exec.Dir.

Description: Individuals and businesses united to promote the motto, "Replace Black on Black crime with Black on Black love" and foster love and respect in all communities where people are, the group believes, inordinately affected by crime. Organizes No Crime Day in various communities and Adopt A Building Program for businesses. Sponsors youth organizations and seminars in schools and communities to educate the public in ways of dealing with crime. Operates charitable program; bestows awards. Maintains speakers' bureau; compiles statistics. **Founded:** 1983. **State Groups:** 6. **Telecommunications Services:** Fax, (312)565-4658.

★309★
National Black Police Association (NBPA)
1919 Pennsylvania Ave., NW, Ste. 300
Washington, DC 20006 Phone: (202)457-0563
Ronald E. Hampton, Exec.Dir.

Description: Male and female Black police officers. Seeks to: improve relationships between police departments and the Black community; recruit minority police officers on a national scale; eliminate police corruption, brutality, and racial discrimination. Bestows awards; maintains speakers' bureau. Operates charitable program. Offers scholarship. **Founded:** 1972. **Members:** 35,000. **Budget:** $95,000. **Regional Groups:** 5. **Local Groups:** 105. **Publications:** Black Police Membership Directory, annual.

★310★
National Black Public Relations Society (BPRS)
c/o Robbie Smith
1209 E. 53rd St., No. 1
Chicago, IL 60615-4023
Robbie Smith, Contact

Description: Black public relations professionals who are either self-employed or employed by advertising agencies, radio and television stations, businesses, or nonprofit organizations. Provides a forum for discussion of topics related to public relations; holds professional development workshops; conducts seminars; maintains speakers' bureau to promote the image of Blacks in business. **Founded:** 1981. **Members:** 100. **Budget:** Less than $25,000. **Publications:** Beepers, quarterly. Newsletter. Also publishes instructional brochures; plans to publish a directory of Black public relations professionals.

★311★
National Black Republican Council (NBRC)
375 S End Ave., Plaza 400-84
New York, NY 10280 Phone: (202)662-1335
Fred Brown, Chm.

Description: Black Republicans in the U.S. Works to elect more Black Republicans to national, state, and local offices. Maintains speakers' bureau. **Founded:** 1972. **Members:** 25,000. **Budget:** $100,000. **Regional Groups:** 4. **State Groups:** 44.

★312★
National Black Sisters' Conference (NBSC)
1001 Lawrence St., NE, Ste. 102
Washington, DC 20017 Phone: (202)529-9250
Sr. Gwynette Proctor, Exec.Dir.

Description: Black religious women. Seeks to develop the personal resources of Black women; challenges society, especially the church, to address issues of racism in the U.S. Activities include: retreats; consulting, leadership, and cultural understanding; formation workshops for personnel. Maintains educational programs for facilitating change and community involvement in inner-city parochial schools and parishes. Operates Sojourner House to provide spiritual affirmation for Black religious and laywomen. Bestows awards; maintains speakers' bureau. **Founded:** 1968. **Members:** 150. **Budget:** $40,000. **Publications:** Signs of Soul, 4/year. Newsletter reporting on Black members of the Catholic church. Includes employment opportunities and obituaries of members.

★313★
National Black Survival Fund (EBSF)
1006 Surrey St.
Lafayette, LA 70501 Phone: (318)232-7672
Rev. A. J. McKnight CS, Chm.

Description: A project of the Southern Development Foundation (see separate entry). Objective is to improve the ability of Black and other minority poor to achieve economic progress through their own effort and initiative. Believes that the economic, cultural, and physical survival of the nation's Black community is endangered due to the recession, discrimination, and the Reagan administration's cutbacks in social assistance programs. Seeks to maintain and increase support for programs that can avert the economic and human catastrophe the fund says will result if the opportunities offered to Blacks are undermined by current assistance cutbacks. Maintains: Food for Survival Program in which landowners and sharecroppers in Mississippi volunteer land, equipment, and labor to provide food and employment for needy families; Health Care for Survival Program, a cooperative low-cost health center in Mississippi; Jobs for Survival Program, which has assisted in providing jobs for Black workers in Alabama in construction, farming, and community service. **Founded:** 1982. **Publications:** Brochures and flyers. **Formerly:** Emergency Black Survival Fund.

★314★
National Black United Front (NBUF)
PO Box 470665
Brooklyn, NY 11247 Phone: (718)467-0258
Elizabeth Butler, Sec.

Description: Purpose is to unite Black people of diverse political ideologies, age groups, socioeconomic backgrounds, and religious beliefs in order to build "a viable force for social transformation." Goals are: the elimination of racism, sexism, bigotry, and racial violence; redistribution of the resources and wealth of the nation to provide abundantly for all citizens; elimination of the "genocidal mis-education system," police brutality, and denial of human rights nationally and internationally. Believes that current conditions in the U.S. threaten the survival of Black people as a whole, and urges Blacks to overlook individual differences by working together for common goals. Addresses such issues as unemployment, police brutality, budget cuts harmful to Black communities, and the resurgence of the Ku Klux Klan. Conducts seminars and forums; maintains speakers' bureau; offers charitable program; sponsors competitions. Plans to organize boycotts, hold demonstrations, engage in electoral politics, and seek new vehicles for change. Hopes to mobilize an effective grass roots Black movement. **Founded:** 1980. **Members:** 2000. **Publications:** The Front Page, quarterly. Newsletter.

★315★
National Black United Fund (NBUF)
50 Park Pl., Ste. 1538
Newark, NJ 07102 Phone: (201)643-5122
William T. Merritt, Pres.

Description: Provides financial and technical support to projects serving the critical needs of Black communities nationwide. Solicits funds through payroll deduction to support projects in the areas of education, health and human services, economic development, social justice, arts and culture, and emergency needs. Programs supported by NBUF emphasize self-help, volunteerism, and mutual aid. Maintains Walter Bremond Memorial Fund campaign. Provides charitable program. **Founded:** 1972. **Members:** 30. **Local Groups:** 15. **Telecommunications Services:** Fax, (201)648-8350; toll-free number, (800)223-0866. **Publications:** Newsletter, quarterly.

★316★
National Black Women's Consciousness Raising Association (BWCR)
1906 N. Charles St.
Baltimore, MD 21218 Phone: (301)727-8900
Dr. Elaine Simon, Exec.Dir.

Description: Black women interested in women's rights and women's issues. Acts as a support group for women. Provides educational and informational workshops and seminars on subjects of concern to Black women and women in general. Annually recognizes individuals, especially for academic achievement. **Founded:** 1975. **Members:** 750. **Budget:** Less than $25,000. **Publications:** BWCR, semiannual. Newsletter.

★317★
National Black Women's Health Project (NBWHP)
1237 Gordon St. SW
Atlanta, GA 30310 Phone: (404)753-0916
Julia R. Scott, Dir.

Description: Encourages mutual and selfhelp activism among women to bring about a reduction in health care problems prevalent among Black women. Urges women to communicate with health care providers, seek out available health care resources, become aware of selfhelp approaches, and communicate with other Black women to minimize feelings of powerlessness and isolation, and thus realize they have some control over their physical and mental health. Points out the higher incidence of high blood pressure, obesity, breast and cervical cancers, diabetes, kidney disease, arteriosclerosis, and teenage pregnancy among Black women than among other racial or socioeconomic groups. Also notes that Black infant mortality is twice that of Whites and that Black women are often victims of family violence because of the life stresses of Blacks. Offers lectures outlining demographic information, chronic conditions, the need for health information and access to services, and possible methods of improving the health status of Black women. Maintains data base and speakers' bureau. Plans to: establish Black women's selfhelp centers; develop Empowerment Though Wellness curriculum. **Founded:** 1980. **Budget:** $750,000. **State Groups:** 98. **Computerized Services:** Mailing list. **Telecommunications Services:** Fax, (404)752-6756; toll-free number, (800)ASK-BWHP. **Publications:** Vital Signs, 3/year. Newsletter. **Formerly:** (1984) Black Women's Health Project.

★318★
National Black Women's Political Leadership Caucus
3005 Bladensburg Rd., NE, No. 217
Washington, DC 20018 Phone: (202)529-2806
Juanita Kennedy Morgan, Dir.

Description: Women interested in understanding their political role and the need for females to work toward equality; auxiliary membership includes men, senior citizens, and youths. Works to educate and incorporate all Black women and youth in the political and economic process through participation. Encourages women to familiarize themselves with the role of city, state, and federal governments. Presents awards for humanitarianism; trains speakers and conducts research on the Black family and on topics concerning politics and economics; compiles statistics. Holds legislative, federal, state, and local workshops. Provides placement service; offers children's services; operates charitable program. **Founded:** 1971. **Regional Groups:** 3. **State Groups:** 33. **Publications:** Newsletter, semiannual. Has published election tabloids.

★319★
National Black Youth Leadership Council (NBYLC)
250 W. 54th St., Ste. 800
New York, NY 10019 Phone: (212)541-7600
Dennis Rahiim Watson, Exec.Dir.

Description: Outreach training and motivation organization. Conducts workshops for groups involved with Black youth and minority student academic and leadership development; works to reduce the number of minority students that do not finish high school. Provides resources, information, skills, and strategies for fostering such development. Advises educators and parents on their role and responsibility to display leadership and success skills to youths they come in contact with; makes available to educational institutions training and expertise on cultural diversity, multiculturalism, and problems of bigotry and racism. Sponsors drug abuse awareness programs. Maintains speakers' bureau and children's services. **Founded:** 1983.

★320★
National Bowling Association (NBA)
377 Park Ave., S., 7th Fl.
New York, NY 10016 Phone: (212)689-8308
Margaret S. Lee, Exec.Sec.-Treas.

Description: Seeks to: foster good sportsmanship, fellowship, and friendship; increase the interests, talents, and skills of adult and youth bowlers; create national awareness and interest in civic and community programs. Participates in and promotes bowling tournaments and other activities. Sponsors fundraising programs for sickle cell anemia and the United Negro College Fund (see separate entry). Bestows bowling awards, annual special bowling and service awards, and annual national and local scholarship awards. Maintains hall of fame; compiles statistics. **Founded:** 1939. **Members:** 26,000. **Local Groups:** 80. **Publications:** Bowler, quarterly. News magazine/paper. Newsletter/Bulletin, monthly. Souvenir Yearbook. Journal. Is preparing the NBA History Book. **Formerly:** (1944) Negro National Bowling Association.

★321★
National Brotherhood of Skiers (NBS)
16900 Hubbell
Detroit, MI 48235
Sam Lawler, Pres.

Description: Minority ski clubs. Promotes winter sports among minorities, with emphasis on youth. Seeks to locate and develop talented ski racers through local, regional, and national competitions. Long-term goal is to develop Olympic-quality minority skiers. Sponsors two-year scholarships and bestows awards. **Founded:** 1974. **Members:** 7000. **Budget:** $75,000. **Regional Groups:** 4. **Local Groups:** 51. **Publications:** Skiers Edge, quarterly.

★322★
National Business League (NBL)
4324 Georgia Ave. NW
Washington, DC 20011 Phone: (202)829-5900
Arthur Teele Jr., Pres.

Description: Organizational vehicle for minority businesspeople. Promotes the economic development of minorities. Encourages minority ownership and management of small businesses and supports full minority participation within the free enterprise system. Maintains file of minority vendors and corporate procurement and purchasing agents. Presents awards; conducts special projects. **Founded:** 1900. **Members:** 10,000. **Budget:** $500,000. **Local Groups:** 127. **Telecommunications Services:** Fax, (202)726-6141. **Publications:** Corporate Guide for Minority Vendors, annual. National Memo, monthly. Membership newsletter. President's Briefs, monthly. Bulletin. **Formerly:** National Negro Business League.

★323★
National Catholic Conference for Interracial Justice (NCCIJ)
3033 4th St. NE
Washington, DC 20017 Phone: (202)529-6480
Jerome B. Ernst, Exec.Dir.

Description: Catholic organization working for interracial justice and social concerns in America. Initiates programs within and outside the Catholic church to end discrimination in community development, education, employment, health care, and housing. Conducts specialized education and research programs; maintains library. **Founded:** 1960. **Publications:** Commitment, quarterly. Newsletter. Also publishes LASER: Creating Unity in Diversity (book), Workshops on Racism (manual), Pentecost: A Feast for all Peoples, Martin Luther King Jr. Holiday Celebration Packet, and pamphlets.

★324★
National Caucus and Center on Black Aged (NCCBA)
1424 K St. NW, Ste. 500
Washington, DC 20005 Phone: (202)637-8400
Samuel J. Simmons, Pres.

Description: Seeks to improve living conditions for low-income elderly Americans, particularly Blacks. Advocates changes in federal and state laws in improving the economic, health, and social status of low-income senior citizens. Promotes community awareness of problems and issues effecting low-income aging population. Operates an employment program involving 2000 older persons in 14 states. Sponsors, owns, and manages rental housing for the elderly. Conducts training and intern programs in nursing home administration, long-term care, housing management, and commercial property maintenance. Bestows scholarships and awards. **Founded:** 1970. **Members:** 3000. **Budget:** $9,000,000. **Local Groups:** 45. **Telecommunications Services:** Fax, (202)347-0895. **Publications:** Golden Page, quarterly. Newsletter reporting developments concerning elderly Blacks; includes association news and legislative update.

★325★
National Center for Neighborhood Enterprise (NCNE)
1367 Connecticut Ave. NW
Washington, DC 20036 Phone: (202)331-1103
Robert L. Woodson Sr., Pres.

Description: Promotes community self-sufficiency through support of effective neighborhood mediating structures in low-income communities. Provides support and technical assistance to enable grass roots organizations to expand their role in the revitalization of urban communities. Objectives are to: recognize, promote, and explain alternative approaches to community development; identify and analyze successful program principles, strategies, and techniques that may be transferable; identify needs for developing neighborhood groups and small business leaders; simplify information technology and encourage grass roots organizations to make greater use of technological gains in solving problems; encourage financial support for programs; educate the public and private sectors; formulate policy recommendations to assist neighborhood revitalization. Conducts Resident Management for Public Housing Seminars; sponsors programs in youth entrepreneurship. **Founded:** 1981. **Budget:** $3,000,000. **Publications:** In the News, periodic. Policy Dispatch, periodic. Also publishes On the Road to Economic Freedom: An Agenda for Black Progress.

★326★
National Center for the Advancement of Blacks in the Health Professions (NCABHP)
PO Box 21121
Detroit, MI 48221 Phone: (313)345-4480
Della McGraw Goodwin, Pres.

Description: Participants belong to organizations including the American Public Health Association, National Urban League, National Black Nurses Association, and the American Hospital Association. Promotes the advancement of Blacks in the health professions. Publicizes the disparity between the health of Black and White Americans and its relationship to the underrepresentation of Blacks in the health professions. (According to the National Center for Health Statistics, Blacks have a higher death rate from cancer, heart disease, stroke, and diabetes than Whites; Blacks also have a higher infant mortality rate.) Acts as clearinghouse. Conducts skills development seminars for college recruiters and employers and empowerment seminars for new graduates. Demonstrates recruitment projects. Bestows Pathfinder Award. **Founded:** 1988. **Computerized Services:** Data base that matches applicants with colleges and universities and graduates with employers. **Publications:** Improving the Health Status of Black Americans, annual. Lists priorities and agenda for the coming year.

★327★
National Center for Urban Ethnic Affairs (NCUEA)
PO Box 20, Cardinal Sta.
Washington, DC 20064 Phone: (202)232-3600
Dr. John A. Kromkowski, Pres.

Description: Develops neighborhood programs and policies that are grounded in an appreciation of ethnic cultural diversity. Encourages and enables urban communities, parishes, and congregations to clarify important policy issues. Aids organized networks of neighbors and neighborhood organizations in achieving their goals and objectives. Creates partnerships among neighborhood organizations, government agencies, and the private sector for neighborhood revitalization, selfhelp development, and cultural programs. Works to improve education, human services, economic opportunities, housing, and culture and heritage for immigrants and in the ethnic and multi-ethnic neighborhoods. Provides technical assistance, advisement training, and workshops. Develops research proposals; assists neighborhood and ethnic organizations seeking financial support; makes available summer internships. **Founded:** 1970. **Publications:** Buildingblocks, periodic. Newsletter. Also publishes Urban Ethnic Policy Series, Neighborhood Strategy Series, and Neighborhood Revitalization Series (books and pamphlets).

★328★
National Center of Afro-American Artists (NCAAA)
300 Walnut Ave.
Boston, MA 02119 Phone: (617)442-8614
Charles Desmond, Pres.

Description: African American artists; institutions; and interested others. Goals are to: promote cultural activites in African American history and culture; encourage the development of artistic and cultural expression within Black communities; increase awareness and appreciation of the achievements of Black artists. Organizes and conducts cultural events, theatrical productions, and concerts. Sponsors workshops on topics such as 19th Century Black America, Introduction to Africa, and the Caribbean. **Founded:** 1968. **Publications:** none.

★329★
National Coalition for Haitian Refugees (NCHR)
16 E. 42nd St., 3rd Fl.
New York, NY 10017 Phone: (212)867-0020
Jocelyn McCalla, Exec.Dir.

Description: Haitian, labor, civil rights, human rights, trade union, and religious organizations united to secure humane treatment, due process of law, and legal status for Haitians seeking asylum in the U.S. Goals are to: ensure that Haitians receive fair treatment in their quest for asylum; convince the public of the need for legal status for the refugees; end U.S. Coast Guard interdiction of Haitian boats on the high seas; deepen the public's understanding of the social, economic, and political causes of Haitian flight from Haiti. Sponsors forums on Haiti. **Founded:** 1982. **Members:** 47. **Budget:** $150,000. **Telecommunications Services:** Fax, (212)867-1668. **Publications:** Haiti Insight, monthly. Newsletter disseminating information and analysis on current events in Haiti. **Formerly:** (1983) National Emergency Coalition for Haitian Refugees.

★330★
National Coalition for Quality Integrated Education (NCQIE)
1201 16th St. NW, Ste. 424
Washington, DC 20036 Phone: (202)822-7708
Dr. Arthur Flemming, Dir.

Description: National organizations committed to desegregating and improving the quality of elementary and secondary schools in the U.S. Serves as a forum for issues and developments pertaining to quality integrated education; encourages and coordinates citizen involvement in legislative developments. Sponsors educational meetings. **Founded:** 1975. **Members:** 25. **Telecommunications Services:** Fax, (202)822-7292. **Formerly:** (1982) National Center for Quality Integrated Education.

★331★
National Coalition of Black Meeting Planners (NCBMP)
50 F St. NW, Ste. 1040
Washington, DC 20001 Phone: (202)628-3952
Howard Mills, Pres.

Description: Black meeting planners. Purposes are to: act as liaison with hotels, airlines, convention centers, and bureaus in an effort to assess the impact of minorities in these fields; assess the needs of the convention industry and how best to meet these needs; enhance members' sophistication in planning meetings; maximize employment of minorities in the convention industry. Maintains speakers' bureau. Conducts educational and research programs and compiles statistics on demographic employment of minorities in the convention industry. Bestows 6 scholarship awards annually. **Founded:** 1983. **Members:** 400. **Telecommunications Services:** Fax, (202)628-3958. **Publications:** Directory, annual. **Formerly:** (1984) National Black Meeting Planners Coalition.

★332★
National Coalition of 100 Black Women
50 Rockefeller Plaza, Concourse Level, Rm. 46
New York, NY 10020 Phone: (212)974-6140
Cara Field, Pres.

Description: Black women actively involved with issues such as economic development, health, employment, education, voting, housing, criminal justice, the status of Black families, and the arts. Seeks to: resolve problems of Black people in cities; foster the growth and development of the community, city, state, and nation; create forums to encourage both young and older women to share experiences; work toward strategies to support Black women and their communities. Encourages other Black women and groups to join the efforts of the coalition. Bestows Candace Awards honoring outstanding Black men and women. **Founded:** 1981. **Members:** 3500. Chapters: 30. **Publications:** National Coalition of 100 Black Women–Statement, periodic. Newsletter reporting on the activities and achievements of Black women.

★333★

National Coalition on Black Voter Participation (NCBVP)
1101 14th St. NW, Ste. 925
Washington, DC 20005 Phone: (202)898-2220
Sonia R. Jarvis, Exec.Dir.

Description: Religious organizations, sororities, fraternities, labor groups, Black caucuses, and government and political groups. Seeks to: increase Black voter registration and participation in electoral voting; develop and fund local independent coalitions that will conduct campaigns to increase nonpartisan voter participation and citizenship empowerment programs. Conducts training programs. Collects and analyzes data; disseminates information on voter education including data on the Black voting age population. Sponsors Operation Big Vote and Black Women's Roundtable on Voter Participation (see separate entries). **Founded:** 1976. **Members:** 86. **Budget:** $700,000. **Publications:** Operation Big Vote Newsletter, bimonthly. Also publishes Black Women Voting Patterns (statistical fact sheet) and How to Organize and Implement a Successful Nonpartisan Voter Participation Campaign (manual).

★334★

National Coalition to End Racism in America's Child Care System (NCERACCS)
22075 Koths
Taylor, MI 48180 Phone: (313)295-0257
Carol Coccia, Pres.

Description: Adoption support groups, child care agencies, state offices of the U.S. Department of Social Services, politicians, members of the news media, and interested individuals. Purpose is to assure that all children requiring placement outside the home, whether through foster care or adoption, are placed in the earliest available home most qualified to meet the child's needs. Believes that in foster care situations, the child should not be moved after initial placement to match the child's race or culture. Encourages recruitment of foster and adoptive homes of all races and cultures; feels that while race and culture should be considered in placements, no child should be denied services on the basis of race. Seeks to educate the public, members of the media, and representatives of the political and legal sectors. Coordinates efforts of individuals and groups and utilizes the media and various legal procedures to accomplish goals of the coalition. Conducts workshops; maintains speakers' bureau. **Founded:** 1984. **Members:** 1000. **Budget:** Less than $25,000. **Publications:** The Children's Voice, quarterly. Newsletter discussing member activites, court decisions and laws, and civil rights information as it pertains to racism in adoption practices.

★335★

National Committee for Independent Political Action (NCIPA)
PO Box 170610
Brooklyn, NY 11217 Phone: (718)643-9603
Ted Glick, Coord.

Description: Individuals who are members of community organizations, civil rights groups, women's organizations, peace groups, and other progressive political groups. Purpose is to bring together grass roots progressive movements into one organized framework in order to represent the political interests of groups not represented by either major political party and to allow independent activists to share strategy and ideas. Goal is to develop independent political and electoral activity aimed at changing society to bring about economic and political democracy. Concerns addressed include labor movement issues, racism, apartheid, women's issues, farm issues, and U.S. intervention in Central America. Maintains speakers' bureau. **Founded:** 1984. **Members:** 10,000. **Publications:** Bulletin, 4/year.

★336★

National Conference of Black Lawyers (NCBL)
126 W. 119th St.
New York, NY 10026 Phone: (212)864-4000
Adjoa Ayetero, Dir.

Description: Attorneys throughout the U.S. and Canada united to use legal skills in the service of Black and poor communities. Maintains projects in legal services to community organizations, voting rights, and international affairs; provides public education on legal issues affecting Blacks and poor people. Researches racism in law schools and bar admissions. Conducts programs of continuing legal education for member attorneys. Maintains general law library. Compiles statistics; maintains lawyer referral and placement services. Provides speakers' bureau on criminal justice issues, international human rights law, and civil rights practice. Presents awards. **Founded:** 1968. **Members:** 1000. **Local Groups:** 15. **Publications:** Notes, quarterly.

★337★

National Conference of Black Mayors (NCBM)
1430 W. Peachtree St. NW, Ste. 700
Atlanta, GA 30309 Phone: (404)892-0127
Michelle D. Kourouma, Exec.Dir.

Description: Nonpartisan organization dedicated to promoting the development of municipalities managed by Black mayors. Objectives are to: improve the executive management capacity and efficiency of member municipalities in the delivery of municipal services; create viable communities within which normal government functions can be performed efficiently; provide the basis upon which new social overhead investments in the infrastructure of municipalities can utilize federal, state, local, and private resources to encourage new industry and increase employment; assist municipalities in stabilizing their population through improvements of the quality of life for residents and, concurrently, create alternatives to outward migration. Facilitates small town growth and development through energy conservation. Bestows awards, including Tribute to a Black American. Offers workshops; compiles demographic statistics. **Founded:** 1974. **Members:** 322. **Budget:** $125,000. **State Groups:** 17. **Telecommunications Services:** Fax, (404)876-4597. **Publications:** Mayors Roster, annual. Directory. Newsletter, monthly. Municipal Watch, quarterly. Press Releases, periodic. Also publishes NCBM Fact Sheet. **Formerly:** (1977) Southern Conference of Black Mayors.

★338★

National Conference of Black Political Scientists (NCOBPS)
c/o Joseph H. Silver
Georgia Bd. of Regents
244 Washington St.
Atlanta, GA 30334 Phone: (404)656-0763
Joseph H. Silver, Pres.

Description: Political and social science faculty, lawyers, and related professionals interested in Black politics and related fields. Seeks to encourage research, publication, and scholarship by Black Americans in political science; and to improve the political life of Black Americans. Maintains graduate assistantship program; bestows awards; compiles statistics on Blacks in politics and political science. **Founded:** 1969. **Members:** 400. **Publications:** National Political Science Review, annual. Contains research articles , symposia proceedings, and book reviews.

★339★

National Conference of Editorial Writers (NCEW)
6223 Executive Blvd.
Rockville, MD 20852 Phone: (301)984-3015
Cora B. Everett, Exec.Sec.

Description: Editorial writers on newspapers of general circulation in the U.S. and Canada; journalism educators. "To stimulate the conscience and the quality of the editorial page." In cooperation with the National Association of Black Journalists and the National Broadcast Editorial Association (see separate entries), bestows Wells Award for Leadership to provide employment for minorities in the field of journalism. Sponsors professional seminars. **Founded:** 1947. **Members:** 560. **Budget:** $100,000. **Publications:** The Masthead, quarterly. Journal covering all aspects of producing a daily newspaper. Includes conference news.

★340★
National Congress of Neighborhood Women (NCNW)
249 Manhattan Ave.
Brooklyn, NY 11211 Phone: (718)388-6666
Deidra Ahran, Exec. Officer

Description: Low-and moderate-income women from diverse ethnic and racial backgrounds united to: bring about neighborhood stabilization and revitalization; raise awareness of women's roles in neighborhood activities and organizations as well as on issues affecting low-income women; provide a voice for a new women's movement that reflects family and neighborhood values while promoting women's empowerment. Current projects include: Neighborhood Women College Program, which offers associate arts degree programs; Project Prepare, which seeks to prepare individuals to get a job through adult education classes, work experience, resume writing, child care, and counseling support. Maintains local advisory board and support groups. Offers speakers' bureau and placement service. Bestows awards. Compiles statistics on women, poverty, and neighborhood development. Maintains library of articles, papers, reports, oral histories, newspapers, letters, and audiovisual materials. **Founded:** 1975. **Budget:** $550,000. **Regional Groups:** 26. **Local Groups:** 26. **Computerized Services:** Mailing list. **Publications:** Neighborhood Women Network News, bimonthly. Also publishes Leadership Training Manual, Neighborhood Women: Putting It Together, articles, and conference reports.

★341★
National Consortium for Black Professional Development (NCBPD)
PO Box 18308
Louisville, KY 40218-0308
Hanford D. Stafford Ph.D., Exec.Dir.

Description: Industrial corporations and business firms (32); universities, including schools of business, science, and math, and public school systems (20); affiliates (5). Goal is to increase substantially, by the year 2000, the number of Black professionals in business administration, communications, applied and natural sciences, engineering, and law. Sponsors a science and engineering competition for Black students and Ph.D. programs in the agricultural sciences and business administration. Maintains clearinghouse and placement bureau for Black professionals seeking employment. Provides recruitment service for universities seeking qualified Black faculty and students. Services several federal contracts. **Founded:** 1974. **Members:** 57. **Publications:** Journal of Minority Employment, monthly. Reports employment information concerning Hispanics, Blacks, Native Americans, and Asians.

★342★
National Consortium for Graduate Degrees for Minorities in Science and Engineering (GEM)
PO Box 537
Notre Dame, IN 46556 Phone: (219)287-1097
Dr. Howard G. Adams, Exec.Dir.

Description: A graduate fellowship program operated by corporate and university representatives involved in increasing the number of minorities with master's degrees in engineering. Formed to provide opportunities for minority students to obtain a master's degree in engineering through a program of paid summer engineering experience and financial aid. Graduate fellowships are awarded to each fellow, which provide for tuition, fees, and a stipend of $6000 per academic year. Sponsors competitions. **Founded:** 1976. **Members:** 135. **Telecommunications Services:** Fax, (219)287-1486. **Publications:** Brochure, annual. Report, semiannual. Newsletter. Also publishes Successfully Negotiating the Gradutate School Process: A Guide for Minority Students. **Formerly:** (1990) National Consortium for Graduate Degrees for Minorities in Engineering.

★343★
National Consortium of Arts and Letters for Historically Black Colleges and Universities (NCALHBCU)
PO Box 19033
Washington, DC 20036 Phone: (202)833-1327
Dr. Walter F. Anderson, Exec.Dir.

Description: Historically and/or predominantly Black colleges and universities; other institutions of higher learning are associate members. Encourages academic excellence with an emphasis on cultural growth. Promotes study of African-American history and culture in the context of the scholarly study of world cultures. Offers no grants, but helps sponsor programs through fundraising efforts. **Founded:** 1984. **Members:** 38. **Publications:** Brochure; also plans to publish quarterly newsletter.

★344★
National Council for Black Studies
Ohio State University
Lincoln Tower, Rm. 1130
1800 Cannon Dr.
Columbus, OH 43229 Phone: (614)292-1035
Jacqueline E. Wade, Exec.Dir.

Description: Faculty members, students, and institutions united to promote and strengthen academic and community programs in Black and/or African-American studies. Bestows awards for scholarly contributions; sponsors undergraduate and graduate student essay contests. Offers professional opportunities referral service; compiles statistics on Black studies activities including information on students, faculty, research, and curricula. **Founded:** 1975. **Members:** 350. **Regional Groups:** 2. **Publications:** Annual Report; Black Studies Chairpersons/Directors, annual; Voices in Black Studies, bimonthly; Newsletter.

★345★
National Council for Culture and Art (NCCA)
1600 Broadway, Ste. 611C
New York, NY 10019 Phone: (212)757-7933
Robert H. LaPrince Ph.D., Exec.Dir. & Pres.

Description: Artists, civic and business leaders, professional performers, and visual arts organizations. Purpose is to provide exposure and employment opportunities for rural Americans, disabled Americans, and other minorities including Blacks, Hispanics, American Indians, and European-Americans. Sponsors arts programs and spring and fall concert series. Operates Opening Night, a cable television show. Bestows annual Monarch Award and President's Award, and sponsors annual Monarch Scholarship Program. Offers children's and placement services; conducts charitable program; maintains hall of fame. Plans to conduct Minority Playwrights Forum, Dance Festival U.S.A., Vocal and Instrumental Competition, Film and Video Festival, and Concerts U.S.A.. **Founded:** 1980. **Members:** 1500. **Budget:** $350,000. **Publications:** Monarch Herald, quarterly. Newsletter.

★346★
National Council of Negro Women (NCNW)
1211 Connecticut Ave., NW, Ste. 702
Washington, DC 20036 Phone: (202)659-0006
Dorothy I. Height, Pres.

Description: A coalition of 31 national organizations and concerned individuals. Assists in the development and utilization of the leadership of women in community, national, and international life. Provides a center of information for and about women in the Black community; stimulates cooperation among women in diverse economic and social interests; acts as a catalyst for constructive advocacy on a number of women's issues. Maintains Women's Center for Education and Career Advancement in New York City, which offers programs designed to aid minority women pursuing nontraditional careers; also maintains the Bethune Museum and Archives for Black Women's History. Operates offices in west and southern Africa, which serve NCNW's international projects and which were designed to improve the social and economic status of rural women in Third World countries. Founded by Mary McLeod Bethune (1875-1955), Black American educator and presidential advisor. **Founded:** 1935. **Members:** 40,000. **Budget:** $1,500,000. **Local Groups:** 240. **Publications:** Black Woman's Voice, periodic. Sisters Magazine, quarterly.

★347★
National Council on Black Aging (NCBA)
Box 51275
Durham, NC 27717 Phone: (919)489-2563
Dr. Jacquelyne J. Jackson, Dir.

Description: Persons interested in research and policies affecting older Blacks and other minorities and in the dissemination of research findings. Maintains speakers' bureau. Conducts lectures on minority aging. **Founded:** 1975. **Publications:** Research findings in Journal of Minority Aging.

★348★
National Dental Assistants Association (NDAA)
c/o Mae L. Eldridge
5506 Connecticut Ave., NW, Ste. 24-25
Washington, DC 20015 Phone: (202)244-7555
Mae L. Eldridge, Pres.

Description: An auxiliary of the National Dental Association (see separate entry). Works to encourage education and certification among dental assistants. Conducts clinics and workshops to further the education of members. Bestows annual Humanitarian Award; offers scholarships. **Founded:** 1964. **Members:** 500. **Publications:** NDAA Journal, annual.

★349★
National Dental Association (NDA)
5506 Connecticut Ave. NW, Ste. 24
Washington, DC 20015 Phone: (202)244-7555
Rosita Stevens Holsey, Exec.Dir.

Description: Professional society for dentists. Aims to provide quality dental care to the unserved and underserved public and promote knowledge of the art and science of dentistry. Advocates the inclusion of dental care services in health care programs on local, state, and national levels. Fosters the integration of minority dental health care providers in the profession, and promotes dentistry as a viable career for minorities through scholarship and support programs. Bestows awards; conducts research programs. Sponsors National Dental Health Poster Contest and working group on high blood pressure. Group is distinct from the former name of the American Dental Association. **Founded:** 1913. **Members:** 2500. **Budget:** $294,050. **Regional Groups:** 6. **State Groups:** 15. **Local Groups:** 31. **Telecommunications Services:** Fax, (202)244-5992. **Publications:** Flossline, quarterly. Contains educational news. **Formerly:** (1932) Interstate Dental Association.

★350★
National Dental Hygienists' Association (NDHA)
5506 Connecticut Ave. NW, Ste. 24-25
Washington, DC 20015 Phone: (202)244-7555
Dr. Andrea Foster, Pres.

Description: Minority dental hygienists. To cultivate and promote the art and science of dental hygiene and to enhance the professional image of dental hygienists. Attempts to meet the needs of society through educational, political, and social activities while giving the minority dental hygienist a voice in shaping the profession. Encourages cooperation and mutual support among minority professionals. Seeks to increase opportunities for continuing education and employment in the field of dental hygiene. Works to improve individual and community dental health. Sponsors annual seminar, fundraising events, and scholarship programs; participates in career orientation programs; counsels and assists students applying for or enrolled in dental hygiene programs. Maintains liaison with American Dental Hygienists' Association. **Founded:** 1932. **Members:** 50. **Budget:** $50,000. **State Groups:** 10. **Publications:** Newsletter, quarterly.

★351★
National Economic Association (NEA)
c/o Alfred L. Edwards
School of Business
University of Michigan
Ann Arbor, MI 48109-1230 Phone: (313)763-0121
Alfred L. Edwards, Sec.-Treas.

Description: Purposes are to: promote the professional life of Blacks within the economics profession; advance the study and understanding of the economic problems confronting the Black community; increase the number of Black economists. Bestows Samuel Z. Westerfield Award to distinguished Black economists. **Founded:** 1969. **Budget:** Less than $25,000. **Telecommunications Services:** Fax, (313)763-5688. **Publications:** Directory of Black Economists, biennial. Job Placement Bulletin, periodic. Review of Black Political Economy, quarterly. Includes book reviews, annual indexes, manuscripts, and editorial correspondence. **Formerly:** (1975) Caucus of Black Economists.

★352★
National Emergency Civil Liberties Committee (NECLC)
175 5th Ave., Rm. 814
New York, NY 10010 Phone: (212)673-2040
Edith Tiger, Dir.

Description: To reestablish in full the traditional freedoms guaranteed under the Constitution and Bill of Rights. Committee "stands uncompromisingly for civil liberties for everyone and every variety of dissent." Legal staff handles test cases in the courts, without charge to the clients. Also functions as information service. **Founded:** 1951. **Publications:** Bill of Rights Journal, annual. Rights, 3/year. Newsletter. **Formerly:** (1968) Emergency Civil Liberties Committee.

★353★
National Florist Association (NFA)
115 W. 2nd Ave.
Franklin, VA 23851 Phone: (804)569-8737
Charlie Williams, Pres.

Description: Black retail florists. Works to: create better relationships with florists and allied trades throughout the U.S.; guide Black florists in the improvement and upgrading of their businesses and to promote among them the wire communication of flower service; create better relationships with funeral directors throughout the country. Awards annual plaques and trophies for the best original flower displays. **Founded:** 1953. **Members:** 500. **Formerly:** (1963) International Flower Association; (1988) International Florists Association.

★354★
National Forum for Black Public Administrators (NFBPA)
777 N. Capitol St. NE, Ste. 801
Washington, DC 20002 Phone: (202)408-9300
Quentin R. Lawson, Exec.Dir.

Description: Black city and county managers and assistant managers; chief administrative officers; agency directors; bureau and division heads; corporate executives; students. Works to promote, strengthen, and expand the role of Blacks in public administration. Seeks to focus the influence of Black administrators toward building and maintaining viable communities. Develops specialized training programs for managers and executives. Provides national public administrative leadership resource and skills bank. Works to further communication among Black public, private, and academic institutions. Addresses issues that affect the administrative capacity of Black managers. Maintains Executive Leadership Institute which grooms mid-level executives for higher positions in government, the Mentor Program which matches aspiring Black managers with seasoned executives over an 8-month period, and the Leadership Institute for Small Municipalities, which provides intensive training for elected and appointed officials from small communities. Sponsors the National Minority Business Development Forum to increase the participation of small and minority businesses in local government procurement and contracting programs. **Founded:** 1983. **Members:** 2600. **Local Groups:** 45. **Telecommunications Services:** Fax, (202)408-8558; jobs hot line, (800)55-FORUM (outside Washington, DC) and (202)39-FORUM (Washington, DC). **Publications:** Adolescent Pregnancy Reduction Task Force Bulletin, quarterly.

★355★
National Funeral Directors and Morticians Association (NFDMA)
1800 E. Linwood
Kansas City, MO 64109 Phone: (816)921-1800
Lawrence Jones, Exec.Dir.

Description: State, district, and local funeral directing and embalming associations and their members. Promotes ethical practices; encourages just and uniform laws pertaining to funeral directing and embalming. **Founded:** 1938. **Members:** 2000. **Budget:** $150,000. **State Groups:** 26. **Formerly:** (1957) National Negro Funeral Directors and Morticians Association.

★356★
National Hook-Up of Black Women (NHBW)
c/o Wynetta Frazier
5117 S. University Ave.
Chicago, IL 60615 Phone: (312)643-5866
Wynetta Frazier, Pres.

Description: Black women from business, professional, and community-oriented disciplines representing all economic, educational, and social levels. Purpose is to provide a communications network in support of Black women who serve in organizational leadership positions, especially those elected or appointed to office and those wishing to elevate their status through educational and career ventures. Works to form and implement a Black Women's Agenda that would provide representation for women, families, and communities and that would help surmount economic, educational, and social barriers. Supports efforts of the Congressional Black Caucus (see separate entry) in utilizing the legislative process to work toward total equality of opportunity in society. Seeks to highlight the achievements and contributions of Black women. Sponsors workshops. Bestows Distinguished Community Service, Distinguished Family Service, Outstanding Leadership, and Hook-Up Member of the Year awards. Operates speakers' bureau. **Founded:** 1975. **Members:** 500. **Regional Groups:** 8. **Local Groups:** 9. **Publications:** Hook-Up News and Views, quarterly. Newsletter.

★357★
National Housewives' League of America for Economic Security (NHLA)
3240 Gilbert
Cincinnati, OH 45207 Phone: (513)281-8822
Magnolia R. Silmond, Pres.

Description: Black women seeking to strengthen the economic base of their communities through a program of positive support for businesses and professions owned and operated by or employing Blacks. Aids stores through increased purchasing; conducts tours of businesses; sponsors high school essay contest on business and economics. Maintains library of newspaper articles, bulletins, and minutes of meetings. Sponsors competitions; conducts research programs. **Founded:** 1933. **Members:** 250. **Budget:** Less than $25,000. **Local Groups:** 7. **Publications:** Publishes souvenir conference program. **Formerly:** (1986) National Housewives' League of America.

★358★
National Hypertension Association (NHA)
324 E. 30th St.
New York, NY 10016 Phone: (212)889-3557
William M. Manger M.D., Chm.

Description: Physicians, medical researchers, and business professionals dedicated to the prevention of the complications of hypertension. Seeks to combat hypertension by developing, directing, and implementing effective programs to educate physicians and the public about the severe, life-threatening dangers of this health disorder. Conducts research on the cause of hypertension through basic laboratory studies. Sponsors seminars and symposia to keep the medical profession abreast of advances in the diagnosis and treatment of hypertension; conducts hypertension and hypercholesterol detection programs. Offers medical consulting to those found to have high blood pressure or hypercholesterolemia. Develops educational materials and participates in radio and television programs. Bestows awards. **Founded:** 1977. Mailing List: 1700. Advisory Committee: 400. **Telecommunications Services:** Fax, (212)447-7032. **Publications:** News Report, annual. Newsletter.

★359★
National Institute Against Prejudice and Violence (NIAPV)
31 S. Greene St.
Baltimore, MD 21201 Phone: (301)328-5170
Joan C. Weiss, Exec.Dir.

Description: Purpose is to study and respond to the problem of violence and intimidation motivated by racial, religious, ethnic, or anti-gay prejudice. Collects, analyzes, produces, and disseminates information and materials on programs of prevention and response. Conducts research on the causes and prevalence of prejudice and violence and their effects on victims and society; provides technical assistance to public agencies, voluntary organizations, schools, and communities in conflict; analyzes and drafts model legislation; conducts educational and training programs; sponsors conferences, symposia, and other forums for information exchange among experts. **Founded:** 1984. **Budget:** $587,900. **Publications:** Forum, quarterly. Newsletter. **Formerly:** (1986) Institute for Prevention and Control of Violence and Extremism.

★360★
National Institute for Women of Color (NIWC)
1301 20th St. NW Ste. 702
Washington, DC 20036 Phone: (202)296-2661
Sharon Parker, Bd.Chm.

Description: Aims to: enhance the strengths of diversity; promote educational and economic equity for Black, Hispanic, Asian-American, Pacific-Islander, American Indian, and Alaskan Native women. Focuses on mutual concerns and needs, bringing together women who have traditionally been isolated. (NIWC uses the phrase "women of color" to convey unity, self-esteem, and political status and to avoid using the term "minority," which the institute feels has a negative psychological and social impact.) Serves as a networking vehicle to: link women of color on various issues or programs; promote women of color for positions on boards and commissions; ensure that women of color are visible as speakers or presenters at major women's conferences, as well as planners or program developers; support and initiate programs; educate women and the public about the status and culture of the various racial/ethnic groups they represent; promote cooperative efforts between general women's organizations and women of color, while raising awareness about issues and principles of feminism. Sponsors seminars and workshops. Provides technical assistance; conducts internship and leadership development programs. Bestows Outstanding Women of Color Awards; compiles statistics. **Founded:** 1981. **Budget:** Less than $25,000. **Publications:** Has published Brown Papers, NIWC Network News, bibliographies, bulletins, fact sheets, and other related resources.

★361★
National Institute of Hypertension Studies (NIHS)
Institute of Hypertension School of Research
13217 Livernois
Detroit, MI 48238 Phone: (313)931-3427
Dr. Herbert R. Lockett, Exec.Dir.

Description: Purposes are: to help find causes of and to help prevent essential hypertension; to educate people concerning essential hypertension; to diagnose, counsel, and refer afflicted individuals for treatment and follow-up activities; to conduct research on hypertension and to extend that research into the areas of crime and drug addiction and psychosocial and occupational stress. Sponsors public seminars and hypertension detection clinics. Offers youth leadership courses. Maintains library. Compiles statistics and disseminates educational materials. Conducts research programs on psychosocial and occupational stress which offer diplomas to those completing the programs; also conducts research on drugs and hypertension. **Founded:** 1975. **Publications:** Magazine, periodic. OHRST Assessment Report Series, annual. **Formerly:** (1977) Institute of Hypertension Studies; (1981) Institute of Hypertension Studies - Institute of Hypertension School of Research.

★362★
National Insurance Association (NIA)
PO Box 53230
Chicago, IL 60653-0230 Phone: (312)924-3308
Josephine King, Pres.

Description: Conducts annual Institute in Agency Management and Institute in Home Office Operations. Sponsors National Insurance Week. **Founded:** 1921. **Members:** 23. **Local Groups:** 8. **Publications:** Member Roster, periodic. **Formerly:** (1954) National Negro Insurance Association.

★363★
National Medical Association (NMA)
1012 10th St. NW
Washington, DC 20001 Phone: (202)347-1895
William C. Garrett, Exec.V.Pres.

Description: Professional society of Black physicians. Bestows awards. Maintains 19 sections representing major specialties of medicine. Plans to establish library and physician placement service. Conducts symposia and workshops. **Founded:** 1895. **Members:** 14,500. **Regional Groups:** 6. **State Groups:** 32. **Local Groups:** 62. **Computerized Services:** Mailing list (for NMA regions and affiliates only). **Publications:** Journal of the National Medical Association, monthly. National Medical Association Newsletter, quarterly.

★364★
National Minority AIDS Council (NMAC)
300 I St., NE, Ste. 400
Washington, DC 20002 Phone: (202)544-1076
Paul A. Kawata, Exec.Dir.

Description: Public health departments and AIDS service organizations. Serves as a clearinghouse of information on AIDS as it affects minority communities in the U.S. Facilitates discussion among national minority organizations about AIDS. Maintains Project Health, Education, and AIDS Leadership, which provides computer usage, strategic planning, financial management, and volunteer program development assistance to AIDS service organizations, and Project Volunteer Information, Technical Assistance, and Leadership, which provides technical assistance in volunteer program development and maintenance. Conducts training conferences. Offers educational and research programs; compiles statistics. Bestows awards; maintains speakers' bureau, biographical archives, and library. **Founded:** 1986. **Members:** 200. **Budget:** $550,000. **Regional Groups:** 1. **State Groups:** 20. **Local Groups:** 160. **Telecommunications Services:** Fax, (202)544-0378; toll-free number, (800)544-0586. **Publications:** Leadership Reprint Series, quarterly. Includes information on strategies for addressing HIV/AIDS and scientific updates.

★365★
National Minority Business Council (NMBC)
235 E. 42nd St.
New York, NY 10017 Phone: (212)573-2385
John F. Robinson, CEO & Pres.

Description: Minority businesses in all areas of industry and commerce. Seeks to increase profitability by developing marketing, sales, and management skills in minority businesses. Acts as an informational source for the national minority business community. Programs include: a legal services plan that provides free legal services to members in such areas as sales contracts, copyrights, estate planning, and investment agreement; a business referral service that develops potential customer leads; an international trade assistance program that provides technical assistance in developing foreign markets; an executive banking program that teaches members how to package a business loan for bank approval; a procurement outreach program for minority and women business owners. Conducts continuing management education and provides assistance in teaching youth the free enterprise system. Bestows awards. **Founded:** 1972. **Members:** 400. **Budget:** $250,000. **Telecommunications Services:** Fax, (212)573-7550. **Publications:** Better Business, semiannual. Magazine. Corporate Minority Vendor Directory, annual. NMBC Business Report, bimonthly. NMBC Corporate Purchasing Directory, periodic.

★366★
National Minority Business Directories (NMBD)
2105 Central Ave., NE
Minneapolis, MN 55418 Phone: (612)781-6819
Liz Kahnk, Exec.Dir.

Description: Objective is to compile and publish minority business directories to acquaint major corporations and government purchasing agents with the products and services of minority firms. Sponsors minority purchasing seminars. **Founded:** 1968. **Telecommunications Services:** Fax, (612)781-0109. **Publications:** Guide to Obtaining Minority Business Directories, annual. Directory listing local and regional directories, organized by state. **Formerly:** (1970) National Buy-Black Campaign; (1984) National Minority Business Campaign.

12/91 no info to public

★367★
National Minority Health Association (NMHA)
PO Box 11876
Harrisburg, PA 17108 Phone: (717)234-3254
Leroy Robinson, Exec.Dir.

Description: Health care providers and associations, consumers, executives and administrators, educators, pharmaceutical and health insurance companies, and other corporations with an interest in health care. Seeks to identify and focus attention on the health needs of minorities. Promotes: more effective research in minority health issues; better training of health care practitioners; development of programs that encourage minorities to pursue careers in the health care industry and educate minority communities on the importance of good health. Initiates discussions with professional health organizations, academic institutions, state and federal governments, and health departments to develop strategies to improve the quality and availability of health care, health delivery systems, and health professionals to minority communities. Bestows National Health Achievement Award annually to individual or group that has made significant contributions in the area of minority health. Maintains speakers' bureau, library, and placement services; conducts research and educational programs; sponsors children's programs; complies statistics. **Founded:** 1987. **Members:** 30,000. **State Groups:** 1. **Computerized Services:** Data base; mailing list. **Publications:** The National Minority Health Association News, quarterly.

★368★
National Minority Supplier Development Council (NMSDC)
15 W. 39th St., 9th Fl.
New York, NY 10018 Phone: (212)944-2430
Harriet Michel, Pres.

Description: Individuals, corporations, associations, foundations, and other organizations who are members of regional purchasing councils or who have agreed to participate in the program. Program provides, exclusively for educational purposes, consultative, advisory, and informational services and technical resources to minority businesses and to regional and local minority purchasing councils. These services include purchasing, product development, marketing, industrial, and managerial operations. Conducts sales training program for minority entrepreneurs, and buyer training program for corporate minority purchasing programs. **Founded:** 1972. **Members:** 160. **Budget:** $3,000,000. **Regional Groups:** 47. **Computerized Services:** MBISYS, Minority Business Information System, an online database of certified minority-owned businesses and qualified vendors to business and industry. **Publications:** Minority Supplier News, 6/year. **Formerly:** (1980) National Minority Purchasing Council.

★369★
National Naval Officers Association (NNOA)
PO Box 46256
Washington, DC 20050 Phone: 800-772-6662
Corp. Anthony Dupree, Exec. Officer

Description: Active, reserve, and retired Naval, Marine, and Coast Guard officers and students in college and military sea service programs. Promotes and assists recruitment, retention, and retirement of minorities in naval service. Conducts specialized education; maintains counseling , referral, and children's services. Makes available non-ROTC grants-in-aid. Sponsors competitions; bestows awards; operates charitable program. **Founded:** 1971. **Members:** 750. **Budget:** Less than $25,000. **Regional Groups:** 4. **Local Groups:** 25. **Computerized Services:** Membership data base. **Telecommunications Services:** Electronic bulletin board. **Publications:** NNOA Annual Conference Program. NNOA Meridian, quarterly. Tabloid covering sea service news and events; includes chapter news, news from other military services, statistics, and information about other organizations.

★370★
National Neighbors (NN)
3130 Mayfield Rd.
Cleveland Heights, OH 44118 Phone: (216)397-9606
Helen Payton, Exec.Dir.

Description: Federation of interracial neighborhoods. Fosters and encourages successful multiracial neighborhoods. Seeks to strengthen interracial neighborhoods and promote open housing through technical assistance and consultant visits in the areas of real estate, open housing, education, and neighborhood safety training. Represents the interests of integrated neighborhoods before government agencies and other national organizations. Serves as an information clearinghouse for individuals seeking to move into interracial neighborhoods. Conducts studies in housing discrimination, exclusionary policies in housing and families with children, redevelopment and stabilization program, and redlining and related discriminatory practices by financial institutions. **Founded:** 1970. **Members:** 2500. **Budget:** $50,000. **Regional Groups:** 27. **State Groups:** 25. **Local Groups:** 225. **Publications:** Current and Pending, periodic. Neighbors, 4/year. Newsletter. Also publishes reports, dictionary, manuals, and guides for and about multiracial neighborhoods.

★371★
National Network of Minority Women in Science (MWIS)
c/o American Association for the
Advancement of Science
Directorate for Educ. and Human
Resources Programs
1333 H St. NW
Washington, DC 20005 Phone: (202)326-6677
Marsha Matyas, Chm.

Description: Asian, Black, Mexican American, Native American, and Puerto Rican women involved in science related professions; other interested persons. Promotes the advancement of minority women in science fields and the improvement of the science and mathematics education and career awareness of minorities. Supports public policies and programs in science and technology that benefit minorities. Compiles statistics; serves as clearinghouse for identifying minority women scientists. Offers writing and conference presentations, seminars, and workshops on minority women in science and local career conferences for students. Local chapters maintain speakers' bureaus and placement services, offer children's services, sponsor competitions, and bestow awards. **Founded:** 1978. **Members:** 400. **Budget:** Less than $25,000. **Regional Groups:** 1. **State Groups:** 2. **Local Groups:** 3. **Publications:** Quarterly. Plans to publish directory.

★372★
National Newspaper Publishers Association (NNPA)
948 National Press Bldg., Rm. 948
Washington, DC 20045 Phone: (202)662-7324
Steve G. Davis, Exec.Dir.

Description: Publishers of daily and weekly newspapers. Presents Distinguished Service Award annually to the Black leader who has made the most significant contribution to Black advancement during the previous year. Maintains hall of fame. Sponsors annual workshop. **Founded:** 1940. **Members:** 178. **Budget:** $215,000. **Computerized Services:** Mailing lists. **Telecommunications Services:** Fax, (202)662-8725. **Publications:** Convention Journal, annual. **Formerly:** (1956) National Negro Newspaper Publishers Association.

★373★
National Office for Black Catholics (NOBC)
3025 4th St. NE
Washington, DC 20017 Phone: (202)635-1778
Walter Hubbard, Dir.

Description: Black priests, sisters, brothers, and laypersons of the Catholic church. Participating organizations: National Black Sisters' Conference; National Black Catholic Clergy Caucus (see separate entries). Serves as a "foundation for the renewal of the credibility of the church in the Black community." Works to coordinate actions designed "to liberate Black people and to serve as a unifying strength." Plans to: have specialists and technicians working within the Black community to coordinate community organization and development; provide leadership training for youth; attack problems of poverty and deprivation; sensitize Blacks to their heritage through historical, cultural, and liturgical experience. Seeks cooperation with groups working toward Black liberation. Concerns include: training Black and White clergy and religious, Catholic, and non-Catholic laity; influencing decisions involving race and the church; monitoring, in order to prevent, manifestations of racism. Sponsors Pastoral Ministry Institute and Afro-American Culture and Worship Workshop; provides evangelization workshops and leadership training for parish councils and parochial schools; maintains 400 volume library. **Founded:** 1970. **Members:** 1,000,000. **Publications:** Freeing the Spirit, quarterly. Impact, 6/year. Newsletter. Also publishes booklets.

★374★
National Optometric Association (NOA)
1489 Livingston Ave.
Columbus, OH 43205 Phone: (614)253-5593
Dr. Clayton Hicks, Exec.Dir.

Description: Optometrists dedicated to increasing minority optometric manpower. Conducts research programs and national recruiting program. Bestows awards; maintains speakers' bureau. Offers specialized education program. **Founded:** 1969. **Members:** 350. **Budget:** Less than $25,000. **Regional Groups:** 5. **Publications:** Newsletter, quarterly.

★375★
National Organization for the Professional Advancement of Black Chemists and Chemical Engineers (NOPABCCE)
525 College St. NW
Washington, DC 20059 Phone: (202)667-1699
Damon Larry, Dir.

Description: Black professionals in science and chemistry. Seeks to aid Black scientists and chemists in reaching their full professional potential; encourages Black students to pursue scientific studies and employment; promotes participation of Blacks in scientific research. Provides volunteers to teach science courses in selected elementary schools; sponsors scientific field trips for students; maintains speakers' bureau for schools; provides summer school for students of the U.S. Naval Academy. Conducts technical seminars in Africa; operates exchange program of scientific and chemical professionals with the People's Republic of China. Sponsors competitions; presents awards for significant achievements to qndividuals in the field. Maintains library of materials pertaining to chemistry, science, and Black history; keeps archive of organization's books and records. Maintains placement service; compiles statistics. **Founded:** 1972. **Members:** 1000. **Budget:** $280,000. **Regional Groups:** 5. **Local Groups:** 14. **Computerized Services:** Records file. **Publications:** Newsmagazine, quarterly. Newsletter. **Formerly:** (1989) National Organization of Black Chemists and Chemical Engineers.

★376★
National Organization of Black College Alumni (NOBCA)
4 Washington Sq. Village, No. 15E
New York, NY 10012 Phone: (212)982-7726
Dr. Jean Gilbert, Coord.

Description: Graduates, friends, and supporters of the 114 historically Black colleges. Works to ensure the survival of Black colleges by addressing their concerns and needs and providing resources to meet these needs. Coordinates and focuses alumni support for Black colleges; strengthens existing alumni associations; urges Black youth to obtain a college education. Facilitates the exchange of information. Provides consultants; holds workshops and seminars. **Founded:** 1982. **State Groups:** 50. **Publications:** NOBCA Newsletter, semiannual.

★377★
National Organization of Black County Officials (NOBCO)
440 1st St., NW, Ste. 500
Washington, DC 20001 Phone: (202)347-6953
Crandall O. Jones, Exec.Dir.

Description: Black county officials organized to provide program planning and management assistance to selected counties in the U.S. Acts as a technical information exchange to develop resolutions to problems on the local and national levels. Promotes the sharing of knowledge and methods of improving resource utilization and government operations. Conducts seminars. Plans to maintain resource file on the achievements and history of Black county officials. **Founded:** 1982. **Members:** 1400. **Telecommunications Services:** Fax, (202)393-6596. **Publications:** County Compass, quarterly. Newsletter; includes calendar of events and member profiles.

★378★
National Organization of Black Law Enforcement Executives (NOBLE)
908 Pennsylvania Ave., SE
Washington, DC 20003 Phone: (202)546-8811
Dr. Elsie Scott, Exec.Dir.

Description: Law enforcement executives above the rank of lieutenant; police educators; academy directors; interested individuals and organizations. Goals are: to provide a platform from which the concerns and opinions of minority law enforcement executives and command-level officers can be expressed; to facilitate the exchange of programmatic information among minority law enforcement executives; to increase minority participation at all levels of law enforcement; to eliminate racism in the field of criminal justice; to secure increased cooperation from criminal justice agencies; to reduce urban crime and violence. Seeks to develop and maintain channels of communication between law enforcement agencies and the community; encourages coordinated community efforts to prevent and abate crime and its causes. Offers on-site technical assistance and training to police departments; develops model policies, practices, and procedures designed to decrease racial and religious violence and harassment. Provides job referral services to organizations seeking minority executives. Conducts research and trainig and offers technical assistance in crime victim assistance, community oriented policing, domestic violence, use of deadly force, reduction of fear of crime, airport security assessment, and minority recruitment. Awards scholarships and offers internships and fellowships to students preparing for careers in law enforcement. Operates 300 volume library. **Founded:** 1976. **Members:** 2000. **Budget:** $800,000. **Regional Groups:** 6. **Local Groups:** 20. **Computerized Services:** Data base on domestic violence resources. **Telecommunications Services:** Fax, (202)544-8351. **Publications:** NOBLE ACTIONS, quarterly. Newsletter reporting on current law enforcement issues and activities. Contains employment opportunities, calendar of events, and legislative information.

★379★
National Organization of Minority Architects (NOMA)
120 Ralph McGill Blvd., Ste. 815
Atlanta, GA 30308 Phone: (404)876-3055
William Stanley, Pres.

Description: Seeks to increase the number and influence of minority architects by encouraging minority youth and taking an active role in the education of new architects. Works in cooperation with other associations, professionals, and architectural firms to promote the professional advancement of members. **Founded:** 1971. **Members:** 250. **Budget:** $25,000. **Publications:** Newsletter, quarterly. Roster of Minority Firms, periodic. **Formerly:** (1973) National Organization of Black Architects.

★380★
National Podiatric Medical Association (NPMA)
c/o Raymond E. Lee, D.P.M.
1638 E. 87th St.
Chicago, IL 60617 Phone: (312)374-1616
Raymond E. Lee D.P.M., Contact

Description: Minority podiatrists, predominately Black. Promotes the science and art of podiatry. Seeks to: improve public health; raise the standards of the podiatric profession and education; stimulate a favorable relationship between all podiatrists; nurture growth and diffusion of podiatric information; stimulate public education concerning public health and features of podiatric medicine. Sponsors proposal of podiatric laws; works to eliminate religious and racial discrimination and segregation in American medical institutions. **Founded:** 1971. **Members:** 200. **Budget:** Less than $25,000. **Publications:** Annual Seminar Ad Book. National Podiatric Medical Association–Newsletter, annual. Includes calendar of events and news from student-affiliated associations. **Formerly:** (1987) National Podiatry Association.

★381★
National Rainbow Coalition, Inc. (The Rainbo)
1110 Vermont Ave. NW
Washington, DC 20005 Phone: (202)728-1180
Rev. Jesse L. Jackson Sr., Pres.

Description: Promotes the creation of a better nation and world by lifting the hope of all Americans and assuring economic justice, peace, human rights, and dignity for all. Works to build a consensus in the areas of civil rights, government, politics, labor, education, religion, business, academia, the environment, health care, and other issues; provides a platform for debate at the national, state, and local levels. Encourages the development of a new political leadership committed to progressive domestic and international policies and programs, leading to a more humane society. Named during the 1984 presidential campaign of the Rev. Jesse L. Jackson, Sr. (1942-), prominent Black civil rights leader and politician. **Founded:** 1984. **Members:** 13,000. **State Groups:** 50. **Telecommunications Services:** Fax, (202) 728-1192. **Formerly:** (1986) Rainbow Coalition.

★382★
National Society of Black Engineers (NSBE)
344 Commerce St.
Alexandria, VA 22314 Phone: (703)549-2207
Florida Morehead, Exec.Dir.

Description: Engineering and science students. Seeks to increase the number of minority graduates in engineering and technology. Bestows awards; sponsors seminars and workshops geared toward preparing students for careers, the industry, and leadership roles. **Founded:** 1975. **Members:** 6600. **Budget:** $1,200,000. **Regional Groups:** 6. **Local Groups:** 168. **Telecommunications Services:** Electronic mail; fax, (703)683-5312. **Publications:** Journal, bimonthly. National Conference Proceedings, annual. Newsletter, bimonthly. Also publishes pamphlet.

★383★
National Society of Certified Public Accountants (NSCPA)
1313 E. Sibley Blvd., Ste. 210
Dolton, IL 60419 Phone: (312)849-0098
Eugene Varnado, Pres.

Description: Black certified public accountants who seek to advance their profession and encourage minority students to pursue careers in the field. Conducts monthly seminar. Maintains scholarship program. **Members:** 200. **Telecommunications Services:** Fax, (708)849-8718. **Publications:** none.

★384★
National Sorority of Phi Delta Kappa
8233 S. Martin Luther King Dr.
Chicago, IL 60619 Phone: (312)783-7379
Edna Murray, Exec.Sec.

Description: Women who teach or who hold administrative positions in education. Five-point program includes educational conferences (Teach-A-Rama), reading and study centers for youth, youth guidance, scholarship awards, and maintenance of a children's library in Liberia. Awards three lifetime memberships annually to members of the National Association for the Advancement of Colored People (see separate entry); offers tutorial programs. **Founded:** 1923. **Members:** 5000. **Regional Groups:** 5. Chapters: 113. **Computerized Services:** Mailing list. **Publications:** Bulletin, quarterly. Directory, annual. Krinon, annual.

★385★
National Technical Association (NTA)
PO Box 27787
Washington, DC 20038-7787 Phone: (202)829-6100
Kathye E. Lewis, Pres.

Description: Persons who have attained proficiency in engineering, architecture, mathematics, and natural sciences. Seeks to: develop and integrate the minority technical input into the total scientific process; give minorities an awareness of their technical contribution to the establishment of the world's societies; provide for technical interchange among minorities; disseminate career opportunity information to minorities; motivate minority youth to consider technical careers; remove barriers against minorities entering into and advancing in technical professions. Compiles statistics; presents awards; maintains speakers' bureau. Conducts national junior and senior high school scientific and technical career awareness programs, and student technical symposia. **Founded:** 1926. **Members:** 1500. Professional Chapters: 40. Student Chapters: 30. **Publications:** Journal, quarterly. Newsletter, quarterly.

★386★
National United Affiliated Beverage Association (NUABA)
PO Box 9308
Philadelphia, PA 19139 Phone: (215)748-5670
Joseph T. Finn, Pres.

Description: Black and minority beverage distributors (42,000); auxiliary members (5000) are interested in the beverage industry. Seeks to broaden opportunities for minorities in the beverage industry. Monitors state and federal liquor laws and informs members of developments. Cooperates with the National Conference of Black Mayors (see separate entry) in an effort to stimulate economic growth in U.S. cities; conducts fundraising activities for the United Negro College Fund (see separate entry). Supports literacy programs; regional groups offer scholarships. **Founded:** 1979. **Members:** 47,000. **Regional Groups:** 22. **Publications:** Corkscrew, monthly. Newspaper. Also publishes souvenir book.

★387★
National United Law Enforcement Officers Association (NULEOA)
256 E. McLemore Ave.
Memphis, TN 38106 Phone: (901)774-1118
Clyde R. Venson, Exec.Dir.

Description: Law enforcement officers from all departments; interested persons from the community. Develops community-based programs designed to improve the relationship between law enforcement officers and the community, with emphasis on the Black community. Provides educational seminars on law enforcement that promote professionalism and improvement of performance standards; emphasizes past contributions by Black officers and encourages potential leadership. Compiles data regarding the history of Blacks in law enforcement. Promotes equal employment and promotional practices for Black officers. Makes available scholarship program for college students. Operates hall of fame; maintains library and biographical archives; provides speakers' bureau; offers children's services. Maintains data base; compiles statistics. Sponsors competitions; bestows awards. **Founded:** 1969. **Members:** 5000. **Budget:** $75,000. **Local Groups:** 250. **Telecommunications Services:** Search for Answers (information hot line); toll-free number, (800)533-4649. **Publications:** Black Chiefs and Elected Law Enforcement Officers, annual. Directory. Blacks in Law Enforcement, semiannual. Journal on law enforcement as it relates to the Black community. Includes membership directory, listings of employment opportunities, research reports, and statistics.

★388★
National United Licensees Beverage Association (NULBA)
7141 Frankstown Ave.
Pittsburgh, PA 15208 Phone: (412)241-9344
Vivian Lane, Exec. Officer

Description: Holders of alcoholic beverage licenses. Purposes are to promote fellowship; develop, strengthen, and improve methods; promote integrity, good faith, and just and equitable principles in business and professional activity; seek uniformity in commercial usages; acquire, preserve, and distribute educational, civic, social, commercial, and economic statistics, and information. Conducts seminars. Awards annual scholarship to a needy high school honor student seeking a business education. **Founded:** 1964. **Members:** 1200. **Publications:** Newsletter, quarterly.

★389★
National Urban Coalition (NUC)
8601 Georgia Ave., Ste. 500
Silver Spring, MD 20910 Phone: (301)495-4999
Ramona H. Edelin Ph.D., CEO

Description: Seeks to improve the quality of life and opportunity for the disadvantaged in urban areas through the combined efforts of leaders among minorities, business, labor, local government, women, youth, and religion. Operates Say Yes to a Youngster's Future Program, which works to increase the participation of Blacks, Hispanics, Native Americans, and females in science, math, and computer education. Provides programs for at-risk minority youth in the areas of science and mathematics; operates AIDS education and information demonstration program for Black teenagers in Washington, DC. Conducts advocacy on behalf of cities and the least advantaged residents of urban areas. Conducts Urban Journalism Competition; bestows awards to individuals who perform outstanding service for urban communities. **Founded:** 1967. **Budget:** $1,800,000. **Local Groups:** 40. **Computerized Services:** National Education Information Exchange data base. **Telecommunications Services:** Fax, (301)587-0868. **Publications:** Urban Education Exchange, quarterly.

★390★
National Urban League (NUL)
500 E. 62nd St.
New York, NY 10021 Phone: (212)310-9000
John E. Jacob, CEO & Pres.

Description: Voluntary nonpartisan community service agency of civic, professional, business, labor, and religious leaders with a staff of trained social workers and other professionals. Aims to eliminate racial segregation and discrimination in the United States and to achieve parity for Blacks and other minorities in every phase of American life. Works to eliminate institutional racism and to provide direct service to minorities in the areas of employment, housing, education, social welfare, health, family planning, mental retardation, law and consumer affairs, youth and student affairs, labor affairs, veterans' affairs, and community and minority business development. Maintains research department in Washington, D C. **Founded:** 1910. **Members:** 50,000. **Budget:** $18,900,000. **Local Groups:** 113. Regional Offices: 5. **Telecommunications Services:** Fax, (212)593-8250. **Publications:** BEEP Newsletter, quarterly. Describes BEEP courses. Includes member news and listing of publications. Community Surveys and Reports, periodic. The Urban League News, quarterly. League program and activities newsletter. **Formerly:** National League on Urban Conditions Among Negroes.

★391★
National Urban/Rural Fellows (NU/RF)
55 W. 44th St., Ste. 600
New York, NY 10036 Phone: (212)921-9400
Luis Alvarez, Pres.

Description: Program designed to make top leadership opportunities in government and rural development available to minority group members. Recipients of the 14-month fellowships are selected competitively and must be U.S. citizens who: have a bachelor's degree or equivalent experience in solving urban or rural problems; have at least three years of employment experience in an administrative or economic development capacity; have demonstrated ability, leadership qualities, and a commitment to the solution of urban or rural problems. Program is aimed at meeting the need for competent urban and rural administrators, particularly minority group members and women, by combining a nine month, on-the-job assignment as special assistant to an experienced practitioner with several kinds of academic work. A master's degree in public administration or regional planning/rural development is awarded to qualified fellows at the end of the fellowship. **Founded:** 1985. Fellows: 530. **Budget:** $1,800,000. **Telecommunications Services:** Fax, (212)921-9572. **Publications:** Annual Report. Bio/Directory of Class, annual.

★392★
National Youth Employment Coalition (NYEC)
1501 Broadway, Rm. 1111
New York, NY 10036 Phone: (212)840-1834
Linda Laughlin, Exec.Dir.

Description: Representatives of community-based organizations, think tanks, corporate interests, and policy analysis organizations. Promotes education, employment, and training opportunities for disadvantaged youth. Encourages local grass roots organizing and information exchange. Conducts forums and training seminars. Maintains speakers' bureau; compiles statistics. **Founded:** 1979. **Members:** 60. **Telecommunications Services:** Fax, (212)768-0963. **Publications:** NYEC Notes, bimonthly. Newsletter; includes statistics.

★393★
Negro Airmen International (NAI)
PO Box 1340
Tuskegee, AL 36088 Phone: (205)727-0721
John W. Hicks Jr., Operations Officer

Description: Individuals holding at least a student pilot license who are active in some phase of aviation; members include both aviation professionals and others who are qualified pilots. Seeks greater participation by Blacks in the field of aviation through the encouragement of broader job opportunities; promotes awareness by government and industry of the needs, attitudes, and interests of Blacks concerning aviation. Encourages Black youth to remain in school and to enter the field of aviation. Maintains Summer Flight Academy for teenagers each July at Tuskegee Institute in Alabama. Sponsors competitions; bestows awards. Operates speakers' bureau, placement service, and library. **Founded:** 1967. **Members:** 912. **Regional Groups:** 10. **Local Groups:** 25. **Computerized Services:** Data base on membership and demographics. **Publications:** Membership Directory, annual. Newsletter, monthly. Also publishes informational brochures, and has produced a film on flight basics for youth.

★394★
New Afrikan People's Organization (NAPO)
13206 Dexter
Detroit, MI 48238 Phone: (313)883-3312
Chokwe Lumumba, Chm.

Description: Works for the foundation of an independent Black nation in the American deep south (Alabama, Georgia, Louisiana, Mississippi, and South Carolina); aims to develop a national consciousness favorable to the group's goals. Monitors legislation it considers repressive; collects and disseminates information; compiles statistics. Operates People's Low Cost Survival Program; establishes youth programs; maintains Malcolm X Community Centers to educate Blacks about the struggle for Black independence. Maintains speakers' bureau. Collects food and clothing for the needy. **Founded:** 1984. **Members:** 125. **Regional Groups:** 4. **State Groups:** 4. **Local Groups:** 4. **Publications:** By Any Means Necessary, monthly. Newspaper.

★395★
Nigerian Students Union in the Americas (NSUA)
c/o Granville U. Osuji
654 Girard St. NW, Apt. 512
Washington, DC 20001 Phone: (202)462-9124
Granville U. Osuji, Contact

Description: Nigerian students at institutions of higher learning in North and South America and neighboring islands. Disseminates information about Nigeria and Africa; cooperates with other African student unions in the Americas and with Nigerian student unions in Nigeria and other parts of the world. Maintains placement service and speakers' bureau. Holds teach-ins, symposia, debates, panel discussions, and lectures. Conducts research; bestows awards. **Founded:** 1962. **Members:** 25,000. **Regional Groups:** 4.

★396★
North American Center on Adoption (NACA)
67 Irving Pl.
New York, NY 10003 Phone: (212)254-7410
Elizabeth S. Cole, Dir.

Description: Resource center dealing with the problems preventing the adoption of older children, minority group children, children with physical, emotional, and/or intellectual problems, and children belonging to a sibling group of three or more. A project of Permanent Families for Children. Works with the media to increase public awareness of the waiting child. Develops training materials and provides technical assistance and consultation to agency staffs and interested groups. Offers resource services and consultation to those interested in establishing or improving state, provincial and regional adoption. Works with specialized agencies. **Founded:** 1974. **Publications:** Permanency Report, quarterly.

★397★
Office for Advancement of Public Black Colleges (OAPBC)
National Association of State Universities and Land Grant Colleges
1 Dupont Circle NW, Ste. 710
Washington, DC 20036-1191 Phone: (202)778-0818
Dr. N. Joyce Payne, Dir.

Description: Collects, organizes, interprets, and disseminates data on 35 predominantly Black public colleges. The colleges, located in 18 states, enroll over 135,000 students. Conducts research programs; bestows awards. Compiles statistics; maintains data bases. **Founded:** 1968. **Members:** 35. **Regional Groups:** 12. **State Groups:** 18. **Publications:** Key Administrative Personnel, annual. Directory. A National Resource, biennial. Newsletter, periodic. Profiles in Success, quarterly. Also publishes books and booklets.

★398★
Omega Psi Phi Fraternity
2714 Georgia Ave., NW
Washington, DC 20001 Phone: (202)667-7158
Dr. John S. Epps, Dir.

Description: Social fraternity. **Founded:** 1911. **Members:** 50,000. Active Chapters: 511. Alumni Chapters: 259. **Publications:** Bulletin, quarterly. The Oracle, quarterly.

★399★
Operation Crossroads Africa (OCA)
475 Riverside Dr.
New York, NY 10115 Phone: (212)242-8550
George Carter, Pres.

Description: Students and professionals, mostly from the U.S., who live and work with African counterparts during July and August on selfhelp community development projects in Africa. Opportunities are provided for interaction with village elders, educators, and political and other community leaders. Emphasizes community growth from within a "Third World" structure. Before departure, participants make an intensive study of Africa; after their return, they give speeches about their experiences. Participants pay part of the cost of the project. Organizes workcamp projects for U.S. high school students in the Caribbean and programs the visits of African and Caribbean leaders to the U.S. Sponsors training and exchange programs. Conducts fundraising and relief activities. Maintains liaison with similar groups abroad. **Founded:** 1958. **Members:** 7800. **Budget:** $3,500,000. **Telecommunications Services:** Toll-free number, (800)422-8742. **Publications:** Annual Report. Crossroads Communique, quarterly. Also publishes brochure.

★400★
Operation PUSH
930 E. 50th St.
Chicago, IL 60615 Phone: (312)373-3366
Rev. Tyrone Crider, Exec.Dir.

Description: National and international human rights organization and movement directed toward educational and economic equity and parity for all, particularly Black, Hispanic, and poor people. Seeks to create an ethical atmosphere; encourages self and community motivation and social responsibility. Uses research, education, negotiation, and direct action to achieve its goals. Sponsors Push for Excellence Program to aid the nation's public schools and restore academic excellence and discipline. Conducts conferences; maintains tape and speech library; operates speakers' bureau. (PUSH stands for People United to Serve Humanity.) **Founded:** 1971. **Budget:** $300,000. **Local Groups:** 50. **Telecommunications Services:** Fax, (312)924-3571. **Publications:** The Push Magazine, quarterly. The Voice of Excellence, bimonthly. Newspaper.

★401★
Operation Sisters United (OSU)
1104 Allison St. NW
Washington, DC 20011 Phone: (202)726-7365
Eleanore Cox, Dir.

Description: A program of the National Council of Negro Women (see separate entry). Aids teenage girls who have had conflicts with the law; seeks to prevent incarceration and institutionalization of these girls, and help them avoid future legal problems. Works to keep teenage girls with their families. Operates cultural enrichment, counseling, sex education, and family planning programs. Conducts parenting classes for teenage parents. Compiles statistics; maintains placement service. Sponsors competitions and bestows awards. **Founded:** 1972.

★402★
Opportunities Industrialization Centers of America (OIC/A)
100 W. Coulter St.
Philadelphia, PA 19144 Phone: (215)951-2200
Elton Jolly, CEO & Pres.

Description: A national technical assistance program funded by both the public and private sector for the disadvantaged, unemployed, and underemployed. Offers vocational skills training and job placement services. Conducts demonstration projects for alternative education that include counseling, remediation, and pre-vocational and vocational training. OIC's professional training arm, the Opportunities Academy of Management Training, offers management, operational, and community economic development training as well as continuing education for adults. Guided by a philosophy of selfhelp, trains more than 50,000 individuals yearly in over 100 skill areas. Bestows ten annual awards; conducts research; promotes community economic development. Maintains library of vocational skills and technical information; sponsors competitions. **Founded:** 1964. **Telecommunications Services:** Fax, (215)951-2227. **Publications:** OIC Key News, quarterly. Newsletter.

★403★
Organization of Black Airline Pilots (OBAP)
PO Box 86, La Guardia Airport
New York, NY 11371 Phone: (201)568-8145
Eddie R. Hadden, Gen.Mgr.

Description: Cockpit crew members of commercial air carriers, corporate pilots, and other interested individuals. Seeks to enhance minority participation in the aerospace industry. Maintains liaison with airline presidents and minority and pilot associations. Conducts lobbying efforts, including congressional examinations into airline recruitment practices. Provides scholarships; cosponsors Summer Flight Academy for Youth at Tuskegee Institute in Alabama. Offers job placement service and charitable program; operates speakers' bureau; compiles statistics on airline hiring practices. **Founded:** 1976. **Members:** 650. **Budget:** Less than $25,000. **Regional Groups:** 5. **Computerized Services:** Job placement bank. **Telecommunications Services:** Fax, (201)568-5178. **Publications:** Convention Journal, annual. Newsletter, bimonthly.

★404★
Pan-African Resource Center (PARC)
PO Box 3307
Washington, DC 20010
Banbose Shango, Chm.

Description: Educational organization that seeks to raise public awareness of the historical development of Pan-Africanism. According to the center, Africa was divided 100 years ago by the Europeans at the Berlin Conference of 1885. Seeks reunion of Africa and believes that Africa's resources should be used by Africans or go toward the betterment of Africa instead of being exploited by Europeans. Works to fight world hunger through programs designed to establish "self-reliance with dignity." Conducts research; compiles statistics. Maintains 43,000 volume library, biographical archives, and speakers' bureau. Bestows awards. **Founded:** 1980. **Members:** 435.

★405★
Panamerican/PanAfrican Association (PPA)
PO Box 143
Baldwinsville, NY 13027 Phone: (315)638-7379
Dr. Robert S. Pritchard, Chm.

Description: Supporters include scholars, diplomats, denominations, African-American and inter-American cultural exchange organizations, and persons who promote intercultural, interracial, and inter-group understanding. Maintains Applecrest in Baldwinsville, NY, headquarters and "think tank" for various cultural groups and activities and site of seminars, educational encounters, art exhibits, and music recitals. Sponsors inter-American, African-American, and Asian-American educational, cultural, and economic exchange, including Festival Sankofa-Masianoke multi-media touring exhibition. Maintains public diplomacy program; promotes artistic endeavors including concerts and recitals; conducts public interest civil and human rights litigation activities; promotes Third World economic development. Administers National and International Black History Month observances each February. Operates library of 2000 items including works from Afro-Brazilian guilds of ecclesiastical music, literature, and specialized studies on multiethnic/multicultural education and curriculum development. **Founded:** 1967. **Telecommunications Services:** Fax, (315)638-2590; toll-free number, (800)287-7868. **Publications:** Panamerican/Panafrican Association–Notes, periodic. Newsletter covering association activities and international ethnic and cultural topics. Includes commentary. **Also known as:** Panamerican Association.

★406★
PanAmerican Women's Association (PAWA)
c/o Frances R. Grant
310 W. End Ave., Apt. 16C
New York, NY 10023 Phone: (212)362-0710
Frances R. Grant, Pres.

Description: Women united to foster greater inter-American understanding. Promotes common action for the well-being of the people of the Western Hemisphere through cultural and educational exchange. Organizes music, art, dance, and student programs; sponsors periodic panel discussions. **Founded:** 1930.

★407★
Parker-Coltrane Political Action Committee (PCPAC)
669 Federal Bldg.
231 W. Lafayette
Detroit, MI 48226 Phone: (313)961-5670
Hansen Clark, Contact

Description: Political action organization supported by financial contributions of individuals. Organized by Congressman John Conyers and others to encourage and help Blacks and progressive candidates to win election to public office in the southern U.S. through direct campaign contributions and technical assistance. Conducts training sessions on methods and techniques of running for office. Initial efforts have been concentrated in Georgia, although the committee now operates throughout the South. Plans to extend operations on a national level. Presently inactive. **Founded:** 1981.

★408★
Partners of the Americas
1424 K St., NW, Ste. 700
Washington, DC 20005 Phone: (202)628-3300
William Reese, Pres.

Description: Volunteer private citizens organized in 60 partnerships linking U.S. states with Latin American and Caribbean countries. Goals are: to encourage innovative, community-based projects and joint planning among local partnerships; to provide a stimulus to local partnerships in generating additional resources for their technical and cultural exchange projects; to assist in the implementation of effective and ongoing development projects in the Latin American, Mexican, and Caribbean partner areas. Partnerships form the basis for exchange projects in agriculture, public health, culture, rehabilitation, community education, sports, and other areas of hemispheric development. Presents grants to partnership projects and travel funds for selected volunteer technicians; bestows awards. **Founded:** 1964. **Members:** 20,000. **Budget:** $6,200,000. **Telecommunications Services:** Electronic mail, TYMNET (CONTYME) DNA.NAPA; fax, (202)628-3306; telex, 6421 NAPAR. **Publications:** Annual Report. Partners, quarterly. Newsletter on technical assistance projects and exchanges between the United States and Latin America in agriculture, public health, education, and development. Also publishes brochures and booklets; makes available A Good Idea That Works (videotape). **Formerly:** (1971) National Association of the Partners of the Alliance.

★409★
PFB Project
c/o Robert B. Fitzpatrick
4801 Massachusetts Ave. NW, Ste. 400
Washington, DC 20016 Phone: (202)364-8710
Robert B. Fitzpatrick, Co-Founder

Description: Seeks humane solutions for victims of pseudofolliculitis barbae (PFB). PFB is a skin disorder peculiar to Black men in which victims suffer from a bump-like rash on the face which is aggravated by shaving. There is no complete cure for the disorder; the least painful solution is for victims to allow their beards to grow. The project believes that individuals who suffer from the disorder and are forced to shave by employers are victims of racial discrimination. Provides legal assistance to those discriminated against because of PFB. Supports research on PFB; maintains library. **Founded:** 1978.

★410★
Phi Beta Sigma Fraternity
145 Kennedy St. NW
Washington, DC 20011 Phone: (202)726-5424
Dr. Lawrence E. Miller, Exec.Dir.

Description: Service fraternity. Seeks to develop and translate into functional realities the ideals of brotherhood, service, and scholarship. Promotes three national programs: Bigger and Better Business; Education; Social Action. Sponsors Sigma Beta Club for high school aged males. **Founded:** 1914. **Members:** 90,000. **Telecommunications Services:** Fax, (202)882-1680. **Publications:** The Crescent, semiannual. The Crescent Extra, periodic. Newsletter.

★411★
Plan of Action for Challenging Times (PACT)
PACT-Educ. Opportunities Clearinghouse
635 Divisadero St.
San Francisco, CA 94117 Phone: (415)922-2550
W. Charlene Folsom, Project Dir.

Description: Program to benefit minority and/or low-income students who have not, in most cases, utilized their educational potential by reason of circumstances inherent in their background, mainly lack of encouragement, motivation, and finances. Serves the city and county of San Francisco, CA; African-Americans represent the greatest percentage of students served. Assists Mexican-Americans, Asians, Native Americans, and low-income Caucasians as often as possible. Students are identified through agency, school, and community referrals offering counseling services, college and financial aid information, and college admissions procedures. Provides college admissions, financial aid, and career counseling services; offers assistance with application forms; organizes campus visits, meetings between college recruiters and students, and visits to corporations and public institutions to observe various professions; conducts financial aid workshops; sponsors presentations to organizations, churches, and clubs. PACT has developed a screening process and a system of commitments from colleges. Supported by U.S. Department of Education under Educational Talent Search Program. **Founded:** 1966.

★412★
Planning and the Black Community (PBC)
Department of the Army
PO Box C-3755
Seattle, WA 98124-2255 Phone: (206)764-3614
Horace H. Foxall Jr., Treas.

Description: Members of the American Planning Association interested in issues related to planning in the Black community. Objectives are to: formulate and articulate positions on national, regional, and statewide policy issues related to Blacks for presentation to the APA and the public; provide a forum for exchange of practical experience and knowledge among Black planners; establish and strengthen liaison with Black professionals and groups such as social workers, economists, lawyers, public administrators, International City Management Association, National Association for the Advancement of Colored People, and National League of Cities. Disseminates employment information and provides a means for employers to address affirmativ e action goals regarding planning and planning-related jobs. Encourages and assists Black planning students and programs; sponsors planning studies research. **Founded:** 1980. **Members:** 125. **Publications:** Newsletter, quarterly.

★413★
The Platters Fan Club (TPFC)
PO Box 39
Las Vegas, NV 89125 Phone: (702)648-3514

Description: Fans of The Platters, a vocal group popular in the mid-1950s. Original members included David Lynch, Herbert Reed, Paul Robi, Zola Taylor, and Tony Williams. Their early hits included The Great Pretender and Only You. **Founded:** 1956. **Members:** 2000. **Telecommunications Services:** Fax, (702)648-2913. **Publications:** The Platters Anthology Songbook (book).

★414★
Potomac Institute (PI)
1400 20th St. NW, Ste. 5
Washington, DC 20036 Phone: (202)331-0087
Harold C. Fleming, Pres. Emeritus

Description: Nonprofit, foundation-funded research organization concerned with developing human resources by expanding opportunities for racial and economically deprived minorities. Provides advisory and research services to government and private agencies involved in the development of programs to increase opportunities for minorities. Sponsors special purpose conferences to explore problems affecting minority groups. Studies, conferences, and publications have covered such areas as affirmative action in employment, state and local civil rights activities, implementation of federal policies for minorities, school desegregation, police and civil rights, disparities in public education funding, development of Black business entrepreneurship, inner-city teacher expectations, and student achievement, inclusionary zoning and housing for lower income families, national youth service, urban growth, and central city technical assistance. Maintains library of 2000 volumes on race relations, civil rights, and urban problems. **Founded:** 1961.

★415★
Project Equality (PE)
1020 E. 63rd St., Ste. 102
Kansas City, MO 64110 Phone: (816)361-9222
Maurice E. Culver, Pres.

Description: A nationwide interfaith program enabling religious organizations, institutions, and others to support equal opportunity employers with their purchasing power. Services include: validation of hotels for conventions and meetings of organizations, validations of suppliers to member organizations and institutions, and consultant and educational services to assist employers in affirmative action and equal employment opportunity programs. **Founded:** 1965. **Members:** 140. **Budget:** $250,000. **State Groups:** 1. **Local Groups:** 3. **Computerized Services:** Mailing list of members, prospective members, and participating employers. **Publications:** PE Action, quarterly. PE EEO News, quarterly. Project Equality–Buyer's Guide, annual. Directory listing employers that have provided current equal employment opportunity data and have been validated by the project.

★416★
Project US
1151 Titus Ave.
Rochester, NY 14617 Phone: (716)544-8605
Evelyn Scott, Dir.

Description: Attempts to handle the problem of school integration through a totally voluntary two-way urban-suburban transfer program. Makes available transfers to both minority and White children. Maintains Operation Enrichment, a program designed to attract suburban students to urban schools through the offering of specialized courses. Serves as a national model for alternatives to busing. Maintains collection of clippings and materials on integration efforts in Monroe County. Is currently operating in the Rochester and Monroe county school districts of New York state. **Founded:** 1965. **Publications:** Handbook. **Also known as:** Urban-Suburban Interdistrict Transfer Program.

★417★
Project Vote!
1424 16th St., Ste. 101
Washington, DC 20036 Phone: (202)328-1500
Sanford A. Newman, Exec.Dir.

Description: Nonpartisan organization working to increase electoral participation among low-income, minority, and unemployed citizens. Organizes local coalitions and hires local staffs and interns; conducts voter registration and education in order to increase turnout; registers individuals door-to-door and as they wait in food stamp and unemployment lines. **Founded:** 1982. **Budget:** $1,000,000. **Local Groups:** 100. **Publications:** How to Develop a Voter Registration Plan, How to Register Voters at a Central Site, and general information flyer; also produces video training tapes. **Also known as:** Americans for Civic Participation.

★418★
PUSH International Trade Bureau (PITB)
930 E. 50th St.
Chicago, IL 60615 Phone: (312)373-0992
McNair Grant, Exec.Dir.

Description: A bureau of Operation PUSH (see separate entry). Minority-owned franchises and small businesses; minority individuals who are self-employed. Seeks the creation of a Black common market in the U.S. Works to facilitate the opening of new markets for Black-owned businesses. Provides technical assistance to members, including market research and analysis, financial counseling, and packaging and marketing services. Negotiates with major U.S. corporations to help create business opportunities for Blacks. Conducts workshops on job hunting and business management. Bestows Black Diamond Award to businesses and individuals who have done the most to improve the economic status of Blacks in the U.S. Maintains archive. **Founded:** 1982. **Members:** 300. **Publications:** Membership List, quarterly. PUSH International Trade Bureau Economic Viewpoint, monthly. Newsletter. Also publishes brochure.

★419★
Radical Women (RW)
523-A Valencia St.
San Francisco, CA 94110 Phone: (415)864-1278
Constance Scott, Organizer

Description: Women with a socialist-feminist political orientation who believe that women's leadership is decisive for basic social change. Works toward reform in the areas of reproductive rights, child care, affirmative action, divorce, police brutality, rape, women of color, lesbians, and working women. Opposes efforts of conservative anti-feminist groups. **Founded:** 1967. **Local Groups:** 9. **Publications:** Papers.

★420★
Rhythm and Blues Rock and Roll Society, Inc. (RBRRSI)
PO Box 1949
New Haven, CT 06510 Phone: (203)924-1079
William J. Nolan, Dir.

Description: Record collectors, disc jockeys, record dealers, performing artists, and others dedicated to the preservation and promotion of rhythm and blues music and its counterparts (blues, gospel, and jazz) as a part of U.S. cultural heritage. Sponsors benefit concerts for prisoners, fundraising programs for amateur talent, and music concerts and festivals. Conducts workshops on R & B culture with lectures and films on the history of Black music. Seeks to encourage the employment of minorities in jobs related to blues music and hopes to offer training programs in the production of educational television shows and films. Sponsors Antique Blues, a cultural radio program presenting, live gospel, blues, and rhythm and blues performing groups. Bestows awards to artists, authors, and writers. Cooperates with the annual W.C. Handy Blues Music Awards ceremony. Maintains international record review panel. Compiles statistics and conducts research. Operates record and tape-book library and archive; plans to maintain hall of fame and museum. **Founded:** 1974. **Members:** 50,000. **Regional Groups:** 13. **Telecommunications Services:** Telephone referral services. **Publications:** Big Beat, periodic. Newsletter; includes reports on the society's concerts, fundraising events, and festivals; also contains calendar of events, interviews with musicians, research news, and record reviews.

★421★
Scott Joplin Ragtime Festival (SJRF)
113 E. 4th St.
Sedalia, MO 65301 Phone: (816)826-2271
John Moore, Festival Coord.

Description: Fans of ragtime composer and musician Scott Joplin (1868-1917) and of ragtime music. Sponsors concerts featuring ragtime artists. Holds annual educational symposium and panel discussions. Offers children's services; conducts annual research trips to other festivals and historically affiliated sites in the U.S. and Canada. Maintains speakers' bureau, biographical archives, museum, and library of subject biographies, videocassettes of past festivals, and research materials. Sponsors competitions; bestows awards. **Founded:** 1974. **Members:** 30. **Budget:** $50,000. **Computerized Services:** Mailing list. **Publications:** none. **Formerly:** (1983) Scott Joplin Ragtime Festival Committee (the committee reactivated in 1983 to coincide with the issuance of a commemorative stamp in Joplin's honor by the U.S. Postal Service); (1966) Scott Joplin Commemorative Committee.

★422★
Sickle Cell Disease Foundation of Greater New York (SCDFGNY)
127 W. 127, Rm. 421
New York, NY 10027 Phone: (212)865-1500
Dick Campbell, Exec.Dir.

Description: Physicians and professionals in allied fields. A voluntary health agency formed to support and conduct research and educational programs aimed at control and, ultimately, eradication of sickle cell anemia. Activities thus far are conducted primarily in the New York City area, but the group also offers information and guidance to organizations in Europe, Africa, South America, Southeast Asia, London, England, and the Caribbean area. Assists in the establishment of local chapters that establish clinics for screening and genetic counseling; sponsors symposia, seminars, and public school programs; offers professional training for screening and counseling programs. Maintains a speakers' bureau; compiles statistics. Maintains extensive files on research being conducted, individuals and organizations working to overcome the disease, and advocacy services available to families and patients with the disease. Programs include: Outreach, an in-service hospital emergency program which informs hospital personnel of the implications of a crisis in a sickle cell anemia patient; a blood bank; referral services; counseling, social services assistance, and employment and aid services. Bestows awards. Maintains library containing updated reports, pamphlets, and backgrounders-research studies. **Founded:** 1972. **Members:** 1500. **Budget:** $150,000. **Local Groups:** 65. **Publications:** Annual Report. Newsletter, quarterly. Also publishes brochures; makes available educational materials and film.

★423★
Sigma Pi Phi Fraternity
99 Hudson St., Ste. 1600
New York, NY 10013 Phone: (212)219-1360
Butler T. Henderson, Exec.Sec.

Description: Social fraternity. Promotes social and intellectual camaraderie; supports designated social programs. Maintains the Boule Foundation. **Founded:** 1904. **Members:** 3000. **Regional Groups:** 5. Active Chapters: 91. **Publications:** Boule Journal, quarterly. Roster, biennial.

★424★
Society of Ethnic and Special Studies (SESS)
Southern University at Edwardsville
Box 1652
Edwardsville, IL 62026 Phone: (618)692-2042
Emil F. Jason, Pres.

Description: Faculty, administrators, students, and others interested in the furtherance and preservation of ethnic, environmental, and special programs in secondary and postsecondary education. Sponsors workshops, seminars, publications, and projects that will further the understanding of problems and issues; evaluates special studies and related programs; encourages joint cooperative efforts within regions. Presents awards; sponsors competitions; maintains speakers' bureau. **Founded:** 1973. **Members:** 400. **State Groups:** 3. **Local Groups:** 1. **Publications:** Journal, semiannual.

★425★
South Africa Foundation (SAF)
1225 19th St., NW, Ste. 700
Washington, DC 20036 Phone: (202)223-5486
Michael Christie, Dir.

Description: Representatives of the private sector of South Africa. Objectives are to: act as a professional international communication network and work with individuals and groups whose decisions affect the lives of South Africans; formulate responses to outside political and commercial pressure that are beneficial to South African life and national economy. Does not enter into defense of South African policies or promote any particular ideology or factional interest; favors peaceful change in South Africa through the private sector. Provides policymakers with analyses of South African trends and events. Operates referral service with representatives from each international group for information exchange, special problem solving, an d tour and visit planning related to interests affecting South Africa. Conducts surveys and provides statistical analyses. **Founded:** 1960. **Members:** 5000. **Regional Groups:** 2. **Publications:** Information Digest, annual. News, monthly. South Africa International, quarterly. Also publishes special reports and analyses.

★426★
South African Military Refugee Aid Fund (SAMRAF)
29 7th Ave.
Brooklyn, NY 11217

Description: Seeks aid for South African military refugees and war resisters. Provides military dissenters with support and seeks asylum for them in the U.S. Maintains speakers' bureau; offers legal assistance and specialized education. Maintains offices in Brooklyn, NY and San Francisco, CA. **Founded:** 1978. **Publications:** News and Notes, bimonthly.

★427★
Southeastern Regional Office National Scholarship Service and Fund for Negro Students (NSSFNS)
965 Martin Luther King, Jr. Dr. NW
Atlanta, GA 30314 Phone: (404)577-3990
Samuel Johnson, Exec.Dir.

Description: Supported by foundation and corporate grants and individual contributions. Provides scholarships to broaden higher education opportunities for Black and other minority and low-income high school students. Maintains a free college advisory and referral service for interested students and those enrolled in Talent Search and Upward Bound projects; offers supplementary scholarship aid to counselees. Sponsors annual Student-College Interview Sessions and workshops for guidance and admissions counselors (dates and sites available upon request). Participates in professional meetings. **Founded:** 1947. **Computerized Services:** Data base of student mailing lists for higher education institutions. **Publications:** Annual Report. Also publishes brochure. **Formerly:** (1987) National Scholarship Service and Fund for Negro Students.

★428★

Southern Africa Media Center (SAMC)

149 9th St., Rm. 420
San Francisco, CA 94103 Phone: (415)621-6196
Cornelius Moore, Dir.

Description: A national project of California Newsreel, a nonprofit educational organization which produces and distributes media materials. Media specialists, educators, religious leaders, and concerned citizens. Objective is to improve the effectiveness of film/video in church, community, and education and action programs centered around southern Africa, particularly concerning human rights in South Africa. Believes that film/video screening can help form attitudes on foreign policy. Provides information on informing and involving the community on current U.S. foreign policy issues about apartheid through film/video screenings and countering lobbying and public relations efforts of the South African Information Service. Sponsors Bring South Africa Into the Classroom, an educational program combining videocassettes and curriculum guides. Maintains film library. **Founded:** 1976. Advisory Board: 26. **Budget:** $165,000. **Computerized Services:** Mailing lists of individuals active in South Africa awareness work. **Telecommunications Services:** Fax, (415)621-6522. **Publications:** Southern Africa Media Center Catalog, annual. Also distributes Together/Against Apartheid (resource and action guide) and Using Films on South Africa (handbook). Makes available films including Mapantsula Generations of Resistance, Chain of Tears, and The Cry of Reason.

★429★

Southern Africa Project (SAP)

c/o Lawyers' Comm. for Civil Rights
Under Law
1400 I St. NW, Ste. 400
Washington, DC 20005 Phone: (202)371-1212
Gay McDougall, Dir.

Description: Purpose is to provide competent legal representation to defendants in political and quasi-political trials in South Africa. Concerns include illegal detention, security legislation, and deviations from the law. Provides U.S. government and U.S. organizations with information on human rights violations and conditions in South Africa. **Founded:** 1967. **Telecommunications Services:** Fax, (202)842-3211. **Publications:** Annual Report. Also publishes Special Reports, reports on trials, and analyses of South African statutes.

★430★

Southern Christian Leadership Conference (SCLC)

334 Auburn Ave. NE
Atlanta, GA 30312 Phone: (404)522-1420
Dr. Joseph E. Lowery, Pres.

Description: Nonsectarian coordinating and service agency for local organizations seeking full citizenship rights, equality, and the integration of African-Americans in all aspects of life in the U.S. and subscribing to the Ghandian philosophy of nonviolence. Works primarily in 16 southern and border states to improve civic, religious, economic, and cultural conditions. Fosters nonviolent resistance to all forms of racial injustice, including state and local laws and practices. Conducts leadership training program embracing such subjects as registration and voting, social protest, use of the boycott, picketing, nature of prejudice, and understanding politics. Sponsors citizenship education schools to teach reading and writing, help persons pass literacy tests for vot ing, and provide information about income tax forms, tax-supported resources, aid to handicapped children, public health facilities, how government is run, and social security. Conducts Crusade for the Ballot, which aims to double the Black vote in the South through increased voter registrations. Sponsors lectures; disseminates literature. **Founded:** 1957. **Publications:** Newsletter, monthly.

★431★

Southern Coalition for Educational Equity (SCEE)

PO Box 22904
Jackson, MS 39225 Phone: (601)355-7398
Winifred Green, Pres.

Description: Coalition of parents, students, teachers, and administrators that operates in Alabama, Georgia, Louisiana, Mississippi, and North Carolina, with plans to include eight additional states. Works toward developing more efficient educational programs and eliminating racism and sexism within southern schools. Has organized projects including: Arkansas Career Resources Project, which provides minorities and single heads of households with marketable skills and jobs; New Orleans Effective Schools Project, which attempts to increase school effectiveness through high expectations, stressing academic achievement, and quality instruction; Project MiCRO, which seeks to provide computer access for, and sharpen analytical skills of, minority students; Summer Program, which focuses on students' reading comprehension skills. **Founded:** 1978. **Publications:** Annual Report.

★432★

Southern Development Foundation (SDF)

1006 Surrey St.
Lafayette, LA 70501 Phone: (318)232-7672
Rev. A. J. McKnight CS, Founder

Description: Combats Black poverty in the South and helps the poor achieve economic independence. Provides, through its affiliates, money and technical assistance to limited resource co-ops and community controlled organizations. Promotes minority co-ops. Helps to form selfhelp projects. Sponsors National Black Survival Fund (see separate entry). **Founded:** 1972. **Telecommunications Services:** Fax, (318)232-5094.

★433★

Southern Education Foundation (SEF)

135 Auburn Ave. NE, 2nd Fl.
Atlanta, GA 30303 Phone: (404)523-0001
Elridge W. McMillan, Pres.

Description: Self-perpetuating, integrated organization created to improve and extend educational opportunities for Southern youth, with special regard to the needs of minorities. Conducts educational programs. **Founded:** 1937. Trustees: 12. **Publications:** Pipeline, quarterly. Newsletter covering issues related to minority teachers; also contains annual report and reviews of educational research publications.

★434★

Southern Poverty Law Center (SPLC)

PO Box 2087
Montgomery, AL 36102 Phone: (205)264-0286
Morris Dees, Exec.Dir.

Description: Seeks to protect and advance the legal and civil rights of poor people, regardless of race, through education and litigation. Does not accept fees from clients. The center is currently involved in several lawsuits representing individuals injured or threatened by activities of the Ku Klux Klan and related groups. Attempts to develop techniques and strategies that can be used by private attorneys. Operates Klanwatch (see separate entry). **Founded:** 1971. **Budget:** $2,000,000. **Publications:** Law Report, 5/year. Klanwatch Intelligence Report, monthly. Also publishes books.

★435★
Southern Regional Council (SRC)
60 Walton St. NW
Atlanta, GA 30303-2199 Phone: (404)522-8764
Stephen T. Suitts, Exec.Dir.

Description: Leaders in education, religion, business, labor, and the professions interested in improving race relations in the South. An interracial research and technical assistance center that addresses issues of social justice and political and economic democracy. Seeks to engage public policy as well as personal conscience in pursuit of equality. Develops educational programs; provides community relations consultation and field services when requested by official and private agencies. Distributes pamphlets pertaining to desegregation of various public facilities and fosters elimination of barriers to Black voting registration. Acts as official sponsor of overseas government officials, leaders, and other visitors who wish to view race relations in the South. Maintains extensive library on civil rights, civil liberties, politics, and suffrage, including the largest newspaper collection on civil rights in U.S. Bestows annual Lillian Smith Book Award for best books on the South. **Founded:** 1944. **Computerized Services:** Mailing lists; redistricting services. **Telecommunications Services:** Fax, (404)522-8791 **Publications:** Legislative Bulletin, quarterly.

★436★
Student National Dental Association (SNDA)
c/o Dr. Robert Knight
Howard University School of Dentistry
600 W. St. NW
Washington, DC 20059 Phone: (202)806-0301
Martin Jordan, Pres.

Description: A section of the National Dental Association (see separate entry). Minority dental students. Addresses the needs of minority dental students; strives to expose and eliminate discriminatory practices encountered by its members. Promotes increased minority enrollment in dental schools. Seeks to improve dental health care delivery to all disadvantaged people. Compiles statistics. **Founded:** 1972. **Members:** 9000. **Budget:** Less than $25,000. **Regional Groups:** 10. **Local Groups:** 46. **Publications:** Convention Bulletin, annual. Help Us to Build Your Dental Career, updated annually. Membership Directory, annual.

★437★
Student National Medical Association (SNMA)
1012 10th St. NW
Washington, DC 20001 Phone: (202)371-1616
Jeffrey E. Sterling, Chm.

Description: Minority medical students and interns. Seeks to help minority students in recruitment, admission, and retention in medical school and publishes information on problems and achievement in this area. Conducts research forums and medical projects. Sponsors competitions; bestows awards. **Founded:** 1964. **Members:** 2500. **Regional Groups:** 10. **Local Groups:** 130. **Publications:** SNMA Journal, quarterly.

★438★
Student National Podiatric Medical Association (SNPMA)
c/o Aurelio Jimenez
Dr. Scholl's Coll. of Podiatric Medicine
Mail Box 430
1001 N. Dearborn
Chicago, IL 60610 Phone: (708)757-5991
Aurelio Jimenez, Pres.

Description: Minorities in the podiatric medical field furthering podiatric medicine. Promotes minority equality in the podiatric colleges and profession. Sponsors competitions; bestows awards; maintains charitable program; provides speakers' bureau; compiles statistics. Holds ethnic festivals, events, and a Christmas program. **Founded:** 1973. **Members:** 300. **Publications:** Newsletter, semiannual.

★439★
Tau Gamma Delta Sorority
c/o Ernestine Belfield
3152 Greenfield Dr.
Rocky Mount, NC 27804 Phone: (919)443-6786
Ernestine Belfield, Pres.

Description: Service sorority - women in business and the professions. Sponsors Tauettes, for girls ages 13-18, to "help instill good character" and expose them to "the finer cultures"; also sponsors Taugadette, an annual arts program to promote young artists ages 19-35. Presents awards; maintains hall of fame; compiles statistics. **Founded:** 1942. **Members:** 1500. **Regional Groups:** 4. **Local Groups:** 60. **Publications:** Roster, annual. The Star, semiannual.

★440★
369th Veterans' Association (TVA)
369th Regiment Armory
1 369th Plaza
New York, NY 10037 Phone: (212)281-3308
Kenneth J. Myles, Pres.

Description: Veterans of World War I, World War II, Korean Conflict, and the Vietnam War. Seeks to support all patriotic endeavors of the U.S., and to assist members and their families through charitable programs and community activities. Donates funds, equipment, and other supplies to children's camps, needy families, religious institutions, Veterans Administration Hospitals, and community and senior citizen centers. Provides children's services, including: sponsoring Little League baseball teams and a basketball team; a tutorial program; donation of awards to elementary school children at graduation; scholarship assistance for children of members. Sponsored the rehabilitation of apartment buildings in New York City, and a four million dollar housing development for senior citizens and the handicapped. Conducts seminars and counseling sessions to assist unemployed veterans, and offers study classes to adults for preparation in Civil Service examinations. Sponsors the annual Dr. Martin Luther King, Jr. Memorial Parade in New York City. Maintains biographical archives. **Founded:** 1953. **Members:** 2500. **State Groups:** 11. **Local Groups:** 10. **Publications:** 369th News Bulletin, quarterly.

★441★
Trade Union Leadership Council (TULC)
8670 Grand River Ave.
Detroit, MI 48204 Phone: (313)894-0303
Hubert Holly, Pres.

Description: Primarily Black trade unionists in Michigan, but membership open to anyone. To eradicate injustices perpetrated upon people because of race, religion, sex, or national origin. Seeks increased leadership and job opportunities for Blacks. Maintains Nelson Jack Edwards Educational Centre. **Founded:** 1957. **Members:** 2500. **Publications:** Vanguard, quarterly.

★442★
Trade Union Women of African Heritage (TUWAH)
530 W. 23rd St., Ste. 428
New York, NY 10011 Phone: (212)929-6449
Thelma Dailey, Pres.

Description: Black women union members. Supports various causes of ethnic working women; participates in community activities; conducts alternative school programs. Maintains Global Women of African Heritage (see separate entry), Maverick Center for Self Development, and Leaders of the 21st Century. Operates speakers' bureau; compiles statistics; conducts research programs. **Founded:** 1969. **Publications:** The Ethnic Woman, periodic. Magazine.

★443★
TransAfrica
545 8th St. SE, Ste. 200
Washington, DC 20003 Phone: (202)547-2550
Randall Robinson, Exec.Dir.

Description: Concerned with the political and human rights of people in Africa and the Caribbean, and those of African descent throughout the world. Attempts to influence U.S. foreign policy in these areas by informing the public of violations of social, political, and civil rights, and by advocating a more progressive attitude in the U.S. policy stance. Supports the work of the United Nations (see separate entry) in Africa. Sponsors TransAfrica Action Alert to mobilize Black opinion nationally on foreign policy issues by contacting influential policymakers. Sponsors TransAfrica Forum (see separate entry), which conducts research and educational activities. **Founded:** 1977. **Members:** 18,000. **Budget:** $300,000. **Telecommunications Services:** Fax, (202)547-7687. **Publications:** TransAfrica News, quarterly.

★444★
TransAfrica Forum (TF)
545 8th St. SE, Ste. 200
Washington, DC 20003 Phone: (202)547-2550
Randall Robinson, Exec.Dir.

Description: Research and education arm of TransAfrica (see separate entry). Seeks to provide an independent review of differing perspectives on political, economic, and cultural issues affecting Black communities globally through its publications. Conducts seminars with scholars and government officials. **Founded:** 1981. **Telecommunications Services:** Fax, (202)547-7687. **Publications:** TransAfrica Forum: A Quarterly Journal of Opinion on Africa and the Caribbean. Journal reporting on economic, foreign policy, political, and social issues affecting Black Africa and the Caribbean. Includes book reviews and conference and seminar transcriptions.

★445★
Tuskegee Airmen, Inc. (TAI)
156 Sugar Tom's Ln.
East Norwich, NY 11732-1153 Phone: (516)922-1198
Nancy Leftenant-Colon, Pres.

Description: Majority of members are Black men and women involved in aviation in the military services, service academies, and ROTC units; former airmen who flew in a segregated U.S. Army Air Corps. Seeks to maintain a relationship among those who fought and served in World War II overseas and at home. Strives to motivate minority students in the proper curriculum for opportunities in high tech society. Provides information about the contributions Black Americans have made to aviation history. Has established a scholarship fund for students interested in aviation or aerospace careers. Bestows awards; maintains speakers' bureau and biographical archives. Operates museum at Historic Fort Wayne in Detroit, MI. **Founded:** 1972. **Members:** 1684. **Budget:** $65,000. **Regional Groups:** 3. **Local Groups:** 32. **Publications:** Tuskegee Airmen, quarterly. Tuskegee Airmen, Inc., Membership Roster, annual. Also publishes The Lonely Eagles (book) and historical biography of members. **Formerly:** Do Do Club.

★446★
Twenty-First Century Foundation (TFCF)
10 E. 87 St.
New York, NY 10128 Phone: (212)427-8100
Robert S. Browne, Pres.

Description: For the development of an endowment for the support of Black charitable institutions. Grants are bestowed in the areas of education and economic development. **Founded:** 1971. **Budget:** $60,000. **Telecommunications Services:** Fax, (212)876-6278.

★447★
United American Progress Association (UAPA)
701 E. 79th St.
Chicago, IL 60619 Phone: (312)268-1873
Webb Evans, Pres.

Description: Businesses, churches, and organizations in the Black community. Promotes and assists Black entrepreneurs. Encourages business owners to agree to supply goods and services to Black communities whose residents support local Black-owned firms. Works in conjunction with Operation PUSH and National Black United Front (see separate entries). **Founded:** 1961. **Members:** 250. **Publications:** Community News, monthly. Newsletter.

★448★
United Black Christians (UBC)
1380 E. Hyde Park Blvd., No. 815
Chicago, IL 60615
Patricia Eggleston, Pres.

Description: To increase the relevance of United Church of Christ in the struggle for liberation and justice. **Founded:** 1970. **Members:** 70,000. **Formerly:** United Black Churchmen.

★449★
United Black Church Appeal (UBCA)
c/o Christ Church
860 Forest Ave.
Bronx, NY 10456 Phone: (212)665-6688
Hon. Wendell Foster, Pres.

Description: Black clergy and laity. Objective is to awaken the power of the Black clergy and the Black church to provide leadership for the liberation of the Black community. Is concerned with Black economic development and political power, and the strengthening of Black families and churches. Believes pastors in Black churches should reestablish legitimate leadership roles within the Black community. Works with troubled Black youths in the community; rallies against drugs in urban areas. Supports community betterment projects including surplus food programs and distribution of food to needy families. Raises funds to alleviate hunger in Puerto Rico, Mexico, Colombia, and Africa. Plans to establish Black Church Center to house a hall of fame, museum, and library dedicated to preserving the history and restoring the importance of the Black church. **Founded:** 1980. **Members:** 500.

★450★
United Church of Christ Commission for Racial Justice (UCCCRJ)
700 Prospect Ave. E., 7th Fl.
Cleveland, OH 44115-1110 Phone: (216)736-2168
Rev.Dr. Benjamin F. Chavis Jr., Exec.Dir.

Description: Seeks to increase the involvement of the United Church of Christ in the human rights struggles of African-Americans and other minorities. Maintains higher education program to provide scholarships to minority college students. **Founded:** 1965. **Telecommunications**

Services: Fax, (216)736-2171. **Publications:** The Civil Rights, weekly. Newsletter. Civil Rights Journal, periodic.

★451★
United Church of Christ Coordinating Center for Women in Church and Society (CCW)
700 Prospect Ave.
Cleveland, OH 44115 Phone: (216)736-2100
Marilyn Breitling, Exec.Dir.

Description: Works to eliminate racism and sexism in the church and society. Promotes advocacy for women's concerns through cooperative projects with United Church of Christ agencies; cooperates in projects by helping to establish a network to respond to legislation affecting women. Promotes consciousness-raising by contributing to other United Church of Christ publications. Maintains 200 volume library on women's issues, theology, economics, and employment. Bestows biennial Antoinette Brown Award to clergy women. Recognizes the contributions of lay women. Provides speakers; conducts workshops. **Founded:** 1980. **Budget:** $495,000. **Publications:** Common Lot, quarterly. Journal. Also publishes Moms Morning Out and Women Pray (books).

★452★
United Church of Christ Ministers for Racial and Social Justice (MRSJ)
National Headquarters of United Church of Christ
700 Prospect Ave.
Cleveland, OH 44115 Phone: (216)736-2160
Benjamin F. Chavis Jr., Exec.Dir.

Description: Ministers of United Church of Christ. To maximize impact of Black constituency of UCC; to increase its relevance to the struggle of the Black and other minority communities. Conducts research and training seminars for ministers and laypeople. Maintains speakers' bureau; offers placement service; bestows awards. **Founded:** 1967. **Members:** 350. **Regional Groups:** 6. **Local Groups:** 4. **Telecommunications Services:** Fax, (216)736-2171. **Publications:** Newsletter, annual.

★453★
United Golfers' Association (UGA)
321 Congress
Indianapolis, IN 46208 Phone: (317)925-8135
Belita Page, Sec.

Description: Golf clubs with predominantly, though not exclusively, Black members. Promotes golf and encourages young people to participate in the sport. Sponsors annual tournament; offers scholarships. **Founded:** 1926. **Members:** 60. **Budget:** Less than $25,000. **Regional Groups:** 7.

★454★
United Mortgage Bankers of America (UMBA)
800 Ivy Hill Rd.
Philadelphia, PA 19150 Phone: (215)242-6060
Gene Hatton, Exec.Dir. & Pres.

Description: Minority mortgage brokers and mortgage bankers. Purpose is to coordinate and channel mortgage money for all Americans regardless of race, creed, or color, on a non-segregated basis. Arranges discussions with top officials of major insurance companies, savings banks, and pension plans throughout the country. Seeks to ascertain the policies of various companies toward making loans through minority bankers. Provides training for new mortgage brokers; conducts workshops; maintains library of 2000 volumes. **Founded:** 1962. **Members:** 1600. **Budget:** $1,200,000. **State Groups:** 8. **Local Groups:** 20. **Telecommunications Services:** Fax, (215)247-1580. **Publications:** News Bulletin, monthly.

★455★
United Nations Centre Against Apartheid (UNCAA)
United Nations Plaza, Rm. S-3577
New York, NY 10017 Phone: (212)963-5511
Sotirios Mousouris, Asst.Sec.Gen.

Description: Assists political bodies concerned with apartheid in executing their policy decisions; acts as a clearinghouse of information for the United Nations and specialized agencies involved in the international campaign against apartheid; promotes assistance to the indigenous people of South Africa and their liberation movements; conducts research. Maintains liaisons with antiapartheid movements, trade unions, religious, student, and youth organizations, and women's groups. Serves the United Nations' Special Committee Against Apartheid, the Advisory Committee on the United Nations Educational and Training Programme for Southern Africa, the International Commission Against Apartheid in Sports, the Intergovernmental Group to Monitor the Supply and Shipping of Oil and Petroleum Products to South Africa, as well as the United Nations General Assembly and Security Council, in their apartheid deliberations. Operates three funds generated by voluntary contributions: the United Nations Trust for South Africa, which is used primarily to provide legal assistance to victims of apartheid and their families; the United Nations Educational and Training Programme for Southern Africa, which provides funds for South Africans seeking postsecondary education outside of South Africa; the Trust Fund for Publicity Against Apartheid, which provides additional means to disseminate publicity material. Provides speakers on apartheid-related issues. **Founded:** 1976. **Telecommunications Services:** Fax, (212)963-5305; telex, 177642. Branches: Committee Servicing and Research; Publicity, Assistance and Promotion of International Action. **Publications:** News Digest, bimonthly. Notes and Documents, 20-25/year. Register of Entertainers, Actors, and Others Who Have Performed in South Africa, semiannual. Register of Sports Contacts with South Africa, semiannual. Also publishes information notes, leaflets, and special reports; makes available posters and films. **bd Formerly:** (1976) Unit on Apartheid.

★456★
United Nations Special Committee Against Apartheid
United Nations
New York, NY 10017 Phone: (212)963-1234
Ibrahim Noor, Sec.

Description: Representatives of member countries of the United Nations. Purposes are to: monitor the racial policies of the South African government and periodically report to the U.N. General Assembly on these issues; provide consulting services on apartheid to other U.N. committees and agencies. Coordinates special studies on the nature, extent, and repercussions of apartheid. Reviews and evaluates the implementation of U.N. resolutions against apartheid; researches methods of mobilizing effective international action to eliminate apartheid. Advocates sanctions against South Africa including: embargo of arms and oil sales; prohibition of nuclear cooperation; cessation of financial collaboration; boycott of cultural and athletic exchanges; institution of general economic and diplomatic sanctions. Encourages and assists South African liberation movements, recognized by the Organization of Africa Unity (see separate entry), namely the African National Congress and Pan Africanist Congress (see separate entries); promotes public observances and opposition campaigns. Investigates the repression of South African opponents of apartheid; seeks the unconditional release of all political prisoners within South Africa. Organizes conferences, seminars, and hearings; compiles statistics; bestows awards. **Founded:** 1962. **Members:** 19. **Telecommunications Services:** Telexes, 232422 UNH UR, 82731, and 62450. **Publications:** Annual Report. Also publishes other reports and documents.

★457★

United Negro College Fund (UNCF)
500 E. 62nd St.
New York, NY 10021 Phone: (212)326-1118
Virgil E. Ecton, CEO & Pres.

Description: Fundraising agency for historically Black private colleges and universities and graduate and professional schools, all of which are private and fully accredited. The UNCF Department of Educational Services offers information on a broad range of educational and administrative programs to the member schools; conducts Premedical Summer Institute; sponsors college fairs for high school and community college students; administers scholarship awards and major corporate and foundation programs. Holds meetings of institutional members. **Founded:** 1944. **Members:** 43. **Regional Groups:** 28. **Publications:** Annual Report. UNCF Journal, semiannual. Also publishes government affairs, research, and statistical reports.

★458★

U.S. Out of Southern Africa Network
PO Box 1819, Madison Square Sta.
New York, NY 10159 Phone: (212)741-0633
Monica Moorehead, Contact

Description: Seeks to educate the public on the role the U.S. plays in southern Africa, particularly in South Africa. Advocates total U.S. withdrawal and divestiture from that area. Stages demonstrations, provides speakers, and shows films. Acts as head office of a network of chapters nationwide. **Founded:** 1985. **Publications:** History of the Struggle (brochure) and fact sheet.

★459★

U.S. South Africa Leader Exchange Program (USSALEP)
1730 M St. NW, Ste. 701
Washington, DC 20036 Phone: (202)293-5410
Robert M. Hoen, Dir.

Description: Supported by private American and South African foundations, corporations, and individuals dedicated to the promotion of a just society through the fostering of communications and interaction across group divisions within and between both countries. A council of American and South African university, business, religious, and civic leaders, a full representation of ethnic, political, vocational, gender, and regional groupings in those countries, supervises the program. Programs include symposia and U.S.-South Africa exchanges by university presidents, jurists, journalists, and other professionals. Assists the midcareer training and counseling of Black South African leaders by offering leadership development and training programs in the professions, business, science, and the arts. Nominates and finances South African participants in annual Nieman Fellowship in journalism at Harvard and a teaching fellowship at John Hopkins University Center for Advanced International Studies. Holds symposia on South African sociopolitical dynamics and U.S.-South Africa relations; sponsors training course for Black journalists in Johannesburg, South Africa. **Founded:** 1958. **Members:** 50. **Budget:** $600,000. **Publications:** Newsletter, annual. Contains program highlights, calendar of events, and organizational news. Also publishes occasional papers, brochures, and books.

★460★

Urban Environment Conference (UEC)
c/o Franklin Wallick
7620 Morningside Dr. NW
Washington, DC 20012 Phone: (202)726-8111
Franklin Wallick, Chm.

Description: National labor, minority, and environmental organizations. Lobbies in Washington, DC and at a grass roots level for strong environmental and occupational health laws. Offers educational programs to enable minorities, workers, and others to participate more effectively in decisions affecting their health and interests. **Founded:** 1971. **Budget:** Less than $25,000. **Telecommunications Services:** Fax, (202)829-6762. **Publications:** America's Forgotten Environment (booklet).

★461★

Visions Foundation (VF)
1538 9th St. NW
Washington, DC 20001 Phone: (202)462-1779
Gary A. Puckrein, Exec.Dir.

Description: To promote understanding of Afro-American culture. Conducts media-related and educational programs to educate the public about the contributions of Blacks to society and culture in the U.S. Bestows awards. **Founded:** 1983. **Members:** 21,000. **Telecommunications Services:** Fax, (202)462-3997. **Publications:** American Visions: The Magazine of Afro-American Culture, bimonthly. Lines of Sight, bimonthly. Newsletter. Also publishes Afro-American Art.

★462★

Voter Education Project (VEP)
604 Beckwith St. SW
Atlanta, GA 30314 Phone: (404)522-7495
Edward Brown, Exec.Dir.

Description: Created as part of the Southern Regional Council (see separate entry) to investigate the causes and remedies of low political participation by southern Blacks. In June 1970, VEP became an independent corporation, operating in 11 southern states. Through direct grants to local groups for voter registration drives, VEP promotes greater participation and documents the problems and progress of their activities. From 1962 to 1984, Black voter registration rose from less than 1,500,000 to more than 5,000,000. Is also concerned with citizenship education and assistance to Black elected officials. Maintains statistics on registration and voting, data on Black elected officials, and other information concerning Black political participation in the South. Undertakes in-depth studies of elections or related events. **Founded:** 1962. **Publications:** Issues publications on political participation, state governments, Black political candidates, elected officials, and other issues pertinent to minorities in the South.

★463★

Washington Office on Africa (WOA)
110 Maryland Ave. NE, Ste. 112
Washington, DC 20002 Phone: (202)546-7961
Arvie McCluchin, Exec.Dir.

Description: To monitor and analyze developments in U.S. policy toward southern Africa and work with national and local groups which support the attainment of majority rule. Lobbies on congressional legislation affecting southern Africa. **Founded:** 1972. **Publications:** Action Alerts, periodic. Legislative Bulletins, periodic. Washington Notes on Africa, quarterly.

★464★

Washington Office on Haiti (WOH)
110 Maryland Ave. NE, Ste. 301
Washington, DC 20002 Phone: (202)543-7095
Fritz Longchamp, Exec.Dir.

Description: Works to support the Haitian people's ongoing movement for democracy, social and economic justice, and self-determination through public education and advocacy. Seeks to generate international response to human and labor rights violations in Haiti and create a responsive support network for victims of these violations. Gathers and disseminates information and documentation on development in, and U.S. policy toward, Haiti. Sponsors delegations from Haiti and public educational events. Provides resource and referral services for Haitian refugees and for attorneys handling political asylum claims. Maintains speakers' bureau and library. **Founded:** 1984. **Members:** 4. **Budget:** $120,000. **Publications:** The Haiti Beat, quarterly. Newsletter providing information on Haiti, including political analysis and resource availability.

★465★
Women for Racial and Economic Equality (WREE)
198 Broadway, Rm. 606
New York, NY 10038 Phone: (212)385-1103
Sally Chaffee Maron, Co-Chair

Description: Multiracial and multinational group of working and working class women. Purposes include: to end race and sex discrimination in hiring, pay, and promotion practices; to support quality integrated public education and federally funded comprehensive child care; to promote peace and solidarity with women of all countries; to work for passage of the Women's Bill of Rights, a program of legislative demands that guarantees economic independence and social equality. Lobbies for equal employment, education, child care, and health issues. Conducts community education and action campaigns, conferences, seminars, forums, leadership training, and research projects. Bestows awards; maintains speakers' bureau. **Founded:** 1975. **Members:** 1600. **Budget:** Less than $25,000. **Local Groups:** 18. **Publications:** Women of the Whole World, quarterly. Magazine reporting on social concerns such as world peace, the militarization of space, the homeless crisis, feminism, and other issues and concerns of the organization. Includes annual index.

★466★
Women of Color Partnership Program (WCPP)
100 Maryland Ave. NE, Ste. 307
Washington, DC 20002 Phone: (202)543-7032
Elizabeth Castro, Dir.

Description: A division of the Religious Coalition for Abortion Rights. Educates women about reproductive health issues such as accessibility and cost of health care, role of the church, male responsibility, sterilization, and medical abuse of women. Conducts forums and workshops. Maintains speakers' bureau. **Founded:** 1985. **Publications:** Common Ground - Different Planes, semiannual. Newsletter.

★467★
Women's Africa Committee of the African-American Institute (WACAAI)
c/o African-Amer. Institute
833 United Nations Plaza
New York, NY 10017 Phone: (212)949-5666
Marian V. Hughes, Sec.-Treas.

Description: Volunteer organization of African and American women. Members seek to become better acquainted through social, educational, and cultural activities. **Founded:** 1959.

★468★
World Africa Chamber of Commerce (WACC)
PO Box 33144
Washington, DC 20033 Phone: (202)223-3244
Ohene Darko, Pres.

Description: Organizations, groups, and individuals interested in advancing the efficiency of commerce between the U.S. and Africa by promoting trade, industrial development, transportation, communication, agricultural development, tourism, and investment. Sponsors trade missions to Africa and seminars to assist members with personal contacts and in gaining knowledge in the market and the needs of the countries they service. Conducts research and development studies on the changing economic developments and attitudes in specific countries and on the continent as a whole. Provides professional consulting in areas including market development, export promotion, joint venture projects, trade finance counseling, and market research studies. Operates trade center to provide facilities for exhibits, meetings, and other activities. Additional services include: assistance with visas and business trip planning; job referrals; clearinghouse on business, political, and cultural information; office and secretarial aid for businessmen and dignitaries traveling abroad. Maintains the Continental Africa Chamber Foundation. **Founded:** 1973. **Publications:** The African Connection, monthly. WACC Network, bimonthly. **Formerly:** (1986) Continental Africa Chamber of Commerce.

★469★
World Institute of Black Communications/CEBA Awards
463 7th Ave.
New York, NY 10018 Phone: (212)714-1508
Adriane T. Gaines, Exec.Dir.

Description: Objectives are to broaden opportunities for Blacks in the communications industry; recognize Black communications contributions; and establish and quantify the value of the Black consumer market to the national advertising community. Sponsors annual Communications Excellence to Black Audience Awards to patronizing corporations and creative entities for most creative, relevant, and professionally executed media efforts. Operates library on advertising directed toward the Black consumer market over the last 13 years and slides on Black American lifestyles. Compiles demographic and marketing research on the Black consumer market. Maintains Black media source directory listing: radio and television stations; newspapers; national publications; advertising agencies; marketing/research companies; photographers; music, sound, and radio recording studios. **Founded:** 1978. **Telecommunications Services:** Fax, (212)714-1563. Award Categories: Cable; Consumer Print; Merchandising and Sales Promotion; Radio; Television; Video. **Publications:** Awards Exhibit Journal, annual.

★470★
World of Michael Jackson (WMJ)
PO Box 1804
Encino, CA 91426
Kate Rapp, Exec. Officer

Description: Individuals interested in the life and career of entertainer Michael Jackson (1959-), formerly of the family musical group the Jackson Five (formed in 1969), and currently one of the best-selling solo pop musicians worldwide.

★471★
Young Black Programmers Coalition (YBPC)
PO Box 1051
Vicksburg, MS 39181 Phone: (601)634-5775
Robert Rosenthal, Mgr.

Description: Black professionals in the communications, broadcasting, and music industries. Provides professional training and offers technical assistance to Black entrepreneurs in the broadcast and music industries. Conducts lobbying activities pertaining to legislation affecting the music industry. Provides scholarships to attend Black colleges and universities. Bestows awards; maintains biographical archives; compiles statistics. **Founded:** 1976. **Members:** 2615. **Budget:** $52,000. **Regional Groups:** 5. **Computerized Services:** Data base; mailing list. **Telecommunications Services:** Hotline, (713)974-2422. **Publications:** Book Programming Radio, triennial. The Programmer: YBPC News Letter, monthly. Reports on the communications, broadcasting, and music industries. Includes information on employment opportunities, research, and industry trends.

★472★
Zeta Phi Beta Sorority
1734 New Hampshire Ave. NW
Washington, DC 20009 Phone: (202)387-3103
Linda Thompson, Exec.Dir.

Description: Service and social sorority. Maintains Zeta Phi Beta Sorority Educational Foundation. Maintains speakers' bureau and charitable program; sponsors competitions and awards scholarships. **Founded:** 1920. **Members:** 75,000. **Regional Groups:** 8. Alumnae and College Chapters: 550. **Telecommunications Services:** Fax, (202)232-4593. **Publications:** Archon, semiannual. Journal; includes listing of employment opportunies.

(2) REGIONAL, STATE, AND LOCAL ORGANIZATIONS

Entries in this chapter are arranged alphabetically by organization name within states. See the User's Guide at the front of this directory for additional information.

Alabama

★473★
Alabama Black Lawyers Association
c/o Brenda Montgomery
3505 23rd St., N.
Birmingham, AL 35207 Phone: (205)254-0608
Brenda Montgomery, Pres.

★474★
Alabama Lawyers Association
2102 6th Ave., N.
Birmingham, AL 35203 Phone: (205)254-3216
LaVeeda Morgan-Battle, Pres.
Affiliated with: National Bar Association.

★475★
American Association of Blacks in Energy
Birmingham Chapter
c/o Ronald Edwardservices
Alabama Gas Corp.
2101 6th Ave., N.
Birmingham, AL 35203 Phone: (205)326-8433
Ronald Edwards, Pres.

★476★
American Civil Liberties Union
Alabama Affiliate
PO Box 447
Montgomery, AL 36104 Phone: (205)262-0304
Olivia Turner, Contact

★477★
Association for the Study of Afro-American Life and History
Birmingham Branch
PO Box 11258
Birmingham, AL 35201 Phone: (205)929-8119
Otis Dismuke, Pres.

★478★
Birmingham Association of Black Journalists
c/o Harold J. Jackson
The News
PO Box 2553
Birmingham, AL 35202 Phone: (205)325-2222
Harold J. Jackson, Pres.
Affiliated with: National Association of Black Journalists.

★479★
Birmingham Brothers
PO Box 55006
Birmingham, AL 35255
Affiliated with: International Association of Black Professional Fire Fighters.

★480★
Birmingham Minority Business Development Center
2100 16th Ave., S., Ste. 203
Birmingham, AL 35205 Phone: (205)930-9254

★481★
Birmingham Urban League
1717 4th Ave., N.
PO Box 11269
Birmingham, AL 35202-1269 Phone: (205)326-0162
James C. Graham Jr., Pres.
Affiliated with: National Urban League.

★482★
Metropolitan Business League
PO Box 1281
Birmingham, AL 35201 Phone: (205)251-0166
Dr. Eddie Woods Jr., Pres.
Affiliated with: National Business League.

★483★
Mobile County Criminal Justice Society
5984 Carlisle Dr., N.
Mobile, AL 36608
Herbert McCants, Pres.
Affiliated with: National Black Police Association.

★484★
Mobile Minority Business Development Center
801 Executive Park Dr., Ste. 102
Mobile, AL 36606 Phone: (205)471-5165

★485★
Mobile Peace Benevolent Association
5928 Heatherwood Ct.
Mobile, AL 36618
Diana Chapman, Pres.
Affiliated with: National Black Police Association.

★486★
Montgomery Minority Business Development Center
770 S. McDonough St., Ste. 207
Montgomery, AL 36104 Phone: (205)834-7598

★487★
National Association of Minority Contractors
Alabama Chapter
401 Belt Line Dr. N.
Mobile, AL 36617 Phone: (205)432-6232
Dr. Anthony Carter, Pres.

★488★
National Black MBA Association
Birmingham Chapter
PO Box 370132
Birmingham, AL 35237
Wayman Powell III, Contact

★489★
North Alabama Chapter of Black Professional Fire Fighters
4307 Patton Rd. SW, No. 13
Huntsville, AL 35805
Affiliated with: International Association of Black Professional Fire Fighters.

★490★
Prichard Police Benevolent Association
PO Box 10592
Prichard, AL 36610
Leslie Nobles, Pres.
Affiliated with: National Black Police Association.

★491★
Tuskegee University
Carver Research Foundation
Tuskegee Institute
Tuskegee, AL 36088 Phone: (205)727-8246
Dr. B. D. Maybarry, Acting Dir.

★492★
United Negro College Fund
Birmingham Office
310 18th St., N., Ste. 400
Birmingham, AL 35023
Territory Includes: Alabama.

Alaska

★493★
Alaska Minority Business Development Center
1577 C St. Plaza, Ste. 200
Anchorage, AK 99501 Phone: (907)274-5400

★494★
American Civil Liberties Union
Alaska Affiliate
PO Box 201844
Anchorage, AK 99520-1844 Phone: (907)276-2258
Jamie Bollenbach, Pres.

★495★
ARCO Alaska, Inc.
700 G St.
PO Box 100360
Anchorage, AK 99510 Phone: (907)265-6123
James M. Posey, Pres.

★496★
Association for the Study of Afro-American Life and History
Marianna Branch
Rte. 2, Box 21
Marianna, AK 72360 Phone: (501)295-3273
Carrie P. Anthony, Pres.

★497★
United Minority Coalition
Box 020014
Juneau, AK 99802 Phone: (907)780-6739
Ben E. Holganza, Pres.

Arizona

★498★
American Civil Liberties Union
Arizona Affiliate
2021 N. Central, No. 301
Phoenix, AZ 85004 Phone: (602)254-3339
Louis L. Rhodes, Pres.

★499★
Arizona Alliance of Black Educators
11640 N. 49th Dr.
Glendale, AZ 85304
Darlene M. White, Pres.
Affiliated with: National Alliance of Black School Educators.

★500★
Arizona Association of Blacks in Criminal Justice
PO Box 3665
Phoenix, AZ 85003
Ida Wilber, Exec. Officer

★501★
Arizona Black Lawyers Association
3602 E. Campbell
Phoenix, AZ 85016 Phone: (602)236-5536
Yvonne Evans, Pres.
Affiliated with: National Bar Association.

★502★
Arizona Black United Fund
P0 Box 24457
Phoenix, AZ 85074 Phone: (602)268-0666
Carolyn Lowery, Exec.Dir.
Affiliated with: National Black United Fund, Inc.

★503★
Heatwaves
PO Box 8834
Phoenix, AZ 85040
Affiliated with: International Association of Black Professional Fire Fighters.

★504★
Operation PUSH
Phoenix Chapter
2006 E. Broadway Rd.
Phoenix, AZ 85040 Phone: (602)268-2512
Rev. Bernard Black, Chairman

★505★
Phoenix Black Chamber of Commerce
623 E. Euclid
Phoenix, AZ 85040 Phone: (602)243-1857
Deborah Ellison

★506★
Phoenix Minority Business Development Center
1661 E. Camelback, Ste. 210
Phoenix, AZ 85016 Phone: (602)277-7707

★507★
Phoenix Urban League
1402 S. 7th Ave.
Phoenix, AZ 85007 Phone: (602)254-5611
Junius A. Bowman, Pres.
Affiliated with: National Urban League.

★508★
Tucson Minority Business Development Center
181 W. Broadway
Tucson, AZ 85702 Phone: (601)629-9744

★509★
Tucson Urban League
2305 S. Park Ave.
Tucson, AZ 85713 Phone: (602)791-9522
Raymond Clarke, Pres.
Affiliated with: National Urban League.

Arkansas

★510★
American Association of Blacks in Energy
Arkansas Chapter
c/o Alma Williams
Arkansas Power & Light Co.
PO Box 551
Little Rock, AR 72203 Phone: (501)377-3555
Alma Williams, Pres.

★511★
American Civil Liberties Union
Arkansas Affiliate
209 W. Capitol, No. 304
Little Rock, AR 72201 Phone: (501)374-2660
Joseph L. Jacobson, Pres.

★512★
Arkansas Alliance of Black School Educators
1823 S. Taylor
Little Rock, AR 72204
Othello Faison, Pres.
Affiliated with: National Alliance of Black School Educators.

★513★
Black Little Rock Police Association
3410 Pinewood Loop
Little Rock, AR 72209
Affiliated with: National Black Police Association.

★514★
Little Rock Minority Business Development Center
1 Riverfront Pl., Ste. 415
North Little Rock, AR 72114 Phone: (501)372-7312

★515★
National Association of Minority Contractors
Arkansas Chapter
PO Box 5121
Little Rock, AR 72119 Phone: (501)375-6262
Wall Caradine, Pres.

★516★
National Black Child Development Institute
Magnolia Affiliate
PO Box 236
Emerson, AR 71740 Phone: (501)547-2950
Mary Hanson, Pres.

★517★
Operation PUSH
North Little Rock Chapter
5205 S. Woodland
North Little Rock, AR 72117 Phone: (501)945-7724
Dee Bennett, Chairman

★518★
Urban League of Arkansas
2200 Main St.
PO Box 164039
Little Rock, AR 72216 Phone: (501)372-3037
Carmelita Smith, Interim Pres.
Affiliated with: National Urban League.

★519★
W. Harold Flowers Law Society
PO Box 2454
Little Rock, AR 72401 Phone: (501)972-2255
Rodney Slater, Pres.
Affiliated with: National Bar Association.

California

★520★
Afro American Community Services Agency
304 N. 6th St.
San Jose, CA 95112 Phone: (408)292-3157

★521★
American Association for Affirmative Action
Region IX
c/o Arthur V.N. Wint
Cal. State Univ.
Fresno, CA 93740-0041 Phone: (209)294-2364
Arthur V.N. Wint J.D., Dir.
Territory Includes: California, Nevada, Arizona, Hawaii, the Trust Territories, American Samoa, Guam, and the Mariannas.

★522★
American Association of Blacks in Energy
Los Angeles Chapter
c/o Ezekiel Patten, Jr.
Patten Energy Enterprises0
9850 Glenoaks Blvd.
Sun Valley, CA 91352 Phone: (818)504-0982
Ezekiel Patten Jr., Pres.

★523★
American Association of Blacks in Energy
San Francisco Chapter
c/o Danielle T. McGrue
Chevron International Oil Co.
555 Market St., Ste. 732
San Francisco, CA 94105 Phone: (415)894-2832
Danelle T. McGrue, Pres.

★524★
American Civil Liberties Union
Northern California Affiliate
1663 Mission St., No. 460
San Francisco, CA 94103 Phone: (415)621-2488
Dorothy M. Ehrlich, Contact

★525★
American Civil Liberties Union
San Diego Affiliate
1202 Kettner Blvd., No. 6200
San Diego, CA 92101 Phone: (619)232-2121
Linda Hills, Pres.

★526★
American Civil Liberties Union
Southern California Affiliate
633 S. Shatto Pl.
Los Angeles, CA 90005 Phone: (213)487-1720
Ramona Ripston, Pres.

★527★
Anaheim Minority Business Development Center
6 Hutton Center Dr., Ste. 1050
Santa Ana, CA 92707 Phone: (714)434-0444

★528★
Association for the Study of Afro-American Life and History
Los Angeles Branch
8947 Gramercy Pl.
Los Angeles, CA 90047 Phone: (213)758-4520
Deloris Nehemiah, Pres.

★529★
Association of Black Personnel in City Government
5462 Crenshaw Blvd.
Los Angeles, CA 90043 Phone: (213)290-3070

★530★
Association of Black Psychologists
Southern California Chapter
3731 Stocker St., No. 107
Los Angeles, CA 90008 Phone: (202)722-0808
Dr. Evelyn Clark, Pres.

★531★
Bakersfield Minority Business Development Center
218 S. H St., Ste. 103
Bakersfield, CA 93304 Phone: (805)837-0291

★532★
Bay Area Association of Black Social Workers
PO Box 15254
San Francisco, CA 92115 Phone: (415)982-2716

★533★
Bay Area Black Consortium for Quality Health Care Inc.
1440 Broadway, Ste. 403
Oakland, CA 94612 Phone: (415)763-1872
Dani Taylor, Acting Exec.Dir.

★534★
Bay Area Black Journalists Association
4536 West St.
Oakland, CA 94608 Phone: (415)338-1689
Austin Long-Scott, Pres.
Affiliated with: National Association of Black Journalists.

★535★
Bay Area Black Media Coalition
PO Box 2382
Oakland, CA 94614
Rudy Marshall, Contact
Affiliated with: National Black Media Coalition.

★536★
Bay Area Black United Fund
1440 Broadway, Ste. 405
Oakland, CA 94612 Phone: (415)763-7270
Arnold Swope, Exec.Dir.
Affiliated with: National Black United Fund, Inc.

★537★
Bay Area Urban League
Kaiser Center Mall
344 20th St., Ste. 211
Oakland, CA 94612 Phone: (415)839-8011
Jesse J. Payne, Pres.

★538★
Berkeley Black Fire Fighters Association
59 Elysian Fields
Berkeley, CA 94605
Affiliated with: International Association of Black Professional Fire Fighters.

★539★
Berkeley Black Officers Association
5067 Hartnett Ave.
Richmond, CA 94804
Drucilla H. Cooper, Pres.
Affiliated with: National Black Police Association.

★540★
Bernard S. Jefferson Law Society
2122 N. Broadway, Ste. 200
Santa Anna, CA 92706-2614 Phone: (714)558-1059
Charlotte Adams, Pres.
Affiliated with: National Bar Association.

★541★
Black Agenda
200 E. Slauson Ave.
Los Angeles, CA 90011 Phone: (213)233-2030

★542★
Black Business and Professional Association
119 E. 8th St.
Long Beach, CA 90813 Phone: (213)499-1038

★543★
Black Christians Political Organizations
PO Box 161659
Sacramento, CA 95816 Phone: (916)363-8583

★544★
Black Federation of San Diego
4291 Dr. Martin Luther King, Jr. Hwy.
San Diego, CA 92102 Phone: (619)263-8161

★545★
Black Journalists Association of Southern California
c/o Linda A. Williams
University of Southern California
Box 25
Los Angeles, CA 90089-0890 Phone: (213)743-5331
Linda A. Williams, Pres.
Affiliated with: National Association of Black Journalists.

★546★
Black on Black Crime Task Force
2104 Orange Ave.
Long Beach, CA 90806 Phone: (213)763-2760

★547★
Black Peace Officers of Fresno
8871 N. Archie
Fresno, CA 93710
Gregory T. Kelly, Pres.
Affiliated with: National Black Police Association.

★548★
Black Peace Officers of Santa Clara County
PO Box 2275
San Jose, CA 95111
Charles Brown, Pres.
Affiliated with: National Black Police Association.

★549★
Black Police Officers Association of San Diego
PO Box 14320
San Diego, CA 92114
Charles Kindred, Pres.
Affiliated with: National Black Police Association.

★550★
Black Radio Exclusive
6353 Hollywood Blvd.
Hollywood, CA 90028 Phone: (213)469-7262

★551★
Black Sacramento Christian Club Organizers
3301 Broadway
Sacramento, CA 95817 Phone: (916)454-3186

★552★
Black Women Lawyers Association of Northern California
State Bar of California
555 Franklin St.
San Francisco, CA 94102
Phyllis Culp, Pres.
Affiliated with: National Bar Association.

★553★
Black Women Lawyers Association of Southern California
State Bar Court
818 W. 7th St.
Los Angeles, CA 90017
E. Jean Gary, Pres.
Affiliated with: National Bar Association.

★554★
Black Women Organize for Educational Development
518 17th St., Ste. 202
Oakland, CA 94612 Phone: (415)763-9501

★555★
Black Women's Forum
PO Box 01702
Los Angeles, CA 90001 Phone: (213)292-3009

★556★
Black Women's Health Project
PO Box 10529
Oakland, CA 94601 Phone: (415)533-6923

★557★
Black Women's Resource Center
518 17th St., Ste. 202
Oakland, CA 94612 Phone: (415)763-9501

★558★
Brotherhood Crusade Black United Fund
200 E. Slauson Ave.
Los Angeles, CA 90011 Phone: (503)231-2171
Danny J. Bakewell Sr., Pres.
Affiliated with: National Black United Fund, Inc.

★559★
Brothers United of San Diego
PO Box 14307
San Diego, CA 92114
Affiliated with: International Association of Black Professional Fire Fighters.

★560★
Business Equity and Development Corporation
1411 W. Olympic Blvd., No. 200
Los Angeles, CA 90015 Phone: (213)385-0351

★561★
California Association of Black Lawyers
3580 Wilshire Blvd., Ste. 1920
Los Angeles, CA 90010 Phone: (213)387-6628
Joan Whiteside Green, Pres.
Affiliated with: National Bar Association.

★562★
California Legislative Black Caucus
State Capitol, Rm. 6011
Sacramento, CA 95814 Phone: (916)445-7498
Curtis Tucker, Chairman

★563★
A Central Place
1212 Broadway, Ste. 830
Oakland, CA 94612 Phone: (415)834-7897

★564★
Charles Houston Bar Association
1901 Harrison St., No. 901
Oakland, CA 94612 Phone: (415)465-0368
Felix Stuckey, Pres.
Affiliated with: National Bar Association.

★565★
Compton Black Fire Fighters
1133 W. Rosecrans St.
Compton, CA 90222
Affiliated with: International Association of Black Professional Fire Fighters.

★566★
Contra Costa Black Chamber of Commerce
3101 MacDonald Ave.
Richmond, CA 94804 Phone: (415)235-9350
Willie L. Williams, Exec. Officer

★567★
Contra Costa Black Fire Fighters Association
PO Box 2571
Antioch, CA 94531
Affiliated with: International Association of Black Professional Fire Fighters.

★568★
Contra Costa Deputies for Better Community Relations
173 Crown Pointe Dr.
Vallejo, CA 94590
Mildred Watkins, Pres.
Affiliated with: National Black Police Association.

★569★
Earl B. Gilliam Bar Association of San Diego County
3841 4th St.
PO Box 199
San Diego, CA 92103 Phone: (619)557-7047
Randy K. Jones, Pres.
Affiliated with: National Bar Association.

★570★
Ethiopian Refugee Project of the Third Baptist Church
1341 McAllister
San Francisco, CA 94115 Phone: (415)922-9100

★571★
Fair Housing Council of Orange County
1522 E. 17th St., Ste. E
Santa Ana, CA 92701 Phone: (714)835-0160
Maya K. Dunne, Dir.

★572★
Fair Housing Council of San Gabriel Valley
1020 N. Fair Oaks Ave., Rm. 301
Pasadena, CA 91103 Phone: (818)791-0211

★573★
FOCUS
PO Box 50134
Oxnard, CA 93033
Affiliated with: International Association of Black Professional Fire Fighters.

★574★
Fresno Minority Business Development Center
2010 N. Fine, Ste.103
Fresno, CA 93727 Phone: (209)252-7551

★575★
Golden State Business League
333 Hagenberger Rd., Ste. 203
Oakland, CA 94021 Phone: (415)635-5900
C.J. Patterson, Pres.
Affiliated with: National Business League.

★576★
Golden State Minority Foundation
1999 W. Adams Blvd.
Los Angeles, CA 90018 Phone: (213)731-7771

★577★
Greater Riverside Area Urban League
5225 Canyon Crest Dr., Bldg. 100, Ste. 105
Riverside, CA 92507 Phone: (714)682-2766
Rose Oliver, Interim Exec.Dir.

★578★
Guardians of Justice
PO Box 163, Sta. A
Richmond, CA 94804
Affiliated with: National Black Police Association.

★579★
Hollywood-Mid Los Angeles Fair Housing Council
7080 Hollywood Blvd., No. 801
Hollywood, CA 90028 Phone: (213)464-1141
Debra Rodriguez, Exec.Dir.

★580★
Independent School Alliance for Minority Affairs
110 S. LaBrea Ave., Ste. 265
Inglewood, CA 90301 Phone: (213)672-5544
Manasa Hekymara, Exec.Dir.

★581★
Inland Alliance of Black School Educators
PO Box 7324
San Bernadino, CA 92411
Harriette L. Moore, Pres.

★582★
Inland Empire Peace Officers Association
PO Box 1784
Victorville, CA 92392
Affiliated with: National Black Police Association.

★583★
John Langston Bar Association
10960 Wilshire Blvd., Ste. 2210
Los Angeles, CA 90024 Phone: (213)470-2804
George Mallory, Pres.
Affiliated with: National Bar Association.

★584★
Long Beach Bar Association
11 Golden Ave.
Long Beach, CA 95240 Phone: (213)432-5913

★585★
Los Angeles Black Media Association
1114 W. 99th St.
Los Angeles, CA 90044
Cassandra Jordan, Contact
Affiliated with: National Black Media Coalition.

★586★
Los Angeles Black Media Coalition
PO Box 48899
Los Angeles, CA 90048
Elaine Pounds, Contact
Affiliated with: National Black Media Coalition.

★587★
Los Angeles Council of Black Professional Engineers
4401 Crenshaw Blvd.
Los Angeles, CA 90043 Phone: (213)295-0867

★588★
Los Angeles Equal Rights Congress
4167 S. Normandie Ave.
Los Angeles, CA 900037 Phone: (213)291-1092

★589★
Los Angeles Minority Business Development Center
3807 Wilshire Blvd., Ste. 700
Los Angeles, CA 90010 Phone: (213)380-9471

★590★
Los Angeles Urban League
3450 Mt. Vernon Dr.
Los Angeles, CA 90008 Phone: (213)299-9660
John W. Mack, Pres.
Affiliated with: National Urban League.

★591★
Minorities Alcoholic Treatment Alternative
1315 Fruitvale Ave.
Oakland, CA 94601 Phone: (415)261-7120

★592★
National Association of Minority Contractors Northern California Chapter
1177 5th St.
Oakland, CA 94607 Phone: (415)268-1505
Alan Dones, Contact

★593★
National Association of Minority Contractors
Southern California Chapter
11910 Steeplechase Dr.
Moreno Valley, CA 92360 Phone: (714)242-9600
Victor Torres, Pres.

★594★
National Black Child Development Institute
East Bay Affiliate
29150 Ruus Rd.
Hayward, CA 94544 Phone: (415)783-0910
Ms. Larmon Buckner, Pres.

★595★
National Black Child Development Institute
Los Angeles/South Bay Affiliate
5105 W. Goldleaf Cir., Ste. 200
Los Angeles, CA 90056
Crystal Stairs, Pres.

★596★
National Black Child Development Institute
Sacramento Affiliate
7505 McMullen Way
Sacramento, CA 95828 Phone: (916)689-2593
Robin Harrison-Philips, Pres.

★597★
National Black Child Development Institute
San Diego Affiliate
6161 El Cajon Blvd., Ste. B-21
San Diego, CA 92115-3922 Phone: (619)264-5239
Gail O. Knight, Pres.

★598★
National Black Child Development Institute
San Francisco Affiliate
1219 Skyline Dr.
Daly City, CA 94015 Phone: (415)756-5382
Bess Ricketts, Pres.

★599★
National Black Community Fund
Los Angeles Chapter
8344 Melrose Ave
Los Angeles, CA 90069 Phone: (213)658-9620

★600★
National Black MBA Association
Los Angeles Chapter
PO Box 43009
Los Angeles, CA 90043 Phone: (213)964-3053
Laurie Murphy, Contact

★601★
National Black MBA Association
San Francisco Chapter
PO Box 3683
San Francisco, CA 94119-3683
Evon Anderson, Contact

★602★
Northern California Black Chamber of Commerce
5741 Telegraph Ave.
Oakland, CA 94609 Phone: (415)601-5741
Oscar J. Coffey Jr., Pres.

★603★
Oakland Black Firefighters Association
4615 Grass Valley Rd.
Oakland, CA 94605 Phone: (415)568-8692
Affiliated with: International Association of Black Professional Fire Fighters.

★604★
Oakland Black Officers Association
1440 Broadway, Ste. 618
Oakland, CA 94612
Leonard White, Pres.
Affiliated with: National Black Police Association.

★605★
Officers for Justice Peace Officers Association
5126 3rd St.
San Francisco, CA 94124
Joe Williams, Pres.
Affiliated with: National Black Police Association.

★606★
Orange County Urban League
12391 Lewis St., Ste. 102
Garden Grove, CA 92648 Phone: (714)748-9976
George L. Williams, Pres.
Affiliated with: National Urban League.

★607★
Oscar Joel Bryant Association
1409 W. Vernon Ave.
Los Angeles, CA 90062
Joseph T. Rouzan III, Pres.
Affiliated with: National Black Police Association.

★608★
Pasadena Black Firefighters Association
5623 Bowersfield St.
Los Angeles, CA 90016
Affiliated with: International Association of Black Professional Fire Fighters.

★609★
Pasadena Interracial Women's Club
Pilgrim Tower, N., No. 710
560 E. Villa
Pasadena, CA 91101 Phone: (818)584-1611
Genevieve Valliere, Pres.

★610★
Peace Officers for Better Community Relations
PO Box 5281
Oakland, CA 94605
Del Coleman, Pres.
Affiliated with: National Black Police Association.

★611★
Pomona Alliance of Black School Educators
PO Box 2274
Pomona, CA 91769
Dr. Leonard Duff, Pres.
Affiliated with: National Alliance of Black School Educators.

★612★
Richmond Black Fire Fighters Association
PO Box 3042
Richmond, CA 94801
Affiliated with: International Association of Black Professional Fire Fighters.

★613★
Riverside Minority Business Development Center
1060 Cooley Dr., Ste. F
Cotton, CA 92324 Phone: (714)824-9695

★614★
Sacramento Alliance of Black School Educators
PO Box 13992
Sacramento, CA 95853
Jerry Payne, Pres.
Affiliated with: National Alliance of Black School Educators.

★615★
Sacramento Black Alcoholism Center
2425 Alhambra Blvd., Ste. F
Sacramento, CA 95817 Phone: (916)454-4242

★616★
Sacramento Black Chamber of Commerce
1009 22nd St.
Sacramento, CA 95816 Phone: (916)447-0234
Edward Phillips, Exec.Dir.

★617★
Sacramento Black Journalists Association
Box 189003
Sacramento, CA 75818 Phone: (916)927-1318
Alisa J. White, Pres.
Affiliated with: National Association of Black Journalists.

★618★
Sacramento Black Women's Network
PO Box 162986
Sacramento, CA 95816 Phone: (916)427-7296

★619★
Sacramento Minority Business Development Center
530 Bercut Dr., Stes. C & D
Sacramento, CA 95814 Phone: (916)443-0700

★620★
Sacramento Urban League
8929 Volunteer Ln., Ste. 220
Sacramento, CA 95826 Phone: (916)368-3280
George H. Dean, Pres.
Affiliated with: National Urban League.

★621★
Salinas Minority Business Development Center
123 Capital St., Ste. B
Salinas, CA 93901 Phone: (408)754-1061

★622★
San Bernardino Black Fire Fighters Association
1189 E. Shamrock Ave.
San Bernardino, CA 92410
Affiliated with: International Association of Black Professional Fire Fighters.

★623★
San Diego Council of Black Engineers
c/o San Diego Engineering Society
PO Box 2733
San Diego, CA 92112 Phone: (619)222-8641

★624★
San Diego Minority Business Development Center
6363 Alvarado Ct., Ste. 225
San Diego, CA 92120 Phone: (619)594-3684

★625★
San Diego Urban League
4261 Market St.
San Diego, CA 92101 Phone: (619)263-3115
Ibrahim Naeem, Exec.Dir.
Affiliated with: National Urban League.

★626★
San Francisco Alliance of Black School Educators
PO Box 27577
San Francisco, CA 94127
Mary Twegdy, Pres.
Affiliated with: National Alliance of Black School Educators.

★627★
San Francisco Black Chamber of Commerce
1426 Filmore St., Ste. 205
San Francisco, CA 94102 Phone: (415)922-8720
Fred Jordan, Pres.

★628★
San Francisco Black Fire Fighters Association
PO Box 12390
San Francisco, CA 94112
Affiliated with: International Association of Black Professional Fire Fighters.

★629★
San Francisco/Oakland Minority Business Development Center No. 1
1 California St., Ste. 2100
San Francisco, CA 94111 Phone: (415)989-2920

★630★
San Francisco/Oakland Minority Business Development Center No. 2
1000 Broadway, Ste. 270
Oakland, CA 94607 Phone: (415)465-6756

★631★
San Jose Minority Business Development Center
150 Almaden Blvd., Ste. 600
San Jose, CA 95150 Phone: (408)275-9000

★632★
Santa Barbara Minority Business Development Center
4141 State St., Ste. B-4
Santa Barbara, CA 93110 Phone: (805)964-1136

★633★
Santa Clara Black Fire Fighters Association
c/o Bobby Dixon
2264 Shiloh Ave.
Milpitas, CA 95035
Affiliated with: International Association of Black Professional Fire Fighters.

★634★
Santa Clara County Alliance of Black School Educators
PO Box 3134
San Jose, CA 95156
Brenda Smith, Pres.
Affiliated with: National Alliance of Black School Educators.

★635★
Santa Clara Valley Urban League
753 N. 9th St., No. 131
San Jose, CA 95112 Phone: (408)971-0117
Susan Logan, Interim Exec.Dir.
Affiliated with: National Urban League.

★636★
Sickle Cell Anemia Disease Research Foundation of the Bay Area
1332 Haight St.
San Francisco, CA 94117 Phone: (415)626-5834
Francis Luster, Pres.

★637★
South Bay Black Fire Fighters Association
PO Box 431722
Los Angeles, CA 90043
Affiliated with: International Association of Black Professional Fire Fighters.

★638★
South Bay Black Lawyers Association
c/o Moore Law Firm, APC
55 S. Market St., No. 1020
San Jose, CA 95110 Phone: (408)286-6431
Rodney G. Moore, Pres.
Affiliated with: National Bar Association.

★639★
Stentorians of Los Angeles City
1409 W. Vernon Ave.
Los Angeles, CA 90062
Affiliated with: International Association of Black Professional Fire Fighters.

★640★
Stentorians of Los Angeles County
1409 W Vernon Ave.
Los Angeles, CA 90062
Affiliated with: International Association of Black Professional Fire Fighters.

★641★
Stockton Black Fire Fighters Association
9343 Cherbourg Way
Stockton, CA 95210
AFF International Association of Black Professional Fire Fighters.

★642★
Stockton Minority Business Development Center
5361 N. Pershing Ave., Ste. F
Stockton, CA 95207 Phone: (209)477-2098

★643★
Stockton-San Joaquin County Black Chamber of Commerce
11 S. San Joaquim St.
Stockton, CA 95202 Phone: (209)466-7222
Claude Brooks, Pres.

★644★
Unitarian Universalist Association Black Concerns Working Group
Pacific Central Chapter
2441 LeConte Ave.
Berkeley, CA 94709 Phone: (415)845-6233
Rev. Robbie L. Cranch, Dist. Exec.

★645★
Unitarian Universalist Association Black Concerns Working Group
Pacific Southwest Chapter
12355 Moorpark St.
Studio City, CA 91604 Phone: (818)769-5917
Constance LaFerriere Ed.D., Dist. Exec.

★646★
United Negro College Fund
Los Angeles Office
2533 W. 3rd St., Ste. 109
Los Angeles, CA 90057
Territory Includes: Los Angeles and San Diego, California; Arizona; Nevada.

★647★
United Negro College Fund
Oakland Office
600 Grand Ave., Ste. 300
Oakland, CA 94610 Phone: (415)839-7360
Territory Includes: Oakland, San Francisco, Sacramento, Fresno, San Jose, Salinas/Monterey, California; the Pacific Islands.

★648★
Unity Fellowship Outreach Program
Minority AIDS Project
5149 W. Jefferson Blvd.
Los Angeles, CA 90016 Phone: (213)936-4949

★649★
Vallejo Black Fire Fighters Association
156 Wildberry Ct.
Vallejo, CA 94591
Affiliated with: International Association of Black Professional Fire Fighters.

★650★
West Los Angeles Community Service Organization
714 California Ave.
Venice, CA 90291 Phone: (213)823-9254
Francisca Rivas, Dir.

★651★
Western States Black Research Center
3617 Montclair St.
Los Angeles, CA 90018 Phone: (213)737-3585
Mayme A. Clayton, Exec.Dir.

★652★
Westside Fair Housing Council
10835 Santa Monica Blvd., Ste. 203
Los Angeles, CA 90025 Phone: (213)475-9671
Stephanie Knapik, Exec.Dir.

★653★
Wiley M. Manuel Bar Association
449 15th St., Ste. 303
Oakland, CA 94612 Phone: (415)465-0203
Thelma B. Bailey, Pres.
Affiliated with: National Bar Association.

★654★
William H. Hastie Lawyers Association
c/o James & Jeffers
870 Market St., Ste. 1200
San Francisco, CA 94102
Clifton R. Jeffers, Pres.
Affiliated with: National Bar Association.

★655★
American Association for Affirmative Action
Region VIII
Efforts to locate an address for this edition were unsuccessful. **Territory Includes:** Colorado, Montana, North Dakota, South Dakota, Utah, and Wyoming.

Colorado

★656★
American Civil Liberties Union
Colorado Affiliate
915 E. 22nd Ave.
Denver, CO 80205 Phone: (303)861-2258
James Jou, Pres.

★657★
American Civil Liberties Union
Mountain States Regional Office
6825 E. Tennessee Ave., Bldg. 2, Ste. 262
Denver, CO 80224 Phone: (303)321-4828
Dorothy Davidson, Pres.

★658★
Colorado Alliance of Black School Educators
PO Box 440474
Aurora, CO 80044
Dr. Betty J. Foshee, Pres.
Affiliated with: National Alliance of Black School Educators.

★659★
Colorado Association of Black Journalists
c/o Ray Metoyer
KUSA-TV
1089 Bannock St.
Denver, CO 80231 Phone: (303)893-9000
Ray Metoyer, Pres.
Affiliated with: National Association of Black Journalists.

★660★
Colorado Association of Black Law Enforcement Officers
4800 Troy
Denver, CO 80239
Lynn Foster, Pres.
Affiliated with: National Black Police Association.

★661★
Colorado Black Chamber of Commerce
517 E. 16th Ave.
Denver, CO 80205 Phone: (303)832-2242
Larry Clayton, Exec.Dir.

★662★
Colorado Black Fire Fighters Association
PO Box 7492
Denver, CO 80277
Affiliated with: International Association of Black Professional Fire Fighters.

★663★
Denver Minority Business Development Center
4450 Morrison Rd.
Denver, CO 80219 Phone: (303)937-1005

★664★
Professional Black Fire Fighters of Colorado Springs
116 Eastcrest Way
Colorado Springs, CO 80916
Affiliated with: International Association of Black Professional Fire Fighters.

★665★
Sam Cary Bar Association
15400 E. 14th Pl.
Aurora, CO 80011
Hon. Robert Russell, Pres.
Affiliated with: National Bar Association.

★666★
Unitarian Universalist Association Black Concerns Working Group
Mountain Desert Chapter
1510 Glen Ayr Dr., Ste. 4
Lakewood, CO 80215 Phone: (303)238-4051
Rev. Sue Turner-Kent, Dist. Exec.

★667★
United Negro College Fund
Aurora Office
15290 E. 6th Ave., Ste. 216
Aurora, CO 80011
Territory Includes: Colorado; Utah; Wyoming; New Mexico.

★668★
Urban League of Metropolitan Denver
1525 Josephine St.
Denver, CO 80206 Phone: (303)388-5861
Thomas Jenkins, Acting Pres.
Affiliated with: National Urban League.

★669★
Urban League of the Pikes Peak Region
324 N. Nevada
Colorado Springs, CO 80903 Phone: (719)634-1525
James E. Miller, Pres.
Affiliated with: National Urban League.

Connecticut

★670★
American Civil Liberties Union
Connecticut Affiliate
32 Grand St.
Hartford, CT 06106 Phone: (203)247-9823
William Olds, Pres.

★671★
Association of Black Psychologists
Connecticut Chapter
152 Way Rd.
Salem, CT 06415 Phone: (203)442-3380
Dr. Willie Coleman, Pres.

★672★
Bridgeport Guardians Association
PO Box 9018
Bridgeport, CT 06640
Affiliated with: National Black Police Association.

★673★
Connecticut Association of Black Communicators
c/o Frances Grandy Taylor
The Courant
285 Broad St.
Hartford, CT 06115 Phone: (203)241-6606
Frances Grandy Taylor, Pres.
Affiliated with: National Association of Black Journalists.

★674★
Connecticut Minority Business Development Center
410 Asylum St., Ste. 243
Hartford, CT 06103 Phone: (203)246-5371

★675★
Danbury Guardians Association
36 Tamarack Ave., Ste. 111
Danbury, CT 06811
Elliot Brevard, Pres.
Affiliated with: National Black Police Association.

★676★
Firebird Society of Bridgeport
231 Penn Ave.
Bridgeport, CT 06610
Affiliated with: International Association of Black Professional Fire Fighters.

★677★
Firebird Society of New Haven
63 Long Meadow Rd.
Hamden, CT 06514
Affiliated with: International Association of Black Professional Fire Fighters.

★678★
George W. Crawford Law Association
PO Box 3291
Hartford, CT 06103 Phone: (203)566-5996
Kimberly Graham, Pres.
Affiliated with: National Bar Association.

★679★
Hartford Guardians
PO Box 1524
Hartford, CT 06144
Carl Henderson, Pres.
Affiliated with: National Black Police Association.

★680★
National Association of Minority Contractors
Connecticut Chapter
PO Box 4280
Hartford, CT 06147 Phone: (203)549-1964
George Milward, Pres.

★681★
New Haven Silver Shields
1 Union Ave.
New Haven, CT 06519
Bennie Smith, Pres.
Affiliated with: National Black Police Association.

★682★
Operation PUSH
Hartford Chapter
53 Sharon St.
Hartford, CT 06112 Phone: (203)527-8440
Theodore Hudson, Pres.

★683★
Phoenix Society
PO Box 12481
Hartford, CT 06112
Affiliated with: International Association of Black Professional Fire Fighters.

★684★
Southern Connecticut Lawyers Association
106 Ledgebrook Dr.
Norwalk, CT 06854
Gary White, Pres.
Affiliated with: National Bar Association.

★685★
United Negro College Fund
Stamford Office
26 6th St., Ste. 305
Stamford, CT 06905
Territory Includes: Connecticut; Albany, Rochester, and Buffalo New York.

★686★
Urban League of Greater Bridgeport
285 Golden Hill St.
Bridgeport, CT 06604 Phone: (203)366-2737
William K. Wolfe, Pres.
Affiliated with: National Urban League.

★687★
Urban League of Greater Hartford
1229 Albany Ave., 3rd Fl.
Hartford, CT 06112 Phone: (203)527-0147
Esther Bush, Pres.
Affiliated with: National Urban League.

★688★
Urban League of Greater New Haven
1184 Chapel St.
New Haven, CT 06511 Phone: (203)624-4168
Martha Wright, Interim Dir.
Affiliated with: National Urban League.

★689★
Urban League of Southwestern Fairfield County
1 Atlantic St., Ste. 619
Stamford, CT 06901 Phone: (203)327-5810
Dr. Curtiss E. Porter, Pres.
Affiliated with: National Urban League.

Delaware

★690★
American Civil Liberties Union
Delaware Affiliate
702 King St., No. 600A
Wilmington, DE 19801 Phone: (302)654-3966
Judith Mellen, Pres.

★691★
Delaware Alliance of Black School Educators
PO Box 185
Wilmington, DE 19899-0185
Dr. Henry Rose, Pres.
Affiliated with: National Alliance of Black School Educators.

★692★
Unitarian Universalist Association Black Concerns Working Group
Joseph Priestly Chapter
730 Halstead Rd.
Wilmington, DE 19803 Phone: (302)478-1018
Rev. Sidney Peterman, Dist. Consultant

District of Columbia

★693★
African American Writers Guild
4108 Arkansas Ave., NW
Washington, DC 20002 Phone: (202)722-2760

★694★
Alliance of Black Federal Officers
PO Box 27773
Washington, DC 20038-7773
Ronald E. Stalling, Pres.
Affiliated with: National Black Police Association.

★695★
American Association of Blacks in Energy
Washington Chapter
c/o John M. Bush
PEPCO
1900 Pennsylvania Ave., NW
Washington, DC 20068-0001 Phone: (202)872-2399
John M. Bush, Pres.

★696★
American Civil Liberties Union
District of Columbia Affiliate
1400 20th St., NW, Ste. 119
Washington, DC 20036 Phone: (202)457-0800

★697★
American Civil Liberties Union
National Prison Project
1875 Connecticut Ave. NW, Ste. 410
Washington, DC 20009 Phone: (202)234-4830
Al Bronstein, Pres.

★698★
Association for the Study of Afro-American Life and History
Capital Branch
1522 Jackson St. NE
Washington, DC 20017 Phone: (202)832-3916
William Steen, Acting Pres.

★699★
Association for the Study of Afro-American Life and History
Charles H. Wesley Branch
3228 Oliver St. NW
Washington, DC 20015 Phone: (202)966-8760
Col. George Haley, Pres.

★700★
Association for the Study of Afro-American Life and History
Far North East/South East Branch
7238 15th Pl. NW
Washington, DC 20012 Phone: (202)882-3792
Mauree Ayton, Pres.

★701★
Association for the Study of Afro-American Life and History
George E.C. Hayes Branch
440 Buchanan St. NW
Washington, DC 20011 Phone: (202)829-0731
Shirley Hayes Ganao, Pres.

★702★
Black Student Fund
3636 16th St., NW
Ste. AG 15-19
Washington, DC 20010 Phone: (202)387-1414
Barbara Patterson, Exec.Dir.

★703★
Bread for the City
1305 14th St., NW
Washington, DC 20005 Phone: (202)332-0440
Charles Parker, Dir.

★704★
Capitol East Children's Center
315 G St., SE
Washington, DC 20003 Phone: (202)546-6966
Judith Fisher, Dir.

★705★
Concerned Black Men
PO Box 33104
Washington, DC 20033 Phone: (202)265-3175
Warner H. Session, Pres.

★706★
District of Columbia Chamber of Commerce
1411 K St., NW, 5th Fl.
Washington, DC 20004 Phone: (202)347-7202
Robert Titus, Pres.
Affiliated with: National Business League.

★707★
District of Columbia City Wide Welfare Rights Organization
PO Box 6951
Washington, DC 20032 Phone: (202)889-3448
Etta Horn Prather, Dir.

★708★
District of Columbia Office of Human Rights
2000 14th St., NW
Washington, DC 20009 Phone: (202)939-8740
Maudine R. Cooper, Dir.

★709★
National Black Child Development Institute
Washington/Metro Affiliate
1316 Rhode Island Ave. NW
Washington, DC 20005 Phone: (202)483-8525
Doll Gordon, Pres.

★710★
National Black MBA Association
Washington Chapter
PO Box 14042
Washington, DC 20044
Lajoy Mosby, Contact

★711★
National Black Police Association
Capitol Police Chapter
PO Box 91907
Washington, DC 20090-1907
Mary J. Rhone, Pres.

★712★
National Urban League
Washington Bureau
1111 14th St., NW, 6th Fl.
Washington, DC 20005 Phone: (202)898-1604

★713★
Progressive Fire Fighters Association of Washington, DC
PO Box 5063
Washington, DC 20019
Affiliated with: International Association of Black Professional Fire Fighters.

★714★
United Negro College Fund
Washington Office
2100 M St. NW, Ste. 405
Washington, DC 20037
Territory Includes: District of Columbia; Maryland.

★715★
Washington Association of Black Journalists
c/o Michelle Norris
Washington Post
1150 15th St., NW
Washington, DC 20071 Phone: (202)334-7313
Michelle Norris, Pres.
Affiliated with: National Urban League.

★716★
Washington Bar Association
1819 H St., NW, Ste. 300
Washington, DC 20006 Phone: (202)659-8510
Wendell W. Webster, Pres.
Affiliated with: National Bar Association.

★717★
Washington Minority Business Development Center
1133-15th St., NW, Ste. 1120
Washington, DC 20005 Phone: (202)785-2886

★718★
Washington Urban League
3501 14th St., NW
Washington, DC 20001 Phone: (202)265-8200
Maudine R. Cooper, Pres.
Affiliated with: National Urban League.

Florida

★719★
American Civil Liberties Union
Florida Affiliate
225 NE 34th St., No. 208
Miami, FL 33137 Phone: (305)576-2336
Robyn Blumner, Pres.

★720★
Association for the Study of Afro-American Life and History
Miami-Dade Branch
c/o Black Archives, History, and Research Foundation of South Florida
5400 NW 22nd Ave., 7th Fl.
Miami, FL 33142 Phone: (305)638-6064
Dorothy Jenkins Fields, Pres.

★721★
Association of Black Psychologists
Greater Fort Lauderdale Chapter
231 Utah Ave.
Fort Lauderdale, FL 33312 Phone: (202)722-0808
Dr. Timothy R. Moragne, Pres.

★722★
Association of Black Psychologists
Jacksonville Chapter
7202 Eudine Dr., N.
Jacksonville, FL 32210 Phone: (904)725-6662
Larry Richardson

★723★
Association of Black Psychologists
North Florida Chapter
909 Oak Knoll
Tallahasse, FL 32312 Phone: (202)722-0808
Dr. Seward Hamilton, Pres.

★724★
Black Historical Preservation Society of Palm Beach County
623 Division Ave.
West Palm Beach, FL 33401 Phone: (407)833-5836

★725★
Black United Fund of Tampa Bay
PO Box 4787
Tampa, FL 33677 Phone: (813)251-0594
Affiliated with: National Black United Fund, Inc.

★726★
Blacks in Communications
Tallahassee Chapter
c/o LaNedra A. Carroll
The Democrat
PO Box 990
Tallahassee, FL 32302 Phone: (904)599-2157
LaNedra A. Carroll, Pres.
Affiliated with: National Association of Black Journalists.

★727★
Broward County Law Enforcement Officers
9620 NW 42nd Court
Sunrise, FL 33321
Diane Ramsey, Pres.
Affiliated with: National Black Police Association.

★728★
Central Florida Association of Black Journalists and Broadcasters
c/o Rosemary Banks-Harris
The Orlando Sentinel
633 N. Orange Ave.
Orlando, FL 32801-1349 Phone: (407)420-5494
Rosemary Banks-Harris, Pres.
Affiliated with: National Association of Black Journalists.

★729★
Florida Association of Voluntary Agencies for Caribbean Action
1311 Exec. Center Dr., No. S-202
Tallahassee, FL 32301 Phone: (904)877-4750
David A. Pasquarelli, Exec.Dir.

★730★
Florida Democratic Black Caucus
PO Box 470518, Martin Luther King, Jr. Station
Miami, FL 33247 Phone: (305)284-1023
Dorothy D. Jackson, Sec.

★731★
Gainesville Guardians Association
205 SE 38th St.
Gainesville, FL 32601 Phone: (904)378-6595
Robert Bryant, Pres.

★732★
Goldcoast Firefighters
PO Box 926
West Palm Beach, FL 33401
Affiliated with: International Association of Black Professional Fire Fighters.

★733★
Greater Tampa Urban League
1405 Tampa Park Plaza
Tampa, FL 33605 Phone: (813)229-8117
Joanna N. Tokley, Pres.
Affiliated with: National Urban League.

★734★
Jacksonville Alliance of Black School Educators
1701 Prudential Dr.
Jacksonville, FL 32207
G. Hall, Contact
Affiliated with: National Alliance of Black School Educators.

★735★
Jacksonville Brotherhood Firefighters
PO Box 2728
Jacksonville, FL 32203
Affiliated with: International Association of Black Professional Fire Fighters.

★736★
Jacksonville Brotherhood of Police Officers
PO Box 41583
Jacksonville, FL 32203
Anthony R. Rodgers, Pres.
Affiliated with: National Black Police Association.

★737★
Jacksonville Minority Business Development Center
333 N. Laura St., Ste. 465
Jacksonville, FL 32202-3502 Phone: (904)353-3826

★738★
Jacksonville Urban League
233 W. Duval St.
Jacksonville, FL 32202 Phone: (904)356-8336
Ronnie A. Ferguson, Pres.
Affiliated with: National Urban League.

★739★
Liberal Fire Fighters of Broward
3871 NW 5th Ct.
Ft. Lauderdale, FL 33311
Affiliated with: International Association of Black Professional Fire Fighters.

★740★
Mary McLeod Bethune Foundation
101 Bethune Village
Daytona Beach, FL 32114 Phone: (904)253-9474
Francis Mobley, Exec.Dir.

★741★
Metropolitan Orlando Urban League
2512 W. Colonial Dr.
Orlando, FL 32804 Phone: (407)841-7654
Shirley J. Boykin, Pres.
Affiliated with: National Urban League.

★742★
Miami Alliance of Black School Educators
14657 SW 94th Ave.
Miami, FL 33176
George M. Koonce Jr., Pres.
Affiliated with: National Alliance of Black School Educators.

★743★
Miami Community Police Benevolent Association
3261 Venice Way
Miramar, FL 33025
Diane Barnes, Pres.
Affiliated with: National Black Police Association.

★744★
Miami/Ft. Lauderdale Minority Business Development Center
1200 NW 78th Ave., Ste. 301
Miami, FL 38103 Phone: (305)591-7355

★745★
Minority Builders Coalition of Broward County
771 NW 22nd Rd.
Fort Lauderdale, FL 33311 Phone: (305)792-1121
Lloyd Brown, Pres.

★746★
Minority Women Business Enterprise
201 S. Rosalind Ave.
Orlando, FL 32801 Phone: (407)836-7317

★747★
National Association of Minority Contractors
Central State Association of Minority Contractors
2900 Granada Blvd.
Kissimmee, FL 32741 Phone: (407)933-1794
Percival Sewell, Pres.

★748★
National Association of Minority Contractors
Student Chapter
School of Bldg. Const., SAC 101
Gainesville, FL 32611 Phone: (904)335-2825
Jose R. Moreno Jr., Pres.

★749★
National Bar Association
Florida Chapter
2 S. Orange Plaza
Orlando, FL 32802 Phone: (407)843-4421
Affiliated with: National Bar Association.

★750★
National Black Child Development Institute
Miami Affiliate
395 NW 1st St., Ste. 207
Miami, FL 33128 Phone: (305)253-0992
Regina M. Grace, Pres.

★751★
National Black MBA Association
South Florida Chapter
PO Box 694154
Miami, FL 33269-4154
Sonia A.S. Johnson, Contact

★752★
National Business League
Florida First Coast Chapter
8905 Castle Blvd.
Jacksonville, FL 32209 Phone: (904)765-2339
George F. Carter, Pres.

★753★
National Business League
Tri-County Chapter
PO Box 1626
West Palm Beach, FL 33402-1828 Phone: (407)996-0465
Virginia Merriett, Pres.

★754★
National Organization of Black Law Enforcement Executives
Florida Chapter
PO Box 4991
Miami, FL 33269 Phone: (305)547-7532
James L. Bryant, Pres.

★755★
New Breed of Firefighters
PO Box 5512
Tampa, FL 33675
Affiliated with: International Association of Black Professional Fire Fighters.

★756★
Operation PUSH
Pensacola Network
Pensacola, FL 32514 Phone: (904)484-1000
Joyce Hopson

★757★
Organization of Minority Correctional Officers
PO Box 470309
Miami, FL 33147-0309
Affiliated with: National Black Police Association,.

★758★
Orlando Minority Business Development Center
132 E. Colonial Dr., Ste. 211
Orlando, FL 32801 Phone: (407)422-6234

★759★
Palm Beach Association of Black Journalists
c/o Kenneth Bohannon
The Palm Beach Post
Box 24700
West Palm Beach, FL 33416-4700 Phone: (407)837-4100
Kenneth Bohannon, Pres.
Affiliated with: National Association of Black Journalists.

★760★
Pinellas County Urban League
333 31st St., N.
St. Petersburg, FL 33713 Phone: (813)327-2081
James O. Simmons, Pres.
Affiliated with: National Urban League.

★761★
Professional Black Fire Fighters Association of Miami
6600 NW 27th Ave., No. 205
Miami, FL 33142
Affiliated with: International Association of Black Professional Fire Fighters.

★762★
Progressive Firefighters Association of Central Florida
PO Box 570966
Orlando, FL 32857
Affiliated with: International Association of Black Professional Fire Fighters.

★763★
Progressive Firefighters Association of Dade County
926 Rutland St.
Opa-Locka, FL 33054
Affiliated with: International Association of Black Professional Fire Fighters.

★764★
Progressive Officers Club
PO Box 680398
Miami, FL 33168
John Pace, Pres.
Affiliated with: National Black Police Association.

★765★
Society for Black Student Engineers
University of Florida
500 Weil Hall
Gainesville, FL 32611 Phone: (904)392-0937
Mark Norton, Pres.

★766★
South Florida Association of Black Journalists
c/o Daniel C. Holly
The Herald
1 Herald Plaza
Miami, FL 33132 Phone: (305)376-3400
Daniel C. Holly, Pres.
Affiliated with: National Association of Black Journalists.

★767★
South Florida Business League
555 NE 15th St., No. 31-A
Miami, FL 33132 Phone: (305)372-3716
Alexis Snyder, Pres.
Affiliated with: National Business League.

★768★
Southeastern Association of Educational Opportunity Program Personnel
Daytona Beach Community College
PO 1111
Daytona, FL 32015 Phone: (904)255-8131
Sue Hawkins, Pres.

★769★
Suncoast Black Communicators
c/o Kevin Washington
St. Petersburg Times
1229 Sand Lake Circle
Tampa, FL 33613 Phone: (813)972-2441
Kevin Washington, Pres.
Affiliated with: National Association of Black Journalists.

★770★
Tallahassee Urban League
923 Old Bainbridge Rd.
Tallahassee, FL 32301 Phone: (904)222-6111
Rev. Ernest Ferrell, Pres.
Affiliated with: National Urban League.

★771★
Tampa/St. Petersburg Minority Business Development Center
4601 W. Kennedy Blvd., Ste. 200
Tampa, FL 33609 Phone: (813)289-8824

★772★
Unitarian Universalist Association Black Concerns Working Group
Florida Chapter
3975 Fruitville Rd.
Sarasota, FL 34232 Phone: (904)371-4974
Rev. John and Mary Louise DeWolf-Hurt, Co-Dist. Execs.

★773★
United Negro College Fund
Miami Beach Office
407 Arthur Godfrey Rd.
Miami Beach, FL 33140
Territory Includes: Miami, Platka, and West Palm Beach, Florida.

★774★
United Negro College Fund
Orlando Office
47 E. Robinson St., Ste. 206
Orlando, FL 32802 Phone: (407)425-3555
Territory Includes: Orlando, Pensacola, Tampa/St. Petersburg, Tallahassee, Gainesville, Jacksonville/Lake City, Florida.

★775★
Urban League of Broward County
11 NW 36th Ave.
Fort Lauderdale, FL 33311 Phone: (305)584-0777
Donald E. Bowen, Exec.Dir.
Affiliated with: National Urban League.

★776★
Urban League of Greater Miami
8500 NW 25th Ave.
Miami, FL 33132 Phone: (305)696-4450
T. Willard Fair, Pres.
Affiliated with: National Urban League.

★777★
Urban League of Palm Beach County
1700 Australian Ave.
West Palm Beach, FL 33407 Phone: (407)833-1461
Percy H. Lee, Pres.
Affiliated with: National Urban League.

★778★
West Palm Beach Minority Business Development Center
2001 Broadway, Ste. 301
Riveria Beach, FL 33404 Phone: (407)393-2530

Georgia

★779★
Afro American Patrolmans League
PO Box 92276
Atlanta, GA 30314
Donald Smith, Pres.
Affiliated with: National Black Police Association.

★780★
Afro-American Police Officers of Augusta
PO Box 5337
Augusta, GA 30906
Affiliated with: National Black Police Association.

★781★
American Association of Blacks in Energy
Atlanta Chapter
c/o Willie J. Green
Georgia Power Co.
333 Piedmont Ave., 6th Fl.
Atlanta, GA 30308 Phone: (404)526-6237
Willie J. Green, Pres.

★782★
American Civil Liberties Union
Georgia Affiliate
233 Mitchell St. SW, No. 200
Atlanta, GA 30303 Phone: (404)523-5398
Ellen Spears, Pres.

★783★
American Civil Liberties Union
Southern Regional Office
44 Forsyth St. NW, Ste. 202
Atlanta, GA 30303 Phone: (404)523-2721
Laughlin McDonald, Pres.

★784★
Apple Corps
250 Georgia Ave., SE
Atlanta, GA 30312 Phone: (404)522-4662

★785★
Association for the Study of Afro-American Life and History
Savannah Chapter
c/o W. W. Law
710 W. Victory Dr.
Savannah, GA 31405 Phone: (912)234-8000
W. W. Law, Pres.

★786★
Association of Black Psychologists
Atlanta Chapter
2114 W. Cedar Lane SW
Atlanta, GA 30311 Phone: (202)722-0808
Dr. Arletta Brinson, Pres.

★787★
Association of Law Enforcement Officers of Dekalb
PO Box 370292
Decatur, GA 30037-0972
Darryl Fauly, Pres.
Affiliated with: National Black Police Association.

★788★
Atlanta Association of Black Journalists
Box 54128
Atlanta, GA 30308 Phone: (404)897-6270
Vic Carter, Pres.
Affiliated with: National Association of Black Journalists.

★789★
Atlanta Business League
818 Washington St.
Atlanta, GA 30315 Phone: (404)584-6126
Valerie Montague, Pres.
Affiliated with: National Business League.

★790★
Atlanta Metropolitan Alliance of Black School Educators
3006 Dodson Dr.
East Point, GA 30344
Dr. Ernest P. Lavender Jr., Pres.
Affiliated with: National Alliance of Black School Educators.

★791★
Atlanta Urban League
100 Edgewood Ave., NE
Atlanta, GA 30303 Phone: (404)659-1150
Lyndon A. Wade, Pres.
Affiliated with: National Urban League.

★792★
Augusta Minority Business Development Center
1208 Laney Walker Blvd.
Augusta, GA 30901-2796 Phone: (404)722-0994

★793★
Black Evangelism and Counseling Association
6635 Doublegate Ln.
Atlanta, GA 30273 Phone: (404)474-0085

★794★
Black Ministerial Association
Statesboro Chapter
c/o Rev. Lee Hunter
135 President Circle
Statesboro, GA 30458 Phone: (912)764-4901
Rev. Lee Hunter, Exec. Officer

★795★
Black United Fund of Atlanta
PO Box 42348
Atlanta, GA 30311 Phone: (404)758-7944
Leonard Tate, Co-Chair
Affiliated with: National Black United Fund, Inc.

★796★
Black Women of Profession
Statesboro Chapter
c/o Carolyn Postell
104 Harris Rd.
Statesboro, GA 30458 Phone: (912)764-4913
Carolyn Postell, Exec. Officer

★797★
Black Women's Coalition of Atlanta
PO Box 11367, Sta. A
Atlanta, GA 30310 Phone: (404)627-6000

★798★
Brother to Brother Firefighters of East Point
2683 Stoneview Terrace
East Point, GA 30344
Affiliated with: International Association of Black Professional Fire Fighters.

★799★
Brothers Combined of Atlanta
7528 Old South Ln.
Jonesboro, GA 30236
Affiliated with: International Association of Black Professional Fire Fighters.

★800★
Brothers United of Valdosta
516 Troupe St.
Valdosta, GA 31601
Affiliated with: International Association of Black Professional Fire Fighters.

★801★
Central Savannah River Area Business League
PO Box 1283
Augusta, GA 30903 Phone: (404)722-0994
Dr. Faye Hargrove, Pres.
Affiliated with: National Business League.

★802★
Columbus Minority Business Development Center
1214 1st Ave., Ste. 430
Columbus, GA 31902-1696 Phone: (404)324-4253

★803★
Dekalb County Minority Firemen's Association
3858 Natalie Court
Ellenwood, GA 30049
Affiliated with: International Association of Black Professional Fire Fighters.

★804★
Dekalb Lawyers Association
PO Box 2403
Decatur, GA 30031-2403 Phone: (404)522-6386
Denise Welch, Pres.
Affiliated with: National Bar Association.

★805★
Fellowship of Fulton County
PO Box 1051
Red Oak, GA 30272
Affiliated with: International Association of Black Professional Fire Fighters.

★806★
Fire Fighters United of Augusta
4306 White Pine Ct.
Augusta, GA 30906
Affiliated with: International Association of Black Professional Fire Fighters.

★807★
Gate City Bar Association
141 Pryor St., SW
Atlanta, GA 30303 Phone: (404)730-8232
Auarita L. Hanson, Pres.
Affiliated with: National Bar Association.

★808★
Metro Columbus Urban League
802 1st Ave.
Columbus, GA 31901 Phone: (404)323-3687
Jessie J. Taylor, Exec.Dir.
Affiliated with: National Urban League.

★809★
Metro Fair Housing Services
1083 Austin Ave.
Atlanta, GA 30307 Phone: (404)221-0147
Dr. William C. Brown, Dir.

★810★
National Association of Minority Contractors
Central Savannah River Chapter
PO Box 1442
Augusta, GA 30903 Phone: (404)724-5310
Sandra Bell, Pres.

★811★
National Association of Minority Contractors
Greater Atlanta Chapter
513 Edgewood Ave.
Atlanta, GA 30344 Phone: (404)522-7727
Thomas Walton, Pres.

★812★
National Black Child Development Institute
Atlanta Affiliate
5867 Sheldon Ct.
College Park, GA 30349 Phone: (404)669-0884
Sherekaa Osorio, Pres.

★813★
National Black MBA Association
Atlanta Chapter
PO Box 158
Atlanta, GA 30301
Henry Hutchins, Contact

★814★
National Black Media Coalition
Altanta Chapter
6375 Elchaudillo Court
College Park, GA 30349
Joan Lewis, Contact

★815★
Operation PUSH
Columbus Chapter
4601 Old Cusseta Rd.
Columbus, GA 31903 Phone: (404)687-4567
William B. Howell

★816★
Progressive Firefighters of Columbus
435 Braselman Ave.
Columbus, GA 31907
Affiliated with: International Association of Black Professional Fire Fighters.

★817★
Savannah Brotherhood Fire Fighters Association
PO Box 22842
Savannah, GA 31403
Affiliated with: International Association of Black Professional Fire Fighters.

★818★
Savannah Minority Business Development Center
31 W. Congress St., Ste. 201
Savannah, GA 31401 Phone: (912)236-6708

★819★
Sickle Cell Foundation of Georgia
2391 Benjamin E. Mays Dr., SW
Atlanta, GA 30311 Phone: (404)755-1641

★820★
Unitarian Universalist Association Black Concerns Working Group
Thomas Jefferson-Mid-South Chapter
1534 N. Decatur Rd., NE
Atlanta, GA 30307 Phone: (404)377-9275
Roger Comstock, Contact

★821★
United Negro College Fund
Atlanta Office
120 Ralph McGill Blvd., NE, Ste. 501
Atlanta, GA 30308 Phone: (404)881-6171
Territory Includes: Georgia; South Carolina; Tennessee.

Hawaii

★822★
American Civil Liberties Union
Hawaii Affiliate
PO Box 3410
Honolulu, HI 96801 Phone: (808)545-1722
Vanessa Y. Chong, Pres.

★823★
Honolulu Minority Business Development Center
1001 Bishop St., Ste. 2900
Honolulu, HI 96813 Phone: (808)536-0066

Idaho

★824★
American Civil Liberties Union
Idaho Affiliate
PO Box 1897
Boise, ID 83701 Phone: (208)344-5243
Jack Van Valkenburg, Pres.

Illinois

★825★
African American Images
9204 S. Commercial Ave., Ste. 306
Chicago, IL 60617 Phone: (312)375-9682

★826★
African-American Police League of Harvey, Illinois
80 W. 150th St.
Harvey, IL 60426
Sylvester Jones, Pres.
Affiliated with: National Black Police Association.

★827★
African American Police League of Lake County
PO Box 9204
Waukegan, IL 60079-9204
Timothy Burch, Pres.
Affiliated with: National Black Police Association.

★828★
Afro-American Fire Fighters of Chicago
9543 S. University St.
Chicago, IL 60628
Affiliated with: International Association of Black Professional Fire Fighters.

★829★
Afro-American Fire Fighters of Peoria
5504 Knoxville St.
Peoria, IL 61614
Affiliated with: International Association of Black Professional Fire Fighters.

★830★
Afro-American Police League
3012 N. Woodbine Terrace, Apt. 2
Peoria, IL 61604
Sandra L. Figaro, Pres.
Affiliated with: National Black Police Association.

★831★
Afro-American Police League
9219 S. Elizabeth St.
Chicago, IL 60620
Patricia Hill, Pres.
Affiliated with: National Black Police Association.

★832★
Afro-American Sheriffs League of Cook County
10219 S. Racine Ave.
Chicago, IL 60643
Ms. Leslie Smith, Pres.
Affiliated with: National Black Police Association.

★833★
American Association of Blacks in Energy
Chicago Chapter
c/o Frank M. Clark
PO Box 278
Lombard, IL 60148 Phone: (708)691-4501
Frank M. Clark, Pres.

★834★
American Civil Liberties Union
Illinois Affiliate
20 E. Jackson Blvd., Ste. 1600
Chicago, IL 60604 Phone: (312)427-7330
Jay Miller, Pres.

★835★
Association for the Study of Afro-American Life and History
Chicago Branch
c/o Jeanette Williams, Asst. Dean of Student Services
Kennedy King College
6800 S. Wentworth Ave.
Chicago, IL 60621 Phone: (312)962-3200
Jeanette Williams, Pres.

★836★
Association of Black Law Enforcement Officers
2006 S. 13th Ave.
Broadview, IL 60153
Ronald Reece, Pres.
Affiliated with: National Black Police Association.

★837★
Black Police Officers Association of Joliet
PO Box 532
Joliet, IL 60434-0532
Affiliated with: National Black Police Association.

★838★
Black Police Officers United for Justice and Equality
7737 S. Phillips Ave.
Chicago, IL 60649
Jerry Crawley, Pres.
Affiliated with: National Black Police Association.

★839★
Chicago Alliance of Black School Educators
5127 Greenwood
Chicago, IL 60615
Ida Cross, Pres.
Affiliated with: National Alliance of Black School Educators.

★840★
Chicago Association of Black Journalists
c/o Renee Turner
Ebony Magazine
810 S. Michigan Ave.
Chicago, IL 60605 Phone: (312)322-9258
Renee Turner, Pres.
Affiliated with: National Association of Black Journalists.

★841★
Chicago Guardians of Police
12609 S. Wentworth
Chicago, IL 60628
Firmin Duplessis, Pres.
Affiliated with: National Black Police Association.

★842★
Chicago Lawyers' Committee for Civil Rights Under Law
c/o Roslyn C. Lieb
220 S. State St., Ste. 300
Chicago, IL 60604 Phone: (312)939-5797
Roslyn C. Lieb, Exec.Dir.

★843★
Chicago Minority Business Development Center No. 1
35 E. Wacker Dr., Ste. 790
Chicago, IL 60601 Phone: (312)977-9190

★844★
Chicago Minority Business Development Center No. 2
700 1 Prudential Plaza
Chicago, IL 60601 Phone: (312)565-4710

★845★
Chicago Urban League
4510 S. Michigan Ave.
Chicago, IL 60653 Phone: (312)285-5800
James W. Compton, Pres.
Affiliated with: National Urban League.

★846★
Chicago Westside Police Association
5052 W. Huron St.
Chicago, IL 60644
Ernestine Dowell, Pres.
Affiliated with: National Black Police Association.

★847★
Coalition of Law Enforcement Officers
5402 Hyde Park Blvd.
Chicago, IL 60615
Jacquelyn Kimber, Pres.
Affiliated with: National Black Police Association.

★848★
Cook County Bar Association
25 E. Washington, No. 1500
Chicago, IL 60602 Phone: (312)726-5444
Affiliated with: National Bar Association.

★849★
Cosmopolitan Chamber of Commerce
1326 S. Michigan Ave.
Chicago, IL 60605 Phone: (312)326-4140
Connie Williams-Pope, Pres.
Affiliated with: National Business League. **Formerly:** Chicago Negro Chamber of Commerce.

★850★
Evanston Black Police Association
PO Bos 5244
Evanston, IL 60204-5244
Diane Elam, Pres.
Affiliated with: National Black Police Association.

★851★
Evanston Brothers
8415 Central Park
Skokie, IL 60076
Affiliated with: International Association of Black Professional Fire Fighters.

★852★
Hope Fair Housing Center
154 S. Main St.
Lombard, IL 60148 Phone: (708)495-4846
Bernard J. Kleina, Exec.Dir.
Formerly: (1981) Hope/West Suburban Fair Housing Center.

★853★
Illinois Black United Fund
2336 E. 71st St.
Chicago, IL 60649 Phone: (312)324-0494
Henry English, Pres.
Affiliated with: National Black United Fund, Inc.

★854★
Illinois Committee on Black Concerns
Southern Illinois University
411 E. Broadway
East St. Louis, IL 62201 Phone: (618)482-6900
Johnetta Haley, Pres.

★855★
Joint Negro Appeal
2400 S. Michigan Ave.
Chicago, IL 60616 Phone: (312)842-6262
Mr. Robert D. Pruden, Pres.

★856★
Lake County Alliance of Black School Educators
PO Box 501
North Chicago, IL 60064
Bettye Johnson, Pres.
Affiliated with: National Alliance of Black School Educators.

★857★
Lake County Urban League
122 Madison St.
Waukegan, IL 60085 Phone: (708)249-3770
Lorraine Hale-Bryant, Pres.
Affiliated with: National Urban League.

★858★
League of Black Women
18 S. Michigan Ave.
Chicago, IL 60603 Phone: (312)368-1329

★859★
Madison County Urban League
210 Williams St.
Alton, IL 62002 Phone: (618)463-1906
Julia Tibbs, Pres.
Affiliated with: National Urban League.

★860★
Martin Luther King, Jr. Coalition
6430 S. Ashland Ave.
Chicago, IL 60636 Phone: (312)925-5250

★861★
National Black Child Development Institute
Chicago Affiliate
11070 S. Western Ave.
Chicago, IL 60643 Phone: (312)445-8207
Dr. George Smith, Pres.

★862★
National Black Child Development Institute
Metro East St. Louis Affiliate
1200 N. 13th St.
East St. Louis, IL 62205 Phone: (618)271-7710
Mary Rhodes, Pres.

★863★
National Black MBA Association
Chicago Chapter
PO Box 8513
Chicago, IL 60680 Phone: (312)373-5100
Mark Smith, Contact

★864★
Neighborhood Fund
1750 E. 71st St.
Chicago, IL 60649 Phone: (312)684-8074

★865★
Neighborhood Institute
1950 E. 71st St.
Chicago, IL 60649 Phone: (312)684-4610

★866★
Oak Park Housing Center
1041 South Blvd.
Oak Park, IL 60302 Phone: (708)848-7150
Roberta L. Raymond, Dir.

★867★
Operation PUSH
Chicago Chapter
PO Box 5432
Chicago, IL 60680 Phone: (312)287-0422
Rev. Charlie Murray

★868★
Operation PUSH
Joliet Chapter
McKinnley & Erie Sts.
Joliet, IL 60436 Phone: (815)723-9445
Rev. Issac Singleton, Pres.

★869★
Quad County Urban League
305 E. Benton St.
Aurora, IL 60505 Phone: (708)897-5335
Peggy S. Hicks, Pres.
Affiliated with: National Urban League

★870★
Society of African American Police
2228 Claremont Dr.
Springfield, IL 62703
Anthony Pettit Sr., Pres.
Affiliated with: National Black Police Association.

★871★
Springfield Urban League
100 N. 11th St.
PO Box 3865
Springfield, IL 62708 Phone: (217)789-0830
Howard R. Veal, Pres.
Affiliated with: National Urban League.

★872★
Tri-County Urban League
317 S. MacArthur Hwy.
Peoria, IL 61605-3892 Phone: (309)673-7474
Frank Campbell, Exec.Dir.
Affiliated with: National Urban League.

★873★
Unitarian Universalist Association Black Concerns Working Group
Central Midwest Chapter
114 S. Marion St.
Oak Park, IL 60302 Phone: (708)383-4344

★874★
United Negro College Fund
Chicago Office
600 S. Federal St., Ste. 704
Chicago, IL 60605
Territory Includes: Illinois.

★875★
Urban League of Champaign County
17 Taylor St.
Champaign, IL 61820 Phone: (217)356-1364
Vernon L. Barkstall, Pres.
Affiliated with: National Urban League.

★876★
Will County Alliance of Black School Educators
417 N. Raven Rd.
Shorewood, IL 60435
Dr. Dillard J.F. Harris, Pres.
Affiliated with: National Alliance of Black School Educators.

Indiana

★877★
American Civil Liberties Union
Indiana Affiliate
445 N. Pennsylvania St., Ste. 991
Indianapolis, IN 46204 Phone: (317)635-4056
Michael Lee Gradison, Pres.

★878★
Association of Black Psychologists
Indiana Chapter
2635 Lincoln Ln.
Indianapolis, IN 46208 Phone: (317)226-4747
Dr. Frankie Cooper, Pres.

★879★
Black Coalition, Recruitment, and Training
625 E. Bellemeade Ave.
Evansville, IN 47713 Phone: (812)423-5291
Bobby Ogburn, Exec.Dir.

★880★
Community Relations Team
2042 S. Meridan St.
Marion, IN 46953
Thomas J. Wise, Pres.
Affiliated with: National Black Police Association.

★881★
Evansville Black Coalition
625 Bellemeade Ave.
Evansville, IN 47713 Phone: (812)423-5291
Bobby Ogbuch, Exec.Dir.

★882★
Fairness in Law Enforcement
6614 Latona Dr.
Indianapolis, IN 46278
Ricky Clark, Pres.
Affiliated with: National Black Police Association.

★883★
Fort Wayne Black Professional Fire Fighters Association
906 Drexel Ave.
Ft. Wayne, IN 46806
Affiliated with: International Association of Black Professional Fire Fighters.

★884★
Fort Wayne Guardians of Police
PO Box 11371
Fort Wayne, IN 46857-1371
Jerome Bostwick, Pres.
Affiliated with: NBPNational Black Police Association.

★885★
Fort Wayne Urban League
Foellinger Community Center
227 E. Washington Blvd.
Fort Wayne, IN 46802 Phone: (219)424-6326
Rick C. Frazier, Pres.

★886★
Gary Minority Business Development Center
567 Broadway
Gary, IN 46402 Phone: (219)883-5802

★887★
Indiana Black Expo, Inc.
3130 Sutherland Ave.
Indianapolis, IN 46205 Phone: (317)925-2702
Rev. Charles Williams, Pres.

★888★
Indianapolis Alliance of Black School Educators
5264 Roxbury Rd.
Indianapolis, IN 46226
Dr. Shirl E. Gilbert, Pres.
Affiliated with: National Alliance of Black School Educators.

★889★
Indianapolis Minority Business Development Center
617 Indiana Ave., Ste. 319
Indianapolis, IN 46204 Phone: (317)685-0055

★890★
Indianapolis Plan for Equal Employment
445 N. Pennsylvania
Indianapolis, IN 46204 Phone: (317)639-4661

★891★
Indianapolis Professional Association
740 E. 52nd St., Ste. 5
Indianapolis, IN 46205 Phone: (317)542-8540
Leslie Hollingsworth, Pres.

★892★
Indianapolis Urban League
850 Meridian St.
Indianapolis, IN 46204 Phone: (317)639-9404
Sam H. Jones, Pres.
Affiliated with: National Urban League.

★893★
James Kimbrough Law Association
1345 Wallace St.
Gary, IN 46402 Phone: (219)949-3585
Karen P. Pulliam, Pres.
Affiliated with: National Bar Association.

★894★
Marion County Bar Association
440 N. East St.
Indianapolis, IN 46204 Phone: (317)637-9111
Larry G. Whitney, Pres.
Affiliated with: National Bar Association.

★895★
Marion Urban League
1221 W. 12th St.
Marion, IN 46953 Phone: (317)664-3933
Arthur N. Banks III, Exec.Dir.
Affiliated with: National Urban League.

★896★
Minority Police Officers Association of South Bend
29763 Roycroft Dr.
South Bend, IN 46614
Lynn C. Coleman, Pres.
Affiliated with: National Black Police Association.

★897★
National Black Child Development Institute
Indianapolis Affiliate
3737 N. Meridian St., Ste. 403
Indianapolis, IN 46208 Phone: (317)291-0595
Cynthia Renea Oda, Pres.

★898★
National Black MBA Association
Indianapolis Chapter
PO Box 2325
Indianapolis, IN 46206-2325
Darlene Sowell, Contact

★899★
Northwest Indiana Alliance of Black School Educators
401 Rutledge St.
Gary, IN 46404
Leola Rule, Pres.
Affiliated with: National Alliance of Black School Educators.

★900★
Operation PUSH
Anderson Chapter
PO Box 853
Anderson, IN 46015 Phone: (317)643-7952
Rev. Jack Samuels

★901★
Operation PUSH
Indianapolis Chapter
1901 N. Hardy
Indianapolis, IN 46202 Phone: (317)631-5946
Rev. Tommy Brown

★902★
Operation PUSH
Michigan City Chapter
PO Box 856
Michigan City, IN 46360 Phone: (219)879-4114
Mamie Davis, Contact

★903★
Unitarian Universalist Association Black Concerns Working Group
Michigan-Ohio Valley Chapter
1010 E. 86th St., 65H
Indianapolis, IN 46240-1875 Phone: (317)844-0933
Rev. Jerry D. Wright, Interim Dist. Consultant

★904★
United Black Fire Fighters of Michigan City
409 Washington Park
Michigan City, IN 46360
Affiliated with: International Association of Black Professional Fire Fighters.

★905★
United Negro College Fund
Indianapolis Office
617 Indiana Ave., Ste. 315
Indianapolis, IN 46202 Phone: (317)638-7477
Territory Includes: Indiana.

★906★
Urban League of Madison County, Inc.
1210 W. 10th St.
PO Box 271
Anderson, IN 46015 Phone: (317)649-7126
Albert B. Simmons, Pres.
Affiliated with: National Urban League.

★907★
Urban League of Northwest Indiana
3101 Broadway
Gary, IN 46408 Phone: (219)887-9621
Eloise Gentry, Pres.
Affiliated with: National Urban League.

★908★
Urban League of South Bend and St. Joseph County, Inc.
1708 High St.
PO Box 1476
South Bend, IN 46624 Phone: (219)287-7261
Affiliated with: National Urban League.

Iowa

★909★
American Civil Liberties Union
Iowa Affiliate
466 Insurance Exchange Bldg.
Des Moines, IA 50309 Phone: (515)243-3576
Cryss D. Farley, Pres.

★910★
Iowa Alliance of Black School Educators
2210 University Ave.
Des Moines, IA 50311
Alice Clinton Boyd, Pres.
Affiliated with: National Alliance of Black School Educators.

★911★
Iowa National Bar Association
c/o Robin Humphrey
State Attorney General's Office
Hoover State Office Bldg.
Des Moines, IA 50319 Phone: (515)281-7055
Robin Humphrey, Pres.
Affiliated with: National Bar Association.

★912★
National Black Child Development Institute
Des Moines Affiliate
1529 19th St.
Des Moines, IA 50314 Phone: (515)282-4037
Evelyn Davis, Pres.

★913★
Operation PUSH
Waterloo Network
PO Box 2211
Waterloo, IA 50765 Phone: (319)233-0803
Anna Weems

Kansas

★914★
Association for the Study of Afro-American Life and History
Dr. Lorenzo Greene Branch of the Greater Kansas City Area
4836 Sortor Dr.
Kansas City, KS 66104 Phone: (913)287-3247
Dr. Gerald W. Hall, Pres.

★915★
Kansas Alliance of Black School Educators
2001 Fairlawn Rd.
Topeka, KS 66604
Dr. Robert McFrazier, Pres.
Affiliated with: National Alliance of Black School Educators.

★916★
Kansas City Bar Association
103 Cross Lines Towers
1021 N. 7th St.
Kansas City, KS 66101-2823 Phone: (913)621-1911
Hosea Ellis Sowell, Pres.
Affiliated with: National Bar Association.

★917★
Kansas City Ethical Police Alliance
6618 Sewell Ave.
Kansas City, KS 66104
Harold L. Simmons, Pres.
Affiliated with: National Black Police Association.

★918★
Minority Press Association
5121 Parallel Pkwy.
Kansas City, KS 66104 Phone: (913)596-1007
Doretha Jordan, Ed.

★919★
National Business League
Wichita Chapter
1125 E. 13th St.
Wichita, KS 67124 Phone: (316)262-5431
Anderson E. Jackson, Pres.

★920★
PRIDE
1726 Quindaro Blvd.
Kansas City, KS 66104
Affiliated with: International Association of Black Professional Fire Fighters.

★921★
Urban League of Wichita
1405 N. Minneapolis
Wichita, KS 67214 Phone: (316)262-2463
Otis G. Milton, Pres.
Affiliated with: National Urban League.

Kentucky

★922★
American Civil Liberties Union
Kentucky Affiliate
425 W. Muhammad Ali Blvd., Ste. 230
Louisville, KY 40202 Phone: (502)581-1181
Jan Phillips, Pres.

★923★
Black Professional Fire Fighters of Louisville
PO Box 11767
Louisville, KY 40211
Affiliated with: International Association of Black Professional Fire Fighters.

★924★
BLOOD
553 Ashbury St.
Lexington, KY 40511
Affiliated with: International Association of Black Professional Fire Fighters.

★925★
Jefferson County Minority Law Enforcement Association
4515 Brewster Ave.
Louisville, KY 40211
Gwen Lyons, Pres.
Affiliated with: National Black Police Association.

★926★
Louisville Association of Black Communicators
c/o David Goodwin
The Courier-Journal
525 W. Broadway
Louisville, KY 40202 Phone: (502)582-7091
David Goodwin, Pres.
Affiliated with: National Association of Black Journalists.

★927★
Louisville Black Police Officers Organization
PO Box 11400
Louisville, KY 40251-0400
Shelby Lanier Jr., Pres.
Affiliated with: National Black Police Association.

★928★
Louisville Minority Business Development Center
835 W. Jefferson St., Ste. 103
Louisville, KY 40202 Phone: (502)589-7401

★929★
Louisville Urban League
1535 W. Broadway
Louisville, KY 40203 Phone: (502)585-4622
Benjamin K. Richard, Pres.
Affiliated with: National Urban League.

★930★
National Bar Association
John W. Rowe Chapter
106 W. Vine St.
Lexington, KY 40507 Phone: (606)255-2424
John McNeill, Pres.
Affiliated with: National Bar Association.

★931★
National Bar Association
Kentucky Chapter
747 S. 5th St., No. 35
Louisville, KY 40203-2161 Phone: (502)582-1942
Rhonda Richardson, Pres.

★932★
Urban League of Lexington-Fayette County
167 W. Main St., Rm. 406
Lexington, KY 40507 Phone: (606)233-1561
Porter G. Peeples, Exec.Dir.
Affiliated with: National Urban League.

Louisiana

★933★
African Chamber of Commerce
3028 Gentilly Blvd.
New Orleans, LA 70122 Phone: (504)948-9769
Emily Williams, Dir.

★934★
American Association of Blacks in Energy
New Orleans Chapter
c/o Phillip R. Snowden
Entergy Operations
PO Box 1559
Gretna, LA 70160 Phone: (504)739-6348
Phillip R. Snowden, Pres.

★935★
American Civil Liberties Union
Louisiana Affiliate
921 Canal St., Ste. 1237
New Orleans, LA 70112 Phone: (504)522-0617
Shirley Pedler, Contact

★936★
BANOFF of New Orleans
4301 Macarthur Blvd.
New Orleans, LA 70114
Affiliated with: International Association of Black Professional Fire Fighters.

★937★
Baton Rouge Minority Business Development Center
2036 Woodale Blvd., Ste. D
Baton Rouge, LA 70806 Phone: (512)476-9700

★938★
Black and White Communications Task Force
610 Texas
Shreveport, LA 71101 Phone: (318)425-8912

★939★
Black Collegiate Services
1240 S. Broad St.
New Orleans, LA 70125 Phone: (504)821-5694

★940★
Black Organization of Police
PO Box 8382
New Orleans, LA 70182
Melvin Howard, Pres.
Affiliated with: National Black Police Association.

★941★
Crescent City Black Journalists
c/o Keith Woods
The Times-Picayune
3800 Howard Ave.
New Orleans, LA 70140-1097 Phone: (504)826-3279
Keith Woods, Pres.
Affiliated with: National Association of Black Journalists.

★942★
Ethnic, Cultural, and Heritage Organization of New Orleans
c/o Rudolph Ramelli
201 St. Charles
New Orleans, LA 70130 Phone: (504)288-5059
Rudolph Ramelli, Exec. Officer

★943★
Louis A. Martinet Legal Society
New Orleans, LA
Angelique Reed, Pres.
Efforts to locate an address for this edition were unsuccessful.
Affiliated with: National Bar Association.

★944★
Magnolia State Peace Officers Association
Lafayette Chapter
348 Josephine St.
Lafayette, LA 70501
Affiliated with: National Black Police Association.

★945★
Magnolia State Peace Officers Association
Shreveport Chapter
PO Box 913
Shreveport, LA 71101
Sammie Robinson, Pres.
Affiliated with: National Black Police Association.

★946★
National Association for Sickle Cell Anemia of Baton Rouge
2301 North Blvd.
Baton Rouge, LA 70806 Phone: (504)346-8434

★947★
National Association of Minority Contractors
North Louisiana Chapter
1134 N. Market St.
Shreveport, LA 71107 Phone: (318)424-4533
Raymond Hill, Pres.

★948★
National Black Child Development Institute
New Orleans Affiliate
5725 Providence Pl.
New Orleans, LA 70126 Phone: (504)283-1841
Gladys Robinson, Pres.

★949★
National Society of Black Physicists
Southern University
Dept. of Physics
Baton Rouge, LA 70810 Phone: (504)771-4130

★950★
New Orleans Alliance of Black School Educators
1400 Camp St.
New Orleans, LA 70130
H. Kenneth Johnson, Pres.
Affiliated with: National Alliance of Black School Educators.

★951★
New Orleans Black Media Coalition
2032 Delachaise St.
New Orleans, LA 70115
C.C. Campbell, Contact
Affiliated with: National Black Media Coalition.

★952★
New Orleans Business League
107 Harbour Circle
New Orleans, LA 70126 Phone: (504)246-1166
Sherman N. Copelin Jr., Pres.
Affiliated with: National Business League.

★953★
New Orleans Minority Business Development Center
1683 N. Claiborne
New Orleans, LA 70116 Phone: (504)947-1491

★954★
Northwest Louisiana Sickle Cell Anemia Foundation and Research Center
2200 Milam St.
Shreveport, LA 71103 Phone: (318)226-8975

★955★
Operation "X" Cell Minority Fire Fighters
5610 Rickover Dr., No. B
Baton Rouge, LA 70811
Affiliated with: International Association of Black Professional Fire Fighters.

★956★
Percy R. Johnson Memorial Fire Fighters Association
2526 Hopewell St.
Shreveport, LA 71104
Affiliated with: International Association of Black Professional Fire Fighters.

★957★
Shreveport Bar Association
501 Texas St.
Shreveport, LA 71101 Phone: (318)222-0720

★958★
Southwest Association of Professional Firefighters
PO Box 92592
Lafayette, LA 70509
Affiliated with: International Association of Black Professional Fire Fighters.

★959★
Southwest Louisiana Law Association
PO Box 92766
Lafayette, LA 70509-2766
Nolton J. Senegal, Pres.
Affiliated with: National Bar Association.

★960★
Total Community Action
1420 S. Jefferson Davis Pkwy.
New Orleans, LA 70125 Phone: (504)821-2000

★961★
United Negro College Fund
New Orleans Office
1000 Howard Ave., Ste. 604
New Orleans, LA 70113
Territory Includes: Louisiana.

★962★
Urban League of Greater New Orleans
1929 Bienville Ave.
New Orleans, LA 70112 Phone: (504)524-4667
Clarence L. Barney, Pres.
Affiliated with: National Urban League.

Maine

★963★
American Civil Liberties Union
Maine Affiliate
97A Exchange St.
Portland, ME 04101 Phone: (207)774-8087
Sally Sutton, Pres.

★964★
Unitarian Universalist Association Black Concerns Working Group
Northeast Chapter
125 Auburn St.
Portland, ME 04103 Phone: (207)797-3246
Rev. Glenn H. Turner, Dist. Minister

Maryland

★965★
Alliance of Black Women Attorneys
Legal Aid Bureau
714 E. Pratt St.
Baltimore, MD 21202 Phone: (301)539-5340
Harriette Taylor, Pres.
Affiliated with: National Bar Association.

★966★
American Civil Liberties Union
Maryland Affiliate
2219 St. Paul St.
Baltimore, MD 21218 Phone: (301)889-8555
Stuart Comstock-Gay, Pres.

★967★
Association for the Study of Afro-American Life and History
Baltimore Branch
PO Box 67582
Baltimore, MD 21215 Phone: (301)484-6686
Richard Andrews, Pres.

★968★
Association for the Study of Afro-American Life and History
Julian Branch
3728 Pikeswood Dr.
Baltimore County, MD 21133 Phone: (301)521-3413
Gloria Marrow, Pres.

★969★
Association of Black Media Workers Baltimore Chapter
c/o Jerry Bembry
The Sun
501 N. Calvert
Baltimore, MD 21278 Phone: (301)332-6000
Clifton Cox, Pres.
Affiliated with: National Association of Black Journalists.

★970★
Baltimore Council for Equal Business Opportunity
1925 Eutaw Pl.
Baltimore, MD 21217 Phone: (301)669-3400

★971★
Baltimore Minority Business Development Center
2901 Druid Park Dr., Ste. 201
Baltimore, MD 21215 Phone: (301)383-2214

★972★
Baltimore Urban League
1150 Mondawmin Concourse
Baltimore, MD 21215 Phone: (301)523-8150
Roger I. Lyons, Pres.
Affiliated with: National Urban League.

★973★
Black Business League of Maryland
PO Box 26443
Woodlawn, MD 21207 Phone: (301)728-0900
W. H. Scott, Exec. Officer

★974★
Black Mental Health Alliance
2901 Druid Pk. Dr., Ste. 300
Baltimore, MD 21215 Phone: (301)523-6670

★975★
Black United Fund of Maryland
10 South St.
Baltimore, MD 21202 Phone: (301)752-8220
Affiliated with: National Black United Fund, Inc.

★976★
Blue Guardians
PO Box 10004
Towson, MD 21285-0004
Richard I. Flichman Jr., Pres.
Affiliated with: National Black Police Association.

★977★
Business League of Baltimore
1831 W. North Ave.
Baltimore, MD 21217 Phone: (301)728-1234
Dr. Chester Gregory, Pres.
Affiliated with: National Business League.

★978★
Citizens for Fair Housing
1004 N. Caroline St.
Baltimore, MD 21205 Phone: (301)522-7474

★979★
Coalition for Open Doors
10 N. Calvert St., No. 405
Baltimore, MD 20202 Phone: (301)576-1103
Susan Goering, Dir.

★980★
Coalition of Black Maryland State Troopers
PO Box 11959
Baltimore, MD 21207
Raymond Grisett, Pres.
Affiliated with: National Black Police Association.

★981★
Coalition of Black Police Officers
PO Box 1863
Rockville, MD 20850
James A. Fenner, Pres.
Affiliated with: National Black Police Association.

★982★
Combined Communities in Action of Prince George's County
6200 Annapolis Rd., Ste. 201
Hyattsville, MD 20784 Phone: (301)772-1777
Cora L. Rice, Dir.

★983★
District of Columbia Afro-American Police Officers Association
900 Cornish St.
Fort Washington, MD 20744
Dewayne Anderson, Pres.
Affiliated with: National Black Police Association.

★984★
District of Columbia Alliance of Black School Educators
8601 Manchester Rd., No. 422
Silver Spring, MD 20901
Sharon Godfrey, Pres.
Affiliated with: National Alliance of Black School Educators.

★985★
Howard County Minority Police Officers
PO Box 1624
Ellicott City, MD 21043
Michael Williams, Pres.
Affiliated with: National Black Police Association.

★986★
J. Franklin Bourne Bar Association
14741 Governor Oden Bowie Dr., Rm. 5121
Upper Marlboro, MD 20772 Phone: (301)952-4028
Sheila R. Tillerson, Pres.
Affiliated with: National Bar Association.

★987★
Maryland Rainbow Coalition
1443 Gorsuch Ave.
Baltimore, MD 21218 Phone: (301)467-9388
Clifford Durand, Co-Chairman

★988★
Metro Baltimore Alliance of Black School Educators
1614 Hartsdale Rd.
Baltimore, MD 21239
Annette Howard Hall, Pres.
Affiliated with: National Alliance of Black School Educators.

★989★
Minority Alliance
1831 W. North Ave.
Baltimore, MD 21217 Phone: (301)769-2445
Jerome Fenwick, Pres.
Affiliated with: National Business League.

★990★
Montgomery County Alliance of Black School Educators
PO Box 10278
Rockville, MD 20850
Gerald Johnson, Pres.
Affiliated with: National Alliance of Black School Educators.

★991★
Monumental City Bar Association
711 Brookwood Rd.
Baltimore, MD 21229 Phone: (301)255-4726
Michael N. Gambrill, Pres.
Affiliated with: National Bar Association.

★992★
National Black Child Development Institute
Prince George's County Affiliate
8922 Hillside Ct.
Landover, MD 20785 Phone: (301)336-5844
Dawn A. Johnson, Pres.

★993★
National Business League
DelMarVa Chapter
821 F Springhill Rd.
Salisbury, MD 21801 Phone: (301)749-8800
Karl V. Binns, Pres.

★994★
National Business League
Montgomery County Chapter
c/o CIS Inc.
8720 Georgia Ave., Ste. 301
Silver Spring, MD 209110 Phone: (301)588-29777
Michelle Dyson, Pres.

★995★
National Business League
Southern Maryland Chapter
9200 Basil Court, No. 210
Landover, MD 20785 Phone: (301)772-3683
Clemon Wesley, Pres.

★996★
Progressive Firefighters Association of Montgomery Country Maryland
PO Box 10011
Silver Spring, MD 20904
Affiliated with: International Association of Black Professional Fire Fighters.

★997★
Students Assistance Project
5000 Pennsylvania Ave., Ste. J
Suitland, MD 20046 Phone: (301)420-9101
Elois G. Hamilton, Dir.

★998★
Suburban Maryland Fair Housing
414 Hungerford Dr., Ste. 216
Rockville, MD 20853 Phone: (201)251-1997
Kathy Muehlberger, Dir.

★999★
United Firefighters TASK
PO Box 3333
Capitol Heights, MD 20791
Affiliated with: International Association of Black Professional Fire Fighters.

★1000★
Vanguard Justice Society
4800 Reisterstown Rd.
Baltimore, MD 21215
Barry W. Powell, Pres.
Affiliated with: National Black Police Association.

★1001★
Vulcan Blazers
2811 Druid Park Dr.
Baltimore, MD 21215
Affiliated with: International Association of Black Professional Fire Fighters.

★1002★
Waring Mitchell Law Society of Howard County
PO Box 651
Columbia, MD 21045 Phone: (301)313-2140
Leslie Turner, Pres.
Affiliated with: National Bar Association.

Massachusetts

★1003★
American Association for Affirmative Action
Region I
c/o James. W. McLain
Boston University
25 Buick St.
Boston, MA 02215 Phone: (617)353-4475
James W. McClain, Dir.
Territory Includes: Maine, Vermont, New Hampshire, Massachusetts, Connecticut, and Rhode Island.

★1004★
American Civil Liberties Union
Massachusetts Affiliate
19 Temple Pl.
Boston, MA 02111 Phone: (617)482-3170
John Roberts, Pres.

★1005★
Association for the Study of Afro-American Life and History
Boston Branch
PO Box 5453
Boston, MA 02102 Phone: (617)265-2323
Robert Hayden, Pres.

★1006★
Black Community Information Center
466 Blue Hill Ave.
Dorchester, MA 02121 Phone: (617)445-3098

★1007★
Black Research and Development Foundation
MBA Research Team
2000 Massachusetts Ave.
Cambridge, MA 02140

★1008★
Boston Association of Black Journalists
PO Box 866
Boston, MA 02199 Phone: (617)787-7351
Alexis Yancy George, Pres.
Affiliated with: National Association of Black Journalists.

★1009★
Boston Lawyers' Committee for Civil Rights Under Law of the Boston Bar
294 Washington St.
Boston, MA 02108 Phone: (617)482-1145
Alan Jay Rom, Interim Dir.

★1010★
Boston Minority Business Development Center
985 Commonwealth Ave.
Boston, MA 02215 Phone: (617)353-7060

★1011★
Boston Society of Vulcans
PO Box 269
Roxbury, MA 02119
Affiliated with: International Association of Black Professional Fire Fighters.

★1012★
Cambridge Afro-American Police Association
PO Box 390987
Cambridge, MA 02139
Garfield A. Morrison Jr., Pres.
Affiliated with: National Black Police Association.

★1013★
Lena Park Community Development Corporation
150 American Legion Hwy.
Dorchester, MA 02124 Phone: (617)436-1900

★1014★
MAMLEO
61 Columbia Rd.
Dorchester, MA 02121
James L. Brown, Pres.
Affiliated with: National Black Police Association.

★1015★
Massachusetts Alliance of Black School Educators
PO Box 1418
Boston, MA 02104
Dr. Clarence Hoover, Pres.
Affiliated with: National Alliance of Black School Educators.

★1016★
Massachusetts Black Caucus
State House, Rm. 127
Boston, MA 02133 Phone: (617)722-2680
Bettye Robinson, Exec.Dir.

★1017★
Massachusetts Black Lawyers Association
PO Box 2411
Boston, MA 02208 Phone: (617)298-4269
Brenda Fluker, Pres.
Affiliated with: National Bar Association.

★1018★
Massachusetts Committee Against Discrimination
Hastings Keith Federal Bldg.
53 N. 6th St.
New Bedford, MA 02740 Phone: (508)997-3191

★1019★
National Association of Minority Contractors
Massachusetts Chapter
PO Box 275
Dorchester, MA 02121 Phone: (617)265-5500
Theodore Webster, Pres.

★1020★
National Black Child Development Institute
Boston Affiliate
c/o Parent Child Center
198 Geneva Ave.
Dorchester, MA 02121

★1021★
National Black MBA Association
Boston Chapter
PO Box 3709, JW McCormack Station
Boston, MA 02101
Carole Copeland Thomas, Contact

★1022★
National Business League
Boston Chapter
500-502A Harrison Ave.
Boston, MA 02118 Phone: (617)247-9141
Bob Winstead, Pres.

★1023★
New England Minority Purchasing Council
4 Copley Pl.
Box 145
Boston, MA 02116 Phone: (617)578-8900
May Ling Tong, Exec.Dir.

★1024★
North Shore Afro-American Police Officers Association
PO Box 455
Lynn, MA 02149
Thaddeus Wheeler, Pres.
Affiliated with: National Black Police Association.

★1025★
Unitarian Universalist Association Black Concerns Working Group
Ballou-Channing Chapter
325 W. Elm St.
Brockton, MA 02401 Phone: (508)559-6650
Rev. Dorothy Boroush, Dist. Exec.

★1026★
Unitarian Universalist Association Black Concerns Working Group
Central Massachusetts-Connecticut Valley Chapter
245 Porter Lake Dr.
Springfield, MA 01106 Phone: (413)788-6140
Rev. William A. DeWolfe, Dist. Exec.

★1027★
Unitarian Universalist Association Black Concerns Working Group
Massachusetts Bay Chapter
110 Arlington St.
Boston, MA 02116 Phone: (617)542-3231
Rev. Timothy Ashton, Dist. Exec.

★1028★
United Negro College Fund
Boston Office
131 State St., Ste. 305
Boston, MA 02109
Territory Includes: Massachusetts; New Hampshire; Maine; Vermont; Rhode Island; Syracuse/Elmira and Binghamton, New York.

★1029★
Urban League of Eastern Massachusetts
88 Warren St.
Roxbury, MA 02119 Phone: (617)442-4519
Joan Wallace-Benjamin Ph.D., Pres.
Affiliated with: National Urban League.

★1030★
Urban League of Springfield
756 State St.
Springfield, MA 01109 Phone: (413)739-7211
Henry M. Thomas III, Pres.
Affiliated with: National Urban League.

Michigan

★1031★
Afro-American Police League
902 Brookhollow Ct., No. 2B
Flint, MI 48503
Doris Roberts-Henry, Pres.
Affiliated with: National Black Police Association.

★1032★
American Association of Blacks in Energy
Michigan Chapter
c/o Walter Starghill, Jr.
Intervale Fuel Corp.
1411 Livernois
Detroit, MI 48238 Phone: (313)933-4110
Walter Starghill Jr., Pres.

★1033★
American Civil Liberties Union
Michigan Affiliate
1249 Washington Blvd., Ste.2910
Detroit, MI 48226-1822 Phone: (313)961-4662
Howard Simon, Pres.

★1034★
Association for the Study of Afro-American Life and History
Detroit Branch
2557 W. McNichols Rd., No. 208
Detroit, MI 48221 Phone: (313)862-1938
Arthur Coar, Pres.

★1035★
Association of Black Psychologists
Michigan Chapter
1451 E. Lansing Dr., Ste. 224
East Lansing, MI 48823 Phone: (517)351-9006
Alton Kirk, Pres.

★1036★
Battle Creek Area Urban League
182 W. Van Buren
Battle Creek, MI 49017 Phone: (616)962-2228
Joyce A. Brown, Pres.
Affiliated with: National Urban League.

★1037★
Black Educators of Pontiac
50 Dakota Dr.
Pontiac, MI 48053 Phone: (313)334-2751
Joanne Walker, Minority Dir.

★1038★
Black Family Development
15231 N. McNichols
Detroit, MI 48235 Phone: (313)272-3500
Jacqueline Jones, Exec.Dir.

★1039★
Black Police Officers Association of Battle Creek
230 S. Woodrow Ave.
Battle Creek, MI 49015
Charles A. Cooper Jr., Pres.
Affiliated with: National Black Police Association.

★1040★
Black Police Officers Association of Kalamazoo
2809 Random Rd.
Kalamazoo, MI 49001
Albert Hampton, Pres.
Affiliated with: National Black Police Association.

★1041★
Black Police Officers Association of Saginaw
3231 S. Auburn St.
Saginaw, MI 48601
Alphonso Jamison, Pres.
Affiliated with: National Black Police Association.

★1042★
Black United Fund of Michigan
2187 W. Grand Blvd.
Detroit, MI 48208 Phone: (313)894-2200
Brenda L. Rayford, Exec.Dir.
Affiliated with: National Black United Fund, Inc.

★1043★
Booker T. Washington Business Association
2885 E. Grand Blvd.
Detroit, MI 48202 Phone: (313)875-4250
Nicholas Hood III, Pres.
Affiliated with: National Business League.

★1044★
Council on Urban League Executives
208 Mack Ave.
Detroit, MI 48201 Phone: (313)832-4600
Roy Levy Williams, Contact

★1045★
Detroit Guardians of Police
14009 Warwick St.
Detroit, MI 48223
Herman Hutson Jr., Pres.
Affiliated with: National Black Police Association.

★1046★
Detroit Minority Business Development Center
65 Cadillac Sq., Ste. 3701
Detroit, MI 48226-2822 Phone: (313)961-2100

★1047★
Detroit Real Estate Brokers Association
15918 W. McNichols
Detroit, MI 48235 Phone: (313)835-2143

★1048★
Detroit Urban League
208 Mack Ave.
Detroit, MI 48201 Phone: (313)832-4600
N. Charles Anderson, Pres.
Affiliated with: National Urban League.

★1049★
Fair Housing Center of Greater Grand Rapids
1514 Wealthy, SE, Rm. 238
Grand Rapids, MI 49506 Phone: (616)451-2980
Lee Nelson Webber, Exec.Dir.

★1050★
Fair Housing Center of Metropolitan Detroit
2230 Witherell, Rm. 601
Detroit, MI 48201 Phone: (313)963-1274
Clifford C. Schrupp, Exec.Dir.

★1051★
Floyd Skinner Bar Association
934 Scibner Ave., NW
Grand Rapids, MI 49504 Phone: (616)774-0003
Stephen R. Drew, Pres.
Affiliated with: National Bar Association.

★1052★
Focus Hope Resource Center
1355 Oakman Blvd.
Detroit, MI 48238 Phone: (313)883-7440

★1053★
Grand Rapids Urban League
745 Eastern St. SE
Grand Rapids, MI 49503 Phone: (616)245-2207
Walter M. Brame Ed.D, Pres.
Affiliated with: NUL.

★1054★
Greater Lansing Urban League
300 N. Washington Sq., Ste. 100
Lansing, MI 48933 Phone: (517)487-3608
Ray Margaret Jackson Ph.D., Interim Exec.Dir.
Affiliated with: National Urban League.

★1055★
Kalamazoo Alliance of Black School Educators
726 Darby Ln.
Kalamazoo, MI 49007
Kai M. Jackson, Pres.
Affiliated with: National Alliance of Black School Educators.

★1056★
Lansing Black Lawyers Association
PO Box 18222
Lansing, MI 48901 Phone: (517)373-1162
Lamont M. Walton, Pres.
Affiliated with: National Bar Association.

★1057★
Mallory, Van-Dyne and Scott Bar Association
432 N. Saganaw, No. 810
Flint, MI 48502 Phone: (313)239-2323
Archie Hayman, Pres.
Affiliated with: National Bar Association.

★1058★
Metro Detroit Alliance of Black School Educators
PO Box 02339, North End Sta.
Detroit, MI 48202
Tommie L. Burton, Pres.
Affiliated with: National Alliance of Black School Educators.

★1059★
Michigan Coalition for Human Rights
4800 Woodward Ave.
Detroit, MI 48201-1399 Phone: (313)833-4407
Rev. Edmund Millet, Chm.

★1060★
Michigan State Association of Colored Women's Clubs
26842 Hopkins
Inkster, MI 48141 Phone: (313)561-4694
Gertrude Warren, Pres.

★1061★
Mid-Michigan Association of Black Journalists
c/o Jonesetta Lassiter
The Chronicle
981 3rd St.
Muskegon, MI 49443 Phone: (616)722-2165
Jonesetta Lassiter, Pres.
Affiliated with: National Association of Black Journalists.

★1062★
National Association of Black Journalists
Detroit Chapter
Box 1293
Detroit, MI 48231 Phone: (313)965-7698
Connie Prater, Pres.

★1063★
National Black Child Development Institute
Metro Detroit Affiliate
11000 W. McNichols, Ste. 124
Detroit, MI 48221 Phone: (313)373-2276
Rep. Alma Stallworth, Pres.

★1064★
National Black Child Development Institute
Washtenaw Affiliate
PO Box 7948
Ann Arbor, MI 48107 Phone: (313)482-7658
Ena L. Weathers, Pres.

★1065★
National Black MBA Association
Detroit Chapter
PO Box 02398
Detroit, MI 48202
Bruce Thompson, Contact

★1066★
New Phoenix of Detroit
PO Box 02022
Detroit, MI 48202
Affiliated with: International Association of Black Professional Fire Fighters.

★1067★
Officers of the Shield
142 Alger St. SE
Grand Rapids, MI 49507
Marvin Smith, Pres.
Affiliated with: National Black Police Association.

★1068★
Operation PUSH
Detroit Chapter
18700 James Couzens Fwy.
Detroit, MI 48325 Phone: (313)861-1300

★1069★
Operation PUSH
Detroit Chapter
1465 Balmorae Dr.
Detroit, MI 48202 Phone: (313)368-3600
Rev. Jim Holley, Pres.

★1070★
Operation PUSH
Muskegon Heights Network
3020 Woodcliffe
Muskegon Heights, MI 49444 Phone: (616)739-5247
Dr. Vivian Witherspoon

★1071★
Pontiac Area Urban League
295 W. Huron St.
Pontiac, MI 48053 Phone: (313)335-8730
Jacquelin E. Washington, Pres.
Affiliated with: National Urban League.

★1072★
Racial Justice Center of Grosse Pointe
17150 Maumee
Grosse Pointe, MI 48230 Phone: (313)882-6464
Jeri Grover, Sec.
Formerly: Grosse Pointe Inter-Faith Center for Racial Justice.

★1073★
Saginaw County Black Fire Fighters Association
PO Box 4838
Saginaw, MI 48601
Affiliated with: International Association of Black Professional Fire Fighters.

★1074★
Society of Afro-American Police
211 Auburn St.
Pontiac, MI 48058
Conway Thompson, Pres.
Affiliated with: National Black Police Association.

★1075★
Society of Minority Fire Fighters
PO Box 4129
Flint, MI 48504
Affiliated with: International Association of Black Professional Fire Fighters.

★1076★
United Negro College Fund
Detroit Office
417 Penobscot Bldg.
Detroit, MI 48226 Phone: (313)965-5550
Territory Includes: Michigan.

★1077★
Urban League of Flint
202 E. Blvd. Dr., 2nd Fl.
Flint, MI 48503 Phone: (313)239-5111
Melvyn S. Brannon, Pres.
Affiliated with: National Urban League.

★1078★
Urban League of Flint
Housing Center
4401 Detroit St.
Flint, MI 48503 Phone: (313)789-8541
James Richardson, Dir.
Affiliated with: National Urban League.

★1079★
Urban League of Greater Muskegon
469 W. Webster Ave.
Muskegon, MI 49440 Phone: (616)722-3736
Gloria Gardner, Interim
Affiliated with: National Urban League.

★1080★
Wolverine Bar Association
656 Lothrop, No. 206
Detroit, MI 48202 Phone: (313)237-5540
Leslie T. Graves, Pres.
Affiliated with: National Bar Association.

Minnesota

★1081★
American Civil Liberties Union
Minnesota Affiliation
1021 W. Broadway
Minneapolis, MN 55411 Phone: (612)522-2423
William South, Pres.

★1082★
Association of Black Psychologists
Minnesota Chapter
590 Iglehart Ave.
St. Paul, MN 55103 Phone: (202)722-0808
Dr. Pearl Bonner II, Pres.

★1083★
Halie Q. Brown/Martin Luther King Center
270 N. Kent St.
St. Paul, MN 55102 Phone: (612)224-4601
Fred Williams, Exec.Dir.

★1084★
Minneapolis Minority Business Development Center
2021 E. Hennepin Ave., LL 35
Minneapolis, MN 55413 Phone: (612)378-0361

★1085★
Minneapolis Urban League
2000 Plymouth Ave., N.
Minneapolis, MN 55411 Phone: (612)521-1099
Gleason Glover, Pres.
Affiliated with: National Urban League.

★1086★
Minnesota Alliance of Black School Educators
701 Printice Ln.
Minneapolis, MN 55411
Joyce A. Lake, Pres.
Affiliated with: National Alliance of Black School Educators.

★1087★
Minnesota Business League
2210 Plymouth Ave., N.
Minneapolis, MN 55411 Phone: (612)673-2205
John Irving, Contact
Affiliated with: National Business League.

★1088★
Minnesota Minority Lawyers Association
PO Box 2754, Loop Sta.
Minneapolis, MN 55402 Phone: (612)340-1822
Jarvis Jones, Pres.
Affiliated with: National Bar Association.

★1089★
National Association of Minority Contractors
Minnesota Chapter
1121 Glenwood Ave.
Minneapolis, MN 55405-1431 Phone: (612)374-5129
Richard A. Copeland

★1090★
National Black MBA Association
Twin Cities Chapter
PO Box 2709
Minneapolis, MN 55402
Gregg Smith, Contact

★1091★
St. Paul Association of Centurions
687 Carroll Ave.
St. Paul, MN 55104
Clifford A. Kelly, Pres.
Affiliated with: National Black Police Association.

★1092★
St. Paul Urban League
401 Selby Ave.
St. Paul, MN 55102 Phone: (612)224-5771
Willie Mae Wilson, Pres.
Affiliated with: National Urban League.

★1093★
State Council of Black Minnesotans
Right Bldg., Ste. 426
2233 University Ave.
St. Paul, MN 55114 Phone: (612)642-0811
Victor Propes, Exec. Officer

★1094★
Twin Cities Black Journalists
Minneapolis-St. Paul Chapter
c/o Sherrie Marshall
The Star Tribune
425 Portland Ave.
St. Paul, MN 55101 Phone: (612)372-4144
Sherrie Marshall, Pres.
Affiliated with: National Association of Black Journalists.

★1095★
Unitarian Universalist Association Black Concerns Working Group
Prairie Star Chapter
122 W. Franklin Ave., Ste. 318
Minneapolis, MN 55404 Phone: (612)870-4823
Rev. Harry C. Green, Dist. Exec.

★1096★
United Negro College Fund
Minneapolis Office
401 2nd Ave., S., Ste. 532
Minneapolis, MN 55401
Territory Includes: Minnesota; Iowa; Nebraska.

Mississippi

★1097★
American Civil Liberties Union
Mississippi Affiliate
921 N. Congress St.
Jackson, MS 39202 Phone: (601)355-6464

★1098★
Bureau of Business and Economic Research
c/o J.B. Burrell
Jackson State Univ. School of Business
PO Box 18525
Jackson, MS 39203 Phone: (601)968-2028
J.B. Burrell, Contact
Affiliated with: National Business League.

★1099★
Firefighters Limited
2650 Livingston Rd., Ste. A
Jackson, MS 39213
Affiliated with: International Association of Black Professional Fire Fighters.

★1100★
Jackson Association of Black Journalists
PO Box 2108
Jackson, MS 39205 Phone: (601)961-7000
Marie T. King, Pres.
Affiliated with: National Association of Black Journalists.

★1101★
Jackson Concerned Officers for Progress
PO Box 31085
Jackson, MS 39206
Affiliated with: National Black Police Association.

★1102★
Jackson County-Pascagoula-Moss Point Negro Senior Club
c/o Roberta Deleah Johnson
5030 Frederick St.
Moss Point, MS 39563 Phone: (601)475-2155
Roberta Deleah Johnson, Pres.

★1103★
Jackson Minority Business Development Center
5285 Galaxie Dr., Ste. 465
Jackson, MS 39206 Phone: (601)362-2260

★1104★
Magnolia Bar Association
4620 D. Chastain Dr.
Jackson, MS 39206 Phone: (601)582-3216
Romaine L. Richards, Pres.
Affiliated with: National Bar Association.

★1105★
Mississippi Action for Community Education
119 S. Theobald St.
Greenville, MS 38701 Phone: (601)335-3523
Larry Farmer, Pres.

★1106★
Natchez Business and Civic League
1044 N. Pine St.
Natchez, MS 39120 Phone: (801)442-6644
Harden Wallace, Pres.
Affiliated with: National Business League.

★1107★
National Association of Minority Contractors
Mississippi Chapter
PO Box 1461
Columbus, MS 39703 Phone: (601)328-0837
Tom Epps, Pres.

★1108★
Operation PUSH
Jackson Chapter
746 Windward Rd.
Jackson, MS 39206 Phone: (601)982-6145
Dr. Leslie McLemore

★1109★
Southern Media Coalition
3322 S. Lamar Blvd.
Oxford, MS 38655
Alvin Chambliss, Contact
Affiliated with: National Black Media Coalition.

★1110★
Urban League of Greater Jackson
3405 Medgar Evers Blvd.
PO Box 11249
Jackson, MS 39213 Phone: (601)981-4211
Affiliated with: National Urban League.

Missouri

★1111★
American Association for Affirmative Action Region VII
c/o Jacqueline A. Lester
State of Missouri
St. Louis, MO 63101 Phone: (314)444-7028
Jacqueline A. Lester, Dir.
Territory Includes: Nebraska, Iowa, Kansas, and Missouri.

★1112★
American Association of Blacks in Energy Kansas/Missouri Chapter
c/o Verneda Gilbert
Kansas Power Light Gas Service
2460 Pershing Rd., 4th Fl.
Kansas City, MO 64108 Phone: (816)346-5504
Verneda Gilbert, Pres.

★1113★
American Civil Liberties Union Eastern Missouri Affiliate
4557 Lacleda Ave.
St. Louis, MO 39202 Phone: (314)361-2111
Joyce Armstrong, Pres.

★1114★
American Civil Liberties Union Kansas and Western Missouri Affiliate
201 Wyandotte St., No. 209
Kansas City, MO 64105 Phone: (816)421-4449
Dick Kurtenbach, Pres.

★1115★
Black Economic Union of Greater Kansas City
1601 E. 18th St., Ste. 300
Kansas City, MO 64108 Phone: (816)474-1080
Sylvester Holmes, Exec.Dir.

★1116★
Black Music Society of Missouri
3701 Grandel Sq.
St. Louis, MO 63108 Phone: (314)534-4344

★1117★
Black United Appeal of Kansas City
3338 Benton Blvd.
Kansas City, MO 64128 Phone: (816)861-1222
Elvis E. Gibson, Pres.
Affiliated with: National Black United Fund, Inc.

★1118★
FIRE
4577 Athlone St.
St. Louis, MO 63115
Affiliated with: International Association of Black Professional Fire Fighters.

★1119★
Greater St. Louis Association of Black Journalists
c/o Mary Cannon
KMOV-TV
1 S. Memorial Dr.
St. Louis, MO 63108 Phone: (314)361-7877
Mary Cannon, Pres.
Affiliated with: National Association of Black Journalists.

★1120★
Kansas City Association of Black Journalists
PO Box 32744
Kansas City, MO 64111 Phone: (913)345-1990
Gromer Jeffers, Pres.
Affiliated with: National Association of Black Journalists.

★1121★
Kansas City Minority Business Development Center
1000 Walnut, Ste. 1000
Kansas City, MO 64106 Phone: (816)221-6504

★1122★
Metro Black Media Coalition
PO Box 5826
St. Louis, MO 63134
Ms. Freddie Lee Thompson, Contact
Affiliated with: National Black Media Coalition.

★1123★
Mound City Bar Association
PO Box 1543
St. Louis, MO 63188 Phone: (314)231-9775
Dorothy White-Coleman, Pres.
Affiliated with: National Bar Association.

★1124★
Mound City Business League
10345 Nashua
Dellwood, MO 63136 Phone: (314)361-2613
Marvin Batey, Pres.
Affiliated with: National Business League.

★1125★
National Black Child Development Institute St. Louis Affiliate
739 Harvest Ln.
St. Louis, MO 63132 Phone: (314)997-0831
Christine Reams, Pres.

★1126★
National Black MBA Association Kansas City Chapter
PO Box 410692
Kansas City, MO 64141
Vernita Turner, Contact

★1127★
National Black MBA Association St. Louis Chapter
PO Box 5296
St. Louis, MO 63115
Kenneth Rowey, Contact

★1128★
Operation PUSH
Kansas City Chapter
2310 E. Linwood Blvd.
Kansas City, MO 64109 Phone: (816)923-3689
Rev. Wallace Hartfields, Pres.

★1129★
Operation PUSH
St. Louis Chapter
1260 Hamilton Ave.
St. Louis, MO 63112 Phone: (314)385-8900
Rev. Garnett Hennings

★1130★
St. Louis Black Fire Chiefs Association
6308 Tennessee St.
St. Louis, MO 63111
Affiliated with: International Association of Black Professional Fire Fighters.

★1131★
St. Louis County Minority Law Enforcement Association
702 W. Caterbury St., Apt. D
University, MO 63132
Craig Franklin, Pres.
Affiliated with: National Black Police Association.

★1132★
St. Louis Ethical Police Society
913 Melvin St.
St. Louis, MO 63137
Rodney Williams, Pres.
Affiliated with: National Black Police Association.

★1133★
St. Louis Minority Business Development Center
500 Washington Ave., Ste. 1200
St. Louis, MO 63101 Phone: (314)621-6232

★1134★
United Minority Media Association
5511 Woodland
Kansas City, MO 64110
M.C. Richardson, Contact
Affiliated with: National Black Media Coalition.

★1135★
United Negro College Fund
St. Louis Office
915 Olive St., Ste. 821
St. Louis, MO 64106
Myra R. Coates, Area Development Dir.
Territory Includes: Missouri; Kansas.

★1136★
Urban League of Kansas City
1710 Paseo
Kansas City, MO 64108 Phone: (816)471-0550
William H. Clark, Pres.
Affiliated with: National Urban League.

★1137★
Urban League of Metropolitan St. Louis
3701 Grandel Sq.
St. Louis, MO 63108 Phone: (314)289-0328
James H. Buford, Pres.
Affiliated with: National Urban League.

Montana

★1138★
American Civil Liberties Union
Montana Affiliate
PO Box3012
Billings, MT 59103 Phone: (403)248-1086
Scott Crichton, Pres.

Nebraska

★1139★
American Civil Liberties Union
Nebraska Affiliate
633 S. 9th St. LL 10
Lincoln, NE 68508 Phone: (402)476-8091
Bill Schats, Pres.

★1140★
Brotherhood of the Midwest Guardians
2505 N. 24th St., Ste. 468
Omaha, NE 68111 Phone: (402)455-2271

★1141★
Malcolm X Memorial Foundation
2019 20th St.
Omaha, NE 68110 Phone: (402)342-4214
Rowena Moore

★1142★
Omaha Association of Black Professional Fire Fighters
PO Box 11053, Ames Sta.
Omaha, NE 68111
Affiliated with: International Association of Black Professional Fire Fighters.

★1143★
Urban League of Nebraska
3022-24 N. 24th St.
Omaha, NE 68110 Phone: (402)453-9730
George H. Dillard, Pres.

Nevada

★1144★
American Civil Liberties Union
Nevada Affiliate
418 S. Maryland Pkwy.
Las Vegas, NV 89101 Phone: (702)366-1226
Chan Kendrick, Pres.

★1145★
Las Vegas Alliance of Black School Educators
2300 Alta Dr.
Las Vegas, NV 89107
Daisey Miller, Pres.
Affiliated with: National Alliance of Black School Educators.

★1146★
Las Vegas Black Fire Fighters
PO Box 5027
Las Vegas, NV 89101
Affiliated with: International Association of Black Professional Fire Fighters.

★1147★
Las Vegas Minority Business Development Center
716 S. 6th St.
Las Vegas, NV 89101 Phone: (702)384-3293

★1148★
National Association of Minority Contractors
Nevada Chapter
4214 Bertsos Dr.
Las Vegas, NV 89106 Phone: (702)876-7699
Claudio Ferreiro, Pres.

★1149★
National Bar Association
Las Vegas Chapter
316 Bridger Ave., No. 144
Las Vegas, NV 89101 Phone: (702)455-4761
Michael L. Douglas, Pres.

★1150★
Nevada Black Chamber of Commerce
1048 W. Owens
Las Vegas, NV 89106 Phone: (702)648-6222
Al O'Neal, Pres.

★1151★
Nevada Black Police Association
PO Box 1834
Las Vegas, NV 89125
Cliff E. Davis Jr., Pres.
Affiliated with: National Black Police Association.

★1152★
Professional Black Fire Fighters of Clark County Nevada
PO Box 15328
Las Vegas, NV 89114
Affiliated with: International Association of Black Professional Fire Fighters.

★1153★
Reno Black Fire Fighters
6091 Banside Way
Reno, NV 89523
Affiliated with: International Association of Black Professional Fire Fighters.

New Hampshire

★1154★
American Civil Liberties Union
New Hampshire Affiliate
11 S. Main St.
Concord, NH 03301 Phone: (603)225-3080
Claire Ebel, Pres.

★1155★
Unitarian Universalist Association Black Concerns Working Group
New Hampshire-Vermont Chapter
41-A S. State St.
Concord, NH 03301 Phone: (603)228-8704
Rev. Deane Starr, Dist. Exec.

New Jersey

★1156★
American Association for Affirmative Action
Region II
c/o Alonzo Carthage, II
Raritan Valley Community College
Somerville, NJ 08876 Phone: (201)218-8873
Alonzo Carthage II, Dir.
Territory Includes: New York, New Jersey, and Puerto Rico.

★1157★
American Civil Liberties Union
New Jersey Affiliate
2 Washington Pl.
Newark, NJ 07102 Phone: (201)642-2084
Ed Martone, Pres.

★1158★
Association for the Study of Afro-American Life and History
Camden County Branch
6 Tulip Ct.
Mt. Laurel, NJ 08054 Phone: (609)235-3758
Christine Blake, Pres.

★1159★
Association for the Study of Afro-American Life and History
Central New Jersey Branch
137 Central Pl.
East Orange, NJ 07050 Phone: (201)674-2676
Evelyn Claiborne, Pres.

★1160★
Association for the Study of Afro-American Life and History
Essex County Branch
1060 Broad St., Apt. 606
Newark, NJ 07102 Phone: (201)824-8736
Odelma Hammond, Pres.

★1161★
Association for the Study of Afro-American Life and History
Franklin/St. John's Branch
260 Meeker Ave.
Newark, NJ 07112 Phone: (201)923-9707
Rev. Lloyd Preston Terrell, Pres.

★1162★
Association for the Study of Afro-American Life and History
South Jersey Branch
PO Box 283
Berlin, NJ 08009 Phone: (609)629-8483
Elvira Bradford, Pres.

★1163★
Association of Black Psychologists
New Jersey Chapter
111 Livingston Ave.
New Brunswick, NJ 08901 Phone: (202)722-0808
Dr. Abisola Gallagher, Pres.

★1164★
Atlantic City Vulcans
PO Box 161
Atlantic City, NJ 08404
Affiliated with: International Association of Black Professional Fire Fighters.

★1165★
Batons
PO Box 974
Newark, NJ 07102
Frank McMickens, Pres.
Affiliated with: National Black Police Association.

★1166★
Black United Fund of New Jersey
50 Park Pl., Ste. 1419
Newark, NJ 07102 Phone: (201)624-0909
Lloyd J. Oxford, Pres.
Affiliated with: National Black United Fund, Inc.

★1167★
Black Youth Organization
308 S. 9th St.
Newark, NJ 07103 Phone: (201)622-1061
W. Leon Moore, Exec.Dir

★1168★
Bronze Shields
PO Box 1144
Newark, NJ 07102
Alonzo Evans, Pres.
Affiliated with: National Black Police Association.

★1169★
Brother Officers Law Enforcement Society
PO Box 914
Trenton, NJ 08606-0914
Ulysses Davis, Pres.
Affiliated with: National Black Police Association.

★1170★
Brotherhood for Unity and Progress
PO Box 641
Camden, NJ 08102
Leonard W. Hall, Pres.
Affiliated with: National Black Police Association.

★1171★
Brotherhood of United Fire Fighters
PO Box 753
Camden, NJ 08101
Affiliated with: International Association of Black Professional Fire Fighters.

★1172★
Brothers in Blue
450 E. 34th St.
Patterson, NJ 07054
Willie Smoot, Pres.
Affiliated with: National Black Police Association.

★1173★
COFFEE
PO Box 2578
Plainfield, NJ 07062
Affiliated with: International Association of Black Professional Fire Fighters.

★1174★
East Orange Kinsmen
PO Box 4075
East Orange, NJ 07017
John W. Lee, Pres.
Affiliated with: National Black Police Association.

★1175★
FAIR
PO Box 99
Montclair, NJ 07042
Affiliated with: International Association of Black Professional Fire Fighters.

★1176★
Federation of Afro-American Police Officers
21 Porter Ave.
Newark, NJ 07102
Ron Arbuckle, Pres.
Affiliated with: National Black Police Association.

★1177★
FLAME
518 Arlington Ave.
East Orange, NJ 07017
Affiliated with: International Association of Black Professional Fire Fighters.

★1178★
Garden State Bar Association
744 Broad St., No. 1514
Newark, NJ 07102 Phone: (201)643-5972
Andrew Manns, Pres.
Affiliated with: National Bar Association.

★1179★
Golden Shields Association
PO Box 74
Irvington, NJ 07111
Mike Chase, Pres.
Affiliated with: National Black Police Association.

★1180★
IMPAC
PO Box 215
Jersey City, NJ 07302
George Wilson, Pres.
Affiliated with: National Black Police Association.

★1181★
Men and Women for Justice
PO Box 1286
Piscataway, NJ 08854
Leonard W. Randolph, Pres.
Affiliated with: National Black Police Association.

★1182★
Minority Opportunities
780 Northfield Ave.
West Orange, NJ 07052 Phone: (201)762-6866

★1183★
Morris County Urban League
27 Market St.
Morristown, NJ 07960 Phone: (201)539-2121
Janice S. Johnson, Pres.
Affiliated with: National Urban League.

★1184★
National Association of Extension Home Economists
Minority Network Committee
2569 E. Landis Ave.
Vineland, NJ 08360 Phone: (609)691-0369
Dianne S. Lennon, Chairman

★1185★
National Association of Minority Contractors
New Jersey Chapter
340 W. 1st Ave.
Roselle, NJ 07203 Phone: (201)241-9500
Tony Singh, Pres.

★1186★
National Black Child Development Institute
Newark/Essex County Affiliate
403 University Ave.
Newark, NJ 07102 Phone: (718)479-4451
Dolores Odom, Pres.

★1187★
National Black MBA Association
Central New Jersey Chapter
PO Box 127
Piscataway, NJ 08854
Donna Johns, Contact

★1188★
National Business League
South Jersey Chapter
PO Box 1382
Atlantic City, NJ 08401 Phone: (609)344-3499
B.A.C. Johnson, Asst. Reg. V.Pres.

★1189★
National Minority Business Council
Newark Extension Office
494 Broad St., Ste. 600
Newark, NJ 07102 Phone: (201)624-3765
William Franklin, Managing Dir.

★1190★
New Brunswick Minority Business Development Center
134 New St., Rm. 102
New Brunswick, NJ 08901 Phone: (201)247-2000

★1191★
New Brunswick Minority Fire Fighters
15 Conger St.
New Brunswick, NJ 08902
Affiliated with: International Association of Black Professional Fire Fighters.

★1192★
New York Metropolitan Business League
20 N. Van Brunt St., Ste. 200
Englewood, NJ 07631 Phone: (201)568-8145
E. R. Hadden, Coord.

★1193★
Newark Alliance of Black School Educators
PO Box 32458
Newark, NJ 07102
Dr. Lorenzo, Grant
Affiliated with: National Alliance of Black School Educators.

★1194★
Newark Minority Business Development Center
60 Park Pl., Ste. 1404
Newark, NJ 07102 Phone: (201)623-7712

★1195★
Operation PUSH
Jersey City Chapter
632 Garfield Ave.
Jersey City, NJ 07305 Phone: (201)332-3158
Rev. Edward Allen, Pres.

★1196★
Plainfield Area Ebony Police Association
PO Box 3158
Plainfield, NJ 07063
Siddeeq W. El-Amin, Pres.
Affiliated with: National Black Police Association.

★1197★
Sentinel Sixteen - 87, Inc.
PO Box 1192
Montclair, NJ 07042
Benjamin Powell, Pres.
Affiliated with: National Black Police Association.

★1198★
Silver Shields Club
23 Williams St.
Newark, NJ 07102
Robert Hubbert, Pres.
Affiliated with: National Black Police Association.

★1199★
United Negro College Fund
Newark Office
24 Commerce St., Ste. 1327
Newark, NJ 07102 Phone: (201)642-1955
Territory Includes: New Jersey.

★1200★
Unity Guardians Association
PO Box 269
Rahway, NJ 07605
Sam Freeman, Pres.
Affiliated with: National Black Police Association.

★1201★
Urban League of Bergen County
106 W. Palisade Ave.
Englewood, NJ 07631 Phone: (201)568-4988
William E. Brown, Pres.
Affiliated with: National Urban League.

★1202★
Urban League of Essex County
3 Williams St., Ste. 300
Newark, NJ 07102 Phone: (201)624-6660
Lawrence E. Pratt, Pres.
Affiliated with: National Urban League.

★1203★
Urban League of Hudson County
779 Bergen Ave.
Jersey City, NJ 07306 Phone: (201)451-8888
Elnora Watson, Pres.
Affiliated with: National Urban League.

★1204★
Urban League of Metropolitan Trenton
209 Academy St.
Trenton, NJ 08618 Phone: (609)393-1512
Paul P. Pintella Jr., Pres.
Affiliated with: National Urban League.

★1205★
Urban League of Union County
272 N. Broad St.
Elizabeth, NJ 07207 Phone: (201)351-7200
Ella S. Teal, Pres.
Affiliated with: National Urban League.

★1206★
Vulcan Pioneers of Hudson County
PO Box 9104
Jersey City, NJ 07309
Affiliated with: International Association of Black Professional Fire Fighters.

★1207★
Vulcan Pioneers of New Jersey
54 N. Munn Ave., No. 12
Newark, NJ 07106
Affiliated with: International Association of Black Professional Fire Fighters.

New Mexico

★1208★
Albuquerque Minority Business Development Center
718 Central SW
Albuquerque, NM 87102 Phone: (505)843-7114

★1209★
American Civil Liberties Union
New Mexico Affiliate
PO Box 80915
Albuquerque, NM 87108 Phone: (505)266-5915
Grace W. Williams, Pres.

★1210★
Black Officers Association of New Mexico
503 Maddox Loop
Belen, NM 87124
Norman Richard, Pres.
Affiliated with: National Black Police Association.

★1211★
New Mexico Black Lawyers Association
1117 Stanford, NE
Albuquerque, NM 87131 Phone: (505)277-5820
Alfred Matthewson, Pres.
Affiliated with: National Bar Association.

New York

★1212★
Abeny Alliance of Black School Educators
GPO Box 1846
Brooklyn, NY 11202
Silverlane Clark, Pres.
Affiliated with: National Alliance of Black School Educators.

★1213★
Afro-American Police Association
735 Humboldt Pkwy.
Buffalo, NY 14208
Nadine Wilson, Pres.
Affiliated with: National Black Police Association.

★1214★
Afro-American Vegetarian Society
PO Box 46, Colonial Park Station
New York, NY 10039 Phone: (914)664-2066
Ron Davis, Pres.

★1215★
Albany Area Urban League
95 Livingston Ave.
Albany, NY 12207 Phone: (518)463-3121
Joseph Griggs, Interim Pres.
Affiliated with: National Urban League.

★1216★
American Association of Blacks in Energy
New York Chapter
c/o Leandra H. Abbott
ConEd Co. of New York
4 Irving Pl., Rm. 1634
New York, NY 10003 Phone: (212)460-6918
Leandra H. Abbott, Pres.

★1217★
American Civil Liberties Union
New York Affiliate
132 W. 43rd St., 2nd Fl.
New York, NY 87108 Phone: (212)382-0557
Norman Siegal, Pres.

★1218★
Associated Black Charities
105 E. 22nd St.
New York, NY 10010 Phone: (212)777-6060

★1219★
Association for the Study of Afro-American Life and History
American Federation of Teachers Branch, Local 2
15 W. 72nd St., No. 33A
New York, NY 10023 Phone: (212)595-0282
Ponsie Hillman, Pres.

★1220★
Association for the Study of Afro-American Life and History
Bronx Branch
3617 Bronxwood Ave.
Bronx, NY 10469 Phone: (212)652-6247
Cheryl Hockaday, Pres.

★1221★
Association for the Study of Afro-American Life and History
Manhattan Branch
25 St. Nicholas Terrace, No. 51
New York, NY 10027 Phone: (212)662-9447
Vincent Baker, Pres.

★1222★
Association for the Study of Afro-American Life and History
Queens Branch
88-34 145th St.
Jamaica, NY 11435 Phone: (718)297-7108
Marie Thomas, Pres.

★1223★
Association for the Study of Afro-American Life and History
Sullivan County Branch
PO Box 1351
South Fallsburg, NY 12779 Phone: (914)434-7481
Dorothy Fields, Pres.

★1224★
Association for the Study of Afro-American Life and History
Westchester Branch
118 N. Everts Ave.
Elmsford, NY 10523 Phone: (914)592-6425
Yvonne Jones, Pres.

★1225★
Association of Black Lawyers of Westchester County
19 Chestnut Hill Ave.
White Plains, NY 10606 Phone: (914)347-2244
Eric Lamar Harris, Pres.
Affiliated with: National Bar Association.

★1226★
Association of Black Psychologists
New York Chapter
3875 Waldo Ave.
Bronx, NY 10463 Phone: (212)447-0900
Lorraine Maxwell

★1227★
Association of Black Women Attorneys
134 W. 32nd St., Ste. 602
New York, NY 10001 Phone: (212)815-0478
Leslie R. Jones, Pres.
Affiliated with: National Bar Association.

★1228★
Association of Minority Business Enterprises of New York
165 40A Baisle Blvd., Ste. 3
Jamaica, NY 11434 Phone: (718)341-0707
Nathaniel Singleton, Pres.

★1229★
Association of Neighborhood Housing Development
236 W. 27th St.
New York, NY 10001 Phone: (212)463-9600

★1230★
Bi-State Shields
PO Box 382, JFK Station
Jamaica, NY 11430
Howard Walcott, Pres.
Affiliated with: National Black Police Association.

★1231★
Black Community Development Project
241 Liberty
Newburgh, NY 12550 Phone: (914)561-2107
Billie McClearn, Exec.Dir.

★1232★
Black Interest Group
Nazareth College
Undergraduate Office
Student Union
4245 East Ave.
Rochester, NY 14618 Phone: (716)586-2525

★1233★
Black Media
Black Resources
231 W. 29th St., Rm. 1205
New York, NY 10001 Phone: (212)967-4000

★1234★
Black New York Action Committee
1878 7th Ave.
New York, NY 10026 Phone: (212)678-0549

★1235★
Black Newspapers Clipping Bureau
68 E. 131st St.
New York, NY 10037 Phone: (212)281-6000

★1236★
Black Radio Network
166 Madison Ave.
New York, NY 10002 Phone: (212)686-6850

★1237★
Black Resources Inc.
410 Central Park W.
New York, NY 10025 Phone: (212)222-3556

★1238★
Black Theatre Fund
c/o*The Black American*
545 8th Ave., 12th Fl.
New York, NY 10018 Phone: (212)594-0179

★1239★
Black United Fund of New York
144 W. 125th St.
New York, NY 10027 Phone: (212)234-1695
Affiliated with: National Black United Fund, Inc.

★1240★
Black Women's Support Group
280 Valiant Dr.
Rochester, NY 14623 Phone: (716)359-2302
Merlina Moore, Exec. Officer

★1241★
Bronx County Black Bar Association
19828 Pompeii Ave.
Queens, NY 11423 Phone: (212)804-1512
Teresa Mason, Pres.
Affiliated with: National Bar Association.

★1242★
Bronx Minority Business Development Center
349 E. 149th St., Ste. 702
Bronx, NY 10451 Phone: (212)665-8583

★1243★
Bronze Shields of Suffolk County, New York
PO Box 544
Calverton, NY 11933
Clement Snell, Pres.
Affiliated with: National Black Police Association.

★1244★
Brooklyn Minority Business Development Center
16 Court St., Rm. 1903
Brooklyn, NY 11201 Phone: (718)522-5880

★1245★
Broome County Urban League
43-45 Carroll St.
Binghamton, NY 13901 Phone: (607)723-7303
Laura C. Keeling, Pres.
Affiliated with: National Urban League.

★1246★
Brothers of the Shield
PO Box 146
Carle Place, NY 11514
Oscar Powell, Pres.
Affiliated with: National Black Police Association.

★1247★
Buffalo Black Media Coalition
225 Hasting St.
Buffalo, NY 14215
John E. Smith, Contact
Affiliated with: National Black Media Coalition.

★1248★
Buffalo Minority Business Development Center
523 Delaware Ave.
Buffalo, NY 14202 Phone: (716)885-0336

★1249★
Buffalo Urban League
15 E. Genessee St.
Buffalo, NY 14203 Phone: (716)854-7625
Leroy R. Coles Jr., Pres.
Affiliated with: National Urban League.

★1250★
Catholic Interracial Council of New York
16 W. 36th St.
New York, NY 10018 Phone: (212)237-8255
Gerald W. Lynch, Pres.

★1251★
Concerned Black Film Makers of New York
20 W. 120th St.
New York, NY 10027 Phone: (212)410-2101

★1252★
Council on Economic Development and Empowerment of Black People
63 W. 125th St.
New York, NY 10027 Phone: (212)722-1922

★1253★
East Upton Harlem Chamber of Commerce
186 E. 116th St.
New York, NY 10029 Phone: (212)996-2288
Henry Calderon, Pres.

★1254★
Ebony Society
15 Linden St.
Coram, NY 11727
Jeanne Goshay, Pres.
Affiliated with: National Black Police Association.

★1255★
Greater New York Business League
491 DeKalb Ave.
Brooklyn, NY 11205 Phone: (718)636-1509
Bryon A. Lee, Pres.
Affiliated with: National Business League.

★1256★
Guardian Association of the Long Island Railroad
339 Midward St.
Brooklyn, NY 11225
Stephen Mears, Pres.
Affiliated with: National Black Police Association.

★1257★
Guardian Association of the New York City Housing Dept.
Manhattanville Sta.
PO Box 1746
New York, NY 10027
Oubey Jefferson, Pres.
Affiliated with: National Black Police Association.

★1258★
Guardians Association of the New York City Corrections Dept.
PO Box 527
Bronx, NY 10451
Ali A. Al-Rahman, Pres.
Affiliated with: National Black Police Association.

★1259★
Guardians Association of the New York City Police Department
120-22E Erskine Pl.
Bronx, NY 10475
Roger L. Abel, Pres.
Affiliated with: National Black Police Association.

★1260★
Guardians Association of the New York State Courts
PO Box 524-021,
New York, NY 10037
Jay Best Sr., Pres.
Affiliated with: National Black Police Association.

★1261★
Harlem Commonwealth Council
361 W. 125th St.
New York, NY 10027 Phone: (212)749-0900

★1262★
Harlem Minority Business Development Center
270 Sylvan Ave.
Englewood Cliffs, NY 07362 Phone: (212)661-8044

★1263★
Harlem Parents Union
271 W. 125th St.
New York, NY 10027 Phone: (212)662-4888

★1264★
Inner-City Scholarship Fund
1011 1st Ave.
New York, NY 10022 Phone: (212)753-8583

★1265★
INTERACE
PO Box 582
Forest Hills, NY 11375 Phone: (718)657-2271
Holly Sheeger, Coord.

★1266★
Long Island Alliance of Black School Educators
729 Wilson
Central Islip, NY 11722
Helen D. Brannon, Pres.
Affiliated with: National Alliance of Black School Educators.

★1267★
Long Island Guardians
PO Box 1313M
Bayshore, NY 11706
Wes Daily, Pres.
Affiliated with: National Black Police Association.

★1268★
Macon B. Allen Bar Association
110-11 225th St.
Queens Village
New York, NY 11429 Phone: (516)829-3190
Mortimer Lawrence, Pres.
Affiliated with: National Bar Association.

★1269★
Manhattan Minority Business Development Center
51 Madison Ave., Ste, 2212
New York, NY 10010 Phone: (212)779-4360

★1270★
Metropolitan Black Bar Association
175 W. 87th St., Apt. 15F
New York, NY 10024 Phone: (212)590-3777
Denise A. Outram, Pres.
Affiliated with: National Bar Association.

★1271★
Minority Bar Association of Western New York
PO Box 211,
Niagara Sq. Sta.
Buffalo, NY 11401-0211
David L. Edmonds, Pres.
Affiliated with: National Bar Association.

★1272★
MOCHA
822 N. French Rd.
North Tonawanda, NY 14120
Affiliated with: International Association of Black Professional Fire Fighters.

★1273★
Nassau County Guardians
PO Box 100
Uniondale, NY 11553
Larry Hill, Pres.
Affiliated with: National Black Police Association.

★1274★
Nassau/Suffolk Minority Business Development Center
150 Broad Hollow Rd., Ste. 304
Melville, NY 11747 Phone: (516)549-5454

★1275★
National Association of Minority Contractors
New York Chapter
PO Box 5371
Albany, NY 12205 Phone: (518)426-2271
Michael Hurt, Pres.

★1276★
National Black Child Development Institute
Buffalo Affiliate
PO Box 452
Buffalo, NY 14214 Phone: (716)832-9172
Odessa Brown, Pres.

★1277★
National Black Child Development Institute
Mid-Hudson Affiliate
PO Box 1383
Newburgh, NY 12550 Phone: (914)297-8933
Linda Melton-Mann, Pres.

★1278★
National Black Child Development Institute
New York Affiliate
c/o New York Urban League
218 W. 40th St., 8th Fl.
New York, NY 10018 Phone: (212)730-5200
Dennis Walcott, Pres.

★1279★
National Black MBA Association
New York Chapter
Grand Central Station
PO Box 1602, Grand Central Station
New York, NY 10163 Phone: (212)978-4333
Jennifer Taylor-Smith, Contact

★1280★
National Black MBA Association
Westchester/Greater Connecticut Chapter
PO BOX 552
White Plains, NY 10602
Charles Wade, Contact

★1281★
National Black MBA Association
Western New York Chapter
PO Box 15697
Rochester, NY 14615-0697
Denise Cornwell, Contact

★1282★
National Council of Negro Women of Greater New York
777 United Nations Plaza, 10th Fl.
New York, NY 10017 Phone: (212)687-5870

★1283★
New American
310 Lenoy Ave.
New York, NY 100127 Phone: (212)427-3880

★1284★
New York Alliance of Black School Educators
PO Box 100-449
Brooklyn, NY 11210
Dr. Ronald Frye, Pres.
Affiliated with: National Alliance of Black School Educators.

★1285★
New York Association of Black Journalists
WPIX-TV
220 E. 42nd St.
New York, NY 10017 Phone: (212)210-2420
Sheila D. Stainback, Pres.
Affiliated with: National Association of Black Journalists.

★1286★
New York Urban Coalition
99 Hudson, 11th Fl.
New York, NY 10013 Phone: (212)219-4500

★1287★
New York Urban League
218 W. 40th St.
New York, NY 10018 Phone: (212)730-5200
Dennis M. Walcott, Pres.
Affiliated with: National Urban League.

★1288★
Niagara Alliance of Black School Educators
PO Box 244 Bridge Sta.
Niagara Falls, NY 14305
Gloria Scott, Pres.
Affiliated with: National Alliance of Black School Educators.

★1289★
One Hundred Black Men
105 E. 22nd
New York, NY 10010 Phone: (212)777-7070

★1290★
Operation PUSH
Buffalo Chapter
184 Goodall St.
Buffalo, NY 14204 Phone: (716)852-4504
B.W. Smith, Pres.

★1291★
Operation PUSH
New York City Chapter
270 Lenox Ave.
New York, NY 10027 Phone: (212)534-6300
Cora Walker

★1292★
Queens Minority Business Development Center
110-29 Horace Harding Expwy.
Corona, NY 11368 Phone: (718)699-2400

★1293★
Rochester Black Media Coalition
700 North St.
Rochester, NY 14605
Charles Hatcher, Contact
Affiliated with: National Black Media Coalition.

★1294★
Rochester Minority Business Development Center
350 North St.
Rochester, NY 14615 Phone: (716)232-6120

★1295★
Suffolk Housing Services
550 Smithtown Bypass, Rm. 220
Hauppauge, NY 11787 Phone: (516)724-6920
David Berenbaum, Exec.Dir.

★1296★
Syracuse Association of Black Journalists
c/o Saundra Smokes
The Herald-Journal
PO Box 4915
Syracuse, NY 13221 Phone: (315)470-3091
Saundra Smokes, Pres.
Affiliated with: National Association of Black Journalists.

★1297★
Syracuse Black Media Coalition
1450 Comstock Ave.
Syracuse, NY 13220
Butch Charles, Contact
Affiliated with: National Black Media Coalition.

★1298★
Unitarian Universalist Association Black Concerns Working Group
Metropolitan New York Chapter
2 Harvard Rd.
Shoreham, NY 11786 Phone: (215)744-0557
Rev. Howell K. Lind, Dist. Exec.

★1299★
Unitarian Universalist Association Black Concerns Working Group
St. Lawrence Chapter
695 Elmwood Ave.
Buffalo, NY 14222 Phone: (716)882-0430
Rev. Wendy L. Colby, Dist. Consultant

★1300★
United Black Appeal
545 8th Ave.
New York, NY 10018 Phone: (212)564-9852

★1301★
United Federation of Black Community Organizations
Child Development Center
474 W. 159th St.
New York, NY 10032 Phone: (212)281-1950

★1302★
Uptown Chamber of Commerce
125th St., Ste. 206
New York, NY 10027 Phone: (212)427-7200
Lloyd Williams, Pres./CEO

★1303★
Urban League of Long Island
221 Broadway, Ste. 207
Amityville, NY 11701 Phone: (516)691-7230
Doris P. Miles, Pres.
Affiliated with: National Urban League.

★1304★
Urban League of Onondaga County
505 E. Fayette St.
Syracuse, NY 13202 Phone: (315)472-6955
Leon E. Modeste, Pres.
Affiliated with: National Urban League.

★1305★
Urban League of Rochester
177 N. Clinton Ave.
Rochester, NY 14604 Phone: (716)325-6530
William A. Johnson Jr., Pres.
Affiliated with: National Urban League.

★1306★
Urban League of Westchester County
61 Mitchell Pl.
White Plains, NY 10601 Phone: (914)428-6300
Ernest S. Prince, Pres.
Affiliated with: 2NUL.

★1307★
Vulcan Society of New York
739 Eastern Pkwy.
Brooklyn, NY 112123
Affiliated with: International Association of Black Professional Fire Fighters.

★1308★
Vulcan Society of Westchester County
PO Box 2179
Mt. Vernon, NY 10551
Affiliated with: International Association of Black Professional Fire Fighters.

★1309★
Westchester Alliance of Black School Educators
1-B Quaker Ridge Rd., No. 101
New Rochelle, NY 10804
Ann Williams, Pres.
Affiliated with: National Alliance of Black School Educators.

★1310★
Westchester Rockland Guardians
PO Box 138
White Plains, NY 10605
Curley Brown, Pres.
Affiliated with: National Black Police Association.

★1311★
Williamsburg/Brooklyn Minority Business Development Center
12 Heywood St.
Brooklyn, NY 11211 Phone: (718)522-5620

North Carolina

★1312★
American Association for Affirmative Action
Region IV
c/o Mary C. Williams
Forsyth Memorial Hospital
Winston-Salem, NC 27103 Phone: (919)760-5469
Mary C. Williams, Dir.
Territory Includes: Kentucky, Tennessee, North Carolina, South Carolina, Georgia, Alabama, Mississippi, and Florida.

★1313★
American Association of Blacks in Energy
Virginia/North Carolina Chapter
c/o Hilda Pinnix-Ragland
Carolina Power & Light Co.
PO Box 207
Raleigh, NC 27602 Phone: (919)546-7567
Hilda Pinnix-Ragland, Pres.

★1314★
American Civil Liberties Union
North Carolina Affiliate
PO Box 28004
Raleigh, NC 27611 Phone: (919)834-3390
James Shields, Pres.

★1315★
Association of Black Psychologists
North Carolina Chapter
c/o Dr. Dennis Chestnut
East Carolina University
Greenville, NC 27834 Phone: (919)757-1531
Dr. Dennis Chestnut, Pres.

★1316★
Black History Research Committee of Henderson County
733 3rd Ave.
Hendersonville, NC 28739 Phone: (704)693-4548
John R. Marable, Dir.

★1317★
Bull City Professional Fire Fighters
1122 Drew St.
Durham, NC 27701
Affiliated with: International Association of Black Professional Fire Fighters.

★1318★
Carolinas Minority Supplier Development Councils
700 E. Stonewall St., Ste. 340
Charlotte, NC 28202 Phone: (704)372-8731

★1319★
Charlotte Area Association of Black Journalists
PO Box 32574
Charlotte, NC 28232 Phone: (704)289-6576
Cliff Harrington, Pres.
Affiliated with: National Association of Black Journalists.

★1320★
Charlotte Meckleburg Urban League
A.M.E. Zion Bldg.
401 E. 2nd St.
Charlotte, NC 28202 Phone: (704)376-9834
Madine Hester Fails, Pres.
Affiliated with: National Urban League.

★1321★
Charlotte Minority Business Development Center
700 E. Stonewall St., Ste. 360
Charlotte, NC 28202 Phone: (704)334-7522

★1322★
Durham Business and Professional Chain
PO Box 1088
Durham, NC 27702 Phone: (919)683-1047
Wallace O. Green, Pres.

★1323★
Fayetteville Business and Professional League
PO Box 1387
Fayettville, NC 28302 Phone: (919)483-6252
David C. Brown, Pres.
Affiliated with: National Business League.

★1324★
Fayetteville Minority Business Development Center
1141/2 Anderson St.
Fayetteville, NC 28302 Phone: (919)483-7513

★1325★
National Association for Sickle Cell Disease
Charlotte Chapter
623 E. Trade St., Ste. 201
Charlotte, NC 28202 Phone: (704)332-4184

★1326★
National Black Child Development Institute
Charlotte Affiliate
5822 Rimerton Dr.
Charlotte, NC 28226 Phone: (704)542-0764
Dr. Arthur Griffin, Pres.

★1327★
National Black Child Development Institute
Durham Affiliate
1118 Hunstman Dr.
Durham, NC 27713 Phone: (919)544-1050
Nellie F. Riley, Pres.

★1328★
National Black Child Development Institute
Greensboro Affiliate
1411 Wayside Dr.
Greensboro, NC 27405 Phone: (919)375-3151
Claudette Burroughs-White, Pres.

★1329★
National Black Child Development Institute
High Point Affiliate
1807 Briarcliff Ct.
High Point, NC 27260 Phone: (919)882-2620
Linda Hanes, Pres.

★1330★
National Black Child Development Institute
Raleigh (Triangle Area) Affiliate
902 Creech Rd.
Garner, NC
Donald Harris, Pres.

★1331★
National Black MBA Association
Raleigh/Durham Chapter
PO Box 728
Durham, NC 27702
Paula Stewart, Contact

★1332★
North Carolina Association of Black Lawyers
c/o Kaye R. Webb
1200 Murchison Rd.
New Bold Station
Lafayetteville, NC 28301-4298 Phone: (919)486-1142
Kaye R. Webb, Pres.
Affiliated with: National Bar Association.

★1333★
Oxford Business and Professional Chain
PO Box 304
Oxford, NC 27565 Phone: (919)693-8874
A. J. McGee Jr., Pres.

★1334★
Progressive Firefighters Association of Charlotte
PO Box 16619
Charlotte, NC 28297
Affiliated with: International Association of Black Professional Fire Fighters.

★1335★
Raleigh/Durham Minority Business Development Center
817 New Bern Ave., Ste. 8
Raleigh, NC 27601 Phone: (919)833-6122

★1336★
Southern Regional Council on Black American Affairs
c/o Dr. David L. Hunter
Central Piedmont Community College
PO Box 35009
Charlotte, NC 28235 Phone: (704)342-6491
Dr. David Hunter, Pres.

★1337★
United Negro College Fund
Winston-Salem Office
310 W. 4th St., Ste. 724
Winston-Salem, NC 27101
Territory Includes: North Carolina.

★1338★
Winston-Salem Urban League
201 W. 5th St.
Winston-Salem, NC 27101 Phone: (919)725-5614
Gregory Bradsher, Interim Pres.
Affiliated with: National Urban League.

Ohio

★1339★
Afro-American Patrolman's League
1001 Indiana
Toledo, OH 43607
Marlon Shockley, Pres.
Affiliated with: National Black Police Association.

★1340★
Akron Alliance of Black School Educators
BOE 70 N. Broadway
Akron, OH 44308
Johnnette Curry, Pres.
Affiliated with: National Alliance of Black School Educators.

★1341★
Akron Association of Blacks in Communication
Box 80188
Akron, OH 44308 Phone: (216)996-3726
Cristal W. Walker, Pres.
Affiliated with: National Association of Black Journalists.

★1342★
Akron Barristers Club
75 E. Market St.
Akron, OH 44308 Phone: (419)867-9028
Orlando Williams, Pres.
Affiliated with: National Bar Association.

★1343★
Akron Community Service Center and Urban League
250 E. Market St.
Akron, OH 44308 Phone: (216)434-3101
Vernon L. Odom, Exec.Dir.
Affiliated with: National Urban League.

★1344★
American Association of Blacks in Energy
Cleveland Chapter
c/o Elizabeth J. Shaw
Centerior Energy Corp.
PO Box 94661
Cleveland, OH 44101-4661 Phone: (216)447-2823
Elizabeth J. Shaw, Pres.

★1345★
American Association of Blacks in Energy
Dayton Chapter
c/o James R. Greene III
Dayton Power & Light Co.
PO Box 8825
Dayton, OH 45401 Phone: (513)259-7114
James R. Greene III, Pres.

★1346★
American Civil Liberties Union
Ohio Affiliate
Cleveland Chapter
1223 W. 6th St., 2nd Fl.
Cleveland, OH 44113 Phone: (216)781-6276
Christine Link, Pres.

★1347★
Association for the Study of Afro-American Life and History
Cleveland Branch
3144 Albion Rd.
Shaker Heights, OH 44120 Phone: (216)921-2530
Gail Rose, Pres.

★1348★
Association for the Study of Afro-American Life and History
Columbus Branch
10581/2 Fair Ave.
Columbus, OH 43205 Phone: (614)252-4563
Floyd Goode, Pres.

★1349★
Association for the Study of Afro-American Life and History
Dayton Branch
1312 Princeton Dr.
Dayton, OH 45406 Phone: (513)274-8362
Margaret E. Peters, Pres.

★1350★
Association for the Study of Afro-American Life and History
Springfield Branch
424 Willow Dr.
Springfield, OH 45505-2521 Phone: (513)325-4040
Charles Beard, Pres.

★1351★
Association for the Study of Afro-American Life and History
Toledo Branch
c/o the Black Historical Society
1104 Mackow Dr.
Toledo, OH 43607 Phone: (419)531-3759
B. Jeanne Palmer, Treas.

★1352★
Association for the Study of Afro-American Life and History
Tri-County Branch
PO Box 382
Wilberforce, OH 45384 Phone: (513)427-1680
Dr. Joseph Lewis, Pres.

★1353★
Association of Black Psychologists
Central Ohio Chapter
PO Box 8451
Columbus, OH 43201 Phone: (614)292-5766
Dr. Dennis Alexander, Pres.

★1354★
Association of Black Psychologists
Cleveland Chapter
20310 Chagrin Blvd.
Shaker Heights, OH 44122 Phone: (216)491-9405
Dr. Willie Williams, Pres.

★1355★
Association of Black Psychologists
Dayton Chapter
4830 Old Hickory Pl.
Dayton, OH 46226 Phone: (513)837-3961
Dr. Michael Williams, Pres.

★1356★
B-FORCE of Cleveland
PO Box 12729
East Cleveland, OH 44112
Affiliated with: International Association of Black Professional Fire Fighters.

★1357★
Black Economic Union of Ohio
10510 Park Lane Dr.
Cleveland, OH 44106 Phone: (216)231-0080

★1358★
Black Elected Democrats of Ohio
37 W. Broad St., Ste. 430
Columbus, OH 43215 Phone: (614)341-6912
Ray Miller, Pres.

★1359★
Black Focus on the Westside
4115 Bridge Ave.
Cleveland, OH 44113 Phone: (216)631-7660
William Griffin, Exec.Dir.

★1360★
Black Knights Police Association
PO Box 2052
Youngstown, OH 44506
Louis Averhart, Pres.
Affiliated with: National Black Police Association.

★1361★
Black Law Enforcement Officers Association
1353 Copley Rd.
Akron, OH 44320
Odell Daniels, Pres.
Affiliated with: National Black Police Association.

★1362★
Black Lawyers Association of Cincinnati
230 E. 9th St., Ste. 200
Cincinnati, OH 45202 Phone: (513)352-4663
Ernest F. McAdams, Pres.
Affiliated with: National Bar Association.

★1363★
Black Shield Police Association
4087 E. 131st St.
Cleveland, OH 44105
Andre Haynesworth, Pres.
Affiliated with: National Black Police Association.

★1364★
Canton Black United Fund
1341 Market Ave., N.
Canton, OH 44714-2605
William Dent, Pres.
Affiliated with: National Black United Fund, Inc.

★1365★
Canton Urban League
Community Center
1400 Sherrick Rd. SE
Canton, OH 44707-3533 Phone: (216)456-3479
Joseph N. Smith, Exec.Dir.
Affiliated with: National Urban League.

★1366★
Cincinnati African-American Fire Fighters
PO Box 29441
Cincinnati, OH 45229
Affiliated with: International Association of Black Professional Fire Fighters.

★1367★
Cincinnati Association of Black Journalists
c/o Chet Fuller
WLWT-TV
140 W. 9th St.
Cincinnati, OH 45202 Phone: (513)352-5011
Chet Fuller, Pres.
Affiliated with: National Association of Black Journalists.

★1368★
Cincinnati Minority Business Development Center
113 W. 4th St., Ste. 600
Cincinnati, OH 45202 Phone: (513)381-4770

★1369★
Cleveland Association of Black Journalists
PO Box 5028
Cleveland, OH 44101 Phone: (216)529-1993
Eric D. Stringfellow, Pres.
Affiliated with: National Association of Black Journalists.

★1370★
Cleveland Business League
2330 E. 79th St.
PO Box 99556
Cleveland, OH 44199 Phone: (216)561-3800
R. Turner-Hickson, Pres.
Affiliated with: National Business League.

★1371★
Cleveland Heights Alliance of Black School Educators
PO Box 18134
Cleveland Hts., OH 44118
Margaret Peacock, Pres.
Affiliated with: National Alliance of Black School Educators.

★1372★
Cleveland Minority Business Development Center No. 1
601 Lakeside, Ste. 335
Cleveland, OH 44114 Phone: (216)664-4150

★1373★
Cleveland Minority Business Development Center No. 2
6200 Frank Rd. NW
Canton, OH 44720-7299 Phone: (216)494-6170

★1374★
Columbus Association of Black Journalists
Box 091123
Columbus, OH 43209 Phone: (614)292-7438
Lynda F. Callahan, Pres.
Affiliated with: National Association of Black Journalists.

★1375★
Columbus Urban League
700 Bryden Rd., Ste. 230
Columbus, OH 43215 Phone: (614)221-0544
Samuel Gresham Jr., Pres.
Affiliated with: National Urban League

★1376★
Council for Economic Opportunities in Greater Cleveland
668 Euclid Ave.
Cleveland, OH 44114 Phone: (216)696-9077

★1377★
Dayton Association of Black Professional Fire Fighters and Paramedics
141 Bank St.
Dayton, OH 45406
Affiliated with: International Association of Black Professional Fire Fighters.

★1378★
Dayton Urban League
United Way Bldg., Rm. 200
184 Salem Ave.
Dayton, OH 45406 Phone: (513)220-6666
Willie F. Walker, Pres.
Affiliated with: National Urban League.

★1379★
East Cleveland Black Police Officers Association
PO Box 12429
East Cleveland, OH 44112 Phone: (216)382-5672
Patricia A. Lane, Pres.
Affiliated with: National Black Police Association.

★1380★
Ebony Police Association of Stark County
377 Hamilton, NE
Canton, OH 44704
John C. Ball, Pres.
Affiliated with: National Black Police Association.

★1381★
Franklin County Alliance of Black School Educators
1850 Bryden Rd.
Columbus, OH 43205
Linda L. Gibson-Tyson, Pres.
Affiliated with: National Alliance of Black School Educators.

★1382★
Greater Cincinnati Alliance of Black School Educators
2133 Crave Ave.
Cincinnati, OH 43205
Dr. Obadiah Williams, Pres.
Affiliated with: National Alliance of Black School Educators.

★1383★
Greater Cleveland Minority Police Officers Association
1869 E. 86th St.
Cleveland, OH 44106
Cheryl M. Tell, Pres.
Affiliated with: National Black Police Association.

★1384★
Hamilton County Association for Minority Law Enforcement Officers
5355 Tompkins Ave., Apt. No. E-11
Cincinnati, OH 45227
Rudolph Stafford, Pres.
Affiliated with: National Black Police Association.

★1385★
Harambee Services to Black Families
1468 E. 55th St.
Cleveland, OH 44103 Phone: (216)391-7044
Iona Willis Hancock, Exec.Dir.

★1386★
Lorain County Alliance of Black School Educators
PO Box 745
Lorain, OH 44053
Deroy Gorham, Pres.
Affiliated with: National Alliance of Black School Educators.

★1387★
Lorain County Minority Law Enforcement Association
PO Box 1096
Lorain, OH 44052-0096
David Wrice, Pres.
Affiliated with: National Black Police Association.

★1388★
Lorain County Urban League
Robinson Bldg.
401 Broad St., Ste. 204-206
Elyria, OH 44035 Phone: (216)323-3364
Delbert L. Lancaster, Pres.
Affiliated with: National Urban League.

★1389★
Massillon Urban League
11 Lincoln Way, W., Ste. 2C
Massillon, OH 44647 Phone: (216)833-2804
Harold I. Glenn, Interim Pres.
Affiliated with: National Urban League.

★1390★
Metro Cleveland Alliance of Black School Educators
PO Box 1083
Shaker Heights, OH 44120
Dr. Shirley S. Seaton, Pres.
Affiliated with: National Alliance of Black School Educators.

★1391★
Minority Association of Cuyahoga County Corrections
3269 Berkshire Rd.
Cleveland Heights, OH 44118
Varno Harris, Pres.
Affiliated with: National Black Police Association.

★1392★
Minority Contracts Assistance Program
12000 Shaker Blvd.
Cleveland, OH 44120 Phone: (216)283-4700

★1393★
National Association of Minority Contractors
Dayton Chapter
1705 Guenther Rd.
Dayton, OH 45427 Phone: (513)854-0281
Warren Wise, Pres.

★1394★
National Association of Minority Contractors
Northern and Central Ohio Chapter
65 E. State St., Ste. 1000
Columbus, OH 43215 Phone: (614)460-3673
Kevin Williams, Pres.

★1395★
National Association of Minority Contractors
Southern Ohio Chapter
1939 Avonlea Ave.
Cincinnati, OH 45237 Phone: (513)351-2114
Sam Moore, Pres.

★1396★
National Black Child Development Institute
Akron Affiliate
c/o Mamie Gardner
Kandy Kane Day Care, Inc.
1310 Superior Ave.
Akron, OH 44307 Phone: (216)836-8009
Mamie Gardner, Pres.

★1397★
National Black Child Development Institute
Cleveland Affiliate
14748 Rider Rd.
Cleveland, OH 44021 Phone: (216)834-4581
Dorothy Cheeks, Pres.

★1398★
National Black Child Development Institute
Lorain Affiliate
PO Box 631
Lorain, OH 44052 Phone: (216)246-6359
Sylvia Duvall, Pres.

★1399★
National Black Independent Political Party
436 Almeda Ave.
Youngstown, OH 44505 Phone: (216)746-5747
Ron Daniels, Chair

★1400★
National Black MBA Association
Cincinnati Chapter
PO Box 3391
Cincinnati, OH 45201 Phone: (513)723-3448
Earl M. Pinkett III, Contact

★1401★
National Black MBA Association
Cleveland Chapter
PO Box 22839
Beachwood, OH 44122
Donald Graham, Contact

★1402★
National Black MBA Association
Dayton Chapter
PO Box 5697
Dayton, OH 45405
Jackie Thornton, Contact

★1403★
National Business League
Dayton Chapter
323 Salem Ave.
Dayton, OH 45406 Phone: (513)222-2889
Bill Littlejohn Esq., Pres.

★1404★
National Business League
Stark County Chapter
2442 14th St., NE
Canton, OH 44705 Phone: (216)454-8081
Norma Mills, Pres.

★1405★
Norman S. Minor Bar Association
8250 Wooster
Cincinnati, OH 45227 Phone: (216)241-6602
Clarence Keller, Pres.
Affiliated with: National Bar Association.

★1406★
Northwest Ohio Black Media Association
Box 9232
Toledo, OH 43697-9232 Phone: (419)245-6088
Clyde Hughes, Pres.
Affiliated with: National Association of Black Journalists.

★1407★
Operation PUSH
Akron Network
Tabernacle Baptist Church
795 Russell Ave.
Akron, OH 44307 Phone: (216)762-8810
Rev. Isiah Paul, Contact

★1408★
Operation PUSH
Cincinnati Chapter
5457 Ehrling Rd.
Cincinnati, OH 45227 Phone: (513)272-3631
Barbara Favors, Sec.

★1409★
Operation PUSH
Cleveland Chapter
8712 Quincy St.
Cleveland, OH 44106 Phone: (216)721-3585
Rev. Otis Moss, Pres.

★1410★
Operation PUSH
Columbus Chapter
7100 Huntly Rd.
Columbus, OH 43229 Phone: (614)431-1195
Linda Sanders, Sec.

★1411★
Operation PUSH
Shaker Heights Chapter
3646 Rollister Rd.
Shaker Heights, OH 44120 Phone: (216)921-0245
Alfred Warren, Pres.

★1412★
Operation PUSH
Springfield Network
1119 W. Liberty
Springfield, OH 45506 Phone: (513)325-0495
Craig Williams, Contact

★1413★
Operation PUSH
Wilberforce Chapter
Central State University
204 Administration Bldg.
Wilberforce, OH 45384 Phone: (513)376-6332
Dr. Arthur Thomas, Pres.

★1414★
Phillis Wheatley Association
4450 Cedar Ave.
Cleveland, OH 44103 Phone: (216)391-4443
Ela H. Becktor, Exec.Dir.

★1415★
Police Officers for Equal Rights
2445 Mason Village Ct.
Columbus, OH 43227
James E. Moss, Pres.
Affiliated with: National Black Police Association.

★1416★
Robert B. Elliot Law Club
c/o Attorney General's Office
65 E. St. No. 708
Columbus, OH 43215 Phone: (614)466-6696
Jenice R. Golson, Pres.
Affiliated with: National Bar Association.

★1417★
Sentinel Police Association
7942 Glen Orchard Dr.
Cincinnatti, OH 45237-1004
Michael Cureton, Pres.
Affiliated with: National Black Police Association.

★1418★
Springfield Area Alliance of Black School Educators
1119 W. Liberty Ave.
Springfield, OH 45506
Craig L. Williams, Pres.
Affiliated with: National Alliance of Black School Educators.

★1419★
Springfield Urban League
521 S. Center St.
Springfield, OH 45506 Phone: (513)323-4603
Donna Brino Ph.D., Interim Admin.
Affiliated with: National Urban League.

★1420★
Stonewall Cincinnati Human Rights Organization
Box 954
Cincinnati, OH 45201 Phone: (513)541-8778
Betsy Gressler, Pres.

★1421★
Thurgood Marshall Law Association
2700 Monroe, Ste. B
Toledo, OH 43606 Phone: (419)241-6282
Lafayette Tolliver, Pres.
Affiliated with: National Bar Association.

★1422★
Thurgood Marshall Law Society
City Hall Municipal Ct.
Dayton, OH 45402 Phone: (513)443-0812
Hon. Alice McCollum, Pres.
Affiliated with: National Bar Association.

★1423★
Unitarian Universalist Association Black Concerns Working Group
Ohio-Meadville Chapter
760 E. Broad St.
Columbus, OH 43205 Phone: (614)224-6688
Rev. Carol Brody, Consultant

★1424★
United Black Fire Fighters of Akron
1020 Winton St.
Akron, OH 44320
AFF International Association of Black Professional Fire Fighters.

★1425★
United Negro College Fund
Cleveland Office
25 W. Prospect
Cleveland, OH 44115 Phone: (216)781-8623
Territory Includes: Cleveland, Akron, Toledo, Ohio; All of West Virginia.

★1426★
United Negro College Fund
Columbus Office
50 W. Broad St., Ste. 1308
Columbus, OH 43215 Phone: (614)488-3222
Territory Includes: Columbus, Dayton, Cincinnati, Ohio; All of Kentucky; South Dakota.

★1427★
Urban League of Greater Cincinnati
2400 Reading Rd.
Cincinnati, OH 45202 Phone: (513)721-2237
Sheila J. Wilson, Exec.Dir.
Affiliated with: National Urban League.

★1428★
Urban League of Greater Cleveland
12001 Shaker Blvd.
Cleveland, OH 44120 Phone: (216)421-0999
Jacqulyn Shropshire, Interim Pres.
Affiliated with: National Urban League.

★1429★
Urban Minority Alcohol Drug Abuse Outreach Program
1323 W. 3rd St.
Dayton, OH 45407 Phone: (513)225-5556
Debra Styles, Prog. Dir.

★1430★
Urban Minority Alcoholism Outreach
2500 E. 61st St.
Cleveland, OH 44104 Phone: (216)881-5533

★1431★
Vanguards of Cleveland
PO Box 1802
Cleveland, OH 44106
Affiliated with: International Association of Black Professional Fire Fighters.

★1432★
Warren-Trumbull Urban League
290 W. Market St.
Warren, OH 44481 Phone: (216)394-4316
Marion V. Perkins, Pres.
Affiliated with: National Urban League.

★1433★
Youngstown Area Urban League
2516 Market St.
Youngstown, OH 44507 Phone: (216)788-6533
Stephen Pressley Jr., Pres.
Affiliated with: National Urban League.

Oklahoma

★1434★
American Association for Affirmative Action
Region VI
c/o Beth Wilson
University of Oklahoma
Norman, OK 73019 Phone: (405)325-3546
Beth Wilson, Dir.
Territory Includes: New Mexico, Texas, Louisiana, Arkansas, and Oklahoma.

★1435★
American Civil Liberties Union
Oklahoma Affiliate
1411 Classen, Ste. 318
Oklahoma City, OK 73106 Phone: (405)524-8511
Joann Bell, Pres.

★1436★
Federation of Colored Women's Clubs
Tulsa Chapter
c/o Fannie Bryant
1612 N. Boston
Tulsa, OK 74106 Phone: (918)584-1546
Fannie Bryant, Sec.

★1437★
Greenwood Chamber of Commerce
130 N. Greenwood Ave.
Tulsa, OK 74120 Phone: (918)585-2084
Alvarez Allen, Pres.

★1438★
Metropolitan Tulsa Urban League
240 E. Apache St.
Tulsa, OK 74106 Phone: (918)584-0001
Rev. Laverne Hill, Exec.Dir.
Affiliated with: National Urban League.

★1439★
National Business League
Oklahoma City Chapter
PO Box 11221
Oklahoma City, OK 73136 Phone: (405)843-6400
Anita Arnold, Pres.

★1440★
Northeast Oklahoma Black Lawyers Association
2400 First National Tower
Tulsa, OK 74103 Phone: (918)586-8562
Hannibal B. Johnson, Pres.
Affiliated with: National Bar Association.

★1441★
Oklahoma City Metro Area Black Officers Association
PO Box 1674
Oklahoma City, OK 73101-1674
J.W. Martin, Pres.
Affiliated with: National Black Police Association.

★1442★
Oklahoma City Metropolitan Alliance of Black School Educators
3468 Parker Dr.
Del City, OK 73135
Jesse Thompson, Pres.
Affiliated with: National Alliance of Black School Educators.

★1443★
Oklahoma City Minority Business Development Center
1500 NE 4th St. Ste. 101
Oklahoma City, OK 73117 Phone: (405)235-0430

★1444★
Operation PUSH
Oklahoma City Chapter
Jesus Church
2201 NE 15th St.
Oklahoma City, OK 73136 Phone: (405)424-3590
Rev. Clarence E. Davis

★1445★
Tulsa Area Alliance of Black School Educators
1164 N. Union Pl.
Tulsa, OK 74127
Fred Latimer, Pres.
Affiliated with: National Alliance of Black School Educators.

★1446★
Tulsa Black Officers Coalition
PO Box 1765
Tulsa, OK 74103
Affiliated with: National Black Police Association.

★1447★
Tulsa Minority Business Development Center
240 E. Apache St.
Tulsa, OK 74106 Phone: (918)592-1995

★1448★
Urban League of Greater Oklahoma City
3017 Martin Luther King Ave.
Oklahoma City, OK 73111 Phone: (405)424-5243
Leonard D. Benton, Pres.
Affiliated with: National Urban League.

Oregon

★1449★
American Association for Affirmative Action
Region X
c/o Stephanie Sanford
Oregon State Univ.
Corvallis, OR 97331 Phone: (503)737-3556
Stephanie Sanford, Dir.
Territory Includes: Washington, Oregon, Idaho, and Alaska.

★1450★
American Civil Liberties Union
Oregon Affiliate
705 Board of Trade Bldg.
310 SW 4th Ave.
Portland, OR 73106 Phone: (503)227-3186
Ms. Stevie Remington, Pres.

★1451★
Black United Fund of Oregon
PO Box 12406
Portland, OR 97212 Phone: (503)282-7973
Amina A. Anderson, Exec.Dir.
Affiliated with: National Black United Fund, Inc.

★1452★
National Association of Minority Contractors
Oregon Chapter
PO Box 11233
Portland, OR 97211 Phone: (503)260-9000
Bruce Broussard, Pres.

★1453★
National Business League
Oregon Chapter
3802 NE Union, Ste. 303
Portland, OR 97212 Phone: (503)249-0711
Chad Debnam, Pres.

★1454★
Oregon Alliance of Black School Educators
PO Box 6067
Portland, OR 97228-6067
Michael L. Grice, Pres.
Affiliated with: National Alliance of Black School Educators.

★1455★
Oxnard Minority Business Development Center
8959 SW Barbur Blvd., Ste. 102
Portland, OR 97219 Phone: (805)483-1123

★1456★
Portland Association of Black Journalists
c/o Ken Bodie
KOIN-TV
5005 NE Emerson Ct.
Portland, OR 97218 Phone: (503)464-0768
Ken Bodie, Pres.
Affiliated with: National Association of Black Journalists.

★1457★
Portland Black Firefighters Association
5630 NE Church St.
Portland, OR 97218
Affiliated with: International Association of Black Professional Fire Fighters.

★1458★
Urban League of Portland
Urban Plaza
10 N. Russell
Portland, OR 97227 Phone: (503)280-2600
Dr. Darryl Tukufu, Pres.
Affiliated with: National Urban League.

Pennsylvania

★1459★
Afro-American Automobile Association
5125 Walnut St.
Philadelphia, PA 19139 Phone: (215)472-4250

★1460★
American Association of Blacks in Energy
Philadelphia Chapter
c/o James Banko'le
Philadelphia Electric Co.
2301 Market St., 58-2
Philadelphia, PA 19146 Phone: (215)841-5675
James Banko'le, Pres.

★1461★
American Association of Blacks in Energy
Pittsburgh Chapter
c/o Sylvia Fields
Duquesne Light Co.
1 Oxford Center
301 Grant St.
Pittsburg, PA 15279 Phone: (412)393-6065
Sylvia Fields, Contact

★1462★
American Civil Liberties Union
Pennsylvania Affiliate
Philadelphia Chapter
PO Box 1161
Philadelphia, PA 19105 Phone: (215)923-4357
Deborah Leavy, Pres.

★1463★
American Civil Liberties Union
Pennsylvania Affiliate
Pittsburgh Chapter
237 Oakland Ave.
Pittsburgh, PA 15213 Phone: (412)681-7736
Marion Demick, Pres.

★1464★
Association for the Study of Afro-American Life and History
Philadelphia Branch
5403 Angora Terrace
Philadelphia, PA 19143 Phone: (215)748-6164
Othella R. Vaughn, Pres.

★1465★
Barristers Association of Philadelphia
4914 Chancellor St.
Philadelphia, PA 19139 Phone: (215)747-4254
Renee Cardwell Hughes, Pres.
Affiliated with: National Bar Association.

★1466★
Black Clergy of Philadelphia and Vicinity
5238 Chestnut
Philadelphia, PA 19139 Phone: (215)476-9111

★1467★
Black Family Services
115 S. 46th St.
Philadelphia, PA 19138 Phone: (215)662-0533

★1468★
Black United Fund of Pennsylvania
4601 Market St.
Philadelphia, PA 19139 Phone: (215)748-0150
Linda Richardson, Pres.
Affiliated with: National Black United Fund, Inc.

★1469★
Business and Professional Association of Pittsburgh
4909 Pennsylvania Ave.
Pittsburgh, PA 15224 Phone: (412)362-5702
Lewis Goodman, Pres.
Affiliated with: National Business League.

★1470★
Central Pennsylvania Association of Black Communicators
1912 Forster St.
Harrisburg, PA 17103 Phone: (717)232-7920
Affiliated with: National Association of Black Journalists.

★1471★
Delaware Valley Alliance of Black School Educators
5425 Wynnefield Ave.
Philadelphia, PA 19131-1323
Dr. Edna McCrae, Pres.
Affiliated with: National Alliance of Black School Educators.

★1472★
Fire Power
704 Ward St.
Chester, PA 19013
Affiliated with: International Association of Black Professional Fire Fighters.

★1473★
Garden State Association of Black Journalists
800 Trenton Rd., No. 95
Longhorne, PA 19047 Phone: (215)741-4673
Pamela E. Judge, Pres.
Affiliated with: National Business League.

★1474★
Greater Pittsburgh Alliance of Black School Educators
6393 Penn Ave., No. 128
Pittsburgh, PA 15206
Dr. Janet Bell, Pres.
Affiliated with: National Alliance of Black School Educators.

★1475★
Guardian Civic League
1516 W. Girard Ave.
Philadelphia, PA 19130
Ronald E. Oliver, Pres.
Affiliated with: National Black Police Association.

★1476★
Guardians of Greater Pittsburgh
PO Box 681
Pittsburgh, PA 15230
Donald G. Page, Pres.
Affiliated with: National Black Police Association.

★1477★
Harrisburg Black Attorneys Association
Harrisburg, PA
Angelique E. Weeks, Pres.
Efforts to locate an address for this edition were unsuccessful.
Affiliated with: National Bar Association.

★1478★
Homer S. Brown Law Association
c/o Horace Payne
People's National Gas Co.
625 Liberty Ave.
Pittsburgh, PA 15222 Phone: (412)497-6633
Horace Payne, Pres.
Affiliated with: National Bar Association.

★1479★
National Bar Association
Erie Chapter
925 French St., Ste. 3
Erie, PA 16501 Phone: (814)454-2139
Melvin T. Toran, Pres.

★1480★
National Black Child Development Institute
Pittsburgh Affiliate
c/o Dr. Joan Clark
Western Pennsylvania School for the Blind
201 Bellefield Ave.
Pittsburgh, PA 15213 Phone: (412)371-1461
Dr. Joan Clark, Pres.

★1481★
National Black MBA Association
Philadelphia Chapter
PO Box 1384
Philadelphia, PA 19105 Phone: (215)472-2622
Charlotte McKines, Contact

★1482★
National Black MBA Association
Pittsburgh Chapter
PO Box 3502
Pittsburgh, PA 15230
Kerry Nelson, Contact

★1483★
Negro Trade Union Leadership Council
929 N. Broad St.
Philadelphia, PA 19108 Phone: (215)787-3600

★1484★
New-Penn-Del Minority Business Resource Council
Monroe Office Center, Ste. 210
1 Winding Dr.
Philadelphia, PA 19131 Phone: (215)578-0964
Thornton Carroll Jr., Pres.

★1485★
Operation PUSH
Philadelphia Chapter
1204 Paper Mill Rd.
Philadelphia, PA 19118 Phone: (215)424-7855
Ima Jean Anderson, Contact

★1486★
Philadelphia Association of Black Journalists
c/o Vanessa Williams
The Philadelphia Inquirer
Philadelphia, PA 19131 Phone: (215)854-2786
Vanessa Williams, Pres.
Affiliated with: National Association of Black Journalists.

★1487★
Philadelphia Black Media Corporation
Temple University
12th & Berks St., Ste. 308
Philadelphia, PA 19122
Molefi Asante, Contact
Affiliated with: National Black Media Coalition.

★1488★
Philadelphia Black Women's Health Project
1415 N. Broad, Rm. 227-D
Philadelphia, PA 19122 Phone: (215)232-1115

★1489★
Philadelphia Federation of Black Business and Professional Organizations
9200 Bustleton Ave.
2112 Lloyd Bldg.
Philadelphia, PA 19115
Barbara C. Merriweather, Pres.

★1490★
Philadelphia Minority Business Development Center
801 Arch St.
Philadelphia, PA 19107 Phone: (215)629-9841

★1491★
Philadelphia Urban Coalition
121 N. Broad St., Ste. 618
Philadelphia, PA 19107 Phone: (215)977-2800

★1492★
Pittsburgh Minority Business Development Center
9 Pkwy. Center, Ste. 250
Pittsburgh, PA 15220 Phone: (412)921-1155

★1493★
Pittsburgh Regional Minority Purchasing Council
1 Oliver Plaza, Ste. 3004
Pittsburgh, PA 15222 Phone: (412)391-4423

★1494★
Squirrel Hill Urban Coalition
5604 Solway
Pittsburgh, PA 15217 Phone: (412)422-7666

★1495★
United Negro College Fund
Philadelphia Office
42 S. 15th St., Ste. 1610
Philadelphia, PA 19102
Territory Includes: Philadelphia, Harrisburg, and Wilkes-Barre, Pennsylvania; Delaware.

★1496★
United Negro College Fund
Pittsburgh Office
5907 Pennsylvania Ave., Ste. 212
Pittsburgh, PA 15206 Phone: (412)361-5300
Territory Includes: Pittsburgh, New Castle, Erie, Pennsylvania.

★1497★
Urban League of Lancaster County
502 S. Duke St.
Lancaster, PA 17602 Phone: (717)394-1966
Milton J. Bondurant, Pres.
Affiliated with: National Urban League.

★1498★
Urban League of Metropolitan Harrisburg
25 N. Front St.
Harrisburg, PA 17101 Phone: (717)234-5925
Kinneth W. Washington, Pres.
Affiliated with: National Urban League.

★1499★
Urban League of Philadelphia
4601 Market St., Ste. 25
Philadelphia, PA 19139 Phone: (215)476-4040
Robert W. Sorrell, Pres.
Affiliated with: National Urban League.

★1500★
Urban League of Pittsburgh
200 Ross St., 2nd Fl.
Pittsburgh, PA 15219 Phone: (412)261-1130
Leon L. Haley Ph.D., Pres.
Affiliated with: National Urban League.

★1501★
Urban League of Shenango Valley
39 Chestnut St.
Sharon, PA 16146 Phone: (412)981-5310
Phillip E. Smith, Pres.
Affiliated with: National Urban League.

★1502★
Valiants of Philadelphia
3021 N. 35th St.
Philadelphia, PA 19132
Affiliated with: International Association of Black Professional Fire Fighters.

Puerto Rico

★1503★
Mayaguez Minority Business Development Center
70 W. Mendez Bigo
Mayaguez, PR 00708 Phone: (809)833-7783

★1504★
Ponce Minority Business Development Center
19 Salud St.
Ponce, PR 00731 Phone: (809)840-8100

★1505★
San Juan Minority Business Development Center
207 O'Neill St.
San Juan, PR 00936 Phone: (809)753-8484

Rhode Island

★1506★
American Civil Liberties Union
Rhode Island Affiliate
212 Union St., Rm. 211
Providence, RI 02903 Phone: (401)831-7171
Steve Brown, Pres.

★1507★
Newport Martin Luther King Center
20 W. Broadway
Newport, RI 02840 Phone: (401)846-4828
Marcia G. Farrar, Exec.Dir.

★1508★
Rhode Island Black Media Coalition
131 Washington St.
Providence, RI 02903
Norman Lincoln, Contact
Affiliated with: National Black Media Coalition.

★1509★
Rhode Island Minority Police Association
950 Eddy St.
Providence, RI 02905
Joseph Almeida, Pres.
Affiliated with: National Black Police Association.

★1510★
Urban League of Rhode Island
246 Prairie Ave.
Providence, RI 02905 Phone: (401)351-5000
B. Jae Clanton, Pres.
Affiliated with: National Urban League.

South Carolina

★1511★
American Association of Blacks in Energy
South Carolina Chapter
c/o Vera Steplight Goodson
South Carolina Electric and Gas
PO Box 764
Columbia, SC 29218 Phone: (803)748-3868
Vera Steplight Goodson, Pres.

★1512★
American Civil Liberties Union
South Carolina Affiliate
Middleburg Plaza, Ste. 104
2712 Middleburg Dr.
Columbia, SC 29204 Phone: (803)799-5151
Steven Bates, Contact

★1513★
Association for the Study of Afro-American Life and History
Orangeburg Branch
781 Whitman St. SE
Orangeburg, SC 29116 Phone: (803)533-1049
Sarah M. Washington, Pres.

★1514★
Columbia Minority Business Development Center
2711 Middleburg Dr., Ste. 114
Columbia, SC 29204 Phone: (803)256-0528

★1515★
Columbia Urban League
1400 Barnwell St.
PO Drawer J
Columbia, SC 29250 Phone: (803)799-8150
James T. McLawhorn Jr., Pres.
Affiliated with: National Urban League

★1516★
Greenville/Spartanburg Minority Business Development Center
300 University Ridge, Ste. 200
Greenville, SC 29601 Phone: (803)271-8753

★1517★
Greenville Urban League
15 Regency Hill Dr.
PO Box 10161
Greenville, SC 29603 Phone: (803)244-3862
Myron F. Robinson, Pres.
Affiliated with: National Urban League.

★1518★
National Black Child Development Institute
Columbia Affiliate
324 Stamford Bridge Rd.
Columbia, SC 29212 Phone: (803)732-1206
Mona Bryant-Shanklin, Pres.

★1519★
Operation PUSH
Charleston Chapter
387 Sumter
Charleston, SC 29403 Phone: (803)556-3736
Rev. Fred Dawson, Pres.

★1520★
Operation PUSH
Marion County Network
Rt. 1, Box 410
Marion, SC 29571 Phone: (803)423-6874
Rev. Joseph Abram Jr.

★1521★
Palmetto State Law Enforcement Officers
PO Box 515
Summerville, SC 29484
Willie L. Johnson, Pres.
Affiliated with: National Black Police Association.

★1522★
Pendleton Foundation for Black History and Culture
PO Box 122
Pendleton, SC 29670 Phone: (803)646-3792
Annie Ruth Morse, Pres.

★1523★
South Carolina Alliance of Black School Educators
103 Bowling Ave.
Columbia, SC 29203
Lemuel C. Stevens, Pres.
Affiliated with: National Alliance of Black School Educators.

★1524★
South Carolina Black Lawyers Association
PO Box 8417
Columbia, SC 29202
Jeremiah Brown, Pres.
Affiliated with: National Bar Association.

★1525★
South Carolina Coastal Association of Black Journalists
c/o Herb Frazier
The News and Courier
134 Columbus St.
Charleston, SC 24903 Phone: (803)577-7111
Herb Frazier, Pres.
Affiliated with: National Association of Black Journalists.

Tennessee

★1526★
Afro-American Police Association
5348 Cosmos Cove
Memphis, TN 38118 Phone: (901)774-5404
Pauline Johnson, Pres.
Affiliated with: National Black Police Association.

★1527★
American Civil Liberties Union
Tennessee Affiliate
PO Box 120160
Nashville, TN 37212 Phone: (615)320-7142
Hedy Weinberg, Pres.

★1528★
Association for the Study of Afro-American Life and History
Rosa McGhee/F. A. Dixon Branch
3031 Wilcox Blvd.
Chattanooga, TN 37411 Phone: (615)266-3424
Rev. J. Lloyd Edwards Jr., Pres.

★1529★
Black Business Association
555 Beale St.
Memphis, TN 38114 Phone: (901)527-2222

★1530★
Brothers United of Chattanooga
3864 Mark Twain Cir.
Chattanooga, TN 37406
Affiliated with: International Association of Black Professional Fire Fighters.

★1531★
Chattanooga Area Urban League
730 Martin Luther King Blvd.
PO Box 11106
Chattanooga, TN 37401 Phone: (615)756-1762
Jerome W. Page, Pres.
Affiliated with: National Urban League.

★1532★
Clarksville Peace Officers Association
4 Chalemagne Blvd.
Clarksville, TN 37040
George F. Elliott, Pres.
Affiliated with: National Black Police Association.

★1533★
Knoxville Area Urban League
2416 Magnolia Ave.
PO Box 1911
Knoxville, TN 37901 Phone: (615)524-5511
Mark Brown, Pres.
Affiliated with: National Urban League.

★1534★
Memphis Alliance of Black School Educators
1844 Kingsview Dr.
Memphis, TN 38114
Dr. James O. Catchings, Pres.
Affiliated with: National Alliance of Black School Educators.

★1535★
Memphis Bar Association
140 Adams Ave.
Memphis, TN 38103 Phone: (901)527-3573

★1536★
Memphis Black Media Coalition
4796 Coventry Mall
Memphis, TN 38118
Gwen Sneed, Pres.
Affiliated with: National Black Media Coalition.

★1537★
Memphis Minority Business Development Center
5 M. 3rd St., Ste. 2000
Memphis, TN 38103 Phone: (901)527-2298

★1538★
Memphis Urban League
2279 Lamar Ave.
Memphis, TN 38114 Phone: (901)327-3591
Herman C. Ewing, Pres.
Affiliated with: National Urban League.

★1539★
Nashville Association of Minority Communicators
c/o Dwight Lewis
The Tennessean
1100 Broadway
Nashville, TN 37203 Phone: 800-351-1752
Dwight Lewis, Pres.
Affiliated with: National Association of Black Journalists.

★1540★
Nashville Bar Association
316 Stahlmar Bldg.
Nashville, TN 37201 Phone: (615)242-9272

★1541★
Nashville Minority Business Development Center
404 J. Robertson Pkwy., Ste. 207
Nashville, TN 37219 Phone: (615)255-0432

★1542★
Nashville Peace Officers Association
PO Box 100109
Nashville, TN 37224
Luther J. Hunter Jr., Pres.
Affiliated with: National Black Police Association.

★1543★
Nashville Urban League
1219 9th Ave.
Nashville, TN 37208 Phone: (615)254-0525
Joseph S. Carroll, Exec.Dir.
Affiliated with: National Urban League.

★1544★
National Bar Association
Ben F. Jones Chapter
60 N. Mid-America Mall, Ste. 200
Memphis, TN 38103 Phone: (901)527-4744
Samuel Perkins, Pres.

★1545★
National Bar Association
Napier/Looby Chapter
District Attorney's Office
402 Metro Courthouse
Nashville, TN 38103 Phone: (615)862-5500
Floyd N. Price, Pres.

★1546★
National Business League
Mid-South Chapter
918 South Pkwy., E.
Memphis, TN 38106 Phone: (901)942-4348
M. La Troy Williams, Pres.

★1547★
Operation PUSH
Chattanooga Chapter
PO Box 6221
Chattanooga, TN 37401 Phone: (615)267-6106
Rev. Virgil E. Caldwell, Chairman

★1548★
Operation PUSH
Memphis Chapter
Monumental Baptist Church
704 South Pkwy., E.
Memphis, TN 38106 Phone: (901)946-2529
Rev. Samuel B. Kyles, Pres.

★1549★
Operation PUSH
Nashville Chapter
Temple Baptist Church
3810 King's Ln.
Nashville, TN 37218 Phone: (615)876-4084
Rev. Michael Graves, Chairman

★1550★
Tennessee Black Caucus
209 War Memorial Bldg.
Nashville, TN 37219 Phone: (615)741-7140

Texas

★1551★
Afro-American Peace Officers Association
PO Box 943
Arlington, TX 76004
James Hawthorne, Pres.
Affiliated with: National Black Police Association.

★1552★
Afro American Police Officers League
4101 San Jacinto, Ste. 225
Houston, TX 77004 Phone: (713)522-2850
Mae Walker, Pres.
Affiliated with: National Black Police Association.

★1553★
American Association of Blacks in Energy
Houston Chapter
c/o Len Taylor
Houston Lighting & Power Co.
PO Box 1700
Houston, TX 77001 Phone: (713)229-7310
Len Taylor, Pres.

★1554★
American Civil Liberties Union
Texas Affiliate
Austin Chapter
1611 E. 1st St.
Austin, TX 78702-4455 Phone: (512)477-5849
Suzanne Donovan, Pres.

★1555★
American Civil Liberties Union
Texas Affiliate
Dallas Chapter
PO Box 215135
Dallas, TX 75221 Phone: (214)823-1555
Joe Cook, Pres.

★1556★
American Civil Liberties Union
Texas Affiliate
Houston Chapter
1236 W. Gray
Houston, TX 77019 Phone: (713)524-5925
Helen M. Gros, Pres.

★1557★
Association for the Study of Afro-American Life and History
Houston Branch
3213 Binz St.
Houston, TX 77004 Phone: (713)522-3264
Pearl C. Suel, Pres.

★1558★
Association of Black Psychologists
Dallas Chapter
3625 Cripple Creek Dr.
Dallas, TX 75224 Phone: (202)772-0808
Dr. Linda W. Watson, Pres.

★1559★
Austin Alliance of Black School Educators
6101 Highland Hills
Austin, TX 78731
Barbara Williams, Pres.
Affiliated with: National Alliance of Black School Educators.

★1560★
Austin Area Urban League
1825 E. 381/2 St.
Austin, TX 78722 Phone: (512)478-7176
Linda Moore Smith, Pres.
Affiliated with: National Urban League

★1561★
Austin Association of Black Communicators
c/o Roxanne J. Evans
The American Statesman
Box 670
Austin, TX 76704 Phone: (512)445-3655
Roxanne J. Evans, Pres.
Affiliated with: National Association of Black Journalists.

★1562★
Austin Black Lawyers Association
150 E. Riverside Dr., Ste. 501
Austin, TX 78704 Phone: (512)448-2911
Velva Price, Pres.
Affiliated with: National Bar Association.

★1563★
Austin Minority Business Development Center
301 Congress Ave., Ste. 1020
Austin, TX 78701 Phone: (512)476-9700

★1564★
Beaumont Minority Business Development Center
550 Fannin, Ste. 106A
Beaumont, TX 77701 Phone: (409)835-1377

★1565★
Black Fire Fighters Association of Dallas
1402 Corinth St., Ste. 113
Dallas, TX 75215
Affiliated with: International Association of Black Professional Fire Fighters.

★1566★
Black Registry
1223 A Rosewood Ave.
Austin, TX 78702 Phone: (512)476-0082

★1567★
Black United Fund of Houston
5151 Martin Luther King Blvd.
Houston, TX 77021 Phone: (713)644-1461
Cleo Glenn-Johnson, Pres.
Affiliated with: National Black United Fund, Inc. **Toll-free phone:** (800)332-BUFH.

★1568★
Black Voters for Republican Congress
2714 West Ave.
San Antonio, TX 78201 Phone: (512)340-2424

★1569★
Brownsville Minority Business Development Center
2100 Boca Chica, Ste. 301
Brownsville, TX 78521-2265 Phone: (512)887-7961

★1570★
Capitol City Chamber of Commerce
5407 N. IH 35, Ste. 304
Austin, TX 78723 Phone: (512)459-1181
Karen Box, Exec.Dir.

★1571★
Corpus Christi Minority Business Development Center
3649 Leopard, Ste. 301
Corpus Christi, TX 78404 Phone: (512)887-7961

★1572★
Dallas Alliance of Black School Educators
PO Box 710464
Dallas, TX 75371
Dr. Frederick D. Todd, Pres.
Affiliated with: National Alliance of Black School Educators.

★1573★
Dallas Black Chamber of Commerce
2838 Martin Luther King, Jr. Blvd.
Dallas, TX 75215 Phone: (214)421-5200
Tom Houston, Exec.Dir.

★1574★
Dallas Black Media Coalition
5807 S. Marsalrs St.
Dallas, TX 75241
George Brewer, Contact
Affiliated with: National Black Media Coalition.

★1575★
Dallas/Fort Worth Association of Black Communicators
c/o John McCaa
WFAA-TV
Communications Center
606 Young St.
Dallas, TX 75202-4810 Phone: (214)748-9631
John McCaa, Pres.
Affiliated with: National Association of Black Journalists.

★1576★
Dallas/Fort Worth Minority Business Development Center
1445 Ross Ave., Ste. 800
Dallas, TX 75202 Phone: (214)855-7373

★1577★
Dallas Urban League
2121 Main St., 4th Fl., Ste. 410
Dallas, TX 75201 Phone: (214)747-4734
Dr. Beverly K. Mitchell-Brooks, Exec.Dir.
Affiliated with: National Urban League.

★1578★
El Paso Minority Business Development Center
1312-A E. Rio Grande St.
El Paso, TX 79902 Phone: (915)544-2700

★1579★
Fort Worth Alliance of Black School Educators
324 Revere Dr.
Fort Worth, TX 76134
Affiliated with: National Alliance of Black School Educators.

★1580★
Fort Worth Black Bar Association
777 Main St., No. 890
Fort Worth, TX 76102-5304 Phone: (817)870-2027
Nelda F. Harris, Pres.
Affiliated with: National Bar Association.

★1581★
Fort Worth Black Fire Fighters
PO Box 19009
Fort Worth, TX 76119
Affiliated with: International Association of Black Professional Fire Fighters.

★1582★
Fort Worth Black Peace Officers Association
PO Box 15907
Fort Worth, TX 76119
Affiliated with: National Black Police Association.

★1583★
Fort Worth Metropolitan Black Chamber of Commerce
2914 E. Rosedale, Ste. 101
Fort Worth, TX 76105 Phone: (817)531-8510
Dezoyd Jennings, Chairman

★1584★
Houston Area Alliance of Black School Educators
PO Box 660
Houston, TX 77001-0660
Edward Cline, Pres.
Affiliated with: National Alliance of Black School Educators.

★1585★
Houston Area Urban League
3215 Fannin
Houston, TX 77004 Phone: (713)526-5127
Sylvia K. Brooks, Pres.
Affiliated with: National Urban League.

★1586★
Houston Black Firefighters Association
4101 San Jacinto St., Ste. 229
Houston, TX 77004 Phone: (713)528-7405
Affiliated with: International Association of Black Professional Fire Fighters.

★1587★
Houston Citizens Chamber of Commerce
2808 Wheeler
Houston, TX 77004 Phone: (713)522-9745
James Hagee, Pres.

★1588★
Houston Lawyers Association
2208 Blodgett St.
Mail Sta. 10, TCB 545
PO Box 2558
Houston, TX 77004-5218 Phone: (713)520-0260
U. Lawrence Boze, Pres.
Affiliated with: National Bar Association.

★1589★
Houston Minority Business Development Center
1200 Smith St., Ste. 2800
Houston, TX 77002 Phone: (713)650-3831

★1590★
J. L. Turner Legal Association
NCNB Oak Cliff Tower
400 S. Zang, 6th Fl.
Dallas, TX 75208 Phone: (214)941-1881
Royce B. West, Pres.
Affiliated with: National Bar Association.

★1591★
Laredo Minority Business Development Center
777 Calledelnorte No. 2
Laredo, TX 78401 Phone: (512)725-5177

★1592★
Lubbock/Midland-Odessa Minority Business Development Center
1220 Broadway, Ste. 509
Lubbock, TX 79401 Phone: (806)762-6232

★1593★
McAllen Minority Business Development Center
1701 W. Bus. Hwy. 83, Ste. 1108
McAllen, TX 78501 Phone: (512)687-5224

★1594★
Men of Color Together
PO 190611
Dallas, TX 72519

★1595★
Minority Assistance National Network
4317 K St.
Houston, TX 77051 Phone: (713)668-0440
Edward Lewis, Exec.Dir.

★1596★
Minority Business Association
625 E. 10th St., Ste. 800
Austin, TX 78701 Phone: (512)473-2606

★1597★
National Association of Minority Contractors Houston Chapter
PO Box 14611
Houston, TX 77221-4611 Phone: (713)661-4160
Edna I.B. Goodie, Pres.

★1598★
National Black Child Development Institute Dallas Affiliate
813 Ryan Rd.
Dallas, TX 75224 Phone: (214)375-8006
Sharon Harris, Pres.

★1599★
National Black Child Development Institute Houston Affiliate
8602 Allwood Ave.
Houston, TX 77016 Phone: (713)633-2752
Odessa Sayles, Pres.

★1600★
National Black MBA Association
Dallas Chapter
PO Box 797174
Dallas, TX 75374-7174 Phone: (214)558-1699
Loretta Barr, Contact

★1601★
National Black MBA Association
Houston Chapter
PO Box 56525
Houston, TX 77256
Arnita Gates, Contact

★1602★
National Business League
Austin Cen-Tex Chapter
2334 Rosewood
Austin, TX 78762 Phone: (512)476-3506
T.L. Wyatt, Pres.

★1603★
National Business League
Dallas Chapter
PO Box 11331
Dallas, TX 75223 Phone: (214)565-7827
Jasper Baccus, Pres.

★1604★
Odessa Black Chamber of Commerce
303 Curver St.
Odessa, TX 79761 Phone: (915)332-5812
Odel Crawford

★1605★
Operation PUSH
Austin Network
Grant Chapel AME Church
1190 Chicon St.
Austin, TX 78702 Phone: (512)472-2827
Rev. William Turner, Contact

★1606★
Operation PUSH
Dallas Chapter
3410 S. Polk St.
Dallas, TX 75224 Phone: (214)372-4543
Rev. E. K. Bailey, Contact

★1607★
Operation PUSH
Fort Worth Chapter
2900 Hunting Dr.
Fort Worth, TX 76119 Phone: (817)535-7861
Walter Day, State Coord.

★1608★
San Antonio Bar Association
Court House
San Antonio, TX Phone: (512)227-8322

★1609★
San Antonio Black Lawyers Association
PO Box 830294
San Antonio, TX 78283-0294 Phone: (512)225-3031
Lamont Jefferson, Pres.
Affiliated with: National Bar Association.

★1610★
San Antonio Black Police Officers Coalition
PO Box 1058
San Antonio, TX 78205
Samuel E. Moore, Pres.
Affiliated with: National Black Police Association.

★1611★
San Antonio Minority Business Development Center
UTSA, Hemisphere Tower
San Antonio, TX 78285 Phone: (512)224-1945

★1612★
Tarrant County Black Historical and Genealogical Society
1020 E. Humbolt
Fort Worth, TX 76104 Phone: (817)332-6049
Don Williams, Pres.

★1613★
Texarkana Black Chamber of Commerce
414 Texas Blvd.
Texarkana, TX 75501 Phone: (903)792-8931
Elridge Robertson, Exec.Vice-Pres.

★1614★
Texas Alliance of Black School Educators
PO Box 271392
Houston, TX 77277-1393
Joseph Drayton, Pres.
Affiliated with: National Alliance of Black School Educators.

★1615★
Texas Black State Troopers Association
PO Box 472524
Garland, TX 75047-2524
Affiliated with: National Black Police Association.

★1616★
Texas Peace Officers Association
PO Box 762353
Dallas, TX 75376-2353
James A. Allen, Pres.
Affiliated with: National Black Police Association.

★1617★
Unitarian Universalist Association Black Concerns Working Group
Southwest Chapter
6471 Waverly Way
Fort Worth, TX 76116 Phone: (817)733-4418
Rev. Dwight Brown, Dist. Exec.

★1618★
United Negro College Fund
Dallas Office
1140 Empire Central, Ste. 310
Dallas, TX 75247
Territory Includes: Dallas, Ft. Worth, Midland/Odessa, Amarillo, Wichita Falls, and Lubbock, Texas; Oklahoma.

★1619★
United Negro College Fund
Houston Office
Riviana Bldg., Ste. 910
2777 Allen Pkwy.
Houston, TX 77019 Phone: (512)224-1674
Territory Includes: Houston, San Antonio, Waco, Beaumont, Hawkins/Longview, Corpus Christi, Tyler, El Paso, Texas.

Utah

★1620★
American Civil Liberties Union
Utah Affiliate
Boston Bldg.
9 Exchange Pl., Ste. 701
Salt Lake City, UT 84111 Phone: (801)521-9289
Michele Parish, Pres.

★1621★
Salt Lake City Minority Business Development Center
350 E. 500 S., Ste. 101
Salt Lake City, UT 84111 Phone: (801)328-8181

★1622★
Utah Alliance of Black School Educators
815 Germaine
Murray, UT 84123
Joyce Gray, Pres.
Affiliated with: National Alliance of Black School Educators.

Vermont

★1623★
American Civil Liberties Union
Vermont Affiliate
100 State St.
Montepelier, VT 05601 Phone: (802)223-6304
Leslie Williams, Pres.

Virgin Islands

★1624★
Virgin Islands Minority Business Development Center
81-AB Princess Gade
St. Thomas, VI 00804 Phone: (809)774-7215

Virginia

★1625★
American Association for Affirmative Action
Region III
c/o Ruth C. Jones
Old Dominion University
Norfolk, VA 23529 Phone: (804)683-3141
Ruth C. Jones, Dir.
Territory Includes: Pennsylvania, West Virginia, Virginia, Maryland, Delaware, and the District of Columbia.

★1626★
American Civil Liberties Union
Virginia Affiliate
6 N. 6th St., Ste. 400
Richmond, VA 23219-2419 Phone: (804)644-8022
Kent Willis, Pres.

★1627★
Association for the Study of Afro-American Life and History
Louisa County Branch
Rte. 4, Box 62A
Louisa, VA 23093 Phone: (703)894-4818
Pearlie R. Askew, Pres.

★1628★
Black Fire Service Professionals of Alexandria
PO Box 25483
Alexandria, VA 22313-5483
Sam Parker, Pres.
Affiliated with: International Association of Black Professional Fire Fighters.

★1629★
Hampton Roads Black Media Professionals
c/o Barbara Clara
WVEC-TV
613 Woodif Ave.
Norfolk, VA 23510 Phone: (804)628-6200
Barbara Clara, Pres.
Affiliated with: National Association of Black Journalists.

★1630★
Housing Opportunities Made Equal
1220 W. Cary St.
Richmond, VA 23220 Phone: (804)648-0116
Constance K. Chamberlin, Exec.Dir.

★1631★
Metropolitan Business League
121 E. Marshall St.
Richmond, VA 23261 Phone: (804)649-7473
Neverett A. Eggleston Jr., Pres.
Affiliated with: National Business League.

★1632★
National Black Child Development Institute
Hampton Affiliate
c/o Bassette Elementary School
671 Bell St.
Hampton, VA 23661

★1633★
National Black Child Development Institute
Williamsburg Affiliate
109 Spring Rd.
Williamsburg, VA 23185 Phone: (804)229-8910
Dr. Elizabeth Morgan, Pres.

★1634★
Newport News Minority Business Development Center
6060 Jefferson Ave., Ste. 6016
Newport News, VA 23605 Phone: (804)245-8743

★1635★
Norfolk Minority Business Development Center
355 Crawford Pkwy., Ste. 608
Portsmouth, VA 23701 Phone: (804)399-0888

★1636★
Northern Virginia Urban League
908 King St., Ste. 302
Alexandria, VA 22314 Phone: (703)836-2858
George H. Lambert Jr., Pres.
Affiliated with: National Urban League.

★1637★
Nothern Virginia Alliance of Black School Educators
12057 Sugarland Valley Dr.
Herndon, VA 22070
Dr. Rudolph V. Wiggins, Pres.
Affiliated with: National Alliance of Black School Educators.

★1638★
Old Dominion Bar Association
2509 E. Broad St.
Richmond, VA 23223 Phone: (804)643-8401
Roger Gregory, Pres.
Affiliated with: National Bar Association.

★1639★
Operation PUSH
Triangle Network
4416 Forestburg Ln.
Triangle, VA 22172
Elsie Queen

★1640★
Progressive Fire Fighters of Fairfax County Virginia
PO Box 404
Fairfax, VA 22030
Affiliated with: International Association of Black Professional Fire Fighters.

★1641★
Richmond Black Police Officers Association
PO Box 27201
Richmond, VA 23261
Willie Jones, Pres.
Affiliated with: National Black Police Association.

★1642★
Richmond Urban League
101 E. Clay St.
Richmond, VA 23219 Phone: (804)649-8407
Randolph C. Kendall Jr., Pres.
Affiliated with: National Urban League.

★1643★
Southside Minority Business League
1781 Anchor Ave.
Petersburg, VA 23261 Phone: (804)649-7473
Bossie Bonner, Pres.
Affiliated with: National Business League.

★1644★
Tidewater Law Enforcement Officers
PO Box 2601
Norfolk, VA 23501
Phillip Sams, Pres.
Affiliated with: National Black Police Association.

★1645★
Tidewater Regional Minority Purchasing Council
142 W. York St., Ste. 611
Norfolk, VA 23510 Phone: (804)627-8471
Bernard Big, Exec.Dir.

★1646★
United Brotherhood Fire Fighters Assocation
PO Box 1734
Norfolk, VA 23501
Affiliated with: International Association of Black Professional Fire Fighters.

★1647★
United Negro College Fund
Richmond Office
1001 E. Main St., Ste. 725
Richmond, VA 23219
Territory Includes: Virginia.

★1648★
Urban League of Hampton Roads
Plume Center West
147 Granby St.
Norfolk, VA 23510 Phone: (804)627-0864
Mary L. Redd, Pres.
Affiliated with: National Urban League.

★1649★
Virginia Regional Minority Supplier Development Council
201 E. Franklin
Richmond, VA 23219 Phone: (804)780-2322
Adele Johnson-Crowley, Exec.Dir.

Washington

★1650★
Black Law Enforcement Association of Washington
PO Box 18493
Seattle, WA 98118
Bob Alexander, Contact
Affiliated with: National Black Police Association.

★1651★
Ethnic Heritage Council of the Pacific Northwest
3123 Eastlake Ave., E.
Seattle, WA 98102 Phone: (206)328-9204
Peter S. Davenport Jr., Exec.Dir.

★1652★
Loren Miller Bar Association
PO Box 4233
Seattle, WA 98104 Phone: (206)722-4061
Leah Cattrell, Pres.
Affiliated with: National Bar Association.

★1653★
Metropolitan Seattle Urban League
105 14th Ave.
Seattle, WA 98122 Phone: (206)461-3792
Rossalind Y. Woodhouse Ph.D., Pres.
Affiliated with: National Urban League.

★1654★
National Black Child Development Institute
Seattle Affiliate
PO Box 22483
Seattle, WA 98122 Phone: (206)723-6593
Yvonne Ervin-Carr, Pres.

★1655★
Port of Seattle Minority Fire Fighters Association
2400 S. 170th St.
Seattle, WA 98188
Affiliated with: International Association of Black Professional Fire Fighters.

★1656★
Seattle Association of Black Journalists
2700 4th Ave., No. 504
Seattle, WA 98121 Phone: (206)448-2208
Rhoda E. McKinney, Pres.
Affiliated with: National Association of Black Journalists.

★1657★
Seattle Black Fire Fighters Association
PO Box 22005
Seattle, WA 98118
Affiliated with: International Association of Black Professional Fire Fighters.

★1658★
Seattle Minority Business Development Center
155 NE 100th Ave., Ste. 401
Seattle, WA 98125 Phone: (206)525-5617

★1659★
Tacoma-Pierce County Business League
1321 S. K St.
PO Box 5076
Tacoma, WA 98405 Phone: (206)272-7498
Frank H. Russell, Pres.
Affiliated with: National Business League.

★1660★
Tacoma Urban League
2550 S. Yakima Ave.
Tacoma, WA 98405 Phone: (206)383-2006
Thomas Dixon, Pres.
Affiliated with: National Urban League.

★1661★
United Negro College Fund
Seattle Office
7 Valley St.
Seattle, WA 98109
Territory Includes: Washington; Montana; Idaho; Alaska; Oregon.

★1662★
Washington State Business League and Chamber of Commerce
PO Box 18528
Seattle, WA 98118 Phone: (206)859-8284
James L. McGhee, Pres.
Affiliated with: National Business League.

West Virginia

★1663★
American Civil Liberties Union
West Virginia Affiliate
PO Box 3952
Charleston, WV 25301 Phone: (304)755-5978

★1664★
Mountain State Bar Association
PO Box 5105
Charleston, WV 25302 Phone: (305)348-0546
Sharon Mullens Jr., Pres.
Affiliated with: National Bar Association.

★1665★
West Virginia Black Law Enforcement Officers United
22431/2 Oakridge Rd.
Charleston, WV 25311
Dallas Staples, Pres.
Affiliated with: National Black Police Association.

Wisconsin

★1666★
Alliance of Black Law Enforcement
3344 N. 39th St.
Milwaukee, WI 53216
Martha Brock, Pres.

★1667★
American Association for Affirmative Action
Region V
c/o Joseph R. Buchanan
Racine County Human Services
Racine, WI 53403 Phone: (414)636-3201
Joseph R. Buchanan, Dir.
Territory Includes: Minnesota, Wisconsin, Michigan, Ohio, Indiana, and Illinois.

★1668★
American Civil Liberties Union
Wisconsin Affiliate
207 E. Buffalo St., No. 325
Milwaukee, WI 53202 Phone: (414)272-4032
Eunice Edgar, Pres.

★1669★
Association for the Study of Afro-American Life and History
Clarence L. and Cleopatra Johnson Branch
3612 N. Rev. Martin Luther King Jr. Dr.
Milwaukee, WI 53212 Phone: (414)265-5300
William Rogers, Pres.

★1670★
League of Martin
PO Box 09628
Milwaukee, WI 53209
Harold Hampton, Pres.
Affiliated with: National Black Police Association.

★1671★
Madison Urban League
151 E. Gorham
Madison, WI 53703 Phone: (608)251-8550
Betty A. Franklin-Hammonds, Exec.Dir.
Affiliated with: National Urban League.

★1672★
Metro Milwaukee Alliance of Black School Educators
PO Box 12520
Milwaukee, WI 53212
Dr. Michael Smith, Pres.
Affiliated with: National Alliance of Black School Educators.

★1673★
Milwaukee Bar Association
605 E. Wisconson Ave.
Milwaukee, WI 53202 Phone: (414)274-6760

★1674★
Milwaukee Black Fire Fighters
6162 N. 35th St., No. 10
Milwaukee, WI 53209
Affiliated with: International Association of Black Professional Fire Fighters.

★1675★
Milwaukee Minority Business Development Center
3929 N. Humboltd Blvd.
Milwaukee, WI 53212 Phone: (414)272-8300

★1676★
Milwaukee Minority Chamber of Commerce
2821 4th St. N., Ste. 302
Milwaukee, WI 53212
J. Paul Jordan, Contact

★1677★
Milwaukee Urban League
2800 W. Wright St.
Milwaukee, WI 53210 Phone: (414)374-5850
Jacqueline J. Patterson, Pres.
Affiliated with: National Urban League.

★1678★
Operation PUSH
Milwaukee Chapter
6985 N. Darien St.
Milwaukee, WI 53209 Phone: (414)447-6644
Rev. Floyd Taylor, Contact

★1679★
Project Equality of Wisconsin
1442 N. Farwell Ave., Ste. 210
Milwaukee, WI 53202 Phone: (414)272-2642
Betty J. Thompson, Exec.Dir.

★1680★
United Negro College Fund
Milwaukee Office
152 W. Wisconsin Ave., Ste. 515
Milwaukee, WI 53203 Phone: (414)277-0330
Territory Includes: All of Wisconsin.

★1681★
Urban League of Racine and Kenosha
718-22 N. Memorial Dr.
Racine, WI 53404 Phone: (414)637-8532
Rodney Brooks, Pres.
Affiliated with: National Urban League.

★1682★
Wisconsin Association of Minority Attorneys
845 N. 11th St.
Milwaukee, WI 53233 Phone: (414)271-8860
Celia M. Jackson, Pres.
Affiliated with: National Bar Association.

Wyoming

★1683★
American Civil Liberties Union
Wyoming Affiliate
PO Box A
Laramie, WY 82070 Phone: (307)742-0945
Laurie Seidenberg, Pres.

(3) RELIGIOUS ORGANIZATIONS

Entries in this chapter are arranged alphabetically by organization name. See the User's Guide at the front of this directory for additional information.

★1684★
African Methodist Episcopal Church
500 8th Ave., S., Ste. 201
Nashville, TN 37203

A short time after the founding of the Methodist Episcopal Church in 1784, friction developed between the Blacks and the Whites of St. George's Church in Philadelphia. The situation was intensified by the erection of a gallery to which the Blacks were relegated. The long-standing grievances came to a head on a Sunday morning in November 1787, when Whites tried to pull several Blacks from their knees at the altar rail. Richard Allen led the group of Blacks out of the church, and they formed a church of their own.

Allen was a former slave whose master had been converted by Freeborn Garrettson (a Methodist preacher). His master allowed Allen to buy his freedom. As a freeman he became a prosperous businessman and a licensed Methodist preacher. After leaving St. George's, Allen purchased an abandoned Blacksmith shop, and in 1744 Methodist Bishop Francis Asbury dedicated it as Bethel Church. In 1799 Allen was ordained a deacon, the first Black so honored.

Differences continued between the leaders of Allen's Bethel Church and St. George's. The former wished to be independent but with a nominal relation to the Methodists. Finally, in 1816, the issues were settled in a court suit when Bethel was granted full independence.

In Baltimore, Blacks at the two White churches formed an independent Colored Methodist Society after they had been put in galleries and not allowed to take communion until after the Whites. In 1801 Daniel Coke arrived in Baltimore and took over the leadership of the Society. Through his work an independent Methodist Church, also named Bethel, was formed. A call was issued in 1816 for a national meeting of Black Methodists for the purpose of forming an African Methodist Episcopal (AME) Church. The *Discipline*, *Articles of Religion*, and *General Rules of the Methodist Episcopal Church* were adopted, and Richard Allen was elected bishop. The AME Church remains close in doctrine, practice and polity to the United Methodist Church, the successor to the Methodist Episcopal Church, with whom it has engaged in some serious merger conversations.

Growth in the church throughout the North and Midwest was steady through 1865. After the Civil War a rapid expansion throughout the South occurred, and conferences were established across the territory of the former confederacy.

A missionary imperative was an early part of African Methodist concern, and in 1827 Scipio Bean was ordained as an elder and sent to Haiti. From that small beginning (and slow growth due to lack of funds), a twentieth-century mission program has emerged with stations in Africa, South America, and the West Indies. The primary work is with other people of African descent.

Publishing was seen as an integral part of the evangelistic, missionary and cultural life of the church from the beginning, and the items published by this church have had a major impact on the Black community. The AME Book Concern was the first publishing house owned and operated by Black people in America. *The Christian Recorder*, a newspaper begun as *The Christian Herald*, published continuously since 1841, is the oldest Black periodical in the world; *The AME Review*, started in 1883, is the oldest magazine published by Black people in the world. Education joined publishing as an early concern, and the first AME affiliated college, Wilberforce University, was established in 1856. Educational concerns have been carried to the mission field as well, and the church has established a number of schools from the primary grades through college for its African membership. West Africa Seminary was founded in Sierre Leone.

The church is governed episcopally. An international general conference meets quadrennially. The church is divided into 18 episcopal districts. Districts 1 through 13 oversee work in the United States, Canada, and Bermuda. The remaining districts oversee foreign work in 20 African countries, Jamaica, Haiti, the Dominican Republic, the Virgin Islands, the Windward Island, Guyana, and Surinam.

The church is a member of both the National Council of Churches and the World Council of Churches. Affiliated congregations in Barbados and the Caribbean are members of the Caribbean Conference of Churches.

★1685★
African Methodist Episcopal Zion Church
Box 32843
Charlotte, NC 28232

In the late 1790s a movement for independence among New York Blacks was begun when a group petitioned Bishop Francis Asbury, the first bishop of the Methodist Episcopal Church, to let them hold separate meetings. They complained of not being allowed to preach or join the conference and itinerate. Asbury granted the request, and meetings were held immediately. In 1801 a charter was drawn up for the "African Methodist Episcopal Church (called Zion Church) of the City of New York." It was to be supplied with a minister from the White John's Street Church. Zion Church was thus assured of regular preaching and the sacraments.

In 1813 Zion Church split and Asbury Church was formed as a second Black Methodist congregation. Both churches were being served by William Stillwell of John's Street Church in 1820, when Stillwell left the Methodist Episcopal Church with about 300 White members. Blacks, afraid of losing their property to the Methodist Episcopal Church, separated themselves from John's Street Church. They also voted not to join the African Methodist Episcopal Church. Several independent Black churches in New Haven and Philadelphia petitioned them for ministers. A *Discipline*, based upon the one of the Methodist Episcopal Church, was drawn up.

Several attempts at reconciliation were made, the most important being a petition to establish the several Black congregations as an annual conference within the Methodist Episcopal Church. This request was refused, and the African Methodist Episcopal Zion (AMEZ) Church emerged. Ordination was accepted from William Stillwell, and in 1822 James Varick was elected the first superintendent.

Doctrinally, the AMEZ Church accepts the Twenty-five Articles of Religion common to Methodists and has an episcopal polity similar to the Methodist Episcopal Church. Church boards implement programs of the quadrennial General Conference. The Publishing House and Book Concern are located in the headquarters complex in Charlotte, North Carolina, and publish a complete line of church school material. The church is a member of both the National Council of Churches and the World Council of Churches.

★1686★
African Orthodox Church
122 W. 129th St.
New York, NY 10027

The Protestant Episcopal Church, like all American denominations with both episcopal leadership and a significant Black membership, faced the problems and pressures related to electing and elevating their first Black member to the bishopric. Within the Episcopal Church the cries for a bishop drawn from among Black members grew even louder after the Civil War. They were refused, the leadership arguing that, since the church did not recognize racial distinctions, it could not elevate a man to the bishopric just because he was Black. A step toward the solution came in 1910 with the creation of Black "suffragan" bishops, bishops without right to succession and without vote in the house of bishops. Among those who complained that suffragans were not enough was Dr. George A. McGuire (1866-1934), an Episcopal priest who had emigrated from the West Indies. In 1921 he left the Protestant Episcopal Church and founded the Independent Episcopal Church. McGuire had had a distinguished career in the Episcopal Church, serving parishes in both the United States and Antigua, and he had been considered for the post of Suffragan Bishop of Arkansas. He declined in order to study medicine at Jefferson Medical College, where he graduated as a Doctor of Medicine in 1910. Upon graduation, he served at St. Bartholomew's Episcopal Church in Cambridge, Massachusetts. He was then called to be the Secretary of the Commission for Work among the Colored People under the Church's Board of Missions.
After several years as Secretary, he moved back to Antigua, where he remained for six years building the church where he was baptized, St. Paul's in Sweets. When fellow West Indian Marcus Garvey formed the United Negro Improvement Association, McGuire returned to the United States to support him. Working with Garvey only strengthened his dissatisfaction in serving a church where Black people were systematically denied positions of leadership, and he became determined to pursue an independent course.
On September 2, 1921, in the Church of the Good Shepherd in New York City, a meeting of independent Black clergy resolved itself into the first Synod of the African Orthodox Church, and designated McGuire as its bishop elect. The Synod then entered into negotiations with the Russian Orthodox Church in America in their search for episcopal orders for their newly elected bishop. The Russians indicated a willingness to consecrate McGuire, but only if they controlled the newly created jurisdiction. The idea of non-Black control had no appeal to either McGuire or his followers. They then turned to the American Catholic Church, headed by Archbishop Joseph Rene Vilatte. Vilatte was willing to confer orders and ask little or nothing in the way of control. On September 29, 1921, Bishop Vilatte, assisted by Carl A. Nybladh, consecrated Dr. McGuire in the Church of Our Lady of Good Death in Chicago.
The Church experienced slow but steady growth, although most of the individual congregations were small. The priests were seldom full-time clergy, although every church was encouraged to contribute something to their support. McGuire emphasized education and led in the organization of a seminary for the training of clergy. The first class numbered fourteen men. The school provided professional training for its students, while accommodating to the generally lower educational level of its applicants. It has not tried to become an accredited degree-granting institution.
Archbishop McGuire led the Church until his death in 1923, and it enjoyed peace and stability. After his death the leadership of the church fell into the hands of Archbishop W.E.J. Robertson. Shortly after his elevation to the archbishopric, dissatisfaction arose among the group of clergy, and a schism, the Holy African Church was created. The dissidents were led by Bishop R.G. Barrow, who had been McGuire's closest associate. In time, Barrow was succeeded by Bishop F.A. Toote and then Bishop Gladstone St. Claire Nurse. Bishop Nurse led the efforts to reunite the two factions. On February 22, 1964, the two bodies joined together under Robertson, who adopted the Patriarchal name of Peter IV. Just prior to the merger he consecrated several bishops, an obvious effort to insure his continued control of the Church. Nurse did not protest Robertson's action, and upon the death of the Patriarch was elected by the bishops to be the new primate of the Church. He quickly brought all the elements of the Church together and upon his death, leadership passed very easily to Archbishop William R. Miller, who served as the Church's Primate from 1976 until August of 1981. At the Annual Synod of the Church, he resigned and was succeeded by Archbishop Stafford J. Sweeting.
The denomination remains small in the United States, but it has affiliated parishes in the West Indies and Africa (Nigeria, Ghana, and Uganda). Recently, the Church lost one of its strongest parishes when Bishop G. Duncan Hinkson of Chicago left to found the African Orthodox Church of the West.

★1687★
African Orthodox Church of the West
c/o Most Rev. G. Duncan Hinkson
St. Augustine's African Orthodox Church
5831 S. Indiana St.
Chicago, IL 60637

In 1984 Bishop G. Duncan Hinkson, a physician and pastor of St. Augustine's African Orthodox Church, on the southside of Chicago, left the African Orthodox Church and formed a new jurisdiction. While following the teachings and ritual of its parent body, it is administratively independent. Bishop Hinkson consecrated Bishop Franzo King to lead work in San Francisco.

★1688★
African Union First Colored Methodist Protestant Church
602 Spruce St.
Wilmington, DE 19801

The origins of the African Union First Colored Methodist Protestant Church can be traced to 1813 and the formation of the Union Church of Africans, an event that present-day church leaders point to with pride. The Union Church of Africans was the first church in the United States to be originally organized by and afterward wholly under the care of Black people.
The Union Church of Africans began in a series of disputes in the Asbury Methodist Episcopal Church, a congregation in Wilmington, Delaware. In 1905, Black members under the leadership of Peter Spencer (1782-1843) and William Anderson (d. 1843) withdrew from what had been an integrated congregation, formed an all Black congregation, Ezion Church, and erected a building. They cited as reasons for their departure the denial of religious privileges and lack of freedom in exercising their "spiritual gifts." The Black members had been segregated in a balcony and made to take communion after White members.
While breaking with the local congregation, Ezion was still a part of the predominantly White Methodist Episcopal Church. However, in 1912, a conflict arose with the White minister who had been assigned to preach to both Wilmington's congregations. The conflict resulted in the minister's dismissing all of Ezion's trustees and class leaders. That action led to a court dispute that ended when the Black members withdrew from the church. In 1913, they reorganized independently and elected Spencer and Anderson as their ministers. By 1837, there were 21 congregations.
In the generation after Spencer and Anderson, two events were most important. First, in 1850, a major schism occurred when a group arose in the Union Church that demanded the adoption of an episcopal polity. That group left to found the Union American Methodist Episcopal Church. The Union Church of Africans emerged from this struggle as the African Union Church. Then, after the Civil War, the church merged with the First Colored Methodist Protestant Church to form the present African Union First Colored Methodist Protestant Church.
The First Colored Methodist Protestant Church was formed about 1840 when members of the African Methodist Episcopal Chruch rejected episcopal leadership and reorganized along the principles of the Methodist Protestant Church, which included no episcopacy and lay representation of local preachers at the general conference. Since the Methodist Protestant Church was very similar to the African Union Church, they united in 1866.
The church accepts the commonly held articles of religion of United Methodism, but it has attached the Apostles' Creed as the first article and deleted the article on "The Rulers of the United States." It has made a few changes in wording, for example, adding the words "and women" to the article on "The Church," which now reads, "The visible church is a congregation of faithful men and women."
The church is organized congregationally. Congregations are grouped into three districts: the Middle District, which includes New Jersey, Pennsylvania, New York, Delaware, and Canada; the Maryland District , which includes Maryland, the District of Columbia, Virginia, and all states south and southwest of Maryland; and the Southern and Western

Missionary District, which includes all the southern and western states. A general conference meets quadrennially.
In 1966, the church moved to replace the titles of general president and general vice president, the two offices elected by the General Conference, with that of senior bishop and junior bishop. In 1971, the office of presiding elder of the combined districts of the church was created, and a second presiding elder was named in 1979.
There is no foreign mission work, and the home mission work is primarily the providence of the women.

★1689★
African Universal Church

Efforts to locate an address for this edition were unsuccessful. The African Universal Church was established in 1927 in Jacksonville, Florida, by Archbishop Clarence C. Addison. The movement which became the African Universal Church was founded in the Gold Coast, West Africa, by a number of tribal chiefs. Among the leaders was Laura Adanka Kauffey, a Christian and daughter-in-law of an African king. Unfortunately, Princess Kauffey was assassinated in 1928 in Miami.
The church is Pentecostal, but believes in four experiences: justification, sanctification, baptism of the Holy Ghost, and baptism with fire. The baptism of the Holy Ghost is for the sanctified. The baptism with fire is seen as a "definite Scriptural experience, obtainable by faith on the part of the Spirit-filled believer." The church also believes in healing and the Second Coming. The church does not baptize with water nor does it use wine in the Lord's Supper.
A subsidiary of the African Universal Church is the Commercial League Corporation formed in 1934. It operates as an insurance company for members and pastors. Its motto, printed on all church literature, is, "You need our protection; we need your cooperation; we protect our members financially as well as spiritually." The League has been an expression of Black nationalism, which Addison constantly preached. He opposed both "civil rights" and integration, but believed in a Black nation in Africa. His anti-integration position made him a popular speaker for conservative White groups such as the Congress of Christian States of America.
The polity of the church is episcopal. There is a general assembly which meets every four years. The church is divided into state districts headed by overseers. Parish mothers (deaconesses) are organized under a senior mother and district mothers.

★1690★
The Afro-American Social Research Association

Efforts to locate an address for this edition were unsuccessful. The Afro-American Social Research Asociation was formed by a Black man who has taken the religious name, The Spirit of Truth. In the 1970s he began to receive messages from the Creator, many of which were incorporated into a book entitled *"The Spirit of Truth." Doom Days!*. The content of the messages was a word of warning and judgment, an important aspect of which was the necessity of doing away with the monetary system. According to The Spirit of Truth, the earth was given as a divine inheritance, but in time the wicked took control of everyone's divine inheritance, the monetary system being a tool in that takeover. He has predicted an astronomic catastrophy in the near future in which a comet will strike the moon which will in turn strike the sun. The earth will then move out of orbit and take a new position in the center of the universe. Most of earth's people will be destroyed in the process and a new world system, the United Countries of the Solar System, will then be established. The New Jerusalem will be built upon the exact spot where the first Jerusalem was built.

★1691★
Ahmadiyya Anjuman Ishaat Islam, Lahore, Inc.

Efforts to locate an address for this edition were unsuccessful. Following the death of Mirza Ghulam Hazrat Ahmad (1835-1908), founder of the Ahmadiyya Movement in Islam, a disagreement arose among his followers concerning the founder's status. Those who followed Ahmad's family proclaimed him a prophet. However, others, led by Maulawi Muhammad Ali, considered Ahmad the Promised Messiah and the greatest *mujaddid*, i.e., renewer of Islam, but denied that Ahmad had ever claimed the special status of "prophet." Ali asserted that Ahmad's use of that term was entirely allegorical. The claim of prophethood for Ahmad has resulted in the assignment of Ahmadiyya Muslims to a status outside of the Muslim community and resulted in their persecution in several Muslim-dominated countries.
Members of the Ahmadiyya branch founded by Ali came to America in the 1970s and incorporated in California.

★1692★
Ahmadiyya Movement in Islam
2141 Leroy Pl., NW
Washington, DC 20008

The Ahmadiyya movement was not brought to the United States with the intention of its becoming a Black man's religion. Ahmadiyya originated in India in 1889 as a Muslim reform movement. It differs from orthodox Islam in that it believes that Hazrat Mirza Ghulam Ahmad (1835-1908) was the promised Messiah, the coming one of all the major faiths of the world. It has, in the years since its founding, developed the most aggressive missionary program in Islam.
Ahmad had concluded, as a result of his studies, that Islam was in a decline and that he had been appointed by Allah to demonstrate its truth, which he began doing by authoring a massive book, *Barahin-i-Ahmaditah*. He assumed the title of *mujaddid*, the renewer of faith for the present age, and declared himself both Madhi, the expected returning savior of Muslims, and the Promised Messiah of Christians. He advocated the view that Jesus had not died on the cross, but had come to Kashmir in his later life and died a normal death there. The second coming is not of a resurrected Jesus, but the appearance of one who bore the power and spirit of Jesus.
Ahmadiyya came to the United States in 1921 and the first center was in Chicago. Its founder, Dr. Mufti Muhammad Sadiq began to publish a periodical, *Muslim Sunrise*. While recruiting some members from among immigrants, the overwhelming majority of converts consisted of Blacks. Only since the repeal of the Asian Exclusion Act in 1965 and the resultant emigration of large numbers of Indian and Pakistani nationals has the movement developed a significant Asian constituency in the United States.
A vast missionary literature demonstrating Islam's superiority to Christianity has been produced. Jesus is widely discussed. He is viewed as a great prophet. He only swooned on the cross. He escaped from the tomb to India and continued many years of ministry. He is buried at Srinagar, India, where the legendary Tomb of Issa (Jesus) is a popular pilgrimage site. The denial of the divinity of Jesus is in line with the assertion of Allah as the one true God. Christianity is seen as tritheistic.
At present, the movement is small. Headquarters were moved to Washington, D.C., in 1950 after a quarter century in Chicago.

★1693★
Alpha and Omega Pentecostal Church of God of America, Inc.
3023 Clifton Ave.
Baltimore, MD 21216

The Alpha and Omega Pentecostal Church of God of America, Inc., was formed in 1945 by the Rev. Magdalene Mabe Phillips, who withdrew from the United Holy Church of America and, with others, organized the Alpha and Omega Church of God Tabernacles, soon changed to the present name. Like the Church of God (Cleveland, Tennessee), the church's doctrine reserves the baptism of The Holy Spirit for the sanctified.

★1694★
American Catholic Church (Syro-Antiochean)

Efforts to locate an address for this edition were unsuccessful. In the late 1930s, Archbishop Daniel C. Hinton, the third primate of the American Catholic Church, resigned in favor of Bishop Percy Wise Clarkson. Clarkson was the founder-pastor of the jurisdiction's most

successful parishes in Laguna Beach, California. However, he had strong theosophical leanings, and strengthened the tendency to move the American Catholic Church into theological alignment with the Liberal Catholic Church. Among those who strongly opposed the direction in which Clarkson was leading was Ernest Leopold Peterson (d. 1959), a Black man who had been consecrated in 1927 by the former primate, Archbishop Frederick E. J. Lloyd. Peterson authored the liturgy used by the church prior to Clarkson's leadership.
Peterson withdrew from Clarkson's jurisdiction and formed the American Catholic Church (Syro-Antiochean), which continued in the faith and practice of the American Catholic Church. In 1950, Peterson consecrated Herbert F. Wilkie, who succeeded as primate in 1959.

★1695★
American Muslim Mission
7330 S. Stony Island
Chicago, IL 60649

Though there are a variety of Muslim groups functioning within the Black community, when one reads in the media or hears mention of "Black Muslims," the most likely reference is to the Nation of Islam, founded by Master Wallace Fard Muhammad and headed for many years by its purported prophet, Elijah Muhammad (1897-1975). After Elijah Muhammad's death the organization's name was changed successively to the World Community of Islam in the West and in 1980 the American Muslim Mission. It is the most successful of the Black Muslim bodies, having spread across the nation in the 1960s during the period of the Black revolution. Its success and that of one dissident member, Malcolm X, led to numerous books and articles about it.
Following the death of Noble Drew Ali, founder of the Moorish Science Temple of America, there appeared in Detroit one W.D. Fard, a mysterious figure claiming to be Noble Drew Ali reincarnated. He proclaimed that he had been sent from Mecca to secure freedom, justice and equality for his uncle (the Negroes) living in the wilderness of North America, surrounded and robbed by the cave man. (The White man was also referred to as the "Caucasian devil" and "Satan.") He established a temple in 1930 in Detroit. Among his many converts was Elijah Poole.
The 1930's were a time of intense recruiting activity and dispute with the Nation of Islam. Within Fard's ranks discussion focused on his divinity, legitimacy and role. In 1934, a second temple was founded in Chicago, and the following year Fard dropped from sight. By this time, Poole, known as Elijah Muhammad, had risen to leadership.
Under Elijah Muhammad's leadership the Black Muslims emerged as a strong, cohesive unit. Growth was slow, due in part to Muhammad's imprisonment during World War II as a conscientious objector. As the new prophet, he composed the authoritative *Message to the Blackman in America*, a summary statement of the Nation of Islam's position. The central teaching of the Nation of Islam can be seen as a more sophisticated version of the Moorish Science study of the Black man's history. According to Muhammad, Yakub, a mad Black scientist, created the White beast, who was then permitted by Allah to reign for six thousand years. That period was over in 1914. Thus the twentieth century is the time for the Nation of Islam to regroup and regain an ascendant position.
Education, economics, and political aspirations were major aspects of the Muslim program. The first University of Islam was opened in 1932, and parochial education (many of the schools being named for Clara Muhammad, Elijah Muhammad's wife) has been a growing and more effective part of the Nation ever since. Besides the common curriculum, Black Muslim history, Islam and Arabic have been stressed. Classes are offered through the twelfth grade. Economically, the Muslims have stressed a work ethic and business development. The weekly newspaper carries numerous ads by businesses owned by Muslims. Politically, Muslims looked to the establishment of a Black nation to be owned and operated by Blacks.
Black Muslims excluded Whites from the movement and imposed a strict discipline on members to accentuate their new religion and nationality. Foods, dress and behavior patterns are regulated; a ritual life based on, but varying from, Orthodox form, was prescribed.
Black Muslims instituted a far-reaching program in furtherance of their aspirations. An evangelizing effort to make the Muslim program known within the Black community was sustained in a weekly newspaper, *Muhammad Speaks.* During the 1960 and into the 1970s, growth was spectacular. By the time of Elijah Muhammad's death there were approximately 70 temples across the nation, including the South, and over 100,000 members.
In 1975 Elijah Muhammad died and was succeeded by his son Wallace D. Muhammad. During the decade of Wallace's leadership, a move toward both Orthodox Islam and decentralization of the organization has occurred. These moves have been reflected in the name changes, the schism of conservatives who have left to found movements continuing the peculiar emphasies of the Nation of Islam prior to 1975, and the beginning of acceptance of the American Muslim Mission by orthodox Muslims. *Muhammad Speaks* was renamed *Bilalian News.*
In 1985 Wallace Muhammad, with the approval of the Council of Imans (ministers), resigned his post as leader of the American Muslim Mission and disbanded the movement's national structure. That move represents the establishment of a fully congregational polity by the Muslims whose local centers are now under the guidance of the Imans rather than the control of the Chicago headquarters. Wallace D. Muhammad, also known as Warith Deen Muhammad, now operates as an independent Muslim lecturer and as a member of the World Council of Masajid which is headquartered in Mecca, Saudi Arabia. His emphasis is upon the proper image of Muslims worldwide.

★1696★
Ansaaru Allah Community

Efforts to locate an address for this edition were unsuccessful. Members of the Ansaaru Allah Community , also known as the Nubian Islaamic Hebrew Mission, believe that the nineteenth century Sudanese leader, Muhammed Ahmed Ibn Abdullah (1845-1885), was the True Mahdi, the predicted Khaliyfah (successor) to the Prophet Mustafa Muhammed Al Amin. After his death, Al Mahdi was buried in the Sudan, and the group he founded (the Ansaars) continued under his successors, mainly: (1) As Sayyid Abdur Rahman Muhammad Al Madhi (the first successor); (2) As Sayyid Al Haadi Abdur Muhammad Rahmaan Al Madhi (the second successor); (3) As Sayyid Al Imaan Isa Al Haadi Al Madhi (the third successor). Presently, the third successor, who is also Al Mahdi's great-grandson, leads the mission.
The Community teaches from the Old Testament (*Tawrah*), the Psalms of David (*Zubuwr*), the New Testament (*Injiyl*), and the *Holy Qur'aan.* The last testament, the *Holy Qur'aan*, was given to the last and seal of the Prophets of the line of Adam, Mustafa Muhammad Al Amin. The group teaches that Allah is Alone in His power, the All (which is Tawhiyd "Oneness"), and does not use the term "God." They believe the Jesus is the Messiah and that Ali (599-661 C.E.) and Faatima (610-633 C.E.) are the succesors to Mustafa Muhammad Al Amin.
Adam and Hawwah (Eve) are believed to have been Nubians. After the flood, during the prophet Nuwh's (Noah) time, his son Ham desired to commit sodomy while looking at his father's nakedness. This act resulted in the curse of leprosy being put upon Ham's fourth son, Canaan, thus turning his skin pale. In such a manner did the pale races come into existence, including the Amorites, Hittites, Jebusites, Sidonites, all the sons of Canaan and their descendants. Mixing the blood with these "subraces" (so-called because they are no longer pure Nubians), is unlawful for Nubians.
From the seed of Ibrahiym (Abraham), two nations were produced, the nation of Isaac, whose descendants later became known as Israelites, through his son Jacob, and the nation of Ishmael, whose descendants are called the Ishmailites and the nation of Midian, whose descendents are known as Midianites from Ketura, Abraham's third wife. The Israelites were enslaved for 430 years in Egypt. The Ishmailites were predicted to be enslaved in a land not of their own for 400 years. The Nubians of the United States, the West Indies and various other places around the world are the seed of Ishmael (and hence Hebrews). Al Madhi taught that all with straight hair and pale skin were Turks; However, this does not include people of color such as the Latins, Japanese, Koreans, Cubans, Sicilians, etc.
Under As Siddid Al Imaan Isa Al Haahi Al Madhi's guidance, the Nubian Islaamic Hebrew Mission was begun in the late 1960s in New York. In 1970, the prophesies of the "Opening of the Seventh Seal" (Revelation 8:1) commenced with the opening of the Ansaaru Allah Community and the publishing of literature to help remove the veil of confusion from Nubians. In 1972, communities were established in Philadlephia, Pennsylvania; Connecticut; Texas; and Albany, New York. The following year centers were opened in Washington, DC; Baltimore, Maryland; North Carolina; South Carolina; Georgia; Michigan; Florida; and Virginia. In the Caribbean, centers were opened in Trinidad, Jamaica, Puerto Rico, Guyana, and Tobago. During the next decade, the movement spread around the world and included South America, Ghana and Hawaii.

The symbol of the community is the six-pointed star (made from two triangles) in an inverted cresent. It is considered to be the seal of Allah.

★1697★
Antioch Association of Metaphysical Science

Efforts to locate an address for this edition were unsuccessful. The Antioch Association of Metaphysical Science is a metaphysical church founded in 1932 by Dr. Lewis Johnson of Detroit, Michigan. It serves a predominantly Black membership.

★1698★
Apostolic Assemblies of Christ, Inc.

Efforts to locate an address for this edition were unsuccessful. The Apostolic Assemblies of Christ was formed in 1970 by former members of the Pentecostal Churches of the Apostolic Faith led by Bishop G.N. Boone. During the term of presiding Bishop Willie Lee, questions of his administrative abilities arose. In the midst of the controversy, he died. In the organizational disarray the church splintered, and one group formed around Bishop Boone and Virgil Oates, the vice-bishop. The new body is congregational in organization and continues in the doctrine of the parent body, since no doctrinal controversy accompanied the split.

★1699★
Apostolic Church of Christ
2044 Stadium Dr.
Winston-Salem, NC 27107

The Apostolic Church of Christ was founded in 1969 by Bishop Johnnie Draft and Elder Wallace Snow, both ministers in the Church of God (Apostolic). Draft, for many years an overseer in the church and pastor of St. Peter's Church, the denomination's headquarters congregation, expressed no criticism of the Church of God (Apostolic); rather, he stated that the Spirit of the Lord brought him to start his own organization. The church differs from its parent body in its development of a centralized church polity. Authority is vested in the executive board, which owns all the church property. Doctrine follows that of the Church of God (Apostolic).

★1700★
Apostolic Church of Christ in God
c/o Bethlehem Apostolic Church
1217 E. 15th St.
Winston-Salem, NC 27105

The Apostolic Church of Christ in God was formed by five elders of the Church of God (Apostolic): J.W. Audrey, J.C. Richardson, Jerome Jenkins, W.R. Bryant, and J.M. Williams. At the time of the split, the Church of God (Apostolic) was formally led by Thomas Cox, but, due to his ill health, Eli N. Neal was acting as presiding bishop. The dissenting elders were concerned with the authoritarian manner in which Neal conducted the affairs of the church as well as with some personal problems that Neal was experiencing. Originally, three churches left with the elders, who established headquarters in Winston-Salem, North Carolina. J.W. Audrey was elected the new presiding bishop.

The new church prospered and in 1952 Elder Richardson was elected as a second bishop. In 1956 Audrey resigned and Richardson became the new presiding bishop. Under his leadershp the Apostolic Church enjoyed its greatest success. He began The *Apostolic Gazette* (later the *Apostolic Journal*) which served the church for many years. He also instituted a program to assist ministers in getting an education. However, his efforts were frustrated by several schisms that cut into the church's growth, most prominently the 1971 schism led by former-bishop Audrey.

The church retained the doctrine and congregational polity of the Church of God (Apostolic).

★1701★
Apostolic Church of Jesus Christ

Efforts to locate an address for this edition were unsuccessful. The Apostolic Church of Jesus Christ is a second body that grew out of the Pentecostal Assemblies of the World after the death of Garfield Thomas Haywood (1880-1931), who founded the "oneness" work in Indianapolis, Indiana. The Church believes in the indispensability of baptism for salvation.

★1702★
Apostolic Faith Mission Church of God

Efforts to locate an address for this edition were unsuccessful. Among the people who visited the early Pentecostal revival which occurred in 1906-08 in Los Angeles was F.W. Williams (d.1932), a Black man from the deep south. He received the Baptism of the Holy Spirit under the ministry of William J. Seymour and returned to Mississippi to establish an outpost of the Apostolic Faith Mission. Not having great success, he moved to Mobile, Alabama, where a revival occurred under his ministry. Among those converted was an entire congregation of the Primitive Baptist Church. The members gave him their building as the first meeting house for the new mission parish. The church was organized on July 10, 1906.

In 1915 Bishop Williams became one of the first to adopt the Oneness or non-Trinitarian theology which had been espoused through Pentecostal circles. He broke with Seymour and renamed his church the Apostolic Faith Mission Church of God. He incorporated the new church on October 9, 1915. The church continues to place a strong emphasis upon divine healing, allows women preachers, and practices footwashing with communion. Baptism is in the name of the "Lord Jesus Christ," and without the use of the name, the baptism is considered void. Intoxicants, especially tobacco, alcohol and drugs are forbidden. Members are admonished to marry only those who have been "saved." The church is headed by the Senior Bishop and a Cabinet of Executive Officers composed of the bishops, overseers and the general secretary.

★1703★
Apostolic Overcoming Holy Church of God
1807 S. Mott Dr.
Mobile, AL 36617

The Apostolic Overcoming Church of God was founded by William Thomas Phillips (1893-1973), the son of a Methodist Episcopal Church minister. However, at a tentmeeting service in Birmingham, Alabama, Phillips was converted to the message of pentecost and holiness under the ministry of Frank W. Williams of the Faith Mission Church of God. Williams ordained Phillips in 1913, and three years later Phillips launched his career as an evangelist in Mobile, Alabama. In 1917, he was selected by the people who had responded to his ministry as the bishop of the Ethiopian Overcoming Holy Church of God. The new organization was incorporated in 1920. It adopted its present name in 1941 in realization that the church was for all people, not just Ethiopians, a popular designation for Black people in the early twentieth century.

The AOH Church of God follows the Oneness theology,. It believes in One God who subsists in the union of Father, Son, and Holy Spirit. The church, however, rejects any hint of tri-theism and believes that the One God bears the name of Jesus, a name that can express the fulness of the Godhead. Out of this belief, the church baptizes members in the name of Jesus. Baptism is by immersion and considered necessary for salvation.

The church teaches that God acts in the believer both to baptize in the Spirit (which will be signified by speaking-in-tongues) and progressively over a lifetime to sanctify (make holy). Besides baptism, there are two other ordinances–the Lord's supper and foot washing. The church also teaches divine healing and exhorts members to tithe.

Though headed by bishops, the AOH Church of God is basically congregational in polity with each church owning its own property and managing its own affairs. Churches are grouped into districts presided over by bishops and overseers. A General Assembly, to which all churches send representatives, convenes annually. It is led by the presiding bishop. After serving the church for 57 years, Bishop Phillips was succeeded by Bishop Jasper Roby, the present senior presiding bishop. He is assisted by five associate bishops. The church's periodicals are published by the church's publishing board. Missions are supported in Haiti and Africa.

★1704★
Associated Churches of Christ (Holiness)

Efforts to locate an address for this edition were unsuccessful. On the West Coast the Church of Christ (Holiness) U.S.A. was formed in 1915 by Bishop William Washington and work was carried on independently of the work in the east and south by the church's founder, C.P. Jones. A few years later, Jones went to Los Angeles and held a revival meeting. At that time the two men worked out an agreement for cooperative endeavor. The agreement was in effect until 1946-47. Because of what the manual of the Associated Churches of Christ (Holiness) calls the "manipulating of some administrative problems in the upper circles of the Church," the West Coast churches withdrew from the Church of Christ (Holiness) U.S.A. They now continue under the original incorporation of Bishop Washington. Doctrine and polity are identical with the Church of Christ (Holiness) U.S.A.

★1705★
Astrological, Metaphysical, Occult, Revelatory, Enlightenment Church

Efforts to locate an address for this edition were unsuccessful. The Astrological, Metaphysical, Occult, Revelatory, Enlightenment Church (AMORE) was formed in 1972 by the Reverend Charles Robert Gordon, formerly a minister of the African Methodist Episcopal Zion Church (AMEZ). His father was Bishop Buford Franklin Gordon of the AMEZ Church. The church is Bible-based and views Jesus as the embodiment of cosmic consciousness. The AMORE Church believes in using the occult arts as a means to enlightenment in the coming Aquarian Age. Headquarters of the AMORE Church were established in Meriden, Connecticut. In recent years the church has moved and no contact has been made. Its present status (1985) is unknown.

★1706★
Ausar Auset Society
c/o Oracle of Thoth, Inc.
Box 281
Bronx, NY 10462

The Ausar Auset Society is a Rosicrucian body serving the Black community of the United States. It was founded in the mid-1970s by R.A. Straughn, also known by the name Ra Un Nefer Amen, formerly head of the Rosicrucian Anthroposophical League in New York City. He is the author of several occult texts in spiritual science, each offering methods drawn from the Kabbalah and eastern religions to facilitate the orderly transition to the enlightened state.
The Society has directed its program to Blacks and *Metu Neter* (formerly *The Oracle of Thoth*) regularly features, alongside of its occult articles, items of general interest and concern to Black people. The Society advocates the appropriation of the positive accomplishments of African ancestors by the contemporary Black community. The Society offers free public classes in a variety of occult topics. Currently such classes are being held in New York City, Brooklyn, Chicago, Philadelphia, New Haven, Washington, DC, and Norfolk, VA.

★1707★
Bible Way Church of Our Lord Jesus Christ World Wide, Inc.
1100 New Jersey Ave., NW
Washington, DC 20001

The Bible Way Church of Our Lord Jesus Christ World Wide, Inc., was formed in 1957 by former members of some seventy churches of the Church of Our Lord Jesus Christ of the Apostolic Faith. Smallwood E. Williams became the presiding bishop. The purpose of organizing the new body was to effect a less autocratic leadership than in the parent body. (Prior to that time, Bishop R.C. Lawson had refused to consecrate other bishops for his church.) Besides Bishop Williams, John S. Beane, McKinley Williams, Winfield A. Showell, and Joseph Moore were also consecrated as bishops. A bishop of the Pentecostal Assemblies of the World officiated at the consecration service. Doctrine remains the same. A general conference meets annually. Williams has become best known for his work on social conditions within the Black community in Washington, DC.

★1708★
Bible Way Pentecostal Apostolic Church

Efforts to locate an address for this edition were unsuccessful. The Bible Way Pentecostal Apostolic Church was founded by Curtis P. Jones. Jones began as a pastor in North Carolina in the Church of God (Apostolic), but left that church to join the Church of Our Lord Jesus Christ of the Apostolic Faith under Robert Clarence Lawson. He became pastor of the St. Paul Apostolic Church in Henry County, Virginia. Jones left during the internal disruption within Bishop Lawson's church in 1957, but did not join with Smallwood E. Williams' Bible Way Church of Our Lord Jesus Christ. Rather, in 1960, with two other congregations in Virginia, he founded a new denomination. A fourth church was soon added.

★1709★
Black Primitive Baptists

Efforts to locate an address for this edition were unsuccessful. Until the Civil War, Blacks were members of the predominantly White Primitive Baptist associations and worshipped in segregated meeting houses. After the Civil War, the Blacks were organized into separate congregations, and associations were gradually formed. In North Alabama, the Indian Creek Association was formed as early as 1869. Among the leaders was Elder Jesse Lee. He was ordained after the War, and in 1868, organized the Bethlehem Church in Washington, Virginia. In 1877, he became the moderator of the newly formed Second Ketocton Association.
Doctrine and practice of the Black Primitive Baptists are like those of the Regulars. They have no periodical. *The Primitive Messenger*, partially underwritten by Elder W.J. Berry, editor of *Old Faith Contender*, lasted only four years in the early 1950s.

★1710★
Center of Being

Efforts to locate an address for this edition were unsuccessful. The Center of Being was formed in 1979 by Baba Prem Ananda, also known as "Anandaji" (b. 1949), and Her Holiness Sri Marashama Devi, affectionately known as "Mataji," an American-born Black woman considered by her followers to be an avatar (a self-realized master of the highest order). Mataji was born fully Enlightened in her present incarnation and retained that state for the first twelve years of her life. She regressed in order to experience the separation from the Divine and the path to re-union. During this twelve-year period, she retained some communion with the Divine and experienced many unusual powers, among them an ability to see Lord Shiva (considered a major deity by Hindus), who functioned as her guru. At the age of twenty-four, she regained the state of Enlightenment and began to teach privately. One of her first disciples, Anandaji, assisted her in the formation of the Center of Being and her public teaching activity. Anandaji also attained the Enlightened state.
Mataji teaches a path of Enlightenment, a spontaneous way of being beyond intellectual rules and answers. Mataji is considered a divine personage with the ability to bestow the grace which leads to Enlightenment. She offers herself in weekly "darshans," sessions in which disciples sit in her presence, and in "grace intensives" (thrice annually). Darshan sessions include lectures by Mataji and question-

and-answer sessions (satsang). "Pujas," devotional worship services directed to the deities and Mataji, are held quarterly.

★1711★

Christian Methodist Episcopal Church
1474 Humber St.
Memphis, TN 38106

From 1844 until the end of the Civil War, slaves formed a large percentage of the membership of the Methodist Episcopal Church. In South Carolina they were in the majority. The proselytizing activity of both the African Methodist Episcopal Church and the African Methodist Episcopal Zion Church claimed many of these former slaves as soon as they were free; others remained with the Methodist Episcopal Church, South (MEC,S), the southern branch of the Methodist Episcopal Church which had split in 1844. Many White Methodists felt that given the Blacks' new freedom, a new relationshp must follow. In 1870, following the wishes of their Black members, the Methodist Episcopal Church, South helped them form a separate church named the Colored Methodist Episcopal Church (CME). In 1954 the church changed its name to the Christian Methodist Episcopal Church.

At the first General Conference nine annual conferences were designated, the of the MEC,S adopted with necessary changes, a publishing house established, and a periodical, *The Christian Index*, begun. Two MEC,S bishops ordained two colored Methodist Episcopal bishops. Throughout its history the Colored Methodist Episcopal Church has been aided financially in its program by the MEC,S and its successor bodies. Today, the church is very similiar to the United Methodist Church in belief and practice.

One of the keys to Colored Methodist Episcopal success was the 41-year episcopate of Isaac Lane. Besides traveling widely and bolstering the poverty-ridden church, he initiated the educational program by founding the CME High School, now Lane College in 1882. Education of former slaves and their children, a major enterprise of all Methodists, has been carried through the CME Church in the establishment of a number of schools across the South. Paine College, established MEC,S has been a traditional focus of CME and MEC,S. Growth and expansion beyond the 200,000 initial members was slowed by lack of funds. Movement northward followed the major migration of Blacks into northern urban centers in the early twentieth century.

The CME Church is a member of both the National Council of Churches and the World Council of Churches.

★1712★

Christ's Sanctified Holy Church (Louisiana)
S. Cutting Ave. at E. Spencer St.
Jennings, LA 70546

In 1903 members of Christ's Sanctified Holy Church (South Carolina) came to West Lake, Louisiana, and proselytized a group of Black people, who in 1904 organized the Colored Church South. Among the leaders were Dempsey Perkins, A. C. Mitchell, James Briller, Sr., and Leggie Pleasant. The church soon changed its name to Christ's Sanctified Holy Church Colored. Over the years the church members dropped the word "Colored" from their title and returned to using the same name as their parent body, Christ's Sanctified Holy Church. The parent body is White and has headquarters in South Carolina, whereas the church under discussion here is headquartered in Louisiana. Organization and doctrine are as in the parent body, except that the ministers in Christ's Sanctified Holy Church (Louisiana) are salaried.

★1713★

Church of Christ (Holiness) U.S.A.
329 E. Monument St.
Jackson, MS 39202

In 1894 C.P. Jones and Charles H. Mason formed the Church of God in Christ as a holiness body, following their exclusion from fellowship with Black Baptists in Arkansas. Mason took most of the body into pentecostalism in 1907. Those who remained were reorganized by Jones as the Church of Christ (Holiness) U.S.A. Jones himself, residing in Jackson, Mississippi, became well known as a composer and publisher of holiness gospel songs. Doctrinally, the Church of Christ (Holiness) U.S.A. is very close to the Church of the Nazarene, with which it almost merged. It follows the *Methodist Articles of Religion* and stresses the second blessing of the Holy Spirit which imparts sanctification to the believer. Race issues prevented close relations between the Church of Christ (Holiness) U.S.A. and predominantly White holiness churches.

The church is episcopal in structure with a senior bishop as the highest official. There are seven dioceses. A convention held every two years is the highest legislative authority. Missionary work is sponsored in Mexico. There is a publishing house in Los Angeles. Present leader of the church is Bishop M.R. Conic.

★1714★

Church of God and Saints of Christ

Efforts to locate an address for this edition were unsuccessful. Elder William S. Crowdy, a Black cook on the Sante Fe Railroad, claimed to have a vision from God calling him to lead his people to the true religion. He left his job and founded the Church of God and Saints of Christ in 1896 at Lawrence, Kansas. In 1900, he moved to Philadelphia, and the first annual assembly was held. Crowdy died in 1908, and Joseph N. Crowdy and William H. Plummer succeeded him as bishops. Joseph N. Crowdy died in 1917, the same year that the headquarters were moved to Bellville, Virginia, where the church had purchased a large farm. In 1931, Calvin S. Skinner, the last leader appointed by the founder, became bishop, but he lived only three months thereafter. He passed the leadership to Howard Z. Plummer, who held it for many years.

The doctrine of the Church of God is a complicated mixture of Judaism, Christianity and Black nationalism. Members are accepted into the church by repentance, baptism by immersion, confession of faith in Christ Jesus, receiving communion of unleavened bread and water, having their feet washed by the elder, and agreeing to keep the Ten Commandments. They must also have been taught how to pray according to *Matthew 6:9-13*, and they must have been breathed upon with a holy kiss. They believe that Black people are the descendants of the ten lost tribes of Israel. They believe in keeping the Ten Commandments and adhering literally to the teachings of both the Old and New testaments as positive guides to salvation. The church observes the Jewish Sabbath and the use of corresponding Hebrew names. The church is a strong advocate of temperance.

The church is headed by its bishop and prophet who is divinely called to his office. He is believed to be in direct communion with God, to utter prophecies, and to perform miracles. When a prophet dies, the office remains vacant until a new call occurs. The prophet presides over the executive board of twelve ordained elders. The church is divided into district, annual, and general assemblies. There are four orders of the ministry: bishops, missionaries, ordained ministers, and nonordained ministers. Deacons care for the temporal affairs of the church. Each local church bears the denominational name and is numbered according to its appearance in the state. The church at Bellville is communalistic, but other churches are not. The Daughters of Jerusalem and Sisters of Mercy is a women's organization whose duty is to look for straying members, to help the sick and needy, and to care for visitors from other local churches.

★1715★

Church of God (Apostolic)
125 Meadow's St.
Beckley, WV 25801

The Church of God (Apostolic) was formed in 1877 by Elder Thomas J. Cox at Danville, Kentucky, as the Christian Faith Band. It was one of a number of independent holiness associations of the late nineteenth century. In 1915, it voted a name change, and in 1919 became the Church of God (Apostolic). In 1943, Cox was succeeded by M. Gravely and Eli N. Neal as co-presiding bishops. Headquarters were moved to Beckley, West Virginia. Two years later Gravely divorced his wife and remarried. He was disfellowshipped from the church. In 1964 Neal was succeeded by Love Odom who died two years later and was succeeded by David E. Smith. These two bishops did much to put the national church in a firm financial condition. They were suceeded by the present general overseer, Ruben K. Hash.

It is a strict church, opposing worldliness and practicing footwashing with the monthly Lord's Supper. Baptism by immersion is in the name of Jesus. The church is headed by a board of bishops, one of whom is designated the general overseer who serves as the church's executive head. There is a general assembly annually.

★1716★
Church of God (Black Jews)

Efforts to locate an address for this edition were unsuccessful. The Church of God (Black Jews) was founded in the early twentieth century by Prophet F.S. Cherry, who claimed to have had a vision calling him to his office as prophet. He was sent to America and began the church in Philadelphia. A self-educated man, Prophet Cherry became conversant in both Hebrew and Yiddish. He became famous for his homiletic abilities, colloquialisms, and biting slang.

The Church of God is open only to Black people, who are identified with the Jews of the Bible. White Jews are viewed as frauds and interlopers. The church does not use the term synagogue, the place of worship of the White Jews (*Rev. 3:9*). The church teaches that Jesus was a Black man. The first men were also Black, the first White man being Gehazi, who received his Whiteness as a curse (*11 Kings 5: 27*). The White man continued to mix with the Black people, and the yellow race resulted. Esau was the first red man (*Gen. 25:25*). God is, of course, Black. Black people sprang from Jacob.

The New Year begins with Passover in April. Saturday is the true Sabbath. Speaking in tongues is considered nonsense. Eating pork, divorce, taking photographs, and observing Christian holidays are forbidden. The end of the period that started with creation is approaching, and the Black Jews will return in 2000 A.D. to institute the millennium.

★1717★
Church of God in Christ
958 Mason St.
Memphis, TN 38103

The church of God in Christ was established in 1894 in Jackson, Mississippi by Charles H. Mason, at that time an independent Baptist minister who four years previously had been affected by the holiness movement and sanctified. With a colleague, Elder C.P. Jones, he had founded the Church of Christ (Holiness) U.S.A. He had as a child of twelve been healed suddenly of a sickness that almost killed him. In 1907, two events further changed his life. Elder Jones convinced him that he did not yet have the fullness of the Holy Spirit, for, if he did, he would have the power to heal the sick, cast out devils, and raise the dead. He also heard of the meetins at Azuse Street in Los Angeles, went there, was baptized in the Spirit and spoke in tongues.

In August, 1908, the new doctrine and experience was presented to the representatives of the Church of Christ (Holiness) U.S.A. convention in Jackson. At a meeting of those who accepted Pentecostalism, a General Assembly of the Church of God in Christ was organized. Mason was elected general overseer. (This brief history is at odds withthe history presented in the item elsewhere in this chapter on teh Churst of Christ (Holiness) U.S.A.; the two churches involved tell two different stories.)

The Church of God in Christ was organized in an ascending hierarchy of overseer (pastor), the state overseer, and general overseer. There are annual state convocations which decide on disputed matters and assign pastors, and a general convocation for matters of the general church. Upon the death of Bishop Mason in 1961, a series of reorganizational steps began. Power reverted to the seven bishops who made up the executive commission. This group was extended to twelve in 1962 and O.T. Jones, Jr., was named "senior bishop." An immediate controversy began over the focus of power and a constitutional convention was scheduled. In 1967, a court in Memphis ruled that the powers of the senior bishop and executive board should remain intact until the constitutional convention in 1968. That year reorganization took place and power was invested in a quadrennial general assembly and a genral board of twelve with a presiding bishop to conduct administration between meetings of the general assembly.

Doctrine is similar to that of the Pentecostal Holiness Church. The group believes in the Trinity, holiness, healing, and the premillennial return of Christ. Three ordinances are recognized: batism by immersion, the Lord's Supper, and foot-washing.

★1718★
Church of God in Christ, Congregational

Efforts to locate an address for this edition were unsuccessful. The Church of God in Christ, Congregational, was formed in 1932 by Bishop J. Bowe of Hot Springs, Arkansas, who argued that the Church of God in Christ should be congregational, not episcopal, in its polity. Forced to withdraw, Bowe organized the Church of God in Christ, Congregational. In 1934, he was joined by George Slack. Slack had been disfellowshipped from the church because of his disagreement with the teaching that if a saint did not pay tithes, he was not saved. He was convinced that tithing was not a New Testament doctrine. He became the junior bishop under Bowe. In 1945, Bowe was wooed back into the Church of God in Christ, and Slack became senior bishop.

Doctrine is like that of the Church of God in Christ, but with disagreements on matters of polity and tithing. Members are conscientious objectors.

★1719★
Church of God in Christ, International

Efforts to locate an address for this edition were unsuccessful. In 1969, following its constitutional convention and reorganization, a major schism of the Church of God in Christ occurred when a group of fourteen bishops led by Bishop Illie L. Jefferson rejected the polity of the reorganized church, left it and formed the Church of God in Christ, International, at Kansas City. The issue was the centralized authority in the organization of the parent body. The new group quickly set up an entire denominational structure. The doctrine of the parent body remained intact.

★1720★
Church of God (Sanctified Church)

Efforts to locate an address for this edition were unsuccessful. In the early years of the Church of Christ (Holiness) U.S.A., discussed elsewhere in this chapter, the church existed as an unincorporated entity called the "Church of God" or the "Holiness Church." It was only after the schism over Pentecostalism in 1907 that the church was incorporated and its present name was adopted. Before the incorporation, one of the ministers, Elder Charles W. Gray, established the church in Nashville, Tennessee, and the surrounding areas. When the Church of Christ (Holiness) U.S.A. incorporated, Gray continued his work independently as the Church of God (Sanctified Church). The doctrine was the same as that of the Church of Christ (Holiness) U.S.A., but the polity was congregational with local churches operating autonomously and appointing their own ministers. The associated churches remained unincorporated. In 1927 there arose a movement within the Church of God (Sanctified Church) to incorporate and to consolidate the work under a board of elders. Among those who constituted the newly incorporated church were Elders J.L. Rucker, R.A. Manter, R.L. Martin, M.S. Sowell, B. Smith, and G.A. Whitley. The move to incorporate led to further controversy and a schism. However, under the incorporation, the elders retained the rights to direct the church, and it continues as the Church of God (Sanctified Church). Elder Gray, founder of the church, withdrew to found the Original Church of God (or Sanctified Church).

The Church of God (Sanctified Church) is headed by a general overseer. The first was Elder Rucker. He has been suceeded by Elder Theopolis Dickerson McGhee (d.1965) and Elder Jesse E. Evans. Mission work is conducted in Jamaica.

★1721★
Church of Hakeem

Efforts to locate an address for this edition were unsuccessful. The Church of Hakeem was founded by Clifton Jones, better known to his followers as Hakeem Abdul Rasheed, in Oakland, California, in January 1978. Jones, a Detroit-born Black man, attended Purdue University as a psychology major. In the mid-1970s he ran a weight-reduction clinic, which was closed in 1976 when the state Board of Medical Quality Assurance reported that he was using "psychology" rather than diet and exercise to treat clients. He was practicing psychology without a license.

Hakeem turned from weight-reduction to religion and assumed his new name. Like his colleague, Rev. Frederick Eikerenkoetter II (Rev. Ike), founder of the United Church and Science of Living Institute, Hakeem built upon New Thought emphases that health, wealth, and happiness came from positive mental attitudes put into positive action. He emphasized positive action as a means to wealth. In contrast to Rev. Ike, however, Hakeem implemented his teachings through a variation of what is known as the Ponsie game, a standard confidence scheme. Members paid into the church with the promise of a 400 percent return within three years. Members would in turn recruit further investors. The early investors receive their promised return. People who joined last receive nothing, not even their original investment. Such schemes are illegal.

In May 1979 Hakeem was indicted and later convicted on six counts of fraud. A group of members signed a class action suit against the church, and the Internal Revenue Service moved against the church for taxes. The cumulative effect of these actions have paralyzed the Church of Hakeem, and its future is doubtful.

★1722★
Church of Our Lord Jesus Christ of the Apostolic Faith

Efforts to locate an address for this edition were unsuccessful. The Church of Our Lord Jesus Christ of the Apostolic Faith was founded in Columbus, Ohio, in 1919 by Robert Clarence Lawson (d. 1961), who as a pastor in the Pentecostal Assemblies of the World had founded churches in Texas and Missouri. At one point in his early life when he was ill he had been taken to the Apostolic Faith Assembly Church, a leading church of the Pentecostal Assemblies, and its pastor, Garfield Thomas Haywood. Healed, Lawson joined the Assemblies, and adopted their non-trinitarian theology. However, in 1913 he left Haywood's jurisdiction and, moving to New York City, founded Refuge Temple, the first congregation in his new independent church. Given Lawson's effective leadership, the organization grew quickly. Other congregations were established and a radio ministry , a periodical, a day nursery, and several businesses were initiated. In 1926 he opened a bible school to train pastors.

In the 1930s, Lawson began a series of trips to the West Indies which led to congregations being formed in Jamaica, Antigua, the Virgin Islands, and Trinidad. His lengthy tenure as bishop of the Church was a time of steady growth, broken only by two schisms by Sherrod C. Johnson, (Church of the Lord Jesus Christ of the Apostolic Faith, 1930) and Smallwood E. Williams, (Bible Way Church of Our Lord Jesus Christ, 1957). Lawson was succeeded by Hubert J. Spencer and by the present presiding apostle, William Bonner.

Doctrine is like the older Pentecostal Assemblies of the World. Footwashing is practiced and the baptism of the Holy Spirit is believed to be necessary for salvation. The church is headed by the presiding apostle, who is assisted by six regional apostles. There is an annual convocation. Affiliated churches can be found in the West Indies, Africa, England and Germany.

★1723★
Church of the Fuller Concept

Efforts to locate an address for this edition were unsuccessful. The Church of the Fuller Concept is a New Thought group headed by Dr. Bernese Williamson, a doctor of metaphysical science. Dr. Williamson teaches that we live in the God dispensation. God is our Father and Mother, our natural parents being God caring for us. God has a body (*I Cor. 11:30*) and is manifested in body-form on earth. Man's body is the image and likeness of God. In recognizing God's body, man can have the blessing of a healthy, whole body. Members of the church do not carry insurance, because in God, where man lives and moves and has his being (which is the body of God), there can be no illness. Dr. Williamson teaches that every meal is a communion and that what one visualizes as he eats and drinks will materialize.

Headquarters of the church are at the Hisacres New Thought Center in Washington, D.C. Members live by a pledge to remember their spiritual nature. They greet each other with the word, "Peace." They adopt spiritual names, because they want to acquire the nature, characteristics and attributes of God. All students sign a pledge to give honest service to their employer for their pay, not accepting tips or vacation-with-pay, nor using intoxicants on the job. This pledge is given to the employers.

★1724★
Church of the Living God (Christian Workers for Fellowship)

Efforts to locate an address for this edition were unsuccessful. The Church of the Living God (Christian Workers for Fellowship) was formed in 1889 by a former slave, the Rev. William Christian (1856-1928) of Wrightsville, Arkansas. Christian was an early associate of Charles H. Mason, also a Baptist minister who left the Baptist Church to form the Church of God in Christ. Christian claimed to have had a revelation that the Baptists were preaching a sectarian doctrine and he left them in order to preach the unadulterated truth. He created the office of "chief." Mrs. Ethel L. Christian succeeded her husband after his death and was, in turn, succeeded by their son, John L. Christian. Mrs. Christian claimed that the original revelation came to both her husband and herself.

The doctrine is trinitarian and somewhat Pentecostal. The group rejects the idea of "tongues" as the initial evidence of the baptism of the Holy Spirit, although "tongues" are allowed. However, "tongues" must be recognizable languages, not "unintelligible utterance." Footwashing is a third ordinance. Salvation is gained by obeying the commandments to hear, understand, believe, repent, confess, be baptized, and participate in the Lord's Supper and in foot-washing.

The Church of the Living God also has a belief that Jesus Christ was of the Black race because of the lineage of David and Abraham. David in *Psalms 119:83* said he became like a bottle in the smoke (i.e., Black). The church members also hold that Job (*Job 30:30*), Jeremiah (*Jer. 8:21*), and Moses' wife (*Numbers 12:11*) were Black. These teachings were promulgated at a time when many Baptists were teaching that Blacks were not human, but the offspring of a human father and female beast. The Church of the Living God countered with the assertion that the saints of the Bible were Black.

The polity is episcopal and the church is modeled along the lines of a fraternal organization. Christian was very impressed with the Masons, and there are reportedly many points of doctrine known only to members of the organization. Tithing is stressed. Churches are called temples.

★1725★
Church of the Living God, the Pillar and Ground of the Truth

Efforts to locate an address for this edition were unsuccessful. The Church of the Living God, the Pillar and Ground of the Truth, Inc. traces its beginning to 1903 when Mary L. Tate (1871-1930), generally referred to as Mother or Saint Mary Magdalena, a Black woman, began to preach first at Steel Springs, Tennessee, and Paducah, Kentucky, and then throughout the South. By 1908, when a number of holiness bands had been formed by people converted under her ministry, she was taken ill. Pronounced beyond cure, she was healed and given the baptism of the Holy Spirit and spoke in tongues. She called an assembly in Greenville, Alabama, during which the Church of the Living God was organized. She became the chief overseer. The church quickly spread to the surrounding states of Georgia, Florida, Tennessee, and Kentucky and by the end of the next decade had congregations across the eastern half of the United States.

In 1919, the first of two major schisms occurred. Led by the church in Philadelphia, Pennsylvania, some members left to found the House of God, Which Is the Church of the Living God, the Pillar and Ground of Truth. Then, in 1931, following Mother Tate's death, the church

reorganized, and three persons were ordained to fill the office of chief overseer. The three chosen were Mother Tate's son F.E. Lewis, M.F.L. Keith (widow of Bishop W.C. Lewis), and B.L. McLeod. These three eventually became leaders of distinct church bodies. Lewis' following is the continuing Church of the Living God, the Pillar and Ground of the Truth, Inc. Keith's group became known as the House of God Which Is the Church of the Living God, the Pillar and Ground of Truth Without Controversy.
Bishop McLeod's organization is known as the Church of the Living God, the Pillar, and Ground of Truth, Inc. affirms the central doctrines of traditional Christianity including the Trinity and salvation through Christ. It teaches that people are justifies and cleansed by faith in Christ and glorified and wholly sanctified by receiving of the Holy Ghost and Fire. Evidence of the reception of the Holy Ghost is speaking in tongues. The unknown tongue is a sign of God's victory over sin. There are three ordinances: baptism by immersion, the Lord's Supper, and foot washing.
The church is headed by a bishop, designated the chief overseer. After the death of Bishop F.E. Lewis in 1968, Bishop Helen M. Lewis, the present head of the church, became the chief overseer. She administers the affairs of the church with the assistance of the general assembly, which meets annually, a board of trustees, and the supreme executive council consisting of the other bishops and seven elders. The New and Living Way Publishing House is the church's publishing arm.

★1726★
Church of the Lord Jesus Christ of the Apostolic Faith (Philadelphia)
Apostolic Sq.
Philadelphia, PA 19146

The Church of the Lord Jesus Christ of the Apostolic Faith was founded in 1933 by Bishop Sherrod C. Johnson, formerly of the Church of Our Lord Jesus Christ of the Apostolic Faith. Johnson protested what he felt were too liberal regulations espoused by Bishop Robert Clarence Lawson in regard to the appearance of female members. Lawson allowed the wearing of jewelry and make-up. Johnson insisted upon female members wearing cotton stockings, calf-length dresses, unstraightened hair and head coverings. Johnson also opposed the observance of Lent, Easter and Christmas. Upon Bishop Johnson's death in 1961, he was succeeded by S. McDowell Shelton, the "Bishop, Apostle, and Overseer of the Church." This church has been most aggressive and has approached its parent body in membership.
The doctrine is a typical "oneness" doctrine, though the church is known for its conservatism. It does demand that baptism must be in the name of the "Lord Jesus" or "Jesus Christ," but not just "Jesus." This exacting formula is to distinguish the Lord Jesus from Bar Jesus (*Acts 13:6*) and Jesus Justas (*Col. 4:11*), two other Biblical characters. The church members also believe one must be filled with the Holy Ghost in order to have the new birth. The church's conservatism is most manifest in its rigid behavior code. Prohibited are women preachers and teachers, remarriage after divorce, dressing like the world, and wearing costly apparel.
The church is episcopal. There is a national convention annually at the national headquarters in Philadelphia. Lay people have an unusually high participation level in the national church, holding most of the top administrative positions. There is an active radio ministry, "*The Whole Truth*," carried on 50 stations. Missions are conducted in Liberia, West Africa, England, Honduras, Jamaica, Haiti, Bahamas, Jordan, Portugal, and the Maldives.

★1727★
Church of Universal Triumph/The Dominion of God

Efforts to locate an address for this edition were unsuccessful. Rivaling Sweet Daddy Grace and Father Divine as charismatic leaders in the Black community was the Rev. James Francis Marion Jones, better known as Prophet Jones (1908-1971). Born in Birmingham, Alabama, the son of a railroad brakeman and a school teacher, he was raised in Triumph the Church and Kingdom of God in Christ. Even as a child, he preached (he did so regularly after his eleventh birthday). In 1938 he was sent to Detroit as a missionary and became successful quickly. Tension with headquarters arose before the year was out, however, when members began to shower Jones with expensive gifts. The headquarters claimed them. Rather than surrender his new affluence, Jones left the church and founded the Church of Universal Triumph/the Dominion of God.
The new church, modeled on the parent body, was built upon Jones' charisma. During the 1940s and 1950s he became known for his wealth. His possessions included a white mink coat, a 54-room French chateau which had been built in 1917 by a General Motors executive, five Cadillacs each with its own chauffeur, jewelry, perfumes, and wardrobe of almost 500 ensembles. Jones claimed to be in direct contact with God, who instructed him in the form of a breeze fanning his ear. Among his practices was dispensing solutions to personal problems after inviting individuals to mount his dais and whisper their problems in his ear. Most of Prophet Jones' wealth came from people grateful for Jones' healing ability. Followers were to be found in all the large northern cities. Jones was titled, "His Holiness the Rev. Dr. James F. Jones, D.D., Universal Dominion Ruler, Internationally known as Prophet Jones."
The Church, like the parent body, is very strict. Members are not allowed to smoke, drink, play games of any kind, use coffee or tea, fraternize with non-Dominionitetry, attend another church, or marry without the consent of the ruler of the church. Women must wear girdles and men health belts. The major theological tenet concerns the beginning of the millennium in 2,000 A.D. All alive at that time will become immortal and live in the heaven on earth.
The upward path of Prophet Jones came to an abrupt end in 1956 when a vice raid on his home led to his arrest and trial for gross indecency. He was acquitted, but the damage had been done and his following declined from that time. During the year prior to his death in 1971, he commuted between Detroit and Chicago. Following his death, his assistant, the Rev. Lord James Schaffer became the Dominion Ruler. He was named by the Dominion Council and Board of Trustees. Some 20 ministers and 5,000 members attended the funeral of Prophet Jones in 1971.

★1728★
Churches of God, Holiness
170 Ashby St., NW
Atlanta, GA 30314

The Churches of God, Holiness, were formed by Bishop King Hezekiah Burruss (d.1963), formerly of the Church of Christ (Holiness) U.S.A. Burruss began a church in Atlanta in 1914 that belonged to that organization, and by 1920, the Atlanta congregation was large enough that it hosted the national convention of the Church of Christ (Holiness) U.S.A. Shortly after that Atlanta meeting, however, Burruss formed his own church. Doctrine is like the doctrine of the parent body.
The highest authority is the national convention. There are also annual state conventions. Practically speaking the government developed during the period of strong leadership exercised by the founding bishop. The bishop appoints the state overseers who assign all pastors. The present bishop is Titus Paul Burruss.

★1729★
Commandment Keepers Congregation of the Living God

Efforts to locate an address for this edition were unsuccessful. The Commandment Keepers Congregation of the Living God emerged among West Indian Blacks who migrated to Harlem. The group began with the Beth B'nai Abraham congregation founded in 1924 by Arnold Josiah Ford, an early Black nationalist and leader in the Universal Negro Improvement Association founded by Marcus Garvey. Ford had repudiated Christianity, adopted Judaism, and learned Hebrew. During the years after the congregation began, Ford met Arthur Wentworth Matthew (1892- 1973). Matthew was born in Lagos, West Africa, in 1892. His family moved to St. Kitts in the British West Indies and then, in 1911, to New York. Matthew became a minister in the Church of the Living God, the Pillar and Ground of Truth, a Black pentecostal church which had endorsed the U.N.I.A. Then in 1919, with eight other men, he organized his own group, the Commandment Keepers: Holy Church of the Living God, over which he became bishop. In Harlem, he had met White Jews for the first time and in the 1920s came to know A.J. Ford. Possibly from Ford, Matthew began to learn Orthodox Judaism and Hebrew and to acquire ritual materials.

Both also learned of the Falashas, the Black Jews of Ethiopia, and began to identify with them. In 1930, Ford's congregation ran into financial trouble. Ford turned over the membership to Matthew's care and left for Ethiopia where he spent the rest of his life. The identification with Ethiopia merely increased through the years. In 1935, when Haile Selassie was crowned emperor, Matthew declared himself the Falashas in America and claimed credentials from Haile Selassie.

The Commandment Keepers believe that the Black men are really the Ethiopian Falashas and the Biblical Hebrews who had been stripped of the knowledge of their name and religion during the slavery era. It is impossible for a Black man to conceive of himself as a "Negro" and retain anything but slave mentality. With other Black Jews, adherents believe the biblical patriarchs to have been Black. Christianity is rejected as the religion of the Gentiles or Whites.

An attempt has been made to align the Commandment Keepers with Orthodox Jewish practice. Hebrew is taught and revered as a sacred language. The Jewish holidays are kept, and the Sabbath services are held on Friday evenings and Saturday mornings and afternoons. Kosher food laws are kept. An Ethiopian Hebrew Rabbinical college trains leaders in Jewish history, the Mishnah, Josephus, the Talmud, and legalism. Elements of Christianity are retained–footwashing, healing, and the gospel hymns. Services are free of what Matthew terms "niggeritions," the loud emotionalism of the holiness groups.

Matthew also taught Kabbalistic Science, a practice derived from conjuring, the folk magic of Southern Blacks. By conjuring, Matthew believed that he could heal and create changes in situations. The conjuring is worked through four angels. In order to get results, one must call upon the right angel.

Matthew was succeeded by his grandson, David M. Dore, a graduate of Yeshiva University.

★1730★
Deliverance Evangelistic Centers

Efforts to locate an address for this edition were unsuccessful. The initial Deliverance Evangelistic Center was formed in Brooklyn, New York in the 1950's by Arturo Skinner (d. 1975). Skinner had been stopped from committing suicide by what he believed to be the voice of God which told him, "Arturo, if you but turn around, I'll save your soul, heal your body, and give you a deliverance ministry." He was twenty-eight years old at the time, and though he had a full gospel background, he had never heard of anything termed a "deliverance ministry." In a period of retreat following his encounter with God, Skinner fasted and had a number of visions and dreams. He also consecrated his life to the ministry to which he had been called. After the founding of the first center, others were founded and pastors ordained to care for them. Women have been accepted into the ordained ministry as both evangelists and pastors.

The statement of belief of the centers includes an affirmation in the authority of the Bible as inspired and infallible, the Trinity, Jesus Christ as redeemer, the Holy Spirit who empowers and baptizes believers, speaking-in-tongues as evidence of the baptism of the Holy Spirit, creation, the necessity of repentence, sanctification, and water baptism by immersion. Skinner was the church's first Apostle. He was succeeded by Ralph Nickels.

★1731★
Ethiopian Zion Coptic Church

Efforts to locate an address for this edition were unsuccessful. The Ethiopian Zion Coptic Church was founded in Jamaica in 1914 by Marcus Garvey and orginially came to America in 1920 as part of his reformist efforts in the Black community. However, the church died out in the United States and became a small body in Jamaica. Then in 1970, several Americans in Jamaica encountered the church, joined it, and brought it back to Star Island, off Miami Beach, Florida. A second center was started in New Jersey. The leader of the group was Thomas Reilly Jr., generally known by his religious name, Brother Louv.

Church members believe in God who is experienced through the smoking of ganja, i.e., marijuana. Smoking marijuana is described as making a burnt sacrifice to the God within. The ceremonies for smoking the ganja utilize a specially made pipe. Coptics smoke ganja in such quantities that they hope it will reorganize their body chemistry around THC, the psycho-active ingredient in the plant, and they will thus survive the end of this world to live in God's new world. The new world is seen as a time in which there will be plenty for all without the necessity of an eight-hour work day. Peace and brotherhood will reign, and life will be lived at the horse-and-buggy pace. Ceremonially smoking ganja is the major sacramental act of church members, and members quote the Bible (*Genesis 1:29; Exodus 3:2-4; Psalm 104:14; and Hebrews 6:7*) in support of their use of marijuana.

Coptics also have a strong code dictating relations between the sexes. Women sit separately for the sacramental service and are not allowed to fill their own pipe. Sexual activity is strongly regulated. Homosexuality, oral sex, birth control, and abortion are prohibited. The only recognized purpose for sex is procreation.

Even prior to the church being granted tax exemption in 1975, it has fought an intense battle with government authorities. As early as 1973, authorities had seized 105 tons of marijuana from the group. In 1977 tax exemption was revoked. The church filed a lawsuit demanding the religious right of its members to smoke marijuana, a case lost in late 1978. Immediately after the court ruling, Reilly and five other church leaders were arrested in a raid on the Star Island headquarters. They were indicted and in 1981 convicted for drug smuggling. In 1982, Reilly, serving time in the Metropolitan Corrections Center in Miami, sued U.S. Attorney General William French Smith for the right to his daily sacrament of at least an ounce of marijuana.

In 1981, a group of approximately 20 members of the church moved to rural Wisconsin and established a settlement in an isolated valley near Soldiers Grove. They had moved from Iowa because of local harassment as a result of their refusal to have their children immunized as required by state law. Investigation stimulated by the group's use of marijuana led to arrests of church leaders in 1985. The arrest and conviction of church leaders has disrupted the life of the church, and the courts in the United States have persistently refused to allow the use of controlled substances by church organizations (apart from the Native American Church). The present status of the church is in doubt.

International headquarters of the church are in White Horses, Jamaica, where it had incorporated in 1976. They operate a 4,000 acre farm in St. Thomas Parish. Leader of the church in Jamaica is Keith Gordon (religious name, "Nyah").

★1732★
Fire-Baptized Holiness Church of God of the Americas

555 Houston St., NE
Atlanta, GA 30312

W.E. Fuller (1875-1958), the only Black man in attendance at the 1898 organizing conference of the Fire-Baptized Holiness Church, became the leader of almost a thousand Black people over the next decade. Feelings of discrimination led to their withdrawal and they organized the Colored Fire-Baptized Holiness Church at Anderson, South Carolina, on May 1, 1908. The White body gave them their accumulated assets and property at this time. Rev. Fuller was elected overseer and bishop. Doctrine is the same as in the International Pentecostal Holiness Church, the body that absorbed the Fire-Baptized Holiness Church. Legislative and executive authority are vested in a general council that meets every four years and in the eleven-member executive council (composed of bishops, district elders, and pastors). Mission work is under one of the bishops.

★1733★
Free Christian Zion Church of Christ

1315 Hutchingson
Nashville, AR 71852

The Free Christian Zion Church of Christ was formed on July 10, 1905, at Redemption, Arkansas, by the Rev. E.D. Brown, a conference missionary of the African Methodist Episcopal Zion Church. He and ministers from other Methodist churches objected to what they considered a taxing of the churches for support of an ecclesiastical system and believed that the primary concern of the church should be the care of the poor and needy.

The doctrine is Wesleyan and the polity Methodist with several minor alterations. The bishop, who is called the chief pastor, presides over the work and appoints the ministers and church officers. Pastors and deacons are the local church officers. There are district evangelists to care for the unevangelized communities.

★1734★
Free Church of God in Christ

Efforts to locate an address for this edition were unsuccessful. The Free Church of God in Christ dates from 1915 when J.H. Morris, a former pastor in the National Baptist Convention of the U.S.A., Inc., and a group of members of his church experienced the baptism of the Holy Spirit and spoke in tongues. The group, mostly members of Morris' family, founded a Pentecostal group which they called the Church of God in Christ. They chose as their leader the founder's son, E.J. Morris, who believed he was "selected" for the role. In 1921, the group united with the larger body led by Bishop Charles H. Mason, which had the same name. The union lasted for only four years, and Morris' group adopted its present name when it again became independent in 1925. It has the same doctrine and polity as the Mason body. By the late 1940's the church had 20 congregations.

★1735★
Fundamental Baptist Fellowship Association

Efforts to locate an address for this edition were unsuccessful. The Fundamental Baptist Fellowship Association was formed in 1962 by Black members of the General Association of Regular Baptist Churches (GARBC). The Black members came into the GARBC as a result of missionary work but felt that the GARBC would not accept them into the full fellowship. They presently cooperate with the Conservative Baptist Association.

★1736★
Glorious Church of God in Christ Apostolic Faith

Efforts to locate an address for this edition were unsuccessful. The Glorious Church of God in Christ Apostolic Faith was founded in 1921 by C.H. Stokes, its first presiding bishop. He was succeeded in 1928 by S.C. Bass who was to head the church for over a quarter of a century. However, in 1952, after the death of his first wife, Bass remarried a woman who was a divorcee. It had been taught for many years that marrying a divorced person was wrong. Bass' actions split the fifty-congregation church in half. Those who remained loyal to Bishop Bass retained the name, but the founding charter was retained by the other group, which took the name Original Glorious Church of God in Christ Apostolic Faith.

★1737★
God's House of Prayer for All Nations

Efforts to locate an address for this edition were unsuccessful. God's House of Prayer for All Nations, Inc., was founded in 1964 in Peoria, Illinois, by Bishop Tommie Lawrence, formerly of the Church of God in Christ. The doctrine is "oneness" Pentecostal, identifying Jesus with the Father, and the polity is strongly episcopal. Great stress is placed on healing as one of the signs of the spirit and there is much fellowship with the churches of the Miracle Revival Fellowship founded by the late A.A. Allen.

★1738★
Gospel Spreading Church

Efforts to locate an address for this edition were unsuccessful. The Gospel Spreading Church, sometimes called Elder Michaux Church of God or the Radio Church of God, was founded by Lightfoot Solomon Michaux (1885-1968), a minister in the Church of God (Holiness). At one point he served as the church's secretary-treasurer. However, he came into conflict with C.P. Jones, founder of the Church of God (Holiness) and left to found an independent church in Hampton, Virginia in 1922, retaining the name he had previously used, the Gospel Spreading Tabernacle Association. In 1928 he moved to Washington, D.C. and established the Church of God and Gospel Spreading Association.
His early success continued in the nation's capital, and he had discovered the potential of radio while in Virginia. In 1929 he began broadcasting on WJSV. Shortly thereafter CBS bought the station and his show expanded through the system. By 1934 he was on over 50 stations nationwide, with an estimated audience of 25,000,000. His show was also carried internationally by shortwave. He was the first Black person to receive such exposure. He mixed holiness themes with positive thinking. His magazine was entitled *Happy News*.
From his radio audience, congregations began to form in Black communities, primarily in the East. However, by the beginning of World War II his radio ministry had declined and he was heard only a few stations, in those cities where congregations had formed. In 1964 he reorganized his followers as the Gospel Spreading Church, but most of the congregations continued to call themselves the Church of God.

★1739★
Hanafi Madh-hab Center, Islam Faith

Efforts to locate an address for this edition were unsuccessful. The Hanafi Madh-hab Center, Islam Faith was formed in 1947 at the time when Hammas Abdul Khaalis (born Ernest Timothy McGee) met his teacher, Dr. Tasibur Uddein Rahman, a Mussulman (or Muslim) from Pakistan, who gave him his new name and taught him the *sunnah* (the tradition and practice) of the Prophet Muhammad. In 1950, Dr. Rahman sent Khaalis into the Nation of Islam (now the American Muslim Mission) to guide the members into Sunni Islam (that faith and practice recognized by the great majority of Muslims). By 1956 Khaalis was the national secretary of the Nation of Islam. He left the Nation of Islam in 1958, after unsuccessfully trying to convince Elijah Muhammad, the leader of the Nation of Islam, to change the direction of the movement. He founded the Hanafi Madh-hab Center in Washington, D.C., located in facilities provided by basketball star Kareem Abdul-Jabbar.
Again at the beginning of 1973, Khaalis wrote letters to the members and leaders of the Nation of Islam asking them to change to Sunni Muslim belief and practice. On January 18, 1973, several individuals came into the center in Washington, D.C., (which also served as Khaalis' home) and murdered six of his children and his stepson. His wife was wounded and is now paralyzed for life. Khaalis accused the Nation of Islam of the shooting, a charge it vehemently denied. Subsequently, five members of the Philadelphia Nation of Islam group were convicted of the murders, only to receive relatively light sentences.
In 1977, Khaalis and other Al-Hanif Musselman men took action against the showing of a motion picture, "*Mohammad, Messenger of God*," due to be released in theatres in America. They took over three buildings in Washington, D.C., and held people hostage for 38 hours. In the process, one man was killed. For this action Khaalis was sentenced to spend from 41 to 120 years in prison, and 11 of his followers were also convicted and sentenced.
The Al-Hanif Hanafi Musselmans believe in a literal interpretation of the *Holy Qur'an* and count themselves among the true followers of Islam in the larger world. They consider themselves to be Hanafi (meaning unconditional and uncompromising) and *Sunni* (obeying all things as laid down by Allah to the Prophet Muhammad). They are guided by the two standards of Islam, the *Holy Qur'an* and the Sunni Hadiths, the body of transmitted actions and sayings of Muhammad. They also follow by way of the 124,000 Prophets major and minor, and believe in all holy books according to Allah's knowledge. The *Holy Qur'an* is the final Seal of All Prophets and Prophecy.
The Hanafi Musselmans have taken a special interest in presenting Islam to so-called Black people and informing them that Islam is a religion that does not recognize distinctions of race or color.
Authority for Al-Hanif Hanafi Musselmans is vested in the chief Iman (teacher), Khalifa Hammas Abdul Khaalis, and each mosque is headed by an Iman appointed by him.

★1740★
Hebrew Israelites
2766 NW 62nd St.
Miami, FL 33147

The Hebrew Israelites, also known as the Temple of Love, was founded by Hulon Mitchell Jr. (b. 1935), known to his followers by his religious name, Moses Israel. Mitchell was raised in the Pentecostal church, where his father was a minister, but later became the leader of a mosque in the Nation of Islam, headed by Elijah Muhammad. The Hebrew Israelites were formed in the 1970's.

Moses Israel teaches that there is one God and Yahweh is his name. He is a Black God with woolly hair (*Daniel 7:9; Deuternomy 7:21*), and has sent his son, Yahweh ben Yahweh, to be the Saviour and Deliverer of his people, the Black race. Black people are believed to be the true lost tribe of Judah and will soon go to Israel. Members renounce their slave name and take the surname Israel. They are also encouraged to make white robes (*Revelation 3:4-5, 18*) to show the world that they know God. All members of the group dress in white. White people are seen as the devil, the adversary of God, the product of Eve's adulterous relation with the serpent in the Garden of Eden.

Since its founding the Temple of Love has expanded in the Miami area. There it has two temples, a school, and a printing plant. It also has a fleet of buses used to send its evangelists around the United States.

★1741★

Highway Christian Church of Christ

432 W St.,NW
Washington, DC 20001

The Highway Christian Church of Christ was founded in 1929 by James Thomas Morris, formerly a minister with the Pentecostal Assemblies of the World. Relations between the two groups remained cordial, and in 1941 Bishop J.M. Turpin of the Assemblies consecrated Morris to the episcopal leadership of the Highway Church. Morris died in 1959 and was succeeded by his nephew, J.V. Lomax, formerly a member of the Church of Our Lord Jesus Christ of the Apostolic Faith.

The Highway Church has a reputation as one of the more conservative Pentecostal church bodies. Members are encouraged to wear only black (suits and skirts) and white (shirts and blouses), and to avoid bright colors as too ostentatious. The church will accept ordained women from other denominations, but will neither ordain females nor allow them to pastor congregations.

★1742★

House of God Which Is the Church of the Living God, The Pillar and Ground of Truth

Efforts to locate an address for this edition were unsuccessful. Not to be confused with the church of the same name which derives from the movement begun by Mary L. Tate known as the Church of the Living God, the Pillar and Ground of Truth. The church presently under discussion derives from the work begun by William Christian. In the early twentieth century, the Church of the Living God (Christian Workers for Fellowship), which Christian founded, was splintered on several occasions. In 1902, a group calling itself the Church of the Living God, Apostolic Church, withdrew and, six years later under the leadership of Rev. C. W. Harris, became the Church of the Living God, General Assembly. It united in 1924 with a second small splinter body. In 1925, a number of churches withdrew from the Church of the Living God (Christian Workers for Fellowship) under the leadership of Rev. E. J. Cain and called themselves the Church of the Living God, the Pillar and Ground of Truth. The Harris group joined the Cain group in 1926 and they later adopted the present name. The Church is one in doctrine with the Church of the Living God (Christian Workers for Fellowship). Polity is episcopal and there is an annual general assembly.

★1743★

House of God, Which Is the Church of the Living God, the Pillar and Ground of Truth, Inc.

Efforts to locate an address for this edition were unsuccessful. In 1919 the Church of the Living God, the Pillar and Ground of Truth founded by Mary L. Tate, experienced a schism led by the congregation in Philadelphia. The new group, the House of God, the Church of the Living God, the Pillar and Ground of Truth continues the doctrine and episcopal polity of the parent body, but is administratively separate. The general assembly meets annually.

★1744★

House of God Which is the Church of the Living God, the Pillar and Ground of Truth without Controversy (Keith Dominion)

Efforts to locate an address for this edition were unsuccessful. In 1931, following the death of founder Bishop Mary L. Tate, the Church of the Living God, the Pillar and Ground of the Truth, Inc., appointed three chief overseers. Eventually, each became the head of a distinct segment of the church and then of an independent body called a dominion. One of the three chief overseers was M.F.L. Keith, widow of Bishop Tate's son, W.C. Lewis. Her dominion became known as the House of God Which is the Church of the Living God the Pillar and Ground of Truth Without Controversy (Keith Dominion).

The church is headed by a Chief Overseer (Bishop J.W. Jenkins succeeded Bishop Keith in that post) and a Supreme Executive Council.

★1745★

House of Judah

Efforts to locate an address for this edition were unsuccessful. The House of Judah is a small Black Israelite group founded in 1965 by Prophet William A. Lewis. Alabama-born Lewis was converted to his Black Jewish beliefs (which are similar to those of the Church of God and Saints of Christ) from a street preacher in Chicago in the 1960s. Throughout the decade he gathered a small following out of a storefront on the southside and in 1971 moved the group to a twenty-two-acre tract near Grand Junction, Michigan. The group lived quietly and little noticed until 1983 when a young boy in the group was beaten to death. The incident focused attention on the group for its advocacy of corporal punishment. The mother of the boy was sentenced to prison for manslaughter. By 1985 the group had resettled in Alabama.

The House of Judah teaches that the Old Testament Jews were Black, being derived from Jacob and his son Judah, who were Black (*Jeremiah 14:2*). Both Solomon and Jesus were Black. Jerusalem, not Africa, is the Black man's land. The White Jew is the devil (*Rev. 2:9*); he occupies the Black man's land but will soon be driven out. The House of Judah awaits a deliverer, whom God will send to take the Black man from the U.S.A. to Jerusalem. He will be a second Moses to lead his people to the promised land. The group lives communally.

★1746★

House of the Lord

Efforts to locate an address for this edition were unsuccessful. The House of the Lord was founded in 1925 by Bishop W.H. Johnson, who established headquarters in Detroit. The doctrine is Pentecostal but departs on several important points. A person who enters the church is born of water and seeks to be born of God by a process of sanctification. The Holy Ghost may be given and is evidenced by speaking in tongues. But sanctification is evidenced by conformity to a very rigid code which includes refraining from worldly amusements, whiskey, policy rackets (the "numbers game"), becoming bell hops, participating in war, swearing, secret organizations, tithing, and life insurance (except as required by an employer). A believer is not sanctified if he owns houses, lands, or goods. Water is used in the Lord's Supper. Members are not to marry anyone not baptized by the Holy Ghost.

The church is governed by a hierarchy of ministers, state overseers, and chief overseer. There is a common treasury at each local church from which the destitute are helped.

★1747★

Imani Temple African-American Catholic Congregation

1134 11th St. NW
Washington, DC 20001 Phone: (202)371-0801

In 1989 Father G. Augustus Stallings, Jr. formed the Imani Temple African-American Congregation in the face of disapproval from Cardinal James Hickey to meet what he felt were the underrecognized needs of

Black Catholics in the Washington, D.C. area. Stallings has said that he is not seeking a schism, but rather wants to form an African-American rite within the Catholic Church that embraces the culture and traditions of Black Americans.

★1748★
Institute of Divine Metaphysical Research

Efforts to locate an address for this edition were unsuccessful. The Institute for Divine Metaphysical Research grew out of a vision of Dr. Henry Clifford Kinley which occurred on June 6, 1931 in Springfield, Ohio. Kinley, a holiness church minister, was given a vision of Yahweh (who others mistakenly call God) and His plan for the ages. He began to give classes on the insight derived from the vision the following year and soon thereafter he founded the Kinley Institute. Among his first students was Carl F. Gross, who became his lifelong associate and president of the institute. In 1958, with approximately seventy of his students, Kinley moved to Los Angeles and incorporated the Institute for Divine Metaphysical Research. In 1961, Elohim the Archetype (Original Pattern of the Universe, the major exposition of the vision) appeared. Copies were immediately sent to a number of prominent world political and religious leaders. In 1971 twelve ministers of the institute were sent out on an Ecclesiastical Peace Mission to countries in Europe and the Middle East. A second such mission to countries on every continent was conducted in 1975.

The intent of the institute has been to spread the message of Kinley's vision as presented in his book. The teachings draw from a variety of sources including both the Sacred Name Movement and theosophy. In the vision he learned the real name of the Holy One of Israel (Yahweh) and of his nature and purposes. Yahweh is Spirit Substance, without form. As Elohim, Yahweh appears in His super incoporeal form and in that form was seen by Moses (*Exodus 24*), Isaiah (*Isaiah 6:1-4*), and the disciples at the Mount of Transfiguration (*Matthew 17:1-2*). Yahweh-Elohim has also taken physical form generally as the material creation (matter is condensed spirit) and specifically as Yahshua the Messiah (generally known as Jesus). After the death and resurrection of Yahshua, Yahweh continued in his physical form as the Comforter or Holy Spirit, and dwells in preachers of the true gospel.

Yahweh-Elohim, as was revealed to Kinley, is the archtypal pattern of the universe, a pattern revealed to Moses and embodied in the Hebrew tabernacle. It is, however, also repeated in numerous earthly structures, among which is the Kaballah, which Kinley terms "theosophy."

Yahweh's purpose is revealed through the ages (i.e., particular periods of history) and dispensations (i.e., the divinely appointed ordering of earthly affairs by Yahweh). The dispensations as recounted by Kinley generally follow that proposed by C.I. Scofield in his reference Bible, and adopt a traditional chronology. The first dispensation begins with Yahweh's covenant with Adam, the second with Noah, the third with Abraham, and the fourth with Noah. Kinley is insistent that the fifth dispensation, that of the "law of the Spirit" or New Testament, this present church age, began not at Jesus' birth but at his resurrection and Pentecost. Most importantly, the present dispensation is swiftly drawing to a close and the next dispensation, that of the Kingdom in Immortality, will begin around the year 2000. The revelation of Yahweh's purposes to Kinley and his work of spreading the information ushered in the last days of the church age.

★1749★
International Council of Community Churches

Efforts to locate an address for this edition were unsuccessful. The International Council of Community Churches was formally organized in 1946, but possesses a history dating from the early nineteenth century when nonsectarian community churches began to appear as an alternative to the formation of separate denominationally affiliated congregations. Such community churches were especially welcomed in communities too small to support more than one viable congregation. Over the years, such congregations have frequently retained a fiercely independent stance. To their number were added other independent congregations that had separated from denominational structures and adopted a nonsectarian stance.

In the wake of the ecumenical movement in the early twentieth century, the most visible symbol being the Federal Council of Churches of Christ formed in 1908, many congregations merged across denominational lines, some forming independent federated or union churches, dropping all denominational affiliation. During this period, some community churches began to see, in light of their years of existence apart from denominational boundaries, that they had a particular role vis-a-vis Christian unity.

A first attempt to build a network of community churches was known as the Community Church Workers of the United States. At a national conference of individuals serving community churches in Chicago in 1923, a committee formed to hold a second conference and outline plans for a national association. Organization occurred the next year and the Rev. Orvis F. Jordan of the Park Ridge (Ill.) Community Church was named as secretary. He later became the first president of the group. The organization continued for over a decade, but died in the 1930's due to lack of support.

A second organization of community churches was also begun in 1923 among predominantly Black congregations. Representatives of five congregations gathered in Chicago, Illinois in the fall of 1923 to form the National Council of the People's Community Churches (incorporated in 1933 as the Biennial Council of the People's Church of Christ and Community Centers of the United States and Elsewhere). The Rev. William D. Cook, pastor of Metropolitan Community Church in Chicago, served as the first president.

Unable to gain recognition from the Federal Council of Churches, the independent community churches began a second attempt at organization in the last days of World War II. The Rev. Roy A. Burkhart, pastor of First Community Church of Columbus, Ohio, led in the formation of the Ohio Association for Community Churches in 1945. The next year representatives from nineteen states and Canada met and formed the National Council of Community Churches.

Almost immediately, the Black and White groups began to work toward a merger. The merger, accomplished in 1950, created the International Council of Community Churches with a charter membership of 160 churches. By 1957, the several foreign congregations had ceased their affiliation with the council and the word "International" was dropped. In 1969, the name was changed to National Council of Community Churches. In 1983, however, foreign congregations in Canada and Nigeria affiliated and in 1984 the original name was again assumed.

There is no doctrinal statement shared by the council or its member churches, though most churches share a liberal, ecumenical-minded, Protestant perspective. The council describes itself as committed to Christian unity and working "toward a fellowship as comprehensive as the spirit and teachings of Christ and as inclusive as the love of God." The council is a loosely organized fellowship of free and autonomous congregations. The national and regional officers facilitate communication between congregations and serve member congregations in various functions, such as representing them at the Consultation on Church Union and coordinating the securing of chaplains in the armed services.

★1750★
International Evangelical Church and Missionary Association

c/o Evangel Temple
610 Rhode Island Ave., NE
Washington, DC 20002

The International Evangelical Church and Missionary Association is a charismatic fellowship of churches formed in the early 1980's under the leadership of John Meares, pastor of Evangel Temple in Washington, D.C. Meares was raised in the Church of God (Cleveland, Tennessee), the nephew of the general overseer. After serving several Church of God congregations, Meares went to Washington, D.C., in 1955 to begin the Revival Center (soon renamed the National Evangelistic Center), a new Church of God outreach for the city. However, he soon encountered controversy within the Church of God because he had started an unlicensed ministry. This led to his disfellowshipping in May 1956. He continued his independent ministry, however, which emerged in new quarters as Evangel Temple in 1957. Membership of the integrated congregation was approximately two-thirds Black.

In the early 1960's, Meares became aware of Bethesda Missionary Temple, one of the principle congregations of the Latter-Rain movement. From his observation of the life of the temple, he picked up a new emphasis on praise and the gift of prophecy which he introduced to Evangel Temple. This coincided with the heightened tensions of the civil rights movement which climaxed for Meares and the temple in the rioting that followed the assassination of Martin Luther King. Most of the White members withdrew, and Meares emerged in the early 1970's as

the White pastor of a largely Black church. Membership dropped to several hundred. The church slowly rebuilt, however, and in 1975 moved into new three million dollar facilities.
During his years in Washington, many independent Pentecostal pastors had begun to look to Meares for leadership and guidance. The International Evangelical Churches and Missionary Association emerged out of that relationship. In 1982, Bishops Benson Idahosa of Nigeria, Robert McAleister of Brazil, and Earl P. Paulk, Jr. of Atlanta, Georgia, all members of the International Communion of Charismatic Churches, consecrated Meares a bishop.
Over the years, Meares and Evangel Temple have become major voices in the Pentecostal community speaking to the issues of racism. Since 1984, Evangel Temple has become the site of an annual national Inner City Pastors' Conferences, attended primarily, but by no means exclusively, by Black Pentecostal pastors from around the United States and Canada. More than 1,000 pastors attended the 1987 conference.

★1751★
Kodesh Church of Emmanuel

Efforts to locate an address for this edition were unsuccessful. The Kodesh Church of Emmanuel is a Black holiness sect that was formed by Reverend Frank Russell Killingsworth when he withdrew from the African Methodist Episcopal Church in 1929 along with 120 followers. In common with other holiness churches, this church emphasizes entire sanctification as a second definite work of grace conditioned upon a life of absolute consecration. The church forbids use of alcohol, tobacco and prideful dress; membership in secret societies; and profaning the Sabbath. In 1934, a merger was effected with the Christian Tabernacle Union of Pittsburgh.
The church is governed by a quadrennial general assembly. Regional assembly assemblies annually. There is mission work in Liberia.

★1752★
Latter House of the Lord for All People and the Church of the Mountain, Apostolic Faith

Efforts to locate an address for this edition were unsuccessful. The Latter House of the Lord for All People and the Church of the Mountain, Apostolic Faith, was founded in 1936 by Bishop L.W. Williams, a former Black Baptist preacher from Cincinnati. The founding followed an enlightenment experience and spiritual blessing realized in prayer. The doctrine is Calvinistic, but adjusted to accommodate Pentecostal beliefs. The Lord's Supper is observed, with water being used instead of wine. The Church members are conscientious objectors. The chief overseer is appointed for life.

★1753★
Miracle Life Fellowship International

Efforts to locate an address for this edition were unsuccessful. Asa Alonzo Allen was born of a poor Arkansas family, saved in a Methodist revival, and later baptized with the Holy Spirit in a Pentecostal meeting. He joined the Assemblies of God and felt called to preach. In the early 1940s, he began to seek a ministry of signs and wonders, particularly healing. He had what amounted to a theological conversion when, during a prayer time, he formulated the thirteen requirements for a powerful ministry. He became convinced that he could do the works of Jesus, and do more than Jesus did; that he could be flawless and perfect (in the Biblical sense), and should believe all the promises. During World War II, his throat became, according to one throat specialist, "permanently ruined," but Allen was healed.
In 1951, he purchased a tent and began the crusade in earnest. Headquarters of A.A. Allen Revivals, Inc., were established in Dallas and *Miracle Magazine* was begun. From that time until his death, Allen was an immensely popular evangelist speaking both to integrated and predominantly Black audiences. As early as 1960, he was holding fully integrated meetings in the South. In 1958, he was given 1,250 acres near Tombstone, Arizona, which were named Miracle Valley and which became the international headquarters. Allen died in 1970 and was succeeded by Don Stewart, who chose the new name for the organization: Miracle Revival Fellowship.
Miracle Valley was created as a totally spiritual community. Allen founded a Bible school and publishing house, located adjacent to radio and television studios, the healing pool of Bethesda, and the headquarters. He also operated a telephone Dial-a-Miracle prayer service. The church seats 2,500. As a result of Allen's accomplishments and success, missionary churches were begun and independent ministers have become associated wtih him. Miracle Revival Fellowship, (now Miracle Life Fellowship International) at first a department of A.A. Allen Revivals, was established as a ministerial fellowship and licensing agency. After Allen's death, the Bible college was turned over to the Central Latin American District Council of the Assemblies of God and is now known as Southern Arizona Bible College. A. A. Allen Revivals became the Don Stewart Association.

★1754★
Moorish Science Temple of America
1316 E. 33rd St.
Baltimore, MD 21201

Timothy Drew (1886-1929), a Black man from North Carolina, had concluded from his reading and travels that Black people were not Ethiopians (as some early Black nationalists were advocating) but Asiatics, specifically Moors. They were descendants of the ancient Moabites and their homeland was Morocco. He claimed that the Continental Congress had stripped American Blacks of their nationality and that George Washington had cut down their bright red flag (the cherry tree) and hidden it in a safe in Independence Hall. Blacks were thus assigned to the role of slaves.
As Noble Drew Ali, Drew emerged in 1913 in Newark, New Jersey, to preach the message of Moorish identity. The movement spread slowly with early centers in Pittsburgh, Detroit and several southern cities. In 1925, Ali moved to Chicago and the following year incorporated the Moorish Science Temple of America. In 1927 he published *The Holy Koran* (not to be confused with the *Koran* or *Qur'aan* used by all orthodox Moslem groups). Ali's *Koran* was a pamphlet-size compilation of Moorish beliefs which drew heavily upon *The Aquarian Gospel of Jesus Christ*, a volume received by automatic writing by Spiritualist Levi Dowling in the 1890s. The *Koran* delineates the creation and fall of the race, the origin of Black people, the opposition of Christianity to God's people and the modern predicament of the Moors.
It was Noble Drew Ali's belief that only Islam could unite the Black man. The Black race is Asiatic, Moroccan, hence Moorrish. Jesus was a Black man who tried to redeem the Black Moabites and was executed by the White Romans. Moorish Americans must be united under Allah and his holy prophet. Marcus Garvey is seen as forerunner to Ali. Friday has been accepted as the holy day. Worship forms, particularly music, have been drawn from popular Black culture and given Islamic content.
Ali died in 1919 and was succeeded by one of his young colleagues, R. German Ali, who still heads the movement. Shortly after Ali's death, one of the members appeared in Detroit as Wallace Fard Muhammad, the reincarnation of Noble Drew Ali, and began the Nation of Islam (now the American Muslim Mission). In spite of the competition from the Nation of Islam, the temple grew in the years after Ali's death, and during the 1940's the temples could be found in Charleston, West Virginia; Hartford, Connecticut; Milwaukee; Richmond, Virginia; Cleveland; Flint, Michigan; Chattanooga, Tennessee; Indianapolis; Toledo and Steubenville, Ohio; Brooklyn; and Indiana Harbor, Indiana. In more recent years, the movement has declined. During the 1970's, the headquarters were moved to Baltimore.

★1755★
Moorish Science Temple, Prophet Ali Reincarnated, Founder

Efforts to locate an address for this edition were unsuccessful. In 1975, Richardson Dingle-El, a member of the Moorish Science Temple of America in Baltimore, proclaimed himself Noble Drew Ali 3d, the reincarnation of Noble Drew Ali (1886-1929), the founder of the Moorish Science Temple of America. As such he claimed succession to Noble Drew Ali 2d (d.1945), who had claimed succession in the 1930s. The followers of Noble Drew Ali 3d have established headquarters in Baltimore and have several temples around the United States. A periodical is published by the temple in Chicago. In most ways it follows the beliefs and practices of the Moorish Science Temple of America.

★1756★
Mount Calvary Holy Church of America
c/o Bishop Harold Williams
1214 Chowan St.
Durham, NC 27713

The Mt. Calvary Holy Church is a small Black holiness church headquartered in Boston, Massachusetts, founded by Bishop Brumfield Johnson. Its doctrine is similar to that of the United Holy Church of America. Churches are located in North Carolina; Baltimore, Maryland; New York; Boston; and other cities on the east coast.

★1757★
Mount Hebron Apostolic Temple of Our Lord Jesus of the Apostolic Faith

Efforts to locate an address for this edition were unsuccessful. The Mount Hebron Apostolic Temple of Our Lord Jesus of the Apostolic Faith was founded in 1963 by George H. Wiley III, pastor of the Yonkers, New York, congregation of the Apostolic Church of Christ in God. As his work progressed, Wiley came to feel that because of his accomplishments for the denomination he should be accorded the office of bishop. He had had particular success in the area of youth work, and his wife, Sister Lucille Wiley, served as president of the Department of Youth Work. However, the board of the Apostolic Church denied his request to become a bishop. He left with his supporters and became bishop of a new Apostolic denomination.
Wiley has placed great emphasis upon youth work and upon radio work, establishing an outreach in New York, one in North Carolina, and another in South Carolina. The temple continues the doctrine and polity of the Apostolic Church of Christ in God and has a cordial relationship with its parent organization.

★1758★
Mount Sinai Holy Church

Efforts to locate an address for this edition were unsuccessful. Ida Robinson grew up in Georgia, was converted at age seventeen, and joined the United Holy Church of America. She moved to Philadelphia where she became the pastor of the Mount Olive Holy Church. Following what she believed to be the command of the Holy Spirit to "Come out on Mount Sinai," she founded the Mount Sinai Holy Church in 1924. Women have played a prominent role in its leadership from the beginning.
The doctrine is Pentecostal, with sanctification a prerequisite for the baptism of the Holy Spirit. One must be converted before becoming a member. Bishop Robinson believed that God ordained four types of human beings: the elect or chosen of God, the compelled (those who could not help themselves from being saved), the "who so ever will" who can be saved, and the damned (ordained for hell). Spiritual healing is stressed. Foot-washing is practiced. Behavior, particularly sexual, is rigidly codified and rules are strictly observed. Short dresses, neckties, and worldly amusements are frowned upon.
The Mount Sinai Holy Church is episcopal in government. Bishop Robinson served as senior bishop and president until her death in 1946. She was succeeded by Bishop Elmira Jeffries, the original vice-president, who was, in turn, succeeded by Bishop Mary Jackson in 1964. Assisting the bishops is a board of presbyteries, composed of the elders of the churches. There are four administrative districts, each headed by a bishop. There is an annual conference of the entire church, and one is held in each district. Foreign missions in Cuba and Guinea are supported.

★1759★
The Nation of Islam (Farrakhan)
734 W. 79th Ave.
Chicago, IL 60620

Of the several factions which broke away from the American Muslim Mission (formerly known as the Nation of Islam and then as the World Community of Islam in the West) and assumed the group's original name, the most successful has been the Nation of Islam headed by Abdul Haleem Farrakhan. Farrakhan was born Louis Eugene Wolcott. He was a nightclub singer in the mid-1950s when he joined the Nation of Islam headed by Elijah Muhammad. As was common among Muslims at that time, he dropped his last name, which was seen as a name imposed by slavery and White society, and became known as Minister Louis X. His oratorical and musical skills carried him to a leading position as minister in charge of the Boston Mosque and, after the defection and death of Malcolm X, to the leadership of the large Harlem center and designation as the official spokesperson for Elijah Muhammad.
In 1975 Elijah Muhammad died. Though many thought Louis X, by then known by his present name, might become the new leader of the nation, Elijah Muhammad's son, Wallace, was chosen instead. At Wallace Muhammad's request, Farrakhan moved to Chicago to assume a national post. During the next three years, the Nation of Islam moved away from many of its distinctive beliefs and programs and emerged as the American Muslim Mission. It dropped many of its racial policies and began to admit White people into membership. It also began to move away from its Black nationalist demands and to accept integration as a proper goal of its programs.
Farrakhan emerged as a leading voice among "purists" who opposed any changes in the major beliefs and programs instituted by Elijah Muhammad. Long-standing disagreements with the new direction of the Black Muslim body led Farrakhan to leave the organization in 1978 and to form a new Nation of Islam. He reinstituted the beliefs and program of the pre-1975 Nation of Islam. He reformed the Fruit of Islam, the internal security force, and demanded a return to strict dress standards.
With several thousand followers, Farrakhan began to rebuild the Nation of Islam. He established mosques and developed an outreach to the Black community on radio. He was only slightly noticed until 1984 when he aligned himself with the U.S. presidential campaign of Jesse Jackson, a Black minister seeking the nomination of the Democratic Party. Jackson's acceptance of his support and Farrakhan's subsequent controversial statements (some claimed by critics to be anti-Semitic) on radio and at press conferences kept Farrakhan's name in the news during the period of Jackson's candidacy and in subsequent months.

★1760★
The Nation of Islam (John Muhammad)
14880 Wyoming
Detroit, MI 48238

John Muhammad, brother of Elijah Muhammad, founder of the Nation of Islam, was among those who rejected the changes in the Nation of Islam and the teachings of Elijah Muhammad which led to its change into the American Muslim Mission. In 1978 he left the mission and formed a continuing Nation of Islam designed to perpetuate the programs outlined in Elijah Muhammad's two books, *Message to the Blackman* and *Our Saviour Has Arrived.* According to John Muhammad, who uses the standard title of Black Muslim leaders, "Minister" Elijah Muhammad was the last Messenger of Allah and was sent to teach the Black man a New Islam.

★1761★
The Nation of Islam (The Caliph)

Efforts to locate an address for this edition were unsuccessful. As significant changes within the Nation of Islam founded by Elijah Muhammad proceeded under his son and successor Wallace D. Muhammad, the Nation of Islam became a more orthodox Islamic organization. It was renamed the American Muslim Mission and dropped many of the distinctive features of its predecessor. Opposition among those committed to Elijah Muhammad's ideas and programs led to several schisms in the late 1970s. Among the "purist" leaders,

Emmanuel Abdullah Muhammad asserted his role as the Caliph of Islam raised up to guide the people in the absence of Allah (in the person of Wallace Fard Muhammad) and his Messenger (Elijah Muhammad). One Islamic tradition insists that a caliph always follows a messenger.
The Nation of Islam under the caliph continues the beliefs and practices abandoned by the American Muslim Mission. A new school, the University of Islam, was begun and the Fruit of Islam, the disciplined order of Islamic men, reinstituted. A new effort aimed at economic self-sufficiency has been promoted, and businesses have been created to implement the program.

★1762★
Nation of Yahweh (Hebrew Israelites)
c/o Temple of Love
2766 NW 62nd St.
Miami, FL 33147

The Nation of Yahweh, also known as the Hebrew Israelites or the Followers of Yahweh, is a movement founded by Yahweh ben (son of) Yahweh. Yahweh ben Yahweh was born Hulon Mitchell, Jr., considered a slave name, and no longer used. He was the son of a Pentecostal minister who at one point joined the Nation of Islam in which he became the leader of one of the mosques. He began to call together the Followers of Yahweh in the 1970s.
Yahweh ben Yahweh teaches that there is one God, whose name is Yahweh. God is Black with woolly hair (*Daniel 7:9; Revelation 1:13-15; Dueteronomy 7:21*), and has sent his son, Yahweh ben Yahweh to be the Savior and Deliverer of His people, the so-called Black people of America. Those who believe in Yahweh ben Yahweh and His name are immortal. Black people are considered the true lost tribe of Judah. They have been chosen by Yahweh, but have yet to be put into their destined office of rulership. Members, upon joining, renounce their slave name and take the surname Israel. Many of them wear white robes as commanded in the Bible (*Ecclesiastes 9:8*). They believe that all people who oppose God are devils, regardless of race or color. The devil is one who is immoral and follows immoral teachings of wickedness and evilness. Many persons, regardless of their race or color are capable of being and actually are the devil.
While the Nation of Yahweh has a special place for the chosen Black people of America, and see White people as especially used by Satan in exercising wicked rulership, in the end salvation is not a matter of color. Any person of any race or color can be saved by faith in Yahweh ben Yahweh.
Along with its particular religious beliefs, the Nation of Yahweh sees itself as establishing a united moral power to benefit the total community of America. It supports voter registration, education, self-help jobs, business opportunities, scholarships for children, health education, better housing, strong family ties, peace, love, and harmony among people regardless of race, creed, or color. Members are taught to practice charity and benevolence, to protect chastity, to respect the ties of blood and friendship, and revere the laws of Yahweh.
The Nation of Yahweh is headed by Yahweh ben Yahweh. In its work, the nation has purchased several hotels and apartment buildings. It owns, through its corporate entity, the Temple of Love, and more than 42 (in 1988) businesses which are used to support the organization and its members.

★1763★
National Baptist Convention of America

Efforts to locate an address for this edition were unsuccessful. In 1915, an issue arose in the National Baptist Convention of the U.S.A., Inc. over the ownership of the publishing house. Early in the Convention's life, the Rev. R.H. Boyd, a brilliant businessman, was made corresponding secretary of the publication board. Under his leadership, the publishing house did over two million dollars in business in the first decade. As time passed, however, some members of the Convention realized that the publishing interest had been built on Boyd's property, and all the materials had been copyrighted in his name. Further, no proceeds were being donated to other Convention activities.
In a showdown, the 1915 Convention moved to correct its mistake by adopting a new charter which clarified the subservient position of the boards. Refusing to comply, Boyd withdrew the publishing house from the Convention and made it the center of a second National Baptist Convention, called the National Baptist Convention of America. Because of its refusal to accept the charter, it is usually referred to as "unincorporated." Missions are carried on in Jamaica, Panama, and Africa. Ten colleges and seminaries are supported.

★1764★
National Baptist Convention of the U.S.A., Inc.
c/o Dr. T.G. Jemison, Pres.
915 Spain St.
Baton Rouge, LA 70802

The National Baptist Convention of the U.S.A. came into existence after the adoption of a resolution before the Foreign Mission Baptist Convention of the U.S.A. to merge itself, the American National Baptist Convention, and the Baptist National Educational Convention. To these three would be added a publications board for Sunday school literature. The Convention was formed in Atlanta, Georgia, in 1895. Elected president and corresponding secretary of foreign missions were Rev. E.C. Morris and Lewis G. Jordan, respectively. Both were able men; the National Baptist Convention's survival, stability, and success were in no small part due to their long terms in office.
Doctrine and government were taken over from the White Baptists. The congregational form of church life allowed a ready adaptation to the Black culture, which used religious forms as a socially accepted way to express their frustration and to protest their conditions. The worship developed a high degree of emotional expression, making little reference to traditional liturgical forms. (While freed from the rituals of their White parents in the faith, the local church developed its own "forms," which seem spontaneous to the occasional visitor. In fact, the Black Baptists allowed themselves to create a new religious culture, the pattern of which they follow weekly in their service.)
Within two years of its founding, the new National Baptist Convention ran into trouble when Jordan moved its offices from Richmond to Louisville. The Virginia Brethren, fearing a loss of power, withdrew support. They formed the Lott Carey Missionary Convention, which still exists as an independent missionary society. A more serious disagreement split the denomination in 1915.
For twenty-nine years (1953-1982) the National Baptists were led by J.H. Jackson. He was succeeded in 1982 by T.J. Jamison, the son of the convention's president from 1941-1953, D.V. Jemison. There is mission work in Africa and the Bahamas. The group operates five colleges, a theological seminary, and a training school for women and girls.

★1765★
National Baptist Evangelical Life and Soul Saving Assembly of the U.S.A.
441 Monroe Ave.
Detroit, MI 48226

The National Baptist Evangelical Life and Soul Saving Assembly of the U.S.A. was founded by A.A. Banks in 1920 in Kansas City, Missouri. It was begun as a city mission and evangelical movement within the National Baptist Convention of America, with which it remained affiliated for 15 years. Differences arose in the mid-1930s, and in 1936 at Birmingham, Alabama, the Assembly declared itself independent. Centers were established in cities across the nation.
No official statements regulate the doctrine of the Assembly, but generally the doctrine follows that of the National Baptist Convention of America. Relief work, charitable activity, and evangelizing are the main concerns of the Association. Each member hopes to add one member to the kingdom annually. Correspondence courses have been developed in evangelism, missions, pastoral ministry, and the work of deacons and laymen. Degrees are awarded for these studies.

★1766★
National Colored Spiritualist Association of Churches
c/o Rev. Nellie Mae Taylor
1245 W. Watkins Rd.
Phoenix, AZ 85007

Shortly after World War I, the growing Black membership in the National Spiritualist Association of Churches separated from the parent body and, in 1922, formed the National Colored Spiritualist Association of Churches. Doctrine and practice follow closely those of the parent body. Churches are located in Detroit, Chicago, Columbus (Ohio), Miami, Charleston (South Carolina), New York City, Phoenix and St. Petersburg.

★1767★
National Primitive Baptist Convention of the U.S.A.
2116 Clinton Ave., W.
Huntsville, AL 35805

Around the turn of the century, there was a movement among the Black Primitive Baptists to organize a national convention. In 1906, Elders Clarence Francis Sams, George S. Crawford, James H. Carey, and others called on their colleagues to join them in a meeting at Huntsville, Alabama, in 1907. Eighty-eight elders from seven Southern states responded. In organizing the convention, of course, the members departed from a main Primitive Baptist concern-that there should be no organization above the loose associations that typically cover several counties.
Doctrinally, the National Primitive Baptist Convention follows the Regular Primitive Baptists. The Convention's creeds profess belief in the "particular election of a definite number of the human race." Footwashing is practiced. The organization is congregational, and at the local level there are two offices-pastor (elder) and deacon or deaconness (mother). The convention meets annually and sponsors Sunday schools and a publishing board.

★1768★
New Bethel Church of God in Christ (Pentecostal)

Efforts to locate an address for this edition were unsuccessful. In 1927, the Rev. A.D. Bradley was admonished by the board of bishops of the Church of God in Christ to refrain from preaching the "Jesus only" doctrine. (The Church of God in Christ was the oldest and among the largest of the predominantly-Black trinitarian Pentecostal churches.) He refused, and with his wife and Lonnie Bates established the New Bethel Church of God in Christ (Pentecostal). Bradley became the church's presiding bishop. Doctrine is similar to other "Jesus only" groups. The three ordinances of baptism, the Lord's Supper, and foot-washing are observed. The group is pacifist but allows alternative noncombatant positions to be held by law-abiding church members. The group disapproves of secret societies and of school activities which conflict with a student's moral scruples.
The presiding bishop is the executive officer and presides over all meetings of the general body. A board of bishops acts as a judicatory body and a general assembly as the legislative body.

★1769★
Original Glorious Church of God in Christ Apostolic Faith

Efforts to locate an address for this edition were unsuccessful. The Glorious Church of God was founded in 1921. However, in 1952 its presiding bishop, S.C. Bass married a divorced woman. Approximately half of the fifty-congregation church rejected Bass and reorganized under the leadership of W.O. Howard and took the name Original Glorious Church of God in Christ Apostolic Faith. The term "Original" signified their claim to the history of the church, demonstrated by their retention of the founding charter. Howard was succeeded by Bishop I.W. Hamiter, under whose leadership the church has grown spectacularly and developed a mission program in Haiti, Jamaica and India. Hamiter has also led in the purchase of a convention center for the church's annual meeting in Columbus, Ohio.

★1770★
Original Hebrew Israelite Nation

Efforts to locate an address for this edition were unsuccessful. The Black Israelites (members of the Original Hebrew Israelite Nation) emerged in Chicago in the 1960's around Ben Ammi Carter (born G. Parker), a Black man who had studied Judaism with a rabbi, and Shaleah Ben-Israel. To the Black Jewish ideas (which were espoused by several groups in Chicago at this time) Carter and Ben-Israel added the concept of Black Zionism and held out the vision of a return to the Holy Land for their members. From headquarters at the A-Beta Cultural Center on Chicago's south side, they began to gather followers. The somewhat anonymous group came into prominence in the late 1960's as a result of their attempts to migrate to Africa and then to Israel. The group moved first to Liberia, seen as analogous to the Hebrew children's wandering in the desert for forty years to throw off the effects of slavery. Soon after their arrival, they approached the Israeli ambassador about a further move to Israel. They were unable to negotiate the move to Israel for members in Liberia. In 1968 Carter and 38 members from Chicago flew directly to Israel. Given temporary sanction and work permits, the group from Liberia joined them. By 1971, when strict immigration restrictions were imposed upon members of the group, over 300 had migrated. Other members of the group continued to arrive, however, using tourist visas which were destroyed upon moving into the colony (which had been established at Dimona). By 1980 between 1,500 and 2,000 had settled in Israel.
The Black Israelites feel they are descendants of the ten lost tribes of Israel and thus Jews by birth. They celebrate the Jewish rituals and keep the Sabbath. However, they are distinguished from traditional Jews by their practice of polygamy (a maximum of seven wives is allowed) and their abandonment of the synagogue structure.
The group is currently headed by Carter, the chief rabbi. He is assisted by a divine council of twelve princes (for each of the twelve ancient tribes of Israel). During the early 1980's, the American following was under the direction of Prince Asiel Ben Israel. Under the princes are seven ministers responsible for providing education, distribution of food, clothing and shelter, economics, transportation, sports, recreation and entertainment, life preservation, and sanitation.
In Israel, the group lives communally. According to most reports, the group (due to lack of legal status), lives under harsh conditions and the continual threat of mass deportation. They have been unable to obtain necessary additional housing (for those many members who immigrated illegally) and the children are not allowed to attend public schools. Within Israel, the group has asked for land to settle in order to create their own community.

★1771★
Original United Holy Church International

Efforts to locate an address for this edition were unsuccessful. The Original United Holy Church International grew out of a struggle between two bishops of the United Holy Church of America. The conflict led to Bishop James Alexander Forbes and the Southern District being severed from the organization. Those put out of the church met and organized on June 29, 1977 at a meeting in Raleigh, North Carolina. The new body remains in essential doctrinal agreement and continues the polity of the United Holy Church
The Original United Holy Church is concentrated on the Atlantic coast from South Carolina to Connecticut, with congregations also found in Kentucky, Texas, and California. Bishop Forbes also serves as pastor of the Greater Forbes Temple of Hollis, New York. The church supports missionary work in Liberia. On January 24, 1979, in Wilmington, North Carolina, an agreement of affiliation between the Original United Holy Church and the International Pentecostal Holiness Church was signed, which envisions a close cooperative relationship between the two churches.

★1772★
Pan African Orthodox Christian Church
13535 Livernois
Detroit, MI 48238

The Pan African Orthodox Christian Church dates to 1953 when 300 members of St. Mark's Presbyterian Church in Detroit walked out and formed Central Congregational Church. In 1957 they moved into facilities at 7625 Linwood in Detroit and over the next decade became intensely involved in community issues, especially those impinging upon the Black community. In 1967, the church's pastor, Albert B. Cleage, Jr. preached what has become a famous sermon calling for a new Black theology and a Black church to articulate it. An eighteen-foot painting of a Black Madonna was unveiled and the Black Christian Nationalist Movement was launched. The church building became known as the Shrine of the Black Madonna. In 1970 a book store and cultural center were opened. Cleage changed his name to Jaramogi Abebe Agyeman. The *Black Nationalist Creed*, printed below, spells out a position which identifies the Black man and the Hebrew Nation:

"I Believe that human society stands under the judgment of one God, revealed to all, and known by many names. His creative power is visible in the mysteries of the universe, in the revolutionary Holy Spirit which will not long permit men to endure injustice nor to wear the shackles of bondage, in the rage of the powerless when they struggle to be free, and in the violence and conflict which even now threaten to level the hills and the mountains."

"I Believe that Jesus, the Black Messiah, was a revolutionary leader, sent by God to rebuild the Black Nation Israel and to liberate Black People from powerlessness and from the oppression, brutality, and exploitation of the White gentile world.

"I Believe that the revolutionary spirit of God, embodied in the Black Messiah, is born anew in each generation and that Black Christian Nationalists constitute that living remnant of God's Chosen People in this day, and are charged by him with responsibility for the Liberation of Black People.

"I Believe that both my survival and my salvation depend upon my willingness to reject INDIVIDUALISM, and so I commit my life to the Liberation Struggle of Black people and accept the values, ethics, morals, and program of the Black Nation defined by that struggle and taught by the Black Christian Nationalist Movement."

During the 1970s the organization expanded significantly. Agyeman composed an ordination service and ordained eight ministers, who were given the title "Mwalimu," Swahili for "teacher." Agyemnan's own name means "liberator, blessed man, savior of the nation." Other congregations and centers were established in Detroit. In 1974 a shrine was opened in Atlanta, Georgia and in 1977 in Kalamazoo, MIchigan. Also in 1974, a BGN training program to prepare leaders for the liberation struggle of Black people was begun.

★1773★
The Peace Mission Movement

Efforts to locate an address for this edition were unsuccessful. The Peace Mission Movement was founded as an organization in the early twentieth century by the Rev. Major J. Divine, better known as Father Divine. He was one of the most colorful and controversial leaders of a new religious movement in American history. By his own choosing, and in accord with his own religious conviction, Father Divine's life and activity are veiled in obscurity until just prior to 1919 in Brooklyn, New York, where he was known to be preaching about Jesus Christ and the coming of the kingdom of God.

From his own writings and the testimonies of those who knew him, it is believed that Father Divine left Brooklyn and went south just after the Jim Crow Law was passed in Grover Cleveland's administration. While in the South, he was in the hands of 32 lynch mobs because of his stand for brotherhood, eternal life, and salvation being free and without the payment of money. The first Mother Divine and others were witnesses of his treatment in the hands of lynch mobs. In the name of the Rev. Major J. Divine, he married Mother Penniah Divine on June 6, 1882. Father Divine appeared as an intinerant preacher on the east coast of the United States who found fellowship with others who were preaching that the Christ could be manifested as God in man. Samuel Morris, known as Father Jehovah, and John Hickerson, known by his followers as Bishop St. John the Divine, were two of these. Because of jealous rivalry, it is believed, Hickerson fabricated the story that Father Divine's name was really George Baker. Hickerson also is responsible for other biographical misinformation.

To remove himself from the turmoil, Father Divine went into seclusion in the little Long Island fishing village of Sayville, New York. It was here that his residence became known as "The Rescue Home for the Poor Only." He attracted those in need of food, clothing, shelter, and employment, as well as seekers who were drawn by the demonstration at the Sayville residence of "supernatural" abundance in the midst of seeming scarcity. Father Divine's work commanded more and more attention, and ever greater numbers flocked to Sayville to banquet with him, listen to his sermons, and receive healings of mind, body, and spirit, all gratis to everyone who came.

The influx of numbers of people into the town disturbed the residents. Their hostility led to a court case against Father Divine in 1931, the events of which created worldwide publicity. Although the local county court convicted Father Divine, fined him, and sent him to jail for 30 days, the appellate court later condemned the proceedings as erroneous and prejudicial.

The vindication notwithstanding, Father Divine chose to move his headquarters to Harlem in 1933, where he could direct his activity to the masses, especially the Black people who had gathered there after World War I. While gaining a large following from the Harlem public, he experienced continual harassment from the authorities, so that in 1942 he moved again, this time to Philadelphia, Pennsylvania.

The Peace Mission Movement is primarily of a religious nature, but its tenets have strong social, economic, and patriotic ramifications. Its members believe in the principles of Americanism, brotherhood, Christianity, democracy, and Judaism, and that all true religions are synonymous. Members believe that Father Divine fulfills the scriptural promise of the Second Coming of Christ, is the personification of God in a bodily form, and that heaven is a state of consciousness. This state is being materialized, in as much as the members believe that America is the birthplace of the Kingdom of God on Earth, which will be realized when everyone lives the life of Christ.

Father Divine founded the church under the Peace Mission Movement which was incorporated in 1940 and 1941. Mother Divine, with the recognition of Father Divine's Ever Presence, became the Spiritual Head in 1965. There are no ministers and no prescribed ritual in the church services. Those in attendance are free to testify, sing, read scripture, repeat the Words of Father Divine or Mother Divine, or offer praise to God as they are led to do from any inner prompting. Services feature congregational singing. The only sacrament is Holy Communion, served daily as a full-course meal to which all are welcome. There are also two holidays: April 29, which is the celebration of Father Divine's marriage to His Spotless Bride (Mother Divine) to bring about the universal brotherhood of man and the propagation of virtue, honesty, and truth; and September 10-12, which is the consecration and dedication of Woodmont to universalize the Woodmont Estate as a symbol of the highest spiritual state of consciousness.

The mission stands for the absolute fatherhood and motherhood of God and the universal brotherhood of man. Its members believe that a person is a person–not a specified race, color, nationality, or religion, and they live integrated together as brothers and sisters in the family of God and as members only of the human race. They avoid all reference to color or race.

Members of the mission live communally in the churches and affiliated sorority and fraternity houses. They are strictly celibate men and women living in separate houses and on separate floors of the larger facilities. They observe Father Divine's International Modest Code which states: "No smoking, No drinking, No obscenity, No vulgarity, No profanity, No undue mixing of sexes, and No receiving of gifts, presents, tips or bribes. " It is understood to include abstinence from all drugs.

The Peace Mission Movement was most active in the post-depression era when Father Divine preached peace, health, happiness, and abundance, and demonstrated that his teachings were practical as he provided food and shelter for all those in need at no cost to them. To others in dire circumstances, but who had a poverty-level income or less, Father Divine offered 15-cent meals and one dollar-per-week shelter, so that they could hold up their heads with a sense of individual worth and independence, since they were able to pay for their sustenance. The same abundance was manifested in the churches and extensions in various countries as well as those in the United States, where elaborate banquets are the custom.

After Father Divine's passing, his wife Edna Rose Ritchings, known to members as Mother Divine, assumed leadership of the movement. She had married Father Divine in 1946, and currently resides at Woodmont. The movement has a long history of being integrated, as was the marriage.

★1774★
Pentecostal Assemblies of the World, Inc.
c/o James A. Johnson, Presiding Bishop
3939 Meadows Dr.
Indianapolis, IN 46205

Oldest of the Apostolic or "Jesus Only" Pentecostal churches, the Pentecostal Assemblies of the World began as a loosely-organized fellowship of trinitarian pentecostals in Los Angeles in 1906. J.J. Frazee (occasionally incorrectly reported as "Frazier") was elected the first general superintendent. Early membership developed along the West Coast and in the Midwest. From 1913 to 1916, the annual convention was held in Indianapolis, soon to become the center of the organization. Growth in the organization was spurred when it became the first group of pentecostals to accept the "Jesus Only" Apostolic theology, which identified Jesus as the Jehovah of the Old Testament and denied the Trinity. Many ministers from other pentecostal bodies joined the Assemblies when the group within which they held credentials rejected Apostolic teachings. In 1918, the General Assemblies of the Apostolic Assemblies, a recently formed Apostolic body, which included such outstanding early movement leaders as D.C.O. Opperman and H.A. Goss, merged into the PAW.

From its beginning the Pentecostal Assemblies of the World was fully integrated racially, though predominantly White in membership. In 1919, following the influx of so many ministers and members, especially the large newly-merged body, the Pentecostal Assemblies reorganized. Four of its twenty-one field superintendents were Black, among whom were Garfield Thomas Haywood, (1880-1931) who would later become presiding bishop. In 1924, most of the White members withdrew to form the Pentecostal Ministerial Alliance, now an integral part of the United Pentecostal Church. The remaining members, not totally, but predominantly Black, reorganized again, created the office of bishop, and elected Haywood to lead them. He remained presiding bishop until his death in 1931.

Shortly after Haywood's death, the Apostolic Churches of Jesus Christ, a name briefly assumed by the former Pentecostal Ministerial Alliance that was then in a phase of consolidatiing various Apostolic groups into a single organization, invited the Assemblies to consider merger. The merger attempt failed, but the Assemblies again lost individual congregations and members to the Apostolic Churches of Jesus Christ, and a large group who formed a new church, the Pentecostal Assemblies of Jesus Christ, as a prelude to the merger which failed. In the face of the new losses, a third reorganization had to occur in 1932. For several years, the church was led by a small group of bishops, enlarged to seven in 1935. Two years later, Samuel Grimes, a former missionary in Liberia, was elected presiding bishop, a post he retained until his death in 1967. Under his guidance, the Pentecostal Assemblies church experienced its greatest era of expansion. Contrary to most Black Pentecostal bishops, Grimes did not also serve a parish, hence he was able to devote himself full-time to his episcopal duties.

Doctrine of the Assemblies is similar to that of the Assemblies of God except that it does not believe in the Trinity. Holiness is stressed and the group believes that for ultimate salvation, it is necessary to have a life wholly sanctified. Wine is used in the Lord's Supper. Healing is stressed and foot-washing practiced. Members are pacifists, though they feel it is a duty to honor rules. There is a strict dress and behavior code. Divorce and remarriage are allowed under certain circumstances.

There is an annual general assembly which elects the bishops and the general secretary. It also designates the presiding bishop, who heads a board of bishops. The church is divided into 30 districts (dioceses) headed by a bishop. The Assemblies are designated joint members of each local board of trustees. A missionary board oversees missions in Nigeria, Jamaica, England, Ghana, and Egypt.

★1775★
Pentecostal Church of God
9244 Delmar
Detroit, MI 48211

The Pentecostal Church of God (not to be confused with the Pentecostal Church of God of America headquartered at Joplin, Missouri) is a predominantly Black Pentecostal body founded by Apostle Willie James Peterson (1921-1969). Peterson grew up in Florida, and though his family attended the Baptist church there, he was never baptized. The course of his life was interrupted in his early adult years by a dream in which he was in the presence of God and His angels. Peterson began a period of prayer, after which God called him to preach. He became an independent evangelist and had come to believe in the Apostolic or non-Trinitarian position. He began to preach that doctrine in 1955 in Meridian, Mississippi, and to raise up congregations across the South. At the time of his death, Peterson was succeeded by the four bishops of the church, William Duren, J.J. Sears, C.L. Rawls, and E. Rice.

It is the belief of the Pentecostal Church of God that Peterson was an apostle, annointed by God for his task through revelation. The essence of the revelation was an understanding of the Kingdom of God. Peterson taught that conversion meant turning away from worldliness (the kingdom of this world ruled by Satan) to godliness (the kingdom of Heaven). Peterson identified the Roman Catholic Church with Babylon, the Mother of Harlots, (*Revelation 17:3-5*). Satanic doctrine was taught in that church and in its daughter churches, Protestantism. To accept the gospel of the kingdom is to turn from the false teachings of the Babylonish churches to God's truths which include repentance as godly sorrow for one's sins; baptism by immersion in the name of Jesus Christ; a rejection of the unbiblical doctrine of the Trinity; an understanding of heaven as the realm of God and his angels and hell as a place of confinement; the nonobservance of holidays such as Christmas, Easter, and New Year's Day; nonparticipation in human government (which includes pacifism, not saluting the flag, and not voting); and holy matrimony performed by a holy minister.

★1776★
Pentecostal Churches of Apostolic Faith

Efforts to locate an address for this edition were unsuccessful. The Pentecostal Churches of Apostolic Faith was formed in 1957 by former members of the Pentecostal Assemblies of the World under the leadership of Bishop Samuel N. Hancock. Hancock was one of the original men selected as a bishop of the Assemblies following its reorganization in 1925. In 1931 he was one of the leaders in the attempt to unite the Assemblies with the predominantly White Pentecostal Ministerial Alliance, and he helped form the Pentecostal Assemblies of Jesus Christ, a body whose polity was more acceptable to the Alliance. Within a few years, Hancock returned to the Assemblies as an elder and was elected as a bishop for the second time.

However, soon after Hancock's return, it was discovered that he had deviated on traditional Apostolic doctrine in that he taught that Jesus was only the son of God, not that he was God. His position forced the Assemblies to issue a clarifying statement of its position, but Hancock's teachings were tolerated. Hancock also felt that he should have become the presiding bishop. Disappointment at not being elected seems to have fueled the discontent felt throughout the 1950's. Hancock carried two other bishops into the new church formed in 1957, including Willie Lee, pastor of Christ Temple Church, the congregation pastored by Garfield Thomas Haywood, the first presiding bishop of the Assemblies. Lee succeeded Hancock as presiding bishop of the Churches upon the latter's death in 1963. The following year, a major schism occurred when the majority of the Churches rejected the doctrinal position held by Hancock and also taught by Lee. Elzie Young had the charter and claimed the support of the Churches to become the new presiding bishop. The church returned to the traditional Apostolic theology.

The Pentecostal Churches of the Apostolic Faith are congregational in polity, and headed by a presiding bishop (Elzie Young) and a council of bishops. Under Young's leadership, the Churches have grown and stablized their original shaky financial condition. A mission program developed, and the Churches support missionaries in Haiti and Liberia, where they have built a school.

★1777★
Progressive National Baptist Convention, Inc.
601 50th St., NE
Washington, DC 20019

The Progressive National Baptist Convention was formed in 1961 following a dispute over the tenure of the presidency at the 1960 meeting of the National Baptist Convention of the U.S.A., Inc. In 1957, Dr. J.H. Jackson, who had been elected president in 1953, declined to step down and ruled the four-year tenure rule out of the Constitution. Prior to the adoption of the rule in 1952, presidents had served for life. At the 1960 Convention session, dissatisfaction came to a head in the attempt to elect Dr. G.C. Taylor as Dr. Jackson's successor. The failure of Dr. Taylor's supporters led in 1961 to the call for a meeting to form a new National Baptist Convention by Dr. L.V. Booth of Zion Baptist Church, Cincinnati, Ohio. He was elected the first president of the new Progressive National Baptist Convention.

Also at issue in the 1961 break was denominational support for the Civil Rights Movement, then gaining momentum in the South. Those who formed the new convention represented the strongest backers of Martin Luther King, who was among those who left to join the Progressives, who in turn gave King their full support.

The Convention is in agreement on doctrine with its parent body, the disagreements being concerned with organization and social policy. It has organized nationally with two-year terms for all officers, except the executive secretary, who has an eight-year term. The women's auxiliary was formed in 1962 and a Department of Christian Education, Home Mission Board, and Foreign Mission Bureau were soon added.

★1778★
Rastafarians

Efforts to locate an address for this edition were unsuccessful. The Rastafarian Movement, a Jamaican Black nationalist movement, grew out of a long history of fascination with Africa in general and Ethiopia in particular among the masses in Jamaica. The movement can be traced directly to the efforts of Marcus Garvey, founder of the Universal Negro Improvement Association, who, among other endeavors, promoted a steamship company that would provide transportation for Blacks going back to Africa. In 1927 Garvey predicted the crowning of a Black king in Africa as a sign that the redemption of Black people from White oppression was near. The 1935 coronation of Haile Selassie as emperor of Ethiopia was seen as a fulfillment of Garvey's words.

Haile Selassie was born Ras Tafari Makonnen out of a lineage claimed to derive from the Queen of Sheba and King Solomon. He proclaimed his title as King of Kings, Lord of Lords, His Imperial Majesty the Conquering Lion of the Tribe of Judah, Elect of God. His name Haile Selassie means "Power of the Holy Trinity." Reading about the coronation, four ministers in Jamaica–Joseph Hibbert, Archibald Dunkley, Robert Hinds, and most prominently, Leonard Howell–saw the new emperor as not only the fulfillment of the Garveyite expectation, but also the completion of Biblical prophecies such as those in *Revelation 5:2-5* and *19:16* which refer to the Lion of the Tribe of Judah and the King of Kings. The four, independently of each other, began to proclaim Haile Selassie the Messiah of the Black people. Their first successes came in the slums of West Kingston, where they discovered each other and a movement began.

Howell began to proselytize around the island. He raised money by selling pictures of Haile Selassie and telling the buyers that they were passports back to Africa. He was arrested and sentenced to two years in jail for fraud. Upon his release he moved into the hill country of St. Catherine's parish and founded a commune, the Pinnacle, which, in spite of government attacks and several moves, became the center of the movement for the next two decades. At the Pinnacle, the smoking of ganga (marijuana) and the wearing of long hair curled to resemble a lion's mane (dread locks) became the marks of identification of the group.

As the Rastafarians matured, they adopted the perspectives of Black Judaism and identified the Hebrews of the Old Testament as Black people. Their belief system was distinctly racial and they taught that the Whites were inferior to the Blacks. More extreme leaders saw Whites as the enemies of Blacks and believed that, in the near future, Blacks will return to Africa and assume their rightful place in world leadership. Haile Selassie is believed to be the embodiment of God and, though no longer visible, he nevertheless still lives. Some Rastafarians believe Selassie is still secretly alive, though most see him as a disembodied spirit.

Relations with White culture have been tense, lived at the point of "dread," a term to describe the confrontation of a people struggling to regain a denied racial selfhood. Most Rastafarians are pacifists, though much support for the movement developed out of intense antiWhite feelings. Violence has been a part of the movement since the destruction of the Pinnacle, though it has been confined to individuals and loosely organized groups. One group, the Nyabingi Rastas, stand apart from most by their espousal of violence.

Rastafarians came to the United States in large numbers as part of the general migration of Jamaicans in the 1960's and 1970's. They have brought with them an image of violence, and frequent news reports have detailed murders committed by individuals identified as Rastafarians. Rastafarian spokespersons have only complained that many young Jamaican-Americans have adopted the outward appearance of Rastafarians (dread locks and ganga-smoking) without adopting Rastafarian beliefs and lifestyle.

A major aspect of Rastafarian life is the unique music developed as its expression. Reaggae, a form of rock music, became popular far beyond Rastafarian circles, and exponents such as Bob Marley and Peter Tosh became international stars. Reggae has immensely helped in the legitimization of Rastafarian life and ideals.

In Jamaica the Rastafarian Movement is divided into a number of organizations and factions, many of which have been brought into the Jamaican community in America. Surveys of American Rastafarians have yet to define the organization in the United States though individual Rastafarians may be found in Black communities across America, most noticably Brooklyn, New York, Miami, Florida, and Chicago, Illinois.

★1779★
Redeemed Assembly of Jesus Christ, Apostolic

Efforts to locate an address for this edition were unsuccessful. The Redeemed Assembly of Jesus Christ, Apostolic was formed by James Frank Harris and Douglas Williams, two bishops of the Highway Christian Church who rejected the leadership of that church by Bishop J.V. Lomax. They complained of his control, bypassing other bishops and pastors and making decisons in conference with the elders of the congregation he headed in Washington, D.C. The new church is headed by a presiding bishop, assistant presiding bishop, and an executive council consisting of the bishops and all the pastors. There was no doctrinal conflict in the split.

★1780★
Reformed Methodist Union Episcopal Church

Efforts to locate an address for this edition were unsuccessful. The Reformed Methodist Union Episcopal Church was formed in 1885 by members of the African Methodist Episcopal Church who withdrew after a dispute concerning the election of ministerial delegates to the Annual Conference. The Rev. William E. Johnson was elected the first president. A strong sentiment approving of the non-episcopal nature of the new church was expressed. However, in 1896, steps were taken to alter the polity, and in 1919 after the death of the Rev. Johnson, E. Russell Middleton was elected bishop. He was consecrated by the Rt. Rev. Peter F. Stevens of the Reformed Episcopal Church. Following Middleton's death, a second bishop was elected and consecrated by the laying on of hands of seven elders of the church.

Doctrine was taken from the Methodist Episcopal Church. The polity has moved in the episcopal direction and was fully adopted in 1916. Class meetings and love feasts are also retained. Class meetings are regular gatherings of small groups for exhortation, discussion, confession and forgiveness, Bible study, and prayer. Love feasts are informal services centering on holy communion but also including a light meal, singing, and a talk by the officiating minister.

★1781★
Reformed Zion Union Apostolic Church

Efforts to locate an address for this edition were unsuccessful. The Reformed Zion Union Apostolic Church was founded by a group from the African Methodist Episcopal Church interested in setting up a religious organization "to aid in bringing about Christian Union, whose fruit will be Holiness unto the Lord." Led by the Rev. James Howell, the group met at Boydton, Virginia, in April 1869, and organized the Zion Union Apostolic Church with the Rev. Howell as the president. Harmony and growth prevailed until 1874, when changes in polity led to the election of the Rev. Howell as bishop with life tenure. Dissatisfaction with this action nearly destroyed the organization, even though Bishop Howell resigned. In 1882 a re-organization was effected, the four-year presidential structure reinstituted, and the present name adopted.

The representative conference structure is maintained with the law-making power invested in the quadrennial General Conference. Over the years the four-year presidency has again been dropped in favor of life-tenure bishops. A Board of Publication has control over church literature and prints the church school material and the *Union Searchlight*, a periodical.

★1782★
Sacred Heart Catholic Church (Arrendale)

Efforts to locate an address for this edition were unsuccessful. The Sacred Heart Catholic Church was founded in 1980 by Archbishop James Augustine Arrendale and other former members of Archbishop James Lashley's American Catholic Church, Archdiocese of New York. Arrendale was consecrated on August 10, 1981 by Bishop Pinachio, who was assisted by Bishops Donald Anthony and William Wren. The group adheres to the teachings of the Seven Ecumenical Councils and the three Ecumenical Creeds. Archbishop Arrendale died in 1985 and the future course of the Archdiocese is in doubt.

★1783★
Second Cumberland Presbyterian Church in U. S.

Efforts to locate an address for this edition were unsuccessful. In the early years of the Cumberland Presbyterian Church, following a pattern of the Methodist Episcopal Church, South, ministers of the Presbyterian Church established a slave mission throughout the South. White ministers served segregated Black congregations as well as segregated White congregations. By 1860 some 20,000 Black members were on the church rolls. Among these was Edmond Weir, who was sent as a missionary to Liberia. After the Civil War, attempts were accelerated to train Black ministers, thus providing Blacks with an adequate ministry. Separate regional synods were established for Black members. Between 1871 and 1874, synods in such states as Tennessee, Kentucky, and Texas organized. By 1874, following again a pattern set by the Methodists, these regional synods established their broader governing unit, the general assembly, and the Colored Cumberland Presbyterian Church became a church separate from the Cumberland Presbyterian Church. The parent church, though, continued moderate financial and educational support of the new church, which is now called the Second Cumberland Presbyterian Church in the U.S.

The church is similar to its parent body in doctrine and organization. The General Assembly meets regularly. There are 19 presbyteries and four synods.

★1784★
Shiloh Apostolic Temple
1500-34 W. Master
Philadelphia, PA 19121

The Shiloh Apostolic Temple was founded in 1953 by Elder Robert O. Doub, Jr., of the Apostolic Church of Christ in God. In 1948 Doub had moved to Philadelphia to organize a new congregation for the Apostolic Church of Christ in God. He not only succeeded in building a stable congregation, Shiloh Apostolic Temple, but assisted other congregations throughout the state to organize. In light of his accomplishments, Doub felt that he should be made a bishop and so petitioned the church. He believed that the state overseer was taking all the credit Doub himself deserved. Doub's petition was denied. He left with but a single congregation in 1953 and incorporated separately in 1954.

The energetic work that characterized Doub's years in the Apostolic Church of Christ in God led Shiloh Apostolic Temple to outgrow its parent body. Doub began a periodical and purchased a camp, Shiloh Promised Land Camp, in Montrose, Pennsylvania. He also took over foreign work in England and Trinidad. The doctrine, not at issue in the schism, remains that of the parent Church of God (Apostolic) from which the Apostolic Church of Christ in God came.

★1785★
Sought Out Church of God in Christ

Efforts to locate an address for this edition were unsuccessful. The Sought Out Church of God in Christ and Spiritual House of Prayer, Inc., was founded in 1947 by Mother Mozella Cook. Mother Cook was converted in a service led by her physical mother, an ecstatic person who was once hauled into court to be examined for lunacy because of her mystical states. Mother Cook's mother seemed to go into trances and was "absent from this world while she talked with God." Mother Cook moved to Pittsburgh and there became a member of the Church of God in Christ founded by Charles H. Mason, but left it to found her own church, which she formed in Brunswick, Georgia, after feeling a divine call.

★1786★
Sunni Muslims

Efforts to locate an address for this edition were unsuccessful. The Islamic world, though concentrated in the Arab nations of the Middle East, stretches from Yugoslavia to Indonesia and includes not only a large part of the U.S.S.R. but a growing community in Africa south of the Sahara. Since 1965, the Islamic community which had been concentrated in the Midwest and a few Eastern urban centers, has blossomed into a significant religious element of American life in every part of the United States. Literally millions of immigrants from Islamic Asia, Africa and Europe have settled in North America and begun the generation-long process of building ethnic community centers and facilities for worship (often the same building).

Unlike much of Christendom, Islam is organized into a number of autonomous centers. Each center (which may be called a community center, a mosque, a musjid) will tend to be dominated by one ethnic community, though outside the largest urban centers where a variety of mosques can be found, centers will have welcomed people of various nationalities into affiliation. Many of the major centers will have a periodical, which has both a primary local audience and a national circulation. The mosque, headed by the imam (minister-teacher) is the basic center of Islam.

Above the level of the local centers, a variety of national and continental organizations have been formed to mobilize the various local Islamic communities, provide the public (largely ignorant of Islam) with information, and coordinate the activities (particularly the propagation of the faith) of the community at large. These organizations, whose members hip will come from a variety of ethnic backgrounds, tend to be divided politically. Each of the different organizations will be ideologically aligned to, for example, different factions in the Middle East, and/or atuned to a more-or-less activist role in support of various concerns of the land from which they immigrated. Political activism is particularly noticeable in those groups which serve the large Muslim community on the nation's campuses. Local centers will often affiliate with several of the competing national associations.

Symbolic of Sunni Muslim presence in America is the Islamic Center in Washington, D.C. Begun in 1949, it took seven years to complete. It was officially opened in 1957. While begun as a center for diplomatic personnel, with financial support from seventeen countries, with the growth of Islam in North America it has become a place to which all American Sunnis look as a visible point of unity in the otherwise decentralized Islamic community. The importance of the Center was dramatically underscored in the early 1980's when it was taken over by a group who supported the Iranian Revolution under the Ayatollah Khomeini and opposed the influence of the ambassadors from Saudi Arabia and other Islamic countries. The takeover disrupted the center for several years and led to the withdrawal of its prominent Iman, Dr. Muhammad Abdul Rauf, a leading Islamic apologist in North America.

Among the oldest of the Canadian-United States organizations is the Federation of Islamic Organizations in the United States and Canada. It was founded in 1952, largely as a result of the efforts of Abdullah Ingram of Cedar Rapids, Iowa. He called a meeting attended primarily by Lebanese Muslims, representative of the older American Muslim centers, and formed the International Muslim Society, which two years later became the Federation. The Federation has as its goals the perpetuation of Islam and of Muslim culture and the dissemination of correct information about Muslim society worldwide. It publishes a periodical, *The Muslim Star*, and holds annual conventions, usually in the Midwest. The Federation accomplishments have been related to the fellowship of various Muslim centers across national and ethnic

boundaries, and more activist groups, while acknowledging the contribution of the Federation, saw the need for further organizations. The Islamic Society of North America emerged in the early 1980's out of the Muslim Students Association originally founded in 1952. It represents a broadening focus of concern by former students who moved into roles of leadership in the Muslim, academic and professional communities in America. The Society is headquartered at the Islamic Teaching Center, a large complex in suburban Indianapolis, from which it oversees the network of subsidiary organizations it has fostered and nurtured.
From its original goals, developed to assist graduate students temporarily in the United States study to survive in a non-Muslim environment, the Society has since 1975 refocused its attention on building Islamic structures among a permanent and growing North American Islamic population and actively propagating the faith among the non-Muslim public. To these ends, the society has established the Islamic Medical Association, the Association of Muslim Social Scientists and the Association of Muslim Scientists and Engineers. It has published numerous books (including the proceedings of the many conferences its sponsors) and pamphlets (especially a set designed to introduce Islam to non-Muslims) and several periodicals, most prominently *Al-Ittihad* and *Islamic Horizons*. The Muslim Student Association continues as one department of the Society. The Islamic Teaching Center is the main structure engaged in *dawah*, the propagation of the faith.
Possibly the most inclusive Islamic organization for Sunni Muslims is the Council of Islamic Organizations of America (both the Federation of Islamic Associations and the Islamic Society of North America are affiliates). The idea of the Council emerged in 1973 at a meeting in Saudi Arabia. Then the Muslim World League, an international Muslim organization with offices in New York City, organized the first Islamic Conference of North America which met April 22-24, 1977 at Newark, New Jersey. The Council was organized at that gathering to meet primary needs for unity and co-ordination of the many Islamic centers in North America. In its lengthy list of goals, it set itself the task of fostering unity, establishing and propagating the faith in its fullness, the perpetuation of modest dress codes, assistance in building mosques and other facilities for Muslims, and the funding of various designated projects of broad Muslim interest.
Also formed in the 1970's, the Council of Imams in North America formed as a continent-wide professional organization for the leaders of the various mosques and Islamic centers.
The several organizations mentioned above are but a few of the many new structures being established in the Muslim Community. All of the organizations have been assisted by the development of Muslim publishing concerns, such as American Trust Publications, affiliated with the Islamic Society of North America; Kazi Publications in Chicago; and The Crescent Publications, Tacoma Park, Maryland. As of the mid-1980s, however, the majority of English-language literature produced for the American Muslim community is still published overseas.

★1787★
Triumph the Church and Kingdom of God in Christ

Efforts to locate an address for this edition were unsuccessful. Triumph the Church and Kingdom of God in Christ was founded by Elder E.D. Smith in 1902. The founding followed by five years a divine revelation given to Smith. According to the literature of the church, the 1902 organization of the church marked the time when the revelation was "speeded to earth." Finally, in 1904, the content of the revelation was announced. Headquarters for the church were established in Baton Rouge, Louisiana, then were moved to Birmingham, Alabama, and later to Atlanta, Georgia. The founder was in charge of the church until 1920, when he moved to Addis Ababa, Ethiopia.
The church follows the holiness beliefs common to holiness churches, but also believes in fire baptism, a spiritual experience of empowerment by the Holy Spirit. Fire baptism was first received by the Apostles in the upper room on Pentecost, when tongues of fire appeared above their heads (*Acts 2*). As practiced by the several nineteenth and twentieth century "fire- baptized" churches, fire baptism is similar to the pentecostal experience of the baptism of the Holy Spirit, except it is typically not accompanied by speaking in tongues. (See separate entry on the Fire-Baptized Holiness Church, Wesleyan.)
Triumph the Church and Kingdom of God in Christ holds a unique view of itself as a church in relation to Christendom, traditionally called the church militant. This view is reflected in the following passage from the church's catechism: *Question* Was there another Church in the earth before Triumph? *answer.* Yes. Church Militant; *Question* Is there any difference between the Triumph Church and Church Militant? *answer* Yes. Church Militant is a Church of warfare, and Triumph is a Church of Peace; *Question* What happened to Church Militant when Triumph was revealed? *answer* God turned it upside down and emptied His Spirit into Triumph; *Question* Is Triumph just a Church only? *answer* No. It has a Kingdom with it.
Polity is episcopal with bishops elected for life. Under the bishops is a hierarchy of state and local workers. Every four years the church holds an International Religious Congress.

★1788★
True Fellowship Pentecostal Church of God of America
4238 Pimlico Rd.
Baltimore, MD 21215

The True Fellowship Pentecostal Church of God of America was formed in 1964 by the secession of the Rev. Charles E. Waters, Sr., a presiding elder in the Alpha and Omega Pentecostal Church of God of America, Inc.. Doctrine is like the Church of God in Christ, differing only in the acceptance of women into the ministry as pastors and elders. Bishop Waters and his wife operate a mission for those in need in Baltimore.

★1789★
True Grace Holy Temple of Christ
205 V St., NW
Washington, DC 20001

In 1960 after Bishop Marcelino Manoel de Graca (Sweet Daddy Grace) died, Walter McCoullough was elected bishop of the United House of Prayer for All People, but approximately six months later criticism was directed at him for his disposal of church monies without explanation to the other church leaders. The elders relieved him of his office and a lawsuit ordered a new election, at which time he was re-elected. Complaints continued that he was assuming false doctrines, such as claiming that he and only he was doing God's work or that he had power to save or condemn people. Shortly after the second election, he dismissed a number of the church leaders. Twelve dissenting members, with Thomas O. Johnson (d. 1970) as their pastor, formed the True Grace Memorial House of prayer in Washington, D.C. (Elder Johnson had been dismissed after 23 years of service as a pastor.) In 1962 the church members adopted a church covenant in which they agreed to assist one another in loving counsel, prayer, and aid in times of sickness and distress; to do all good to all, in part, by assisting them to come under the ministry of the church; to avoid causes of divisions, such as gossip; and to refrain from any activity that might bring disgrace on the cause of Christ. The present head of the church is Elder William G. Easton.
Formerly: True Grace Memorial House of Prayer.

★1790★
True Vine Pentecostal Churches of Jesus

Efforts to locate an address for this edition were unsuccessful. Dr. Robert L. Hairston had been a pastor in several trinitarian Pentecostal groups and had been a co-founder with Willaim Monroe Johnson of the True Vine Pentecostal Holiness Church. However, in 1961 Hairston accepted the Apostolic "Jesus Only" teachings. He left the church he had founded and formed the True Vine Penetcostal Churches of Jesus. Also causal factors in the formation of the new denomination were differences between Hairston and Johnson over church polity and Hairston's marital situation. Hairston rejected the idea of local congregations being assessed to pay for the annual convocation of the church. Also, he had divorced his first wife and remarried, an action frowned upon in many Pentecostal circles.
The Church follows standard Apostolic teachings. Women are welcome in the ministry. Growth of the group was spurred in 1976 by the addition of several congregations headed by Bishop Thomas C. Williams.

★1791★
Unification Association of Christian Sabbath Keepers
255 W. 131st St.
New York, NY 10027

In the early 1940's in Manhattan a movement was started among Black Adventists to unite independent Sabbath-keeping congregations. It was begun by Thomas I.C. Hughes, a former minister in the Seventh-Day Adventist Church and pastor of the Advent Sabbath Church, formed in 1941 in Manhattan. The missionary-minded Hughes conceived the idea of both home and foreign endeavors and began to gather support from his congregation. In 1956, the Unification Association of Christian Sabbath Keepers was formed, bringing together Hughes's parish and the New York United Sabbath Day Advent Church. Others joined, including the Believers in the Commandments of God.
There is a wide range of doctrinal belief in the various churches. Immersion is practiced and the Sabbath kept. A general adventist theology prevails. The polity is congregational. There are annual meetings for fellowship and general conferences every four years for business. At the second general conference, the title "bishop" was created, but there is no episcopal authority accompanying that title. A twenty-three member board of evangelism operates between general conferences.
The Unification Association is very missionary-minded. Missions had been established by its founders even before the Association was formed. Affiliated fellowships can be found in Nigeria, Liberia, Jamaica, Antigua and Trinidad.

★1792★
United Church and Science of Living Institute

Efforts to locate an address for this edition were unsuccessful. The United Church and Science of Living Institute was formed in 1966 by the Rev. Frederick Eikerenkotter II, a former Baptist minister, popularly known as Rev. Ike. The Church has become the major Thrust of New Thought into the Black community. After graduating from the American Bible School in Chicago in 1956, Rev. Ike spent a time in evangelism and faith healing and became influenced by New Thought. "Science of Living" is the term used to describe the teachings of Rev. Ike, which focus upon the prosperity theme in New Thought thinking. He believes the lack of money is the root of all evil.
Rev. Ike emphasizes the use of mind-power. Members are urged to rid the self of attitudes of "pie-in-the-sky," and postponed rewards. Instead, they should begin thinking of God as the real man in the self. Turning one's attention to the self allows God to work. Believing in God's work allows one to see the self as worthy of God's success. Visualization is a popular technique to project desires into the conscious mind as a first step to the abundant life. A prosperity "blessing plan" emphasizes believing, giving, and prospering. Rev. Ike developed an extensive media ministry and is heard over 89 radio and 22 television stations in the Eastern half of the United States and in California and Hawaii.

★1793★
United Church of Jesus Christ (Apostolic)
c/o Monroe Saunders, Presiding Bishop
2226 Park Ave.
Baltimore, MD 21229

The United Church of Jesus Christ (Apostolic) dates to 1945 when Randolph Carr left the Pentecostal Assemblies of the World to found the Church of God in Christ (Apostolic). During the 1960s, Monroe Saunders, chief assistant to Carr, criticized him for contradicting in action his stated position on divorce and remarriage. Carr asked Saunders to leave the Church, and most of the group followed him. They reorganized as the United Church and elected Saunders the presiding bishop. Doctrine stresses the authority of the Bible and the unity of the Godhead. There are three ordinances, including foot-washing.
The Church is headed by a presiding bishop, a vice-bishop, and three other bishops. As presiding bishop, Saunders, who completed his post-graduate education, has led the church in emphasizing an educated ministry, and with the development of The Center for a More Abundant Life, which provides a variety of social services to people living in Baltimore. Missions are supported in Mexico, Trinidad, Jamaica, and other West Indian Islands.

★1794★
United Churches of Jesus, Apostolic

Efforts to locate an address for this edition were unsuccessful. The United Churches of Jesus, Apostolic was formed by several bishops of the Apostle Church of Christ in God who rejected the leadership of presiding bishop J. C. Richardson Sr. Richardson had married a divorced woman. The church is headed by a general bishop, J. W. Ardrey (one of the founders of the Apostle Church) and a board of bishops. Doctrine is like the parent body.

★1795★
United Free-Will Baptist Church
Kinston College
1000 University St.
Kinston, NC 28501

Racial division did not escape the Free Will Baptists, but did wait until the twentieth century. The predominantly Black United Free Will Baptist Church was established in 1901. Like its parent body, it is Arminian in theology and practices footwashing and anointing the sick with oil. The congregational polity was modified within a system of district, quarterly, annual, and general conferences. The local church is autonomous in regard to business, elections, and form of government, but the conferences have the power to decide the questions of doctrine.

★1796★
United Hebrew Congregation

Efforts to locate an address for this edition were unsuccessful. The United Hebrew Congregation was the name of about a half dozen congregations of Black Jews which during the mid-1970s were centered upon the Ethiopian Hebrew Culture Center in Chicago, which were headed by Rabbi Naphtali Ben Israel. It was this group's belief that Ham's sons were Black. Included were the Hebrews of which one reads in the Bible. Abraham came from Chaldea, and the ancient Chaldeans were Black. The congregation members believe Solomon was Black (*Song of Solomon 1:5*). Sabbath services were held on Saturday. No sign of their continuance into the 1980's has been found.

★1797★
United Holy Church of America

Efforts to locate an address for this edition were unsuccessful. The United Holy Church of America was formed as the outgrowth of a holiness revival conducted by the Rev. Isaac Cheshier at Method, North Carolina (near Raleigh), in 1886. In 1900, the group became known as the Holy Church of North Carolina (and as growth dictated, the Holy Church of North Carolina and Virginia). In the early twentieth century, the church became Pentecostal and adopted a theology like the Church of God (Cleveland, Tennessee). The present name was chosen in 1916.

★1798★
United House of Prayer for All People
1314 H St., NE
Washington, DC 20005

Sweet Daddy Grace, as Bishop Marcelino Manoel de Graca (1884-1960) was affectionately known by his followers, was born in 1884 on Brava, Cape Verde Islands, and was a former railroad cook who began preaching in 1925. He founded the United House of Prayer for All

People, which in the 1930s and 1940s was one of the most famous religious groups in the Black community.
In doctrine, the church resembles the holiness Pentecostal bodies. It teaches the three experiences-conversion, sanctification, and baptism with the Holy Spirit. There is a strict behavior code. What sets the House of Prayer apart is the role that Daddy Grace assumed in the group, i.e., that of a divine being. In an often repeated quote, he was heard to have admonished his worshippers:
Never mind about God. Salvation is by Grace only...Grace has given God a vacation, and since God is on His vacation, don't worry Him...If you sin against God, Grace can save you, but if you sin against Grace, God cannot save you.
Thus, while the House of Prayer derives from and continues to grow in relation to the Pentecostal framework, the framework was significantly changed by Grace's assumption of deific powers. Grace reigned supreme as an autocrat until his death. He appointed the ministers and all church officials. A line of Daddy Grace Products included soap, toothpaste, writing paper, face powder, shoe polish, and cookies. There is an annual convocation.
Grace died in 1960 and, after a period of court fights, Bishop Walter McCoullough was acknowledged as head of the church. He has assumed Grace's powers, if not his divine claims. Under his leadership, the church has assumed more traditional Pentecostal stance. In 1974, it launched a $1.5 million housing project in Washington, D.C.

★1799★
United Way of the Cross Churches of Christ of the Apostolic Faith

Efforts to locate an address for this edition were unsuccessful. The United Way of the Cross Churches of Christ of the Apostolic Faith was founded by Bishop Joseph H. Adams of the Way of the Cross Church of Christ and Elder Harrison J. Twyman of the Bible Way Church of Our Lord Jesus Christ World Wide, Inc. The new church was formed when the two founders, both pastors of congregations in North Carolina, discovered that God had given each a similar vision to form a new church. Also, Adams, a bishop in North Carolina for the Way of the Cross Church of Christ, had developed some concerns with the administrative procedures of the church. The church grew, in part, from the addition of pastors and their congregations who had previously left other Apostolic bodies.

★1800★
Universal Christian Spiritual Faith and Churches for All Nations

Efforts to locate an address for this edition were unsuccessful. The Universal Christian Spiritual Faith and Churches for All Nations was founded in 1952 by the merger of the National David Spiritual Temple of Christ Church Union (Inc.) U.S.A., St. Paul's Spiritual Church Convocation, and King David's Spiritual Temple of Truth Association. National David Spiritual Temple of Christ Church Union (Inc.) U.S.A. had been founded at Kansas City, Missouri, in 1932 by Dr. David William Short, a former Baptist minister. He became convinced that no man had the right or spiritual power "to make laws, rules or doctrines for the real church founded by Jesus Christ" and that the "denominational" churches had been founded in error and in disregard of the apostolic example. Bishop Short claimed that the temple was the true church, and hence dated to the first century.
The merged church differs from many Pentecostal churches in that it denies that only those who have spoken in tongues have received the Spirit. It does insist, however, that a full and complete baptism of the Holy Ghost is always accompanied by both the gift of "tongues" and other powers. The members of the church rely on the Holy Spirit for inspiration and direction. The church is organized according to I Corinthians 12:1-31 and Ephesians 4:11. It includes pastors, archbishops, elders, overseers, divine healers, deacons, and missionaries. Bishop Short is the chief governing officer. In 1952, he became archbishop of the newly merged body. He is assisted by a national executive board which holds an annual assembly.

★1801★
Universal Church, the Mystical Body of Christ

Efforts to locate an address for this edition were unsuccessful. The Universal Church, the Mystical Body of Christ, is an interracial Pentecostal group which emerged in the 1970's. It is distinguished by its belief that in order to serve God freely, members must come out of a corrupt government, society, and churches of this land, and establish a separate government on another continent where a theocratic system can be constructed. Only then, can perfection exist in society. Members call upon all Christians to join them. They believe that these are the end-times and that God is calling together his 144,000 mentioned in Revelation.
The church has a strict moral code and disapproves of short dresses for women, long hair for men, and women preachers and elders. Women cover their heads during worship. The group fasts, uses wine and unleavened bread at the Lord's Supper, and believes in baptism for the remission of sins, divine healing, speaking in tongues, and the unity of the church. The Universal Church is headed by Bishop R.O. Frazier. Members do not think of themselves as another denomination, but as the one true body of Christ.

★1802★
Universal Foundation for Better Living
11901 S. Ashland Ave.
Chicago, IL 60643

The Universal Foundation for Better Living was founded in 1974 but grew out of the ministry begun in Chicago, Illinois, in 1956 by the Rev. Johnnie Coleman, then a minister with the Unity School of Christianity and one of the first Black New Thought ministers. In 1953 she learned that she had an incurable disease. She moved to Kansas City and enrolled in the Unity School of Christianity. In a few months she was healed and she stayed at Unity to become the first Black person ordained as a Unity minister (1956). Moving to Chicago, she founded the Christ Unity Temple, which first met in the Y.M.C.A. building on South Cottage Grove. She became a prominent Unity minister and was the first Black to be elected president of the Association of Unity Churches. However, in 1974 she withdrew from the association and renamed her congregation Christ Universal Temple. That same year she founded the Johnnie Coleman Institute as an educational arm of the church for both lay and professional education. The first ministers were graduated and ordained in 1978. In 1981 she began a television ministry with the "*Better Living with Johnnie Coleman*" show that airs on 13 stations across the United States.
In 1985 the growing ministry reached a major plateau with the opening of the Christ Universal Temple complex on the far south side of Chicago. The church, which also serves as headquarters from the foundation and institute, seats 3,500 in its sanctuary, the largest in Chicago. The building also houses the UFBL Bookstore and the Prayer Ministry, which offers a 24-hour call-in service for those in need.
The beliefs of the foundation are largely in harmony with that of the Unity School of Christianity, the break being largely a matter of social policy, not doctrine. A statement of belief emphasizes that it is God's will for everyone to live a healthy, happy, and prosperous life and that such a life is attainable for each person. The kingdom within can be brought to visible expression by following the principles of Jesus, the Wayshower. The key is right thinking followed by right action. Specifically cited is a belief that rather than making a primary effort to provide for the needy, the church should provide the teaching which will allow each person to provide for themselves.
The foundation is a member of the International New Thought Alliance.

★1803★
Universal Peace Mission Movement

Efforts to locate an address for this edition were unsuccessful. The Universal Peace Mission Movement was founded in the early twentieth century by Father Major J. Divine, one of the most colorful and controversial founders of a new religious movement in American history. Father Divine (George Baker) was a Black man born in Georgia soon after the Civil War. As a young man he was sentenced to six months on a chain gang for opening a mission and proclaiming himself the "son of righteousness." In 1906 he became associated with Samuel Morris, known by his followers as "Father Jehovah." As "Father Jehovah's messenger," Baker traveled to Valdosta, Georgia, but was expelled from the state. He moved to Harlem and became associated with John Hickerson, known to his followers as "Bishop St. John the Divine." Baker soon left Hickerson and became the leader of a communal group in Brooklyn which grew to become the Universal Peace Mission Movement. There he took the name of Father Major J. Divine.

In 1919 the commune moved to Sayville, Long Island, New York, where it prospered. Father Divine became revered and even worshipped by his followers. In 1931-32 a series of events made him nationally famous: he was arrested for blasphemy, convicted, fined $500.00, and sent to jail for a year. Three days after sentencing the judge died, after which Divine was quoted as saying, "I hated to do it." Further attempts at legal action by detractors of the movement led him to move the headquarters to New York City and in 1941 to Philadelphia, where a suburban estate, Woodmont, had been donated to him by a wealthy disciple.

Members of the movement believe that Father Divine fulfilled both the second coming of Christ and the Messianic expectations of Judaism. Members recognize one Father and one Mother–one God–personified in Father Divine and Mother Divine. True religion is faith in the one, invisible God. Heaven is considered a state of consciousness which is being materialized as the kingdom of God on earth. America is called the birthplace of the kingdom, which will be fully realized when everyone lives by the principles of Americanism, democracy, Christianity, Judaism, and true religion.

Church services in the movement have little ritual. The Lord's Supper is served daily as a meal to which all are welcome. Members live together in church centers. They practice a celibate existence; refrain from the use of tobacco, alcohol, and drugs; and avoid using profane language. The height of the movement was in the post-depression years when Father Divine staged elaborate feasts for his followers in the Black ghetto. Buildings which served as headquarters for the associated communes (called "heavens") were scattered along the East Coast during Father Divine's lifetime. These heavens offered members and prospective members inexpensive meals and rooms for the poor.

After Father Divine's passing, his wife, Edna Rose Ritchings, known to members as Mother Divine, assumed leadership of the movement. A White woman, she married Father Divine in 1949 and currently resides at Woodmont. Approximately one-fourth of the movement is White and it has had a long history as a functionally-integrated movement.

★1804★
Vedantic Center

Efforts to locate an address for this edition were unsuccessful. The Vedantic Center was founded in 1975 in Los Angeles by Alice Coltrane (b. 1937), a former student of Swami Satchidananda, founder of the Integral Yoga Institute, with whom she journeyed in India and Sri Lanka. Raised in Detroit, Coltrane devoted her early life to music, as did her late husband, jazz musician John Coltrane, and like him attained a high level of success and fame. In 1968 at the age of 21, she entered a period described as a time of both spiritual isolation and re-awakening. Directly from the Supreme Lord, she also received an initiation into the renounced order of sannyas, but was instructed not to don the ochre robe, symbolic of the renounced life, until 1975. During the early 1970s she did a series of records expressing her spiritual pilgrimage and devotional life.

In 1975 Coltrane emerged as Swami Turiyasangitananda. A few months later, she organized the Vedantic Center. She authored several books, including *Monument Eternal* and *Endless Wisdom*, and began to build a following. In 1983 the center purchased 48 acres of land in rural southern California near the town of Agoura and established a community, Shanti Anantam, for the center's members.

The Vedantic Center is unique in that it is one of the very few Hindu organizations drawing members predominantly from the American Black community and led by a Black person (though there are predominantly Black centers within large and otherwise predominantly non-Black Hindu groups). While beginning with the yoga system passed to her by Swami Satchidananda, Turiyasangitananda has developed an ecletic blend of Hinduism which draws upon other spiritual traditions as well. She teaches that the purpose of human life is to advance spiritually. The highest stage of life is devotional service (bhakti yoga), rendered unto the Supreme Lord (known in his three aspects as Brahma, Vishnu or Krishna, and Siva). In this light, devotional singing has attained an important role at the ashram, and Turiyasangitananda has composed new music with a decidedly Western flavor for the traditional bhajans (devotional songs).

The weekly schedule at Shanti Anantam begins with worship, including satang discourses by Swami Turiyasangitananda, on Sunday afternoons. An additional satsang occurs on Wednesday evening. Hatha yoga classes are held several times during the week. The center operates a vegetarian restaurant in Westlake Village, California, and a bookstore at the entrance to the ashram grounds. A television show, "*Eternity's Pillar*", is seen weekly on one station in southern California.

★1805★
Way of the Cross Church of Christ
332 9th St., NE
Washington, DC 20003

The Way of the Cross Church of Christ was founded in 1927 by Henry C. Brooks, an independent Black Pentecostal minister. Brooks had founded a small congregation in Washington, D.C. which became part of the Church of Our Lord Jesus Christ of the Apostolic Faith founded by R.C. Lawson. At that time there was another small congregation under Bishop Lawson in Washington headed by Smallwood E. Williams, and Lawson wanted Brooks' congregation to join Williams'. Brooks rejected the plan, left Lawson's jurisdiction and founded a separate organization. A second congregation in Henderson, North Carolina became the first of several along the East Coast. Brooks pastored the mother church for forty years and built a membership of over 3,000. The Way of the Cross Church is headed by a presiding bishop. John L. Brooks, the son of the founder, succeeded to that post. He is assisted by twelve other bishops. Missions are supported in Ghana and Liberia.

★1806★
Yahweh's Temple

Efforts to locate an address for this edition were unsuccessful. Yahweh's Temple was founded in 1947 as the Church of Jesus and has through the decades of its existence sought the name that best expressed its central doctrinal concern of identifying Jesus with the God of the Old Testament. In 1953 the Church became The Jesus Church, and it adopted its present name in 1981. The Temple is headed by Samuel E. Officer, its bishop and moderator, a former member of the Church of God (Cleveland, Tennessee). The Temple follows the "oneness" doctrine generally, but has several points of difference from other bodies. From the Sacred Name Movement it has accepted the use of the Hebrew transliterations of the names of the Creator. It also keeps the Saturday Sabbath. It derives its name from a belief that Jesus is the "new and proper name of God, Christ, and the church." Specifically rejected are names such as "Church of God," "Pentecostal," and "Churches of Christ." The organization of the Temple is based upon an idea that all the members have a special place to work in a united body. From *Ezekiel 10:10*, a model of four wheels within wheels has been constructed. Each wheel consists of a hub of elders, spokes of helpers, a band for service, and the rim of membership. At the center is the international bishop, who exercises episcopal and theocratic authority. There are national and state bishops, and local deacons.

(4) LIBRARY COLLECTIONS

Entries in this chapter are arranged alphabetically by institution name. See the User's Guide at the front of this directory for additional information.

★1807★
Africa News Service, Inc.
Library
PO Box 3851
Durham, NC 27702 Phone: (919)286-0747

Subjects: African news - politics, economics, foreign affairs, culture, media, women, sports. **Holdings:** 2000 books; 136 VF drawers of news clippings, documents, radio transcriptions, and other materials. **Subscriptions:** 300 journals and other serials. **Computerized Information Services:** Internal database. **Remarks:** Telex: 3772229.

★1808★
African-American Institute
Africa Policy Information Center
833 United Nations Plaza
New York, NY 10017 Phone: (212)949-5666
Daphne Topovzis, Asst.Ed.

Staff: Prof 1. **Subjects:** Africa - commodities, oil, U.S. foreign policy, United Nations, development. **Special Collections:** News clippings from American, European, and African publications, 1974 to present. **Holdings:** Magazines; conference reports; Africa Report (a complete set of the institute's publication). **Subscriptions:** 200 journals and other serials; 50 newspapers. **Services:** Copying; center open to the public. **Remarks:** FAX: (212)682-6421. Telex: 666 565.

★1809★
African American Museum
Library
1765 Crawford Rd.
Cleveland, OH 44106 Phone: (216)791-1700
Dr. Eleanor Engram, Dir./Cur.

Founded: 1953. **Staff:** Prof 3. **Subjects:** African and African-American history and culture. **Special Collections:** African-American music; Blacks in aviation; Black theology; Black church in Cleveland. **Holdings:** 200 books; 200 bound periodical volumes; 10,000 negatives; 100 paintings; 100,000 news clippings; 500 slides; 100 audiotapes; 50 pieces of art; 15 proclamations; 3 Reconstruction maps. **Services:** Library open to the public with restrictions.

★1810★
African Literature Association
Library
Africana Studies & Research Center
Cornell University
310 Triphammer Rd.
Ithaca, NY 14853 Phone: (607)255-2000
Prof. Anne Adams

Staff: Prof 1. **Subjects:** African literature. **Holdings:** 5 VF drawers of business and editorial archives. **Publications:** *Directory*, annual; *Annual Selected Conference Papers*. **Remarks:** Archival materials 5 years and older are on deposit in Northwestern University - Melville J. Herskovits Library of African Studies (see separate entry).

★1811★
Alabama A&M University
J. F. Drake Memorial Learning Resources Center
Box 489
Normal, AL 35762 Phone: (205)851-5760
Dr. Birdie O. Weir, Dir.

Founded: 1904. **Staff:** Prof 8; Other 14. **Subjects:** Education, business and economics, agriculture, the sciences, computer science, literature. **Special Collections:** Black Collection (3236 items); Archival Collection (2965 items); Curriculum Collection (5313 items); Children's Collection (5560 items); Schomburg Collection; Carnegie-Mydral Collection; J. F. Kennedy Memorial Collection; International Studies Collection (1496 items). **Holdings:** 256,521 books; 19,711 bound periodical volumes; 4417 AV programs; 14,884 periodicals on microfilm. **Subscriptions:** 1512 journals and other serials; 92 newspapers; 650 microfilm subscriptions. **Services:** Interlibrary loan; copying; videotaping; center open to the public; courtesy card must be purchased for check out of materials by persons not enrolled at the university or at one of the cooperating institutions. **Automated Operations:** Computerized public access catalog, cataloging, and Interlibrary loan. **Computerized Information Services:** DIALOG Information Services. Performs searches on fee basis. Contact Person: Prudence W. Bryant, Supv., Ref. & Info.Serv. **Networks and Consortia:** Member of Network of Alabama Academic Libraries (NAAL), Alabama Library Exchange, Inc. (ALEX), SOLINET. **Publications:** *Mixed Media* (newsletter), annual; *In the News* (newsletter) - for internal distribution only; *LRC Fast Facts*; *LRC Handbook of Programs and Services*; brochures. **Remarks:** FAX: (205)851-5768. **Also known as:** Alabama Agricultural and Mechanical University.

★1812★
Alabama State University
University Library & Learning Resources
Archives & Special Collections
Levi Watkins Learning Center
915 S. Jackson St.
Montgomery, AL 36195-0301 Phone: (205)293-4106
Rubye J. Sullivan, Spec.Coll.Libn.

Staff: Prof 1; Other 6. **Subjects:** Afro-Americans. **Special Collections:** Atlanta University's Black Culture Collection (181 reels of microfilm);

George W. Carver Correspondence Collection (67 reels of microfilm); Bibliography of Doctoral Research on the Negro, 1933-1966; E. D. Nixon Collection; Alabama Statewide Oral History Project (10 volumes of transcribed interviews); Montgomery, Alabama Bus Boycott, 1955-1957 (4 volumes). **Holdings:** 11,980 books; 600 bound periodical volumes; 384 reels of microfilm; 435 microfiche; 305 16mm films, cassettes, filmstrip/cassette sets; 2 vertical files of clippings; 200 phonograph records, slides, audiotapes; 1690 theses. **Subscriptions:** 50 journals and other serials; 30 newspapers. **Services:** Copying; collections open to the public. **Special Indexes:** Index to Periodicals by and about Negroes (book); Indexes to Vertical Files (card); Index to Black Cultural Collection (book); Index to Doctoral Research on the Negro (card).

★1813★
Alternative Press Center
Library
Box 33109
Baltimore, MD 21218 Phone: (301)243-2471
Elizabeth O'Lexa, Coord.

Founded: 1969. **Staff:** Prof 3. **Subjects:** Liberation - women's, gay, Black; Third World movement; ecology; alternative life styles. **Holdings:** 420 volumes. **Subscriptions:** 120 journals and other serials; 180 newspapers. **Services:** Library open to the public. **Publications:** *Alternative Press Index*, quarterly.

★1814★
American Baptist Theological Seminary
T. L. Holcomb Library
1800 White's Creek Pike
Nashville, TN 37207 Phone: (615)228-7877
Dorothy B. Lucas, Libn.

Founded: 1924. **Staff:** Prof 1; Other 48. **Subjects:** Bible, religion, theology, Black studies. **Holdings:** 34,857 books; 706 bound periodical volumes; 2576 vertical file materials; 562 AV programs. **Subscriptions:** 220 journals and other serials. **Services:** Interlibrary loan; copying; library open to the public for reference use only.

★1815★
American Civil Liberties Union
ACLU/CNSS Library
122 Maryland Ave., NE
Washington, DC 20002 Phone: (202)544-1681
Tamara Silver, Libn.

Founded: 1979. **Staff:** Prof 1; Other 2. **Subjects:** Civil rights, religious freedom, reproductive freedom, alien rights and immigration, national security, criminal justice, freedom of speech. **Holdings:** 2500 books; 100 reports. **Subscriptions:** 2000 journals and other serials. **Services:** Interlibrary loan; copying; library open to the public. **Publications:** *First Principles: National Security and Civil Liberties.* **Remarks:** FAX: (202)546-0738.

★1816★
American Civil Liberties Union
Library/Archives
132 W. 43rd St.
New York, NY 10036 Phone: (212)944-9800
Ava Chamberlain, Libn.

Founded: 1920. **Staff:** Prof 1. **Subjects:** Civil liberties, law. **Holdings:** 5000 books; 50 files of ACLU board and committee minutes and reports, affiliate mailings, press releases; annual reports; ACLU pamphlets and newsletters, 1920 to present. **Services:** Copying; library open to the public for research only. **Remarks:** Archives housed at Princeton University.

★1817★
Amistad Research Center
Library/Archives
Tulane University
6823 St. Charles Ave.
New Orleans, LA 70118 Phone: (504)865-5535
Dr. Clifton H. Johnson, Exec.Dir.

Founded: 1966. **Staff:** Prof 6; Other 14. **Subjects:** Ethnic minorities of America, Afro-American history and culture, civil rights, Africa, abolitionism, United Church of Christ. **Special Collections:** Manuscript collections (8 million items); Aaron Douglas Art Collection (200 items); Victor DuBois Art Collection (81 items). **Holdings:** 17,500 books; 1600 bound periodical volumes; 15,000 pamphlets; 210 dissertations on microfilm; 2100 reels of microfilm; 500,000 clippings. **Subscriptions:** 650 journals and other serials; 31 newspapers. **Services:** Interlibrary loan; copying; library open to the public. **Computerized Information Services:** OCLC. **Networks and Consortia:** Member of SOLINET. **Publications:** *Amistad Reports* (newsletter), quarterly; *Amistad Log* (magazine), annual; *Historical Source Research Materials on Microfilm*, irregular - all free upon request; *Amistad Research Center Manuscipt Holdings*, irregular - for sale. **Special Catalogues:** Catalog of the American Missionary Association Archives.

★1818★
Association for the Study of Afro-American Life and History
Carter G. Woodson Library
1407 14th St., NW
Washington, DC 20005 Phone: (202)667-2822
Karen A. Robinson, Exec.Dir.

Founded: 1915. **Staff:** 3. **Subjects:** Afro-American history. **Special Collections:** Rare books on Black involvement in America prior to 1865 (200 books). **Holdings:** 4200 books; 88 bound periodical volumes.

★1819★
Atlanta-Fulton Public Library
Special Collections Department
1 Margaret Mitchell Sq.
Atlanta, GA 30303 Phone: (404)730-1700
Janice White Sikes, Mgr.

Founded: 1925. **Staff:** Prof 5; Other 3. **Subjects:** African-American studies, genealogy, Georgia history and literature, oral history, Margaret Mitchell. **Special Collections:** Hattie Wilson High Memorial Genealogical Collection (6800 books, 372 bound periodical volumes, 129 unbound periodicals, 214 city directories, 1200 maps, 160 reels of microfilm); Samuel Williams Collection of materials by and about Afro-Americans (40,000 books, 1600 bound periodical volumes, 2100 reels of microfilm, 1000 microfiche); Margaret Mitchell Collection (1766 items); Atlanta-Fulton Public Library Archives; rare books. **Holdings:** 54,300 books; 3930 bound periodical volumes; 4396 reels of microfilm; 11,000 microfiche; 300 audiocassettes; 790 other cataloged items. **Subscriptions:** 350 journals and newsletters; 15 newspapers. **Services:** Copying; department open to the public for reference use only. **Publications:** Bibliographies and guides. **Remarks:** FAX: (404)730-1989.

★1820★
Beloit College
Colonel Robert H. Morse Library
731 College St.
Beloit, WI 53511 Phone: (608)363-2481
Dennis W. Dickinson, Lib.Dir.

Founded: 1847. **Staff:** Prof 5; Other 7.5. **Subjects:** Anthropology, economics, Shakespeare, international relations, geology, sociology. **Special Collections:** Includes Martin Luther King, Jr. Collection. **Holdings:** 178,516 books; 39,679 bound periodical volumes; 4548 reels of microfilm. **Subscriptions:** 809 journals and other serials; 19 newspapers. **Services:** Interlibrary loan; library open to the public for reference use only. **Computerized Information Services:** DIALOG Information Services, CAS ONLINE, Knowledge Index. Performs searches. Contact Person: Christine Nelson, Pub.Serv.Libn. **Remarks:** FAX: (608)363-2487.

★1821★
Bennett College
Thomas F. Holgate Library
Special Collections
900 E. Washington
Campus Box M
Greensboro, NC 27401 Phone: (919)273-4431

Special Collections: Afro-American Women's Collection (480 books; 2 VF drawers); Norris Wright Cuney Papers (personal and business correspondence, diaries, and newspaper clippings); College Archives (51 boxes; 3 file cabinets; 28 shelves; 1 bookcase). **Services:** Copying; collections open to the public by appointment. **Networks and Consortia:** Member of CCLC.

★1822★
Bienville Historical Society
Cleveland Prichard Memorial Library
4559 Old Citronelle Hwy.
Prichard, AL 36613 Phone: (205)457-5242
Johnnie Andrews, Jr., Dir.

Founded: 1955. **Staff:** Prof 3; Other 2. **Subjects:** City of Mobile and Alabama; genealogy; history of Louisiana, Florida, Mississippi, Georgia, and South Carolina; French, Spanish, and English colonial history; Black history. **Special Collections:** Manuscripts; early church records dating from 1594 from numerous colonial towns; art collection, 1717 to present (1000 prints, etchings, and paintings); Blakeley, Alabama ghost town papers (5000 pages); Pensacola, Florida papers, 1559-1763 (7000 pages); Africa Town, Alabama papers (1000 pages); descriptive catalog of library collection from 1978-1988. **Holdings:** 24,000 books; 1500 colonial manuscripts; 200 Overby photo manuscripts; 300 railroad manuscripts; 300 early maps; 5000 pamphlets; 50,000 clippings in vertical files; 5000 photographs, 1855 to present; 20,000 copies of colonial archives. **Subscriptions:** 137 journals and other serials; 20 newspapers. **Services:** Copying; translation of holdings; library open to the public by appointment only. **Publications:** 60 publications on Gulf South history and genealogy. **Special Indexes:** Card indexes to library holdings of local history collections in 170 Southern libraries; Index of 150,000 Gulf Coast area residents from 1559-1876 (card).

★1823★
Birmingham Public and Jefferson County Free Library
Linn-Henley Library for Southern Historical Research
Department of Archives and Manuscripts
2100 Park Pl.
Birmingham, AL 35203 Phone: (205)226-3645
Marvin Y. Whiting, Archv./Cur., Mss.

Founded: 1976. **Staff:** Prof 2; Other 1. **Subjects:** Birmingham, Alabama - history, civil rights, real estate development, politics and government, private utilities, industry, civic organizations, photographic history, women's history. **Special Collections:** Birmingham Municipal Records (500 linear feet); Jefferson County Public Records (1550 linear feet); Civil Rights in Alabama (85 linear feet and microforms); Robert Jemison, Jr. papers (250 linear feet); Birmingham Water Works Company Records (180 linear feet); Southern Women's Archives (500 linear feet). **Holdings:** 1040 books; 230 bound periodical volumes; 9000 linear feet of archives and manuscripts; 875 reels of microfilm of archives and manuscripts; 2106 microfiche; 600 oral history cassette tapes; 230,000 photographic prints and negatives. **Subscriptions:** 12 journals and other serials; 23 newspapers. **Services:** Interlibrary loan; copying; department open to the public for reference use only. **Computerized Information Services:** OCLC; internal databases. **Publications:** *A Guide to the Collections of the Department of Archives and Manuscripts, Linn-Henley Research Library* - for sale. **Special Catalogues:** Preliminary and Descriptive Inventories for Manuscript Collections and Archival Records Groups, Sub-groups, & Series. **Special Indexes:** Subject file index to photographic collections (card). **Remarks:** FAX: (205)226-3743.

★1824★
Birmingham Public and Jefferson County Free Library
Linn-Henley Library for Southern Historical Research
Tutwiler Collection of Southern History and Literature
2100 Park Pl.
Birmingham, AL 35203 Phone: (205)226-3665
Anne F. Knight, Dept.Hd.

Founded: 1927. **Staff:** Prof 4; Other 8. **Subjects:** Birmingham and Alabama history and literature; Southeastern genealogy; Civil War and Reconstruction history; slave history. **Special Collections:** State, county, and municipal documents. **Holdings:** 62,000 books; 7100 bound periodical volumes; 11,200 reels of microfilm; 1800 pamphlets; 6000 microforms; 154 VF drawers. **Subscriptions:** 353 journals and other serials. **Services:** Collection open to the public for reference use only. **Automated Operations:** Computerized cataloging, acquisitions, and serials. **Computerized Information Services:** DIALOG Information Services, OCLC. **Networks and Consortia:** Member of SOLINET. **Publications:** *George B. Ward: Birmingham's Urban Statesman*; *Research in Black History*; *Genealogical Research in the Tutwiler Collection*; *Bibliography of Birmingham, Alabama, 1872-1972* (book); *Contemporary Literature in Birmingham.* **Special Indexes:** Index to the Birmingham News-Birmingham Post Herald, 1978 to present (microfiche). **Remarks:** FAX: (205)226-3743.

★1825★
Boston University
Department of Special Collections
771 Commonwealth Ave.
Boston, MA 02215 Phone: (617)353-3696
Dr. Howard B. Gotlieb, Dir.

Founded: 1963. **Staff:** Prof 3; Other 9. **Subjects:** Literature - English, American, Afro-American; military history; private presses; Spanish history and literature. **Special Collections:** Twentieth century archives: papers of over 1200 individuals, including Dr. Martin Luther King, Jr. (180 boxes). **Holdings:** 87,000 books; 30,000 boxes of manuscripts. **Subscriptions:** 35 journals and other serials. **Services:** Copying (limited); department open to the public by appointment. **Automated Operations:** Computerized cataloging and serials. **Networks and Consortia:** Member of Boston Library Consortium (BLC). **Publications:** *Special Collections at Boston University* (1981); *Some Notable Recent Gifts to the Twentieth Century Archives* (1984; brochure); *Manuscripts Sacred and Secular* (1985). **Special Catalogues:** Catalogs to manuscript collections (card); catalogs of printers, presses, illustrators, association copies, and provenance (card). **Special Indexes:** Index to individual collections. **Remarks:** FAX: (617)353-2838.

★1826★
California State University, Fullerton
Oral History Program
The Library
800 N. State College Blvd.
Fullerton, CA 92634 Phone: (714)773-3580
Shirley E. Stephenson, Assoc.Dir./Archv.

Founded: 1968. **Staff:** Prof 2. **Subjects:** Local, community, and family history; ethnic groups: Japanese Americans, Chinese Americans, African Americans, Native Americans, Mexican Americans, Swedish Americans; biography; political and university history. **Holdings:** 750 volumes; 3050 interviews (audio); 10 masters' thesis. **Subscriptions:** 4 journals and other serials. **Services:** Program open to the public by appointment. **Special Catalogues:** Catalog of Oral History Collection.

★1827★
Caribbean Culture Center
Library
408 W. 58th St.
New York, NY 10019 Phone: (212)307-7420
Laura G. Moreno, Asst.Dir.

Founded: 1976. **Staff:** 1. **Subjects:** Influence of African traditions in the cultures of the Americas. **Holdings:** Photographs; videotapes. **Services:** Copying; library open to the public by appointment. **Publications:** *Caribe Magazine*; occasional publications. **Remarks:** FAX: (212)315-1086.

★1828★
Carnegie Public Library of Clarksdale and Coahoma County
Delta Blues Museum Collection
114 Delta Ave.
Box 280
Clarksdale, MS 38614 Phone: (601)624-4461
Sid F. Graves Jr., Dir.

Founded: 1914. **Staff:** Prof 6; Other 5. **Subjects:** Blues music; history - local, state, regional, Black. **Holdings:** 15,000 books, periodicals, phonograph records, photographs, videotapes. **Services:** Interlibrary loan; copying; collection open to the public with restrictions. **Publications:** *Clarksdale & Coahoma County: A History*, 1982. **Remarks:** FAX: (601)627-7263.

★1829★
Center for Cultural Survival
Library
11 Divinity Ave.
Cambridge, MA 02138 Phone: (617)496-0786
Jason W. Clay, Dir. of Res./Ed.

Staff: 3. **Subjects:** Indigenous populations, ethnic minorities, human rights, development, social impact, culture change. **Holdings:** 10,000 clippings; 500 unpublished social impact assessments; 1000 reports and documents. **Subscriptions:** 150 journals and other serials; 20 newspapers. **Services:** Library open to the public. **Publications:** Quarterly magazine; occasional reports. **Remarks:** FAX: (617)496-8787. Center is the research division of Cultural Survival, Inc.

★1830★
Center for Southern Folklore
Archives
152 Beale St.
Memphis, TN 38103 Phone: (901)525-3655
Richard Raichelson, Folklorist

Founded: 1972. **Staff:** Prof 8. **Subjects:** Folklife and ethnic cultures of the Mid-South, folk music and religion, folktales, crafts, folk art and architecture, occupational lore, blues music, ethnic culture, Memphis and Mississippi River history. **Special Collections:** The Reverend L. O. Taylor Collection (documentation of Memphis Black community from the late 1920s to 1977); oral histories of Beale Street entertainers and businessmen, and of the Memphis Jewish community. **Holdings:** 1000 books; 3500 unbound periodical volumes; 2000 newsletters; 1200 phonograph records; 40,000 slides; 200,000 feet of film; 40,000 photographs; 5000 hours of audiotapes. **Services:** Copying; archives open to the public by appointment. **Publications:** *Images of the South: Visits with Eudora Welty and Walker Evans* (first in the series); *Center for Southern Folklore Update*, quarterly - to members and media. **Special Catalogues:** American Folklore Films and Videotapes: A Catalog, volume 2. **Special Indexes:** American Folklore Films and Videotapes: An Index, volume 1. **Remarks:** This is "a nonprofit multimedia folklife center documenting the people and traditions of the South and producing films, records, illustrated books, slide and tape programs, concert series, conferences, and folklife festivals which present these people and traditions to large general audiences, educators, and public media."

★1831★
Central Michigan University
Clarke Historical Library
Mt. Pleasant, MI 48859 Phone: (517)774-3352

Founded: 1955. **Staff:** Prof 3; Other 4. **Subjects:** Michigan, Old Northwest Territory, early travel in the Midwest, Afro-Americana, history of slavery, Native Americans, children's literature, angling. **Special Collections:** Lucile Clarke Memorial Children's Library (6768 volumes); Wilbert Wright Collection Afro-Americana (5000 volumes); Reed T. Draper Angling Collection (1261 volumes); Presidential Campaign Biography Collection (778 volumes); university archives. **Holdings:** 60,000 books; 1440 maps; 3274 manuscripts; 1100 broadsides; 26,400 photographs; 8072 microforms; 3564 pieces of sheet music; 900 newspapers; 12,000 pieces of ephemera; 50 tape recordings; 100 phonograph records. **Subscriptions:** 103 journals and other serials. **Services:** Library open to the public. **Automated Operations:** Computerized public access catalog and cataloging. **Networks and Consortia:** Member of Michigan Library Consortium (MLC). **Publications:** Annual report - to mailing list; Resource Guides; occasional books and bibliographies; Michigan Historical Review, semiannual - by subscription. **Special Indexes:** Indexes to: newspapers on microfilm; Mt. Pleasant death records; manuscripts on microfilm; women's history; Twain Collection. **Remarks:** FAX: (517)774-4499.

★1832★
Cheyney University of Pennsylvania
Leslie Pinckney Hill Library
Special Collections
Cheyney, PA 19319 Phone: (215)399-2203
Kay Ridout-Harper, Act.Dir., Lib.Serv.

Holdings: Afro-American Collection (3534 volumes); Cheyney Archives and the William Dorsey Collection of Notebooks and Books on Afro-American History (2500 items). **Subscriptions:** 1016 journals and other serials; 31 newspapers. **Services:** Interlibrary loan; copying; collections open to the public with restrictions. **Automated Operations:** Computerized cataloging. **Computerized Information Services:** BRS Information Technologies. Performs searches on fee basis. **Networks and Consortia:** Member of Tri-State College Library Cooperative (TCLS), PALINET, State System of Higher Education Libraries Council (SSHELCO). **Remarks:** FAX: (215)399-2491.

★1833★
Chicago Public Library
Carter G. Woodson Regional Library
Vivian G. Harsh Research Collection of Afro-American History & Literature
9525 S. Halsted St.
Chicago, IL 60628 Phone: (312)881-6910
Robert Miller, Cur.

Founded: 1932. **Staff:** Prof 4; Other 1. **Subjects:** Afro-Americans - history, religion, sociology, art, literature, music. **Special Collections:** Illinois Writers Project; Heritage Press Archives; Carl Sang Collection of Afro-American History, 1684 to present; Charlemae Hill Rollins Collection of Children's Literature; Era Bell Thompson Collection; Ben Burns Collection; David P. Ross Collection of Reprints in Afro-Americana and Africana; Horace Revells Cayton Collection. **Holdings:** 65,000 books; 565 bound periodical volumes; 5000 linear feet of other cataloged items; 10,180 pamphlets; 1146 phonograph records; 1500 cassette tapes; 10,170 reels of microfilm. **Subscriptions:** 70 journals and other serials; 13 newspapers. **Services:** Interlibrary loan; copying; library open to the public. **Automated Operations:** Computerized cataloging. **Computerized Information Services:** OCLC. **Networks and Consortia:** Member of ILLINET. **Publications:** *Serials Holding List*, biennial; *Malcolm X, a Selected Bibliography2*, biennial; *Richard Wright,* *a Selected Bibliography*; *Harold Washington, a Selected Bibliography*; *Microfilm Holdings*, annual; *Dr. Martin Luther King, Jr., a Selected Bibliography*, biennial; *Jazz at Harsh*, biennial. **Special Catalogues:** The Dictionary Catalog of the Vivian G. Harsh Collection; Afro-American History & Literature (book); The Chicago Afro-American Union Analytic Catalog (book); Union Catalog of Black Music Holdings in Selected Chicago Libraries (online). **Remarks:** FAX: (312)881-3396.

★1834★
Clark Atlanta University
Robert W. Woodruff Library
Division of Archives and Special Collections
111 James P. Brawley Dr., SW
Atlanta, GA 30314 Phone: (404)522-8980
Wilson Flemister, Dir.

Founded: 1982. **Staff:** Prof 5; Other 3. **Subjects:** The Afro-American Experience; Afro-Americana in the southeastern United States; materials by and about peoples of African descent. **Special Collections:** Thayer-Lincoln Collection (125 manuscripts, pictures, and artifacts recording the career of Abraham Lincoln); manuscript collections representing outstanding persons in Afro-American history including Arthur Ashe, Clarence A. Bacote, John Brown, Thomas Clarkson, Paul Laurence Dunbar, Grace Towns Hamilton, C. Eric Lincoln, Rose McLendon, Paul and Eslanda Goode Robeson, Henry O. Tanner, George A. Towns, Andrew Young; Countee Cullen-Harold Jackman Collection (Black artists and writers); Maud Cuney Hare Music and Musicians Manuscript Collection; Henry P. Slaughter Collection (pre-mid-20th century Afro-American history); archival holdings for academic institutions in the Atlanta University Center consortium (Atlanta University, Clark College, The Interdenominational Theological Center) and component seminaries: Gammon Theological Seminary (Methodist), Morehouse School of Religion (Baptist), Charles H. Mason Theological Seminary (Church of God in Christ), Phillips School of Theology (Christian Methodist Episcopal), Johnson C. Smith Seminary, Inc. (Presbyterian), Turner Theological Seminary (African Methodist Episcopal), Morehouse College, Morris Brown College, and Spelman College; archival holdings from race relations and socioeconomic organizations in the South: the Neighborhood Union in Atlanta, Commission on Interracial Cooperation, Association of Southern Women for the Prevention of Lynching, Southern Regional Council, Southern Conference for Human Welfare (manuscripts and archives total approximately 5000 cubic feet); American Missionary Association papers; George Washington Carver papers, 1864-1943; Freedman's Bureau correspondence; Hoyt Fuller Collection on the Afro-American Experience; John and Lugenia Burns Hope Papers, 1888-1947; Martin Luther King, Jr. Memorabilia Collection, 1954 to present; Carl Van Vechten Photograph Collection of internationally known persons of African descent; Black Abolitionists papers, 1830-1865 (microfilm); slavery and antislavery pamphlets from the libraries of Salmon P. Chase and John P. Hale, 1840s and 1850s (microfilm); papers of the Congress of Racial Equality (CORE), records of the Fair Employment Practice Committee, 1941-1946 (microfilm); Johnstown Archeological Collection, 1912-1982 (microfilm); Pennsylvania Abolition Society papers, 1775-1975 (microfilm); Gerrit Smith papers, 1775-1924 (microfilm); Peter Smith papers, 1763-1850 (microfilm); papers of the Student Nonviolent Coordinating Committee (SNCC), 1959-1972 (microfilm); Tuskegee Institute News Clipping File, 1899-1966 (microfilm). **Holdings:** 22,000 books; 1000 bound periodical volumes; 313 college and university catalogs; 94 VF drawers of subject files; 59 audiotapes; 76 microfiche; dissertations on Negros, 1931-1966 on microfilm; Atlanta University and The Interdenominational Theological Center graduate theses and dissertations; pamphlets. **Services:** Interlibrary loan; copying (limited); library open to the public for reference use only for a fee. **Computerized Information Services:** DIALOG Information Services, BRS Information Technologies. **Networks and Consortia:** Member of CCLC, University Center in Georgia, Inc., Georgia Library Information Network (GLIN). **Publications:** *Graduate Theses of Atlanta University*; *Guide to Manuscripts and Archives in the Negro Collection of Trevor Arnett Library*.

★1835★
Clark Atlanta University
School of Library & Information Studies
Library
223 James P. Brawley Dr., SW
Atlanta, GA 30314 Phone: (404)880-8691
Almeta Gould Woodson, Libn.

Founded: 1941. **Staff:** Prof 1; Other 8. **Subjects:** Library and information sciences. **Special Collections:** Children's books; Afro-American studies; ethnic studies. **Holdings:** 22,384 books; 3442 bound periodical volumes; 12 VF drawers; microfilm; microcards; filmstrips; motion pictures; tapes; phonograph records. **Subscriptions:** 143 journals and other serials. **Services:** Interlibrary loan; library open to the public with restrictions. **Remarks:** Electronic mail address(es): ATLANTA.SLIS; ALA0300.

★1836★
Clark Atlanta University
Southern Center for Studies in Public Policy
Research Library
240 Chestnut St.
Atlanta, GA 30314 Phone: (404)880-8000
Mrs. Ollye G. Davis, Res.Libn.

Founded: 1968. **Staff:** Prof 2; Other 2. **Subjects:** Economic development, public policy, transportation, employment and labor, Blacks and civil rights, poverty. **Holdings:** 5000 books; 325 bound periodical volumes; 6 VF drawers of clippings; 10 tapes each of the National Longitudinal Survey, the Panel Study of Income Dynamics, 1980 Census Report. **Subscriptions:** 185 journals and other serials; 6 newspapers. **Services:** Interlibrary loan; copying; library open to the public for reference use only. **Automated Operations:** Computerized cataloging. **Computerized Information Services:** DIALOG Information Services. **Networks and Consortia:** Member of Georgia Library Information Network (GLIN). **Special Indexes:** Index of journal articles dealing with public policy issues. **Remarks:** FAX: (404)880-8222.

★1837★
Cleveland Public Library
Fine Arts and Special Collections Department
John G. White Collection and Rare Books
325 Superior Ave.
Cleveland, OH 44114-1271 Phone: (216)623-2818
Alice N. Loranth, Dept.Hd.

Founded: 1869. **Staff:** Prof 2; Other 2. **Subjects:** History, linguistics, religion, folklore, archaeology. **Special Collections:** Includes Margaret Klipple Memorial Archives of African Folktales; Black Names in America; Religious Beliefs of the Southern Negro. **Holdings:** 133,199 volumes; 1500 bound manuscripts; 315 boxes and 90 VF drawers of clippings and pictorial material on chess; 147 tapes; 2551 reels of microfilm. **Subscriptions:** 795 journals and other serials. **Services:** Interlibrary loan; copying; exhibits; lectures; collection open to the public with valid identification. **Automated Operations:** Computerized public access catalog, cataloging, acquisitions, and circulation. **Computerized Information Services:** OCLC, DIALOG Information Services, BRS Information Technologies, OhioPI (Ohio Public Information Utility), Hannah Information Systems, U.S. Patent Classification System, Pergamon ORBIT InfoLine, Inc., WILSONLINE; CD-ROMs (CIRR, ABI/INFORM). **Networks and Consortia:** Member of OHIONET, NEOMARL, Cleveland Area Metropolitan Library System (CAMLS), North Central Library Cooperative (NCLC). **Publications:** Descriptive pamphlets of holdings, irregular; John G. White Department of Folklore, Orientalia and Chess (2nd ed., 1978). **Special Catalogues:** Black Names in America: Origin and Usage (1975).

★1838★
Cleveland Public Library
History and Geography Department
325 Superior Ave.
Cleveland, OH 44114-1271 Phone: (216)623-2864
JoAnn Petrello, Dept.Hd.

Founded: 1869. **Staff:** Prof 4; Other 6. **Subjects:** History - ancient, medieval, modern; includes Black history. **Special Collections:** Photograph Collection (900,337); British learned society serials; 19th century travel narratives; English parish register collection. **Holdings:** 205,820 volumes; 12,322 bound periodical volumes. **Subscriptions:** 934 journals and other serials. **Services:** Interlibrary loan; copying; department open to the public. **Automated Operations:** Computerized public access catalog, cataloging, acquisitions, and circulation. **Computerized Information Services:** OCLC, DIALOG Information Services, BRS Information Technologies, OhioPI (Ohio Public Information Utility), Hannah Information Systems, U.S. Patent Classification System, Pergamon ORBIT InfoLine, Inc., WILSONLINE; CD-ROMs (CIRR, ABI/INFORM). **Networks and Consortia:** Member of OHIONET, NEOMARL, Cleveland Area Metropolitan Library System (CAMLS), North Central Library Cooperative (NCLC).

★1839★
Columbia University
Oral History Research Office
Butler Library
Box 20
New York, NY 10027 Phone: (212)854-2273
Ronald J. Grele, Dir.

Founded: 1948. **Staff:** Prof 3; Other 10. **Subjects:** National affairs, New York history, international relations, culture and the arts, social welfare, business and labor, philanthropy, Afro-American community, law, medicine, education, journalism, religion. **Special Collections:** Includes United Negro College Fund (2500 pp.). **Holdings:** 6000 volumes of edited transcript; 3400 reels and cassettes of tapes, 1963 to present; microforms of one third of the collection; supporting papers accompany some memoirs; data on other oral history holdings and centers worldwide. **Services:** Research service available; copying (limited); collection open to the public with restrictions. The office provides books on oral history - for sale. **Automated Operations:** Computerized cataloging. **Computerized Information Services:** RLIN. **Networks and Consortia:** Member of RLG.

★1840★
Commission on Civil Rights
National Clearinghouse Library
1121 Vermont Ave., NW
Washington, DC 20425 Phone: (202)376-8110
Barbara J. Fontana, Libn.

Founded: 1957. **Staff:** Prof 1; Other 1. **Subjects:** Civil rights, economics, education, sex discrimination, sociology, law. **Special Collections:** The aged and the handicapped; commission publications. **Holdings:** 65,000 books; 1100 bound periodical volumes; 1200 state and federal codes and statutes; 110 legal periodical titles; 500 reels of microfilm of minority periodicals; 300 journals on microfiche. **Subscriptions:** 300 journals and newspapers. **Services:** Interlibrary loan; copying; library open to the public for reference use only. **Automated Operations:** Computerized cataloging. **Computerized Information Services:** DIALOG Information Services, OCLC. **Publications:** monthly acquisitions list; bibliographies.

★1841★
Community College of Baltimore
Libraries/Media Services
Bard Library
2901 Liberty Heights Ave.
Baltimore, MD 21215 Phone: (301)396-0432
Bruce Carroll

Founded: 1947. **Staff:** Prof 4; Other 6. **Subjects:** Black history, health science, Baltimore and Maryland history, technology. **Holdings:** 100,000 books; 120,000 pamphlets (uncataloged); 12,000 reels of microfilm; 20,000 nonprint materials. **Subscriptions:** 500 journals and other serials. **Services:** Interlibrary loan; copying; library open to the public for reference use only. **Automated Operations:** Computerized acquisitions, circulation, and shelflist files. **Computerized Information Services:** Microcat (internal database); CD-ROM (Academic Index). **Remarks:** Includes holdings of Business & Industry Center Library located at Lombard at Market Place, Baltimore, MD 21202; phone: (301)396-1860.

★1842★
Compton Community College
Library
Black History Collection
1111 E. Artesia Blvd.
Compton, CA 90221 Phone: (213)637-2660
Saul J. Panski, Hd.Libn.

Founded: 1927. **Staff:** Prof 2; Other 1.5. **Subjects:** Black history. **Holdings:** 43,465 books; 6664 microforms. **Subscriptions:** 219 journals and other serials; 5 newspapers. **Services:** Interlibrary loan; collection open to the public for reference use only. **Remarks:** FAX: (213)608-3721.

★1843★
Cornell University
John Henrik Clarke Africana Library
310 Triphammer Rd.
Ithaca, NY 14850-2599 Phone: (607)255-5229
Thomas Weissinger, Libn.

Founded: 1972. **Staff:** Prof 1; Other 3. **Subjects:** African, Afro-American, Caribbean peoples - history, culture, lifestyles, and economic, social, and political development. **Special Collections:** Civil Rights Microfilm Collection (940 reels of microfilm), 250 video cassettes. **Holdings:** 13,200 books; 800 bound periodical volumes; 12 file drawers of clippings. **Subscriptions:** 104 journals and other serials; 15 newspapers. **Services:** Interlibrary loan; library open to the public. **Automated Operations:** Computerized public access catalog, cataloging, acquisitions, and circulation. **Computerized Information Services:** DIALOG Information Services, RLIN; (internal database). **Networks and Consortia:** Member of RLG. **Remarks:** Alternate telephone number(s): (607)255-0789.

★1844★
Council for Alternatives to Stereotyping in Entertainment
Library
139 Corson Ave.
Staten Island, NY 10301 Phone: (718)720-5378

Subjects: Entertainment - stereotyping, self-image, reality perception, receptivity to accurate performance feedback. **Holdings:** 1000 volumes.

★1845★
County of Los Angeles Public Library
Black Resource Center
150 E. El Segundo Blvd.
Los Angeles, CA 90061 Phone: (213)538-3350
Fannie Love, Commun.Lib.Mgr.

Founded: 1974. **Staff:** Prof 1; Other 2. **Subjects:** Afro-American history and culture, Black music and musical artists. **Special Collections:** Pictures/posters of famous Black Americans (208). **Holdings:** 7200 books; 65 bound periodical volumes; 3150 clippings; 2490 reels of microfilm; 1174 microfiche; 207 video cassettes; 272 audio cassettes; 385 phonograph records. **Subscriptions:** 120 journals and other serials; 20 newspapers. **Services:** Interlibrary loan; copying; center open to the public for reference use only. **Automated Operations:** Computerized public access catalog. **Remarks:** FAX: (213)327-0824. **Also known as:** A. C. Bilbrew Library.

★1846★
Detroit Public Library
Film Department
5201 Woodward Ave.
Detroit, MI 48202 Phone: (313)833-1495
Grace Larson, Chf.

Founded: 1947. **Staff:** Prof 3; Other 3. **Subjects:** Film - educational, children's, feature, Black studies. **Holdings:** 13,000 video cassettes. **Subscriptions:** 5 journals and other serials. **Services:** Library open to the public. **Automated Operations:** Computerized circulation. **Computerized Information Services:** VIDSTAR (internal database). SCA Video Catalog.

★1847★
Detroit Public Library
Music and Performing Arts Department
5201 Woodward Ave.
Detroit, MI 48202 Phone: (313)833-1460
Agatha Pfeiffer Kalkanis, Chf.

Founded: 1921. **Staff:** Prof 5; Other 2. **Subjects:** Music, theater, moving pictures, radio and television, broadcasting, dance, bullfighting, circus, rodeo. **Special Collections:** E. Azalia Hackley Collection (Blacks in the performing arts); Michigan Collection (music by Michigan composers or with Michigan associations). **Holdings:** 40,000 books; 7787 bound periodical volumes; 56,000 scores; 30,000 recordings; 20,000 popular sheet music titles; 150 VF drawers; 6 VF drawers of photographs; 2000 cassettes; 1033 reels of microfilm. **Subscriptions:** 344 journals and other serials. **Services:** Interlibrary loan; copying; department open to the public. **Computerized Information Services:** DIALOG Information Services, VU/TEXT Information Services.

★1848★
District of Columbia Public Library
Black Studies Division
Martin Luther King Memorial Library
901 G St., NW
Washington, DC 20001 Phone: (202)727-1211
Alice B. Robinson, Chf.

Founded: 1971. **Staff:** Prof 3. **Subjects:** Slavery in the U.S. and Caribbean, biography, business, social conditions, literature, history, science, technology, civil rights. **Special Collections:** Beatrice Murphy Foundation (1860 books); Juvenile Reference Collection (709 books). **Holdings:** 19,348 books; 24 bound periodical volumes; 149 reels of microfilm; 30 VF drawers. **Subscriptions:** 106 journals and other serials; 58 newspapers. **Services:** Copying; division open to the public for reference use only. **Publications:** Booklists on special subject, irregular - free. **Special Indexes:** Index of Black literary magazines (card).

★1849★
Divine Word Seminary of St. Augustine
Library
199 Seminary Dr.
Bay St. Louis, MS 39520 Phone: (601)467-6414

Founded: 1923. **Subjects:** Afro-American history and literature, ethnology, theology, social sciences, pure and applied sciences, literature, geography, history. **Holdings:** 8000 volumes; 500 bound periodical volumes. **Services:** Library open to the public for research purposes only. **Remarks:** Includes the holdings of St. Augustine Retreat Center - Library, telephone: 467-9837.

★1850★
DuSable Museum of African American History
Library
740 E. 56th Pl.
Chicago, IL 60637 Phone: (312)947-0600
Useni Perkins, Dir.

Founded: 1961. **Staff:** Prof 2; Other 3. **Subjects:** Black history, sociology, politics, religion, fiction, biography; Africana. **Holdings:** 3000 volumes; 500 other cataloged items; 100 oral history tapes; 50 manuscripts; 85 VF drawers of clippings. **Services:** Library not open to the public. **Publications:** *Calendar*, annual.

★1851★
East Texas State University
James Gilliam Gee Library
Oral History Program
James Gilliam Gee Library
E. Texas Sta.
Commerce, TX 75429-2953 Phone: (214)886-5738
Dr. James Conrad, Coord. of Oral Hist.

Founded: 1968. **Staff:** Prof 1; Other 1. **Subjects:** History of East Texas - railroad, cotton, Blacks, medicine; Texas social work; institutional history. **Special Collections:** Senator A. M. Aikin, Jr. project; Fletcher Warren project; Southwest Dairy project; Dallas Mayors project; Caddo Lake project. **Holdings:** 205 volumes; 800 cassette tapes of interviews. **Subscriptions:** 3 journals and other serials. **Services:** Copying; program open to the public with restrictions. **Automated Operations:** Computerized cataloging. **Special Catalogues:** Oral history catalog. Alternate telephone number(s): (214)886-5737.

★1852★
Eastern Baptist Theological Seminary
Library
Lancaster Ave. & City Ave.
Philadelphia, PA 19151 Phone: (215)645-9318
Dr. William J. Hand, Act.Dir.

Founded: 1925. **Staff:** Prof 2; Other 2. **Subjects:** Theology and allied subjects. **Special Collections:** Russell H. MacBride Collection of Philosophy, Religion and Classical Literature (3750 volumes); J. Pius Barbor Collection in Black Church Studies (1065 volumes); Hispanic Studies Collection (2223 volumes). **Holdings:** 109,082 books; 11,116 bound periodical volumes. **Subscriptions:** 483 journals and other serials. **Services:** Interlibrary loan; copying; library open to graduate students and ministers. **Automated Operations:** Computerized cataloging and acquisitions. **Computerized Information Services:** OCLC. **Networks and Consortia:** Member of PALINET, Southeastern Pennsylvania Theological Library Association (SEPTLA). **Remarks:** FAX: (215)649-3834.

★1853★
Ecumenical Music & Liturgy Resource Library
8000 Hickory Lane
PO Box 30221
Lincoln, NE 68503-0221 Phone: (402)488-1668
Judy H. Barrick, Dir.

Founded: 1975. **Staff:** 1. **Subjects:** History, theology, and practice of worship in the Judeo-Christian traditions. **Special Collections:** Special needs and contributions of Asian, Black, Hispanic, Native American, aging, disabled, single, and women worshippers. **Holdings:** 5000 books; 125 audio cassettes, filmstrips, kits; 125 sets of choir music; unbound periodicals. **Subscriptions:** 25 journals and other serials. **Services:** Interlibrary loan; copying (limited); library open to the public on fee basis. **Publications:** Informational brochure; price list; acquisitions list - available on request. **Also known as:** EMLR Library.

★1854★
Elma Lewis School of Fine Arts
Library
122 Elmhill Ave.
Dorchester, MA 02121

Founded: 1969. **Subjects:** Dance, art, drama, music, costuming, wardrobe, Afro-American and African history, Third World. **Special Collections:** African, Afro-American, and Caribbean art (3000 slides); African artifacts. **Holdings:** Figures not available. **Remarks:** Currently inactive.

★1855★
Enoch Pratt Free Library
Audio-Visual Department
400 Cathedral St.
Baltimore, MD 21201 Phone: (301)396-4616
Marc Sober

Founded: 1949. **Staff:** Prof 1; Other 13. **Subjects:** History of film, experimental film, music, art, social sciences, other arts and crafts, religion, Black history/culture, children's films. **Special Collections:** Maryland and Baltimore history. **Holdings:** 5194 16mm films; 161 super and standard 8mm films; 486 filmstrips; 36,805 slides; 926 videotapes; 120 videodiscs; 412 audiotape cassettes. **Subscriptions:** 14 journals and other serials. **Services:** Interlibrary loan (within Maryland only); department open to the public. **Special Catalogues:** Audio-visual catalog. **Remarks:** FAX: (301)396-5837.

★1856★
ERIC Clearinghouse on Urban Education
Institute for Urban and Minority Education
Teachers College, Columbia University
Box 40
New York, NY 10027 Phone: (212)678-3433
Dr. Erwin Flaxman, Dir.

Founded: 1965. **Staff:** Prof 8; Other 4. **Subjects:** Education of urban and minority children and youths; psychology; sociology. **Holdings:** 1000 books; 15,500 reports, manuscripts, and other documentation; 205,000 titles in ERIC microfiche collection. **Subscriptions:** 60 journals and other serials. **Services:** Reference services by mail in the form of prepared bibliographies and other ERIC/CUE publications; clearinghouse open to the public by appointment. **Computerized Information Services:** DIALOG Information Services, Pergamon ORBIT InfoLine, Inc., BRS Information Technologies, CD-ROM (SilverPlatter). Performs searches on fee basis. Contact Person: Dr. Michael Webb, Assoc. Dir. **Publications:** Trends and Issues Series - for sale; Urban Diversity Series, irregular - for sale; ERIC/CUE Digests, irregular - single copies free upon request with a self-addressed stamped envelope. **Remarks:** FAX: (212)678-4048. **Also known as:** ERIC/CUE.

★1857★
Ethnic American Council
Library
820 Lathrop
River Forest, IL 60305 Phone: (708)366-1000
Michael Burny

Founded: 1984. **Staff:** 1. **Subjects:** American ethnic groups, politics and government, liberty, communism, free market economics, entrepreneurship. **Special Collections:** Austrian economics collection. **Holdings:** 500 books; 25 reports. **Subscriptions:** 15 journals and other serials; 5 newspapers. **Services:** Library open to the public by appointment; must apply in writing.

★1858★
Fisk University
Special Collections Department
17th at Jackson St.
Nashville, TN 37203 Phone: (615)329-8646
Ann Allen Shockley, Assoc.Libn./Archv.

Founded: 1866. **Staff:** Prof 2. **Special Collections:** Negro Collection; Fiskiana Collection (9 VF drawers); Yorkshire Collection; George Gershwin Collection; Langston Hughes Phonograph Collection; Black Oral History Collection (700 tapes); audiotape collection (183 tapes). **Holdings:** 52,000 books; 1565 bound periodical volumes; 3050 reels of microfilm of information by and about Blacks; 2000 phonograph records; 4 VF drawers of pictures; 2 VF drawers of newspaper clippings; 4 VF drawers of biographical information by or about Blacks; 878 Fisk University masters' theses; 95 archival and manuscript collections. **Subscriptions:** 48 journals and other serials; 7 newspapers. **Services:** Copying; department open to the public with restrictions. **Special Catalogues:** Dictionary catalog on the Negro Collection; catalog to Oral History Collection; shelf lists for archives and manuscripts collections. **Remarks:** Alternate telephone number(s): (615)329-8580.

★1859★
Friends of the Third World Inc.
Whole World Books
611 W. Wayne St.
Fort Wayne, IN 46802 Phone: (219)422-6821
Marian R. Waltz, Rsrc.Coord.

Staff: Prof 1; Other 2. **Subjects:** Hunger, population, international politics and economics, U.S. minorities, food and nutrition, international and national poverty issues, American lifestyles and the environment. **Special Collections:** Alternative periodicals and newsletters; research files on Third World Handicraft production (600). **Holdings:** 800 books; 2000 pamphlets and periodicals; 24 VF drawers. **Subscriptions:** 30 journals and other serials. **Services:** Copying; open to the public for reference use only; requests for information or referral are answered by mail. **Computerized Information Services:** Internal database; Dialcom Inc. (electronic mail service). **Publications:** *Alternative Trading News*, quarterly - for sale. **Remarks:** Telex: 4900005862. Electronic mail address(es): TCN 225 (Dialcom, Inc.); FOTW (PEACENET).

★1860★
Great Plains Black Museum
Library
2213 Lake St.
Omaha, NE 68110 Phone: (402)345-2212
Bertha Calloway, Founder/Dir.

Founded: 1976. **Staff:** Prof 2; Other 10. **Subjects:** Blacks in Nebraska and the Midwest. **Holdings:** 2000 books; photographs; archival materials. **Subscriptions:** 12 journals and other serials. **Services:** Library open to the public.

★1861★
Hampton Institute
Collis P. Huntington Memorial Library
Special Collections
Hampton, VA 23668 Phone: (804)727-5371
Jason C. Grant, III, Libn.

Founded: 1904. **Special Collections:** George Foster Peabody Collection of Negro Literature and History; Hampton University Archives (4 million items); U.S. Government documents (partial depository). **Holdings:** 31,748 volumes. **Services:** Interlibrary loan; copying; collections open to the public with restrictions on circulation. **Automated Operations:** Computerized cataloging. **Computerized Information Services:** DIALOG Information Services, OCLC. Performs searches on fee basis. Contact Person: Mary Marks, Acq.. **Networks and Consortia:** Member of SOLINET, Council on Botanical Horticultural Libraries. **Special Catalogues:** Dictionary Catalog of the George Foster Peabody Collection of Negro Literature and History, 1972.

★1862★
Harris-Stowe State College
Library
3026 Laclede Ave.
St. Louis, MO 63103 Phone: (314)533-3366
Martin Knorr, Dir.

Founded: 1857. **Staff:** Prof 3; Other 4. **Subjects:** Education. **Special Collections:** Elementary education; Education of Exceptional Children; Black Studies; Juvenile Literature; Civil Rights. **Holdings:** 90,000 books; 2400 reels of microfilm of periodicals. **Subscriptions:** 325 journals and other serials; 9 newspapers. **Services:** Interlibrary loan; library open to teachers and education professionals with courtesy card. **Automated Operations:** Computerized circulation. **Computerized Information Services:** DIALOG Information Services. **Networks and Consortia:** Member of St. Louis Regional Library Network. **Remarks:** FAX: (314)533-0916.

★1863★
Hatch-Billops Collection, Inc.
Library
491 Broadway, 7th Fl.
New York, NY 10012 Phone: (212)966-3231
Camille Billops, Pres.

Founded: 1975. **Staff:** Prof 1. **Subjects:** Afro-Americana, theater, visual arts. **Special Collections:** Oral history interviews (1100); art slides (10,000); Owen and Edith Dodson Memorial Collection (plays, manuscripts, photos, and letters); Charles and Ellyce Weir Griffin Collection (400 black and white film stills; lobby cards); Theodore Ward plays. **Holdings:** 4000 books; 1000 black/white photographs; 300 posters; 1200 playbills; 300 art catalogs. **Subscriptions:** 12 journals and other serials. **Services:** Copying; collection open to the public by appointment. **Computerized Information Services:** Internal database (playbills, manuscripts, theater articles). **Publications:** *Artist and Influence*. **Special Catalogues:** Catalog of oral history holdings with abstracts; catalog of African American theater history; catalog of African American playbills.

★1864★
Hempstead Public Library
Special Collections
115 Nichols Court
Hempstead, NY 11550 Phone: (516)481-6990
Irene A. Duszkiewicz, Dir.

Founded: 1898. **Special Collections:** Walt Whitman; Long Island Collection; Foreign Language Collection for Children and Adults; New York State History; Job and Education Information Center; Career Counseling; New York State Documents Reference Center; Black studies. **Holdings:** 180,000 books. **Subscriptions:** 400 journals and other serials; 75 newspapers. **Services:** Interlibrary loan; copying; collections open to the public. **Automated Operations:** Computerized cataloging, acquisitions, and circulation. **Computerized Information Services:** DIALOG Information Services. Performs searches free of charge for village residents only. **Networks and Consortia:** Member of Nassau Library System. **Remarks:** FAX: (516)481-6719.

★1865★
Historical Research Repository, Inc.
Library
868 Penobscot Bldg.
Detroit, MI 48226-4004 Phone: (313)822-9027
John M. Green, Archv.

Founded: 1968. **Staff:** Prof 1. **Subjects:** Black history, Michigan Black history. **Special Collections:** Pre-1940 postcards of Blacks (115); African American U.S. postal stamps (complete set). **Holdings:** 85 books. **Services:** Library not open to the public. **Publications:** *Black Nobel Prize Winners*; *Michigan Black History Review*. **Remarks:** Library has access to International Afro-American Sports Hall of Fame and Gallery newspapers, photographs, and films.

★1866★
Historical Society of Pennsylvania
Library
1300 Locust St.
Philadelphia, PA 19107 Phone: (215)732-6201
Thomas Jay Kemp, Lib.Dir.

Founded: 1824. **Staff:** Prof 16. **Subjects:** History - U.S., 1783-1865, Colonial, Revolutionary, Pennsylvania; genealogy; Afro-Americana. **Holdings:** 564,000 volumes; 6 million manuscripts; 2800 microcards; 17,200 microfiche; 16,700 reels of microfilm; maps; prints; drawings; paintings; newspapers; ephemera. **Subscriptions:** 4000 journals and other serials. **Services:** Copying; library open to the public on fee basis. **Automated Operations:** Computerized cataloging. **Computerized Information Services:** OCLC, RLIN. **Networks and Consortia:** Member of PALINET, RLG, Area Consortium of Special Collections Libraries. **Publications:** *The Pennsylvania Magazine of History and Biography*, quarterly; *The Pennsylvania Correspondent* (newsletter), 5/year - to members. **Remarks:** FAX: (215)732-2680.

★1867★
Houston Public Library
Houston Metropolitan Research Center
500 McKinney Ave.
Houston, TX 77002 Phone: (713)247-1661
Louis J. Marchiafava, Ph.D., Archv.

Founded: 1975. **Staff:** Prof 5; Other 1. **Subjects:** Houston - business, politics, architecture, church records, city and county government, agencies. **Special Collections:** Includes Houston African-American Collection. **Holdings:** 18,000 linear feet of archival material. **Services:** Copying; center open to the public. **Remarks:** Alternate telephone number(s): (713)247-3562. FAX: (713)247-3531.

★1868★
Houston Public Library
Special Collections Department
500 McKinney Ave.
Houston, TX 77002 Phone: (713)236-1313

Subjects: U.S. slavery and Civil War, Salvation Army, religious history, 19th century travel. **Special Collections:** Milsaps Collection (8642 titles; 3000 pamphlets; 900 18th century book titles); Annette Finnigan Collection (fine press books; 60 volumes); Mark Twain, Alice Books, limited editions; Historical Juvenile Literature Collection: Reynolds Room (700 rare books) and Julia Ideson Stacks (1527 historical books); St.

Nicholas Magazine collection; British and American Chapbooks of the 18th and 19th Century (500); New England Primers, late 18th-early 19th century (73); American Dictionary Collection, 1780 to present (emphasis on slang); manuscripts and early printing, 1100-1800. **Holdings:** 22,091 books. **Services:** Library open to the public by appointment - contact Texas & Local History Department. **Networks and Consortia:** Member of Houston Area Research Library Consortium (HARLIC).

★1869★
Howard University
African-American Resource Center
2400 6th St., NW
Box 746
Washington, DC 20059 Phone: (202)806-7242
Mr. E. Ethelbert Miller, Dir.

Founded: 1969. **Staff:** Prof 1. **Subjects:** Black studies, economics, history, political science, literature, international relations. **Holdings:** 20,000 books. **Subscriptions:** 50 journals and other serials; 10 newspapers. **Services:** Copying; center open to the public. **Remarks:** Library located at Founders Library, 500 Howard Place, 3rd Fl., Rm. 300, Washington D.C.

★1870★
Howard University
Allen Mercer Daniel Law Library
2900 Van Ness St., NW
Washington, DC 20008 Phone: (202)806-8045
Judy Dimes-Smith, Law Libn. & Assoc.Prof.

Founded: 1867. **Staff:** Prof 14; Other 4. **Subjects:** Law. **Special Collections:** Civil rights. **Holdings:** 190,000 volumes; 59,269 microforms; 44 motion pictures; 269 audio cassettes; 126 video cassettes. **Subscriptions:** 1426 journals and other serials. **Services:** Interlibrary loan; copying; library open to the public. **Automated Operations:** Computerized public access catalog and cataloging. **Computerized Information Services:** LEXIS, WESTLAW; internal databases. **Networks and Consortia:** Member of CAPCON, Consortium of Universities of the Washington Metropolitan Area. **Publications:** Acquisitions list, monthly. **Special Indexes:** Index of microform holdings; Checklist of U.S. Congress Committee Hearings & Committee Prints; Checklist of United Nations Documents; Legislative Research Documents: state; Subject List of Legal Lectures on Tape (all pamphlets). **Remarks:** FAX: (202)686-0740.

★1871★
Howard University
Architecture & Planning Library
6th St. & Howard Pl., NW
Washington, DC 20059 Phone: (202)806-7773
Gertis Fenuku, Libn.

Staff: Prof 1; Other 2. **Subjects:** Architectural history, construction and design, city planning, environmental design. **Holdings:** 24,894 books; 4705 bound periodical volumes; 33,921 slides, filmstrips, lantern frames; 1666 reels of microfilm; 428 maps. **Subscriptions:** 425 journals and other serials. **Services:** Interlibrary loan; library open to the public. **Automated Operations:** Computerized cataloging, acquisitions, and serials. **Computerized Information Services:** DIALOG Information Services. Performs searches on fee basis. **Networks and Consortia:** Member of CAPCON, Consortium of Universities of the Washington Metropolitan Area. **Publications:** *SLIDEX* (a system for indexing, filing, and retrieving slides); *About the A&P Library*; *Resources for Architects and Planners in Washington, DC and Metropolitan Area*; recent acquisitions.

★1872★
Howard University
Center for Economic Education
Library
Department of Economics
Washington, DC 20059 Phone: (202)806-6733
Dr. E.E. Ghartey, Lecturer

Subjects: Macro- and microeconomics, economics education, economic development, labor markets, international economics. **Holdings:** 8000 volumes. **Subscriptions:** 38 journals and other serials. **Publications:** Reports.

★1873★
Howard University
Channing Pollock Theatre Collection
500 Howard Pl., NW
Founders Library Bldg., Rm. 213
Washington, DC 20059 Phone: (202)806-7259
Jean Church, Cur.

Founded: 1950. **Staff:** Prof 2; Other 1. **Subjects:** Theater, drama, performing arts. **Special Collections:** William Warren I journals, 1796-1831; William Warren II diaries, dramatic scrapbooks, letters, and promptbooks (the American Stage and the Boston Museum, 1847-1888; 4 diaries; 2 scrapbooks). **Holdings:** 16,334 books; 2695 bound periodical volumes; 1904 other cataloged items; 90,548 clippings; 38,651 articles; 1923 autograph letters; autograph letter signatures, card autographs, and archive autographs; 12,377 Carte de visite/Cabinet photographs; 6603 photographs; 260 manuscripts; 1493 pieces of sheet music; 2240 prints; 12,594 playbills; 485 rare programs; 516 souvenir programs; 1137 reels of microfilm; 5571 microcards; 5067 microfiche. **Subscriptions:** 382 journals and other serials; 5 newspapers. **Services:** Copying; collection open to the public with identification. **Automated Operations:** Computerized cataloging, acquisitions, and serials. **Networks and Consortia:** Member of CAPCON, Consortium of Universities of the Washington Metropolitan Area. **Special Indexes:** Indexes to scrapbooks - Olga Nethersole Collection (9 volumes of scrapbooks), Percy G. Williams Collection (Novelty Theatre, Brooklyn, programs), Alfred H. Woods Collection (theatrical contracts), Roland Reed Collection (playbills), Albert Berkowitz Collection (photographs of the Old Vic Company), Channing Pollock Collection (complete library and his writings), Harvard/Radcliff Program Collection.

★1874★
Howard University
Health Sciences Library
600 W St., NW
Washington, DC 20059 Phone: (202)806-6433
Salvador Waller, Assoc.Dir.

Founded: 1927. **Staff:** Prof 7; Other 11. **Subjects:** Medicine, dentistry, nursing, and allied health sciences. **Special Collections:** Sickle cell anemia (2 drawers of clippings and pamphlets); Negroes in medicine, dentistry, and psychiatry (2 drawers; 20 boxes). **Holdings:** 204,558 books; 79,257 bound periodical volumes; 515 bibliographies; 121 shelves of AV programs; 20 VF drawers of disease, health, medicine files; 6 VF drawers of biographical files; 115 drawers of microfilm. **Subscriptions:** 5026 journals and other serials. **Services:** Interlibrary loan; copying; SDI; library open to the public for reference use only. **Automated Operations:** Computerized cataloging, acquisitions, serials, and circulation. **Computerized Information Services:** MEDLARS, DIALOG Information Services. Performs searches on fee basis. Contact Person: Howertine Farrell-Duncan, Libn./Supv., Ref. **Networks and Consortia:** Member of CAPCON, Consortium of Universities of the Washington Metropolitan Area, Consortium of Academic Health Science Libraries of the District of Columbia, District of Columbia Health Sciences Information Network (DOCHSIN). **Special Catalogues:** Sickle cell anemia; hypertension among Negroes (both card).

★1875★
Howard University
Health Sciences Library
Annex (Pharmacy)
2300 4th St.
Washington, DC 20059 Phone: (202)806-6545
Mr. Jei Whan Kim, Libn.

Staff: Prof 1; Other 2. **Subjects:** Pharmacy, pharmacology, pharmacognosy, biomedicinal chemistry. **Holdings:** 16,337 books; 4943 bound periodical volumes; 974 reels of microfilm; 415 cassettes; 4001 slides; 31,480 microfiche. **Subscriptions:** 448 journals and other serials. **Services:** Interlibrary loan; copying; library open to the public with restrictions. **Automated Operations:** Computerized cataloging, acquisitions, serials, and circulation. **Computerized Information Services:** DIALOG Information Services, NLM. Performs searches on fee basis. **Networks and Consortia:** Member of CAPCON, Consortium of Universities of the Washington Metropolitan Area.

★1876★
Howard University
Moorland-Spingarn Research Center
Library Division
500 Howard Pl., NW
Washington, DC 20059 Phone: (202)806-7260
Elinor Desverney Sinnette, Chf.Libn.

Founded: 1914. **Staff:** Prof 10. **Subjects:** Afro-Americana, Africana, Caribbeana, Latin Americana. **Holdings:** 150,000 books; 9564 bound periodical volumes; 10,852 microforms; 563 dissertations. **Subscriptions:** 531 journals and other serials; 130 newspapers. **Services:** Copying; division open to the public. **Networks and Consortia:** Member of CAPCON, Consortium of Universities of the Washington Metropolitan Area. **Remarks:** FAX: (202)636-6405.

★1877★
Howard University
Moorland-Spingarn Research Center
Manuscript Division
500 Howard Pl., NW
Washington, DC 20059 Phone: (202)806-7480
Karen L. Jefferson, Cur.

Founded: 1914. **Staff:** Prof 5; Other 2. **Subjects:** Afro-Americana, Africana, Caribbeana. **Special Collections:** Ralph J. Bunche Oral History Collection (individuals involved in 1960s civil rights activities; 700 tapes and transcripts); Music Collection (4000 pieces of sheet music); Prints and Photographs (24,000, including Rose McClendon Collection of Photographs of Celebrated Negroes by Carl Van Vechten, Mary O. H. Williamson Collection, Griffith Davis Collection). **Holdings:** 2000 linear feet of processed manuscripts; 4800 linear feet of unprocessed manuscripts. **Services:** Copying; division open to qualified researchers. **Publications:** *Guide to Processed Collections in the Manuscript Division of the Moorland-Spingarn Research Center.* **Remarks:** FAX: (202)806-6405.

★1878★
Howard University
School of Business and Public Administration
Library
2600 6th St., NW, Rm. 120
Washington, DC 20059 Phone: (202)806-1561
Lucille B. Smiley, Libn.

Staff: Prof 2; Other 5. **Subjects:** Business administration, public administration, health services administration, management, accounting, real estate, insurance, marketing, finance, computer-based management information systems, hotel/motel management, international business. **Holdings:** 60,991 books; 5780 bound periodical volumes; 82 technical assistance reports; 17,633 reels of microfilm; 308,814 10K reports on microfiche. **Subscriptions:** 3139 journals and other serials; 75 newspapers. **Services:** Interlibrary loan; copying; library open to the public for reference use only. **Automated Operations:** Computerized cataloging, acquisitions, serials, and circulation. **Computerized Information Services:** DIALOG Information Services, Dow Jones News/Retrieval, Dun & Bradstreet Corporation, LEXIS, NEXIS. Performs searches on fee basis. **Networks and Consortia:** Member of CAPCON, Consortium of Universities of the Washington Metropolitan Area. **Publications:** *Accessions*, 10/year; *The Negro in the Field of Business*, an annotated bibliography.

★1879★
Howard University
School of Divinity Library
1240 Randolph St., NE
Washington, DC 20017 Phone: (202)806-0760
Irene Owens, Libn.

Founded: 1932. **Staff:** Prof 1; Other 2. **Subjects:** Theology. **Special Collections:** Afro-American religious studies. **Holdings:** 104,041 books; 11,247 bound periodical volumes. **Subscriptions:** 492 journals and other serials. **Services:** Interlibrary loan; copying; library open to the public with restrictions on circulation. **Automated Operations:** Computerized cataloging, acquisitions, serials, and circulation. **Networks and Consortia:** Member of CAPCON, Consortium of Universities of the Washington Metropolitan Area, Washington Theological Consortium. **Publications:** *Biographical Directory of Negro Ministers; Afro-American Religious Studies and supplements; The Howard University Bibliography of African and Afro-American Religious Studies.* **Special Indexes:** Alphabetical name index of 1800 Negro ministers with addresses.

★1880★
Howard University
Social Work Library
6th St. & Howard Pl., NW
Washington, DC 20059 Phone: (202)806-7316
Julia C. Player, Libn.

Founded: 1971. **Staff:** Prof 1; Other 2. **Subjects:** Social work theory and practice; social policy, planning, administration; social welfare problems of Black community; urban-oriented problems; human development; women's issues; gerontology. **Holdings:** 37,607 books; 8880 bound periodical volumes. **Subscriptions:** 804 journals and other serials. **Services:** Interlibrary loan; copying; library open to the public for reference use only. **Automated Operations:** Computerized cataloging, acquisitions, serials, and circulation. **Computerized Information Services:** DIALOG Information Services, OCLC. Performs searches on fee basis. **Networks and Consortia:** Member of CAPCON, Consortium of Universities of the Washington Metropolitan Area.

★1881★
Indiana Historical Society
William Henry Smith Memorial Library
315 W. Ohio St.
Indianapolis, IN 46202-3299 Phone: (317)232-1879
Bruce L. Johnson, Dir.

Founded: 1934. **Staff:** Prof 14; Other 6. **Subjects:** History of Indiana and Old Northwest. **Special Collections:** Architectural history (including Burns & Burns, Bohlen Meyer & Gibson Russ, and Harrison, James & Associates, Rubush and Hunter, and Fenstermaker collections; 161,356 items); Black history (including Mme. C. J. Walker, Elijah Roberts, and Herbert Heller manuscript collections, Emmett Brown photograph collection; 6000 items); railroads (including Kauffman Photograph Collection, Preston Collection; 6000 items); Indiana in the Civil War (including Lew Wallace, D. E. Beem, and Jefferson C. Davis manuscript collections; 15,000 items); 19th century Indiana politics (including Charles Fairbanks, William H. English, and John G. Davis manuscript collections; 10,000 items); Old Northwest Territory history (600 manuscripts);William Henry Harrison and Indiana Territory history (500 manuscripts); charitable organizations (including Family Service Association, Pleasant Run Children's Home, and Jewish Welfare Federation manuscript collections; 85,000 items). **Holdings:** 65,000 books; 150 bound periodical volumes; 4 million manuscripts; 1000 maps; 1600 reels of microfilm; 1.5 million pictures. **Subscriptions:** 360 journals and other serials. **Services:** Copying; library open to the public. **Computerized Information Services:** OCLC; ARCHIE (internal database). Performs searches free of charge. **Networks and Consortia:** Member of INCOLSA. **Publications:** *Indiana Historical Society Annual Report* (accessions); *Black History News and Notes*, quarterly. **Special Catalogues:** Manuscript catalog. **Remarks:** FAX: (317)233-3109.

★1882★
Indiana University
Archives of Traditional Music
Morrison Hall
Bloomington, IN 47405 Phone: (812)855-4679
Ruth M. Stone, Dir.

Founded: 1936. **Staff:** Prof 3; Other 7. **Subjects:** Ethnic music, folk music, oral data, ethnomusicology, discography, early jazz. **Special Collections:** Hoagy Carmichael Collection (manuscripts; recordings; photographs; memorabilia). **Holdings:** 35,000 tape recordings; 6300 cylinder recordings; 36,600 disc recordings; 209 wire recordings. **Subscriptions:** 5 journals and other serials. **Services:** Copying; archives open to the public. **Automated Operations:** Computerized cataloging. **Computerized Information Services:** OCLC; internal database. **Networks and Consortia:** Member of INCOLSA. **Publications:** Resound, quarterly - by subscription. **Special Catalogues:** A Catalog of Phonorecordings of Music and Oral Data Held by the Archives of Traditional Music; African Music and Oral Data, 1902-1975; Native North American Music and Oral Data, A Catalogue of Sound Recordings, 1893-1976; Early Field Recordings (1987). **Special Indexes:** Indiana Folk Music and Oral Data (typescript). **Remarks:** Includes the Center for African Oral Data and Archives of Languages of the World.

★1883★
Indiana University
Black Culture Center
Library
109 N. Jordan Ave.
Bloomington, IN 47405 Phone: (812)335-9271
Wilmer H. Baatz, Libn.

Founded: 1972. **Staff:** Prof 1; Other 2. **Subjects:** Blacks - history, reference works, music, literature, drama; Black-oriented novels. **Special Collections:** The Arno Press Collection (250 titles). **Holdings:** 2200 books; 75 bound periodical volumes; 100 cassette tapes; 170 titles on 285 tapes; pamphlet files. **Subscriptions:** 22 journals and other serials; 12 newspapers. **Services:** Library open to the public. **Publications:** Shelf list of additions to the Afro-American Collections, 1985-1986.

★1884★
Indiana University
Music Library
School of Music
Bloomington, IN 47405 Phone: (812)855-8541
Dr. David Fenske, Hd.

Founded: 1939. **Staff:** Prof 5; Other 9. **Subjects:** Music. **Special Collections:** Apel Collection (photocopies of early keyboard music compiled by Professor Willi Apel; 200 volumes); Black music; Latin American music; opera; piano pedagogy. **Holdings:** 337,000 volumes; 82,000 scores; 15,000 microforms; 65,000 phonograph records; 50,000 audiotapes. **Subscriptions:** 543 journals and other serials. **Services:** Interlibrary loan; copying; library open to the public. **Automated Operations:** Computerized cataloging. **Computerized Information Services:** OCLC; BITNET (electronic mail service). **Networks and Consortia:** Member of INCOLSA. **Remarks:** FAX: (812)855-3843. Electronic mail address(es): FENSKE@IUBACS (BITNET).

★1885★
Inner City Cultural Center
Langston Hughes Memorial Library
1308 S. New Hampshire Ave.
Los Angeles, CA 90006 Phone: (213)387-1161

Founded: 1967. **Staff:** Prof 2; Other 2. **Subjects:** Ethnic groups, performing and visual arts. **Holdings:** 6500 uncataloged books; 300 bound periodical volumes; 100 manuscripts; 100 sound recordings and tapes; 250 clippings; 175 reports; 200 photographs. **Subscriptions:** 10 journals and other serials. **Services:** Library not open to the public. **Remarks:** Center also maintains Inner City Press, which publishes *Innerview* (newsletter), books, and recordings.

★1886★
Intercultural Development Research Association (IDRA)
Library
5835 Callaghan Rd., Ste. 350
San Antonio, TX 78228 Phone: (512)684-8180
Karen J. Diaz

Founded: 1973. **Subjects:** Education - minority, bilingual, compensatory, early childhood; school finance. **Holdings:** 20,000 cataloged materials. **Services:** Library not open to the public. **Remarks:** FAX: (512)684-5389.

★1887★
Jazz Composers Orchestra Association
New Music Distribution Service
Library
500 Broadway
New York, NY 10012 Phone: (212)925-2121
John Baskind, Exec.Dir.

Subjects: Music industry. **Holdings:** 2000 recordings from 350 record companies. **Remarks:** Library specializes in independent label recordings of experimental music. FAX: (212)925-1689.

★1888★
Johnson Publishing Co., Inc.
Library
820 S. Michigan Ave.
Chicago, IL 60605 Phone: (312)322-9320
Pamela Cash Mensies, Libn.

Founded: 1949. **Staff:** Prof 2; Other 1. **Subjects:** Afro-Americana; Black history, literature, biography; Africa. **Special Collections:** Newspaper clippings, 1940s to present; Black newspapers, 1846 to present, on microfilm. **Holdings:** 10,000 books; 1000 bound periodical volumes; 300 drawers of newspaper clippings; pamphlets; company publications. **Subscriptions:** 150 journals and other serials; 50 newspapers. **Services:** Library not open to the public.

★1889★
Joint Center for Political and Economic Studies
Office of Information Resources
1301 Pennsylvania Ave., NW, Ste. 400
Washington, DC 20004 Phone: (202)626-3530
Auriel J. Pilgrim, Dir.

Founded: 1979. **Staff:** Prof 1; Other 2. **Subjects:** Blacks - political participation, social and economic conditions, demographic studies; public, education, and economic policies concerning minorities. **Special Collections:** Black elected officials; Blacks in the military; Black voting and voter registration statistics. **Holdings:** 3500 volumes; 2700 unbound materials; 340 unpublished reports; 60 VF drawers of clippings and archival material; 5 drawers of AV programs. **Subscriptions:** 238 journals and other serials; 4 newspapers. **Services:** Interlibrary loan; copying; office open to the public by appointment for reference use only. **Automated Operations:** Computerized cataloging and acquisitions. **Computerized Information Services:** DIALOG Information Services, NEXIS. **Publications:** Periodical table of contents bulletin, weekly - for internal distribution only. **Remarks:** FAX: (202)626-8774.

★1890★
Kennedy-King College
Library
6800 S. Wentworth Ave.
Chicago, IL 60621 Phone: (312)962-3200
Noel R. Grego, Ch.

Founded: 1934. **Staff:** Prof 4; Other 6. **Subjects:** Black studies - history, sociology, current issues, nursing. **Holdings:** 42,000 volumes. **Subscriptions:** 400 journals and other serials; 12 newspapers. **Services:** Interlibrary loan; copying; library open to the public with restrictions. **Computerized Information Services:** OCLC. **Networks and Consortia:** Member of ILLINET.

★1891★
Kent State University
Center for the Study of Ethnic Publications and Cultural Institutions
University Library, Rm. 318
Kent, OH 44242 Phone: (216)672-2782
Dr. Lubomyr Wynar, Dir.

Staff: Prof 1. **Subjects:** Ethnic bibliography, history, education, and press; ethnic libraries, archives, and museums. **Special Collections:** Ethnic reference files. **Holdings:** 1000 books; 500 pamphlets. **Subscriptions:** 200 journals and other serials. **Services:** Center open to the public with permission. **Publications:** *Ethnic Forum: Journal of Ethnic Studies and of Ethnic Bibliography*, 2/year - by subscription; *Ethnic, Nationality, and Foreign-Language Broadcasting and Telecasting in Ohio* (1981); *Slavic Ethnic Libraries, Museums and Archives in the United States: A Guide and Directory* (1980); *Guide to Ethnic Press* (1986). **Remarks:** FAX: (216)672-7965.

★1892★
Langston University
Melvin B. Tolson Black Heritage Center
Langston, OK 73050 Phone: (405)466-2231
Ronald Keys, Act.Cur.

Founded: 1969. **Staff:** Prof 1. **Subjects:** Afro-American experience in the U.S., Afro-Americans in the humanities and arts since 1900, African history. **Special Collections:** African Art Collection (93 items); Langston University Archives (brochures; programs; yearbooks; presidential papers); Melvin B. Tolson Collection (books; personal items; pictures; awards). **Holdings:** 13,000 books; 1200 bound periodical volumes; 750 recordings; 600 audio cassettes; 150 video cassettes; 100 films; 10,000 VF materials. **Subscriptions:** 90 journals and other serials; 50 newspapers. **Services:** Interlibrary loan; copying; center open to the public. **Publications:** *Acquisitions List*, monthly; newsletter, quarterly. **Special Indexes:** Biography index; periodical articles index.

★1893★
Lawrence Johnson & Associates, Inc.
Library
4545 42nd St., NW, Ste. 100
Washington, DC 20016 Phone: (202)537-6900
Mrs. Tish Nearon, Hd., Adm.Serv.

Staff: Prof 4; Other 3. **Subjects:** Psychology, race relations, human relations development, child welfare, human factors, education. **Special Collections:** Race relations in the military services (50 volumes). **Holdings:** 2000 books; 2500 technical reports; 700 unbound periodicals; 150 boxes of unpublished manuscripts and dissertations; 200 vuegraphs, slides, audiotapes. **Subscriptions:** 50 journals and other serials; 5 newspapers. **Services:** Interlibrary loan; library not open to the public.

★1894★
Library Company of Philadelphia
1314 Locust St.
Philadelphia, PA 19107 Phone: (215)546-3181
John C. VanHorne, Libn.

Founded: 1731. **Staff:** Prof 6; Other 7. **Subjects:** Pre-1860 Americana, Philadelphia and Pennsylvania, pre-1820 medical material, Black history before 1906. **Special Collections:** Early printed books from Girard College and Christ Church (on deposit). **Holdings:** 450,000 books; 50,000 prints and photographs; 160,000 manuscripts. **Subscriptions:** 130 journals and other serials. **Services:** Interlibrary loan; copying; library open to the public for research. **Computerized Information Services:** RLIN. **Networks and Consortia:** Member of RLG. **Publications:** Annual reports; newsletters - both free to libraries and individuals on request. **Special Catalogues:** Afro-Americana, 1553-1906 in collections of the Library Company and the Historical Society of Pennsylvania; The Library of James Logan; Quarter of a Millennium: The Library Company of Philadelphia, 1731-1981; occasional catalogs of special exhibitions; American Education, 1622-1860; Agriculture in America, 1622-1860; Natural History in America, 1609-1860; American Philanthropy, 1731-1860 (4 volume set covering the collections of the Library Company, Historical Society of Pennsylvania, and the American Philosophical Society). **Remarks:** FAX: (215)546-5167.

★1895★
Library of Congress
African & Middle Eastern Division
John Adams Bldg., Rm. 1015
Washington, DC 20540 Phone: (202)707-7937
Dr. Julian W. Witherell, Chf.

Remarks: The Library of Congress has extensive holdings of books, newspapers, manuscripts, periodicals, and other material relating to nations of Africa and the Middle East. Detailed reference services on the 650,000 western-language volumes relating to this area in the library's general collections are provided by the division's African, Hebraic, and Near East sections. In addition, the Hebraic Section has custody of over 131,000 volumes in Hebrew, Yiddish, and cognate languages covering such topics as the Bible, ancient Middle East, and Jews and Judaism throughout the world. The Near East Section has holdings of more than 148,000 volumes in Arabic, Turkish, Persian, and other languages of an area of responsibility that extends from Afghanistan to Morocco, excluding Israel. The African Section, with primary responsibility for Africa south of the Sahara, has a small reference collection and extensive pamphlet files. Both the Hebraic and Near East sections maintain union catalogs relating to their respective areas of responsibility, while the African Section has a card index of citations to Africana periodical literature. The phone numbers for the 3 sections of this Division are as follows: African Section 707-5528; Hebraic Section 707-5422; Near East Section 707-5421.

★1896★
Library of Congress
American Folklife Center
Thomas Jefferson Bldg. - G152
Washington, DC 20540 Phone: (202)707-6590
Alan Jabbour, Dir.

Founded: 1976. **Staff:** Prof 11; Other 5. **Subjects:** American folklife with emphasis on research, public programs, and technical assistance; oral history and the Federal Cylinder Project; folksong; folk music; folklore; folklife; ethnomusicology; oral history. **Special Collections:** Archive of Folk Culture; manuscript collections (100,000 pages); Smithsonian Institution/Frances Densmore American Indian Collection (3700 cylinders). **Publications:** *Folklife Center News*, quarterly; mailing list composed of folklife organizations, institutions, and individuals - additions made upon request; *Folklife Sourcebook: A Directory of Folklife Resources in the United States and Canada* - for sale.

★1897★
Library of Congress
General Reading Rooms Division
Microform Reading Room Section
Thomas Jefferson Bldg. - LJ-140B
Washington, DC 20540 Phone: (202)707-5471
Betty Culpepper, Hd.

Subjects: Early state records; includes American and British Black journals; Schomburg clipping file on Black history. **Holdings:** 3.5 million reels and strips of microfilm, microfiche, and micro-opaques. **Services:** Reading room is open to persons above high school age. **Remarks:** A guide to selected microform sets is available on request.

★1898★
Library of Congress
Manuscript Division
James Madison Memorial Bldg., LM 101-102
Washington, DC 20540 Phone: (202)707-5383
James H. Hutson, Chf.

Subjects: Collections of the papers of most of the Presidents, from George Washington through Calvin Coolidge, other political, military, scientific, and literary leaders, and records of numerous enterprises and institutions, totaling more than 45 million pieces. Among them: Records of the Virginia Company of London, the American Colonization Society, National American Woman Suffrage Association, National Association for the Advancement of Colored People, National Urban League, National Women's Party, the League of Women Voters, Frederick Douglass, A. Philip Randolph, Roy Wilkins. **Services:** Reading room is open to adults; open to high school students with a letter of introduction from faculty advisors.

★1899★
Library of Congress
Rare Book & Special Collections Division
Thomas Jefferson Bldg., Rm. 204
Washington, DC 20540 Phone: (202)707-5434
Larry E. Sullivan, Chf.

Subjects: Aeronautics and ballooning, almanacs, Americana, anarchism, early American architecture, Bibles, book arts, children's literature, dime novels, English printing (1478-1640), early French literature, gastronomy, genealogy, illustrated books, incunabula, magic and the occult, Medieval and Renaissance manuscripts, miniature books, Anglo-American 18th and 19th century pamphlets, playbills, Presidents' books, private press books, radicalism, Shakers, Slavic studies, Spanish-American printing (1543-1820), woman's suffrage, World War II. **Special Collections:** Includes Daniel Murray Collection (pamphlets by Afro-American authors). **Holdings:** 619,000 items, including the largest collection of incunabula (more than 5600) in the Western Hemisphere.

★1900★
Lincoln National Life Insurance Company
Lincoln Museum
Library
1300 S. Clinton St.
Fort Wayne, IN 46801 Phone: (219)455-3031
Dr. Mark E. Neely Jr., Dir.

Founded: 1928. **Staff:** Prof 3; Other 1. **Subjects:** Lincolniana; 19th century American history, biography, and politics; Civil War; slavery; reconstruction. **Special Collections:** Association books (books similar to those Lincoln read; 400); manuscripts; philatelic Lincolniana; metallic Lincolniana; pictorial Lincolniana (original paints, rare lithographs, engravings, original photographs, and prints). **Holdings:** 20,000 volumes; 10,000 pieces of Lincolniana; 9600 collateral books. **Subscriptions:** 36 journals and other serials. **Services:** Interlibrary loan (by special request); copying; library open to researchers and students. **Publications:** *Lincoln Lore*, monthly; *R. Gerald McMurty Lecture*, annual - available on request. **Remarks:** FAX: (219)455-6922. **Formerly:** Louis A. Warren Lincoln Library and Museum.

★1901★
Lincoln University
Langston Hughes Memorial Library
Special Collections
Lincoln University, PA 19352-0999 Phone: (215)932-8300
Ella Forbes, Spec.Coll.Libn.

Staff: Prof 1; Other 2. **Subjects:** Black studies - fine arts, history, civil rights, education; African studies - economics, history, political science, language, literature; antislavery. **Special Collections:** Personal library of Langston Hughes (3300 items); manuscripts of Pennsylvania Colonization Society and Young Men's Colonization Society (6 volumes); rare books (850); rare antislavery pamphlets (200); personal library of Dr. Therman B. O'Daniel (4000 items). **Holdings:** 18,350 books; 1060 bound periodical volumes; 772 reels of microfilm; 100 phonograph records; 250 historical pictures of Black performers; 6000 unbound periodicals; 1595 microfiche; 1300 African Government documents; 2500 VF materials; 6000 archival materials and miscellanea. **Subscriptions:** 180 journals and other serials; 7 newspapers. **Services:** Interlibrary loan; copying; collections open to the public for reference use only. **Automated Operations:** Computerized cataloging and Interlibrary loan. **Computerized Information Services:** OCLC. **Networks and Consortia:** Member of PALINET, Tri-State College Library Cooperative (TCLC). **Publications:** Selected bibliography on Malcolm X; bimonthly accessions lists - both free upon request. **Special Catalogues:** Catalog of the Special Negro and African Collection (2 volumes and supplement, 1970); Computer Output Microfilm Catalog, July 1970 - June 1977; A Survey of the Special Negro Collections; Reference Handbook of Special Collections - all for sale; mimeographed list of periodicals in the African collection; mimeographed reference handbook. **Remarks:** FAX: (215)932-8317.

★1902★
Lincoln University (Missouri)
Inman E. Page Library
Jefferson City, MO 65101 Phone: (314)681-5512
Elizabeth A. Wilson, Dir.

Founded: 1866. **Staff:** Prof 6; Other 6. **Subjects:** Liberal arts; elementary and secondary education; nursing; corrections and law enforcement. **Special Collections:** Pro-slavery and antislavery tracts; pre- and post-Civil War period; Black and ethnic collections (7000 books). **Holdings:** 134,169 books; 9000 bound periodical volumes; 74,670 government documents; 230 theses and dissertations; 30 VF drawers; 4 VF drawers of pictures; 91,945 titles in microform. **Subscriptions:** 705 journals and other serials; 53 newspapers. **Services:** Interlibrary loan; faxing; copying; SDI; library open to the public with restrictions. **Computerized Information Services:** BRS Information Technologies; ALANET (electronic mail service). Performs online searches on fee basis; performs CD-ROM searches at no charge. Contact Person: Oi-Chi Hui, Ref., 681-5512. **Networks and Consortia:** Member of Missouri Library Network Corp. (MLNC). **Publications:** *Lincoln's Page*, irregular; *Bibliography of Books By and About Blacks*, annual supplement; *Monthly Checklist* (selected); *Newsletter*; *Students Handbook*; *Annual Report*; *Library Manual*. **Remarks:** FAX: (314)681-5511. Electronic mail address(es): ALA 2931 (ALANET).

★1903★
Livingstone College
American Black and African Studies Collection
Andrew Carnegie Library
701 W. Monroe St.
Salisbury, NC 28144 Phone: (704)638-5629

Founded: 1908. **Staff:** Prof 5; Other 2. **Special Collections:** Africans and American Blacks; African Methodist Episcopal Zion Church; Ecumenical Methodist Conference, 1881-1956; Livingstone College. **Holdings:** 75,000 books; 4415 bound periodical volumes; 37,226 microfiche; 2752 reels of microfilm. **Subscriptions:** 258 journals and other serials; 28 newspapers. **Services:** Interlibrary loan; copying; collection open to the public. **Computerized Information Services:** DIALOG Information Services. **Remarks:** FAX: (704)638-5646.

★1904★
Long Beach City College
Pacific Coast Campus Library Special Collections
1305 E. Pacific Coast Hwy.
Long Beach, CA 90806 Phone: (213)599-8028
John L. Ayala, Assoc.Prof./Libn.

Founded: 1947. **Staff:** Prof 3; Other 1. **Special Collections:** Vocational education; ethnic materials (Chicano, Black, American Indian); English as a second language. **Services:** Interlibrary loan; copying; library open to the public for reference use only. **Remarks:** Alternate telephone number(s): 599-8029.

★1905★
Long Island University
B. Davis Schwartz Memorial Library
Greenvale, NY 11548 Phone: (516)299-2880
David A. Jasen, Dir.

Founded: 1954. **Staff:** Prof 1. **Subjects:** American popular music, ragtime, jazz. **Special Collections:** Sheet music (50,000); sound recordings (20,000); piano rolls (800); photographs (1000); playbills (500). **Holdings:** 2000 books. **Services:** Copying; library open to the public with restrictions. **Publications:** Brochure.

★1906★
Los Angeles Public Library
Social Sciences, Philosophy and Religion Department
630 W. 5th St.
Los Angeles, CA 90071 Phone: (213)612-3250
Marilyn C. Wherley, Dept.Mgr.

Staff: Prof 11; Other 17. **Subjects:** Philosophy, religion, psychology, social problems, government, foreign affairs, international relations, law, criminology, education, women's movements, family relations, ethnic groups, psychology, interpersonal relations. **Special Collections:** California, U.S., and U.N. documents depository; Black history; Mexican-American Affairs; women; education; the occult; cults and sects; Eastern religions. **Holdings:** 389,000 volumes. **Subscriptions:** 2850 journals and other serials. **Services:** Interlibrary loan; copying; department open to the public. **Automated Operations:** Computerized public access catalog. **Computerized Information Services:** DIALOG Information Services, LEXIS, NEXIS. Performs searches on fee basis. **Networks and Consortia:** Member of Metropolitan Cooperative Library System (MCLS). **Special Indexes:** Superstition; mythology; cults and sects; psychics; metaphysical societies; crime; current affairs; elections; statistics. **Remarks:** Library located at 433 S. Spring St., Los Angeles, CA 90013. FAX: (213)612-0536.

★1907★
Louisiana State University
Special Collections
Hill Memorial Library
Baton Rouge, LA 70803-3300 Phone: (504)388-6551
Robert S. Martin, Asst.Dir. of Libs.

Founded: 1985. **Staff:** Prof 10; Other 10. **Subjects:** Louisiana, southern history and politics, natural history, Civil War, book arts, history of printing, ornithology, botany, slavery, steamboats, exploration and travel. **Special Collections:** E.A. McIlhenny Natural History Collection (10,000 volumes); Warren L. Jones Lincoln Collection (1500 volumes); Oliver P. Carriere Collection of Poker and Hoyle (1200 volumes); Bruce Rogers Collection (1000 volumes); Norman Steamboat Collection (1100 items). **Holdings:** 100,000 books; 7 million manuscript pieces; 2000 maps; 600,000 photographs; 20,000 reels of microfilm; dissertations; porcelain and metal sculptures; wood and stone carvings; paintings; prints. **Services:** Copying; collections open to the public with identification. **Automated Operations:** Computerized cataloging, acquisitions, and serials. **Computerized Information Services:** BITNET (electronic mail service). **Special Catalogues:** Unpublished finding aids for manuscript collections. **Remarks:** FAX: (504)388-6992. Electronic mail address(es): @LSUVM (BITNET).

★1908★
Lower Merion Library Association
Ardmore Library
Gate Collection on the Black Experience
108 Ardmore Ave.
Ardmore, PA 19003 Phone: (215)642-5187
Maryam W. Puller, Dir.

Founded: 1899. **Staff:** Prof 1; Other 3. **Subjects:** Black experience - history, literature, personalities. **Holdings:** 500 books. **Subscriptions:** 65 journals and other serials; 5 newspapers. **Services:** Interlibrary loan; copying; SDI; collection open to nonresidents with valid Access Pennsylvania affiliation. **Automated Operations:** Computerized cataloging, acquisitions, and circulation.

★1909★
Martin Luther King, Jr. Center for Nonviolent Social Change, Inc.
King Library and Archives
449 Auburn Ave.
Atlanta, GA 30312 Phone: (404)524-1956

Founded: 1968. **Staff:** Prof 1; Other 2. **Subjects:** Dr. Martin Luther King, Jr., civil rights movement, African-American history, nonviolence, African-American religion, African-American politics. **Special Collections:** Bilingual materials by Martin Luther King, Jr.; organizational records of the SCLC (1954-1970); SNCL (1959-1972); CORE (1944-1968); MFDP (1964-1965); Delta Ministry (1963-1971); National Lawyers Guild (1936-1968); ESCRU (1959-1970); CCCO (1964-1968); USNSA (1957-1969); Personal papers of Martin Luther King, Jr. (1954-1968); Fred Shuttleworth (1953-1969); Johnnie Carr (1956-1979); Julian Bond (1964-1968). **Holdings:** 4000 books; over 1 million documents focusing primarily on the American civil rights movement. **Services:** Copying; library open to the public. **Publications:** *Martin Luther King Center Newsletter*, quarterly; library holdings and services brochures. **Remarks:** Archives are dedicated to the documentation of the post-1954 Civil Rights Movement with emphasis on the life and work of Martin Luther King, Jr. and the nonviolent movement which continues.

★1910★
Mary Holmes Junior College
Barr Library
Oral History Collection
Hwy. 50, W.
Box 1257
West Point, MS 39773 Phone: (601)494-6820
Gail Davis-Peyton, Contact

Founded: 1967. **Staff:** 6. **Subjects:** History, sociology, folklore. **Special Collections:** Taped interviews and transcriptions of conversations with rural Black Mississippians 70 years of age and older (600). **Holdings:** 14 volumes. **Subscriptions:** 115 journals and other serials; 13 newspapers. **Services:** Interlibrary loan; copying; collection open to the public for reference use only. **Computerized Information Services:** InfoTrac. **Remarks:** FAX: (601)494-5319.

★1911★
Maryland State Archives
Library
350 Rowe Blvd.
Annapolis, MD 21401 Phone: (301)974-3915
Shashi P. Thapar, Lib.Dir.

Founded: 1935. **Staff:** Prof 1; Other 1. **Subjects:** History - Maryland, American, Black, other states; genealogy; biography. **Special Collections:** Works Project Administration Historical Records Survey Publications; Maryland State Publications and Reports; Laws of Maryland; Maryland House and Senate Journals. **Holdings:** 15,000 books; 450 bound periodical volumes; reports; manuscripts; archives. **Subscriptions:** 100 journals and other serials. **Services:** Copying; library open to the public for reference use only. **Automated Operations:** Computerized cataloging. **Computerized Information Services:** Internal databases. Performs searches on fee basis. **Networks and Consortia:** Member of Maryland Interlibrary Organization (MILO). **Publications:** Irregular publications; *Maryland Manual*, biennial; serials and periodicals list. **Remarks:** FAX: (301)974-3895. Contains the holdings of the former Maryland State Department of Natural Resources - Library.

★1912★
Maxwell Museum Association
Maxwell Museum of Anthropology
Clark Field Archive
Maxwell Museum
University of New Mexico
Albuquerque, NM 87131 Phone: (505)277-8675
Garth Bawden, Dir.

Staff: Prof 1; Other 3. **Subjects:** Anthropology, archeology, ethnology, linguistics, biological anthropology, museology. **Special Collections:** Stanley S. Newman Field Collection; Harry Basehart Collection of African Ethnology; Florence Hawley Ellis Collection. **Holdings:** 8000 books; 1500 bound periodical volumes; 60 dissertations. **Subscriptions:** 20 journals and other serials. **Services:** Copying; archive open to the public for reference use only. **Remarks:** Alternate telephone number(s): 277-4404.

★1913★
McKinney Job Corps
Library
1501 N. Church St.
Box 750
McKinney, TX 75069 Phone: (214)542-2623
Dr. Reagan Carr, Libn.

Founded: 1964. **Staff:** Prof 1; Other 1. **Subjects:** Negro history, special education, self-improvement, psychology, careers, guidance and counseling. **Holdings:** 10,500 books; 390 phonograph records. **Subscriptions:** 19 journals and other serials. **Services:** Library not open to the public.

★1914★
Medford Historical Society
Library
10 Governor's Ave.
Medford, MA 02155 Phone: (617)395-7863
Michael Bradford, Cur.

Founded: 1896. **Staff:** Prof 1. **Subjects:** Local history. **Special Collections:** Lydia Maria Child Collection; Civil War Collection; slave trade (mid-18th century). **Holdings:** Books; manuscripts; letters. **Services:** Library open to the public for reference use only. **Publications:** *Medford on the Mystic*, 1980.

★1915★
Medical College of Pennsylvania
Archives and Special Collections on Women in Medicine
3300 Henry Ave.
Philadelphia, PA 19129 Phone: (215)842-7124
Janet Miller, Dir./Archv.

Founded: 1977. **Staff:** Prof 3; Other 1. **Subjects:** Women physicians, health care for women, Medical College of Pennsylvania, education, medicine. **Special Collections:** College archives; women in medicine; Black Women Physicians Collection; Oral History Project (43 interviews); American Women's Hospitals Records (25 linear feet); Medical Women's International Association Records (10 linear feet). **Holdings:** 1000 books; 6000 reprints; 14,000 photographs; 1300 linear feet of archival materials and manuscripts; memorabilia. **Services:** Copying; photograph and slide reproduction; archives open to the public. **Automated Operations:** Computerized cataloging. **Publications:** *Newsletter*, biannual - available on request; *Guide to Collections in the Archives & Special Collections on Women in Medicine.* **Special Indexes:** An Inventory to the Records of the American Women's Hospitals: 1917-1982. **Remarks:** FAX: (215)844-1380.

★1916★
Meharry Medical College
Library
1005 D.B. Todd
Nashville, TN 37208 Phone: (615)327-6728
Cheryl Hamberg, Dir.

Founded: 1942. **Staff:** Prof 12; Other 13. **Subjects:** Medicine, dentistry, public health, medical technology, health care administration. **Special Collections:** Black Medical History Collection (500 books; 20 manuscripts); Meharry Archives Collection (200 books; 59 dissertations; 150 boxes of manuscripts; 50 VF drawers). **Holdings:** 20,954 books; 51,889 bound periodical volumes; 514 audio cassettes; 559 video cassettes; 150 slide/tape sets. **Subscriptions:** 1607 journals and other serials. **Services:** Interlibrary loan (fee); copying; SDI; library open to the public. **Automated Operations:** Computerized cataloging, acquisitions, circulation, and serials. **Computerized Information Services:** MEDLINE, OCLC, DIALOG Information Services; CD-ROMs; electronic mail service. Performs searches on fee basis. **Special Catalogues:** Library guide. **Remarks:** FAX: (615)327-6448.

★1917★
Meiklejohn Civil Liberties Institute
Library
Box 673
Berkeley, CA 94701 Phone: (415)848-0599
Ann Fagan Ginger, Exec.Dir.

Founded: 1965. **Staff:** Prof 2; Other 4. **Subjects:** Peace law, civil rights and liberties, due process, sex discrimination, juries, police misconduct.

Special Collections: Peace Law Brief and Issues Bank; Angela Davis case (20,000 pages); Pentagon Papers Case (35,000 pages); official repository for National Lawyers Guild Archives; Draft and Military Law Collection (188 microfiche). **Holdings:** 200 books; legal documents from over 9000 cases. **Subscriptions:** 130 journals and other serials; 20 newspapers. **Services:** Copying; library open to the public. **Publications:** *Human Rights Organizations and Periodicals Directory*, biennial - for sale; list of other publications - available upon request. **Special Catalogues:** Pentagon Papers Case Collection (book); Angela Davis Collection (book). **Special Indexes:** Meiklejohn Library Acquisitions Index, 1968-1972; Human Rights Casefinder, 1953-1969; index to National Lawyers Guild Periodicals, 1937-1970; The Legal Struggle to Abolish the House Un-American Activities Committee. **Remarks:** Library located at 1715 Francisco St., Berkeley, CA 94703.

★1918★
Memphis State University
Libraries
Special Collections
Memphis, TN 38152 Phone: (901)678-2210
Michelle Fagan, Cur.

Founded: 1964. **Staff:** Prof 1; Other 2. **Subjects:** Lower Mississippi Valley - history, culture, literature. **Special Collections:** Memphis multimedia project (race relations); ; university archives (250,000 archival materials); assassination of Martin Luther King, Jr; manuscript collections (315 collections; 6.7 million items). **Holdings:** 31,316 volumes; 2782 pamphlets; 758,196 photographs; 6270 pieces of sheet music; 722 maps; 2890 oral histories on audiotape; 472 videotapes; 247 reels of 16mm film; 77 records. **Services:** Copying; collections open to the public. **Automated Operations:** Computerized cataloging. **Computerized Information Services:** OCLC. **Networks and Consortia:** Member of SOLINET. **Publications:** *Brister Library Monograph; Campus Tower News*, both irregular - both on exchange. **Special Catalogues:** Registers and inventories to collections.

★1919★
Metropolitan Council for Educational Opportunity
Library
55 Dimock St.
Roxbury, MA 02119 Phone: (617)427-1545
J. Marcus Mitchell, P.R. Off.

Founded: 1966. **Staff:** Prof 1. **Subjects:** Quality integrated education, Afro-American history. **Special Collections:** Scrapbooks of clippings on Greater Boston school systems and Boston's desegregation case (40). **Holdings:** 1260 books; dissertations; 24 annual financial reports; 10 unpublished reports; films; photographs. **Subscriptions:** 20 journals and other serials; 10 newspapers. **Services:** Copying; library open to the public. **Automated Operations:** Computerized cataloging. **Computerized Information Services:** Online systems. **Publications:** *New Images Newsletter*, quarterly; *METCO Parent Handbook*. **Special Catalogues:** Student enrollment, transportation and routes (both computer printouts).

★1920★
Michigan Civil Rights Department
Civil Rights Library
1200 6th St., 7th Fl.
Detroit, MI 48226 Phone: (313)256-2622
Ellen B. McCarthy

Founded: 1964. **Staff:** Prof 1. **Subjects:** Civil rights; discrimination - employment, housing; minority groups. **Holdings:** 10,000 books; 13,000 microfiche; unbound periodicals. **Subscriptions:** 200 journals and other serials; 10 newspapers. **Services:** Interlibrary loan; library open to the public by appointment. **Computerized Information Services:** DIALOG Information Services, VU/TEXT Information Services, ELSS (Electronic Legislative Search System), WILSONLINE, WESTLAW, LEXIS, NEXIS, Hannah Information Systems, OCLC, Questor, Washington Alert Service, CQ Bill Status. **Remarks:** FAX: (313)256-2680.

★1921★
Michigan State University
Africana Library
W-316 University Libraries
East Lansing, MI 48824 Phone: (517)355-2366
Mrs. Onuma Ezera, Hd.

Founded: 1964. **Staff:** Prof 2; Other 1. **Subjects:** Sub-Saharan Africa. **Special Collections:** African languages, linguistics, and literature; socioeconomic development in the Sahel; Colonial Zaire; Ethiopian materials; archival resources on the slave trade; British Colonial and Foreign Office archival materials on Africa (microform); Kenya National Archives (microform). **Holdings:** 150,000 volumes; 27,200 pamphlets; 6610 sheet maps; 32,200 titles in microform. **Subscriptions:** 1700 journals and other serials. **Services:** Interlibrary loan; copying; main collection open to the public. **Computerized Information Services:** BITNET (electronic mail service). **Publications:** *Africana - Select Recent Acquisitions*, 4/year; *Women in Africa: Selected Acquisitions at MSU since 1975* (1988); *A Guide to Africana Materials in the Michigan State University Libraries* (1982). **Special Catalogues:** Card catalog for Africa; card catalog of area studies pamphlet collections. **Remarks:** FAX: (517)336-1445. Electronic mail address(es): 20676AFR (BITNET). The Africana Library is responsible for the development of the collections for African studies needed for teaching and research; provides bibliographic advisory service to faculty and students engaged in the study of this area; and provides consultation service for the university's several African projects.

★1922★
Military Order of the Loyal Legion of the United States
The Civil War Library & Museum
1805 Pine St.
Philadelphia, PA 19103 Phone: (215)735-8196
Russ A. Pritchard, Dir.

Founded: 1888. **Staff:** 2. **Subjects:** Civil War, slavery, politics, Reconstruction. **Special Collections:** Abraham Lincoln Collection (750 books and pamphlets). **Holdings:** 14,000 books; 100 bound periodical volumes; pamphlets; manuscripts; photographs; archives; portraits. **Services:** Copying; library open to the public. **Publications:** *Loyal Legion Historical Journal*, 4/year; quarterly newsletter.

★1923★
Millersville University of Pennsylvania
Helen A. Ganser Library
Special Collections
Millersville, PA 17551 Phone: (717)872-3624
Robert E. Coley, Univ.Archv./Spec.Coll.Libn.

Founded: 1855. **Staff:** Prof 1; Other 1. **Special Collections:** Includes Carl Van Vechten Memorial Collection of Afro-American Arts and Letters (700 items). **Holdings:** 16,000 books; 600 manuscripts; 3600 linear feet of archives; 100 microfiche; 400 reels of microfilm. **Subscriptions:** 15 journals and other serials. **Services:** Copying; collections open to the public. **Automated Operations:** Computerized cataloging. **Computerized Information Services:** DIALOG Information Services; Dynix (internal database). **Networks and Consortia:** Member of PALINET, Association of College Libraries of Central Pennsylvania (ACLCP). **Special Indexes:** Indices to the various collections maintained in department. **Remarks:** FAX: (717)872-3854.

★1924★
Minneapolis Public Library & Information Center
Special Collections Department
300 Nicollet Mall
Minneapolis, MN 55401-1992 Phone: (612)372-6648
Edward R. Kukla, Dept.Hd.

Founded: 1987. **Staff:** Prof 4; Other 2. **Special Collections:** Includes Huttner Abolition and Anti-Slavery Collection (Abolitionist movement, slavery, Black writers and reformers; 550 books; 50 letters and documents; 250 pamphlets, broadsides, newspapers); 19th Century American Studies Collection (materials by and about 19th century American writers, antislavery movement, New England descriptive and historical writings; Truman Nelson letters; John Greenleaf Whittier-Evelina Bray Downey correspondence; manuscript "Ode to France," James Russel Lowell; 4500 books; 200 bound periodical volumes; 150 pamphlets; 150 autograph letters; 150 pictures; 250 unbound periodicals, pamphlets, newspapers; 1 VF drawer of clippings); Hoag Mark Twain Collection (250 books and pamphlets). **Services:** Copying; collections open to the public with restrictions. **Computerized Information Services:** DataTimes; Photos I (internal database).

★1925★
Minority Business Information Institute (MBII)
Library
130 5th Ave., 10th Fl.
New York, NY 10011 Phone: (212)242-8000
Ms. Bene L. Durant, Info.Spec.

Founded: 1971. **Staff:** Prof 1; Other 1. **Subjects:** Minority economic development, minority groups, business. **Special Collections:** Directories of minority businesses. **Holdings:** 2100 volumes; 14 VF drawers of pamphlets and clippings. **Subscriptions:** 110 journals and other serials. **Services:** Library not open to the public. **Computerized Information Services:** Dow Jones News/Retrieval; internal database. **Networks and Consortia:** Member of New York Metropolitan Reference and Research Library Agency. **Publications:** Bibliographies and reference lists, irregular. **Special Indexes:** Complete index to *Black Enterprise* magazine (card). **Remarks:** FAX: (212)989-8410. **Also known as:** MBII.

★1926★
Mystic River Historical Society
William A. Downes Archives
74 High St.
PO Box 245
Mystic, CT 06355 Phone: (203)536-4779
Judith A. Hicks, Pres.

Subjects: Mystic River history. **Special Collections:** Mary Lee Jobe Akeley Collection (African explorer; 2200 magic lantern slides, letters, photographs, memorabilia); Juliet Haley Collection (letters and memorabilia of Captain George Gates, a Mystic sea captain). **Holdings:** Figures not available. **Services:** Copying; archives open to the public by appointment.

★1927★
National Adoption Center
Information Services
1218 Chestnut St.
Philadelphia, PA 19107 Phone: (215)925-0200

Founded: 1980. **Staff:** Prof 1; Other 1. **Subjects:** Adoption, foster care, child welfare. **Special Collections:** Special needs adoption; Black adoption recruitment; foster care; searching for birthparents; adoption legislation; employee adoption benefits information. **Holdings:** 5000 books; 180 unbound materials; 60 AV programs. **Subscriptions:** 130 journals and newsletters; 5 newspapers. **Services:** Interlibrary loan; SDI; copying; services open to the public. **Computerized Information Services:** National Adoption Network. **Publications:** Adoption information packet for libraries. List of other publications - available on request. **Remarks:** Toll-free telephone number(s): is (800)862-3678.

★1928★
National Archives & Records Administration
Still Picture Branch
8th St. & Pennsylvania Ave., NW
NNSP-18N
Washington, DC 20408 Phone: (202)501-5455
Elizabeth L. Hill, Chf.

Founded: 1935. **Staff:** Prof 9; Other 14. **Subjects:** AV materials; still photography; posters; United States - history, politics, government. **Special Collections:** Included in the wide-ranging files are historical photographs from such agencies as: the Harmon Foundation Collection of Photographs, 1922-1966 (art works by Black American and African artists; prominent Black Americans; foreign art objects; activities of Blacks on campuses of southern colleges; exhibits of Black artists' works and art workshops). **Holdings:** 7 million archival photographs from U.S. Federal Government agencies which document American and world cultural, social, environmental, economic, technological, political history of a nongovernmental nature as well as activities of military and civilian governmental agencies; historical photographs of precursors of contemporary governmental activity. **Services:** Copying; branch open to the public for reference use only. **Computerized Information Services:** TextBank (internal database). **Publications:** *Guide to the Holdings of the Still Pictures Branch of the National Archives* (1990). **Special Catalogues:** War and Conflict: Selected Images from the National Archives, 1795-1970.

★1929★
National Association for the Advancement of Colored People
NAACP Legal Defense and Educational Fund
Law Library
99 Hudson St., 16th Fl.
New York, NY 10013 Phone: (212)219-1900
Donna Gloeckner

Subjects: Civil rights law - discrimination against Blacks, other racial minorities, and women in employment, education, housing, and other areas. **Holdings:** 15,000 volumes.

★1930★
National Baseball Hall of Fame and Museum, Inc.
National Baseball Library
Box 590
Cooperstown, NY 13326 Phone: (607)547-9988
Thomas R. Heitz, Libn.

Founded: 1939. **Staff:** Prof 1; Other 8. **Subjects:** Baseball. **Special Collections:** August Hermann correspondence; A.G. Mills correspondence; George Weiss; Lou Perini Collection; Negro baseball collection; official records of the major leagues. **Holdings:** 10,000 books; 750 bound periodical volumes; 1500 pamphlets; 25,000 player data cards; 150,000 photographs; 150 VF drawers of biographical clippings; 1000 videotapes; 700 reels of microfilm; 1100 reels of motion picture film. **Subscriptions:** 85 journals and other serials; 9 newspapers. **Services:** Copying; 16mm film rental library; genealogical research; inquiries answered; library open to the public by appointment. **Computerized Information Services:** Museum and Library Accession Records (internal database). **Networks and Consortia:** Member of South Central Research Library Council (SCRLC). **Publications:** *Bibliographies*, occasional. **Remarks:** FAX: (607)547-5980.

★1931★
National Minority AIDS Council
Library
300 I St., NE, Ste. 400
Washington, DC 20002 Phone: (202)544-1076
Tomas Gomez

Staff: 1. **Subjects:** AIDS issues relating to minorities population. **Holdings:** 30 books; 40 reports. **Subscriptions:** 20 journals and other serials; 5 newspapers. **Services:** Library open to the public. **Remarks:** FAX: (202)544-0378. Telex: 940103 WU PUBTLX BSN.

★1932★
National Urban League
Research Department
Library
1111 14th St., NW, Ste. 600
Washington, DC 20005 Phone: (202)898-1604
Billy Tidwell, Dir. of Res.

Subjects: U.S. social and economic conditions, Blacks, poor minorities. **Holdings:** 1000 volumes. **Services:** Library not open to the public. **Remarks:** FAX: (202)408-1965.

★1933★
New York City Technical College of the City University of New York
Library
300 Jay St.
Brooklyn, NY 11201 Phone: (718)260-5470
Darrow Wood, Chf.Libn. & Dept.Chm.

Founded: 1947. **Staff:** Prof 14; Other 7. **Subjects:** Paramedical sciences, graphic arts, hotel and restaurant management, Afro-American studies, engineering technology, business fields. **Holdings:** 158,372 books; 5156 bound periodical volumes; 108 VF drawers of pamphlet material; 3 VF drawers of menus; 15 VF drawers of pictures; 15 VF drawers of career material; 15 VF drawers of company history; 9051 reels of microfilm; 1934 phonograph records; 797 8mm film loops; 327 audio tapes; 743 video cassettes. **Subscriptions:** 934 journals and other serials; 15 newspapers. **Services:** Interlibrary loan; copying; library open to the public for reference use only. **Automated Operations:** Computerized public access catalog and cataloging. **Computerized Information Services:** OCLC, BRS Information Technologies, ACADEMIC INDEX, MAGAZINE ASAP. **Networks and Consortia:** Member of New York Metropolitan Reference and Research Library Agency, Academic Libraries of Brooklyn (ALB). **Publications:** Library Notes, irregular; *Library Basics*; *Library Alert*, irregular - all to faculty and to others on request.

★1934★
New York Office of Parks, Recreation & Historic Preservation
John Jay Homestead State Historic Site
Library
Box AH
Katonah, NY 10536 Phone: (914)232-5651
Linda M. Connelly, Mgr.

Founded: 1959. **Staff:** Prof 2. **Subjects:** Jay Family, New York State history, antislavery, Westchester County history. **Special Collections:** Antislavery pamphlets of William Jay and John Jay II; archival materials from the Jay family, 18th-20th centuries (5000 items). **Holdings:** 4000 volumes. **Services:** Special arrangements can be made for use of the material by qualified scholars at the site. **Remarks:** The bulk of this collection consists of the library of John Jay (first Chief Justice of the United States) and four generations of his descendants.

★1935★
New York Public Library
Countee Cullen Regional Branch Library
Ethnic Heritage Collection
104 W. 136th St.
New York, NY 10030 Phone: (212)491-2070
Phyllis G. Mack, Reg.Libn.

Founded: 1905. **Staff:** Prof 5; Other 5.5. **Subjects:** Ethnic heritage, African and African-American heritage and culture. **Special Collections:** James Weldon Johnson Collection of Children's Books on the Black Experience. **Holdings:** 44,420 books; 2257 recordings; 728 video cassettes. **Subscriptions:** 95 journals and other serials; 12 newspapers. **Services:** Interlibrary loan; copying; library open to the public. **Remarks:** FAX: (212)491-6541.

★1936★
New York Public Library
Schomburg Center for Research in Black Culture
Library
515 Malcolm X Blvd.
New York, NY 10037-1801 Phone: (212)491-2200
Howard Dodson, Chf.

Founded: 1926. **Staff:** Prof 30; Other 33. **Subjects:** Social sciences, humanities, the Black experience throughout the world. **Special Collections:** Haitian Collection; African and Caribbean music; works of Harlem Renaissance authors and artists. **Holdings:** 102,000 volumes; 3200 archival record groups; 10,000 recordings; 300,000 photographs; 600 videotapes; 5000 hours of oral history; 30,000 reels of microfilm; 40,000 microfiche; paintings; sculpture; drawings; prints; African artifacts. **Subscriptions:** 1000 journals and other serials. **Services:** Copying; center open to adults for reference use. **Computerized Information Services:** RLIN. **Networks and Consortia:** Member of RLG, New York Metropolitan Reference and Research Library Agency, New York State Interlibrary Loan Network (NYSILL). **Publications:** *The Schomburg Center Journal*, quarterly. **Special Indexes:** Kaiser Index to Black Resources, 1940 to present (card, online); clipping files (microfiche); local data bases; vertical file holdings, 1925-1974 (microfiche), 1975 to present (paper). **Remarks:** The Center sponsors two Scholar-in-Residency Programs supported by the Ford Foundation and NEH, as well as the bi-annual Clarence L. Holte Literary Prize. FAX: (212)491-6760.

★1937★
New York Theological Seminary
Library
5 W. 29th St.
New York, NY 10001 Phone: (212)532-4012
Eleanor Soler, Libn.

Founded: 1900. **Staff:** Prof 1; Other 1. **Subjects:** Bible, theology, pastoral counseling, parish ministry, African-American church studies, women in the church. **Holdings:** 20,000 volumes; 700 audio cassettes; 20 video cassettes; 300 Spanish books; 200 Korean books; 2 drawers of periodicals on microfiche. **Subscriptions:** 40 journals and other serials. **Services:** Interlibrary loan; copying; library open to the public for reference use only.

★1938★
Newark Public Library
Humanities Division
5 Washington St.
Box 630
Newark, NJ 07101-0630 Phone: (201)733-7820
Sallie Hannigan, Supv.Libn.

Staff: Prof 6; Other 2. **Subjects:** Literature, language, literary criticism, biography, bibliography, religion, philosophy, history, geography, psychology, librariana, travel, film, theater, television, sports and recreation, encyclopedias, dictionaries. **Special Collections:** Black literature, history, and biography; Granger Collection of Poetry and Anthologies; Puerto Rican Reference Collection; Travel Collection (books; pamphlets; clippings). **Holdings:** 130,000 books; 1000 bound periodical volumes; 1000 maps; dictionaries and encyclopedias in Spanish, Italian, French, German, Russian; information file. **Subscriptions:** 630 journals and other serials. **Services:** Interlibrary loan; copying; telephone and in-person reference available in Spanish; division open to the public. **Automated Operations:** Computerized cataloging and acquisitions. **Computerized Information Services:** BRS Information Technologies, DIALOG Information Services, ORBIT Search Service, VU/TEXT Information Services, NEXIS, WILSONLINE, OCLC, DataTimes. Performs searches on fee basis. **Networks and Consortia:** Member of New Jersey Library Network, Essex Hudson Regional Library Cooperative. **Remarks:** FAX: (201)733-5648.

★1939★
Newark Public Library
Popular Library Division
5 Washington St.
Box 630
Newark, NJ 07101-0630 Phone: (201)733-7784
Wilma Grey, Supv.Libn.

Staff: Prof 7; Other 8. **Subjects:** General fiction, popular nonfiction, Black studies, foreign languages, job and career information. **Special Collections:** African American room, Sala Hispanoamericana; French, German, Italian, Polish, Portuguese, Russian, and Yiddish language collections; 20,000 volumes in Spanish. **Holdings:** 60,000 books; 30 films; 2000 video cassettes; 500 phonograph records; 1500 audio cassettes; 550 large print titles. **Subscriptions:** 25 journals and other serials; 10 newspapers. **Services:** Interlibrary loan; copying; division open to the public. **Automated Operations:** Computerized cataloging and acquisitions. **Computerized Information Services:** DIALOG Information Services, BRS Information Technologies, NEXIS, OCLC, ORBIT Search Service, VU/TEXT Information Services, WILSONLINE, DataTimes. Performs searches on fee basis. Contact Person: James Capuano, Prin.Libn., 733-7814. **Networks and Consortia:** Member of New Jersey Library Network, Essex Hudson Regional Library Cooperative. **Publications:** Monthly film list - to registered borrowers. **Special Indexes:** Index of books into films. **Remarks:** FAX: (201)733-5648.

★1940★
North Carolina A&T State University
F. D. Bluford Library
1601 E. Market St.
Greensboro, NC 27411 Phone: (919)334-7782
Alene C. Young, Dir., Lib.Serv.

Founded: 1894. **Staff:** Prof 17; Other 24. **Subjects:** Agriculture, nursing, engineering, education. **Special Collections:** Collections of Black Studies; Film Collection; Chemistry Library. **Holdings:** 410,170 volumes; 271,590 microforms; archival materials; government documents; theses; pictures; maps; modules. **Subscriptions:** 1716 journals and other serials. **Services:** Interlibrary loan; copying; cooperative lending; library open to the public. **Automated Operations:** Computerized cataloging and circulation. **Computerized Information Services:** OCLC, DIALOG Information Services, LS/2000. Performs searches on fee basis. Contact Person: Euthena Newman, 334-7617. **Networks and Consortia:** Member of SOLINET. **Special Indexes:** Local newspaper index (online). **Remarks:** FAX: (919)334-7783.

★1941★
North Carolina Central University
School of Library and Information Science
Library
J.E. Shepard Library
Durham, NC 27707 Phone: (919)560-6400
Alice S. Richmond, Libn.

Staff: Prof 2; Other 1. **Subjects:** Librarianship, children's literature. **Special Collections:** William Tucker Collection (materials for children by Black authors and illustrators; 302 items; 190 volumes); Black Librarians' Collection (1200 items). **Holdings:** 23,800 books; 4390 bound periodical volumes; 455 reels of microfilm; 15,000 microfiche; 15 VF drawers. **Subscriptions:** 420 journals and other serials. **Services:** Interlibrary loan; library open to the public with restrictions. **Automated Operations:** Computerized public access catalog and cataloging. **Computerized Information Services:** DIALOG Information Services, WILSONLINE. **Networks and Consortia:** Member of SOLINET. **Publications:** Acquisitions list, irregular - for internal distribution only. **Remarks:** FAX: (919)560-6402.

★1942★
North Carolina Museum of Art
Art Reference Library
2110 Blue Ridge Blvd.
Raleigh, NC 27607 Phone: (919)833-1935
Dr. Anna Dvorak, Libn.

Founded: 1956. **Staff:** Prof 1; Other 1. **Subjects:** Painting, sculpture, architecture, drawing, prints, decorative arts, graphics, pre-Columbian and African art. **Holdings:** 26,000 volumes; 20,000 slides of museum's holdings; 68 VF drawers of artist clippings; 30 VF drawers of museum and subject files. **Subscriptions:** 80 journals. **Services:** Interlibrary loan; copying; library open to the public.

★1943★
Northeastern Illinois University
Ronald Williams Library
5500 N. St. Louis Ave.
Chicago, IL 60625-4699 Phone: (312)794-2615
Bradley F. Baker, Univ.Libn.

Founded: 1961. **Staff:** Prof 21; Other 53. **Subjects:** Education, business and management, social sciences, literature and languages. **Special Collections:** U.S. and Illinois document depositories; Illinois Regional Archive Depository (IRAD) for Chicago and Cook County; African-American literature; William Gray Reading Collection; curriculum guides; textbooks. **Holdings:** 532,415 books; 62,930 bound periodical volumes; 1198 linear feet of archival materials; 27,327 reels of microfilm; 28,024 pamphlets; 794,068 microfiche. **Subscriptions:** 6902 journals and other serials; 44 newspapers. **Services:** Interlibrary loan; copying; library open to the public. **Automated Operations:** Computerized public access catalog, acquisitions, and serials. **Computerized Information Services:** DIALOG Information Services, OCLC, BRS Information Technologies, WILSONLINE, EPIC, CARL UnCover; InfoTrac; CD-ROM (ERIC, PAIS on CD-ROM, CIRR on Disc, MLA International Bibliography, SPORT Discus, General Science Index, Disclosure Incorporated, PsycLIT); BITNET (electronic mail service). Performs searches on fee basis. Contact Person: Mary Jane Hilburger, Hd.Ref.Libn., 794-2614. **Networks and Consortia:** Member of Interlibrary loanINET. **Publications:** Annual Report; departmental bibliographies and handouts. **Special Catalogues:** Library shelf lists for special collections, documents, and curriculum materials. **Special Indexes:** Periodicals holding list. **Remarks:** FAX: (312)794-2550. Electronic mail address(es): PROFS (BITNET).

★1944★
Northwestern University
Melville J. Herskovits Library of African Studies
University Library
Evanston, IL 60208-2300 Phone: (708)491-7684
Hans E. Panofsky, Cur. of Africana

Founded: 1955. **Staff:** Prof 4.5; Other 2. **Subjects:** Africa - anthropology, exploration and travel, history, linguistics, literature, bibliography, statistics, geography, sociology, political science, economics. **Special Collections:** African language publications (9000); Dennis Brutus papers (3 feet); Arabic/Hausa Manuscripts from Kano (3000); G.M. Carter/T. Karis Collection on South African Politics (80 feet); African Studies Association (100 feet); African Literature Association (35 feet); Economic Survey of Liberia papers (3 feet); Vernon McKay papers (50 feet); Claude Barnett clipping files (18 feet); A. Abdurahman and Z. Gool papers (2 feet); Leo Kuper papers (8 feet); Alex Hepple (5 feet); Gwendolen M. Carter papers (40 feet); Program of African Studies Records (10 feet). **Holdings:** 214,000 volumes; 3670 feet of vertical files; 11,000 pamphlets; 1600 posters; 1000 phonograph records; 1.3 million feet of tape recordings; 9728 map sheets. **Subscriptions:** 4713 journals and other serials; 138 African newspapers. **Services:** Interlibrary loan; copying; library open to the public with restrictions. **Automated Operations:** Computerized public access catalog, cataloging, acquisitions, serials, and circulation (NOTIS). **Computerized Information Services:** OCLC; LTAP (internal database). **Networks and Consortia:** Member of Center for Research Libraries (CRL) Consortia, ILLINET, RLG, North Suburban Library System (NSLS). **Publications:** *Joint Acquisitions List of Africana (JALA)*, 6/year - by subscription; *Cumulation of JALA on microfiche, 1978-1988.* **Special Catalogues:** Catalog of the Melville J. Herskovits Library of African Studies, Northwestern University Library and Africana in selected libraries (1972; 8 volumes); Supplement (1978; 6 volumes); Censuses in the Melville J. Herskovits Library (1990); Development Plans in the Melville J. Herskovits Library of African Studies (1990); Africana Archives on Microform at Northwestern University Library (1982). **Special Indexes:** The Africana Conference Paper Index (1982; 2 volumes). **Remarks:** FAX: (708)491-5685.

★1945★
Oakland Public Library
History/Literature Division
125 14th St.
Oakland, CA 94612 Phone: (415)273-3136

Staff: Prof 4; Other 3. **Subjects:** History, travel, biography, English and foreign languages and literature, genealogy, maps. **Special Collections:** Includes Schomberg Collection of Black Literature and History (in microform); Negroes of New York, 1939 (Writers Program; in microform); Library of American Civilization (in microform). **Holdings:** 100,663 books; genealogy microfilms. **Subscriptions:** 114 journals and other serials. **Services:** Interlibrary loan; copying; division open to the public. **Networks and Consortia:** Member of Bay Area Library and Information System (BALIS). **Publications:** *New Releases.* **Special Indexes:** Indexes for Drama, Short Story, Poetry, Literary Criticism (on cards); local newspapers, 1978 to present; Local History.

★1946★
Oberlin College
Library
Special Collections Department
Oberlin, OH 44074-1532 Phone: (216)775-8285
Dina Schoonmaker, Spec.Coll.Cur.

Founded: 1833. **Staff:** Prof 1. **Special Collections:** Includes Antislavery (2500 abolitionist books and pamphlets published prior to the Emancipation Proclamation). **Holdings:** 28,000 books; 2500 bound periodical volumes; 1000 manuscripts. **Subscriptions:** 8 journals and other serials. **Services:** Department open to the public on a limited schedule. **Computerized Information Services:** Internal database; BITNET InterNet (electronic mail service). **Remarks:** FAX: (216)775-8739. Electronic mail address(es): PSCHOONMAKER@OBERLIN; PSCHOONMAKER@OCVAXA.CC.OBERLIN.EDU.

★1947★
Oberlin College
Library
Archives
420 Mudd Center
Oberlin, OH 44074-1532 Phone: (216)775-8014
Roland M. Baumann, Coll.Archv.

Founded: 1966. **Staff:** Prof 2; Other 1. **Subjects:** Higher education, 19th century reform, temperance, women's history, Black education, architecture, Ohio history. **Special Collections:** Missions, the antislavery movement, and temperance in Oberlin; papers of Oberlin College faculty and graduates; Oberlin municipal government records; photographs of Oberlin College and Oberlin. **Holdings:** 4000 linear feet of manuscripts and archival materials. **Subscriptions:** 6 journals and other serials. **Services:** Copying; archives open to the public. **Automated Operations:** Computerized public access catalog, cataloging, acquisitions, serials, and circulation. **Computerized Information Services:** DIALOG Information Services, BRS Information Technologies. Performs searches free of charge. Contact Person: Cynthia Comer, Assoc.Hd., Ref.. **Networks and Consortia:** Member of NEOMARL, OHIONET. **Special Catalogues:** Catalog of the Antislavery Collection. **Remarks:** FAX: (216)775-8739.

★1948★
Ohio State University
Black Studies Library
1858 Neil Ave.
Columbus, OH 43210-1286 Phone: (614)292-2393
Eleanor M. Daniel, Hd.Libn.

Founded: 1971. **Staff:** Prof 1; Other 1. **Subjects:** African-American studies, African studies. **Special Collections:** Schomburg Collection; Atlanta University Black Culture Collection; Black Newspaper Collection (Bell & Howell); Tuskegee Institute News Clipping File; Martin Luther King, Jr. Assassination File; W. E. B. DuBois papers; Black Biographical Dictionaries; papers of the National Association for the Advancement of Colored People (NAACP), parts 1-8; papers of the Congress of Racial Equality, 1941-1967. **Holdings:** 30,000 books; 13,000 microforms; 70 major Black U.S. newspapers. **Subscriptions:** 173 journals and other serials; 16 newspapers. **Services:** Interlibrary loan; collection open to the public. **Automated Operations:** Computerized cataloging, serials, and circulation. **Computerized Information Services:** Online systems; BITNET (electronic mail service). **Publications:** *Selected List of Titles Received by the Black Studies Library*, monthly. **Remarks:** FAX: (614)292-7859. Electronic mail address(es): EDANIEL@OHSTMVSA.ACS.OHIO.STATE.EDU (BITNET).

★1949★
Old Slave Mart Library
Box 446
Sullivan's Island, SC 29482 Phone: (803)883-3797
Judith Wragg Chase, Dir.

Subjects: Slavery, Black history, Civil War, Charleston, South Carolina. **Special Collections:** Miriam B. Wilson Collection; Chase/Graves Collection. **Holdings:** 1100 volumes; 1800 photographs; 850 slides; 130 photocopies of documents and 80 original documents; 800 realia; 300 paintings, flatwork, prints; 40 feet of uncataloged record boxes; 35 VF drawers; 10 map case drawers; 500 slides, records, tapes; 65 years of archival records; manuscripts of founder. **Services:** Library open to the public for reference use only on a fee basis.

★1950★
Pacifica Foundation
Pacifica Program Service
Pacifica Radio Archive
3729 Cahuenga Blvd. W.
North Hollywood, CA 91604 Phone: (818)506-1077
Bill Thomas, Dir.

Founded: 1968. **Staff:** Prof 5; Other 2. **Subjects:** Politics and government, social sciences, Third World, minorities, women's studies, philosophy. **Special Collections:** Noncommercial radio programs, 1950 to present. **Holdings:** 28,000 magnetic audiotapes. **Services:** Copying; archive open to the public by appointment. **Automated Operations:** Computerized cataloging and acquisitions. **Special Catalogues:** Collection catalog (microfiche).

★1951★
Pan-African Resource Center
Library
PO Box 3307
Washington, DC 20010

Subjects: Africa - reunification, history, resources; world hunger. **Special Collections:** Biographical archives. **Holdings:** 43,000 volumes.

★1952★
Payne Theological Seminary
R. C. Ransom Memorial Library
PO Box 474
Wilberforce, OH 45384 Phone: (513)376-2946
J. Dale Balsbaugh, Dir. of the Lib.

Founded: 1844. **Staff:** Prof 1; Other 1. **Subjects:** Philosophy, Biblical studies, pastoral theology, doctrinal theology, Black studies, African Methodist Episcopal Church history. **Special Collections:** Arno Press Black Studies Program - The American Negro, His History and Literature (150 volumes). **Holdings:** 20,000 books; 500 archival materials. **Subscriptions:** 2 journals and other serials; 2 newspapers. **Services:** Interlibrary loan; copying; library open to the public. **Special Catalogues:** Union Serials List of Seminaries, every 4 years.

★1953★
Popular Culture Association
Library
Popular Culture Center
Bowling Green State University
Bowling Green, OH 43403 Phone: (419)372-7861

Subjects: Popular culture - television, motion pictures, editorial cartoons, pulp fiction, underground culture, folklore, American humor, popular and protest music, Black culture, Indian and Chicano popular culture, social significance of the soap opera. **Holdings:** 200,000 volumes; 300,000 records; statistics.

★1954★
Portsmouth Public Library
Local History Room
601 Court St.
Portsmouth, VA 23704 Phone: (804)393-8501
Mrs. Brooke Maupin, Lib.Asst.

Staff: 1. **Subjects:** Local history, lighthouses and lightships, genealogy. **Special Collections:** Judge White Collection; Lee Rogers Collection (photographs of Portsmouth's Black community, 1920s-1960s; 6 scrapbooks). **Holdings:** 4000 books; 200 bound periodical volumes; 70 maps; 350 documents; 21,400 photographs; Norfolk County and Portsmouth wills and deeds, 1637-1820. **Services:** Interlibrary loan; copying; room open to the public. **Automated Operations:** Computerized public access catalog, cataloging, acquisitions, and circulation. **Special Indexes:** Portsmouth and Norfolk County Documents; Emmerson Papers (abstracts of local newspapers, 1700-1880); Butt papers (17th century land holdings in Norfolk county; all on cards). **Remarks:** FAX: (804)393-5107.

★1955★
Prairie View A&M University
Special Collections/University Archives
John B. Coleman Library, Rm. 505
Prairie View, TX 77446 Phone: (409)857-3119
Joyce K. Thornton, Interim Lib.Dir.

Founded: 1912. **Staff:** 2. **Special Collections:** T.K. Lawless Collection; Black Heritage of the West Collection; university archives; rare books collection; Blacks in the Military Collection. **Holdings:** 2059 books; 74 bound periodical volumes; 761 reels of microfilm; VF drawers; 1254 folders, pictures, memorabilia; 164 cubic feet of official records; 114 cubic feet of papers; 44 cubic feet of university publications; 19 cubic feet of clippings and pamphlets. **Services:** Interlibrary loan; copying; collections open to the public. **Automated Operations:** Computerized public access catalog (NOTIS) and cataloging. **Computerized Information Services:** DIALOG Information Services, OCLC; internal databases. Performs searches on fee basis. **Networks and Consortia:** Member of Houston Area Research Library Consortium (HARLIC), AMIGOS Bibliographic Council, Inc.. **Publications:** *Annual Report*. **Special Catalogues:** Record series control (card). **Remarks:** FAX: (409)857-2755.

★1956★
Prince George's County Memorial Library System
Sojourner Truth Room
6200 Oxon Hill Rd.
Oxon Hill, MD 20745 Phone: (301)839-2400
Teresa M. Stakem, Libn. II

Founded: 1968. **Staff:** Prof 2. **Subjects:** African American history - women, family, slavery, civil rights; literary criticism; military. **Special Collections:** Slave narratives (30). **Holdings:** 4200 books; 130 bound periodical volumes; 12 VF drawers of clippings, pamphlets, government documents; 100 reels of microfilm and 35 microfiche of periodicals. **Subscriptions:** 31 journals and other serials. **Services:** Copying; room open to the public with restrictions. **Automated Operations:** Computerized circulation. **Computerized Information Services:** CLSI (internal database).

★1957★
Providence College
Phillips Memorial Library
River Ave. at Eaton St.
Providence, RI 02918 Phone: (401)865-2377
Jane Jackson, Dir. of Archv.

Founded: 1917. **Staff:** Prof 7; Other 35. **Subjects:** Works of St. Thomas Aquinas, Thomistic philosophy and theology, Dominican Order. **Special Collections:** Includes Rhode Island Urban League Papers (200,000 items); Black Regiment Collection (600 pieces); Black Newspapers, 1932-1957 (8 reels of microfilm); National Association for the Advancement of Colored People Collection (pending). **Holdings:** 242,845 books; 50,349 bound periodical volumes; 111,577 government documents; 25,554 microforms; 1137 AV items. **Subscriptions:** 1862 journals and other serials; 43 newspapers. **Services:** Interlibrary loan (books only); copying; library open to the public for reference use only. **Automated Operations:** Computerized cataloging, acquisitions, and Interlibrary loan. **Computerized Information Services:** DIALOG Information Services, BRS Information Technologies, OCLC. **Networks and Consortia:** Member of Consortium of Rhode Island Academic and Research Libraries, Inc. (CRIARL), NELINET, Inc.. **Remarks:** FAX: (401)865-2057.

★1958★
Providence Public Library
150 Empire St.
Providence, RI 02903 Phone: (401)455-8021
Ms. Dale Thompson

Founded: 1878. **Staff:** Prof 1. **Special Collections:** Daniel Berkeley Updike Printing Collection (7000 volumes; 500 letters; engraved portraits; ephemera; 3 presses); C. Fiske Harris Collection on the Civil War and Slavery (5000 pamphlets; 1500 books; 100 volumes of newspaper clippings; 107 volumes of bound newspapers; boxes and albums of songs and ballads; prints; manuscripts; photographs; broadsides). **Holdings:** 24,500 books; 1000 bound periodical volumes; 42 linear feet of archival materials. **Services:** Copying; collections open to the public. **Remarks:** FAX: (401)455-8080.

★1959★
Prudence Crandall Museum
Library
Box 47
Canterbury, CT 06331 Phone: (203)546-9916
Kazimiera Kozlowski, Musm.Cur.

Staff: Prof 1. **Subjects:** Black history, life of Prudence Crandall, state and local history, women's history. **Holdings:** 1000 books. **Services:** Library open to the public by appointment for reference use only. **Remarks:** Maintained by Connecticut Historical Commission.

★1960★
Queens Borough Public Library
History, Travel & Biography Division
89-11 Merrick Blvd.
Jamaica, NY 11432 Phone: (718)990-0762
Deborah Hammer, Hd.

Founded: 1930. **Staff:** Prof 6; Other 3. **Subjects:** History, Indians of North America, biography, geography, travel, exploration. **Special Collections:** Carter G. Woodson Collection of Afro-American Culture and Life; Schomburg microfilm collection; U.S. Geographic Survey topographic maps (10,300); physical/thematic maps of countries of the world (126); nautical charts (8 kits); jet/ocean/world navigation charts (520); national forest maps (75); Latin American topographic maps (97); New York State planimetric maps (968); New York state, county, road maps (78); railroad transportation zone maps (82); historic/city maps (442). **Holdings:** 139,000 books; 3500 bound periodical volumes; 6550 microforms; 1 drawer of microfiche; 36 VF drawers of pamphlets; New York Daily News, 1950 to present; newspapers on microfilm. **Subscriptions:** 95 journals and other serials; 32 newspapers. **Services:** Interlibrary loan; copying; division open to the public. **Automated Operations:** Computerized cataloging and circulation. **Computerized Information Services:** ALANET (electronic mail service). **Special Indexes:** Collective biography analytics (card). **Remarks:** FAX: (718)658-8312; (718)658-8342.

★1961★
Queens Borough Public Library
Library Action Committee of Corona-East Elmhurst, Inc.
Langston Hughes Community Library and Cultural Center
102-09 Northern Blvd.
Corona, NY 11368 Phone: (718)651-1100
Andrew P. Jackson, Exec.Dir.

Founded: 1969. **Staff:** Prof 14; Other 34. **Subjects:** Third World, children's literature. **Special Collections:** Langston Hughes Collection (books by and about the author); Black Heritage Reference Collection; Langston Hughes Music Collection. **Holdings:** 110,000 books; 150 documents, manuscripts, reels of microfilm. **Subscriptions:** 105 journals and other serials; 15 newspapers. **Services:** Copying; library open to the public. **Publications:** *Library Center Brochure.*

★1962★
Queens College of the City University of New York
Ethnic Materials Information Exchange
Graduate School of Lib. & Info. Studies
NSF 300
65-30 Kissena Blvd.
Flushing, NY 11367 Phone: (718)997-3790
David Cohen, Prog.Dir.

Founded: 1980. **Staff:** Prof 1; Other 1. **Subjects:** Ethnic studies resources, minority groups in America, multicultural librarianship. **Holdings:** 2000 volumes; 40 filmstrips; 10 tapes; 250 pamphlets; curriculum materials; vertical file of clippings for each group and information area. **Subscriptions:** 6 journals and other serials. **Services:** Center open to the public. **Remarks:** Alternate telephone number(s): 997-3626. FAX: (718)793-8049.

★1963★
Radcliffe College
Arthur and Elizabeth Schlesinger Library on the History of Women in America
10 Garden St.
Cambridge, MA 02138 Phone: (617)495-8647
Dr. Patricia M. King, Dir.

Founded: 1943. **Staff:** Prof 10; Other 4. **Subjects:** Women - suffrage, medicine, education, law, social service, labor, family, organizations; history of American women in all phases of public and private life. **Special Collections:** Includes Black Women Oral History Project; **Holdings:** 30,000 volumes; 3000 bound periodical volumes; 850 major collections of papers on individual American women, families, women's organizations; 9500 reels of microfilm; 2250 magnetic tapes; 70 VF drawers; 2500 reels of audio- and videotapes; 6500 linear feet of manuscripts; 50,000 photographs. **Subscriptions:** 495 journals and other serials. **Services:** Interlibrary loan; copying; library open to the public. **Automated Operations:** Computerized public access catalog, cataloging and serials. **Publications:** *Occasional Reports*, sent on request. **Special Catalogues:** Manuscript Inventories; Catalogs of the Manuscripts, Books and Periodicals, 1984 (10 volumes). **Remarks:** Library located at 3 James St., Cambridge, MA, 02138.

★1964★
Richmond Public Library
Special Collections
325 Civic Center Plaza
Richmond, CA 94804 Phone: (415)620-6561
Adelia Lines, Dir.

Founded: 1905. **Special Collections:** Local history; job information center; AV collection (film; video cassettes); motor manuals; art prints; Afro-American history; LEAP (literacy program). **Services:** Interlibrary loan; collections open to the public. **Automated Operations:** Computerized cataloging and circulation. **Computerized Information Services:** DIALOG Information Services, WILSONLINE; CLSI (internal database); OnTyme Electronic Message Network Service (electronic mail service). Performs searches on fee basis. Contact Person: Douglas Holtzman. **Networks and Consortia:** Member of Bay Area Library and Information Network, Bay Area Library and Information System (BALIS).

★1965★
Rockefeller University
Rockefeller Archive Center
15 Dayton Ave.
Pocantico Hills
North Tarrytown, NY 10591 Phone: (914)631-4505
Dr. Darwin H. Stapleton, Dir.

Founded: 1975. **Staff:** Prof 10; Other 6. **Subjects:** American philanthropy; Rockefeller family; education; medicine; physical, natural, and social sciences; public health; arts; humanities; agriculture; Black history; international relations and economic development; labor; politics; population; religion; social welfare; women's history. **Holdings:** 23,000 cubic feet of archival and manuscript collections; 250,000 photographs; 4000 microfiche; 1600 films. **Services:** Copying; center open to scholars by appointment. **Computerized Information Services:** RLIN. **Networks and Consortia:** Member of RLG. **Publications:** occasional papers. **Special Catalogues:** A Guide to Archives and Manuscripts at the Rockefeller Archive Center, 1989 (pamphlet); Photograph Collections in the Rockefeller Archive Center, 1986. **Remarks:** FAX: (914)631-6017.

★1966★
Rowland E. Robinson Memorial Association
Rokeby Museum
Library
RD 1
Ferrisburg, VT 05456 Phone: (802)877-3406
Karen E. Petersen, Musm.Dir.

Founded: 1963. **Subjects:** Family history, abolition, reform, agriculture, Quakerism. **Special Collections:** Robinson/Sterns Family Papers Collection (30 cubic feet). **Holdings:** 2000 books; 30 cubic feet of archival materials; 60 reels of microfilm; 1000 unbound periodicals. **Services:** Library open to the public by appointment.

★1967★
St. Joseph's Seminary
Library
1200 Varnum St., NE
Washington, DC 20017 Phone: (202)526-4231
Laurence A. Schmitt, Libn.

Founded: 1930. **Staff:** Prof 1; Other 1. **Subjects:** Philosophy and theology, Black studies. **Holdings:** 24,000 volumes. **Subscriptions:** 75 journals and other serials. **Services:** Interlibrary loan (limited); library open to the public by appointment.

★1968★
St. Louis Community College at Forest Park
Instructional Resources
Special Collections
5600 Oakland Ave.
St. Louis, MO 63110 Phone: (314)644-9209
Carol S. Warrington, Contact

Founded: 1968. **Staff:** Prof 5.5; Other 20.5. **Subjects:** African Americans, allied health, tourism. **Services:** Interlibrary loan; collection open to the public. **Automated Operations:** Computerized cataloging (NOTIS). **Computerized Information Services:** DIALOG Information Services, BRS Information Technologies, WILSONLINE. Performs searches. Contact Person: Carol Shahriary, Ref.Libn. **Remarks:** Interlibrary loan requests should be directed to 5460 Highland Pk. Dr., St. Louis, MO 63110. FAX: (314)644-9240.

★1969★
St. Mary's Hospital of Brooklyn
Medical Library
170 Buffalo Ave.
Brooklyn, NY 11213 Phone: (718)774-3600
Elsa Sansaricq, Dir.

Staff: 1. **Subjects:** Medicine, allied health sciences, nursing, sickle cell anemia, administration, drug addiction. **Holdings:** 1000 books; 100 administrative materials; Audio-Digest tapes. **Subscriptions:** 112 journals and other serials. **Services:** Interlibrary loan; copying; library open to paramedical personnel and others with proper identification. **Computerized Information Services:** MEDLINE; DOCLINE (electronic mail service). **Networks and Consortia:** Member of Brooklyn-Queens-Staten Island Health Sciences Librarians (BQSI), Medical & Scientific Libraries of Long Island (MEDLI), BHSL. **Publications:** *CMC Newsletter*, quarterly.

★1970★
San Diego Public Library
Social Sciences Section
820 E St.
San Diego, CA 92101 Phone: (619)236-5564
Jean C. Hughes, Supv.

Staff: Prof 4; Other 4.5. **Subjects:** Sociology, education, political science, law, economics, finance, conservation, transportation, military service, folklore. **Holdings:** 67,500 books; 5 VF drawers of corporation annual reports; 5 VF drawers of vocational pamphlets; 19 VF drawers of miscellaneous pamphlets; 5000 college catalogs on microfiche; corporation annual reports, 1978 to present, on microfiche; talking books and cassette tapes for the visually handicapped. **Subscriptions:** 520 journals and other serials. **Services:** Interlibrary loan; copying; section open to the public. **Automated Operations:** Computerized cataloging and circulation. **Computerized Information Services:** DIALOG Information Services; InfoTrac. Performs searches free of charge. **Networks and Consortia:** Member of Serra Cooperative Network, CLASS. **Publications:** Booklists, irregular. **Special Indexes:** Black American Firsts File (card); Women Firsts File (card).

★1971★
Seattle Public Library
Douglass-Truth Branch Library
2300 E. Yesler Way
Seattle, WA 98122 Phone: (206)684-4704
Irene Haines, Team Ldr.

Founded: 1965. **Staff:** Prof 3; Other 4. **Subjects:** Afro-American history and literature - the African-American experience in the Pacific Northwest, the portrayal of Blacks in children's literature. **Special Collections:** Afro-American Collection; Children's Literature Reference Collection. **Holdings:** 6020 books; 346 bound periodical volumes; 5 VF drawers of pictures and pamphlets; 95 sound recordings; 3 boxes of microfiche; 200 video recordings. **Subscriptions:** 17 journals and other serials; 6 newspapers. **Services:** Interlibrary loan; copying; library open to the public. **Automated Operations:** Computerized public access catalog, serials, and circulation. **Computerized Information Services:** InfoTrac. **Networks and Consortia:** Member of Western Library Network (WLN). **Special Indexes:** Afro-American History Index (card). **Remarks:** FAX: (206)684-4346.

★1972★
South Africa as the Fifty-first State Library
4845 S. Raymond
Seattle, WA 98118 Phone: (206)725-7417
William H. Davis, Libn.

Founded: 1986. **Staff:** Prof 1. **Subjects:** Events which will cause the "White Tribe" to favor union; cultural conditions to which Blacks from South Africa would have to adjust; winter resort possibilities. **Holdings:** 40 books; 22 scrapbooks; Proceedings of South African tricameral Parliamentary sessions, 1988-1990 (32 volumes). **Services:** Interlibrary loan; copying; library open to the public. **Publications:** Leaflets, bimonthly - available on request.

★1973★
South Carolina State College
Miller F. Whittaker Library
South Carolina State College Historical Collection
College Ave.
Box 1991
Orangeburg, SC 29117 Phone: (803)536-7045
Barbara Williams Jenkins, Ph.D.

Subjects: College history, 1897 to present. **Special Collections:** Black Collection (by and about Blacks). **Holdings:** College records; presidential papers; photographs; blueprints; college publications; yearbooks; newspapers; oral history recordings; documents concerning the development of South Carolina State College. **Subscriptions:** 1104 journals and other serials; 45 newspapers. **Services:** Copying; collection open to the public with restrictions. **Computerized Information Services:** DIALOG Information Services, BRS Information Technologies, VU/TEXT Information Services, ALANET, OCLC. **Networks and Consortia:** . **Remarks:** FAX: (803)536-8902.

★1974★
Southern California Library for Social Studies and Research
6120 S. Vermont Ave.
Los Angeles, CA 90044 Phone: (213)759-6063
Sarah Cooper, Dir.

Founded: 1963. **Staff:** Prof 3; Other 8. **Subjects:** Labor; Marxism; socialism; Black, Chicano, and women's movements; Southern California grassroots organizations. **Special Collections:** Civil Rights Congress (Los Angeles area) archival records; Harry Bridges papers on deportation trials; Los Angeles Committee for the Protection of the Foreign Born records; personal manuscript collections from Charlotta A. Bass, Richard Gladstein, Robert W. Kenny, and Earl Robinson. **Holdings:** 35,000 books; 30,000 pamphlets; 3500 tapes; 500,000 news clippings; 3000 periodicals titles; files from labor, peace, and civil rights organizations, 1930s to present; 100 documentary films, 1930s-1970s. **Services:** Copying; library open to the public. **Publications:** *Heritage* (newsletter), quarterly.

★1975★
Southern Poverty Law Center
Klanwatch
Library
Box 2087
Montgomery, AL 36102-2087 Phone: (205)264-0286
Danny Welch, Dir.

Founded: 1980. **Staff:** 8. **Subjects:** Ku Klux Klan, neo-Nazi organizations, other right-wing extremists, anti-KKK information. **Holdings:** 50 books; 100 legal documents; 30,000 news clippings; 100 audio- and videotapes; 1000 letters. **Subscriptions:** 30 journals and other serials. **Services:** Copying; library open to the public with restrictions. **Publications:** *Klanwatch Intelligence Report*, bimonthly - for internal distribution only; *Klanwatch Law Report*; *The Ku Klux Klan: A History of Racism and Violence, Decade Review*. **Remarks:** FAX: (205)264-0629.

★1976★
Southern Regional Council
Reference Library
60 Walton St., NW, 2nd Fl.
Atlanta, GA 30303-2199 Phone: (404)522-8764
Stephen T. Suitts, Exec.Dir.

Subjects: Civil rights, civil liberties, poverty, politics, suffrage. **Holdings:** 1200 books; civil rights movement newspaper collection on microfilm; newsclip collection, 1946-1975; special studies. **Services:** Copying; library open to the public with restrictions. **Computerized Information Services:** EasyLink (electronic mail service). **Publications:** *Southern Changes*, bimonthly - by subscription; *SRC House Record, Voting Rights Review, Legislative Bulletin* - all quarterly; *Special Reports and Studies*. **Remarks:** FAX: (404)522-8791.

★1977★
Southern University
Law Center
Library
Southern Branch Post Office
Box 9294
Baton Rouge, LA 70813 Phone: (504)771-2315
Alvin A. Roche Jr., Law Libn.

Founded: 1947. **Staff:** Prof 4; Other 9. **Subjects:** Law - civil, general, medical, international; political science. **Special Collections:** Civil rights; Federal and Louisiana State documents. **Holdings:** 175,015 books; 27,000 bound periodical volumes; 109,012 volumes of microfiche; 24,725 volumes of microfilm. **Subscriptions:** 540 journals and other serials; 15 newspapers. **Services:** Interlibrary loan; copying; library open to the public on a limited schedule. **Automated Operations:** Computerized cataloging and acquisitions. **Computerized Information Services:** OCLC, WESTLAW, LEXIS. **Networks and Consortia:** Member of SOLINET. **Publications:** Periodical list, annual; acquisitions list, quarterly; subject bibliographies, monthly. **Remarks:** FAX: (504)771-2474.

★1978★
State Community College
Senator Kenneth Hall Learning Resource Center
Special Collections
601 James R. Thompson Blvd.
East St. Louis, IL 62203 Phone: (618)583-2573
Dr. W.J. Van Grunsven

Founded: 1969. **Staff:** Prof 3; Other 4. **Subjects:** African-Americans - general, history. **Holdings:** 31,250 books; 2305 reels of microfilm; bound periodical volumes. **Subscriptions:** 99 journals and other serials; 11 newspapers. **Services:** Interlibrary loan; copying; library open to the public for reference use only. **Networks and Consortia:** Member of ILLINET. **Remarks:** FAX: (618)583-2660.

★1979★
State University of New York at New Paltz
Sojourner Truth Library
Special Collections
New Paltz, NY 12561 Phone: (914)257-3676
William E. Connors, Dir.

Founded: 1833. **Staff:** 35. **Subjects:** Sojourner Truth. **Holdings:** Africa and Asia collections; New Paltz collection; college archives; U.S. Government documents (selective); New York State documents (1989); Early American Imprints (Readex); Early English Books (Readex microprint). **Subscriptions:** 1350 journals and other serials. **Services:** Interlibrary loan; copying; collections open to the public. **Automated Operations:** Computerized public access catalog, cataloging, circulation, and Interlibrary loan. **Computerized Information Services:** DIALOG Information Services; BITNET (electronic mail service). Performs searches on fee basis. Contact Person: Gerlinde Barley, 257-3702. **Networks and Consortia:** Member of SUNY/OCLC Library Network, Southeastern New York Library Resources Council (SENYLRC). **Remarks:** FAX: (914)257-3670. Electronic mail address(es): CONNORSW@SNYNEWVM.

★1980★
State University of New York at Syracuse
Syracuse Educational Opportunity Center
Paul Robeson Library
100 New St.
Syracuse, NY 13202 Phone: (315)472-0130
Florence Beer, Dir.

Founded: 1969. **Staff:** Prof 2. **Subjects:** Afro-Americans, job preparation, women, African fiction, business skills, minorities. **Special Collections:** Frazier Library of Afro-American Books (500 volumes); National Archives Collection of Afro-American Artists (23 trays of slides). **Holdings:** 11,000 books and bound periodical volumes; 40 VF drawers. **Subscriptions:** 139 journals and other serials; 20 newspapers. **Services:** Interlibrary loan; copying; library open to the public. **Networks and Consortia:** Member of Central New York Library Resources Council (CENTRO). **Publications:** Periodical Holdings, annual - for internal distribution only; New Acquisitions Listings, semiannual. **Special Catalogues:** Catalog to audiovisual collection.

★1981★
Staten Island Institute of Arts and Sciences
Archives and Library
75 Stuyvesant Pl.
Staten Island, NY 10301 Phone: (718)727-1135
John-Paul Richiuso, Archv./Hist.

Founded: 1881. **Staff:** Prof 2; Other 1. **Subjects:** Natural history, Staten Island history, archeology, Black history, women's history, urban planning. **Special Collections:** Architecture; N. L. Britton; G. W. Curtis; J. P. Chapin; W. T. Davis (total of 1000 cubic feet); photographs and prints of old Staten Island; local Black history; repository for U.S. Geological Survey publications; complete list of special collections available on request. **Holdings:** 12,000 books; 22,000 bound periodical volumes; 3000 maps; 1200 prints; 50,000 photographs; 1500 art museum and gallery catalogs; 1500 cubic feet of manuscripts, letters, and documents; 80 reels of microfilm of Staten Island newspapers. **Subscriptions:** 200 journals and other serials. **Services:** Copying; library open to the public by appointment. **Special Indexes:** Guide to Institute Archives, 2 vol umes; indexes to newspapers, iconography of Staten Island, special collections (all on cards). **Remarks:** Basic library has been divided into two sections, a Science Library and a History Library.

★1982★
Suffolk University
Mildred F. Sawyer Library
Collection of Afro-American Literature
8 Ashburton Pl.
Boston, MA 02108 Phone: (617)573-8532
E.G. Hamann, Dir.

Staff: Prof 6; Other 6. **Subjects:** Afro-American literature - bibliography, history, biography, literary criticism; New England Afro-American writers. **Holdings:** 5000 books; 200 bound periodical volumes. **Subscriptions:** 20 journals and other serials. **Services:** Interlibrary loan; copying; collection open to the public for reference use only. **Automated Operations:** Computerized cataloging and indexing. **Networks and Consortia:** Member of NELINET, Inc., Fenway Library Consortium (FLC). **Publications:** *Black Writers in New England, a Bibliography,* 1985 - for sale; acquisitions list, annual - free upon request.

★1983★
Talladega College
Savery Library
Historical Collections
627 W. Battle St.
Talladega, AL 35160 Phone: (205)362-0206
Frances Baker Dates, Dir.

Founded: 1939. **Staff:** 6. **Subjects:** American Blacks; missions in Angola, Mozambique, Zaire, and South Africa; the Black church; civil rights; education. **Special Collections:** College archives (includes the activities of Talladega alumni); Historical Collections (the Black church, African missions, southern Africa, civil rights, education). **Holdings:** 120 linear feet of archival items. **Subscriptions:** 4 journals and other serials. **Services:** Interlibrary loan; copying; collections open to serious researchers and noncampus undergraduates with letter from supervising faculty. **Computerized Information Services:** NCS (internal database). **Publications:** *A Guide to the Archives of Talladega College,* 1981; *A Guide to the Collections,* 1981. **Remarks:** FAX: (205)362-2268.

★1984★
Temple University
Charles L. Blockson Afro-American Historical Collection
Sullivan Hall, 1st Fl.
Philadelphia, PA 19122 Phone: (215)787-6632
Charles L. Blockson, Cur.

Founded: 1983. **Staff:** Prof 1; Other 2. **Subjects:** Afro-American history, literature, and religion; African history; Blacks in sports; Caribbean; sociology; education. **Special Collections:** History of Blacks in Pennsylvania; underground railroad; John Mosley Photo Collection; Paul Robeson Collection; Bishop R. R. Wright, Jr. Collection. **Holdings:** 20,000 books; 169 bound periodical volumes; 20,000 other cataloged items. **Subscriptions:** 22 journals and other serials. **Services:** Copying; collection open to the public for reference use only. **Automated Operations:** Computerized cataloging and circulation. **Computerized Information Services:** RLIN. **Publications:** *Afro-Americana: An Exhibition of Selected Books, Manuscripts & Prints,* 1984.

★1985★
Tennessee Department of Economic & Community Development
Library
Rachel Jackson Bldg., 8th Fl.
Nashville, TN 37219 Phone: (615)741-1995
Edith Snider, Libn.

Founded: 1973. **Staff:** Prof 1. **Subjects:** Industrial development, economics, minority business enterprise. **Special Collections:** Department Archives. **Holdings:** 3000 books; 300 documents; 750 file folios of corporation annual reports from Fortune 500 companies and major Tennessee companies. **Subscriptions:** 210 journals and other serials. **Services:** Interlibrary loan; copying; library open to the public with restrictions.

★1986★
Tennessee Department of Employment Security
Research & Statistics Division
500 James Robertson Pkwy., 11th Fl.
Nashville, TN 37245-1000 Phone: (615)741-2284
Joe Cummings, Dir., Res. & Stat.

Staff: 1. **Subjects:** Data - labor market, census, economic. **Holdings:** Publications of the U.S. Bureau of Census, the U.S. Department of Labor, and the Department of Employment Security. **Services:** Copying; section open to the public for reference use only. **Publications:** Includes *Minorities in Tennessee*; *Tennessee Data for Affirmative Action Plans* 1984 (main publication); *Tennessee Data for Affirmative Action Plans* (current supplement). **Remarks:** FAX: (615)741-3203.

★1987★
Tennessee Human Rights Commission
Resource Library
Capitol Blvd. Bldg., Ste. 602
226 Capitol Blvd.
Nashville, TN 37243-0745 Phone: (615)741-5825

Staff: 1. **Subjects:** Race relations; discrimination in employment, housing, and public accommodations; legislation and decisions rendered in discrimination cases. **Holdings:** 60 books; 500 bound periodical volumes; commission-related materials. **Subscriptions:** 10 journals and other serials. **Services:** Library open to the public with restrictions.

★1988★
Texas Southern University
Library
Heartman Collection
3100 Cleburne St.
Houston, TX 77004 Phone: (713)527-7149
Dorothy H. Chapman, Libn.

Staff: Prof 2; Other 1. **Subjects:** Black culture and history, slavery. **Special Collections:** Barbara Jordan Archives (24 square feet); Texas Southern University Archives (12 square feet); Jazz Archives; Traditional African Art Gallery. **Holdings:** 35,000 books; 487 bound periodical volumes; 10,000 pamphlets; 66 VF drawers of clippings; 1 VF drawer of pictures; 1 VF drawer of sheet music. **Subscriptions:** 163 journals and other serials; 26 newspapers. **Services:** Interlibrary loan; copying; collection open to the public. **Automated Operations:** Computerized cataloging and acquisitions. **Remarks:** FAX: (713)639-1875.

★1989★
Tri-County Technical College
Learning Resource Center
Box 587
Pendleton, SC 29670 Phone: (803)646-8361
Nancy C. Griese, Hd.Libn.

Founded: 1963. **Staff:** Prof 2; Other 6. **Special Collections:** Includes Black studies (300 items). **Holdings:** 39,439 books; 4565 bound periodical volumes; 3868 AV programs. **Subscriptions:** 170 journals and other serials; 12 newspapers. **Services:** Interlibrary loan; copying; comprehensive audiovisual production services; center open to residents of Anderson, Oconee, and Pickens Counties, South Carolina. **Computerized Information Services:** OCLC. **Networks and Consortia:** Member of South Carolina Library Network. **Publications:** Quarterly and annual reports. **Special Catalogues:** Printed catalog of AV materials.

★1990★
Trinity College
Watkinson Library
300 Summit St.
Hartford, CT 06106 Phone: (203)297-2268
Dr. Jeffrey H. Kaimowitz, Cur.

Founded: 1857. **Staff:** Prof 5; Other 2. **Subjects:** Americana (especially 19th century), American Indians, Black history, U.S. Civil War, British history and topography, folklore, witchcraft, graphic arts, history of printing, natural history, horology, philology (especially American Indian languages), early voyages and travels, maritime history. **Special Collections:** Includes American music (including jazz and blues and 18th and 19th century religious and secular works in printed and manuscript form; 1100 song sheets; 26,000 pieces of sheet music). **Holdings:** 165,000 books and bound periodical volumes; atlases; 500 maps; printed ephemera including 100 indexed scrapbooks, advertisements, fashion plates, music and theater programs, and valentines. **Subscriptions:** 40 journals and other serials. **Services:** Copying; library open to the public for reference use only. **Automated Operations:** Computerized cataloging. **Computerized Information Services:** OCLC. **Networks and Consortia:** Member of NELINET, Inc. **Publications:** Bibliographies, irregular. **Special Catalogues:** Exhibition catalogs. **Remarks:** FAX: (203)297-2251.

★1991★
Tuskegee University
Architecture Library
Willcox Bldg. A
Tuskegee, AL 36088 Phone: (205)727-8351
Linda K. Harvey, Hd.Libn.

Founded: 1964. **Staff:** Prof 1; Other 6. **Subjects:** Architecture, construction, science management, planning, historic preservation. **Special Collections:** Rare architectural book collection (520); African-American architects and architecture. **Holdings:** 8100 books; 525 bound periodical volumes; 89 theses; 22,678 slides; microfiche. **Subscriptions:** 125 journals and other serials. **Services:** Interlibrary loan; copying; SDI; library open to the public for reference use only. **Computerized Information Services:** Access to DIALOG Information Services. Performs searches on fee basis. Contact Person: Edna L. Williams, 727-8892. **Networks and Consortia:** Member of SOLINET. **Special Catalogues:** Library's Periodical Holdings (book). **Special Indexes:** Index to African-American architects and architecture collection.

★1992★
Tuskegee University
Hollis Burke Frissell Library
Archives
Tuskegee, AL 36088 Phone: (205)727-8888
Daniel T. Williams, Archv.

Staff: Prof 1; Other 1. **Subjects:** African-American history, Tuskegee University history, civil rights, oral history. **Special Collections:** Washington Collection; Tuskegee University archives; Booker T. Washington papers (155 containers); George W. Carver papers (159 containers). **Holdings:** 25,000 books; 625 bound periodical volumes; 101 cabinets of Tuskegee University clipping files. **Subscriptions:** 39 journals and other serials; 19 newspapers. **Services:** Interlibrary loan; library open to the public on a limited schedule. **Computerized Information Services:** OCLC. **Networks and Consortia:** Member of Network of Alabama Academic Libraries (NAAL), CCLC. **Publications:** *A Guide to the Special Collection and Archives of Tuskegee University* (1974). **Remarks:** FAX: (205)727-9282.

★1993★
Tuskegee University
School of Engineering Library
Tuskegee, AL 36088 Phone: (205)727-8901
Frances F. Davis, Libn.

Founded: 1962. **Staff:** Prof 1; Other 1. **Subjects:** Engineering - electrical, mechanical, chemical, aerospace. **Holdings:** 14,500 books; 3700 bound periodical volumes; 19,000 Atomic Energy Commission materials; Energy Research Abstracts and Indexes. **Subscriptions:** 205 journals and other serials. **Services:** Library open to the public with restrictions. **Computerized Information Services:** DIALOG Information Services. **Networks and Consortia:** Member of Network of Alabama Academic Libraries (NAAL), SOLINET. **Remarks:** FAX: (205)727-8484.

★1994★
Tuskegee University
Veterinary Medicine Library
Patterson Hall
Tuskegee, AL 36088 Phone: (205)727-8307
F. Nell Thomas, Libn.

Founded: 1949. **Staff:** Prof 2; Other 3. **Subjects:** Anatomy, physiology, pathology, pharmacology, microbiology, radiology. **Special Collections:** Small and large animal medicine and surgery. **Holdings:** 15,565 volumes; 194 reels of microfilm; 447 slide programs; 478 video programs; 49 filmstrips; 20 tape programs. **Subscriptions:** 420 journals and other serials. **Services:** Interlibrary loan (fee); copying; library open to the public for reference use only. **Computerized Information Services:** DIALOG Information Services, MEDLINE. Performs searches on fee basis. Contact Person: Mrs. Shana K. Siddique, Lib.Asst. **Networks and Consortia:** Member of CCLC, Network of Alabama Academic Libraries (NAAL). **Publications:** Library Newsletter, semiannual - for internal distribution only. **Special Catalogues:** Tuskegee University School of Veterinary Medicine AV/AT Catalog of Programs. **Remarks:** FAX: (205)724-9236.

★1995★
United Mortgage Bankers of America
Library
800 Ivy Hill Rd.
Philadelphia, PA 19150 Phone: (215)242-6060
Gene Hatton, Exec.Dir.

Founded: 1962. **Subjects:** Minority mortgage brokering and banking. **Holdings:** 2000 volumes. **Remarks:** United Mortgage Bankers of America, Inc., a National Trade Association, seeks to provide members with the information and technical assistance necessary to enhance their businesses. The UMBA sponsors training sessions and educational programs in order to accomplish this goal. FAX: (215)247-1580.

★1996★
United Negro College Fund
Department of Archives and History
500 E. 62nd St.
New York, NY 10021 Phone: (212)326-1285
Paula Williams, Asst.Archv.

Staff: Prof 3. **Subjects:** Higher education for Blacks, history of philanthropy and fund raising. **Holdings:** 750 cubic feet. **Services:** Copying; department open to the public with restrictions.

★1997★
U.S. Department of Justice
Civil Rights Branch Library
10th & Pennsylvania Ave., NW, Rm. 7618
Washington, DC 20530 Phone: (202)514-4098
Catherine D. Harman, Libn.

Staff: Prof 1; Other 1. **Subjects:** Civil rights, constitutional law, demographics. **Holdings:** 8000 volumes. **Subscriptions:** 50 journals and other serials. **Services:** Interlibrary loan; library not open to the public. **Automated Operations:** Computerized cataloging and acquisitions. **Computerized Information Services:** JURIS, WESTLAW, LEXIS, NEXIS, DIALOG Information Services, LEGI-SLATE, VU/TEXT Information Services, DataTimes, Washington Alert Service, DATALIB, OCLC. **Networks and Consortia:** Member of FEDLINK. **Remarks:** A branch library is maintained at 320 1st St., NW, Rm. 1066, Washington, DC 20530.

★1998★
U.S. Equal Employment Opportunity Commission
Library
1801 L St., NW, Rm. 6502
Washington, DC 20507 Phone: (202)663-4630
Susan D. Taylor, Lib.Dir.

Founded: 1964. **Staff:** Prof 2; Other 3. **Subjects:** Employment discrimination, minorities, women, aged, handicapped, testing, labor law, civil rights. **Special Collections:** Equal Employment Opportunity Commission Publications. **Holdings:** 25,000 books. **Subscriptions:** 300 journals and other serials; 8 newspapers. **Services:** Interlibrary loan; copying; SDI; library open to the public by appointment. **Computerized Information Services:** LEXIS, DIALOG Information Services, WESTLAW, LEGI-SLATE, OCLC. **Networks and Consortia:** Member of FEDLINK. **Publications:** *Library Service and Selected Bibliographies*, brochure. **Remarks:** FAX: (202)663-4629. **Also known as:** EEOC.

★1999★
U.S. National Park Service
Booker T. Washington National Monument
Library
Rte. 3, Box 310
Hardy, VA 24101 Phone: (703)721-2094
Richard Saunders, Chf.Interp. & Rsrcs.Mgt.

Subjects: Booker T. Washington, Black history, local agriculture in the mid-19th century, Appalachian culture. **Special Collections:** Correspondence and documents relating to Burroughs plantation, birthplace of Booker T. Washington. **Holdings:** 600 books; photographs. **Services:** Interlibrary loan; copying (limited); library open to the public.

★2000★
U.S. National Park Service
George Washington Carver National Monument
Library
Box 38
Diamond, MO 64840 Phone: (417)325-4151
Rebecca Harriett, Chf. Ranger

Staff: Prof 1. **Subjects:** George Washington Carver, Black history, national parks. **Special Collections:** Carver Collection (3019 archives and artifacts); original Carver letters (97 items). **Holdings:** 246 books; 130 documents and technical reports; 50 maps and charts; 1505 pictures and study prints; 16 VF drawers of park administrative records. **Subscriptions:** 14 journals and other serials. **Services:** Interlibrary loan; copying; library open to the public for historic research. **Publications:** *Monumental News* (newsletter), quarterly - free upon request. **Special Catalogues:** Carver Collection.

★2001★
U.S. National Park Service
Harpers Ferry National Historical Park
Library
Box 65
Harpers Ferry, WV 25425 Phone: (304)535-6163

Founded: 1962. **Staff:** 1. **Subjects:** John Brown, Armory, Civil War, Black history of education, local and general U.S. history, natural science, military science. **Holdings:** 2168 books; 230 historical newspapers; 224 research reports on historic structures, sites, archeology, and related histories; 53 college catalogs; 58 binders of unpublished correspondence and papers; booklet and document file; historic and modern photographs; 166 reels of microfilm. **Services:** Interlibrary loan; library open to the public by appointment and for reference use only. **Remarks:** FAX: (304)535-6244.

★2002★
U.S. National Park Service
Martin Luther King, Jr. National Historic Site and Preservation District
Library
522 Auburn Ave., NE
Atlanta, GA 30312 Phone: (404)331-3920
Peggy Scherbaum, Pk. Ranger

Subjects: Dr. Martin Luther King, Jr., Civil Rights Movement, Black history, Black Atlanta history, historic preservation. **Holdings:** 200 books. **Services:** Library not open to the public.

★2003★
U.S. Smithsonian Institute
National Museum of African Art
Eliot Elisofon Archives
950 Independence Ave., SW
Washington, DC 20560 Phone: (202)357-4654
Christaud M. Geary, Cur. of Photo.Coll.

Staff: Prof 3. **Subjects:** Africa, African art. **Special Collections:** Eliot Elisofon Collection (1943-1973); Historic Photograph Collection (1860-1930s). **Holdings:** 220,000 color slides; 80,000 Black/White negatives; 70 feature films; 160,000 feet of unedited outtakes, 1860 to present; 30 video cassettes. **Services:** Copying; archives open to the public by appointment. **Computerized Information Services:** Internal databases. **Remarks:** FAX: (202)357-4879.

★2004★
University of Alabama
William Stanley Hoole Special Collections Library
Box 870266
Tuscaloosa, AL 35487-0266 Phone: (205)348-5512
Joyce H. Lamont, Asst. Dean, Spec.Coll.

Founded: 1947. **Staff:** Prof 5; Other 3. **Subjects:** Alabamiana, travels in the South East, southern Americana, early imprints, state documents. **Special Collections:** Rare books (12,500); manuscripts (14 million); university archives (4 million items); Alabamiana (35,000 volumes); Black folk music (250 magnetic tapes); oral history (875 magnetic tapes); maps (15,000). **Holdings:** 46,000 books; 10,000 theses, dissertations, and pamphlets. **Subscriptions:** 135 journals and other serials. **Services:** Interlibrary loan; copying; library open to the public. **Automated Operations:** NOTIS. **Computerized Information Services:** OCLC. **Networks and Consortia:** Member of SOLINET, Network of Alabama Academic Libraries (NAAL), Center for Research Libraries (CRL) Consortia. **Special Indexes:** Finding aids for manuscripts and archival collections. **Remarks:** FAX: (205)348-8833.

★2005★
University of Arkansas, Pine Bluff
John Brown Watson Memorial Library
N. University Blvd.
U.S. Hwy. 79
Pine Bluff, AR 71601 Phone: (501)541-6825
E.J. Fontenette, Libn.

Founded: 1938. **Staff:** 1. **Subjects:** History and biography, emigration, sociology, literature, slavery and emancipation, education, music, religion, economics. **Special Collections:** Afro-American Literature; Paul Laurence Dunbar papers (9 reels of microfilm). **Holdings:** 4615 books; 65 bound periodical volumes; 73 reels of microfilm of the Pittsburgh Courier; 4 recordings; 4 films; 18 overhead transparencies; periodicals on microfilm. **Subscriptions:** 41 journals and other serials; 10 newspapers. **Services:** Interlibrary loan; copying; library open to the public. **Computerized Information Services:** OCLC. **Networks and Consortia:** Member of AMIGOS Bibliographic Council, Inc.

★2006★
University of California, Berkeley
Music Library
240 Morrison Hall
Berkeley, CA 94720 Phone: (415)642-2623
John H. Roberts, Hd.

Founded: 1947. **Staff:** Prof 3; Other 5. **Subjects:** History of Western music; history of opera; 18th century instrumental music; contemporary American and European music; ethnomusicology; Afro-American, Indic, Indonesian, and Japanese music; historiography of music. **Holdings:** 140,000 volumes; 25,000 sound recordings; 6000 early music manuscripts; 11,500 microforms. **Subscriptions:** 1200 journals and other serials. **Services:** Interlibrary loan (through 307 General Library); copying; library open to the public for reference use; circulation available to users with valid borrower's cards. **Automated Operations:** Computerized cataloging. **Computerized Information Services:** RLIN, DIALOG Information Services, OCLC; internal database; InterNet (electronic mail service). **Networks and Consortia:** Member of RLG. **Special Catalogues:** Duckles and Elmer Thematic Catalog of a Manuscript Collection of 18th Century Italian Instrumental Music, 1963; Catalog of the Opera Collections (UCB & UCLA), 1983; Catalog of Pre-1900 Vocal Manuscripts in the Music Library, 1988. **Remarks:** FAX: (415)643-7891. Electronic mail address(es): MUSI@LIBRARY.BERKELEY.EDU (InterNet).

★2007★
University of California, Los Angeles
Center for Afro-American Studies
Library
1232 Campbell Hall
405 Hilgard Ave.
Los Angeles, CA 90024-1545 Phone: (213)825-6060
Dr. M. Belinda Tucker, Act.Dir.

Founded: 1969. **Staff:** Prof 1; Other 4. **Subjects:** Afro-American studies. **Special Collections:** Black history photograph collection (250 items). **Holdings:** 4900 books and bound periodical volumes; 540 35mm slides; 280 photographs; 55 videotapes; 300 audio cassettes; 2050 pamphlets. **Subscriptions:** 52 journals and other serials; 19 newspapers. **Services:** Copying; library open to the public. **Publications:** *Afro-American Library Resources at UCLA*, 1980; *Graduate Research in Afro-American Studies, 1942-1980.*

★2008★
University of California, Los Angeles
Department of Special Collections
University Research Library, Fl. A
Los Angeles, CA 90024-1575 Phone: (213)825-4988
David Zeidberg, Hd.Libn.

Founded: 1946. **Staff:** Prof 6; Other 16. **Subjects:** Includes Blacks in entertainment and literature; **Holdings:** 182,555 volumes; 19.7 million manuscripts; 632 volumes of newspapers; 238,409 pieces of ephemera and clippings; 46,730 pamphlets; 673,225 pictorial items; 2188 historical maps; 12,684 reels of microfilm; 205 sound recordings; 4719 slides; 3028 videotapes. **Subscriptions:** 339 journals and other serials. **Services:** Copying (limited); department open to the public for reference use only. **Automated Operations:** Computerized cataloging, acquisitions, serials, and circulation. **Computerized Information Services:** OCLC; ORION (internal database); BITNET (electronic mail service). Performs searches free of charge. **Publications:** Bibliographies of Henry Miller, Kenneth Rexroth, and Lawrence Durrell. **Remarks:** Alternate telephone number(s): 825-4879. FAX: (213)206-1864. Electronic mail address(es): ECZ5DAV@UCLAMVS. (BITNET).

★2009★
University of California, Santa Barbara
Black Studies Library Unit
Santa Barbara, CA 93106 Phone: (805)893-2922
Sylvia Y. Curtis, Black Studies Libn.

Founded: 1971. **Staff:** Prof 1; Other 1. **Subjects:** African-American studies, African area studies, Caribbean studies, Black literature and history. **Holdings:** 7000 books; 5 VF drawers of newspaper clippings; 5 VF drawers of pamphlets; 100 posters; catalogs from Black colleges and universities. **Subscriptions:** 101 journals and other serials. **Services:** Interlibrary loan; SDI; library open to the public. **Automated Operations:** Computerized cataloging, acquisitions, serials, and circulation. **Computerized Information Services:** DIALOG Information Services, BRS Information Technologies, WILSONLINE; BITNET (electronic mail service). Performs searches on fee basis to members of the University of California community. **Publications:** *New Acquisitions List & Announcements* - to researchers, patrons, and on request. **Remarks:** FAX: (805)893-4676. Electronic mail address(es): SYCSB@UCCMUSA. (BITNET).

★2010★
University of Kansas
Kansas Collection
220 Spencer Research Library
Lawrence, KS 66045-2800 Phone: (913)864-4274
Sheryl K. Williams, Cur.

Founded: 1892. **Staff:** Prof 4; Other 3. **Subjects:** Kansas and Great Plains - social movements, business and economic history, social and cultural history, politics, travel; regional African-American history. **Special Collections:** Overland diaries; Kansas State documents depository; J. J. Pennell Collection of photographs and negatives, 1891-1923 (40,000 items); Wilcox Collection of Contemporary Political Movements, 1960 to present (5000 books; 4000 serials; 80,000 pieces of ephemera); Jules Bourquin Collection of photographs, 1898-1959 (30,000); J. B. Watkins Land Mortgage Company Records, 1864-1946 (627 linear feet) regional African-American history. **Holdings:** 97,323 volumes; 7849 linear feet of manuscripts; 1.1 million photographs; 79,770 glass negatives; 9368 sheets and volumes of maps; 4260 cartoons. **Subscriptions:** 1575 journals and other serials; 50 newspapers. **Services:** Interlibrary loan; copying; collection open to the public. **Automated Operations:** Computerized cataloging and serials. **Computerized Information Services:** OCLC; BITNET (electronic mail service). **Networks and Consortia:** Member of Bibliographical Center for Research, Rocky Mountain Region, Inc. (BCR), Kansas Library Network. **Remarks:** Electronic mail address(es): SWILLIAM@UKANVM (BITNET).

★2011★
University of Maine
Raymond H. Fogler Library
Special Collections Department
Orono, ME 04469 Phone: (207)581-1686
Muriel Sanford, Spec.Coll.Libn.

Founded: 1970. **Staff:** Prof 1.5; Other 2. **Subjects:** State of Maine, maritime history. **Special Collections:** Includes ; O'Brien Collection of American Negro History and Culture (1600 items). **Holdings:** 35,000 books; 475 bound periodical volumes; 1700 archive boxes of manuscripts on Maine; 2500 maps of Maine; 5600 reels of microfilm. **Subscriptions:** 75 journals and other serials; 36 Maine newspapers. **Services:** Interlibrary loan; copying; library open to the public. **Automated Operations:** Computerized public access catalog, acquisitions, serials, and indexing. **Special Catalogues:** A Catalog of the Clinton L. Cole Collection (1972). **Special Indexes:** Maine Times Index; Down East Magazine Index; Maine Campus Index; Elderberry Times Index; Maine Fish and Wildlife Index (each in card or book form); Shaker Quarterly Index. **Remarks:** FAX: (207)581-1653.

★2012★
University of Massachusetts at Amherst
Library
Special Collections and Archives
Amherst, MA 01003 Phone: (413)545-2780

Staff: Prof 1; Other 2. **Subjects:** History of botany and entomology to 1900; historical geography and cartography of Northeastern United States to 1900; history of Massachusetts and New England; antislavery movement in New England; travel and tourism in New England, New York, and eastern Canada; Massachusetts; Afro-American studies; labor and business history. **Special Collections:** Alspach Yeats Collection (600 items); Federal Land Bank Collection (cartography, county maps and atlases; 270 items); Robert Francis Collection (100 items); Binet French Revolution Collection (1524 items); Massachusetts Pamphlet Collection (985 items); Benjamin Smith Lyman Collection (Japan; 2000 items); Papers of W. E. B. Du Bois, Horace Mann Bond, Erasmus Darwin Hudson, John Haigis, Maurice Donahue, Sol Barkin, J. William Belanger, Kenyon Butterfield, Harvey Swados, Robert Francis, Joseph Obrebski, Thomas Copeland; Records of American Writing Paper Co., Northampton Cutlery Co., George H. Gilbert Co., Rodney HuntCo., Granite Cutters International Association, Carpenters unions of Western Massachusetts, New England Joint Board of Textile Workers Union of America, American Dialect Society, Renaissance Diplomatic Documents, University of Massachusetts. **Holdings:** 19,000 books; 6000 linear feet of records, manuscripts, clippings, photographs, maps, building plans, microfilm, audiotapes. **Services:** Copying; collections open to the public. **Computerized Information Services:** OCLC.

★2013★
University of Michigan
Center for the Education of Women
Library
330 E. Liberty
Ann Arbor, MI 48104-2289 Phone: (313)998-7080

Founded: 1965. **Staff:** Prof 1; Other 1. **Subjects:** Women - minorities, employment, education, status, counseling. **Special Collections:** Women's organizations collection (3 cubic feet); women in science series (20 audio- and videotapes). **Holdings:** 700 books; 2600 organizational reports, government publications, dissertations, manuscripts, unpublished papers; 200 bibliographies classified by subject; 3 cubic feet of vocational files; 1 cubic foot of clippings; Michigan Occupational Information System computer software and microfiche. **Subscriptions:** 50 journals and other serials. **Services:** Copying; library open to the public. **Computerized Information Services:** BRS Information Technologies, MERIT/UMNET; electronic mail service. **Publications:** Acquisition list, quarterly; library flyer; *The Job Search*, a selected annotated bibliography; selected topical bibliographies - all free upon request; *Directory of Special Collections/Libraries Independent of the University of Michigan Library System*, irregular. **Remarks:** FAX: (313)936-7787.

★2014★
University of Minnesota
Special Collections and Rare Books Library
466 Wilson Library
309 19th Ave., S.
Minneapolis, MN 55455 Phone: (612)624-3855
Austin J. McLean, Cur.

Staff: Prof 2; Other 1. **Subjects:** History, literature, philosophy, astronomy, 17th century England and Holland, private press books, fortification, Scandinavian travel. **Special Collections:** Includes Black literature (3000 volumes). **Holdings:** 89,665 books and bound periodical volumes. **Subscriptions:** 20 journals and other serials. **Services:** Copying; library open to the public for reference use only. **Networks and Consortia:** Member of RLG. **Special Indexes:** Card indexes to places, dates, printers of books before 1700; card index to private press books by press, printer, designers; card indexes of provenance, manuscripts, signed bindings.

★2015★
University of Mississippi
Archives & Special Collections/Mississippiana
J.D. Williams Library
University, MS 38677 Phone: (601)232-7408
Dr. Thomas M. Verich, Univ.Archv.

Founded: 1975. **Staff:** Prof 1; Other 3. **Subjects:** Mississippi and Southern subjects and authors, Afro-American fiction. **Special Collections:** Lumber archives of lumber industry of southern Mississippi (268 linear feet); William Faulkner Collection (2000 volumes); Wynn Collection of Faulkner editions; Senator Pat Harrison Collection (51 linear feet including photographs); Arthur Palmer Hudson Folklore Collection (5 linear feet); David L. Cohn Collection (12 linear feet); Stark Young Collection (3.5 linear feet); Revolutionary War Letters (1 linear foot); Rayburn Collection of Paper Americana (36 linear feet); Herschel Brickell Collection (4000 manuscript items; 3400 volumes; 150 linear feet); William Faulkner Rowan Oak Literary Manuscript Collection; literary papers of Ellen Douglas, Barry Hannah, and Beth Henley (33 linear feet); James Silver papers (20 linear feet); Aldrich Collection (10 linear feet); William R. Ferris Collection (350 linear feet). **Holdings:** 32,000 books; 3000 bound periodical volumes; 2000 manuscripts; 525 linear feet of University of Mississippi archival materials; 221 linear feet of Thomas G. Abernathy papers; 67 linear feet of Carroll Gartin papers, 1913-1966; 485 linear feet of John E. Rankin papers, 1882-1960; 164 linear feet of William M. Whittington papers, 1878-1962; 180 linear feet of William M. (Fishbait) Miller papers (all papers are unprocessed); 9.5 linear feet of Henry H. Bellamann papers, 1882-1945; 80 linear feet of James W. Garner papers. **Subscriptions:** 150 journals and other serials. **Services:** Copying; archives open to the public.

★2016★
University of Pittsburgh
Afro-American Library
Hillman Library, 1st Fl.
Pittsburgh, PA 15260 Phone: (412)648-7713
P. Wilkins, Interim Hd.

Founded: 1969. **Staff:** Prof 1; Other 1. **Subjects:** History, political science, literature, literary criticism, social sciences, culture and the arts, Blacks in Western Pennsylvania. **Special Collections:** Atlanta University Black Culture Collection (microfilm); W. E. B. Dubois papers (microfilm); papers of the Congress of Racial Equality (microfilm); Black history and landmarks in Western Pennsylvania (80 slides). **Holdings:** 15,860 volumes; 6 VF drawers of clippings and pamphlets. **Subscriptions:** 85 journals and other serials; 27 newspapers. **Services:** Interlibrary loan; library open to the public; service desk open 9-5 only. **Automated Operations:** Computerized public access catalog, cataloging, acquisitions, serials, and circulation. **Networks and Consortia:** Member of Pittsburgh Regional Library Center (PRLC), Oakland Library Consortium. **Remarks:** FAX: (412)648-1245.

★2017★
University of Rochester
Government Documents and Microtext Center
Rush Rhees Library
Rochester, NY 14627 Phone: (716)275-4484
Kathleen E. Wilkinson, Govt.Docs.Libn.

Staff: Prof 1; Other 4. **Subjects:** Documents - U.S. Congress, U.S. Bureau of the Census, New York State, women's studies, Black studies, North American Indians, American and British literature. **Special Collections:** Goldsmiths'-Kress Collection (economic literature); slavery; papers of William Henry Seward and of the National Association for the Advancement of Colored People (NAACP); Early English Books; American Fiction; History of Women; Early British Periodicals. **Holdings:** 380 books; 391,000 uncataloged government documents in paper; 914,200 uncataloged government documents in microform; 2.4 million other microforms. **Services:** Interlibrary loan; copying; center open to the public. **Computerized Information Services:** DIALOG Information Services, BRS Information Technologies. **Remarks:** FAX: (716)473-1906.

★2018★
University of the District of Columbia
Georgia/Harvard Campus
Harvard Street Library
1100 Harvard St., NW
Washington, DC 20009 Phone: (202)673-7018
Melba Broome, Supv.

Staff: Prof 3; Other 1. **Subjects:** Education, human ecology. **Special Collections:** Trevor Arnett Library of Black Culture (8000 reels of microfilm); Miner-Wilson Collection (2000 rare books); legislative history of Federal City College. **Holdings:** 111,000 books; 10,000 bound periodical volumes; 150,000 microforms; archives. **Subscriptions:** 500 journals and other serials; 6 newspapers. **Services:** Interlibrary loan; copying; library open to the public with restrictions. **Networks and Consortia:** Member of Consortium of Universities of the Washington Metropolitan Area. **Special Catalogues:** Catalog of Miner-Wilson Collection; District of Columbia Teachers College Library (book catalog).

★2019★
University of the District of Columbia
Learning Resources Division
4200 Connecticut Ave., NW
MB 4102
Washington, DC 20008 Phone: (202)282-7536
Albert J. Casciero, Dir.

Staff: 68. **Special Collections:** Human Relations Area Files (microfiche); African/Afro-Hispanic/American Media Collection (25 films; 97 books; 2 VF drawers of clippings); Atlanta University Black Culture Collection; Water Resources (625 items); University of D.C. archives (513 linear feet); slavery source materials (962 microfiche); Schombury Clipping File (9500 microfiche). **Holdings:** 491,530 books; 564,738 microfiche. **Subscriptions:** 2769 journals and other serials; 25 newspapers. **Services:** Interlibrary loan; copying; SDI; division open to the public with restrictions. **Automated Operations:** Computerized cataloging and circulation. **Computerized Information Services:** DIALOG Information Services, OCLC. Performs searches on fee basis. Contact Person: Eva-Maria Vidaeus, 282-3091. **Networks and Consortia:** Member of CAPCON, Washington Research Library Consortium. **Publications:** Access brochures. **Remarks:** FAX: (202)282-3102.

★2020★
University of Toledo
Ward M. Canaday Center
William S. Carlson Library
Toledo, OH 43606 Phone: (419)537-4480
Richard W. Oram, Dir.

Staff: Prof 3; Other 2. **Subjects:** 20th century American poetry, Southern authors, and Black American literature; university history; history of books and printing; Toledo glass industry. **Special Collections:** Ezra Pound Collection (400 volumes); William Faulkner Collection (500 volumes); Black American Poetry, 1920 to present (1000 volumes); William Dean Howells Collection (150 volumes); Herbert W. Martin Collection (15 feet); Etheridge Knight Collection (10 feet); Libbey-Owens-Ford Corporation archives (150 feet); Richard T. Gosser Collection (20 feet); Jean Gould Collection (11 feet); university archives (2000 feet); J. H. Leigh Hunt (100 volumes); Scott Nearing (50 volumes); T. S. Eliot (200 volumes); William Carlos Williams (75 volumes); Marianne Moore (75 volumes); Broadside Press (200 items); Women's Social History, 1840-1920 (1200 volumes). **Holdings:** 25,000 books; 3000 linear feet of archives and manuscripts. **Services:** Copying; center open to the public. **Automated Operations:** Computerized public access catalog and cataloging. **Computerized Information Services:** BITNET (electronic mail service). **Publications:** *Friends of the University of Toledo Libraries*; exhibition catalogs. **Special Catalogues:** Catalog to special collections (card). **Remarks:** FAX: (419)537-2726. Electronic mail address(es): FAC1734@UOFT1 (BITNET).

★2021★
Virginia State University
Johnston Memorial Library
Special Collections
Box JJ
Petersburg, VA 23803 Phone: (804)524-5040
Catherine V. Bland, Dean, Lib.Serv.

Founded: 1882. **Special Collections:** U.S. Government document depository; Black studies; instructional materials; manuscripts. **Holdings:** Figures not available. **Services:** Interlibrary loan; copying; collections open to the public with restrictions. **Automated Operations:** Computerized cataloging. **Computerized Information Services:** DIALOG Information Services, OCLC. **Networks and Consortia:** Member of SOLINET.

★2022★
Virginia Union University
William J. Clark Library
Special Collections
1500 N. Lombardy St.
Richmond, VA 23220 Phone: (804)257-5820
Vonita W. Dandridge, Libn.

Founded: 1865. ST 6. **Special Collections:** Afro-American materials, with emphasis on Richmond Black history. **Holdings:** 8,765 volumes. **Services:** Interlibrary loan; copying; collections open to the public with special permit for reference use only. **Automated Operations:** Computerized cataloging, acquisitions, circulation, and serials. **Computerized Information Services:** Cooperative College Library Center (CCLC). **Remarks:** FAX: (804)257-5818.

★2023★
Wayne State University
Folklore Archive
448 Purdy Library
Detroit, MI 48202 Phone: (313)577-4053
Janet L. Langlois, Dir.

Founded: 1939. **Staff:** Prof 1; Other 2. **Subjects:** Oral, customary, and material culture of urban, occupational, and ethnic groups. **Special Collections:** Includes Afro-American Folklore Collections; International Library of African Music (authentic tribal music); Urban Legends: Video Anecdotes of Contemporary Folklore; **Holdings:** 200 books; 3000 manuscripts, 1000 audiotape recordings, 460 phonograph records. **Services:** Copying; archive open to the public.

★2024★
West Virginia Library Commission
Film Services Department
Science and Cultural Center
Charleston, WV 25305 Phone: (304)348-3976
Steve Fesenmaier, Hd. Film Serv.

Founded: 1976. **Staff:** Prof 2; Other 4. **Special Collections:** Includes Black history and culture (200 films). **Holdings:** 5000 16mm sound films. **Subscriptions:** 12 journals and other serials. **Services:** Interlibrary loan (within state); department open to the public. **Publications:** *WVLC Film Services Newsletter*, quarterly - to WV public libraries; *Pickflick Papers* (online). **Special Catalogues:** Video Catalog, 1989.

★2025★
Western Historical Manuscript Collection
State Historical Society of Missouri Manuscripts Joint Collection
Thomas Jefferson Library
University of Missouri
8001 Natural Bridge Rd.
St. Louis, MO 63121 Phone: (314)553-5143
Ann Morris, Assoc.Dir.

Founded: 1968. **Staff:** Prof 2; Other 2. **Subjects:** History - state and local, women's, Afro-American, ethnic, education, immigration; socialism; 19th century science; environment; peace; religion; Missouri politics; social reform and welfare; photography; journalism; business; labor. **Holdings:** 4500 linear feet of manuscripts, photographs, oral history tapes, and university archives. **Services:** Interlibrary loan (limited); copying of manuscripts, tape recordings, and photographs; library open to the public with restricted circulation. **Special Indexes:** Unpublished inventories to collections in repository. **Remarks:** Collection contains the manuscript holdings of both the University of Missouri and the State Historical Society of Missouri. Offices are located at the four branches of the University of Missouri. Materials may be loaned among the four branches.

★2026★
Western Interstate Commission for Higher Education Library
Drawer P
Boulder, CO 80301 Phone: (303)541-0285
Eileen Conway, Cons.Dir.

Founded: 1955. **Staff:** Prof 1; Other 1. **Subjects:** Higher education, mental health and human services, nursing, minority education. **Holdings:** 7000 books and documents; 1000 volumes of unbound periodicals; 2000 documents on microfiche. **Subscriptions:** 280 journals and other serials; 10 newspapers. **Services:** Interlibrary loan; copying; SDI; library open to the public. **Automated Operations:** Computerized public access catalog, serials, and circulation. **Computerized Information Services:** DIALOG Information Services. Performs searches on fee basis. **Publications:** acquisitions list, monthly - for internal distribution only.

★2027★
Wilberforce University
Rembert Stokes Learning Center
Archives and Special Collections
Wilberforce, OH 45384-1003 Phone: (513)376-2911
Jean Mulhern, Lib.Dir.

Staff: Prof 2; Other 3. **Subjects:** African Methodist Episcopal (A.M.E.) Church history; books by and about Blacks, 19th century; history of Wilberforce University. **Special Collections:** A.M.E. Church conference minutes; papers of Bishop Reverdy Cassius Ransom, university president W. S. Scarborough, and Wilberforce professor Milton S. J. Wright. **Holdings:** 2000 books; 20 reels of microfilm; 10,000 uncataloged items. **Services:** Copying; collections open to the public by appointment. **Networks and Consortia:** Member of Southwest Ohio Council for Higher Education (SOCHE). **Publications:** Printed guides to some parts of collection.

★2028★
Women's History Research Center, Inc.
Women's History Library
2325 Oak St.
Berkeley, CA 94708 Phone: (415)524-1582
Laura X, Dir.

Founded: 1968. **Staff:** Prof 2; Other 20. **Subjects:** Women's health and mental health, women and law, Black and Third World women, female artists, children, films by and/or about women, Soviet women. **Special**

Collections: International Women's History Archive (850 periodical titles on microfilm). **Holdings:** 2000 books; 300 tapes; 54 reels of microfilm on health and law; 90 reels of microfilm of women's periodicals in Herstory Collection. **Services:** Library not open to the public. **Publications:** *Directory of Films by and/or about Women; Female Artists Directory; Women & Health/Mental Health, Women & Law, and Herstory* serials (microfilm) - all for sale.

★2029★
Women's Resource and Action Center
Sojourner Truth Women's Resource Library
130 N. Madison
Iowa City, IA 52242 Phone: (319)335-1486
Laura K. Stokes, Libn.

Founded: 1976. **Staff:** Prof 1; Other 5. **Subjects:** Feminism. **Special Collections:** Complete holdings of *Ain't I A Woman*, 1970-1973 (feminist periodical). **Holdings:** 1700 books. **Subscriptions:** 100 journals and other serials. **Services:** Library open to the public. **Publications:** *Women's Resource & Action Center News*, monthly - by subscription and free local distribution.

★2030★
Women's Resource Center Library
250 Golden Bear Ctr.
University of California
Berkeley, CA 94720 Phone: (415)643-8367
Dorothy Lazard, Lib.Coord.

Founded: 1973. **Staff:** Prof 1; Other 2. **Subjects:** Women's studies, women and work, financial aid, comparable worth, women of color, international issues. **Special Collections:** Catherine Scholten Collection on Women in American History (100 books); Bea Bain Collection on the Women's Movement (100 books); Margaret Monroe Drews Collection of Working Papers (the status of women in the U.S., 1950-1970; 12 VF drawers). **Holdings:** 3000 books; 20,000 other uncataloged items. **Subscriptions:** 60 journals and other serials. **Services:** Library open to the public for reference use only. **Computerized Information Services:** GLADIS, MELVYL (internal databases). **Publications:** Acquisitions list, quarterly; bibliographies, irregular. **Special Catalogues:** Tape catalog; journal and newsletter catalog (both on cards). **Special Indexes:** Vertical file index. **Remarks:** Alternate telephone number(s): (415)643-5727.

★2031★
Yale University
African Collection
Sterling Memorial Library, Rm. 317
New Haven, CT 06520 Phone: (203)432-1883
J. Moore D. Crossey, Cur.

Founded: 1963. **Staff:** Prof 1; Other 2. **Subjects:** Africa - languages, literature, history, ethnography, anthropology, art, politics, government, religion, education, economics, law, social conditions, civilizations, philosophy, natural history, big game hunting, travel, topography, mining. **Special Collections:** Howell Wright Collection of Rhodesiana and South Africana (5000 volumes). **Holdings:** 90,000 books; 85,000 bound periodical volumes; 150 manuscript collections (original and microform); 1800 reels of microfilm of newspapers, pamphlet collections, government documents; photographs; posters; postcards; pamphlets; broadsides; maps. **Subscriptions:** 1000 journals and other serials; 35 newspapers. **Services:** Interlibrary loan; copying; collection open to the public with restrictions. **Automated Operations:** Computerized cataloging, acquisitions, serials, and circulation. **Networks and Consortia:** Member of RLG, Center for Research Libraries (CRL) Consortia, Hartford Consortium for Higher Education. **Special Catalogues:** Catalog of Africa-related materials (1965 to present) arranged by African countries and/or subjects (card).

★2032★
Yale University
Beinecke Rare Book and Manuscript Library
Wall & High Sts.
New Haven, CT 06520 Phone: (203)432-2977
Ralph W. Franklin, Dir.

Founded: 1963. **Staff:** Prof 20; Other 20. **Subjects:** Includes Afro-American arts and letters. **Special Collections:** Includes Langston Hughes, Richard Wright. **Holdings:** 495,279 volumes; 2.25 million manuscripts. **Services:** Copying; library open to the public. **Automated Operations:** Computerized index (ZyIndex). **Networks and Consortia:** Member of RLG, Center for Research Libraries (CRL) Consortia, Hartford Consortium for Higher Education. **Publications:** Yale University Library Gazette. **Remarks:** FAX: (203)432-4047.

(5) MUSEUMS AND OTHER CULTURAL ORGANIZATIONS

Entries in this chapter are arranged alphabetically by organization name within states. See the User's Guide at the front of this directory for additional information.

Alabama

★2033★
George Washington Carver Museum
1212 Old Montgomery Rd.
PO Drawer 10
Tuskegee Institute, AL 36088 Phone: (205)727-6390
Willie C. Madison, Superintendent and CEO
Remarks: Collections include awards, furnishings and personal items of Dr. George Washington Carver.

★2034★
Macon County Fine Arts Manifesto
104 Frazier St.
Tuskegee, AL 36083 Phone: (205)727-3029
Barbara Danner, Pres.
Remarks: Provides workshops in dance, drama, and the visual arts.

★2035★
Tuskegee Institute National Historic Site
1212 Old Montgomery Rd.
PO Drawer 10
Tuskegee Institute, AL 36088 Phone: (205)727-6390
Willie C. Madison, Superintendent
Remarks: Collections include items pertaining to Dr. George Washington Carver and Booker T. Washington.

Arizona

★2036★
Black Theater Troupe
333 E. Portland St.
Phoenix, AZ 85004 Phone: (602)258-8128
Remarks: Presents four to five productions a year. Conducts workshops and an eight week workshop/touring program in the summer.

California

★2037★
African American Drama Company of California
394 5th Ave.
San Francisco, CA 94118 Phone: (415)386-2832

★2038★
African-American Historical & Cultural Society
Fort Mason Center, Bldg. C
San Francisco, CA 94123 Phone: (415)441-0640
Charles Mason, Man.

★2039★
African American Historical Society
Fort Mason Center Bldg. C, No. 165
San Francisco, CA 94123 Phone: (415)441-0640
Remarks: Interested in the role of the African American in art and history. Houses a museum and gallery.

★2040★
Afro American Cultural Center
2560 W. 54th St.
Los Angeles, CA 90058 Phone: (213)299-6124

★2041★
Black Repertory Group
3201 Adeline St.
Berkeley, CA 94703 Phone: (415)652-2120
Remarks: Presents five productions a year by Black playwrights and presents a series of one-act plays by local writers. Conducts workshops in acting, dance, and creative writing.

★2042★
Brockman Gallery
4334 Degnan Blvd.
Los Angeles, CA 90008 Phone: (213)294-3766
Alonzo Davis, Dir.

★2043★
California Afro-American Museum
600 State Dr., Exposition Park
Los Angeles, CA 90037 Phone: (213)744-7432
Bridget Cullerton, Dir.
Remarks: Exhibitions include items relating to Afro-American heritage.

★2044★
Center for Afro-American History
5606 San Pablo Ave.
Oakland, CA 94608 Phone: (415)658-3158
Lawrence Crouchett, Dir.
Remarks: Researches national and international Black history. Collections include books, pictures, documents, and artifacts.

★2045★
Ebony Museum of Art
30 Jack Londo Blvd., Ste. 209
Oakland, CA 94607 Phone: (415)763-0141
Aissatoui Vernita, Exec.Dir.
Remarks: Black oriented exhibitions.

★2046★
Harambee Dance Ensemble
3026 57th Ave.
Oakland, CA 94605 Phone: (415)532-8558
Akili Denianke, Dir.
Remarks: Perfoms African dance and music from the west coast of Africa, the Caribbean, and the United States.

★2047★
Museum of African American Art
4005 Crenshaw Blvd., 3rd Fl.
Los Angeles, CA 90008 Phone: (213)294-7071
Joyce Henderson, Acting Dir.
Remarks: Exhibits art of Africans and African decendants. Collections include: traditional sculpture from Southeast, West and East Africa; paintings, prints, and sculptures of contemporary American artists; and Harlem Renaissance art.

★2048★
Oakland Ensemble Theater
1615 Broadway, Ste. 800
Oakland, CA 94612 Phone: (415)763-7774
Remarks: Explores contemporary American life through the sensibilities, idiom, and world-view of Black Americans.

Colorado

★2049★
Black American West Museum and Heritage Center
3091 California St.
Denver, CO 80207 Phone: (303)292-2566
Joe Mangrum, Dir.
Remarks: Collections include items relating to Black culture.

★2050★
EDEN Theatrical Workshop
1570 Gilpin St.
Denver, CO 80218 Phone: (303)321-2320
Lucy M. Walker, Pres.
Remarks: Provides funds in support of visual, performing, and literary arts projects with an emphasis on Black culture.

Connecticut

★2051★
Connecticut Afro-American Historical Society
444 Orchard St.
New Haven, CT 06511
George Bellinger, Pres.
Remarks: Museum exhibits reflect the Afro-American cultural experience.

★2052★
Talking Drums
400 Plaza Middlesex
Middletown, CT 06457 Phone: (203)347-4304
Wes Brown, Administrative Dir.
Remarks: West African music and dance company. Presents performances, classes, workshops, lectures, and demonstrations of traditional and contemporary West African music and dance.

Delaware

★2053★
Afro-American Historical Society of Delaware
512 E. 4th St.
Wilmington, DE 19801 Phone: (302)984-1421
Harmon R. Carey, Pres.

District of Columbia

★2054★
African Cultural Foundation
731 Rock Creek Church Rd., NW
Washington, DC 20010 Phone: (202)882-2232

★2055★
African Heritage Center for African Dance and Music (AHCADM)
4018 Minnesota Ave. NE
Washington, DC 20019 Phone: (202)399-5252
Melvin Deal, Founding Dir.
Remarks: Serves as a multicultural center for instruction and training in traditional West African dance, music, and dramatic ritualistic forms; also serves as institution for cross-cultural workshops between ethnic groups. Receives traveling artists from abroad for workshops and exchange. Presents concerts; conducts lecture demo-performances. Teaches modern and jazz dance. Maintains art gallery and a collection of traditional African musical instruments. Provides children's services; sponsors charitable program.

★2056★
Anacostia Museum
1901 Fort Pl., SE
Washington, DC 20020 Phone: (202)287-3183
John R. Kinard, Dir.
Remarks: Explores American history in relation to the Afro-American experience and culture.

★2057★
Andrew Cacho African Drummers and Dancers
PO Box 15282
Washington, DC 20003 Phone: (202)889-0350
Andrew Cacho, Dir.

★2058★
Association for the Study of Afro-American Life and History
Carter G. Woodson Center
1407 14th St., NW
Washington, DC 20005 Phone: (202)667-2822
Karen Robinson, Exec.Dir.

★2059★
Bethune Museum-Archives
National Historic Site
1318 Vermont Ave., NW
Washington, DC 20005 Phone: (202)332-1233
Dr. Bettye Collier-Thomas, Exec.Dir.
Remarks: Offers permanent and changing exhibitions and preserves the records of Black women and their organizations. Interested in promoting the role of Black women in America through educational programs.

★2060★
Black Film Institute
University of the District of Columbia
Carnegie Bldg.
8th St. & Mt. Vernon Pl., NW
Washington, DC 20001 Phone: (202)727-2396
Remarks: Exhibition and discussion forum on Blacks and the Third World. Shows films and presents lectures on campus and at community sites, prisons, schools, and senior centers.

★2061★
Evans-Tibbs Collection
1910 Vermont Ave., NW
Washington, DC 20001 Phone: (202)234-8164
Thurlow E. Tibbs Jr., Dir.

★2062★
Frederick Douglass National Historic Site
1411 W. St., SE
Wahington, DC 20020 Phone: (202)426-5961
Carnell Poole, Site Man.
Remarks: Furnishings, documents, and personal items of Frederick Douglass.

★2063★
Howard University
Gallery of Art
2455 6th St., NW
Washington, DC 20059 Phone: (202)806-7070
Tritobi Benjamin, Dir.
Remarks: Collections include Afro-American paintings, sculpture, and graphic art.

★2064★
Pin Points Theater
4353 Dubois Pl., SE
Washington, DC 20019 Phone: (202)582-0002
Ersky Freeman Jr., Pres.
Remarks: Uses academic subjects such as biology, history, and math and puts them into theatrical formats that "edu-train." The play "1001 Black Inventions" illustrates the lives of Black inventors.

★2065★
Sign of the Times Cultural Workshop & Gallery, Inc.
605 56th St., NE
Washington, DC 20019 Phone: (202)399-3400
George S. Martin, Dir.

★2066★
U.S. Smithsonian Institute
National Museum of African Art
950 Independence Ave., SW
Washington, DC 20560 Phone: (202)357-4600
Sylvia H. Williams, Dir.
Remarks: Collections include film footage on African art and culture, wood metal, ceramic, ivory, and fiber objects of African art.

Florida

★2067★
Afro-Carib American Cultural Center
4511 NW 25th Pl.
Lauderhill, FL 33313 Phone: (305)739-1015
Aina Olomo, Dir.

★2068★
Appleton Museum of Art/The Appleton Cultural Center
4333 E. Silver Springs Blvd.
Ocala, FL 32670 Phone: (904)236-5050
Sandra Talarico, Dir.
Remarks: Collections include African arts.

★2069★
Black Archives Research Center and Museum
c/o Florida A&M University
PO Box 809
Tallahassee, FL 32307 Phone: (904)599-3020
James N. Eaton, Exec.Dir.
Remarks: Collections include documents and other items relating to the Afro-Americann experience.

★2070★
Black Heritage Museum
PO Box 570327
Miami, FL 33257-0327 Phone: (305)252-3535
Mrs. Priscilla G. Stephens Kruize, Pres.

★2071★
Gallery Antiqua
5138 Biscayne Blvd.
Miami, FL 33137 Phone: (305)759-5355
Caleb A. Davis, Dir.

Georgia

★2072★
Herndon Home
587 University Pl., NW
Atlanta, GA 30314 Phone: (404)581-9813
Carole Merritt, Dir.

★2073★
Jomandi Productions
1444 Mayson St., NE
Atlanta, GA 30308 Phone: (404)876-6346
Gloria Lockhart, Managing Dir.
Remarks: Presents four productions a year on universal themes viewed from the Black perspective.

★2074★
Just Us Theater Company
1058 Oglethorpe Ave., SW
Atlanta, GA 30303 Phone: (404)753-2399
Remarks: Presents and tours works by Black dramatists.

★2075★
Uncle Remus Museum (URM)
PO Box 184
Eatonton, GA 31024 Phone: (404)485-6856
Madeleine Gooch, Sec.
Remarks: Persons interested in Joel Chandler Harris (1848-1908) and his folklore tales of Uncle Remus. Purposes are to: honor the memory of Harris; keep his works before the public; distribute the Uncle Remus stories. Maintains museum in an old slave cabin depicting an antebellum Southern plantation and the imaginary world of Uncle Remus.

★2076★
U.S. National Park Service
Martin Luther King, Jr. National Historic Site and Preservation District
522 Auburn Ave., NE
Atlanta, GA 30312 Phone: (404)331-5190
Randolph Scott, Superintendent
Remarks: Neighborhood of Dr. Martin Luther King, Jr.; includes birthplace, childhood home, church, and gravesite, Research is carried out on the Civil Rights Movement and Black history.

Illinois

★2077★
African-American Arts Alliance of Chicago
7558 S. Chicago Ave.
Chicago, IL 60619 Phone: (312)288-5100
Remarks: Consortium of art groups and individuals. Publishes a newsletter, provides technical assistance, and sponsors performances.

★2078★
Afro-American Genealogical & Historical Society
DuSable Museum of African-American History
740 E. 56th Pl.
Chicago, IL 60637 Phone: (312)947-0600
Hezekiah Baker, Pres.
Remarks: Collections include African and Afro-American art, sculpture, photographs, and books.

★2079★
Chicago City Theater Company/Joel Hall Dancers
1225 W. School
Chicago, IL 60657 Phone: (312)880-1002
Joel Hall, Co-Dir.
Remarks: Multi-racial, ethnic dance and theater companies featuring jazz and contemporary styles. Features new works by Black choreographers.

★2080★
Downstate Afro-American Hall of Fame—Museum
309 S. DuSable
Peoria, IL 61605 Phone: (309)673-2206
Harlan Neal, Pres.

★2081★
Malcolm X College
1900 W. Van Buren St.
Chicago, IL 60612 Phone: (312)738-5832
Remarks: Houses African cultural artifacts.

Indiana

★2082★
Indiana University
Art Museum
Bloomington, IN 47405 Phone: (812)855-5445
Adelheid M. Gealt, Dir.
Remarks: Curatorial and student research is conducted in major areas represented by the Museum collections: ancient art, Asian art, Western art, photography, African art, Oceanic art, and art of the Americas.

★2083★
Madame Walker Urban Life Center
617 Indiana Ave.
Indianapolis, IN 46202 Phone: (317)236-2099
Josephine Weathers, Dir.
Remarks: Now a historic landmark, originally this structure housed Madame Walker's cosmetic company.

Iowa

★2084★
Gateway Dance Theater
1225 Stephenson Way
Des Moines, IA 50314 Phone: (515)282-8696
Lee Furgerson, Dir.
Remarks: A Black dance group that presents performances and workshops.

Kansas

★2085★
First National Black Historical Society of Kansas
601 N. Water
Wichita, KS 67201 Phone: (316)262-7651
Ruby Parker, Dir.
Remarks: Exhibits include African and historical artifacts, a doll collection, and paintings by John Allen. Also offers traveling exhibitions.

Louisiana

★2086★
Alliance for Community Theaters
3936 Magazine St.
New Orleans, LA 70115 Phone: (504)897-0411
Deborah Smith
Remarks: Acts as a support organization for local Black theater programs.

Maryland

★2087★
Baltimore's Black American Museum
1765 Carswell St.
Baltimore, MD 21218 Phone: (301)243-9600
Frank Richardson, Dir.

★2088★
Banneker-Douglass Museum
84 Franklin St.
Annapolis, MD 21401 Phone: (301)974-2893
Steven Newsome, Dir.
Remarks: Exhibits art dealing with the Black experience in America.

★2089★
Great Blacks in Wax Museum
1603 E. North Ave.
Baltimore, MD 21213 Phone: (301)563-3404
Tulani Salahu-din, Dir.

★2090★
Maryland Museum of African Art
8510 Vantage Point Rd.
Ellicott City, MD 21043 Phone: (301)730-7105
Doris Ligon, Dir.

Massachusetts

★2091★
Harriet Tubman Gallery and Resource Center
United SouthEnd Settlement
566 Columbus Ave.
Boston, MA 02118 Phone: (617)536-8610
Frieda Garcia, Dir.
Remarks: Exhibits items relating to Afro-American history during Harriet Tubman's lifetime.

★2092★
Museum of Afro-American History
Abiel Smith School
46 Joy St.
Boston, MA 02114 Phone: (617)742-1854
Monica A. Fairbairn, Dir.
Remarks: A charitable nonprofit institution established "to locate, collect, conserve, preserve, and secure for exhibition and research, historical material pertaining to the life, thought, material culture, and heritage of Afro-Americans in New England." The majority of the collection pertains to 19th and 20th century history. Maintains library of films and filmstrips on Afro-American history. Provides guided tours of a 19th century Black neighborhood (the Black Heritage Trail) and a 20th century Black community (Roxbury Heritage Trail).

★2093★
National Center of Afro-American Artists
300 Walnut Ave.
Boston, MA 02119 Phone: (617)442-8014
Edmund B. Gaither, Dir. and Curator
Remarks: Multi-media art center featuring dance, theater, visual arts, film, and educational programs. Collections include paintings, prints, and graphics of Afro-American artists.

★2094★
Parting Ways; The Museum of Afro-American Ethnohistory
130 Court St., Rear
Plymouth, MA 02361 Phone: (617)746-6028
Diane Haynes, Exec.Dir.
Remarks: Black history collections include documents and photographs of an early Black family in the Plymouth area, underground railroad collection, and a manuscript collection.

★2095★
Wendell Street Gallery
17 Wendell St.
Cambridge, MA 02138 Phone: (617)864-9294
Remarks: Features the work of distinguished Black artists.

Michigan

★2096★
Afro American Studio Theater
17138 Hickory
Detroit, MI 48205 Phone: (313)527-0277
Remarks: Offers performances exploring the concerns of the area's Black community.

★2097★
Black Theatre Network
PO Box 11502, Fisher Bldg. Sta.
Detroit, MI 48211
Addell Austin Anderson, Pres.

★2098★
Detroit Black Arts Alliance
13217 Livernois
Detroit, MI 48238-3162 Phone: (313)931-3427
David Rambeau, Dir.

★2099★
Detroit Historical Museum
African-American Businesses in Detroit Exhibit
5401 Woodward
Detroit, MI 48202 Phone: (313)833-1805
Thomas Dietz, Curator of Urban History
Remarks: Exhibit of historical artifacts and memorabilia from early Black businesses in Detroit; one-year exhibit opens February 1992.

★2100★
Graystone International Jazz Museum
3000 E. Grand Blvd.
Detroit, MI 48202 Phone: (313)871-0234
James T. Jenkins, Pres.

★2101★
Harmonie Park Playhouse and Actors Lab
279 E. Grand River
Detroit, MI 48226 Phone: (313)965-2480
Maggie Porter, Founder/Exec.Dir.
Remarks: Offers studio workshops for a professional interracial acting ensemble. Minority playwrights are highlighted, although all works are considered.

★2102★
Historic Fort Wayne
6325 W. Jefferson
Detroit, MI 48207 Phone: (313)297-9360
Remarks: An 83-acre former military post which includes the National Museum of the Tuskegee Airmen.

★2103★
McCree Theater and Performing Arts Center
115 E. Pierson Rd.
Flint, MI 48505 Phone: (313)785-3475
Remarks: Conducts workshops in the arts serving the area's Black community.

★2104★
Michigan Ethnic Heritage Center
60 Farnsworth
Detroit, MI 48202 Phone: (313)832-7400

★2105★
Michigan Opera Theater
6519 2nd Ave.
Detroit, MI 48202 Phone: (313)874-7850
Remarks: Offers a Black outreach program for schools, audiences, and teachers. Program explores the Black Heritage in western music.

★2106★
Motown Museum Historical Foundation
2648 W. Grand Blvd.
Detroit, MI 48208 Phone: (313)867-0991
Remarks: Exhibits include photographs of Black recording artists and other Motown memorabilia.

★2107★
Museum of African American History
301 Frederick Douglass St.
Detroit, MI 48202 Phone: (313)833-9800
Marian J. Moore, Exec.Dir.
Remarks: Dedicated to preserving, documenting, interpreting, and exhibiting the cultural heritage of African-Americans and their ancestors. Serves as a learning and resource center; collects and documents contributions of Black people. Offers permanent and traveling exhibits. Conducts workshops, seminars, and lecture series. Maintains reference library containing books, films and audiotapes of African world history, art, and culture.

★2108★
TABS Center
3721 S. Westnedge Ave., Ste. 222
Kalamazoo, MI 49008 Phone: (616)342-1382
LeAndre Jones, Dir.
Remarks: Presents four theater and TV programs for community organizations. Goal is to build morale and encourage talent in the Black community.

★2109★
Your Heritage House
110 E. Ferry
Detroit, MI 48202 Phone: (313)871-1667
Josephine H. Love, Dir.
Remarks: Exhibits a Black heritage collection.

Minnesota

★2110★
Gospel Workshop of America
3029 3rd Ave., S.
Minneapolis, MN 55408 Phone: (612)823-8706
K. L. Robinson, Chap. Rep.
Remarks: Presents five major gospel concerts a year highlighting mostly Black gospel composers. A division of the Gospel Music Workshop of America.

★2111★
Pillsbury House/Cultural Arts
3501 Chicago Ave., S.
Minneapolis, MN 55407 Phone: (612)824-0708
David T. Anderson, Dir.
Remarks: Provides art programming for predominately Black neighborhoods.

★2112★
Whittier Writers' Workshop
PO Box 1042
Minneapolis, MN 55440 Phone: (612)872-8694
Carolyn Holbrook-Montgomery, Dir.
Remarks: Offers specialized programming for Black American writers in the Minneapolis-St. Paul area.

Mississippi

★2113★
Black Arts Music Society
PO Box 3214
Jackson, MS 39207 Phone: (601)354-1049
John Reese, Pres.
Remarks: Books jazz concerts featuring top regional artists.

★2114★
Smith Robertson Museum and Cultural Center
PO Box 3259
Jackson, MS 39207 Phone: (601)960-1457
Jessie Mosley, Dir.
Remarks: Collections include artwork with Afro-American themes and artwork of Black artists.

Missouri

★2115★
Black Archives of Mid-America
2033 Vine St.
Kansas City, MO 64108 Phone: (816)483-1300
Horace M. Peterson III, Dir.
Remarks: Collections include Black art, paintings, and sculptures.

★2116★
Black Repertory Company
634 N. Grand
St. Louis, MO 63106 Phone: (314)534-3807
Remarks: Offers theater and dance performances. Sponsors acting and dance classes and tours.

★2117★
Charlie Parker Memorial Foundation
Academy of the Arts
4605 The Paseo
Kansas City, MO 64110 Phone: (816)924-2200
Eddie Baker, Exec.Dir.
Remarks: Preserves jazz heritage through studies, performances, and workshops by internationally recognized artists. Offers youth study programs.

★2118★
St. Louis Science Center
5050 Oakland
St. Louis, MO 63110 Phone: (314)289-4400
Dwight S. Crandell, Exec.Dir.
Remarks: Collections include ethnic miniatures.

★2119★
Vaughn Cultural Center
1408 N. Kings Hwy., Ste. 205
St. Louis, MO 63113 Phone: (314)361-0111
Robert Watson, Dir.

Nebraska

★2120★
Emmy Gifford Children's Theater
3504 Center St.
Omaha, NE 68105 Phone: (402)345-4849
Nancy K. Duncan, Exec.Dir.
Remarks: Presents original productions by Black performers and playwrights.

★2121★
Great Plains Black Museum
2213 Lake St.
Omaha, NE 68110 Phone: (402)345-2212
Bertha Calloway, Exec.Dir.
Remarks: Founded by the Negro Historical Society. Contains gallery rooms and offers special exhibits, lectures, tours, and resource material.

New Jersey

★2122★
African Art Museum of the S.M.A. Fathers
23 Bliss Ave.
Tenafly, NJ 07670 Phone: (201)567-0450
Rev. Thomas Conlon S.M.A, Dir.
Remarks: Explores the transition of African art to the Americas. Exhibits sculpture, masks, textiles, household utensils, musical instruments, and other items from more than 40 West African groups.

★2123★
Afro-American Historical & Cultural Society of Jersey City, Inc.
1841 Kennedy Blvd.
Jersey City, NJ 07305 Phone: (201)547-5262
Theodore Brunson, Pres.

★2124★
Afro-One Dance, Drama, and Drum Theater
Park Plaza Mall, Rt. 130 S.
Willingboro Plaza
Willingboro, NJ 08046 Phone: (609)871-8340
Patricia Reid-Bookhart, Founder and Artistic Dir.
Remarks: Presents performances depicting the Black experience in America featuring dancers, drummers, and poets.

★2125★
Carter G. Woodson Foundation
PO Box 1025
Newark, NJ 07102 Phone: (201)242-0500
Phillip Thomas, Dir.

★2126★
Crossroads Theater Company
320 Memorial Pkwy.
New Brunswick, NJ 08901 Phone: (908)249-5581
Rick Khan, Exec.Dir.
Remarks: A professional Black company that produces mainstage productions and co-productions with TV and New York theater.

★2127★
Merabash Museum
PO Box 752
Willingboro, NJ 08046 Phone: (609)877-3177
Mark Henderson Jr., Exec.Dir.

★2128★
Newark Museum
43-49 Washington St.
Newark, NJ 07101 Phone: (201)596-6550
Anne Spencer, Curator of Ethnology
Remarks: Exhibits an ethnology collection. Also sponsors the Newark Black Film Festival comprised of films by Black filmmakers and films about the history and culture of Black people.

New York

★2129★
African-American Cultural Center of Buffalo
350 Masten Ave.
Buffalo, NY 14209 Phone: (716)884-2013
Remarks: Exhibits items pertaining to Afro-American history and art.

★2130★
African-American Culture and Arts Network
2090 Adam Clayton Powell, Jr. Blvd.
New York, NY 10027 Phone: (212)749-4408

★2131★
African-American Institute
Museum
833 United Nations Plaza
New York, NY 10017 Phone: (212)949-5666
Donald B. Easum, Pres.
Remarks: Displays loan exhibitions of traditional and contemporary African arts and crafts. Museum also houses an African affairs library.

★2132★
African American Museum of Nassau County
110 N. Franklin St.
Hempstead, NY 11550
Shirley Darkeh, Dir.
Remarks: Exhibits and programs reflect the history and culture of Afro-Americans in the Long Island area.

★2133★
Afrikan Poetry Theater
176-03 Jamaica Ave.
Jamaica, NY 11423 Phone: (718)523-3312
John Watusi Branch, Exec.Dir.
Remarks: A predominantly Black, multicultural center which offers poetry readings and workshops, musical and cultural performances, lecturers, educational programs, and a children's workshop.

★2134★
Afro-American Cultural Foundation
Black History Museum
c/o Westchester Community College
75 Grasslands Rd.
Valhalla, NY 10595 Phone: (914)285-6600
Remarks: In honor of Black businesswoman Madam C.J. Walker (1867-1919).

★2135★
Afro-American Historical Society of the Niagara Frontier
Erie County Public Library
Layfayette Sq.
Buffalo, NY 14203 Phone: (716)858-8900

★2136★
Alonzo Players
317 Clermont Ave.
Brooklyn, NY 11205
Remarks: Black theatrical group.

★2137★
Artists Doing Business Worldwide
874 Brooklyn Ave.
Brooklyn, NY 11203 Phone: (718)693-1274
Al Browne, Dir.
Remarks: Offers entertainment skills of talented Black performing artists.

★2138★
Aunt Len's Doll and Toy Museum
6 Hamilton Terr.
New York, NY 10031 Phone: (212)926-4172
Lenon H. Hoyte, Dir.
Remarks: Collection of national and international dolls.

★2139★
Bedford-Stuyvesant Restoration Center for Arts and Culture
1368 Fulton, Ste. 4G
Brooklyn, NY 11216 Phone: (718)636-6948
Ted Barnett, Pres.
Remarks: Offers special cultural events, community programs, workshops, and outreach activities which delve into the American Black-African experience. Exhibitions held on a continual basis.

★2140★
Bedford-Stuyvesant Restoration Center for Arts and Culture
Billie Holiday Theater
1368 Fulton St.
Brooklyn, NY 11216 Phone: (718)636-0919
Marjorie Moon, Exec.Dir.
Remarks: Produces a 40-week season of original work by Black playwrights. Presents a Little Folk series of performances for children, workshops, and a college internship program.

★2141★
Black Experience Ensemble
5 Homestead Ave.
Albany, NY 12203 Phone: (518)482-6683
Mars Hill, Exec.Dir.
Remarks: Conducts drama and dance workshops 12-30 weeks per year and produces 1-3 plays per year.

★2142★
Black Experimental Theater
47 McKeever Pl., No. 6H
Brooklyn, NY 11225 Phone: (718)735-4290
Van Fisher, Pres./Artistic Dir.
Remarks: Presents theater productions using community members. Performs plays and musicals dealing with Caribbean and Black American culture.

★2143★
Black Fashion Museum
157 W. 126 St.
New York, NY 10027 Phone: (212)666-1320
Lois K. Alexander, Founder-Dir.
Remarks: Presents two exhibitions per year of costumes and other fashion memorabilia designed, made, or worn by Blacks in the U.S.

★2144★
Black Filmmaker Foundation
375 Greenwich St., Ste, 600
New York, NY 10013 Phone: (212)941-3944
Susan Christian, Exec.Dir.
Remarks: Media arts center established to support the independently produced work of Black media artists. Programs and services include production, distribution, exhibition, programming, newsletter, and membership screenings.

★2145★
Black Spectrum Theater Co.
119 Roy Wilkins Park
Jamaica, NY 11434 Phone: (718)723-1800
Carl Clay, Exec.Dir.
Remarks: Presents works that are socially significant to the Black community. Company performs four to five productions per year. Conducts acting and technical classes and produces original films.

★2146★
Boys Choir of Harlem
127 W. 127th St.
New York, NY 10027 Phone: (212)749-1717
Walter J. Turnbull, Founder and Exec.Dir.
Remarks: A touring choir of boys, ranging in ages from nine to nineteen. Choristers study voice and piano with a program of counseling and academic tutoring.

★2147★
Center for African Art
52-54 E. 68th St.
New York, NY 10021 Phone: (212)861-1200
Remarks: Exhibits include historic art originating in Africa.

★2148★
Charles Moore Dance Theater
1043 President St.
Brooklyn, NY 11225 Phone: (718)467-7127
Pam Mitchell, Man.
Remarks: Performs African, Caribbean, and other Black related dance in concert in the U.S., Puerto Rico and West Indies. Researches dance and dance styles from the past and operates a school for dance in New York.

★2149★
Chuck Davis Dance Co.
819 E. 168th St.
Bronx, NY 10013 Phone: (212)589-0400
Bess Pruitt, Company Man.
Remarks: Performs ethnic African dance and modern works. Tours nationally and internationally.

★2150★
The Cinque Gallery
560 Broadway
New York, NY 10012 Phone: (212)966-3464
Remarks: Exhibits the works of Afro-American artists.

★2151★
Community Folk Art Gallery
2223 E. Genessee St.
Syracuse, NY 13210 Phone: (315)424-8487
Herbert Williams, Dir.

★2152★
Dance Theater of Harlem
466 W. 152nd St.
New York, NY 10031 Phone: (212)690-2800
Arthur Mitchell, Exec.Dir.
Remarks: A ballet company which performs an annual New York Season and tours nationally and internationally. Operates a school of classical ballet for children three years and older.

★2153★
Frederick Douglass Creative Arts Center
168 W. 46th St.
New York, NY 10036 Phone: (212)944-9870
Fred Hudson, Pres., Artistic Dir.
Remarks: Holds writing workshops. Features Off-Broadway Equity Showcases and the Black Roots Festival of Poetry and Music.

★2154★
Genesis II Museum of International Black Culture
509 Cathedral Pwy.
New York, NY 10025 Phone: (212)666-7222
Andi Owens, Dir.

★2155★
Grinnell Gallery
800 Riverside Dr.
New York, NY 10032 Phone: (212)927-7941
Ademola Olugebefola, Co-Dir.

★2156★
Harlem Cultural Council
215 W. 125 St.
New York, NY 10027 Phone: (212)316-6277
Edward K. Taylor Jr., Exec.Dir.
Remarks: Sponsors a Dancemobile, Black filmaking projects, and poetry festivals. Offers technical assistance in securing grants to artists and arts organizations.

★2157★
Harlem Institute of Fashion
157 W. 126th St.
New York, NY 10027 Phone: (212)666-1320
Lois K. Alexander, Founder-Dir.
Remarks: Offers courses in dressmaking, millinery, tailoring, and related fashion courses. Conducts workshops with an emphasis on the above subjects, as well as reading, math, ethnic studies, and computer technology as it relates to fashion.

★2158★
Harlem School of the Arts
645 St. Nicholas Ave.
New York, NY 10030 Phone: (212)926-4100
Betty Allen, Exec.Dir.
Remarks: Exposes children to the arts and offers professional arts training. Provides classical arts education (music, dance, drama, and visual arts) primarily to minority youngsters.

★2159★
Hatch-Billops Collection, Inc.
491 Broadway
New York, NY 10012 Phone: (212)966-3231
Remarks: Concerned with the collection and preservation of historical and contemporary articles relating to the cultural experiences of Afro-Americans.

★2160★
Henry Street Settlement Arts for Living Center
466 Grand St.
New York, NY 10002 Phone: (212)598-0400
Steven Tennen Woodie King Jr., Producers
Remarks: Presents six predominatly Black and four Ethinic Heritage productions each season. Offers workshop in Black theater for adults and drama classes for children.

★2161★
International Agency for Minority Artists Affairs Inc.
352 W. 71st St.
New York, NY 10023 Phone: (212)873-5040
Gregory Javan Mills, Chairman
Remarks: Provides technical and arts managerial training to Black artists. Sponsors a year-round Black Film Festival.

★2162★
Ladji Camara African Music Dance Ensemble
1706 Davidson Ave., Ste. 513
Bronx, NY 10453 Phone: (212)716-4711
Ladji Camara, Dir.
Remarks: Offers instruction and performances in vocal and instrumental music and dance of African ritual ceremonies, portrayed in costumes of African tribes. Free workshops offered.

★2163★
Langston Hughes Institute
25 Hugh St.
Buffalo, NY 14203 Phone: (716)881-3266
Keith Baird, Dir.

★2164★
Museum of African and African-American Art and Antiquities
11 E. Utica St.
Buffalo, NY 14209 Phone: (716)882-7676
Glendora Johnson, Dir.
Remarks: Collections include items relative to Afro-American heritage.

★2165★
National Black Theater
2033 5th Ave.
New York, NY 10035 Phone: (212)427-5615
Remarks: Organizes workshops in acting and creative development in the theater. Tours in the East. Operates a children's school and develops children's plays.

★2166★
National Black Touring Circuit
417 Convent Ave.
New York, NY 10031 Phone: (212)283-0974
Remarks: Produces Black theater and film. Co-produces and assists other organizations with touring projects.

★2167★
Negro Ensemble Co., Inc.
155 W. 46 St.
New York, NY 10036 Phone: (212)575-5860
Leon Denmark, Producing Dir.
Remarks: Black professional theater company that produces new plays based on the Black experience. Sponsor playwrighters' workshops to foster the development of new plays.

★2168★
New Muse Community Museum of Brooklyn
1530 Bedford Ave.
Brooklyn, NY 11216 Phone: (718)774-2900
Remarks: Permanent exibitions, traveling exhibits, numerous workshops, and classes in music, dance, and the arts. Special events in the cultural center are dedicated to the Black experience in America.

★2169★
Society for the Preservation of Weeksville and Bedford-Stuyvesant History
1698 Bergen
Brooklyn, NY 11213 Phone: (718)756-5250
Joan Maynard, Exec.Dir.
Remarks: Working to develop a neighborhood museum of African-American history at a New York City national register site. Films and slide-lecture presentation available.

★2170★
Studio Museum in Harlem
144 W. 125th St.
New York, NY 10027 Phone: (212)864-4500
Kinshasha H. Conwill, Exec.Dir.
Remarks: Presents exhibitions featuring Black artists, conducts research in Black art, publishes exhibition catalogues, schedules tours, workshops, lectures, symposia, seminars, and concerts.

★2171★
Wayne County Minority Performing Arts Series
PO Box 156
Alton, NY 14413 Phone: (315)483-4092
Remarks: Plans a series of arts events representing Black-American and Haitian cultures.

★2172★
"Where We At" Black Women Artists
1452 Bedford Ave.
Brooklyn, NY 11216 Phone: (718)398-3871
Remarks: Includes artists of varied disciplines presenting exhibitions, seminars, and outreach workshops in centers, prisons, and other community facilities. Sponsors folk arts and steel bank presentations.

North Carolina

★2173★
Afro-American Cultural Center
401 N. Myers St.
Spirit Sq.
Charlotte, NC 28202 Phone: (704)374-1565
Vanessa Greene, Exec.Dir.
Remarks: Preserves, promotes, and presents Afro-American culture and history. Provides multicultural, multiethnic, and multifaceted programming.

★2174★
Black Artists' Guild
400 N. Queen St.
PO Box 2162
Kinston, NC 28501 Phone: (919)523-0003
Gary Dove, Exec.Dir.
Remarks: Seeks to alleviate problems concerning Black artists and to preserve Afro-American heritage.

★2175★
Harambee Arts Festival
Lenoir Recreation Department
PO Box 958
c/o Viewmont Community Center
Lenoir, NC 28645 Phone: (704)754-3278
Remarks: Promotes a greater awareness of Black culture through the performing arts, art exhibits, and crafts.

★2176★
North Carolina Black Repertory Company
610 Coliseum Dr.
Winston-Salem, NC 27106 Phone: (919)723-7907
Larry Leon Hamlin, Artistic Dir.
Remarks: Produces four mainstage and two second stage productions per year. Offers a four-year acting training program and a children's Acting for Television Commercials Workshop.

★2177★
North Carolina Central University Art Museum
PO Box 19555
Durham, NC 27707 Phone: (919)560-6211
Norman E. Pendergraft, Dir.
Remarks: Exhibits contemporary Afro-American art. Collection includes work of R.S. Duncanson, Henry Tanner, and Elizabeth Catlett.

★2178★
Somerset Place State Historic Site
Rt. 1
Creswell, NC 27928 Phone: (919)797-4560
Leisa M. Brown, Site Man.
Remarks: Collections include plantation slave records. Conducts research on Afro-American history.

★2179★
Young Men's Institute Cultural Center
PO Box 7301
Asheville, NC 28802 Phone: (704)252-4614
Wanda Coleman, Dir.

Ohio

★2180★
African American Museum
1765 Crawford Rd.
Cleveland, OH 44106 Phone: (216)791-1700
Dr. Eleanor Engram, Dir.
Remarks: Persons in the Cleveland area who are interested in building a national Afro-American history museum in that city. Goals are: to promote genealogical research; to study the Afro-American and minority race achievements and contributions; to bring about a harmonious relationship between the races through better understanding. Furnishes speakers for school and civic organizations; holds history classes and workshops. Maintains library of 1200 volumes and Alexander E. Pushkin exhibit.

★2181★
Afro-American Cultural and Historical Society Museum
1765 Crawford Rd.
Cleveland, OH 44106 Phone: (216)791-1700
Dr. Eleanor Engram, Dir.
Remarks: Promotes genealogical research and studies Afro-American and minority race relations. Also furnishes speakers for school and civic organizations and holds history classes and workshops.

★2182★
Afro-American Cultural Center
Cleveland State University
Black Studies Program
2121 Euclid Ave., UC 103
Cleveland, OH 44115 Phone: (216)687-3655
Professor Curtis Wilson, Dir.

★2183★
Afro American Music Hall of Fame and Museum
1870 Goleta
Youngstown, OH 44504 Phone: (216)783-9922
Frank Halssacre, Dir.
Remarks: Exhibits items relating to the lives of Black musicians and composers.

★2184★
Art for Community Expressions
772 N. High St.
Columbus, OH 43215 Phone: (614)252-3036
Remarks: Sponsors art exhibitions featuring Afro-American artists. Offers two annual projects.

★2185★
Black Historical Museum of Fashion Dolls
National Association of Fashion and Accessory Designers
2180 E. 93rd St.
Cleveland, OH 44106 Phone: (216)231-0375
Beatrice Spencer, Pres.

★2186★
Cincinnati Art Museum
Eden Park
Cincinnati, OH 45202 Phone: (513)721-5204
Millard F. Rogers Jr., Dir.
Remarks: Exhibits primitive art of Africa.

★2187★
Dunbar House State Memorial
219 Summitt St.
Dayton, OH 45407 Phone: (513)224-7061
Eva F. Peterson, Dir.

★2188★
Karamu House
2355 E. 89th St.
Cleveland, OH 44106 Phone: (216)795-7070
Milton C. Morris, Exec.Dir.
Remarks: Black theater featuring a resident acting company, classes, and a music series focusing on Black artists. Provides workshops and gallery spaces.

★2189★
National Afro-American Museum and Cultural Center
PO Box 578
Wilberforce, OH 45384 Phone: (513)376-4944
Dr. John E. Fleming, Dir.
Remarks: Separately incorporated, nonprofit organization affiliated with the Ohio Historical Society, operating under a state and general board. Studies the role of the Afro-American in America through preservation and conservation of Afro-American culture. Colletions include manuscripts and rare books on Black history and culture and art and historical objects.

★2190★
National Conference of Artists
1624 Grand Ave.
Dayton, OH 45407 Phone: (513)278-6793
Remarks: Goals include the promotion, production, and encourangement of Black visual artists working in diverse media. Sponsors exhibits of Black African-American visual artists. Offers free public workshops, seminars, and artist demonstrations.

★2191★
Resident Art and Humanities Consortium
1515 Linn St.
Cincinnati, OH 45214 Phone: (513)381-0645
Anthony Davis, Dir.

★2192★
Watkins Academy Museum of Cultural Arts
724 Mineola Ave.
Akron, OH 44320 Phone: (216)864-0673
James Watkins, Dir.

Oklahoma

★2193★
Kirkpatrick Center Museum Complex
2100 NE 52nd
Oklahoma City, OK 73111 Phone: (405)427-5461
Mary Ann Haliburton, Exec.Dir.
Remarks: Exhibits African art and sponsors ethnic festivals.

★2194★
NTU Art Association
2100 N. 52nd St.
Oklahoma City, OK 73111 Phone: (405)424-7760
Mary Ann Haliburton, Dir.

★2195★
Theater North
PO Box 6255
Tulsa, OK 74148 Phone: (918)587-8937
Remarks: Black community theater producing dramatic presentations, gospel, and jazz concerts. Screens films with an emphasis on Black culture.

Pennsylvania

★2196★
Africamerica Festival
2247 N. Broad
Philadelphia, PA 19132 Phone: (215)232-2900

★2197★
African American Heritage, Inc.
4601 Market St.
Philadelphia, PA 19139 Phone: (215)748-7817

★2198★
African Cultural Art Forum
237 S. 60 St.
Philadelphia, PA 19139 Phone: (215)476-0680
Remarks: Interested in promoting Black artists and their work.

★2199★
Afro-American Historical and Cultural Museum
701 Arch St.
Philadelphia, PA 19106 Phone: (215)574-0380
Rowena Stewart, Exec.Dir.
Remarks: Conducts research on Black history in Pennsylvania 1660-1976. Collections include prints and sculptures, African sculpture and artifacts, and artifacts pertaining to the American Revolution and slave trade.

★2200★
Avante Theater Company
Manaheim & Pulaski
Philadelphia, PA 19144 Phone: (215)848-9099
John R. Giugliano, Artistic Dir.
Remarks: Presents productions by Black playwrights. Available for touring, workshops, and residences in the Mid-Atlantic states.

★2201★
Minority Arts Resource Council
1421 W. Girard Ave.
Philadelphia, PA 19130 Phone: (215)236-2688
Curtis E. Brown, Exec.Dir.
Remarks: Consortium for Black and Hispanic professional arts groups. Sponsors performances and exhibitions throughout the Delaware Valley.

★2202★
New Freedom Theater
1346 N. Board St.
Philadelphia, PA 19121 Phone: (215)765-2793

Rhode Island

★2203★
Rhode Island Black Heritage Society
1 Hilton St.
Providence, RI 02905 Phone: (401)751-3490
Linda Avant Coleman, Dir.
Remarks: Exhibits documents, photographs, and an art collection pertaining to the Afro-American in Rhode island; organizes touring exibitions, lecture series, and arts workshops.

South Carolina

★2204★
Avery Research Center for Afro-American History and Culture
125 Bull St.
College of Charleston
Charleston, SC 29424 Phone: (803)792-5742
Dr. Myrtle Glascoe, Dir.
Remarks: Collections include materials, manuscripts, and artifacts illustrating the history and culture of the Afro-American in South Carolina.

★2205★
Mann-Simons Cottage: Museum of African-American Culture
1403 Richland St.
Columbia, SC 29201 Phone: (803)252-3964
Henry Cauthen, Dir.
Remarks: An historic house museum which is also operated as a cultural center or the preservation of African-American culture.

★2206★
Museum of African-American Culture
1403 Richard St.
Columbia, SC 29201 Phone: (803)252-1450
Henry Calhoun, Dir.
Remarks: Features African-American artwork by local artists; African-American historical (c. 1850) furnishings, literature, and artifacts.

★2207★
South Carolina State College
I. P. Stanback Museum and Planetarium
South Carolina State College
Orangeburg, SC 29117 Phone: (803)536-7174
Dr. Leo F. Twiggs, Exec.Dir.
Remarks: Exhibits include contemporary African and Afro-American art including 300-400 photographs, Harlem On My Mind Exhibit, and over 60 pieces from Cameroon and parts of Western Africa.

★2208★
Umoja Dance Company
35 Harvey Ave.
Charleston, SC 29405 Phone: (803)744-5834
Cheryl West
Remarks: Emphasizes African and Afro-American history and culture through dance.

Tennessee

★2209★
Beck Cultural Exchange Center
1927 Dandridge Ave.
Knoxville, TN 37915 Phone: (615)524-8461
Robert J. Booker, Exec.Dir.
Remarks: Explores local Black history. Collections include Black weekly newspapers, books, and artwork by local artists.

★2210★
Blues City Cultural Center
415 S. Main
Memphis, TN 38114 Phone: (901)525-3031
Levi and Deborah Frazier, General Mans.
Remarks: Exhibits and produces original and historic works related to the Southern Black experience.

★2211★
Memphis Black Arts Alliance
985 S. Bellevue Blvd.
Memphis, TN 38174 Phone: (901)948-9522
Helen Dickerson, Exec.Dir.
Remarks: Houses a gallery, theater/dance studio, classrooms, and offices; and provides a slide registry, directory, and administrative services.

★2212★
Tennessee State University
Institute for African Affairs
Tennessee State University
PO Box 828
Nashville, TN 37209 Phone: (615)320-3035
Dr. Levi Jones, Dir.
Remarks: Disseminates information about African nations, including lifestyles, religious values, and culture.

Texas

★2213★
African American Cultural Heritage Center
Nolan Estes Educational Plaza
3434 S.R.L. Thornton Fwy.
Dallas, TX 75224 Phone: (214)375-7530
Robert Edison, Dir.
Remarks: Sponsored by the Dallas Independent School District. Facilities include a small history museum.

★2214★
Black Art Gallery
5408 Almeda Rd.
Houston, TX 77004 Phone: (713)529-7900

★2215★
Black Arts Alliance
1157 Navasota St.
Austin, TX 78702 Phone: (512)477-9660
Annell Williams, Dir.
Remarks: Arts organization serving both artists and communities in Texas with a visual and performing arts registry, multi-arts performances, workshops, and exhibitions of Texas artists.

★2216★
Black Texan Cultural Museum and Hall of Fame
920 E. 11th St.
Austin, TX 78702 Phone: (512)472-5731

★2217★
Community Music Center of Houston
5613 Almeda
Houston, TX 77004 Phone: (713)523-9710
Remarks: Conducts research on Afro-American music and seeks to educate the community through performances of Afro-American music.

★2218★
George Washington Carver Museum and Cultural Center
1165 Angelina St.
Austin, TX 78702 Phone: (512)472-4809
Clarence Anthony Brisco, Interim Dir.
Remarks: Collections include manuscripts, maps, books, and photographs documenting the history of Blacks.

★2219★
Museum of African-American Life and Culture
PO Box 26153
Dallas, TX 75226 Phone: (214)565-9026
Dr. Harry Robinson, Dir.
Remarks: Sponsors approximately six exhibitions per year, including a Youth Symphony Orchestra, a biannual Black Woman's Conference, and the Annual Southwest Black Art Exhibition.

Virginia

★2220★
Alexandria Black History Resource Center
20 N. Washington St.
Alexandria, VA 22314 Phone: (703)838-4577
Marjorie D. Tallichet, Dir.

★2221★
Black Historical Museum and Cultural Center
122 W. Leigh St.
Richmond, VA 23220 Phone: (804)780-9093
Anthony J. Binga Sr., Pres.

★2222★
Harrison Museum of African American Culture
523 Harrison Ave.
Roanoke, VA 24016 Phone: (703)345-4818
Freeland O. Tendleton Jr., Pres.
Remarks: Repository for the history of Blacks in the Roanoke Valley.

★2223★
Task Force on Historical Preservation and Minority Communities
500 N. 3rd St.
Richmond, VA 23219 Phone: (804)788-1709
Preddy Ray, Dir.

★2224★
Virginia Museum for Black History and Archives
PO Box 61052
Richmond, VA 23261 Phone: (804)780-9093
Remarks: Commemorates accomplishments of Black people through community education efforts.

Wisconsin

★2225★
Hedzoleh African Dance Troupe
2630 Smithfield Dr.
Madison, WI 53701 Phone: (608)274-9769
Malzern Akyea, Artistic Dir.
Remarks: African drum and dance company choreographing West African dance by recreating events and rituals of traditional African society. Offers lecture-demonstrations, performances, and residencies.

★2226★
Ko-Thi Dance Company
PO Box 1093
Milwaukee, WI 53201 Phone: (414)442-6844
Sandra Jordan, Office Man.
Remarks: Professional Black ensemble specializing in traditional and contemporary African-American performing arts. Offers concerts, lecture-demonstrations, and master classes.

(6) COLLEGES AND UNIVERSITIES

Entries in this chapter are arranged alphabetically by institution name. See the User's Guide at the front of this directory for additional information.

★2227★
Alabama A&M University
PO Box 285
Normal, AL 35762 Phone: (205)851-5245
Dr. Carl Harris Marbury, Interim Pres.

Founded: 1875. State-supported university. **Cost:** $3,284.00 in-state; $4,272.00 out-of-state. **Application Deadline:** Rolling admissions policy. **Number of Students:** 4500. **Tests Required:** SAT or ACT. **Admissions Director:** James O. Heyward.

★2228★
Alabama State University
915 S. Jackson St.
Montgomery, AL 36195 Phone: (205)293-4291
Dr. Leon Howard, Pres.

Founded: 1874. State-supported university. **Cost:** $1,160.00 in-state; $2,320.00 out-of-state. **Application Deadline:** July 31 (fall). **Number of Students:** 3,600. **Tests Required:** SAT or ACT. **Admissions Director:** Arthur D. Barnett. **Toll-free phone:** (800)354-8865 (Alabama only).

★2229★
Albany State College
504 College Dr.
Albany, GA 31705-2797
Dr. Billy C. Black, Pres.

Founded: 1903. State-supported college. **Cost:** $4,146.00 in-state; $6,198.00 out-of-state. **Application Deadline:** September 1 (fall). **Number of Students:** 2307. **Tests Required:** SAT (preferred) or ACT. **Admissions Director:** Patricia Price. **Toll-free phone:** (800)822-7267 (Georgia only).

★2230★
Alcorn State University
PO Box 359
Lorman, MS 39096 Phone: (601)877-6147
Dr. Walter Washington, Pres.

Founded: 1871. State-supported university. **Cost:** $3,600.00 in-state; $4,782.00 out-of-state. **Application Deadline:** August 15 (fall). **Number of Students:** 2847. **Tests Required:** SAT or ACT. **Admissions Director:** Albert Z. Johnson. **Toll-free phone:** (800)222-6790 (Mississippi only).

★2231★
Allen University
1530 Harden St.
Columbia, SC 29204 Phone: (803)254-9735
Dr. Collie Coleman, Pres.

Founded: 1870. Independent university. **Cost:** $6,590.00. **Application Deadline:** Rolling admissions policy. **Number of Students:** 272. **Tests Required:** Open admissions policy. **Admissions Director:** Mrs. L. S. Grady.

★2232★
Arkansas Baptist College
1600 Bishop St.
Little Rock, AR 72202 Phone: (501)374-7856
Dr. William Keaton, Pres.

Founded: 1884. Independent four-year college. **Cost:** $3,870.00. **Application Deadline:** Rolling admissions policy. **Number of Students:** 268. **Tests Required:** Open admissions policy. **Admissions Director:** Annie A. Hightower.

★2233★
Atlanta Metropolitan College
1630 Stewart Ave., SW
Atlanta, GA 30310 Phone: (404)756-4441
Dr. E.A. Thompson, Pres.

Founded: 1974. State-supported two-year college. **Cost:** $933.00 in-state; $2,718.00 out-of-state. **Application Deadline:** September 6 (fall). **Number of Students:** 1570. **Tests Required:** SAT. **Admissions Director:** Verle V. Wilson.

★2234★
Barber-Scotia College
145 Cabarrus Ave.
Concord, NC 28025 Phone: (704)786-5171
Dr. Joel Nwagbaraocha, Pres.

Founded: 1867. Independent four-year college affiliated with the Presbyterian Church. **Cost:** $5,850.00. **Application Deadline:** Rolling admissions policy. **Number of Students:** 383. **Tests Required:** SAT or ACT. **Admissions Director:** Mrs. Jonyrma Elliott.

★2235★
Benedict College
Harden & Blanding Sts.
Columbia, SC 29204 Phone: (803)256-4220
Dr. Marshall C. Grigsby, Pres.

Founded: 1870. Private college. **Cost:** $6,851.00. **Application Deadline:** Rolling admissions policy. **Number of Students:** 1,616. **Tests**

Required: SAT or ACT. **Admissions Director:** Virginia McKee. **Toll-free phone:** (800)868-6598 (South Carolina only).

★2236★
Bennett College
900 E. Washington St.
Greensboro, NC 27401-3239 Phone: (919)370-8624
Dr. Gloria R. Scott, Pres.

Founded: 1873. Private undergraduate women's college. **Cost:** $7,480.00. **Application Deadline:** Rolling admissions policy. **Number of Students:** 572. **Tests Required:** SAT or ACT. **Admissions Director:** Gwen Sellers. **Toll-free phone:** (800)338-2366.

★2237★
Bethune-Cookman College
640 2nd Ave.
Daytona Beach, FL 32015 Phone: (904)255-1401
Dr. Oswald B. Bronson, Pres.

Founded: 1904. Independent four-year Methodist college. **Cost:** $6,679.00. **Application Deadline:** July 30 (fall). **Number of Students:** 2145. **Tests Required:** SAT or ACT. **Admissions Director:** Gloria Bartley. **Toll-free phone:** (800)448-0228.

★2238★
Bishop State Community College
351 N. Broad St.
Mobile, AL 36690 Phone: (205)690-6800
Dr. Yvonne Kennedy, Pres.

Founded: 1927. State-supported junior college. **Cost:** $650.00 in-state; $1,050.00 our-of-state. **Application Deadline:** Rolling admissions policy. **Number of Students:** 1857. **Tests Required:** Open admissions policy. **Toll-free phone:** (800)523-7235.

★2239★
Bowie State University
Jericho Park Rd.
Bowie, MD 20715-9465 Phone: (301)464-6563
Dr. James E. Lyons Sr., Pres.

Founded: 1865. State-supported university. **Cost:** $5,321.00 in-state; $6,982.00 out-of-state. **Application Deadline:** April 1 (fall); November 1 (spring). **Number of Students:** 3748. **Tests Required:** SAT. **Admissions Director:** Lawrence A. Waters.

★2240★
Central State University
1400 Brush Row Rd.
Wilberforce, OH 45384-3002 Phone: (513)376-6478
Dr. Arthur E. Thomas, Pres.

Founded: 1887. State-supported university. **Cost:** $5,878.00 in-state; [illegible]230.00 out-of-state. **Application Deadline:** Rolling admissions [illegible] **Number of Students:** 2550. **Tests Required:** ACT. **Admissions** [illegible] Robert E. Johnson. **Toll-free phone:** (800)624-4958.

★2241★
Charles R. Drew University of Medicine and Science
1621 E. 120th St.
Los Angeles, CA 90059 Phone: (213)563-4960
Dr. Henry S. Williams, Interim Pres.

Founded: 1978. Federally funded private university. **Cost:** $10,230.00 in-state; $15,230.00 out-of-state. **Application Deadline:** November 15 (fall). **Number of Students:** 24. **Tests Required:** MCAT. **Admissions Director:** Dr. Alice Faye-Singleton.

★2242★
Cheyney University of Pennsylvania
Cheyney & Creek Rds.
Cheyney, PA 19319 Phone: (215)399-2275
Dr. LeVerne McCummings, Pres.

Founded: 1837. State-supported university. **Cost:** $4,954.00 in-state; $6,590.00 out-of-state. **Application Deadline:** Rolling admissions policy. **Number of Students:** 1646. **Tests Required:** SAT or ACT. **Admissions Director:** Gwendolyn Miller.

★2243★
Chicago State University
95th St. at King Dr.
Chicago, IL 60628 Phone: (312)995-2513
Dr. George E. Ayers, Pres.

Founded: 1867. State-supported university. **Cost:** $1,772.00 in-state; $4,716.00 out-of-state. **Application Deadline:** Three weeks prior to the beginning of each term. **Number of Students:** 6034. **Tests Required:** SAT or ACT. **Admissions Director:** Romi Lowe.

★2244★
Claflin College
College Ave., NE
Orangeburg, SC 29115 Phone: (803)534-2710
Dr. Oscar A. Rogers Jr., Pres.

Founded: 1869. Independent, four-year United Methodist college. **Cost:** $6,008.00. **Application Deadline:** Rolling admissions policy. **Number of Students:** 850. **Tests Required:** SAT. **Admissions Director:** George F. Lee.

★2245★
Clark Atlanta University
240 James P. Brawley Dr., SW
Atlanta, GA 30314 Phone: (404)880-8018
Dr. Thomas W. Cole Jr., Pres.

Founded: 1869. Independent four-year college affiliated with the United Methodist Church. **Cost:** $9,370.00. **Application Deadline:** May 1 (fall); December 1 (spring). **Number of Students:** 3339. **Tests Required:** SAT or ACT. **Admissions Director:** Clifton B. Rawles.

★2246★
Clinton Junior College
1020 Crawford Rd.
PO Box 968
Rock Hill, SC 29731 Phone: (803)327-5587
Dr. Sallie V. Moreland, Pres.

Founded: 1894. Private two-year college. **Cost:** $2,885.00. **Application Deadline:** Rolling admissions policy. **Number of Students:** 87. **Tests**

Required: Open admissions policy. **Admissions Director:** Patrice Dixon.

★2247★
Coahoma Community College
Rt. 1, Box 616
Clarksdale, MS 38614 Phone: (601)627-2571
Dr. McKinley C. Martin, Pres.

Founded: 1949. Independent two-year Southern Baptist college. **Cost:** $700.00 area; $1,100.00 in-state; $2,100.00 out-of-state. **Number of Students:** 1478. **Admissions Director:** Rita Hanfor.

★2248★
Concordia College
1804 Green St.
Selma, AL 36701 Phone: (205)874-5736
Dr. Julius Jenkins, Pres.

Founded: 1922. Private four-year college. **Cost:** $3,000.00. **Application Deadline:** Rolling admissions policy. **Number of Students:** 343. **Tests Required:** ACT. **Admissions Director:** Evelyn Pickens.

★2249★
Coppin State College
2500 W. North Ave.
Baltimore, MD 21216 Phone: (301)333-5990
Dr. Calvin W. Burnett, Pres.

Founded: 1900. State-supported college. **Cost:** $2,096.00 in-state; $3,3564.00 out-of-state. **Application Deadline:** July 30 (fall). **Number of Students:** 2229. **Tests Required:** SAT. **Admissions Director:** Allen D. Mosley, Acting Dir.

★2250★
Delaware State College
1200 N. Dupont Hwy.
Dover, DE 19901 Phone: (302)736-4917
Dr. William B. DeLauder, Pres.

Founded: 1891. State-supported college. **Cost:** $4,026.00 in-state; $5,841.00 out-of-state. **Application Deadline:** June 1 (fall); December 1 (spring). **Number of Students:** 2610. **Tests Required:** SAT (preferred) or ACT. **Admissions Director:** Jethro C. Williams.

★2251★
Denmark Technical College
PO Box 327
Denmark, SC 29042 Phone: (803)793-3301
Dr. Curtis E. Bryan, Pres.

Founded: 1948. State-supported four-year college. **Cost:** $1,162.00 per quarter in-state; $1,412.00 per quarter out-of-state. **Application Deadline:** Rolling admissions policy. **Number of Students:** 800. **Tests Required:** Open admissions policy. **Admissions Director:** Dr. Iris D. Bomar, Associate Dean of Student Services.

★2252★
Dillard University
2601 Gentilly Blvd.
New Orleans, LA 70122 Phone: (504)283-8822
Dr. Samuel Cooke, Pres.

Founded: 1869. Independent, interdenominational four-year college. **Cost:** $8,250.00. **Application Deadline:** July 15 (fall). **Number of Students:** 1668. **Tests Required:** SAT or ACT. **Admissions Director:** Vernese B. O'Neal.

★2253★
Edward Waters College
1658 Kings Rd.
Jacksonville, FL 32209 Phone: (904)355-3030
Dr. Robert L. Mitchell, Pres.

Founded: 1866. Private four-year college. **Cost:** $6,656.00. **Application Deadline:** Two weeks prior to the beginning of each semester. **Number of Students:** 686. **Tests Required:** Open admissions policy. **Admissions Director:** Jerome Goodwin.

★2254★
Elizabeth City State University
1704 Weekszill Rd.
Elizabeth City, NC 27909 Phone: (919)335-3305
Dr. Jimmy R. Jenkins, Pres.

Founded: 1891. State-supported four-year college. **Cost:** $4,210.00 in-state; $7,488.00 out-of-state. **Application Deadline:** August 1 (fall); December 1 (spring). **Number of Students:** 1694. **Tests Required:** SAT or ACT. **Admissions Director:** William T. Byrd; PO Box 901, ECSU, Elizabeth City, NC 27909.

★2255★
Fayetteville State University
Murchison Rd.
Fayetteville, NC 28301 Phone: (919)486-1371
Dr. Lloyd V. Hackley, Pres.

Founded: 1867. State-supported institution; part of the University of North Carolina System. **Cost:** $2,670.00 in-state; $5,962.00 out-of-state. **Application Deadline:** Rolling admissions policy. **Number of Students:** 3034. **Tests Required:** SAT. **Admissions Director:** Charles A. Darlington. **Toll-free phone:** (800)672-6667 (North Carolina only); (800)222-2594 (out-of-state).

★2256★
Fisk University
1000 17th Ave., N.
Nashville, TN 37203-4501 Phone: (615)329-8665
Dr. Henry Ponder, Pres.

Founded: 1866. Independent university affiliated with the United Church of Christ. **Cost:** $6,950.00. **Application Deadline:** June 15 (fall). **Number of Students:** 891. **Tests Required:** SAT or ACT. **Admissions Director:** Harrison F. DeShields, Jr.

★2257★
Florida A&M University
Tallahassee, FL 32307 Phone: (904)599-3796
Dr. Frederick S. Humphiries, Pres.

Founded: 1887. State-supported university. **Cost:** $3,613.00 in-state; $6,372.00 out-of-state. **Application Deadline:** June 1 (fall). **Number of Students:** 7469. **Tests Required:** SAT or ACT. **Admissions Director:** Daisy O. Young.

★2258★
Florida Memorial College
15800 NW 42nd Ave.
Miami, FL 33054 Phone: (305)623-4145
Dr. Willie C. Robinson, Pres.

Founded: 1879. Independent four-year college affiliated with the Baptist Church. **Cost:** $6,650.00. **Application Deadline:** Rolling admissions policy. **Number of Students:** 2000. **Tests Required:** SAT or ACT. **Admissions Director:** Peggy Kelly. **Toll-free phone:** (800)822-1362.

★2259★
Fort Valley State College
1005 State College Dr.
Fort Valley, GA 31030-3298 Phone: (912)825-6307
Dr. Luther Burse, Pres.

Founded: 1895. State-supported college. **Cost:** $4,089.00 in-state; $6,132.00 out-of-state. **Application Deadline:** September 1 (fall). **Number of Students:** 2097. **Tests Required:** SAT. **Admissions Director:** Della W. Taylor.

★2260★
Grambling State University
PO Box 864
Grambling, LA 71245 Phone: (318)274-2435
Dr. Joseph B. Johnson, Pres.

Founded: 1901. State-supported university. **Cost:** $4,412.00 in-state; $5,962.00 out-of-state. **Application Deadline:** Rolling admissions policy. **Number of Students:** 6205. **Tests Required:** SAT or ACT. **Admissions Director:** Karen C. Lewis.

★2261★
Hampton University
Hampton, VA 23668 Phone: (804)727-5328
Dr. William R. Harvey, Pres.

Founded: 1868. Private university. **Cost:** $8,042.00. **Application Deadline:** February 15 (fall). **Number of Students:** 5342. **Tests Required:** SAT or ACT. **Admissions Director:** Dr. Ollie M. Bowman. **Toll-free phone:** (800)624-3328.

★2262★
Harris-Stowe State College
3026 Laclede Ave.
St. Louis, MO 63103-2136 Phone: (314)533-3000
Dr. Henry Givens Jr., Pres.

Founded: 1857. State-supported four-year college. **Cost:** $1,391.00 in-state; $2,767.00 out-of-state. **Application Deadline:** August 1 (fall); January 1 (spring). **Number of Students:** 1881. **Tests Required:** SAT or ACT. **Admissions Director:** Valerie A. Beeson.

★2263★
Hinds Community College—Utica Campus
Utica, MS 39715 Phone: (601)885-6062
Dr. George Barnes, V.Pres.

Founded: 1903. State-supported two-year college. **Application Deadline:** August 23 (fall); January 10 (spring). **Number of Students:** 1030. **Admissions Director:** Ellestene Turner, Registrar.

★2264★
Howard University
2400 6th St., NW
Washington, DC 20059 Phone: (202)636-6150
Dr. Franklyn G. Jenifer, Pres.

Founded: 1867. Private university. **Cost:** $8,705.00. **Application Deadline:** April 1 (fall). **Number of Students:** 11,452. **Tests Required:** SAT or ACT. **Admissions Director:** Emmett R. Griffin, Jr. **Toll-free phone:** (800)822-6363.

★2265★
Huston-Tillotson College
1820 E. 8th St.
Austin, TX 78702 Phone: (512)476-7421
Dr. Joseph T. McMillan Jr., Pres.

Founded: 1875. Independent religious four-year college. **Cost:** $7,460.00. **Application Deadline:** Rolling admissions policy. **Number of Students:** 695. **Tests Required:** SAT or ACT. **Admissions Director:** Paul K. Kimbrough.

★2266★
Interdenominational Theological Center
671 Beckwith St., SW
Atlanta, GA 30314 Phone: (404)527-7709
Dr. James H. Costen, Pres.

Founded: 1958. Private graduate center. **Cost:** $5,754.00. **Application Deadline:** August 1 (fall). **Number of Students:** 300. **Tests Required:** None (GRE required for file). **Admissions Director:** Dr. Edith D. Thomas.

★2267★
Jackson State University
1400 John R. Lynch St.
Jackson, MS 39217 Phone: (601)968-2100
Dr. James A. Hefner, Pres.

Founded: 1877. State-supported university. **Cost:** $3,824.00 in-state; $5,000.00 out-of-state. **Application Deadline:** Rolling admissions policy. **Tests Required:** SAT or ACT. **Admissions Director:** Walter L. Crockett. **Toll-free phone:** (800)682-5390.

★2268★
Jarvis Christian College
Hwy. 80 W.
Drawer G
Hawkins, TX 75765 Phone: (214)769-2174
Dr. Julius Nimmons, Pres.

Founded: 1912. Independent four-year college affiliated with the Christian Church. **Cost:** $6,343.00. **Application Deadline:** Rolling admissions policy. **Number of Students:** 543. **Tests Required:** ACT. **Admissions Director:** Edward Thomas.

★2269★
Johnson C. Smith University
100-152 Beatties Ford Rd.
Charlotte, NC 28216 Phone: (704)378-1010
Dr. Robert L. Albright Jr., Pres.

Founded: 1867. Independent four-year Presbyterian college. **Cost:** $7,323.00. **Application Deadline:** August 1 (fall); December 1 (spring). **Number of Students:** 1310. **Tests Required:** SAT or ACT. **Admissions Director:** Wilburn M. Sanders.

★2270★
Kentucky State University
E. Main St.
Frankfort, KY 40601
Raymond M. Burse, Pres.

Founded: 1886. State-supported university. **Cost:** $3,780.00 in-state; $6,008.00 out-of-state. **Application Deadline:** Rolling admissions policy. **Number of Students:** 2190. **Tests Required:** SAT or ACT. **Admissions Director:** Tava T. Clay. **Toll-free phone:** (800)633-9415 (Kentucky only); (800)325-1716 (out-of-state).

★2271★
Knoxville College
901 College St., NW
Knoxville, TN 37921 Phone: (615)524-6525
Dr. Dennis Spelmann, Exec. V.Pres.

Founded: 1875. Private undergraduate college. **Cost:** $8,290.00. **Application Deadline:** Rolling admissions policy. **Number of Students:** 1225. **Tests Required:** SAT or ACT. **Admissions Director:** Earl Nash. **Remarks:** Knoxville College acquired Morristown College, Morristown, TN, in the fall of 1988.

★2272★
Lane College
545 Lane Ave.
Jackson, TN 38301 Phone: (901)424-4600
Dr. Alex A. Chambers, Pres.

Founded: 1882. Private four-year college. **Cost:** $6,242.00. **Application Deadline:** Rolling admissions policy. **Number of Students:** 525. **Tests Required:** SAT or ACT. **Admissions Director:** E. Ruth Maddox.

★2273★
Langston University
PO Box 907
Langston, OK 73050 Phone: (405)466-2231
Dr. Ernest L. Holloway, Pres.

Founded: 1897. State-supported four-year college. **Application Deadline:** Rolling admissions policy. **Number of Students:** 2500. **Admissions Director:** La Cressa Trice, Admissions Counselor.

★2274★
Lawson State Community College
3060 Wilson Rd., SW
Birmingham, AL 35221 Phone: (205)925-2515
Dr. Perry Ward, Pres.

Founded: 1973. State-supported two-year college. **Cost:** $645.00 in-state; $1,200.00 out-of-state. **Application Deadline:** Rolling admissions policy. **Number of Students:** 1470. **Tests Required:** Asset placement. **Admissions Director:** James E. Edwards.

★2275★
Le Moyne-Owen College
807 Walker Ave.
Memphis, TN 38126 Phone: (901)942-7302
Dr. Doris Weathers, Pres.

Founded: 1870. Private four-year college. **Cost:** $3,600.00. **Application Deadline:** Rolling admissions policy. **Number of Students:** 1130. **Tests Required:** ACT. **Admissions Director:** Frankie Jeffries.

★2276★
Lewis College of Business
17370 Meyer Rd.
Detroit, MI 48235 Phone: (313)862-6300
Dr. Marjorie Harris, Pres.

Founded: 1929. Independent two-year college. **Cost:** $2,250.00. **Application Deadline:** Rolling admissions policy. **Number of Students:** 346. **Tests Required:** Open admissions policy. **Admissions Director:** Janice Carrington, Admissions Secretary.

★2277★
Lincoln University
Lincoln University, PA 19352 Phone: (215)932-8300
Dr. Niara Sudarkasa, Pres.

Founded: 1854. State-related university. **Cost:** $5,015.00 in-state; $5,765.00 out-of-state. **Application Deadline:** Rolling admissions policy. **Number of Students:** 1304. **Tests Required:** SAT or ACT. **Admissions Director:** Dr. Charles A. Edington.

★2278★
Lincoln University (Missouri)
820 Chestnut St.
Jefferson City, MO 65101 Phone: (314)681-5599
Dr. Wendell G. Rayburn, Pres.

Founded: 1866. State-supported university. **Cost:** $4,018.00 in-state; $5,338.00 out-of-state. **Number of Students:** 3063. **Tests Required:** ACT. **Admissions Director:** Charles E. Glasper.

★2279★
Livingstone College
Hood Theological Seminary
701 W. Monroe St.
Salisbury, NC 28144 Phone: (704)638-5502
Dr. Bernard W. Franklin, Pres.

Founded: 1879. Private seminary. **Cost:** $6,242.00. **Number of Students:** 558. **Tests Required:** SAT or ACT. **Admissions Director:** Lula N. Holloway.

★

Mary Holmes Junior College
Hwy. 50 W.
PO Box 1257
West Point, MS 39773 Phone: (601)494-6820
Dr. Sammie Potts, Pres.

Founded: 1892. Private two-year college. **Cost:** $8,590.00. **Application Deadline:** Rolling admissions policy. **Number of Students:** 619. **Tests Required:** None (ACT suggested). **Admissions Director:** Geraldine Lee. **Toll-free phone:** (800)634-2749 (Mississippi only).

★2281★

Medgar Evers College of City University of New York
1650 Bedford Ave.
Brooklyn, NY 11225 Phone: (718)735-1948
Dr. Edgar O. Jackson, Pres.

Founded: 1969. State-supported four-year college. **Cost:** $1,776.00 in-state; $2,576.00 out-of-state. **Application Deadline:** Rolling admissions policy. **Number of Students:** 2660. **Tests Required:** Open admissions policy. **Admissions Director:** Roberta Dannenfeiser; 1150 Carroll St., Brooklyn, NY 11225.

★2282★

Meharry Medical College
1005 D. B. Todd Blvd.
Nashville, TN 37208 Phone: (615)327-6223
Dr. David Satcher, Pres.

Founded: 1876. Private professional college. **Cost:** $21,000.00. **Application Deadline:** December 15 (fall). **Number of Students:** 683. **Tests Required:** MCAT, DAT, or GRE. **Admissions Director:** Ottie L. West.

★2283★

Miles College
PO Box 3800
Birmingham, AL 35208 Phone: (205)923-2771
Dr. Albert Sloan II, Pres.

Founded: 1905. Independent, four-year Christian Methodist Episcopal college. **Cost:** $6,000.00. **Application Deadline:** Rolling admissions policy. **Number of Students:** 620. **Tests Required:** SAT or ACT. **Admissions Director:** A. Lois Williams.

★2284★

Mississippi Valley State University
Itta Bena, MS 38941 Phone: (601)254-9041
Dr. William W. Sutton, Pres.

Founded: 1946. State-supported university. **Cost:** $3,425.00. **Application Deadline:** Rolling admissions policy. **Number of Students:** 1691. **Tests Required:** SAT or ACT (preferred). **Admissions Director:** Sara C. White; PO Box 61, MVSU, Itta Bena, MS 38941. **Toll-free phone:** (800)821-2743 (Mississippi only).

★2285★

Morehouse College
830 Westview Dr., SW
Atlanta, GA 30314 Phone: (404)681-2800
Dr. Keith Leroy, Pres.

Founded: 1867. Independent four-year men's college. **Cost:** $9,150.00. **Application Deadline:** March 15 (fall); November 1 (spring). **Number of Students:** 2620. **Tests Required:** SAT or ACT. **Admissions Director:** Sterling H. Hudson, III.

★2286★

Morehouse School of Medicine
720 Westview Dr., SW
Atlanta, GA 30310-1495 Phone: (404)752-1500
Dr. James A. Goodman, Pres.

Founded: 1975. Independent graduate institution. **Cost:** $12,700.00. **Application Deadline:** December 1. **Number of Students:** 137. **Admissions Director:** Dr. Angela Franklin, Assistant Dean for Student Affairs.

★2287★

Morgan State University
Cold Spring Ln. & Hillen Rd.
Baltimore, MD 21239 Phone: (301)444-3430
Dr. Earl S. Richardson, Pres.

Founded: 1867. State-supported university. **Cost:** $5,220.00 in-state; $6,656.00 out-of-state. **Application Deadline:** April 15 (fall); December 15 (spring). **Number of Students:** 4399. **Tests Required:** SAT or ACT. **Admissions Director:** Chelseia Harold-Miller. **Toll-free phone:** (800)444-6674.

★2288★

Morris Brown College
643 Martin Luther King Dr., NW
Atlanta, GA 30311 Phone: (404)525-7831
Calvert H. Smith, Pres.

Founded: 1881. Private four-year college. **Cost:** $9,290.00. **Application Deadline:** November 1 (fall); May 1 (spring). **Number of Students:** 1805. **Tests Required:** Open admissions policy. **Admissions Director:** Col. Tyrone P. Fletcher.

★2289★

Morris College
N. Main St.
Sumter, SC 29150 Phone: (803)775-9371
Dr. Luns C. Richardson, Pres.

Founded: 1908. Private four-year college. **Cost:** $5,795.00. **Application Deadline:** Rolling admissions policy. **Number of Students:** 796. **Tests Required:** Open admissions policy. **Admissions Director:** Queen W. Spann.

★2290★

Natchez College
1010 N. Union St.
Natchez, MS 39120 Phone: (601)445-9702
Dr. James E. Gray Sr., Pres.

Founded: 1885. Private two-year college. **Application Deadline:** September 15 (fall); January 15 (spring). **Number of Students:** 100.

Tests Required: Open admissions policy. **Admissions Director:** L. G. Rucker.

★2291★
Norfolk State University
2401 Corprew Ave.
Norfolk, VA 23504 Phone: (804)683-8391
Dr. Harrison B. Wilson, Pres.

Founded: 1935. State-supported university. **Cost:** $5,380.00 in-state; $7,810.00 out-of-state. **Application Deadline:** Rolling admissions policy. **Number of Students:** 7721. **Tests Required:** SAT or ACT. **Admissions Director:** Dr. Frank Cool.

★2292★
North Carolina A&T State University
815 W. Market St.
Greensboro, NC 27411 Phone: (919)334-7946
Dr. Edward B. Fort, Chancellor

Founded: 1891. State-supported university. **Cost:** $3,325.00 in-state; $7,697.00 out-of-state. **Application Deadline:** June 1 (fall). **Number of Students:** 6536. **Tests Required:** SAT or ACT. **Admissions Director:** Clenton A. Blount, Jr.

★2293★
North Carolina Central University
PO Box 19717
Durham, NC 27707 Phone: (919)560-6066
Dr. Tyronza R. Richmond, Chancellor

Founded: 1910. State-supported university. **Cost:** $5,158.00 in-state; $9,078 out-of-state. **Application Deadline:** May 1 (fall, in-state); March 1 (fall, out-of-state). **Number of Students:** 5343. **Tests Required:** SAT or ACT. **Admissions Director:** Nancy R. Rowland.

★2294★
Oakwood College
Oakwood Rd., NW
Huntsville, AL 35896 Phone: (205)837-1630
Dr. Benjamin F. Reaves, Pres.

Founded: 1896. Private four-year college. **Cost:** $8,883.00. **Application Deadline:** Rolling admissions policy. **Number of Students:** 1223. **Tests Required:** SAT or ACT. **Admissions Director:** Hattie D. Mims. **Toll-free phone:** (800)544-4183 (Alabama only); (800)824-5312 (out-of-state).

★2295★
Paine College
1235 15th St.
Augusta, GA 30910 Phone: (404)722-4471
Dr. Julius S. Scott, Pres.

Founded: 1882. Private four-year college. **Cost:** $7,535.00. **Application Deadline:** July 15 (fall); December 1 (spring). **Number of Students:** 580. **Tests Required:** SAT or ACT. **Admissions Director:** Lacius H. Pitts. **Toll-free phone:** (800)476-7703.

★2296★
Paul Quinn College
1020 Elm Ave.
Waco, TX 76704 Phone: (817)753-6415
Dr. Warren W. Morgan, Pres.

Founded: 1872. Independent, four-year African Methodist Episcopalian college. **Cost:** $5,650.00. **Application Deadline:** Rolling admissions policy. **Number of Students:** 577. **Tests Required:** Open admissions policy. **Admissions Director:** Marilyn Marshall.

★2297★
Philander-Smith College
812 W. 13th
Little Rock, AR 72202 Phone: (501)375-9845
Dr. Myer L. Titus, Pres.

Founded: 1877. Independent, four-year United Methodist college. **Cost:** $3,300.00. **Application Deadline:** Rolling admissions policy. **Number of Students:** 620. **Tests Required:** SAT or ACT. **Admissions Director:** Annie Carson.

★2298★
Prairie View A&M University
PO Box 2818
Prairie View, TX 77446 Phone: (409)857-2618
Gen. Julius W. Becton Jr., Pres.

Founded: 1876. State-supported university. **Cost:** $4,198.00 in-state; $4,682.00 out-of-state. **Application Deadline:** Rolling admissions policy. **Number of Students:** 5686. **Tests Required:** SAT or ACT. **Admissions Director:** Mary Gooch; PO Box 2610, Prarie View, TX 77446. **Toll-free phone:** (800)635-4859.

★2299★
Prentiss Normal & Industrial Institute
PO Box 1107
Prentiss, MS 39474
Dr. Sidney J. James, Pres.

Founded: 1907. Independent two-year college. **Number of Students:** 150. **Tests Required:** None (ACT strongly recommended). **Admissions Director:** Lulla Myles.

★2300★
Roxbury Community College
1234 Columbus Ave.
Roxbury Crossing, MA 02120 Phone: (617)541-5310
Dr. Walter C. Howard, Pres.

Founded: 1973. State-supported two-year college. **Cost:** $1,200.00. **Application Deadline:** Rolling admissions policy. **Number of Students:** 2300. **Tests Required:** Open admissions policy. **Admissions Director:** Rosie Quashie.

★2301★
Rust College
1 Rust Ave.
Holly Springs, MS 38635 Phone: (601)252-4461
Dr. William A. McMillan, Pres.

Founded: 1866. Private, four-year college. **Cost:** $5,052.00. **Application Deadline:** July 15 (fall); December 15 (spring). **Number of**

Students: 925. **Tests Required:** SAT or ACT. **Admissions Director:** Jo Ann Scott.

★2302★
St. Augustine's College
1315 Oakwood Ave.
Raleigh, NC 27610-2298 Phone: (919)828-4451
Dr. Prezell R. Robinson, Pres.

Founded: 1867. Independent, four-year Episcopalian college. **Cost:** $7,100.00. **Application Deadline:** August 10 (fall). **Number of Students:** 1885. **Tests Required:** SAT. **Admissions Director:** Wanzo Hendrix.

★2303★
St. Paul's College
406 Windsor Ave.
Lawrenceville, VA 23868 Phone: (804)848-3984
Dr. Thomas M. Law, Pres.

Founded: 1888. Independent, four-year Episcopalian college. **Cost:** $7,143.00. **Application Deadline:** Rolling admissions policy. **Number of Students:** 735. **Tests Required:** SAT. **Admissions Director:** Larnell R. Parker. **Toll-free phone:** (800)678-7071.

★2304★
Savannah State College
State College Branch
PO Box 2029
Savannah, GA 31404 Phone: (912)356-2181
Dr. Ann Brock, Acting Pres.

Founded: 1890. State-supported college. **Cost:** $3,576.00 in-state; $5,958.00 out-of-state. **Application Deadline:** September 1 (fall). **Number of Students:** 2075. **Tests Required:** SAT. **Admissions Director:** David E. Foye.

★2305★
Selma University
1501 Lapsley
Selma, AL 36701 Phone: (205)872-2533
Dr. B. W. Dawson, Pres.

Founded: 1878. Independent, four-year Baptist college. **Cost:** $4,015.00. **Application Deadline:** August 20 (fall). **Number of Students:** 207. **Tests Required:** Open admissions policy. **Admissions Director:** Ovetta C. Williams.

★2306★
Shaw University
118 E. South St.
Raleigh, NC 27611 Phone: (919)546-8200
Dr. Talbert O. Shaw, Pres.

Founded: 1865. Independent, four-year Baptist college. **Cost:** $7,500.00. **Application Deadline:** August 10 (fall). **Number of Students:** 1507. **Tests Required:** SAT or ACT. **Admissions Director:** Louise Lewis.

★2307★
Shorter College
604 Locust St.
North Little Rock, AR 72114 Phone: (501)374-6305
Dr. Katherine Mitchell, Pres.

Founded: 1886. Private two-year college. **Cost:** $3,990.00. **Application Deadline:** Rolling admissions policy. **Number of Students:** 150. **Tests Required:** Open admissions policy, Internal Basic Skills. **Admissions Director:** Delores Voliber.

★2308★
Simmons Bible College
1811 Dumesnil St.
Louisville, KY 40210 Phone: (502)776-1443
Dr. W. J. Hodge, Pres.

Founded: 1879. Denomination-supported four-year college. **Cost:** $900.00. **Application Deadline:** September 1 (fall); January 26 (spring). **Number of Students:** 115. **Tests Required:** Open admissions policy. **Admissions Director:** Charles E. Price.

★2309★
Sojourner-Douglass College
500 N. Caroline St.
Baltimore, MD 21205 Phone: (301)276-0306
Dr. Charles W. Simmons, Pres.

Founded: 1972. Independent four-year college. **Cost:** $1,595.00. **Application Deadline:** Rolling admissions policy. **Number of Students:** 350. **Tests Required:** Open admissions policy. **Admissions Director:** Brenda D. Jackson.

★2310★
South Carolina State College
300 College St., NE
Orangeburg, SC 29117 Phone: (803)536-7185
Dr. Albert E. Smith, Pres.

Founded: 1896. State-supported college. **Cost:** $4,036.00 in-state; $5,766.00 out-of-state. **Application Deadline:** July 30 (fall); November 30 (spring). **Number of Students:** 4399. **Tests Required:** SAT or ACT. **Admissions Director:** Dorothy L. Brown.

★2311★
Southern University
J.S. Clark Administration Bldg.
Baton Rouge, LA 70813 Phone: (504)771-2430
Dr. Dolores R. Spikes, Pres. and Chancellor

Founded: 1880. State-supported college; part of the Southern University System. **Cost:** $3,424.00 in-state; $4,946.00 out-of-state. **Application Deadline:** August 26 (fall). **Number of Students:** 9811. **Tests Required:** SAT or ACT. **Admissions Director:** Clip Carroll.

★2312★
Southern University—New Orleans
6400 Press Dr.
New Orleans, LA 70126 Phone: (504)282-4401
Dr. Robert Gex, Chancellor

Founded: 1959. State-supported college; part of the Southern University System. **Cost:** $1,452.00 in-state; $3,018.00 out-of-state.

Application Deadline: July 1 (fall). **Number of Students:** 3650. **Tests Required:** ACT. **Admissions Director:** Melvin Hodges, Registrar.

★2313★
Southern University—Shreveport
3050 Martin Luther King, Jr. Dr.
Shreveport, LA 71107 Phone: (318)674-3342
Dr. Robert H. Smith, Chancellor

Founded: 1964. State-supported two-year college; part of the Southern University System. **Cost:** $800.00 in-state; $1,830.00 out-of-state. **Application Deadline:** Rolling admissions policy. **Number of Students:** 1042. **Tests Required:** ACT. **Admissions Director:** Clifton Jones.

★2314★
Southwestern Christian College
PO Box 10
Terrell, TX 75160 Phone: (214)563-3341
Dr. Jack Evans, Pres.

Founded: 1949. Private two-year college. **Cost:** $5,156.00. **Application Deadline:** September 1 (fall); January 2 (spring). **Number of Students:** 250. **Tests Required:** SAT or ACT. **Admissions Director:** Gerald E. Lee.

★2315★
Spelman College
350 Spelman Ln., SW
Atlanta, GA 30314
Dr. Johnnetta Cole-Robinson, Pres.

Founded: 1881. Private, four-year women's college. **Cost:** $9,989.00. **Application Deadline:** February 1 (fall); November 15 (spring). **Number of Students:** 1789. **Tests Required:** SAT or ACT. **Admissions Director:** Aline A. Rivers. **Toll-free phone:** (800)282-2625 (Alabama only); (800)241-3421 (out-of-state).

★2316★
Stillman College
PO Box 1430
Tuscaloosa, AL 35403
Dr. Cordell Wynn, Pres.

Founded: 1876. Private four-year college. **Cost:** $6,010.00. **Application Deadline:** August 1 (fall); December 15 (spring). **Number of Students:** 745. **Tests Required:** SAT or ACT (preferred). **Admissions Director:** Mason Bonner. **Toll-free phone:** (800)523-6331 (Alabama only); (800)841-5722 (out-of-state).

★2317★
Talladega College
627 W. Battle St.
Talladega, AL 35160 Phone: (205)362-0206
Dr. Joseph Johnson, Pres.

Founded: 1867. Private four-year college. **Cost:** $6,198.00. **Application Deadline:** Rolling admissions policy. **Number of Students:** 615. **Tests Required:** ACT. **Admissions Director:** Ardie Riveria. **Toll-free phone:** (800)762-2468 (Alabama only); (800)633-2440 (out-of-state).

★2318★
Tennessee State University
3500 John Merritt Blvd.
Nashville, TN 37203 Phone: (615)320-3420
Dr. James Hefner, Pres.

Founded: 1912. State-supported university. **Cost:** $3,576.00 in-state; $6,530.00 out-of-state. **Application Deadline:** August 1 (fall). **Number of Students:** 8270. **Tests Required:** SAT or ACT. **Admissions Director:** Dr. Robert Boone.

★2319★
Texas College
2404 N. Grand Ave.
Tyler, TX 75702 Phone: (214)593-8311
Dr. David H. Johnson, Pres.

Founded: 1894. Independent four-year college affiliated with the Christian Methodist Episcopalian Church. **Cost:** $5,580.00. **Application Deadline:** August 15 (fall). **Number of Students:** 440. **Tests Required:** ACT. **Admissions Director:** Dr. M. E. Surry-Fingal.

★2320★
Texas Southern University
3100 Cleburne Ave.
Houston, TX 77004 Phone: (713)527-7070
Dr. William H. Harris, Pres.

Founded: 1947. State-supported university. **Application Deadline:** August 1 (fall); January 2 (spring). **Number of Students:** 9198. **Tests Required:** SAT or ACT. **Admissions Director:** Collie Chambers, Coordinator of Recruitment.

★2321★
Tougaloo College
Tougaloo, MS 39174 Phone: (601)956-4941
Dr. Adib Shakir, Pres.

Founded: 1869. Private four-year college. **Cost:** $5,429.00. **Application Deadline:** Rolling admissions policy. **Number of Students:** 948. **Tests Required:** SAT or ACT. **Admissions Director:** George Johnson.

★2322★
Tuskegee University
Office of Admissions and Enrollment Services
Carnegie Hall, 4th Fl.
Tuskegee, AL 36088 Phone: (205)727-8500
Dr. Benjamin F. Payton, Pres.

Founded: 1881. Independent university. **Cost:** $8,050.00. **Application Deadline:** April 30 (fall). **Number of Students:** 3510. **Tests Required:** SAT or ACT. **Admissions Director:** Ann R. Ware.

★2323★
University of Arkansas, Pine Bluff
University Dr.
PO Box 4038
Pine Bluff, AR 71601 Phone: (501)541-6559
Dr. Charles A. Walker, Chancellor

Founded: 1873. State-supported four-year university. **Cost:** $3,326.00 in-state; $4,938.00 out-of-state. **Application Deadline:** August 10 (fall);

December 10 (spring). **Number of Students:** 3077. **Tests Required:** ACT. **Admissions Director:** Kwurly M. Floyd.

★2324★
University of Maryland—Eastern Shore
Princess Anne, MD 21853 Phone: (301)651-2200
Dr. William P. Hytche, Pres.

Founded: 1886. State-supported university. **Cost:** $5,468.00 in-state; $8,842.00 out-of-state. **Application Deadline:** Rolling admissions policy. **Number of Students:** 1828. **Tests Required:** SAT. **Admissions Director:** Edwina Morse, Assistant Director.

★2325★
University of the District of Columbia
4200 Connecticut Ave., NW
Washington, DC 20008 Phone: (202)282-8637
Rafael L. Cortada, Pres.

Founded: 1976. State- and locally-supported university. **Cost:** $600.00 in-state; $2,464.00 out-of-state. **Application Deadline:** August 1 (fall). **Number of Students:** 12,000. **Tests Required:** Rolling admissions policy. **Admissions Director:** Alfred Taylor.

★2326★
Virginia State University
Petersburg, VA 23803 Phone: (804)524-5900
Dr. Wesley Cornelious McClure, Pres.

Founded: 1882. State-supported university. **Cost:** $4,697.00 in-state; $8,437.00 out-of-state. **Application Deadline:** May 1 (fall); October 1 (spring). **Number of Students:** 4073. **Tests Required:** SAT (preferred) or ACT. **Admissions Director:** Hope N. Walton; PO Box 18, Petersburg, VA 23803.

★2327★
Virginia Union University
1500 N. Lombardy St.
Richmond, VA 23220 Phone: (804)257-5885
Dr. S. Dallas Simmons, Pres.

Founded: 1865. Private university. **Cost:** $8,850.00. **Application Deadline:** Rolling admissions policy. **Number of Students:** 1200. **Tests Required:** SAT. **Admissions Director:** Gil Powell. **Toll-free phone:** (800)368-3227.

★2328★
Voorhees College
Voorhees Rd.
Denmark, SC 29042 Phone: (803)793-3351
Dr. Leonard E. Dawson, Pres.

Founded: 1897. Private four-year college. **Cost:** $8,194.00. **Application Deadline:** Rolling admissions policy. **Number of Students:** 590. **Tests Required:** Open admissions policy. **Admissions Director:** Francine English Cayruth.

★2329★
West Virginia State College
Institute, WV 25112 Phone: (304)766-3221
Dr. Hazo W. Carter, Pres.

Founded: 1891. State-supported four-year college. **Cost:** $3,810.00 in-state; $5,610.00 out-of-state. **Application Deadline:** August 10 (fall); December 15 (spring). **Number of Students:** 3374. **Tests Required:** ACT. **Admissions Director:** James M. Huffman; PO Box 336, Institute, WV 25112.

★2330★
Wilberforce University
1055 N. Bickett Rd.
Wilberforce, OH 45384 Phone: (513)376-2911
Dr. John L. Henderson, Pres.

Founded: 1856. Independent four-year college affiliated with the African Methodist Episcopalian Church. **Cost:** $9,262.00. **Application Deadline:** June 1 (fall); November 15 (spring). **Number of Students:** 800. **Tests Required:** SAT or ACT. **Admissions Director:** Robert A. Thomas. **Toll-free phone:** (800)367-8565 (Ohio only); (800)367-8568 (out-of-state).

★2331★
Wiley College
711 Wiley Ave.
Marshall, TX 75670 Phone: (214)938-8341
Dr. David L. Beckley, Pres.

Founded: 1873. Private four-year college. **Cost:** $6,490.00. **Application Deadline:** March 15 (fall); October 15 (spring). **Number of Students:** 400. **Tests Required:** SAT or ACT recommended. **Admissions Director:** Edward Morgan.

★2332★
Winston-Salem State University
Martin Luther King Blvd.
Winston-Salem, NC 27110
Dr. Cleon F. Thompson Jr., Pres.

Founded: 1892. State-supported four-year university. **Cost:** $3,362.00 in-state; $7,204.00 out-of-state. **Application Deadline:** Rolling admissions policy. **Number of Students:** 2576. **Tests Required:** SAT or ACT. **Admissions Director:** Dr. J. A. Mootz.

★2333★
Xavier University of Louisiana
7325 Palmetto St.
New Orleans, LA 70125 Phone: (504)486-7411
Dr. Norman C. Francis, Pres.

Founded: 1915. Private university. **Cost:** $7,900.00. **Application Deadline:** July 15 (fall); December 15 (spring). **Number of Students:** 2900. **Tests Required:** SAT or ACT. **Admissions Director:** Winston D. Brown.

(7) BLACK STUDIES PROGRAMS

Entries in this chapter are arranged alphabetically by institution name within three categories: Two-year Colleges; Four-year Colleges; and Graduate Programs. See the User's Guide at the front of this directory for additional information.

Two-Year Colleges

★2334★
Bronx Community College of the City University of New York
Cultural Affairs
181st & University Ave.
Bronx, NY 10453 Phone: (212)220-6343
Harvey Erdsneker, Registrar

★2335★
City College of Chicago - Olive-Harvey College
Black Studies Progam
Chicago, IL 60628 Phone: (312)568-3700
Richard Hazley, Dir. of Adm.

★2336★
City College of San Francisco
Black Studies Program
San Francisco, CA 94112 Phone: (415)239-3291
Mira D. Sina, Dean of Adm.

★2337★
Contra Costa College
Black Studies Program
San Pablo, CA 94806 Phone: (415)235-7800
Dean Eaton, Dir. of Adm.

★2338★
East Los Angeles College
Black Studies Program
Monterey Park, CA 91754 Phone: (213)265-8712
Maria Elena Martinez, Asst. Dean of Adm.

★2339★
El Camino College
Black Studies Program
Torrance, CA 90506 Phone: (213)532-3670
William Robinson, Registrar

★2340★
Essex County College
Black Studies Program
Office of the Dean of Academic Affairs
Newark, NJ 07102 Phone: (201)877-3115
Vivian O. Jones, Dir. of Enrollment Svc.

★2341★
Laney College
Ethnic Studies Department
Oakland, CA 94607 Phone: (415)466-7368
Henry Fort, Dist. Dean of Adm.

★2342★
Los Angeles City College
Black Studies Program
Los Angeles, CA 90029 Phone: (213)669-4382
Myra B. Siegel, Asst. Dean of Adm.

★2343★
Los Angeles Harbor College
Black Studies Program
Wilmington, CA 90744 Phone: (213)518-1000
Luis Rosas, Asst. Dean of Adm.

★2344★
Los Angeles Valley College
Afro-American Studies
Van Nuys, CA 91401 Phone: (818)781-1200
John T. Barnhart, Asst. Dean of Adm.

★2345★
Merritt College
Black Studies Program
Oakland, CA 94619 Phone: (415)436-2477
Dr. George Herring, Dean of Students

★2346★
Mira Costa College
Black Studies Program
Oceanside, CA 92056 Phone: (619)757-2121
Norma L. Cooper, Registrar

★2347★
Nassau Community College
Afro-American Studies Department
Garden City, NY 11530 Phone: (516)222-7352
Bernard Iantosa, Dir. of Adm.

★2348★
Prairie State College
Black Studies Program
Chicago Heights, IL 60411 Phone: (708)756-3110
Carol Cleator, Adm. Office Supr.

★2349★
Rancho Santiago College
Black Studies Program
Santa Ana, CA 92706 Phone: (714)667-3016
Dr. Harold Bateman, Dean of Adm.

★2350★
St. Louis Community College at Forest Park
Black Studies Program
St. Louis, MO 63110 Phone: (314)644-9131
Bart S. Devoti, Registrar/Dir. of Adm.

★2351★
San Diego City College
Black Studies Program
San Diego, CA 92101 Phone: (619)230-2475
Leticia Peters, Student Svc. Tech.

★2352★
San Diego Mesa College
Black Studies Program
San Diego, CA 92111 Phone: (619)560- 2689
Wiletta Tomlinson, Adm. Officer

★2353★
Santa Barbara City College
Ethnic Studies Department
Santa Barbara, CA 93109 Phone: (805)965-0581
Jane G. Craven, Asst. Dean of Adm.

★2354★
Solano Community College
Black Studies Program
Suisun City, CA 94585 Phone: (707)864-7113
Gerald Fisher, Asst. Dean of Adm.

★2355★
Southwestern College
Black Studies Program
Chula Vista, CA 92010 Phone: (619)421-6700
Georgia Copeland, Dir. of Adm.

★2356★
Thornton Community College
Black Studies Program
South Holland, IL 60473 Phone: (312)596-2000
William J. Hafer, Dean of Adm.

★2357★
Triton College
School of Arts and Sciences
Black Studies Program
River Grove, IL 60171 Phone: (312)456-0300
Gwen E. Kanelos, Dean of Students

★2358★
Yuba College
Black Studies Program
Marysville, CA 95901 Phone: (916)741-6705
Susan Singhas, Assoc. Dean of Adm.

Four-Year Colleges and Universities

★2359★
Amherst College
Department of Black Studies
Amherst, MA 01002 Phone: (413)542-2328
Jane E. Reynolds, Dean of Adm.

★2360★
Ball State University
Afro-American Studies
Muncie, IN 47306 Phone: (317)285-8288
Ruth Vedvik, Dir. of Adm.

★2361★
Bowdoin College
Afro-American Studies Program
Brunswick, ME 04011 Phone: (207)725-3100
William R. Mason, Dir. of Adm.

★2362★
Bowling Green State University
Ethnic Studies Department
Bowling Green, OH 43403 Phone: (419)372-2086
John W. Martin, Dir. of Adm.

★2363★
Brandeis University
Department of African and Afro-American Studies
Waltham, MA 02254 Phone: (617)736-2000
David L. Gould, Dean of Adm.

★2364★
Brown University
Afro-American Studies Program
Providence, RI 02912 Phone: (401)863-2378
Eric Widmer, Dir. of Adm.

★2365★
California State University, Dominquez Hills
African-American Studies Program
Carson, CA 90747 Phone: (213)516-3600
Anita Gash, Dir. of Adm.

★2366★
California State University, Fullerton
Department of Afro-Ethnic Studies
Fullerton, CA 92634 Phone: (714)773-2370
William Gowler, Adm. Dir.

★2367★
California State University, Hayward
Afro-American Studies Program
Hayward, CA 94542 Phone: (415)881-3817
Glenn Perry, Dir. of Adm.

★2368★
California State University, Long Beach
Department of Black Studies
Long Beach, CA 90840 Phone: (213)498-4141
James F. Menzel, Dir. of Adm.

★2369★
California State University, Los Angeles
Department of Pan-African Studies
Los Angeles, CA 90032 Phone: (213)224-2180
Kevin M. Browne, Adm. Officer

★2370★
California State University, Northridge
Pan-African Studies Department
Northridge, CA 91330 Phone: (818)885-3700
Lorraine Newlon, Dir. of Adm.

★2371★
California State University, Sacramento
Pan-African Studies Program
Sacramento, CA 95819 Phone: (916)278-6763
Larry Glasmire, Adm. Officer

★2372★
Central State University
Department of Political Science
African and Afro-American Studies
Wilberforce, OH 45384 Phone: (513)376-6011
Robert Johnson, Dir. of Adm.

★2373★
Central Washington University
Black Studies Program
Ellensburg, WA 98926 Phone: (509)963-1211
Jim Maraviglia, Dir. of Adm.

★2374★
Chatham College
Black Studies Program
Pittsburgh, PA 15232 Phone: (412)365-1290
Miriam King-Watts, Dean of Enrollment

★2375★
City College of City University of New York
Department of African and Afro-American Studies
New York, NY 10031 Phone: (212)690-6977
Leonard Jeffries Jr., Chairman

★2376★
Cleveland State University
Black Studies Program
Cleveland, OH 44115 Phone: (216)791-1700
Professor Curtis Wilson, Dir.

★2377★
Coe College
Afro-American Studies
Cedar Rapids, IA 52402 Phone: (319)399-8000
Michael White, Dean of Adm.

★2378★
College of Staten Island of City University of New York
Institute for African-American Studies
Staten Island, NY 10301 Phone: (718)390-7557
Ramon H. Hulsey, Dir. of Adm.

★2379★
College of Wooster
Black Studies Program
Wooster, OH 44691 Phone: (216)263-2000
Dr. William Baird, Dean of Adm.

★2380★
Columbia College
Department of Afro-American Studies
New York, NY 10027 Phone: (212)854-2521
Lawrence Momo, Dir. of Adm.

★2381★
Cornell University
Africana Studies and Research Center
Ithaca, NY 14853 Phone: (607)255-5241
Nancy Hargrave Meislahn, Dean of Adm.

★2382★
Dartmouth College
African and Afro-American Studies Program
Hanover, NH 03755 Phone: (603)646-2875
Karl M. Furstenberg, Dir. of Adm.

★2383★
Denison University
Center for Black Studies
Granville, OH 43023 Phone: (614)587-0810
Richard F. Boyden, Dir. of Adm.

★2384★
Duke University
Black Studies
2138 Campus Dr.
Durham, NC 27706 Phone: (919)684-3214
Harold M. Wingood, Assoc. Undergrad. Adm. Dir.

★2385★
Earlham College
African and African-American Studies
Richmond, IN 47374 Phone: (317)983-1200
Robert de Veer, Dean of Adm.

★2386★
Eastern Illinois University
Afro-American Studies
Charleston, IL 61920 Phone: (217)581-2223
Dale Wolf, Dir. of Adm.

★2387★
Eastern Michigan University
Department of Afro-American Studies
Ypsilanti, MI 48197 Phone: (313)487-0239
James Olsen, Adm. Coor.

★2388★
Edinboro University of Pennsylvania
History Department
African History
Edinboro, PA 16444 Phone: 800-626-2204
Terry Carlin, Adm. Dir.

★2389★
Elizabeth City State University
African-American Studies Program
Elizabeth City, NC 27909 Phone: (919)335-3305
William Byrd, Dir. of Adm.

★2390★
Emory University
African and African American Studies Program
Atlanta, GA 30322 Phone: (404)727-6036
Daniel C. Walls, Dean of Adm.

★2391★
Florida A&M University
Afro-American Studies
Tallahassee, FL 32307 Phone: (904)599-3796
Daisy O. Young, Deputy Registrar

★2392★
Fordham University
Afro-American Studies Department
Bronx, NY 10458 Phone: (212)579-2133
Richard A. Avitabile, Dir. of Adm.

★2393★
Friends World College
African Studies
Huntington, NY 11743 Phone: (516)549-1102
Arthur Meyer, Dir. of Adm.

★2394★
Goucher College
Black Studies Program
Baltimore, MD 21204 Phone: (301)337-6100
Elsie A. Seraydarian, Dir. of Adm.

★2395★
Grambling State University
Afro-American Studies Program
Grambling, LA 71245 Phone: (318)274-2487
Karen Lewis, Dir. of Adm.

★2396★
Grinnell College
Afro-American Studies
Grinnell, IA 50112-0807 Phone: (515)269-3600
John R. Hopkin, Dir. of Adm.

★2397★
Hamilton College
African-American Studies Program
Clinton, NJ 13323 Phone: (315)859-4421
Douglas C. Thompson, Dean of Adm.

★2398★
Hampshire College
Black Studies
Amherst, MA 01002 Phone: (413)549-4600
Olga Euben, Dir. of Adm.

★2399★
Harvard University
Afro-American Studies Department
Cambridge, MA 02138 Phone: (617)495-1551
Dr. William R. Fitzsimmons, Dean of Adm.

★2400★
Hobart College
Black Studies Program
Geneva, NY 14456 Phone: (315)789-5500
Leonard A. Wood Jr., Dir. of Adm.

★2401★
Howard University
Department of Afro-American Studies
Washington, DC 20059 Phone: (202)636-6200
Emmett R. Griffin Jr., Dir. of Adm.

★2402★
Hunter College of City University of New York
New York, NY 10021 Phone: (212)772-4479
Dr. Kenneth Kleinrock, Dir. of Adm.

★2403★
Indiana State University
Center for Afro-American Studies
Terre Haute, IN 47809 Phone: (812)237-2121
Richard Riehl, Dir. of Adm.

★2404★
Indiana University
Afro-American Studies Department
814 E. 3rd St.
Bloomington, IN 47405 Phone: (812)335-0661
Robert S. Magee, Dir. of Adm.

★2405★
Indiana University
Department of Minority Studies
Gary, IN 46408 Phone: (219)980-6821
William D. Lee, Dir. of Adm.

★2406★
Kent State University
Institute of African American Affairs
Black Studies Program
Kent, OH 44242 Phone: (216)672-2444
Bruce L. Riddle, Dir. of Adm.

★2407★
Knox College
Black Studies Department
Galesburg, IL 61401 Phone: (309)343-0112
Karen Ruedi Crowell, Dir. of Adm.

★2408★
Lehman College of City University of New York
Black Studies Department
Bronx, NY 10468 Phone: (212)960-8131
Jane Herbert, Dir. of Enrollment

★2409★
Loyola Marymount University
Department of Afro-American Studies
Los Angeles, CA 90045 Phone: (213)642-2750
M.E. L'Heureux, Dir. of Adm.

★2410★
Loyola University of Chicago
Afro-American Studies Program
Chicago, IL 60626 Phone: (312)915-6500
Allen V. Lentino, Dir. of Adm.

★2411★
Luther College
African-American Studies
Decorah, IA 52101 Phone: (319)387-1287
Dennis R. Johnson, Dean of Enrollment

★2412★
Mercer University
Afro-American Studies
Macon, GA 31207 Phone: (404)986-3000
William Muller, Dean of Enrollment

★2413★
Metropolitan State College
Department of Afro-American Studies
Denver, CO 80204 Phone: (303)556-3977
Thomas R. Gray, Asst. Dean of Adm.

★2414★
Miami University
Afro-American Studies
Oxford, OH 45056 Phone: (513)529-2531
Charles R. Schuter, Dir. of Adm.

★2415★
Morgan State University
Department of History
Baltimore, MD 21239 Phone: (301)444-3430
Chelseia Harold, Dir. of Adm.

★2416★
Mount Holyoke College
Black Studies Department
South Hadley, MA 01075 Phone: (413)538-2023
Susan P. Staggers, Dean of Adm.

★2417★
New York University
Department of History
New York, NY 10012 Phone: (212)598-3591
David Finney, Dir. of Adm.

★2418★
North Carolina Central University
Black Studies Program
Durham, NC 27707 Phone: (919)683-6298
Nancy R. Rowland, Dir. of Adm.

★2419★
Northeastern University
Department of African and Afro-American Studies
Boston, MA 02115 Phone: (617)437-2222
Philip R. McCabe, Dean of Adm.

★2420★
Northwestern University
African American Studies Department
Evanston, IL 60201 Phone: (312)491-7271
Carol Lunkenheimer, Dir. of Adm.

★2421★
Oberlin College
Black Studies Department
Oberlin, OH 44074 Phone: (216)775-8411
Thomas C. Hayden, Dir. of Adm.

★2422★
Occidental College
Department of History
Los Angeles, CA 90041 Phone: (213)259-2700
Charlene Liebau, Dir. of Adm.

★2423★
Ohio State University
Department of Black Studies
Columbus, OH 43210 Phone: (614)292-3980
Dr. James J. Mager, Dir. of Adm.

★2424★
Ohio University
Afro-American Studies
Athens, OH 45701 Phone: (614)593-4100
Dr. James C. Walters, Dir. of Adm.

★2425★
Ohio Wesleyan University
Cross-Cultural Programs
Delaware, OH 43015 Phone: (614)369-4431
Michael Kennedy, Dir. of Adm.

★2426★
Purdue University
Afro-American Studies Center
West Lafayette, IN 47907 Phone: (317)494-1776
William J. Murray, Dir. of Adm.

★2427★
Rhode Island College
African and Afro-American Studies Program
Providence, RI 02908 Phone: (401)456-8234
Patricia A. Sullivan, Dean of Adm.

★2428★
Roosevelt University
African, Afro-American, and Black Studies
Chicago, IL 60605 Phone: (312)341-3515
Barbara Gianneschi, Dean of Adm.

★2429★
Rutgers State University of New Jersey
Camden College of Arts and Sciences
Camden, NJ 08102 Phone: (201)932-3770
Deborah Bowles, Asst. V.Pres., Adm.

★2430★
Rutgers State University of New Jersey
Douglas College
Africana Studies
New Brunswick, NJ 08903 Phone: (201)932-3770
Dr. Elizabeth Mitchell, Asst. V.Pres., Adm.

★2431★
Rutgers State University of New Jersey
Livingston College
Black Studies Program
New Brunswick, NJ 08903 Phone: (201)932-3770
Dr. Elizabeth Mitchell, Asst. V.Pres., Adm.

★2432★
Rutgers State University of New Jersey
New Brunswick College
Africana Studies
New Brunswick, NJ 08903 Phone: (201)932-7276
William Callahan, Asst. Dir.

★2433★
Rutgers State University of New Jersey
Newark College
Afro-American and African Studies Department
Newark, NJ 07102 Phone: (201)932-3770
John Scott, Dir. of Adm.

★2434★
Rutgers State University of New Jersey
Rutgers College
Africana Studies
New Brunswick, NJ 08903 Phone: (201)932-3770
Dr. Elizabeth Mitchell, Asst. V.Pres., Adm.

★2435★
St. Olaf College
American Minority Studies Program
Northfield, MN 55057 Phone: (507)663-3025
John Ruohoniemi, Dir. of Adm.

★2436★
San Diego State University
Department of Afro-American Studies
San Diego, CA 92182 Phone: (619)265-5384
Nancy C. Sprotte, Dir. of Adm.

★2437★
San Francisco State University
Black Studies
San Francisco, CA 94132 Phone: (415)469-2163
Dr. Corwin Bjonerud, Dir. of Adm.

★2438★
San Jose State University
Afro-American Studies Department
San Jose, CA 95192 Phone: (408)277-2200
Edgar A. Chambers, Assoc. Exec. V.Pres.

★2439★
Scripps College
Black Studies Program
Claremont, CA 91711 Phone: (714)621-8149
Leslie Miles, Dean of Adm.

★2440★
Seton Hall University
African American Studies
South Orange, NJ 07079 Phone: (201)761-9332
Patricia L. Burgh, Dean of Adm.

★2441★
Shaw University
Afro-American Studies
Raleigh, NC 27611 Phone: (919)755-4804
Gloria Smith, Dir. of Adm.

★2442★
Sierra University
Black Studies Program
Costa Mesa, CA 92626 Phone: (714)545-1133

★2443★
Simmons College
Afro-American Studies Program
Boston, MA 02115 Phone: (617)738-2107
Debra Wright, Assoc. Dean of Adm.

★2444★
Smith College
Department of Afro-American Studies
Northampton, MA 01063 Phone: (413)584-0515
Lorna R. Blake, Dir. of Adm.

★2445★
Sonoma State University
Black Studies Program
Rohnert Park, CA 94928 Phone: (707)664-2326
Dr. Frank Tansey, Dean of Adm.

★2446★
Southern Illinois University
Black American Studies Program
Carbondale, IL 60091 Phone: (618)536-4405
Thomas McGinnis, Dir. of Adm.

★2447★
Southern Methodist University
Department of Anthropology
Dallas, TX 75275 Phone: (214)692-2058
Andrew L. Bryant, Dir. of Adm.

★2448★
Stanford University
African and Afro-American Studies Program
Stanford, CA 94305 Phone: (415)725-0104
Horace Porter, Chair

★2449★
State University of New York at Albany
African and Afro-American Studies
Albany, NY 12222 Phone: (518)442-5435
Dr. Allen Ballard, Chair

★2450★
State University of New York at Binghamton
Afro-American and African Studies Department
Binghamton, NY 13901 Phone: (607)777-2171
Geoffrey D. Gould, Dir. of Adm.

★2451★
State University of New York at Brockport
Department of African and Afro-American Studies
Brockport, NY 14420 Phone: (716)395-2751
Marsha R. Gottovi, Dir. of Adm.

★2452★
State University of New York at Buffalo
Department of African-American Studies
Buffalo, NY 14222 Phone: (716)878-5511
Deborah K. Renzi, Dir. of Adm.

★2453★
State University of New York at Cortland
Black Studies Program
Cortland, NY 13045 Phone: (607)753-4711
Michael K. McKeon, Dir. of Adm.

★2454★
State University of New York at Geneseo
Black Studies Program
Geneseo, NY 14454 Phone: (716)245-5571
Janet M. Graeter, Dean of Adm.

★2455★
State University of New York at New Paltz
Black Studies Department
New Paltz, NY 12561 Phone: (914)257-2414
Robert J. Seaman, Dean of Adm.

★2456★
State University of New York at Oneonta
Department of Black and Hispanic Studies
Oneonta, NY 13820 Phone: (607)431-2524
Richard Burr, Dir. of Adm.

★2457★
Syracuse University
Afro-American Studies Department
Syracuse, NY 13244 Phone: (315)423-2300
David C. Smith, Dean of Adm.

★2458★
Temple University
Pan-African Studies
Philadelphia, PA 19122 Phone: (215)787-7200
Dr. Sarah Banks, Dir. of Undergrad. Adm.

★2459★
Tougaloo College
Black Studies Program
Tougaloo, MS 39174 Phone: (601)956-4941
Dr. George Johnson, Asst. Dir. of Student Enrollment

★2460★
Towson State University
African-American Studies
Towson, MD 21204 Phone: (301)321-2112
Linda J. Collins, Dir. of Adm.

★2461★
Trenton State College
African-American Studies
Hillwood Lakes, CN4700
Trenton, NJ 08625 Phone: (609)771-2138
Gloria H. Dickinson, Dir.

★2462★
Tufts University
Africa and the New World Program
Medford, MA 02155 Phone: (617)381-3170
David Cuttino, Dean of Adm.

★2463★
Tuskegee University
Black Studies Program
Tuskegee, AL 36088 Phone: (205)727-8500
Ann Ware, Dir. of Adm.

★2464★
University of California, Berkeley
Afro-American Studies Department
Berkeley, CA 94720 Phone: (415)642-0200
Dr. Robert L. Bailey, Dir. of Adm.

★2465★
University of California, Davis
Afro-American Studies Program
Davis, CA 95616 Phone: (916)752-2971
Dr. Gary Tudor, Dir. of Adm.

★2466★
University of California, Los Angeles
Center for Afro-American Studies
Los Angeles, CA 90024 Phone: (213)825-3101
Dr. Rae Lee Siporin, Dir. of Adm.

★2467★
University of California, Santa Barbara
Department of Black Studies
Santa Barbara, CA 93106 Phone: (805)961-2485
William Villa, Dir. of Adm.

★2468★
University of Cincinnati
Afro-American Studies
Cincinnati, OH 45221 Phone: (513)475-3427
Robert W. Neal, Dir. of Adm.

★2469★
University of Colorado—Boulder
Black Studies Program
Boulder, CO 80309 Phone: (303)492-6301
Millard Storey, Dir. of Adm.

★2470★
University of Hartford
African-American Studies
West Hartford, CT 06117 Phone: (203)243-4296
Richard A. Zeiser, Dir. of Adm.

★2471★
University of Illinois at Chicago
Black Studies Program
Chicago, IL 60680 Phone: (312)996-4350
Marge Gockel, Assoc. Dir. of Adm.

★2472★
University of Illinois at Urbana-Champaign
Afro-American Studies and Research Center
Urbana, IL 61801 Phone: (217)333-0302
Martha H. Moore, Asst. Dir. of Adm.

★2473★
University of Iowa
African-American World Studies Program
Iowa City, IA 52242 Phone: (319)335-3847
Darwin T. Turner, Chair

★2474★
University of Kansas
African and African American Studies Department
Lawrence, KS 66045 Phone: (913)864-3054
Arthur D. Drayton, Chair

★2475★
University of Maryland
Afro-American Studies
College Park, MD 20742 Phone: (301)454-5550
Dr. Linda M. Clement, Dir. of Adm.

★2476★
University of Maryland
Department of African-American Studies
Cantonsville, MD 21228 Phone: (301)455-2291
Mindy Hand, Assoc. Dir. of Adm.

★2477★
University of Massachusetts at Amherst
W.E.B. DuBois Department of Afro-American Studies
Amherst, MA 01003 Phone: (413)545-0222
Dr. Timm Rinehart, Dir. of Freshman Adm.

★2478★
University of Massachusetts at Boston
Black Studies
Boston, MA 02125 Phone: (617)929-8000
Ronald Ancrum, Dir. of Adm.

★2479★
University of Michigan
Center for Afroamerican and African Studies
Black Studies Program
Ann Arbor, MI 48109 Phone: (313)764-7433
Dr. Richard Shaw, Dir. of Adm.

★2480★
University of Michigan, Flint
Afro-American and African Studies Program
Flint, MI 48502 Phone: (313)762-3300
Melba Moore, Dir.

★2481★
University of Minnesota
Afro-American and African Studies Program
Minneapolis, MN 55455 Phone: (612)625-5000
Leo D. Abbott, Dir. of Adm.

★2482★
University of Missouri, Columbia
Black Studies Program
Columbia, MO 65211 Phone: (314)882-7651
Dr. Gary L. Smith, Dir. of Adm.

★2483★
University of Nebraska, Lincoln
Anthropology Department
Black Studies Program
Lincoln, NE 68588 Phone: (402)472-2480
Richard Hitchcock, Dir.

★2484★
University of New Mexico
African-American Studies Department
1130 Mesa Vista Hall
Albuquerque, NM 87131 Phone: (505)277-3430
Shiame Okunor, Dir.

★2485★
University of North Carolina at Chapel Hill
Afro-American Studies
Chapel Hill, NC 27514 Phone: (919)966-3621
Richard G. Cashwell, Dir. of Adm.

★2486★
University of North Carolina at Charlotte
Afro-American and African Studies
Charlotte, NC 28223 Phone: (704)547-2211
Kathi Baucom, Dir. of Adm.

★2487★
University of North Carolina at Greensboro
Anthropology Department
Black Studies Program
Greensboro, NC 27412 Phone: (919)334-5243
Willie Baber, Dir.

★2488★
University of Northern Colorado
Afro-American Studies
Greeley, CO 80639 Phone: (303)351-2881
Gary Gullickson, Dir. of Adm.

★2489★
University of Pennsylvania
Afro-American Studies Program
Philadelphia, PA 19104 Phone: (215)898-7507
Willis J. Stetson Jr., Dean of Adm.

★2490★
University of Pittsburgh
Department of Black Studies
Pittsburgh, PA 15260 Phone: (412)624-7488
Dr. Betsy A. Porter, Dir. of Adm.

★2491★
University of South Carolina at Columbia
Afro-American Studies
Columbia, SC 29208 Phone: (803)777-7700
Deborah C. Haynes, Dir. of Adm.

★2492★
University of South Florida
Department of African and Afro-American Studies
Tampa, FL 33620 Phone: (813)974-3350
Vicki W. Ahrens, Dir. of Adm.

★2493★
University of Tennessee at Knoxville
Afro-American Studies Program
Knoxville, TN 37996 Phone: (615)974-2184
Richard Griffin, Acting Dir. of Adm.

★2494★
University of Texas at Austin
African and AfroAmerican Studies & Research Center
Black Studies Program
Austin, TX 78712 Phone: (512)471-1711
Shirley Binder, Dir. of Adm.

★2495★
University of the Pacific
Department of Black Studies
Stockton, CA 95211 Phone: (209)946-2211
Ms. Pat Peters, Dir. of Adm.

★2496★
University of Toledo
Minority Affairs
Toledo, OH 43606 Phone: (419)537-2696
Richard J. Eastop, Dean of Adm.

★2497★
University of Virginia
Carter G. Woodson Institute for AfroAmerican and African Studies
Charlottesville, VA 22903 Phone: (804)924-3109
Armistad Robinson, Dir.

★2498★
University of Washington
Afro-American Studies Program
Seattle, WA 98195 Phone: (206)543-9686
Stephanie Preston, Asst. Dir. of Adm.

★2499★
University of Wisconsin—Madison
Department of Afro-American Studies
Madison, WI 53706 Phone: (608)262-3961
David E. Vinson, Dir. of Adm.

★2500★
University of Wisconsin—Milwaukee
Afro-American Studies Department
Milwaukee, WI 53201 Phone: (414)229-1122
Beth L. Weckmueller, Dir. of Adm.

★2501★
Upsala College
Black Studies
East Orange, NJ 07019 Phone: (201)266-7191
George Lynes, Dir. of Adm.

★2502★
Vanderbilt University
Black Studies Program
Nashville, TN 37240 Phone: (615)322-2561
Dr. Neill Sanders, Dean of Adm.

★2503★
Washington State University
Heritage House
Pullman, WA 99164 Phone: (509)335-5586
Terry Flynn, Acting Dir. of Adm.

★2504★
Washington University
Black Studies
St. Louis, MO 63130 Phone: (314)889-6000
Dr. Charles S. Nolan, Dean of Adm.

★2505★
Wayne State University
Black Americana Studies Center
Detroit, MI 48202 Phone: (313)577-3501
Michael Martin, Dir.

★2506★
Wellesley College
Black Studies Department
Wellesley, MA 02181 Phone: (617)235-0320
Natalie Aharonian, Dir. of Adm.

★2507★
Wesleyan University
Center for Afro-American Studies
Middletown, CT 06457 Phone: (203)347-9411
Karl M. Furstenberg, Dean of Adm.

★2508★
Western Illinois University
African-American Studies Program
Currens Hall, Rm. 500
Macomb, IL 61455 Phone: (309)298-1181
Dr. Abdi Sheik-Abdi, Dir.

★2509★
Western Michigan University
Black Americana Studies Center
Black Studies Program
Kalamazoo, MI 49008 Phone: (616)387-2000
Leroy Ray, Dir.

★2510★
William Paterson College of New Jersey
Department of African and Afro-American Studies
Wayne, NJ 07470 Phone: (201)595-2126
Leo DeBartolo, Dir. of Adm.

★2511★
Williams College
African-American Studies Program
Williamstown, MA 01267 Phone: (413)597-3131
Dennis Dickerson, Chair

★2512★
Yale University
Afro-American Studies Department
New Haven, CT 06520 Phone: (203)432-1900
David Worth, Dean of Adm.

★2513★
York College of City University of New York
Afro-American Studies
9420 Guy R. Brewer Blvd.
Jamaica, NY 11451 Phone: (718)262-2165
Ronnie Levitt, Dir. of Adm.

★2514★
Youngstown State University
Black Studies Program
Youngstown, OH 44555 Phone: (216)742-3158
James R. Kraynak, Dir. of Adm.

Graduate Programs

★2515★
Atlanta University
Department of Afro-American Studies
Atlanta, GA 30314 Phone: (404)681-0251
Peggy Wade, Registrar/Dir. of Adm.

★2516★
Boston University
Afro-American Studies Program
Boston, MA 02215 Phone: (617)353-2693
Wislon J. Moses Ph.D., Dir.

★2517★
Clark Atlanta University
Center for Afro-American Studies
Atlanta, GA 30314-4389 Phone: (404)880-8784
Caroline Fowler Ph.D., Chair.

★2518★
Cornell University
Africana Studies and Research Center
Ithaca, NY 14853 Phone: (607)255-4884
Robert Brashear, Dir. of Grad. Adm.

★2519★
Emory University
African and African American Studies Program
Atlanta, GA 30322 Phone: (404)727-6036
Dr. Walter Adamson, Dir., Grad. Lib. Arts

★2520★
Morgan State University
Afro-American Studies
Baltimore, MD 21239 Phone: (301)444-3185
James E. Waller, Adm. Officer

★2521★
North Carolina A&T State University
English and Afro-American Literature Program
Greensboro, NC 27411 Phone: (919)379-7771
Dr. James Williams, Chair, Dept. of Eng.

★2522★
Ohio State University
Department of Black Studies
Columbus, OH 43210 Phone: (614)292-3700
Dr. Manning Marable, Chair

★2523★
Princeton University
Afro-American Studies Program
Princeton, NJ 08544 Phone: (609)452-3000
Howard F. Taylor, Dir.

★2524★
San Francisco State University
School of Ethnic Studies
Black Studies Department
San Francisco, CA 94132 Phone: (415)338-1693
Dr. Jim Okutsu, Grad. Coor.

★2525★
State University of New York at Albany
African and Afro-American Studies
Albany, NY 12222 Phone: (518)442-4730
Dr. Allen Ballard, Chair

★2526★
Temple University
African American Studies
Philadelphia, PA 19122 Phone: (215)787-7200

★2527★
University of California, Los Angeles
Afro-American Studies Program
Los Angeles, CA 90024 Phone: (213)825-7462
Claudia Mitchell-Kernan, Chair

★2528★
University of Iowa
African-American World Studies Program
Iowa City, IA 52242 Phone: (319)335-0317
Darwin T. Turner, Chair

★2529★
University of Wisconsin—Madison
Department of Afro-American Studies
Madison, WI 53706 Phone: (608)263-1642
F. Wilson, Chair

★2530★
Yale University
African and Afro-American Studies Program
New Haven, CT 06520 Phone: (203)432-1170
John Blassingame, Chair

(8) RESEARCH CENTERS

Entries in this chapter are arranged alphabetically by center name. See the User's Guide at the front of this directory for additional information.

★2531★
Amistad Research Center
Tulane University
6823 St. Charles Ave.
New Orleans, LA 70118 Phone: (504)865-5535
Dr. Clifton H. Johnson, Dir.

Founded: 1966. **Research Activities and Fields:** Collects primary source materials pertaining to the history of American ethnic minorities, race relations, civil rights, and various religious denominations. **Publications:** *Amistad Reports* (quarterly). **Library:** Maintains a reference collection of about 17,500 books, 1,000 serials, 30,000 pamphlets, 1,500,000 press clippings, and 2,400 reels of microfilm; Kenneth Coleman, contact.

★2532★
Association for the Study of Afro-American Life and History
1407 14th St., NW
Washington, DC 20005 Phone: (202)667-2822
Karen Robinson, Exec.Dir.

Founded: 1915. **Research Activities and Fields:** Afro-American life and history. Collects historical manuscripts and materials relating to Black people and promotes study of Black history through schools, colleges, churches, homes, fraternal groups, and clubs. Publishes books on Afro-American life and history and originated Negro History Week (now observed as Afro-American History Month each February). **Publications:** *Journal of Negro History* (quarterly); *Negro History Bulletin* (bimonthly). **Meetings/Educational Activities:** Holds professional conferences and conventions annually. Cosponsors the H. Council Trenholm Memorial Writing Contest for high school students in cooperation with the National Education Association. **Library:** Private collection of 2,100 volumes on Black history and culture. **Formerly:** Association for Study of Negro Life and History.

★2533★
Balch Institute for Ethnic Studies
18 S. 7th St.
Philadelphia, PA 19106 Phone: (215)925-8090
Dr. M. Mark Stolarik, Pres.

Founded: 1971. **Research Activities and Fields:** Immigration and ethnicity. Activities focus on documenting and interpreting the American multicultural experience. **Publications:** *New Dimensions* (semiannually). Also publishes monographs on the history of immigration and ethnic groups in North America. Maintains a press in cooperation with associated universities. **Meetings/Educational Activities:** Sponsors occasional conferences. Offers educational programs to the public. **Library:** 50,000 volumes on American ethnic groups.

★2534★
Black Music Archives
1130 S. Michigan Ave., No. 3204
Chicago, IL 60605-2322
Dr. Dominique-Rene de Lerma, Dir.

Founded: 1976. **Research Activities and Fields:** Identification, documentation, and bibliographic and discographic registration of various manifestations of Black music cultures and Black composers, including books, scores and parts, journals, recordings, letters, photographs, and similar items. Cooperates with other departments and divisions of the University and the city and serves as nucleus for recording, publication, concert, and broadcasting projects. Provides public reference services for educators, researchers, and performers. **Publications:** *Sonorities in Black Music* (irregularly). **Meetings/Educational Activities:** Holds National Black Music Symposia (annually in February) in association with the Peabody Conservatory of Music at Johns Hopkins University, open to registrants. **Library:** 30,000 books, records, and scores on Black music (international). **Formerly:** Morgan Center for Black Music Research (1978); Sonorities in Black Music (1985).

★2535★
Black Periodical Literature Project, 1827-1940
Department of English
Duke University
Durham, NC 27706 Phone: (919)684-3769
Prof. Henry Louis Gates Jr., Dir.

Founded: 1981. **Research Activities and Fields:** Collects periodical fiction and poetry, book reviews, and obituaries published in African-American periodicals between 1827 and 1940. **Formerly:** Black Periodical Fiction Project (1987).

★2536★
Black Research and Resource Center
253 W. 72nd St., Ste. 211A
New York, NY 10023 Phone: (212)496-2234
Robert Hess, Exec.Dir.

Founded: 1986. **Research Activities and Fields:** History, careers, literature, culture, and education of Black people.

★2537★
Boston Sickle Cell Center
Boston City Hospital
818 Harrison Ave., FGH 2
Boston, MA 02118 Phone: (617)424-5727
Dr. Lillian E.C. McMahon, Dir.

Founded: 1973. **Research Activities and Fields:** Sickle cell trait and sickle cell anemia/disease, including molecular, cellular, tissue, and organ studies. Investigates glucose 6-phosphate dehydrogenase deficiency, coagulation and carbomylation of hemoglobin S, anti-sickling compounds, red cell membrane alterations, fetal jeopardy, fetal hemoglobin synthesis, cardiac manifestations, lung function, and infection. Conducts ultrastructural and clinical studies and seeks to translate basic and clinical research to improved health care at the community level. **Publications:** Educational Booklets. **Meetings/Educational Activities:** Holds Annual Directors Conference, sponsored by National Institutes of Health for staff members from participating centers. Offers initial training and on-going, weekly, in-service training to the Center's staff. **Library:** BSCC Audio-Visual Library, containing a variety of films, slide collections, and slide-tape presentations.

★2538★
Boston University
African Studies Center
125 Bay State Rd.
Boston, MA 02215 Phone: (617)353-3674
Dr. Allan Hoben, Dir.

Founded: 1953. **Research Activities and Fields:** Anthropology, archeology, economics, geography, history, sociology, and political science as related to basic facets of African life. Also studies African art, literature, and law, with particular emphasis placed upon areas of health care delivery, rural development, and population distribution and migration. **Publications:** *International Journal of African Historical Studies* (quarterly); *African Economic History* (annual journal); *Discussion Papers in the African Humanities*. **Meetings/Educational Activities:** Provides a program of instruction in African languages, including Hausa and Swahili through third year level, Yoruba and Sesotho/Setwsana through second year, and less commonly taught African languages on demand. Sponsors seminars on African history, politics, and problems of population and administration in relation to development in Africa. **Library:** 30,000 volumes, 22,000 documents, 2,000 pamphlets, 700 periodicals, and 120 newspapers on anthropology, economics, history, sociology, geography, political sciences, education, languages, and religion; Gretchen Walsh, head.

★2539★
Boston University
Center for Health and Advanced Policy Studies
232 Bay State Rd.
Boston, MA 02215 Phone: (617)353-2770
Prof. John B. McKinlay, Dir.

Research Activities and Fields: Application of knowledge to the study of contemporary policy and program issues, including health and health services, aging, minority issues, criminal justice, community organization and development, intergroup relations, and education. **Formerly:** Center for Applied Social Science.

★2540★
Brooklyn College of City University of New York
Africana Research Center
3105 James Hall Bldg.
Brooklyn, NY 11210 Phone: (718)780-5597
Dr. George Cunningham, Head

Founded: 1968. **Research Activities and Fields:** History, economics, sociology, psychology, education, political science, and the arts as they relate to Black people. Studies are being conducted on African-American history, Southern Africa, and the Caribbean. **Publications:** *Black Prism* (annually). **Formerly:** Africana Research Institute (1985).

★2541★
Brown University
Center for Race and Ethnicity
82 Waterman, Box 1886
Providence, RI 02912 Phone: (401)863-3080
John Ladd, Acting Dir.

Research Activities and Fields: Racial and ethnic minorities in America, focusing on African Americans, Asian Americans, Latinos, and native Americans. Conducts cross-disciplinary studies on issues relating to race, ethnicity, and intergroup relations. **Meetings/Educational Activities:** Sponsors public lectures and faculty seminars.

★2542★
Brown University
Institute for International Studies
2 Stimson Ave.
Box 1970
Providence, RI 02912 Phone: (401)863-2809
Howard R. Swearer, Dir.

Founded: 1986. **Research Activities and Fields:** North-South/East-West relations, regional security, transnational organization, U.S.-Soviet relations, security studies, world hunger, population, comparative study of development, geographical medicine, primary health care, Latin American studies, Portuguese and Brazilian studies, Afro-American studies, East Asian studies, and South Asian studies. **Publications:** *Annual Report*; *Newsletters*; *Conference Reports*; *Occasional Papers*; also publishes books. **Meetings/Educational Activities:** Offers international relations undergraduate major, and foreign exchange programs for faculty and students. Sponsors selected teaching positions in academic departments, conferences, seminars, and lectures.

★2543★
Brown University
Rites and Reason
Box 1148
Providence, RI 02912 Phone: (401)863-3558
Karen Baxter, Managing Dir.

Founded: 1970. **Research Activities and Fields:** Examines Afro-American issues and culture and seeks to investigate and portray the realities of Black life in the Americas. **Publications:** *The Langston Hughes Review* (journal); *Plantation Society* (journal). **Meetings/Educational Activities:** Offers courses in the arts, humanities, and social sciences dealing with Africa, the Caribbean, South America, and the United States.

★2544★
Center for Applied Jurisprudence
Pacific Research Institute for Public Policy
177 Post St., Ste. 500
San Francisco, CA 94108 Phone: (415)989-0833
William H. Mellor III, Pres.

Founded: 1986. **Research Activities and Fields:** Civil rights, property rights, First Amendment, and litigation strategy development.

★2545★
Center for Blood Research
800 Huntington Ave.
Boston, MA 02115 Phone: (617)731-6470
Dr. Chester A. Alper, Scientific Dir.

Founded: 1953. **Research Activities and Fields:** Human blood, including multidisciplinary studies on heart disease, diabetes, cancer,

AIDS, hemophilia, sickle cell anemia, mental illness, hepatitis, Rh factor in pregnancy, serum proteins, blood collection methods, preservation of formed elements, methods of plasma fractionation, and characterization of plasma components. **Library:** Maintains a reference collection of current journals. **Formerly:** Until 1967 known as the Protein Foundation and subsequently as Blood Research Institute until its merger in 1972 with Blood Grouping Laboratory, formed in 1942.

★2546★
Center for the Study of Social Policy
1250 I St. NW, Ste. 503
Washington, DC 20005 Phone: (202)371-1565
Tom Joe, Dir.

Founded: 1979. **Research Activities and Fields:** Social policy, including studies on children and youth, income support, long-term care, health, disability, and minorities. **Formerly:** Center for the Study of Welfare Policy (1982).

★2547★
Charles R. Drew University of Medicine and Science
Hypertension Research Center
1621 E. 120th St., M.P. No. 11
Los Angeles, CA 90274 Phone: (213)563-5927
Clarence E. Grim M.D., Dir.

Founded: 1984. **Research Activities and Fields:** Epidemiology, causes, and treatment of high blood pressure in Blacks. Analyzes twin studies to assess genetic and environmental factors in blood pressure variations. Conducts cross-cultural studies in Barbados and Nigeria. **Meetings/Educational Activities:** Offers pre- and postdoctoral training in hypertension research.

★2548★
Children's Hospital Oakland Research Institute
747 52nd St.
Oakland, CA 94609 Phone: (415)428-3502
Dr. Bertram Lubin, Dir. of Medical Research

Founded: 1959. **Research Activities and Fields:** Special research focuses include problems in sickle cell anemia, cystic fibrosis, cancer gene markers, nutritional/metabolic analytical method, and toxic chemical exposure. **Library:** Separate reference library of over 2,500 volumes on medical and biochemical subjects. **Formerly:** Children's Hospital Research Laboratory (1986).

★2549★
City University of New York
Center for Social Research
33 W. 42nd St.
New York, NY 10036 Phone: (212)642-1600
Dr. William Kornblum, Dir.

Founded: 1966. **Research Activities and Fields:** Basic and applied research in such areas as art, culture, mass media, race and ethnicity, political economy, urban politics and anthropology, women, and comparative social research.

★2550★
Clark Atlanta University
Southern Center for Studies in Public Policy
Brawley & Fair Sts., SW
Atlanta, GA 30314 Phone: (404)880-8085
Dr. Robert A. Holmes, Dir.

Founded: 1968. **Research Activities and Fields:** Labor market, education, welfare, rural transportation, and rural political and economic development studies emphasizing strategies, policies, and programs to improve the political and economic position of Black and minority populations. **Publications:** *Monographs*; *Newsletter*, *Occasional Papers*; *Research Reports*. **Library:** Maintains a research library of 12,000 volumes, a microfiche collection, and computer tapes.

★2551★
Clemson University
Center for the Study of the Black Experience in Higher Education
E-103 Martin Hall
Clemson, SC 29634-5404 Phone: (803)656-0313
Herman G. Green, Dir.

Founded: 1988. **Research Activities and Fields:** Issues related to the recruitment and retention of graduate and undergraduate African-American students and African-American faculty and staff at institutions of higher education in South Carolina and the southeastern and southern regions of the U.S. Promotes access and equity at all educational levels. **Publications:** *Challenge* (quarterly newsletter). **Meetings/Educational Activities:** Sponsors seminars, roundtables, and symposia.

★2552★
College of Staten Island of City University of New York
Institute for African American Studies
130 Stuyvesant Pl.
Staten Island
New York, NY 10301 Phone: (718)390-7990
Dr. Calvin B. Holder, Professor

Founded: 1969. **Research Activities and Fields:** African and Afro-American studies, including selected aspects of African civilization, sociocultural and political institutions, contributions of Afro-Americans to American civilization, and role of Afro-Americans in the U.S. **Publications:** *Research Review* (semiannually). **Meetings/Educational Activities:** Provides instruction. **Formerly:** Institute for Afro-American Studies.

★2553★
Columbia University
Center for American Culture Studies
603 Lewisohn Hall
New York, NY 10027 Phone: (212)854-8253
Jack Salzman, Dir.

Founded: 1982. **Research Activities and Fields:** American culture studies, with special emphasis on ethnic communities. **Publications:** *Prospects: An Annual of American Cultural Studies*; *The Dispatch* (biennial newsletter). Coordinating the Encyclopedia of African American Culture and History (five volumes). **Meetings/Educational Activities:** Sponsors conferences, lectures, and panel discussions; also sponsors international scholars.

★2554★
Columbia University
Comprehensive Sickle Cell Center
Harlem Hospital
506 Lenox Ave.
Rm. 6146 Sickle Cell Department
New York, NY 10037 Phone: (212)491-8074
Dr. Jeanne A. Smith, Dir.

Founded: 1972. **Research Activities and Fields:** Sickle cell disease, including studies of pathophysiological and biochemical aspects, rheological studies of the blood, studies on intellectual growth and development of children with sickle cell and allied diseases, biochemical factors involved in the clinical severity of the disease, and synthesis of normal hemoglobin in vitro.

★2555★
Columbia University
ERIC Clearinghouse on Urban Education
Institute for Urban and Minority Education
Box 40, Teachers College
New York, NY 10027 Phone: (212)678-3433
Dr. Erwin Flaxman, Dir.

Founded: 1965. **Research Activities and Fields:** Information collection and dissemination regarding urban education, with an aim to better serve the populations in urban school districts, including education of minorities, women, immigrants, and refugees. **Publications:** *Monographs*; *Fact Sheets*; *Urban Diversity Series*; *Trends and Issues Series*; *ERIC/CUE Digests*. Enters documents into ERIC educational database, indexed in published volumes of Resources in Education and Current Index to Journals in Education. **Meetings/Educational Activities:** Offers workshops on using the ERIC system. **Library:** Maintains a complete ERIC microfiche collection and a library of more than 16,000 items. **Formerly:** ERIC Clearinghouse for the Urban Disadvantaged; IUME/ERIC Clearinghouse on Urban Education.

★2556★
Columbia University
Institute of African Studies
420 W. 118th St.
New York, NY 10027 Phone: (212)854-4633
Dr. George Bond, Dir.

Research Activities and Fields: African politics, history, anthropology, art history, linguistics, literature, economic development, and education. **Meetings/Educational Activities:** Offers students instruction on peoples and problems of the African continent, particularly those of tropical Africa.

★2557★
Comprehensive Sickle Cell Center
Children's Hospital Research Foundation
Elland & Bethesda Aves.
Cincinnati, OH 45229 Phone: (513)559-4543
Donald Rucknagel M.D.,, Dir.

Founded: 1972. **Research Activities and Fields:** Sickle cell disease, including molecular, cellular, tissue, and organ studies. Conducts clinical trials and seeks to translate research to improved health care. **Meetings/Educational Activities:** Offers postgraduate training courses and continuing medical education.

★2558★
Cornell University
Africana Studies and Research Center
310 Triphammer Rd.
Ithaca, NY 14850 Phone: (607)255-5218
Prof. Robert Harris, Dir.

Founded: 1969. **Research Activities and Fields:** Africa, America, and Caribbean. **Publications:** *Monograph Series*. Sponsors postdoctoral faculty humanities fellowships in African cultural studies. **Meetings/Educational Activities:** Offers lectures and graduate and undergraduate instruction. **Library:** Houses a collection of reference materials and research guides.

★2559★
Designs for Change
220 S State St., Ste. 1900
Chicago, IL 60604 Phone: (312)922-0317
Dr. Donald R. Moore, Exec.Dir.

Founded: 1977. **Research Activities and Fields:** Improving the quality of public schools, particularly for low-income, minority, and handicapped children. Projects include studies of misclassification of minority children in classes for the educable mentally handicapped in the Chicago area, placement and grouping in big city high schools, reading scores and dropout scores analysis, and qualitative research on effective schools, school finance, and staff development combining qualitative and quantitative methods. **Publications:** *Reports*; *All Our Kids Can Learn to Read: A Guide to Parent and Citizen Action* (in English and Spanish); *Caught in the Web: Misplaced Children in Chicago's Classes for the Mentally Retarded*; *Child Advocacy and the Schools: Past Impact and Potential for the 1980's*; *Helping Schools Change: Ideas for Assistance Groups*.

★2560★
Duke University
Comprehensive Sickle Cell Center
Medical Center
Box 3934 Morris Bldg.
Durham, NC 27710 Phone: (919)684-3724
Wendell F. Rosse M.D., Dir.

Research Activities and Fields: Sickle cell disease, including molecular, cellular, tissue, and organ studies. Conducts clinical trials. Seeks to translate basic and clinical research to improved health care at the community level.

★2561★
Equality Center
1223 Girard St., NW
Washington, DC 20009-5325 Phone: (202)546-6706
Margaret Dunkle, Exec.Dir.

Founded: 1982. **Research Activities and Fields:** Civil rights programs applicable to education, health, and social services. Research topics include teenage pregnancy, equity in athletics for women, and health care for males and females. **Meetings/Educational Activities:** Sponsors seminars for special projects.

★2562★
Florida International University
Center for Multilingual & Multicultural Studies
University Park Campus, DM 274
Miami, FL 33199 Phone: (305)348-3207
Dr. Tanya Saunders-Hamilton, Acting Dir.

Founded: 1981. **Research Activities and Fields:** Migration, language policy, ethnicity, cross-cultural education, multicultural communication, linguistics, and international studies. Employs basic, field, survey, historical, and analytical research methods. **Publications:** *FIU Special Language Series*; *Haitian Publications*; *Paper Series*; *Cuban Heritage* (magazine). **Meetings/Educational Activities:** Sponsors Hispanic conference (biennially in February), African-New World Studies conference (biennially in March or April), Haitian conference (annually), and Native American conference (annually).

★2563★
Florida State University
Black Abolitionist Papers Project
Department of History
Tallahassee, FL 32306 Phone: (904)644-4527
Dr. C. Peter Ripley, Dir.

Founded: 1976. **Research Activities and Fields:** Conducts research and collects documents on free Blacks and fugitive slaves in the U.S., Canada, and the British Isles who worked to promote the emancipation of enslaved fellow Blacks from 1830 to 1865. **Publications:** *Black Abolitionist Papers*, a five volume letterpress series.

★2564★
Fordham University
Langenfeld Research and Demonstration Center
Graduate School of Social Service
Fordham at Lincoln Center
New York, NY 10023 Phone: (212)841-5275
Dr. Eugene B. Shinn, Dir.

Founded: 1968. **Research Activities and Fields:** Develops and implements social research methodologies related to gerontology, international social service policy, and family, children, and minority services, substance abuse, and family violence. **Formerly:** Research Center-Graduate School of Social Service; Research and Demonstration Center.

★2565★
Harvard University
W.E.B. DuBois Institute for AfroAmerican Research
44 Brattle St.
Cambridge, MA 02138 Phone: (617)495-4192
Peter J. Gomes, Acting Dir.

Founded: 1975. **Research Activities and Fields:** Postdoctoral research on Afro-American history and culture, emphasizing the humanities, social sciences, and an international perspective. **Publications:** *The Newsletter of the Afro-American Religious History Group* (semiannually); brochures and application procedures available upon request. **Meetings/Educational Activities:** Sponsors working groups and research conferences.

★2566★
Howard University
African Studies and Research Program
Washington, DC 20059 Phone: (202)806-7115
Sulayman S. Nyang Ph.D., Dir.

Founded: 1953. **Research Activities and Fields:** Africa, with particular reference to social science, language training studies, professional sciences, and natural sciences, including studies of African development, policy planning, and history. **Publications:** *African Monograph Series*. **Meetings/Educational Activities:** Sponsors a noon seminar series, a monthly seminar series, a rural/urban development conference, and one national conference per year. **Formerly:** Formed by merger of former African Studies Program and African Language and Area Center.

★2567★
Howard University
Bureau of Educational Research
Box 311
Washington, DC 20059 Phone: (202)806-8120
Dr. Faustine C. Jones-Wilson, Dir.

Founded: 1932. **Research Activities and Fields:** Education of Black Americans.

★2568★
Howard University
Center for Sickle Cell Disease
2121 Georgia Ave. NW
Washington, DC 20059 Phone: (202)806-7930
Dr. Oswaldo Castro, Dir.

Founded: 1972. **Research Activities and Fields:** Sickle cell disease, including basic and clinical investigations of its nature, causes, effects, and potential control. Develops and implements high quality total care for victims of the disease. Develops and evaluates methods of prevention through screening for sickle and other abnormal hemoglobins and participates in the Mid-Atlantic Regional Genetic Counseling Program. **Publications:** *Newsletter* (semiannually); *Annual Report*. **Meetings/Educational Activities:** Offers educational and training programs for medical professionals and allied health personnel, including bimonthly staff meetings, an annual symposium on sickle cell disease and other related abnormal hemoglobins, an annual postgraduate conference, monthly scientific seminars, and sickle cell grand rounds. **Library:** 230 volumes on sickle cell, hemoglobins, and pediatrics; Sheilla Bailey, librarian.

★2569★
Howard University
Housing and Community Development Studies Center
Institute for Urban Affairs and Research
2900 Van Ness St., NW
Washington, DC 20008 Phone: (202)806-8770
Dr. G. McRae, Project Dir.

Founded: 1983. **Research Activities and Fields:** Conducts research on high priority problems in the area of housing and community development, including current research methods of study of the homeless, housing characteristics of Black female householders, and a survey of housing alternatives for the elderly.

★2570★
Howard University
Institute for Urban Affairs and Research
2900 Van Ness St., NW
Washington, DC 20008 Phone: (202)686-6770
Lawrence E. Gary Ph.D., Dir.

Founded: 1972. **Research Activities and Fields:** Psychology, sociology, social work, demography, and public health studies in the urban environment. Specific areas of research include the following: life satisfaction among dual-career couples; correlates of depressive symptoms among Black Americans; prevalence of drug abuse and mental illness among the homeless; economic stability among the elderly; stress among retired eldery; mental health of Black Americans; Black family life; and infant mortality. **Publications:** *Newsletter* (semiannually); *Occasional Papers*; *Monographs*; books; resource guides and directories. Disseminates information and bibliographies upon request. **Meetings/Educational Activities:** Series of conferences covering such topics as Black fathers, stress at the workplace, and Black families; open to lay persons and professionals. **Library:** 10,000 volumes on mental health, administration of justice, social support networks, child abuse and neglect, and human resources development.

★2571★
Howard University
Moorland-Spingarn Research Center
500 Howard Pl., NW
Washington, DC 20059 Phone: (202)806-5726
Dr. Elinor DesVerney Sinnette, Chief Librarian

Founded: 1914. **Research Activities and Fields:** Repository for collections documenting history and culture of people of African descent in the Americas, Africa, and Europe. **Library:** 150,000 volumes on Afro-American history and culture, Africa, the Caribbean and Afro-Brazilian culture, also artifacts, manuscripts, newspapers, photographs, prints, recordings, and other materials documenting from antiquity to the present the history and culture of Black people in Africa, Europe, Latin America, the Caribbean, and United States. **Formerly:** Moorland Foundation (1946); Moorland-Spingarn Collection (1973).

★2572★
Indiana University
African Studies Program
Bloomington, IN 47405 Phone: (812)855-6825
Dr. Patrick O'Meara, Dir.

Founded: 1961. **Research Activities and Fields:** Emerging nations of sub-Saharan Africa, including interdisciplinary studies in anthropology and ethnography, comparative literature, economics, fine arts, music and folklore, geography, government, history, politics, and linguistics, with emphasis on West Africa and southern Africa. **Meetings/Educational Activities:** Provides graduate and undergraduate instruction. Holds semiannual series of seminars on problems of contemporary Africa. **Library:** 76,000 volumes in the University's library collection.

★2573★
Indiana University
AfroAmerican Arts Institute
109 N. Jordan Ave.
Bloomington, IN 47405 Phone: (812)855-9501
Dr. Charles Sukes, Exec.Dir.

Founded: 1974. **Research Activities and Fields:** Afro-American performing arts: Black dance, Black choral music, and urban popular music. Reflects upon the historical development of Black people through research and performance. Consists of three performance groups which present live performances and lecture-demonstrations. **Meetings/Educational Activities:** Supports undergraduate curriculum in Afro-American studies. **Library:** 1,000 volumes on Black studies.

★2574★
Institute for American Pluralism
55 E. Jackson Blvd., Ste. 1880
Chicago, IL 60604 Phone: (312)663-5400
David Roth, Dir.

Founded: 1967. **Research Activities and Fields:** Issues affecting American pluralism in areas such as the humanities, communications, immigration, foreign and coalition building, leadership, and education. Research topics chosen by Institute's staff and leaders of Illinois Ethnic Consultation, affiliated with the Institute. Professionals from across the country conduct the research. **Formerly:** Institute on Pluralism and Group Identity.

★2575★
Institute for New Enterprise Development
25 Highland Ave.
Cambridge, MA 02233-1021 Phone: (617)491-0203
Dr. Stewart E. Perry, Pres.

Founded: 1971. **Research Activities and Fields:** Assesses specialized resources for community economic development; analyzes problems and potential problems of minorities, younger workers, women, and the elderly in relation to local economic revitalization; analyzes the differences in entrepreneurial patterns related to the ethnicity of a community; develops community based ventures, especially in the field of energy; and evaluates federal, state, and municipal policies for economic development.

★2576★
Institute for Policy Studies
1601 Connecticut Ave., NW
Washington, DC 20009 Phone: (202)234-9382
Marcus Raskin, Codirector

Founded: 1963. **Research Activities and Fields:** National security, foreign policy, human rights, international economic order, knowledge and politics, and domestic reconstruction, including studies of the security alternatives in the 1990s, U.S./U.S.S.R. exchange on disarmament, Europe, nuclear and conventional arms, crisis monitoring, intervention and revolution, human rights in Latin America, women in developing countries, feminism and socialism, transnational corporations, international aid, race and class, science and technology, and Blacks and Hispanics in the U.S. **Meetings/Educational Activities:** Sponsors a network of study groups which explores elements of ethical inquiry into current disciplines and myths of value-free science while formulating alternatives.

★2577★
Institute for Public Policy Advocacy
1730 Rhode Island Ave. NW, Ste. 600
Washington, DC 20036-3118 Phone: (202)659-8475
David Cohen, Codirector

Founded: 1984. **Research Activities and Fields:** Conducts research on the role of public interest advocacy, especially in the areas of civil, children, and human rights, public health, arms control, foreign affairs, environment, consumerism, tax justice, and economic opportunity. **Publications:** *Advocate's Advocate* (monthly newsletter). **Meetings/Educational Activities:** Conducts workshops and seminars on advocacy skills.

★2578★
Institute for Scientific Analysis
2235 Lombard St.
San Francisco, CA 94123 Phone: (415)921-4987
Dr. Dorothy L. Miller, Pres.

Founded: 1966. **Research Activities and Fields:** Fulfills research contracts for public or private agencies, and oversees research projects on social problems in the fields of education, social welfare, criminology, alcoholism, drug addiction, mental health, population, runaways, child rearing, status of women and ethnic minorities, and transportation.

★2579★
Institute for Southern Studies
PO Box 531
Durham, NC 27702 Phone: (919)688-8167
Meredith Emmett, Exec.Dir.

Founded: 1970. **Research Activities and Fields:** Labor, civil rights, energy, land use, environment, banking and finance, campaign finances, and social change movements in the South. **Publications:** *Southern Exposure* (quarterly); *Special Reports.*

★2580★
Institute for the Preservation and Study of African-American Writing
PO Box 50172
Washington, DC 20004 Phone: (202)628-0454
Joseph Jordan, Dir.

Founded: 1978. **Research Activities and Fields:** Local African-American authors and the history of African-American writing in Washington, D.C. (1800-present). **Publications:** *Bywords* (quarterly newsletter); *Monographs*; *Anthologies.* **Meetings/Educational Activities:** Sponsors creative writing workshops, photo-literary exhibits, and fall, winter, and spring colloquiums, open to the public.

★2581★
Institute for Women's Policy Research
1400 20th St., NW, Ste. 104
Washington, DC 20036 Phone: (202)785-5100
Heidi I. Hartmann Ph.D., Dir.

Founded: 1987. **Research Activities and Fields:** Causes and consequences of women's poverty, particularly of minority women; costs and benefits of family and work policies; pay equity; wages and employment opportunities; and impact of tax policy on women and families. Specific issues include the impact of the Pregnancy Discrimination Act, pay equity in 20 state civil service systems, and the wage gap between women of color and white women. **Meetings/Educational Activities:** Offers workshops, conferences, and speeches.

★2582★
Institute of Comparative Social and Cultural Studies
6935 Wisconsin Ave., Ste. 500
Chevy Chase, MD 20815 Phone: (301)656-7996
Dr. Lorand B. Szalay, Dir.

Founded: 1976. **Research Activities and Fields:** Tests and compares the differences in perceptions and values of different cultural groups in the U.S. and abroad using the Associative Group Analysis Technique, and other empirical methods. Produces new perceptual and motivational insights into psycho-cultural dispositions, which shape people's views and behavior without their conscious awareness, for utilization in international education, substance abuse treatment and prevention programs, mental health service, conflict resolution, cross-cultural problem solving, and management in multi-cultural settings.

★2583★
Intercultural Development Research Association
5835 Callaghan Rd., Ste. 350
San Antonio, TX 78228 Phone: (512)684-8180
Jose A. Cardenas, Exec.Dir.

Founded: 1973. **Research Activities and Fields:** Minority and bilingual education, school finance, desegregation, and compensatory education. **Publications:** *IDRA Newsletter* (monthly). **Meetings/Educational Activities:** Sponsors conferences, seminars, and workshops for school and related personnel. **Library:** 20,000 items on minority, compensatory, and early childhood education and school finance.

★2584★
International Organization for the Study of Group Tensions, Inc.
240 E. 76th St., Apt. 1-B
New York, NY 10021 Phone: (212)628-1797
Dr. Benjamin B. Wolman, Pres.

Founded: 1970. **Research Activities and Fields:** Causes of and solutions to human conflict and violence. Members' professions include anthropology, economics, history, political science, psychiatry, psychoanalysis, psychology, and sociology. **Publications:** *International Journal of Group Tensions* (quarterly). **Meetings/Educational Activities:** Sponsors or cosponsors international conferences; topics have included the college campus of the future as a source of multicultural experience, and problems of racial, ethnic, and other special groups from both national and international perspectives.

★2585★
Investor Responsibility Research Center, Inc.
1755 Massachusetts Ave., NW, Ste. 600
Washington, DC 20036 Phone: (202)234-7500
Margaret Carroll, Exec.Dir.

Founded: 1972. **Research Activities and Fields:** Social, public policy, and corporate governance issues and their impact on major corporations and institutional investors. Issues studied have included anti-takeover measures, U.S. and foreign business in South Africa, energy and the environment, the electric utility industry, military contracting, executive compensation, South Africa-related divestment, business in northern Ireland, plant closings, global shareholder rights, animal testing, and voting and other actions by institutional investors. Also offers consulting and contract research. **Publications:** *News for Investors* (monthly); *Corporate Governance Bulletin* (bimonthly); *South Africa Reporter* (quarterly); and reports by the Center's Social Issues Service, Corporate Governance Service, and South Africa Review Service. **Meetings/Educational Activities:** Sponsors seminars, briefing and workshops.

★2586★
James N. Gamble Institute of Medical Research
2141 Auburn Ave.
Cincinnati, OH 45219 Phone: (513)369-2582
Gilbert M. Schiff M.D., Pres.

Founded: 1927. **Research Activities and Fields:** Virology and immunology, including studies on rubella and rubella vaccines, role of complement in sickle cell disease and burn wounds, and basic and clinical studies on rotaviruses, hepatitis, and human immunodeficiency virus. **Library:** 5,200 volumes, 280 current journal titles, and 10,000 bound journal volumes on virology, immunology, medicine, and surgery. **Formerly:** Christ Hospital Institute of Medical Research (1984).

★2587★
Joint Center for Political and Economic Studies
1301 Pennsylvania Ave. NW, Ste. 400
Washington, DC 20004 Phone: (202)626-3500
Milton Morris, V.Pres. of Research

Founded: 1970. **Research Activities and Fields:** Politics and public policy, including issues which have impact on minorities and the disadvantaged. Collects, analyzes, and disseminates data on all aspects of Black political participation. Also works with minority elected officials and pinpoints resources that can be used to solve problems besetting socially and economically disadvantaged communities. **Publications:** *Focus* (monthly); *Roster of Black Elected Officials* (annually). **Meetings/Educational Activities:** Holds forums, seminars, and conferences. **Library:** Reference and periodical library, including 4,000 volumes on Black politics and urban affairs; Auriel Pilgrim, information director.

★2588★
Kent State University
Center for the Study of Ethnic Publications and Cultural Institutions
School of Library Science
Kent, OH 44242-0001 Phone: (216)672-2782
Prof. Lubomyr R. Wynar, Dir.

Founded: 1971. **Research Activities and Fields:** Promotes bibliographical and historical research on ethnic publications and cultural institutions in the U.S. in cooperation with various scholarly, professional, and governmental organizations and agencies. Surveys ethnic press as well as ethnic serials, books, libraries, archives, and museums. Activities focus on developing a curriculum for library schools, emphasizing library services to ethnic communities and ethnic publicatons. **Publications:** *Ethnic Forum*; *Journal of Ethnic Studies and Ethnic Bibliography* (semiannually); *Monographs*. **Library:** 1,200 volumes on major ethnic studies. **Formerly:** Program for Study of Ethnic Publications (1980); Center for the Study of Ethnic Publications (1988).

★2589★
Kent State University
Institute for African American Affairs
18 Ritchie Hall
Kent, OH 44240 Phone: (216)672-2300
Dr. Mohan Kaul, Dir.

Founded: 1969. **Research Activities and Fields:** African and American affairs. **Publications:** *Monograph Series*; *Kitabu Newsletter*; *Occasional Papers*. **Meetings/Educational Activities:** Offers teacher training workshops, public forums on Black community issues, biweekly research-in-progress colloquia, grantsmanship seminars, and a speakers bureau.

★2590★
Louisiana State University
Center for French and Francophone Studies
Department of French and Italian
225 Prescott Hall
Baton Rouge, LA 70803 Phone: (504)388-6589
Prof. Edouard Glissant, Dir.

Founded: 1983. **Research Activities and Fields:** French and francophone culture of the southern U.S., Caribbean, and Caribbean coast of Latin America, including studies of the mores and customs, work, law and commerce, slave trade, role of women in the system, Creole languages, musics of silence, and literature in the South and Caribbean. In association with the French Education Project in the College of Education, the Center supports research on the teaching of the French language in Louisiana and throughout the world.

★2591★
Louisiana State University
Public Administration Institute
3171 CEBA
Baton Rouge, LA 70803 Phone: (504)388-6743
James A. Richardson, Dir.

Research Activities and Fields: Public administration, including studies on health policy, minority health care, economics and taxes, state and local governments, and public finance. **Meetings/Educational Activities:** Offers graduate instruction and administers a master's degree program.

★2592★
Martin Luther King, Jr. Center for Nonviolent Social Change, Inc.
449 Auburn Ave., NE
Atlanta, GA 30312 Phone: (404)524-1956
Coretta Scott King, Pres.

Founded: 1968. **Research Activities and Fields:** Nonviolence, violence, resolution of conflict, current social and economic issues, and civil rights leader Martin Luther King, Jr. (1929-1968). **Publications:** *Annual Report*. **Meetings/Educational Activities:** Sponsors King Week (annually); Youth and Adult Workshops on Nonviolence (annually in July); Kingfest; Gandhi Day, in honor of the Indian nationalist, spiritual leader, and nonviolent activist whom Dr. King emulated; "I have a Dream" Celebration, in memory of noted speech by Dr. King; and over 20 other programs, including continuing education seminars, conferences, and workshops on nonviolent conflict resolution. **Library:** Collection of reference material on Dr. Martin Luther King, Jr.

★2593★
Medical College of Georgia
Comprehensive Sickle Cell Center
1435 Laney-Walker Blvd.
Augusta, GA 30912-2200 Phone: (404)721-3091
Dr. Titus H.J. Huisman, Dir.

Founded: 1972. **Research Activities and Fields:** Hemoglobinopathy detection, identification, and characterization, including studies of factors determining severity of sickle cell anemia in adults and the young child, cardiac evaluation of children with sickle cell anemia, thalassemia in association with sickle cell syndromes, biochemical studies in sickle cell anemia and related disorders with special emphasis on heterogeneity of Hb F, immunological identification, DNA gene mapping of hemoglobin variants, nucleotide sequence, and thalassemia genes, and characterization of hemoglobin variants. **Publications:** *SPHERE* (six times per year); *Hemoglobin: International Journal for Hemoglobin Research* (six times per year). **Meetings/Educational Activities:** Sponsors Hemoglobin Research Club (semimonthly), open to interested personnel, and a weekly conference on DNA research for personnel involved. Sponsors three workshops per year in basic hemoglobin techniques, HPLC methodology, and DNA mapping. **Library:** 3,000 volumes on hemoglobinopathies and related topics.

★2594★
Meiklejohn Civil Liberties Institute
PO Box 673
Berkeley, CA 94701 Phone: (415)848-0599
Prof. Ann Fagin Ginger, Pres.

Founded: 1965. **Research Activities and Fields:** Constitutional, international, U.N. Charter, First Amendment, and peace law. Collects and documents material for attorneys and non-attorneys. **Publications:** *Newsletter* (semiannually); *Studies in Law and Social Change* (book series); *Human Rights Organizations and Periodicals Directory* (Annually); *Peace Law Docket* (Annually). **Meetings/Educational Activities:** Sponsors annual symposium on civil liberties and peace law issues.

★2595★
Memphis State University
Center for Research on Women
Clement Hall-339
Memphis, TN 38152 Phone: (901)678-2770
Lynn Weber Cannon, Dir.

Founded: 1982. **Research Activities and Fields:** Southern women and women of color (Black, Latina, Asian American, and Native American) in the U.S., including critical examination of the intersection of gender, class, and racial oppression; perception of class among Americans; mobility strategies of minority women; working class women in the South; rural poverty; and comparative study of Black and White professional and managerial women in the Memphis area. **Publications:** *Newsletter* (three times per year); *Southern Women: The Intersection of Race, Class and Gender* (co-sponsored with the Duke University–University of North Carolina Women's Studies Research Center); *Research Papers Curriculum Integration Publications*; a printed version of the database (updated annually). **Meetings/Educational Activities:** Sponsors Workshop on Women in the Curriculum (annually) and summer research institutes (occasionally).

★2596★
Memphis State University
Center for Voluntary Action Research
Memphis, TN 38152 Phone: (901)678-2080
Dr. Stanley E. Hyland, Contact

Founded: 1981. **Research Activities and Fields:** Provides research assistance to groups, agencies, and industries interested in developing collaborative social science projects. Activities include establishing neighborhood associations for the transfer of information, developing mutual aid societies, investigating minority and small business concerns, analyzing urban renewal, evaluating community health, studying alcoholism and minorities, establishing a neighborhood health association for Shelby County Health Department, and weatherization in low-income neighborhoods and rural areas. **Publications:** *Journal for Voluntary Action Research* (quarterly).

★2597★
Michigan State University
African Studies Center
East Lansing, MI 48824-1035 Phone: (517)353-1700
David Wiley, Dir.

Founded: 1960. **Research Activities and Fields:** Coordinates and fosters teaching/research and public service programs in African area studies throughout the University and the region. Courses offered through departments of the University include 25 African languages, African anthropology, art history, sociology, geography, history, linguistics, literature, political science, economics, agricultural economics, business, education, ecology, agriculture, tropical agriculture, public health, animal science and veterinary medicine, medicine, criminal justice, tropical medicine, and communication, with emphasis on sub-Saharan Africa, including islands and Republic of South Africa. Administers Title VI, South African, and Zimbabwean fellowships for African language and area studies at the graduate level. **Publications:** *African Urban Studies* (quarterly journal); *Rural Africana* (quarterly journal); *Northeast African Studies* (quarterly journal); *ASC Newsletter*, *Africana: Select Recent Acquisitions* (three times yearly). The Center also publishes an *Africana Monograph Series* and a *Monograph Series in Northeast African Studies.* **Meetings/Educational Activities:** Sponsors annual national conference on Africa and an African Cultural Festival. **Library:** Maintains African collection of 170,000 volumes; Onuma Ezera, head.

★2598★
Michigan State University
Center for Urban Affairs
East Lansing, MI 48824 Phone: (517)353-9035
Dr. Marvel Lang, Dir.

Founded: 1968. **Research Activities and Fields:** Problems of urban communities, with particular emphasis on improvement of life chances for poor and disadvantaged minorities, including studies on fiscal affairs and urban development. Also urban research designed to generate new knowledge about the changing condition of cities and to aid private and public policy decisions that will affect the future of urban areas. Initiates experimental community action and development programs and develops cooperative relationship with other University programs and community groups. **Publications:** *Monographs*; *Research Papers* (series).

★2599★
National Black Child Development Institute
1463 Rhode Island Ave. NW
Washington, DC 20005 Phone: (202)387-1281
Evelyn K. Moore, Dir.

Founded: 1970. **Research Activities and Fields:** Policy issues affecting Black children, with emphasis on child care, child welfare, health, and education. Studies foster care and tutoring/mentoring programs, include after-school care, teenage pregnancy, health care policy, and juvenile justice. **Publications:** *Black Child Advocate* (quarterly newsletter); *Child Health Talk* (quarterly newsletter); Reports. **Meetings/Educational Activities:** Sponsors an annual conference and convenes forums.

★2600★
National Caucus and Center on Black Aged
1424 K St., NW, Ste. 500
Washington, DC 20005 Phone: (202)637-8400
Samuel J. Simmons, Pres.

Founded: 1970. **Research Activities and Fields:** Elderly Black Americans, including studies on job placement, medical services in the Southwest U.S., and older women in the workplace. **Publications:** reports. **Meetings/Educational Activities:** Sponsors National Conference (annually in June).

★2601★
National Institute Against Prejudice and Violence
31 S. Greene St.
Baltimore, MD 21201 Phone: (301)328-5170
Howard J. Ehrlich Ph.D., Contact

Founded: 1984. **Research Activities and Fields:** Causes of prejudice and violence and their effects on individuals and society, including studies of the news media. Special focus is on college campus, housing, and workplace violence involving race, religion, ethnicity, gender, or sexual orientation. **Publications:** *Forum* (newsletter); reports. **Meetings/Educational Activities:** Sponsors conferences and workshops.

★2602★
National Institute for Women of Color
1301-20th St., NW, Ste. 202
Washington, DC 20036 Phone: (202)296-2661
Sharon Parker, Chair, Board of Dirs.

Founded: 1981. **Research Activities and Fields:** Women of color, including studies on demographic trends, education, sports, and sex equity. Assists in the formulation and implementation of public policy.

Publications: *NIWC Network News.* **Meetings/Educational Activities:** Developed and distributes a resource packet on reproductive freedom for women of color.

★2603★
National Urban Coalition
8601 Georgia Ave., Ste. 500
Silver Spring, MD 20910 Phone: (301)495-4999
Ramona H. Edelin, Pres.

Founded: 1967. **Research Activities and Fields:** Housing and neighborhood revitalization, employment, youth employment, urban education, income maintenance, and economic development. **Publications:** *Alert* (monthly); *Neighborhood Exchange* (quarterly); *Urban Policy Watch* (quarterly); and *Network* (annual magazine). **Meetings/Educational Activities:** Sponsors workshops, and seminars, by invitation only. **Library:** 1,000 volumes.

★2604★
National Urban League
Research Department
1111 14th St., NW, 6th Fl.
Washington, DC 20005 Phone: (202)898-1604
Dr. Billy J. Tidwell, Dir. of Research

Research Activities and Fields: U.S. social and economic conditions, Blacks, and poor minorities. Studies are undertaken from a Black perspective and are directed at influencing policy. Answers inquiries and makes referrals. **Publications:** *Urban League Review* (semiannually); *Monographs*; papers; *Quarterly Report on the Social and Economic Condition of Black Americans.* **Meetings/Educational Activities:** The National Urban League Conference (annually in July/August), open to public.

★2605★
New York Public Library
Schomburg Center for Research in Black Culture
515 Malcolm X Blvd.
New York, NY 10037-1801 Phone: (212)491-2200
Howard Dodson, Chief

Founded: 1925. **Research Activities and Fields:** Collects and preserves materials on Black people, including books, rare books, microforms, photographs, oral histories, video tapes, manuscripts, archives, paintings, sculpture, and U.S. Census reports (1790-1900). **Publications:** *Schomburg Center Journal* (quarterly). **Meetings/Educational Activities:** Sponsors scholar-in-residence program, forums, exhibitions, and book parties. **Library:** 100,000 volumes, available to the public. **Formerly:** Schomburg Collection of Negro Literature and History (1972).

★2606★
Niagara University
Center for the Study and Stabilization of the Black Family
PO Box 367
Niagara Falls, NY 14109 Phone: (716)285-1212
Umeme Sababu, Dir.

Research Activities and Fields: Black family, including studies on moral values, academic achievements, educational goals, parenting skills, and social relationships.

★2607★
North Carolina Central University
Institute on Desegregation
214 Taylor Education Bldg.
Durham, NC 27707 Phone: (919)560-6367
Dr. Beverly W. Jones, Dir.

Founded: 1972. **Research Activities and Fields:** Desegregation and postsecondary education, including studies on housing, health, employment, and private and public secondary education. **Publications:** *Journal on Desegregation* (semiannually). **Meetings/Educational Activities:** Sponsors annual conference on desegregation, open to the public.

★2608★
North Carolina Central University
Office of Research, Evaluation and Planning
Fayetteville St.
Durham, NC 27707 Phone: (919)560-6367
Dr. Linda K. Pratt, Assoc. Vice Chancellor

Founded: 1951. **Research Activities and Fields:** Higher education, including institutional studies with particular reference to attitudes and achievements of students attending predominantly Black colleges, evaluation of remedial instruction, curriculum evaluation, institutional goals, and planning. **Formerly:** Bureau of Educational Research.

★2609★
Northern Illinois University
Center for Black Studies
DeKalb, IL 60115 Phone: (815)753-1709
Dr. Admasu Zike, Dir.

Founded: 1970. **Research Activities and Fields:** All areas of interest and concern affecting Blacks and other minorities, including Afro-American history, Afro-American education, multicultural education, African political systems, African history, and African oral and written literature. **Publications:** reports. **Meetings/Educational Activities:** Sponsors lectures, seminars, and conferences, open to the public. **Library:** 6,000 volumes on Afro-American studies, Black education, and African studies; Rob Ridinger, librarian. **Formerly:** Center for Minority Studies.

★2610★
Northwestern University
Center for Urban Affairs and Policy Research
2040 Sheridan Rd.
Evanston, IL 60208-4100 Phone: (708)491-3395
Burton A. Weisbrod, Dir.

Founded: 1968. **Research Activities and Fields:** Interdisciplinary public policy studies, including programs on (1) poverty, race, and inequality (housing, education, crime, unemployment, and the family); (2) community and neighborhood development; (3) law, society, and the economy; and (4) alternatives to government (privatization, nonprofits, and voluntarism). **Publications:** *Working Paper Series*; *Monographs*; *Biennial Report*; *Center Research & Policy Reports*; *Urban Affairs News* (a periodic newsletter). **Formerly:** Center for Urban Affairs.

★2611★
Northwestern University
Program of African Studies
620 Library Pl.
Evanston, IL 60208 Phone: (708)491-7323
David William Cohen, Dir.

Founded: 1948. **Research Activities and Fields:** Economics, political science, anthropology, history, performance studies, sociology, art history, music, literature, education, law, and African languages and linguistics, including interdisciplinary study of African peoples and cultures in the past and in their contemporary settings. Research program maintains a regional emphasis on Africa south of the Sahara. Activities are centered in Africa House on the University campus; library and field research are conducted in Africa by faculty and graduate students. **Publications:** *P.A.S. News and Events*; *Arabic Literature in Africa*; *Fontes*; *Asantesem: The Asante Collective Biography Project*; *Newsletter*. **Meetings/Educational Activities:** Provides graduate and undergraduate instruction and research opportunities at the University. Holds research seminars and public lecture series during the academic year, an annual interdisciplinary seminar on approaches to study of Africa, and national conferences. **Library:** Maintains a special collection of 187,000 volumes in University library and 2,000 periodicals dealing with Africa, as well as most newspapers from Africa; Hans Panofsky, curator.

★2612★
Ohio University
African Studies Program
56 E. Union St.
Athens, OH 45701 Phone: (614)593-1834
Prof. Gifford Doxsee, Dir.

Founded: 1964. **Research Activities and Fields:** Politics, geography, history, economics, philosophy, and literature of Africa. Provides instruction in these fields at the University. **Publications:** *African Studies Series* (four per year).

★2613★
Ohio University
Center for AfroAmerican Studies
300 Lindley Hall
Athens, OH 45701 Phone: (614)593-4546
Dr. Vattel T. Rose, Dir.

Founded: 1969. **Research Activities and Fields:** Afro-American politics, education, family, and culture. Studies include urban politics, comparison analyses of Afro-American and African political thought, multicultural education issues, socialization patterns, impact of technology, strength of the family structure, single parent families, portrayal of Black males in media and effects on the family, race and ethnicity, and aesthetics in Black media, film, and literature. **Meetings/Educational Activities:** Sponsors conferences (annually).

★2614★
Purdue University
Afro-American Studies Center
326 Stone Hall
West Lafayette, IN 47907 Phone: (317)494-5680
Carolyn E. Johnson Ph.D., Dir.

Founded: 1974. **Research Activities and Fields:** African, Afro-American, and Caribbean studies. **Publications:** *NOMMO* (quarterly). **Meetings/Educational Activities:** Holds Martin Luther King Lecture Series (spring).

★2615★
Queens College of the City University of New York
Africana Studies and Research Institute
65-30 Kissena Blvd.
Flushing, NY 11367 Phone: (718)520-7545
Prof. Omayemi Agbeyebe, Dir.

Founded: 1973. **Research Activities and Fields:** Promotes Africana scholarship and publications, supports the teaching of African studies at the College, and related academic research and teaching to the needs and interests of the Black community. **Meetings/Educational Activities:** Offers an interdisciplinary curriculum with a major, minor, and electives in Africana studies. Sponsors monthly seminars, open to students, faculty, staff, and the public. **Library:** Maintains volumes on African, African-American, and Caribbean studies.

★2616★
Rutgers State University of New Jersey
Douglas College
Institute for Research on Women
PO Box 270
Douglass College
New Brunswick, NJ 08903 Phone: (201)932-9072
Carol H. Smith, Dir.

Founded: 1976. **Research Activities and Fields:** Gender and class, global feminism, gender integration and curricular reform, reproductive laws, women and war and peace, Black women writers, gender issues and creativity, and feminist theory and methodology. **Publications:** *NETWORC* (semiannual newsletter); *Women, War & Peace Bibliography and Filmography*. **Meetings/Educational Activities:** Sponsors Consortium for Educational Equity, Thinking About Women Seminar Series (monthly), and a Celebration of Our Work Conference (annually, open to the public). **Formerly:** Women's Studies Institute (1982).

★2617★
San Diego State University
Bureau of Business and Economic Research
School of Business Administration
San Diego, CA 92182 Phone: (619)594-6838
Dr. Oliver Galbraith III, Dir.

Founded: 1957. **Research Activities and Fields:** Business administration and health economics, particularly studies of minority business and small business in the Pacific coast and the southwest.

★2618★
Seton Hall University
Center for African American Studies
400 S. Orange Ave.
South Orange, NJ 07079 Phone: (201)761-9411
Julia A. Miller, Dir.

Founded: 1970. **Research Activities and Fields:** Community designated projects on African Americans, conducted by students of the University for credit. **Publications:** *Booklet* (annually). **Meetings/Educational Activities:** Tucker/Fahy Lecture Series, which sponsors Black scholars to relate the lessons of Black experience to the problem of formulating viable social policy to meet the needs of inner cities. **Formerly:** Black Studies Center.

★2619★
Sickle Cell Association of the Texas Gulf Coast
2626 S Loop W., Ste. 245
Houston, TX 77054 Phone: (713)666-0300
Rebecca Jasso, Exec.Dir.

Founded: 1971. **Research Activities and Fields:** Performs laboratory tests to identify persons with sickle cell disease. **Publications:** *Sickle Cell Anemia Fast Facts.* **Meetings/Educational Activities:** Conducts support groups and offers sickle cell anemia education programs on request. Holds residential summer camp programs and tutorial programs. **Formerly:** Sickle Cell Disease Research Foundation of Texas, Inc. (1990).

★2620★
Social Science Research Council
605 3rd Ave.
New York, NY 10158 Phone: (212)661-0280
David L. Featherman, Pres.

Founded: 1923. **Research Activities and Fields:** Seeks to advance research in the social sciences by providing fellowships and grants such as the MacArthur Foundation Fellowship in International Security, Public Policy Research on Contemporary Hispanic Issues, and Research on the Urban Underclass. Maintains the following committees with the American Council of Learned Societies (ACLS): African Studies, Chinese Studies, Eastern Europe Studies, Japanese Studies, Korean Studies, Latin American Studies, South Asian Studies, Southeast Asian Studies, Soviet Studies, Western Europe Studies, and Scholarly Communication with the People's Republic of China. **Publications:** *Items* (quarterly); Annual Report.

★2621★
South Dakota State University
Census Data Center
Brookings, SD 57007 Phone: (605)688-4132
Dr. James Satterlee, Dir.

Founded: 1981. **Research Activities and Fields:** Population census, agriculture census, minorities, and migration. The Center responds to out-state needs of public and private agencies for census data and is a repository for all census data for South Dakota. Participates in the U.S. Census Bureau State Data Center program. **Publications:** *Update Series*; monthly *Newsletter*. Sponsors Census Users Workshops (two or three per year). **Library:** Maintains a collection of census data on microfiche, computer tape, and print; Don Arwood, librarian.

★2622★
Spelman College
Women's Research and Resource Center
Box 115
Atlanta, GA 30314 Phone: (404)681-3643
Dr. Beverly Guy-Sheftall, Dir.

Founded: 1981. **Research Activities and Fields:** Black women, particularly history, literature, higher education, and health care studies. Coordinates curriculum development project in Black women's studies at selected southern colleges. **Publications:** *Exhibit Catalogs*; *Sage: A Scholarly Journal on Black Women* (semiannually). **Meetings/Educational Activities:** Sponsors conferences on Black women and brown bag luncheon seminars (monthly).

★2623★
State University of New York at Albany
Center for Women in Government
Draper 310
135 Western Ave.
Albany, NY 12222 Phone: (518)442-3900
Florence Bonner, Dir.

Founded: 1978. **Research Activities and Fields:** Brings together unions, women's organizations, advocacy organizations, and government officials to address public sector employment issues of interest to women and minorities, including studies on career ladders, promotion processes, pay equity, and other barriers preventing full participation of women and minorities in public service. Other areas of study include access to public sector jobs for economically disadvantaged, and inner city women. **Publications:** *Monographs*; *Working Paper Series*; *News on Women in Government* (newsletter); *Technical Reports*; *Guidebooks*. **Meetings/Educational Activities:** Sponsors seminars and special programs, including training seminars. Conducts a fellows program which places graduate student interns in state department and state legislative offices.

★2624★
State University of New York at Binghamton
Fernand Braudel Center for the Study of Economies, Historical Systems and Civilizations
Binghamton, NY 13902-6000 Phone: (607)777-4924
Prof. Immanuel Wallerstein, Dir.

Founded: 1976. **Research Activities and Fields:** Center is organized into research working groups, which study the following topics: hegemony and rivalry in the world-system, 1500-2025; commodity chains; world labor; southern Africa and the world-system, 1975-2000; institutionalization of the social sciences; households and labor force formation in the world economy; and gender, race, and ethnicity in the world-system. **Publications:** *Review* (quarterly journal); *Studies in Modern Capitalism* (book series); *Southern Africa* (pamphlet series); *Annual Newsletter*; *Newsletter on Long Waves*; *Research Bulletin on Southern Africa*. **Meetings/Educational Activities:** Sponsors conferences in coordination with research programs and monthly seminars.

★2625★
State University of New York Health Science Center at Brooklyn
Sickle Cell Center
450 Clarkson Ave., Box 20
Brooklyn, NY 11203 Phone: (212)735-2249
Dr. R.F. Rieder, Prog. Dir.

Founded: 1972. **Research Activities and Fields:** Sickle cell disease, including studies on natural history of sickle cell disease, and genetic basis for variations in disease severity.

★2626★
Thomas Jefferson University
Cardeza Foundation for Hematologic Research
1015 Walnut St.
Philadelphia, PA 19107 Phone: (215)955-7786
Sandor S. Shapiro M.D., Dir.

Founded: 1939. **Research Activities and Fields:** Conducts basic and clinical hematologic research. Maintains a blood bank, hemophilia and sickle cell centers, and a photographic unit. **Meetings/Educational Activities:** Sponsors weekly seminars for interested workers in the field. **Library:** 1,500 volumes on hematology; Doris Riso, librarian.

★2627★
Tuskegee University
Division of Behavioral Science Research
1506 Franklin Rd.
Tuskegee, AL 36088 Phone: (205)727-8575
Dr. Paul L. Wall, Dir.

Founded: 1967. **Research Activities and Fields:** Race relations and problems of the South, student attitudes and aspirations, problems related to poverty and its alleviation, Black migration, informal adoption, Black oral history, patterns of intercultural adaptation, nutrition, and public housing. Evaluates rural community education programs. Microfilming projects include compilation of the George Washington Carver Papers and a newsclipping file concerning Blacks in America. **Publications:** *Monographs*; *Census News* (six times per year). **Library:** 5,000 books and periodicals on the South, Black community, and race relations.

★2628★
University of Alabama
Center for Southern History and Culture
PO Box 870342
University, AL 35487-0342 Phone: (205)348-7467
Dr. Robert J. Norrell, Dir.

Founded: 1976. **Research Activities and Fields:** History and culture of the South, including regional and urban studies, economic history, and race relations. Supports research and writing and aids the University library in discovering and preserving important documents. **Publications:** *The Alabama Review* (quarterly) for the Alabama Historical Association; *Alabama Heritage* (popular history magazine). **Meetings/Educational Activities:** Trains students in research and writing. Conducts teacher education activities, including in-service workshops and residential institutes. **Formerly:** Center for the Study of Southern History and Culture.

★2629★
University of Alabama
Institute of Higher Education Research and Services
PO Box 870302
Tuscaloosa, AL 35487 Phone: (205)348-7770
Prof. David Masoner, Dir.

Founded: 1970. **Research Activities and Fields:** Development of postsecondary education, with special attention given to Alabama and surrounding states, including institutional self-studies and long-range planning activities, studies of interinstitutional cooperative arrangements, single and multi-institution goal-setting efforts, postsecondary educational needs by state or area within state, international education, and Black community in Alabama. **Publications:** *Progress Report* (annually, mimeographed). **Meetings/Educational Activities:** Trains college teachers and administrators in working with work with disadvantaged students. Holds periodic seminars for college administrators and faculty members, also workshops on community services, developing human potential, and improvement of instruction.

★2630★
University of California, Berkeley
Institute for the Study of Social Change
2420 Bowditch St.
Berkeley, CA 94720 Phone: (415)642-0813
Prof. Troy Duster, Dir.

Founded: 1975. **Research Activities and Fields:** Mechanisms of social change, development of techniques and methods to assist direction of social change, and social stratification and differentiation, including condition of both economically and politically depressed minorities as well as the more privileged strata, social and cultural anthropology, sociology, and social psychology, plus allied fields of architecture, city planning, education, economics, and political science. Ongoing projects include studies on effects of technological innovation on longshoring community, social and political implications of AIDS antibody testing and health policies, reconstruction of culture through oral histories, facilitation of public and private partnerships in local economic development, development of a community mobilization approach to juvenile delinquency population, social and political implications of new technology in mass screening for defective genes, and corporate culture and the structure of decision making within corporations, particularly as it relates to productivity of American industry. **Publications:** *Institute Working Papers*; *Annual Report*. **Meetings/Educational Activities:** Offers a predoctoral training program to teach graduate students in social sciences about institutional processes and the power-based negotiations of normality and illness (mental and physical). **Library:** 4,000 volumes on sociology, architecture, and political science. **Formerly:** Institute of Race and Community Relations (1977).

★2631★
University of California, Los Angeles
African Studies Center
405 Hilgard Ave.
Los Angeles, CA 90024-1310 Phone: (213)825-3779
Prof. Merrick Posnansky, Dir.

Founded: 1959. **Research Activities and Fields:** Countries of Africa, especially social and humanistic studies. Facilitates communication and collaboration among African study scholars in social sciences, fine and performing arts, film, humanities, law, education, linguistics, and public health. Growing interest in francophone and lusophone Africa. Assists research efforts that involve field work or travel in Africa. Special research projects in African agriculture and development studies. **Publications:** *African Arts* (quarterly); *Ufahamu* (three times per year); *Journal of African Studies* (quarterly); *Studies in African Linguistics* (three times per year). **Meetings/Educational Activities:** Develops and coordinates teaching programs on Africa. Sponsors annual interdisciplinary colloquia, public lectures, seminars, and annual summer institute for school teachers. **Library:** Extensive holdings on Africa and resident Africana bibliographer.

★2632★
University of California, Los Angeles
Center for Afro-American Studies
160 Haines Hall
405 Hilgard Ave.
Los Angeles, CA 90024-1545 Phone: (213)825-7403
Dr. M. Belinda Tucker, Acting Dir.

Founded: 1969. **Research Activities and Fields:** Conducts and coordinates academic and research programs in Afro-American studies designed to expand the knowledge of the history, life styles, and sociocultural systems of persons of African descent and to investigate problems that have bearing on the psychological, social, and material well-being of Afro-Americans throughout the Western Hemisphere. Current research includes examination of the impact of sex ratio imbalance on social structure and social psychological adaptation, the socioeconomic well-being of ethnic communities in Los Angeles, social support and well-being among mildly retarded Black adults, experiences of Black men in the labor market, and Afro-American sociolinguistics. **Publications:** *Afro-American Culture and Society Monograph Series*; the *Community Classic Series*; *CAAS Special Publication Series*; *Annual Report*; *CAAS Newsletter* (semiannually). **Meetings/Educational Activities:** Administers B.A. and M.A. degree programs and provides fellowships and scholarships. Sponsors a wide variety of scholarly and cultural programs with Afro-American themes, including Thurgood Marshall Lecture (annually), symposia, exhibits, and concerts. **Library:** 5,000 volumes on Black history, literature, and culture, plus subscriptions to leading Black newspapers and video cassettes of events affecting the Afro-American experience; Reynoir Lewis, assistant.

★2633★
University of California, Los Angeles
Higher Education Research Institute
Graduate School of Education
Los Angeles, CA 90024 Phone: (213)825-1925
Dr. Alexander W. Astin, Dir.

Founded: 1973. **Research Activities and Fields:** Higher education institutions, federal and state policy assessment, minority access to higher education, student and faculty development, retention, and women, leadership, and values in higher education. Conducts the Annual Survey of American College Freshmen. Survey data is collected on 280,000 freshmen from 600 institutions each fall. Follow-up surveys on each cohort are conducted after 2-4 years. **Publications:** *American Freshman: National Norms for Fall* (annually).

★2634★
University of California, Los Angeles
National Study of Black College Students
Dept. of Sociology
405 Hilgard Ave.
Los Angeles, CA 90024-1551 Phone: (213)206-7107
Prof. Walter R. Allen, Dir.

Research Activities and Fields: Analyzes experiences of Black students attending predominantly White or predominantly Black schools, including studies of psychological stress and social groups.

★2635★
University of California, Los Angeles
Research Center on the Psychobiology of Ethnicity
D-2 Annex
1000 W. Carson St.
Torrance, CA 90504 Phone: (213)212-4266
Keh-Ming Lin Ph.D., Dir.

Founded: 1990. **Research Activities and Fields:** Role of ethnicity (including culture) and biological variables in the mental health of ethnic minority populations. Conducts studies using pharmacokinetical, pharmacodynamical, and pharmacogenetical research techniques to examine ethnic and individual differences in responses to psychotropic drugs. **Meetings/Educational Activities:** Provides research training to psychiatric residents and other trainees.

★2636★
University of California, San Francisco
Comprehensive Sickle Cell Center
San Francisco General Hospital
1001 Potrero Ave., 6J5
San Francisco, CA 94110 Phone: (415)821-5169
William C. Mentzer M.D., Dir.

Research Activities and Fields: Sickle cell disease, including molecular, cellular, tissue, and organ studies. Conducts clinical trials. Seeks to translate research on sickle cell disease to improved health care at the community level. **Formerly:** Comprehensive Sickle Cell Center.

★2637★
University of California, Santa Barbara
Center for Black Studies
Santa Barbara, CA 93106 Phone: (805)893-3914
Dr. Gerald C. Horne, Acting Dir.

Founded: 1969. **Research Activities and Fields:** Social, historical, political, and economic forces that have affected African people throughout the world. Sponsors a faculty development program, which supports dissertation research.

★2638★
University of Chicago
Committee on African and African-American Studies
5828 S. University Ave.
Chicago, IL 60637 Phone: (312)702-8344
Prof. Jean Conaroff, Chairman

Research Activities and Fields: Serves as a supporting and coordinating body for research on African and African-American history, culture, economy, and society conducted by faculty and students of the University. **Formerly:** Committee on African Studies (1986).

★2639★
University of Colorado—Boulder
Center for Comparative Politics
Dept. of Political Science, CB 333
Boulder, CO 80309 Phone: (303)492-7064
William Safran, Dir.

Founded: 1983. **Research Activities and Fields:** Ethnic and class-based groups, social and economic policies, growth of state powers and resources, ethnic conflicts, political terrorism and revolution, political institutions, and group-institution relationships in democratic, authoritarian, and revolutionary situations. Projects conducted on the global level, including areas of western Europe, Latin America, and Africa.

★2640★
University of Colorado—Boulder
Center for Studies of Ethnicity and Race in America
Ketchum 30
Campus Box 339
Boulder, CO 80309-0339 Phone: (303)492-8852
Dr. Evelyn Hu-DeHart, Dir.

Founded: 1988. **Research Activities and Fields:** Comparative race and ethnicity and specific ethnic groups, including Afro-American, American Indian, Asian-American, and Chicano studies; African and Asian diasporal studies. **Meetings/Educational Activities:** Offers public lectures, art exhibits, and conferences.

★2641★
University of Connecticut
Women's Center
417 Whitney Rd., Box U-118
Storrs, CT 06268 Phone: (203)486-4738

Research Activities and Fields: Conducts institutional research and other activities related to women's and gender issues, including Connecticut PEER (Project for Equal Education Rights) to improve K-12 math and science education for female and minority students; the Vocational Equity Research, Evaluation and Training Center, to examine gender equity in vocational education. Other areas of interest include gender harassment, sexual harassment and violence, abortion, job discrimination, women's economic status, status of women of color, the legal meaning of marriage, sexual abuse of children, eating disorders, and Black women under apartheid. **Publications:** *Annual Report*; *VERTEC Newsletter*; *Research Briefs*. Also publishes various informational pamphlets, fact sheets, and brochures. **Meetings/Educational Activities:** Conducts monthly informal lectures (open to the public), invites guest speakers to campus, and conducts various conferences, seminars, and training programs. **Library:** Maintains a collection of books, magazines, and reference information.

★2642★
University of Florida
Center for African Studies
470 Grinter Hall
Gainesville, FL 32611 Phone: (904)392-2183
Dr. Peter R. Schimdt, Dir.

Founded: 1964. **Research Activities and Fields:** Directs and coordinates African studies at the University, including tropical rural development, constitutionality and governance, food supply, languages and literature, prehistory, agroforestry, and wildlife ecology. **Publications:** Annual volume based on its Carter Lecture Series. **Meetings/Educational Activities:** Offers certificates at the undergraduate, M.A., and Ph.D. levels. Sponsors Carter Lecture Series, conferences, and seminars. **Library:** 75,000 volumes, 500 periodicals, and an extensive map collection; Peter Malanchuk, Africana bibliographer.

★2643★
University of Florida
Urban and Regional Research Center
2326 Turlington
Gainesville, FL 32611 Phone: (904)392-2351
Prof. A. LaGreca, Dir.

Founded: 1967. **Research Activities and Fields:** General community and urban problems, with emphasis given to social perspectives, formation of urban subcommunities, residential segregation, elderly in the city, the consequences of neighborhood deterioration, retirement communities in America, and the elderly and their use/non-use of alcohol.

★2644★
University of Houston
African and AfroAmerican Studies Program
College of Humanities and Fine Arts
Agnes Arnold Hall
Houston, TX 77204-3784 Phone: (713)749-2900
Lawrence Curry, Assoc. Dean

Founded: 1969. **Research Activities and Fields:** Black operated and inner city businesses, including studies designed to isolate problems inherent in these businesses and to develop guidelines for a business symposium in East, Central, and Southern Africa. **Meetings/Educational Activities:** Provides instruction emphasizing cultural and historical heritage of Black Americans, analyzing and critically examining sociological, psychological, economic, and political aspects of Black community as it exists in the U.S. and Africa. **Library:** 800 volumes; Audrey Taylor, librarian. **Formerly:** Afro-American Studies Program (1977).

★2645★
University of Illinois
AfroAmerican Studies and Research Program
1204 W. Oregon
Urbana, IL 61801 Phone: (217)333-7781
Prof. Alice A. Deck, Acting Dir.

Founded: 1969. **Research Activities and Fields:** Subjects related to Afro-Americans, including the African diaspora in the Americas, educational policy, intellectual history, curriculum development, critical social theory, social sciences, and the humanities. **Publications:** *Afro-Americanist Newsletter*. Sponsors colloquia. **Library:** Maintains a reference collection.

★2646★
University of Illinois
Center for African Studies
1208 W. California, Rm. 101
Urbana, IL 61801 Phone: (217)333-6335
Dr. D.E. Crummey, Dir.

Founded: 1970. **Research Activities and Fields:** Coordinates research, instructional, and outreach activities at the University in Sub-Saharan Africa, including agriculture, education, social science, language studies, and the humanities. **Meetings/Educational Activities:** Offers a noon lunch series, including guest lecturers, on topical political matters and current research. Sponsors a spring symposium. **Library:** Yvette Scheven, librarian. **Formerly:** African Studies Program.

★2647★
University of Illinois at Chicago
Sickle Cell Eye Center
UIC Eye Center
Rm. L111
1905 W. Taylor St.
Chicago, IL 60612 Phone: (312)996-7831
Steven B. Cohen M.D., Dir.

Research Activities and Fields: Clinical trials to compare methods of treating sickle cell retinopathy.

★2648★
University of Massachusetts at Boston
William Monroe Trotter Institute for the Study of Black Culture
Harbor Campus
Boston, MA 02125-3393 Phone: (617)287-5880
Wornie L. Reed, Dir.

Founded: 1984. **Research Activities and Fields:** Black issues nationally and locally, including economics, history, Black service institutions, demographic and political trends, community development, Black artists, housing, education, Africa, women, family, criminal justice, Black image in media, and psychology. **Publications:** *Trotter Institute Review* (quarterly); *Research Report Series*; *Occasional Paper Series*. **Meetings/Educational Activities:** Sponsors weekly Institute Forums and panel discussions.

★2649★
University of Miami
Innovation and Entrepreneurship Institute
PO Box 249117
Coral Gables, FL 33124 Phone: (305)284-4692
Carl McKeney, Exec.Dir.

Founded: 1984. **Research Activities and Fields:** Entrepreneurship and innovation in Florida, including studies on high-technology ventures and Black and Cuban-American entrepreneurs. Promotes interaction of entrepreneurs and capital and service providers. **Publications:** *Research Report Series*; *Friends of the Forum Directory*. **Meetings/Educational Activities:** Sponsors the University of Miami Venture Council Forum, a series of programs to assist small entrepreneurial companies that include company case studies, seminars, workshops, and lectures.

★2650★
University of Michigan
Center for AfroAmerican and African Studies
Rm. 200 W. Engineering Bldg.
550 E. University
Ann Arbor, MI 48109-1092 Phone: (313)764-5514
Prof. Earl Lewis, Interim Dir.

Founded: 1970. **Research Activities and Fields:** Conducts interdisciplinary studies on the Black experience in Africa and throughout the diaspora. Projects include a national study of Black college students, immigration and acculturation of Falashas in Israel, comparative Black family organization, Africa's triple heritage, urban political systems and racial transitions in Detroit, west African women, African agriculture and trade, and post-emancipation societies in the Caribbean and North America. **Publications:** *CAAS Newsletter* (twice yearly). **Meetings/Educational Activities:** Sponsors the Dubois-Mandela-Rodney Postdoctoral Fellowship Program (a four-year undergraduate honors program), the Zora Neale Hurston Speakers Series, and the Speakers Colloquia.

★2651★
University of Michigan
Program for Research on Black Americans
5118 Institute for Social Research
426 Thompson St.
PO Box 1248
Ann Arbor, MI 48106 Phone: (313)763-0045
Prof. James S. Jackson, Dir.

Founded: 1976. **Research Activities and Fields:** Aging and human development of Black Americans, including race and cultural factors in marital formation and dissolution, race and sociocultural factors in productive activities across the life course, and health and coping in elderly Blacks. Studies race attitudes and political behavior, including a national Black election study. Evaluates psychiatric epidemiology and mental health of Blacks, including a probability survey of risk factors, mental health status, and treatment in Michigan prisons. Activities include investigations on the correlation of religious participation and family and friendship networks of Black Americans. **Meetings/Educational Activities:** Provides education and research opportunities at the undergraduate, graduate, and postdoctoral levels.

★2652★
University of Missouri, Kansas City
Center for Study of Metropolitan Problems in Education
5100 Rockhill Rd.
Kansas City, MO 64110 Phone: (816)276-2251
Dr. Daniel U. Levine, Dir.

Founded: 1964. **Research Activities and Fields:** Educational problems in metropolitan areas, including studies on relation between census data and school achievement. Emphasizes studies involving compensatory education and desegregation.

★2653★
University of North Carolina at Charlotte
Urban Institute
Charlotte, NC 28223 Phone: (704)547-2307
Dr. William J. McCoy, Dir.

Founded: 1969. **Research Activities and Fields:** Economic development and planning, survey research, and small business and low income neighborhood development. The Institute maintains a Small Business and Technology Development Center, which studies marketing, capital formation, business planning, and technological development, and a Survey Center, which analyzes retail marketing, housing needs, medical insurance availability, recycling, and hazardous waste systems. Also works as an affiliate with the Social Science Research Working Group, focusing on community organizations, career socialization among minority students, age discrimination, utilization of public health clinics, and missing children. **Publications:** *Annual Report*; *Newsletter*; *Research and News*. **Meetings/Educational Activities:** Employs graduate assistants from the University and provides support services for summer internships for students.

★2654★
University of Notre Dame
Institute for Urban Studies
Law School
Notre Dame, IN 46556 Phone: (219)239-8129
Dr. Thomas F. Broden, Dir.

Founded: 1969. **Research Activities and Fields:** Neighborhoods in the U.S., minority educational opportunity, and minority community development, including Hispanic community development in the Midwest. **Library:** Maintains a small collection on neighborhoods, youth advocacy, social indicators, and urban affairs; Theodessa Earles, librarian.

★2655★
University of Oklahoma
Center for Research on Minority Education
601 Elm Ave., Rm. 146
Norman, OK 73019-0315 Phone: (405)325-4529
Prof. Wanda Ward, Dir.

Founded: 1986. **Research Activities and Fields:** Needs of and opportunities for minorities in education and the nature of minority participation in education and the workforce. Activities focus on higher education, including minority graduate education, effect of various admission standards upon minority student access, factors affecting academic success and the cultural identity of minority students on college and university campuses, and minority faculty career development. **Publications:** *Cultural Diversity* (newsletter). **Meetings/Educational Activities:** Administers senior scholar and postdoctoral scholar programs.

★2656★
University of Pennsylvania
Center for Cultural Studies
420 Williams Hall
Philadelphia, PA 19104 Phone: (215)898-6836
Dr. Gerald Prince, Codirector

Founded: 1986. **Research Activities and Fields:** Cross-disciplinary studies of systems of cultural expression. Activities focus on anthropology, art history, communications, literature, folklore, linguistics, Black studies, women's studies, musicology, psychology, American studies, drama, film, history, and history of science.

★2657★
University of Pennsylvania
Institute for Research on Higher Education
4200 Pine St., 5th Fl.
Philadelphia, PA 19104-4090 Phone: (215)898-4585
Dr. Robert Zemsky, Dir.

Founded: 1979. **Research Activities and Fields:** Enrollment planning, demographic research, and minority participation in higher education. Also conducts collegiate curriculum analysis, strategic planning, postsecondary education finance studies, and research on institutional decision making. **Publications:** *Policy Perspectives* (quarterly). **Meetings/Educational Activities:** Sponsors a higher education seminar.

★2658★
University of Southern California
Comprehensive Sickle Cell Center
1200 N. State St., Box 305
Los Angeles, CA 90033 Phone: (213)226-7116
Dr. L. Julian Haywood, Dir.

Founded: 1972. **Research Activities and Fields:** Sickle cell disease, including studies on molecular biology of red cells, fetal hemoglobin identification, and renal, cardiovascular, and endocrine functions.

★2659★
University of Tennessee
Clinical Research Center
951 Court Ave., Rm. 329B
Memphis, TN 38163 Phone: (901)528-5802
Abbas E. Kitabchi Ph.D.,, Prog. Dir.

Founded: 1965. **Research Activities and Fields:** Provides general clinical research facilities for controlled inpatient and outpatient studies on human subjects with various disorders, including sickle cell anemia, diabetes mellitus, hyperandrogenism and other endocrine disorders, kidney disease, liver disorders, hypertension, brain tumors, muscular dystrophy, obesity, metabolic bone diseases, psychiatric disorders, osteoporosis, Reye's syndrome, hirsutism, sexual disorders, problems of reproduction, thyroid disorders, cancer of the breast, and leukemia. **Publications:** *Annual Report*. **Meetings/Educational Activities:** Holds scientific advisory committee meetings and investigators conferences, to which all faculty members of the College are invited. Provides training to science students in community colleges and conducts lectures for students interested in health science careers. **Library:** Maintains all research publications generated by the Center.

★2660★
University of Texas at Austin
African and AfroAmerican Studies & Research Center
Jester A232A
Austin, TX 78705 Phone: (512)471-1784
Prof. John Sibley Butler, Acting Dir.

Founded: 1969. **Research Activities and Fields:** African and Afro-American cultures, including studies in African geography and history. Studies include African-American history, literature, historical figures, music, institutional racism, roles of African-American women, the Black family, minority education, entrepreneurial activities in the community, Black movements in the Caribbean, sociological perspectives of Black Americans, and Black English (linguistics). **Publications:** *Newsletter* (bimonthly); *Working Paper Series*; *Reprint Series*. **Meetings/Educational Activities:** Sponsors Heman Sweatt Symposium on Civil Rights (annually in spring).

★2661★
University of Virginia
Carter G. Woodson Institute for AfroAmerican and African Studies
1512 Jefferson Park Ave.
Charlottesville, VA 22903 Phone: (804)924-3109
Prof. Armstead L. Robinson, Dir.

Founded: 1981. **Research Activities and Fields:** African studies, including persons of African descent in the Americas, Europe, and the Caribbean, across the spectrum of social science and humanistic disciplines. **Formerly:** Institute for Afro-American Studies and African Studies (1982).

★2662★
University of Wisconsin—La Crosse
Office of Minority Affairs
223 Main Hall
1725 State
La Crosse, WI 54601 Phone: (608)785-8225
Julian Sanchez, Dir.

Founded: 1981. **Research Activities and Fields:** Student retention and prediction equations for student success. **Library:** Carol Miller, librarian. **Formerly:** Institute of Minority Studies.

★2663★
University of Wisconsin—Madison
African Studies Program
1454 Van Hise Hall
1220 Linden Dr.
Madison, WI 53706 Phone: (608)262-2380
Prof. Edris Makward, Dir.

Founded: 1961. **Research Activities and Fields:** Individually determined studies on Africa by 48 faculty members in 21 departments of the University, including African art, African languages and literature, Afro-American studies, economics, educational policy, curriculum and instruction, geography, history, journalism, law, music, politics, sociology, anthropology, and agricultural and development sciences. **Publications:** *News and Notes* (semiannually); *Occasional Paper Series*. Also publishes bibliographies and language materials. **Meetings/Educational Activities:** Provides instruction, with emphasis on postgraduate studies on Africa and outreach assistance to kindergarten through twelfth grade teachers in Wisconsin and other states of the upper Midwest. Holds weekly Africanist seminars and occasional conferences for educators in schools and colleges. **Library:** Uses collection of 60,000 Africana volumes and 600 periodicals and newspapers in the University's Memorial Library.

★2664★
Urban Institute
2100 M St., NW
Washington, DC 20037 Phone: (202)833-7200
William Gorham, Pres.

Founded: 1968. **Research Activities and Fields:** Domestic, social, and economic affairs, including multidisciplinary studies and government program evaluations in the areas of tax and budget reform, health policy, housing and community development, human resources, income security and pension, international activities, public finance, productivity and economic development, social services, and immigration. Also conducts research programs on employment and training, children's issues and family policy, minorities and social policy, poverty, state and local governments, transportation, and community impact and demography. **Publications:** *Policy and Research Report* (three times yearly); *Annual Report*; *Policy Bites* (bimonthly); supplements and summaries of reports, papers, reprints, and other communications of the Institute. **Meetings/Educational Activities:** Conducts press briefings, policy seminars, and interdisciplinary conferences. **Library:** 32,000 volumes, 650 journals, and 5,000 reels of microfilm on social and economic issues; Camille Motta, librarian.

★2665★
Wayne State University
Comprehensive Sickle Cell Center
Curricular Affairs Office
540 E. Canfield
Rm. 1206 Scott Hall
Detroit, MI 48201 Phone: (313)577-1546
Charles F. Whitten M.D., Dir.

Research Activities and Fields: Sickle cell disease, including molecular, cellular, tissular, and organic studies. Seeks to apply sickle cell research to improved health care at the community level.

★2666★
Wayne State University
Folklore Archive
Purdy Library, Rm. 448
Detroit, MI 48202 Phone: (313)577-4053
Janet L. Langlois, Dir.

Founded: 1939. **Research Activities and Fields:** Folklore and urban tradition, especially of Michigan and Detroit, including oral traditions in urban centers and among ethnic and occupational groups. Sponsors collection, classification, and cross-indexing of field data, maintains and prepares collections for use by researchers, solicits field collections from individuals and institutions, develops questionnaires and forms for use by collectors, provides consulting services for the mass media, and advises institutions developing folklore archive materials. **Publications:** *Urban Folklore and Anthropology Series*; *Annotated Holdings List* (occasionally); *Annual Report*. **Library:** 200 volumes on folklore, ethnographic data, and history of Michigan and Detroit. **Formerly:** Folklore Archive and Center for Study of Urban Tradition; merged with the University's Archive of Ethnomusicology (1966).

★2667★
Wellesley College
Center for Research on Women
Wellesley, MA 02181 Phone: (617)431-1453
Dr. Susan M. Bailey, Dir.

Founded: 1974. **Research Activities and Fields:** Social science, applied, and policy research on women, including studies on adolescent girls' development, child care, the economic condition of Black women, stress in the lives of women and men, and curriculum revision. **Publications:** *Working Papers Series*; *Research Report* (occasional newsletter); *Annual Report*; *Women's Review of Books*. **Meetings/Educational Activities:** Sponsors seminars and colloquia on current research topics.

★2668★
Western Michigan University
Black Americana Studies Center
814 Sprau Tower
Kalamazoo, MI 49008 Phone: (616)387-2661
Dr. Leroi Ray Jr., Dir.

Research Activities and Fields: Black Americans, particularly students.

★2669★
Western Washington University
American Cultural Studies
Bellingham, WA 98225 Phone: (206)647-4861
Dr. Jesse Hiraoka, Dir.

Founded: 1969. **Research Activities and Fields:** Conducts theoretical studies of ethnic groups. **Publications:** *U Journal of Ethnic Studies* (quarterly). **Formerly:** Program in Ethnic Studies (1987).

★2670★
William O. Douglas Institute
PO Box 45745, University Station
Seattle, WA 98145 Phone: (206)522-2388
Prof. Hubert G. Locke, Dir.

Founded: 1972. **Research Activities and Fields:** Race and ethnicity, social pathology, democratic theory, the administration of justice, and the quality of urban life. The Institute's current program focuses on the problems that were dominant under German national socialism and which persist as critical issues in contemporary America: economic instability, race, technology, ideological extremism, and the integrity of the political process. **Publications:** *Occasional Papers*. **Meetings/Educational Activities:** Holds annual seminar for leaders of public service employee associations. **Library:** 1,000 volumes on race and ethnicity and law and justice. **Formerly:** The Institute for the Study of Contemporary Social Problems.

★2671★
Wisconsin Public Policy Research Institute, Inc.
3107 N. Shepard Ave.
Milwaukee, WI 53211 Phone: (414)963-0600
James A. Miller, Exec.Dir.

Founded: 1987. **Research Activities and Fields:** State public policy issues focusing on education, including minority education, educational finance, and programs for gifted and talented children. Also studies welfare reform, criminal justice, and economic development.

(9) AWARDS, HONORS, AND PRIZES

Entries in this chapter are arranged alphabetically by name of sponsoring organization. See the User's Guide at the front of this directory for additional information.

★2672★

A. Philip Randolph Institute
c/o Mary E. Pearce, Admin. Dir.
260 Park Ave., S.
New York, NY 10010 Phone: (212)533-8000

Achievement Award
For recognition of a ranking Black trade unionist who has achieved high excellence and has made a major contribution to the improvement of the lives of workers. Candidate must hold a high ranking responsible position in the American trade union movement. A medallion is presented annually. Established in 1968 by A. Philip Randolph and Bayard Rustin.
A. Philip Randolph/Bayard Rustin Freedom Award
For recognition of outstanding contributions to the advancement of human rights and civil rights nationally and internationally. A bust of A. Philip Randolph is presented annually. Established in 1968 by A. Philip Randolph and Bayard Rustin to honor A. Philip Randolph. **Formerly:** A. Philip Randolph Freedom Award.
Rosina Tucker Award
For recognition of the contribution to the strengthening of the Black-labor alliance in the spirit of A. Philip Randolph. Nomination is by the Executive Committee of the Institute and approval by the National Board. A plaque is awarded annually. Established in 1989 in honor of Rosina Tucker, former President of Ladies' Auxillary of the Brotherhood of Sleeping Car Porters.

★2673★

Actors' Equity Association
c/o H. Feldman
165 W. 46th St.
New York, NY 10036 Phone: (212)869-8530

Rosetta LeNoire Award
To recognize those theatres and producing organizations under an Equity contract which are exemplary in the hiring of ethnic minority and female actors through affirmative action, multi-racial and non-traditional casting. Nominations of a theatre producing organization are accepted by October 31.

★2674★

African Studies Association (ASA)
c/o Dr. Edna Bay, Exec. Sec.
Credit Union Bldg.
Emory University
Atlanta, GA 30322 Phone: (404)329-6410

Herskovits Award
To recognize the author of a distinguished work on Africa published or distributed in the United States during the preceding year. The winning work must be an original scholarly publication. Edited collections, symposia, new editions of previously published books, bibliographies, and dictionaries are not eligible. A monetary prize is awarded annually.
James H. Robinson Award
To foster involvement in short-term volunteer activity and visitations to the continent of Africa. Individuals may present a creative work based upon a first-time visit of less than six months to Africa. A monetary award of $250 is presented during the ASA Annual Meeting. Established in 1983 by the African Studies Association and Operation Crossroads Africa, Inc., in honor of Rev. James H. Robinson, founder of Operation Crossroads Africa, Inc.

★2675★

Afro-American Police League (AAPL)
c/o Edgar Gosha, Exec. Officer
PO Box 49122
1525 E. 53rd St.
Chicago, IL 60619 Phone: (312)753-9454

National Law and Social Justice Leadership Award
To recognize individuals who, on a national level, best exemplify dedication to social justice. A plaque is awarded annually. Established in 1971.

★2676★

Alpha Kappa Alpha Sorority (AKA)
c/o Ms. Alison A. Harris
5656 S. Stony Island Ave.
Chicago, IL 60637 Phone: (312)684-1282

National Achievement Awards
To honor women who have distinguished themselves in their fields, rendered unselfish and outstanding service to humanity, and demonstrated Alpha Kappa Alpha's belief in "Service To All Mankind." Members may submit nominations by February 15. The following awards are presented: (1) Anna Eleanor Roosevelt Medallion of Honor; (2) Founders' Graduate Service Award; (3) Founders' Undergraduate Service Award; (4) International Service Award to a Foreign Woman; and (5) Septima Poinsette Clark Award. A plaque is awarded biennially at the National Convention in even-numbered years. Established in 1964.

★2677★

American Alliance for Health, Physical Education, Recreation, and Dance (AAHPRED)
1900 Association Dr.
Reston, VA 22091 Phone: (703)476-3436

Charles D. Henry Award
For recognition of essential contributions of its members who, through distinguished service to the Alliance (or its component structures): (1) increase involvement of ethnic minorities in AAHPERD; (2) increase communication with greater numbers of ethnic minority members; and (3) extend meaningful services to AAHPERD ethnic minorities. Members who have held such membership for at least five years and have served professionally in school (preschool, elementary, secondary), college, or

community programs in AAHPERD for a period of at least five years may be nominated. A plaque is presented annually in a ceremony at the National Convention. Not more than one award is given each year. Established in 1984.

★2678★
American Association for Counseling and Development
c/o Ginger Burns, Dir./Member Public Relations
5999 Stevenson Ave.
Alexandria, VA 22304 Phone: (703)823-9800

Kitty Cole Human Rights Award
To honor a member who has made significant contributions in one or more areas of the broad spectrum of human rights. Human rights contributions include, but are not limited to, services to people with special needs or handicaps, abused and neglected children, minority groups, economically disadvantaged, or other underserved populations. Nominees should have contributed to the field of human rights either through a special project, direct services, or a life's work and role. Nominees should have contributed a significant amount of time and effort to the area or project for which they were nominated, thus demonstrating a long-term commitment to the field of human rights. Nominations of current members must be submitted by December 15. Awarded annually. Established in honor of Kitty Cole, an active leader in the counseling and human development profession.

★2679★
American Association of State Colleges and Universities
c/o Rosemary Lauth, Dir. Annual Meeting
1 Dupont Circle, NW, Ste. 700
Washington, DC 20036-1192 Phone: (202)293-7070

AASCU/Christa McAuliffe Showcase for Excellence Awards
To highlight the pivotal role state colleges and universities play in the preparation of teachers and to provide educators with program models for improving and enhancing the teaching profession. Nominations are invited for programs in ten categories: (1) Attracting more talented students as majors in the field of education; (2) Developing more innovative curricula in teacher preparation programs; (3) Strengthening relationships with local school districts; (4) Building and sustaining new strategies for involving the entire university in teacher preparation programs and enhancing the institutional climate for teaching and learning; (5) Creating new strategies for ensuring the quality of graduates in the field of education; (6) Initiating innovative applied research projects in education and disseminating the findings to schools and other campuses, as well as throughout the institution; (7) Discovering new ways of training teachers to work with disadvantaged youth; (8) Providing professional leadership to influence state policies affecting the field of teacher ecucation; (9) Discovering new ways of attracting minority youth to enter the teaching profession; and (10) Creating new strategies for attracting minority faculty members to schools and colleges of education. Awarded annually. Established in 1985. Renamed to honor the late teacher/astronaut Christa McAuliffe, who received her bachelor's degree from Framingham State College in Massachusetts and her master's degree from Bowie State University in Maryland, both AASCU institutions. Additional informaion is available from Louis M. Barsi, Director, The Center for Educational Opportunity and Achievement, phone: (202) 293-7070.

★2680★
American Association of University Professors (AAUP)
c/o Iris Molotsky
1012 14th St., NW, Ste. 500
Washington, DC 20005 Phone: (202)737-5900

Beatrice G. Konheim Award
To recognize a chapter of the Association for distinctive achievement in advancing the objectives of AAUP in academic freedom, student rights and freedoms, the status of academic women, the elimination of discrimination against minorities, or the establishment of equal opportunity for members of college and university faculties. A monetary prize of $1,000 is awarded annually. Established in 1974.

★2681★
American College Theatre Festival
John F. Kennedy Center for the Performing Arts
Washington, DC 20566 Phone: (202)254-3437

Lorraine Hansberry Playwriting Award
To recognize an outstanding, original play on the Black experience in America written by a student in an undergraduate or graduate program. The following monetary prizes are awarded: first prize - $2,500 to the playwright and $750 to the drama department presenting the play; and second prize - $1,000 and $500 to the Theatre Departments of the college(s) and university(ies) producing the play. Awarded annually. Established in 1977. Funded by Penn State University.

★2682★
American Fund for Dental Health
211 E. Chicago Ave., Ste. 1630
Chicago, IL 60611 Phone: (312)787-6270

American Fund for Dental Health Dental Scholarships for Minority Students
To provide for a dental scholarship program for minority students. Applicants must be resident citizens of the United States from one of the following minority groups currently under-represented in the dental profession: American Indian, Black American, Mexican-American, and Puerto Rican. Applicants must be accepted by a dental school in the United States which is accredited by the Commission on Dental Accreditation. Students selected under this program may receive up to $2,000 for their first year of dental school.

★2683★
American Heart Association (AHA)
7320 Greenville Ave.
Dallas, TX 75231-4599 Phone: (214)373-6300

Louis B. Russell, Jr., Memorial Award
For recognition of leadership in promoting and enhancing the relationship between the American Heart Association and the minority or low-income community. The nominee should be an active member or volunteer of the Association. Established in 1977 in memory of Louis B. Russell, Jr., who, as a volunteer, gave willingly and freely of himself to benefit others.

★2684★
American Library Association (ALA)
Office for Library Personnel Resources
c/o Margaret Myers, Staff Liaison, Scholarship Juries
50 E. Huron St.
Chicago, IL 60611 Phone: (312)944-6780

Louise Giles Minority Scholarship
To provide funds for a U.S. or Canadian minority student to begin an MLS Degree in ALA-accredited program. A monetary award of $3,000 is presented. Established in 1977.

★2685★

American Library Association (ALA)
Reference and Adult Services Division

c/o Andrew M. Hansen, Executive Director
50 E. Huron St.
Chicago, IL 60611 Phone: (312)944-6780

Denali Press Award
To recognize achievement in creating reference works, outstanding in quality and significance, that provide information about ethnic and minority groups in the United States. Contributions are judged on accuracy, scope, usefulness, format, special features, and access, as well as the gap in the literature filled by the work. A monetary award of $500 and a citation are presented annually, at the ALA Conference. Established in 1989 by Denali Press, Alan Edward Schorr, President.

★2686★

American Library Association (ALA)
Social Responsibilities Round Table

50 E. Huron St.
Chicago, IL 60611 Phone: (312)944-6780

Coretta Scott King Book Award
To recognize African American authors and illustrators for outstanding contributions which promote better understanding and appreciation of the culture and contribution of all peoples to the realization of the American Dream. The noted book must be published in the calendar year preceding the year of award presentation. The deadline for nominations is December 31. The winners are announced during Black History Month in February and presented with an honorarium, a plaque, and a set of Encyclopedia Britannica or World Book Encyclopedias. Certificates are awarded to those chosen for Honorable Mention. Presented yearly at the Annual Conference of the American Library Association. Established in 1969 by Glyndon Flynt Greer to commemorate the life and works of Dr. Martin Luther King, Jr., and to honor Mrs. Coretta Scott King for her courage and determination to continue the work for peace and world brotherhood.

★2687★

American Nurses Association (ANA)

c/o Karen A. Keithley, Coor.
2420 Pershing Rd.
Kansas City, MO 64108 Phone: (816)474-5720

Honorary Human Rights Award
For recognition of an outstanding commitment to human rights and exemplifying the essence of nursing's philosophy about mankind. The deadline for nominations is October. Awarded biennially.

Mary Mahoney Award
To honor an individual or group of nurses for significant contributions to opening and advancing equal opportunities in nursing to members of minority groups and who have also made a significant contribution to nursing. The deadline for nominations is October. Awarded biennially. Established in 1936 in honor of Mary Eliza Mahoney, the first Black graduate nurse in the United States, and her efforts to raise the status of Black nurses in professional life.

SNA Affirmative Action Award
To recognize a constituent state nurses' association demonstrating outstanding development in implementation of affirmative action policy and programming which encourages the elimination of all barriers preventing the full participation of minorities in the total organizational programming. The deadline for nominations is October. Established in 1988.

★2688★

American Physical Therapy Association (

c/o Ree Birner, Administrative Assistant
1111 N. Fairfax St.
Alexandria, VA 22314 Phone: (

Minority Achievement Award
To recognize continuous achievement by an entry-level accredited physical therapy program in the recruitment, admission, retention, and graduation of minority students. The applicant must be accredited by the American Physical Therapy Association. The efforts for minority students must have been ongoing for at least three years. The deadline for entry is December 1. A certificate and monetary award of $1,000 are presented. Established in 1984.

Minority Initiatives Award
To recognize the efforts of a physical therapy education program in the initiation and/or improvement of recruitment, admission, retention, and graduation of minority students, and the provision of services for students from racial and ethnic minority groups. Eligible applicants are accredited education programs in physical therapy and physical therapy education programs which have been granted accreditation candidacy status. The deadline for entry is December 1. A monetary prize of $1,000 and a certificate are awarded. Established in 1984.

★2689★

American Planning Association (APA)

c/o Dir. of Public Information
1776 Massachusetts Ave., NW
Washington, DC 20036 Phone: (202)872-0611

APA Planning Fellowship
To increase the participation of minority group members (Black, Hispanic or Native American) in the planning profession. Awarded annually. Established in 1970.

★2690★

American Political Science Association (APSA)

c/o Jean Walen
1529 New Hampshire Ave., NW
Washington, DC 20036 Phone: (202)483-2512

Ralph J. Bunche Award
For recognition of the best scholarly work in political science published within the previous year that explores the phenomenon of ethnic and cultural pluralism. Books must be nominated by the publisher. A monetary prize of $500 is awarded annually. Established in 1978 in memory of Ralph J. Bunche, a prominent Black world statesman and diplomat.

★2691★

American Psychiatric Association (APA)

c/o Terry Tropin, Achievement Awards Depart.
1400 K St., NW
Washington, DC 20005 Phone: (202)682-6032

Solomon Carter Fuller Award
To recognize a Black citizen who has pioneered in an area which has significantly benefited the quality of life for Black people. The winner is selected by the Committee of Black Psychiatrists. An honorarium of $500 and a plaque, with travel expenses paid for nonmember winners, are awarded. The winner presents a lecture at the APA Annual Meeting. Established in 1969.

★2692★
American Psychological Association (APA)
1200 17th St., NW
Washington, DC 20036 Phone: (202)955-7710

Distinguished Professional Contributions to Public Service
To recognize psychologists who have made outstanding contributions in serving the public through their knowledge and practical skills. Such contributions must be seen as directed to and on behalf of the public. Consideration is given to psychologists whose professional involvement has resulted in a major benefit to the public as well as those who have made significant contributions to special populations such as those who have disabilities, are disadvantaged or underprivileged, or are are members of a minority group. Psychologists who are active in legislative, legal, political, organizational and other areas that are directed at providing benefits to the public also are considered. The deadline for nominations is February 1. Additional information is available from Darian Dreyfuss, APA Practice Directorate, phone: (202) 955-7648.

★2693★
American Red Cross
c/o Gwen T. Jackson, Nat'l Chairman of Volunteers
17th & D Sts., NW
Washington, DC 20006 Phone: (202)639-3270

Cultural Diversity Outreach Award
To recognize Red Cross unit excellence in achieving reciprocity with local minority communities through outreach efforts, programs, and services. The award is made in recognition of the chairman's and manager's teamwork that led the unit in pursuit of excellence. Established in 1987.

★2694★
American Society for Engineering Education (ASEE)
c/o Barbara Ramey
11 Dupont Circle, NW, Ste. 200
Washington, DC 20036 Phone: (202)293-7080

Vincent Bendix Minorities in Engineering Award
For outstanding achievements by an engineering educator to increase participation by minority and/or women students in the engineering curricula. The following prizes are awarded: a monetary prize of $1,500, a certificate, and a grant of $500 for travel expenses to the ASEE Annual Conference. Established in 1979. Funded by Allied Corporation Foundation.

★2695★
American Society for Microbiology
c/o Juliet Jacobsen, Prog. Asst.
1325 Massachusetts Ave., NW
Washington, DC 20005 Phone: (202)737-3600

American Society for Microbiology Fellowships
Predoctoral Minority Fellowship - To support graduate students in microbiology who are members of recognized racial and ethnic minorities in the population of the United States. A Fellow must be a citizen of the United States, a member of a minority as defined by the National Institutes of Health Minority Access to Research Careers (MARC) program, and formally admitted for a graduate academic degree in microbiology in an accredited institution of higher learning in the United States. A stipend up to $5,000 and an additional amount up to $5,000 to cover tuition and fees at the institution chosen by the awardee are awarded annually. Grants are renewable.

★2696★
Audience Development Committee (AUDELCO)
c/o Jeri Small
290 Lennox Ave.
New York, NY 10027 Phone: (212)534-8776

AUDELCO Recognition Award
For recognition of outstanding contributions to Black theater. Awards are given in the following categories: (1) Lighting Design; (2) Sound Design; (3) Scenic Design; (4) Costume Design; (5) Director/Dramatic Production; (6) Director/Musical Production; (7) Choreography; (8) Playwright; (9) Supporting Actress; (10) Supporting Actor; (11) Outstanding Performance in a Musical/Female; (12) Outstanding Performance in a Musical/Male; (13) Outstanding Musical Creator; (14) Musical Production of the Year; (15) Lead Actress in a Dramatic Role; (16) Lead Actor in a Dramatic Role; and (17) Dramatic Production of the Year. Eligibility is limited to productions mounted by professional, not-for-profit organizations, in existence at least two years and providing a minimum of 500 hours of rehearsal, performance, and/or training. To be eligible, productions must have been performed 12 or more times between September 1 and August 31. Friends of AUDELCO, in good financial standing, receive ballots reflecting the final list of nominations in each category from the Nominating Committee. They are eligible to vote only in categories in which they have seen at least three of the nominees. The AUDELCO Awards Selection Committee evaluates, counts, and makes a final tally of the ballots. Plaques are awarded annually. Established in 1973.

★2697★
Berea College
PO Box 2317
Berea, KY 40404 Phone: (606)986-9341

Carter G. Woodson Award
For recognition of efforts to foster either the development of unity, culture or research of Black communities, or equality and understanding in interracial and multicultural education. Individuals from the United States with special emphasis on the Southern Appalachian region and adjacent urban areas are eligible for consideration. A plaque is awarded annually in February (Black History Month). Established in 1983 in memory of Carter G. Woodson, Berea alumnus and founder of Black History Month. Additional information is available from Andrew Baskin, Director of the Black Cultural Center, Berea College, PO Box 134, Berea, KY 40404.

★2698★
B'nai B'rith International
Don King Center for Black-Jewish Relations
c/o Jeffrey M. Green, Dept. of Public Affairs
1640 Rhode Island Ave., NW
Washington, DC 20036 Phone: (202)857-4993

Martin Luther King/Abraham Joshua Heschel Award
To recognize individuals for continuing commitment to the advancement of equality, human rights and a meaningful relationship between the Black and Jewish communities. A plaque is awarded periodically. Established in 1988 to honor Martin Luther King and Abraham Joshua Heschel, two distinguished clergymen from the Black and Jewish communities who struggled together in the American civil rights movement.

★2699★
Career Communications Group
729 E. Pratt St., Ste. 504
Baltimore, MD 21202 Phone: (301)244-7101

Black Engineer of the Year Awards
To recognize Black engineers who have excelled in their field. Awards are given in the following categories: (1) Black Engineer of the Year; (2)

Technical Contribution; (3) Outstanding Acheivement in Government; (4) President's Award; (5) Lifetime Achievement; (6) Entrepreneur; (7) Promotion of Engineering Education; (8) Affirmative Action; (9) Most Promising Engineer; (10) Higher Education; (11) Student Leadership; (12) Community Service; (13) Professional Achievement; and (14) Honorable Mention. Trophies are awarded in each category annually at the Award Conference. Established in 1987. Co-sponsored by Mobil, *US Black Engineer* magazine, and the Council of Engineering Deans of the Historically Black Colleges and Universities.

★2700★
Caribbean Review
9700 SW 67th Ave.
Miami, FL 33156 Phone: (305)284-8466

Caribbean Review Award
To honor an individual who has contributed to the advancement of Caribbean intellectual life. The award recognizes individual effort irrespective of field, ideology, national origin, or place of residence. A plaque is awarded annually. Established in 1980. Co-sponsored by the Caribbean Studies Association.

★2701★
Caribbean Studies Association (CSA)
c/o Angel Calderon-Cruz, Sec.-Treas.
1078 Calle 5
Villa Nevares, Puerto Rico, PR 00927 Phone: (809)763-4128

Distinguished Service Award
To recognize an individual for distinguished contributions to the advancement of the Association's goals and objectives. Leadership within the organization or outside personal services or support, material or otherwise are considered. A plaque is presented in a public ceremony, usually at the annual conference. Established in 1985. Additional information is available from Gilberto Arroyo, Secretary-Treasurer, c/o Department of Social Sciences, Inter American University, San German, Puerto Rico 00753, phone: (809) 892-1095.

★2702★
Catholic Interracial Council of New York
c/o P. Maull
John Jay College
889 10th Ave.
New York, NY 10019 Phone: (212)237-8255

James J. and Jane Hoey Award for Interracial Justice
To recognize outstanding contributions in the cause of human rights and social justice. Engraved silver medals are presented to Catholic and non-Catholic recipients annually. Established in 1942.
John LaFarge Memorial Award for Interracial Justice
To recognize outstanding contributions for furthering interracial justice. Outstanding public figures are eligible. A hand-lettered scroll is awarded annually. Established in 1965 in memory of Father John LaFarge, founder of the Council.

★2703★
Cleveland Foundation
c/o Alicia M. Ciliberto, Admin. Asst.
1422 Euclid Ave., Ste. 1400
Cleveland, OH 44115 Phone: (216)861-3810

Anisfield/Wolf Book Award in Race Relations
For recognition of the authors of outstanding published books in the following two categories: (1) an outstanding scholarly work in the field of race relations; and (2) the best book concerned with racial problems in the field of creative literature, such as fiction, drama, poetry, biography or autobiography. Books in any field which in any way contribute to the betterment of race relations or to a clearer understanding of the mechanisms or injustices of racism are eligible for an award. A copy of the book in published form may be submitted by January 31. Monetary prizes of $3,000 are presented in each category. Awarded annually. Established by Edith Anisfield Wolf in memory of her father, John Anisfield, and her husband, Eugene E. Wolf, in 1934 and 1942, respectively. Originally sponsored by *Saturday Review*. Additional information is available from Ashley Montague, 321 Cherry Hill Road, Princeton, NJ 08540.

★2704★
Columbia University
Graduate School of Journalism
c/o Judith L. Leynse, Assoc. Dir.
Office of Public Information
304 Low Library
116th & Broadway
New York, NY 10027 Phone: (212)280-5573

Paul Tobenkin Memorial Award
To honor reporting excellence in a United States newspaper in the fight against racial and religious intolerance and bigotry, in the tradition of Paul Tobenkin. Newspaper journalists in the United States are eligible. A monetary award and a certificate are awarded annually. Honorable Mentions and Special Presentations are also given. Established in 1960 in memory of Paul Tobenkin who died in 1959 after a 25-year career with the *New York Herald Tribune*.

★2705★
Congressional Black Caucus Foundation
1004 Pennsylvania Ave., SE
Washington, DC 20003 Phone: (202)675-6735

George W. Collins Award
To recognize the individual or group of individuals on the local level who exemplify the dedication and work styles of the late Honorable George W. Collins in the areas of young people, senior citizens and minorities. An engraved ebony plaque is awarded annually. Established in 1973.
William L. Dawson Award
To recognize an individual who has made significant research, organizational and leadership contributions in the development of legislation that addresses the needs of minorities in the United States. A plaque is awarded annually. Established in 1981.
Humanitarian Award
To recognize an individual for exceptional work in the struggle for human rights and social justice. A plaque is awarded annually.
Adam Clayton Powell Award
To recognize an individual in the political arena who has contributed substantially to Black political awareness and empowerment. A plaque is awarded annually. Established in 1972.
Harold Washington Award
To recognize an individual who has demonstrated excellence in coalition building. Established in 1988 in memory of Harold Washington.

★2706★
Eastern Music Festival
c/o Susan W. Black, Dir. of Adm.
PO Box 22026
Greensboro, NC 27420 Phone: (919)272-9575

Wynton Marsalis Scholarship
To provide funds for a Black trumpet player to attend the Eastern Music Festival. United States citizens between the ages of 13 and 20 are eligible. One full scholarship is awarded annually. For six weeks, the recipient performs weekly in orchestral concerts, plays in a coached chamber music group, studies with a private teacher, and is given the opportunity to attend various classes in music theory, literature and analysis, conducting, etc. Established in 1986 by Wynton Marsalis.

★2707★
Fellowship of Reconciliation
c/o Nancy Mainland
PO Box 271
523 N. Broadway
Nyack, NY 10960 Phone: (914)358-4601

Martin Luther King, Jr. Award
To recognize a person or group working quietly but effectively for peace, justice and nonviolence in the tradition of Martin Luther King, Jr. Nominations are accepted. The winners are selected by a panel of seven judges which includes past Martin Luther King, Jr. Award winners. A monetary award and a plaque are presented annually on the eve of Dr. King's birthday. Established in 1979.

★2708★
Gospel Music Association
c/o Donald W. Butler, Sr., Exec. Dir.
38 Music Square W.
PO Box 23201
Nashville, TN 37202 Phone: (615)242-0303

Dove Award
For recognition of excellence and/or significant accomplishments in the quality and means of spreading the true word through gospel music. Awards are presented in the following categories: (1) Song of the Year; (2) Songwriter of the Year; (3) Male Vocalist of the Year; (4) Female Vocalist of the Year; (5) Group of the Year; (6) Artist of the Year; (7) New Artist of the Year; (8) Metal Recorded Song of the Year; (9) Rock Recorded Song of the Year; (10) Contemporary Recorded Song of the Year; (11) Inspirational Recorded Song of the Year; (12) Southern Gospel Recorded Song of the Year; (13) Country Recorded Song of the Year; (14) Contemporary Black Gospel Recorded Song of the Year; (15) Traditional Black Gospel Recorded Song of the Year; (16) Metal Album of the Year; (17) Rock Album of the Year; (18) Contemporary Gospel Album of the Year; (19) Inspirational Album of the Year; (20) Southern Gospel Album of the Year; (21) Country Gospel Album of the Year; (22) Contemporary Black Gospel Album of the Year; (23) Traditional Black Gospel Album of the Year; (24) Children's Music Album of the Year; (25) Recorded Music Packaging of the Year; (26) Short Form Video of the Year; (27) Long Form Video of the Year; (28) Instrumental Album of the Year; (29) Worship & Praise Album of the Year; (30) Musical Album of the Year; and (31) Choral Collection Album of the Year. Bronze sculptures of a dove perched on a harp are presented annually. Established in 1969.

★2709★
Indiana Black Expo, Inc.
c/o Rev. Charles R. Williams, President
3130 Sutherland Ave.
Indianapolis, IN 46205 Phone: (317)925-2702

Freedom Award
To recognize the individual whom Indiana Black Expo, Inc. feels has contributed the most effective service in promoting goodwill to all mankind through performance, accomplishments and contributions to our world. Awarded annually. Established in 1981.

★2710★
InterFuture
51 E. 42nd St., Ste. 417
New York, NY 10117-5404 Phone: (212)385-0005

Paul W. Conner Memorial Scholarship
To further diversify each year's class of InterFuture students; and to encourage comparative study projects in third world countries and representation of minority groups whose heritage and interests lie outside Western Europe. Students who fulfill all the requirements of an interfuture scholar are eligible. A monetary award applicable toward payment of the Interfuture fee is presented annually. Established in 1984 in memory of Paul W. Conner, founder and past president. Additional information is available from Prof. David Robbins, Dean, Department of History, Suffolk University, 8 Ashburton Place, Boston, MA 02108.

★2711★
International Black Writers (IBWC)
c/o Mable Terrell
PO Box 1030
Chicago, IL 60690 Phone: (312)995-5195

Alice C. Browning Award
To recognize excellence in writing and to assist a promising young Black writer in his/her attempts to master the craft of writing. Published writers 18 years or older who are members of the organization are eligible. A plaque is presented annually at the Conference in June. Established in 1985 in honor of Alice C. Browning, founder of the International Black Writers Conference.

★2712★
International City Management Association (ICMA)
c/o Sonya Yates, Prog. Mgr.
777 N. Capitol St., NE, Ste. 500
Washington, DC 20002-4201 Phone: (202)962-3596

Workplace Diversity Professional Development Award
To recognize an administrator who has established outstanding career development programs that assist minorities and women in local government. ICMA Corporate Members are eligible.

★2713★
J. Morris Anderson Production Co.
c/o Mr. Maurice Smith
PO Box 25668
Philadelphia, PA 19144 Phone: (215)844-8872

Miss Black America
To recognize outstanding pageant participants in the categories of swimwear, talent, and personality projection. Cash awards, merchandise, trips, and public appearances are awarded annually. Established in 1968. Sponsored by Luster Products.

★2714★
Jackie Robinson Foundation
80 8th Ave., 20th Fl.
New York, NY 10011 Phone: (212)675-1511

Jackie Robinson Foundation Award for Achievement in Industry
To recognize outstanding corporate leaders who have worked to improve the plight of minorities in economic development. Chief executive officers who have guided their company to improve the plight of minorities in economic development are eligible. A trophy/plaque is awarded annually at the Awards Dinner Dance. Established in 1980 in memory of Jackie Robinson.

★2715★
Jane Addams Peace Association
777 United Nations Plaza
New York, NY 10017 Phone: (212)682-8830

Jane Addams Children's Book Award
To promote the cause of peace, social justice, world community, and the equality of the sexes and all races. Children's books published in English in the preceding year are eligible. A certificate is awarded annually in September. Established in 1953 by Marta Teele of Ithaca,

NY. Co-sponsored by the Women's International League for Peace and Freedom.

★2716★
Johnson Publishing Co., Inc.
c/o Sharon Minor
820 S. Michigan Ave.
Chicago, IL 60605 Phone: (312)322-9352

American Black Achievement Awards
To honor Black accomplishment in the fields of public service, religion, dramatic arts, fine arts, music, business and the professions, and athletics. The awards are open to any persons who have achieved monumental success in their field during a given year. A trophy is awarded in the following categories: (1) Jackie Robinson Award for Athletics; (2) Business and the Professions Award; (3) Dramatic Arts Award; (4) Fine Arts Award; (5) Music Award; (6) Martin Luther King Jr. Award For Public Service: (7) Religion Award; (8) *EBONY* Lifetime Achievement Award; (9) Trailblazer Award; and (10) Thurgood Marshall Black Education Fund Educational Achievement Award. Awarded annually in the fall in Hollywood. Established in 1978. Sponsored by *Ebony*. Additional information is available from Lydia J. Davis.
Gertrude Johnson Williams Writing Contest To recognize short stories by Black Americans. Monetary awards of $5,000 for the winning story and $1,000 for each of five runners-up are presented annually. Established in 1988 in honor of *EBONY* editor and publisher John H. Johnson's late mother.

★2717★
Leadership Conference on Civil Rights
2027 Massachusetts Ave., NW
Washington, DC 20036 Phone: (202)667-1780

Hubert H. Humphrey Civil Rights Award
For recognition of selfless devotion to the cause of equality. Recipients of the award are selected by officers of the organization with suggestions made by the Executive Committee. A medallion, encased in lucite, is presented at the Annual Meeting. Established in 1978 in memory of Hubert H. Humphrey, a former Minnesota Senator and Vice President of the United States.

★2718★
Lincoln University (Missouri)
Department of Communications
201 Elliff Hall
Jefferson City, MO 65101 Phone: (314)681-5436

Unity Awards in Media
To recognize the media for excellence in reporting on issues affecting minorities and the disadvantaged, and to emphasize the national goals the media serves in improving understanding among all peoples. In the past, the Human Relations Citation was basically restricted to coverage of the Black American. Entries may be submitted from print and broadcast media in the United States in the following categories: (1) Reporting of Economics; (2) Reporting of Education; (3) Investigative Reporting; (4) Reporting of Politics; (5) Editorial Writing; and (6) Public Affairs/Social Issues Reporting. The contest is open to any print or broadcast person working for a recognized daily, weekly, monthly or quarterly publication including newspapers and magazines as well as radio and television stations. Submissions are evaluated in both regional and national categories. The deadline for submission is January 6. A trophy is presented annually at a gala awards ceremony. Established in 1949 by Armistead S. Pride, Professor Emeritus of Journalism and former Head of the Department. Sponsored by the Anheuser-Busch Companies and the Philip Morris Companies.

★2719★
Martin Luther King, Jr. Center for Nonviolent Social Change, Inc.
449 Auburn Ave., NE
Atlanta, GA 30312 Phone: (404)524-1956

Martin Luther King, Jr., Nonviolent Peace Prize
This, the highest award of the Center, is given to honor those persons and/or organizations whose continuing activities have made outstanding contributions to nonviolent social change in the spirit and tradition of Martin Luther King, Jr. The prize recognizes achievements in the eradication of poverty and racism, and the successful quest for alternatives to war. A monetary award of $1,000, a medal depicting Dr. King, a diploma and a citation are awarded annually. Established in 1973 and presented during the celebration of Dr. King's birthday.
Labor, Management, Government Social Responsibility Award
To recognize persons in the Trade Union Movement who have made and are making outstanding contributions to the cause of economic justice, freedom, and nonviolence. An inscribed plaque, with the Center's logo and labor symbol, is awarded annually during the celebration of Dr. King's birthday. **Formerly:** (1989) Labor Social Responsibility Award.
Community Service Award
To recognize persons who would normally be overlooked for their service to others in the spirit of Dr. King. Awarded during the annual observance of Dr. King's birthday.
Martin Luther King, Jr. Humanitarian Award
For recognition of those very few persons and special drum majors for justice who use their life service and giving impact institutions and institutional changes, and who promote and advance human welfare and social reform regardless of nations, cultures, races, religions or other barriers which tend to separate peoples who share a common humanity. An International Humanitarian Award is presented to an individual who, through a race, religion and economic circumstance and who, in Dr. King's spirit, has demonstrated a belief that poverty, racism, and violence can be eliminated and that we can achieve Dr. King's Beloved Community.

★2720★
McDonald's Corp.
Literary Achievement Awards
c/o Phyllis Banks
Burrell Public Relations
20 N. Michigan Ave.
Chicago, IL 60602 Phone: (312)443-8739

McDonald's Literary Achievement Awards for Writing on the Black Experience in America
To recognize and reward literary excellence for writing about the Black experience in America. Winners are selected in three categories - playwriting, poetry and fiction writing. Entries submitted by June 1 must meet the following requirements: (1) fiction - up to 50 pages of a long work or two short works, with information on publication; (2) poetry - not more than 20 pages, with information on publication; and (3) playwriting - at least 20 pages, with information on productions. Winners in each category receive an honorarium of $2,000, a trip to New York to participate in a celebrity reading of their work and a literary reception.Established in 1977. Additional information is available from Mike Gordon, McDonald's Corp., phone: (312) 575-7676.

★2721★
McKnight Programs in Higher Education
201 E. Kennedy Blvd., Ste. 1510
Tampa, FL 33602 Phone: (813)221-2772

McKnight Black Doctoral Fellowship Program in Arts and Sciences, Mathematics, Business and Engineering
To provide up to $5,000 in tuition and fees plus an annual tax-free stipend of $10,000 to 25 Black American citizens to pursue Ph.D. degrees at participating Florida universities. Applicants must hold or be receiving a bachelor's degree from a regionally-accredited college or university. The deadline for applications is January 15. Contingent upon successful academic progress, the maximum length of awards is f

years. The McKnight Program in Higher Education funds the first three years and the student's university continues funding at the same level of support, if required, for a fourth year.

★2722★

National Association for the Advancement of Colored People (NAACP)
1025 Vermont Ave., NW, Ste. 730
Washington, DC 20005 Phone: (202)638-2269

Kelly M. Alexander, Sr., NAACP State Conference President's Award
To recognize a State Conference president for outstanding achievement in the following areas: (1) programs; (2) membership; (3) fund raising; (4) growth of branches; (5) leadership; and (6) youth and college leadership development. Nominations may be submitted by December 31. A monetary award of $1,000 and a gold medal are awarded annually. Established in 1987 to honor Kelly M. Alexander, Sr., who served as a State Conference President for 27 years and chairman of the NAACP Board of Directors.

William Edward Burghardt Du Bois Medal
To recognize individuals who are not citizens of the United States for exceptional contributions to the protection of human rights and furtherance of international understanding, fraternity and fundamental freedoms. Men or women whose lives exemplify the tradition of service to mankind; who perform extraordinary acts of moral courage; and whose work promotes civil rights and democratic principles are eligible. Nominations may be submitted by May 15. A medal is awarded annually. Established in 1985.

Image Awards
To recognize entertainers and sports figures who have made positive contributions to minority images in movies, television, the music business and sports. Awarded annually by the Hollywood California Chapter of NAACP. Established in 1979. Additional information is available from the Press Office, (213)734-6108.

Spingarn Medal
To recognize the highest achievement of an American Negro. The purpose of the medal is twofold: to call the attention of the American people to the existence of distinguished merit and achievement among American Negroes; and to serve as a reward for such achievement, and as a stimulus to the ambition of colored youth. Men and women of African descent and American citizenship who shall have made the highest achievement during the preceding year or years in any honorable field of human endeavor are eligible. A gold medal is presented at the annual convention of the National Association for the Advancement of Colored People, and the presentation speech is delivered by a distinguished citizen. Recommendations should be submitted by January 1 of each year. Established in 1914 by the late J.E. Spingarn, then Chairman of the Board of Directors of the National Association for the Advancement of Colored People.

★2723★

National Association of Black Journalists
11600 Sunrise Valley Dr.
Reston, VA 22091 Phone: (703)648-1270

National Association of Black Journalists Salute to Excellence Awards
To recognize outstanding contributions by Black journalists. Awards are given in the following categories: (1) Radio Reporting; (2) Print International Reporting; (3) Print General News; (4) Print Feature; (5) Special Black History Awards; (6) Print Sports; (7) Print Commentary; (8) Print Photojournalism; (9) Television International Reporting; (10) Spot News; (11) Television News Segment; (12) Television News Series; (13) Tele[illegible] Features; (14) Television Sports; (15) Television D[illegible]ry; (16) Photojournalism Television; and (17) Radio. The [illegible]cial awards are also presented: (1) Internship Awards; (2) [illegible]ards; (3) Journalist of the Year Awards; and (4) Lifetime [illegible]ard. Established in 1975. Additional information is [illegible]l E. Morris, Sr., Executive Director, Box 17212, [illegible]41, (703) 648-1270.

★2724★

National Association of Black Women Attorneys (NABWA)
c/o Mabel D. Haden, Pres.
3711 Macomb St., NW
Washington, DC 20016 Phone: (202)966-9693

Hall of Fame Award
For recognition of civic and community leadership. Contributions to the Black community are considered. Induction into the Hall of Fame is awarded annually at the Red Dress Ball at the Convention. Established in 1987.

Scholarship Award
To provide a scholarship for Black women law students. Several scholarships are presented annually at the Red Dress Ball at the Convention. Established in 1978 by Attorney Mabel D. Haden, Washington, DC, with contributions from various businesses, lawyers and concerned citizens.

★2725★

National Association of Dramatic and Speech Arts (NADSA)
c/o Dr. H.D. Flowers, II
PO Box 20984
Greensboro, NC 27420 Phone: (919)697-7034

S. Randolph Edmonds Playwriting Award
To honor the best play written on the Black experience. Established in 1975 by S. Randolph Edmonds, Founder of NADSA.

★2726★

National Association of Negro Business and Professional Women's Clubs
c/o Ellen Graves
1806 New Hampshire Ave., NW
Washington, DC 20009 Phone: (202)483-4206

National Achievement Award
For recognition of achievement by a woman. A plaque is awarded annually at the convention.

National Appreciation Award
For recognition for service to the Association. Members are eligible. Awarded annually at the Convention.

National Community Service Award
To recognize an oustanding woman, non-member, who resides in the city where the convention is held for a contribution to the community. A plaque is awarded annually at the convention.

National Scholarship Award
To encourage professional development. Members are eligible. A plaque is awarded annually at the convention.

National Youth Award
For recognition of achievement. Outstanding young women under 30 years of age are eligible. A plaque is awarded annually at the Convention.

★2727★

National Association of Recording Merchandisers (NARM)
c/o Dana Kornbluth, Dir., Press Relations/Public Affair
3 Eves Dr., Ste. 307
Marlton, NJ 08053 Phone: (609)596-2221

NARM Best Seller Awards
For recognition by the industry of actual over-the-counter sales to the consumer of records and pre-recorded tapes. Nominations may be made by NARM regular members for the best selling product in the calendar year beginning January 1 and ending December 31. The deadline for ballots is February 1. Awards are given in the following categories: (1) Best Selling Single (45 RPM); (2) Best Selling Single (12 inch); (3) Best Selling Movie or TV Soundtrack; (4) Best Selling Original

Cast Album; (5) Best Selling Country Album by a Male Artist; (6) Best Selling Country Album by a Female Artist; (7) Best Selling Country Album by a Group; (8) Best Selling Black Music Album by a Male Artist; (9) Best Selling Black Music Album by a Female Artist; (10) Best Selling Black Music Album by a Group; (11) Best Selling Jazz Album; (12) Best Selling Gospel/Spiritual Album; (13) Best Selling Classical Album; (14) Best Selling Children's Product; (15) Best Selling Album by a Female Artist; (16) Best Selling Album by a Male Artist; (17) Best Selling Album by a Group; (18) Best Selling Album; (19) Best Selling Album by a New Artist; (20) Best Selling Foreign Language Album; (21) Best Selling Videocassette merchandised as Music Video; (22) Best Selling Comedy Album; and (23) Best Selling Rap Album. Plaques are awarded annually at the convention.

★2728★
National Bar Association (NBA)
1225 11th St., NW
Washington, DC 20001-4217 Phone: (202)842-3900

Gertrude E. Rush Award
To recognize individuals who have demonstrated leadership ability in the community within their profession; a pioneer spirit in the pursuit of civil and human rights; and excellence in legal education and perseverance in the law, public policy or social activism. Nominations are accepted. A trophy is awarded annually during the NBA Mid-Year Conference. Established in 1982 in honor of Gertrude Rush, NBA's only woman co-founder.

C. Francis Stradford Award
To recognize a person who has performed outstanding service in the furtherance of the Association's objectives. Nominations are accepted by June 1. A plaque is presented at the NBA Annual Convention each summer. Awarded in honor of C. Francis Stradford, NBA co-founder.

★2729★
National Black Programming Consortium
c/o Mabel Haddock, Exec. Dir.
929 Harrison Ave., Ste. 104
Columbus, OH 43215 Phone: (614)299-5355

Prized Pieces Competition
For recognition of superior artistic achievement in the development, production, and presentation of programming that depicts Black people and their cultures from throughout the world positively. Awards are given in the following categories: (1) Public Affairs/News; (2) Cultural Affairs; (3) Children/Teens; (4) Drama; (5) Documentary; (6) Innovative; and (7) Comedy. Producers, distributors or individuals may submit any Black-oriented television programs with Blacks in primary roles that enrich the understanding of lifestyles, culture, and the concerns of Blacks. The deadline is October 3. Monetary prizes and plaques are awarded annually at the Prized Pieces Awards Ceremony. Established in 1981.

★2730★
National Caucus and Center on Black Aged
c/o Toni Quarles, Management Analyst
1424 K St., NW, Ste. 500
Washington, DC 20005 Phone: (202)637-8400

Living Legacy Award
To honor Black Americans for outstanding contributions to society and for achievement in the arts, sciences and humanities. Candidates must be 60 years of age or older and U.S. citizens. Nominations may be submitted by national, state or local civic or non-profit organizations. A plaque is presented annually to six awardees at the Living Legacy Awards Banquet in Washington, D.C. Hotel and travel expenses for awardees are paid by NCBA. Established in 1979.

★2731★
National Coalition of 100 Black Women
50 Rockefeller Plaza
New York, NY 10020 Phone: (212)974-6140

Candace Award
To recognize the achievements of Black women in various fields of endeavor.

★2732★
National Council for Black Studies (NCBS)
c/o Dr. Joseph J. Russell, Exec. Dir.
Memorial Hall W. 105
Indiana University
Bloomington, IN 47405 Phone: (812)855-6581

Bertha Maxwell Award
To recognize and facilitate outstanding student scholarship through National Student Essay Contest participation. Undergraduate and graduate students at a university or college are eligible to participate in both creative and scholastic writing categories. The deadline varies from year to year. A monetary prize of $500, a plaque, and publication of the noted essays in a leading journal of Black studies are awarded. First and second prizes are awarded annually at the convention. Established in 1978 in honor of Dr. Bertha Maxwell, first chairperson of NCBS.

★2733★
National Council for the Social Studies
3501 Newark St., NW
Washington, DC 20016 Phone: (202)966-7840

Carter G. Woodson Book Award
To encourage the writing, publishing, and dissemination of outstanding social science books for young readers, which treat topics related to ethnic minorities and race relations sensitively and accurately. Authors of social science books appropriate for young readers, which depict ethnicity in the United States, are eligible. A plaque is awarded annually for an elementary book and a secondary book. Established in 1973 in honor of Carter G. Woodson, the Black historian and educator, who founded and edited the *Journal of Negro History*.

★2734★
National Economic Association
c/o Dr. Alfred L. Edwards, Sec.-Treas.
University of Michigan
School of Business
Ann Arbor, MI 48109-1234 Phone: (313)763-0121

Samuel Z. Westerfield Award
To recognize and encourage scholarly work by Black economists. Selection is based on outstanding contributions as both a scholar and an economist. A plaque is awarded periodically, usually every two years.

★2735★
National Foundation for Infectious Diseases
4733 Bethesda Ave., Ste. 750
Bethesda, MD 20814 Phone: (301)656-0003

NFID Minority Postdoctoral Fellowship in Tropical Disease Research
To encourage and assist a qualified minority researcher to become a specialist and investigator in the field of tropical diseases. Black Americans, American Indians, Hispanic Americans, and Pacific Islanders are eligible. Applications may be submitted by January 15. The applicant must hold a doctorate from a recognized university and be a permanent resident or citizen of the United States, or a spouse of a citizen or permanent resident of the United States. A fellowship of $24,000 for the

year and an additional $3,000 for travel and supplies are awarded. Sponsored by the Rockefeller Foundation.

★2736★
National Medical Fellowships
254 W. 31st St., 7th Fl.
New York, NY 10001-2183 Phone: (212)714-0933

Hugh J. Andersen Memorial Scholarships
To provide need-based scholarships for outstanding leadership and community service. These scholarships are available to rising second-, third-, or fourth-year minority students attending Minnesota medical schools. In addition to demonstrating leadership and community involvement, students must have financial need. Up to seven new scholarships are presented each year. Students must be nominated by their medical school deans. Stipends of $2,500 to $4,000 and certificates are awarded. Nominations are requested in August. Established in 1982 with an endowment from the Andersen family of Minnesota to honor the memory of Hugh J. Andersen, a long-time contributor and active member of NMF's Minneapolis/St. Paul Advisory Committee.
William and Charlotte Cadbury Award
To recognize the outstanding achievement of a fourth year minority medical student. Academic achievement, leadership, and social consciousness are criteria for the award. A monetary prize of $2,000 and a certificate of merit are awarded annually. Established in 1977 by Dr. Irving Graef in honor of the organization's former Executive Director and Staff Associate.
Commonwealth Fund Medical Fellowship Program
To encourage academically outstanding minority medical students to pursue careers in biomedical research and academic medicine. The program fosters mentor relationships between these students and prominent biomedical scientists. NMF annually names up to twenty minority medical students as Commonwealth Fund Medical Fellows. Competition is open to minority students attending accredited U.S. medical schools who have demonstrated outstanding academic achievement and show promise for careers in research and academic medicine. Candidates must be nominated by the medical school deans. Up to twenty $5,000 fellowships are awarded annually. Each Fellow spends eight to twelve weeks working in a major research laboratory under the tutelage of a well-known biomedical scientist. Established in 1983 with grant support from The Commonwealth Fund of New York, New York.
Fellowship Program in Health Policy and Management for Minority Medical Students
To encourage minority medical students to enter careers in health policy and management. Blacks, mainland Puerto Ricans, Mexican-Americans, and American Indians who are U.S. citizens attending M.D. degree-granting programs in the United States accredited by the Liaison Committee on Medical Education of the Association of American Medical Colleges, or in D.O. degree-granting programs at colleges of osteopathic medicine in the United States accredited by the Bureau of Professional Education of the American Osteopathic Association, are eligible. Deans of medical schools may nominate up to two candidates. Five funded fellowships of $4,000 each to rising second-, third-, or fourth-year minority students are awarded. Each fellow studies a policy issue which is of particular concern to the Health and Hospitals Corporation, and works with high-level administrators in the New York City Health and Hospitals Corporation's central office, or with executive directors or designees of HHC's municipal hospitals. Additional information is available from: Maritza E. Myers.
Irving Graef Memorial Scholarship
To recognize a third-year minority medical student for outstanding academic achievement, leadership and community service. Candidates must demonstrate outstanding academic achievement and leadership as well as financial need. Nominations are usually requested in the fall. One new scholarship is awarded each year. This honor includes a certificate of merit and annual stipend of $2,000.00. Established in 1978, and permanently endowed by the Irving Graef Medical Fund in 1980, to honor the memory of one of NMF's most active board members who was associate professor of Medicine at New York University School of Medicine.
William T. Grant Behavior Development Research Fellowship Program
To foster minority student research interest in the areas of stress and coping among school-age children. The program also encourages pursuit of academic careers in child psychiatry, behavior development research, and health policy. The fellowship competition is open to minority students attending accredited U.S. medical schools who are in good academic standing and show promise for careers in child psychiatry, behavior development research, or mental health policy. Candidates must be nominated by the medical school deans by September. National Medical Fellowships annually selects five students through a national competition. Fellows will spend eight to twelve weeks working with senior staff of the Prevention Research Center, a project of the Department of Mental Hygiene at The Johns Hopkins University School of Hygiene and Public Health in Baltimore, Maryland. Five fellowships of $3,500 each are presented annually. Established in 1986 with grant support from the William T. Grant Foundation of New York, New York.
Henry G. Halladay Awards
To recognize the achievement of Black males in the first year of medical school who have overcome significant obstacles to obtain a medical education. Five supplemental scholarships of $760 each are awarded annually. Established in 1970 by an endowment from Mrs. Henry G. Halladay in memory of her husband.
George Hill Memorial Scholarship Program
To recognize a Black medical student from Westchester County, New York for outstanding academic achievement, leadership and community service. Black residents of Westchester County, New York, who have been accepted into first-year classes of accredited U.S. medical schools are eligible to apply. One new scholarship is awarded each year. The Hill Scholar receives $4,000 annually for the length of undergraduate medical education. Established in 1975 by Cheesebrough-Pond's Inc. of Westport, Connecticut, in memory of the Black physician who pioneered in the testing, screening and counseling of persons suffering from sickle-cell anemia.
Henry J. Kaiser Family Foundation Merit Awards
To recognize the achievements of about 25 outstanding graduating minority medical students. Students are nominated by medical schools on the basis of academic achievement, leadership, social consciousness, and potential for significant contributions to the medical profession. Monetary awards and certificates of merit are awarded annually. Established in 1980. Sponsored by the Henry J. Kaiser Family Foundation, Menlo Park, California.
Franklin C. McLean Award
This, the oldest and most prestigious honor of NMF, is given to recognize a senior minority medical student for distinguished academic achievement, leadership ability, and community service. A monetary prize of $3,000 and a certificate of merit are awarded annually. Established in 1968 in memory of NMF's founder, Franklin C. McLean.
Metropolitan Life Foundation Award Program for Academic Excellence in Medicine
To recognize and reward minority medical students for outstanding academic achievement and demonstrated leadership. Candidates must be second- or third-year students enrolled in accredited, degree-granting programs leading to the M.D. or D.O. degrees, and must be members of minority groups considered to be underrepresented in medicine by the Association of American Medical Colleges: Blacks, American Indians, Mexican-Americans and mainland Puerto Ricans. Medical schools may nominate one candidate for these awards by January 16. Criteria for selection include: (1) Outstanding academic achievement; (2) Leadership; (3) Potential for Distinguished Contributions to Medicine; and (4) Documented Financial Need. Minority students must attend medical school or have legal residence in the following cities or designated surrounding areas: San Francisco, CA; Tampa, FL; Atlanta, GA; Aurora, IL; Wichita, KS; New York, NY; Tulsa, OK; Pittsburgh, PA; Scranton, PA; Warwick, RI; Greenville, SC; and San Antonio, TX. Up to ten need- based awards, valued at $2,500 each, are awarded.
National Medical Fellowships/New York City Health and Hospitals Corporation Health Policy and Management Fellowship Program To encourage minority medical students to enter careers in health policy, planning, and management. Competition for fellowships is open to minority students attending accredited U.S. medical schools who are in good academic standing and show promise for leadership positions in health policy, planning, and management. Candidates must be nominated by the medical school deans. Nominations are requested in the summer. Five $4,000 fellowships are presented annually. Fellows spend eight to twelve weeks working with top-level executives of the New York City Health and Hospitals Corporation or with executive directors of HHC municipal hospitals. Established in 1985 with grant support from the Medical Trust of Philadelphia, Pennsylvania and the Booth Ferris Foundation of New York, New York.
James H. Robinson, M.D. Memorial Prizes in Surgery
To recognize senior, minority medical students selected in a national competition for outstanding performance in surgery. Eligible candidates

must be minority students enrolled in accredited U.S. schools of medicine who will graduate during the academic year in which the awards are made available. Students must be nominated by medical school deans and the chairmen of the departments of Surgery at the medical schools in which they are enrolled by December. Each prize includes a certificate of merit and a $500 stipend. Established in 1986 in memory of James H. Robinson, M.D. who was clinical professor of Surgery and associate dean of Student Affairs at Jefferson Medical College of Thomas Jefferson University in Philadelphia, Pennsylvania.

Aura E. Severinghaus Award To recognize and honor an outstanding minority medical student at Columbia University College of Physicians and Surgeons for outstanding academic achievement, leadership, and community service. A $2,000 stipend and a certificate of merit are awarded annually. Established in 1975 by Mr. Chauncey Waddell and the Charles Evans Hughes Memorial Foundation, Inc., in memory of Aura E. Severinghaus, a long-time NMF Board member and Associate Dean Emeritus of Columbia University's College of Physicians and Surgeons.

★2737★

National Newspaper Publishers Association (NNPA)
c/o Steve G. Davis, Exec. Dir.
948 National Press Bldg.
529 14th St., NW
Washington, DC 20045 Phone: (202)662-7324

Merit Awards
To recognize excellence and to stimulate improvements in the quality of the Black press. Awards are given in the following categories: (1) John H. Sengstacke General Excellence; (2) Robert S. Abbott Best Editorial Awards; (3) Emory O. Jackson Best Column Writing; (4) Carl Murphy Community Service Awards - campaign or crusade series; (5) best news story; (6) Frank L. Stanley, Sr., Best Feature Story Awards; (7) best news pictures - news or feature; (8) Wilbert L. Holloway Best Editorial Cartoon Awards; (9) Robert L. Vann Best Typography and Make-up; (10) Leon H. Washington Best Special Edition; (11) W.A. Scott, II Best Circulation Promotion; (12) best women's sectionl (13) best youth section; (14) E. Washington Rhodes Best Original Advertising; (15) best use of photographs; (16) best church page; (17) best sports page; (18) best business section; and (19) Armstrong-Ellington Best Entertainment section. NNPA-member newspapers are eligible. The John B. Russwurm Trophy and $1,000 are awarded to the newspaper judged the overall best; and plaques and monetary prizes are awrded in each category. In addition, Publisher-of-the Year and a Distinguished Service Award are presented. Established in 1971.

★2738★

National Research Council (NRC)
2101 Constitution Ave., NW
Washington, DC 20418 Phone: (202)334-2860

Ford Foundation Postdoctoral Fellowships for Minorities
To provide for one-year postdoctoral fellowships to teacher-scholars preparing for or already engaged in college or university teaching and research. Awards are made in the behavioral and social sciences, humanities, engineering, mathematics, physical sciences, and biological sciences, or for interdisciplinary programs comprised of two or more eligible disciplines. Applicants must be U.S. citizens or nationals who are members of the following minority groups: American Indian or Alaskan Native (Eskimo or Aleut), Black American, Mexican American/Chicano, Native Pacific Islander (Micronesian or Polynesian), and Puerto Rican. A stipend of $22,500 for Postdoctoral Fellows; and $26,000 for Senior Postdoctoral Fellows are awarded. The National Research Council also offers the Ford Foundation Predoctoral and Dissertation Fellowships for Minorities.

★2739★

National Urban League (NUL)
c/o Faith V. Williams, Asst. Dir.,
Communications Dept.
500 E. 62nd St.
New York, NY 10021 Phone: (212)310-9000

Equal Opportunity Day Award
To recognize contributions made by individuals, corporations, labor unions and other organizations. A plaque is awarded annually. Established in 1957.

Labor Affairs Award
To recognize organized labor's commitment to forging links and strengthening bonds between the trade union movement and the Black community. Two plaques are awarded annually. Established in 1986.

Living Legends Award
To recognize Black Americans who have made a significant contribution in their particular field of endeavor. Ten trophies are awarded annually. In addition, Special Legend Awards are presented posthumously. Established in 1987.

Ann Tanneyhill Award
To recognize an employee of the National Urban League with ten years or more of service for excellence and extraordinary commitment to the Urban League Movement. A monetary award of $1,000 and a plaque are presented annually. Established in 1970.

★2740★

New York Urban League
218 W. 40th St., 6th Fl.
New York, NY 10018 Phone: (212)730-5200

Frederick Douglass Award
To recognize New Yorkers for distinguished leadership in the fight for equal opportunity. Three engraved medallions are awarded annually. Established in 1966 to honor Frederick Douglass, father of the Protest Movement.

Whitney M. Young, Jr. Memorial Football Classic Award
To recognize an individual for the ideals of leadership, character, and sportsmanship that honor the memory of Whitney M. Young, Jr. A plaque is awarded at the Annual Football Classic in the fall. Established in 1971. Sponsored by the New York Yankees in association with the New York Urban League and the New York Daily News. The proceeds from the Football Classic help support scholarships at the participating schools - Grambling and North Carolina Central - and fund the New York Urban League's Whitney M. Young Jr. Memorial Scholarship Program, which was established in 1978. Traditionally ten students are awarded scholarships of $1,500 each.

★2741★

Newark Black Film Festival
c/o Jane Rappaport
The Newark Museum
49 Washington St.
PO Box 540
Newark, NJ 07101 Phone: (201)596-6637

Paul Robeson Awards
For recognition of excellence in independent filmmaking. The Festival screens films by Black filmmakers and films featuring the history and culture of Black people in America and elsewhere. Films completed in the two-year period between awards may be entered in the following categories: (1) documentary; (2) long narrative; (3) short narrative; and (4) experimental. A monetary prize is awarded biennially. Established in 1985 in honor of Paul Robeson. Sponsored by The Newark Museum; Newark Public Library; New Jersey Institute of Technology; Rutgers, The State University, Newark Campus; and Newark Symphony Hall.

★2742★
Penumbra Theatre Company
The Martin Luther King Bldg.
270 N. Kent St.
Saint Paul, MN 55102 Phone: (612)224-4601

Cornerstone: A National Black Playwrighting Competition
To encourage the development of plays and playwrights which, and who are directly concerned with the Afro-American experience as it relates to realistic portrayals on the American stage. Entries must address the Afro-American experience, and may be submitted by July 15. The winning play and playwright receive a monetary award of $1,000, a workshop-reading of the play, and a full production as part of Penumbra's mainstage season. Established in 1984. Partially sponsored by The Jerome Foundation.

★2743★
Phelps-Stokes Fund
10 E. 87th St.
New York, NY 10028 Phone: (212)427-8100

Aggrey Medal
To recognize individuals who have made significant contributions in one of the charter areas of interest of the Phelps-Stokes Fund, i.e., education for Africans, Black Americans, and American Indians. A silver medal is awarded from time to time by the Board of Trustees of the Phelps-Stokes Fund. Established in 1986.
Clarence L. Holte Literary Prize
To recognize a living writer for a significant contribution to the cultural heritage of Africa and the African diaspora made through published writings in the humanities. Nominations for this international prize are open to the public. A monetary prize of $7,500 is awarded biennially from the earnings of an endowment established anonymously in 1977 in honor of Clarence L. Holte, a writer and editor who is a collector of books about the African heritage and diaspora. The prize was conceived by Cliff Lashley, scholar, book collector, and former Jamaican diplomat. Co-sponsored by the Schomburg Center for Research in Black Culture, the New York Public Library, and the Fund. Additional information is available from Harold Anderson, Schomburg Center, (212) 862-4000.

★2744★
St. Martin de Porres Guild Inc.
c/o Rev. Damian R. Myett, O.P., Dir.
141 E. 65th St.
New York, NY 10021 Phone: (212)744-2410

St. Martin de Porres Award for Interracial Justice
For recognition of a contribution that promotes social and interracial justice. A monetary award, a statue, and a certificate are awarded from time to time. Established in 1982.

★2745★
Seattle Group Theatre Company
3940 Brooklyn Ave., NE
Seattle, WA 98105 Phone: (206)545-4969

Multi-Cultural Playwrights' Festival
To develop new plays and to nurture young playwrights. American citizens of Asian, Black, Chicano, Hispanic or Native American descent may submit previously unproduced scripts. A monetary award of $1,000, travel expenses and a three week residency with a workshop production of the winning play are awarded annually to two playwrights. Established in 1984. Sponsored by the Lila Wallace Reader's Digest Fund.

★2746★
Unitarian Universalist Association
25 Beacon St.
Boston, MA 02108 Phone: (617)742-2100

Holmes/Weatherly Award
For recognition of that person or group whose pursuit of social justice best exemplifies the spirit of John Haynes Holmes and Arthur L. Weatherly. A monetary prize of $250 is awarded annually. Established in 1951 in honor of two ministers who were the founders in 1908 of the Unitarian Fellowship for Social Justice: Rev. John Haynes Holmes and Rev. Arthur L. Weatherly.

★2747★
United Methodist Church
Board of Global Ministries, Health and Welfare Ministries Division
c/o Charles P. Kellogg
475 Riverside Dr., Ste. 350
New York, NY 10115 Phone: (212)870-3872

Affirmative Action Award of the Year
To give national recognition to an individual who has made noteworthy achievement in affirmative action. Awarded at the Honors Luncheon.

★2748★
U.S. Department of State
c/o Kay Smith, Rm. 2429
Washington, DC 20520 Phone: (202)647-7236

Equal Employment Opportunity Award
For recognition of outstanding contributions toward improving employment opportunities for minorities and women. It is given to an employee of the Department of State who has made the most significant achievements in the futherance of affirmative action and equal employment opportunity. The award consists of a certificate signed by the Secretary and $5,000 in cash. Awarded annually.

★2749★
U.S. Small Business Administration
c/o Office of Public Communicators
1441 L St., NW
Washington, DC 20416 Phone: (202)653-6365

Small Business Advocates of the Year
To recognize individuals in various professions who have significantly increased awareness of small business concerns or created opportunities for small business to succeed. Advocates of the Year are recognized in each of the 50 states, the District of Columbia, and Puerto Rico for their efforts in the following areas of importance to small businesses: (1) accountant advocate; (2) banker advocate; (3) media advocate; (4) minority advocate; (5) veteran advocate; and (6) women in business advocate. State winners are then eligible for national recognition. The criteria for selection are: engaging in civic and community activities that promote small business; volunteering services to assist small firms experiencing management, financial, or legal problems; sponsoring or participating in legislative or regulatory initiatives; communicating publicly through speech or the written word; actively participating in small business organizations; or pursuing initiatives that will help a large number of small businesses. Nominations are accepted. Awards are presented during Small Business Week in May. Established in 1978.

★2750★
University of Kansas
William Allen White School of Journalism
c/o Prof. Samuel L. Adams, Curator
207-B, Stauffer-Flint Hall
Lawrence, KS 66045 Phone: (913)864-4744

Ida B. Wells Award
For recognition of exemplary leadership in providing minorities with employment opportunities in journalism. Applications or nominations showing the leadership and achievements reflected in the purpose of the award are accepted from anyone. An original bust of Ida B. Wells with inscription of the winner's exemplary achievements is awarded. Scholarships in the name of the winner are awarded for journalism training of minority students. Awarded annually at the convention of one of the three sponsoring organizations: National Association of Black Journalists; National Conference of Editorial Writers; and National Broadcast Editorial Association. Established in 1983 by Michael Richardson and Samuel Adams. The award honors Ida B. Wells (1866-1932), pioneer Black editor and anti-lynching leader. She was co-owner of a newspaper, a candidate for Congress, and a founding member of the NAACP.

★2751★
Western Political Science Association
c/o Department of Political Science
University of Utah
Salt Lake City, UT 84112 Phone: (916)278-7737

Western Political Science Association Awards
To recognize outstanding unpublished papers in the field of political science. Award by Committee on the Status of Blacks - $100 for an outstanding paper discussing issues and problems which concern most Black Americans. Entries must be submitted by January 15. Established in 1976.

★2752★
World Institute of Black Communications
c/o Adriane Gaines
10 Columbus Circle
New York, NY 10019 Phone: (212)586-1771

CEBA Awards (Communications Excellence to Black Audiences)
To recognize excellence in communications directed at Black audiences. Awards are presented in the following categories: (1) Consumer Print - newspapers, campaign, consumer magazine, public service, and public relations; (2) Radio - product messages, public relations, campaign, public service, non-entertainment programming; (3) Television - product message, campaign, public service; (4) Film and Video - single feature segments, interview, public relations, dramatic productions, music videos; and (5) Merchandizing and Sales Promotion - posters, album covers, brochures, newsletters, sales promotion, etc. A bronze statuette designed by Valerie Maynard is awarded annually. Established in 1978 by the National Black Network.

(10) FEDERAL GOVERNMENT AGENCIES

Entries in this chapter are arranged alphabetically by name of parent agency. See the User's Guide at the front of this directory for additional information.

★2753★
U.S. Commission on Civil Rights
1121 Vermont Ave., NW
Washington, DC 20425 Phone: (202)523-5571
Arthur A. Fletcher, Chairman

★2754★
U.S. Commission on Civil Rights
Central Region
Old Federal Bldg.
911 Walnut St., Rm. 3100
Kansas City, MO 64106 Phone: (816)426-5253
Melvin Jenkins, Reg. Dir.
Territory Includes: Alabama, Arkansas, Illinois, Indiana, Kansas, Kentucky, Louisiana, Michigan, Minnesota, Mississippi, Missouri, Nebraska, Ohio, Tennessee, and Wisconsin.

★2755★
U.S. Commission on Civil Rights
Eastern Region
1121 Vermont Ave., NW, Rm. 710
Washington, DC 20425 Phone: (202)523-5264
John I. Binkley, Reg. Dir.
Territory Includes: Connecticut, Delaware, District of Columbia, Florida, Georgia, Maine, Maryland, Massachusetts, New Hampshire, New Jersey, New York, North Carolina, Pennsylvania, Rhode Island, South Carolina, Vermont, Virginia, and West Virginia.

★2756★
U.S. Commission on Civil Rights
Western Region
3660 Wilshire Blvd., Ste. 810
Los Angeles, CA 90010 Phone: (213)894-3437
Philip Montez, Reg. Dir.
Territory Includes: Alaska, Arizona, California, Colorado, Hawaii, Idaho, Montana, Nevada, New Mexico, North Dakota, Oklahoma, Oregon, South Dakota, Texas, Utah, Washington, and Wyoming.

★2757★
U.S. Department of Agriculture
Food and Nutrition Service
Northeast Regional OfficeCivil Rights/Equal Employment Opportunity
10 Causeway St., Rm. 501
Boston, MA 02222-1071 Phone: (617)565-6424
Beverly Hayes, Contact

★2758★
U.S. Department of Agriculture
Office of Advocacy and Enterprise
Equal Opportunity
14th St. & Independence Ave., SW, Ste. 1345
Washington, DC 20250 Phone: (202)447-5681
William C. Payne, Deputy Assoc. Dir.

★2759★
U.S. Department of Agriculture
Office of Small and Disadvantaged Business Utilization
14th St. & Independence Ave., SW, Rm. 127W
Washington, DC 20250 Phone: (202)447-7117
Luther Burse, Assoc. Dir.

★2760★
U.S. Department of Commerce
Economic Development Administration
Office of Program Support
Compliance Review Division— Civil Rights
14th St. & Constitution Ave., NW, Rm. 7221
Washington, DC 20230 Phone: (202)377-5575
David E. Lasky, Chief

★2761★
U.S. Department of Commerce
Minority Business Development Agency
Herbert Clark Hoover Bldg.
14th St. & Constitution Ave., NW, Rm. 5053
Washington, DC 20230 Phone: (202)377-5061
Jose Lira, Acting Dir.

★2762★
U.S. Department of Commerce
Minority Business Development Agency
Atlanta Region
401 Peachtree, St. 1930
Atlanta, GA 30308-3516 Phone: (404)730-3300
Carlton L. Eccles, Reg. Dir.
Territory Includes: Alabama, Florida, Georgia, Kentucky, Mississippi, North Carolina, South Carolina, and Tennessee.

★2763★
U.S. Department of Commerce
Minority Business Development Agency
Chicago Region
55 E. Monroe St., Ste. 1440
Chicago, IL 60630 Phone: (202)377-3007
David Vega, Reg. Dir.
Territory Includes: Illinois, Indiana, Iowa, Kansas, Michigan, Minnesota, Missouri, Nebraska, Ohio, and Wisconsin.

★2764★
U.S. Department of Commerce
Minority Business Development Agency
Dallas Region
1100 Commerce St., Rm. 7-B23
Dallas, TX 75242 Phone: (214)767-8001
Melba C. Cabrera, Reg. Dir.
Territory Includes: Arkansas, Colorado, Louisiana, Montana, New Mexico, North Dakota, Oklahoma, South Dakota, Texas, Utah, and Wyoming.

★2765★
U.S. Department of Commerce
Minority Business Development Agency
New York Region
26 Federal Plaza, Rm. 3720
New York, NY 10278 Phone: (212)264-3262
John F. Inglehart, Reg. Dir.
Territory Includes: Connecticut, Maine, Massachusetts, New Hampshire,New Jersey, New York, Puerto Rico, Rhode Island, Vermont, and Virgin Islands.

★2766★
U.S. Department of Commerce
Minority Business Development Agency
San Francisco Region
221 Main St., Rm. 1280
San Francisco, CA 94105 Phone: (415)744-3001
Xavier Mena, Reg. Dir.
Territory Includes: Alaska, American Samoa, Arizona, California, Hawaii, Idaho, Nevada, Oregon, Washington.

★2767★
U.S. Department of Commerce
Minority Business Development Agency
Washington, DC Region
Herbert Clark Hoover Bldg.
14th St. & Constitution Ave., NW
Washington, DC 20230 Phone: (202)377-8275
Georginia A. Sanchez, Reg. Dir.
Territory Includes: Delaware, District of Columbia, Maryland, Pennsylvania, Virginia, and West Virginia.

★2768★
U.S. Department of Commerce
Office of Civil Rights
14th St. & Constitution Ave., NW, Rm. 6010
Washington, DC 20230 Phone: (202)377-3940
Gerald R. Lucas, Dir.

★2769★
U.S. Department of Commerce
Office of Civil Rights
Equal Employment Opportunity Programs
14th St. & Constitution Ave., NW
Washington, DC 20230 Phone: (202)377-5691

★2770★
U.S. Department of Commerce
Office of Small and Disadvantaged Business Utilization
14th St. & Constitution Ave., NW, Rm. 6411
Washington, DC 20230 Phone: (202)377-3387
James P. Maruca, Dir.

★2771★
U.S. Department of Education
Civil Rights Office
Region I, Boston
McCormack Post Office & Courthouse, Rm. 222
Boston, MA 02109 Phone: (617)223-9667
Thomas Habino, Reg. Dir.
Territory Includes: Connecticut, Maine, Massachusetts, New Hampshire, Rhode Island, and Vermont.

★2772★
U.S. Department of Education
Civil Rights Office
Region II, New York
26 Federal Plaza, Rm. 36-118
New York, NY 10278 Phone: (212)264-4633
Paula Kuebler, Reg. Dir.
Territory Includes: New Jersey, New York, Puerto Rico, and the Virgin Islands.

★2773★
U.S. Department of Education
Civil Rights Office
Region III, Philadelphia
3535 Market St., Rm. 16350
Philadelphia, PA 19104 Phone: (215)596-6787
Dr. Robert Smallwood, Reg. Dir.
Territory Includes: Delaware, District of Columbia, Maryland, Pennsylvania, Virginia, and West Virginia.

★2774★
U.S. Department of Education
Civil Rights Office
Region IV, Atlanta
101 Marietta Tower Bldg.
Atlanta, GA 30323 Phone: (404)331-2954
Jesse Hugh, Reg. Dir.
Territory Includes: Alabama, Florida, Georgia, Kentucky, Mississippi, North Carolina, South Carolina, and Tennessee.

★2775★
U.S. Department of Education
Civil Rights Office
Region V, Chicago
401 S. State St.
Chicago, IL 60605 Phone: (312)886-3456
Kenneth Mines, Reg. Dir.
Territory Includes: Illinois, Indiana, Michigan, Minnesota, Ohio, and Wisconsin.

★2776★
U.S. Department of Education
Civil Rights Office
Region VI, Dallas
1200 Main Tower Bldg., Rm. 2125
Dallas, TX 75202 Phone: (214)767-3959
Taylor D. August, Reg. Dir.
Territory Includes: Arkansas, Louisiana, New Mexico, Oklahoma, and Texas.

★2777★
U.S. Department of Education
Civil Rights Office
Region VII, Kansas City
10220 N. Executive Hills Blvd.
Kansas City, MO 61453 Phone: (816)891-8026
Territory Includes: Iowa, Kansas, Missouri, and Nebraska.

★2778★
U.S. Department of Education
Civil Rights Office
Region VIII, Denver
1961 Stout, Rm. 308
Denver, CO 80294 Phone: (303)844-5695
Lilliam Tutiernc, Reg. Dir.
Territory Includes: Colorado, Montana, North Dakota, South Dakota, Utah, and Washington.

★2779★
U.S. Department of Education
Civil Rights Office
Region IX, San Francisco
50 United Nations Plaza, Rm. 205
San Francisco, CA 94102 Phone: (415)227-8040
John E. Palomino, Reg. Dir.
Territory Includes: Arizona, California, Hawaii, Nevada, American Samoa, Guam, and Pacific Islands.

★2780★
U.S. Department of Education
Civil Rights Office
Region X, Seattle
915 2nd Ave., Rm. 3362
Seattle, WA 98174-1099 Phone: (206)442-6811
Gary Jackson, Reg. Dir.
Territory Includes: Alaska, Idaho, Oregon, and Washington.

★2781★
U.S. Department of Education
Office of Assistant Secretary for Postsecondary Education
Higher Education Programs
Minorities and Women/Howard University
7th & D Sts., SW, Rm. 3915
Washington, DC 20202 Phone: (202)732-5656
William C. Young, Liaison

★2782★
U.S. Department of Education
Office of Assistant Secretary for Postsecondary Education
Higher Education Programs
Minority Science Improvement Program
400 Maryland Ave., SW, Rm. 3514
Washington, DC 20202 Phone: (202)708-4662
Angelia Velez-Rodriquez, Sr. Science Education Officer

★2783★
U.S. Department of Education
Office of Assistant Secretary for Postsecondary Education
Historically-Black Colleges and Universities
7th & D Sts., SW, Rm. 3682
Washington, DC 20202 Phone: (202)708-8667
Robea K. Goodwin, Exec. Staff Dir.

★2784★
U.S. Department of Education
Office of Intergovernmental and Interagency Affairs
Civil Rights Reviewing Authority
330 C St., SW, Rm. 4044
Washington, DC 20202 Phone: (202)245-0425
Richard Slippen, Staff Dir.

★2785★
U.S. Department of Education
Office of Small and Disadvantaged Business Utilization
400 Maryland Ave., SW, Rm. 3120
Washington, DC 20202 Phone: (202)708-9820
Daniel L. Levin, Dir.

★2786★
U.S. Department of Education
Office of the Secretary
Assistant Secretary for Civil Rights
330 C St., SW, Rm. 5000
Washington, DC 20202 Phone: (202)732-1213
Michael L. Williams, Asst. Sec.

★2787★
U.S. Department of Energy
Office of Administration and Human Resource Management
Office of Equal Opportunity
Affirmative Action Programs Division
Forrestal Bldg.
1000 Independence Ave., SW, Rm. 4B-058
Washington, DC 20585 Phone: (202)586-2272
Craig K. Zane, Divisional Dir.

★2788★
U.S. Department of Energy
Office of Minority Economic Impact
Forrestal Bldg.
1000 Independence Ave., SW, Rm. 5B-110
Washington, DC 20585 Phone: (202)586-5876
Melva G. Wray, Dir.

★2789★
U.S. Department of Energy
Office of Small and Disadvantaged Business Utilization
Forrestal Bldg.
1000 Independence Ave., SW, Rm. 905
Washington, DC 20585 Phone: (202)586-8201
Leo V. Miranda, Dir.

★2790★
U.S. Department of Health and Human Services
Assistant Secretary for Management and Budget
Office of Management and Acquisition
Office of Equal Employment Opportunity
330 Independence Ave., SW, Rm. 4317
Washington, DC 20201 Phone: (202)619-1564
Barbara Aulenbach, Dir.

★2791★
U.S. Department of Health and Human Services
Civil Rights Office
200 Independence Ave., SW, Rm. 5400
Washington, DC 20201 Phone: (202)619-0403
Edward Mercado, Dir.

★2792★
U.S. Department of Health and Human Services
Civil Rights Office
Equal Employment Opportunity/Affirmative Action
300 Independence Ave., SW, Rm. 5400
Washington, DC 20201 Phone: (202)619-0585
Mary Martin, Coord.

★2793★
U.S. Department of Health and Human Services
Civil Rights Office
Region I, Boston
2411 J.F. Kennedy Federal Bldg.
Boston, MA 02203 Phone: (617)565-1340
Caroline Chang, Reg. Man.

★2794★
U.S. Department of Health and Human Services
Civil Rights Office
Region II, New York
J.K. Javits Federal Bldg., Ste. 3835
New York, NY 10278 Phone: (212)264-3313
Frank Cedo, Reg. Man.

★2795★
U.S. Department of Health and Human Services
Civil Rights Office
Region III, Philadelphia
Gateway Bldg.
PO Box 13716
Philadelphia, PA 19101 Phone: (215)596-1262
Paul Cushing, Reg. Man.

★2796★
U.S. Department of Health and Human Services
Civil Rights Office
Region IV, Atlanta
101 Marietta Tower
Atlanta, GA 30323 Phone: (404)331-2779
Marie A. Chretien, Reg. Man.

★2797★
U.S. Department of Health and Human Services
Civil Rights Office
Region V, Chicago
105 W. Adams, 16th Fl.
Chicago, IL 60603 Phone: (312)886-2359
Charlotte Irons, Reg. Man.

★2798★
U.S. Department of Health and Human Services
Civil Rights Office
Region VI, Dallas
1200 Main Tower Bldg.
Dallas, TX 75202 Phone: (214)767-4056
Davis Sanders, Reg. Man.

★2799★
U.S. Department of Health and Human Services
Civil Rights Office
Region VII, Kansas City
601 E. 12th St.
Federal Bldg.
Kansas City, MO 64106 Phone: (816)426-7277
Lois Carter, Reg. Man.

★2800★
U.S. Department of Health and Human Services
Civil Rights Office
Region VIII, Denver
Federal Bldg.
1961 Stout St.
Denver, CO 80294 Phone: (330)844-3372
Vada Kyle-Holmes, Reg. Man.

★2801★
U.S. Department of Health and Human Services
Civil Rights Office
Region IX, San Francisco
50 United Nations Plaza
San Francisco, CA 94102 Phone: (415)556-8586
Virginia Apodaca, Reg. Man.

★2802★
U.S. Department of Health and Human Services
Civil Rights Office
Region X, Seattle
2201 6th Ave.
Seattle, WA 98121 Phone: (206)442-0473
Carmen Rockwell, Reg. Man.

★2803★
U.S. Department of Health and Human Services
Office of Human Development Services
Head Start Bureau
330 C St., SW, Rm. 2058
Washington, DC 20201 Phone: (202)245-0572
James Kolb, Dir.

★2804★
U.S. Department of Health and Human Services
Office of Human Development Services
Office of Equal Opportunity and Civil Rights
200 Independence Ave., SW, Rm. 338
Washington, DC 20201 Phone: (202)245-1787
David L. Shorts, Dir.

★2805★
U.S. Department of Health and Human Services
Office of Human Development Services
Office of Equal Opportunity and Civil Rights
Small and Disadvantaged Business Utilization and Civil Rights
200 Independence Ave., SW, Rm. 338F
Washington, DC 20201 Phone: (202)245-1787
Cynthia Haile Selassie, Specialist

★2806★
U.S. Department of Health and Human Services
Office of the General Counsel
Civil Rights Division
330 Independence Ave., SW, Rm. 5061
Washington, DC 20201 Phone: (202)245-6900
Grover G. Hankins, Assoc. General Counsel

★2807★
U.S. Department of Health and Human Services
Public Health Service
Centers for Disease Control
Minority Health
1600 Clifton Rd., NE, Rm. 2122
Atlanta, GA 30333 Phone: (404)639-3703
Rueben Warren, Asst. Dir.

★2808★
U.S. Department of Health and Human Services
Public Health Service
Food and Drug Administration
Office of Equal Employment and Civil Rights
Park Lawn Bldg., Rm. 11E06
5600 Fisher's Ln.
Rockville, MD 20857 Phone: (301)443-3310
Rose Melia T. De la Rocha, Dir.

★2809★
U.S. Department of Health and Human Services
Public Health Service
National Institutes of Health
Equal Opportunity Division
9000 Rockville Pike, Bldg. 31
Bethesda, MD 20892 Phone: (301)496-6301
Diane E. Armstrong, Dir.

★2810★
U.S. Department of Health and Human Services
Public Health Service
National Institutes of Health
Office of Minority Health
9000 Rockville Pike, Bldg. 31
Bethesda, MD 20892 Phone: (301)402-1366
John Ruffin, Assoc. Dir.

★2811★
U.S. Department of Health and Human Services
Public Health Service
Office of Equal Opportunity and Civil Rights
Park Lawn Bldg., Rm. 14-25
5600 Fisher's Ln.
Rockville, MD 20857 Phone: (202)443-5636
J. Calvin Adams, Admin.

★2812★
U.S. Department of Housing and Urban Development
Assistant Secretary for Community Planning and Development
Office of Block Grant Assistance
451 7th St., SW, Rm. 7286
Washington, DC 20410 Phone: (202)708-3587
Don Patch, Dir.

★2813★
U.S. Department of Housing and Urban Development
Assistant Secretary for Fair Housing and Equal Opportunity
451 7th St., SW, Rm. 5100
Washington, DC 20410 Phone: (202)708-4242
Gordon H. Mansfield, Asst. Sec.

★2814★
U.S. Department of Housing and Urban Development
Office of Fair Housing and Equal Opportunity
Region I, Boston
O'Neill Federal Bldg, Rm. 309
10 Causeway St.
Boston, MA 02222 Phone: (617)565-5304
Robert W. Laplante, Dir.

★2815★
U.S. Department of Housing and Urban Development
Office of Fair Housing and Equal Opportunity
Region II, New York
26 Federal Plaza
New York, NY 10278-0068 Phone: (212)264-1290
Stanley Seidenfeld, Dir.

★2816★
U.S. Department of Housing and Urban Development
Office of Fair Housing and Equal Opportunity
Region III, Philadelphia
105 S. 7th St.
Philadelphia, PA 19106 Phone: (215)597-1052
Raymond Solecki, Dir.

★2817★
U.S. Department of Housing and Urban Development
Office of Fair Housing and Equal Opportunity
Region IV, Atlanta
75 Spring St., SW
Atlanta, GA 30303 Phone: (404)331-5140
Donnie Murray, Dir.

★2818★
U.S. Department of Housing and Urban Development
Office of Fair Housing and Equal Opportunity
Region V, Chicago
626 W. Jackson, Rm. 718
Chicago, IL 60606 Phone: (312)353-7776
Thomas Higginbothan, Dir.

★2819★
U.S. Department of Housing and Urban Development
Office of Fair Housing and Equal Opportunity
Region VI, Dallas
PO Box 2905
Fort Worth, TX 76113 Phone: (817)885-5491
John E. Wright, Dir.

★2820★
U.S. Department of Housing and Urban Development
Office of Fair Housing and Equal Opportunity
Region VII, Kansas City
1103 Grand Ave.
Kansas City, MO 64106 Phone: (816)374-6457
J. B. Littlejohn, Dir.

★2821★
U.S. Department of Housing and Urban Development
Office of Fair Housing and Equal Opportunity
Region VIII, Denver
1405 Curtis St.
Denver, CO 80202 Phone: (303)844-4751
Lloyd R. Miller, Dir.

★2822★
U.S. Department of Housing and Urban Development
Office of Fair Housing and Equal Opportunity
Region IX, San Francisco
450 Golden Gate Ave.
PO Box 36003
San Francisco, CA 94102 Phone: (415)556-6826
LaVera Gillespie, Dir.

★2823★
U.S. Department of Housing and Urban Development
Office of Fair Housing and Equal Opportunity
Region X, Seattle
1321 2nd
Mailstop 10-E
Seattle, WA 98101 Phone: (206)442-0226
James Brown, Dir.

★2824★
U.S. Department of Housing and Urban Development
Office of Small and Disadvantaged Business Utilization
Minority Business
451 7th St., SW, Rm. 10232
Washington, DC 20410 Phone: (202)708-3350
Elaine Dudley, Acting Dir.

★2825★
U.S. Department of Housing and Urban Development
Office of the Secretary
Martin Luther King, Jr. Federal Holiday Commission
451 7th St., SW, Rm. 5182
Washington, DC 20410 Phone: (202)755-1005
Coretta Scott King, Chair

★2826★
U.S. Department of Justice
Civil Rights Division
10th St. & Constitution Ave., NW, Rm. 5643
Washington, DC 20530 Phone: (202)514-2151
John R. Dunne, Asst. Attorney General

★2827★
U.S. Department of Justice
Justice Management Division
Office of Small and Disadvantaged Business Utilization
601 D St., NW, Rm. 7014
Washington, DC 20530 Phone: (202)501-6271
Enos E. Roberts, Dir.

★2828★
U.S. Department of Labor
Assistant Secretary for Administration and Management
Directorate of Civil Rights
200 Constitution Ave., NW
Washington, DC 20210 Phone: (202)523-8927
Annabelle T. Lockhart, Dir.

★2829★
U.S. Department of Labor
Assistant Secretary for Administration and Management
Directorate of Civil RightsOffice of Equal Employment Opportunity and Affirmative Action
200 Constitution Ave., NW
Washington, DC 20210 Phone: (202)523-6362
Andre C. Whisenton, Division Chief

★2830★
U.S. Department of Labor
Civil Rights Office
Region I, Boston
J.F. Kennedy Bldg.
Boston, MA 02203 Phone: (617)565-2011
Jane Daugherty, Dir.

★2831★
U.S. Department of Labor
Civil Rights Office
Region II, New York
201 Varick St.
New York, NY 10014 Phone: (212)337-2218
Charles Mason, Dir.

★2832★
U.S. Department of Labor
Civil Rights Office
Region III, Philadelphia
3535 Market St., Rm. 14120
Philadelphia, PA 19104 Phone: (215)596-6751
Jerome Hines, Dir.

★2833★
U.S. Department of Labor
Civil Rights Office
Region IV, Atlanta
1371 Peachtree St., NE
Atlanta, GA 30367 Phone: (404)347-2195
Alice Ahlers, Dir.

★2834★
U.S. Department of Labor
Civil Rights Office
Region IX, San Francisco
71 Stevenson St.
San Francisco, CA 94105 Phone: (415)766-6683
Lee Makapagal, Dir.

★2835★
U.S. Department of Labor
Civil Rights Office
Region V, Chicago
230 S. Dearborn St.
Chicago, IL 60604 Phone: (312)353-4670
Herb Roth, Dir.

★2836★
U.S. Department of Labor
Civil Rights Office
Region VI, Dallas
735 Federal Bldg.
525 Griffin St.
Dallas, TX 75202 Phone: (214)767-4136
Jim Lyke, Dir.

★2837★
U.S. Department of Labor
Civil Rights Office
Region VII, Kansas City
911 Walnut St.
Kansas City, MO 64106 Phone: (816)426-6171
Donna Porter, Dir.

★2838★
U.S. Department of Labor
Civil Rights Office
Region VIII, Denver
c/o Region VII
911 Walnut St.
Kansas City, MO 64106 Phone: (816)426-3891
Donna Porter, Dir.

★2839★
U.S. Department of Labor
Civil Rights Office
Region X, Seattle
909 1st Ave.
Seattle, WA 98174 Phone: (203)442-2767
Bill Page, Dir.

★2840★
U.S. Department of Labor
Office of Small and Disadvantaged Business Utilization
200 Constitution Ave., NW
Washington, DC 20210 Phone: (202)523-9148
Walter C. Terry, Dir.

★2841★
U.S. Department of State
Bureau of Human Rights and Humanitarian Affairs
2201 C St., NW
Washington, DC 20520 Phone: (202)647-2126
Richard Schifter, Asst. Sec.

★2842★
U.S. Department of State
Office of Small and Disadvantaged Business Utilization
SA-6, Rm. 633
Washington, DC 20520 Phone: (703)875-6823
Robert A. Cooper Jr., Dir.

★2843★
U.S. Department of State
Office of the Secretary
Equal Employment Opportunity and Civil Rights Office
2201 C St., NW, Rm. 4216
Washington, DC 20520 Phone: (202)647-9294
Audrey Morton, Deputy Asst. Sec.

★2844★
U.S. Department of State
Office of the Secretary
Equal Employment Opportunity and Civil Rights Office
2201 C St., NW, Rm. 4216
Washington, DC 20520 Phone: (202)647-7824
Gloria J. Jackson, Coord.

★2845★
U.S. Department of the Interior
Policy, Management, and Budget
Office of Equal Opportunity
C St. between 18th & 19th Sts., NW
Washington, DC 20240 Phone: (202)208-5693
Carmen R. Maymi, Dir.

★2846★
U.S. Department of the Interior
Policy, Management, and Budget
Office of Historically Black College and University Programs and Job Corps
C St between 18th & 19th Sts., NW
Washington, DC 20240 Phone: (202)208-2403
Ira J. Hutchison, Dir.

★2847★
U.S. Department of the Interior
Policy, Management, and Budget
Office of Small and Disadvantaged Business Utilization
C St. between 18th & 19th Sts., NW
Washington, DC 20240 Phone: (202)208-8493
Kenneth Kelly, Dir.

★2848★
U.S. Department of Transportation
Coast Guard, United States
Office of AcquisitionContract Support Division—Small and Minority Business
2100 2nd St., SW, Rm. 5216
Washington, DC 20593 Phone: (202)267-2499
Dan Sturdivant, Branch Chief

★2849★
U.S. Department of Transportation
Coast Guard, United States
Office of Civil Rights
2100 2nd St., SW, Rm. 2400
Washington, DC 20593 Phone: (202)267-1562
Walter R. Somerville, Chief

★2850★
U.S. Department of Transportation
Federal Aviation Administration
Assistant Administrator for Civil Rights
800 Independence Ave., SW, Rm. 1030G
Washington, DC 20590 Phone: (202)267-3254
Leon C. Watkins, Asst. Admin.

★2851★
U.S. Department of Transportation
Federal Aviation Administration
Assistant Administrator for Civil Rights
Historically Black Colleges and Universities
800 Independence Ave., SW, Rm. 1030
Washington, DC 20590 Phone: (202)267-3267
George Thomas, Prog. Man.

★2852★
U.S. Department of Transportation
Federal Highway Administration
Office of Civil Rights
400 7th St., SW, Rm. 4132
Washington, DC 20590 Phone: (202)366-0693
Edward W. Morris Jr., Dir.

★2853★
U.S. Department of Transportation
Federal Highway Administration
Office of Civil Rights
Title VI and Minority Business Enterprise
400 7th St., SW, Rm. 4132
Washington, DC 20590 Phone: (202)366-1586
George F. Duffy, Division Chief

★2854★
U.S. Department of Transportation
Federal Railroad Administration
Office of the Administrator
Civil Rights
400 7th St., SW, Rm. 5420
Washington, DC 20590 Phone: (202)366-9753
Miles S. Washington Jr., Officer

★2855★
U.S. Department of Transportation
National Highway Traffic Safety Administration
Office of Civil Rights
400 7th St., SW, Rm. 5312
Washington, DC 20590 Phone: (202)366-4762
Hanley J. Norment, Dir.

★2856★
U.S. Department of Transportation
Office of Civil Rights
400 7th St., SW, Rm. 10215
Washington, DC 20590 Phone: (202)366-4648
William T. Hudson, Dir.

★2857★
U.S. Department of Transportation
Office of Civil Rights
Historically Black Colleges and Universities
400 7th St., SW, Rm. 10215
Washington, DC 20590 Phone: (202)366-5997
Wilbur Williams, Prog. Man.

★2858★
U.S. Department of Transportation
Office of Small and Disadvantaged Business Utilization
Minority Business Resource Center
400 7th St., SW, Rm. 9410
Washington, DC 20590 Phone: (202)366-1930
Wendell K. Harbour, Chief

★2859★
U.S. Department of Transportation
Research and Special Programs Administration
Office of Civil Rights
400 7th St., SW, Rm. 8406
Washington, DC 20590 Phone: (202)366-9638
Bernice D. Vandervalk, Dir.

★2860★
U.S. Department of Transportation
Urban Mass Transportation Administration
Office of Civil Rights
400 7th St., SW, Rm. 7412
Washington, DC 20590 Phone: (202)366-4018
Robert G. Owens, Dir.

★2861★
U.S. Environmental Protection Agency
Office of Civil Rights
401 M St., SW, Rm. W206
Washington, DC 20460 Phone: (202)382-4575
Nathaniel Scurry, Dir.

★2862★
U.S. Environmental Protection Agency
Office of Civil Rights
National Black Employment Program
401 M St., SW, Rm. W206
Washington, DC 20460 Phone: (202)382-4595
Ronald Blakely, Man.

★2863★
U.S. Environmental Protection Agency
Office of Small and Disadvantaged Business Utilization
401 M St., SW, Rm. 1108 CM-2
Washington, DC 20460 Phone: (703)557-7777

★2864★
U.S. Equal Employment Opportunity Commission
1801 L St., NW
Washington, DC 20507 Phone: (202)663-4001
Evan J. Kemp, Chairman

★2865★
U.S. Equal Employment Opportunity Commission
Atlanta District Office
75 Piedmont Ave., NE, Ste. 1100
Atlanta, GA 30335 Phone: (404)331-6093
Harris A. Williams, Dir.

★2866★
U.S. Equal Employment Opportunity Commission
Birmingham District Office
1900 3rd Ave., N.
Birmingham, AL 35203 Phone: (205)731-0083
Warren A. Bullock, Dir.

★2867★
U.S. Equal Employment Opportunity Commission
Charlotte District Office
5500 Central Ave.
Charlotte, NC 28212 Phone: (704)567-7100
Curtiss P. Todd, Dir.

★2868★
U.S. Equal Employment Opportunity Commission
Cleveland District Office
1375 Euclid Ave., Rm. 600
Cleveland, OH 44115 Phone: (216)522-2001
Harold Ferguson, Dir.

★2869★
U.S. Equal Employment Opportunity Commission
Dallas District Office
8303 Elmbrook Dr., 2nd Fl.
Dallas, TX 75247 Phone: (214)767-7015
Jacqueline R. Bradley, Dir.

★2870★
U.S. Equal Employment Opportunity Commission
Denver District Office
1845 Sherman St., Rm. 201
Denver, CO 80203 Phone: (303)866-1300
Francisco J. Flores, Dir.

★2871★
U.S. Equal Employment Opportunity Commission
Detroit District Office
477 Michigan Ave.
Detroit, MI 48226 Phone: (313)226-7636
A. William Schukar, Dir.

★2872★
U.S. Equal Employment Opportunity Commission
District of Columbia District Office
1400 L St., NW, Ste. 200
Washington, DC 20006 Phone: (202)275-6365
Susan Reilly, Dir.

★2873★
U.S. Equal Employment Opportunity Commission
Florida Office
1 NE 1st St., 6th Fl.
Miami, FL 33132 Phone: (305)536-4491
Frederico Costales, Dir.

★2874★
U.S. Equal Employment Opportunity Commission
Fresno Office
1313 P St., Ste. 103
Fresno, CA 93721 Phone: (209)487-5793
David Rodriguez, Dir.

★2875★
U.S. Equal Employment Opportunity Commission
Illinois Office
536 S. Clark St., Rm. 930-A
Chicago, IL 60605 Phone: (312)353-2713
Marsha Drane, Dir.

★2876★
U.S. Equal Employment Opportunity Commission
Indiana Office
46 E. Ohio St., Rm. 456
Indianapolis, IN 46204 Phone: (317)269-7212
Thomas P. Hadfield, Dir.

★2877★
U.S. Equal Employment Opportunity Commission
Los Angeles District Office
3660 Wilshire Blvd., 5th Fl.
Los Angeles, CA 90010 Phone: (213)251-7278
Dr. Dorothy Porter, Dir.

★2878★
U.S. Equal Employment Opportunity Commission
Maryland Office
111 Market Pl., Ste. 4000
Baltimore, MD 21202 Phone: (301)962-3932
Chris Roggerson, Dir.

★2879★
U.S. Equal Employment Opportunity Commission
Memphis District Office
1407 Union Ave., Ste. 621
Memphis, TN 38104 Phone: (901)521-2617
Walter S. Grabon, Dir.

★2880★
U.S. Equal Employment Opportunity Commission
Missouri Office
625 N. Euclid St., 5th Fl.
St. Louis, MO 63108 Phone: (314)425-6585
Lynn Bruner, Dir.

★2881★
U.S. Equal Employment Opportunity Commission
New Orleans District Office
701 Loyola Ave., Ste. 600
New Orleans, LA 70113 Phone: (504)589-2329
Patricia F. Bivins, Dir.

★2882★
U.S. Equal Employment Opportunity Commission
New York Office
90 Church St., Rm. 1501
New York, NY 10007 Phone: (212)264-7161
Spencer H. Lewis, Dir.

★2883★
U.S. Equal Employment Opportunity Commission
Oakland Office
Wells Fargo Bank Bldg.
1333 Broadway, Rm. 430
Oakland, CA 94612 Phone: (415)273-7588
Deborah Randall, Dir.

★2884★
U.S. Equal Employment Opportunity Commission
Office of Program Operations
Federal Sector Programs
Affirmative Employment Programs Division
2401 E St., NW, Rm. 8219
Washington, DC 20507 Phone: (202)663-7039
Clayton G. Boyd, Dir.

★2885★
U.S. Equal Employment Opportunity Commission
Pennsylvania Office
1421 Cherry St., 10th Fl.
Philadelphia, PA 19102 Phone: (215)597-7784
Johnny J. Butler, Dir.

★2886★
U.S. Equal Employment Opportunity Commission
Phoenix District Office
4520 N. Central Ave., Ste. 300
Phoenix, AZ 85012 Phone: (602)261-3882
Charles D. Burtner, Dir.

★2887★
U.S. Equal Employment Opportunity Commission
San Antonio District Office
5410 Fredericksburg Rd., Ste. 200
San Antonio, TX 78229 Phone: (512)229-4810
Pedro Esquivel, Dir.

★2888★
U.S. Equal Employment Opportunity Commission
San Francisco District Office
901 Market St., Ste. 500
San Francisco, CA 94103 Phone: (415)995-5049
Paul Montanez, Dir.

★2889★
U.S. Equal Employment Opportunity Commission
San Jose Office
U.S. Court House & Federal Bldg.
280 S. 1st St., Ste. 4150
San Jose, CA 95113 Phone: (408)291-7352
Charles Carattini, Dir.

★2890★
U.S. Equal Employment Opportunity Commission
Seattle District Office
2815 2nd Ave., Ste. 500
Seattle, WA 98121 Phone: (206)442-0968
Jeanette Leino, Dir.

★2891★
U.S. Equal Employment Opportunity Commission
Texas Office
1919 Smith St., 7th Fl.
Houston, TX 77002 Phone: (713)653-3320
Harriet J. Ehrlich, Dir.

★2892★
U.S. Equal Employment Opportunity Commission
Wisconsin Office
310 W. Wisconsin Ave., Ste. 800
Milwaukee, WI 53203 Phone: (414)291-1111
Chester V. Bailey, Dir.

★2893★
U.S. General Accounting Office
Civil Rights Office
441 G St., NW, Rm. 3027
Washington, DC 20001 Phone: (202)275-6388
Nilda Aponte, Dir.

★2894★
U.S. Information Agency
Bureau of Management
Office of Equal Employment Opportunity and Civil Rights
301 4th St., SW, Rm. 365
Washington, DC 20547 Phone: (202)619-5151
Marilyn B. Thompson, Dir.

★2895★
U.S. National Aeronautics and Space Administration
Office of Equal Opportunity Programs
400 Maryland Ave., SW
Washington, DC 20546 Phone: (202)453-2167
Harriett G. Jenkins, Asst. Admin.

★2896★
U.S. National Aeronautics and Space Administration
Office of Equal Opportunity Programs
Affirmative Action and Evaluation Division
400 Maryland Ave., SW
Washington, DC 20546 Phone: (202)453-2175
Alfonso J. Ludi, Dir.

★2897★
U.S. National Aeronautics and Space Administration
Office of Equal Opportunity Programs
Discrimination Complaints Division
400 Maryland Ave., SW
Washington, DC 20546 Phone: (202)453-2180
Oceola S. Hall, Dir.

★2898★
U.S. National Aeronautics and Space Administration
Office of Equal Opportunity Programs
Minority University Research and Education Programs
400 Maryland Ave., SW, Rm. F611
Washington, DC 20546 Phone: (202)453-2171

★2899★
U.S. National Aeronautics and Space Administration
Office of Equal Opportunity Programs
Minority University Research and Education Programs
Historically Black Colleges and Universities
400 Maryland Ave., SW, Rm. F6111
Washington, DC 20546 Phone: (202)453-2173
Orlando Guitierrez, Prog. Man.

★2900★
U.S. National Aeronautics and Space Administration
Office of Equal Opportunity Programs
Minority University Research and Education Programs
Other Minority Universities
400 Maryland Ave., SW, Rm. F6111
Washington, DC 20546 Phone: (202)453-2173
Bettie L. White, Prog. Man.

★2901★
U.S. National Aeronautics and Space Administration
Office of Small and Disadvantaged Business Utilization
Minority Businesses
400 Maryland Ave., SW
Washington, DC 20546 Phone: (202)453-2088
Rae C. Martel, Advisor

★2902★
U.S. Office of Personnel Management
Office of Equal Employment Opportunity
Equal Employment Opportunity Division
1900 E St., NW, Rm. 5457
Washington, DC 20415 Phone: (202)606-2460
Teresa Alzamora del Rio, Asst. Dir.

★2903★
U.S. Small Business Administration
Associate Deputy Administrator for Management and Administration
Office of Civil Rights Compliance
1441 L St., NW
Washington, DC 20416 Phone: (202)653-6054
J. Arnold Feldman, Chief

★2904★
U.S. Small Business Administration
Minority Small Business and Capital Ownership Development
Region I, Boston
155 Federal St., 9th Fl.
Boston, MA 02110 Phone: (617)223-2036
Samuel W. Brown, Asst. Admin.

★2905★
U.S. Small Business Administration
Minority Small Business and Capital Ownership Development
Region III, Philadelphia
475 Allendale Rd., Ste. 201
King of Prussia, PA 19406 Phone: (215)962-3758
Delores Ellis, Asst. Admin.

★2906★
U.S. Small Business Administration
Minority Small Business and Capital Ownership Development
Region IV, Atlanta
1375 Peachtree St., NE
Atlanta, GA 30367 Phone: (404)347-4089
Isaiah Washington, Asst. Admin.

★2907★
U.S. Small Business Administration
Minority Small Business and Capital Ownership Development
Region IX, San Francisco
71 Stevenson St., 20th Fl.
San Francisco, CA 94105 Phone: (415)774-6429
R. Stephen Bangs, Asst. Admin.

★2908★
U.S. Small Business Administration
Minority Small Business and Capital Ownership Development
Region V, Chicago
230 S. Dearborn St., Rm. 570
Chicago, IL 60604 Phone: (312)353-4361
Gary Peele, Asst. Admin.

★2909★
U.S. Small Business Administration
Minority Small Business and Capital Ownership Development
Region VI, Dallas
8625 King George Dr., Bldg. C
Dallas, TX 75235 Phone: (214)767-7631
Lavan Alexander, Asst. Admin.

★2910★
U.S. Small Business Administration
Minority Small Business and Capital Ownership Development
Region VII, Kansas City
911 Walnut St., 13th Fl.
Kansans City, MO 64106 Phone: (816)426-3516
Art Seibert, Asst. Admin.

★2911★
U.S. Small Business Administration
Minority Small Business and Capital Ownership Development
Region VIII, Denver
999 18th St., Ste. 701
Denver, CO 80202 Phone: (303)294-7076
Gerald Martinez, Asst. Admin.

★2912★
U.S. Small Business Administration
Minority Small Business and Capital Ownership Development
Region X, Seattle
2615 4th Ave., Ste. 440
Seattle, WA 98121 Phone: (206)553-0391
Carol Colpitts, Asst. Admin.

★2913★
U.S. Small Business Administration
Minority Small Business and Capital Ownership Development
Region II, New York
26 Federal Plaza, Rm. 3108
New York, NY 10278 Phone: (212)264-1046
Larry Gaunt, Asst. Admin.

★2914★
U.S. Smithsonian Institute
National Museum of African Art
950 Independence Ave., SW
Washington, DC 20560 Phone: (202)357-4858
Sylvia H. Williams, Dir.

★2915★
U.S. Smithsonian Institute
National Museum of American History
Department of Social and Cultural HistoryBlack American Culture
14th St. & Constitution
Washington, DC 20560 Phone: (202)357-2385
Bernice Reagan, Curator

★2916★
U.S. Smithsonian Institute
National Museum of American History
Department of Social and Cultural History
Black History and Civil Rights
14th St. & Constitution
Washington, DC 20560 Phone: (202)357-2008
Lonnie G. Bunch, Curator

★2917★
U.S. Smithsonian Institute
Office of Equal Opportunity
1000 Jefferson Dr., SW, Ste. 915
Washington, DC 20560 Phone: (202)357-4505
Will Douglas Jr., Dir.

★2918★
U.S. Smithsonian Institute
Office of Equal Opportunity
Affirmative Action Program
1000 Jefferson Dr., SW, Ste. 915
Washington, DC 20560 Phone: (202)357-3508
Diane Cook-Lee, Man.

(11) FEDERAL DOMESTIC ASSISTANCE PROGRAMS

Entries in this chapter are arranged alphabetically by name of sponsoring agency. See the User's Guide at the front of this directory for additional information.

★2919★
U.S. Commission on Civil Rights
Clearinghouse Services, Civil Rights Discrimination Complaints (29.001)
1121 Vermont Ave., NW
Washington, DC 20425 Phone: (202)376-8177

Types of Assistance: Dissemination of technical information. **Applicant Eligibility:** Anyone can seek information; no criteria must be satisfied. **Beneficiary Eligibility:** General public. **Range and Average of Financial Assistance:** Not applicable.

★2920★
U.S. Department of Agriculture
Office of Advocacy and Enterprise
Minority Research and Teaching Program Grants (10.140)
14th & Independence Ave. SW
Washington, DC 20250 Phone: (202)447-2019
Dr. Ezra Naughton, Contact

Types of Assistance: Project Grants, Advisory Services, and Counseling. **Applicant Eligibility:** Public, private, state, and other colleges, universities and related institutions of higher learning whose activities meet the required criteria of encouraging minority participation in agricultural sciences. **Beneficiary Eligibility:** Same as above. **Range and Average of Financial Assistance:** Not applicable.

★2921★
U.S. Department of Commerce
Economic Development Administration
Economic Development - Business Development Assistance (11.301)
Herbert C. Hoover Bldg., Rm. H7844
Washington, DC 20230 Phone: (202)377-5067
Steven R. Brennen, Deputy Asst. Sec., Loan Prog.

Types of Assistance: Loan guarantees/grants. **Applicant Eligibility:** Private lending institutions lending to private borrowers whose projects have been approved for assistance by the state or political sub-division in which the project to be financed is located. **Beneficiary Eligibility:** The project funded must provide more than a temporary alleviation of unemployment and/or underemployment within the area wherein the project is or will be located. **Range and Average of Financial Assistance:** $500,000.00 to $111,100,000.00; $2,000,000.00.

★2922★
U.S. Department of Commerce
Economic Development Administration
Economic Development - Grants for Public Works and Development Facilities (11.300)
Public Works Division
Herbert C. Hoover Bldg., Rm. H7326
Washington, DC 20230 Phone: (202)377-5265
David L. McIlwain, Dir.

Types of Assistance: Project grants. **Applicant Eligibility:** States, cities, counties, and other political subdivisions, and private or public nonprofit organizations or associations representing a redevelopment area or a designed Economic Development Center are eligible to receive grants. Corporations and associations organized for profit are not eligible. **Beneficiary Eligibility:** Unemployed and underemployed persons and/or members of low-income families. **Range and Average of Financial Assistance:** No specific minimum or maximum project amount - $56,000.00 to $1,800,000.00; $560,000.00.

★2923★
U.S. Department of Commerce
Economic Development Administration
Special Economic Development and Adjustment Assistance Program - Sudden and Severe Economic Dislocation and Long-term Economic Deterioration (11.307)
Economic Adjustment Division
Herbert C. Hoover Bldg., Rm. H7327
Washington, DC 20230 Phone: (202)377-2659
David L. McIlwain, Dir.

Types of Assistance: Project grants. **Applicant Eligibility:** States, cities, counties or other political subdivisions of a State, consortia of such political subdivisions, public or private nonprofit organizations representing redevelopment areas designated under the Public Works and Economic Development Act of 1965. **Beneficiary Eligibility:** SSED grants may be used in direct expenditures by the eligible recipient or through redistribution by the recipient to public and private entities, in the form of grants, loans, loan guarantees, or other appropriate assistance except that grants may not be made to for-profit entities. LTED grants may only be redistributed by the recipient in the form of loans and loan guarantees. **Range and Average of Financial Assistance:** No specific minimum or maximum size.

★2924★
U.S. Department of Commerce
Minority Business Development Agency
Minority Business and Industry Association - Minority Chambers of Commerce (11.802)
Office of Program Development, Rm. 5096
14th & Constitution Ave., NW
Washington, DC 20230 Phone: (202)377-5770
Georgina Sanchez, Dir.

Types of Assistance: Project grants (cooperative agreements). **Applicant Eligibility:** Restricted to established business, industry, professional and trade associations, and chambers of commerce. **Beneficiary Eligibility:** Same as above. **Range and Average of Financial Assistance:** $25,000.00 to $320,000.00.

★2925★
U.S. Department of Commerce
Minority Business Development Agency
Minority Business Development Centers (11.800)
Office of Program Development, Rm. 5096
14th & Constitution Ave., NW
Washington, DC 20230 Phone: (202)377-5770
Georgina Sanchez, Asst. Dir.

Types of Assistance: Project grants (cooperative agreements). **Applicant Eligibility:** No restrictions. **Beneficiary Eligibility:** Recipient is to provide assistance to minority-owned businesses or minorities interested in starting a business. **Range and Average of Financial Assistance:** $165,000.00 to $622,000.00; $212,000.00.

★2926★
U.S. Department of Education
Office of Assistant Secretary for Elementary and Secondary Education
Desegregation Assistance, Civil Rights Training, and Advisory Service (84.004)
Division of Discretionary Grants
400 Maryland Ave., SW
Washington, DC 20202 Phone: (202)732-4342
Sylvia Wright, Contact

Types of Assistance: Project grants. **Applicant Eligibility:** State and educational agencies, desegregation assistance centers, any private nonprofit organization or any public agency (other than SEA or school board). **Beneficiary Eligibility:** Educational personnel and elementary and secondary students in eligible local school districts. **Range and Average of Financial Assistance:** $500,000.00 to $1,020,000.00; $820,000.00; for SEAs $77,500.00 to $800,000.00; $296,980.00.

★2927★
U.S. Department of Education
Office of Assistant Secretary for Elementary and Secondary Education
Magnet Schools Assistance (84.165)
Division of Discretionary Grants
Mail Stop 6264 FOB6
400 Maryland Ave., SW, Rm. 2040, FB6
Washington, DC 20202 Phone: (202)732-4360
Sylvia Wright, Contact

Types of Assistance: Project grants. **Applicant Eligibility:** Local educational agencies. **Beneficiary Eligibility:** Same as above. **Range and Average of Financial Assistance:** $183,705.00 to $4,000,000.00.

★2928★
U.S. Department of Education
Office of Assistant Secretary for Postsecondary Education
Grants to Institutions to Encourage Minority Participation in Graduate Education (84.202)
Division of Higher Education Incentive Programs
Washington, DC 20202 Phone: (202)732-4393
Walter T. Lewis, Contact

Types of Assistance: Project grants. **Applicant Eligibility:** Accredited institutions of higher education. **Beneficiary Eligibility:** Institutions receiving the awards will provide direct fellowship aid to graduate students accepted and approved by the institution. **Range and Average of Financial Assistance:** Estimated range of awards: $12,904.00 to $120,000.00; $77,244.00.

★2929★
U.S. Department of Education
Office of Assistant Secretary for Postsecondary Education
Minority Science Improvement (84.120)
Division of Higher Education Incentive Programs
Washington, DC 20202 Phone: (202)732-4396
Argelia Velez-Rodriguez, Contact

Types of Assistance: Project grants. **Applicant Eligibility:** Private and public accredited two- and four-year institutions of higher education whose enrollments are predominantly (50% or more) American Indian, Alaskan Native, Black (not Hispanic origin), Hispanic, Pacific Islander, or any combination of these or other disadvantaged ethnic minorities who are underrepresented in science and engineering. Proposals may also be submitted by professional scientific societies, and all nonprofit accredited colleges and universities. **Beneficiary Eligibility:** Same as above; also nonprofit science-oriented societies, and all nonprofit accredited colleges and universities. **Range and Average of Financial Assistance:** $19,000.00 to $500,000.00; $250,000.00 for institutional and Cooperative Projects, $19,000.00 for Design Projects, and $47,000.00 for Special Projects.

★2930★
U.S. Department of Education
Office of Assistant Secretary for Postsecondary Education
Upward Bound (84.047)
Division of Student Services
Education Outreach Branch
400 Maryland Ave., SW, Rm. 3060
Regional Office Bldg. 3
Washington, DC 20202 Phone: (202)732-4804
Goldia Hogdon, Contact

Types of Assistance: Project grants. **Applicant Eligibility:** Institutions of higher education, public and private agencies and organizations, and in exceptional cases, secondary public schools. **Beneficiary Eligibility:** Low-income individuals and potential first generation college students who have a need for academic support in order to successfully pursue a program for postsecondary education. Two-thirds of the participants must be low-income individuals who are also potential first generation college students. The remaining participants must be either low-income individuals or potential first generation college students. Except for veterans, who can be served regardless of age, project participants must be between 13 and 19 years old and have completed the eighth grade, but have not entered the twelfth grade (exceptions allowed). **Range and Average of Financial Assistance:** $90,809.00 to $511,745.00; $196,000.00.

★2931★
U.S. Department of Energy
Office of Minority Economic Impact
Management and Technical Assistance for Minority Business Enterprises (81.082)
Forrestal Bldg., Rm. 5B-110
Washington, DC 20585 Phone: (202)586-1594
Joe Easton, Contact

Types of Assistance: Advisory services and counseling. **Applicant Eligibility:** Minority business enterprises. **Beneficiary Eligibility:** Minority business enterprises wanting to do business with the Department of Energy. **Range and Average of Financial Assistance:** Not applicable.

★2932★
U.S. Department of Energy
Office of Minority Economic Impact
Minority Educational Institution Assistance (81.094)
Forrestal Bldg., Rm. 5B-110
Washington, DC 20585 Phone: (202)586-1593
Isiah O. Sewell, Contact

Types of Assistance: Project grants. **Applicant Eligibility:** Educational institutions with more than 50% minority enrollment. **Beneficiary Eligibility:** Public and private minority educational institutions. **Range and Average of Financial Assistance:** $120,000.00 to $180,000.00; $140,000.00.

★2933★
U.S. Department of Energy
Office of Minority Economic Impact
Minority Educational Institution Research Travel Fund (81.083)
Forrestal Bldg., Rm. 5B-110
Washington, DC 20585 Phone: (202)896-1593
Isiah O. Sewell, Contact

Types of Assistance: Direct payments for specified use. **Applicant Eligibility:** Minority postsecondary educational institutions. **Beneficiary Eligibility:** Faculty members and graduate students involved in an energy research related planning project. **Range and Average of Financial Assistance:** $200.00 to $800.00; $500.00.

★2934★
U.S. Department of Energy
Office of Minority Economic Impact
Minority Honors Training and Industrial Assistance Program (81.084)
Forrestal Bldg., Rm. 5B-110
Washington, DC 29585 Phone: (202)896-1593
Isiah O. Sewell, Contact

Types of Assistance: Project grants. **Applicant Eligibility:** Limited minority honor students attending institutions offering degree progrms in at least four energy-related areas of study. **Beneficiary Eligibility:** Financially needy minority honor students. **Range and Average of Financial Assistance:** $33,000.00 to $78,500.00; $59,000.00.

★2935★
U.S. Department of Energy
Office of Minority Economic Impact
National Minority Energy Information Clearinghouse (81.085)
Forrestal Bldg., Rm. 5B-110
Washington, DC 20585 Phone: (202)586-5876
Effie A. Young, Contact

Types of Assistance: Dissemination of technical information. **Applicant Eligibility:** No restrictions. **Beneficiary Eligibility:** Scholars and members of organizations doing energy-related research and minority business enterprises. **Range and Average of Financial Assistance:** Not applicable.

★2936★
U.S. Department of Energy
Office of Minority Economic Impact
Office of Minority Economic Impact Loans (81.063)
Forrestal Bldg., Rm. 5B-110
Washington, DC 20585 Phone: (202)586-1594
Joe Easton, Contact

Types of Assistance: Direct loans. **Applicant Eligibility:** A firm, including sole proprietorship, corporation, association, or partnership, which is at least 50% owned or controlled by a member of a minority or a group of members of a minority. Control means direct or indirect possession of the power to direct or cause the direction of management and policies, whether through the ownership of voting securities, by contract or otherwise. **Beneficiary Eligibility:** Minority business enterprises. **Range and Average of Financial Assistance:** $1,000.00 to $25,000.00; $5,000.00.

★2937★
U.S. Department of Health and Human Services
Family Support Administration
Work Incentive Program (13.790)
Office of Family Assistance
Washington, DC 20201 Phone: (202)535-0174
Ronald E. Putz, Exec.Dir.

Types of Assistance: Formula grants. **Applicant Eligibility:** WIN services are available in all States as well as in Washington DC, Puerto Rico, the Virgin Islands, and Guam. **Beneficiary Eligibility:** Applicants and recipients of Aid to Families with Dependent Children (AFDC) who are required by law to register with WIN or who choose to register voluntarily. **Range and Average of Financial Assistance:** $94,000.00 to $12,677,000.00; $1,713,907.00.

★2938★
U.S. Department of Health and Human Services
National Institutes of Health Public Health Service
Minority Access to Research Careers (13.880)
National Institute of General Medical Sciences
Bethesda, MD 20892 Phone: (301)496-7941
Elward Bynum, Prog. Dir.

Types of Assistance: Project grants. **Applicant Eligibility:** Any nonfederal public or private nonprofit four-year university or college with substantial enrollment of ethnic minority students may apply for the institutional National Service Awards. To be eligible for funding, a proposal must first receive favorable recommendations from a scientific review committee and a national advisory council. Individual National Research Service awardees must be nominated and sponsored by a public or nonprofit private institution having staff and facilities appropriate to the proposed research training program. All awardees must be citizens or have been admitted to the United States for permanent residence. **Beneficiary Eligibility:** Same as above. **Range and Average of Financial Assistance:** $9,889.00 to $406,944.00; $67,512.00.

★2939★
U.S. Department of Health and Human Services
National Institutes of Health, Public Health Service
Minority Biomedical Research Support (13.375)
National Institutes of Health
Division of Research Resources
Bethesda, MD 20892 Phone: (301)496-6745
Dr. Ciriaco Gonzales, Dir.

Types of Assistance: Project grants. **Applicant Eligibility:** Four-year colleges, universities, and health professional schools with over 50% minority enrollment; four-year institutions with significant, but not necessarily over 50% minority enrollment, provided they have a history of encouragement and assistance to minorities; two-year colleges with 50% minority enrollment. **Beneficiary Eligibility:** Minority students and faculty, and investigators at eligible institutions. **Range and Average of Financial Assistance:** $100,000.00 to $1,500,000.00 per year for three to four years.

★2940★
U.S. Department of Health and Human Services
National Institutes of Health Public Health Service
Office of the Assistant Secretary For Health (13.137) Minority Community Health Coalition Demonstration
Hubert H. Humphrey Bldg., Rm. 118 F
200 Independence Ave., SW
Washington, DC 20201 Phone: (202)245-0020
Betty Lee Hawks, Contact

Types of Assistance: Project grants. **Applicant Eligibility:** Public organizations, private nonprofit organizations, and for-profit organizations. **Beneficiary Eligibility:** Members of the four major minority groups: Asian/Pacific Islanders, Blacks, Hispanics, Native Americans, or a subgroup of any of these groups. **Range and Average of Financial Assistance:** $130,000.00 to $200,000.00; $182,000.00 (two-year awards).

★2941★
U.S. Department of Health and Human Services
Office of Human Development Services
Administration for Children, Youth, and Families - Head Start (13.600)
PO Box 1182
Washington, DC 20013 Phone: (202)245-0569

Types of Assistance: Project grants. **Applicant Eligibility:** Any local government, federally-recognized Indian tribe, or private nonprofit agency which meets the requirements may apply for a grant. Grantee agencies may subcontract with other child-serving agencies to provide service to Head Start children. **Beneficiary Eligibility:** Full-year Head Start programs are primarily for children from age 3 up to the age when the child enters the school system, but may include some younger children. No less than 10% of the total enrollment opportunities in Head Start programs in each State shall be available for handicapped children. **Range and Average of Financial Assistance:** $51,311.00 to $41,013,050.00.

★2942★
U.S. Department of Health and Human Services
Office of the Secretary
Civil Rights Compliance Activities (13.675)
Office of Director
5032 Cohen Bldg.
330 Independence Ave., SW
Washington, DC 20201 Phone: (202)245-6403

Types of Assistance: Investigation of complaints; dissemination of technical information. **Applicant Eligibility:** Anyone who believes he or she has been discriminated against and recipients of Federal financial assistance who desire technical assistance and information on the purpose of assuring their compliance with nondiscrimination laws. **Beneficiary Eligibility:** Individual subject to discrimination and recipients who require technical assistance and information. **Range and Average of Financial Assistance:** Not applicable.

★2943★
U.S. Department of Housing and Urban Development
Community Planning and Development
Rehabilitation Loans (14.220)
Office of Urban Rehabilitation
451 7th St., SW
Washington, DC 20410 Phone: (202)755-0367

Types of Assistance: Direct loans. **Applicant Eligibility:** Owners of residential and non-residential property in eligible Community Development Block Grant areas and Section 810 Urban Homesteading Areas. Applicant must have ability to repay loan and security offered for loan must be adequate. Priority is provided to applicants who are low to moderate income owner-occupants of single family property. **Beneficiary Eligibility:** Property owners. **Range and Average of Financial Assistance:** Loan limit maximum of $33,500.00/dwelling unit; $100,000.00 for non-residential properties; average: $27,121.00 for single-family loans; $313,672.00/loan for loans on multi-family, non-residential and mixed use loans.

★2944★
U.S. Department of Housing and Urban Development
Office of Fair Housing and Equal Opportunity
Equal Opportunity in Housing (14.400)
Asst. Sec. for Fair Housing and Equal Opportunity
Washington, DC 20410 Phone: (202)755-7252

Types of Assistance: Investigation of complaints. **Applicant Eligibility:** Any individual aggrieved by a discriminatory housing practice because of race, color, religion, sex, or national origin may file a complaint with the Department of Housing and Urban Development. Litigation may be initiated by the individual aggrieved and under certain conditions by the Attorney General. **Beneficiary Eligibility:** Individuals. **Range and Average of Financial Assistance:** Not applicable.

★2945★
U.S. Department of Housing and Urban Development
Office of Fair Housing and Equal Opportunity
Fair Housing Assistance Program - State and Local (14.401)
Asst. Sec. for Fair Housing and Equal Opportunity
451 7th St., SW
Washington, DC 20410 Phone: (202)755-0455

Types of Assistance: Project grants (cooperative agreements). **Applicant Eligibility:** State and local governments administering State and local fair housing laws and ordinances which have been recognized by HUD as providing substantially equivalent rights and remedies as those provided by Title VII of the Civil Rights Act of 1968, and which have executed formal Memoranda of Understanding with HUD to process Title VII complaints. **Beneficiary Eligibility:** Any person or group of persons aggrieved by a discriminatory housing practice because of race, color, religion, sex, or national origin. **Range and Average of Financial Assistance:** Contribution for capacity building and complaint processing - $20,000.00 to $250,000.00; training - $4,000.00; Incentive funds - $30,000.00 to $100,000.00.

★2946★
U.S. Department of Housing and Urban Development
Office of Fair Housing and Equal Opportunity
Non-Discrimination in Federally Assisted Programs (14.405)
451 7th St., SW
Washington, DC 20410 Phone: (202)755-5904
Peter Kaplan, Contact

Types of Assistance: Investigation of complaints. **Applicant Eligibility:** Any individual feeling aggrieved because of an alleged discriminatory action on the basis of race, color, or national origin may file a complaint with the Department of Housing and Urban Development. **Beneficiary Eligibility:** Aggrieved individuals. **Range and Average of Financial Assistance:** Not applicable.

★2947★
U.S. Department of Housing and Urban Development
Office of Fair Housing and Equal Opportunity
Non-Discrimination in the Community Development Block Grant Program (14.406)
451 7th St., SW
Washington, DC 20410 Phone: (202)755-5904
Peter Kaplan

Types of Assistance: Investigation of complaints. **Applicant Eligibility:** Any individual feeling aggrieved because of an alleged discriminatory action in a Title I program on the basis of race, color, national origin, handicap, or age may file a complaint with the Department of Housing and Urban Development. **Beneficiary Eligibility:** Aggrieved individuals. **Range and Average of Financial Assistance:** Not applicable.

★2948★
U.S. Department of Justice
Civil Rights Division
Desegregation of Public Education (16.100)
Educational Opportunities Litigation Section
Washington, DC 20530 Phone: (202)633-2019
Deborah Burstion-Wade, Contact

Types of Assistance: Provision of specialized services. **Applicant Eligibility:** Parent or group of parents in the case of public schools. An individual or his/her parents in the case of a public college. **Beneficiary Eligibility:** Same as above. **Range and Average of Financial Assistance:** Not applicable.

★2949★
U.S. Department of Justice
Civil Rights Division
Equal Employment Opportunity (16.101)
Employment Litigation Section
Washington, DC 20530 Phone: (202)633-2019
Deborah Burstion-Wade, Contact

Types of Assistance: Provision of specialized services. **Applicant Eligibility:** All persons. **Beneficiary Eligibility:** All persons. **Range and Average of Financial Assistance:** Not applicable.

★2950★
U.S. Department of Justice
Civil Rights Division
Fair Housing and Equal Credit Opportunity (16.103)
Housing & Civil Enforcement
Washington, DC 20530 Phone: (202)633-4713
Deborah Burstion-Wade, Contact

Types of Assistance: Provision of specialized services. **Applicant Eligibility:** All U.S. citizens of voting age. **Beneficiary Eligibility:** Same as above. **Range and Average of Financial Assistance:** Not applicable.

★2951★
U.S. Department of Justice
Civil Rights Division
Protection of Voting Rights (16.104)
Voting Section
Washington, DC 20530 Phone: (202)633-2019
Deborah Burstion-Wade, Contact

Types of Assistance: Provision of specialized services. **Applicant Eligibility:** All U.S. citizens of voting age. **Beneficiary Eligibility:** Same as above. **Range and Average of Financial Assistance:** Not applicable.

★2952★
U.S. Department of Justice
Community Relations Service (16.200)
Washington, DC 20530 Phone: (301)492-5929

Types of Assistance: Provision of specialized services. **Applicant Eligibility:** Any person, group, community, or State or local governmental unit that seeks to alleviate tensions related to race, color, or national origin may be considered for CRS assistance. **Beneficiary Eligibility:** Same as above. **Range and Average of Financial Assistance:** Not applicable.

★2953★
U.S. Department of Labor
Employment Standards Administration
Non-discrimination and Affirmative Action By Federal Contractors and Federal Contractors Assisted Construction Contractors (17.301)
Office of Federal Contract Compliance Programs
Washington, DC 20210 Phone: (202)523-9475

Types of Assistance: Dissemination of technical information and investigation of complaints. **Applicant Eligibility:** Complaints against Federal contractors and federally assisted construction contractors which allege class-type employment discrimination on the basis of race, sex, religion, or national origin may be filed. **Beneficiary Eligibility:** Employees, former employees, or applicants with a Government contractor or federally involved contractor, including construction contractors. **Range and Average of Financial Assistance:** Not applicable.

★2954★
U.S. Department of Transportation
Urban Mass Transportation Administration
Human Resource Programs (20.511)
Dir. of Civil Rights
400 7th St., SW, Rm. 7412
Washington, DC 20590 Phone: (202)366-4018

Types of Assistance: Project grants (cooperative agreements) and dissemination of technical information. **Applicant Eligibility:** Grants and cooperative agreements; public bodies, State and local agencies, other legally constituted public agencies, institutions of higher learning, nonprofit institutions; Contracts: the same as for grants and cooperative agreements, as well as for-profit business endeavors. **Beneficiary Eligibility:** All public and private sector bodies and organizations, universities, and individuals. **Range and Average of Financial Assistance:** None established.

★2955★
U.S. Equal Employment Opportunity Commission
Employment Discrimination - Equal Pay Act (30.010)
Office of Communications & Legislative Affairs
Public Information Unit
1801 L St., NW
Washington, DC 20507 Phone: 800-872-3362

Types of Assistance: Advisory services and counseling; investigation of complaints. **Applicant Eligibility:** Individuals who believe they have been paid in violation of the Equal Pay Act or who believe that other persons are being paid in violation of the Act in any State or the United States, the District of Columbia, or any territory or possession of the United States. **Beneficiary Eligibility:** Individuals covered by the Fair Labor Standards Act of 1938, as amended. **Range and Average of Financial Assistance:** Not applicable.

★2956★
U.S. Equal Employment Opportunity Commission
Employment Discrimination - Private Bar Program (30.005)
1801 L St., NW
Washington, DC 20507 Phone: (202)663-4780
Johnnie L. Johnson Jr., Sr. Trial Attorney

Types of Assistance: Provision of specialized services. **Applicant Eligibility:** Any individual who has received a notice of right to sue from the Commission. **Beneficiary Eligibility:** Same as above. **Range and Average of Financial Assistance:** Not applicable.

★2957★
U.S. Equal Employment Opportunity Commission
Employment Discrimination - State and Local Anti-discrimination Agency Contracts (30.002)
Program Development & Coordination Division
Systemic Investigation & Individual Compliance Programs
1801 L St., NW, Rm. 8054
Washington, DC 20507 Phone: (202)663-4862
Robert L. Walker, Contact

Types of Assistance: Direct payments for specified use. **Applicant Eligibility:** Official State and local government agencies charged with the administration and enforcement of fair employment practices laws. **Beneficiary Eligibility:** Employees, potential employees, and former employees covered by Title VII of the Civil Rights Act of 1964 as amended, or the Age of Discrimination in Employment Act of 1967. **Range and Average of Financial Assistance:** $9,640.00 to $1,776,000.00; $228,718.00.

★2958★
U.S. Equal Employment Opportunity Commission
Employment Discrimination - Title VII of the Civil Rights Act of 1964 (30.001)
Public Information Unit
Office of Communications & Legislative Affairs
1801 L St., NW
Washington, DC 20507 Phone: 800-USA-EEOC

Types of Assistance: Investigation of complaints. **Applicant Eligibility:** Any aggrieved individual or individuals, labor union, association, legal representative, or unincorporated organization, filing on behalf of an aggrieved individual who has reason to believe that an unlawful employment practice within the meaning of Title VII, as amended, has been committed by an employer with more than 15 employees, employment agency, labor organization, or joint labor-management committee. **Beneficiary Eligibility:** Potential employees, employees and former employees of the named respondents in a charge who have been subject to unlawful employment practices. **Range and Average of Financial Assistance:** Not applicable.

★2959★
U.S. General Services Administration
Business Services (39.001)
Office of Small & Disadvantaged Business Utilization
Washington, DC 20405 Phone: (202)566-1021

Types of Assistance: Advisory services and counseling. **Applicant Eligibility:** Any business concern is eligible. **Beneficiary Eligibility:** Business concerns. **Range and Average of Financial Assistance:** Not applicable.

★2960★
U.S. Office of Personnel Management
Federal Employment for Disadvantaged Youth - Part-time (27.003)
Research & Development Division
Office of Affirmative Recruiting & Employment
Career Entry & Employment Development Group
1900 E St., NW
Washington, DC 20415 Phone: (202)632-0604
Yolanda Wilson, Contact

Types of Assistance: Federal employment. **Applicant Eligibility:** Disadvantaged young people 16 years of age and older; must be accepted for or enrolled in an accredited secondary school or institution of higher learning and pursuing an education no higher than a baccalaureate level; maintain an acceptable school standing; and meet the financial need criterion of the program which is divided into income levels based upon the Federal Poverty Level. **Beneficiary Eligibility:** Disadvantaged youth 16 years of age and older. **Range and Average of Financial Assistance:** Not applicable.

★2961★
U.S. Office of Personnel Management
Federal Employment for Disadvantaged Youth - Summer (27.004)
Office of Affirmative Recruiting & Employment
Career Entry & Employee Development Group
1900 E St., NW
Washington, DC 20415 Phone: (202)632-0604

Types of Assistance: Federal employment. **Applicant Eligibility:** Youth must meet the program's economic needs criteria, which are divided into income levels based upon the Federal Poverty Level. **Beneficiary Eligibility:** Disadvantaged youth 16 years of age and older. **Range and Average of Financial Assistance:** Not applicable.

★2962★
U.S. Small Business Administration
Management and Technical Assistance for Socially and Economically Disadvantaged Businesses (59.007)
Assoc. Admin. for Minority Small Businesses
1441 L St., NW, Rm. 602
Washington, DC 20416 Phone: (202)653-6407

Types of Assistance: Project grants (cooperative agreements). **Applicant Eligibility:** State and local governments, education institutions, public or private organizations that have the capability to provide the necessary assistance. **Beneficiary Eligibility:** Businesses or potential businesses which are economically and socially disadvantaged, or participants in the 8(a) program. **Range and Average of Financial Assistance:** $1,800.00 to $388,000.00; $78,620.00.

★2963★
U.S. Small Business Administration
Minority Business Development - Procurement Assistance (59.006)
Office of AA/MSBDCOD
1441 L St., NW, Rm. 602
Washington, DC 20416 Phone: (202)653-6407

Types of Assistance: Provision of specialized services. **Applicant Eligibility:** Qualification as a socially and economically disadvantaged person on the basis of clear and convincing evidence. **Beneficiary Eligibility:** Socially and economically disadvantaged individuals. **Range and Average of Financial Assistance:** Not applicable.

★2964★
U.S. Small Business Administration
Small Business Investment Companies (59.011)
Dir., Office of Investment
1441 L St., NW
Washington, DC 20416 Phone: (202)653-6584

Types of Assistance: Direct loans, guaranteed and insured loans, and advisory services and counseling. **Applicant Eligibility:** Any chartered small business investment company having a combined paid-in capital and paid-in surplus of not less than $1,000,000.00 having qualified management, and giving evidence of sound operation, and establishing the need for SBIC financing in the geographic area in which the applicant proposes to operate. **Beneficiary Eligibility:** Individual businesses (single proprietorship, partnership, or corporation) which satisfy the established criteria of a small business. MESBICs beneficiary must also be a business owned and operated by socially or economically disadvantaged individuals. **Range and Average of Financial Assistance:** Guarantee loans: $50,000.00 to $35,000,000.00; $1,000,000.00.

(12) STATE AND LOCAL GOVERNMENT AGENCIES

Entries in this chapter are arranged alphabetically within states. See the User's Guide at the front of this directory for additional information.

Alabama

★2965★
Alabama Attorney General
Civil Rights Division
11 S. Union St.
Montgomery, AL 36130 Phone: (205)242-7300
Milt Belcher, Dir.

★2966★
Alabama Department of Public Health
Division of Primary Care and Minority Health
434 Monroe St.
Montgomery, AL 36130 Phone: (205)242-2807
Sharon Rose, Dir.

★2967★
Alabama Employment Service
Industrial Relations Dept.
Work Incentive Program
649 Monroe St.
Mobile, AL 36130 Phone: (205)242-8003

Alaska

★2968★
Alaska Department of Administration
Personnel and Equal Employment Opportunity Office
PO Box CE
Juneau, AK 99811 Phone: (907)465-3570
David Otto, Dir.

★2969★
Alaska Office of the Governor
Human Rights Commission
800 A St., Ste. 202
Anchorage, AK 99501-3628 Phone: (907)276-7474
Paula Haley, Exec.Dir.

Arizona

★2970★
Arizona Attorney General
Civil Rights Division
1275 W. Washington
Phoenix, AZ 85007 Phone: (602)542-5263
Philip A. Austin, Dir.

★2971★
Arizona Department of Administration
Affirmative Action Office
1700 W. Washington
State Capitol, WW, Rm. 104
Phoenix, AZ 85007 Phone: (602)542-3711
Brenda J. Smith, Dir.

★2972★
Arizona Department of Commerce
Community Block Grant
3800 N. Central
Phoenix, AZ 85012 Phone: (602)280-1300
Rivco Knox, Dir.

★2973★
Arizona Department of Health Services
Affirmative Action Office
1740 W. Adams
Phoenix, AZ 85007 Phone: (602)542-1030
David Goldberg, Dir.

★2974★
Arizona Department of Health Services
Office of Planning and Health Status Monitoring
1740 W. Adams St., Rm. 312
Phoenix, AZ 85007 Phone: (602)542-1216
Stan Kliner, Chief Planner

★2975★
Maricopa County Social Services Department
3335 W. Durango St.
Phoenix, AZ 85009 Phone: (602)261-5911

★2976★
Phoenix Economic Security Department
Equal Employment Opportunity Office
550 W. Washington St.
Phoenix, AZ 85003 Phone: (602)262-7716

★2977★
Phoenix Equal Opportunity Department
Affirmative Action Department
Minority Business Enterprise Program
550 W. Washington St.
Phoenix, AZ 85003 Phone: (602)262-6790

★2978★
Phoenix Equal Opportunity Department
Community Relations Committee
Fair Housing Services
550 W. Washington St.
Phoenix, AZ 85003 Phone: (602)261-8242

★2979★
Scottsdale Human Resources Department
7575 E. Main St.
Scottsdale, AZ 85251 Phone: (602)994-2491

★2980★
Tucson Civil Rights Investigations
Human Relations Division
110 E. Pennington
Tucson, AZ 85701 Phone: (602)791-4593
Robert McKnight, Dir.

★2981★
Tucson Minority Business Enterprise
110 E. Pennington
PO Box 27210
Tucson, AZ 85726 Phone: (602)791-4593
Wayne Casper, Dir.

Arkansas

★2982★
Arkansas Corrections Department
Equal Employment Opportunity Grievance Office
PO Box 8707
Pine Bluff, AR 71611 Phone: (501)247-1800
Jane Manning, Dir.

★2983★
Arkansas Education Department
Affirmative Action
Bldg. 4, Capitol Mall
Little Rock, AR 72201-1071 Phone: (501)682-4204
Fred Dawson, Dir.

★2984★
Arkansas Industrial Development Commission
Minority Business Division
1 Capitol Mall
Little Rock, AR 72201 Phone: (501)682-5060
James Hall, Dir.

California

★2985★
California Community Colleges
Civil Rights Office
1107 9th St., Ste. 600
Sacramento, CA 95814 Phone: (916)327-5491
Nancy Davenport, Dir.

★2986★
California Department of Health Services
Primary Health Services Development Program
714 P St., Rm. 599
Sacramento, CA 95814 Phone: (916)322-1355
Arthur E. Jordan, Chief

★2987★
California Education Department
Affirmative Action Office
PO Box 944272
Sacramento, CA 94244-2720 Phone: (916)322-9636
Sharon Felix, Dir.

★2988★
California Fair Employment and Housing Department
322 W. 1st St.
Los Angeles, CA 90802 Phone: (213)620-2610

★2989★
California Health and Welfare Agency
1600 9th St., Rm. 450
Sacramento, CA 95814 Phone: (916)445-6951

★2990★
California Health and Welfare Agency
Employment Development Department
Equal Employment Opportunity Office
800 Capitol Mall
PO Box 826880
Sacramento, CA 95814 Phone: (916)445-7777
Roberto Gracia, Dir.

★2991★
California Health and Welfare Agency
Mental Health Department
Affirmative Action Division
1600 9th St., Rm. 151
Sacramento, CA 95814 Phone: (916)323-9163
Olivia Cortez, Dir.

★2992★
California State and Consumer Services Agency
Fair Employment and Housing Commission
1390 Market St., Ste. 410
San Francisco, CA 94102 Phone: (415)557-1180
Steve Owyang, Dir.

★2993★
California State and Consumer Services Agency
Small and Minority Business Office
1808 14th St., Ste. 100
Sacramento, CA 95814 Phone: (916)322-1847
Alice Flissinger, Chief

★2994★
California State and Consumer Services Agency
State Personnel Board
Affirmative Action and Merit Oversight Division
PO Box 944201
Sacramento, CA 94244-2010 Phone: (916)322-1436
Laura Aguilera, Dir.

★2995★
California Work Incentive Program
1925 Brush
Oakland, CA 94612 Phone: (415)464-0484

Colorado

★2996★
Colorado Department of Health
Alcohol and Drug Abuse Division
4210 E. 11th Ave.
Denver, CO 80220 Phone: (303)331-6530
Linda Garrett, Minority Resource Information Specialist

★2997★
Colorado Regulatory Agencies Department
Civil Rights Division
1525 Sherman St., Rm. 110
Denver, CO 80203 Phone: (303)866-2621
Jack Langymarquez, Dir.

Connecticut

★2998★
Connecticut Human Rights and Opportunities Commission
90 Washington St.
Hartford, CT 06106 Phone: (203)566-4895
Lewis Martin, Dir.

Delaware

★2999★
Delaware Community Affairs Department
Human Relations Division
820 N. French St.
Wilmington, DE 19801 Phone: (302)571-3485
Andrew J. Turner Jr., Dir.

★3000★
Delaware Labor Department
Industrial Affairs Division
Discrimination Review Board
820 N. French St.
Wilmington, DE 19801 Phone: (302)577-2877
John F. Kirk Jr., Dir.

★3001★
Delaware Transportation Department
Equal Employment Opportunity and Civil Rights Officer
Transportation Administration Bldg.
PO Box 778
Dover, DE 19903 Phone: (202)739-4359
Willie Jones, Dir.

District of Columbia

★3002★
District of Columbia Arts and Humanities Commission
Human Rights and Minority Business Opportunity Commission
2000 14th St., NW
Washington, DC 20009 Phone: (202)939-8740
Loretta S. Caldwell, Dir.

★3003★
District of Columbia Arts and Humanities Commission
Human Rights Commission
1350 Pennsylvania Ave., NW, Rm. 202
Washington, DC 20004 Phone: (202)727-0656
Patricia Grace Smith, Chair

★3004★
District of Columbia Human Services Department
801 N. Capitol St., NE
Washington, DC 20002 Phone: (202)727-0310
Dr. Robert A. Washington, Dir.

★3005★
District of Columbia Human Services Department
Social Services Commission
801 N. Capitol St., NE
Washington, DC 20002 Phone: (202)727-5930
Barbara Burke Tatum, Dir.

Florida

★3006★
Florida Administration Department
Human Relations Commission
325 John Knox Rd.
Tallahassee, FL 32301 Phone: (904)488-7082
Ronald McElrath, Dir.

★3007★
Florida Health and Rehabilitative Services Department
Civil Rights Office
1317 Winewood Blvd.
Tallahassee, FL 32399-0700 Phone: (904)487-1901
Melvin Herring, Dir.

★3008★
Hillsborough County Equal Opportunity Office
412 Madison, Ste. 1200
Tampa, FL 33602 Phone: (813)272-5969
Spencer Albert, Dir.

★3009★
Jacksonville Purchasing Department
Minority Business Coordinator
220 E. Bay St., Rm. 301
Jacksonville, FL 32202 Phone: (904)630-1165
Connell Heyward, Dir.

★3010★
Tampa Administration Department
Equal Employment Opportunity Office
306 E. Jackson St.
Tampa, FL 33602 Phone: (813)223-8192

Georgia

★3011★
Georgia Fair Employment Practices Office
156 Trinity Ave., SW, Ste. 208
Atlanta, GA 30303 Phone: (404)656-1736
Carla A. Ford, Admin.

Hawaii

★3012★
Hawaii Human Services Department
PO Box 339
Honolulu, HI 96809 Phone: (808)548-6260
Winona E. Rubin, Dir.

★3013★
Hawaii Labor and Industrial Relations Department
Equal Employment Opportunity Office
830 Punchbowl St.
Honolulu, HI 96813 Phone: (808)548-4533
Alice Hong, Dir.

★3014★
Hawaii Office of the Governor
Affirmative Action Coordinator
5th Fl. State Capitol
Honolulu, HI 96813 Phone: (808)548-3432

Idaho

★3015★
Idaho Human Rights Commission
450 W. State St.
Boise, ID 83720 Phone: (208)334-2873
Marilyn T. Shuler, Dir.

Illinois

★3016★
Illinois Central Management Services Department
Minority and Female Business Enterprises Office
715 William Stratton Bldg.
Springfield, IL 62706 Phone: (217)814-4190
Sharon Matthews, Dir.

★3017★
Illinois Commerce and Community Affairs Department
Equal Employment Opportunity and Affirmative Action
620 E. Adams
Springfield, IL 62701 Phone: (217)785-7360
Victoria Benn, Dir.

★3018★
Illinois Department of Public Health
Office of Health Services
Center for Health Promotion
525 W. Jefferson, 3rd Fl.
Springfield, IL 62761 Phone: (217)785-2060
Shirley Randolph, Deputy Dir.

★3019★
Illinois Employment Security Department
Equal Employment Opportunity/Affirmative Action Office
401 S. State St.
Chicago, IL 60605 Phone: (312)793-4305
Juliette Hurtz, Dir.

★3020★
Illinois Human Rights Department
100 W. Randolph, Ste. 10-100
Chicago, IL 60601 Phone: (312)814-6245
Rosemary Bombela, Dir.

★3021★
Illinois Revenue Department
Equal Employment Opportunity Office
101 W. Jefferson
Springfield, IL 62708 Phone: (217)782-4708
Sherry Meady, Dir.

★3022★
Illinois Secretary of State
Affirmative Action Officer
213 Capitol Bldg.
Springfield, IL 62756 Phone: (217)782-3405

Indiana

★3023★
Indiana Administration Department
Minority Business Development Division
Indiana Government Center, S.
402 W. Washington St., Ste. W-461
Indianapolis, IN 46204 Phone: (317)232-3061

★3024★
Indiana Civil Rights Commission
32 E. Washington St., Ste. 900
Indianapolis, IN 46204 Phone: (317)232-2612
Karen M. Freeman, Dir.

★3025★
Indiana Employment and Training Services Department
Equal Employment Opportunity and Compliance Secretary
10 N. Senate Ave., Rm. 103
Indianapolis, IN 46204 Phone: (317)232-7482
David Shaheed, Dir.

★3026★
Indiana Human Services Department
ISTA Bldg.
PO Box 7083
Indianapolis, IN 46207 Phone: (317)232-1139
Jeff Richardson, Dir.

★3027★
Indiana State Board of Health
Bureau of Family Health Services
Interagency Council on Black and Minority Health
1330 W. Michigan St., Rm. 232
Indianapolis, IN 46206 Phone: (317)633-0683
Valarie Rochester, Minority Health Consultant

★3028★
Indianapolis Equal Opportunity Division
129 E. Market St., Ste. 300
Indianapolis, IN 46204 Phone: (317)236-5262
Robert Ransom, Dir.

Iowa

★3029★
Iowa Attorney General
Civil Rights Division
Hoover State Office Bldg., 2nd Fl.
Des Moines, IA 50319 Phone: (515)281-4121
Teresa Baustian, Dir.

★3030★
Iowa Civil Rights Commission
Grimes Bldg., 2nd Fl.
211 E. Maple St.
Des Moines, IA 50319 Phone: (515)281-4121
Lone G. Shaddock, Exec.Dir.

★3031★
Iowa Human Rights Department
Lucas State Office Bldg.
321 12th St.
Des Moines, IA 50319 Phone: (515)281-5960
Almo Hawkins, Dir.

★3032★
Iowa Human Rights Department
Status of Blacks Division
Lucas State Office Bldg.
321 12th St.
Des Moines, IA 50319 Phone: (515)281-7283
Gary Lawson, Admin.

★3033★
Iowa Human Services Department
Equal Opportunity and Affirmative Action Bureau
Hoover State Office Bldg., 5th St.
Des Moines, IA 50319 Phone: (515)281-6090
Barb Oliver Hall, Dir.

Kansas

★3034★
Kansas Administration Department
Equal Employment Opportunity Division
Rm. 263-E, State Capitol
Topeka, KS 66612 Phone: (913)296-4278
Clyde Howard, Dir.

★3035★
Kansas Civil Rights Commission
900 SW Jackson St., Ste. 851-S
Topeka, KS 66612-1258 Phone: (913)296-3206
Joanne Hurst, Exec.Dir.

★3036★
Kansas Commerce Department
Minority Business Office
400 SW 8th St., 5th Fl.
Topeka, KS 66603 Phone: (913)296-2954
Tony Augusto, Dir.

★3037★
Kansas Human Resources Department
401 Topeka Ave.
Topeka, KS 66603 Phone: (913)296-7474
Michael L. Johnston, Sec.

★3038★
Kansas Human Resources Department
Equal Employment Opportunity Office
401 Topeka Ave.
Topeka, KS 66603 Phone: (913)296-5233
Hobart Hayes, Dir.

★3039★
Kansas Social and Rehabilitation Services Department
Civil Rights/Equal Employment Opportunity Office
Docking State Office Bldg.
Topeka, KS 66612 Phone: (913)296-4766
Gene Wilson, Dir.

Kentucky

★3040★
Kentucky Economic Development Cabinet
Minority Business Development Division
Capitol Plaza Tower
Frankfort, KY 40601 Phone: (502)564-2064
Floyd C. Taylor, Dir.

★3041★
Kentucky Human Rights Commission
832 Capital Plaza Tower
Frankfort, KY 40601 Phone: (502)564-3550
Leonard W. Clark, Exec.Dir.

★3042★
Kentucky Human Rights Commission
Louisville Office
332 W. Broadway
PO Box 69
Louisville, KY 40201 Phone: (502)588-4024
John Kelsey, Compliance Dir.

★3043★
Kentucky Justice Cabinet
Minority Recruitment Division
417 High St.
Frankfort, KY 40601 Phone: (502)564-6712
Jane Driskell, Dir.

★3044★
Kentucky Transportation Cabinet
Minority Affairs and Equal Employment Opportunity Office
State Office Bldg.
Frankfort, KY 40622 Phone: (502)564-3601
Bill Colfield, Dir.

Louisiana

★3045★
Kenner Office of the Mayor
Minority Affairs
2000 18th St.
Kenner, LA 70062 Phone: (504)468-7295
Joseph James, Dir.

★3046★
Louisiana Office of the Governor
Minority Business Development Office
PO Box 94095
Baton Rouge, LA 70804 Phone: (504)342-5373
Angelisa Harris, Dir.

★3047★
Louisiana Social Services Department
Civil Rights Division
PO Box 3776
Baton Rouge, LA 70821-1532 Phone: (504)342-0286
George Clark, Dir.

★3048★
New Orleans Human Resources Policy and Planning Administrative UnitHuman Rights
1300 Perdido St.
City Hall Rm. 1W-06
New Orleans, LA 70112 Phone: (504)565-7120
Tommie Lockhart, Dir.

Maine

★3049★
Maine Human Rights Commission
State House Sta. 51
Augusta, ME 04333 Phone: (207)289-2326
Patricia Ryan, Exec.Dir.

★3050★
Maine Transportation Department
Equal Opportunity Secretary
State House Sta. 16
Augusta, ME 04333-0016 Phone: (207)289-3576
Jane Gilbert, Dir.

Maryland

★3051★
Baltimore City Housing Authority
Fair Housing and Equal Opportunity
417 E. Fayette St.
Baltimore, MD 21202 Phone: (301)396-3246
Dr. Robert Hearn, Commissioner

★3052★
Baltimore Social Services Department
1510 Guilford Ave.
Baltimore, MD 21202 Phone: (301)361-2222

★3053★
Maryland Department of Health and Mental Hygiene
Public Health Service
201 W. Preston St., Rm. 519A
Baltimore, MD 21201 Phone: (301)225-6541
Leslie McMillan, Coord. of Special Progs.

★3054★
Maryland Economic and Employment Development Department
Equal Employment Opportunity Office
217 E. Redwood St., Ste. 1123
Baltimore, MD 21202 Phone: (301)333-6626
Dale Webb, Dir.

★3055★
Maryland Education Department
Equal Opportunity Office
200 W. Baltimore St.
Baltimore, MD 21201 Phone: (301)333-2228
Woodrow Grant, Dir.

★3056★
Maryland Higher Education Commission
Equal Educational Division
16 Francis St., Jeffrey Bldg.
Annapolis, MD 21401 Phone: (301)974-2971

★3057★
Maryland Human Relations Commission
20 E. Franklin St.
Baltimore, MD 21202 Phone: (301)333-1715
Jennifer Burdick, Exec.Dir.

★3058★
Maryland Human Resources Department
Equal Opportunity Division
311 W. Saratoga St.
Baltimore, MD 21201 Phone: (301)333-0350
Harry Hamrick, Dir.

☆3059★
Maryland Personnel Department
Equal Opportunity Officer
301 W. Preston St.
Baltimore, MD 21201 Phone: (301)225-4792
Celeste Morgan, Dir.

Massachusetts

★3060★
Arlington Civil Rights Committee
c/o Ruth Ann Putnam
116 Winchester Rd.
Arlington, MA 02174 Phone: (617)646-3387
Ruth Ann Putnam, Pres.

★3061★
Boston Fair Housing Office
Boston City Hall, Rm. 957
Boston, MA 02201 Phone: (617)725-4408

★3062★
Cambridge Affirmative Action Office
795 Massachusetts Ave.
Cambridge, MA 02139 Phone: (617)349-4332

★3063★
Massachusetts Administration and Finance Executive Office
Affirmative Action Central Regional Office
455 Main St.
City Hall
Worcester, MA 01608 Phone: (508)799-1186

★3064★
Massachusetts Administration and Finance Executive Office
Affirmative Action Office
1 Ashburton Pl., Rm. 303
Boston, MA 02108 Phone: (617)727-7441
Linda Lynn-Weaver, Dir.

★3065★
Massachusetts Administration and Finance Executive Office
Boston Commission Against Discrimination
1 Ashburton Pl., 6th Fl.
Boston, MA 02108 Phone: (617)727-3990

★3066★
Massachusetts Administration and Finance Executive Office
Personnel Administration Department
Equal Employment Practices Office
1 Ashburton Pl., Rm. 213
Boston, MA 02108 Phone: (617)727-3777
Eugene H. Rooney Jr., Dir.

★3067★
Massachusetts Administration and Finance Executive Office
Revenue Department
Affirmative Action Bureau
100 Cambridge St., Rm. 806
Boston, MA 02204 Phone: (617)727-0193
Virginia Johnson, Dir.

★3068★
Massachusetts Administration and Finance Executive Office
Springfield Commission Against Discrimination
145 State St., Rm. 506
Springfield, MA 01103 Phone: (413)739-2145

★3069★
Massachusetts Attorney General
Civil Rights and Civil Liberties Division
1 Ashburton Pl., Rm. 2010
Boston, MA 02108 Phone: (617)727-2200
Richard Cole, Dir.

★3070★
Massachusetts Bay Transportation Authority
Affirmative Action and Equal Employment Opportunity Division
10 Park Plaza, Rm. 4810
Boston, MA 02116 Phone: (617)722-3305
Mary A. Fernandes, Dir.

★3071★
Massachusetts Economic Affairs Executive Office
Minority Business Development Division
100 Cambridge St., 13th Fl.
Boston, MA 02202 Phone: (617)727-3220
Jose Perez, Asst. Sec.

★3072★
Massachusetts Education Equity Department
1385 Hancock St.
Quincy, MA 02169 Phone: (617)770-7530

★3073★
Massachusetts Human Services Executive Office
Corrections Department
Affirmative Action Office
100 Cambridge St.
Boston, MA 02202 Phone: (617)727-1238
Carole Montalto, Dir.

★3074★
Massachusetts Minority Business Development and Employment Office
State Office of Minority and Women Business Assistance
100 Cambridge St., 13th Fl.
Boston, MA 02202 Phone: (617)727-3220
Mukiya Baker-Gomez, Asst.

★3075★
Massachusetts Office of Personnel Management
Affirmative Action Program
City Hall Plaza, Rm. 612
1 City Hall Square
Boston, MA 02201 Phone: (617)725-3361
Roscoe Marvis, Dir.

Michigan

★3076★
Michigan Attorney General
Civil Rights Division
PO Box 30212
Lansing, MI 48909 Phone: (313)256-2557
Robert Willis, Dir.

★3077★
Michigan Civil Rights Department
303 W. Kalamazoo, 4th Fl.
Lansing, MI 48913 Phone: (517)335-3165
John Roy Castillo, Dir.

★3078★
Michigan Civil Rights Department
Minority/Woman Business Certification
State Plaza Bldg.
1200 6th Ave.
Detroit, MI 48226 Phone: (313)335-3165
Winifred Avery, Dir.

★3079★
Michigan Department of Public Health
Office of Minority Health
3423 Martin Luther King Blvd.
Box 30195
Lansing, MI 48909 Phone: (517)335-9287
Cheryl Anderson-Small, Chief

★3080★
Michigan Social Services Department
Affirmative Action and Equal Opportunity Office
235 S. Grand Ave.
Lansing, MI 48909 Phone: (517)373-8520
James Newsom, Dir.

Minnesota

★3081★
Minneapolis Civil Rights Department
350 S. 5th St.
City Hall, Rm. 239
Minneapolis, MN 55415 Phone: (612)673-3012
Emma Hixson, Dir.

★3082★
Minneapolis Community Development Agency
331 2nd Ave., S. Ste. 600
Minneapolis, MN 55401 Phone: (612)348-7100

★3083★
Minnesota Attorney General
Human Rights Division
State Capitol Bldg., Rm. 102
75 Constitution Ave.
St. Paul, MN 55155 Phone: (612)296-9412
Carl Warren, Dir.

★3084★
Minnesota Education Department
Affirmative Action Office
Capitol Square Bldg.
550 Cedar St.
St. Paul, MN 55101 Phone: (612)296-0342

★3085★
Minnesota Employee Relations Department
Equal Opportunity Division
3rd Fl., 520 Lafayette Rd.
St. Paul, MN 55155 Phone: (612)296-8272
Elsa Vega-Perez, Dir.

★3086★
Minnesota Human Rights Department
500 Bremer Tower
7th Pl. & Minnesota
St. Paul, MN 55101 Phone: (612)296-5665
Pamela B. Kelly, Commissioner

★3087★
Minnesota Human Rights Department
Equal Employment Opportunity Commission Office
500 Bremer Tower
7th Pl. & Minnesota
St. Paul, MN 55101 Phone: (612)296-9061
Karen Ferguson, Dir.

★3088★
Minnesota Human Services Department
Affirmative Action Office
444 Lafayette Rd.
St. Paul, MN 55155 Phone: (612)296-3510
Mary Jean Anderson, Dir.

★3089★
Minnesota Human Services Department
Civil Rights Office
444 Lafayette Rd.
St. Paul, MN 55155 Phone: (612)296-4638
Roberto Reyna, Dir.

★3090★
Minnesota Jobs and Training Department
Affirmative Action Office
390 N. Robert St.
St. Paul, MN 55101 Phone: (612)296-1823
Linda Sloan, Dir.

Mississippi

★3091★
Mississippi Human Services Department
421 W. Pascagoula
Jackson, MS 39203 Phone: (601)960-4246
Bea Branch, Commissioner

★3092★
Mississippi Office of the Governor
Health and Human Services Specialist Assistant
PO Box 139
Jackson, MS 39215 Phone: (601)359-3100
Jesse Buie, Dir.

★3093★
Mississippi State Department of Health
Office of Health Education and Health Promotion
2423 N. State St.
PO Box 1700
Jackson, MS 39215 Phone: (601)960-7499
Ellen Jones, Dir.

Missouri

★3094★
Missouri Administration Office
Affirmative Action Office
PO Box 809
Jefferson City, MO 65102 Phone: (314)751-1856
Jacqueline Lester, Dir.

★3095★
Missouri Administration Office
Minority Business Development Commission
PO Box 809
Jefferson City, MO 65102 Phone: (314)751-2249
Mark Miller, Dir.

★3096★
Missouri Department of Health
Office of Minority Health
1738 E. Elm St.
PO Box 570
Jefferson City, MO 65102 Phone: (314)751-6064
Jacquelin Horton, Chief

★3097★
Missouri Housing Development Commission
Human Rights Commission
3770 Broadway
Kansas City, MO 64111 Phone: (816)756-4126

★3098★
Missouri Labor and Industrial Relations Department
Human Rights Commission
315 Ellis Blvd.
PO Box 1129
Jefferson City, MO 65102 Phone: (314)751-3325
Alvin A. Plummer, Exec.Dir.

★3099★
St. Louis Civil Rights Enforcement Agency
Civil Courts Bldg., 10 N.
St. Louis, MO 63101 Phone: (314)622-3301

★3100★
St. Louis Human Resources Department
121 S. Merrimac
St. Louis, MO 63105 Phone: (314)889-3453

Montana

★3101★
Montana Labor and Industry Department
Human Rights Division
PO Box 1728
Helena, MT 59624 Phone: (406)444-2884
Ann MacIntyre, Dir.

Nebraska

★3102★
Nebraska Equal Opportunity Commission
PO Box 94934
Lincoln, NE 68509 Phone: (402)471-2024
Lawrence R. Myers, Exec.Dir.

Nevada

★3103★
Nevada Equal Rights Commission
1515 E. Tropicana Ave., Ste. 590
Las Vegas, NV 89109 Phone: (702)486-7161
Delia E. Martinez, Exec.Dir.

★3104★
Nevada Human Resources Department
505 E. King St., Rm. 600
Carson City, NV 89710 Phone: (702)687-4400
Jerry Griepentrog, Dir.

New Hampshire

★3105★
New Hampshire Human Rights Commission
163 Louden Rd.
Concord, NH 03301 Phone: (603)271-2767
Raymond S. Perry Jr., Exec.Dir.

New Jersey

★3106★
New Jersey Commerce and Economic Development Department
Minority Business Enterprise
20 W. State St., CN 820
Trenton, NJ 08625-0820 Phone: (609)292-0500
Shakira Abdul-Ali, Dir.

★3107★
New Jersey Commerce and Economic Development Department
Small, Minority, and Women-Owned Business Development Office
CN 820, 20 W. State St.
Trenton, NJ 08625-0820 Phone: (609)292-3860
Leland S. McGee, Dir.

★3108★
New Jersey Human Services Department
Economic Assistance Division
6 Quacker Bridge Plaza
CN716
Trenton, NJ 08625 Phone: (609)588-2401
Marion Reitz, Dir.

★3109★
New Jersey Law and Public Safety Department
Civil Rights Division
1100 Raymond Blvd., Rm. 400
Newark, NJ 07102-0860 Phone: (201)648-2700
C. Gregory Stewart, Dir.

★3110★
New Jersey Personnel Department
Equal Employment Opportunity Affirmative Action Division
44 S. Clinton Ave.
Trenton, NJ 08625 Phone: (609)777-0919
Howard Woodson, Dir.

★3111★
New Jersey State Legislature Senate
Institutions, Health and Welfare Committee
State House Annex CN-068
Trenton, NJ 08625 Phone: (609)292-1646
Eleanor Seel, Chair

★3112★
New Jersey Transit Corporation
Civil Rights Division
PO Box 10009
Newark, NJ 07101 Phone: (201)643-4323
Alvin Stokes, Dir.

New Mexico

★3113★
Albuquerque Affirmative Action Office
Minority Business Enterprises
PO Box 1293
Albuquerque, NM 87103 Phone: (505)768-3540

★3114★
New Mexico Labor Department
Human Rights Division
1596 Pacheco St.
Santa Fe, NM 87501 Phone: (505)827-6838
Lenton Malry, Exec.Dir.

New York

★3115★
New York Agriculture and Markets Department
Affirmative Action Program
Capital Plaza
1 Winners Circle
Albany, NY 12235 Phone: (518)457-2737
James Burnes, Dir.

★3116★
New York Alcoholism and Alcohol Abuse Division
Affirmative Action Bureau
194 Washington Ave.
Albany, NY 12210 Phone: (518)474-5418
Henry Gonzales, Dir.

★3117★
New York Committee to Improve Minority Health by the Year 2000
Harlem Hospital Center
506 Lennox Ave.
New York, NY 10037 Phone: (212)491-1234
Warren Dandridge, Dir. of Public Relations

★3118★
New York Division of Human Rights
Albany Regional Office
PO Box 7063
State Office Bldg.
Albany, NY 12225 Phone: (518)474-2705
Carol Praylor, Dir.

★3119★
New York Division of Human Rights
Binghamton Regional Office
State Office Bldg. Annex
164 Hawley St.
Binghamton, NY 13901 Phone: (607)773-7713
John H. Peterson, Dir.

★3120★
New York Division of Human Rights
Buffalo Regional Office
65 Court St., Ste. 506
Buffalo, NY 14202 Phone: (716)847-7632
Richard E. Clark, Dir.

★3121★
New York Division of Human Rights
Nassau County Regional Office
100 Main St.
Hempstead, NY 11550 Phone: (516)538-1360
Ralph Seskine, Dir.

★3122★
New York Division of Human Rights
New York City (Brooklyn-Staten Island) Regional Office
555 Hanson Pl.
Brooklyn, NY 11217 Phone: (718)260-2856
Susanna Moquette, Reg. Coord.

★3123★
New York Division of Human Rights
New York City (Lower Manhattan) Regional Office
State Office Bldg., 9th Fl.
270 Broadway
New York, NY 10007 Phone: (212)417-5041
John A. Cooper, Dir.

North Carolina

★3124★
North Carolina Department of Environment, Health and Natural Resources
State Health Director's Office
PO Box 27867
Raleigh, NC 27611-7687 Phone: (919)733-4984
Phillys Gray, Special Asst.

★3125★
North Carolina Office of the Governor
Human Relations Council
121 W. Jones St.
Raleigh, NC 27603 Phone: (919)733-7996
Jim Stowe, Dir.

★3126★
North Carolina State Personnel Office
Equal Employment Opportunity Services Division
116 W. Jones St.
Raleigh, NC 27603-8004 Phone: (919)733-0205
Nelly Riley, Dir.

North Dakota

★3127★
North Dakota Human Services Department
600 E. Blvd.
State Capitol
Bismarck, ND 58505 Phone: (701)224-2310
John A. Graham, Exec.Dir.

Ohio

★3128★
Cleveland Human Services Department
Office of Human Resources
Equal Employment Opportunity Division
30 E. Broad St.
Columbus, OH 43266-0423 Phone: (216)466-2455

★3129★
Ohio Administrative Services Department
Equal Employment Opportunity Division
65 E. State St., 8th Fl.
Columbus, OH 43266 Phone: (614)466-8380
Gilbert Price, Deputy Dir.

★3130★
Ohio Attorney General
Civil Rights Section
50 W. Broad St.
Columbus, OH 43215 Phone: (614)466-7900
Sherrie Passmore, Chief

★3131★
Ohio Civil Rights Commission
Columbus Chapter
220 Parsons Ave.
Cleveland, OH 43206-0543 Phone: (614)466-2785
Joseph Carmichaels, Exec.Dir.

★3132★
Ohio Commerce Department
Equal Employment Opportunity Office
77 S. High St., 23rd Fl.
Columbus, OH 43266-0544 Phone: (614)466-3636
Joyce Frazier, Dir.

★3133★
Ohio Commission on Minority Health
Vern Risse Government Center
77 S. High St., Ste. 745
Columbus, OH 43266-0377 Phone: (614)466-4000
Cheryl Boyce, Exec.Dir.

★3134★
Ohio Education Department
Equal Employment Opportunity Division
65 S. Front St.
Columbus, OH 43266-0308 Phone: (614)466-3304
Hazel Flowers, Dir.

★3135★
Ohio Employment Services Bureau
Affirmative Action Office
145 S. Front St.
Columbus, OH 43216 Phone: (614)481-5797

★3136★
Ohio Industrial Relations Department
Equal Employment Opportunity Office
2323 W. 5th Ave.
PO Box 825
Columbus, OH 43266 Phone: (614)644-2229
Lynnette Riley, Dir.

★3137★
Ohio Natural Resources Department
Contract Compliance and Equal Employment Opportunity Office
Fountain Square
Columbus, OH 43224-1387 Phone: (614)265-6872
Phyllis Hart, Dir.

Oklahoma

★3138★
Oklahoma Education Department
Human Relations Services
2500 N. Lincoln Blvd.
Oklahoma City, OK 73105 Phone: (405)521-2841
Annette Murphy, Dir.

★3139★
Oklahoma Employment Security Commission
Equal Employment Opportunity Office
2401 N. Lincoln Blvd.
Oklahoma City, OK 73105 Phone: (405)557-7255
Barbara Williams, Dir.

★3140★
Oklahoma Health Department
Affirmative Action Division
1000 NE 10th St.
PO Box 53551
Oklahoma City, OK 73152 Phone: (405)271-4171
Charles Smith, Dir.

★3141★
Oklahoma Human Rights Commission
2101 N. Lincoln Blvd., Rm. 480
Oklahoma City, OK 73105 Phone: (405)521-3441
Ronald L. Johnson, Dir.

★3142★
Oklahoma State Department of Health
1000 NE 10th St.
PO Box 53551
Oklahoma City, OK 73152 Phone: (405)271-4026
Patricia Hawkins, Aministrative Officer

Oregon

★3143★
Oregon Human Resources Department
Affirmative Action Unit
417 Public Service Bldg.
Salem, OR 97310 Phone: (503)378-3687
Linda Topping, Personnel Officer

★3144★
Oregon Labor and Industries Bureau
Civil Rights Division
1400 SW 5th Ave., Ste. 409
Portland, OR 97201 Phone: (503)229-6600
Raleigh Lewis, Dir.

★3145★
Oregon Office of the Governor
Affirmative Action Director
State Capitol Bldg., Rm. 254
Salem, OR 97310 Phone: (503)378-5336
Jeanne Pai, Dir.

★3146★
Oregon State Health Division
Department of Human Services
Field Services Section
508 State Office Bldg.
1400 SW 5th Ave.
PO Box 231
Portland, OR 97207 Phone: (503)229-5691
Barbara Taylor, Minority Health Coord.

★3147★
Oregon Transportation Department
Civil Rights Section
135 Transportation Bldg.
Salem, OR 97310 Phone: (503)378-8077
Harold Lasley, Dir.

Pennsylvania

★3148★
Allegheny County Welfare Rights Organizations
1835 Centre Ave.
Pittsburgh, PA 15219 Phone: (412)471-0180

★3149★
Pennsylvania Commerce Department
Bureau of Minority Business Development
1400 Spring Garden St.
Philadelphia, PA 17120 Phone: (215)560-3236
Karim A. Nalik, Reg. Rep.

★3150★
Pennsylvania Commerce Department
Minority Business Development Authority
404 Forum Bldg.
Harrisburg, PA 17120 Phone: (717)783-1127
Aquid Sabur, Dir.

★3151★
Pennsylvania Corrections Department
Affirmative Action Office
PO Box 598
Camp Hill, PA 17011 Phone: (717)975-4906
Eugene Smith, Dir.

★3152★
Pennsylvania General Services Department
Minority Construction Information Center
210 S. Bouquet St.
Pittsburgh, PA 15213 Phone: (412)565-2365

★3153★
Pennsylvania General Services Department
Minority Development Office
Rm. 515, N. Office Bldg.
Harrisburg, PA 17125 Phone: (717)787-7629
Brenda Blake, Dir.

★3154★
Pennsylvania Human Relations Commission
PO Box 3145
Harrisburg, PA 17105 Phone: (717)787-4410
Homer Floyd, Exec.Dir.

★3155★
Pennsylvania Human Relations Commission
Harrisburg Regional Office
Uptown Shopping Center
2971E N. 7th St.
Harrisburg, PA 17110 Phone: (717)787-9780
Howard L. Tucker Jr., Reg. Dir.

★3156★
Pennsylvania Human Relations Commission
Philadelphia Regional Office
711 State Office Bldg.
1400 Spring Garden St.
Philadelphia, PA 19130 Phone: (215)560-2496
Sandra Holman Bacote, Reg. Dir.

★3157★
Pennsylvania Human Relations Commission
Pittsburgh Regional Office
State Office Bldg., Ste. 1100
300 Liberty Ave.
Pittsburgh, PA 15222 Phone: (412)565-5395
George A. Simmons, Reg. Dir.

★3158★
Pennsylvania Minority Business Enterprise Council
1401 Arch St.
Philadelphia, PA 19102 Phone: (215)686-6372

★3159★
Pennsylvania Office of the Governor
Administration Office
Affirmative Action Bureau
207 Finance Bldg.
Harrisburg, PA 17120 Phone: (717)783-1130
Richard James, Dir.

★3160★
Pennsylvania Public Welfare Department
Affirmative Action Office
PO Box 2675
Harrisburg, PA 17105 Phone: (717)787-3336
Mary Majors, Dir.

Rhode Island

★3161★
Rhode Island Administration Department
Equal Opportunity Office
1 Capitol Hill
Providence, RI 02908 Phone: (401)277-3090
A. Vincent Igliozzi, Dir.

★3162★
Rhode Island Human Rights Commission
10 Abbott Park Pl.
Providence, RI 02903 Phone: (401)277-2661
Margurita Beaubien, Chair

South Carolina

★3163★
South Carolina Department of Health and Environmental Control
Office of Minority Health
c/o Division of Maternal Health
2600 Bull St.
Columbia, SC 29201 Phone: (803)737-4000
Gardenia Ruff, Dir.

★3164★
South Carolina Health and Human Services Finance Commission
PO Box 8206
Columbia, SC 29202-8206 Phone: (803)253-6100
Eugene A. Laurent, Dir.

★3165★
South Carolina Human Affairs Commission
PO Box 11009
Columbia, SC 29211 Phone: (803)253-6336
James E. Clyburn, Commissioner

South Dakota

★3166★
South Dakota Commerce and Regulations Department
Human Rights Division
910 E. Sioux
State Capitol
Pierre, SD 57501 Phone: (605)773-4493
Beth Pay, Dir.

★3167★
South Dakota Personnel Bureau
Equal Employment Opportunity
500 E. Capitol
Pierre, SD 57501 Phone: (605)773-4919
Douglas Decker, Dir.

Tennessee

★3168★
Tennessee Department of Economic and Community Development
Minority Business Enterprise Division
320 6th Ave., N., 8th Fl.
Nashville, TN 37243-0405 Phone: (615)741-2545
John Birdsong, Dir.

★3169★
Tennessee Human Rights Commission
226 Capitol Blvd., Ste. 602
Nashville, TN 37243-0745 Phone: (615)741-5825
Warren Moore, Exec.Dir.

★3170★
Tennessee Human Services Department
400 Deaderick St.
Nashville, TN 37248-0001 Phone: (615)741-3241
Robert A. Grunow, Commissioner

Texas

★3171★
Houston Affirmative Action Office
500 Jefferson
Houston, TX 77002 Phone: (713)658-3800

★3172★
Houston Housing and Community Development Office
Fair Housing Section
601 Sawyer St., 4th Fl.
Houston, TX 77002 Phone: (713)868-8480
Annie R. Hill, Admin.

★3173★
Texas Employment Commission
Equal Employment Opportunity Division
Congress & 15th St.
Austin, TX 78778 Phone: (512)475-1173
David Laurel, Dir.

★3174★
Texas Human Services Department
Civil Rights Division
701 W. 51st St.
Box 2960
Austin, TX 78769 Phone: (512)450-3630

Utah

★3175★
Utah Community and Economic Development Department
Black Affairs Division
324 S. State St.
Salt Lake City, UT 84111 Phone: (801)538-8200
Betty Sawyer, Dir.

★3176★
Utah Department of Health
Division of Community Health Services
Ethnic Minority Health Committee Program
288 N. 1460, W.
PO Box 660
Salt Lake City, UT 84116-0660 Phone: (801)538-6305
Mary Ellen Warstler, Coord.

Vermont

★3177★
Vermont Human Rights Commission
PO Box 997
Montpelier, VT 05601 Phone: (802)828-2480
Susan Sussman, Exec.Dir.

Virginia

★3178★
Virginia Administration Office
Personnel and Training Department
Equal Employment Opportunity Services
Monroe Bldg.
101 N. 14th St.
Richmond, VA 23219 Phone: (804)225-3303
George Gardner, Dir.

★3179★
Virginia Department of Health
PO Box 2448
Richmond, VA 23218 Phone: (804)786-3561
Sue Roland, Acting Legislative Liason

★3180★
Virginia Economic Development
Minority Business Enterprises
200-202 9th St. Office Bldg., 11th Fl.
Richmond, VA 23219 Phone: (804)786-5560
Esther Vassar, Dir.

★3181★
Virginia Health and Human Resources Office
Health Department
Equal Employment Opportunity Division
109 Governor St., Rm. 400
Richmond, VA 23219 Phone: (804)225-4059
Vaughn M. Cunningham, Dir.

★3182★
Virginia Health and Human Resources Office
Social Services Department
Civil Rights Coordinator
8007 Discovery Dr.
Richmond, VA 23229-8699 Phone: (804)662-9236

★3183★
Virginia Human Rights Council
PO Box 717
Richmond, VA 23206 Phone: (804)225-2292

Washington

★3184★
King County Affirmative Action
Minority/Women's Business Enterprise
406 S. Water
Olympia, WA 98504 Phone: (206)753-9693

★3185★
King County Office of Civil Rights and Complaints
Fair Employment Office
King County Courthouse, Rm. E-224
516 3rd Ave.
Seattle, WA 98104-2312 Phone: (206)296-7594

★3186★
King County Office of Civil Rights and Complaints
Fair Housing Office
King County Courthouse, Rm. E-224
516 3rd Ave.
Seattle, WA 98104-2312 Phone: (206)296-7652

★3187★
King County Office of Human Resource Management
Affirmative Action
King County Courthosue, Rm. 214
500 4th St.
Seattle, WA 98104 Phone: (206)296-7340

★3188★
Washington Affirmative Action Policy Committee
PO Box 1789, FE-11
Olympia, WA 98507 Phone: (206)753-3758
Roy Standifer, Prog. Admin.

★3189★
Washington Human Rights Commission
711 S. Capitol Way, FJ41
Olympia, WA 98504 Phone: (206)753-6770
Kathryn Friedt, Exec. Sec.

★3190★
Washington Human Rights Commission
Seattle Office
1516 2nd Ave.
Seattle, WA 98101 Phone: (206)464-6500

★3191★
Washington Human Rights Commission
Spokane Office
W. 905 Riverside, Ste. 416
Spokane, WA 99201 Phone: (509)456-4473

★3192★
Washington Human Rights Commission
Yakima Office
32 N. 3rd St., Ste. 441
Yakima, WA 98901 Phone: (509)575-2772

★3193★
Washington Social and Health Services Department
Equal Opportunity Office
MS OB-44
Olympia, WA 98504 Phone: (206)753-4070
Dan Lundsford, Dir.

West Virginia

★3194★
West Virginia Attorney General
Civil Rights Deputy Attorney General
State Capitol 26 E.
Charleston, WV 25305 Phone: (304)348-0546
Mike Kelly, Dir.

★3195★
West Virginia Commerce, Labor, and Environmental Resources Department
Community and Industrial Development
Economic Opportunity Office
1426 Kanawha Blvd., Bldg. E
Charleston, WV 25301 Phone: (304)348-8860
Joe Barker, Dir.

★3196★
West Virginia Commerce, Labor, and Environmental Resources Department
Minority and Small Business Development Agency
1500 Virginia St., E.
Charleston, WV 25301 Phone: (304)348-2960
Eloise Jack, Dir.

★3197★
West Virginia Human Rights Commission
1321 Plaza E. Rm. 104-106
Charleston, WV 25301 Phone: (304)348-2616
Quewannocoii C. Stephens, Exec.Dir.

Wisconsin

★3198★
Wisconsin Employment Relations Department
Affirmative Action Division
PO Box 7855
Madison, WI 53707-7855 Phone: (608)266-3017
Arley Gonnering, Dir.

★3199★
Wisconsin Health and Social Services Department
Affirmative Action/Civil Rights Office
PO Box 7850
Madison, WI 53707 Phone: (608)266-3465
Georgina Taylor, Dir.

★3200★
Wisconsin Industry Labor and Human Relations Department
PO Box 7946
Madison, WI 53707 Phone: (608)266-7552
Carol Skornicka, Sec.

★3201★
Wisconsin Industry Labor and Human Relations Department
Equal Rights Division
PO Box 8928
Madison, WI 53708 Phone: (608)266-0946
Sheehan Donoghue, Admin.

Wyoming

★3202★
Wyoming Employment Security Commission
Equal Employment Opportunity Division
Herschler Bldg., 2nd Fl. E.
Cheyenne, WY 82002 Phone: (307)777-7672
Dean Pratt, Dir.

★3203★
Wyoming Labor Standards/Fair Employment Division
Herschler Bldg., 2nd Fl. E.
Cheyenne, WY 82002 Phone: (307)777-6381
Dave Simonton, Dir.

(13) BUSINESSES (TOP 100 COMPANIES)

Entries in this chapter are listed in descending rank based on total sales. See the User's Guide at the front of this directory for additional information.

★3204★
TLC Beatrice International Holdings, Inc.
99 Wall St., 16th Fl.
New York, NY 10005 Phone: (212)233-5109
Reginald F. Lewis, CEO

Founded: 1987. **Staff:** 5,000. **Type of Business:** Processing and distribution of food products. **1990 Sales (in millions of dollars):** 1496.000. **Current Rank:** 1. **Rank in 1990:** 1.

★3205★
Johnson Publishing Co., Inc.
820 S. Michigan Ave.
Chicago, IL 60605 Phone: (312)322-9200
John H. Johnson, CEO

Founded: 1942. **Staff:** 2,382. **Type of Business:** Publishing; broadcasting; cosmetics; hair-care. **1990 Sales (in millions of dollars):** 252.187. **Current Rank:** 2. **Rank in 1990:** 2.

★3206★
Philadelphia Coca-Cola Bottling Co., Inc.
Erie Ave. & G St.
Philadelphia, PA 19134 Phone: (215)427-4500
J. Bruce Llewellyn, CEO

Founded: 1985. **Staff:** 1,000. **Type of Business:** Soft-drink bottling. **1990 Sales (in millions of dollars):** 251.300. **Current Rank:** 3. **Rank in 1990:** 3.

★3207★
H. J. Russell & Co.
504 Fair St. SW
Atlanta, GA 30313 Phone: (404)330-1000
Herman J. Russell, CEO

Founded: 1958. **Staff:** 668. **Type of Business:** Construction and development; food services. **1990 Sales (in millions of dollars):** 143.295. **Current Rank:** 4. **Rank in 1990:** 4.

★3208★
Soft Sheen Products, Inc.
1000 E. 87th St.
Chicago, IL 60619-6391 Phone: (312)978-0700
Edward G. Gardner, CEO

Founded: 1964. **Staff:** 532. **Type of Business:** Hair-care products manufacturer. **1990 Sales (in millions of dollars):** 92.100. **Current Rank:** 5. **Rank in 1990:** 6.

★3209★
Barden Communications, Inc.
1249 Washington Blvd.
Detroit, MI 48226 Phone: (313)963-5010
Don H. Barden, CEO

Founded: 1981. **Staff:** 308. **Type of Business:** Communications and real estate development. **1990 Sales (in millions of dollars):** 86.000. **Current Rank:** 6. **Rank in 1990:** Not in Top 100.

★3210★
Trans Jones, Inc./Jones Transfer Co.
300 Jones Ave.
Monroe, MI 48161 Phone: (313)241-4120
Gary L. White, CEO

Founded: 1986. **Staff:** 1,189. **Type of Business:** Transportation services. **1990 Sales (in millions of dollars):** 75.000. **Current Rank:** 7. **Rank in 1990:** 7.

★3211★
Garden State Cable TV
1250 Haddonfield-Bekin Rd.
Box 5025
Cherry Hill, NJ 08034 Phone: (609)354-1880
J. Bruce LLewellyn, CEO

Founded: 1989. **Staff:** 300. **Type of Business:** Cable TV broadcasting. **1990 Sales (in millions of dollars):** 74.000. **Current Rank:** 8. **Rank in 1990:** Not in Top 100.

★3212★
Stop Shop and Save
4514 Edmondson Ave.
Baltimore, MD 21229 Phone: (301)233-7152
Henry T. Baines, CEO

Founded: 1978. **Staff:** 600. **Type of Business:** Supermarkets. **1990 Sales (in millions of dollars):** 65.000. **Current Rank:** 9. **Rank in 1990:** Not in Top 100.

★3213★
The Bing Group
1130 W. Grand Blvd.
Detroit, MI 48208 Phone: (313)895-3400
Dave Bing, CEO

Founded: 1980. **Staff:** 173. **Type of Business:** Steel processing and metal stamping operations. **1990 Sales (in millions of dollars):** 61.000. **Current Rank:** 10. **Rank in 1990:** 8.

★3214★
Technology Applications, Inc.
6101 Stevenson Ave.
Alexandria, VA 22304-3599 Phone: (703)461-2000
James I. Chatman, CEO

Founded: 1977. **Staff:** 800. **Type of Business:** Information systems integration. **1990 Sales (in millions of dollars):** 59.739. **Current Rank:** 11. **Rank in 1990:** Not in Top 100.

★3215★
Advanced Consumer Marketing Corp.
810 Burlway Rd.
Burlingame, CA 94010 Phone: (415)340-7134
Harry W. Brooks Jr., CEO

Founded: 1985. **Staff:** 250. **Type of Business:** Information systems integration; mail-order products. **1990 Sales (in millions of dollars):** 51.250. **Current Rank:** 12. **Rank in 1990:** 13.

★3216★
Community Foods, Inc.
336 E. 25th St.
Baltimore, MD 21218 Phone: (301)235-9800
Oscar A. Smith Jr., CEO

Founded: 1970. **Staff:** 430. **Type of Business:** Supermarkets. **1990 Sales (in millions of dollars):** 47.500. **Current Rank:** 13. **Rank in 1990:** 14.

★3217★
The Maxima Corp.
2101 E. Jefferson St.
Rockville, MD 20852 Phone: (301)230-2000
Joshua I. Smith, CEO

Founded: 1978. **Staff:** 785. **Type of Business:** Systems engineering and computer facilities management. **1990 Sales (in millions of dollars):** 45.804. **Current Rank:** 14. **Rank in 1990:** 9.

★3218★
The Thacker Organization
5400 Truman Dr.
Decatur, GA 30035 Phone: (404)981-9820
Floyd G. Thacker, CEO

Founded: 1970. **Staff:** 115. **Type of Business:** Construction and management; engineering. **1990 Sales (in millions of dollars):** 45.600. **Current Rank:** 15. **Rank in 1990:** 17.

★3219★
Crescent Distributing Co., Inc.
5733 Citrus Blvd.
Harahan, LA 70123-1662 Phone: (504)733-8705
Stanley S. Scott, CEO

Founded: 1988. **Staff:** 170. **Type of Business:** Beer distributor. **1990 Sales (in millions of dollars):** 45.250. **Current Rank:** 16. **Rank in 1990:** 15.

★3220★
Network Solutions, Inc.
505 Huntmar Park Dr.
Herndon, VA 22070-5100 Phone: (703)742-0400
Emmit J. McHenry, CEO

Founded: 1979. **Staff:** 450. **Type of Business:** Systems integration. **1990 Sales (in millions of dollars):** 43.000. **Current Rank:** 17. **Rank in 1990:** 11.

★3221★
Granite Broadcasting Corp.
245 E. 47th St.
New York, NY 10017 Phone: (212)826-2530
W. Don Cornwell, CEO

Founded: 1988. **Staff:** 356. **Type of Business:** TV broadcasting. **1990 Sales (in millions of dollars):** 42.614. **Current Rank:** 18. **Rank in 1990:** 18.

★3222★
Essence Communications, Inc.
1500 Broadway, 6th Fl.
New York, NY 10036-4071 Phone: (212)642-0600
Edward Lewis, CEO

Founded: 1969. **Staff:** 80. **Type of Business:** Magazine publishing; TV production; direct-mail catalog. **1990 Sales (in millions of dollars):** 42.392. **Current Rank:** 19. **Rank in 1990:** 19.

★3223★
Integrated Systems Analysts, Inc.
2800 Shirlington Pl., Ste. 1100
Arlington, VA 22206 Phone: (703)824-0700
C. Michael Gooden, CEO

Founded: 1980. **Staff:** 600. **Type of Business:** Engineering; technical support; electronic repair. **1990 Sales (in millions of dollars):** 42.000. **Current Rank:** 20. **Rank in 1990:** 12.

★3224★
Systems Management American Corp.
254 Monticello Ave.
Norfolk, VA 23510-2397 Phone: (804)627-9331
Herman E. Valentine, CEO

Founded: 1970. **Staff:** 273. **Type of Business:** Computer systems integration. **1990 Sales (in millions of dollars):** 40.260. **Current Rank:** 21. **Rank in 1990:** 20.

★3225★
Surface Protection Industries, Inc.
3411 E. 15th St.
Los Angeles, CA 90023-3800 Phone: (213)269-9231
Robert C. Davidson Jr., CEO

Founded: 1978. **Staff:** 175. **Type of Business:** Paint and specialty coatings manufacturer. **1990 Sales (in millions of dollars):** 40.000. **Current Rank:** 22. **Rank in 1990:** 23.

★3226★
Wesley Industries, Inc.
c/o Flint Coatings Inc.
40221 James P. Cole Blvd.
Flint, MI 48505 Phone: (313)787-3077
Delbert W. Mullens, CEO

Founded: 1983. **Staff:** 340. **Type of Business:** Industrial coatings and grey iron foundry products. **1990 Sales (in millions of dollars):** 36.400. **Current Rank:** 23. **Rank in 1990:** 22.

★3227★
Pro-Line Corp.
2121 Panoramic Circle
PO Box 223706
Dallas, TX 75222 Phone: (214)631-4247
Isabel P. Cottrell, CEO

Founded: 1970. **Staff:** 290. **Type of Business:** Hair-care products manufacturer and distributor. **1990 Sales (in millions of dollars):** 35.416. **Current Rank:** 24. **Rank in 1990:** 25.

★3228★
Westside Distributors
2405 Southern Ave.
South Gate, CA 90280 Phone: (213)758-3133
Edison R. Lara Sr., CEO

Founded: 1974. **Staff:** 115. **Type of Business:** Beer and snack foods distributor. **1990 Sales (in millions of dollars):** 35.400. **Current Rank:** 25. **Rank in 1990:** 27.

★3229★
Johnson Products Co., Inc.
8522 S. Lafayette Ave.
Chicago, IL 60620-1301 Phone: (312)483-4100
Eric G. Johnson, CEO

Founded: 1954. **Staff:** 232. **Type of Business:** Hair and personal care products manufacturer. **1990 Sales (in millions of dollars):** 34.000. **Current Rank:** 26. **Rank in 1990:** 24.

★3230★
Beauchamp Distributing Co.
1911 S. Santa Fe Ave.
Compton, CA 90221 Phone: (213)639-5320
Patrick L. Beauchamp, CEO

Founded: 1971. **Staff:** 110. **Type of Business:** Beer distributor. **1990 Sales (in millions of dollars):** 31.600. **Current Rank:** 27. **Rank in 1990:** 28.

★3231★
Brooks Sausage Co., Inc.
4545 S. Racine Ave.
Chicago, IL 60609 Phone: (312)927-4141
Frank B. Brooks, CEO

Founded: 1985. **Staff:** 145. **Type of Business:** Sausage manufacturer. **1990 Sales (in millions of dollars):** 31.100. **Current Rank:** 28. **Rank in 1990:** 39.

★3232★
The Gourmet Companies
c/o Gourmet Services, Inc.
1100 Spring St., Ste. 450
Atlanta, GA 30367 Phone: (404)876-5700
Nathaniel R. Goldston III, CEO

Founded: 1975. **Staff:** 1,395. **Type of Business:** Food service management. **1990 Sales (in millions of dollars):** 30.210. **Current Rank:** 29. **Rank in 1990:** 32.

★3233★
Calhoun Enterprises
810 W. South Blvd.
Montgomery, AL 36105 Phone: (205)288-2996
Greg Calhoun, CEO

Founded: 1984. **Staff:** 520. **Type of Business:** Supermarkets. **1990 Sales (in millions of dollars):** 30.000. **Current Rank:** 30. **Rank in 1990:** Not in Top 100.

★3234★
Superb Manufacturing, Inc.
1200 Woodland St.
Detroit, MI 48211 Phone: (313)867-3700
Dave Bing, CEO

Founded: 1985. **Staff:** 130. **Type of Business:** Automotive parts supplier. **1990 Sales (in millions of dollars):** 28.400. **Current Rank:** 31. **Rank in 1990:** 43.

★3235★
Orchem, Inc.
10925 Reed Hartman Hwy.
Cincinnati, OH 45242 Phone: (513)984-0990
Oscar Robertson, CEO

Founded: 1981. **Staff:** 55. **Type of Business:** Specialty chemicals manufacturer. **1990 Sales (in millions of dollars):** 27.000. **Current Rank:** 32. **Rank in 1990:** 34.

★3236★
Commonwealth Holding Co., Inc.
361 W. 125th St.
New York, NY 10027 Phone: (212)749-0900
James H. Dowdy, CEO

Founded: 1967. **Staff:** 286. **Type of Business:** Real estate and manufacturing. **1990 Sales (in millions of dollars):** 26.900. **Current Rank:** 33. **Rank in 1990:** 30.

★3237★
Trumark, Inc.
1820 Sunset St.
Lansing, MI 48917 Phone: (517)482-0795
Carlton L. Guthrie, CEO

Founded: 1985. **Staff:** 205. **Type of Business:** Metal stampings and products manufacturer; welding. **1990 Sales (in millions of dollars):** 26.400 **Current Rank:** 34. **Rank in 1990:** 29.

★3238★
Parks Sausage Co.
3330 Park Circle Dr.
Baltimore, MD 21215 Phone: (301)664-5050
Raymond V. Haysbert Sr., CEO

Founded: 1951. **Staff:** 245. **Type of Business:** Sausage manufacturer. **1990 Sales (in millions of dollars):** 26.037. **Current Rank:** 35. **Rank in 1990:** 40.

★3239★
Queen City Broadcasting, Inc.
30 Rockefeller Plaza, 29th Fl.
New York, NY 10112 Phone: (212)698-7700
J. Bruce Llewellyn, CEO

Founded: 1985. **Staff:** 160. **Type of Business:** TV broadcasting. **1990 Sales (in millions of dollars):** 26.000. **Current Rank:** 36. **Rank in 1990:** 34.

★3240★
Yancy Minerals
1768 Litchfield Tpke.
Woodbridge, CT 06525 Phone: (203)624-8067
Earl J. Yancy, CEO

Founded: 1977. **Staff:** 8. **Type of Business:** Industrial metals, minerals and coal distributor. **1990 Sales (in millions of dollars):** 25.840. **Current Rank:** 37. **Rank in 1990:** 15.

★3241★
Crest Computer Supply
7855 Gross Point Rd., Ste. H-1
Skokie, IL 60077 Phone: (708)982-1030
Gale Sayers, CEO

Founded: 1984. **Staff:** 45. **Type of Business:** Computer hardware and software supplier. **1990 Sales (in millions of dollars):** 25.000. **Current Rank:** 38. **Rank in 1990:** 48.

★3242★
Inner City Broadcasting Corp.
801 2nd Ave.
New York, NY 10017 Phone: (212)953-0300
Pierre Sutton, CEO

Founded: 1972. **Staff:** 200. **Type of Business:** Radio, TV and cable TV broadcasting. **1990 Sales (in millions of dollars):** 25.000. **Current Rank:** 38. **Rank in 1990:** 26.

★3243★
Summa-Harrison Metal Products, Inc.
401 S. Lafayette
Royal Oak, MI 48067 Phone: (313)548-1210
Charlie J. Harrison Jr., CEO

Founded: 1978. **Staff:** 170. **Type of Business:** Engineering and metal stampings manufacturer. **1990 Sales (in millions of dollars):** 25.000 **Current Rank:** 38. **Rank in 1990:** Not in Top 100.

★3244★
H. F. Henderson Industries, Inc.
45 Fairfield Plaza
West Caldwell, NJ 07006-6202 Phone: (201)227-9250
Henry F. Henderson Jr., CEO

Founded: 1954. **Staff:** 181. **Type of Business:** Industrial process controls and defense electronics. **1990 Sales (in millions of dollars):** 24.100. **Current Rank:** 41. **Rank in 1990:** 37.

★3245★
Restoration Supermarket Corp.
1360 Fulton St.
Brooklyn, NY 11216 Phone: (718)636-6900
Roderick B. Mitchell, CEO

Founded: 1977. **Staff:** 116. **Type of Business:** Supermarket and drugstore. **1990 Sales (in millions of dollars):** 24.000. **Current Rank:** 42. **Rank in 1990:** 38.

★3246★
Regal Plastics Co., Inc.
15700 Common Rd.
PO Box 246
Roseville, MI 48066 Phone: (313)772-7120
William F. Pickard, CEO

Founded: 1985. **Staff:** 250. **Type of Business:** Custom plastic ejection molding. **1990 Sales (in millions of dollars):** 22.369. **Current Rank:** 43. **Rank in 1990:** Not in Top 100.

★3247★
National Capital Systems, Inc.
5205 Leesburg Pike, Ste. 400
Falls Church, VA 22041-3898 Phone: (703)671-3360
Sy O. Smith, CEO

Founded: 1976. **Staff:** 260. **Type of Business:** ADP professional services; health care. **1990 Sales (in millions of dollars):** 22.000. **Current Rank:** 44. **Rank in 1990:** Not in Top 100.

★3248★
Input Output Computer Services, Inc.
400 Totten Pond Rd.
Waltham, MA 02254 Phone: (617)890-2299
Thomas A. Farrington, CEO

Founded: 1969. **Staff:** 200. **Type of Business:** Computer software and systems integrations. **1990 Sales (in millions of dollars):** 21.000. **Current Rank:** 45. **Rank in 1990:** 44.

★3249★
African Development Public Investment Corp.
1635 N. Cahuenga Blvd.
Hollywood, CA 90028 Phone: (213)461-0390
Dick Griffey, CEO

Founded: 1985. **Staff:** 8. **Type of Business:** African commodities and air charter service. **1990 Sales (in millions of dollars):** 20.550. **Current Rank:** 46. **Rank in 1990:** 52.

★3250★
Dick Griffey Productions
1635 N. Cahuenga Blvd.
Hollywood, CA 90028 Phone: (213)461-0390
Dick Griffey, CEO

Founded: 1975. **Staff:** 74. **Type of Business:** Entertainment. **1990 Sales (in millions of dollars):** 20.000. **Current Rank:** 47. **Rank in 1990:** 10.

★3251★
Viking Enterprises Corp.
4027 N. Kedzie Ave.
Chicago, IL 60618 Phone: (312)588-4300
Fletcher E. Allen, CEO

Founded: 1990. **Staff:** 170. **Type of Business:** Color separations and commercial printing. **1990 Sales (in millions of dollars):** 20.000. **Current Rank:** 47. **Rank in 1990:** Not in Top 100.

★3252★
Delta Enterprises, Inc.
819 Main St.
PO Box 588
Greenville, MS 38701 Phone: (601)335-5291
Harold L. Hall, CEO

Founded: 1969. **Staff:** 300. **Type of Business:** Electronics, railroad parts, apparel, and lumber manufacturer. **1990 Sales (in millions of dollars):** 19.500. **Current Rank:** 49. **Rank in 1990:** 36.

★3253★
Dual & Associates, Inc.
2101 Wilson Blvd., Ste. 600
Arlington, VA 22201 Phone: (703)527-3500
J. Fred Dual Jr., CEO

Founded: 1983. **Staff:** 210. **Type of Business:** Engineering and technical services. **1990 Sales (in millions of dollars):** 19.339. **Current Rank:** 50. **Rank in 1990:** Not in Top 100.

★3254★
Simmons Enterprises
c/o Simmons Carvel Insurance Agency
7781 Cooper Rd.
Cincinnati, OH 45242 Phone: (513)791-4446
Carvel E. Simmons, CEO

Founded: 1970. **Staff:** 80. **Type of Business:** Insurance, daycare, and trucking. **1990 Sales (in millions of dollars):** 19.250. **Current Rank:** 51. **Rank in 1990:** 42.

★3255★
Accurate Information Systems, Inc.
3000 Hadley Rd.
South Plainfield, NJ 07080 Phone: (201)754-7714
Stephen Yelity, CEO

Founded: 1983. **Staff:** 110. **Type of Business:** Software development and systems integration. **1990 Sales (in millions of dollars):** 18.300. **Current Rank:** 52. **Rank in 1990:** 67.

★3256★
Bronner Brothers
600 Truseo Way SW
Atlanta, GA 30310 Phone: (404)577-4321
Nathaniel Bronner Sr., CEO

Founded: 1947. **Staff:** 250. **Type of Business:** Hair-care products manufacturer. **1990 Sales (in millions of dollars):** 18.200. **Current Rank:** 53. **Rank in 1990:** 46.

★3257★
V-Tech, Inc.
270 E. Bonita Ave.
Pomona, CA 91767 Phone: (714)596-7741
James E. Parker, CEO

Founded: 1982. **Staff:** 248. **Type of Business:** Biomedical test products manufacturer. **1990 Sales (in millions of dollars):** 18.000. **Current Rank:** 54. **Rank in 1990:** 51.

★3258★
Metters Industries, Inc.
8200 Greensboro Dr., Ste. 500
McLean, VA 22102 Phone: (703)821-3300
Samuel Metters, CEO

Founded: 1981. **Staff:** 303. **Type of Business:** Systems engineering; computer science; telecommunications. **1990 Sales (in millions of dollars):** 16.960. **Current Rank:** 55. **Rank in 1990:** Not in Top 100.

★3259★
Telephone Advertising Corp. of America, Inc.
6 Piedmont Center, Ste. 610
Atlanta, GA 30305 Phone: (404)261-1038
Herbert H. Hamlett Sr., CEO

Founded: 1988. **Staff:** 16. **Type of Business:** Advertising kiosks for telephone companies. **1990 Sales (in millions of dollars):** 16.832. **Current Rank:** 56. **Rank in 1990:** Not in Top 100.

★3260★
Keys Group Co.
23828 W. 7 Mile
Detroit, MI 48219 Phone: (313)533-5397
Brady Keys Jr., CEO

Founded: 1967. **Staff:** 1,400. **Type of Business:** Fast food. **1990 Sales (in millions of dollars):** 16.100. **Current Rank:** 57. **Rank in 1990:** 45.

★3261★
Earl G. Graves, Ltd.
130 5th Ave., 10th Fl.
New York, NY 10011-4306 Phone: (212)242-8000
Earl G. Graves, CEO

Founded: 1970. **Staff:** 62. **Type of Business:** Magazine publishing. **1990 Sales (in millions of dollars):** 16.000. **Current Rank:** 58. **Rank in 1990:** 50.

★3262★
Williams-Russell and Johnson, Inc.
771 Spring St., NW
Atlanta, GA 30308 Phone: (404)853-6800
Pelham C. Williams CEO

Founded: 1976. **Staff:** 210. **Type of Business:** Construction and waste management; engineering. **1990 Sales (in millions of dollars):** 15.300. **Current Rank:** 59. **Rank in 1990:** 68.

★3263★
C. H. James & Co.
PO Box 10170, Sta. C
Charleston, WV 25357 Phone: (304)744-1531
Charles H. James III, CEO

Founded: 1883. **Staff:** 25. **Type of Business:** Wholesale food distribution. **1990 Sales (in millions of dollars):** 15.056. **Current Rank:** 60. **Rank in 1990:** 73.

★3264★
Terry Manufacturing Co., Inc.
924 South St.
PO Box 648
Roanoke, AL 36274-0648 Phone: (205)863-2171
Roy D. Terry, CEO

Founded: 1963. **Staff:** 280. **Type of Business:** Apparel manufacturing. **1990 Sales (in millions of dollars):** 15.000. **Current Rank:** 61. **Rank in 1990:** Not in Top 100.

★3265★
Mandex, Inc.
8003 Forbes Pl.
Springfield, VA 22151 Phone: (703)321-0200
Carl A. Brown, CEO

Founded: 1974. **Staff:** 270. **Type of Business:** Telecommunications, computer and engineering services. **1990 Sales (in millions of dollars):** 14.961. **Current Rank:** 62. **Rank in 1990:** 47.

★3266★
American Development Corp.
1930 Hanahan Rd.
North Charleston, SC 29406-2068 Phone: (803)572-0010
W. Melvin Brown Jr., CEO

Founded: 1972. **Staff:** 187. **Type of Business:** Manufacturing and sheet metal fabrication. **1990 Sales (in millions of dollars):** 14.819. **Current Rank:** 63. **Rank in 1990:** 33.

★3267★
Burns Enterprises
1631 W. Hill St.
Louisville, KY 40210 Phone: (502)585-4548
Tommie Burns Jr., CEO

Founded: 1969. **Staff:** 450. **Type of Business:** Janitorial services; light manufacturing and supermarkets. **1990 Sales (in millions of dollars):** 14.800 **Current Rank:** 64. **Rank in 1990:** 61.

★3268★
Consolidated Beverage Corp.
235 W. 154th St.
New York, NY 10039 Phone: (212)926-5865
Albert N. Thompson, CEO

Founded: 1978. **Staff:** 20. **Type of Business:** Wholesaler; Caribbean exporter and bottler. **1990 Sales (in millions of dollars):** 14.500. **Current Rank:** 65. **Rank in 1990:** 57.

★3269★
Powers & Sons Construction Co., Inc.
2636 W. 15th Ave.
Gary, IN 46404 Phone: (219)944-3000
Mamon Powers Sr., CEO

Founded: 1967. **Staff:** 60. **Type of Business:** Construction. **1990 Sales (in millions of dollars):** 14.464. **Current Rank:** 66. **Rank in 1990:** 54.

★3270★
Ozanne Construction Co., Inc.
1635 E. 25th St.
Cleveland, OH 44114 Phone: (216)696-2876
Leroy Ozanne, CEO

Founded: 1956. **Staff:** 40. **Type of Business:** General construction and management. **1990 Sales (in millions of dollars):** 14.000. **Current Rank:** 67. **Rank in 1990:** Not in Top 100.

★3271★
James T. Heard Management Corp.
16627 S. Valley View Ave.
Cerritos, CA 90703 Phone: (213)926-2293
Lonear Heard, CEO

Founded: 1971. **Staff:** 490. **Type of Business:** Fast food. **1990 Sales (in millions of dollars):** 13.965. **Current Rank:** 68. **Rank in 1990:** 55.

★3272★
Am-Tech Export Trading Co., Inc.
Detroit, MI
Robert E. Ellis Sr., CEO

Efforts to locate an address for this edition were unsuccessful. **Founded:** 1984. **Staff:** 14. **Type of Business:** High technology products and systems engineering services. **1990 Sales (in millions of dollars):** 13.600. **Current Rank:** 69. **Rank in 1990:** Not in Top 100.

★3273★
TEM Associates, Inc.
1900 Powell St.
Emeryville, CA 94608 Phone: (415)655-6576
Berah D. McSwain, CEO

Founded: 1981. **Staff:** 150. **Type of Business:** Technical, management and computer support services. **1990 Sales (in millions of dollars):** 13.400 **Current Rank:** 70. **Rank in 1990:** 58.

★3274★
Systems Engineering & Management Associates, Inc.
5205 Leesburg Pike
Falls Church, VA 22041 Phone: (703)486-0440
James C. Smith, CEO

Founded: 1985. **Staff:** 194. **Type of Business:** ADP technical support services. **1990 Sales (in millions of dollars):** 13.250. **Current Rank:** 71. **Rank in 1990:** 95.

★3275★
A Minority Entity, Inc.
PO Box 117
Norco, LA 70079 Phone: (504)764-2422
Burnell K. Molerie, CEO

Founded: 1978. **Staff:** 1,000. **Type of Business:** Janitorial and food services; temporary employment services. **1990 Sales (in millions of dollars):** 12.939. **Current Rank:** 72. **Rank in 1990:** 69.

★3276★
Carter Industrial Services, Inc.
2501 Fairview
Anderson, IN 46016 Phone: (317)644-6601
Will J. Carter, CEO

Founded: 1976. **Staff:** 241. **Type of Business:** Shipping containers repair and trucking. **1990 Sales (in millions of dollars):** 12.586. **Current Rank:** 73. **Rank in 1990:** 76.

★3277★
Best Foam Fabricators, Inc.
9633 S. Cottage Grove
Chicago, IL 60628 Phone: (312)721-1006
Keith A. Hasty, CEO

Founded: 1981. **Staff:** 105. **Type of Business:** Corrugated boxes and cushioning materials manufacturer. **1990 Sales (in millions of dollars):** 12.500. **Current Rank:** 74. **Rank in 1990:** 81.

★3278★
NBN Broadcasting & Companies
463 7th Ave.
New York, NY 10018-7604 Phone: (212)714-1000
Sydney L. Small, CEO

Founded: 1973. **Staff:** 105. **Type of Business:** Radio broadcasting and telephone communications. **1990 Sales (in millions of dollars):** 12.500. **Current Rank:** 74. **Rank in 1990:** 61.

★3279★
Management Assistance Corp. of America
8600 Boeing
PO Box 4856
El Paso, TX 79914 Phone: (915)772-4975
Louise E. Johnson, CEO

Founded: 1979. **Staff:** 190. **Type of Business:** High technology and technical support services. **1990 Sales (in millions of dollars):** 12.000. **Current Rank:** 76. **Rank in 1990:** 66.

★3280★
Stephens Engineering Co., Inc.
6301 Ivy Ln.
Greenbelt, MD 20770 Phone: (301)220-0470
Wallace O. Stephens, CEO

Founded: 1979. **Staff:** 120. **Type of Business:** Systems integration, facility and computer maintenance. **1990 Sales (in millions of dollars):** 12.000. **Current Rank:** 76. **Rank in 1990:** Not in Top 100.

★3281★
Eltrex Industries
65 Sullivan St.
Rochester, NY 14605 Phone: (716)423-5960
Matthew Augustine, CEO

Founded: 1968. **Staff:** 155. **Type of Business:** Office products distribution; printing and custom packaging. **1990 Sales (in millions of dollars):** 11.950. **Current Rank:** 78. **Rank in 1990:** 80.

★3282★
Williams & Richardson Co., Inc.
660 Woodward Ave., Ste. 1625
Detroit, MI 48226 Phone: (313)961-5590
Eddie C. Williams Sr., CEO

Founded: 1978. **Staff:** 40. **Type of Business:** General contracting and construction management. **1990 Sales (in millions of dollars):** 11.500. **Current Rank:** 79. **Rank in 1990:** 41.

★3283★
Black River Manufacturing, Inc.
2625 20th St.
Port Huron, MI 48060 Phone: (313)982-9812
Isaac Lang Jr., CEO

Founded: 1977. **Staff:** 87. **Type of Business:** Auto parts supplier. **1990 Sales (in millions of dollars):** 11.400. **Current Rank:** 80. **Rank in 1990:** 72.

★3284★
Ellis Electronics, Inc.
Detroit, MI
Robert E. Ellis Sr., CEO

Efforts to locate an address for this edition were unsuccessful. **Founded:** 1984. **Staff:** 24. **Type of Business:** Environmental engineering development; defense research and development. **1990 Sales (in millions of dollars):** 11.400. **Current Rank:** 80. **Rank in 1990:** Not in Top 100.

★3285★
Drew Pearson Enterprises, Inc.
15006 Beltway Dr.
Addison, TX 75001 Phone: (214)702-8055
Drew Pearson, CEO

Founded: 1985. **Staff:** 16. **Type of Business:** Sports licensing and sportswear manufacturer. **1990 Sales (in millions of dollars):** 11.257. **Current Rank:** 82. **Rank in 1990:** 74.

★3286★
Texcom, Inc.
4550 Forbes Blvd.
Lanham, MD 20706 Phone: (301)794-8836
Clemon H. Wesley, CEO

Founded: 1981. **Staff:** 93. **Type of Business:** Telecommunication services. **1990 Sales (in millions of dollars):** 10.774. **Current Rank:** 83. **Rank in 1990:** 49.

★3287★
Burrell Communications Group
20 N. Michigan Ave., Ste. 300
Chicago, IL 60602-4899 Phone: (312)443-8600
Thomas J. Burrell, CEO

Founded: 1971. **Staff:** 120. **Type of Business:** Advertising; public relations; consumer promotions. **1990 Sales (in millions of dollars):** 10.684. **Current Rank:** 84. **Rank in 1990:** 71.

★3288★
Specialized Packaging International, Inc.
100 Crown St.
New Haven, CT 06510 Phone: (203)777-8561
Carlton L. Highsmith, CEO

Founded: 1983. **Staff:** 6. **Type of Business:** Packaging design and engineering consulting. **1990 Sales (in millions of dollars):** 10.680. **Current Rank:** 85. **Rank in 1990:** 78.

★3289★
Watiker & Son, Inc.
1233 Maple Ave.
Zanesville, OH 43701 Phone: (614)454-7958
Al Watiker Jr., CEO

Founded: 1973. **Staff:** 130. **Type of Business:** Heavy construction and mine reclamation. **1990 Sales (in millions of dollars):** 10.538. **Current Rank:** 86. **Rank in 1990:** 64.

★3290★
Production Dynamics of Chicago, Inc.
1339 S. Michigan Ave.
Chicago, IL 60605 Phone: (312)939-3220
Charlie Banks, CEO

Founded: 1985. **Staff:** 10. **Type of Business:** Wholesale electrical, industrial and contractor supplier. **1990 Sales (in millions of dollars):** 10.425. **Current Rank:** 87. **Rank in 1990:** 86.

★3291★
Correction Connection, Inc.
2227 Bryn Mawr Ave.
Philadelphia, PA 19131 Phone: (215)578-3100
Larry D. Depte, CEO

Founded: 1987. **Staff:** 30. **Type of Business:** Health products manufacturer. **1990 Sales (in millions of dollars):** 10.100. **Current Rank:** 88. **Rank in 1990:** 74.

★3292★
Highbeam Business Systems, Inc.
280 S. Harrison St.
East Orange, NJ 07018-1398 Phone: (201)673-2800
Henry E. Davis Jr., CEO

Founded: 1978. **Staff:** 115. **Type of Business:** Business equipment dealership. **1990 Sales (in millions of dollars):** 10.100 **Current Rank:** 88. **Rank in 1990:** 53.

★3293★
Jet-A-Way, Inc.
123 Magazine St.
PO Box 861
Roxbury, MA 02119 Phone: (617)288-7131
Eddie Jeter, CEO

Founded: 1969. **Staff:** 56. **Type of Business:** Rubbish removal and material recycling. **1990 Sales (in millions of dollars):** 10.000. **Current Rank:** 90. **Rank in 1990:** Not in Top 100.

★3294★
Universal Software, Inc.
28260 Franklin Rd.
Southfield, MI 48034 Phone: (313)356-7890
Shirley F. Moulton, CEO

Founded: 1983. **Staff:** 28. **Type of Business:** Computer reseller; imaging; networks. **1990 Sales (in millions of dollars):** 10.000. **Current Rank:** 90. **Rank in 1990:** Not in Top 100.

★3295★
Michael Alan Lewis Co.
17816 Washington St.
Union, IL 60180 Phone: (815)923-2127
Wayne Embry Sr., CEO

Founded: 1978. **Staff:** 86. **Type of Business:** Automotive interior trim components manufacturer. **1990 Sales (in millions of dollars):** 9.880 **Current Rank:** 92. **Rank in 1990:** 82.

★3296★
RPM Supply Co., Inc.
621 N. 2nd St.
Philadelphia, PA 19123 Phone: (215)627-7106
Robert P. Mapp, CEO

Founded: 1977. **Staff:** 19. **Type of Business:** Electrical and electronic distributor. **1990 Sales (in millions of dollars):** 9.820. **Current Rank:** 93. **Rank in 1990:** Not in Top 100.

★3297★
Apex Construction Co., Inc.
61 Arborway
PO Box 255
Boston, MA 02130 Phone: (617)524-7300
Jack E. Robinson, CEO

Founded: 1983. **Staff:** 230. **Type of Business:** General construction. **1990 Sales (in millions of dollars):** 9.700. **Current Rank:** 94. **Rank in 1990:** 94.

★3298★
William Cargile Contractor, Inc.
2008 Freeman Ave.
Cincinnati, OH 45214 Phone: (513)381-2442
William Cargile III, CEO

Founded: 1956. **Staff:** 63. **Type of Business:** Construction; real estate development. **1990 Sales (in millions of dollars):** 9.700. **Current Rank:** 94. **Rank in 1990:** 96.

★3299★
The Mingo Group
228 E. 45th St.
New York, NY 10017 Phone: (212)697-4515
Samuel J. Chisholm, CEO

Founded: 1977. **Staff:** 45. **Type of Business:** Advertising; public relations; marketing communications. **1990 Sales (in millions of dollars):** 9.450. **Current Rank:** 96. **Rank in 1990:** 60.

★3300★
C. G. Enterprises, Inc.
27704 Franklin Ave.
Southfield, MI 48034 Phone: (313)352-5151
Phillip M. Ingram, CEO

Founded: 1982. **Staff:** 35. **Type of Business:** Computer products sales and service. **1990 Sales (in millions of dollars):** 9.448. **Current Rank:** 97. **Toll-free phone:** (800)522-8671. **Rank in 1990:** 77.

★3301★
Uniworld Group, Inc.
1250 Broadway, 36th Fl.
New York, NY 10001 Phone: (212)564-0066
Byron E. Lewis, CEO

Founded: 1969. **Staff:** 80. **Type of Business:** Advertising. **1990 Sales (in millions of dollars):** 9.392. **Current Rank:** 98. **Rank in 1990:** 79.

★3302★
Solo Construction Corp.
15251 NE 18th Ave.
North Miami Beach, FL 33162 Phone: (305)944-3922
Randy Pierson, CEO

Founded: 1978. **Staff:** 37. **Type of Business:** Underground engineering construction. **1990 Sales (in millions of dollars):** 9.362. **Current Rank:** 99. **Rank in 1990:** Not in Top 100.

★3303★
Compliance Corporation
34 Essex, S.
Lexington Park, MD 20653 Phone: (301)863-8070
Harold Thomas Herndon, CEO

Founded: 1980. **Staff:** 170. **Type of Business:** Computer software, hardware design and facility management. **1990 Sales (in millions of dollars):** 9.200. **Current Rank:** 100. **Rank in 1990:** Not in Top 100.

(14) PUBLICATIONS

Entries are arranged alphabetically by publication title within four categories: Newspapers; Periodicals; Newsletters; and Directories. See the User's Guide at the front of this directory for additional information.

Newspapers

★3304★
Afro-American
429 Central Ave.
East Orange, NJ 07108 Phone: (201)672-9102
Black community newspaper. **Contact(s):** Robert Queen, Editor.

★3305★
The Afro American
Afro American Newspapers
628 N. Eutaw St.
Baltimore, MD 21201 Phone: (301)728-8200
Newspaper serving the Black community. **Established:** 1892. **Column Depth:** 301 agate lines. **Frequency:** Weekly (Sat.). **Print Method:** Letterpress. **Number of Columns Per Page:** 6. **Column Width:** 24 nonpareils. **Contact(s):** Robert W. Matthews III, Publisher. **Subscription:** $26. **Circulation:** 5,500.

★3306★
Afro-American Times
1360 Fulton
Brooklyn, NY 11216 Phone: (718)636-9500
Black community newspaper. **Frequency:** Weekly. **Contact(s):** Thomas H. Watkins, Jr., Editor and Publisher.

★3307★
Afro-Americans in New York Life and History
Afro-American Historical Assn. of the
Niagara Frontier, Inc.
PO Box 1663, Hertle Sta.
Buffalo, NY 14216 Phone: (716)878-5412
Established: 1977. **Column Depth:** 7 1/2 in. **Frequency:** 2x/yr. **Print Method:** Offset. **Trim Size:** 6 x 9. **Number of Columns Per Page:** 1. **Column Width:** 4 1/2 in. **Contact(s):** Monroe Fordham, Editor. **ISSN:** 0364-2437. **Subscription:** $8. $5 single issue. **Circulation:** 600.

★3308★
The Akron Reporter
1134 S. Main St.
PO Box 2042
Akron, OH 44309 Phone: (216)253-0007
Black community newspaper. **Established:** 1969. **Frequency:** Weekly (Thurs.). **Contact(s):** William R. Ellis, Sr., Editor and Publisher. **Circulation:** 17,000.

★3309★
The Alexandria News Weekly
PO Box 608
Alexandria, LA 71301 Phone: (318)443-7664
General newspaper for the Black community. **Established:** 1975. **Column Depth:** 294 agate lines. **Frequency:** Weekly (Thurs.). **Print Method:** Offset. **Number of Columns Per Page:** 6. **Column Width:** 26 nonpareils. **Contact(s):** Rev. C.J. Bell, Editor; H. Nicholas Stull, Publisher and Advertising Mgr. **Subscription:** $15. **Circulation:** 13,750.

★3310★
Amsterdam News
2340 Fredrick Douglas Blvd.
New York, NY 10027 Phone: (212)932-7400
Black community newspaper. **Established:** 1909. **Column Depth:** 200 agate lines. **Frequency:** Weekly (Sat.). **Print Method:** Offset. **Number of Columns Per Page:** 6. **Column Width:** 18 nonpareils. **Contact(s):** William Egyir, Publisher. **Subscription:** $18. **Circulation:** 34,915.

★3311★
Arizona Informant
1746 E. Madison, No. 2
Phoenix, AZ 85034 Phone: (602)257-9300
Black community newspaper. **Established:** 1958. **Column Depth:** 116 agate lines. **Frequency:** Weekly (Wed.). **Print Method:** Web offset. **Trim Size:** 9 3/4 x 16. **Number of Columns Per Page:** 6. **Column Width:** 20 nonpareils. **Contact(s):** Charles R. Campbell, Editor and Publisher; Cloves C. Campbell, Sr., Publisher; Cloves C. Campbell, Jr., Advertising Mgr. **ISSN:** 051-770. **Subscription:** $15; $18 out of area. **Circulation:** 10,000.

★3312★
Arkansas State Press
PO Box 164037
Little Rock, AR 72216 Phone: (501)371-9991
Black community newspaper. **Established:** 1941. **Column Depth:** 13 in. **Frequency:** Weekly (Wed.). **Print Method:** Offset. **Number of Columns Per Page:** 5. **Column Width:** 1 1/2 in. **Contact(s):** Janis Kearney Lunon, Publisher. **Subscription:** $20.

★3313★
Atlanta Daily World
145 Auburn Ave. NE
Atlanta, GA 30335 Phone: (404)659-1110
Black community newspaper. **Established:** 1928. **Column Depth:** 21 in. **Frequency:** 4x/wk. (Tues., Thurs., Fri., and Sun.). **Print Method:** Offset. **Number of Columns Per Page:** 6. **Column Width:** 1 5/8 in. **Contact(s):** C.A. Scott, Editor and Publisher. **Subscription:** $65. **Circulation:** 20,000.

★3314★
The Atlanta Inquirer
947 Martin Luther King Jr. Dr. NW
Atlanta, GA 30314 Phone: (404)523-6086
Black community newspaper. **Established:** 1960. **Frequency:** Weekly (Thurs.). **Contact(s):** Mzee O. Adjanaku, Editor; John B. Smith, Publisher and CEO. **Circulation:** 55,000.

★3315★
The Atlanta Tribune
L & L Communications, Inc.
875 Old Roswell Rd., Ste. C-100
Roswell, GA 30076 Phone: (404)587-0501
Black community newsmagazine. **Established:** 1986. **Frequency:** Monthly. **Print Method:** Web offset. **Trim Size:** 9 13/16 x 13 7/8. **Number of Columns Per Page:** 4. **Column Width:** 2 5/16 in.

Contact(s): Adrienne Harris, Mng. Editor; Patricia Lottier, Publisher. **Subscription:** $10.

★3316★
The Atlanta Voice
PO Box 92487
Atlanta, GA 30314 Phone: (404)524-6426
Black community newspaper. **Established:** 1966. **Column Depth:** 21 1/2 in. **Frequency:** Weekly (Thurs.). **Number of Columns Per Page:** 6. **Contact(s):** J. Lowell Ware, Editor and Publisher. **Subscription:** $39. **Circulation:** 103,000.

★3317★
Bakersfield News Observer
1219 20th St.
Bakersfield, CA 93301 Phone: (805)324-9466
Black community newspaper. **Frequency:** Weekly (Wed.). **Contact(s):** Opal Buchanan, Managing Editor; Joseph L. Coley, Publisher.

★3318★
Baltimore Afro-American
Afro-American Newspapers
628 N. Eutaw St.
Baltimore, MD 21201 Phone: (301)728-8200
Black community newspaper. **Established:** 1892. **Column Depth:** 301 agate lines. **Frequency:** 2x/wk. (Tues. and Sat.). **Print Method:** Letterpress. **Number of Columns Per Page:** 6. **Column Width:** 24 nonpareils. **Contact(s):** Robert Matthews, Editor; John J. Oliver, Jr., Publisher; Thomas Gaines, Advertising Mgr. **Subscription:** $26.

★3319★
Baton Rouge Community Leader
1010 North Blvd.
Baton Rouge, LA 70802 Phone: (504)343-0544
Black and religious-oriented community newspaper. **Established:** 1952. **Frequency:** Weekly (Thurs.). **Print Method:** Offset. **Contact(s):** Carl Lankster, Editor; Al Lankster, Publisher. **Subscription:** $15. **Circulation:** 21,700.

★3320★
Bay State Banner
925 Washington St.
Dorchester, MA 02124 Phone: (617)288-4900
Newspaper serving the Black community. **Established:** 1965. **Column Depth:** 224 agate lines. **Frequency:** Weekly (Thurs.). **Print Method:** Offset. **Number of Columns Per Page:** 5. **Column Width:** 23 nonpareils. **Contact(s):** Melvin B. Miller, Editor and Publisher; Kim Rogers, Advertising Mgr. **Subscription:** $15. **Circulation:** 11,500.

★3321★
Bayou Talk
Jo Val, Inc.
PO Box 712
Moreno Valley, CA 92337-0712 Phone: (714)247-1316
Cajun Creole community newspaper. **Frequency:** Monthly (first Thurs.). **Contact(s):** Velma V. Conant Metoyer, Editorial Advisor.

★3322★
Berkeley Tri City Post
The Alameda Publishing Corp.
630 20th St.
PO Box 1350
Oakland, CA 94612 Phone: (415)763-1120
Black community newspaper. **Established:** 1963. **Column Depth:** 21 1/2 in. **Frequency:** 2x/wk. (Wed. and Sun.). **Print Method:** Offset. **Number of Columns Per Page:** 6. **Column Width:** 1 1/16 in. **Contact(s):** Gail Berkley, Editor; Thomas Berkley, Publisher; Donald V. Welcher, Advertising Mgr. **Subscription:** $42. **Circulation:** 20,000.

★3323★
Big Red News
155 Water St.
Brooklyn, NY 11201 Phone: (718)852-6001
Black community newspaper. **Established:** 1976. **Column Depth:** 196 agate lines. **Frequency:** Weekly (Sat.). **Print Method:** Offset. Uses mats. **Number of Columns Per Page:** 5. **Column Width:** 26 nonpareils. **Contact(s):** Walter Smith, Jr., Publisher. **Subscription:** $26.50. **Circulation:** 53,766.

★3324★
Birmingham Times
The Birmingham Times Publishing Co.
115 3rd Ave. W.
PO Box 10503
Birmingham, AL 35202 Phone: (205)251-5158
Black community newspaper. **Established:** February 1964. **Column Depth:** 21 in. **Frequency:** Weekly. **Print Method:** Offset. **Number of Columns Per Page:** 6. **Column Width:** 13 picas. **Contact(s):** James E. Lewis, Editor and Publisher; Jesse J. Lewis, Sr., Advertising Mgr. **Subscription:** Free; $20 (mail).

★3325★
Birmingham World
407 15th St. N.
Birmingham, AL 35203-1877
Black community newspaper. **Established:** April 1930. **Frequency:** Weekly. **Print Method:** Offset. **Number of Columns Per Page:** 6. **Column Width:** 2 4/5 in. **Contact(s):** Joe N. Dickson, Editor and Publisher. **ISSN:** 0006-3754. **Subscription:** $26. **Circulation:** 11,500.

★3326★
Black American
Cool Magazine, Inc.
310 Lenox Ave., No. 304
New York, NY 10027-4411 Phone: (212)564-5110
Black-oriented newspaper reporting on movies, theatre, African and local politics, and interviews. **Established:** 1960. **Column Depth:** 14 1/4 in. **Frequency:** Weekly (Thurs.). **Print Method:** Offset. **Trim Size:** 10 1/4 x 14 1/4. **Number of Columns Per Page:** 5. **Column Width:** 2 in. **Contact(s):** Hope Offord, Editor; Carl Offord, Publisher; Carlton Brown, Advertising Mgr. **ISSN:** 0890-5983. **Subscription:** $33.

★3327★
The Black Chronicle
PO Box 17498
Oklahoma City, OK 73136 Phone: (405)424-4695
Black community newspaper. **Established:** April 1979. **Column Depth:** 301 agate lines. **Frequency:** Weekly. **Print Method:** Offset. **Trim Size:** 12 1/2 x 21 1/2. **Number of Columns Per Page:** 8. **Column Width:** 10 picas. **Contact(s):** Albert J. Lindsey, Editor; Russell M. Perry, Publisher. **Circulation:** 28,803.

★3328★
Black Miami Weekly
PO Box F
Miami, FL 33147
Black community newspaper. **Contact(s):** Joel B. Dyer, Publisher.

★3329★
Black Voice/Carta Boricua
Rutgers University
Student Activities Center
Box 28
Geroge St.
New Brunswick, NJ 08903 Phone: (201)828-9554
Black hispanic collegiate newspaper. **Established:** 1969. **Column Depth:** 224 agate lines. **Frequency:** Weekly (Tues.). **Print Method:** Offset. **Number of Columns Per Page:** 5. **Column Width:** 21 nonpareils. **Contact(s):** Rebecca Roberts, Editor-in-Chief; Arrigo Rogers, Bus. Mgr. **Subscription:** Free; $10 (mail). **Circulation:** 4,000.

★3330★
Black Voice News
PO Box 1581
Riverside, CA 92502 Phone: (714)682-6070
Newspaper serving the Black communities of Riverside, Moreno Valley, Perris, Banning, Palm Springs, San Bernardino, Ontario, Redlands, and Fontana westend. **Established:** 1972. **Column Depth:** 294 agate lines. **Frequency:** Weekly (Thurs.). **Print Method:** Offset. **Number of Columns Per Page:** 6. **Column Width:** 24 nonpareils. **Contact(s):** Hardy Brown, Publisher. **Subscription:** $25; $29 out of area. **Circulation:** 7,500.

★3331★
Boston Greater News
PO Box 497
Roxbury, MA 02119-0004 Phone: (617)445-7063
Black community newspaper. **Established:** September 1983. **Column Depth:** 14 in. **Frequency:** Weekly. **Print Method:** Offset. **Trim Size:** 11 x 15. **Number of Columns Per Page:** 5. **Column Width:** 2 in. **Contact(s):** Fred J. Clark, Editor and Publisher; Edwin Sumpter, Advertising Mgr. **Subscription:** $18.

★3332★
Brooklyn New York Recorder
86 Bainbridge
Brooklyn, NY 11207 Phone: (212)493-4616
Black community newspaper. **Contact(s):** Thomas Watkins, Publisher.

★3333★
The Buckeye Review
William Publishing Co.
620 Belmont Ave.
Youngstown, OH 44502 Phone: (216)743-2250
Black community newspaper. **Established:** 1937. **Column Depth:** 182 agate lines. **Frequency:** Weekly (Fri.). **Print Method:** Offset. **Number of Columns Per Page:** 5. **Column Width:** 24 nonpareils. **Contact(s):** Crystal A. Williams, Editor. **Subscription:** $15.

★3334★
Buffalo Criterion
623-625 William St.
Buffalo, NY 14206 Phone: (716)882-9570
Black community newspaper. **Established:** 1925. **Frequency:** Weekly (Thurs.). **Print Method:** Offset. **Trim Size:** 13 x 19 1/2. **Number of Columns Per Page:** 8. **Column Width:** 1 7/8 in. **Contact(s):** Frank E. Merriweather, Editor and Publisher. **Subscription:** $14.95; $19.95 out of area.

★3335★
The Bulletin
2490 Dr. M.L. King, Jr. Way
PO Box 2560
Sarasota, FL 34230-2560 Phone: (813)953-3990
Black community newspaper. **Established:** 1959. **Column Depth:** 126 agate lines. **Frequency:** Weekly (Fri.). **Print Method:** Offset. **Number of Columns Per Page:** 6. **Column Width:** 2 1/16 in. **Contact(s):** Richard Wright, Editor; Rosalind J. Bacon, Mng. Editor; Fred L. Bacon, Publisher; Johnny Hunter, Advertising Mgr. **Subscription:** $26. $.25 single issue. **Circulation:** 19,000.

★3336★
California Advocate
452 Fresno St.
PO Box 11826
Fresno, CA 93775 Phone: (209)268-0941
Black community newspaper. **Established:** 1967. **Frequency:** 2x/mo. **Contact(s):** Pauline Kimber, Editor; Lesly H. Kimber, Publisher. **Circulation:** 22,500.

★3337★
California Voice
2956 Sacramento St., Ste. C
Berkeley, CA 94702 Phone: (415)644-2446
Black community newspaper. **Established:** 1919. **Frequency:** Weekly (Fri.). **Print Method:** Letterpress. Uses mats. **Contact(s):** Dr. Ruth C. Love, Editor and Publisher. **Subscription:** $9. **Circulation:** 37,325.

★3338★
Call
PO Box 410-477
Kansas City, MO 64141 Phone: (816)842-3804
Black community newspaper. **Established:** 1919. **Column Depth:** 294 agate lines. **Frequency:** Weekly (Fri.). **Print Method:** Offset. **Number of Columns Per Page:** 8. **Column Width:** 18 nonpareils. **Contact(s):** Lucille Bluford, Editor and Publisher. **Subscription:** $17.50.

★3339★
Call and Post
1949 E. 105 St.
PO Box 6237
Cleveland, OH 44101 Phone: (216)791-7600
Black community newspaper. **Established:** 1919. **Column Depth:** 294 agate lines. **Frequency:** Weekly (Thurs.). **Print Method:** Letterpress and offset. **Number of Columns Per Page:** 6. **Column Width:** 26 nonpareils. **Contact(s):** Harry Alexander, Editor and Publisher. **Subscription:** $20. **Circulation:** 43,283.

★3340★
Campus Digest
Tuskegee University
Tuskegee, AL 36083 Phone: (205)727-8263
Black collegiate newspaper. **Established:** 1931. **Column Depth:** 196 agate lines. **Frequency:** Weekly (Fri.). **Print Method:** Offset. **Number of Columns Per Page:** 6. **Column Width:** 20 nonpareils. **Contact(s):** Tanya Cross, Editor. **Subscription:** $3.50.

★3341★
Capital Outlook
1501 E. Park
PO Box 11335
Tallahassee, FL 32301 Phone: (904)878-3895
Black community newspaper. **Established:** 1964. **Frequency:** Weekly (Thurs.). **Contact(s):** Geraldine Williams Smith, Editor and Publisher; Walter Smith, Editor and Publisher. **Circulation:** 11,333.

★3342★
Carolina Peacemaker
PO Box 20853
Greensboro, NC 27420 Phone: (919)274-6210
Black community newspaper. **Established:** April 3, 1967. **Column Depth:** 301 agate lines. **Frequency:** Weekly (Thurs.). **Print Method:** Offset. **Number of Columns Per Page:** 6. **Column Width:** 26 nonpareils. **Contact(s):** John Marshall Kilimanjaro, Editor and Publisher; Thomas E. Price, Advertising Mgr. **Subscription:** $15; $18 out of state. **Circulation:** 5,490.

★3343★
The Carolina Times
923 Old Fayetteville St.
Durham, NC 27701 Phone: (919)682-2913
Black community newspaper. **Established:** 1926. **Column Depth:** 301 agate lines. **Frequency:** Weekly (Thurs.). **Print Method:** Offset. **Number of Columns Per Page:** 6. **Column Width:** 24 nonpareils. **Contact(s):** Mrs. V. A. Edmonds, Editor and Publisher; Kenneth W. Edmonds, Advertising Mgr. **Subscription:** $12.60; $18.90 out of area. **Circulation:** 5,300.

★3344★
The Carolinian
518 E. Martin St.
PO Box 25308
Raleigh, NC 27601 Phone: (919)834-5558
Black community newspaper. **Established:** October 1940. **Column Depth:** 294 agate lines. **Frequency:** 2x/wk. (Mon. and Thurs.). **Print Method:** Offset. **Number of Columns Per Page:** 6. **Column Width:** 25 nonpareils. **Contact(s):** P.R. Jervay, Sr., Editor and Publisher; Paul Jervay, Jr., Advertising Mgr. **Subscription:** $25.

★3345★
Carson Bulletin
Rapid Publishing
PO Box 4248
Compton, CA 90224 Phone: (213)774-0018
Black community newspaper. **Column Depth:** 21 1/2 in. **Frequency:** Weekly (Wed.). **Number of Columns Per Page:** . 6. **Column Width:** 12 1/2 picas. **Contact(s):** O. Ray Watkins, Publisher.

★3346★
The Catholic Mentor
Winston Derek Publishers, Inc.
PO Box 90883
Nashville, TN 37209 Phone: (615)321-0535
Newspaper for Black Catholics. **Established:** 1986. **Frequency:** 6x/yr. **Contact(s):** James W. Peebles, Editor-in-Chief.

★3347★
Central Star/Journal Wave
Central News-Wave Publications
2621 W. 54th St.
Los Angeles, CA 90043 Phone: (213)290-3000
Black community newspaper. **Established:** 1919. **Column Depth:** 21 1/2 in. **Frequency:** Weekly (Wed.). **Print Method:** Offset. **Trim Size:** 13 3/4 x 21 1/2. **Number of Columns Per Page:** 6. **Column Width:** 5 nonpareils. **Contact(s):** C. Z. Wilson, Publisher. **Subscription:** $78. **Circulation:** 39,900.

★3348★
The Challenger
1303 Fillmore Ave.
Buffalo, NY 14211 Phone: (716)897-0442
Black community newspaper featuring political editorials. **Established:** 1963. **Column Depth:** 196 agate lines. **Frequency:** Weekly (Wed.). **Print Method:** Offset. **Number of Columns Per Page:** 5. **Column Width:** 22 nonpareils. **Contact(s):** Barbara Banks, Editor and Publisher. **Subscription:** $15. **Circulation:** 10,000.

★3349★
Charleston Black Times
1310 Harden
Columbia, SC 29204 Phone: (803)799-5252
Black community interest newspaper. **Established:** 1970. **Column Depth:** 224 agate lines. **Frequency:** Weekly (Wed.). **Print Method:** Offset. **Number of Columns Per Page:** 6. **Column Width:** 24 nonpareils. **Contact(s):** Zack Weston, Editor; Isaac Washington, Publisher; Cynthia Bowden, Advertising Mgr. **Subscription:** $25. **Circulation:** 6,883.

★3350★
The Charleston Chronicle
Chronicle Communications Corp.
534 King St.
PO Box 20548
Charleston, SC 29403-0548 Phone: (803)723-2785
Black community newspaper. **Established:** 1971. **Column Depth:** 294 agate lines. **Frequency:** Weekly (Wed.) **Print Method:** Offset. **Number of Columns Per Page:** 6. **Column Width:** 26 nonpareils. **Contact(s):** J. John French, Editor and Publisher. **Subscription:** $18.

★3351★
The Charlotte Post
1531 Camden Rd.
PO Box 30144
Charlotte, NC 28230 Phone: (704)376-0496
Black community newspaper. **Established:** 1887. **Column Depth:** 301 agate lines. **Frequency:** Weekly (Thurs.). **Print Method:** Offset. **Number of Columns Per Page:** 6. **Column Width:** 25 nonpareils. **Contact(s):** Herbert White, Editor; Gerald Johnson, Publisher; Bob Johnson, Publisher; Fran Farrer-Bradley, Advertising Mgr. **Subscription:** $21; $18 senior citizens. **Circulation:** 11,500.

★3352★
Chatham-Southeast Citizen
Citizen Newspapers
412 E. 87th St.
Chicago, IL 60619 Phone: (312)487-7700
Newspaper serving Chicago's Black community. **Established:** 1965. **Column Depth:** 196 agate lines. **Frequency:** Weekly (Thurs.). **Print Method:** Offset. **Number of Columns Per Page:** 5. **Column Width:** 25 nonpareils. **Contact(s):** William Garth, Publisher and Advertising Mgr. **Subscription:** $15.

★3353★
Chicago Citizen
Citizen Newspapers
412 E. 87th St.
Chicago, IL 60619
Black community newspaper. **Established:** 1965. **Frequency:** Weekly (Thurs.). **Contact(s):** John Williams, Jr., Editor; William A. Garth, Publisher.

★3354★
Chicago Crusader
Crusader Newspapers
6429 S. Martin Luther King Dr.
Chicago, IL 60637 Phone: (312)752-2500
Black community newspaper (tabloid). **Established:** June 1940. **Column Depth:** 14 in. **Frequency:** Weekly (Sat.). **Print Method:** Offset. **Trim Size:** 10 x 14. **Number of Columns Per Page:** 5. **Column Width:** 2 in. **Contact(s):** Dorothy R. Leavell, Editor and Publisher; John Smith, Advertising Mgr. **Subscription:** $12. **Circulation:** 48,000.

★3355★
Chicago Independent Bulletin
2037 95th St.
Chicago, IL 60643 Phone: (312)783-1040
Black community newspaper. **Established:** 1958. **Frequency:** Weekly (Thurs.). **Contact(s):** Hurley Green, Sr., Editor and Publisher. **Circulation:** 64,000.

★3356★
Chicago Metro News
2600 S. Michigan Ave., No. 308
Chicago, IL 60616 Phone: (312)842-5950
Newspaper for the Black community. **Established:** 1965. **Column Depth:** 301 agate lines. **Frequency:** Weekly (Sat.). **Print Method:** Offset. **Number of Columns Per Page:** 6. **Column Width:** 26 nonpareils. **Contact(s):** Ruth Armstrong, Editor and Publisher; Judith M. Armstrong, Advertising Mgr.; Patricia Armstrong, Advertising Mgr. **Subscription:** $20; $10.50 (6 months).

★3357★
Chicago Shoreland News
AJA Enterprise
11740 S. Elizabeth
Chicago, IL 60643 Phone: (312)568-7091
Black community newspaper. **Established:** 1974. **Column Depth:** 14 in. **Frequency:** Weekly (Thurs.). **Print Method:** Offset. **Trim Size:** 9 3/4 x 14. **Number of Columns Per Page:** 5. **Column Width:** 11 picas. **Contact(s):** Al Johnson, Publisher; Donna Weathersby, Editor **Subscription:** $21.

★3358★
Chicago South Shore Scene
7426 S. Constance
Chicago, IL 60649 Phone: (312)363-0441
Community newspaper (Black). **Established:** 1959. **Column Depth:** 224 agate lines. **Frequency:** Weekly (Thurs.). **Print Method:** Offset. **Number of Columns Per Page:** 4. **Column Width:** 18 nonpareils. **Contact(s):** Dr. Claudette McFarland, Editor and Publisher. **Subscription:** $50.

★3359★
Chicago Standard News
Standard Newspapers
615 S. Halsted
Chicago Heights, IL 60411 Phone: (708)755-5021
Black community newspaper. **Established:** 1984. **Column Depth:** 16 in. **Frequency:** Weekly. **Print Method:** Offset. **Number of Columns Per Page:** 5. **Column Width:** 12 picas. **Contact(s):** Lorenzo Martin, Editor and Publisher; Pat Rush Martin, Advertising Mgr. **Subscription:** $30. **Circulation:** 10,000.

★3360★
Chicago Weekend
Citizen Newspapers
412 E. 87th St.
Chicago, IL 60619 Phone: (312)487-7700
Weekend newspaper serving Chicago's Black community. **Established:** 1974. **Column Depth:** 196 agate lines. **Frequency:** Weekly (Thurs.). **Print Method:** Offset. **Number of Columns Per Page:** 5. **Column Width:** 25 nonpareils. **Contact(s):** William Garth, Editor and Publisher. **Subscription:** $15.

★3361★
Cincinnati Herald
Porter Publishing
836 Lincoln Ave.
Cincinnati, OH 45206 Phone: (513)221-5440
Black community newspaper. **Established:** 1955. **Column Depth:** 294 agate lines. **Frequency:** Weekly. **Print Method:** Offset. **Trim Size:** 15 x 22. **Number of Columns Per Page:** 6. **Column Width:** 2 3/16 in. **Contact(s):** Donald Anthony, Editor; Marjorie B. Parham, Publisher; Jermaine Hill, Advertising and Promotion Dir. **Subscription:** $18. **Circulation:** 24,500.

★3362★
Citizen
PO Box 216
Benton Harbor, MI 49022 Phone: (616)927-1527
Black community newspaper. **Contact(s):** Charles Kelly, Publisher.

★3363★
The City Sun
The City Sun Publishing Co., Inc.
GPO 560
Brooklyn, NY 11202 Phone: (718)624-5959
Newspaper with Black orientation. **Established:** June 6, 1984. **Column Depth:** 198 agate lines. **Frequency:** Weekly (Wed.). **Print Method:** Letterpress. **Number of Columns Per Page:** 6. **Column Width:** 9 1/2 picas. **Contact(s):** Utrice C. Leid, Editor; Andrew W. Cooper, Publisher and Advertising Mgr. **Subscription:** $26. **Circulation:** 20,000.

★3364★
The Coastal Times
701 E. Bay St.
B & C Box 1407
Charleston, SC 29403 Phone: (803)723-5318
Community newspaper (Black oriented). **Established:** July 1983. **Column Depth:** 21 in. **Frequency:** Weekly (Wed.). **Print Method:** Offset. **Number of Columns Per Page:** 6. **Column Width:** 2 1/16 in. **Contact(s):** Mignon Clyburn, Editor; James E. Clyburn, Publisher. **Subscription:** $15.

★3365★
Columbia Black News
Ju Ju Publishing
PO Box 11128
Columbia, SC 29211 Phone: (803)799-5252
Black community newspaper. **Established:** 1970. **Column Depth:** 224 agate lines. **Frequency:** Weekly (Wed.). **Print Method:** Offset. **Number of Columns Per Page:** 6. **Column Width:** 24 nonpareils. **Contact(s):** Issac Washington, Publisher; Earl Kennedy, Advertising Mgr. **Subscription:** $25. **Circulation:** 22,834.

★3366★
The Columbus Times
2230 Buena Vista Rd.
PO Box 2845
Columbus, GA 31993-2999 Phone: (404)324-2404
Black community newspaper. **Established:** 1970. **Column Depth:** 21.5 in. **Frequency:** Weekly (Wed.). **Print Method:** Offset. Broadsheet. **Trim Size:** 13 x 21.5. **Number of Columns Per Page:** 6. **Column Width:** 2 1/16 in. **Contact(s):** Carol Gerdes, Editor; Ophelia Devore Mitchell, Publisher; Helmut Gerdes, Advertising Mgr. **Subscription:** $15.60. **Circulation:** 20,000.

★3367★
Communicade
Okang Communications Corp.
104 Magnolia St.
PO Box 60739
Rochester, NY 14606 Phone: (716)235-6695
Regional newspaper (Black). **Established:** 1972. **Column Depth:** 224 agate lines. **Frequency:** Every other week. **Print Method:** Offset. **Number of Columns Per Page:** 5. **Column Width:** 24 nonpareils. **Contact(s):** Frank B. Willis, Editor. **Subscription:** $4.95.

★3368★
Community Leader
1210 North Blvd.
Baton Rouge, LA 70802
Black community newspaper. **Contact(s):** Alfonso Lankster, General Manager.

★3369★
Compton Bulletin
Rapid Publishing
349 W. Compton
PO Box 4248
Compton, CA 90224 Phone: (213)774-0018
Black community newspaper. **Column Depth:** 21 1/2 in. **Frequency:** Weekly (Wed.). **Number of Columns Per Page:** 6. **Column Width:** 12 1/2 picas. **Contact(s):** O. Ray Watkins, Publisher.

★3370★
Compton/Carson Wave
Central News-Wave Publications
2621 W. 54th St.
Los Angeles, CA 90043 Phone: (213)290-3000
Black community newspaper. **Column Depth:** 21 1/2 in. **Frequency:** Weekly (Wed.). **Print Method:** Offset. **Trim Size:** 13 3/4 x 21 1/2. **Number of Columns Per Page:** 6. **Column Width:** 5 nonpareils. **Contact(s):** C.Z. Wilson, Publisher. **Subscription:** $78. **Circulation:** 38,200.

★3371★
Culver City/Westchester Wave
Central City-Wave Publications
2621 W. 54th St.
Los Angeles, CA 90043 Phone: (213)290-3000
Black community newspaper. **Established:** 1980. **Column Depth:** 21 1/2 in. **Frequency:** Weekly (Wed.). **Print Method:** Offset. **Number of Columns Per Page:** 6. **Column Width:** 5 nonpareils. **Contact(s):** C.Z. Wilson, Publisher. **Subscription:** $78. **Circulation:** 33,750.

★3372★
Dallas Examiner
424 Centre St.
Dallas, TX 75208 Phone: (214)948-9175
Black community newspaper. **Established:** 1986. **Frequency:** Weekly (Thurs.). **Contact(s):** Charles O'Neal, Editor; Finch Belt, Publisher. **Circulation:** 50,000.

★3373★
Dallas Post Tribune
2726 S. Beckley
Dallas, TX 75224 Phone: (214)946-7678
Black community newspaper. **Established:** 1962. **Column Depth:** 294 agate lines. **Frequency:** Weekly (Thurs.). **Print Method:** Offset. **Number of Columns Per Page:** 6. **Column Width:** 24 nonpareils. **Contact(s):** Alison Hines-Boney, Editor; James A. Washington, Publisher; Shaun Angles, Advertising Mgr. **Subscription:** $12. **Circulation:** 30,000.

★3374★
The Dallas Weekly Newspaper
Ad-Mast Publishing, Inc.
Anthony T. Davis Bldg.
3101 Martin Luther King, Jr. Blvd.
Dallas, TX 75215 Phone: (214)428-8958
Black community newspaper. **Established:** 1955. **Column Depth:** 175 agate lines. **Frequency:** Weekly (Thurs.). **Print Method:** Offset. **Trim Size:** 10 1/4 x 12 1/4. **Number of Columns Per Page:** 5. **Column Width:** 143 agate lines. **Contact(s):** Steven Scott, Gen. Mgr.; James Washington, Publisher. **ISSN:** 0895-1271. **Subscription:** Free; $20 (mail); $32 out of state.

★3375★
Daytona Times
Daytona Times, Inc.
429 S. Dr. M. L. King Blvd.
PO Box 1110
Daytona Beach, FL 32115 Phone: (904)253-0321
Black community newspaper. **Established:** August 1978. **Column Depth:** 21 in. **Frequency:** Weekly (Thurs.). **Print Method:** Offset. **Number of Columns Per Page:** 6. **Column Width:** 2 1/16 in. **Contact(s):** Charles W. Cherry II, Editor and Publisher. **Subscription:** $20. **Circulation:** 20,150.

★3376★
Decatur Voice
625 E. Wood St.
Decatur, IL 62523-1152 Phone: (217)423-2231
Black community newspaper. **Established:** 1968. **Column Depth:** 16 in. **Frequency:** Weekly. **Print Method:** Offset. **Trim Size:** 10 x 16. **Number of Columns Per Page:** 5. **Column Width:** 2 in. **Contact(s):** Horace G. Livingston, Jr., Publisher; Mildred Covington, Advertising Mgr. **Subscription:** $20.

★3377★
The Defender
1702 Locust St.
Wilmington, DE 19802 Phone: (302)656-3252
Black community newspaper. **Established:** 1962. **Column Depth:** 14 in. **Frequency:** Weekly. **Print Method:** Offset. **Trim Size:** 10 x 17. **Number of Columns Per Page:** 5. **Column Width:** 1 3/4 in. **Contact(s):** Earl Brown, Publisher.

★3378★
Denver Weekly News
PO Box 38939
Denver, CO 80238-0939 Phone: (303)839-5800
Black community newspaper serving Denver and surrounding areas. **Frequency:** Weekly (Thurs.). **Contact(s):** F. Cosmo Harris, Editor and Publisher; Ms. Tommie Thomas, Advertising Mgr. **Circulation:** 17,500.

★3379★
East St. Louis Crusader
2206 Missouri Ave.
East Saint Louis, IL 62205 Phone: (618)271-0565
Black community newspaper. **Contact(s):** Joe Lewis, Sr., Publisher.

★3380★
East St. Louis Monitor
East St. Louis Monitor Publishing, Inc.
1501 State St.
Box 2137
East Saint Louis, IL 62205 Phone: (618)271-0468
Black community newspaper. **Established:** 1963. **Column Depth:** 21 1/2 in. **Frequency:** Weekly. **Print Method:** Offset. **Trim Size:** 13 1/8 x 21 1/2. **Number of Columns Per Page:** 6. **Column Width:** 2 in. **Contact(s):** Vivian Hamer, Acting Editor; Anne E. Jordan, Publisher; George Laktzian, Advertising Mgr. **Subscription:** $21.80. **Circulation:** 22,500.

★3381★
Ecorse Telegram
4122 10th St.
PO Box 4585
Ecorse, MI 48229 Phone: (313)928-2955
Black community newspaper. **Established:** 1945. **Column Depth:** 16 in. **Frequency:** Weekly. **Print Method:** Offset. Uses mats. **Number of Columns Per Page:** 5. **Column Width:** 23 nonpareils. **Contact(s):** J.C. Wall, Editor and Publisher; Dorothy Wall, Advertising Mgr. **Subscription:** $25. **Circulation:** 12,000.

★3382★
The Evening Whirl
PO Box 5088 Nagel Sta.
Saint Louis, MO 63115 Phone: (314)383-3875
Black community newspaper. **Established:** 1938. **Column Depth:** 294 agate lines. **Frequency:** Weekly (Tues.). **Print Method:** Offset. **Number of Columns Per Page:** 8. **Column Width:** 21 nonpareils. **Contact(s):** A.C. Clay, Editor; Benjamin Thomas, Publisher. **Subscription:** $30. **Circulation:** 40,000.

★3383★
Every Wednesday
Afro-American Newspapers
628 N. Eutaw St.
Baltimore, MD 21201 Phone: (301)728-8200
Black community newspaper. **Established:** 1984. **Frequency:** Weekly (Wed.). **Print Method:** Offset. **Trim Size:** 11 x 14. **Number of Columns Per Page:** 2. **Contact(s):** Robert Matthews, Editor; John Oliver, Publisher; Marsha White, Advertising Mgr. **Circulation:** 45,854.

★3384★
Facts News
2803 Cherry St.
PO Box 22015
Seattle, WA 98122 Phone: (206)324-0552
Black community newspaper. **Established:** 1961. **Column Depth:** 224 agate lines. **Frequency:** Weekly. **Print Method:** Offset. **Number of Columns Per Page:** 6. **Column Width:** 20 nonpareils. **Contact(s):** Fitzgerald Beaver, Editor and Publisher. **Subscription:** $40.

★3385★
The Famuan
Florida A&M University
Tallahassee, FL 32307 Phone: (904)599-3159
College newspaper. **Column Depth:** 196 agate lines. **Frequency:** Weekly. **Print Method:** Offset. **Trim Size:** 11 1/2 x 14 1/2. **Number of Columns Per Page:** 4. **Column Width:** 26 nonpareils. **Contact(s):** Gale A. Workman, Faculty Adviser. **Subscription:** Free; $15 (mail). **Circulation:** 4,000.

★3386★
The Fayetteville Black Times
The Black Press, Inc.
108 Webb St.
PO Box 863
Fayetteville, NC 28302
Black community newspaper. **Frequency:** Weekly (Wed.). **Number of Columns Per Page:** 6. **Contact(s):** Thelma H. Kinney, Sharing Editor; Dr. Johnny Gaston, Contributing Editor; Bro. J. D. Marshall, Contributing Editor.

★3387★
Fine Print News
Box 57 Ellicott Sta.
Buffalo, NY 14205 Phone: (716)886-0041
Black community newspaper. **Contact(s):** Ronald H. Fleming, Publisher.

★3388★
Firestone Park News/Southeast News Press
PO Box 19027A
Los Angeles, CA 90019 Phone: (213)291-9486
Newspaper serving the Black community of L.A. **Established:** 1924. **Column Depth:** 294 agate lines. **Frequency:** Weekly (Thurs.). **Print Method:** Offset. **Trim Size:** 13 x 21 1/2. **Number of Columns Per Page:** 6. **Column Width:** 29 nonpareils. **Contact(s):** Lela Ward Oliver, Editor; John H. Holoman, Publisher; Eric L. Holoman, Advertising Mgr. **ISSN:** 8550-2038. **Subscription:** $20; $40 national.

★3389★
Fisk News
Fisk University
1000 17th Ave. N.
Nashville, TN 37203 Phone: (615)329-8710
Black collegiate newspaper. **Established:** 1950. **Column Depth:** 84 agate lines. **Frequency:** Weekly. **Print Method:** Offset. **Number of Columns Per Page:** 2. **Column Width:** 36 nonpareils. **Circulation:** 1,000.

★3390★
Florence Black Sun
1310 Harden
Columbia, SC 29204 Phone: (803)799-5252
Black community interest newspaper. **Established:** 1970. **Column Depth:** 224 agate lines. **Frequency:** Weekly (Wed.). **Print Method:** Offset. **Number of Columns Per Page:** 6. **Column Width:** 24 nonpareils. **Subscription:** $18. **Circulation:** 5,734.

★3391★
Florida Sentinel-Bulletin
2207-21st Ave.
PO Box 3363
Tampa, FL 33601 Phone: (813)248-1921
Black community newspaper (tabloid). **Established:** 1945. **Column Depth:** 15 in. **Frequency:** 2x/wk. (Tues. and Fri.). **Print Method:** Offset. **Trim Size:** 10 x 15. **Number of Columns Per Page:** 5. **Column Width:** 2 in. **Contact(s):** C. Blythe Andrews, Jr., Publisher; Sybil Andrews Wells, Gen. Mgr. **Subscription:** $31. **Circulation:** 23,345.

★3392★
Florida Star Times
PO Box 40629
Jacksonville, FL 32203
Black community newspaper. **Contact(s):** Eric O. Simpson, Editor.

★3393★
Florida Sun Review
LMH Publications
702 18th St.
PO Box 2348
Orlando, FL 32802 Phone: (407)423-1156
Black-oriented newspaper. **Established:** 1931. **Column Depth:** 231 agate lines. **Frequency:** Weekly (Thurs.). **Print Method:** Offset. **Number of Columns Per Page:** 6. **Column Width:** 19 nonpareils. **Contact(s):** James A. Madison, Editor and Publisher; James W. Macon, Publisher. **Subscription:** $7.50. **Circulation:** 16,500.

★3394★
Ft. Pierce Chronicle
1527 Ave. D
Fort Pierce, FL 34950 Phone: (407)416-7093
Black community newspaper. **Established:** 1957. **Frequency:** Weekly (Wed.). **Contact(s):** C.E. Bolen, Editor and Publisher. **Circulation:** 10,500.

★3395★
Fort Valley Herald
Atlantic Communications of Georgia, Inc.
315 N. Camellia Blvd.
PO Box 899
Fort Valley, GA 31030 Phone: (912)825-7000
Black community newspaper. **Established:** 1986. **Frequency:** Weekly (Wed.). **Print Method:** Offset. **Trim Size:** 13 x 21 1/2 in. **Number of Columns Per Page:** 6. **Column Width:** 2 in. **Contact(s):** Robert E. James, Editor and Publisher. **Subscription:** $15; $17 out of state. **Circulation:** 6,000.

★3396★
Frost Illustrated
Frost, Inc.
3121 S. Calhoun
Fort Wayne, IN 46807-1901 Phone: (219)745-0552
Black community newspaper. **Established:** November 1968. **Column Depth:** 13. **Frequency:** Weekly (Wed.). **Print Method:** Offset. **Number of Columns Per Page:** 5. **Contact(s):** Edna M. Smith, Editor; Edward N. Smith, Sr., Publisher; Edward N. Smith, Jr., Advertising Mgr. **Subscription:** $12; $15 out of state.

★3397★
Gary American
2268 Broadway
Gary, IN 46402 Phone: (219)883-4903
Black community newspaper. **Established:** 1927. **Column Depth:** 224 agate lines. **Frequency:** Weekly (Fri.). **Print Method:** Offset. **Number of Columns Per Page:** 5. **Column Width:** 27 nonpareils. **Contact(s):** Red Harris, Editor and Publisher. **Subscription:** $12; $16 out of state.

★3398★
Gary New Crusader
1549 Broadway
Gary, IN 46407 Phone: (219)885-4357
Black community newspaper. **Established:** 1961. **Frequency:** Weekly (Thurs.). **Contact(s):** Dorothy R. Leavell, Editor and Publisher. **Circulation:** 9,000.

★3399★
The Grand Rapids Times
PO Box 7258
Grand Rapids, MI 49510 Phone: (616)245-8737
Newspaper targeted for Black population in Grand Rapids, Muskegon, Battle Creek and Kalmazoo, Michigan. **Established:** 1959. **Column Depth:** 15 in. **Frequency:** Weekly. **Print Method:** Web offset. **Trim Size:** 9 5/16 x 15. **Number of Columns Per Page:** 5. **Column Width:** 2 in. **Contact(s):** Patricia Pulliam, Editor and Publisher; Yergan Pulliam, Publisher and Advertising Mgr. **Subscription:** $12.

★3400★
Greene County Democrat
Greene County Newspaper Co.
PO Box 598
Eutaw, AL 35462 Phone: (205)372-3373
Black community newspaper. **Established:** 1890. **Column Depth:** 294 agate lines. **Frequency:** Weekly (Wed.). **Print Method:** Offset. **Number of Columns Per Page:** 6. **Column Width:** 21 nonpareils. **Contact(s):** John Zippert, Publisher; Carol Zippert, Publisher; Laddi Jones, Advertising Mgr. **ISSN:** 0889-518X. **Subscription:** $15; $17 out of area; $20 out of state. **Circulation:** 3,500.

★3401★
Greenville Black Star
1310 Harden
Columbia, SC 29204 Phone: (803)799-5252
Black community interest newspaper. **Column Depth:** 224 agate lines. **Frequency:** Weekly (Wed.). **Print Method:** Offset. **Number of Columns Per Page:** 6. **Column Width:** 24 nonpareils. **Contact(s):** Zack Weston, Editor; Isaac Washington, Publisher; Cynthia Bowden, Advertising Mgr. **Subscription:** $25. **Circulation:** 6,849.

★3402★
Hartford Inquirer
3281 Main St.
Hartford, CT 26120 Phone: (203)522-1462
Black community newspaper. **Established:** 1975. **Contact(s):** Edward Laiscell, Editor; William R. Hales, Publisher. **Circulation:** 125,000.

★3403★
The Herald
1803 Barnard St.
PO Box 486
Savannah, GA 31402 Phone: (912)232-4505
Black community newspaper. **Established:** 1945. **Frequency:** Weekly (Wed.). **Print Method:** Offset. **Number of Columns Per Page:** 6. **Contact(s):** Floyd Adams, Editor and Publisher. **Subscription:** $15.75. **Circulation:** 6,200.

★3404★
The Herald
Texas Southern University
3100 Cleburen
Houston, TX 77004 Phone: (713)527-7315
Collegiate newspaper (Black). **Established:** 1947. **Column Depth:** 210 agate lines. **Frequency:** Weekly. **Print Method:** Letterpress and offset. Uses mats. **Trim Size:** 15 x 22. **Number of Columns Per Page:** 6. **Column Width:** 24 nonpareils.

★3405★
Herald Dispatch
3860 Crenshaw Blvd., Ste. 110
PO Box 19027A
Los Angeles, CA 90008 Phone: (213)291-9486
Black community newspaper. **Established:** 1952. **Column Depth:** 294 agate lines. **Frequency:** Weekly (Thurs.). **Print Method:** Offset. **Number of Columns Per Page:** 6. **Column Width:** 29 nonpareils. **Contact(s):** Lela Ward Oliver, Editor; John H. Holoman, Publisher. **Subscription:** $20. **Circulation:** 35,000.

★3406★
Houston Defender
PO Box 8005
Houston, TX 77288 Phone: (713)663-7716
Black community newspaper. **Established:** October 1930. **Column Depth:** 294 agate lines. **Frequency:** Weekly (Wed.). **Print Method:** Offset. **Number of Columns Per Page:** 6. **Column Width:** 25 nonpareils. **Contact(s):** Lucious New, Editor; Sonceria Messiah-Jiles, Publisher; Sonny Jiles, Advertising Mgr. **Subscription:** $30.

★3407★
Houston Forward Times
4411 Almeda Rd.
PO Box 8346
Houston, TX 77004 Phone: (713)526-4727
Black community newspaper. **Established:** 1960. **Column Depth:** 303 agate lines. **Frequency:** Weekly (Sat.). **Print Method:** Offset. **Number of Columns Per Page:** 6. **Column Width:** 20 nonpareils. **Contact(s):** Bud Johnson, Editor; Lenora Carter, Publisher; Henrietta Smith, Advertising Mgr. **Subscription:** $25. **Circulation:** 52,260.

★3408★
Houston Informer
PO Box 3086
Houston, TX 77253 Phone: (713)527-8261
Black community newspaper. **Established:** 1893. **Frequency:** Weekly (Tues.). **Contact(s):** George McElroy, Editor and Publisher. **Circulation:** 23,000.

★3409★
Houston Sun
2322 Blodgett St.
PO Box 600603
Houston, TX 77206-5218 Phone: (713)524-4474
Black community newspaper. **Established:** 1983. **Column Depth:** 21 in. **Frequency:** Weekly (Thurs.). **Print Method:** Web offset. **Number of Columns Per Page:** 6. **Column Width:** 11 picas. **Contact(s):** Doris Ellis, Editor and Publisher. **Subscription:** Free; $35 (mail). **Circulation:** 80,000.

★3410★
Hudson Valley Black Press
PO Box 2160
Newburgh, NY 12550 Phone: (914)562-1313
Black community newspaper. **Established:** 1983. **Column Depth:** 224 agate lines. **Frequency:** Weekly (Wed.). **Print Method:** Offset. **Number of Columns Per Page:** 6. **Column Width:** 18 nonpareils. **Contact(s):** Chuck Stewart, Editor and Publisher. **Subscription:** $18. **Circulation:** 42,500.

★3411★
Hyde Park Citizen
Citizen Newspapers
412 E. 87th St.
Chicago, IL 60619 Phone: (312)487-7700
Newspaper serving Chicago's Black community. **Established:** 1987. **Column Depth:** 196 agate lines. **Frequency:** Weekly (Thurs.). **Print Method:** Offset. **Number of Columns Per Page:** 5. **Column Width:** 25 nonpareils. **Contact(s):** William Garth, Editor and Publisher. **Subscription:** $15. **Circulation:** 15,000.

★3412★
The Indianapolis Recorder
The George P. Stewart Printing, Inc.
2901 N. Tacoma Ave.
PO Box 18267
Indianapolis, IN 46218 Phone: (317)924-5143
Black community newspaper. **Established:** 1895. **Column Depth:** 298 agate lines. **Frequency:** Weekly (Thurs.). **Print Method:** Offset. **Number of Columns Per Page:** 6. **Column Width:** 13 picas. **Contact(s):** Eunice Trotter, Editor; Bill Mays, Publisher; Pam Beene, Advertising Mgr. **Subscription:** $23; $20 out of area. **Circulation:** 11,212.

★3413★
Info
Info Printing & Publishing, Inc.
1953 Broadway
Gary, IN 46407 Phone: (219)882-5591
Black newspaper with a Democratic orientation. **Established:** 1963. **Column Depth:** 14 in. **Frequency:** Weekly (Thurs.). **Print Method:** Offset. **Trim Size:** 10 1/2 x 14 1/2. **Number of Columns Per Page:** 6. **Column Width:** 1 5/8 in. **Contact(s):** Imogene Harris, Editor and Publisher; Huston Pugh, Advertising Mgr. **Subscription:** $12.

★3414★
Inglewood/Hawthorne Wave
Central News-Wave Publications
2621 W. 54th St.
Los Angeles, CA 90043 Phone: (213)290-3000
Black community newspaper. **Established:** 1978. **Column Depth:** 21 1/2 in. **Frequency:** Weekly (Wed.). **Print Method:** Offset. **Number of Columns Per Page:** 6. **Column Width:** 5 nonpareils. **Contact(s):** C.Z. Wilson, Publisher. **Subscription:** $78. **Circulation:** 44,075.

★3415★
Inglewood Tribune
Rapid Publishing
349 W. Compton
PO Box 4248
Compton, CA 90244 Phone: (213)774-0018
Black community newspaper. **Column Depth:** 21 1/2 in. **Frequency:** Weekly (Wed.). **Number of Columns Per Page:** 6. **Column Width:** 12 1/2 picas. **Contact(s):** O. Ray Watkins, Publisher.

★3416★
Inner City News
Inner City Enterprises, Inc.
PO Box 1545
Mobile, AL 36633-1545 Phone: (205)473-2767
African-American community-oriented newspaper. **Established:** January 1977. **Column Depth:** 21 1/2 in. **Frequency:** Weekly (Thurs.). **Print Method:** Offset. **Trim Size:** 13 x 23. **Number of Columns Per Page:** 6. **Column Width:** 2 in. **Contact(s):** Charles W. Porter, Editor and Publisher. **Subscription:** $20. **Circulation:** 8,000.

★3417★
Iredell County News
PO Box 407
Statesville, NC 28677
Black community newspaper. **Established:** 1980. **Column Depth:** 21 1/2 in. **Frequency:** Weekly. **Print Method:** Offset. **Number of Columns Per Page:** 6. **Column Width:** 12 1/2 picas. **Contact(s):** Mason McCullough, Publisher. **Subscription:** $15.

★3418★
Jackson Advocate
PO Box 3708
Jackson, MS 39207 Phone: (601)948-4122
Black community newspaper. **Established:** 1937. **Column Depth:** 21 in. **Frequency:** Weekly. **Print Method:** Offset. **Number of Columns Per Page:** 6. **Column Width:** 2 1/8 in. **Contact(s):** Charles W. Tisdale, Editor and Publisher; Alice Thomas, Advertising Mgr. **Subscription:** $20.

★3419★
Jackson Blazer
PO Box 806
Jackson, MI 49204 Phone: (517)787-0450
Black community newspaper. **Established:** 1963. **Column Depth:** 224 agate lines. **Frequency:** Weekly (Wed.). **Print Method:** Offset. **Number of Columns Per Page:** 5. **Column Width:** 23 nonpareils. **Contact(s):** Ruth Wade, Editor; Ben Wade, Publisher. **Subscription:** $15. **Circulation:** 6,100.

★3420★
Journal & Guide
3535 Tidewater Dr., Ste. F
Norfolk, VA 23509 Phone: (804)625-3686
Black community newspaper. **Established:** 1900. **Column Depth:** 129 agate lines. **Frequency:** Weekly (Wed.). **Print Method:** Offset. **Number of Columns Per Page:** 6. **Column Width:** 2 1/16 in. **Contact(s):** Brenda Andrews, Publisher; Martha Pritchard, Advertising Mgr. **Subscription:** $18.20. **Circulation:** 25,000.

★3421★
Kansas City Globe
PO Box 090410
Kansas City, MO 64109 Phone: (816)531-5253
Black community newspaper. **Established:** 1972. **Frequency:** Weekly (Fri.). **Contact(s):** Marion Jordan, Editor and Publisher. **Circulation:** 30,000.

★3422★
The Kansas City Voice
2727 N. 13th St.
Kansas City, KS 66104 Phone: (913)371-0303
Black community newspaper. **Contact(s):** Gladys Adams, Publisher.

★3423★
The Lincolnian
Lincoln University
English Dept
Lincoln University, PA 19352 Phone: (215)932-8300
Collegiate newspaper. **Established:** 1929. **Frequency:** 14x/yr. (during the academic year). **Print Method:** Letterpress and offset. **Trim Size:** 17 x 22. **Number of Columns Per Page:** 5. **Contact(s):** Students of Lincoln University, Publisher. **Subscription:** $12. **Circulation:** 1,300.

★3424★
Los Angeles Sentinel
1112 E. 43rd St.
PO Box 11456
Los Angeles, CA 90011 Phone: (213)232-3261
Black community newspaper. **Established:** January 26, 1934. **Column Depth:** 294 agate lines. **Frequency:** Weekly (Thurs.). **Print Method:** Offset. **Trim Size:** 13 x 22 1/2. **Number of Columns Per Page:** 6. **Column Width:** 26 nonpareils. **Contact(s):** Kenneth R. Thomas, Editor; Ruth Washington, Publisher. **Subscription:** $25. **Circulation:** 28,000.

★3425★
Louisiana Weekly
616 Baronne St.
New Orleans, LA 70150 Phone: (504)524-5563
Black community newspaper. **Established:** September 25, 1925. **Column Depth:** 21 in. **Frequency:** Weekly (Sat.). **Print Method:** Offset. Uses mats. **Number of Columns Per Page:** 6. **Column Width:** 2 1/8 in. **Contact(s):** C.C. Dejoie, Jr., Publisher. **Subscription:** $15. **Circulation:** 8,000.

★3426★
Louisville Defender
PO Box 2557
Louisville, KY 40201 Phone: (502)772-2591
Black community newspaper. **Established:** March 1933. **Column Depth:** 21 1/2 in. **Frequency:** Weekly (Thurs.). **Print Method:** Offset. **Trim Size:** 13 x 21 1/2. **Number of Columns Per Page:** 6. **Column Width:** 2 1/16 in. **Contact(s):** Yvonne D. Coleman, Acting Editor; Clarence Leslie, Advertising Mgr./Exec. V.P. **Subscription:** $16; $18 out of state.

★3427★
Lubbock Southwest Digest
510 E. 23rd St.
Lubbock, TX 79404 Phone: (806)762-3612
Black community newspaper. **Established:** September 8, 1977. **Column Depth:** 22 1/2 in. **Frequency:** Weekly (Thurs.). **Print Method:** Letterpress and offset. **Trim Size:** 13 x 22 1/2. **Number of Columns Per Page:** 6. **Column Width:** 1 3/4 in. **Contact(s):** T.J. Patterson, Editor and Publisher; Eddie P. Richardson, Publisher. **Subscription:** $15.

★3428★
Lynwood Journal
Rapid Publishing
349 W. Compton
PO Box 4248
Compton, CA 90224 Phone: (213)774-0018
Black community newspaper. **Column Depth:** 21 1/2 in. **Frequency:** Weekly (Wed.). **Number of Columns Per Page:** 6. **Column Width:** 12 1/2 picas. **Contact(s):** O. Ray Watkins, Publisher.

★3429★
Lynwood Wave
Central News-Wave Publications
2621 W. 54th St.
Los Angeles, CA 90043 Phone: (213)290-3000
Black community newspaper. **Established:** 1919. **Column Depth:** 21 1/2 in. **Frequency:** Weekly (Wed.). **Print Method:** Offset. **Number of Columns Per Page:** 6. **Column Width:** 5 nonpareils. **Contact(s):** C.Z. Wilson, Publisher. **Subscription:** $78. **Circulation:** 24,020.

★3430★
Memphis Silver Star News
1277 Worthington St.
PO Box 38114-0445
Memphis, TN 38114-0445 Phone: (901)272-3986
Black community newspaper. **Frequency:** Weekly (Wed.). **Contact(s):** J. Delnoah Williams, Editor and Publisher.

★3431★
Mesa Tribune Wave
Central News-Wave Publications
2621 W. 54th St.
Los Angeles, CA 90043 Phone: (213)290-3000
Black community newspaper. **Established:** 1919. **Column Depth:** 21 1/2 in. **Frequency:** Weekly (Wed.). **Print Method:** Offset. **Number of Columns Per Page:** 6. **Column Width:** 5 nonpareils. **Contact(s):** C.Z. Wilson, Publisher. **Subscription:** $78. **Circulation:** 30,100.

★3432★
Metro Chronicle
529 14th St., Ste. 1143
Washington, DC 20045 Phone: (202)347-1114
Black commmunity newspaper. **Contact(s):** Paris D. Davis, Publisher.

★3433★
Metro County Courier
PO Box 2385
Augusta, GA 30903 Phone: (404)724-6556
Black community newspaper. **Established:** 1983. **Column Depth:** 294 agate lines. **Frequency:** Weekly (Wed.). **Print Method:** Offset. **Trim Size:** 6 x 21. **Number of Columns Per Page:** 6. **Column Width:** 24 nonpareils. **Contact(s):** Barbara A. Gordon, Editor and Publisher. **Subscription:** $20. **Circulation:** 29,900.

★3434★
Metro Reporter
1366 Turk St.
San Francisco, CA 94115 Phone: (415)931-5778
Black community newspaper. **Established:** 1973. **Column Depth:** 21 in. **Frequency:** Weekly (Sun.). **Print Method:** Offset. **Number of Columns Per Page:** 6. **Column Width:** 2 1/16 in. **Contact(s):** Donald R. Young, Editor; Carlton B. Goodlett, Publisher. **Subscription:** $10. **Circulation:** 108,895.

★3435★
Metro Star
42353 47th St. W.
Quartz Hill, CA 93534
Black community newspaper. **Contact(s):** Leon Hudson, Publisher.

★3436★
Metro Times Newspaper
PO Box 1935
Goldsboro, NC 27533 Phone: (919)734-0302
Black community newspaper. **Established:** November 1978. **Column Depth:** 8 in. **Frequency:** Weekly. **Print Method:** Offset. **Trim Size:** 15 1/4 x 21. **Number of Columns Per Page:** 8. **Column Width:** 1 3/4 in. **Contact(s):** Ken Plummer, Editor; Pauline Swinson, Publisher. **Subscription:** $12.

★3437★
Metropolitan Gazette
PO Box 93275
Pasadena, CA 91109 Phone: (818)791-7239
Black community newspaper serving Los Angeles, Compton, Carson, Pasadena, Lynwood, and North Long Beach. **Established:** 1966. **Column Depth:** 294 agate lines. **Frequency:** Weekly (Thurs.). **Print Method:** Offset. **Trim Size:** 13 x 21 1/2. **Number of Columns Per Page:** 8. **Column Width:** 22 nonpareils. **Contact(s):** Beverly Hamm, Editor; Victoria V. Turner, Publisher; Stephen Mack, Publisher. **Subscription:** $25. **Circulation:** 25,000.

★3438★
Miami Republican
Miami County Publishing
121 S. Pearl St.
PO Box 389
Paola, KS 66071 Phone: (913)294-2311
Black community newspaper. **Established:** 1866. **Column Depth:** 21 in. **Frequency:** Weekly (Wed.). **Print Method:** Offset. **Number of Columns Per Page:** 6. **Column Width:** 2 1/6 in. **Contact(s):** Phil McLaughlin, Editor; Marjorie H. McLaughlin, Publisher; Donald Henry, Advertising Mgr. **Subscription:** $18.99.

★3439★
The Miami Times
900 NW 54th St.
Miami, FL 33127 Phone: (305)757-1147
Black community newspaper. **Established:** September 1, 1923. **Column Depth:** 21 in. **Frequency:** Weekly (Thurs.). **Print Method:** Offset. **Trim Size:** 13 3/4 x 22. **Number of Columns Per Page:** 6. **Column Width:** 2 1/16 in. **Contact(s):** Rachel J. Reeves, Executive Editor; Mohamed Hamaludin, Managing Editor; Garth C. Reeves, Publisher. **Subscription:** $35.

★3440★
Michigan Chronicle
479 Ledyard St.
Detroit, MI 48201 Phone: (313)963-5522
Black community newspaper. **Established:** 1936. **Column Depth:** 294 agate lines. **Frequency:** Weekly (Sat.). **Print Method:** Offset. **Number of Columns Per Page:** 6. **Column Width:** 26 nonpareils. **Contact(s):** John H. Stengstacke, Publisher. **Subscription:** $16. **Circulation:** 24,294.

★3441★
Michigan Citizen
New Day Publishing Enterprises
12541 2nd
Highland Park, MI 48203 Phone: (313)869-0033
Newspaper serving African-American communities in Michigan. **Established:** November 25, 1978. **Column Depth:** 14 in. **Frequency:** Weekly. **Print Method:** Offset. **Trim Size:** 10 1/2 x 15. **Number of Columns Per Page:** 5. **Column Width:** 11 picas. **Contact(s):** Teresa Maxwell-Kelly, Editor; Charles D. Kelly, Publisher/Advertising Mgr. **Subscription:** $16; $25 two years.

★3442★
Milwaukee Community Journal
Community Journal, Inc.
3612 N. Martin Luther King Dr.
Milwaukee, WI 53212 Phone: (414)265-5300
Black community newspaper. **Established:** 1976. **Column Depth:** 189 agate lines. **Frequency:** 2x/wk. (Wed. and Fri.). **Print Method:** Offset. **Number of Columns Per Page:** 6. **Column Width:** 20 nonpareils. **Contact(s):** Mikel Holt, Editor; Patricia O'Flynn Thomas, Publisher; Robert Thomas, Gen. Mgr. **Subscription:** Free; $15 (mail).

★3443★
Milwaukee Courier
2431 W. Hopkins St.
Milwaukee, WI 53206 Phone: (414)449-4866
Black community newspaper. **Established:** 1964. **Column Depth:** 126 agate lines. **Frequency:** Weekly (Sat.). **Print Method:** Offset. **Number of Columns Per Page:** 6. **Column Width:** 21 nonpareils. **Contact(s):** Joni Alston, Mng. Editor; Carole Geary, Publisher. **Subscription:** $12.50. **Circulation:** 15,000.

★3444★
Milwaukee Star
3815 N. Teutonia Ave.
Milwaukee, WI 53206 Phone: (414)449-4870
Black community newspaper. **Established:** 1961. **Frequency:** Weekly (Thurs.). **Print Method:** Offset. **Contact(s):** Joni Alston, Editor; Carole Geary, Publisher; Faithe Colas, Assoc. Publisher. **Subscription:** Free; $9.50 (mail). **Circulation:** 25,000.

★3445★
Milwaukee Times
PO Box 16489
Milwaukee, WI 53216 Phone: (414)444-8611
Black community newspaper. **Frequency:** Weekly. **Contact(s):** Nathan Conyers, Publisher.

★3446★
Minneapolis Spokesman
3744 4th Ave., S.
Minneapolis, MN 55409 Phone: (612)827-4021
Black community newspaper. **Established:** 1934. **Column Depth:** 218 agate lines. **Frequency:** Weekly (Thurs.). **Print Method:** Offset. **Number of Columns Per Page:** 6. **Column Width:** 21 nonpareils. **Contact(s):** Launa Newman, Editor and Publisher; Lynda Jackman, Advertising Mgr. **Subscription:** $14; $19 other states.

★3447★
The Mississippi Enterprise
540 1/2 N. Farish St.
PO Box 87236
Chicago, IL 60630-0236
Black community newspaper. **Established:** July 7, 1933. **Column Depth:** 21 in. **Frequency:** Weekly (Fri.). **Print Method:** Offset. **Number of Columns Per Page:** 8. **Column Width:** 11 picas. **Contact(s):** Lee Lyon, Editor and Advertising Mgr.; LeFloris Lyon, Publisher. **Subscription:** $17.

★3448★
Mississippi Memo Digest
2511 5th St.
Box 5782
Meridian, MS 39301 Phone: (601)693-2372
Black community newspaper. **Established:** January 14, 1961. **Column Depth:** 13 in. **Frequency:** Weekly (Wed.). **Print Method:** Offset. **Number of Columns Per Page:** 6. **Column Width:** 9 1/2 picas. **Contact(s):** Robert E. Williams, Editor and Publisher; Mary Jones, Advertising Mgr. **Subscription:** $9.80. **Circulation:** 3,050.

★3449★
Mobile Beacon
2311 Costarides St.
PO Box 1407
Mobile, AL 36633 Phone: (205)479-0629
Black community newspaper. **Established:** 1943. **Column Depth:** 21 in. **Frequency:** Weekly (Sat.). **Print Method:** Offset. **Number of Columns Per Page:** 6. **Column Width:** 2 1/8 in. **Contact(s):** Cleretta T. Blackmon, Editor/Advertising Mgr.; Lancie M. Thomas, Publisher. **Subscription:** $19. **Circulation:** 4,971.

★3450★
Montgomery-Tuskegee Times
3900 Birmingham Hwy.
Montgomery, AL 36108 Phone: (205)264-7149
Black community newspaper. **Established:** 1977. **Frequency:** Weekly. **Contact(s):** Rev. Alvin Dixon, Editor. **Circulation:** 10,000.

★3451★
Muslim Journal
Muslim Journal, Inc.
910 W. Van Buren St., No. 100
Chicago, IL 60607-3523
International Islamic newspaper. **Established:** 1961. **Column Depth:** 208 agate lines. **Frequency:** Weekly (Fri.). **Print Method:** Offset. **Number of Columns Per Page:** 5. **Column Width:** 22 nonpareils. **Contact(s):** Ayesha K. Mustafaa, Editor; Daa'iyah A. Muhaimin, Advertising Mgr. **Subscription:** $20.85. **Circulation:** 40,000.

★3452★
New Bayview
Double Rock Press
1624 Oakdale Ave.
PO Box 24477
San Francisco, CA 94124-0477 Phone: (415)822-6123
Black community newspaper (tabloid). **Established:** September 1, 1976. **Column Depth:** 14 in. **Frequency:** Weekly. **Print Method:** Offset. **Number of Columns Per Page:** 5. **Column Width:** 1 7/8 in. **Contact(s):** Muhammad Al-Kareem, Editor and Publisher. **Subscription:** $15.

★3453★
The New Iowa Bystander
PO Box 762
Des Moines, IA 50303
Newspaper serving the Black community. **Established:** 1893. **Column Depth:** 210 agate lines. **Frequency:** Weekly (Thurs.). **Print Method:** Offset. **Number of Columns Per Page:** 6. **Column Width:** 21 nonpareils. **Contact(s):** Loren T. Sampson, Editor and Publisher. **Subscription:** $7.50.

★3454★
New Jersey Afro-American
PO Box 22162
Newark, NJ 07103 Phone: (201)242-5364
Black community newspaper. **Established:** 1892. **Frequency:** Weekly. **Print Method:** Offset. **Number of Columns Per Page:** 6. **Contact(s):** Deborah P. Smith, Editor and Advertising Mgr.; Frances Murphy Draper, Publisher (301/728-8200). **Subscription:** $26. **Circulation:** 20,000.

★3455★
New Observer
811 Florida Ave. NW
Washington, DC 20001 Phone: (202)232-3060
Black community newspaper. **Contact(s):** Michael Angelo Graham, Editor.

★3456★
New Orleans Data News Weekly
Data Enterprises, Inc.
1001 Howard Ave., Ste. 2309
PO Box 51933
New Orleans, LA 70151 Phone: (504)522-1418
Black community newspaper. **Established:** 1966. **Column Depth:** 14 in. **Frequency:** Weekly (Sat.). **Print Method:** Offset. **Number of Columns Per Page:** 5. **Column Width:** 2 in. **Contact(s):** Terry Jones, Editor and Publisher; Keith Brown, Circulation Mgr. **ISSN:** 1043-4445. **Subscription:** $13.

★3457★
New Pittsburgh Courier
315 E. Carson St.
Pittsburgh, PA 15219 Phone: (412)481-8302
Black community newspaper. **Established:** 1910. **Column Depth:** 294 agate lines. **Frequency:** 2x/wk. (Wed. and Sat.). **Print Method:** Offset. **Number of Columns Per Page:** 6. **Column Width:** 26 nonpareils. **Contact(s):** Ed Davis, Mng. Editor; John H. Sehgstacke, Publisher; Rod Doss, V.P./Gen. Mgr.; Stephan A. Broadus, Advertising Mgr. **Subscription:** $35. **Circulation:** 30,000.

★3458★
The New Times
The New Times Group, Inc.
156 S. Broad St.
Mobile, AL 36602-0356 Phone: (205)432-0356
Black community newspaper. **Established:** 1981. **Column Depth:** 294 agate lines. **Frequency:** Weekly (Thurs.). **Print Method:** Offset. **Number of Columns Per Page:** 6. **Column Width:** 26 nonpareils. **Contact(s):** Vivian Davis Figures, Editor/Advertising Mgr. **Subscription:** Free; $11 (mail).

★3459★
NY Carib News
28 W. 39th St.
New York, NY 10018 Phone: (212)944-1991
Newspaper (tabloid) with Black orientation, providing Caribbean news and features. **Established:** June 29, 1982. **Column Depth:** 194 agate lines. **Frequency:** Weekly (Wed.). **Print Method:** Offset. **Trim Size:** 11 1/2 x 15. **Number of Columns Per Page:** 6. **Column Width:** 18 nonpareils. **Contact(s):** Marcia Keizs, Editor; Karl B. Rodney, Publisher; Jaye A. Rodney, Advertising Mgr. **Subscription:** $26.

★3460★
The New York Voice
75-43 Parsons Blvd.
Flushing, NY 11366 Phone: (718)591-6600
Black community newspaper. **Established:** 1959. **Column Depth:** 200 agate lines. **Frequency:** Weekly (Fri.). **Print Method:** Offset. **Number of Columns Per Page:** 4. **Column Width:** 32 nonpareils. **Contact(s):** Tom Sinclair, Editor; Kenneth Drew, Publisher. **Subscription:** $25. **Circulation:** 90,000.

★3461★
News Reporter
1610 N. Howard Ave.
Tampa, FL 33607
Black community newspaper. **Contact(s):** James Jackson, Editor.

★3462★
The Northwest Dispatch
PO Box 5637
Tacoma, WA 98405 Phone: (206)272-7587
Black community newspaper. **Established:** July 1982. **Column Depth:** 16 in. **Frequency:** Weekly. **Print Method:** Offset. **Number of Columns Per Page:** 5. **Column Width:** 2 1/16 in. **Contact(s):** Lu Taylor, Editor; Virginia Taylor, Publisher; Harold Johnson, Advertising Mgr. **Subscription:** $20.

★3463★
Oakland Post
The Alameda Publishing Corp.
630 20th St.
PO Box 1350
Oakland, CA 94604 Phone: (415)763-1120
Black community newspaper. **Established:** 1963. **Column Depth:** 21 1/2 in. **Frequency:** 2x/wk. (Wed. and Sun.). **Print Method:** Offset. **Number of Columns Per Page:** 6. **Column Width:** 1 1/16in. **Contact(s):** Gail Berkley, Editor; Thomas Berkley, Publisher; Donald V. Welcher, Advertising Mgr. **Subscription:** $42. **Circulation:** 62,496.

★3464★
Observer
6040 S. Harper St.
Chicago, IL 60637 Phone: (312)288-5840
Black community newspaper. **Established:** 1964. **Column Depth:** 196 agate lines. **Frequency:** Weekly (Thurs.). **Print Method:** Offset. **Number of Columns Per Page:** 5. **Column Width:** 24 nonpareils. **Contact(s):** Leon D. Finney, Jr. Publisher; Carolyn Fortier, Advertising Mgr. **Subscription:** $8. **Circulation:** 30,000.

★3465★
Ocean State Grapevine
106 Reservoir Ave.
Providence, RI 02907-3416
Black community newspaper. **Contact(s):** Douglas Terry, Editor.

★3466★
The Oklahoma Eagle
PO Box 3267
Tulsa, OK 74101 Phone: (918)582-7124
Black community newspaper. **Established:** 1921. **Column Depth:** 21 1/2 in. **Frequency:** Weekly (Thurs.). **Print Method:** Offset. **Number of Columns Per Page:** 6. **Column Width:** 2 1/16 in. **Contact(s):** James O. Goodwin, Publisher. **Subscription:** $21. **Circulation:** 12,800.

★3467★
Orangeburg Black Voice
1310 Harden
Columbia, SC 29204 Phone: (803)799-5252
Black community interest newspaper. **Established:** 1970. **Column Depth:** 224 agate lines. **Frequency:** Weekly (Wed.). **Print Method:** Offset. **Number of Columns Per Page:** 6. **Column Width:** 24 nonpareils. **Contact(s):** Zack Weston, Editor; Isaac Washington, Publisher; Cynthia Bowden, Advertising Mgr. **Subscription:** $25. **Circulation:** 5,365.

★3468★
The Orlando Times
4403 Vineland Rd., Ste. B-5
Orlando, FL 32811 Phone: (407)841-3710
Black community newspaper. **Established:** 1975. **Frequency:** Weekly (Thurs.). **Contact(s):** Lottie Collins, Editor; Calvin Collins, Jr., President and Publisher. **Circulation:** 5,710.

★3469★
Pensacola Voice
213 E. Yonge St.
Pensacola, FL 32503 Phone: (904)434-6963
Black community newspaper. **Established:** 1966. **Column Depth:** 21 in. **Frequency:** Weekly. **Number of Columns Per Page:** 6. **Column Width:** 2 in. **Subscription:** $10. **Circulation:** 35,896.

★3470★
Philadelphia New Observer
1930 Chestnut St., Ste. 900
Philadelphia, PA 19103 Phone: (215)922-5220
Newspaper (tabloid) with features for Black and Hispanic audience. **Established:** 1975. **Column Depth:** 224 agate lines. **Frequency:** Weekly (Wed.). **Print Method:** Offset. **Trim Size:** 11 x 17 **Number of Columns Per Page:** 6. **Column Width:** 1 9/16 in. **Contact(s):** J. Hugo Warren III, Editor and Publisher. **Subscription:** $30.

★3471★
The Philadelphia Tribune
524-526 S. 16th St.
Philadelphia, PA 19146 Phone: (215)893-4050
Newspaper with a Democratic orientation (Black). **Established:** 1884. **Column Depth:** 200 agate lines. **Frequency:** 3x/wk. (Tues., Thurs., and Fri.). **Print Method:** Offset. **Number of Columns Per Page:** 6. **Column Width:** 25 nonpareils. **Contact(s):** Paul A. Bennett, Editor; Robert W. Bogle, President. **Subscription:** $36.

★3472★
The Philadelphia Tribune (Metro Edition)
Philadelphia Tribune Co.
524-526 S. 16th St.
Philadelphia, PA 19146 Phone: (215)893-4050
Black community newspaper. **Established:** 1978. **Column Depth:** 182 agate lines. **Frequency:** Weekly (Thurs.). **Print Method:** Offset. **Number of Columns Per Page:** 5. **Column Width:** 25 nonpareils. **Contact(s):** Paul A. Bennett, Editor; Robert W. Bogle, Pres. **Circulation:** 73,000.

★3473★
Portland Observer
PO Box 3137
Portland, OR 97211 Phone: (503)288-0015
Black community newspaper. **Frequency:** Weekly (Thurs.). **Contact(s):** A.L. Henderson, Editor and Publisher. **Circulation:** 10,000.

★3474★
The Portland Skanner
PO Box 5455
Portland, OR 97228 Phone: (503)287-3562
Black community newspaper. **Established:** 1975. **Column Depth:** 224 agate lines. **Frequency:** Weekly (Wed.). **Print Method:** Offset. **Number of Columns Per Page:** 6. **Column Width:** 20 nonpareils. **Contact(s):** Bernard V. Foster, Editor and Publisher. **Subscription:** $20. **Circulation:** 20,000.

★3475★
Precinct Reporter
1677 W. Baseline St.
San Bernardino, CA 92411 Phone: (714)889-0597
Black community newspaper. **Established:** July 26, 1965. **Column Depth:** 294 agate lines. **Frequency:** Weekly (Thurs.). **Print Method:** Offset. **Number of Columns Per Page:** 6. **Column Width:** 18 nonpareils. **Contact(s):** Brian Townsend, Publisher. **Subscription:** $15. **Circulation:** 55,000.

★3476★
The Public Post
PO Box 1951
Laurinburg, NC 28352 Phone: (919)875-8938
Black community interest newspaper. **Established:** 1981. **Column Depth:** 21 in. **Frequency:** Weekly (Wed.). **Print Method:** Offset. **Number of Columns Per Page:** 6. **Column Width:** 2 1/16 in. **Contact(s):** Roosevelt McPherson, Editor and Publisher. **Subscription:** $10.

★3477★
Richmond Afro-American
Afro-American Newspapers
628 N. Eutaw St.
Baltimore, MD 21201 Phone: (301)728-8200
Black community newspaper. **Established:** 1882. **Column Depth:** 308 agate lines. **Frequency:** Weekly (Wed.). **Print Method:** Letterpress and offset. **Number of Columns Per Page:** 6. **Column Width:** 25 nonpareils. **Contact(s):** Robert Matthews, Editor; Frances L. Draper, Publisher; Kenneth O. Wilson, Advertising Mgr. **Subscription:** $23. **Circulation:** 3,250.

★3478★
Richmond Post
The Alameda Publishing Corp.
630 20th St.
PO Box 1350
Oakland, CA 94604-1350 Phone: (415)763-1120
Black community newspaper. **Established:** 1963. **Column Depth:** 21 1/2 in. **Frequency:** 2x/wk. (Wed. and Sun.). **Print Method:** Offset. **Number of Columns Per Page:** 6. **Column Width:** 2 1/16 in. **Contact(s):** Gail Berkley, Editor; Thomas Berkley, Publisher; Donald V. Welcher, Advertising Mgr. **Subscription:** $42. **Circulation:** 13,661.

★3479★
Roanoke Tribune
PO Box 6021
Roanoke, VA 24017 Phone: (703)343-0326
Black community newspaper. **Established:** 1938. **Column Depth:** 294 agate lines. **Frequency:** Weekly (Thurs.). **Print Method:** Offset. **Number of Columns Per Page:** 6. **Column Width:** 25 nonpareils. **Contact(s):** Claudia A. Whitworth, Editor and Publisher. **Subscription:** $10. **Circulation:** 5,200.

★3480★
Rock Hill Black View
1310 Harden
Columbia, SC 29204 Phone: (803)799-5252
Black community interest newspaper. **Established:** 1970. **Column Depth:** 224 agate lines. **Frequency:** Weekly (Wed.). **Print Method:** Offset. **Number of Columns Per Page:** 6. **Column Width:** 24 nonpareils. **Contact(s):** Zack Weston, Editor; Isaac Washington, Publisher; Cynthia Bowden, Advertising Mgr. **Subscription:** $25. **Circulation:** 4,882.

★3481★
Sacramento Observer
The Observer Newspapers
3540 4th Ave.
PO Box 209
Sacramento, CA 95817 Phone: (916)452-4781
Black Community newspaper. **Established:** 1962. **Frequency:** Weekly (Thurs.). **Print Method:** Offset. **Trim Size:** 10 x 15. **Number of Columns Per Page:** 5 and 6. /CLD 21 in. **Contact(s):** Kathryn C. Lee, Mng. Editor; Dr. William H. Lee, Publisher. **Subscription:** $20. **Circulation:** 49,090.

★3482★
The St. Louis American
American Publishing Co.
4144 Lindell Blvd.
Saint Louis, MO 63108 Phone: (314)533-8000
Black community newspaper. **Established:** 1928. **Column Depth:** 194 agate lines. **Frequency:** Weekly (Thurs.). **Print Method:** Offset. **Trim Size:** 13 1/2 x 22 3/4. **Number of Columns Per Page:** 6. **Column Width:** 26 nonpareils. **Contact(s):** Dr. Donald M. Suggs, Publisher. **Subscription:** $12.50.

★3483★
St. Louis Argus
4595 Martin Luther King Dr.
St. Louis, MO 63113 Phone: (314)531-1323
Black community newspaper. **Frequency:** Weekly. **Contact(s):** Donald Thompson, Editor; Dr. Eugene Mitchell, Publisher. **Circulation:** 15,000.

★3484★
St. Louis Crusader
4371 Finney Ave.
St. Louis, MO 63113 Phone: (314)531-5860
Black community newspaper. **Frequency:** Weekly. **Contact(s):** William P. Russell, Pres./Chm. of the Board.

★3485★
St. Louis Sentinel Newspaper
Woods Publications
2900 N. Market
St. Louis, MO 63106 Phone: (314)531-2691
Black newspaper with a Republican orientation. **Established:** April 1968. **Column Depth:** 21 1/2 in. **Frequency:** Weekly (Thurs.). **Print Method:** Offset. **Trim Size:** 13 x 21 1/2. **Number of Columns Per Page:** 6. **Column Width:** 2 1/16 in. **Contact(s):** Michael Williams, Editor; Jane E. Woods, Publisher; Robert Ware, Advertising Mgr. **Subscription:** $20.

★3486★
St. Paul Recorder
3744 4th Ave., S.
Minneapolis, MN 55409
Black community newspaper. **Contact(s):** Cecil Newman, Editor.

★3487★
The San Bernardino American News
PO Box 7010
San Bernardino, CA 92411-0010 Phone: (714)889-7677
Black community newspaper. **Established:** 1969. **Column Depth:** 294 agate lines. **Frequency:** Weekly (Thurs.). **Print Method:** Offset. **Number of Columns Per Page:** 6. **Column Width:** 26 nonpareils. **Contact(s):** Samuel Martin, Publisher. **Subscription:** $12. **Circulation:** 5,000.

★3488★
The San Diego Voice and Viewpoint
PO Box 95
San Diego, CA 92112 Phone: (619)238-0933
Black and Mexican American newspaper. **Established:** 1960. **Column Depth:** 224 agate lines. **Frequency:** Weekly (Thurs.). **Print Method:** Offset. Uses mats. **Number of Columns Per Page:** 5. **Column Width:** 23 nonpareils. **Contact(s):** Earl Davis, Jr., Editor and Publisher. **Subscription:** $20. **Circulation:** 13,000.

★3489★
San Francisco Post
The Alameda Publishing Corp.
630 20th St.
PO Box 1350
Oakland, CA 94604 Phone: (415)763-1120
Black community newspaper. **Established:** 1963. **Column Depth:** 21 1/2 in. **Frequency:** 2x/wk.(Wed. and Sun.). **Print Method:** Offset. **Number of Columns Per Page:** 6. **Column Width:** 1 1/16 in. **Contact(s):** Gail Berkley, Editor; Thomas Berkley, Publisher; Donald V. Welcher, Advertising Mgr. **Subscription:** $42. **Circulation:** 18,289.

★3490★
The Savannah Tribune
916 Montgomery St.
PO Box 2066
Savannah, GA 31402 Phone: (912)233-6128
Black community newspaper. **Established:** 1875. **Column Depth:** 21 1/2 in. **Frequency:** Weekly (Thurs.). **Print Method:** Offset. **Trim Size:** 13 x 21 1/2. **Number of Columns Per Page:** 6. **Column Width:** 2 in. **Contact(s):** Shirley B. James, Editor and Publisher. **Subscription:** $15; $17 out of area.

★3491★
Seaside Post News-Sentinel
The Alameda Publishing Corp.
1244A Broadway Ave.
PO Box 670
Seaside, CA 93955 Phone: (408)394-6632
Black community newspaper. **Established:** 1947. **Column Depth:** 301 agate lines. **Frequency:** Weekly (Wed.). **Print Method:** Offset. Uses mats. **Number of Columns Per Page:** 6. **Column Width:** 26 nonpareils. **Contact(s):** Willie L. Harrell, Editor and Publisher. **Subscription:** $20.

★3492★
Seattle Medium
2600 S. Jackson
Seattle, WA 98144 Phone: (206)323-3070
Black community newspaper. **Established:** 1970. **Frequency:** Weekly (Wed.). **Contact(s):** Angela Jenkins, Editor; Chris Bennett, Publisher. **Circulation:** 37,000.

★3493★
Shoals News Leader
PO Box 427
Florence, AL 35631 Phone: (205)766-5542
Black community newspaper. **Established:** 1980. **Frequency:** Weekly. **Contact(s):** William R. Liner, Editor and Publisher. **Circulation:** 10,000.

★3494★
The Shreveport Sun
The Shreveport Sun, Inc.
PO Box 9328
Shreveport, LA 71139-9328 Phone: (318)631-6222
Black community newspaper. **Established:** 1920. **Column Depth:** 301 agate lines. **Frequency:** Weekly (Wed.). **Print Method:** Offset. **Number of Columns Per Page:** 6. **Column Width:** 25 nonpareils. **Contact(s):** Sonya Collins Landry, Editor; Ronald Collins, Advertising Mgr. **Subscription:** $15.

★3495★
South East Times
3249 E. 137th St.
Cleveland, OH 44120 Phone: (216)921-2788
Black community newspaper. **Contact(s):** Michael L. Potts, President.

★3496★
South End Citizen
Citizen Newspapers
412 E. 87th St.
Chicago, IL 60619 Phone: (312)487-7700
Newspaper serving Chicago's Black community. **Established:** 1966. **Column Depth:** 196 agate lines. **Frequency:** Weekly (Thurs.). **Print Method:** Offset. **Number of Columns Per Page:** 5. **Column Width:** 25 nonpareils. **Contact(s):** William Garth, Publisher/Advertising Mgr. **Subscription:** $15.

★3497★
South Suburban Citizen
Citizen Newspapers
412 E. 87th St.
Chicago, IL 60619 Phone: (312)487-7700
Newspaper serving Chicago's suburban Black community. **Established:** 1983. **Column Depth:** 196 agate lines. **Frequency:** Weekly (Thurs.). **Print Method:** Offset. **Number of Columns Per Page:** 5. **Column Width:** 25 nonpareils. **Contact(s):** William Garth, Editor and Publisher. **Subscription:** $15.

★3498★
South Suburban Standard
615 S. Halsted
Chicago Heights, IL 60411 Phone: (708)755-5021
Black community newspaper. **Established:** 1979. **Column Depth:** 225 agate lines. **Frequency:** Every other week. **Print Method:** Offset. **Number of Columns Per Page:** 6. **Column Width:** 19 nonpareils. **Contact(s):** Charles R. Gordon, Editor; Lorenzo Martin, Publisher; Pat Rush Martin, Advertising Mgr. **Subscription:** $30. **Circulation:** 25,000.

★3499★
Southeastern News
PO Box 461
Cordele, GA 31015
Black community newspaper. **Contact(s):** Eugene Rutland, General Manager.

★3500★
Southwest News Wave
Central News-Wave Publications, Inc.
2621 W. 54th St.
Los Angeles, CA 90043 Phone: (213)290-3000
Black community newspaper. **Established:** 1919. **Column Depth:** 21 1/2 in. **Frequency:** Weekly (Wed.). **Print Method:** Offset. **Trim Size:** 13 3/4 x 21 1/2. **Number of Columns Per Page:** 6. **Column Width:** 5 nonpareils. **Contact(s):** C.Z. Wilson, Publisher. **Subscription:** $78. **Circulation:** 40,450.

★3501★
Southwest Topics/Sun Wave
Central News-Wave Publications
2621 W. 54th St.
Los Angeles, CA 90043 Phone: (213)290-3000
Black community newspaper. **Established:** 1919. **Column Depth:** 21 1/2 in. **Frequency:** Weekly (Wed.). **Print Method:** Offset. **Trim Size:** 13 3/4 x 21 1/2. **Number of Columns Per Page:** 6. **Column Width:** 5 nonpareils. **Contact(s):** C. Z. Wilson, Publisher. **Subscription:** $78. **Circulation:** 30,000.

★3502★
Speakin' Out News
1333 Meridian St. NW
PO Box 2826
Huntsville, AL 35804 Phone: (205)536-3539
Black community newspaper. **Established:** 1980. **Column Depth:** 15 in. **Frequency:** Weekly (Wed.). **Print Method:** Offset. **Trim Size:** 10 1/4 x 15. **Number of Columns Per Page:** 6. **Column Width:** 1 1/2 in. **Contact(s):** William Smothers, Editor and Publisher. **Subscription:** $15. **Circulation:** 16,500.

★3503★
Star of Zion
A.M.E. Zion Publishing House
PO Box 31005
Charlotte, NC 28231-1005 Phone: (704)377-4329
Religious newspaper (tabloid) for the Black community. **Established:** October 1876. **Column Depth:** 140 agate lines. **Frequency:** Weekly (Thurs.). **Print Method:** Offset. **Number of Columns Per Page:** 4. **Column Width:** 26 nonpareils. **Contact(s):** Dr. Morgan W. Tann, Editor; Gregory Smith, Advertising Mgr. **Subscription:** $22.

★3504★
Sumter Black Post
1310 Harden
Columbia, SC 29204 Phone: (803)799-5252
Black community interest newspaper. **Established:** 1970. **Column Depth:** 224 agate lines. **Frequency:** Weekly (Wed.). **Print Method:** Offset. **Number of Columns Per Page:** 6. **Column Width:** 24 nonpareils. **Contact(s):** Zack Weston, Editor; Isaac Washington, Publisher; Cynthia Bowden, Advertising Mgr. **Subscription:** $25. **Circulation:** 5,355.

★3505★
Sun-Reporter
Reporter Publications
1366 Turk St.
San Francisco, CA 94115 Phone: (415)931-5778
Black community newspaper (tabloid). **Established:** 1943. **Column Depth:** 14 in. **Frequency:** Weekly (Wed.). **Print Method:** Offset. **Number of Columns Per Page:** 5. **Column Width:** 2 1/16 in. **Contact(s):** Amelia-Ashley Ward, Editor; Carlton B. Goodlett, Ph.D., M.D., Publisher; Jack Kisbey, Advertising Mgr. **Subscription:** $11. **Circulation:** 11,187.

★3506★
The Suspension Press
1002 Geenup St.
Covington, KY 41011 Phone: (606)491-6106
Black community newspaper. **Established:** August 21, 1982. **Column Depth:** 210 agate lines. **Frequency:** Every other week. **Print Method:** Offset. **Number of Columns Per Page:** 5. **Column Width:** 22 nonpareils. **Contact(s):** Pamela Mullins, Editor; Patricia Humphries Fann, Publisher; Robert Humphries, Advertising Mgr. **Subscription:** $12.

★3507★
Tacoma True Citizen
2600 S. Jackson
Jackson, WA 98144 Phone: (206)627-1103
Black community newspaper. **Frequency:** Weekly (Thurs.). **Contact(s):** Connie Cameron, Editor; Chris Bennett, Publisher. **Circulation:** 13,500.

★3508★
The Toledo Journal
3021 Douglas St.
PO Box 2536
Toledo, OH 43606 Phone: (419)472-4521
African-American newspaper. **Established:** 1975. **Frequency:** Weekly (Wed.). **Print Method:** Offset. **Trim Size:** 10 1/4 x 16. **Number of Columns Per Page:** 6. **Contact(s):** Myron A. Stewart, Editor; Sandra R. Stewart, Publisher. **Subscription:** $25. **Circulation:** 17,000.

★3509★
Tri-City Journal
8 S. Michigan Ave., Ste. 1111
Chicago, IL 60603 Phone: (312)346-8123
Black community newspaper. **Established:** 1978. **Column Depth:** 14 in. **Frequency:** Weekly (Thurs.). **Print Method:** Offset. **Trim Size:** 10 x 14 in. **Number of Columns Per Page:** 5. **Column Width:** 11 1/2 in. **Contact(s):** Ibn Sharrieff, Editor and Publisher. **Circulation:** 50,000.

★3510★
Tri-State Defender
124 E. Calhoun Ave.
Memphis, TN 38101 Phone: (901)523-1818
Black community newspaper. **Established:** 1951. **Column Depth:** 21 in. **Frequency:** Weekly (Thurs.). **Print Method:** Web offset. **Trim Size:** 13 1/2 x 22 1/2. **Number of Columns Per Page:** 6. **Column Width:** 2 1/16 in. **Contact(s):** Audrey McGee, Editor; John H. Sengstacke, Publisher. **Subscription:** $15. **Circulation:** 15,000.

★3511★
Tundra Times
Eskimo, Indian, Aleut Publishing Co.
PO Box 104480
Anchorage, AK 99510-4480 Phone: (907)274-2512
Statewide Native American newspaper. **Established:** 1962. **Column Depth:** 210 agate lines. **Frequency:** Weekly (Mon.). **Print Method:** Offset. **Trim Size:** 11 x 17. **Number of Columns Per Page:** 4. **Column Width:** 2 1/4 in. **Contact(s):** A.J. McClanahan, Editor and Publisher; Michael F. Chase, Advertising Mgr. **ISSN:** 0049-4801. **Subscription:** $20; $35 other countries.

★3512★
Twin Cities Courier
84 S. 6th St., Ste. 501
Minneapolis, MN 55402 Phone: (612)332-3211
Black community newspaper. **Contact(s):** Mary J. Kyle, Editor.

★3513★
View South News
PO Box 1849
Orangeburg, SC 29116 Phone: (803)531-1662
Black community newspaper (tabloid). **Established:** 1979. **Frequency:** Weekly. **Trim Size:** 11 x 16. **Number of Columns Per Page:** 4. **Contact(s):** Cecil J. Williams, Editor and Publisher. **Circulation:** 5,000.

★3514★
The Villager
Black Registry Publishing Co.
1223-A Rosewood Ave.
Austin, TX 78702 Phone: (512)476-0082
Black community newspaper. **Established:** May 13, 1973. **Column Depth:** 294 agate lines. **Frequency:** Weekly (Fri.). **Print Method:** Offset. **Trim Size:** 13 x 21. **Number of Columns Per Page:** 6. **Column Width:** 26 nonpareils. **Contact(s):** Bobbie J. Hall, Managing Editor; T. L. Wyatt, Publisher and Advertising Mgr. **Subscription:** $15. **Circulation:** 6,000.

★3515★
Voice of the Wildcats
Bethune-Cookman College
640 2nd Ave.
Daytona Beach, FL 32115 Phone: (904)255-1401
Black collegiate newspaper. **Established:** 1974. **Column Depth:** 196 agate lines. **Frequency:** Quarterly (during the academic year). **Print Method:** Offset. **Trim Size:** 11 x 14. **Number of Columns Per Page:** 4. **Column Width:** 22 nonpareils. **Contact(s):** Valerie Whitney, Editor and Advertising Mgr. **Subscription:** $5. **Circulation:** 2,000.

★3516★
The Waco Messenger
Smith Printing Co.
PO Box 2087
Waco, TX 76703 Phone: (817)799-6911
Black community newspaper. **Established:** 1929. **Column Depth:** 20 in. **Frequency:** Weekly (Fri.). **Print Method:** Letterpress. **Trim Size:** 22 x 30. **Number of Columns Per Page:** 6. **Column Width:** 13 picas. **Contact(s):** M. P. Harvey, Editor and Publisher. **Subscription:** $10; $12.75 out of state. **Circulation:** 3,000.

★3517★
Washington Afro-American Tribune
2002 11th St. NW
Washington, DC 20001 Phone: (202)332-0080
Newspaper (Black). **Established:** 1933. **Column Depth:** 315 agate lines. **Frequency:** 2x/wk. (Tues. and Sat.). **Print Method:** Letterpress and offset. **Number of Columns Per Page:** 8. **Column Width:** 20 nonpareils. **Contact(s):** Frances L. Murphy, Publisher. **Subscription:** $20.

★3518★
The Washington Capital Spotlight Newspaper
1158 National Press Bldg.
Washington, DC 20045 Phone: (202)628-0700
Black community newspaper. **Established:** 1953. **Column Depth:** 14 in. **Frequency:** Weekly (Thurs.). **Print Method:** Offset. **Number of Columns Per Page:** 6. **Column Width:** 1 9/16 in. **Contact(s):** Barry Murray, Editor; Ike Kendrick, Publisher. **Subscription:** $25. **Circulation:** 60,000.

★3519★
The Washington Informer
3117 Martin Luther King Jr. Ave., SE
Washington, DC 20032 Phone: (202)561-4100
Newspaper (tabloid) serving Washington's metropolitan area Black community. **Established:** October 16, 1964. **Column Depth:** 12 1/2 in. **Frequency:** Weekly (Thurs.). **Print Method:** Offset. **Number of**

Columns Per Page: 6. **Column Width:** 1 1/2 in. **Contact(s):** Calvin W. Rolark, Editor and Publisher. **Subscription:** $15. **Circulation:** 27,000.

★3520★
The Washington New Observer
811 Florida Ave. NW
Washington, DC 20001 Phone: (202)232-3060
Black community newspaper. **Established:** 1957. **Column Depth:** 196 agate lines. **Frequency:** Weekly (Thurs.). **Print Method:** Tabloid. Offset. **Number of Columns Per Page:** 5. **Column Width:** 24 nonpareils. **Contact(s):** Robert T. Newton, Editor; Lauren Newton Johnson, Advertising Mgr. **Subscription:** $24. **Circulation:** 20,000.

★3521★
Watts Star Review
PO Box 19027A
Los Angeles, CA 90019 Phone: (213)291-9486
Black community newspaper. **Established:** 1875. **Column Depth:** 194 agate lines. **Frequency:** Weekly (Thurs.). **Print Method:** Offset. **Number of Columns Per Page:** 6. **Column Width:** 29 nonpareils. **Contact(s):** Lela Ward Oliver, Editor; John H. Holoman, Publisher. **Subscription:** $20. **Circulation:** 30,000.

★3522★
The Weekly Challenger
2500 9th St. S.
Saint Petersburg, FL 33705
Black community newspaper. **Established:** September 1967. **Column Depth:** 21 1/2 in. **Frequency:** Weekly. **Print Method:** Offset. **Trim Size:** 8 x 21 1/2. **Number of Columns Per Page:** 8. **Column Width:** 1 1/2 in. **Contact(s):** Cynthia Armstrong, Editor; Cleveland Johnson, Publisher; William Blackshear, Advertising Mgr. **Subscription:** $15; $22 out of county. **Circulation:** 32,000.

★3523★
West Virginia Beacon Digest
900 Maccorkle Ave., SW
South Charleston, WV 25303-1319 Phone: (304)342-4600
Black community newspaper. **Established:** 1957. **Column Depth:** 21 1/4 in. **Frequency:** Weekly. **Print Method:** Web press. **Number of Columns Per Page:** 6. **Column Width:** 2 in. **Contact(s):** Stephen R. Starks, Editor and Publisher. **Subscription:** $13. **Circulation:** 35,861.

★3524★
Westchester County Press
1 Prospect Ave.
White Plains, NY 10607 Phone: (914)684-0006
Newspaper directed to the total community, with special emphasis on the positive issues about the Black community. **Established:** 1928. **Column Depth:** 14 in. **Frequency:** Weekly (Thurs.). **Print Method:** Offset. Uses mats. **Trim Size:** 11 x 14. **Number of Columns Per Page:** 4. **Column Width:** 2 3/8 in. **Contact(s):** Orial A. Redd, Exec. Editor; Tanya Lewis Mng. Editor; Alvin J. Nall, Editor; M. Paul Redd, Publisher; Paula A. Zeman, Advertising Mgr. **ISSN:** 0043-3373. **Subscription:** $25. **Circulation:** 20,000.

★3525★
Westchester Observer
542 E. 3rd St.
Mount Vernon, NY 10553
Black community newspaper. **Contact(s):** Ben Anderson, Editor.

★3526★
Western Spirit
Miami County Publishing
121 S. Pearl St.
Paola, KS 66071 Phone: (913)294-2311
Black community newspaper. **Established:** 1871. **Column Depth:** 21 in. **Frequency:** Weekly (Mon.). **Print Method:** Offset. **Number of Columns Per Page:** 6. **Column Width:** 2 11/6 in. **Contact(s):** Phil McLaughlin, Editor; Marjorie H. McLaughlin, Publisher; Donald Henry, Advertising Mgr. **Subscription:** $18.99.

★3527★
Westside Gazette
PO Box 5304
Fort Lauderdale, FL 33310 Phone: (305)523-5115
Black community newspaper. **Established:** 1971. **Column Depth:** 294 agate lines. **Frequency:** 2x/wk. (Thurs. and Sun.). **Print Method:** Offset. **Number of Columns Per Page:** 6. **Column Width:** 24 nonpareils. **Contact(s):** Yvonne Henry, Editor; Levi Henry, Jr., Publisher. **Subscription:** $20.

★3528★
Wilmington Beacon
Rapid Publishing
349 W. Compton
PO Box 4248
Compton, CA 90224 Phone: (213)774-0018
Black community newspaper. **Column Depth:** 21 1/2 in. **Frequency:** Weekly (Wed.). **Number of Columns Per Page:** 6. **Column Width:** 12 1/2 picas. **Contact(s):** O. Ray Watkins, Publisher.

★3529★
The Wilmington Journal
412 S. 7th St.
Wilmington, NC 28401 Phone: (919)762-5502
Black community newspaper. **Established:** 1927. **Column Depth:** 294 agate lines. **Frequency:** Weekly (Thurs.). **Print Method:** Offset. **Number of Columns Per Page:** 6. **Column Width:** 25 nonpareils. **Contact(s):** T. C. Jervay, Editor and Publisher. **ISSN:** 0049-7649. **Subscription:** $15. **Circulation:** 8,600.

★3530★
Winston-Salem Chronicle
617 N. Liberty St.
PO Box 3154
Winston-Salem, NC 27102 Phone: (919)722-8624
Black community newspaper. **Established:** 1974. **Column Depth:** 294 agate lines. **Frequency:** Weekly (Thurs.). **Print Method:** Offset. **Number of Columns Per Page:** 6. **Column Width:** 24 nonpareils. **Contact(s):** Ernest H. Pitt, Publisher. **Subscription:** $18.52. **Circulation:** 5,036.

Periodicals

★3531★
A&T Register
North Carolina Agricultural & Technical University
Box E25
Greensboro, NC 27411 Phone: (919)334-7700
Collegiate magazine with a Black orientation. **Established:** 1892. **Column Depth:** 210 agate lines. **Frequency:** Weekly (Fri.). **Print Method:** Offset. **Number of Columns Per Page:** 5. **Column Width:** 22 nonpareils. **Contact(s):** Esther Woods, Editor; Warren McNeill, Advertising Mgr. **Subscription:** $12.

★3532★
About...Time
About...Time Magazine, Inc.
283 Genesee St.
Rochester, NY 14611 Phone: (716)235-7150
Magazine providing a chronicle of minority history and achievement. **Established:** December 1972. **Frequency:** Monthly. **Print Method:** Offset. **Trim Size:** 8 1/2 x 11. **Number of Columns Per Page:** 2 and 3. **Contact(s):** Carolyne S. Blount, Editor; James M. Blount, Publisher and Advertising Mgr. **Subscription:** $11.

★3533★
Africa Today
Africa Today Associates
G.SI.S University of Denver
Denver, CO 80208 Phone: (303)871-3678
Journal on political, social, and economic conditions in Africa. **Established:** March 1954. **Column Depth:** 119 agate lines. **Frequency:** Quarterly. **Print Method:** Offset. **Trim Size:** 5 x 8. **Number of Columns**

Per Page: 1. Column Width: 66 nonpareils. Contact(s): Edward A. Hawley, Editor. ISSN: 0001-9887. Subscription: $40.

★3534★
Aim—America's Intercultural Magazine
Aim Publications
7308 S. Eberhart Ave.
Chicago, IL 60619 Phone: (312)874-6184
Magazine promoting intercultural awareness and understanding in America. **Established:** 1974. **Frequency:** Quarterly. **Trim Size:** 8 1/2 x 11. **Number of Columns Per Page:** 3. **Contact(s):** Myron Apilado, Mng. Editor; Ruth Apilado, Editor and Publisher. **Subscription:** $8.

★3535★
Alternative Press Index
PO Box 33109
Baltimore, MD 21218 Phone: (301)243-2471
Alternative index including Black, Hispanic, and women's listings. **Established:** 1969. **Column Depth:** 130 agate lines. **Frequency:** 4x/yr. **Print Method:** Offset. **Trim Size:** 8 1/2 x 11. **Number of Columns Per Page:** 3. **Column Width:** 27 nonpareils. **Contact(s):** M. D. Adamo, Editor. **ISSN:** 0002-662X. **Subscription:** $30; $125 institutions.

★3536★
American Visions: The Magazine of Afro-American Culture
Warwick Communications
Carter G. Woodson House
Smithsonian Institution
Washington, DC 20560 Phone: (202)462-1779
Established: January 1986. **Column Depth:** 50 picas. **Frequency:** 6x/yr. **Print Method:** Offset. **Trim Size:** 8 1/4 x 10 7/8. **Number of Columns Per Page:** 3. **Column Width:** 13 picas. **Contact(s):** Gary Puckrein, Editor-in-Chief and Publisher; Joanne Harris, Editor. **ISSN:** 0884-9390. **Subscription:** $18.

★3537★
AUC Digest
Atlanta University Center
PO Box 3191
Atlanta, GA 30302 Phone: (404)523-6136
Collegiate magazine (tabloid). **Established:** 1973. **Column Depth:** 196 agate lines. **Frequency:** Weekly (Mon.). **Print Method:** Offset. **Number of Columns Per Page:** 4. **Column Width:** 27 nonpareils. **Contact(s):** Lo Jelks, Editor and Publisher; Tim Williams, Advertising Mgr. **Subscription:** $12.

★3538★
Black American Literature Forum
Dept. of English
Indiana State University
Terre Haute, IN 47809 Phone: (812)237-2968
Journal presenting Black American essays, interviews, poems, and book reviews. **Established:** Fall 1967. **Column Depth:** 44 picas. **Frequency:** 4x/yr. **Print Method:** Offset. **Trim Size:** 6 x 9. **Number of Columns Per Page:** 1. **Column Width:** 26 1/2 picas. **Contact(s):** Joseph Weixlmann, Editor. **ISSN:** 0148-6179. **Subscription:** $20; $32 institutions; $25 foreign; $37 institutions, foreign.

★3539★
BLACK CAREERS
Project Magazine, Inc.
PO Box 8214
Philadelphia, PA 19101-8214 Phone: (215)387-1600
Business news magazine for minority college graduates and working professionals in business, industry, and government. **Established:** 1965. **Column Depth:** 140 agate lines. **Frequency:** 6x/yr. **Print Method:** Offset. **Trim Size:** 8 1/2 x 11. **Number of Columns Per Page:** 3. **Column Width:** 27 nonpareils. **Contact(s):** Emory W. Washington, Editor and Publisher; Herbert Bass, Advertising Mgr.; D. Gooden, Circulation Mgr.. **Subscription:** $20.

★3540★
Black College Sports Review
617 N. Liberty St.
Winston-Salem, NC 27102 Phone: (919)723-9026
Magazine covering Black college sports. **Contact(s):** Ernest H. Pitt, Publisher.

★3541★
The Black Collegian
Black Collegiate Services, Inc.
1240 S. Broad St.
New Orleans, LA 70125-2091 Phone: (504)821-5694
Career and job oriented publication. **Established:** 1970. **Column Depth:** 9 in. **Frequency:** 4x/yr. **Print Method:** Offset. **Trim Size:** 8 x 10 3/4. **Number of Columns Per Page:** 3. **Column Width:** 13 1/2 picas. **Contact(s):** Kuumba Ferrouillett, Editor; Preston J. Edwards, Publisher; Melba Lemieux, Advertising Mgr. **ISSN:** 0192-3757. **Subscription:** $10; $5 students. $2.50 single issue.

★3542★
Black Enterprise
Earl Graves Publishing
130 5th Ave.
New York, NY 10011 Phone: (212)242-8000
Black-oriented business magazine. **Established:** 1970. **Column Depth:** 134 agate lines. **Frequency:** Monthly. **Print Method:** Offset. **Trim Size:** 8 1/8 x 10 7/8. **Number of Columns Per Page:** 3. **Column Width:** 27 nonpareils. **Contact(s):** Earl G. Graves, Editor and Publisher. **Subscription:** $12.95. $1.95 single issue. **Circulation:** 230,000.

★3543★
Black Family
Kent Enterprises, Inc.
Box 1046
Herndon, VA 22070-1046
Magazine focusing and shaping positive lifestyles for middle to upper-middle income Black consumers. **Established:** 1980. **Column Depth:** 140 agate lines. **Frequency:** 6x/yr. **Print Method:** Offset. **Trim Size:** 8 1/8 x 10 7/8. **Number of Columns Per Page:** 3. **Contact(s):** Evelyn Ivery, Managing Editor; Frank C. Kent, Publisher; Mai Ling Poole, Advertising Mgr.

★3544★
Black Health
Altier & Maynard Communications, Inc.
6 Farmingville Rd.
Ridgefield, CT 06877 Phone: (203)431-3454
Established: 1988. **Frequency:** 4x/yr. **Trim Size:** 8 1/8 x 10 3/4. **Contact(s):** Bonnie Maynard, Publisher; Carlos Maynard, Publisher. **Subscription:** Free; $10 institutions (mail). $2.50 single issue.

★3545★
Black News Digest
U.S. Dept. of Labor
Office of Information & Public Affairs
200 Constitution Ave. NW
Washington, DC 20210 Phone: (202)523-7323
Government publication containing news and feature material about the U.S. Department of Labor and its programs for Black Americans. **Frequency:** Weekly. **Trim Size:** 8 1/2 x 11. **Contact(s):** Sue Blumenthal, Editor; Paul S. Williams, Chief, Division of Media and Editorial Services. **Subscription:** Free.

★3546★
The Black Scholar
Black World Foundation
PO Box 2869
Oakland, CA 94609 Phone: (415)547-6633
Established: November 1969. **Frequency:** 6x/yr. **Print Method:** Offset. **Trim Size:** 5 3/4 x 8 1/2. **Number of Columns Per Page:** 2. **Contact(s):** Robert Chrisman, Editor and Publisher. **ISSN:** 0006-4246. **Subscription:** $30; $40 institutions; $50 foreign. $5 single issue.

★3547★
Black Tennis Magazine
PO Box 210767
Dallas, TX 75211 Phone: (214)339-7370
Sports magazine featuring Black tennis players, clubs, and parks. **Established:** August 1977. **Column Depth:** 140 agate lines. **Frequency:** Monthly. **Print Method:** Offset. **Trim Size:** 8 1/2 x 11. **Number of Columns Per Page:** 3. **Column Width:** 27 nonpareils. **Contact(s):** Marcus A. Freeman, Jr., Editor and Publisher. **Subscription:** $15; $28 two years. **Circulation:** 5,000.

★3548★
The Black Writer
Terrell Associates
PO Box 1030
Chicago, IL 60690 Phone: (312)995-5195
Magazine offering information to Afro-American writers and serving as a forum for publishing works by Black writers. **Established:** 1974. **Frequency:** Quarterly. **Print Method:** Offset. **Trim Size:** 8 1/2 x 11. **Number of Columns Per Page:** 2. **Contact(s):** Mable Terrell, Editor and Publisher; Cary D. Boykin, Advertising Mgr. **Subscription:** $19; $15.20 institutions.

★3549★
Botswana Review
PO Box 278
Ivoryton, CT 06442
Pan-African scholarly journal dealing with cultural matters. **Established:** 1989. **Column Depth:** 9 1/2 in. **Frequency:** Quarterly. **Trim Size:** 8 1/2 x 11. **Number of Columns Per Page:** 1. **Column Width:** 7 1/4 in. **Contact(s):** William C. Bendig, Editor; Dan Claffey, Managing Editor; Nicholas Russell, Publisher. **Subscription:** $85. $25 single issue.

★3550★
Callaloo
The Johns Hopkins University Press
701 W. 40th St., Ste. 275
Baltimore, MD 21211 Phone: (301)338-6983
Publishing original works and critical studies by Black writers worldwide. **Established:** 1978. **Column Depth:** 45 picas. **Frequency:** Quarterly. **Print Method:** Offset. **Trim Size:** 6 7/8 x 10. **Number of Columns Per Page:** 1. **Column Width:** 30 picas. **Contact(s):** Charles Rowell, Editor (University of Virginia); Tara Dorai, Advertising Mgr. **ISSN:** 0161-2492. **Subscription:** $20; $41 institutions. **Circulation:** 1,200.

★3551★
Caribbean Review
9700 SW 67th Ave.
Miami, FL 33156 Phone: (305)284-8466
Magazine dedicated to the Caribbean, Latin America, and their emigrant groups. **Established:** January 1969. **Frequency:** Quarterly. **Print Method:** Offset. **Trim Size:** 8 1/2 x 11. **Number of Columns Per Page:** 3. **Contact(s):** Barry B. Levine, Editor and Publisher. **Subscription:** $20.

★3552★
Chocolate Singles
Chocolate Singles Enterprises, Inc.
PO Box 333
Jamaica, NY 11413 Phone: (212)624-6247
Magazine for Black singles. **Contact(s):** Barbara Miles, Publisher.

★3553★
The Christian Index
The Christian Methodist Episcopal Church
PO Box 665
Memphis, TN 38101 Phone: (901)358-7000
Religious magazine fcovering the predominantly Black Christian Methodist Episcopal denomination. **Established:** 1868. **Frequency:** 2x/mo. **Print Method:** Letterpress and offset. **Trim Size:** 8 1/2 x 11. **Number of Columns Per Page:** 2 and 3. **Contact(s):** Lawrence L. Reddick III, Editor and Publisher. **ISSN:** 0744-4060. **Subscription:** $15; $28 two years. **Circulation:** 6,000.

★3554★
Class Magazine
27 Union Sq. W.
New York, NY 10003 Phone: (212)741-1330
Magazine serving Black America. **Established:** 1979. **Frequency:** Monthly. **Print Method:** Web offset. **Trim Size:** 5 3/8 x 7 3/4. **Contact(s):** Rene John-Sandy, Publisher; Beverly Coley-Morris, Advertising Mgr.; Kim Malcolm, Circulation Mgr. and Vice President. **ISSN:** 0747-3826. **Subscription:** $15; $20 foreign. $2 single issue.

★3555★
Clubdate Magazine
13726 Kinsman Rd.
Cleveland, OH 44120 Phone: (216)752-8410
Magazine for upper income Blacks. **Established:** 1979. **Column Depth:** 140 agate lines. **Frequency:** 6x/yr. **Print Method:** Web offset. **Trim Size:** 8 1/2 x 11. **Number of Columns Per Page:** 3. **Column Width:** 27 nonpareils. **Contact(s):** Madelyne B. Blunt, Publisher; Carol Evyans, Advertising Mgr. **Subscription:** $14. $2.50 single issue.

★3556★
CORPORATE HEADQUARTERS
HQ Publications
516 North Ave., E.
Westfield, NJ 07090 Phone: (201)233-8837
Magazine for Black professionals; containing personal, professional, and career development editorial. **Established:** July 1985. **Frequency:** Quarterly. **Trim Size:** 8 1/2 x 11. **Contact(s):** Mrs. Terri Fisher, Editor; Dr. Harold E. Fisher, Publisher. **Subscription:** $12.

★3557★
The Crisis
NAACP/Crisis Publishing
260 5th Ave., 6th Fl.
New York, NY 10001-6408 Phone: (212)481-4100
Magazine covering civil rights, current events, and the arts. **Established:** November 1910. **Frequency:** Monthly. **Print Method:** Offset. **Trim Size:** 8 1/2 x 11. **Number of Columns Per Page:** 3. **Column Width:** 13 picas. **Contact(s):** Fred Beauford, Editor; Benjamin L. Hooks, Publisher; Kevin Moss, Advertising Mgr. **Subscription:** $10. **Circulation:** 350,000.

★3558★
Cultural Survival Quarterly
Cultural Survival, Inc.
11 Divinity Ave.
Cambridge, MA 02138 Phone: (617)495-2562
Magazine for general public and policy makers intended to stimulate action for ethnic minorities. **Established:** 1976. **Frequency:** Quarterly. **Trim Size:** 8 1/2 x 11. **Contact(s):** Jason W. Clay, Editor; Leslie Baker, Associate Editor. **Subscription:** $25. $3 single issue.

★3559★
Daily Challenge
PO Box 4295
Brooklyn, NY 11247 Phone: (718)636-9500
Black community newspaper. **Contact(s):** Thomas H. Watkins, Jr., Publisher.

★3560★
Dollars & Sense Magazine
7853 S. Stony Island Ave.
Chicago, IL 60649 Phone: (312)376-6800
Magazine covering Black history and development in business and other professions. **Established:** 1973. **Column Depth:** 54 picas. **Frequency:** 7x/yr. **Print Method:** Offset. **Trim Size:** 8 1/8 x 10 7/8. **Number of Columns Per Page:** 3. **Column Width:** 13 picas. **Contact(s):** Cheryl Evans, Editorial Dir. **Subscription:** $24.95. **Circulation:** 286,000.

★3561★
Ebony
820 S. Michigan Ave.
Chicago, IL 60605 Phone: (312)322-9200
General editorial magazine geared toward African-Americans. **Established:** 1945. **Column Depth:** 140 agate lines. **Frequency:** Monthly. **Print Method:** Offset **Number of Columns Per Page:** 3 **Column Width:** 30 nonpareils. **Contact(s):** John H. Johnson, Publisher. **Subscription:** $16. single issue. **Circulation:** 1,819,042.

★3562★
EM: Ebony Man
Johnson Publishing Co.
820 S. Michigan Ave.
Chicago, IL 60605 Phone: (312)322-9200
Black men's magazine featuring regular columns on health, fashion, and sports. **Frequency:** Monthly. **Contact(s):** Ooloong J. Smith, Editor; John H. Johnson, Publisher; Errol Griffiths, Advertising Dir. **ISSN:** 0884-4879. **Subscription:** $16. $2 single issue. **Circulation:** 200,000.

★3563★
Emerge
Emerge Communications
599 Broadway
New York, NY 10012 Phone: (212)941-8811
General interest magazine for sophisticated Black readers. **Established:** 1989. **Column Depth:** 66 picas. **Frequency:** 10x/yr. **Print Method:** Web offset. **Trim Size:** 8 1/8 x 10 7/8. **Number of Columns Per Page:** 3. **Column Width:** 13 picas. **Contact(s):** Wilmer C. Ames, Jr., Editor-in-Chief; Everett R. Staten, Advertising Mgr. **ISSN:** 0899-1154. **Subscription:** $11.97. $1.95 single issue.

★3564★
Essence
Essence Communications, Inc.
1500 Broadway
New York, NY 10036 Phone: (212)642-0600
Magazine for contemporary Black women. **Established:** 1970. **Column Depth:** 140 agate lines. **Frequency:** Monthly. **Print Method:** Offset. **Trim Size:** 8 x 10 7/8. **Number of Columns Per Page:** 3. **Column Width:** 26 nonpareils. **Contact(s):** Susan Taylor, Editor-in-Chief; Edward Lewis, Publisher/CEO; Clarence O. Smith, President. **ISSN:** 0014-0880. **Subscription:** $14. $1.75 single issue. **Circulation:** 850,116.

★3565★
The Final Call
757 W. 79th St., Ste. 316
Chicago, IL 60620 Phone: (312)483-8600
Magazine serving the Black community. **Contact(s):** Abdul Wali Muhammed, Editor.

★3566★
Gladiator
142 W. 72nd St., No. 2A
New York, NY 10023 Phone: (212)769-8423
Magazine featuring professional Black athletes. **Established:** April 1989. **Frequency:** Quarterly. **Print Method:** Web offset. **Trim Size:** 8 1/2 x 11 1/2. **Contact(s):** Vinette Pryce, Editor; Flo Anthony, Publisher. **Subscription:** $14 two years. $2 single issue. **Circulation:** 30,000.

★3567★
Impartial Citizen
PO Box 98
433 S. Warren St.
Syracuse, NY 13205 Phone: (315)635-1122
Magazine for the Black community. **Established:** September 1980. **Column Depth:** 294 agate lines. **Frequency:** 2x/mo. **Print Method:** Offset. **Trim Size:** 14 x 23. **Number of Columns Per Page:** 6. **Column Width:** 24 nonpareils. **Contact(s):** Antoine J. Polgar, Editor and Advertising Mgr.; Robert S. Pritchard, Publisher. **ISSN:** 0738-9116. **Subscription:** $15.

★3568★
In a Word
Society of the Divine Word
Bay Saint Louis, MS 39520 Phone: (601)467-1097
Magazine on Black Catholics in the U.S.A. **Established:** 1983. **Frequency:** Monthly. **Contact(s):** Rev. James A. Pawlicki, S.U.D., Editor. **Circulation:** 38,500.

★3569★
International Journal of Intercultural Relations
Pergamon Press, Inc.
Maxwell House
Fairview Pk.
Elmsford, NY 10523 Phone: (914)592-7700
Frequency: Quarterly. **Contact(s):** Dan Landis, Editor. **Subscription:** $60; $180 institutions.

★3570★
The International Review of African American Art
Museum of African American Art
4005 Crenshaw Blvd., 3rd Fl.
Los Angeles, CA 90008-2534 Phone: (213)294-7071
Magazine disseminating information about the contemporary Black artist internationally. **Frequency:** Quarterly. **Contact(s):** Samella Lewis, Ph.D., Art Editor.

★3571★
Interracial Books for Children Bulletin
Council on Interracial Books for Children
1841 Broadway
New York, NY 10023 Phone: (212)757-5339
Journal concerning itself with elimination of racism, sexism, and other bias in children's books. **Established:** 1967. **Column Depth:** 9 1/2 in. **Frequency:** 8x/yr. **Print Method:** Offset. **Trim Size:** 8 1/4 x 10 7/8. **Number of Columns Per Page:** 3. **Column Width:** 2 1/4 in. **Contact(s):** Melba Kgositsile, Executive Director. **ISSN:** 0146-5562. **Subscription:** $20; $28 institutions; $64 foreign, air mail. **Circulation:** 5,000.

★3572★
Ivy Leaf
Alpha Kappa Alpha Sorority, Inc.
5656 S. Stony Island Ave.
Chicago, IL 60637 Phone: (312)684-1282
Sorority publication for Black women. **Established:** December 1921. **Column Depth:** 140 agate lines. **Frequency:** Quarterly. **Print Method:** Offset. **Trim Size:** 8 1/2 x 11. **Number of Columns Per Page:** 3. **Column Width:** 14 picas. **Contact(s):** Alison A. Harris, Executive Director. **ISSN:** 0021-3276. **Subscription:** $10. **Circulation:** 34,000.

★3573★
Jet
Johnson Publishing Co., Inc.
820 S. Michigan Ave.
Chicago, IL 60605 Phone: (312)786-7665
Newsmagazine for the Black community. **Established:** 1951. **Column Depth:** 90 agate lines. **Frequency:** Weekly (Mon.). **Print Method:** Offset. **Number of Columns Per Page:** 2. **Column Width:** 30 nonpareils. **Contact(s):** John H. Johnson, Publisher. **Subscription:** $36. $1.25 single issue. **Circulation:** 892,006.

★3574★
Journal of Black Studies
Sage Periodicals Press
2111 W. Hillcrest Dr.
Newbury Park, CA 91320 Phone: (805)499-0721
Journal containing economic, historical, and philosophical research on Black people. **Established:** 1970. **Column Depth:** 100 agate lines. **Frequency:** Quarterly. **Print Method:** Offset. **Trim Size:** 5 1/2 X 8 1/2. **Number of Columns Per Page:** 1. **Column Width:** 50 nonpareils. **Contact(s):** Molefi K. Asante, Editor; Sara Miller McCune, Publisher; Nancy Hillegeist, Circulation Mgr.. **ISSN:** 0021-9347. **Subscription:** $34; $92 institutions; $68 two years; $184 two years, institutions. $11 single issue; $26 single issue, institutions.

★3575★
Journal of Ethnic Studies
Western Washington University
Bellingham, WA 98225 Phone: (206)647-4861
Journal covering interdisciplinary scholarship, opinion, and creative expression in ethnic matters. **Established:** Spring 1973. **Frequency:** Quarterly. **Print Method:** Offset. **Trim Size:** 6 x 8 1/4. **Number of Columns Per Page:** 1. **Contact(s):** Jesse Hiraoka, Editor. **ISSN:** 0091-3219. **Subscription:** $12; $15 institutions and libraries.

★3576★
Journal of Intergroup Relations
National Assn. of Human Rights Workers
Annex Bldg., 2nd Fl.
115 S. Andrews Ave.
Fort Lauderdale, FL 33301 Phone: (305)357-6046
Magazine focusing on civil rights and race relations issues. **Established:** 1960. **Column Depth:** 112 agate lines. **Frequency:** 4x/yr. **Print Method:** Letterpress. **Number of Columns Per Page:** 1. **Column Width:** 60 nonpareils. **Contact(s):** Dr. Fred Cloud, Editor; Gloria J. Battle, Publisher/Advertising Mgr. **ISSN:** 0047-2492. **Subscription:** $15; $17.50 institutions. $4.50 single issue.

★3577★
Journal of Modern African Studies
Cambridge University Press
40 W. 20th St.
New York, NY 10011 Phone: (914)937-9600
Journal surveying politics, economics, and related topics in contemporary Africa. **Frequency:** Quarterly. **Contact(s):** David Kimble, Editor; Alan Winter, Press Dir., U.S. **ISSN:** 0022-278X. **Subscription:** $49; $114 institutions. $32 single issue.

★3578★
The Journal of Negro Education
Bureau of Educational Research, Howard University Press
Howard University
PO Box 311
Washington, DC 20059 Phone: (202)806-6713
Educational research journal devoted to Black and minority education. **Established:** 1932. **Column Depth:** 18 in. **Frequency:** Quarterly. **Print Method:** Letterpress. **Trim Size:** 7 x 10. **Number of Columns Per Page:** 1. **Column Width:** 5 in. **Contact(s):** Dr. Faustine C. Jones-Wilson, Editor; Mahmoud Gudarzi, Advertising Mgr. **ISSN:** 0022-2984. **Subscription:** $16; $20 institutions; $24 foreign. $6 single issue.

★3579★
Journal of Negro History
Assn. for the Study of Afro-American Life and History
Morehouse College
Box 721
Atlanta, GA 30314 Phone: (404)681-2650
Afro-American history journal. **Established:** 1916. **Column Depth:** 112 agate lines. **Frequency:** Quarterly. **Print Method:** Offset. **Number of Columns Per Page:** 1. **Column Width:** 51 nonpareils. **Contact(s):** Dr. Alton Hornsby, Jr., Editor. **Subscription:** $30.

★3580★
Journal of the National Medical Association
Slack, Inc.
6900 Grove Rd.
Thorofare, NJ 08086-9447 Phone: (203)838-1000
Journal on specialized clinical research related to the health problems in the urban environment; recognizing significant contributions by Black physicians and others towards inner city health care improvement. **Established:** 1909. **Column Depth:** 140 agate lines. **Frequency:** Monthly. **Print Method:** Web offset. **Trim Size:** 8 1/8 x 10 7/8. **Number of Columns Per Page:** 3 and 2. **Column Width:** 27 and 42 nonpareils. **Contact(s):** Calvin C. Sampson, M.D., Editor; Richard N. Roash, V.P./Publisher; George Jankowski, Natl. Advertising Sales Mgr. **ISSN:** 0027-9684. **Subscription:** $55; $85 foreign and institutions. $8 single issue.

★3581★
Journal of the National Technical Association
Black Collegiate Services, Inc.
1240 S. Broad St.
New Orleans, LA 70125-2091 Phone: (504)821-5694
Black-oriented journal emphasizing jobs, careers, and technical interchange for experienced Black technical professionals. **Established:** 1926. **Column Depth:** 140 agate lines. **Frequency:** 4x/yr. **Print Method:** Offset. Uses mat. **Trim Size:** 8 x 10 7/8. **Number of Columns Per Page:** 3. **Column Width:** 26 nonpareils. **Contact(s):** Sonya Stinson, Editor; Melba R. Lemieux, Publisher; Ron Markham, Advertising Mgr. **ISSN:** 0271-776X. **Subscription:** $30; $50 for two years. **Circulation:** 20,000.

★3582★
Lincoln Review
The Lincoln Institute for Research and Education, Inc.
1001 Connecticut Ave. NW, Ste. 1135
Washington, DC 20036 Phone: (202)223-5112
Black public policy journal. **Established:** 1979. **Frequency:** Quarterly. **Print Method:** Offset. **Trim Size:** 6 x 9. **Number of Columns Per Page:** 1. **Contact(s):** J. A. Parker, Editor and Publisher. **ISSN:** 0192-5083. **Subscription:** $12. **Circulation:** 7,000.

★3583★
Living Blues
Center for the Study of Southern Culture
University of Mississippi
University, MS 38677 Phone: (601)232-5518
Magazine covering the Black American blues tradition. **Established:** 1970. **Column Depth:** 60 picas. **Frequency:** 6x/yr. **Print Method:** Offset. **Trim Size:** 8 1/2 x 11. **Number of Columns Per Page:** 3. **Column Width:** 14 picas. **Contact(s):** Peter Lee, Editor; Brett Bonner, Advertising Mgr. **ISSN:** 0024-5232. **Subscription:** $18. $3 single issue. **Circulation:** 10,000.

★3584★
Message Magazine
Review and Herald Publishing Assn.
55 Oak Ridge Dr.
Hagerstown, MD 21740 Phone: (301)791-7000
Religious magazine for Blacks. **Established:** 1898. **Column Depth:** 9 1/4 in. **Frequency:** 6x/yr. **Print Method:** Offset. **Trim Size:** 8 1/8 x 10 5/8. **Number of Columns Per Page:** 3. **Column Width:** 2 1/8 in. **Contact(s):** Delbert W. Baker, Editor; Mark Thomas, Advertising Mgr. **ISSN:** 0026-0231. **Subscription:** $11.95.

★3585★
Minorities and Women in Business
Venture X, Inc.
PO Drawer 210
Burlington, NC 27216 Phone: (919)229-1462
Magazine networks with major corporations and small businesses owned and operated by minority and female entrepreneurs. **Established:** October 1984. **Frequency:** 6x/yr. **Trim Size:** 8 3/8 x 10 3/4. **Number of Columns Per Page:** 3. **Column Width:** 2 1/2 in. **Contact(s):** John D. Enoch, Editor and Publisher; Sherry A. Poole, Managing Editor; Jim Warren, Advertising Mgr. **Subscription:** $15; $36 three years.

★3586★
Minority Business Entrepreneur
924 N. Market St.
Inglewood, CA 90302 Phone: (213)673-9398
Business magazine for the Ethnic Minority Business owner. **Established:** Fall 1984. **Column Depth:** 10 in. **Frequency:** 6x/yr. **Print Method:** Offset. **Trim Size:** 8 x 10 7/8. **Number of Columns Per Page:** 3. **Column Width:** 13 picas. **Contact(s):** Jeanie M. Barnett, Editor; Ginger Conrad, Publisher. **Subscription:** Free to qualified subscribers; $12. **Circulation:** 27,000.

★3587★
Minority Business Social and Cultural Directory
PO Box 10112
Augusta, GA 30901 Phone: (404)722-7327
Minority directory. **Established:** 1989. **Column Depth:** 13 in. **Frequency:** Quarterly. **Print Method:** Web offset. **Trim Size:** 10 1/4 x 13. **Column Width:** 2 in. **Contact(s):** Frederick Benjamin, Editor; Charles W. Walker, Publisher; Tanya Barnhill, Mktg. Mgr. **Subscription:** $11.75.

★3588★
Minority Engineer
Equal Opportunity Publications, Inc.
44 Broadway
Greenlawn, NY 11740 Phone: (516)261-8899
Affirmative action recruitment magazine serving college-graduating and professional minority engineers. **Established:** 1980. **Column Depth:** 136 agate lines. **Frequency:** 4x/yr. **Print Method:** Offset. **Trim Size:** 8 x 10 3/4. **Number of Columns Per Page:** 3. **Column Width:** 26 nonpareils. **Contact(s):** James Schneider, Editor; John Miller III, Publisher/Advertising Mgr. **ISSN:** 0884-1829. **Subscription:** $17. **Circulation:** 16,000.

★3589★
National Scene Magazine
22 E. 41st St.
New York, NY 10017 Phone: (212)862-3700
Magazine serving Black Americans. **Contact(s):** William Decker Clarke, Publisher.

★3590★
The Negro Educational Review
The Negro Educational Review, Inc.
Box 2895, General Mail Center
Jacksonville, FL 32203 Phone: (904)646-2860
Education journal. **Established:** 1950. **Frequency:** Quarterly. **Contact(s):** R. Lloyd, Editor. **Subscription:** $15. **Circulation:** 5,000.

★3591★
The Negro History Bulletin
The Assn. for the Study of Afro-American Life & History, Inc.
1407 14th St. NW
Washington, DC 20005 Phone: (202)667-2822
Magazine profiling Black history through feature articles and biographies. **Established:** 1937. **Frequency:** Quarterly. **Trim Size:** 8 1/2 x 11. **Contact(s):** Karen Robinson, Exec. Dir. **ISSN:** 0028-2529. **Subscription:** $25. **Circulation:** 10,000.

★3592★
Network Africa
PO Box 81, Pratt Sta.
Brooklyn, NY 11205
Magazine featuring African studies and cross-cultural experiences. **Established:** 1982. **Frequency:** Quarterly. **Trim Size:** 8 1/2 x 11. **Contact(s):** Shirley Ademu-John, Editor; Ekundayo Ademu-John, Assoc. Editor. **Subscription:** $10. $2.50 single issue.

★3593★
The New Research Traveler & Conventioneer
11717 S. Vincennes Ave.
Chicago, IL 60643 Phone: (312)881-3712
Magazine containing travel and convention news for Black professionals. **Established:** November 1942. **Column Depth:** 133 agate lines. **Frequency:** 6x/yr.. **Print Method:** Offset. **Trim Size:** 8 1/2 x 11 1/4. **Number of Columns Per Page:** 3. **Column Width:** 27 nonpareils. **Contact(s):** C. M. Markham, Jr., Editor and Publisher; C.M. Markham III, Advertising Mgr. **Subscription:** $7.50. **Circulation:** 88,550.

★3594★
New Visions
5007 Superior Ave.
Cleveland, OH 44103 Phone: (216)881-4112
Magazine covering Cleveland's Black community developments, activities, and leaders. **Established:** July 1989. **Frequency:** 6x/yr. **Contact(s):** Jane Littleton, Editor; Rodney Reynolds, Publisher. **Subscription:** $7.50. $2.50 single issue.

★3595★
Nightmoves
Nightmoves Publishing Co.
105 W. Madison, Ste. 1100
Chicago, IL 60602
Black newspaper (tabloid): half politics, and half entertainment. **Established:** July 1980. **Column Depth:** 13 in. **Frequency:** 2x/mo. **Print Method:** Offset. **Trim Size:** 10 1/4 x 13. **Number of Columns Per Page:** 4. **Column Width:** 2 1/4 in. **Contact(s):** Lise Wilson, Editor; Gloria Golden, Publisher; Tom Drake, Advertising Mgr. **Subscription:** $18. **Circulation:** 100,000.

★3596★
Northwest Ethnic News
Ethnic Heritage Council of the Pacific Northwest
3123 Eastlake Ave., E.
Seattle, WA 98102 Phone: (206)726-0357
Newspaper (tabloid) for local ethnic communities, presenting calendar of events, listings of ethnic art on exhibit, and profiles of ethnic individuals/businesses/organizations. **Established:** 1984. **Column Depth:** 224 agate lines. **Frequency:** Monthly. **Print Method:** Web offset. **Trim Size:** 11 1/2 x 17 1/2. **Number of Columns Per Page:** 5. **Column Width:** 22 nonpareils. **Contact(s): Subscription:** $10.

★3597★
NSBE Magazine
NSBE Publications
National Society of Black Engineers
344 Commerce St.
Alexandria, VA 22314 Phone: (703)549-2207
Journal providing information on engineering careers, self-development, and cultural issues for recent graduates with technical majors. **Established:** October 1985. **Column Depth:** 140 agate lines. **Frequency:** 5x/yr. **Print Method:** Offset. **Trim Size:** 8 x 10 3/4. **Number of Columns Per Page:** 3. **Column Width:** 13 picas. **Contact(s):** Norris Hite, Publisher. **ISSN:** 0888-0573. **Subscription:** $10. $2 single issue.

★3598★
PHYLON
Atlanta University
223 James P. Brawley Dr. SW
Atlanta, GA 30314 Phone: (404)681-0251
Race and culture review magazine. **Established:** 1940. **Column Depth:** 105 agate lines. **Frequency:** Quarterly. **Print Method:** Letterpress. **Number of Columns Per Page:** 1. **Column Width:** 58 nonpareils. **Contact(s):** Wilbur H. Watson, Editor. **Subscription:** $14; $24 institutions. **Circulation:** 2,200.

★3599★
Players
Players International Publications
8060 Melrose Ave.
Los Angeles, CA 90046 Phone: (213)653-8060
Entertainment magazine for the 18-40 year old Black American male. **Established:** 1973. **Column Depth:** 10 in. **Frequency:** Monthly. **Print Method:** Web offset. **Trim Size:** 8 1/8 x 10 7/8. **Number of Columns Per Page:** 3. **Column Width:** 2 1/4 in. **Contact(s):** H. L. Sorrell, Editor. **Subscription:** $45; $36 institutions; $46 foreign. $3.75 single issue. **Circulation:** 175,000.

★3600★
Review of Black Political Economy
Transaction Periodicals Consortium
Rutgers - The State University
New Brunswick, NJ 08903 Phone: (201)932-2280
Journal of economics and Black studies. **Established:** 1970. **Column Depth:** 101 agate lines. **Frequency:** Quarterly. **Print Method:** Offset. **Trim Size:** 6 x 9. **Number of Columns Per Page:** 1. **Column Width:** 54 nonpareils. **Contact(s):** James Stewart, Editor; Mary E. Curtis, Sr. V.P./Publisher; Alicja Garbie, Advertising Mgr. **ISSN:** 0034-6446. **Subscription:** $30; $50 institutions; $40 other countries. **Circulation:** 1,100.

★3601★
Right On!
Lexington Library, Inc.
355 Lexington Ave.
New York, NY 10017 Phone: (221)949-6850
Black young adult entertainment magazine. **Established:** October 1971. **Frequency:** Monthly. **Print Method:** Offset. **Trim Size:** 8 1/2 x 11. **Number of Columns Per Page:** 3. **Contact(s):** Cynthia Horner, Editor; John Plunkett, Publisher. **ISSN:** 0048-8305. **Subscription:** $17.99. $2.25 single issue. **Circulation:** 350,000.

★3602★
SISTERS
National Council of Negro Women, Inc.
1211 Connecticut Ave. NW, Ste. 702
Washington, DC 20036 Phone: (202)659-0006
Magazine covering diverse issues that affect the Black woman and her community. **Established:** 1988. **Frequency:** Quarterly. **Print Method:** Offset. **Trim Size:** 8 1/4 x 11. **Contact(s):** Altoria Bell, Editor; Gayla Cook, Editor-in-Chief and Publisher; Florence Amate, Marketing/Advertising Mgr. **ISSN:** 0899-935X. **Subscription:** $20. $5 single issue.

★3603★
Sophisticate's Black Hairstyles and Care Guide
Associated Publications, Inc.
1165 N. Clark St., No. 607
Chicago, IL 60610 Phone: (312)266-8680
Black hairstyle magazine. **Established:** 1984. **Frequency:** 6x/yr. **Print Method:** Web Offset. **Contact(s):** James Spurlock, Publisher; Bonnie L. Krueger, Publishing Director, Cynthia Hill, Advertising Mgr. **Subscription:** $15.36. $3.25 single issue. **Circulation:** 182,250.

★3604★
U.S. Black Engineer
Career Communications Group, Inc.
729 E. Pratt St., Ste. 504
Baltimore, MD 21202 Phone: (301)244-7101
Professional magazine for Black engineers. **Established:** 1980. **Frequency:** 5x/yr. **Print Method:** Offset. **Trim Size:** 8 1/2 x 11. **Contact(s):** Grady Wells, Editor; Tyrone Taborn, Publisher; Leon Capers, Jr., Advertising Mgr. **Subscription:** $15. **Circulation:** 15,000.

★3605★
Voice of Missions
475 Riverside Dr., Rm 1926
New York, NY 10115 Phone: (212)870-2258
Black Methodist Episcopal Church magazine. **Established:** 1898. **Column Depth:** 133 agate lines. **Frequency:** 6x/yr. **Print Method:** Uses mats. Letterpress. **Number of Columns Per Page:** 2. **Column Width:** 27 nonpareils. **Contact(s):** Frederick Harrison, Publisher. **Subscription:** $10.

★3606★
Washington View
1101 14th St. NW, Ste. 1050
Washington, DC 20005 Phone: (202)371-1313
Magazine for upscale Blacks living in the Washington area. **Established:** June 1989. **Frequency:** 6x/yr. **Contact(s):** Effie Upshaw, Managing Editor; Malcolm Beech, Publisher. **Subscription:** $5. $1.95 single issue. **Circulation:** 30,000.

★3607★
The Western Journal of Black Studies
Washington State University Press
Pullman, WA 99164-5910 Phone: (509)335-8681
Journal covering the universal Black experience. **Established:** 1977. **Column Depth:** 113 agate lines. **Frequency:** Quarterly. **Print Method:** Offset. **Trim Size:** 8 x 10. **Number of Columns Per Page:** 2. **Column Width:** 36 nonpareils. **Contact(s):** Prof. Talmadge Anderson, Editor; Fred C. Bohm, Advertising Mgr.; Nancy Grunewald, Circulation Mgr.. **ISSN:** 0197-4327. **Subscription:** $20; $30 two years; $30 institutions; $45 institutions two years. $7.50 single issue.

Newsletters

★3608★
AALC Reporter
African-American Labor Center
1400 K St., 7th Fl.
Washington, DC 20005 Phone: (202)789-1020
Edited by: John T. Sarr. **Description:** Covers activities of the AALC for the promotion of free and democratic trade unions on the African continent. **Illustrations:** Includes black and white photographs. **First published:** 1965. **Frequency:** Bimonthly. **Size:** 4-6 pages. **Price:** Free. **Circulation:** 3,800. **Remarks:** Also available in French and Arabic.

★3609★
ACAS Bulletin
Association of Concerned Africa Scholars
4205 SE Ramona
Portland, OR 97206
Edited by: Allan Cooper. **Description:** Concerned with U.S. policy toward Africa, particularly Southern Africa. Relates the Association's intent to formulate and communicate alternatives to U.S. Africa policies and to develop a communication action network among Africa scholars. Recurring features include book reviews, news of research, reports on political action, and notes and resources. **First published:** 1977. **Frequency:** 3/yr. **Size:** 8-1/2 x 11, 12-16 pages. **Price:** Included in membership. **Circulation:** 350.

★3610★
ACOA Action News
American Committee on Africa
198 Broadway
New York, NY 10038 Phone: (212)962-1210
Edited by: Jennifer Davis. **Description:** Reports on the activities of the Committee, which supports African independence and majority rule. Carries news of events in Africa, news of members, and brief descriptions of recent publications from The African Fund. **Illustrations:** Includes black and white photographs. **Frequency:** Semiannually. **Size:** 8-1/2 x 11, 4 pages. **Price:** $25/yr. **Circulation:** 5,000.

★3611★
Affirmative Action Compliance Manual for Federal Contractors
Bureau of National Affairs, Inc.
1231 25th St., NW
Washington, DC 20037 Phone: (202)452-4200
Edited by: Susan L. Sala. **Description:** Provides information on developments concerning the Office of Federal Contract Compliance Programs. **First published:** 1975. **Frequency:** Monthly. **Size:** 8-1/2 x 11. **Price:** $248/yr. **ISSN:** 0148-8147. **Remarks:** Fax number is (202)822-8092. Telex number is 285656 BNAI WSH.

★3612★
Africa Catalyst
Matthews Associates
Box 53398, Temple Heights Sta.
Washington, DC 20009 Phone: (202)332-1622
Subtitle: A Monthly Report on U.S.-African Business and Economic Relations. **Description:** Specializes in political analysis and foreign relations between Africa and the U.S. Covers economic growth, trade, markets and industry, debt, loans, gold and precious metals, energy, regional economic initiatives, sanctions, disinvestment, and the

environment. Includes news of speakers, meetings, and conferences. **Frequency:** Monthly. **Price:** $48/yr. for individuals; $75 for nonprofit and African institutions; $125 for corporations, U.S.; $73 for individuals; $100 for nonprofit and African institutions; $150 for corporations elsewhere.

★3613★
Africa Insider
Matthews Associates
Box 53398, Temple Heights Sta.
Washington, DC 20009 Phone: (202)332-1622
Edited by: Dan Matthews. **Description:** Reports on U.S.-African affairs, with special emphasis on developments in Washington, DC. Focuses on Congress and Africa, and the American media and Africa. **First published:** 1984. **Frequency:** Semimonthly. **Size:** 8-1/2 x 11, 8 pages. **Price:** $75/yr. for individuals; $150 for non-profit organizations and African institutions, $300 for corporations, U.S. and Canada; $180 for non-profit organizations, individuals, and African institutions, $330 for corporations elsewhere. **ISSN:** 0748-4356.

★3614★
Africa News
Africa News Service, Inc.
720 9th St.
PO Box 3851
Durham, NC 27702 Phone: (919)286-0747
Edited by: Reed Kramer. **Description:** Covers political, economic, and other news about the continent of Africa. Focuses particularly on U.S. policy and relations with African nations and personalities. Recurring features include reports from correspondents in Africa, statistics, book reviews, and background material. **Illustrations:** Includes black and white graphics. **First published:** June 1973. **Frequency:** Semimonthly. **Size:** 8-1/2 x 11, 12 pages. **Price:** $30/yr. for individuals; $48 for institutions. **ISSN:** 0191-6521. **Circulation:** 3,800. **Online through:** NewsNet Inc., 945 Haverford Rd., Bryn Mawr, PA 19010, (215) 527-8030. **Remarks:** The fax number is (919) 286-0747.

★3615★
African American Museum—Newsletter
African American Museum
The Icabod Flewellen Bldg.
Cleveland, OH 44106 Phone: (216)791-1700
Edited by: H.E. Murray. **Description:** Informs members about activities at the Museum. Seeks to stimulate interest in African and African American history and culture. **Frequency:** Bimonthly. **Size:** 8-1/2 x 11, ca. 4 pages. **Price:** Included in membership.

★3616★
African Presence Newsletter
Associated Publishers
1401 14th St., NW
Washington, DC 20005 Phone: (202)265-1441
Edited by: Paul P. Cooke, Ed.D. **Subtitle:** *Annual Black History Month Kickoff Newsletter.* **Description:** Focuses on critical issues in the development of programs for Black History Month. Discusses the role of the church in the economic, political, and social development of Black society. Recurring features include interviews and notices of publications available. **Illustrations:** Includes black and white graphics. **Editorial policies:** Considers articles for publication. **First published:** October 1988. **Frequency:** Annually. **Size:** 8-1/2 x 11. **Price:** $15/yr., U.S.; $18, Canada; $22 elsewhere for individuals; $25, U.S.; $28, Canada; $32 elsewhere for institutions.

★3617★
African Studies Center—Newsletter
Michigan State University
African Studies Center
100 Center for International Programs
East Lansing, MI 48824 Phone: (517)353-1700
Edited by: David Bloch. **Description:** Provides current news and information on Africa and African studies. Contains news of faculty, new courses in African studies, outreach activities, sources of funding information, and grants and awards. Recurring features include announcements of employment, travel, and educational opportunities. **First published:** October 21, 1976. **Frequency:** 3/yr. **Size:** 8-1/2 x 11, 10-16 pages. **Price:** Free. **Circulation:** 1,400. **Former Title(s):** *Michigan Information on Africa-Newsletter*, 1979.

★3618★
African Studies Center—Outreach Newsletter
African Studies Center
270 Bay State Rd.
Boston, MA 02215 Phone: (617)353-7303
Edited by: Jo Sullivan. **Description:** Promotes various activities, programs, and workshops focused on Africa. Describes available resources in the field. Recurring features include list of new acquisitions of the Center, news of museum exhibits, book reviews, and sample lesson plans. **Editorial policies:** Considers articles for publication. **First published:** 1979. **Frequency:** 3/yr. **Size:** 8-1/2 x 11, 8-10 pages. **Price:** $5/yr. **Circulation:** 800.

★3619★
Africana Libraries Newsletter
Main Library E660
Indiana University
Bloomington, IN 47405 Phone: (812)855-1481
Edited by: Nancy J. Schmidt. **Description:** Concerned with librarianship in African studies. Announces recent publications and other African resources, particularly those "not readily available through regular trade channels." Recurring features include news of professionals in the field, inquiries from readers, and reports from the African Studies Association, its Archives-Library Committee, and the Cooperative Africana Microform Project. **First published:** July 1975. **Frequency:** Quarterly. **Size:** 8-1/2 x 11, 8 pages. **Price:** Free. **ISSN:** 0148-7868. **Circulation:** 600. **Remarks:** Fax number is (812)855-8229.

★3620★
The Afro-Americanist Newsletter
University of Illinois
Afro-American Studies and Research Program
1204 W. Oregon
Urbana, IL 61801 Phone: (217)333-7781
Edited by: Teresa Savage. **Description:** Focuses on issues and research concerning the Afro-American community. **Illustrations:** Includes photographs. **First published:** 1986. **Frequency:** 3/yr. **Size:** 8-12 pages. **Price:** Free. **Circulation:** 1,000. **Online through:** Contact publisher.

★3621★
Alliance Report Newsletter
National Alliance of Third World Journalists
PO Box 43208
Washington, DC 20010 Phone: (202)387-1662
Edited by: Gwen McKinney. **Description:** Functions as an arm of the Alliance, "an organization of Black, Hispanic and other Third World journalists in the United States dedicated to bringing accurate information and analysis about the struggles and progress of Third World people" to their respective constituencies. Covers international and U.S. news as well as reports on U.S. foreign policy. Emphasizes the national liberation struggles of South Africa, Latin America, and the Middle East. Recurring features include job listings, news of chapter activities, and notices of resource publications. **Illustrations:** Includes black and white graphics. **First published:** May 1981. **Frequency:** Quarterly. **Size:** 8-1/2 x 11, 8 pages. **Price:** $6/yr. **Circulation:** 500.

★3622★
ASA News
African Studies Association
ASA
Credit Union Bldg.
Emery University
Atlanta, GA 30322 Phone: (404)329-6410
Edited by: Eric D. Wright and John Distefano. **Description:** Reports news of interest to Africanists. Includes notices of employment opportunities, Association activities, grants and awards, meetings, publications, and information about foreign research institutes. **First published:** 1967. **Frequency:** Quarterly. **Size:** 6 x 9, 32-64 pages. **Price:** Included in membership. **Circulation:** 2,400. **Former Title(s):** African Studies Newsletter.

★3623★
ASC Newsletter
African Studies Center
Michigan State University
East Lansing, MI 48824 Phone: (517)353-1700
Description: Provides news of activities of the Center. **Frequency:** Biennially. **Size:** Semiannually. **Price:** Free. **Circulation:** 1,000.

★3624★
BEEP Newsletter
National Urban League, Inc.
Black Executive Exchange Program
500 E. 62nd St.
New York, NY 10021 Phone: (212)310-9195
Edited by: Renee Du Jean. **Description:** Describes BEEP courses at Black universities in which Black executives serve as professors to link the classroom with the working world. Recurring features include news of members, notices of publications available, and a column titled The Inside Line. **Illustrations:** Includes black and white graphics. **First published:** September 1970. **Frequency:** Quarterly. **Size:** 8-1/2 x 11, 4-6 pages. **Price:** Free. **Circulation:** 5,000.

★3625★
Black Americans for Life Newsletter
National Right to Life Committee
Black Americans for Life
419-7th St., NW, Ste. 500
Washington, DC 20004-2205
Edited by: Michele F. Jackson. **Description:** Seeks to "inform America that African Americans support the right to life of the unborn, older people, and people with disabilities." Recurring features include a calendar of events. **Illustrations:** Includes black and white photographs and graphics. **First published:** 1985. **Size:** 8-1/2 x 11, ca. 8 pages.

★3626★
Black Caucus Newsletter
Four-G Publishers
PO Box 2249
Winter Park, FL 32790-2249 Phone: (305)646-2676
Edited by: Dr. George C. Grant. **Description:** Reports news of interest about Black librarians in library work and library education. Recurring features include notices of professional opportunities and activities of individuals within the Caucus and the American Library Association. **Illustrations:** Includes black and white graphics. **Editorial policies:** Accepts advertising. Considers articles for publication. **First published:** June 1972. **Frequency:** Bimonthly. **Size:** 8-1/2 x 11, 8 pages. **Price:** Included in membership; $7.50/yr. for nonmembers. **ISSN:** 8755-9277. **Circulation:** 900. **Remarks:** Fax number is (407)646-1515.

★3627★
Black Child Advocate
National Black Child Development Institute
1463 Rhode Island Ave., NW
Washington, DC 20005 Phone: (202)387-1281
Edited by: Noreen Yazejian. **Description:** Discusses current issues facing the Black child and family. Also contains public policy updates and internal news of the Institute, and promotes publications and conferences. Recurring features include letters to the editor, interviews, book reviews, and issues analyses. **Illustrations:** Includes black and white photographs, tables, and charts. **Editorial policies:** Accepts display advertising. **First published:** 1972. **Frequency:** Quarterly. **Size:** 8-1/2 x 11, 8 pages. **Price:** Included in membership. **Circulation:** 3,500. **Remarks:** Fax number is (202)234-1738.

★3628★
Black Congressional Monitor
Len Mor Publications
PO Box 75035
Washington, DC 20013 Phone: (202)488-8879
Edited by: Lenora Moragne, Ph.D. **Subtitle:** A Monthly Report of Legislative Initiatives From the U.S. Congress. **Description:** Reports on legislative initiatives. Covers the activities of African-Americans in Congress and provides information regarding set-aside legislation and regulation for minorities. **First published:** 1987. **Frequency:** Monthly. **Size:** 8-1/2 x 11, 8 pages. **Price:** $15.95/yr. **ISSN:** 0895-1780.

★3629★
Black Data Processing Associates—Journal
Black Data Processing Associates
PO Box 7466
Philadelphia, PA 19101
Edited by: Stan Seymore. **Description:** Details chapter activities, which are "dedicated to strengthening the expertise of minority members in the field of data processing, and ...to cultivate computer literacy in the Black community as a whole." Includes informational articles and items of interest concerning data and information processing. Recurring features include editorials, news of members, and a calendar of events. **Illustrations:** Includes black and white graphics. **Editorial policies:** Accepts advertising. Considers articles for publication. **First published:** 1975. **Frequency:** Quarterly. **Size:** 8-1/2 x 11, 20 pages. **Price:** Included in membership. **Circulation:** 3,000. **Former Title(s):** Data News.

★3630★
Black Issues in Higher Education
Cox, Matthews, & Associates, Inc.
10521 Warwick Ave., Ste. B-8
Fairfax, VA 22030 Phone: (703)385-2981
Description: Reports on news affecting minorities and major issues in U.S. higher education. Includes articles on school reform proposals, profiles of successful educators and students, summaries of research reports on ethnicity and education, employment opportunities, and analysis of critical trends and developments in academic and related environments. **Frequency:** Biweekly. **Online through:** NewsNet Inc., 945 Haverford Rd., Bryn Mawr, PA 19010, (215) 527-8030.

★3631★
Black Theater Network—Newsletter
Black Theatre Network
PO Box 11502
Fisher Bldg. Sta.
Detroit, MI 48211
Edited by: Gary Anderson. **Description:** "Dedicated to increasing the awareness, appreciation, and production of Black Theatre in the African diaspora."

★3632★
BNA's Employee Relations Weekly
Bureau of National Affairs, Inc.
1231 25th St., NW
Washington, DC 20037 Phone: (202)452-4200
Edited by: Susan J. Sala. **Description:** Monitors employee and labor relations cases. Follows developments in compensation, health benefits, Equal Employment Opportunity (EEO), labor economics, legislation, and regulatory issues. Recurring features include a calendar of events. **First published:** September 5, 1983. **Frequency:** Weekly. **Size:** 8-1/2 x 11, 32 pages. **Price:** $744/yr. **ISSN:** 0739-3016. **Online through:** Human Resource Information Network, 9585 Valparaiso Court, Indianapolis, IN 46268; (317)872-2045.

★3633★
Building Blocks
National Center for Urban Ethnic Affairs
Box 20, Cardinal Sta.
Washington, DC 20044-0020 Phone: (202)635-5128
Edited by: Jack Whitehurst. **Description:** Provides community action information. **Circulation:** 16,000.

★3634★
Building Concerns
National Association of Minority Contractors
806 15th St., NW, Ste. 340
Washington, DC 20005 Phone: (202)347-8259
Edited by: Ralph C. Thomas, III. **Description:** Concentrates on national and regional news regarding minority construction contractors. Contains articles on issues generally affecting the industry–especially issues affecting minorities–including topics such as legislative and regulatory activity and reports on major corporation developments. Recurring features include reports of meetings, news of educational opportunities, a calendar of events, and news of NAMC chapters and members. **Editorial policies:** Accepts feature articles for publication. **First**

published: 1981. **Frequency:** Monthly. **Size:** 8-1/2 x 11, 8 pages. **Price:** Included in membership. **Circulation:** 3,500.

★3635★
CAAS Newsletter
University of California, Los Angeles
Center for Afro-American Studies
3111 Campbell Hall
Los Angeles, CA 90024 Phone: (213)825-7403
Edited by: M. Belinda Tucker, and N. Cherie Francis. **Description:** Features news of the Center and its work in Afro-American Studies. Covers news of research; information on visiting professors, programs, and awards; and special Center programs. Recurring features include notices of publications available. **Illustrations:** Includes black and white graphics. **First published:** Ca. 1977. **Frequency:** Semiannually. **Size:** 8-1/2 x 11, 20 pages. **Price:** Free. **ISSN:** 0197-5579. **Circulation:** 6,600.

★3636★
CAAS Newsletter
Center for Afroamerican and African Studies
University of Michigan
200 W. Engineering Bldg.
550 E. University
Ann Arbor, MI 48109-1092 Phone: (313)764-5513
Edited by: Susanne Kocsis. **Description:** Contains news of the Center and its faculty. Covers projects of particular interest to the academic community. Recurring features include editorials, news of research, and columns titled CAAS Profile and Project Notes. **Illustrations:** Includes black and white photographs. **First published:** October 1984. **Frequency:** 3/yr. **Size:** 8-1/2 x 11, 28 pages. **Price:** Free. **Circulation:** 2,000.

★3637★
CALC Report
Clergy and Laity Concerned (CALC)
PO Box 1987
Decateur, GA 30031
Edited by: Mark Reeve. **Description:** Provides information about the disarmament movement in the U.S. and internationally and about U.S. military presence around the world. Addresses human rights issues in the U.S., Central America and the Caribbean, South Africa, the Phillipines, and the Middle East. Recurring features include news of the association. **Illustrations:** Includes black and white graphics. **First published:** Fall 1975. **Frequency:** 6/yr. **Size:** 8-1/2 x 11, 24 pages. **Price:** Included in membership. **Circulation:** 17,000. **Former Title(s):** *CALC Report/TWC Bulletin.*

★3638★
Career Opportunities News
Garrett Park Press
PO Box 190
Garrett Park, MD 20896 Phone: (301)946-2553
Edited by: Robert Calvert, Jr. **Description:** Examines career trends and occupations of the future, as well as current career opportunities. Carries information on job leads, information sources, salaries and comparable worth, internships, and grant programs. Recurring features include news of research, book reviews, a calendar of events, sections titled Useful Resources for Women, Women's Interest, Minority Interest, and the supplement 50 Ways to Learn About and Get Jobs. **Illustrations:** Includes black and white graphics and tables. **First published:** 1983. **Frequency:** 6/yr. **Size:** 8-1/2 x 11, 12 pages. **Price:** $30/yr., U.S. and Canada. **ISSN:** 0739-5043. **Circulation:** 3,000.

★3639★
Caribbean Update
Kal Wagenheim
52 Maple Ave.
Maplewood, NJ 07040 Phone: (201)762-1565
Edited by: Kal Wagenheim. **Description:** Contains news of economic developments in the Caribbean and Central America. Provides country-by-country coverage, as well as regional items. Recurring features include news of research, book reviews, and a calendar of events. **Illustrations:** Includes tables. **Editorial policies:** Considers articles for publication. **First published:** February 1985. **Frequency:** Monthly. **Size:** 8-1/2 x 11, 24 pages. **Price:** $120/yr. **ISSN:** 8756-324X. **Remarks:** Fax number is (201)762-9585.

★3640★
Catholic League Newsletter
Catholic League for Religious and Civil Rights
1100 W. Wells St.
Milwaukee, WI 53233 Phone: (414)289-0170
Edited by: John C. Pantuso. **Description:** Discusses Catholic perspectives on social, moral, and ethical issues. **Illustrations:** Includes black and white graphics. **First published:** 1973. **Frequency:** Monthly. **Price:** Included in membership. **Circulation:** 26,000.

★3641★
Center for Democratic Renewal—Monitor
Center for Democratic Renewal
PO Box 50469
Atlanta, GA 30302 Phone: (404)221-0025
Edited by: Daniel Levitas. **Description:** Reports on Ku Klux Klan activities and anti-Klan movements around the U.S. Carries commentary on racial and religious violence and bigotry. Recurring features include highlights of legislative and police actions, news of research, and letters to the editor. **Illustrations:** Includes black and white graphics. **Editorial policies:** Accepts advertising. Considers articles for publication. **First published:** 1980. **Frequency:** Bimonthly. **Size:** 8 x 10-1/2, 16 pages. **Price:** Included in membership; $15/yr. for nonmembers. **Circulation:** 7,000.

★3642★
Center for Sickle Cell Disease—Newsletter
Center for Sickle Cell Disease
Howard University
2121 Georgia Ave., NW
Washington, DC 20059 Phone: (202)636-7930
Edited by: Roland B. Scott, M.D. **Description:** Focuses on sickle cell disease. Reports on research, fundraising and community activities, and people in the field. Recurring features include news of the Center and its staff, letters from readers, profiles of sickle cell patients, reports of seminars and appointments, and notices of awards and continuing education opportunities. **Illustrations:** Includes black and white graphics. **Editorial policies:** Considers articles for publication. **First published:** January 1973. **Frequency:** Quarterly. Cumulative index issued quarterly. **Size:** 8-1/2 x 11, 6 pages. **Price:** Free. **Circulation:** 8,000.

★3643★
The Chicago Reporter
Community Renewal Society
332 S. Michigan Ave.
Chicago, IL 60604 Phone: (312)427-4830
Edited by: Roy Larson. **Description:** Serves as a voice for Chicago's poor. Includes issues on race relations, ethnic stereotypes, and health hazards and sanitation problems in public housing. **First published:** 1972. **Frequency:** Monthly. **Size:** 12 pages. **Circulation:** 3,500.

★3644★
Child Health Talks
National Black Child Development Institute
1463 Rhode Island Ave., NW
Washington, DC 20005 Phone: (202)387-1281
Edited by: Noreen Yazajian. **Description:** Provides information and guidance to parents on health issues facing Black children. **Frequency:** Quarterly. **Size:** 8-1/2 x 11, 8 pages. **Remarks:** Fax number is (202)234-1738.

★3645★
The Children's Voice
National Coalition to End Racisim in America's Child Care System
22075 Koths
Taylor, MI 48180 Phone: (313)295-0257
Edited by: Frank Ehlers. **Description:** Reflects the aims of the Coalition, whose purpose is to assure that all children requiring placement outside the home through foster care or adoption are placed in the earliest

available home most qualified to meet the child's needs. Encourages recruitment of foster and adoptive homes of all races and cultures. Recurring features include news of legislation, foster care and adoptive programs, and legal advancements. **Frequency:** Quarterly. **Price:** Included in membership. **Circulation:** 1,000.

★3646★
Civil Liberties
American Civil Liberties Union Foundation
132 W. 43rd St.
New York, NY 10036 Phone: (212)944-9800
Edited by: Jean Carey Bond. **Description:** Supplies news of the legal defense, research, and public education projects of the ACLU, conducted to enable citizens to know and assert their rights. Focuses on civil liberties issues relating to freedom of expression, due process of law, equality, and privacy. Recurring features include news of significant legislation. **First published:** June 1931. **Frequency:** Quarterly. **Size:** Tabloid. **Price:** Included in membership. **ISSN:** 0009-790X. **Circulation:** 275,000.

★3647★
Come Unity
Margo Yazell
PO Box 41532
St. Petersburg, FL 33743
Edited by: Margo Yazell. **Description:** "Dedicated to the preservation and enhancement of human rights–civil, political, economic, social, and cultural." Contains articles on such topics as abortion rights, sex discrimination, the death penalty, and poverty. Recurring features include cartoons and letters to the editor. **Illustrations:** Includes black and white graphics. **Editorial policies:** Considers articles for publication. **First published:** December 1971. **Frequency:** Periodic. **Size:** 11-1/2 x 17, 12 pages. **Price:** $5/yr. **Circulation:** 2,000.

★3648★
Commission for the Catholic Missions Among the Colored People and Indians—Quarterly
Commission for the Catholic Missions Among the Colored People and the Indians
2021 H St., NW
Washington, DC 20006 Phone: (202)331-8542
Edited by: Monsignor Paul A. Lenz. **Description:** Concerned with evangelism in church programs for the Black and Indian communities in the U.S. Publishes news and updates the financial status of the Commission. Reports the ordination of priests and the activities of individuals from Black and Indian communities. Recurring features include a letter from the editor and statistics. **Illustrations:** Includes black and white graphics. **Frequency:** Quarterly. **Size:** 8-1/2 x 11, 4 pages. **Price:** Free. **Circulation:** 40,000. **Remarks:** (202)331-8544.

★3649★
Con Brio
Music Educators National Conference
National Black Music Caucus
c/o Dr. Willis Patterson
University of Michigan
2308 More St.
Ann Arbor, MI 48109 Phone: (313)764-0586
Description: Monitors the activities of the Caucus, whose purpose is to foster the creation, study, and promotion of Black derived music in education. Helps to heighten awareness of the problems faced by Black music educators and students and provides a forum for the discussion of concerns. Recurring features include reports on regional conferences, collegiate and high school gospel choir competitions, and news of members. **Frequency:** Quarterly. **Price:** Included in membership.

★3650★
The Corporate Examiner
Interfaith Center on Corporate Responsibility
475 Riverside Dr., Rm. 566
New York, NY 10115 Phone: (212)870-2293
Edited by: Diane Bratcher. **Description:** Examines "policies and practices of major U.S. corporations with regard to: South Africa, labor, environment, equal employment, minorities, women, military production, government, and foreign investment." Recurring features include editorials, news of research, news of members, news of corporate activities, reviews of resource materials, and a supplement titled ICCR Brief. **Illustrations:** Includes black and white graphics. **Editorial policies:** Considers articles for publication upon editor's request. **First published:** 1971. **Frequency:** 10/yr. **Size:** 8-1/2 x 11, 8 pages. **Price:** Included in membership; $35/yr. for nonmembers, U.S. and Canada; $40 elsewhere. **Circulation:** 1,500.

★3651★
The Correspondent
Congress of Racial Equality
1457 Flatbush Ave.
Brooklyn, NY 11210 Phone: (718)434-2673
Edited by: George W. Holmes. **Description:** Preserves and promotes the philosophical tenets initiated by Marcus Garvey (1887-1940), the Jamaican-born Black nationalist leader. Provides news and information concerning the right of Black people to govern themselves in areas which are demographically and geographically defined as theirs. Emphasizes the inspirational role of Africa and social concerns such as drug abuse, education, employment, housing, prison reform, and senior citizens. Recurring features include news of members, and news of Congress programs and activities. **First published:** January 1980. **Frequency:** Quarterly. **Size:** 11 x 17. **Price:** Included in membership. **Circulation:** 50,000.

★3652★
County Compass
National Organization of Black County Officials
c/o National Association of Counties
440 1st St., NW
Washington, DC 20001 Phone: (202)347-6953
Edited by: Rosemary Davis. **Description:** Provides information and technical assistance on a range of economic development and other issues. **Illustrations:** Includes photographs. **First published:** 1984. **Frequency:** Quarterly. **Size:** 8 pages. **Price:** Included in membership. **Circulation:** 1,200.

★3653★
Courier
Caribbean American Intercultural Organization
PO Box 27099
Washington, DC 20038 Phone: (202)829-7468
Edited by: Shirley Hamburg and Helen Madison-Kinard. **Description:** Intended to promote, encourage, and maintain intercultural relations between the various peoples of the Caribbean and the people of the U.S. Profiles outstanding individuals of Caribbean ancestry who have made significant contributions to the development of the U.S., Caribbean, or Third World. Recurring features include announcements of exhibitions, forums, and audiovisual educational programs sponsored by the Organization. **First published:** 1968. **Frequency:** Quarterly. **Size:** 8-1/2 x 11. **Price:** Included in membership. **Circulation:** 400. **Remarks:** Fax number is (202)842-0215.

★3654★
CTS Network
Morgan State University
Center for Transportation
PO Box 924
Baltimore, MD 21239 Phone: (301)444-3394
Edited by: Mrs. Vernessa P. Woods. **Description:** Serves as an information exchange among HBCUs (Historically Black Colleges and Universities) concerning issues in transportation education and research. Recurring features include information on the Center's studies, projects, and educational programs, plus reports on other research of interest; notices of symposia, workshops, internships, and research assistantships; a calendar of events; and columns titled Workshop Development, Minority Job Bank in Transit, and Faculty, Student, and Alumni News. **Illustrations:** Includes two-color and black and white graphics. **Editorial policies:** Considers articles for publication. **First published:** Summer 1984. **Frequency:** Semiannually. **Size:** 8-1/2 x 11, 4 pages. **Price:** Free. **Circulation:** 1,500.

★3655★
Educating in Faith
Catholic Negro-American Mission Board
2021 H St., NW
Washington, DC 20006 Phone: (202)331-8542
Edited by: Monsignor Paul A. Lenz. **Description:** Publishes news and concerns of the Board and of the schools and programs they sponsor. Focuses on the needs of the Black community in the U.S., including daycare and other educational programs. Recurring features include a letter from the editor, news of meetings, and a calendar of events. **Illustrations:** Includes black and white graphics. **Frequency:** Quarterly. **Size:** 8-1/2 x 11, 4 pages. **Price:** Free. **Circulation:** 20,000. **Remarks:** Fax number is (202)331-8544.

★3656★
EEO News
Project Equality
1020 E. 63rd St., Ste. 102
Kansas City, MO 64110 Phone: (816)361-9222
Edited by: Maurice E. Culver. **Description:** Reports on issues related to the achievement of equal employment opportunity. Features news of court cases, information concerning elimination of employment barriers, and tips on recruiting, selecting, training, and promoting employees. **Illustrations:** Includes black and white graphics, charts, and graphs. **First published:** 1974. **Frequency:** Quarterly. **Price:** $10/yr.

★3657★
EEOC Compliance Manual
Bureau of National Affairs, Inc.
1231 25th St., NW
Washington, DC 20037 Phone: (202)452-4200
Edited by: Susan J. Sala. **Description:** Summarizes and analyzes policies, procedures, and standards followed by the staff of the Equal Employment Opportunity Commission (EEOC). Contains text of compliance procedures, interpretive manual, conciliation standards, and EEOC general counsel manual. Supplemented with official information as issued by the Commission. **First published:** 1975. **Frequency:** Periodic. **Size:** 8-1/2 x 11. **Price:** $248/yr.

★3658★
EMIE Bulletin
American Library Association
Ethnic Materials & Information Exchange
Round Table
Queens College, NSF 300
Flushing, NY 11367 Phone: (718)520-7139
Edited by: David Cohen. **Description:** Reports on programs and activities of the Round Table and news of related ethnic organizations. Presents articles by members on ethnicity and librarianship topics. Recurring features include book reviews. **Editorial policies:** Considers articles for publication. **First published:** 1983. **Frequency:** Quarterly. **Size:** 8-1/2 x 11, 12 pages. **Price:** Included in membership; $10/yr. for nonmembers. **ISSN:** 0737-9021. **Circulation:** 600.

★3659★
The Equal Employer
Y.S. Publications, Inc.
PO Box 2172
Silver Spring, MD 20915 Phone: (301)649-1231
Edited by: Gilbert Ginsburg and Donald P. Miller. **Description:** "Contains concise, accurate and complete digests of the latest critical decisions of all courts and United States government agencies bearing on employment discrimination." Analyzes recent developments in fair employment practices, especially within the Equal Employment Opportunity Commission (EEOC) and the Office of Federal Contract Compliance Programs (OFCCP). Recurring features include columns titled Cases and Decisions and Miscellany. **First published:** 1977. **Frequency:** Biweekly. **Size:** 8-1/2 x 11, 8 pages. **Price:** $245/yr. **Circulation:** 200.

★3660★
Fair Employment Practices
Bureau of National Affairs, Inc.
1231 25th St., NW
Washington, DC 20037 Phone: (202)452-4200
Edited by: Bill L. Marville. **Description:** Provides a notification and reference service covering developments affecting fair employment practices. Includes federal laws, orders, and regulations; policy guides and ground rules; and state and local fair employment practice laws. Recurring features include sections titled Fair Employment Practice Manual and Fair Employment Practice Cases. **First published:** July 2, 1965. **Frequency:** Biweekly. **Size:** 6 x 9. **Price:** $454/yr. **Toll-free phone:** (800)372-1033. **ISSN:** 0149-2683. **Online through:** DIALOG Information Services, Inc., 3460 Hillview Ave., Palo Alto, CA 94304; (415)858-3785. **Remarks:** Fax number is (202)822-8092. Telex number is 285656 BNAI WSH. **Former Title(s):** *Fair Employment Practice Service.*

★3661★
Fair Employment Practices Guidelines
Bureau of Business Practice
24 Rope Ferry Rd.
Waterford, CT 06386 Phone: (203)442-4365
Edited by: Emily Mitchell. **Description:** Provides information on legislative, administrative, and judicial developments in the fair employment practices field. Covers one specific fair employment case per issue, and includes three in-depth court cases regarding that topic. **Frequency:** Monthly. **Size:** 8 pages. **Price:** $84/yr. **Toll-free phone:** (800)243-0876. **ISSN:** 0093-7630. **Remarks:** Fax number is (203)434-3341.

★3662★
Fair Employment Practices Summary of Latest Developments
Bureau of National Affairs, Inc.
1231 25th St., NW
Washington, DC 20037 Phone: (202)452-4200
Edited by: Bill L. Manville. **Description:** Highlights developments in employment opportunity and affirmative actions, and affirmative action programs. Reports on federal and state court decisions, Equal Employment Opportunity Commission (EEOC) rulings and Office of Federal Contract Compliance Programs (OFCCP) decisions, new laws, regulations, and agency directives. Also provides information on special programs for minorities, the handicapped, women, and older workers. Recurring features include sections titled Fair Employment Practice Manual and Fair Employment Practice Cases. **First published:** March 4, 1965. **Frequency:** Biweekly. **Size:** 8-1/2 x 11, 6 pages. **Price:** $96/yr. **Toll-free phone:** (800)372-1033. **ISSN:** 0525-2156. **Online through:** HRIN, Executive Telecom System, Inc., College Park N., 9585 Valparaiso Ct., Indianapolis, IN 46268; (317)872-2045. **Remarks:** Fax number is (202)822-8092; telex number is 285656 BNA I WSH.

★3663★
Fair Employment Report
Business Publishers, Inc.
951 Pershing Dr.
Silver Spring, MD 20910 Phone: (301)587-6300
Edited by: Steve Lash. **Description:** Focuses on developments on the state and national levels regarding employment practices and discrimination. Emphasizes important legal decisions and governmental activities, particularly those of the Equal Employment Opportunity Commission, the Civil Rights Commission, and the Office of Federal Contract Compliance. **First published:** 1964. **Frequency:** Biweekly. **Size:** 8-1/2 x 11, 8-10 pages. **Price:** $194.72/yr. **ISSN:** 0014-6919. **Former Title(s):** *Civil Rights Employment Reporter.*

★3664★
For the People
Congressional Black Caucus
House Annex 2, Rm. 344
Washington, DC 20515 Phone: (202)226-7790
Description: Designed to address the legislative concerns of Black and other underrepresented citizens. Discusses legislative agenda items that the Caucus supports, including national health care, education, minority business assistance, urban revitalization, rural development, welfare reform, and international affairs. **Frequency:** Quarterly. **Price:** Included in membership.

★3665★
From the State Capitals: Civil Rights
Wakeman/Walworth, Inc.
300 N. Washington St., Ste. 204
Alexandria, VA 22314 Phone: (703)549-8606
Edited by: Keyes Walworth. **Description:** Provides a perspective of states' regulatory actions affecting ethnic and racial discrimination, desegregation, affirmative action programs, discrimination compensation, and civil rights of the disabled. **Frequency:** Monthly. **Price:** $79/yr. **ISSN:** 0741-353X. **Online through:** WESTLAW, a service of West Publishing Company, 50 W. Kellogg Blvd., PO Box 64526, St. Paul, MN 55164-0526; (612) 228-2500. **Remarks:** Fax number is (703)549-1372.

★3666★
The Gallery
Museum of African American History
301 E. Frederick Douglas
Detroit, MI 48202-4024 Phone: (313)899-2500
Description: Designed for persons interested in developing the national, public-sponsored Black Historical Museum, which is dedicated to preserving and exhibiting the cultural heritage of African-Americans and their ancestors. Describes and carries interpretive articles on the Museum's exhibits and acquisitions. Recurring features include listings of workshops, seminars, and lecture series conducted by the Museum. **Frequency:** Quarterly. **Price:** Included in membership. **Circulation:** Ca. 5,000.

★3667★
Heritage
Southern California Library for Social Studies and Research
6120 S. Vermont Ave.
Los Angeles, CA 90044 Phone: (213)759-6063
Description: Reports news of the Library, "a leading resource center specializing in radical, progressive, labor and minorities literature." Provides information on Library-sponsored conferences and programs, new collections, research services, and plans for future development. Recurring features include news of research and a calendar of events. **Editorial policies:** Considers articles for publication. **First published:** Fall 1982. **Frequency:** Quarterly. **Size:** 7 x 8-1/2, 4 pages. **Price:** Donation requested. **Circulation:** 3,600.

★3668★
HMP Newsletter
Georgetown University
Center for Immigration Policy and Refugee Assistance
Hemispheric Migration Project
Box 2298. Hoya Sta.
Georgetown University
Washington, DC 20057 Phone: (202)687-7074
Edited by: Mary Ann Larkin. **Description:** Reviews the progress and results of research projects concerning international migration, refugee flows, and related policy issues throughout North America, Latin America, and the Caribbean. Includes news of members, a calendar of events, and recent bibliography. **Illustrations:** Includes black and white photographs. **Editorial policies:** Considers articles for publication. **First published:** December 1, 1984. **Frequency:** Quarterly. **Size:** 8-1/2 x 11, 10 pages. **Price:** Free. **Circulation:** Ca. 600. **Remarks:** Fax number is (202)687-6988.

★3669★
IDRA Newsletter
Intercultural Development Research Association
5835 Callaghan Rd., Ste. 350
San Antonio, TX 78228 Phone: (512)684-8180
Edited by: Jose A. Cardenas. **Description:** Furnishes educational and social policy concepts emphasizing advocacy for minority groups. Focuses on research and technological implementation related to education and the delivery of other human services. Concentrates on the particular educational needs of children in Texas. Recurring features include news of research. **Illustrations:** Includes black and white graphics and tables. **Editorial policies:** Considers articles for publication. **First published:** May 1973. **Frequency:** Monthly. **Size:** 8-1/2 x 11, 8-12 pages. **Price:** Free. **Circulation:** 6,000. **Former Title(s):** *Tee Newsletter*, September 1974.

★3670★
Indialantic
Tuskegee Airmen Inc.
288 Sand Dollar Rd.
Indialantic, FL 32903 Phone: (305)777-5646
Edited by: John D. Silvera. **Description:** Contains news of reunions and other member activites of the Tuskegee Airmen. **Illustrations:** Includes Black and White photographs. **Frequency:** Quarterly. **Size:** 8-10 pages. **Circulation:** 1,400.

★3671★
Interracial Family Alliance—Communique
Interracial Family Alliance
PO Box 16248
Houston, TX 77222 Phone: (713)454-5018
Edited by: Elizabeth Radcliffe. **Description:** Promotes the purposes of the IFA, which seeks to "strengthen and support the interracial family unit and promote its acceptance by the public." Explores the concerns of interracial families and proposes positive solutions to problems. Focuses on the development of self-esteem in biracial children. Recurring features include editorials, news of members, letters to the editor, news of members, book reviews, a calendar of events, and columns titled A Closer Look, Have You Read, and Adoption. **Illustrations:** Includes black and white photographs and tables. **Editorial policies:** Considers articles for publication. **First published:** December 1, 1983. **Frequency:** Quarterly. **Size:** 8-1/2 x 11, 8 pages. **Price:** Included in membership; $15/yr. for nonmembers. **Circulation:** 150.

★3672★
Iowa Civil Rights Communicator
Iowa Civil Rights Commission
211 E. Maple St., 2nd Fl.
Des Moines, IA 50319 Phone: (515)281-4121
Edited by: Carol L. Groh. Serves as the official newsletter of the Commission, which seeks to "eliminate discrimination and to establish equality and justice for all persons within the state through civil rights enforcement and advocacy." Features news of civil rights legislation and court decisions. Identifies civil rights issues of particular interest to Iowa residents, as well as discussing issues of general interest. Includes articles written by civil rights professionals. **Illustrations:** Includes black and white photographs, charts, and graphs. **First published:** 1980. **Frequency:** Quarterly. **Size:** 8-1/2 x 11, 6 pages. **Price:** Free. **Toll-free phone:** (800)457-4416. **Circulation:** 3,000. **Remarks:** Fax number is (515) 242-5840.

★3673★
Jack and Jill of America Foundation—Intercom
Jack and Jill of America Foundation, Inc.
PO Drawer 3689
Chattanooga, TN 37404 Phone: (615)624-6097
Description: Furnishes information about the Foundation and its chapters, which "increases opportunities for children in the areas of education, cultural growth and civic responsibility for minority youth." Provides news of Foundation activities and reports on the fundraising events of various chapters. Recurring features include editorials, news of research, news of members, a calendar of events, and columns titled President's Message, Chapter Contributions, and National Projects. **Illustrations:** Includes black and white photographs and charts. **First published:** 1973. **Frequency:** Biennially. **Size:** 8-1/2 x 11, 8-10 pages. **Price:** Free. **Circulation:** Ca. 8,000.

★3674★
Joint Center for Political and Economic Studies—Focus
Joint Center for Political and Economic Studies
1301 Pennsylvania Ave., NW, Ste. 400
Washington, DC 20004 Phone: (202)626-3500
Edited by: David Ruffin. **Description:** Reports on Black and other minority participation in electoral politics. Offers public policy analysis on other issues that affect minorities. Recurring features include announcements of available publications, a column titled Perspective, and a supplement titled Political TrendLetter. **Illustrations:** Includes

black and white graphics. **First published:** November 1970. **Frequency:** Monthly. **Size:** 8-1/2 x 11, 8-12 pages. **Price:** $15/yr. **Circulation:** 11,500. **Former Title(s):** *Joint Center for Political Studies–Focus.*

★3675★
Latin American and Caribbean Center—Newsletter
Florida International University
Latin American and Caribbean Center
University Park
Miami, FL 33199 Phone: (305)348-2894
Edited by: Richard Tardanico, Rene Remos and Sofia Lopez. **Description:** Reviews the activities of Latin American and Caribbean Center. **Frequency:** Semiannually. **Size:** 16 pages. **Circulation:** 5,000. **Remarks:** Fax number is (305)348-3593.

★3676★
Latin American Index
Welt Publishing Company
1413 K St., NW, Ste. 800
Washington, DC 20005 Phone: (202)371-0555
Edited by: Barbara Annis. **Description:** Reports on political, economic, and social events of the preceding 15 days in South America, Central America, and the Caribbean. Monitors U.S. administration policy and congressional action affecting Latin America. Includes topics such as security and defense, economic aid, industry and trade, refugees and immigration, and terrorism. Recurring features include columns titled People, Economic Notes, and News Briefs. **Editorial policies:** Accepts advertising. **First published:** January 1, 1973. **Frequency:** Semimonthly. **Size:** 8-1/2 x 11, 4 pages. **Price:** $249/yr.; $199 for nonprofit organizations. **ISSN:** 0090-9416. **Remarks:** This publication is a member of the Inter-American Press Association. Fax number is (202)682-5833.

★3677★
Lawyers' Committee for Civil Rights Under the Law—Committee Report
Lawyers' Committee for Civil Rights Under Law
1400 I St., NW, Ste. 400
Washington, DC 20005 Phone: (202)371-1212
Edited by: Douglas B. Farquhar. **Description:** Discusses Supreme, Federal, and State Court cases that concern the rights of minorities and the poor. Covers civil rights litigation in numerous areas such as education, voting rights, employment discrimination, and equalization of municipal services and other governmental services and benefits. Informs readers of legislation and new programs that affect the civil rights of American citizens and about anti-apartheid work in South Africa and Namibia. Contains information on the Committee's activities and staff members as well as other civil rights issues. **First published:** November 1970. **Frequency:** Quarterly. **Size:** 8-1/2 x 11, 4-14 pages. **Price:** $20/yr. **Circulation:** 5,000.

★3678★
Leaves of Twin Oaks
Twin Oaks Community
Box 169, Rte. 4
Louisa, VA 23093 Phone: (703)894-5126
Edited by: Kat Kinkade. **Description:** Promotes the Community's aim "to maintain and expand a community which values cooperation and equality; which is not violent, racist, or sexist; which treats people fairly; and which provides for the basic physical and social needs of its members." Provides nonresidents with a view of current conditions at Twin Oaks, e.g., financial situation, daily life, health, special events, and cottage industries. Contains interviews with Community members and publishes occasional position papers on current debates. **Illustrations:** Includes black and white graphics. **Frequency:** Quarterly. **Size:** 7 x 8-1/2, 16-30 pages. **Price:** $3/4 issues, U.S.; $6 elsewhere and for institutions. **ISSN:** 0023-9836. **Circulation:** 300.

★3679★
Let's Be Human
National Labor Service
11 Wedgewood Ln.
Wantagh, NY 11793 Phone: (516)731-3069
Edited by: Harry Fleischman. **Description:** Presents articles on labor and civil rights. **First published:** August 1953. **Frequency:** Quarterly. **Size:** 8-1/2 x 11. **Price:** $10/yr. **Circulation:** 2,100.

★3680★
Making Success Happen Newsletter
National Association of Black Women Entrepreneurs
PO Box 1375
Detroit, MI 48231 Phone: (313)341-7400
Description: Acts as a national support system for Black businesswomen in the U.S. and focuses on the unique problems they face. Promotes the Association's objective to enhance business, professional, and technical development of both present and future Black businesswomen. Recurring features include announcements of symposia, workshops, and forums aimed at increasing the business awareness of Black women, profiles of successful Black businesswomen, and news of resources available. **Frequency:** Bimonthly. **Price:** Included in membership. **Circulation:** Ca. 1,760.

★3681★
Michigan Civil Rights Commission—Newsletter
Michigan Civil Rights Commission
Information Division
Department of Civil Rights
303 W. Kalamazoo, 4th Fl.
Lansing, MI 48913 Phone: (517)334-6079
Edited by: James H. Horn. **Description:** Informs the public of specific issues affecting the Civil Rights Commission's jurisdiction, including legislative developments. Covers news of the Commission regarding elections and appointments. Recurring features include notices of publications. **Illustrations:** Includes black and white graphics, charts, and graphs. **First published:** 1970. **Frequency:** Quarterly. **Size:** 8-1/2 x 11, 4 pages. **Price:** Free. **Circulation:** 7,000. **Remarks:** Fax number is (517)334-6075.

★3682★
Minorities in Business Insider
CD Publications
8204 Fenton St.
Silver Spring, MD 20910 Phone: (301)588-6385
Description: Covers affirmative action, employment, government contracting, and education in relation to minorities in business. **First published:** 1987. **Frequency:** Semimonthly. **Size:** 8-1/2 x 11, 8-10 pages. **Price:** $250/yr.

★3683★
Minorities in the Newspaper Business
Task Force on Minorities in the Newspaper Business
PO Box 17401
Dulles Airport
Washington, DC 20041 Phone: (703)648-1285
Edited by: Walterene Swanston. **Description:** Provides a forum for articles and points of view on promotion, retention, management, and education issues throughout the newspaper industry. Keeps readers abreast of industry trends and programs relating to Asians, African-Americans, Hispanics, and Native Americans. **Editorial policies:** Considers articles for publication. **Frequency:** Quarterly. **Size:** 8-1/2 x 11. **Price:** Free. **Circulation:** 15,000.

★3684★
Minority Markets Alert
Alert Publications, Inc.
399 W. Fullerton Pkwy.
Chicago, IL 60614 Phone: (312)525-7594
Description: Provides information on consumer trends, demographics, lifestyle patterns, and attitudes and priorities among Hispanic, Black, and Asian Americans. **Frequency:** Monthly. **Online through:** NewsNet Inc., 945 Haverford Rd., Bryn Mawr, PA 19010, (215)527-8030.

★3685★
Minority Publishers Exchange
Praxis Publications, Inc.
2215 Atwood Ave.
Madison, WI 53704 Phone: (608)244-5633
Edited by: Charles Taylor. **Subtitle:** A bimonthly newsletter for networking with independent minority owned self-publishers. **Description:** Offers advice on selling books, networking, improving efficiency, computerizing the office, and growing. **Illustrations:** Includes black and white graphics. **Editorial policies:** Accepts classified advertising. **First published:** November 1989. **Frequency:** Bimonthly. **Size:** 8-1/2 x 11, ca. 4 pages. **Price:** $12/yr. for individuals; $18 for businesses. **Circulation:** 500. **Former Title(s):** *Praxis Publishing Pointers.*

★3686★
The Minority Trendsletter
Center for Third World Organizing
3861 Martin Luther King Way
Oakland, CA 94609 Phone: (415)654-9601
Edited by: John Anner and Gary Delgado. **Description:** Analyzes issues and trends of particular concern in the Black, Asian, Latino, and Native American communities by surveying "mainstream" media coverage and issuing a different perspective. **Frequency:** Quarterly. **Size:** 24 pages. **Price:** $20/yr. for individuals, U.S.; $50 for institutions. **Circulation:** 15,000. **Former Title(s):** *Third Force.*

★3687★
Montgomery Business Exchange
R&D Village
Montgomery County
Office of Economic Development
101 Monroe St., Ste. 1500
Rockville, MD 20850 Phone: (301)217-2345
Edited by: DeVance Walker, Jr. **Description:** Contains information on services, programs, and technical assistance for small and minority-owned businesses. **Illustrations:** Includes black and white photographs. **Editorial policies:** Accepts advertising and classified advertising. **First published:** January 1988. **Frequency:** Monthly. **Size:** 11-1/2 x 15, 4-8 pages. **Price:** Free.

★3688★
Multicultural Leader
Educational Materials and Services Center
144 Railroad Ave., Ste. 107
Edmonds, WA 98020 Phone: (206)775-3582
Description: Contains articles on multiculturalism. Includes book reviews, news of research, and reports. **Frequency:** 4/yr. **Price:** $35/yr.

★3689★
NAFEO Inroads
National Association for Equal Opportunity
in Higher Education
400 12th St., NE
Washington, DC 20002 Phone: (202)543-9111
Edited by: Johnson Niba. **Description:** Focuses on "research on Blacks in higher education." **First published:** June 1986. **Frequency:** Bimonthly. **Size:** 16-28 pages. **Price:** Included in membership; $30/yr. for nonmembers. **Circulation:** Ca. 1000. **Remarks:** Fax number is (202) 543-9113. **Former Title(s):** *Inroads.*

★3690★
National Association for the Advancement of Black Americans in Vocational Education—Newsletter
National Association for the Advancement
of Black Americans in Vocational
Education
c/o Dr. Ethel O. Washington
5057 Woodward, Rm. 976
Detroit, MI 48202 Phone: (618)692-2131
Edited by: Dr. Ethel O. Washington. **Description:** Provides a forum for the expression of minority concerns within the American Vocational Association. Discusses equity issues and successful programs in vocational education. Facilitates the exchange of Chapter news among states. Recurring features include meeting announcements, notice of job vacancies, and a commentary. **Illustrations:** Includes black and white graphics. **Editorial policies:** Considers articles for publication. **First published:** Spring 1980. **Frequency:** Quarterly. **Size:** 8-1/2 x 11, 4-6 pages. **Price:** $10/yr. **Circulation:** 600.

★3691★
National Association of Black Accountants—News Plus
National Association of Black Accountants
900 2nd St., NE, Ste. 205
Washington, DC 20002 Phone: (202)682-0222
Edited by: Linda Gaston. **Description:** Addresses concerns of Black business professionals, especially in the accounting profession. Reports on accounting education issues, developments affecting the profession, and the Association's activities on the behalf of minorities in the accounting profession. Recurring features include member profiles, job listings, reports of meetings, news of research, and a calendar of events. **Editorial policies:** Accepts classified advertising. Accepts "technical notes" on topics such as tax issues for publication. **Frequency:** Bimonthly. **Size:** 8-1/2 x 11, 4-6 pages. **Price:** Included in membership; $20/yr. for nonmembers. **Circulation:** 2,000. **Remarks:** Fax number is (202)682-3322.

★3692★
National Association of Investment Companies—Newsletter
1111 14th St., Ste. 700
Washington, DC 20005 Phone: (202)347-8600
Description: Presents "issues, events and trends of vital concern to the MESBIC industry and to minority small business." Focuses on legislative trends and actions. **First published:** 1976. **Frequency:** Monthly. **Size:** 8-1/2 x 11, 2 pages. **Price:** $38.64/yr. **Former Title(s):** *National Association of Minority Enterprise Small Business Investment Companies-Perspective.*

★3693★
The National Bar Bulletin
National Bar Association
1225 11th St., NW
Washington, DC 20001-4217 Phone: (202)842-3900
Edited by: Christine McKee. **Description:** Covers new developments in law and the activities of the National Bar Association. Carries information on civil rights issues. Recurring features include news of affiliates and special convention issues. **Illustrations:** Includes Black and White graphics. **Editorial policies:** Accepts advertising. **Frequency:** Monthly. **Size:** 8-1/2 x 11, 8-16 pages. **Price:** $60/yr. **Circulation:** 10,000. **Former Title(s):** *The National Bar Association-News.*

★3694★
National Black MBA Association—Newsletter
National Black MBA Association
180 N. Michigan, Ste. 1820
Chicago, IL 60601 Phone: (312)236-2622
Edited by: Joleen Spencer and Eyvette Jones. **Description:** Serves as a communication network for member Blacks who hold masters degrees in business administration. Reports on chapter activities, other national MBA programs, and on the efforts of the Association to further the skills of the minority manager through continuing business education. Recurring features include news of research, a calendar of events, reports of meetings, and columns titled MBAs on the Move, Letter From the National President, and Message From the Editor-In-Chief. **Illustrations:** Includes black and white photographs. **Editorial policies:** Accepts advertising. Accepts for publication items on chapter activities or national business programs. **Frequency:** Bimonthly. **Size:** 8-1/2 x 11, 8 pages. **Price:** Free. **Circulation:** 3,500. **Remarks:** Fax number is (312)236-4131.

★3695★
National Business League—National Memo
National Business League
4324 Georgia Ave., NW
Washington, DC 20011 Phone: (202)829-5900
Edited by: Barry L. Hudson. **Description:** Discusses minority business development, especially the role of the League in furthering continued advances. Features news about economic trends, government policies and issues, private sector trends, minority business trade association activity, and chapter activities. Recurring features include reports of meetings, news of educational opportunities, book reviews, notices of

publications available, a calendar of events, and a column titled From the President's Desk. **Illustrations:** Includes Black and White graphics. **Editorial policies:** Accepts advertising. Considers articles for publication. **First published:** 1963. **Frequency:** Quarterly. **Size:** 8-1/2 x 11, 8 pages. **Price:** Included in membership. **Circulation:** 5,000.

★3696★
NBPA Advocate
National Black Police Association
1919 Pennsylvania Ave., NW, No. 300
Washington, DC 20006 Phone: (202)457-0563
Edited by: Fran L. Lassiter. **Description:** Furthers the Association's goals to improve relationships between police departments and the Black community; to recruit minority police officers on a national scale; and to eliminate police corruption, brutality, and racial discrimination. Recurring features include profiles of outstanding Black police officers and news of research. Audience: Male and female Black police officers. **First published:** 1987. **Frequency:** Quarterly. **Price:** Included in membership. **Circulation:** Ca. 35,000. **Remarks:** Fax number is (202) 223-6739. **Former Title(s):** *Grapevine Newsletter*; *NBPA Newsletter*.

★3697★
New Images
Metropolitan Council for Educational Opportunity
55 Dimock St.
Roxbury, MA 02119 Phone: (617)427-1545
Edited by: J. Marcus Mitchell. **Description:** Reports on the Council's integration program placing Black children from Boston, Massachusetts, in suburban schools. Discusses educational and integration issues and promotes quality integrated education for urban children, new learning experiences for suburban children, and cooperation between parents and other citizens. **First published:** April 1978. **Frequency:** Quarterly. **Size:** 8-1/2 x 11, 4 pages. **Price:** Free. **Circulation:** 3,000.

★3698★
New York African Studies Association—Newsletter
New York African Studies Association
301 Old Main Bldg.
State University College
New Paltz, NY 12561 Phone: (914)257-2888
Edited by: Thomas E. and Corinne E. Nyquist. **Description:** Acts as an information exchange that promotes African studies at all educational levels and among concerned New York State agencies. Contains news of the Association and its members, special reports, and summaries of past and current events in Africa. Recurring features include notices of work, study, and travel opportunities, poetry, book reviews, a calendar of events, news of members, papers, and columns titled African Studies in New York, Africana Materials, People and Events, and NYASA Guide. **Illustrations:** Includes black and white graphics, charts, and tables. **First published:** Spring 1974. **Frequency:** 3/yr. **Size:** 8-1/2 x 11, 8 pages. **Price:** Included in membership; $10/yr. for nonmembers. **ISSN:** 0148-7264. **Circulation:** Ca. 250. **Remarks:** Fax number is (914) 257-3670. **Also known as:** *NYASA Newsletter*.

★3699★
NMRLS Notes
North Mississippi Rural Legal Services
PO Box 767
Oxford, MS 38655 Phone: (601)234-8731
Edited by: Joseph D. Delaney, Jr. **Description:** Reports on health, housing, economics, education, and other social and legal issues affecting clients of NMRLS. Examines new federal and state laws and court decisions that affect minorities and the poor. Includes news of staff members and of NMRLS conferences and events. **Illustrations:** Includes black and white graphics. **Editorial policies:** Considers articles for publication. **First published:** November 1976. **Frequency:** Bimonthly. **Size:** 8 x 11, 4-6 pages. **Price:** Free. **Circulation:** 1,500. **Remarks:** Fax number is (601)236-3263.

★3700★
Nommo: The Power of the Word
Purdue University
Afro-American Studies Center
326 Stone Hall
West Lafayette, IN 47907 Phone: (317)494-5680
Edited by: Carolyn E. Johnson. **Description:** Reports on and discusses significant events, guest lectures, community matters, and activities in the arts related to Afro-American studies. Recurring features include summaries of Center activities, listings of course offerings and of other educational and professional opportunities, and columns titled What's the Word, Women's Desk, News From Africa, and Caribbean. **Illustrations:** Includes black and white graphics. **First published:** 1976. **Frequency:** 3/academic yr. **Size:** 8-1/2 x 11, 8-12 pages. **Price:** Free. **Circulation:** 1,500.

★3701★
The Nonviolent Activist
War Resisters League
339 Lafayette St.
New York, NY 10012 Phone: (212)228-0450
Edited by: Ruth Benn. **Description:** Monitors League activities and the peace movement in general. Analyzes issues of concern from a pacifist perspective, including disarmament, civil rights, feminism, and various political philosophies. Recurring features include letters to the editor, book reviews, and member news. **Illustrations:** Includes black and white graphics, tables, and graphs. **Editorial policies:** Accepts advertising. Considers articles for publication. **First published:** November 1984. **Frequency:** 8/yr. **Size:** 8-1/2 x 11, 24 pages. **Price:** $15/yr. for individuals; $25 for institutions. **ISSN:** 8755-7428. **Circulation:** 15,000.

★3702★
NOW Newsletter
Black Methodists for Church Renewal
601 W. Riverview Ave.
Dayton, OH 45406 Phone: (513)227-9460
Description: Addresses concerns of Black clergy and lay members of the United Methodist Church. Discusses issues such as revival of the Black church, involvement of Blacks within the structure of the church, the church's social and political position, community approach to the drug crisis through the Church, and support for Black education. Recurring features include news of the organization and its members. **Frequency:** 11/yr. **Price:** Included in membership. **Circulation:** 3,000.

★3703★
Operation Big Vote Newsletter
National Coalition on Black Voter Participation
1101 14th St., NW, Ste. 925
Washington, DC 20005 Phone: (202)898-2220
Description: Focuses on Operation Big Vote, a program to increase Black voter registration and participation in electoral voting. Also reports on the local independent coalitions developed and funded by the Coalition to increase nonpartisan voter participation and citizenship empowerment programs. Recurring features include news of research and information on voter education. **First published:** 1983. **Frequency:** Periodic. **Size:** 8-1/2 x 11. **Price:** Free. **Circulation:** 2,000.

★3704★
The Organizer
National Alliance Against Racist and Political Repression
11 John St., Rm. 702
New York, NY 10038 Phone: (212)406-3330
Edited by: Mike Welch. **Description:** Reports on the activities of task forces within the Alliance concerned with issues such as repressive legislation, political prisoners, police crimes, labor rights, prisoners' rights, racism, and political repression. Recurring features include information on the Alliance's national priority cases and activities planned around each case. **Illustrations:** Includes black and white graphics. **First published:** 1973. **Frequency:** Quarterly. **Size:** 8-1/2 x 11, 8 pages. **Price:** Included in membership; $7/yr. for nonmembers. **Circulation:** 10,000.

★3705★
Outreach Legislative Alert
Unitarian Universalist Association of
Churches in North America
100 Maryland Ave., NE
Washington, DC 20002 Phone: (202)547-0254
Edited by: Robert Z. Alpern. **Description:** Monitors public policy and legislative developments concerning the military budget, arms control and disarmament, human and civil rights, religious liberties, and economic justice. **First published:** 1976. **Frequency:** Periodic. **Size:** 8-1/2 x 11, 4 pages. **Price:** Free. **Circulation:** 2,000. **Former Title(s):** *Outreach*.

★3706★
Peacework
American Friends Service Committee
2161 Massachusetts Ave.
Cambridge, MA 02140 Phone: (617)661-6130
Edited by: Pat Farren. **Subtitle:** *A New England Peace Movement Newsletter*. **Description:** Concerned with social issues such as disarmament, peace and social justice, anti-draft and anti-nuclear movements, alternative economics, feminism, civil liberties, racial equality, community empowerment, and nonviolence. Recurring features include news items, book and resource listings, and a calendar of events. **Illustrations:** Includes black and white graphics and maps. **Editorial policies:** Considers articles for publication. **First published:** June 1972. **Frequency:** Monthly. **Size:** 8-1/2 x 11, 16 pages. **Price:** $12/yr. **ISSN:** 0748-0725. **Circulation:** 2,500.

★3707★
Police Misconduct and Civil Rights Law Report
Clark Boardman Company, Ltd.
375 Hudson St.
New York, NY 10014 Phone: (212)929-7500
Edited by: Elizabeth Brooks. **Description:** Monitors current research and court cases related to police misconduct and civil rights law. **First published:** April 1983. **Frequency:** 6/yr. **Size:** 8-1/2 x 11, 12 pages. **Price:** $75/yr. **ISSN:** 0738-0623. **Circulation:** 2,500. **Remarks:** Fax number is (212)924-0460. Prepared under the auspices of the National Lawyers Guild Civil Liberties Committee.

★3708★
Profits
Howard University
Small Business Development Center
PO Box 748
Washington, DC 20059 Phone: (202)806-2075
Edited by: Mary E. Merchant. **Description:** Carries news of current programs in the public and private sectors relating to minority business assistance. Also covers the activities of the Center. **Illustrations:** Includes black and white graphics. **First published:** 1970. **Frequency:** Periodic. **Size:** 8-1/2 x 11, 8 pages. **Price:** Free. **Circulation:** 2,000.

★3709★
Project Equality of Wisconsin—Newsletter
Project Equality of Wisconsin, Inc.
1442 N. Farwell Ave., Ste. 210
Milwaukee, WI 53202 Phone: (414)272-2642
Edited by: Betty J. Thompson. **Description:** Reports news of the interfaith community-sponsored program to achieve and evaluate equal opportunities for employment. Focuses on nonparticipating vendors, promotes equal employment opportunity (EEO) and affirmative action (AA) in the workplace through spending power of inter-religious community, and covers court rulings and government actions affecting affirmative action programs and equal opportunity employment. Recurring features include news of members, announcements of meetings and seminars, and listings of job opportunities. **Illustrations:** Includes black and white graphics. **First published:** 1969. **Frequency:** Quarterly. **Size:** 8-1/2 x 11, 8 pages. **Price:** Included in membership. **Circulation:** Ca. 3,000.

★3710★
Psych Discourse
Association of Black Psychologists
PO Box 55999
Washington, DC 20040 Phone: (202)289-3663
Description: Publishes news of the Association, whose aim is to "address the long neglected needs of Black professionals and begin to positively impact upon the mental health of the national Black community by means of planning, programs, services, training, and advocacy." Recurring features include editorials, news of research, letters to the editor, a calendar of events, and columns titled Social Actions, Chapter News, Publications, and Members in the News. **Illustrations:** Includes black and white graphics. **Editorial policies:** Accepts advertising. Considers articles for publication. **First published:** 1970. **Frequency:** Bimonthly. **Size:** 8-1/2 x 11, 24 pages. **Price:** Included in membership; $16/yr. for nonmembers, U.S. and Canada; $20 elsewhere. **Circulation:** 1,500. **Former Title(s):** *Association of Black Psychologists–Newsletter*; *Psych Dialogue*.

★3711★
Public Investment and South Africa Newsletter
American Committee on Africa
198 Broadway
New York, NY 10038 Phone: (212)962-1210
Edited by: Rob Jones. **Description:** Monitors the progress of the campaign for passage of state and municipal legislation concerning divestment of public funds from corporations supporting racism in South Africa. Provides state by state updates. **First published:** 1981. **Frequency:** Semiannually. **Size:** 8-1/2 x 11, 14 pages. **Price:** $1/yr. **Circulation:** 1,200.

★3712★
Rights
National Emergency Civil Liberties
Committee
175 5th Ave., Rm. 814
New York, NY 10160 Phone: (212)673-2040
Edited by: Jeff Kisseloff. **Description:** Focuses on civil liberties and rights issues. Discusses legislation and other pertinent national developments, and carries book reviews. **Illustrations:** Includes Black and White photographs and cartoons. **Editorial policies:** Considers articles for publication. **First published:** 1953. **Frequency:** 3/yr. **Size:** 8-1/4 x 11, 16 pages. **Price:** Included in membership. **Circulation:** 8,500.

★3713★
Rural Southern Voice for Peace—Newsletter
Rural Southern Voice for Peace/FOR
1901 Hannah Branch Rd.
Burnsville, NC 28714 Phone: (704)675-5933
Edited by: Clare Hanrahan and Ron Wetteroth. **Description:** Promotes the work of the organization, which seeks to "affirm our common humanity and protect our environment by creatively resolving conflict, promoting positive alternatives and affirming the wisdom and power of grassroots people as they work for nonviolent social change ... in the work for justice, peace, and a healthy environment." Recurring features include news of research, editorials, letters to the editor, news of members, book reviews, a calendar of events, and a column titled From the Homeplace. **Illustrations:** Includes black and white graphics. **First published:** November 1981. **Frequency:** Bimonthly. **Size:** 8-1/2 x 11, 16 pages. **Price:** Donation requested. **Circulation:** 2,500. **Remarks:** Affiliated with Fellowship of Reconciliation.

★3714★
Save Our Sons and Daughters—Newsletter
Save Our Sons and Daughters (SOSAD)
453 Martin Luther King Blvd.
PO Box 32421
Detroit, MI 48201 Phone: (313)833-3030
Edited by: Grace Lee Boggs. **Description:** Serves as a forum for the organization, a group of parents and supporters of children killed in street violence who began working together "to create positive alternatives for young people." Provides commentaries, news of neighborhood coalitions, concerts, rallies, and other social activities. **Illustrations:** Includes black and white graphics. **Size:** 8-1/2 x 11, 8 pages.

★3715★
Sickle Cell Disease Foundation of Greater New York—Newsletter
Sickle Cell Disease Foundation of Greater New York
127 W. 127th St., Rm. 421
New York, NY 10027 Phone: (212)865-1500
Subtitle: *Authoritative Sickle Cell News.* **Description:** Provides information on sickle cell anemia and the Foundation's programs and services. Recurring features include editorials, news of research, news of members, and a calendar of events. **Illustrations:** Includes black and white photographs. **First published:** 1972. **Frequency:** Quarterly. **Size:** 8-1/2 x 11, 8 pages. **Price:** Free. **Circulation:** 15,000. **Online through:** Contact publisher.

★3716★
South Africa as the Fifty-first State Library Newsletter
PO Box 45195
Seattle, WA 98145
Description: Discusses political events and information involving South African Blacks. **Frequency:** Monthly.

★3717★
South Africa Reporter
Investor Responsibility Research Center, Inc.
1755 Massachusetts Ave., NW, Ste. 600
Washington, DC 20036 Phone: (202)939-6500
Edited by: Meg Voorhes. **Description:** Reports on events and trends that will shape the future of South Africa and analyzes how these developments affect U.S. corporations with investments in South Africa. **First published:** February 1983. **Frequency:** 4/yr. **Size:** 8-1/2 x 11, 16 pages. **Price:** $100/yr. **Circulation:** 1,250.

★3718★
Southern Poverty Law Center—Law Report
Southern Poverty Law Center
PO Box 548
Montgomery, AL 36101-0548 Phone: (205)264-0286
Edited by: Sara Bullard and Dave Watson. **Description:** Reviews advances in the legal rights of the poor, monitors Ku Klux Klan and militant right-wing group activities nationwide, and provides model statutes for municipalities or states seeking to regulate racial and religious violence or violations of citizens' civil rights. Recurring features include summaries of significant law suits and court decisions, notices of publications available, and occasional state-by-state surveys of relevant legislation. **Illustrations:** Includes black and white graphics. **First published:** March 1981. **Frequency:** Bimonthly. **Size:** 8-1/2 x 11, 8 pages. **Price:** $15/yr. **Circulation:** 140,000. **Also known as:** *Intelligence Report.*

★3719★
Spotlight on Africa
American-African Affairs Association
1001 Connecticut Ave., NW, No. 1135
Washington, DC 20036 Phone: (202)223-5110
Description: Supports the aim of the Association, which is "to further the cause of knowledge concerning Africa among the people of the United States." Covers such topics as foreign involvement in Africa, famine relief, and African economic issues. **Frequency:** Bimonthly. **Size:** 8-1/2 x 11, 4 pages. **Price:** $10/yr.

★3720★
Statement
National Coalition of 100 Black Women
50 Rockefeller Plaza, Ste. 46
New York, NY 10020 Phone: (212)974-6140
Description: Reports on the activities and achievements of Black women involved with such issues as economic development, health, employment, education, voting, housing, criminal justice, the status of Black families, and the arts. Comments on the problems encountered by Blacks in cities and operates as a forum for the exchange of ideas on improving the conditions for Black communities. **Frequency:** Periodic. **Price:** Included in membership. **Circulation:** 3,500.

★3721★
Trends in Housing
1629 K St., NW, Ste. 802
Washington, DC 20006 Phone: (202)833-4456
Edited by: Natalie P. Shear. **Description:** Covers developments in fair housing issues, with articles on financing, redlining, low-income projects, consequences of regulations and legislation, and related subjects. Serves national, metropolitan, and local fair-housing advocacy and other civil rights groups. **Illustrations:** Includes black and white graphics. **First published:** August 1950. **Frequency:** Bimonthly. **Size:** 8-1/2 x 11, 8-12, pages. **Price:** $18/yr. **Circulation:** 20,000. **Remarks:** Fax number is (202)775-7465.

★3722★
The Tuskegee Airmen
Tuskegee Airmen Inc.
PO Box 1623
Melbourne, FL 32902 Phone: (305)727-3772
Edited by: Col. John D. Silvera. **Subtitle:** *Official National Publication.* **Description:** Promotes the recognition of the role of Blacks in military and civilian aviation. Profiles the careers of prominents Blacks who served in the armed forces. Recurring features include news items of interest to members in Tuskegee's 36 chapters, a calendar of events, research news, and a column titled Along the Tai Line. **Illustrations:** Contains black and white photographs and graphics. **Editorial policies:** Accepts display and classified advertising. Considers articles for publication. **First published:** 1978. **Frequency:** Quarterly. **Size:** 8-1/2 x 11, 8 pages. **Price:** Included in membership. **Circulation:** 1,800.

★3723★
UCC Courage in the Struggle for Justice and Peace
United Church of Christ
Office for Church in Society
110 Maryland Ave.
Washington, NY 20002
Edited by: Russell G. Claussen. **Description:** Monitors congressional legislation in the areas of current social issues. Considers such topics as U.S. involvement in Central America, the role of women and Blacks in the elections, tax relief for the disabled, and the fight of clerical and pastoral groups against racism. Reports on denominational justice and peace activities nationally, regionally, and locally. **Illustrations:** Includes black and white graphics. **First published:** 1977. **Frequency:** Monthly. **Size:** 8-1/2 x 11, 4 pages. **Price:** Free to UCC members. **Circulation:** 15,000. **Former Title(s):** *UCC Network; UCC Peace Priority.*

★3724★
The Urban Banker
National Association of Urban Bankers
122 C St., NW, Ste. 580
Washington, DC 20001 Phone: (202)783-4743
Description: Monitors trends in the provision of financial services products for member minority professionals in the banking industry and related fields. Provides coverage of legislative and regulatory actions affecting the industry, of Association programs, and of the professional accomplishments of members. Recurring features include chapter updates, reports on national and regional conferences and expositions, a calendar of events, results of financial industry surveys, and news of educational opportunities. Also includes the column Message From the President. **Illustrations:** Includes black and white photographs. **Editorial policies:** Accepts summaries of chapter activities for publication. **Frequency:** Quarterly. **Size:** 8-1/2 x 11, 4-6 pages. **Price:** Free. **Circulation:** 1,500. **Remarks:** Fax number is (202)628-3543.

★3725★
The Urban Libraries Exchange
Urban Libraries Council
3101 W. Coulter St.
Philadelphia, PA 19129 Phone: (215)848-3550
Edited by: Roy H. Millenson. **Description:** Covers federal, state, and local developments concerning urban libraries. Reports projects and programs undertaken by urban libraries and items of interest to Council members. **First published:** April 1984. **Frequency:** Monthly. **Price:** Included in membership. **Circulation:** 250. **Former Title(s):** *The Lamp.*

★3726★
Urban Research Review
Institute for Urban Affairs and Research
2900 Van Ness St., NW
Washington, DC 20008 Phone: (202)686-6770
Edited by: Dr. Lula A. Beatty. **Description:** Publishes research findings related to physical and mental health, violence and criminal justice, human resource development, community services, religion, and education, focusing primarily on Blacks. Recurring features include statistical data, interviews with research scholars, book reviews, reference citations, listings of educational and job opportunities, and announcements of research grants, conferences, workshops, and other events. **Illustrations:** Includes black and white graphics. **Editorial policies:** Considers articles for publication. **First published:** March 1974. **Frequency:** Semiannually. **Size:** 8-1/2 x 11, 12-16 pages. **Price:** Free. **Circulation:** 3,000.

★3727★
Vital Signs
National Black Women's Health Project
1237 Gordon St., SW
Atlanta, GA 30310 Phone: (404)753-0916
Edited by: Valerie Boyd. **Description:** Encourages mutual and self-help activism among women to bring about a reduction in health care problems prevalent among African-American women. Reports on research conducted on the health problems of Black women and discusses Black women's health issues. Recurring features include news of upcoming conferences and lectures sponsored by the Project. **First published:** 1984. **Frequency:** Quarterly. **Price:** Included in membership. **Circulation:** 10,000.

Directories

★3728★
Access and Outreach: A Directory of Organizations Serving Women and Minorities in the Chicago Area
Chicago Urban League
Research and Planning Dept.
4510 S. Michigan Ave.
Chicago, IL 60653 Phone: (312)285-5800
Description: About 325 nonprofit organizations serving minority groups and women in metropolitan Chicago. **Entries include:** Organization name, address, phone, name and title of contact, year founded, description of organization's history, purpose, and primary activities. **Arrangement:** Classified by minority group served. **Indexes:** Organization name, type of service provided, geographical. **Pages (approx.):** 240. **Frequency:** Irregular; latest edition 1989. **Price:** $25.00.

★3729★
Affirmative Action Register
Affirmative Action, Inc.
8356 Olive Blvd.
St. Louis, MO 63132 Phone: (314)991-1335
Description: In each issue, about 300 positions at a professional level (most requiring advanced study) available to minorities, veterans, and the handicapped; listings are advertisements placed by employers with affirmative action programs. **Entries include:** Company or organization name, address, contact name; description of position including title, requirements, duties, application procedure, salary, etc. **Arrangement:** Classified by profession. **Pages (approx.):** 50. **Frequency:** Monthly. **Editor(s):** Warren H. Green. **Price:** $1.50 per issue; distributed free to minority and handicapped candidate sources (ISSN 0146-2113). **Toll-free phone:** (800)537-0655. **Fax:** (314)997-1788.

★3730★
Africa: A Directory of Resources
Third World Resources
464 19th St.
Oakland, CA 94612 Phone: (415)835-4692
Description: Organizations and publishers of books, periodicals, audiovisuals, and other materials on Africa. **Entries include:** Organization or company name, address, phone, materials available. **Arrangement:** Geographical. **Indexes:** Organization, name, book title. **Pages (approx.):** 160. **Frequency:** Published fall 1987. **Price:** $9.95. **Other Information:** Part of a 12 volume series (published at the rate of 4 per year), each volume covering a single region or issue.

★3731★
Africa: Human Rights Directory and Bibliography
Human Rights Internet
Harvard Law School
Pound Hall, Rm. 401
Cambridge, MA 02138 Phone: (617)495-9924
Description: Approximately 300 human rights organizations in Africa and organizations worldwide concerned with human rights in Africa. **Entries include:** Organization name, address, phone, names and titles of key personnel, names and titles of key personnel, description of services and activities. **Arrangement:** Geographical. **Indexes:** Organization name/acronym, subject, publication title. **Pages (approx.):** 300. **Frequency:** Published February 1989. **Editor(s):** Laurie S. Wiseberg and Laura Reiner. **Price:** $35.00. **Fax:** (617)495-4110. **Also Includes:** Bibliographies of related materials available in each country, indexed by subject, author's name, and publishing organization.

★3732★
African-American Blackbook International Reference Guide
National Publications Sales Agency, Inc.
1610 E. 79th St.
Chicago, IL 60649 Phone: (312)375-6800
Description: About 4,000 African-American businesses and organizations; African-Americans on boards of major corporations; African-Americans in the food, beverage, and tobacco industries; African-American elected officials. **Entries include:** Firm name, address, phone, key personnel, history. **Pages (approx.):** 300. **Frequency:** Annual, March. **Editor(s):** Donald C. Walker. **Price:** $9.95, plus $3.00 shipping. **Other Information:** Supersedes "Blackbook Business and Reference Guide," which covered only Chicago, Illinois. **Former Title(s):** *Blackbook International Reference Guide*; *Blackbook National Resource Guide*.

★3733★
The African Studies Companion: A Resource Guide and Directory
Hans Zell Publisher
K.G. Saur
245 W. 17th St.
New York, NY 10011 Phone: (212)337-7023
Description: Listings of libraries, documentation centers, magazines, and journals in the field of African studies. **Entries include:** For libraries and documentation centers–Name, address, phone, telex, fax number, electronic mail address, name of person in charge of collection, hours, access, loan and reference/referral services/facilities, size of collection, on-line data base services and accessibility to outside users, publications and finding-aids issued, and brief description of collection. For magazines and journals–Title, publisher name, address, phone, telex, fax number, electronic mail address, year first published, ISSN, frequency, circulation, subscription rates, name of editor, name of book review editor, brief outline of contents and scope and special features; information whether journal welcomes contributions and articles, and in which particular areas, payment offered if any, and/or number of free copies or offprints provided to contributors, and editorial requirements. **Editor(s):** Hans M. Zell. **Fax:** (212)242-6781. **Other Information:** Includes annotated listings of reference works on African studies.

★3734★
African Studies Information Resources Directory
K. G. Saur
R. R. Bowker Company
245 W. 17th St.
New York, NY 10011 Phone: (212)982-1302
Description: Nearly 440 institution and organization archives and libraries with collections dealing with African studies. **Entries include:** Organization or library name, address, phone, name and title of contact, description of collections and information services provided. **Pages (approx.):** 575. **Frequency:** Irregular; latest edition 1986. **Editor(s):** Jean E. Meeh Gosenrink. **Price:** $88.00.

★3735★
Alabama's Black Heritage: A Tour of Historic Sites
Alabama Bureau of Tourism & Travel
532 S. Perry St.
Montgomery, AL 36104 Phone: (205)242-4169
Description: Sites of significance in Black American history in Alabama. **Frequency:** Every four years. **Price:** Free. **Other Information:** Formerly published by DCI.

★3736★
American League of Financial Institutions Directory of Members and Associate Members
U.S. League of Financial Institutions
1709 New York Ave., NW, Ste. 201
Washington, DC 20006 Phone: (202)628-5624
Description: About 80 minority owned savings and loan associations in 25 states and the District of Columbia. **Entries include:** Association name, address, phone, name of principal executive. **Arrangement:** Geographical. **Pages (approx.):** 5. **Frequency:** Irregular; previous edition August 1986; latest edition June 1988. **Editor(s):** John Harshaw. **Price:** $3.50. **Other Information:** Former association name is American Savings and Loan League. Previously cited as "American League of Financial Institutions-Membership Roster." **Formerly:** Directory of Minority Owned Savings and Loan Institutions.

★3737★
ArtSourceBook Minority Artists and Organizations in Pennsylvania
Pennsylvania Council on the Arts
Finance Bldg., Rm. 216
Harrisburg, PA 17120 Phone: (717)787-6883
Description: About 1,100 minority artists in Pennsylvania, including visual artists, filmmakers, performing arts companies, individual performing artists, and literary artists; also includes more than 550 sponsors of the arts and approximately 155 publishers. **Entries include:** For artists - Name, medium, accomplishments, education, address, and phone. For others - Name, address, phone. **Arrangement:** Artists are classified by medium; sponsors are geographical by region; publishers are alphabetical. **Pages (approx.):** 140. **Frequency:** Every four years; latest edition October 1988. **Editor(s):** S. Damon Kletzien. **Price:** Free. **Also Includes:** Bibliography of resource publications.

★3738★
Black Americans Information Directory
Gale Research Inc.
835 Penobscot Bldg.
Detroit, MI 48226-4094 Phone: (313)961-2242
Description: Sources of information on a variety of aspects of Black American life and culture, including national, state, and local organizations; publishers of newspapers, periodicals, newsletters, and other publications and videos; television and radio stations; traditionally Black colleges and universities; library collections; museums and other cultural institutions; Black studies programs and research centers; federal and state government agencies; Black religious organizations; and awards, honors, and prizes. **Entries include:** Name, address, phone, name and title of contact, description of services, activities, etc. **Arrangement:** Classified by type of organization, activity, service, etc. **Indexes:** Name/keyword. **Pages (approx.):** 475. **Frequency:** Biennial, 2nd edition published August 1991. **Editor(s):** Julia C. Furtaw. **Price:** $75.00. **Toll-free phone:** (800)877-GALE. **Fax:** (313)961-6241.

★3739★
Black Clergy Directory
Episcopal Commission for Black Ministries
Episcopal Church
815 2nd Ave.
New York, NY 10017 Phone: (212)867-8400
Description: About 495 Black Episcopal clergy. **Entries include:** Name, address, phone, diocese. **Arrangement:** Alphabetical. **Pages (approx.):** 60. **Frequency:** Annual, January. **Editor(s):** Reverend Canon Harold T. Lewis. **Price:** Free.

★3740★
Black Directory
Urban League of Greater Cleveland
12001 Shaker Blvd.
Cleveland, OH 44120 Phone: (216)421-0999
Description: About 1,500 firms offering professional, commercial, and industrial products and services; churches, associations, and Black public officials. **Entries include:** For firms and organizations - Firm name, address, phone, name of owner or manager. For individuals - Name, address, phone. **Arrangement:** Classified by line of business or activity. **Indexes:** Name. **Pages (approx.):** 25. **Frequency:** Irregular; latest edition 1989; suspended indefinitely. **Editor(s):** Edward Young. **Price:** $5.00.

★3741★
Black Elected Officials: A National Roster
University Press of America
4720 Boston Way
Lanham, MD 20706 Phone: 800-323-5277
Description: Over 6,600 Black Americans who hold elective public office in all 50 states, the District of Columbia, and the Virgin Islands. **Entries include:** Name, title, address, jurisdiction in which person serves, date term ends. **Arrangement:** Geographical, by state; then by level of office. **Pages (approx.):** 470. **Frequency:** Reported as annual; latest edition February 1989. **Editor(s):** Carolyn Barnett-Jones, Research Analyst. **Price:** $22.50 (ISSN 8564-5982). **Fax:** (202)626-8774. **Other Information:** Formerly published by Joint Center for Political Studies. **Former Title(s):** National Roster of Black Elected Officials.

★3742★
Black Enterprise—Top Black Businesses Issue
Earl G. Graves Publishing Company
130 5th Ave., 10th Fl.
New York, NY 10011 Phone: (212)242-8000
Description: Lists of 100 Black-owned industrial/service companies with sales of $5 million or above, more than 35 banks with total assets of $1.6 billion or more, nearly 35 savings and loan associations with total assets of $1.15 billion or more, about 30 insurance companies with total assets of about $830 million or more, and 100 auto dealers with sales of $10 million or above. **Entries include:** Company name, city and state, name of chief executive, year founded, number of employees, financial data. **Arrangement:** In categories, with rankings by financial size. **Frequency:** Annual, June. **Editor(s):** Earl G. Graves. **Price:** $3.75; back issues $4.50 each. **Toll-free phone:** (800)727-7777 (subscriptions only). **Fax:** (212)989-8410. **Also Includes:** Analyses of the lists and of the industries in which firms listed operate. **Other Information:** Cover title, *Black Enterprise-The Top 100 Businesses Issue.*

★3743★
Black Genesis: An Annotated Bibliography for Black Genealogical Research
Gale Research Inc.
835 Penobscot Bldg.
Detroit, MI 48226-4094 Phone: (313)961-2242
Description: Descriptions, with addresses, of about 250 important archival and other sources for Black genealogy. **Frequency:** Published fall 1978. **Editor(s):** James M. Rose and Alice Eicholz. **Price:** $68.00. **Toll-free phone:** (800)877-GALE. **Fax:** (313)961-6241. **Also Includes:** General information on types and usefulness of the various sources available to the Black genealogist and annotated bibliographical notes on general references, publications, the value of oral history, migratory patterns, etc. **Other Information:** *Volume 1 of the Gale Genealogy and Local History Series.*

★3744★
Black Graduates of Kentucky
Kentucky Commission on Human Rights
500 Mural St., Ste. 832
Frankfort, KY 40601 Phone: (502)564-3550
Description: Approximately 240 Black graduates of Kentucky colleges and universities. **Entries include:** Personal name, address, phone, biographical data. **Arrangement:** Classified by academic major. **Pages (approx.):** 35. **Frequency:** Annual, April. **Editor(s):** Eric George. **Price:** Free.

★3745★
Black Resource Guide
Black Resource Guide, Inc.
501 Oneida Pl., NW
Washington, DC 20011 Phone: (202)291-4373
Description: Over 3,000 organizations especially relevant to or comprised primarily of Black Americans, including adoption agencies, business and bar associations, colleges, public administrators, book publishers, church denominations, financial institutions, hospitals, museums, embassies and consulates, and others; also included are Blacks in federal elected and appointed positions; individuals chosen for their prominence in athletics, entertainment, and politics. **Entries include:** Generally, listings show name, address, and phone; name and title of chief executive officer may also be included. **Arrangement:** Classified by line of business or activity. **Pages (approx.):** 285. **Frequency:** Annual, January. **Editor(s):** R. Benjamin Johnson and Jacqueline L. Johnson, Publishers. **Price:** $50.00, plus $1.50 shipping. **Also Includes:** Population, business, and health statistics.

★3746★
Black Student's Guide to Colleges
Beckham House Publishers
PO Box 177
Hampton, VA 23669 Phone: (804)728-9303
Description: Nearly 200 colleges, including about 75 considered to be "the most selective residential colleges," 25 historically Black colleges, and others selected for general popularity, etc. **Entries include:** Name, location, number of Black students, number of Black faculty, total number of faculty, library holdings, tuition, costs, majors often selected by Black students, support services specifically for Black students, and comments by recent alumni or current Black students regarding the general atmosphere and environment of the college. **Arrangement:** Alphabetical. **Indexes:** Geographical. **Pages (approx.):** 510. **Frequency:** Biennial. **Editor(s):** Barry Beckham. **Price:** $15.95. **Fax:** (804)723-8761. **Other Information:** A library edition containning additional indexes is also available; $35.00. Formerly published by E. P. Dutton, Inc.

★3747★
Black Student's Guide to Scholarships
Beckham House Publishers, Inc.
PO Box 177
Newport News, VA 23602 Phone: (804)728-9303
Description: Providers of financial aid for Black students pursuing a college education. **Entries include:** Organization name, address, phone, name and title of contact, eligibility requirements, description of award or grant. **Arrangement:** By category. **Pages (approx.):** 35. **Frequency:** Irregular; previous edition 1985; latest edition August 1990. **Editor(s):** Barry Beckham, President. **Price:** $5.95. **Fax:** (804)723-8761. **Former Title(s):** *75 Scholarships Every Black High School Student Should Know About.*

★3748★
Black Theatre Directory
Audience Development Committee
Box 30
Manhattanville Station
New York, NY 10027 Phone: (212)534-8776
Description: Nearly 1,000 individuals interested in or pursuing a career in Black theater.

★3749★
Black Writers
Gale Research Inc.
835 Penobscot Bldg.
Detroit, MI 48226 Phone: (313)961-2242
Description: Over 400 Black authors of the twentieth century from the United States or of interest to American readers. Entries are selected and updated from "Contemporary Authors". **Entries include:** Author's name; home and office addresses, agent's name and address; date and place of birth, names of parents, spouse, and children, colleges attended and degrees earned, political beliefs; description of career, awards and honors, memberships; chronological bibliography of books written, list of other notable publications such as screenplays and periodical articles; description of works in progress; "Sidelights" section discussing author's literary development, personal interests and attitudes, and reception of author's works by critics; list of publications containing more information on aut[illegible] **Pages (approx.):** 600. **Frequency**[illegible] **Editor(s):** Linda Metzger, Senior Edit[illegible] (800)877-GALE. **Fax:** (313)961-624[illegible]

★3750★
Burrelle's Black Media Directory
Burrelle's Media Directories
75 E. Northfield Rd.
Livingston, NJ 07039 Phone: (201)992-6600
Description: Newspapers, magazines, newsletters, radio and television programs, and other media serving the interests of the Black population. **Entries include:** Publication or station name, address, phone, names and titles of key personnel, description of publication or program. **Arrangement:** Geographical. **Indexes:** Geographical. **Pages (approx.):** 295. **Frequency:** Irregular; latest edition 1989. **Price:** $50.00, plus $3.75 shipping.

★3751★
Buyers' Guide to Minority Business
Arizona Minority Supplier Development Council
5151 N. 16th St., Ste. F-136
Phoenix, AZ 85016 Phone: (602)277-8559
Description: Minority commercial and industrial firms in Arizona. **Entries include:** Company name, address, phone, name of contact, date established, number of employees, facilities, product or service provided, references. **Arrangement:** Classified by line of business. **Indexes:** Alphabetical. **Pages (approx.):** 300. **Frequency:** Twice a year; latest edition July 1991. **Editor(s):** Patsy DiRuzza. **Price:** $50.00, plus $3.50 shipping.

★3752★
Caribbean/American Directory
Caribbean/American Directory, Inc.
Cooper/Lang Communications, Inc.
1377 K St, NW
Washington, DC 20005
Description: 4,500 American business firms and organizations with interests in the Caribbean, Central America (does not include Mexico), the Virgin Islands, and Puerto Rico. **Entries include:** Company name, address, phone, name of parent company (if applicable), type of business, purpose and activities, key personnel, location of business interests in the Caribbean, annual sales. **Arrangement:** Separate sections for corporations and nonprofit organizations. **Indexes:** Industry/line of business, Caribbean country in which active, geographical list of headquarters in the United States, company name. **Pages (approx.):** 600. **Frequency:** Irregular; previous edition September 1986; latest edition July 1987. **Price:** $100.00, plus $3.00 shipping, including update. **Other Information:** This is second in a series describing United States business interests abroad. Other volumes cover South America and Mexico, Europe, the Arab world, the Far East, and the Soviet Union.

★3753★
Caribbean Business Directory & Yellow Pages
Caribbean Publishing Company
4135 Laguna St.
Coral Gables, FL 33146 Phone: (305)445-1919
Description: 40,000 business firms, government offices, and medical and legal practices in 24 Caribbean countries; also includes listings in Miami, Florida. **Entries include:** Name of firm, address, phone, telex, fax. **Arrangement:** Classified by type of firm. **Indexes:** Product/service. **Pages (approx.):** 900. **Frequency:** Annual, September. **Editor(s):** Christine McEvoy, Production Manager. **Price:** $45.00, plus $4.75 shipping. **Send orders to:** Caribbean Imprint Directory Services, 410 W. Falmouth Hwy., Falmouth, MA 02574 (508-540-5378). **Former Title(s):** *Caribbean Telephone Directory*; *Caribbean Business Directory.*

★3754★
Caribbean Exporters, Importers and Business Services Directory
Caribbean Business Development Group, Inc.
67 Wall St., Ste. 2411
New York, NY 10005 Phone: (212)323-7952
Description: Over 5,500 exporters, importers, and business service companies in 23 Caribbean countries. **Entries include:** Company name, address, phone, phone, telex, name and title of contact, number of employees, line of business. **Arrangement:** Classified by product or service. **Indexes:** Standard Industrial Classification (SIC) code, geographical. **Pages (approx.):** 400. **Frequency:** Annual, December. **Editor(s):** Lloyd Pilgrim Spooner and Courtney Jackson. **Price:** $59.95. **Toll-free phone:** (800)638-2000. **Fax:** (212)432-9366.

★3755★
Certified Minority Business Enterprises & Women Business Enterprises in Rhode Island
Rhode Island Department of Economic Development
Small Business Division
7th Jackson Walkway
Providence, RI 02903 Phone: (401)277-2601
Description: About 180 professional, commercial, industrial, and consumer firms. **Entries include:** Company name, address, phone, name of principal officer, line of business, certification and recertification dates. **Arrangement:** Classified by line of business. **Indexes:** Alphabetical. **Pages (approx.):** 25. **Frequency:** Quarterly **Editor(s):** Charles Newton, Coordinator. **Price:** Free. **Other Information:** Publishing office was formerly the Business and Industry Division. **Former Title(s):** *Rhode Island Minority Businesses*; *Rhode Island Minority Business Enterprises*.

★3756★
Cleveland Ethnic Directory Ohio
Nationalities Services Center of Cleveland
1715 Euclid Ave., Ste. 200
Cleveland, OH 44115 Phone: (216)781-4560
Description: Several thousand ethnic organizations, societies, cultural and political organizations, and performing groups in the Cleveland, Ohio area. **Entries include:** Organization name, address, phone, names and titles of key personnel, subsidiary and branch names and locations. **Arrangement:** Classified by nationality. **Indexes:** Subject. **Frequency:** Irregular; latest edition 1990. **Price:** $10.00, plus $2.00 shipping.

★3757★
Community of People: A Multi-Ethnic Bibliography
Portland Public Schools
Educational Media Department
501 N. Dixon St.
Portland, OR 97227 Phone: (503)249-2000
Description: List of community groups that have facilities and services for schools engaged in multicultural education in the Portland, Oregon area. **Entries include:** Group name, address, phone, facilities available. **Arrangement:** Classified by subject. **Frequency:** Irregular; previous edition 1984; latest edition 1988. **Editor(s):** Chris Poole et al. **Price:** $5.00.

★3758★
Contemporary Black American Playwrights & Their Plays: A Biographical Directory & Dramatic Index
Greenwood Publishing, Inc.
88 Post Rd. W.
Westport, CT 06881 Phone: (203)226-3571
Frequency: Latest edition May 1988. **Editor(s):** Bernard L. Peterson, Jr. **Price:** $75.00.

★3759★
Dallas/Fort Worth Black Pages
Dallas/Fort Worth Black Pages
3606 Marvin D. Love Fwy., Ste. 130
Dallas, TX 75224 Phone: (214)375-5200
Description: About 3,000 minority firms offering professional, commercial, and industrial products and services in the greater Dallas/Ft. Worth, Texas area. **Entries include:** Firm name, address, phone, name and title of owner or chief executive, products or services. **Arrangement:** Alphabetical. **Indexes:** Product/service. **Frequency:** Annual, February. **Editor(s):** Arnette D. French. **Price:** Free.

★3760★
Dayton Area Minority & Female Business Directory
Dayton Human Relations Council
40 S. Main St., Ste. 721
Dayton, OH 45402 Phone: (513)228-7277
Description: About 300 firms offering professional, commercial, industrial, and consumer products and services. **Entries include:** Company name, address, phone, name of contact, line of business. **Arrangement:** In separate sections for minority and women-owned businesses. **Indexes:** Line of business. **Pages (approx.):** 50. **Frequency:** Irregular; latest edition 1989. **Price:** Free. **Former Title(s):** *Dayton Area Minority Business Directory*; *Dayton and Surrounding Area Minority Busines Directory*.

★3761★
Directory of African American Religious Bodies
Howard University School of Divinity Research Center
1400 Shepherd St., NE
Washington, DC 20017 Phone: (202)269-1122
Description: Approximately 900 African American religious denominations; resource and service agencies that serve the African American community; religious educational institutions, research organizations, and professional religious organizations; African American colleges and universities founded by religious bodies; African American religious scholars. **Entries include:** For religious denominations–Institution name, address, phone, names and titles of key personnel, description of institution, group type, year founded, number of members, publications, meeting dates. For resource and service agencies–Company name, address, phone. For religious educational institutions, research organizations, and professional religious organizations–Organization name, address, phone, name and title of contact, description of organization. For colleges and universities–School name, address, phone. For individuals–Personal name, address, phone, biographical data. **Arrangement:** Separate sections for religious denominations, resource and service agencies; religious educational institutions, research organizations, and professional religious organizations; colleges and universities, and scholars. **Indexes:** Religious bodies, personal name, geographical, group type, and religious category. **Pages (approx.):** 400. **Frequency:** First edition expected 1990. **Editor(s):** Dr. Wardell J. Payne, Research Director. **Fax:** (202)686-2255 (orders only). **Send orders to:** Howard University Press, 2900 Van Ness St., N.W., Washington, DC 20009 (202-686-6696).

★3762★
Directory of African and Afro-American Studies in the United States
African Studies Association
Credit Union Bldg.
Emory University
Atlanta, GA 30322 Phone: (404)329-6410
Description: About 625 institutions offering programs in African and Afro-American studies; about 300 other institutions have briefer listings. **Entries include:** For principal institutions–Name, address, courses offered, faculty, library collections available, financial aid, and area of specialized study. For other institutions–Name, address, and courses offered. **Arrangement:** Geographical. **Indexes:** Institution name, faculty and staff, program, title and degree offerings, African language. **Pages (approx.):** 275. **Frequency:** Irregular; previous edition 1981; latest edition spring 1988; new edition expected 1991. **Editor(s):** Hamit M. Rana. **Price:** $20.00, plus $2.00 shipping; payment with order. **Former Title(s):** *Directory of Third World Studies in the United States*.

★3763★
Directory of Black Americans in Political Science
American Political Science Association
1527 New Hampshire Ave., NW
Washington, DC 20036 Phone: (202)483-2512
Description: Over 500 Black advanced graduate students, academics, and professionals in the field of political science. A list of about 75 predominantly Black colleges and universities with political science programs is included. **Entries include:** For individuals–Name, title,

affiliation, address, degree, fields of specialization, publications. For colleges–Name, address; many listings also include phone. **Arrangement:** Alphabetical. **Indexes:** Field of interest. **Pages (approx.):** 200. **Frequency:** Irregular; previous edition 1977 (out of print); latest edition January 1988. **Editor(s):** Maurice C. Woodard. **Price:** $15.00.

★3764★
Directory of Black Design Firms
San Francisco Redevelopment Agency
939 Ellis St.
San Francisco, CA 94109 Phone: (415)771-8800
Description: Nearly 90 architectural, engineering, planning and landscape design firms. **Entries include:** Firm name, address, phone. **Arrangement:** Alphabetical. **Pages (approx.):** 10. **Frequency:** Annual, December. **Editor(s):** Benson Hattem. **Price:** Free. **Former Title(s):** *Directory of Black Architects and Engineers in the West*; *Directory of Black Design Firms in the West.*

★3765★
Directory of Black Economists
National Economic Association
c/o Dr. Alfred L. Edwards
School of Business
University of Michigan
Ann Arbor, MI 48109-1234 Phone: (313)763-0121
Description: About 400 economists. **Entries include:** Name, professional affiliation, address, phone, areas of specialization. **Arrangement:** Alphabetical. **Pages (approx.):** 25. **Frequency:** Irregular; latest edition March 1988. **Editor(s):** Lynn Burbridge, Barbara A.P. Jones. **Price:** $15.00. **Fax:** (313)763-5688. **Other Information:** Variant title *National Economic Association–Membership Directory.*

★3766★
Directory of Certified Minority and Women-Owned Business Enterprises
Minority and Women's Business Division
Government Office & Minority Women's Business Department
Empire Plaza, Box 2072
Albany, NY 12220 Phone: (212)417-2263
Description: Officially certified minority-owned and woman-owned construction, professional, service, manufacturing, distributing, and retail firms in New York state. Certification identifies companies that meet state government procurement requirements. **Entries include:** Firm name, address, phone, contact name, Standard Industrial Classification (SIC) number, products or services, sales figure. **Arrangement:** Classified in two-digit SIC categories named, then in four-digit SIC code order (numerical). **Indexes:** Company name, product/service (separate two- and four-digit SIC). **Pages (approx.):** 400. **Frequency:** Annual. **Editor(s):** Jacqueline Hieves, Development Specialist. **Price:** $59.00. **Other Information:** Variant title, *Directory of Minority and Women-Owned Business Enterprises.* **Former Title(s):** *Register of Minority and Women-Owned Business Enterprise*; *Registry of Business Enterprise.*

★3767★
Directory of Certified Minority Business Enterprises
Minority Business Opportunity Commission
2000 14th St., NW
Washington, DC 20009 Phone: (202)939-8780
Description: About 550 suppliers of professional, commercial, and industrial products and services, and construction services, all firms in which minority ownership and control has been certified by the District of Columbia Minority Business Opportunity Commission in accordance with D.C. Law I-95. **Entries include:** Firm name, address, phone, name and title of owner or chief executive, products or services. **Arrangement:** Alphabetical. **Indexes:** Product/service, personal name. **Pages (approx.):** 140. **Frequency:** Twice a year. **Editor(s):** Faith Roland. **Price:** Free.

★3768★
Directory of Certified State and Federal Minority and Women's Business Enterprises
Washington Office of Minority and Women's Business Enterprises
406 S. Water, MS: FK-11
Olympia, WA 98504 Phone: (206)753-9693
Description: More than 3,500 professional, commercial, industrial, and consumer firms. **Entries include:** Company name, address, phone, name of contact, status of certification as a minority- or woman-owned firm, product or service provided. **Arrangement:** Classified by commodity code. **Pages (approx.):** 200. **Frequency:** Annual, July; three addenda per year. **Editor(s):** Diane Bailey. **Price:** $35.00 per year; payment must accompany order. **Other Information:** Combines four previously separate directories which were published by the City of Seattle Human Rights Department, King County Minority & Women's Business Enterprises Business Program, City of Spokane - Affirmative Action Department, and the above office. **Former Title(s):** *Minority Business Enterprises in Washington State.*

★3769★
Directory of Ethnic Minority Professionals in Psychology
American Psychological Association
Office of Ethnic Minority Affairs
1200 17th St., NW
Washington, DC 20036 Phone: (202)955-7600
Description: Nearly 600 ethnic minority psychologists nationwide and in Puerto Rico. **Entries include:** Company name, address, phone. **Arrangement:** Classified by race/ethnicity. **Indexes:** Name, gender. **Pages (approx.):** 115. **Frequency:** Latest edition July 1988; new edition expected 1990. **Price:** $15.00. **Former Title(s):** *Ethnic Minority Directory of Professionals in Psychology.*

★3770★
Directory of Financial Aids for Minorities
Reference Service Press
1100 Industrial Rd., Ste. 9
San Carlos, CA 94070 Phone: (415)594-0743
Description: Over 2,000 financial aid programs and awards available to members of minority groups; includes scholarships, fellowships, loans, grants, awards, and internships; state government agencies with related information. **Entries include:** Program title, sponsor name, address, phone, eligibility requirements, purpose, duration, application deadline, financial data, etc. **Arrangement:** Programs are classified by type of aid, then by minority group; state agencies are geographical. **Indexes:** Program title, sponsor name, geographical, subject, month of application deadline. **Pages (approx.):** 525. **Frequency:** Biennial, January of odd years. **Editor(s):** Gail Ann Schlachter. **Price:** $45.00, plus $2.50 shipping. **Fax:** (415)594-0743. **Other Information:** Former publisher, ABC-Clio Information Services.

★3771★
Directory of Intercultural Education Newsletters
Information Consulting Associates
185 Kenneth St.
Hackensack, NJ 07601 Phone: (201)343-8833
Description: Over 190 newsletters concerned with travel and intercultural education at all levels. **Entries include:** Publication title, publisher or editor, address, frequency, price, number of pages, size, codes for format and circulation. **Arrangement:** Alphabetical by publication title. **Pages (approx.):** 100. **Frequency:** Latest edition January 1987; suspended indefinitely. **Editor(s):** Muriel Wall. **Price:** $10.00, postpaid, payment with order.

★3772★
Directory of Minority- and Women-Owned Business Enterprises
New York City Office of Business Development
17 John St., 10th Fl.
New York, NY 10038-6357 Phone: (212)513-6466
Description: About 600 New York city businesses that are at least 51% owned by women or members of minority groups. **Entries include:** Company name, address, phone, name and title of contact, description of products or services. **Arrangement:** Classified by line of business.

Indexes: Alphabetical. **Pages (approx.):** 100. **Frequency:** Annual, January. **Editor(s):** Edmund Yu. **Price:** Free. **Fax:** (212)267-2598.

★3773★

Directory of Minority and Women Owned Businesses
Louisiana Office of Minority and Women's Business Enterprise
Department of Economic Development
Box 94185
Baton Rouge, LA 70804-9185 Phone: (504)342-5373
Description: Firms offering professional, commercial, and industrial products and services. **Entries include:** Firm name, address, phone, name and title of contact, number of employees, products or services, geographical area served, financial data, Standard Industrial Classification (SIC) code. **Arrangement:** Alphabetical. **Pages (approx.):** 250. **Frequency:** Annual. **Editor(s):** Angelisa M. Harris, Executive Director. **Price:** $25.00. **Former Title(s):** *Minority Entrepreneur Directory*; *Minority and Women's Business Directory*.

★3774★

Directory of Minority and Women-Owned Engineering and Architecural Firms
American Consulting Engineers Council
1015 15th St., NW, Ste. 802
Washington, DC 20005 Phone: (202)347-7474
Description: Approximately 525 minority and women-owned engineering and architectural firms. **Entries include:** Firm name, address, phone; owners' names including percentage of ownership, sex, and race of each; registered professionals, size of staff, description of activities, minority status, branches; local, state, and federal MBE/WBE certification, if applicable. **Arrangement:** Geographical. **Indexes:** Firm name, area of experience. **Pages (approx.):** 115. **Frequency:** Irregular; previous edition 1983; latest edition June 1986; new edition possible 1990. **Editor(s):** Gregory B. Coleman, Vice President. **Price:** $10.00. **Fax:** (202)898-0068. **Former Title(s):** *Directory of Minority Architectural and Engineering Firms* (1980).

★3775★

Directory of Minority and Women-Owned Investment Bankers
San Francisco Redevelopment Agency
939 Ellis St.
San Francisco, CA 94109 Phone: (415)771-8000
Description: About 15 minority-owned investment banking firms. **Entries include:** Company name, address, phone, owner's name and title. **Arrangement:** Alphabetical. **Frequency:** Latest edition 1988. **Editor(s):** Benson I. Hattem.

★3776★

Directory of Minority Arts Organizations
Civil Rights Division
National Endowment for the Arts
1100 Pennsylvania Ave., NW, Rm. 812
Washington, DC 20506 Phone: (202)682-5454
Description: Almost 1,000 performing groups, presenters, galleries, art and media centers, literary organizations, and community centers with significant arts programming which have leadership and constituency that is predominantly Asian-American, Black, Hispanic, Native American, or multi-racial. **Entries include:** Organization name, address, phone, name and title of contact, description of activities. **Arrangement:** Geographical. **Indexes:** Organization name, activity. **Pages (approx.):** 120. **Frequency:** Irregular; previous edition 1982; latest edition February 1987. **Editor(s):** Nellie Fowler. **Price:** Free.

★3777★

Directory of Minority Business in Wisconsin
Wisconsin Office of Minority Business Enterprise
Box 7970
Madison, WI 53707 Phone: (608)267-9550
Description: About 300 non-retail minority firms. **Entries include:** Name, address, phone, name of chief executive or contact, type of minority, year established, number of employees, employer's identification number, Standard Industrial Classification (SIC) code, description of business, including history, capabilities, major customers, geographic territory covered, annual gross sales or income. **Arrangement:** Classified by service. **Pages (approx.):** 100. **Frequency:** Approximately annual; previous edition June 1987; latest edition May 1988. **Price:** Free. **Former Title(s):** *Minority Architectural-Engineering Firms and Construction Supply Distributors in Wisconsin*; *Wisconsin Minority Business Directory* (1981).

★3778★

Directory of Minority Businesses in Tennessee
Office of Minority Business Enterprise
Tennessee Department of Economic and Community Development
320 6th Ave. N., 7th Fl.
Nashville, TN 37219 Phone: (615)741-2545
Entries include: Firm name, address, phone, products or services. **Arrangement:** By Standard Industrial Classification code. **Indexes:** Standard Industrial Classification (SIC) code. **Frequency:** Annual. **Editor(s):** Brenda T. Logan. **Price:** Free. **Toll-free phone:** (800)251-8594. **Former Title(s):** *Tennessee Minority Business Directory* (1988).

★3779★

Directory of Minority Construction Contractors and Subcontractors
San Francisco Redevelopment Agency
770 Golden Gates Ave.
San Francisco, CA 94102 Phone: (415)749-2400
Description: Over 1,000 firms in northern California which offer products and services to the construction industry. **Entries include:** Company name, address, phone, license number, name of contact. **Arrangement:** Classified by product or trade. **Pages (approx.):** 115. **Frequency:** Triennial. **Editor(s):** Benson Hattem. **Price:** $15.00.

★3780★

Directory of Minority Investment Bankers
San Francisco Redevelopment Agency
770 Golden Gates Ave.
San Francisco, CA 94102 Phone: (415)749-2400
Description: Investment bankers in northern California. **Entries include:** Firm name, address, phone, name and title of contact, services. **Arrangement:** Alphabetical. **Frequency:** Annual. **Editor(s):** Benson I. Hattem, Affirmative Action Officer. **Price:** Free.

★3781★

Directory of Minority Management Consulting Firms
San Francisco Redevelopment Agency
770 Golden Gates Ave.
San Francisco, CA 94102 Phone: (415)749-2400
Description: More than 70 management and tax consultants and appraisers. **Entries include:** Firm name, address, phone, name and title of contact, services, clients. **Arrangement:** Alphabetical. **Pages (approx.):** 10. **Frequency:** Annual. **Editor(s):** Benson I. Hattem, Affirmative Action Officer. **Price:** Free.

★3782★

Directory of Minority Media
San Francisco Redevelopment Agency
770 Golden Gates Ave.
San Francisco, CA 94102 Phone: (415)749-2400
Description: More than 50 radio stations, television stations, and publications oriented to Asian Americans, Blacks, Native Americans, and Spanish-speaking people in northern California. **Entries include:** Name of medium, name of contact, address, phone. **Arrangement:** Classified by medium. **Pages (approx.):** 5. **Frequency:** Annual, February. **Price:** Free.

★3783★

Directory of Minority Public Relations Professionals
Public Relations Society of America
33 Irving Pl., 3rd Fl.
15th & 16th Sts.
New York, NY 10003 Phone: (212)995-2230
Description: About 190 minority individuals in the field of public relations. **Entries include:** Individual name, title, company name, address, phone. **Arrangement:** Geographical. **Pages (approx.):** 15. **Frequency:** Irregular; latest edition 1990. **Price:** $10.00.

★3784★
Directory of Minority Suppliers
Indiana Regional Minority Supplier
Development Council
PO Box 44801
Indianapolis, IN 46244-0801 Phone: (317)923-2110
Description: About 450 firms offering professional, commercial, and industrial products and services. **Entries include:** Firm name, address, phone, name of contact, services, capabilities. **Arrangement:** Alphabetical. **Indexes:** Product/service. **Pages (approx.):** 80. **Frequency:** Every four months. **Editor(s):** Jeffery L. Donald, Business Development Specialist. **Price:** $15.00, plus $2.00 shipping. **Also Includes:** List of local and national minority assistance agencies.

★3785★
Directory of Minority Truckers
San Francisco Redevelopment Agency
770 Golden Gates Ave.
San Francisco, CA 94102 Phone: (415)749-2400
Entries include: Company name, address, phone, license number, name of contact, list of equipment. **Arrangement:** Alphabetical. **Pages (approx.):** 30. **Frequency:** Every four years; latest edition 1989. **Editor(s):** Benson Hattem. **Price:** $3.00.

★3786★
Directory of Operating Small Business Investment Companies
Small Business Administration
1441 L St., NW, Rm. 808
Washington, DC 20416 Phone: (202)653-6672
Description: About 570 operating small business investment companies holding regular licenses and licenses under the section of the Small Business Investment Act covering minority enterprise SBICs. **Entries include:** Company name, address, phone, branch offices, type of ownership, date licensed by SBA, license number, amount of obligation to the Small Business Administration, amount of private capital held, and type of investments made. **Arrangement:** Separate geographical sections for each type of license. **Pages (approx.):** 90. **Frequency:** Semiannual, June and December. **Editor(s):** John R. Wilmeth. **Price:** Free.

★3787★
Directory of Private Fair Housing Organizations
United States Commission on Civil Rights
Washington, DC 20425 Phone: (202)376-8312
Description: Over 1,500 private fair housing organizations offering counseling and legal assistance to minorities who are victims of discrimination or are searching for fair housing in their area; 160 community housing resource boards (CHRB) funded by the Department of Housing and Urban Development. **Entries include:** For organizations–Organization name, address, phone, name of director, year established, geographic coverage, description of activities, number of staff. For CHRBs–Name of contact, name of board, address. **Arrangement:** Separate geographical sections for private organizations and CHRBs. **Pages (approx.):** 175. **Frequency:** Published April 1986. **Price:** Free.

★3788★
Directory of Special Programs for Minority Group Members: Career Information Services, Employment Skills Banks, Financial Aid Sources
Garrett Park Press
Box 190F
Garrett Park, MD 20896 Phone: (301)946-2553
Description: About 2,000 private and governmental agencies offering financial aid, employment assistance, and career guidance programs for minorities. **Entries include:** Organization or agency name, address, phone, contact name, type of organization, purpose, description of services and activities in the equal opportunity employment area. **Arrangement:** Alphabetical. **Indexes:** Alphabetical, type of program. **Pages (approx.):** 350. **Frequency:** Irregular; latest edition April 1990. **Editor(s):** Willis L. Johnson. **Price:** $27.00, payment with order; $20.00, billed (current edition).

★3789★
Ebony—100 Most Influential Black Americans Issue
Johnson Publishing Company, Inc.
820 S. Michigan Ave.
Chicago, IL 60605 Phone: (312)332-9200
Entries include: Name, profession, brief career notes. **Frequency:** Annual, May. **Editor(s):** John H. Johnson. **Price:** $2.00.

★3790★
Editor & Publisher International Year Book
Editor & Publisher Company, Inc.
11 W. 19th St.
New York, NY 10011 Phone: (212)675-4380
Description: Daily and Sunday newspapers in the United States and Canada; weekly newspapers; foreign daily newspapers; special service newspapers; newspaper syndicates; news services; journalism schools; foreign language and Black newspapers in the United States; news, picture, and press services; feature and news syndicates; comic and magazine services; advertising clubs; trade associations; clipping bureaus; house organs; journalism awards; also lists manufacturers of equipment and supplies. **Entries include:** For daily papers–Publication name, address, phone, names of executives and departmental editors (business, financial, book, food, etc.), circulation and advertising data, production information including format of paper and equipment used. Similar but less detailed information for other publications. **Arrangement:** Publications and schools are geographical; most other lists are alphabetical. **Pages (approx.):** 600. **Frequency:** Annual, March. **Editor(s):** Orlando Velez. **Price:** $75.00. **Fax:** (212)929-1259.

★3791★
EEO Resource Directory: Technical Assistance Guide for Southern California Personnel Practitioners Equal Employment Opportunity
Institute of Industrial Relations
1001 Gayley Ave., 2nd Fl.
Los Angeles, CA 90024-1478 Phone: (213)825-9191
Description: About 180 agencies, organizations, subscription and information service companies, sponsors of seminars, and suppliers of audiovisual or printed materials related to equal employment opportunity issues, such as affirmative action, recruitment, sexual harassment, the handicapped, and age discrimination. **Entries include:** Company, organization, or agency name, address, phone, name and title of contact, geographical area served, subsidiary and branch names and locations, description of services or products. **Arrangement:** Classified by subject area. **Pages (approx.):** 65. **Frequency:** Annual. **Editor(s):** Rosalind Schwartz, Assistant Director, Management Resources & Education. **Price:** $3.00, plus $1.00 shipping. **Also Includes:** State and federal laws related to equal employment opportunity issues.

★3792★
Ethnic Genealogy: A Research Guide
Greenwood Press, Inc.
Congressional Information Service, Inc.
88 Post Rd. W.
Westport, CT 06881 Phone: (203)226-3571
Description: Genealogical organizations and societies, and libraries and historical societies with significant collections for research in genealogy of American Indians, Asian Americans, Black Americans, Hispanic Americans, and other ethnic groups. **Frequency:** Published November 1983. **Editor(s):** Jessie Carney Smith. **Price:** $45.00; payment must accompany orders from individuals.

★3793★
Ethnic Groups in California: A Guide to Organizations and Information Resources
California Institute of Public Affairs
517 19th St.
PO Box 189040
Sacramento, CA 95818 Phone: (916)442-CIPA
Description: Organizations that provide services and information to ethnic groups in California; publishers of related publications. **Entries include:** Organization or publisher name, address, product or service. **Arrangement:** Classified by ethnic group. **Pages (approx.):** 80. **Frequency:** Irregular; previous edition 1981; latest edition 1988. **Price:** $21.50. **Fax:** (916)442-2478.

★3794★
Fair Housing Directory
Virginia Department of Commerce
3600 W. Broad St., 5th Fl.
Richmond, VA 23230-4917 Phone: (804)367-8530
Description: About 55 local government offices overseeing fair housing ordinances in Virginia communities, and other public and private organizations dealing with fair-housing matters. **Entries include:** Office or organization name, address, phone, name and title of contact, description of activities, including procedures for filing complaints, number of complaints handled per year, and geographical area served. **Arrangement:** Geographical. **Pages (approx.):** 60. **Frequency:** Published 1987. **Price:** Free.

★3795★
Financial Aid for Minorities in...Series on Occupations
Garrett Park Press
Box 190F
Garrett Park, MD 20896 Phone: (301)946-2553
Description: In 6 volumes, sources of financial aid for minorities. Volume 1 covers health occupations; volume 2 covers business and law; volume 3 covers education; volume 4 covers engineering and science; volume 5 covers journalism and mass communications; volume 6 covers financial aid for students with any major. **Entries include:** Organization, institution, or agency name, address, type of assistance, amounts available, application deadline and procedures. **Arrangement:** Alphabetical. **Pages (approx.):** 70 per volume. **Frequency:** Irregular; previous edition 1987; new edition 1989-90. **Price:** $4.00 per volume; $20.00 per set; postpaid.

★3796★
Free Money for Small Businesses and Entrepreneurs
John Wiley & Sons, Inc.
605 3rd Ave.
New York, NY 10158 Phone: (212)850-6418
Description: Federal government programs and charitable organizations that are possible sources of funding for small businesses. **Pages (approx.):** 230. **Frequency:** Latest edition 1989. **Price:** $14.95. **Toll-free phone:** (800)526-5368.

★3797★
Gebbie Press All-in-One Directory
Gebbie Press, Inc.
Box 1000
New Paltz, NY 12561 Phone: (914)255-7560
Description: 1,700 daily newspapers, 8,500 weekly newspapers, 7,000 radio stations, 900 television stations, 250 general-consumer magazines, 430 professional business publications, 2,900 trade magazines, 320 farm publications, list of the Black press and radio, Hispanic press and radio, and a list of news syndicates. **Entries include:** For periodicals–Name, address, phone, frequency, editor, circulation, readership. For newspapers–Name, address, phone, circulation. For radio and television stations–Call letters, address, phone, network affiliations. **Arrangement:** Classified. **Pages (approx.):** 510. **Frequency:** Annual, November. **Editor(s):** Amalia Gebbie. **Price:** $73.00, payment with order; $80.00, billed.

★3798★
Gospel Music Association Official Resource Guide
Gospel Music Association
38 Music Square W.
Nashville, TN 37203 Phone: (615)242-0303
Description: Gospel musicians, composers, and artists; recording companies, studios, and production companies; talent agencies; publishers; performing rights organizations; television and radio broadcasting stations; and book stores, Bible supply stores, and other retailers. **Entries include:** All listings include name, address; some listings include phone. Broadcasting station listings include contact, program title, format (television) or number of hours devoted to gospel music. **Arrangement:** Broadcasting stations and retailers are geographical; others are alphabetical. **Pages (approx.):** 130. **Frequency:** Biennial, even years. **Editor(s):** Don Butler, Executive Director. **Price:** $14.95. **Fax:** (615)254-9755. **Former Title(s):** *Gospel Music Directory & Yearbook* (1979); *Gospel Music.*

★3799★
Greater Detroit Chamber of Commerce—Detroit Buyers' Guide
Greater Detroit Chamber of Commerce
600 W. Lafayette
Detroit, MI 48226 Phone: (313)964-4000
Description: About 4,000 professional and retail firms which are members, and about 500 Detroit minority business, professional, and retail firms. **Entries include:** Firm name, address, phone, name of contact, number of employees, type of business. **Arrangement:** Member firms are alphabetical. **Pages (approx.):** 225. **Frequency:** Annual, March. **Editor(s):** Louise Rallis. **Price:** $27.60. **Fax:** (313)964-0531. **Former Title(s):** *Greater Detroit Chamber of Commerce - Business Register* (1980).

★3800★
Guide to Multicultural Resources
Praxis Publications, Inc.
2215 Atwood Ave.
Madison, WI 53704
Description: Minority and multicultural organizations and associations involved with the Asian, Black, Hispanic, and Native American communities. **Entries include:** Organization name, address, phone, contact names, description of organization, information or publications available, whether willing to network with other groups. **Arrangement:** Classified by racial/minority group. **Indexes:** Alphabetical. **Pages (approx.):** 500. **Frequency:** Biennial, January of odd years. **Editor(s):** Charles Taylor, Publisher. **Price:** $58.00.

★3801★
Guide to Obtaining Minority Business Directories
National Minority Business Directoriess
2105 Central Ave. NE
Minneapolis, MN 55418 Phone: (612)781-6819
Description: About 115 organizations which publish directories of minority businesses; includes local directories covering commercial, industrial, professional, and/or retail business in all lines, and directories of wider geographical scope which tend to cover single lines of business. **Entries include:** Publisher or source name, address, phone, type of publication, date of publication. **Arrangement:** City and state directories are geographical; others listed randomly in separate section. **Pages (approx.):** 15. **Frequency:** Annual, January. **Editor(s):** Liz Kahnk, Executive Director. **Price:** $10.00, plus $1.00 shipping. **Toll-free phone:** (800)627-4347. **Fax:** (612)781-0109. **Former Title(s):** *Guide to Minority Business Directories.*

★3802★
Higher Education Opportunities for Minorities and Women: Annotated Selections
Office of Postsecondary Education
Department of Education
400 Maryland Ave., Rm. 3915
Washington, DC 20202-5151 Phone: (202)732-5656
Description: Programs of public and private organizations and state and federal government agencies which offer loans, scholarships, and fellowship opportunities for women and minorities. **Entries include:** Organization name, address, brief description of program. **Arrangement:** Classified by subject. **Pages (approx.):** 125. **Frequency:** Irregular; previous edition December 1985; latest edition 1989; new edition expected 1991. **Editor(s):** William C. Young and Edward L. Hicks. **Price:** $5.00. **Send orders to:** Superintendent of Documents, U.S. Government Printing Office, Washington, DC 20402 (202-783-3238). **Former Title(s):** *Selected List of Postsecondary Education Opportunities for Minorities and Women.*

★3803★
How and Where to Research Your Ethnic-American Cultural Heritage
Robert D. Reed
18581 McFarland Ave.
Saratoga, CA 95070 Phone: (415)494-1112
Description: Historical societies, cultural institutes, libraries, archives, publishers, and other sources for genealogical research into German, Russian, Native American, Polish, Black, Japanese, Jewish, Irish, Mexican, Italian, Chinese, and Scandinavian backgrounds; separate volumes for each ethnic group. **Pages (approx.):** 30. **Frequency:** Most

volumes first published 1979. **Editor(s):** Robert D. Reed. **Price:** $3.50, plus $1.00 shipping per volume.

★3804★

Human Rights Directory: Latin America and the Caribbean

Human Rights Internet (HRI)
Harvard Law School
Pound Hall, Rm. 401
Cambridge, MA 02138 Phone: (617)495-9924

Description: More than 700 organizations and movements concerned with the human rights situation in Latin America and the Caribbean, both those based in the region and elsewhere. **Entries include:** Organization name, address, phone, names and titles of key personnel, project descriptions. **Arrangement:** Geographical. **Indexes:** Organization name, subject, geographical. **Pages (approx.):** 400. **Frequency:** Irregular; previous edition 1981; new edition expected early 1990. **Editor(s):** Laurie S. Wiseberg. **Price:** $50.00, Latin America and the Caribbean (1990 edition); $22.50, Latin America, Africa , Asia (1981 edition); add $10.00 for overseas orders. **Fax:** (617)495-1110. **Other Information:** Supersedes *Human Rights Directory: Latin America.*

★3805★

Illinois Minority and Female Business Enterprise Directory

Minority and Female Business Enterprise Division
Illinois Department of Central Management Services
801 Stratton Bldg., N. End
Springfield, IL 62706 Phone: (217)785-4320

Description: About 900 firms offering professional, commercial, and industrial products and services. **Entries include:** Firm name, address, phone, name and title of owner or chief executive, products or services, year established. **Arrangement:** Alphabetical. **Pages (approx.):** 810. **Frequency:** Annual. **Price:** Restricted circulation.

★3806★

In Black and White Articles on Black Americans

Gale Research, Inc.
835 Penobscot Bldg.
Detroit, MI 48226-4094 Phone: (313)961-2242

Description: An index to articles concerning more than 15,000 (7,500 more in supplement) notable and newsworthy Blacks, both contemporary and historical, appearing in magazines, newspapers, and books. **Entries include:** Name, birth and/or death dates, occupation and/or other identification, and a list of publications where more information may be found, with full citations. **Arrangement:** Alphabetical. **Indexes:** Occupation. **Pages (approx.):** 1,280 (in two volumes). **Frequency:** Irregular; latest edition 1980; supplement, August 1985; new edition possible 1991. **Editor(s):** Mary Mace Spradling. **Price:** Base edition, $125.00; supplement, $88.00. **Toll-free phone:** (800)877-GALE. **Fax:** (313)961-6241.

★3807★

In Whose Interest?: A Guide to U.S. South Africa Relations

Institute for Policy Studies
1601 Connecticut Ave., NW
Washington, DC 20009 Phone: (202)234-9382

Description: List of government agencies, publishers, and other sources of information on the political and economic relations between South Africa and the United States. **Entries include:** Organization name, address, description. **Frequency:** Published June 1985. **Price:** $11.95. **Also Includes:** Annotated bibliography, maps, glossary. **Other Information:** Principal content of the volume is a discussion of relations between South Africa and the United States.

★3808★

International Business in South Africa

Investor Responsibility Research Center
1755 Massachusetts Ave., NW
Washington, DC 20036 Phone: (202)939-6500

Description: European, Japanese, Australian, Canadian, and other foreign companies with direct investment in South Africa. **Entries include:** Name and address of parent company; whether it is a signatory to the Statement of Principles and, if so, its recent rating of compliance; line of business, names and locations of South African subsidiaries. Many entries include size of sales and assets in South Africa, number of employees there by race, name and title of contact, and policies. **Arrangement:** Alphabetical. **Indexes:** Subsidiary company name, company by assets, company by number of employees, industry sector, company headquarters location. **Pages (approx.):** 375. **Frequency:** Published October 1989. **Price:** $200.00. **Also Includes:** Lists of companies that sell to the South African government; companies that have signed recognition agreements with Black trade unions in South Africa; companies that do business in South Africa but do not own any assets there; companies that have recently left South Africa.

★3809★

Jazz Referral Service

Arts Midwest
528 Hennepin Ave., Ste. 310
Minneapolis, MN 55403 Phone: (612)341-0755

Description: Over 400 jazz musicians and ensembles, support organizations and presenters, educators, radio and television stations that program jazz, jazz writers and publications, and record stores and distributors in Illinois, Indiana, Iowa, Michigan, Minnesota, North Dakota, Ohio, South Dakota, and Wisconsin. **Entries include:** Company, organization, or personal name, address, phone; name and title of contact, biographical data, description of services or products. **Arrangement:** Geographical. **Pages (approx.):** 500. **Editor(s):** Linda Carlson, Program Associate. **Price:** $50.00 (inside Midwest region); $65.00 (outside Midwest region). **Fax:** (612)341-0902.

★3810★

Kansas Minority Business Directory

Office of Minority Business
Kansas Department of Commerce
400 SW 8th St., 5th Fl.
Topeka, KS 66603-3957 Phone: (913)296-3957

Description: Over 900 minority businesses and professional firms. **Entries include:** Company name, address, phone, name of principal executive, code for number of employees, line of busines, product or service, code indicatng ethnic group. **Arrangement:** Classified by product or service. **Indexes:** Geographical, alphabetical. **Pages (approx.):** 75. **Frequency:** Annual, April. **Editor(s):** Antonio Augusto. **Price:** Free. **Other Information:** Publisher was formerly named Kansas Department of Economic Development. **Former Title(s):** *Directory of Kansas Minority Businesses.*

★3811★

Kentucky Directory of Black Elected Officials

Kentucky Commission on Human Rights
The Heyburn Bldg., 7th Fl.
332 W. Broadway
Louisville, KY 40202 Phone: (502)588-4024

Description: About 75 Blacks serving in elective positions in Kentucky. **Entries include:** Name, party affiliation, personal and career data, photograph. **Arrangement:** Classified by office held. **Pages (approx.):** 40. **Frequency:** Annual. **Editor(s):** Eric George. **Price:** Free. **Toll-free phone:** (800)292-5566.

★3812★

Kentucky Minority Purchasing Guide

Minority Business Division
Kentucky Commerce Cabinet
2201 Capital Plaza Tower
Frankfort, KY 40601 Phone: (502)564-2064

Description: About 170 commercial and industrial firms. **Entries include:** Company name, address, phone, name of contact, product or service provided. **Arrangement:** Classified by product or service. **Pages (approx.):** 90. **Frequency:** Annual. **Editor(s):** Floyd C. Taylor, Director. **Price:** $11.85 postpaid. **Former Title(s):** *Kentucky Modified Minority Purchasing Guide.*

★3813★

Latin America and Caribbean: A Directory of Resources

Orbis Books
Maryknoll, NY 10545 Phone: (914)941-7590

Description: Organizations or companies that publish, compile, or distribute publications, audiovisual productions, and other information resources about Latin America and the Caribbean; international organizations with interests in Latin America and the Caribbean. **Entries include:** Publisher, supplier, or organization name, address, phone, description of publication, production, or purpose, geographical area covered, price, distributor name, branch office or subsidiaries. **Arrangement:** Classified by type of organization or resource. **Indexes:** Organization name, individual name, title, geographical, subject. **Pages (approx.):** 160. **Frequency:** Published 1986. **Editor(s):** Tom Fenton and Mary Heffron. **Price:** $9.95, plus $1.50 shipping. **Send orders to:** Third World Resources, 464 19th Street, Oakland, CA 94612 (415-835-4692).

★3814★
List of 8(a) Approved Contractors
Seattle Regional Office
Small Business Administration
2615 4th Ave., Rm. 440
Seattle, WA 98121 Phone: (206)442-2872
Description: More than 150 minority contractors offering industrial and commercial services and products in the Region Ten district of Anchorage, Alaska; Boise, Idaho; Portland, Oregon; and Seattle and Spokane, Washington. **Entries include:** Company name, address, phone, name of contact, line of business. **Arrangement:** Geographical. **Pages (approx.):** 35. **Frequency:** Semiannual, January and June. **Editor(s):** Christina Fischer. **Price:** Free.

★3815★
List of Minority Firms in North & South Carolina
Carolinas Minority Supplier Development Councils
700 E. Stonewall, Ste. 340
Charlotte, NC 28202 Phone: (704)372-8731
Description: About 430 minority-owned firms offering professional, commercial, and industrial products and services. **Entries include:** Firm name, address, phone, name and title of owner or chief executive, products or services, year established. **Arrangement:** Alphabetical by company name. **Indexes:** Product/service. **Pages (approx.):** 75. **Frequency:** Annual. **Editor(s):** Ardrey Y. Massey, Administrative Assistant. **Price:** $50.00. **Fax:** (704)334-5739. **Former Title(s):** *National List of Minority Firms.*

★3816★
List of 96 Ethnic and Religious Genealogical and Historical Societies and Archives
Summit Publications
Box 222
Munroe Falls, OH 44262
Frequency: Irregular; latest edition March 1989. **Editor(s):** J. Konrad. **Price:** $4.00, postpaid.

★3817★
Maryland/DC Minority Supplier Development Council Minority Business Directory
Maryland/DC Minority Supplier Development Council
9150-5B Rumsey Rd.
Columbia, MD 21045 Phone: (301)997-7599
Description: Approximately 500 businesses in the District of Columbia and Maryland. **Entries include:** Company name, address, phone, name and title of contact, subsidiary and branch names and locations, description of products and services. **Arrangement:** Classified by product or service. **Indexes:** Product/service, company name, subject. **Pages (approx.):** 100. **Frequency:** Annual, July. **Editor(s):** Arthur W. Murphy, Executive Director. **Price:** Free. **Fax:** (301)997-2040.

★3818★
MBE/WBE Directory
Detroit Chapter
Associated General Contractors of America
18100 Schaefer Hwy.
Detroit, MI 48235 Phone: (313)948-0000
Description: About 250 women-owned business enterprises (WBE) and minority-owned business enterprises (MBE) offering construction-related services and products in metropolitan Detroit and Michigan. **Entries include:** Company name, address, phone. **Arrangement:** Classified by line of business/service. **Indexes:** Alphabetical. **Pages (approx.):** 20. **Frequency:** Biennial, Spring of even years. **Editor(s):** Ann Smith, Director of Public Relations. **Price:** Free.

★3819★
MEPs/USA: The Directory of Precollege and University Minority Engineering Programs
National Action Council for Minorities in Engineering
3 W. 35th St.
New York, NY 10001-2281 Phone: (212)279-2626
Description: More than 150 precollege and university engineering programs for minority students. **Entries include:** Program name, address, phone, names and titles of key officials. **Arrangement:** Geographical. **Indexes:** Personal name, program, acronym. **Pages (approx.):** 45. **Frequency:** Irregular; latest edition 1990. **Editor(s):** Ronni Denes, Vice President of Communications and Public Relations. **Price:** $12.00. **Fax:** (212)629-5178. **Other Information:** Supersedes *Pre-College Program Directory.*

★3820★
Michigan Ethnic Organizations Directory
Michigan Ethnic Heritage Studies Center
Rackham Bldg.
60 Farnsworth, Rm. 120
Detroit, MI 48202 Phone: (313)832-7400
Description: About 2,000 ethnic organizations and institutions in Michigan. **Entries include:** Organization name, address, phone, name and title of contact, number of members, description of activities and purpose. **Arrangement:** Classified by ethnic group. **Indexes:** Organization name. **Pages (approx.):** 100. **Frequency:** Irregular; previous edition 1983; new edition expected October 1991. **Editor(s):** O. Feinstein. **Price:** $10.00. **Other Information:** Also cited as *Peoples of Michigan: A Two Volume Guide to Ethnic Michigan.*

★3821★
Minorities and Women: A List of Major Organizations in Librarianship
Office for Library Personnel Resources
American Library Association (ALA)
50 E. Huron St.
Chicago, IL 60611 Phone: (312)280-4277
Description: About 10 minority and women librarian organizations. **Entries include:** Organization name, address, phone, names and titles of key personnel, publications. **Arrangement:** Classified by interest group. **Frequency:** Annual, summer. **Price:** Free. **Toll-free phone:** (800)545-2433. **Fax:** (312)440-9374.

★3822★
Minority and Female Business Directory of Chicago Area Contractors, Subcontractors, and Construction Suppliers
Builders Association of Chicago, Inc.
1647 Merchandise Mart
Chicago, IL 60653 Phone: (312)644-6670
Description: Over 200 suppliers of equipment and services to the construction industry in Chicago, Illinois that are at least 51% minority or female owned. **Entries include:** Company name, address, phone, name and title of contact, financial data, minority ownership status, description of products and services. **Arrangement:** Alphabetical. **Indexes:** Product/service. **Pages (approx.):** 130. **Frequency:** Irregular; latest edition 1986; suspended indefinitely. **Price:** Free. **Fax:** (312)644-9791.

★3823★
Minority and Women Business Directory
Massachusetts Office of Minority and Women Business Assistance
100 Cambridge St., Rm. 1305
Boston, MA 02202 Phone: (617)727-8692
Description: About 1,000 minority- and women-owned firms offering professional, commercial, and industrial products and services; includes contractors and national firms operating in Massachusetts. **Entries include:** Firm name, address, phone, name of owner or chief executive, line of business, whether minority- or woman-owned. **Arrangement:** Alphabetical. **Indexes:** Product/service. **Pages (approx.):** 125. **Frequency:** Annual, October; quarterly supplements. **Price:** $5.00 plus $1.75 shipping. free to federal and state purchasing agents. **Send**

orders to: Massachusetts State Book Store, Room 116, Boston, MA 02133. **Former Title(s):** *Minority Business Directory.*

★3824★
Minority & Women-Owned Business Enterprise Directory: Architects/Engineers/Planners & Related Services
Human Rights Commission of San Francisco
1170 Market St., 5th Fl.
San Francisco, CA 94102 Phone: (415)252-2500
Description: About 300 firms offering architectural, engineering, planning, and related services. **Entries include:** Firm name, address, phone, key personnel, services, year established. **Arrangement:** Classified by service. **Indexes:** Alphabetical. **Pages (approx.):** 340. **Frequency:** Annual, June. **Price:** $30.00.

★3825★
Minority Biomedical Support Program: A Research Resources Directory
Department of Health and Human Services
National Institutes of Health
Division of Research Resources
Bethesda, MD 20892 Phone: (301)984-2876
Description: Institutions granting research awards to minority faculty and students engaged in biomedical research. **Entries include:** Institution name, name of program director, address, phone, names of individual project investigators, number of student participants, projects, equipment available. **Arrangement:** Geographical. **Pages (approx.):** 90. **Frequency:** Latest edition January 1988; suspended indefinitely. **Editor(s):** Edward Post, Director of Research Resources Information Center. **Price:** Free. **Send orders to:** Research Resources Information Center, 1601 Research Blvd., Rockville, MD 20850.

★3826★
Minority Business & Professional Directory
Minority Business & Professional Directory, Inc.
1763 Vine St.
Denver, CO 80206 Phone: (303)369-7100
Description: About 1,500 firms offering professional, commercial, and industrial products and services. **Entries include:** Firm name, address, phone. **Arrangement:** Alphabetical. **Indexes:** Product/service. **Pages (approx.):** 100. **Frequency:** Annual, June. **Editor(s):** Marcellus Jackson. **Price:** $2.75.

★3827★
Minority Business Development Agency Directory of Regional & District Offices and Funded Organizations
Minority Business Development Agency
Department of Commerce
Washington, DC 20230 Phone: (202)377-2414
Description: About 10 regional and district offices of the Minority Business Development Agency; approximately 110 agency-funded minority business development centers which offer business services for a nominal fee to current and prospective minority business operators. **Entries include:** For regional offices–Office name, address, phone, states served, director name. For district offices–Office address and phone, names of district officers. For development centers–Center name, address, phone, project director name. **Arrangement:** Separate geographical lists for regional offices, district offices, and development centers. **Pages (approx.):** 15. **Price:** Free.

★3828★
Minority Business Directory
Minority Supplier Development Council
300 Careau Tower
441 Vine St.
Cincinnati, OH 45202 Phone: (513)579-3132
Description: About 200 firms offering professional, commercial, and industrial products and services in the Cincinnati, Ohio, metropolitan area. **Entries include:** Firm name, address, phone, name and title of owner or chief executive, products or services, year established, number of employees. **Arrangement:** Alphabetical. **Indexes:** Product/service. **Pages (approx.):** 210. **Frequency:** Annual. **Editor(s):** Janet Young, Executive Director. **Price:** Free to member corporations only.

★3829★
Minority Business Directory
Nevada Economic Development Commission
701 E. Bridger, Ste. 701
Las Vegas, NV 89101 Phone: (702)369-2339
Description: About 500 firms offering professional, commercial, and industrial products and services. **Entries include:** Firm name, address, phone; name and title of owner, chief executive, or contact; line of business, corporate structure, product or service, number of employees, year established. **Arrangement:** Alphabetical. **Indexes:** Product/service. **Pages (approx.):** 75. **Frequency:** Annual. **Editor(s):** Janis Stevenson, President. **Price:** Free.

★3830★
Minority Business Directory
Minority and Women Business Development
Indiana Department of Commerce
1 N. Capitol, Ste. 501
Indianapolis, IN 46204 Phone: (317)232-3061
Description: About 300 firms offering professional, commercial, industrial, and consumer products and services. **Entries include:** Company name, address, phone, name of contact or owner, services or products, area covered. **Arrangement:** Classified by service or line of business, then geographical. **Pages (approx.):** 70. **Frequency:** Annual. **Editor(s):** Andrew Thomas, Jr., Construction Manager Engineer. **Price:** Free. **Other Information:** Publisher was formerly named Office of Minority Business Enterprise. **Former Title(s):** *Minority Purchasing Guide*; *Indiana Minority Business Directory.*

★3831★
Minority Business Information System (MBISYS) Database
National Minority Supplier Development Council (NMSDC)
15 W. 39th St., 9th Fl.
New York, NY 10018 Phone: (212)944-2430
Description: Approximately 15,000 companies that are certified by the NMSDC as minority owned. **Entries include:** Company name, address, phone, parent company name, Standard Industrial Classification (SIC) code, description of products and services, year founded, ownership structure, number of employees; name, title, ethnicity, and sex of owners; major customers, annual sales, geographical area served, most recent certification date and accrediting council. **Frequency:** Updated as needed. **Editor(s):** Anne Ashton, Director, Communications & Conferences. **Other Information:** Previously cited as *National Minority Purchasing Council Data Bank–Minority Vendor Information Service* and *Supplier Development Council.* **Former Title(s):** *Minority Business Enterprise Network* (MBENET) (1988).

★3832★
Minority Consultants and Minority-Owned Consulting Firms
Atlantic Coast Publishing
2000 Greenway Ave., Ste. 1B
Charlotte, NC 28204 Phone: (704)375-8225
Description: Over 1,000 consultants and consulting firms specializing in over 36 professions. **Entries include:** Firm name, address, phone, name and title of contact, number of employees, geographical area served, description of services, year established, number of principals, ethnic classification. **Arrangement:** Classified by service. **Indexes:** Subject, contact name, firm/consultant name, geographical. **Pages (approx.):** 245. **Frequency:** Annual, February. **Editor(s):** Charles Kelly. **Price:** $125.00. **Toll-free phone:** (800)634-3745.

★3833★
Minority CPAs
San Francisco Redevelopment Agency
770 Golden Gates Ave.
San Francisco, CA 94102 Phone: (415)749-2400
Description: Over 90 Spanish-speaking, Asian, Black or Native American certified public accounting (CPA) firms in northern California; minority CPA associations. **Entries include:** For firms - Name, address, phone. For associations - Name, address, phone, name of president. **Arrangement:** Alphabetical. **Pages (approx.):** 5. **Frequency:** Annual. **Price:** Free. **Fax:** (415)771-3005.

★3834★
Minority Employment Report
Federal Communications Commission
1919 M St., NW
Washington, DC 20554 Phone: (202)632-7000
Description: Television and radio stations with ten or more full-time employees. **Entries include:** Station name (call letters or channel), city and state, class of station; total, female, and minority full-time employment in higher and lower pay occupations, and part-time employment for previous five years. **Arrangement:** By state and community. **Pages (approx.):** 1,480. **Frequency:** Annual, December. **Price:** Free.

★3835★
Minority Engravers, Graphic Artists and Printers
San Francisco Redevelopment Agency
770 Golden Gates Ave.
San Francisco, CA 94102 Phone: (415)749-2400
Description: About 50 minority firms in northern California. **Entries include:** Firm name, address, phone, contact name. **Arrangement:** Alphabetical. **Frequency:** Annual. **Price:** Free. **Fax:** (415)771-3005.

★3836★
Minority Law Firms
San Francisco Redevelopment Agency
770 Golden Gates Ave.
San Francisco, CA 94102 Phone: (415)771-8800
Description: Over 200 Spanish-speaking, Asian, Black, or Native American law firms and lawyers in northern California; minority bar associations. **Entries include:** For firms - Name, address, phone. For associations - Name, address, phone, name of president. **Arrangement:** Alphabetical. **Frequency:** Annual. **Price:** Free. **Fax:** (415)771-3005.

★3837★
Minority Organizations: A National Directory
Garrett Park Press
Box 190F
Garrett Park, MD 20896 Phone: (301)946-2553
Description: Over 7,700 groups composed of or intended to serve members of minority groups, including Alaska Natives, American Indians, Blacks, Hispanics, and Asian Americans. **Entries include:** Organization name, address, description of activities, purpose, publications, etc. **Arrangement:** Classified by minority group. **Indexes:** Organization name, geographical, program, defunct organization. **Pages (approx.):** 690. **Frequency:** Irregular; previous edition 1987; latest edition 1991. **Editor(s):** Robert Calvert, Jr. **Price:** $36.00, payment with order; $40.00, billed.

★3838★
Minority Purchasing Guide for the Louisville Area
Louisville Area Chamber of Commerce
1 Riverfront Plaza
Louisville, KY 40202 Phone: (502)566-5000
Frequency: Annual; quarterly updates. **Price:** $50.00.

★3839★
Minority Student Enrollments in Higher Education: A Guide to Institutions with...Asian, Black, Hispanic, and Native American Students
Garrett Park Press
Box 190F
Garrett Park, MD 20896 Phone: (301)946-2553
Description: About 500 colleges and universities at which one or more minority (Asian, Black, Hispanic, or Native American) constitutes at least 20% of the student body. **Entries include:** Institution name, address, phone, total enrollment, highest level of degree offered, partial list of major programs offered, minority groups representing at least one-fifth of the total enrollment. **Arrangement:** Alphabetical. **Indexes:** Major programs offered. **Pages (approx.):** 80. **Frequency:** Latest edition 1988. **Price:** $14.00, payment with order; $15.00, billed. **Also Includes:** Statistical summary on the number of minorities graduating in with degrees in selected fields; bibliography of related books.

★3840★
Minority Student Opportunities in United States
Association of American Medical Colleges (AAMC)
1 Dupont Circle, NW, Ste. 200
Washington, DC 20036 Phone: (202)828-0400
Description: Programs for minority group students at nearly 130 medical schools. **Entries include:** Name of school, name of parent institution, if applicable, address, phone, name of contact; descriptions of recruitment, admissions, financial aid, and academic assistance programs for the minority student; statistical table on minority admissions and enrollment. **Arrangement:** Geographical. **Indexes:** School name, geographical. **Pages (approx.):** 325. **Frequency:** Biennial, August of even years. **Editor(s):** Mary T. Cureton-Russell, Staff Associate. **Price:** $7.50, plus $2.50 shipping; payment must accompany order. **Fax:** (202)785-5027. **Also Includes:** List of schools offering summer programs.

★3841★
Minority Supplier Directory
New Penn Del Regional Minority Supplier Purchasing Council, Inc.
Monroe Office Center
1 Winding Dr., Ste. 210
Philadelphia, PA 19131 Phone: (215)578-0964
Description: More than 600 firms in Pennsylvania, New Jersey, and Delaware that have been certified as having a minimum of 51% minority ownership and the ability to supply products and services to major corporations. **Frequency:** Irregular; previous edition 1985; latest edition 1988. **Fax:** (215)878-2832. **Other Information:** Prepared in conjunction with Allied Corporation.

★3842★
Minority Supplier Directory
Rio Grande Minority Purchasing Council
5000 Marble, NE, Ste. 108
Albuquerque, NM 87110 Phone: (505)265-7677
Description: About 460 firms offering professional, commercial, and industrial products and services. **Entries include:** Company name, address, phone, name of contact, capability number and description of product, number of employees, date established. **Arrangement:** Classified. **Indexes:** Product/service. **Pages (approx.):** 70. **Frequency:** Semi-annual. **Editor(s):** C. M. Davis, Associate Director. **Price:** $25.00, including updates, to New Mexico residents; $35.00 to others (current and 1989 editions). **Other Information:** Former name of publisher, New Mexico Minority Supplier Development Council. **Former Title(s):** *New Mexico Minority Suppliers Directory.*

★3843★
Minority Supplier Directory
Michigan Minority Business Development Council
2990 W. Grand Blvd., Ste. 408
Detroit, MI 48202 Phone: (313)873-3200
Description: Firms offering professional, commercial, and industrial products and services. **Entries include:** Firm name, address, phone, name and title of owner or chief executive, products or services, year established, etc. **Arrangement:** Alphabetical. **Indexes:** Product/service. **Pages (approx.):** 100. **Frequency:** Quarterly. **Price:** $5.00.

★3844★
Minority Vendor Directory
New England Minority Purchasing Council
Copley Pl. 4
Boston, MA 02116 Phone: (617)578-8900
Description: Over 300 firms offering professional, commercial, and industrial products and services in Maine, Massachusetts, New Hampshire, Rhode Island, and Vermont. **Entries include:** Firm name, address, phone, name and title of contact, number of employees, geographical area served, product or service, year established, Standard Industrial Classification (SIC) code. **Arrangement:** Alphabetical. **Indexes:** Product/service. **Pages (approx.):** 85. **Frequency:** Annual, Fall. **Editor(s):** May Ling Tong, Executive Director. **Price:** $45.00, postpaid. **Former Title(s):** *Minority Firms in New England.*

★3845★
Minority-Women Business Directory
City Manager's Office
City of San Diego
202 C St.
San Diego, CA 92101 Phone: (619)236-6363
Description: About 300 firms owned by women or members of a minority race which offer professional, commercial, and industrial products and services. **Entries include:** Firm name, address, phone, name of contact or chief executive, product or service. **Arrangement:** Classified by line of business. **Indexes:** Product/service. **Pages (approx.):** 700. **Frequency:** Irregular; previous edition November 1986; latest editon January 1988. **Editor(s):** Elizabeth A. Moore, Management Assistant to City Manager. **Price:** Free. **Former Title(s):** *Southern California Minority Vendor Directory.*

★3846★
NACME Students' Guide to Engineering Schools
National Action Council for Minorities in Education (NACME)
3 W. 35th St.
New York, NY 10001 Phone: (212)279-2626
Description: Engineering colleges and universities in the United States with at least one curriculum accredited by the Accreditation Board for Engineering and Technology. **Entries include:** Institution name, location, financial data, outline of admission dates and requirements, minority enrollment, engineering curricula offered, description of program, and support activities. **Arrangement:** Alphabetical. **Pages (approx.):** 45. **Frequency:** Biennial, odd years. **Price:** $10.00 per 30 copies; $25.00 per 100. **Fax:** (212)629-5178.

★3847★
National Association of College Deans, Registrars and Admissions Officers—Directory
National Association of College Deans, Registrars and Admissions Officers
917 Dorsett Ave.
Albany, GA 31701 Phone: (912)435-4945
Description: About 325 member deans, registrars, and admissions officers at nearly 90 predominantly Black schools. **Entries include:** Institution name, address, phone, names and titles of key personnel, enrollment, whether a public or private institution. **Arrangement:** Alphabetical. **Pages (approx.):** 15. **Frequency:** Annual, February. **Editor(s):** Helen M. Mayes, Executive Secretary. **Price:** $5.00.

★3848★
National Association of Investment Companies—Membership Directory
National Association of Investment Companies
111 14th St., NW, Ste. 700
Washington, DC 20005 Phone: (202)289-4336
Description: About 150 venture capital firms for minority small businesses; licensed by the Small Business Administration. **Entries include:** Company name, address, phone, president; investment policy, industry preference, preferred limit of loans and investments. **Arrangement:** Geographical. **Pages (approx.):** 20. **Frequency:** Annual, June. **Editor(s):** Benita M. Gore, Publications Director. **Price:** $3.65, postpaid. **Fax:** (202)289-4329. **Other Information:** Association formerly named American Association of Minority Enterprise Small Business Investment Companies.

★3849★
National Bankers Association—Roster of Minority Banking Institutions
National Bankers Association
122 C St., NW, Ste. 580
Washington, DC 20001 Phone: (202)783-3200
Description: About 140 banks owned or controlled by minority group persons or women. **Entries include:** Bank name, address, phone, name of one executive. **Arrangement:** Geographical. **Pages (approx.):** 15. **Frequency:** Updated as needed. **Editor(s):** John P. Kelly, Jr., President. **Price:** $50.00.

★3850★
National Black Health Leadership Directory
NRW Associates
1315 Hamlin St., NE
Washington, DC 20017 Phone: (202)635-4804
Edited by: Nathaniel Wesley, Jr. **Description:** Covers more than 400 Black health professionals serving in leadership roles in both the public and private sectors of the U.S. health industry. **Entries include:** Name and title, organization name, address, and phone. **Arrangement:** Alphabetical. **Pages (approx.):** 212. **Frequency:** Annual, September. **Price:** $65.00.

★3851★
National Black Media Directory
Alliance Publishers
Box 25004
Fort Lauderdale, FL 33320 Phone: (305)722-5361
Description: Over 1,300 newspapers, radio stations, television stations, and other media. **Entries include:** Company name, address, phone, names and titles of key personnel, description of contents, publishing dates, and circulation figures. **Arrangement:** Geographical. **Indexes:** Geographical. **Pages (approx.):** 250. **Frequency:** First edition January 1989. **Editor(s):** Martin Pollack. **Price:** $100.00, postpaid.

★3852★
National Black Talent Directory
Shooting Gallery Co.
6223 Sunset Blvd.
Hollywood, CA 90028 Phone: (213)463-8033
Description: More than 1,700 Black screen actors, athletes, singers, models, commentators, and those involved in production and promotion in the entertainment industry. **Entries include:** Personal name, name and phone of contact, professional society memberships. **Arrangement:** Classified by typical role or line of business, then alphabetical. **Pages (approx.):** 450. **Frequency:** Semiannual; first edition August 1988. **Editor(s):** J. J. Jones, Publisher. **Price:** $65.00. **Other Information:** Publisher also cited as The National Black Talent Directory, Inc.

★3853★
National Directory of Minority-Owned Business Firms
Business Research Services, Inc.
2 E. 22nd St., Ste. 202
Lombard, IL 60148 Phone: (708)495-8787
Description: Over 35,000 minority-owned businesses. **Entries include:** Company name, address, phone, name and title of contact, minority group, certification status, date founded, number of employees, description of products or services, sales volume government contracting experience, references. **Arrangement:** Alphabetical. **Indexes:** Standard Industrial Classification (SIC) code, geographical. **Pages (approx.):** 1,350. **Frequency:** Irregular; previous edition May 1988; latest edition January 1990. **Editor(s):** JoAnn Frasca and Carollynn Barnes. **Price:** $195.00, plus $5.00 shipping (ISSN 0886-3881). **Toll-free phone:** (800)325-8720. **Fax:** (708)495-8791. **Other Information:** Library edition available from Gale Research Inc., 835 Penobscot Building, Detroit, MI 48226 (800-887-GALE).

★3854★
National Insurance Association—Member Roster
National Insurance Association
PO Box 53230
Chicago, IL 60653-0230 Phone: (312)924-3308
Description: About 25 insurance companies owned or controlled by Blacks. **Entries include:** Company name, address, phone, date founded, states in which licensed, officers. **Arrangement:** Alphabetical. **Pages (approx.):** 10. **Frequency:** Irregular; previous edition January 1987; latest edition April 1989. **Editor(s):** Josephine King, President-Elect. **Price:** Free.

★3855★
National Minority Chamber Directory
National Association of Black and Minority Chambers of Commerce
5741 Telegraph Ave.
Oakland, CA 94609 Phone: (415)601-5741
Description: About 100 affiliated minority chambers of commerce. **Frequency:** Annual.

★3856★
Nationwide Black Radio Directory
CDE
Box 310551
Atlanta, GA 30331 Phone: (404)344-7621
Description: About 500 Black-owned radio stations, broadcasting firms, radio stations with Black programming, Black college radio stations, syndicated radio shows, music organizations, Black music publications, and other music and broadcasting companies with strong Black influence or ownership. **Entries include:** Company name, address, phone. **Arrangement:** Classified by line of business. **Pages (approx.):** 35. **Frequency:** Annual, fall. **Editor(s):** Charles Edwards, Publisher. **Price:** $50.00, plus $2.50 shipping.

★3857★
Navy Small Business Personnel Directory
Office of the Secretary of the Navy
Department of the Navy
Department of Defense
Crystal Plaza 5, Rm. 120
Washington, DC 20360 Phone: (202)692-7122
Description: Navy Department personnel and offices that can be contacted to help small and disadvantaged businesses compete for Navy procurement contracts. **Entries include:** Office name, address, phone; names and titles of key personnel. **Arrangement:** By area of responsibility (research and development, procurement, subcontracting, etc.). **Pages (approx.):** 30. **Frequency:** Biennial, September of even years. **Price:** Free. **Former Title(s):** *Navy Small and Disadvantaged Business Personnel Directory.*

★3858★
The Negro Almanac: A Reference Work on the African American
Gale Research Inc.
835 Penobscot Bldg.
Detroit, MI 48226-4094 Phone: (313)961-2242
Description: Human rights organizations and Black power advocates; African Americans in law, politics; highly capitalized Black companies; support progarams; predominantly Black colleges and universities in the U.S., community and state colleges with Black administrative heads; Blacks in the military; outstanding Black athletes, literary figures, artists, scientific pioneers, astronauts, scientists, entertainers, publishers, and journalists; leaders of slave revolts in the U.S., etc. **Entries include:** Contact information, biography where applicable. **Arrangement:** Chapters by major subjects. **Indexes:** Name. **Pages (approx.):** 1,625. **Frequency:** Expected to be triennial; latest edition December 1989. **Editor(s):** Harry A. Ploski and James Williams. **Price:** $110.00. **Toll-free phone:** (800)877-GALE. **Fax:** (313)961-6241. **Other Information:** Principal content of publication is an all-in-one resource to significant dates, movements, legislation, and people in African American history and culture in America.

★3859★
Network of Small Businesses—Membership Directory
Network of Small Businesses (NSB)
5420 Mayfield Rd., Ste. 205
Lyndhurst, OH 44124 Phone: (216)442-5600
Description: Owners and others involved in small businesses (defined as 500 employees or less). **Entries include:** Company name, address, phone, names and titles of key personnel. **Arrangement:** Classified by product or service. **Indexes:** Company name. **Pages (approx.):** 55. **Frequency:** Approximately annual; latest edition December 1989. **Editor(s):** Irwin Friedman, Chairman. **Price:** $18.00 for annual subscription; $395.00 for mailing list, plus $4.00 shipping. **Also Includes:** Inventors, innovators, engineers, and scientists are also listed.

★3860★
NUCEA Directory of Black Professionals in Continuing Higher Education
National University Continuing Education Association (NUCEA)
1 Dupont Circle, NW, Ste. 615
Washington, DC 20036 Phone: (202)659-3130
Description: Covers Black continuing higher education professionals employed in NUCEA institutions. **Entries include:** Name, address, phone. **Price:** $6.00.

★3861★
Ohio Minority Business Directory
Ohio Department of Development
Minority Business Development Division
77 S. High St., 28th Fl.
Box 1001
Columbus, OH 43266-0101 Phone: (614)466-5700
Description: More than 5,500 minority firms in Ohio offering professional, commercial, construction, industrial, and consumer products and services. **Entries include:** Company name, address, phone, name and ethnic origin of owner, state certification, geographical area served, product or service codes. **Arrangement:** Classified by product or service, then geographical. **Indexes:** Product/service. **Pages (approx.):** 1,450. **Frequency:** Irregular; latest edition February 1990. **Editor(s):** Margie Montgomery. **Price:** $30.00. **Toll-free phone:** (800)282-1085 (in Ohio); (800)848-1300 (elsewhere). **Other Information:** Also cited as *Ohio Minority Business Guide.*

★3862★
Planning Consultant Roster
American Planning Association
1313 E. 60th St.
Chicago, IL 60637 Phone: (312)955-9100
Description: Firms which specialize in, or are active in, planning. Also includes women or minority owned planning firms. **Entries include:** Firm name, address, phone, names of principal executives, identification of minority group(s) in control, number of employees, years of employee experience, geographic area covered, services provided, subsidiary and branch names and locations, year founded. **Arrangement:** Alphabetical. **Indexes:** Geographical, women or minority owned firm name. **Pages (approx.):** 50. **Editor(s):** Jim Hecimovich. **Price:** $16.00. **Former Title(s):** *Minority and Women Planning Consultant Roster* (1987).

★3863★
Regional Directory of Minority & Women-Owned Business Firms
Business Research Services, Inc.
2 E. 22nd St., Ste. 202
Lombard, IL 60148 Phone: (708)495-8787
Description: Published in 5 regional volumes: Northeastern, with 10,000 listings; Southeastern, with 8,000 listings; North Central, with 15,000 listings; South Central, with 10,000 listings; and Western, with 18,000 listings. Based on *National Directory of Minority-Owned Business Firms* and *National Directory of Women-Owned Business Firms* (see separate entries). **Entries include:** Company name, address, phone, name and title of contact, minority group, certification status, date founded, number of employees, description of products or services, sales volume, government contracting experience, references. **Arrangement:** Alphabetical. **Indexes:** Standard Industrial Classification (SIC) code, geographical. **Frequency:** Irregular; previous editions May 1988; latest editions January 1990. **Editor(s):** JoAnn Frasca and Carollynn Barnes. **Price:** $95.00 each, plus $5.00 shipping. **Toll-free phone:** (800)325-8720. **Fax:** (708)495-8791. **Other Information:** Library editions available from Gale Research Inc., 835 Penobscot Building, Detroit, MI 48226 (800-877-GALE).

★3864★
Roster of Minority Financial Institutions
Applications Management Branch
Department of the Treasury
401 14th St., SW
Washington, DC 20227 Phone: (202)287-0580
Description: About 190 commercial, minority-owned financial institutions participating in the Department of the Treasury's Minority Bank Deposit Program. **Entries include:** Name of institution, name and title of chief officer, address, phone. **Arrangement:** Geographical. **Frequency:** Annual, December; quarterly updates. **Editor(s):** Kathryn Vadenoff. **Price:** Free.

★3865★
Small Business Network—National Directory
Small Business Network
Box 30149
Baltimore, MD 21270 Phone: (301)356-4167
Description: Businesses involved in assisting the development and support of small businesses. **Frequency:** Annual, summer. **Price:** Available to members only.

★3866★
Small Business Reference Guide
Bluechip Books
134 Main St. Putney
Stratford, CT 06497 Phone: (203)375-1233
Description: Over 350 firms, associations, and government agencies offering products and services of assistance to small businesses. **Entries include:** Organization name, address, phone; most listings also include description of services, products, or activities. **Arrangement:** Classified by product, service, or activity. **Indexes:** Book title, magazine title, publisher name, company name/subject. **Pages (approx.):** 65. **Frequency:** Irregular; previous edition January 1988; latest edition 1991. **Price:** $14.95.

★3867★
Small Disadvantaged Business Directory
Small Business Office
Defense Contract Administration Services
Region, Chicago
Defense Logistics Agency
Department of Defense
O'Hare International Airport, Box 66475
Chicago, IL 60666 Phone: (312)694-6020
Description: About 200 firms owned or managed by socially and economically disadvantaged individuals offering professional, commercial, and industrial products and services for Department of Defense needs in northern Illinois, Indiana, and Wisconsin. **Entries include:** Firm name, address, phone, name of contact, product or service. **Arrangement:** Classified by product or service. **Indexes:** Alphabetical. **Pages (approx.):** 40. **Frequency:** Annual, spring. **Price:** Free. **Also Includes:** Maps. **Other Information:** Publishing office was formerly named Small Disadvantaged Business Utilization Office. **Former Title(s):** *Minority Business Enterprise Directory of Firms in Northern Illinois, Indiana, and Wisconsin.*

★3868★
Small Disadvantaged Business Enterprises
Defense Contract Administration Services
Region, Boston
Defense Logistics Agency
Department of Defense
495 Summer St.
Boston, MA 02210 Phone: (617)451-4318
Description: About 350 firms offering professional, commercial, and industrial services. **Entries include:** Company name, address, phone, contact, list of products or services. **Arrangement:** Alphabetical. **Indexes:** Product/service. **Pages (approx.):** 50. **Frequency:** Irregular; previous edition 1981; latest edition October 1987. **Editor(s):** Mary Ellen Maitin. **Price:** Free. **Former Title(s):** *Minority Business Enterprises.*

★3869★
Smaller Business Association of New England—Membership Directory & Buyers' Guide
Smaller Business Association of New England
69 Hickory Dr.
Waltham, MA 02254 Phone: (617)890-9070
Entries include: Company name, address, phone, fax, names of chief executives, list of products or services. **Arrangement:** Classified by line of business. **Indexes:** Company name, contact name. **Pages (approx.):** 200. **Frequency:** Annual, August. **Editor(s):** Sara L. Walpert. **Price:** $75.00. **Toll-free phone:** (800)368-6803. **Fax:** (617)890-4567.

★3870★
Society of Newspaper Design—Internship Project
Society of Newspaper Design
The Newspaper Center
Dulles International Airport
Box 17290
Washington, DC 20041 Phone: (703)620-1083
Description: About 75 organizations offering 150 internships in the graphic arts and design fields, including paid and minority internships; limited international coverage. **Entries include:** Organization name, address, phone, name and title of contact. **Arrangement:** Geographical. **Pages (approx.):** 15. **Frequency:** Annual, fall. **Price:** Free. **Fax:** (703)620-4557.

★3871★
Standard Rate & Data Service—Newspaper Rates & Data
Standard Rate & Data Service, Inc.
Macmillan, Inc.
3004 Glenview Rd.
Wilmette, IL 60091 Phone: (312)441-2237
Description: More than 1,700 newspapers and newspaper groups, including newspaper-distributed magazines, nationally and locally edited comics, religious newspapers, Black newspapers, and specialized newspapers. **Entries include:** Publication name, address, phone, names and titles of key personnel, advertising rates, special features, contract and copy regulations, mechanical requirements, and circulation. Information on classified advertising for each publication in separate section. Circulation breakdown in *Newspaper Circulation Analysis*, a separate volume published annually. **Arrangement:** Geographical. **Pages (approx.):** 780. **Frequency:** Monthly; *Newspaper Circulation Analysis* included with November issue; updated by *Weekly Change Bulletin.* **Editor(s):** Bob Parzy. **Price:** $389.00 per year; weekly bulletin (optional), $70.00; additional copies of *Newspaper Circulation Analysis*, $112.00. **Toll-free phone:** (800)323-4601. **Also Includes:** Market and census data.

★3872★
Student National Dental Association—Directory
Student National Dental Association
c/o Martin Jordan
Howard University School of Dentistry
600 W St., NW
Washington, DC 20059 Phone: (202)328-5600
Description: About 1,000 minority dental students. **Entries include:** Name, address, phone, minority classification. **Arrangement:** Alphabetical. **Pages (approx.):** 50. **Frequency:** Annual. **Price:** Available to members only. **Other Information:** Affiliated with the National Dental Association.

★3873★
Talent Roster of Outstanding Minority Community College Graduates
College Entrance Examination Board
45 Columbus Ave.
New York, NY 10023 Phone: (212)713-8000
Description: 1,200 minority graduates of two-year colleges selected on the basis of grade point average by their colleges. **Entries include:** Name, address, grade point average, intended major. **Arrangement:** Geographical, then by name of college presently attending. **Pages (approx.):** 40. **Frequency:** Annual, April. **Price:** Free.

★3874★
Try Us: National Minority Business Directory
National Minority Business Directories
2105 Central Ave., NE
Minneapolis, MN 55418 Phone: (612)781-6819
Description: Over 5,600 minority-owned companies capable of supplying their goods and services on national or regional levels. **Entries include:** Company name, address, phone, name of principal executive, number of employees, date established, trade and brand names, financial keys, products or services, names of three customers, certification status, minority identifcation, gross sales. **Arrangement:** Classified by product or service, then geographical and alphabetical. **Indexes:** Company, product/service. **Pages (approx.):** 500. **Frequency:** Annual, January. **Editor(s):** Liz Kahnk, Executive Director. **Price:** $37.00, plus $3.00 shipping. **Toll-free phone:** (800)627-4347. **Fax:** (612)781-0109.

★3875★
U.S. Directory of Small and Disadvantaged Businesses
Federal Procurement Research Corporation
Seaboard St.
Bladenboro, NC 28320
Description: Approximately 555 businesses having annual revenues of less than $50 million, minority-owned businesses, women-owned businesses, and firms in the Small Business Administration (SBA) 8(a) program that meet subcontracting requirements of prime defense contractors. **Entries include:** Company name, address, phone, fax, names and titles of key personnel, number of employees, geographical

area served, financial data, description of services, Standard Industrial Classification (SIC) code. **Arrangement:** Classified by type of business, then geographical. **Indexes:** Company name, product/service, Standard Industrial Classification (SIC) code. **Pages (approx.):** 350. **Frequency:** Annual, January. **Editor(s):** Vicky S. Wolcott. **Price:** $70.00 (ISSN 1040-7251).

★3876★
Venture Capital Directory 12/91 being updated
Forum Publishing Company
383 E. Main St.
Centerport, NY 11721 Phone: (516)754-5000
Description: Over 400 members of the Small Business Administration and the Small Business Investment Company that provide funding for small and minority businesses. **Entries include:** Company name, address, phone, names and titles of key personnel, geographical area served, financial data, branch office or subsidiary names, description of services and projects. **Arrangement:** Alphabetical. **Pages (approx.):** 50. **Frequency:** Annual. **Editor(s):** Raymond Lawrence. **Price:** $9.95.

★3877★
West Virginia Minority Business Directory
West Virginia Small Business Development Center
115 Virginia St. E.
Charleston, WV 25301 Phone: (304)348-2960
Description: Over 150 firms offering professional, commercial, and industrial products and services; coverage is not limited to West Virginia. **Entries include:** Firm name, address, phone, name and title of owner or chief executive, product or service, minority ownership classification. **Arrangement:** Alphabetical. **Indexes:** Product/service. **Pages (approx.):** 50. **Frequency:** Updated continuously, printed as requested. **Editor(s):** Juanita D. Graves. **Price:** Free.

★3878★
Who's What and Where: A Directory and Reference Book of Minority Journalists in America
Who's What and Where Company
Box 273
Columbia, MO 65205 Phone: (314)443-4519
Description: About 6,000 minority journalists. **Entries include:** Name, office address and phone, area of occupational specialization; personal, career, and education data. **Arrangement:** Alphabetical. **Pages (approx.):** 740. **Frequency:** Irregular; latest edition August 1988; new edition expected August, 1991. **Editor(s):** Ben Johnson and Mary Bullard-Johnson. **Price:** $34.95 (current edition); $44.95 (1991 edition); plus $3.40 shipping. **Former Title(s):** *Who's What and Where: A Directory of Black Journalists in America.*

★3879★
Who's Who Among Black Americans
Gale Research Inc.
835 Penobscot Bldg.
Detroit, MI 48226-4094 Phone: (313)961-2242
Description: Over 18,000 African-American leaders in government, business, education, religion, communications, civic affairs, the arts, law, medicine, science, sports, and entertainment. **Entries include:** Name, home and/or business address (at listees' discretion), education, career, and personal data; organizational affiliations; honors, awards, and special achievements. **Arrangement:** Alphabetical. **Indexes:** Geographical, occupational. **Pages (approx.):** 1,500. **Frequency:** Biennial, odd years. **Editor(s):** Iris Cloyd, Editor, and William C. Matney, Consulting Editor. **Price:** $110.00. **Toll-free phone:** (800)877-GALE. **Fax:** (313)961-6241. **Also Includes:** Obituary section. **Other Information:** Formerly published by Educational Communications, Inc.

★3880★
Who's Who in Business, A Guide for Doing Business in St. Croix, U.S. Virgin Islands
St. Croix Chamber of Commerce
PO Box 4369
Kings Hill, VI 00851 Phone: (809)773-1435
Description: About 1,600 member businesses and professionals in St. Croix, U.S. Virgin Islands. **Entries include:** Company or individual name, address, phone. **Arrangement:** Alphabetical. **Indexes:** Product/service. **Pages (approx.):** 105. **Frequency:** Latest edition 1988. **Price:** $10.00.

★3881★
Who's Who in Music
Mid-South Management, Inc.
Box 1051
Vicksburg, MS 39181 Phone: (601)634-7067
Description: About 20,000 musicians, singers, music associations, broadcasting organizations, record companies, producers, representatives, and others in the Black music industry. **Entries include:** Individual, organization, or company name, address, phone, key personnel; listings for individuals include biographical data. **Arrangement:** Alphabetical. **Indexes:** Subject. **Pages (approx.):** 210. **Frequency:** Irregular; latest edition 1987; new edition expected September 1990. **Editor(s):** Robert Rosenthal. **Price:** $40.00, plus $2.00 shipping. **Former Title(s):** *Who's Who in Black Music.*

★3882★
Who's Who of Black Millionaires
Who's Who of Black Millionaires, Inc.
PO Box 12092
Fresno, CA 93776 Phone: (209)266-5438
Description: Black Americans whose net worth is approximately $1 million or more. **Entries include:** Personal name, location, biographical and financial data. **Arrangement:** Classified by line of profession. **Indexes:** Personal name. **Pages (approx.):** 185. **Frequency:** Irregular; previous edition 1984; latest edition 1991. **Editor(s):** Frank Johnson, President. **Price:** $9.95.

★3883★
Women's and Minorities' Pages for Greater Fargo-Moorhead-West Fargo North Dakota
Fargo Chamber of Commerce
Box 2443
Fargo, ND 58108 Phone: (701)237-5678
Description: About 180 businesses in the greater Fargo, North Dakota area, including Moorhead, Minnesota, which are owned or operated by women or by members of a minority group. **Entries include:** Company name, address, phone, number of employees, type of business, description of products or services, minority status, whether private or publicly owned. **Arrangement:** Alphabetical. **Pages (approx.):** 60. **Frequency:** Annual, spring. **Price:** $5.00. **Fax:** (701)232-3233.

★3884★
World Directory of Minorities
St. James Press
233 E. Ontario, Ste. 600
Chicago, IL 60611 Phone: (312)787-5800
Description: Major minorities that are, by definition, a numerically inferior portion of a national population differing from the majority in ethno-religio-linguistic ways; worldwide coverage. **Entries include:** Description of the minority including population, percentage of national population, location, language, religion. **Arrangement:** Geographical. **Indexes:** Subject and keyword. **Pages (approx.):** 430. **Frequency:** Published 1990. **Price:** $85.00. **Also Includes:** Maps; bibliographies of further references.

(15) PUBLISHERS

Entries in this chapter are arranged alphabetically by publisher's name. See the User's Guide at the front of this directory for additional information.

★3885★
A. J. Muste Memorial Institute
339 Lafayette St.
New York, NY 10012 Phone: (212)533-4335

Description: Reprints classical and modern writings on non-violence, disarmament, race, labor, and women's issues. Reaches market through direct mail and advertising. **Principle Officers and Managers:** Murray Rosenblith, Executive Director. **Discounts:** Universal Schedule - 40%. **Percentage of Sales to:** Bookstores - 20%; Non-Book Retail Outlets - 30%; Individuals - 50%. **Selected Titles:** *Peace Agitator: The Story of A. J. Muste* by Nat Hentoff; *Three Essays* by Martin Luther King, Jr.; *On Civil Disobedience* by H. D. Thoreau.

★3886★
Adrienne Publications
123 Cheshire Rd.
Bethany, CT 06525 Phone: (203)393-2323

Principle Officers and Managers: Richard Kaletsky, President and Treasurer; Laurie Kaletsky, Vice-President and Secretary. **Discounts:** Bookstores - 40%. **Percentage of Sales to:** Libraries - 5%; Bookstores - 20%; Individuals - 75%. **Selected Titles:** *Ali and Me: Through the Ropes* by Richard Kaletsky.

★3887★
Afram Press
181 Northampton Dr.
Willingboro, NJ 08046 Phone: (609)871-0639

Description: Publishes on the Afro-American experience. Also produces newsletters, greeting cards, calendars, and a magazine for Black children. Reaches market through commission representatives, direct mail, and trade sales. **Principle Officers and Managers:** Albert Pitts, Publisher; Yahya Karim, Editor; Linda Richardson, Office Manager. **Discounts:** Bookstores - 40% (10). **Percentage of Sales to:** Bookstores - 80%; Non-Book Retail Outlets - 10%; Individuals - 10%. **Selected Titles:** *Haitian Creole Cookery, Ethiopian Cookery, Afro-Brazilian Cookery, Yoruba Names, Baby Book, Swahili Coloring Book.*

★3888★
The Africa Fund
198 Broadway, 4th Fl.
New York, NY 10038 Phone: (212)962-1210

Description: Conducts research and publishes resources on southern Africa concerning apartheid and colonialism. Distributes International Defense & Aid Fund (London) and Catholic Institute for International Relations. Also publishes *Southern Africa Perspectives*. Offers *ACOA Action News* and *Student Anti-Apartheid Newsletter.* **Principle Officers and Managers:** Jennifer Davis, Executive Secretary; Richard Knight, Literature Director. **Discounts:** Please inquire. **Selected Titles:** *Black Dispossession in South Africa: The Myth of Bantustan Independence* by Richard Knight; *Unified List of United States Companies Doing Business in South Africa and Namibia* by Richard Knight and Roger Walke; *A Woman's Place Is in the Struggle–Not Behind Bars* by the Federation of Transvaal Women; *Apartheid Whitewash: South African Disinformation in the United States* by Richard Leonard; *Brutal Force: The Apartheid War Machine* by Gavin Cawthra.

★3889★
Africa World Press
PO Box 1892
Trenton, NJ 08607 Phone: (609)695-3766

Description: A nonprofit, educational organization concerned with the social, political, and economic development, problems, and prospects of Africa. Also distributes publications of Zed Press. Reaches market through direct mail, reviews, and trade sales. **Principle Officers and Managers:** Kassahun Checole, Publisher and President; Pamela A. Sims, Administrative Assistant. **Number of New Titles:** 1988 - 15, 1989 - 30; Total Titles in Print - 60. **Discounts:** Bookstores - 40%. **Percentage of Sales to:** Libraries - 5%; Bookstores - 30%; Individuals - 60%. **Selected Titles:** *Essays on African History* by Jean Suret-Canale; *Myth, Realism and the West African Writer* by Richard K. Priebe; *The Ties that Bind: African-American Consciousness of Africa* by Richard Magubane; *Operation Timber: Pages from the Savimbi Dossier* edited by William Minter; *Prophetic Fragments* by Cornel West; *Fulcrums of Change: Origins of Racism in the Americas and Other Essays* by Jan Carew.

★3890★
African-American Institute
833 United Nations Plaza
New York, NY 10017 Phone: (212)949-5666

Description: Promotes African-American understanding and assists African development. Conducts conferences, facilitative and informational services, cultural projects, and educational and development training programs. Reports and documents available from the organization directly. Also offers a bimonthly magazine on African political and economic development and U.S.-African policy analysis. **Principle Officers and Managers:** Vivian Lowery Derryck, President. **Selected Titles:** *Toward a New Africa Policy, Africa Policy in the 1980's*, both by Margaret A. Novicki; *African Development and Policy Issues: Implications for California*; *Higher Education and Rural Development in Africa.*

★3891★
African Bibliographic Center
PO Box 13096
Washington, DC 20009

Description: Publishes on foreign affairs, with emphasis on U.S. relations with Africa. **Principle Officers and Managers:** Daniel Matthews, Executive Director; Linda Fink Matthews, Administrative Director; Francis A. Kornegay, Jr., Research Director and Senior Information Specialist; Constance Burr, Publications Editor. **Discounts:** Bookstores & Libraries - 20%. **Selected Titles:** *American-Southern African Relations: Bibliographic Essays*; *AF-LOG II: African Affairs in Washington, DC, 1980-81*; *Washington and Africa: Reagan, Congress, and an African Affairs Constituency* by Francis Kornegay, Jr.; *Dictionary of Afro-Latin American Civilization* by Benjamin Nunez; *African Refugees: A Guide to Contemporary Information Sources* by Gail Kostinkos.

★3892★
Afro-Am Publishing Co., Inc.
819 S. Wabash Ave., Ste. 610
Chicago, IL 60605 Phone: (312)922-1147

Description: Publishes African and Afro-American educational materials for grades pre-kindergarten through high school. Distributes Black-oriented titles for grades kindergarten through twelve, from Harper & Row, Random House, Chelsea House, and Doubleday. Reaches market through direct mail. **Principle Officers and Managers:** Eugene Winslow, President; Loretta Rivers, Secretary-Treasurer. **Subjects:** Black studies. **Discounts:** Bookstores - 20-40%; Libraries - 15%; Catalog Jobbers - 40%. **Percentage of Sales to:** Libraries - 10%; Bookstores - 5%; Individuals - 5%; Educational Institutions - 80%. **Selected Titles:** *Great Negroes, Past and Present* by Russell Adams; *Afro-Americans '76* by Eugene Winslow.

★3893★
Afro-American Research Center, Inc.
Eastport PO Box 4444
Annapolis, MD 21403-6444 Phone: (301)263-4844

Description: Concentrates on publications by and about persons of African descent throughout the world. Reaches market through Cornell University Press, University Press of America and Black-oriented media. **Principle Officers and Managers:** Phaon Sundiata, President; Harrison D. Jones, Jr., Vice-President; Swederai Kumusha Ticharwa, Secretary-Treasurer. **Discounts:** Please inquire. **Percentage of Sales to:** Libraries - 20%; Bookstores - 5%; Individuals - 20%; Universities - 55%. **Selected Titles:** *Checklist for Black Genealogical Researchers* by Sundiata; *How to Organize One Million Blacks*; *Black Manhood: Building of Civilization by the Black Man of the Nile*; both by Phaon Goldman; *A People Feared from the Beginning Onwards* by Sebutan *Statements by Men-of-Science on African Sexuality* by Sekhem-Re-Khu-towy; *A Narrative Chart Highlighting Members of the Eighteenth Dynasty of Ancient Eqypt with Emphasis on Those Noted by Various Authorities As Having African Affinities* by Tarharka. **Formerly:** Tarharka Publishing Co. Mail returned from address above; no forwarding address available.

★3894★
Akili Books of America
PO Box 1291
South Gate, CA 90280 Phone: (213)635-7191

Description: Publishes books concerning cultural heritage of African-Americans, adults and children alike, on any subject. **Principle Officers and Managers:** Issy K. Tindimwebwa, Publishing Manager. **Subjects:** Folklore, philosophy, traditions. **Discounts:** Bookstores - Please inquire; Libraries - 20% (10); Others - Please inquire. **Selected Titles:** *Names from East Africa, Meaning and Pronounciation* by I. K. Tindimwebwa and H. McCkinzie; *A Book of African Sayings and Their Meanings*, *Children's Stories from Africa*, both by Issy K. Tindimwebwa.

★3895★
Alpha Kappa Alpha Sorority
5656 S. Stony Island Ave.
Chicago, IL 60637 Phone: (312)684-1282

Description: Publishes on education and reading. Also publishes *Ivy Leaf Magazine*. **Principle Officers and Managers:** Nan Johnson, Executive Director; Janet J. Ballard, National President. **Selected Titles:** *Reading and the Black Child* by M. Tamao Denniston; *When Is Reading Reading* by Mattie Claybrook Williams; *Toward a Better Start in Reading* by Dorothy S. Strickland; *Teen-Age Reading: Achieving Competence in Written Communication* by Carolyn Troupe; *The 3M Crisis: Miseducating Millions of Minorities* by Shirley A. Jackson.

★3896★
American Civil Liberties Union
132 W. 43rd St.
New York, NY 10036 Phone: (212)944-9800

Description: An organization which defends individual rights guaranteed by the Constitution through litigation, legislative lobbying, and public education. Publishes *ACLU Rights Handbook Series* consisting of thirty titles, Civil Liberties, a quarterly newsletter and periodic pamphlets and brochures. **Principle Officers and Managers:** Ira Glasser, Executive Director; Colleen A. O'Connor, Director of Public Education. **Selected Titles:** *Covert Operations and the Democratic Process: The Implications of the Iran/Contra Affair*, *Justice Evicted: An Inquiry into Housing Court Problems*; *Immigration Reform Act: Employer Sanctions and Discrimination Prohibitions*; *Parental Notice Laws: Their Catastrophic Impact on Teenagers' Right to Abortion.*

★3897★
Amulefi Publishing Co.
11 E. Utica St.
Buffalo, NY 14209 Phone: (716)882-7676

Principle Officers and Managers: Molefi K. Asante, Vice-President and Secretary. **Subjects:** Afro-American studies, poetry, occult, communication, dance. **Discounts:** Bookstores & Libraries - 20%. **Percentage of Sales to:** Libraries - 40%; Bookstores - 50%; Non-Book Retail Outlets - 5%; Individuals - 5%. **Selected Titles:** *Afrocentricity* by Molefi Asante; *Textured Women, Cowrie Shells, Beetle Sticks* by Kariamu Welsh.

★3898★
Andre's and Co.
289 Varick St.
Jersey City, NJ 07302 Phone: (201)451-3804

Description: "Grew out of a need in the Black academic community for a place to publish (unabriged) works dealing with new (Black) prospectives in the psychological, anthropological, economic, and political realms." Concerns are academic, not exclusively Black. **Principle Officers and Managers:** Andre Joseph, President and Editor; Lawrence C. Joseph, Vice-President; Reginald L. Ardrey, Associate Editor; Vincent Thompson, Copy Editor. **Subjects:** Black concerns, math, English, poetry. **Discounts:** Bookstores & Libraries - 10%. **Selected Titles:** *The Psycho-mathematical Basic Skills Learning Workbooklet*, *The Psycho-mathematical Mini Math Packs*, *The White Lie: Black Inferiority* all by Andre Joseph; *Basic College Writing: A Workbook* by Bessie Waites-Black.

★3899★
Associated Publishers, Inc.
1407 14th St. NW
Washington, DC 20005-3704 Phone: (202)265-1441

Description: Publishes on Afro-American life and history. Also produces Annual Black History Kits. Reaches market through exhibits and direct mail. **Principle Officers and Managers:** Edgar A. Toppin, President; Willie L. Miles, Managing Director; Janet Sims-Wood, Treasurer; Roland McConnell, Secretary. **Discounts:** Bookstores - 25%; Libraries & Schools - 20%. **Percentage of Sales to:** Libraries - 20%; Bookstores - 25%; Non-Book Retail Outlets - 20%; Individuals - 5%. **Selected Titles:** *History of Negro Church*, *Negro in Our History*, both by Carter G Woodson, revised by C. H. Wesley; *Black Americans in Cleveland* by Russell H. Davis; *Economic Development: International and African Perspectives* by Andrew F. Brimmer; *R. Nathaniel Dett: His Life and Works, 1882-1943* by Vivian Flagg McBrier; *Women Builders* by Sadie Daniels.

★3900★
Balamp Publishing
PO Box 02367
N. End
Detroit, MI 48202 Phone: (313)491-1950

Principle Officers and Managers: James M. Jay, President. **Subjects:** Biographies, autobiographies. **Discounts:** Bookstores - 40% (trade); Libraries - 10%. **Selected Titles:** *Robeson: Labor's Forgotten Champion* by Charles H. Wright; *You Don't Look Like a Musician* by Bud Freeman; *Walk Quietly through the Night and Cry Softly* by Burniece Avery; *Eubie Blake: Keys of Memory* by Lawrence T. Carter; *My World of Reality* by Hildrus A. Poindexter; *Black American Scholars: Study of Their Beginnings* by Horace Mann Bond.

★3901★
Benin Publishing Co.
802 Columbus Dr.
Teaneck, NJ 07666 Phone: (201)837-8641

Description: Publishes business books for minorities. Reaches market through direct mail. **Principle Officers and Managers:** Robert M. Waite, President. **Discounts:** Bookstores - 30%. **Percentage of Sales to:** Bookstores - 100%. **Selected Titles:** *Daddy Big Bucks* by Robert Waite.

★3902★
Best Western Press
PO Box 494
Bakersfield, CA 93302 Phone: (805)323-0738

Description: Publishes a book on Black history. Reaches market through direct mail. Annual Sales: $1200. **Principle Officers and Managers:** Samuel Barnes, President; William McCulland, Sales Manager. **Discounts:** Please inquire. **Selected Titles:** *Identity* by Samuel Barnes.

★3903★
Black-a-Moors
2339 N. Fairhill St.
Philadelphia, PA 19133 Phone: (215)634-1440

Description: Strives to enhance Black culture through Black literature. Reaches market through direct mail, reviews, and wholesalers. Mail returned from address above; no forwarding address available. **Principle Officers and Managers:** Darlene M. Jackson, Owner; Theresa B. Janrary, Myongsoon Park, Representatives. **Subjects:** Political science, drama, poetry, religion, fiction, nonfiction. **Discounts:** Bookstores - 40%; Libraries - 25%. **Selected Titles:** *Self-Deception*; *The Immigrant*; *The Plan of the Snake: A Look at Our Government Today*; *Of Love, Life and Childhood Days*; *Answer to the Play "For Colored Girls. The Virtue of the Black Female Sex*, all by James A. Fisher; *The Exciting Sex Life of a Widower*, by Shina Sabbu.

★3904★
Black Artists in America
39 Wilshire Dr.
Spring Valley, NY 10977 Phone: (205)435-2678

Description: Makes available wide-ranging information on Black art resources which are normally unavailable. **Principle Officers and Managers:** Oakley N. Holmes, Jr., Author. **Discounts:** Bookstores - 16%. **Selected Titles:** *Complete Annotated Resource Guide to Black American Art* by Oakley Holmes, Jr.

★3905★
Black Caucus of the American Library Association Publications Committee
499 Wilson Library
University of Minnesota Libraries
Minneapolis, MN 55455 Phone: (612)373-3097

Description: Publishes a quarterly newsletter and a biennial directory. Reaches market through direct mail and reviews. **Principle Officers and Managers:** Barbara Williams-Jenkins, Black Caucus Chairor; Thomas Weissinger, Chairor, Publications Committee. **Selected Titles:** *A.L.A. Black Caucus Directory*.

★3906★
Black Classic Press
PO Box 13414
Baltimore, MD 21203 Phone: (301)728-4595

Description: Publishes African and American studies. "Our intent is to bring to light obscure and significant works by and about people of African descent." Reaches market through direct mail and reviews. **Principle Officers and Managers:** W. Paul Coates, Director. **Number of New Titles:** 1988 - 5, 1989 - 2, 1990 (est.) - 5; Total Titles in Print - 21. **Discounts:** Bookstores - 10-40%. **Selected Titles:** *African Glory* by J. C. DeGraft-Johnson; *100 Years of Lynchings* by Ralph Ginzburg; *The Life and Adventure of Nat Love* by Nat Love; *Coltrane* by C. O. Simpkins; *Black Man of the Nile* by Yosef ben-Jochannan; *Your History*; *From the Beginning of Time to the Present* by JA Rogers.

★3907★
Black Entrepreneurs Press
4502 S. Congress Ave., Ste. 254
Austin, TX 78745 Phone: (512)444-9962

Description: Publishes self-help books for African-Americans in business. Offers a newsletter, *Black Entrepreneur's Wealth Builders*. Reaches market through direct mail and Baker & Taylor. **Principle Officers and Managers:** Derek A. Broadnax, President. **Number of New Titles:** 1989 - 1, 1990 - 2. **Subjects:** Personal finance. **Discounts:** Bookstores - 20%, 25% (2-9), 40% (10-99), 45% (100); Libraries - 10%. **Percentage of Sales to:** Libraries - 5%; Bookstores - 1%; Individuals - 94%. **Selected Titles:** *The Black Entrepreneur's Guide to Money*, *The Black Entrepreneur's Guide to Starting and Building a Million Dollar Business of Your Own!*, *Directory of African-American Owned Savings and Loan Institutions*, *What Every Black American Should Know to Gain Financial Success in the 90's*, all by Derek A. Broadnax.

★3908★
Black Graphics International
PO Box 732, Linwood Sta.
Detroit, MI 48206 Phone: (313)890-1128

Description: Publishers and distributors of revolutionary literature and art. **Principle Officers and Managers:** Ibn Pori, Publisher and Editor; Julian Richardson, Publisher; Adebayo Ni Youn, Public Relations. **Discounts:** Bookstores - 30%. **Selected Titles:** *Fire Music* by Rob Backus; *Assassin Poems* by Vajava Mogumbo and Brothers.

★3909★
Black Resource Guide, Inc.
501 Oneida Pl. NW
Washington, DC 20011 Phone: (202)291-4373

Description: Performs research for organizations interested in making contact with various elements in the national Black community. Publishes an annual directory and offers mailing labels of prominent members of the Black community. Audience includes educational institutions, members of the media, and general public. Reaches market through commission representatives, direct mail, reviews, telephone sales, trade sales, and wholesalers. **Principle Officers and Managers:** Robert B. Johnson, President; Jacqueline L. Johnson, Secretary-Treasurer. **Number of New Titles:** 1991 (est.) - 1; Total Titles in Print - 8. **Discounts:** Bookstores - 40%; Libraries - 20% (10 prepaid). **Percentage of Sales to:** Libraries - 35%; Bookstores - 20%; Individuals - 45%. **Selected Titles:** *The Black Resource Guide: A National Black Directory.*

★3910★
Blacklight Fellowship
2859 W. Wilcox St.
Chicago, IL 60612 Phone: (312)722-1441

Description: Publishes Black Christian biblical literature. Offers seminars. Accepts unsolicited manuscripts. Reaches market through direct mail, trade sales, and Baker & Taylor. **Principle Officers and Managers:** Rev. Walter Arthur McCray, Director. **Number of New Titles:** 1989 - 1, 1990 - 2, 1991 (est.) - 3; Total Titles in Print - 7. **Discounts:** Bookstores - 40%; Libraries - None. **Percentage of Sales to:** Libraries - 5%; Bookstores - 70%; Individuals - 20%. **Selected Titles:** *The Black Presence in the Bible, How to Stick Together During Times of Tension, Reaching and Teaching Black Young Adults,* all by McCray; *By Your Traditions* by Arthur D. Griffin.

★3911★
Broadside Press
PO Box 04257
Detroit, MI 48204 Phone: (313)934-1231

Description: Publishes poetry by Black authors. Reaches market through direct mail, telephone sales, and Baker & Taylor. Annual Sales: $12,000. Formerly Broadside/Crummel Press. **Principle Officers and Managers:** Hilda Vest, Publisher; Donald Vest, Business Manager; Gloria House, Editor; Willie D. Williams, Photographer; Ernest Janks, Board Member. **Number of New Titles:** 1988 - 1, 1989 - 4; Total Titles in Print - 40. **Subjects:** Poetry, criticism. **Discounts:** Bookstores - 40%; Wholesalers - 50%; Libraries - None. **Percentage of Sales to:** Libraries - 15%; Bookstores - 80%; Individuals - 5%. **Selected Titles:** *Upside Down Tapestry Mosaic History* by Leslie Reese; *Report from Part One* by Gwendolyn Brooks; *Safari of African Cooking* by Bill Odarty; *Abstract Blues* by Rayfield Waller; *Island Images* by Michele Gilolos; *Rainrituals* by Aneb Kgositsile.

★3912★
Calaloux Publications
22 Belair Rd.
Wellesley, MA 02181 Phone: (617)237-2230

Description: Publishes original works or noteworthy reprints of important works by or about Caribbean, African-American, African, and other Third World people. Offers brochures, videotapes of interviews, and documentaries. Distributes for New Beacon Books and Aquarela Galleries. Accepts unsolicited manuscripts. Annual Sales: $20,000. **Principle Officers and Managers:** Selwyn R. Cudjoe, President; Gwendolyn M. Long-Cudjoe, Vice-President; Ronald Thomas, Secretary. **Number of New Titles:** 1988 - 2, 1989 - 2; Total Titles in Print - 10. **Discounts:** Bookstores - 35%. **Selected Titles:** *Movement of the People, A Just and Moral Society,* both by Selwyn R. Cudjoe; *Labour Law in Trinidad and Tobago* by Roy D. Thomas; *Growing Up with Miss Milly* by Sybil Seaforth; *Those that Be in Bondage* by A. R. F. Webber; *The Still Cry* by Noor Kumar Mahabir.

★3913★
Cape of Good Hope Foundation
1201 E. California
Pasadena, CA 91125 Phone: (818)356-4469

Description: Reaches market through direct mail. Formerly listed as California Institute of Technology, Munger Africana Library. **Principle Officers and Managers:** Edwin S. Munger, President; Helga Harrison, Financial Officer. **Subjects:** Higher education, Southern Africa. **Discounts:** Bookstores - 20%. **Selected Titles:** *The Hunter and His Art* by Jalmar and Ione Rudner; *Africana Byways* by Anna H. Smith; *Touched* by Africa by Ned Munger; *IMVO News*, Issues 1-5 (annual).

★3914★
Capitol Press
6 Kennedy St.
Alexandria, VA 22305 Phone: (703)836-2649

Description: Publishes on the history of Blacks in sports. Reaches market through reviews and baseball organizations. Annual Sales: $1000. Presently inactive. **Principle Officers and Managers:** John B. Holway, President. **Discounts:** Please inquire. **Percentage of Sales to:** Individuals - 100%. **Selected Titles:** *Bullet Joe and the Monarchs, Smokey Joe and the Cannonballs,* both by John B. Holway.

★3915★
Carib House (USA)
11305 Goleta St.
Los Angeles, CA 91342 Phone: (818)890-1056

Description: Publishes and distributes books on all subjects relevant to the Caribbean region; manuscripts also solicited. **Principle Officers and Managers:** Rupert Singh, Owner and Manager; P. D. Sharma, Editor; Lynn Franklin, Sales and Promotion. **Discounts:** Bookstores - 50%; Libraries - 25%; Distributors - 60%. **Selected Titles:** *The New Caribbean Man* by P. D. Sharma.

★3916★
Carver Publishing, Inc.
41 Cornelius Dr.
Hampton, VA 23666 Phone: (804)838-1244

Description: Publishes the history of contributions of Black men and women to U.S. military defense since 1619. **Principle Officers and Managers:** Jesse J. Johnson LTC, Ret., Publisher. **Subjects:** Military history. **Selected Titles:** *Ebony Brass, A Pictorial History of the Black Soldier in the United States in Peace and War, A Pictorial History of Black Servicemen, Black Armed Forces Officers, Roots of Two Black*

Marine Sergeants Major, Black Women in the Armed Forces, all by Jesse J. Johnson. **Formerly:** Ebony Publishing Inc.

★3917★
Center for African Studies
710 West End Ave.
New York, NY 10025 Phone: (212)678-7184

Description: Publishes the Journal of African Economy. Reaches market through direct mail. Annual Sales: $59,000. **Principle Officers and Managers:** Linus A. Bassey, Executive Director. **Subjects:** African policy, African fables. **Discounts:** Bookstores - 40%; Libraries - 20%; Others - 2%. **Percentage of Sales to:** Libraries - 40%; Bookstores - 55%; Non-Book Retail Outlets - 2%; Individuals - 3%. **Selected Titles:** *African Economic and Business Reports*, *African Fables*, *Africa with Facts and Figures*, all by L. A. Bassey; *Stability and Instability: Nigeria and Cameroon* by D. Afiaja; *A General Book of Readings on Africa*; *A General Book of Readings on West Africa*.

★3918★
Change for Children
879 Douglass St.
San Francisco, CA 94114

Description: Develops and distributes educational materials aimed at reducing stereotypes of race and sex. Mail returned from address above; no forwarding address available. **Principle Officers and Managers:** Irene Kane, Materials Coordinator. **Discounts:** Bookstores - 35%; Others - 20% (20). **Selected Titles:** *We Can Change It* by Kane Shargell.

★3919★
Chatham Bookseller
8 Green Village
Madison, NJ 07940 Phone: (201)822-1361

Description: Publishes hardcover reprints of novels by Black writers. **Principle Officers and Managers:** Frank Deodene, President. **Discounts:** Bookstores - 20%. **Selected Titles:** *The Heat's On*, *Pinktoes*, *Run Man Run*, all by Chester Himes; *Banana Bottom* by Claude McKay; *One for New York* by John A. Williams; *Savage Holiday* by Richard Wright.

★3920★
Cobblestone Communications
PO Box 552
Malden, MA 02148 Phone: (617)322-3998

Description: Publishes an African-American travel guide resource and business directory. **Principle Officers and Managers:** Linda Cline, Publisher. **Number of New Titles:** 1990 - 1. **Selected Titles:** *Access: The Black Patron's Directory of Metropolitan Boston's Business*, Professional, and Specialized Services.

★3921★
Council on Interracial Books for Children
1841 Broadway
New York, NY 10023 Phone: (212)757-5339

Description: Publishes "to identify–and more recently to counteract–racism, sexism, and other anti-human values in children's learning materials and in society." Offers books, maps, filmstrips, catalogs, and booklists. Reaches market through direct mail. **Principle Officers and Managers:** Melba Kgositsile, Executive Director. **Discounts:** Bookstores - 20%. **Percentage of Sales to:** Libraries - 20%; Bookstores - 10%; Individuals - 20%; Schools & Universities - 50%. **Selected Titles:** *Embers: Stories for a Changing World*; *Guidelines for Selecting Bias-Free Textbooks and Storybooks*; *Stereotypes, Distortions and Omissions in U.S. History Textbooks*; *Violence, the Ku Klux Klan and the Struggle for Equality*, all by the CIBC.

★3922★
Cultural Survival, Inc.
11 Divinity Ave.
Cambridge, MA 02138 Phone: (617)495-2562

Description: A nonprofit organization founded by a group of social scientists concerned with the fate of tribal peoples and ethnic minorities around the world. Publications serve to inform the general public, educators, and policy makers in the U.S. and abroad to stimulate action on behalf of these societies. Reaches market through direct mail and distributors. **Principle Officers and Managers:** David Maybury-Lewis, President; Jason W. Clay, Editor and Director of Research. **Subjects:** Human rights, anthropology, social sciences. **Discounts:** Bookstores - 40%; Colleges - 20%; Libraries - None.

★3923★
Davida Alake Lewis Publishing
1099 Van Dyke, Ste. 402
Detroit, MI 48226 Phone: (313)822-7922

Description: Publishes on African-Americans. Offers posters, prints, greeting cards, postcards, and booklets. Reaches market through commission reprsentatives, direct mail, trade sales, and Flat Surface. **Principle Officers and Managers:** James Lewis, Vice-President. **Number of New Titles:** 1989 - 2, 1990 - 2; Total Titles in Print - 7. **Discounts:** Bookstores - 50%. **Percentage of Sales to:** Bookstores - 5%; Non-Book Retail Outlets - 95%. **Selected Titles:** *The Miracle of Dr. George Washington Carver* by Davida Smith; *Picking Cotton* by S. Jill Miller; *Hannible* by Alake Lewis; *African Astrology* by Robert Williams; *Directory of African-American Prints, Posters and Craft Dealers*, *Southern Life*, both by James Lewis.

★3924★
Dayton Human Relations Council
40 S. Main St., Ste. 721
Dayton, OH 45402 Phone: (513)225-5336

Description: Makes large segment of the community aware of the services and programs of the Human Relations Council. Reaches market through direct mail and distribution points. **Principle Officers and Managers:** Jerald L. Steed, Executive Director. **Subjects:** Unlawful discriminatory practices in employment, public accommodations, housing, credit transactions. **Discounts:** All publications are free to the general public. **Selected Titles:** *Rules and Regulations for Filing a Complaint of Alleged Discrimination*; *Your Rights Are Protected by Law*; *Human Relations Council Ordinances Prohibiting Discrimination*; *Guide to Complainant*; *Guide to Respondent*.

★3925★
Dr. Cassagnol Institute of Research, Inc.
PO Box 5454
Bossier City, LA 71111-5454 Phone: (318)742-1985

Description: Aim is to provide better quality educational/entertainment materials to the Afro/Hispanic-American population in the United States and targeted markets in Third World communities. Offers greeting cards, high-tech products, art prints, and software packages. Reaches market through direct mail and wholesalers. Annual Sales: $400,000. **Principle Officers and Managers:** Dr. Francois Cassagnol, President, Chairor, and Publisher; Dr. Guito W. Cassagnol, Executive Assistant to Publisher; Dr. Wanda J. W. Cassagnol, International Executive and Representative; Marie D. Cassagnol, Executive Assistant to President,

Overseas Projects; Kathy A. Cassagnol, International Executive and Corporate Secretary. **Number of New Titles:** 1989 - 10; Total Titles in Print - 26. **Selected Titles:** *National Entrepreneurial Training and MBE/WBE Incubation Program*; *A Conceptual Representation of Dr. Cassagnol Institute of Research's Multilingual/Multicultural Model*, both by Dr. Francois Cassagnol.

★3926★
Edward Vaughn and Associates
12135 Dexter
Detroit, MI 48206 Phone: (313)933-1380

Description: Mail returned from address above; no forwarding address available. **Principle Officers and Managers:** Edward Vaughn, Owner. **Subjects:** Black history, African history, Black culture and poetry. **Discounts:** Bookstores - 40%; Libraries - 20%; Distributors - 50%. **Selected Titles:** *Red, Black, and Green: The History of the Black Liberation Flag* by Edward Vaughn.

★3927★
Eliza Washington, Publisher
614 Wilshire Ave.
Waterloo, IA 50701 Phone: (319)234-1460

Percentage of Sales to: Individuals - 100%. **Selected Titles:** *Tomorrow Is Another Day: Hope of a Better Future for Black Americans* by Eliza Washington.

★3928★
Fire!! Press
241 Hillside Rd.
Elizabeth, NJ 07208 Phone: (201)964-8476

Description: Publishes works from the Harlem Renaissance. Reaches market through direct mail. Annual Sales: $2,000. **Principle Officers and Managers:** Thomas H. Wirth, Publisher. **Number of New Titles:** 1991 (est.) 1; Total Titles in Print - 1. **Subjects:** African-American literature. **Discounts:** Bookstores - 40%. **Percentage of Sales to:** Libraries - 20%; Bookstores - 20%; Non-Book Retail Outlets - 10%; Individuals - 50%. **Selected Titles:** *Fire!!* edited by Wallace Thurman.

★3929★
Georgian Press Co.
2620 SW Georgian Pl.
Portland, OR 97201 Phone: (503)223-9899

Description: Publishes books on Portland history (business and politics) and Black history. Reaches market through direct mail, reviews, and Pacific Pipeline. **Principle Officers and Managers:** E. Kimbark MacColl, President and Treasurer; Leeanne G. MacColl, Vice-President; E. Kimbark MacColl, Jr., Secretary. **Discounts:** Bookstores - 40% (no returns); Libraries - 20%; Others - 20% (with the option to return). **Percentage of Sales to:** Libraries - 20%; Individuals - 10%. **Selected Titles:** *A Peculiar Paradise: A History of Blacks in Oregon* by Elizabeth McLagan.

★3930★
Graphics-Communication Associates
PO Box 10549
Tallahassee, FL 32302 Phone: (904)385-0711

Description: Mail returned from address above; no forwarding address available. **Principle Officers and Managers:** James C. Payne II, President and C.E.O. **Subjects:** Black rhetoric, Black history. **Discounts:** Bookstores & Libraries - 10%. **Percentage of Sales to:** Libraries - 99%; Individuals - 1%. **Selected Titles:** *The Anatomy of Black Rhetoric* by James C. Payne II.

★3931★
Gumbs & Thomas Publishers, Inc.
142 W. 72nd St., Ste. 9
New York, NY 10023 Phone: (212)870-0969

Description: Publishes materials on Black history and culture from around the world. Reaches market through direct mail. Distributes for Col-Bob Associates, Inc. Annual Sales: $60,000. **Principle Officers and Managers:** Bob Gumbs, President; Verl Thomas, Vice-President. **Number of New Titles:** 1988 - 1, 1989 - 1, 1990 (est.) - 1; Total Titles in Print - 4. **Discounts:** Bookstores - 30-45%. **Percentage of Sales to:** Libraries - 30%; Bookstores - 25%; Individuals - 20%; Wholesalers - 25%. **Selected Titles:** *Kwanzaa: Everything You Always Wanted to Know but Didn't Know Where to Ask* by Cedric McClester; *Harlem Today: A Cultural and Visitors Guide* by A. Peter Bailey; *Let's Celebrate Kwanzaa: An Activity Book for Young Readers* by Helen Davis Thompson; *On the Real Side* by Shirley Riley.

★3932★
Heritage Press
PO Box 18625
Baltimore, MD 21216 Phone: (301)728-8521

Description: Publishes books on the Black perspective of life in America. **Principle Officers and Managers:** Wilbert L. Walker, President. **Discounts:** Bookstores - 40% (2); Libraries - 30%; Others - Up to 50% (quantity). **Selected Titles:** *Stalemate at Panmunjon, We Are Men: Memoirs of World War II and the Korean War, Servants of All, The Deputy's Dilemma*, all by Wilbert L. Walker.

★3933★
Holistic Exchange
433 Cleveland St., Ste. 115
Clearwater, FL 34615

Description: Publishes books on holistic health, women, and Black studies. Offers a quarterly newsletter Nature's Aid First Aid Kits. Also offers herbs, vitamins, and health products. Distributes for Nature's Sunshine, PASE Publications, Carlton Press, and ETD Consultants. Reaches market through direct mail and trade sales. **Principle Officers and Managers:** Melvia Miller, President. **Number of New Titles:** 1988 - 1, 1989 - 1. **Discounts:** Bookstores - 20% (12). **Percentage of Sales to:** Libraries - 10%; Bookstores - 40%; Individuals - 50%. **Selected Titles:** *Black History Comic Books* by Baylor; *Mama's Baby, Papa's Maybe*; *An Apple A Day*; *Road to Riches*; *New and Different Friends*, all by Miller.

★3934★
Holloway House Publishing Co.
8060 Melrose Ave.
Los Angeles, CA 90046 Phone: (213)653-8060

Description: Publishes books written by Blacks, about the Black lifestyle, and history. Reaches market through commission representatives and telephone sales. **Principle Officers and Managers:** Ralph Weinstock, President; Mitchell Neal, General Manager; Marc K. Morriss, Systems Manager; Mrian O'Farrell, Operations Vice-President. **Percentage of Sales to:** Libraries - 12%; Bookstores - 30%; Individuals - 2%; Mass Market Outlets - 54%. **Selected Titles:** *Trick Baby* by Robert Beck; *Daddy Cool* by Donald Goines; *How to Win* by Mike Goodman; *Paul Robeson, Richard Pryor*, both by Joe Nazel; *Passion's Surrender* by K. Norton.

★3935★
Indiana University
African Studies Program
Woodburn Hall 221
Bloomington, IN 47405 Phone: (812)335-6825

Description: Publishes monographs, papers, and lecture texts by scholars in the field of African studies. Reaches market through wholesalers, reviews, and library exchange. Annual Sales: $2000. **Principle Officers and Managers:** Patrick O'Meara, Director; N. Brian Winchester, Associate Director. **Subjects:** African studies, including political science, folklore, anthropology, fine arts, music, linguistics, history. **Discounts:** Bookstores - 10% (10, single title). **Percentage of Sales to:** Bookstores - 40%; Non-Book Retail Outlets - 40%; Individuals - 10%. **Selected Titles:** *Security Problems: An African Predicament* by Francis Deng; *Short Time to Stay: Comments on Time, Literature, and Oral Performance* by Ruth Finnegan; *Films on Africa* by Paul Lazar.

★3936★
Investor Responsibility Research Center, Inc. (IRRC)
1755 Massachusetts Ave., NW
Ste. 600
Washington, DC 20036 Phone: (202)234-7500

Description: An independent, nonprofit corporation that conducts research and publishes reports on contemporary business and public policy issues that affect corporations and institutional investors. Offers four newsletters, *News for Investors, Corporate Governance Bulletin, South Africa Reporter, and Global Shareholder.* Accepts manuscripts. Reaches market through direct mail. **Principle Officers and Managers:** Margaret Carroll, Executive Director; Carolyn Mathiasen, Social Issues Director; David P. Hauck, South Africa Director; Peg O'Hara, Corporate Governance Director; David Popper, Director, Marketing. **Number of New Titles:** 1988 - 10, 1989 - 12, 1990 (est.) - 18; Total Titles in Print - 45. **Discounts:** Please inquire. **Percentage of Sales to:** Individuals - 10%; Libraries - 30%; Corporations - 70%. **Selected Titles:** *U.S. and Canadian Business in South Africa, 1987*; *Black South Africans' Views on Sanctions.*

★3937★
James H. Boykin
1260 NW 122nd St.
Miami, FL 33167 Phone: (305)681-7663

Description: Publishes on history. Reaches market through commission representatives, reviews, trade sales, and wholesalers. Annual Sales: $250. **Principle Officers and Managers:** James H. Boykin, Author and Publisher. **Number of New Titles:** 1988 - 1, 1990 (est.) - 1; Total Titles in Print - 8. **Subjects:** History, adult, professional. **Discounts:** Please inquire. **Percentage of Sales to:** Libraries - 8%; Individuals - 5%; Bookstores - 87%. **Selected Titles:** *World Blacks: Self Help and Achievement*, *Black Jews*, *Thank God for Black Power*, all by James H. Boykin.

★3938★
Joint Center for Political and Economic Studies
1301 Pennsylvania Ave., NW
Washington, DC 20004 Phone: (202)626-3530

Description: Conducts programs in research, training, technical assistance, and information, with the aim of increasing the effectiveness of Black elected officials specifically, and Black Americans generally, in all aspects of governance. Offers *Focus*, a monthly newsletter. Reaches market through direct mail. Annual Sales: $32,000. **Principle Officers and Managers:** Eddie N. Williams, President; Eleanor Farrar, Vice-President; Milton Morris, Director, Research; Auriel Pilgrim, Director, Information Resources. **Discounts:** Universal Schedule - 20% (2). **Selected Titles:** *A Horse of a Different Color: Media and the Jackson Campaign* by C. Anthony Broh; *How to Use Section 5 of the Voting Rights Act*, 3rd. ed. by Barbara Y. Phillips; *The Impact of the Black Electorate* by Thomas E. Cavanagh; *Minority Vote Dilution* edited by Chandler Davidson; *Journey to Work* by William P. O'Hare; *Who Defends America* edited by Edwin Dorn.

★3939★
Just Us Books, Inc.
301 Main St., Ste. No. 22-24
Orange, NJ 07050 Phone: (201)672-7701

Description: Publishes books and learning materials for children that focus on the African-American experience. Offers T-shirts, sweat shirts, audio cassettes, posters, and reward certificates. Plans a children's newspaper. Accepts unsolicited manuscripts with a query and self-addressed stamped envelope. Reaches market through direct mail, trade sales, Baker & Taylor, Quality Books, Inc., Warner Books, and Inland Book Co. **Principle Officers and Managers:** Wade Hudson, President and Chief Executive Officer; Cheryl Willis-Hudson, Vice-President and Publisher; Opal Newton, Customer Service Representative. **Number of New Titles:** 1988 - 2, 1989 - 2, 1990 (est.) - 6; Total Titles in Print - 3. **Discounts:** Bookstores - 40-47%. **Percentage of Sales to:** Libraries - 10%; Bookstores - 55%; Non-Book Retail Outlets - 5%; Individuals - 15%; Schools - 15%. **Selected Titles:** *Afro-Bets ABC Book*, *Afro-Bets 123 Book*, both by Cheryl Willis Hudson; *Afro-Bets Activity and Coloring Book* by Dwayne Ferguson; *Afro-Bets First Book About Africa* by Veronica Freeman Ellis; *Afro-Bets Book of Black Heroes from A to Z* by Hudson and Wesley; *Afro-Bets Activity and Enrichment Handbook.*

★3940★
Lambeth Press
143 E. 37th St.
New York, NY 10016 Phone: (212)679-0163

Description: Publishes scholarly books with popular appeal. Reaches market through direct mail and reviews. **Subjects:** Religion, Afro-Americana. **Selected Titles:** *Lemuel Heynes: A Bio-Bibliography*, *Afro-American Education: A Bibliographic Index*, both by Richard Newman.

★3941★
Life Signs: Words & Images
PO Box 663
El Cerrito, CA 94530 Phone: (415)540-7767

Description: Publishes African American literature, including the magazine *Genetic Dancers.* Reaches market through direct mail and advertising. Mail returned from address above; no forwarding address available. **Principle Officers and Managers:** Peter Harris, Project Director. **Discounts:** Bookstores - 40%; Libraries - 10% (10). **Percentage of Sales to:** Libraries - 1%; Bookstores - 5%; Individuals - 90%; Mail Order - 4%. **Selected Titles:** *Six Soft Sketches of a Man*, *Wherever Dreams Live*, both by Peter Harris.

★3942★
LSM Press
PO Box 2077
Oakland, CA 94604

Description: Publishes information on revolutionary political movements in Southern Africa through interviews with guerilla leaders, autobiographical life histories of rank-and-file militants, and first-hand accounts by correspondents. Mail returned from above address; no forwarding address available. **Principle Officers and Managers:** Steve Goldfield, Manager. **Selected Titles:** *South Africa: From Shantytowns to Forest* by Dennis and Ginger Mercer.

★3943★
M. L. Williams Publishing Co., Inc.
PO Box 53552
1315 Walnut St., Ste. 1624
Philadelphia, PA 19105 Phone: (215)735-1121

Description: Publishes titles on African-Americans in legal and related professions. Offers services and products to assist minority lawyers in marketing legal services. Also offers audio cassettes, informational pamphlets, a biannual mid-year supplement, and a quarterly newsletter. Accepts unsolicited manuscripts. Reaches market through direct mail and trade sales. **Principle Officers and Managers:** Marshall L. Williams, Publisher,Editor, and Chairor; Dennis Jemmerson, Subscription Director. **Number of New Titles:** 1989 - 1, 1990 - 2; Total Titles in Print - 3. **Discounts:** Bookstores - 35% (3-10), 50% (11); Libraries - 20% (2-5), 40% (6). **Percentage of Sales to:** Libraries - 70%; Bookstores - 10%; Corporations - 10%; Individuals - 10%. **Selected Titles:** *National Directory of Black Law Firms* by G. Ware; *1991-92 National Directory of Minority Law Firms,*, *Directory of Black Lawyers in Pennsylvania, Delaware, and New York, Marketing Legal Services and Increasing Profitability*, all by M. L. Williams.

★3944★
Majority Press
PO Box 538
Dover, MA 02030 Phone: (508)655-1631

Description: Specializes in college texts and adult nonfiction in Afro-American, Caribbean, and African studies. Reaches market through direct mail, reviews, and trade sales. Telephone number for placing orders only: (617) 828-8450. **Principle Officers and Managers:** E. L. Zabo. **Number of New Titles:** 1988 - 3, 1989 - 4, 1990 (est.) - 4; Total Titles in Print - 13. **Discounts:** Bookstores - 20% (1-10), 30% (11-49), 40% (50); School Bookstores - 20%. **Selected Titles:** *Literary Garveyism: Garvey, Black Arts, and the Harlem Renaissance*; *Marcus Garvey: Hero*; *The Pan-African Connection*, all by Tony Martin; *Race First*; *Philosophy and Opinions of Marcus Garvey* edited by Amy Jacques Garvey; *Brazil: Mixture or Massacre* by Abdias do Nascimento.

★3945★
Melvett Chambers, Author/Publisher
PO Box 390174
Denver, CO 80239 Phone: (303)363-7429

Description: Publishes books on the history of Black Americans, past and present. Also offers calendars. Reaches market through direct mail, trade sales, and Baker & Taylor. **Principle Officers and Managers:** Malvett G. Chambers, Author and Publisher; Emma F. Chambers, Vice-President. **Number of New Titles:** 1988 - 2, 1990 (est.) - 1; Total Titles in Print - 3. **Discounts:** Universal Schedule - 20% (1-4), 40% (5-24), 42% (25-99), 44% (100-499), 46% (500-999), 47% (1000). **Percentage of Sales to:** Libraries - 30%; Bookstores - 40%; Individuals - 30%. **Selected Titles:** *The Black History Trivia Quiz Book*, by Melvett G. Chambers.

★3946★
Multicultural Resources
PO Box 2945
Stanford, CA 94306 Phone: (415)493-6729

Description: Provides bibliographic materials, especially dealing with Black, Spanish-speaking, Asian American, Native American, and Pacific Island cultures. Mail returned from address above; no forwarding address available. **Principle Officers and Managers:** Margaret S. Nichols, President; Peggy O'Neill, Vice-President and Secretary; H. S. Van Norman, Treasurer. **Discounts:** Bookstores & Libraries - 20%. **Selected Titles:** *Multicultural Resources for Children, Preschool through Elementary School: Bibliography in the Areas of Black, Spanish-Speaking, Asian American, Native American and Pacific Island Cultures* by Margaret S. Nichols and Peggy O'Neill.

★3947★
Muslim Broadcasting Syndicate
520 Feura Bush Rd.
PO Box 71
Glenmont, NY 12077 Phone: (518)475-0437

Description: Publisher of books about African Americans and the Muslim faith. **Principle Officers and Managers:** Warithu-Deen Umar, Pres. **Selected Titles:** *The Name Game: The Book of Lost Names*, by Warithu-Deen Umar.

★3948★
National Center for Urban Ethnic Affairs
PO Box 20
Washington, DC 20064 Phone: (202)232-3600

Description: Established to develop neighborhood programs and policies which are grounded in the appreciation of ethnic cultural diversity. **Principle Officers and Managers:** John A. Kromkowski, President. **Selected Titles:** *Reclaiming the Inner City, Reversing Urban Decline*, both by Ed Marciniak; *Community Development Credit Union Handbook* by Steve Schanback; *A Guide to the Language of Neighborhoods* by William Watman; *The Self-Help Bridge: A Manual for Support Groups for the Jobless* by Ellie Wegener; *Non-Profits with Hard Hats: Building Affordable Housing* by Kelly, Kuehn, and Marciniak.

★3949★
Network Communications, Inc.
9880 Via Pasar, Ste. F
San Diego, CA 92126-4558 Phone: (619)566-2324

Description: Publishes on affirmative action and equal employment opportunity. Reaches market through direct mail. Annual Sales: $108,000. **Principle Officers and Managers:** David J. Miramontes, President. **Discounts:** Bookstores - 40%; Libraries - 25%; Distributors - 40%. **Percentage of Sales to:** Libraries - 20%; Bookstores - 25%; Non-Book Retail Outlets - 35%; Individuals - 20%.

★3950★
New Day Press, Inc.
Karamu House
2355 E. 89th St.
Cleveland, OH 44106 Phone: (216)795-7070

Description: Publishes books on Black history and biography for children and young adults. Accepts unsolicited manuscripts. Reaches market through direct mail. **Principle Officers and Managers:** Ebraska Ceasor, President; Charlotte Durant, Vice-President; Carl Boyd, Treasurer; Shirley Hayes, Secretary. **Number of New Titles:** 1990 - 1; Total Titles in Print - 15. **Discounts:** Universal - 20% (2-5), 30% (6-30). **Percentage of Sales to:** Libraries - 40%; Bookstores - 1%; Individuals - 19%; Schools - 40%. **Selected Titles:** *Blacks in Ohio* by Mary Shepard et al.; *Ouladah the African Boy* by Suzanne Hartman; *The First Freedom Ride* by Martha L. Smith; *Walk in My Footsteps* by Martha Grooms; *Henry Box Brown* by Pamela Pruitt and Brenda Johnston; *Black Image Makers* by Edith Gaines et al.

★3951★
Open Hand Publishing Inc.
PO Box 22048
Seattle, WA 98122 Phone: (206)323-3868

Description: A literary/political press dedicated to the promotion of social change. Offers postcards. Distributes for Africa World Press. Reaches market through direct mail, reviews, and wholesalers. **Principle Officers and Managers:** P. Anna Johnson, President. **Subjects:** African-American studies, bilingual children's literature.

Discounts: Bookstores - 25% (1-4), 40% (5-49), 42% (50-99), 43% (100); Libraries - 10%; College Bookstores - 20%. **Percentage of Sales to:** Libraries - 40%; Bookstores - 40%; Non-Book Retail Outlets - 5%; Individuals - 15%. **Selected Titles:** *Mississippi to Madrid: Memoir of a Black American in the Abraham Lincoln Brigade* by James Yates; *Self-Determination: An Examination of the Question and Its Application to the African-American People, The Making of Black Revolutionaries, Sammy Younge, Jr.: The First Black College Student to Die in the Black Liberation Movement*, all by James Forman; *The Black West* by William Loren Katz; *The Invisible Empire: Impact of the Klu Klux Klan on History* by William Loren Katz.

★3952★
Paul G. Partington
7320 S. Gretna Ave.
Whittier, CA 90606 Phone: (213)695-7960

Description: Self-publisher on Black studies. **Principle Officers and Managers:** Paul G. Partington, President. **Discounts:** Please inquire. **Percentage of Sales to:** Libraries - 90%; Individuals - 10%. **Selected Titles:** *W. E. B. DuBois: A Bibliography of His Published Writings* by P. G. Partington.

★3953★
Rev. Dr. Charles L. Hoskins
St. Matthew's Episcopal Church
1401 W. Broad St.
Savannah, GA 31401 Phone: (912)234-8126

Selected Titles: *Black Episcopalians in Georgia: Strife, Struggle and Salvation*; *Been in the Storm So Long: Black Savannahians in the 1930's*, both by Charles L. Hoskins.

★3954★
Rumble, Inc.
PO Box 22151
Sacramento, CA 95822 Phone: (916)427-8705

Description: Publishes on interpersonal relationships of the Black experience. Offers the newsletter Rumble. **Principle Officers and Managers:** Grace Douglas, Publisher. **Number of New Titles:** 1988 - 1; Total Titles in Print - 1. **Discounts:** Bookstores - 40% (3). **Percentage of Sales to:** Libraries - 25%; Bookstores - 10%; Non-Book Retail Outlets - 2%; Individuals - 63%. **Selected Titles:** *The Griot: An Anthology of African Necromancers* by Grace Carter-Douglas.

★3955★
Southern Africa Project
1400 I St., NW, Ste. 400
Washington, DC 20005 Phone: (202)628-6700

Description: Private, nonprofit organization working to aid political prisoners in South Africa and to promote awareness in the U.S. of human rights violations in South Africa. **Principle Officers and Managers:** Gay McDougall, Director. **Selected Titles:** *Southern Africa: A Special Report*; *Deaths in Detention and South Africa's Security Laws; South Africa 1985: Maritial Law in the Townships.*

★3956★
Studio Museum in Harlem
Museum Shop
144 W. 125th St.
New York, NY 10027 Phone: (212)864-4500

Description: Publishes African and African-American fine arts exhibition catalogs. Reaches market through direct mail. Annual Sales: $5000. **Principle Officers and Managers:** Joan Deroko, Shop Manager; Claudette Brown, Assistant Manager. **Discounts:** Bookstores - 40% (5); Libraries - 15%. **Percentage of Sales to:** Libraries - 1%; Bookstores - 10%; Non-Book Retail Outlets - 10%; Individuals - 79%. **Selected Titles:** *Tradition and Conflict: Images of a Turbulent Decade 1963-1973* by Campbell; *Faith Ringgold: 20 Years of Painting, Sculpture, etc.* edited by M. Wallace; *Jack Whiten: Ten Years* by Henry Gelzahler; *Harlem Hey Day: The Photography of J. Vanderzee* by Dawson and Thomas; *Ritual and Myth: A Survey of African American Art* by Driskell and Hammond; *Howardena Pindell: Odyssey* by Terrie Rouse.

★3957★
Synthesis Publications, Inc.
PO Box 40099
San Francisco, CA 94140 Phone: (415)550-1284

Description: Publishes and distributes books and journals for classroom and personal use on domestic and international politics, world economy, women, criminology, and other social issues from a critical social perspective. Reaches market through direct mail. Annual Sales: $150,000. **Principle Officers and Managers:** Richard Schauffler, Business Manager and Editor; Elizabeth Sutherland Martinez, Senior Editor. **Discounts:** Bookstores - 40%; University Bookstores - 20%; Distributors - by arrangement. **Percentage of Sales to:** Libraries - 19%; Bookstores - 32%; Individuals - 42%; Classrooms - 7%. **Selected Titles:** *The New Black Vote: Politics and Power in Four American Cities* edited by Rod Bush; *Black Socialist Preacher: The Teachings of Rev. George Washington Woodbey* edited by Philip S. Foner.

★3958★
Tivoli Publishing Co.
2718 Brooklyn Ave.
PO Box 412164
Kansas City, MO 64141 Phone: (816)923-2546

Description: Publishes works by African-Americans. Accepts unsolicited manuscripts. Reaches market through direct mail and Baker & Taylor. Annual Sales: $1500. **Principle Officers and Managers:** Telester F. Powell, Owner. **Number of New Titles:** 1990 - 1, 1991 (est.) - 1; Total Titles in Print - 2. **Subjects:** Poetry, short stories, folktales. **Percentage of Sales to:** Libraries - 3%; Bookstores - 15%; Non-Book Retail Outlets - 10%; Individuals - 50%; Others - 22%. **Selected Titles:** *The Awakening, Awaiting Your Arrival, Trials and Tribulations: Looking for a Miracle*, all by Telester F. Kelly-Powell; *Modern Marriage: How They Keep It Together* by Rose S. Bell.

★3959★
Unicorn/Fitzgerald
808 Charlotte St.
Fredericksburg, VA 22401 Phone: (703)371-3253

Principle Officers and Managers: Ruth Coder Fitzgerald, General Manager. **Subjects:** Local history. **Discounts:** Bookstores - 40% (in lots of 10). **Percentage of Sales to:** Libraries - 25%; Bookstores - 10%; Non-Book Retail Outlets - 30%; Individuals - 25%; Mail Orders - 10%. **Selected Titles:** *A Different Story: A Black History of Fredericksburg, Stafford, and Spotsylvania, Virginia* by Ruth Coder Fitzgerald.

★3960★
Universal Black Writer Press
PO Box 5, Radio City Sta.
New York, NY 10101-0005 Phone: (718)774-4379

Description: Publishes historical and cultural information, books, audio tapes, and materials for Black writers and readers of Black literature. Also publishes the works of contemporary African-descended writers, Black history quizzes, and a black travel newsletter. Conducts seminars and offers consultation on small press publishing. Reaches market through direct mail and reviews. **Principle Officers and Managers:** Linda Cousins, Publisher and Editor; Shola Akintolayo, Marketing Director; Sonia Diaz, Associate Editor. **Number of New Titles:** 1988 - 3, 1989 - 6; Total Titles in Print - 6. **Discounts:** Bookstores - 40%; Libraries - 20%. **Percentage of Sales to:** Libraries - 35%; Bookstores - 15%; Individuals - 50%. **Selected Titles:** *Ancient Black Youth and Elders Reborn: Poetry, Short Stories, Oral Histories, and Deeper Thoughts of African American Youth and Elders* edited by Linda Cousins; *Ancestral Poetsong: Poetworks of Black History, Love, Laughter, and Life* (tape), *A Son Born from Jim-Lee and Me* (tape), both by Linda Cousins.

★3961★
University of California, Los Angeles
Center for Afro-American Studies
3111 Campbell Hall
Los Angeles, CA 90024 Phone: (213)825-3528

Description: The publication program's primary purpose is to guarantee wider access to writing and research on issues that are relevant to Afro-Americans. Also publishes CAAS Newsletter, Minority Economic Development Paper Series, and offers notecards. Accepts unsolicited manuscripts. Reaches market through direct mail and reviews. Annual Sales: $40,000. **Principle Officers and Managers:** Claudia Mitchell-Kernan, Academic Editor; Mona Dallas Merideth, Managing Editor; Ross Steiner, Assistant Editor. **Number of New Titles:** 1988 - 2, 1989 - 1, 1990 (est.) - 3; Total Titles in Print - 11. **Discounts:** Bookstores - 20% (1-4), 30% (5-49), 35% (50); Textbook Sales - 20%. **Percentage of Sales to:** Libraries - 25%; Bookstores - 65%; Individuals - 10%. **Selected Titles:** *Castro, the Blacks, and Africa* by Carlos Moore; *Deep South* by Allison Davis, Burleigh and Mary Gardner; *Workers and Workplace Dynamics in Reconstruction Era Atlanta* by Jonathan W. Mcleod; *Black Folk Hear and There,* Vols. 1-2 by St. Clair Drake; *Black Character in the Brazilian Novel* by Giorgio Marotti; *Minority Economic Development Series.*

★3962★
University Place Book Shop
821 Broadway
New York, NY 10003 Phone: (212)254-5998

Description: Publishes mostly reprints on Blacks, Africa, and chess. **Principle Officers and Managers:** Walter Goldwater, Owner; William P. French, Manager. **Discounts:** Bookstores - 20% (single copies).

★3963★
Vera Pigee
2234 Edison St.
Detroit, MI 48206 Phone: (313)883-6618

Description: Self-publisher of books on the history of the civil rights movement. Reaches market through commission representatives, direct mail, and telephone sales. **Principle Officers and Managers:** Vera Pigee, Author, Manager. **Selected Titles:** *The Struggle of Struggles,* Parts I-II by Vera Pigee.

★3964★
Who's Who in Black Corporate America
1629 K St., NW, Ste. 596
Washington, DC 20006 Phone: (202)244-2100

Description: Mail returned from address above; no forwarding address available. **Principle Officers and Managers:** William Reed, Publisher; Edna Duggett, Editor; Wylie Wilson, Managing Editor. **Percentage of Sales to:** Libraries - 50%; Individuals - 40%; Organizations - 10%. **Selected Titles:** *Who's Who in Black Corporate America* by Edna D. Doggett.

★3965★
Wyndham Hall Press, Inc.
PO Box 1129
52857 C.R. 21
Bristol, IN 46507 Phone: (219)848-7920

Description: An academic/scholarly publisher of college and university monographs. Accepts unsolicited manuscripts that are typed. Reaches market through direct mail, distributors, and wholesalers. Annual Sales: $150,000. **Principle Officers and Managers:** John H. Morgan, President. **Number of New Titles:** 1988 - 25, 1989 - 40, 1990(est.) - 20; Total Titles in Print - 165. **Subjects:** Ethnic studies, social-behavioral-political sciences, history, religion, philosophy, education. **Discounts:** Bookstores - 20%; Libraries - None. **Percentage of Sales to:** Libraries - 50%; Bookstores - 40%; Individuals - 10%. **Selected Titles:** *The American School and the Melting Pot* by Isser and Schwartz; *Black Theatre* by Molette and Molette; *Single Parents in Black America* by Annie S. Barnes.

(16) BROADCAST MEDIA

Entries in this chapter are arranged alphabetically by call letters or network name within states and divided into three categories: Networks, Radio Stations, and Television Stations. See the User's Guide at the front of this directory for additional information.

NETWORKS

★3966★
Black Entertainment Television (BET)
1899 9th St. NW
Washington, DC 20018 Phone: (202)636-2400
Robert L. Johnson, Pres.

★3967★
National Black Network
10 Columbus Cir.
New York, NY 10019 Phone: (212)586-0610
Sydney L. Small, Chairman

★3968★
Sheridan Broadcasting Network
1 Times Sq. Plaza, 18th Fl.
New York, NY 10036 Phone: (212)575-0099
E.J. "Jay" Williams Jr., Pres.

RADIO STATIONS

Alabama

★3969★
WAGG-AM
424 16th St., N.
Birmingham, AL 35203 Phone: (205)324-3356
Frequency: 1320. **Network Affiliation:** Independent. **Format:** Religious. **Operating Hours:** Sunrise-Sunset. **Key Personnel:** Kirkwood Balton, Gen.Mgr. **Owner:** Booker T. Washington Broadcasting Service, Inc.

★3970★
WAPZ-AM
Rte. 6, Box 43
Wetumpka, AL 36092 Phone: (205)567-2251
Frequency: 1250. **Network Affiliation:** National Black. **Format:** Gospel; Rhythm & Blues. **Operating Hours:** 6 a.m.-8 p.m. **Key Personnel:** Robert Henderson, Gen. Mgr. **Owner:** J&W Promotion.

★3971★
WATV-AM
Radio Plaza on Ensley Ave.
Birmingham, AL 35208 Phone: (205)780-2014
Frequency: 900. **Network Affiliation:** ABC. **Format:** Full Service/Eclectic. **Operating Hours:** Continuous. **Key Personnel:** Erskine R. Fausch, Pres./Gen.Mgr. **Owner:** Birmingham Ebony Broadcasting, Inc.

★3972★
WAYE-AM
1408 3rd Ave., W.
Birmingham, AL 35208 Phone: (205)786-9293
Frequency: Network Affiliation: Independent. **Format:** Religious (Black Gospel). **Operating Hours:** Continuous. **Key Personnel:** Toni King, Gen.Mgr. **Owner:** Willis Broadcasting.

★3973★
WBIL-FM
PO Box 666
Tuskegee, AL 36083 Phone: (205)727-2100
Frequency: 95.9. **Format:** Adult Contemporary; Rhythm & Blues; News; Urban Contemporary. **Operating Hours:** Continuous. **Key Personnel:** George Clay, Gen. Mgr.; Joanna Williams, Office Mgr.; Costee McNair, Program Dir. **Owner:** New World Communications.

★3974★
WBTG-FM
1605 Gospel Rd.
PO Box 518
Sheffield, AL 35660 Phone: (205)381-6800
Frequency: 106.3. **Network Affiliation:** USA Radio. **Format:** Southern Gospel. **Operating Hours:** 5 a.m.-midnight; 10% network, 90% local. **Key Personnel:** Paul Slatton, Owner/Gen. Mgr.; Chad Payne, News Dir.; Tomette Boston, Program Dir.; Jerimy Edgils, Music Dir.; Johny Lee Edgils, Sales Mgr.; Don McFall, Promotions Mgr. **Owner:** Slatton & Associates Broadcasters Inc.

★3975★
WENN-FM
424 16th St., N.
Birmingham, AL 35203 Phone: (205)324-3356
Frequency: 107.7 **Network Affiliation:** Independent. **Format:** Urban Contemporary. **Operating Hours:** Continuous. **Key Personnel:** Kirkwood Balton, Gen.Mgr. **Owner:** Booker T. Washington Broadcasting Service, Inc.

★3976★
WMMV-FM
1050 Government St.
Mobile, AL 36604 Phone: (205)433-9577
Frequency: 105.5. **Network Affiliation:** CBS Radio; Sheridan Broadcasting. **Format:** Urban Contemporary. **Operating Hours:** Continuous. **Key Personnel:** W.H. Phillips, Gen. Mgr.; Sonny Love, Operations; Gwin Chesnutt, Sales Mgr. **Owner:** Faulkner-Phillips Media Inc.

★3977★
WNPT-FM
229 3rd St.
Northport, AL 35476 Phone: (205)758-3311
Frequency: 102.9 & 100.1. **Network Affiliation:** NBC Radio. **Format:** Talk; News; Sports; Rhythm & Blues. **Operating Hours:** Continuous; 10% network, 90% local. **Key Personnel:** Ellis J. Parker, Gen. Mgr.; Don Hartley, News Dir.; Jeff Christian, Sports Dir. **Owner:** W.A.N.R., Inc.

★3978★
WTQX-AM
1 Valley Creek Circle
Selma, AL 36701 Phone: (205)872-1570
Frequency: 1570. **Format:** Rhythm & Blues; Gospel. **Operating Hours:** Sunrise-sunset. **Key Personnel:** Bob Bailey, Gen. Mgr. **Owner:** WTQX Radio.

★3979★
WTSK-AM
142 Skyland Blvd.
Tuscaloosa, AL 35405 Phone: (205)345-7200
Frequency: 790. **Network Affiliation:** National Black. **Format:** Black traditional. **Operating Hours:** Continuous. **Key Personnel:** Houston Pearce, Gen. Mgr.

★3980★
WTUG-FM
142 Skyland Blvd.
Tuscaloosa, AL 35405 Phone: (205)345-7200
Frequency: 92.7. **Network Affiliation:** National Black. **Format:** Urban Contemporary. **Operating Hours:** Continuous. **Key Personnel:** Houston Pearce, Gen. Mgr.

★3981★
WZZA-AM
1570 Woodmont Dr.
Tuscumbia, AL 35674 Phone: (205)381-1862
Frequency: 1410. **Network Affiliation:** National Black. **Format:** Urban Contemporary; Talk; News; Soul Top 40; Gospel. **Operating Hours:** Continuous; 10% network, 90% local. **Key Personnel:** Bob Carl Bailey, Pres./Gen., Program and Promotions Mgr.; Delesa Garner, Music Dir.; Odessa Bailey, Mgr. **Owner:** Muscle Shoals Broadcasting.

Arizona

★3982★
KJZZ-FM
1435 S. Dobson Rd.
Mesa, AZ 85202 Phone: (602)834-5627
Frequency: 91.5. **Network Affiliation:** National Public Radio (NPR). **Format:** Jazz; News. **Operating Hours:** Continuous; 30% network, 70% local. **Key Personnel:** Carl Matthusen, Gen. Mgr.; Scott Williams, Program Dir.; Gordon Helm, News Dir.; Bill Shedd, Music Dir.; Bob Glazar, Development Dir. **Owner:** Maricopa Community College District.

Arkansas

★3983★
KCAT-AM
1207 W. 6th St.
Pine Bluff, AR 71602 Phone: (501)534-5000
Frequency: 1340. **Network Affiliation:** Southern Broadcasting; National Black. **Format:** Urban Contemporary; Religious. **Operating Hours:** Continuous; 90% network, 10% local. **Key Personnel:** J.B. Scanlon, Owner/Gen. Mgr. **Owner:** J.B. Scanlon.

★3984★
KELD-AM
2525 Northwest Ave.
El Dorado, AR 71730 Phone: (501)863-6162
Frequency: 1400. **Network Affiliation:** NBC Radio. **Format:** Urban Contemporary. **Operating Hours:** 5 a.m.-midnight. **Key Personnel:** Bob Parks, Gen. Mgr.; Jim Lewis, News Dir. **Owner:** Noalmark Broadcasting Corp.

★3985★
KITA-AM
723 W. 14th St.
Little Rock, AR 72202 Phone: (501)375-1440
Frequency: 1440. **Network Affiliation:** International Broadcasting; Ambassador Inspirational Radio; Moody Broadcasting. **Format:** Talk; Ethnic; Religious. **Operating Hours:** 6 a.m.-1:30 a.m.; 15% network, 85% local. **Key Personnel:** Gary Vaile, Gen. Mgr.; Jim Yoder, Program Dir.; Ulysses Robinson, Music Dir.; Kenneth Robinson, Program Mgr. **Owner:** Kita Ltd. Partnership.

★3986★
KJWH-AM
214 Van Buren
Camden, AR 71701 Phone: (501)836-9393
Frequency: 1450. **Network Affiliation:** Arkansas; ABC Radio. **Format:** News; Religious; Urban Contemporary. **Operating Hours:** 10% network, 90% local. **Key Personnel:** Gary Coates, Owner; Don Jackson, News Director; Carna Coates, Bookkeeper.

★3987★
KLRC-FM
John Brown University
PO Box 3100
Siloam Springs, AR 72761 Phone: (501)524-3131
Frequency: 101.1. **Network Affiliation:** USA Radio. **Format:** Jazz; Religious (Contemporary Christian). **Operating Hours:** 6 a.m.-midnight; 8% network, 92% local. **Key Personnel:** Mike Flynn, Mgr.; Rick Sparks, Program Dir. **Owner:** John Brown University.

★3988★
KMTL-AM
2808 E. Kiehl Ave.
North Little Rock, AR 72116 Phone: (501)835-1554
Frequency: 760. **Format:** Gospel. **Operating Hours:** Sunrise-sunset. **Key Personnel:** George Domrese, Owner.

★3989★
KMZX-FM
314 Main St., Ste. 106
North Little Rock, AR 72114 Phone: (501)376-1063
Frequency: 106.3. **Network Affiliation:** National Black. **Format:** Urban Contemporary (Adult). **Operating Hours:** Continuous. **Key Personnel:** Jon K. Bonadies, Gen. Mgr.; Don Michaels, Operations Dir. **Owner:** Lonoke Broadcasting, Inc.

★3990★
KNEA-AM
603 W. Matthews
Jonesboro, AR 72401 Phone: (501)932-8381
Frequency: 970. **Network Affiliation:** Arkansas. **Format:** Gospel Top 40. **Operating Hours:** 6 a.m.-10 p.m.; 20% network, 80% local. **Key Personnel:** Paul R. Boden, Gen. Mgr.; Donna K. Rogers, Station Mgr.; Jerry Jay, Program Dir.; Greg Dills, Music Dir.; Patsy O'Brien, Sales Mgr. **Owner:** Paul R. Boden.

★3991★
KXAR-FM
Hwy. 29 at I-30
Hope, AR 71801 Phone: (501)777-3601
Frequency: 101.7. **Network Affiliation:** Sheridan Broadcasting. **Format:** Urban Contemporary. **Operating Hours:** Continuous; 5% network, 95% local. **Key Personnel:** Bill Hoglund, Pres.; Dorian Cox, News Dir.; W.A. "Big Daddy" Griffin, Program Dir. **Owner:** KdB, Inc.

★3992★
WJAK-AM
1504 Dogwood Dr.
Jacksonville, AR 72076
Frequency: 1460. **Network Affiliation:** National Black. **Format:** Religious. **Operating Hours:** Sunrise-sunset; 25% network, 75% local. **Key Personnel:** Bishop Harold H. Allen, Owner/Program Dir.; Martha Campbell, Gen. Mgr./Program Dir. **Owner:** Bishop Harold H. Allen.

California

★3993★
KACE-FM
161 N. LaBrea Ave.
Inglewood, CA 90301 Phone: (213)330-3100
Frequency: 103.9. **Network Affiliation:** Independent. **Format:** Urban Contemporary. **Operating Hours:** Continuous. **Key Personnel:** Willie Davis, Pres.; Anne Davis, Gen. Mgr. **Owner:** All Pro Broadcasting Inc.

★3994★
KBFN-AM
601 Ashby Ave.
Berkeley, CA 94710 Phone: (415)848-7713
Frequency: 1400. **Network Affiliation:** Money Radio. **Format:** Financial News. **Operating Hours:** Continuous. **Key Personnel:** Harvey Stone, Gen.Mgr. **Owner:** Inner City Broadcasting Corp. **Formerly:** KBLX-AM.

★3995★
KBLX-FM
601 Ashby Ave.
Berkeley, CA 94710 Phone: (415)848-7713
Frequency: 102.9 **Network Affiliation:** Independent. **Format:** Jazz; Ethnic. **Operating Hours:** Continuous. **Key Personnel:** Harvey Stone, Gen.Mgr. **Owner:** Inner City Broadcasting Corp. **Formerly:** KRE-FM.

★3996★
KDAY-AM
1700 N. Alvarado Blvd.
Los Angeles, CA 90026 Phone: (213)665-1105
Frequency: 1580. **Network Affiliation:** ABC Radio; National Black; Unistar. **Format:** Urban Contemporary. **Operating Hours:** Continuous. **Key Personnel:** Ed Kerby, Gen. Mgr.; Rochelle Lucas, Gen. Sales Mgr.; Jack Patterson, Program Dir.; Ron Russ, Chief Engineer. **Owner:** Heritage Media Corp.

★3997★
KDIA-AM
100 Swan Way
Oakland, CA 94621 Phone: (415)633-2548
Frequency: 1310. **Network Affiliation:** Independent. **Format:** Full Service/Eclectic. **Operating Hours:** Continuous. **Key Personnel:** Aleta Dwyer-Carpenter, V.Pres./Gen.Mgr. **Owner:** Ragan Henry. **Formerly:** KWBR-AM.

★3998★
KEST-AM
1231 Market St.
San Francisco, CA 94103 Phone: (415)626-5585
Frequency: 1450. **Network Affiliation:** Independent. **Format:** New Age; Talk; Ethnic. **Operating Hours:** Continuous. **Key Personnel:** Allan Schultz, Gen.Mgr. **Owner:** Douglas Broadcasting.

★3999★
KGFJ-AM
1100 S. LaBrea Ave.
Los Angeles, CA 90019 Phone: (213)930-9090
Frequency: 1230. **Network Affiliation:** Sheridan Broadcasting. **Format:** Urban Contemporary; Oldies. **Operating Hours:** Continuous. **Key Personnel:** Edward Evans, Gen. Sales Mgr.; Darryl Cox, Program Dir.; Shirley Jackson, Operations Mgr.; William Shearer, Gen. Mgr.; Licia Shearer, Public Service; Theresa Randle Price, Retail Sales Mgr. **Owner:** East-West Broadcasting.

★4000★
KJAZ-FM
1131 Harbor Bay Pkwy.
Alameda, CA 94501 Phone: (415)769-4800
Frequency: 92.7. **Network Affiliation:** Independent. **Format:** Jazz. **Operating Hours:** Continuous; 100% local. **Key Personnel:** Jack Sweeney, Gen. Sales Mgr.; Peter McCoy, Gen. Mgr.; Tim Hodges, Program Dir.; Bob Parlocha, Music Dir.; Denise Culver-Nelson, Promotions Dir. **Owner:** Ronald H. Cowan.

★4001★
KJLH-FM
3847 Crenshaw Blvd.
Los Angeles, CA 90008 Phone: (213)299-5960
Frequency: 102.3. **Network Affiliation:** ABC Radio. **Format:** Urban Contemporary. **Operating Hours:** Continuous. **Key Personnel:** Carl Farley, Gen. Sales Mgr.; Karen Slade, Gen. Mgr.; Eleanor Williams, Promotions Dir. **Owner:** Stevland Morris.

★4002★
KKAM-AM
2020 E. McKinley Ave.
Fresno, CA 93703 Phone: (209)266-9448
Frequency: 1340. **Network Affiliation:** CBS Radio. **Format:** Sports; Rhythm & Blues. **Operating Hours:** Continuous. **Key Personnel:** Ed Prince, Gen. Mgr.; Jeff Davis, Program Dir. **Owner:** Radio Fresno Inc.

★4003★
KKBT-FM
6735 Yucca St.
Hollywood, CA 90028 Phone: (213)466-9566
Frequency: 92.3. **Format:** Urban Contemporary. **Operating Hours:** Continuous. **Key Personnel:** Jim de Castro, Pres./Gen. Mgr.; Liz Kiley, Operations Mgr.; Mike Stradford, Program Dir.; Frank Miniaci, Music Dir.; Shirley Clark, News Dir. **Owner:** Evergreen Media Corp.

★4004★
KKGO-FM
1500 Cotner
Los Angeles, CA 90025 Phone: (213)478-5540
Frequency: 105.1. **Network Affiliation:** Independent. **Format:** Jazz. **Operating Hours:** Continuous. **Key Personnel:** Saul Levine, Gen. Mgr. **Owner:** Mount Wilson FM Broadcasters, Inc.

★4005★
KMJC-AM
4875 N. Harbor Dr.
San Diego, CA 92106-2304
Frequency: 910. **Network Affiliation:** Independent. **Format:** Talk; Ethnic; Religious; Urban Contemporary. **Operating Hours:** Continuous; 100% local. **Key Personnel:** Carl W. James, Station Mgr.; Dick Warren, Chief Engineer; David Manzi, Public Service and Music Dir.; Roger Good, Public Affairs Dir. **Owner:** Bartell Hotels.

★4006★
KMYX-FM
255 W. Stanley Ave.
Ventura, CA 93002 Phone: (805)653-5111
Frequency: 105.5. **Format:** Urban Contemporary. **Operating Hours:** Continuous. **Key Personnel:** Bob Richards, Program Dir. & Dir. of Operations; John Meyerholz, Sports Dir., News Dir.; Rick Hoffman, Gen. Sales Mgr. **Owner:** Eric/Chandler Communications of Ventura.

★4007★
KRML-AM
PO Box 22440
Carmel, CA 93922 Phone: (408)624-6431
Frequency: 1410. **Network Affiliation:** Independent. **Format:** Jazz. **Operating Hours:** 6 a.m.-midnight. **Key Personnel:** Gilbert Wisdom, Gen. Mgr.; Ed Crankshaw, Operations Manager. **Owner:** Gilbert Wisdom.

★4008★
KSDS-FM
1313 12th Ave.
San Diego, CA 92101 Phone: (619)234-1062
Frequency: 88.3. **Network Affiliation:** Independent. **Format:** Jazz. **Operating Hours:** 6 a.m.-midnight Sun.-Thur., 6 a.m.-2 a.m. Fri.-Sat.; 100% local. **Key Personnel:** James Dark, Gen. Mgr.; Hope Shaw, Station Mgr.; Tony Sisti, Program Dir.; Phyllis Hegeman, Music and Promotions Dir.; Stephanie Donavon, News Dir.; Fred Lewis, Sports Dir. **Owner:** San Diego Community College District. Ylvisaker; Precolonial Senegal: The Jolof Kingdom by Eunice Charles; Nama/Namibia: The Diary and Letters of Nama Chief Hendrik Witbooi edited by Georg M.

Gugelberger; Discovering the African Past: Essays in Honor of Daniel McCall edited by Norman Bennett; Agrarian Reform in Ethiopia by Allan Hober.

★4009★
KSOL-FM
1730 S. Amphlett Blvd.
San Mateo, CA 94402 Phone: (415)341-8177
Frequency: 107.7. **Network Affiliation:** Independent. **Format:** Urban Contemporary. **Operating Hours:** Continuous. **Key Personnel:** Ken Shubat, Vice President and Gen. Mgr.; Bernie Moody, Operations Manager. **Owner:** United Broadcasting Co. State Programs and Services for California's Elderly; The Black Family: Legislative Hearing.

★4010★
KUOR-FM
1200 E. Colton Ave.
Redlands, CA 92374 Phone: (714)792-0721
Frequency: 89.1. **Network Affiliation:** Independent. **Format:** Jazz. **Operating Hours:** Continuous. **Key Personnel:** William Bruns, Gen. Mgr.; Scott Sterl, Bus. Dir. **Owner:** University of Redlands.

Connecticut

★4011★
WKND-AM
544 Windsor Ave.
PO Box 1480
Windsor, CT 06095 Phone: (203)688-6221
Frequency: 1480. **Network Affiliation:** Sheridan Broadcasting. **Format:** Full Service; Urban Contemporary. **Operating Hours:** 6 a.m.-6 p.m. during winter; 6 a.m.-8:30 p.m. during summer. **Key Personnel:** Byron McClanahan, Gen. Sales Mgr.; Melonae McLean, Program Dir.; Lloyd Wimbish, News Dir.; Marion Thornton, Gen. Mgr.; John Henry, Sales Mgr. **Owner:** Hartcom Inc.

★4012★
WNHC-AM
112 Washington Ave.
North Haven, CT 06473 Phone: (203)234-1340
Frequency: 1340. **Format:** Urban Contemporary; Adult Contemporary. **Operating Hours:** Continuous; 100% local. **Key Personnel:** Edith Acabbo-Willis, Pres./Gen. Mgr.; Stan Boston, Program Dir. **Owner:** Willis Communications, Inc.

★4013★
WQQQ-FM
100 Prospect St.
Stamford, CT 06901 Phone: (203)327-1400
Frequency: 96.7. **Format:** Jazz. **Operating Hours:** Continuous. **Key Personnel:** Warren Lada, V.P./Gen. Mgr.; Kevin Collins, Gen. Sales Mgr.; Bob Marrone, Program Dir. **Owner:** Chase Broadcasting. et al.; Holding Youth Accountable by Reed and Stevens; Split Second Decisions: Shootings by and of Chicago Police by Geller and Karales; You've Got to Be Strong: A Report on the Cook County Experimental Domestic Violence Court by Kantor et al.

★4014★
WYBC-FM
165 Elm St.
New Haven, CT 06520 Phone: (203)432-4116
Frequency: 94.3. **Network Affiliation:** Independent. **Format:** Jazz; Urban Contemporary; Alternative/New Music/Progressive. **Operating Hours:** Continuous. **Key Personnel:** Elizabeth Bermel, Exec. Dir. **Owner:** Yale Broadcasting Co. Inc.

District of Columbia

★4015★
WDCU-FM
4200 Connecticut Ave. NW
Washington, DC 20008 Phone: (202)282-7588
Frequency: 90.1. **Network Affiliation:** Independent. **Format:** Jazz; Public Radio. **Operating Hours:** Continuous. **Key Personnel:** Edith Smith, Gen. Mgr.; Stephanie Jordan, Promotions Dir.; Ernest White, Community and Public Affairs Dir.; Faunee, Asst. Program Dir. **Owner:** University of the District of Columbia.

★4016★
WHUR-FM
529 Bryant St. NW
Washington, DC 20059 Phone: (202)806-3500
Frequency: 96.3. **Format:** Urban Contemporary. **Operating Hours:** Continuous. **Key Personnel:** Millard J. Watkins, III, Gen. Mgr.; Bobby Bennett, Program Dir.; S. Jeannett Tyce, Gen. Sales Mgr.; Ellis Terry, Jr., Operations Dir.; Barbara Jacobs, Traffic Mgr.; Patrick Ellis, Production Dir.; Bill Christian, News Dir. **Owner:** Howard University.

★4017★
WKYS-FM
4001 Nebraska Ave., NW
Washington, DC 20015 Phone: (202)686-9300
Frequency: 93.9 **Network Affiliation:** Independent. **Format:** Adult Contemporary; Contemporary Hit Radio (CHR); Urban Contemporary. **Operating Hours:** Continuous. **Key Personnel:** Skip Finley, Pres. **Owner:** Albimar Communications.

★4018★
WMMJ-FM
400 H St. NE
Washington, DC 20015 Phone: (202)675-4800
Frequency: 102.3. **Network Affiliation:** NBC Radio; Sheridan Broadcasting. **Format:** Adult Urban Contemporary. **Operating Hours:** Continuous. **Key Personnel:** Alfred Liggins, Gen. Mgr.; Paul Porter, Gen. Mgr.; Bob Alston, National Sales Mgr. **Owner:** Almic Broadcasting.

★4019★
WOL-AM
400 H St. NE
Washington, DC 20015 Phone: (202)675-4800
Frequency: 1450. **Network Affiliation:** NBC Radio; Sheridan Broadcasting. **Format:** Adult Urban Contemporary; Talk. **Operating Hours:** Continuous. **Key Personnel:** Alfred Liggins, Gen. Mgr.; J.J. Starr, Program Dir.; Bob Alston, National Sales Mgr. **Owner:** Almic Broadcasting.

★4020★
WUST-AM
815 V St. NW
Washington, DC 20001 Phone: (202)462-0011
Frequency: 1120. **Network Affiliation:** National Black. **Format:** Gospel. **Operating Hours:** Sunrise-sunset. **Key Personnel:** Lou Hankins, Gen. Mgr./Program Dir.

★4021★
WYCB-AM
529 14th St. NW, Ste. 228
Washington, DC 20045 Phone: (202)737-6400
Frequency: 1340. **Network Affiliation:** Mutual Broadcasting System. **Format:** Gospel and Inspirational. **Operating Hours:** Continuous. **Key Personnel:** Karen Jackson, Gen. Mgr.; Don Miller, Program Dir.; Steven Grice, Traffic Mgr.

Florida

★4022★
WAMF-FM
Florida A&M University
314 Tucker Hall
Tallahassee, FL 32307 Phone: (904)599-3083
Frequency: 90.5. **Network Affiliation:** Independent. **Format:** Jazz; Ethnic; Urban Contemporary. **Operating Hours:** 7 a.m.-1 p.m. Sun.-Thur., 7 a.m.-4 p.m. Fri. and Sat.; 100% local. **Key Personnel:** Phillip Jeter, Gen. Mgr.; Phillip Keirstead, News Dir. **Owner:** Florida A&M University. by Peggy A. Moore; Detroit '64 by Harry M. Anderson; How to Celebrate Kwanza; Through Ebony Eyes.

★4023★
WANM-AM
300 W. Tennessee
Box 10174
Tallahassee, FL 32302 Phone: (904)222-1070
Frequency: 1070. **Format:** Urban Contemporary. **Operating Hours:** Sunrise-sunset. **Key Personnel:** Bob Badger, Gen. Mgr.

★4024★
WAVS-AM
4124 SW 64th Ave.
Davie, FL 33314 Phone: (305)584-1170
Frequency: 1170. **Network Affiliation:** Independent. **Format:** Ethnic (Caribbean); Urban Contemporary. **Operating Hours:** 6 a.m.-midnight; 100% local. **Key Personnel:** Dr. Roy H. Bresky, Pres.; Winsome Charlton, Office and Traffic Mgr.; Winston Barnes, Program and News Dir.; Tony Blair, Sales Mgr.; Ray A. Hooper, Gen. Mgr. **Owner:** Radio WAVS, Inc.

★4025★
WCGL-AM
70 Sherwood Sq.
Jacksonville, FL 32208-1862 Phone: (904)766-9955
Frequency: 1360. **Network Affiliation:** Independent. **Format:** Gospel. **Operating Hours:** Daytime. **Key Personnel:** Emily Timmons, Gen. Mgr.; Melvin Grace, Program Dir. **Owner:** Bob Bell.

★4026★
WEDR-FM
Box 551748
Opa-Locka, FL 33055 Phone: (305)623-7711
Frequency: 99.1. **Network Affiliation:** Independent. **Format:** Urban Contemporary. **Operating Hours:** Continuous. **Key Personnel:** Jerry Rushin, V.P./Gen. Mgr. **Owner:** WEDR Inc.

★4027★
WEXY-AM
412 W. Oakland Blvd.
Fort Lauderdale, FL 33311-1712 Phone: (305)561-1520
Frequency: 1520. **Format:** Religious; Urban Contemporary. **Operating Hours:** Continuous.

★4028★
WHJX-FM
10592 E. Balmoral Circle
Jacksonville, FL 32218 Phone: (904)696-1015
Frequency: 101.5. **Network Affiliation:** ABC Radio. **Format:** Urban Contemporary. **Operating Hours:** Continuous. **Key Personnel:** Walter G. Berry, Jr., V.P./Gen. Mgr.; Bruce Demps, Gen. Sales Mgr. **Owner:** Eagle Broadcasting Co.

★4029★
WHOG-AM
707 Dade St.
Box 496
Fernandina Beach, FL 32034 Phone: (904)261-6157
Frequency: 1570. **Network Affiliation:** Independent. **Format:** Country; Urban Contemporary after 5 p.m. **Operating Hours:** 7 a.m.-midnight. **Key Personnel:** Mark Hogan, Gen. Mgr./Program Dir. **Owner:** Northeast Florida Broadcasting, Inc.

★4030★
WHQT-FM
3200 Ponce de Leon Blvd.
Coral Gables, FL 33134 Phone: (305)445-5411
Frequency: 105.1. **Network Affiliation:** Independent. **Format:** Contemporary Hit Radio (CHR)/Urban Contemporary. **Operating Hours:** Continuous. **Key Personnel:** Chuck Goldmark, Gen. Mgr.

★4031★
WIQI-FM
345 Office Plaza
Tallahassee, FL 32301-2729
Frequency: 101.7. **Network Affiliation:** National Black; Southern Broadcasting. **Format:** Urban Contemporary. **Operating Hours:** Continuous. **Key Personnel:** Lee Clear, Gen. Mgr.

★4032★
WJHM-FM
434 Sanlando Center, No. 124
Longwood, FL 32779-4299 Phone: (407)788-1400
Frequency: 101.9. **Network Affiliation:** NBC Radio. **Format:** Urban Contemporary. **Operating Hours:** Continuous; 3% network, 97% local. **Key Personnel:** Greg Reed David Donahue, Gen. Mgr.; Scott Farkas, Gen. Sales Mgr.; Duff Lindsay, Program Dir.; Cedric Hollywood, Music Dir.; Rebecca Randall, News Dir.; Steve Williamson, Promotions Dir. **Owner:** Beasley Broadcast Group.

★4033★
WJST-FM
3101 W. Hwy. 98
Panama City, FL 32401 Phone: (904)785-9594
Frequency: 94.5. **Network Affiliation:** Florida Radio. **Format:** Southern Gospel. **Operating Hours:** Continuous; 10% network, 90% local. **Key Personnel:** Ron Kight, Gen. Mgr.; Clif Desmond, Program Dir. **Owner:** Asterisk Broadcasting, Inc.

★4034★
WLIT-AM
3033 Riviera Dr., No. 200
Naples, FL 33940-4134 Phone: (803)248-9040
Frequency: 1330. **Format:** Urban Contemporary. **Operating Hours:** 6 a.m.-midnight; 10% network, 90% local. **Key Personnel:** Randall Ramsey, Station Mgr.; Michael Burgess, Program Dir.; Rahim Akram, Music Dir.; Cherly Hall, Promotional Director. **Owner:** Beasley Broadcast Group.

★4035★
WLOQ-FM
170 W. Fairbanks Ave.
PO Box 2085
Winter Park, FL 32789 Phone: (407)647-5557
Frequency: 103.1. **Network Affiliation:** Independent. **Format:** Jazz. **Operating Hours:** Continuous; 5% network, 95% local. **Key Personnel:** Bob Church, Program Dir.; John Gross, Music Dir.; Annetta Wilson, Promotions Dir.; M.F. Kershner, Gen. Sales Mgr. **Owner:** Herb Gross.

★4036★
WLQY-AM
2741 N. 29th Ave.
Hollywood, FL 33020 Phone: (305)921-5995
Frequency: 1320. **Format:** Religious; Hispanic; Ethnic (Haitian, Jamaican). **Operating Hours:** Continuous. **Key Personnel:** Sandra B. Herzberg, Gen. Mgr. **Owner:** Genesis Commmunications II Inc.

★4037★
WLTG-AM
1821 N. East Ave., Ste. H
Panama City, FL 32405 Phone: (904)784-9873
Frequency: 1430. **Network Affiliation:** Independent. **Format:** Urban Contemporary; Religious (Contemporary Christian). **Operating Hours:**

5:30 a.m.-9 p.m.; 100% local. **Key Personnel:** John Gay, Gen. Mgr./PSA Dir.; Peggy Gay, Office Mgr./Music Dir. **Owner:** John Gay.

★4038★
WLVJ-AM
400 J Royal Commerce Rd.
Royal Palm Beach, FL 33411 Phone: (407)793-5555
Frequency: 640. **Network Affiliation:** USA Radio; Sun Radio; CNN Radio. **Format:** Gospel; Talk; Adult Contemporary; News;. **Operating Hours:** 6 a.m-1 a.m. 32% network, 12% local. **Key Personnel:** Stanley Smelt, Program Dir.; Wayne Nauman, Gen. Mgr. **Owner:** South Florida Radio.

★4039★
WMBM-AM
814 1st St.
Miami Beach, FL 33139 Phone: (305)672-1100
Frequency: 1490. **Network Affiliation:** National Black. **Format:** Urban Contemporary. **Operating Hours:** Continuous. **Key Personnel:** Edward Margolis, Gen. Mgr.; Michael Norman, Program Dir. **Owner:** Margolis Broadcasting Co. Ltd.

★4040★
WPOM-AM
5800 N. Military Trail
West Palm Beach, FL 33407 Phone: (407)686-8000
Frequency: 1600. **Format:** Urban Contemporary. **Operating Hours:** Continuous; 100% local. **Key Personnel:** Steve Nettere, Gen. Mgr. **Owner:** WPOM Partners, Inc.

★4041★
WPUL-AM
Box 4010
South Daytona, FL 32021 Phone: (904)767-1131
Frequency: 1590. **Network Affiliation:** Independent. **Format:** Jazz; Urban Contemporary; Oldies. **Operating Hours:** 6 a.m.-9 p.m. **Key Personnel:** Charles W. Cherry, Station Manager. **Owner:** PSI Communications Inc.

★4042★
WRBD-AM
4431 Rock Island Rd.
Fort Lauderdale, FL 33319 Phone: (305)731-4800
Frequency: 1470. **Network Affiliation:** Southern Broadcasting; National Black. **Format:** Classic Rhythm & Blues/Black. **Operating Hours:** Continuous. **Key Personnel:** John Ruffin, Pres./Gen. Mgr.; Ross Alan, Program Dir.; Steven Moostry, V.P. Sales. **Owner:** John Ruffin.

★4043★
WRFA-AM
800 SE 8th Ave.
Largo, FL 34641 Phone: (813)581-7800
Frequency: 820. **Network Affiliation:** USA Radio. **Format:** Southern Gospel. **Operating Hours:** Continuous. **Key Personnel:** Norman Bie, Owner/Pres.; Eddie Bie, Station and Program Mgr.; Jim White, Music Dir.; Norma Jean Padley, News Dir.; Charles Lewallen, Sales Mgr. **Owner:** Norman Bie.

★4044★
WRXB-AM
3000 34th St. S., Ste. 206B
St. Petersburg, FL 33711 Phone: (813)864-1515
Frequency: 1590. **Network Affiliation:** Independent. **Format:** Urban Contemporary. **Operating Hours:** Continuous. **Key Personnel:** J. Eugene Danzey, Gen. Mgr.; Michael Danzey, V.P.; Brenda Facyson, Station Mgr.; John Harmon, III, Program Dir. **Owner:** J. Eugene Danzey.

★4045★
WSVE-AM
4343 Spring Grove Rd.
Jacksonville, FL 32209-3629
Frequency: 1280. **Network Affiliation:** Southern Broadcasting. **Format:** Religious. **Operating Hours:** Continuous. **Key Personnel:** Walter A. Brickhouse, V.Pres. **Owner:** Willis Broadcasting Corp. **Formerly:** WEXI-AM.

★4046★
WSWN-AM
2001 State Rd. 715
PO Box 1505
Belle Glade, FL 33430 Phone: (407)996-2063
Frequency: 900. **Network Affiliation:** ABC Radio; Florida Radio. **Format:** Urban Contemporary. **Operating Hours:** 6 a.m.-midnight; 2% network, 98% local. **Key Personnel:** Vern Thacker, Gen. Mgr.; Joe Fisher, Program Dir. **Owner:** Dee Rivers Group.

★4047★
WTMP-AM
PO Box 1101
Tampa, FL 33601 Phone: (813)626-4108
Frequency: 1150. **Network Affiliation:** Sheridan Broadcasting. **Format:** Urban Contemporary. **Operating Hours:** Continuous. **Key Personnel:** Paul Major, Gen. Mgr.; Chris Turner, Program Dir.; Pat Shaw, Gen. Sales Mgr. **Owner:** Westervile Communications.

★4048★
WTOT-AM
140 W. Lafayette St., Ste. A
PO Box 569
Marianna, FL 32446 Phone: (904)482-3046
Frequency: 980. **Network Affiliation:** NBC Radio; Florida Radio. **Format:** Urban Contemporary. **Operating Hours:** 5 a.m.-midnight; 10% network, 90% local. **Key Personnel:** Lina M. Parish, Gen. Mgr./Sports Dir.; Don Moore, News Dir.

★4049★
WTWB-AM
PO Box 7
Auburndale, FL 33823 Phone: (813)967-1570
Frequency: 1570. **Network Affiliation:** ABC Radio. **Format:** Southern Gospel. **Operating Hours:** Sunrise-sunset. **Key Personnel:** Richard Boyce, Gen. Mgr. **Owner:** L.M. Hughey.

★4050★
WVIJ-FM
3279 Sherwood Rd.
Port Charlotte, FL 33980 Phone: (813)624-5000
Frequency: 91.7. **Network Affiliation:** USA Radio. **Format:** News; Southern Gospel; Eclectic. **Operating Hours:** Continuous; 25% network, 75% local. **Key Personnel:** Dan Kolenda, Jr., Pres./Gen. Mgr.; John Kolenda, Program Dir.; James Kolenda, Production Dir. **Owner:** Port Charlotte Educational Broadcasting Foundation Inc.

★4051★
WWAB-AM
PO Box 65
Lakeland, FL 33802 Phone: (813)646-2151
Frequency: 1330. **Network Affiliation:** National Black. **Format:** Urban Contemporary; Rhythm & Blues. **Operating Hours:** Sunrise-sunset. **Key Personnel:** Dee Van Pelt, Gen. Mgr. **Owner:** WWAB Radio, Inc.

★4052★
WYFX-AM
400 Gulfstream Blvd.
Delray Beach, FL 33444 Phone: (407)737-1040
Frequency: 1040. **Network Affiliation:** Southern Broadcasting. **Format:** Urban Contemporary. **Operating Hours:** Continuous. **Key Personnel:** Gary Lewis, Pres./Gen. Mgr.; Chico Wesley, Program Dir.

★4053★
WZAZ-AM
2611 WERD Radio Dr.
Jacksonville, FL 32204 Phone: (904)389-1111
Frequency: 1400. **Network Affiliation:** Southern Broadcasting. **Format:** Urban Contemporary. **Operating Hours:** Continuous. **Key Personnel:** Mark Picus, Program Dir.; Nat Jackson, Music Dir.; J.C. Sims, Sports

Dir.; Jay Paschall, Public Service Dir.; Joe Bailey, News Dir.; Kathy Jalbert, Promotions Dir. and Office Mgr.

Georgia

★4054★
WCLK-FM
111 James P. Brawley Dr. SW
Atlanta, GA 30314 Phone: (404)880-8273
Frequency: 91.9. **Network Affiliation:** National Public Radio (NPR). **Format:** Jazz. **Operating Hours:** Continuous; 30% network, 70% local. **Key Personnel:** Tony Phillips, Sports and News Dir.; Reggie Hicks, Gen. Mgr.; Stan Washington, Public Affairsd Dir.; Amy Ward, Development Dir.; Claude Mottal, Music Dir. **Owner:** Clark Atlanta University. Muhammed on African American, all by Alexander; Cheikh Anta Diop: On History, Culture, and Technology.

★4055★
WDCY-AM
8451 S. Cherokee Blvd., Ste. B
Douglasville, GA 30134 Phone: (404)920-1520
Frequency: 1520. **Network Affiliation:** Georgia Radio. **Format:** Southern Gospel. **Operating Hours:** Sunrise-sunset; 100% local. **Key Personnel:** Jim O'Neal, Program Dir.; Delores Barker, Office Mgr.; Fred Brewer, News Dir. **Owner:** William Dunn.

★4056★
WDDO-AM
544 Mulberry St.
Macon, GA 31201 Phone: (912)746-6286
Frequency: 1240. **Network Affiliation:** National Black; Mutual Broadcasting System. **Format:** Gospel. **Operating Hours:** Continuous; 1% network, 99% local. **Key Personnel:** Fred L. Newton, Pres./Gen. Mgr.; Oscar Leverette, Station Mgr.; Willie Collins, Program Dir.

★4057★
WFXA-AM
Box 1584
Augusta, GA 30903 Phone: (803)279-2330
Frequency: 1550. **Network Affiliation:** ABC Radio; CBS Radio. **Format:** Religious; Urban Contemporary. **Operating Hours:** Continuous. **Key Personnel:** William S. Jaeger, Gen. Mgr.; Carl Conner, Jr., Natl. Program Dir.; Carroll Redd, Operations Mgr.; William Lawson, Gen. Sales Mgr. **Owner:** Davis Broadcasting Inc.

★4058★
WFXM-FM
369 2nd St.
PO Box 4527
Macon, GA 31208 Phone: (912)742-2505
Frequency: 100.1. **Format:** Urban Contemporary. **Operating Hours:** Continuous. **Key Personnel:** Gregory Davis, Pres.; Jess Branson, Sales Mgr.

★4059★
WGML-AM
Box 15
Hinesville, GA 31313 Phone: (912)368-3399
Frequency: 990. **Format:** Ethnic; Religious. **Operating Hours:** Daytime. **Key Personnel:** E.D. Steele, Mgr.

★4060★
WGOV-AM
Hwy. 84 W.
PO Box 1207
Valdosta, GA 31601 Phone: (912)242-4513
Frequency: 950. **Format:** Urban Contemporary. **Operating Hours:** Continuous; 100% local. **Key Personnel:** Jay Clark, Gen. Mgr.; Elizabeth Wisenbaker, Sales Mgr.; Harvey Moore, Program Dir.; Misty King, Traffic Dir. and Business Office Mgr.; Lamar Freeman, Public Affairs. **Owner:** Dee Rivers Group.

★4061★
WGUN-AM
PO Box 67
Decatur, GA 30031 Phone: (404)373-2521
Frequency: 1010. **Network Affiliation:** Independent. **Format:** Southern Gospel. **Operating Hours:** 6 a.m.-midnight; 100% local. **Key Personnel:** Dick Schroede. **Owner:** Dee Rivers Group.

★4062★
WHCJ-FM
Box 31404
Savannah, GA 31402 Phone: (912)356-2399
Frequency: 88.5. **Format:** Jazz. **Operating Hours:** 8 a.m.-9 p.m. Mon. through Thur.; 8 a.m.-midnight Fri. **Key Personnel:** Carol Gordon, Gen. Mgr.

★4063★
WHGH-AM
PO Box 2218
Thomasville, GA 31799 Phone: (912)228-4124
Frequency: 840. **Network Affiliation:** National Black. **Format:** Urban Contemporary. **Operating Hours:** Sunrise-sunset; 9% network, 91% local. **Key Personnel:** Curtis T. Thomas, Gen. Mgr.; Sheryl D. Walden, Office Mgr.; Arvin L. Berry, Program/Music Dir. **Owner:** Gross Broadcasting Co.

★4064★
WIGO-AM
1532 Howell Mill Rd.
Atlanta, GA 30318 Phone: (404)352-3943
Frequency: 1340. **Network Affiliation:** Sheridan Broadcasting. **Format:** Urban Contemporary; Oldies. **Operating Hours:** Continuous; 5% network, 95% local. **Key Personnel:** Dorothy Brunson, Owner; Vern Catron, Gen. Mgr. **Owner:** Dorothy Brunson.

★4065★
WIQN-AM
1826 Wynnton Rd.
Columbus, GA 31901 Phone: (404)576-3000
Frequency: 1460. **Network Affiliation:** ABC Radio. **Format:** Rhythm & Blues. **Operating Hours:** Continuous; 65% network, 35% local. **Key Personnel:** Jim Martin, Mgr.; Jerry Northington, Sales Mgr. **Owner:** JRM Broadcasting.

★4066★
WJGA-FM
PO Box 3878
Jackson, GA 30233 Phone: (404)775-3151
Frequency: 92.1. **Network Affiliation:** Independent. **Format:** Adult Contemporary 6 a.m. to 6 p.m.; Urban Contemporary 6 p.m. to 1 a.m. **Operating Hours:** 6 a.m.-1 a.m. **Key Personnel:** Don Earnhart, Gen. Mgr. **Owner:** Tarkenton Broadcasting Inc.

★4067★
WKIG-AM
226 E. Bolton St.
Glennville, GA 30427 Phone: (912)654-3580
Frequency: 1580. **Format:** Gospel. **Operating Hours:** Sunrise-sunset; 98% network, 2% local. **Key Personnel:** Judy W. Cobb, Mgr.; Keith Cobb, Program Dir. **Owner:** Tattnall County Broadcasting Co.

★4068★
WKZK-AM
No. 2 Milledge Rd.
Augusta, GA 30904 Phone: (404)738-9191
Frequency: 1600. **Network Affiliation:** Sheridan Broadcasting. **Format:** Black Gospel. **Operating Hours:** 6 a.m.-sunset. **Key Personnel:** Garfield Turner, Program Mgr.; Walter B. Robinson, Jr., Owner and Gen. Mgr.; Dora Clayton, Rep. **Owner:** Gospel Radio Inc.

★4069★
WLOV-AM
823 Berkshire Dr.
Box 400
Washington, GA 30673 Phone: (404)678-2125
Frequency: 1370. **Network Affiliation:** Satellite Music; Gannett News. **Format:** Adult Contemporary; News; Sports; Agricultural; Rhythm & Blues; Urban Contemporary. **Operating Hours:** 18 hours daily; 60% network, 40% local. **Key Personnel:** Van Bufford, Jr., Program Mgr. **Owner:** B.L. Williamson.

★4070★
WLOV-FM
823 Berkshire Dr.
Box 400
Washington, GA 30673 Phone: (404)678-2125
Frequency: 100.1. **Network Affiliation:** Satellite Radio. **Format:** Adult Contemporary; News; Sports; Agricultural; Rhythm & Blues; Urban Contemporary. **Operating Hours:** 6 a.m.-midnight; 60% network, 40% local. **Key Personnel:** Van Bufford, Program Manager. **Owner:** B.L. Williamson.

★4071★
WPGA-FM
404 Gen. C. Hodges Blvd.
PO Drawer 980
Perry, GA 31069 Phone: (912)987-2980
Frequency: 100.9. **Network Affiliation:** Independent. **Format:** Urban Contemporary. **Operating Hours:** Continuous. **Key Personnel:** Lowell Register, Gen. Mgr.; Janice Register, Bookkeeper. **Owner:** Radio Perry Inc.

★4072★
WQVE-FM
Box 434
Camilla, GA 31730 Phone: (912)294-0010
Frequency: 105.5. **Network Affiliation:** Georgia Radio. **Format:** Urban Contemporary. **Operating Hours:** Continuous; 75% network, 25% local. **Key Personnel:** Ron Allen, Gen. Mgr.; Lee Sherman, Jr., Program Dir. **Owner:** W.H. Nesmith, Jr.

★4073★
WRDW-AM
Box 1405
Augusta, GA 30903 Phone: (404)724-1480
Frequency: 1480. **Network Affiliation:** National Black. **Format:** Urban Contemporary. **Operating Hours:** Continuous. **Key Personnel:** Carl Burroughs, Gen. Mgr. **Owner:** Val-Tel Inc.

★4074★
WRDW-FM
Box 1405
Augusta, GA 30903 Phone: (404)724-1480
Frequency: 96.7. **Network Affiliation:** National Black. **Format:** Urban Contemporary. **Operating Hours:** Continuous. **Key Personnel:** Carl Burroughs, Gen. Mgr. **Owner:** Val-Tec Inc.

★4075★
WROM-AM
710 Turner-McCall Blvd., Box 1546
Rome, GA 30162 Phone: (404)291-9766
Frequency: 710. **Format:** Gospel. **Operating Hours:** Sunrise-sunset. **Key Personnel:** Parnick Jennings, Pres.; Delmas Franklin, Gen. Mgr.; Jim McRee, Sales Mgr. **Owner:** Inspiration Radio, Inc.

★4076★
WSNT-AM
PO Box 150
Sandersville, GA 31082 Phone: (912)552-5182
Frequency: 1490. **Network Affiliation:** NBC Radio. **Format:** Urban Contemporary; Country. Simulcast with WSNT-FM. **Operating Hours:** 6:00 a.m.-midnight; 10% network, 90% local. **Key Personnel:** James C. Whaley, Mgr.; Curtis Parsons, Sports Dir.; Michael Howell, News Dir. **Owner:** Cleatus Brazzell.

★4077★
WSNT-FM
PO Box 150
Sandersville, GA 31082 Phone: (912)552-5182
Frequency: 93.5. **Network Affiliation:** NBC Radio. **Format:** Urban Contemporary; Country. Simulcast with WSNT-AM. **Operating Hours:** 6:00 a.m.-midnight; 10% network, 90% local. **Key Personnel:** James C. Whaley, Mgr.; Curtis Parsons, Sports Dir.; Michael Howell, News Dir. **Owner:** Cleatus Brazzell.

★4078★
WSOK-AM
24 W. Henry St.
Savannah, GA 31401 Phone: (912)232-3322
Frequency: 1230. **Network Affiliation:** National Black; Southern Broadcasting; ABC Radio. **Format:** Religious. **Operating Hours:** Continuous; 16% network, 84% local. **Key Personnel:** Daniel Gorby, Gen. Mgr.; Jay Bryant, Operations Mgr.; Paige Grady, Gen. Sales Mgr. **Owner:** Opus Media Group.

★4079★
WTJH-AM
2146 Dodson Dr.
East Point, GA 30364 Phone: (404)344-2235
Frequency: 1260. **Network Affiliation:** National Black; Southern Broadcasting. **Format:** Religious. **Operating Hours:** 50% network, 50% local. **Key Personnel:** Judy Laney, Station Mgr.; Patricia Harris, Traffic Director; Carol Joyce, Program Manager. **Owner:** Willis Broadcasting.

★4080★
WVEE-FM
120 Ralph McGill Blvd.
Atlanta, GA 30365-6901 Phone: (404)898-8900
Frequency: 103.3. **Network Affiliation:** NBC Radio. **Format:** Urban Contemporary. **Operating Hours:** Continuous. **Key Personnel:** C.B. Rik Rogers, V.P. and Gen. Mgr.; Ralph Crossley, Gen. Sales Mgr.; Howard Foole, Assistant Gen. Mgr. Lee L. Moore edited by S. B. Jones-Hendrickson.

★4081★
WXAG-AM
2145 S. Milledge Ave.
Athens, GA 30605 Phone: (404)549-1470
Frequency: 1470. **Network Affiliation:** Sheridan Broadcasting. **Format:** Jazz; Ethnic; Urban Contemporary. **Operating Hours:** 6 a.m.-midnight. 15% network, 85% local. **Key Personnel:** Patrick J. Hogan, Sr., Gen. Mgr. and Sales Mgr.; Craig Norman, Program and News Dir. **Owner:** Larry Blount/Classical Communications Ltd.

★4082★
WXKO-AM
Hwy. 341 N.
PO Box 1150
Fort Valley, GA 31030 Phone: (912)825-5547
Frequency: 1150. **Network Affiliation:** Satellite Music. **Format:** Religious; Ethnic. **Operating Hours:** 6 a.m.-sunset. **Key Personnel:** Lamar Studstill, Gen. Mgr.; Jarrett Raegan, ., News Dir.; Rudy Carson, Sales Mgr.; Joe Willis, Program Dir. **Owner:** S and M Communications.

★4083★
WXRS-AM
Box 1590
Swainsboro, GA 30401 Phone: (912)237-1590
Frequency: 1580. **Network Affiliation:** Satellite Music. **Format:** Urban Contemporary. **Operating Hours:** Continuous; 50% network, 50% local. **Key Personnel:** Bobby Gardner, Music Dir.; Roy A. Thompson, News Dir.; Jeff Wiggins, Program Dir./Sports Dir. **Owner:** Cross Roads Radio, Inc.

★4084★
WYZE-AM
1111 Blvd. SE
Atlanta, GA 30312 Phone: (404)622-7802
Frequency: 1480. **Network Affiliation:** Georgia Radio. **Format:** Jazz; Gospel. **Operating Hours:** 6 a.m.-midnight. **Key Personnel:** Helen J. Humphries, Chief Financial Officer. **Owner:** GHB Broadcasting Corp.

Illinois

★4085★
WBEE-AM
400 E. Sibley Blvd.
Harvey, IL 60426 Phone: (708)210-3231
Frequency: 1570. **Network Affiliation:** Independent. **Format:** Jazz. **Operating Hours:** Continuous. **Key Personnel:** Charles Sherrell, Gen. Mgr. **Owner:** Mariner Broadcasters, Inc.

★4086★
WCFJ-AM
1000 Lincoln Hwy.
Ford Heights, IL 60411 Phone: (708)758-8600
Frequency: 1470. **Network Affiliation:** Independent. **Format:** Gospel; Urban Contemporary. **Operating Hours:** Continuous. **Key Personnel:** Gary Dozier, Gen. Mgr.; Darryl Chavers, Operations Mgr.;, Jr. **Owner:** Liberty Temple Full Gospel Church.

★4087★
WESL-AM
149 S. 8th St.
East St. Louis, IL 62201 Phone: (618)271-1490
Frequency: 1490. **Network Affiliation:** Sheridan Broadcasting. **Format:** Gospel. **Operating Hours:** Continuous. **Key Personnel:** Frank Davis, Pres./Gen. Mgr.; Angel Ski Morris, Program Dir.; Betty Robinson, Office Mgr. **Owner:** WESL Gateway Communications.

★4088★
WGCI-FM
332 S. Michigan Ave., Ste. 600
Chicago, IL 60604 Phone: (312)984-1400
Frequency: 107.5. **Network Affiliation:** Independent. **Format:** Urban Contemporary. **Operating Hours:** Continuous. **Key Personnel:** Marv Dyson, Gen. Mgr. **Owner:** Gannet Co.

★4089★
WJPC-AM
820 S. Michigan Ave.
Chicago, IL 60605 Phone: (312)322-9400
Frequency: 950. **Network Affiliation:** Independent. **Format:** Adult Urban Contemporary. **Operating Hours:** Continuous. Simulcast with WLNR-FM. **Key Personnel:** Lillian Terrell, Oper.Mgr. **Owner:** Johnson Communications.

★4090★
WKDC-AM
130 N. York St.
Box 1530
Elmhurst, IL 60126 Phone: (708)530-1530
Frequency: 1530. **Network Affiliation:** ABC Radio. **Format:** Jazz; Ethnic. **Operating Hours:** 6 a.m.-sundown; 15% network, 85% local. **Key Personnel:** Frank Blotter, Pres.

★4091★
WKRO-AM
Rte. 1, US-51
Box 311
Cairo, IL 62914 Phone: (618)734-1490
Frequency: 1490. **Network Affiliation:** ABC Radio. **Format:** Country; Urban Contemporary. **Operating Hours:** 6 a.m.-10 p.m.; 7% network, 93% local. **Key Personnel:** William T. Crain, Owner/Gen. Mgr.

★4092★
WLNR-FM
2915 Bernice Rd.
Lansing, IL 60438 Phone: (708)895-1400
Frequency: 106.3 **Network Affiliation:** Independent. **Format:** Adult Urban Contemporary. **Operating Hours:** Continuous. Simulcast with WJPC-AM. **Key Personnel:** Lillian Terrell, Oper.Mgr. **Owner:** Johnson Communications.

★4093★
WLUV-FM
Box 2201
Loves Park, IL 61131 Phone: (815)877-9588
Frequency: 96.7. **Network Affiliation:** ABC Radio; Satellite Music. **Format:** Sports; Urban Contemporary (Soul); The Heat. **Operating Hours:** Continuous. **Key Personnel:** Angelo Joseph Salvi, Gen. Mgr.; Virgie Laymeyer, Office Mgr. **Owner:** Angelo Joseph Salvi.

★4094★
WPNA-AM
408 S. Oak Park Ave.
Oak Park, IL 60302 Phone: (708)524-9762
Frequency: 1490. **Network Affiliation:** Independent. **Format:** Ethnic; News; Religious. **Operating Hours:** Continuous; 100% local. **Key Personnel:** C. Chris Gulinski, Gen. Mgr.; Chet Gulinski, Sales Mgr.; Len Petrulis, Public Affairs Dir. **Owner:** Alliance Communications, Inc.

★4095★
WSBC-AM
4949 W. Belmont Ave.
Chicago, IL 60641 Phone: (312)282-9722
Frequency: 1240. **Format:** Black Gospel; Ethnic. **Operating Hours:** 6 a.m.-8:30 a.m., 10 a.m.-11 a.m., 2 p.m.-3:30 p.m., 8 p.m.-10 p.m., 11 p.m.-midnight. **Key Personnel:** Daniel R. Lee, Pres.; Roy J. Bellavia, Gen. and Program Mgr.; Mark Nielsen, Chief Engineer. **Owner:** Diamond Broadcasting, Inc.

★4096★
WSIE-FM
Southern Illinois University
Box 1773
Edwardsville, IL 62026 Phone: (618)692-2228
Frequency: 88.7. **Network Affiliation:** National Public Radio (NPR); American Public Radio (APR). **Format:** Jazz; News. **Operating Hours:** Continuous; 10% network, 90% local. **Key Personnel:** Roy Gerritsen, Gen. Mgr.; Michael Leland, News/Public Affairs Dir.; Vito Lucido, Music Dir.; David Caires, Chief Engineer. **Owner:** Southern Illinois University.

★4097★
WVON-AM
3350 S. Kedzie Ave.
Chicago, IL 60623 Phone: (312)247-6200
Frequency: 1450. **Network Affiliation:** Mutual Broadcasting System; National Black. **Format:** Talk; Religious. **Operating Hours:** 10 p.m.-1 p.m. **Key Personnel:** Wesley W. South, Gen. Mgr.; Verlene Blackburn, Station Mgr.; Melody Spann, Program Dir.; Vincent Micknes, Sales Mgr.; Perri Small, Exec. Producer. **Owner:** Midway Broadcasting.

★4098★
WXAN-FM
Rte. 2, Box 213A
Ava, IL 62907 Phone: (618)426-3308
Frequency: 103.9. **Network Affiliation:** USA Radio; Illinois News; Tribune. **Format:** Southern Gospel. **Operating Hours:** Continuous; 5% network, 95% local. **Key Personnel:** Doug Apple, Mgr./Program Dir.; Daren Payne, Music Dir.; Tim Richards, Sales Mgr. **Owner:** Harold L. Lawder.

Indiana

★4099★
WPZZ-FM
4475 Allisonville Rd., Ste. 525
Indianapolis, IN 46205 Phone: (317)736-4040
Frequency: 95.9. **Network Affiliation:** Southern Broadcasting. **Format:** Urban Contemporary. **Operating Hours:** Continuous; 10% network, 90% local. **Key Personnel:** Eric Blakey, Program Dir.; John C. Asher, Operations Dir.; Kevin Simmons, Sales Mgr.; Pam Coomer, Business Mgr. **Owner:** Willis Broadcast Co.

★4100★
WSLM-FM
Radio Ridge
Hwy. 56 E.
PO Box 385
Salem, IN 47167 Phone: (812)883-5750
Frequency: 98.9. **Network Affiliation:** Independent. **Format:** Gospel; Sports. **Operating Hours:** 6 a.m.-midnight; 100% local. **Key Personnel:** Don H. Martin, Owner/General Manager; Les Arms, News Director; Becky Lynn Coomer, Program Director; John Wood, Sports Director; Elmo Brough, Advertising Manager. Aging and Elders by Eldridge; Tower of Babel: The Nuclear Power Industry by Overton; Through the Hoop: The Sporting South by Wood and Okun.

★4101★
WTLC-FM
2126 N. Meridan St.
Indianapolis, IN 46202 Phone: (317)923-1456
Frequency: 105.7. **Network Affiliation:** Independent. **Format:** Urban Contemporary. **Operating Hours:** Continuous. **Key Personnel:** Amos Brown, Gen. Mgr. **Owner:** Panache Broadcasting.

★4102★
WWCA-AM
545 Broadway
Gary, IN 46402-1983 Phone: (219)886-9171
Frequency: 1270. **Network Affiliation:** Bishop Levi Willis Broadcasting. **Format:** Gospel. **Operating Hours:** Continuous. **Key Personnel:** James Lewis, Gen. Mgr.; Marcus Johns, Program Dir.; Karen Clark, Office Mgr. **Owner:** Willis Broadcasting.

Iowa

★4103★
KBBG-FM
527 Cottage St.
Waterloo, IA 50703 Phone: (319)234-1441
Frequency: 88.1. **Network Affiliation:** National Public Radio (NPR). **Format:** Gospel; Jazz; Urban Contemporary. **Operating Hours:** 5:30 a.m.-midnight Mon. through Thur.; 5:30 a.m.-2 a.m. Fri.; 5:30-midnight Sat.; 6 a.m-midnight Sun. **Key Personnel:** Jimmie Porter, Dir.

★4104★
KCCK-FM
6301 Kirkwood Blvd. SW
Cedar Rapids, IA 52406 Phone: (319)398-5446
Frequency: 88.3. **Network Affiliation:** American Radio. **Format:** Jazz. **Operating Hours:** 5 a.m.-midnight Mon. through Fri., Continuous Sat. and Sun.; 16% network, 84% local. **Key Personnel:** Steve Carpenter, Mgr./Program Dir.; George Dorman, News Dir.; Dave Becker, Music Dir. **Owner:** Kirkwood Community College.

★4105★
KIGC-FM
William Penn College
N. Market & Trueblood Aves.
Oskaloosa, IA 52577 Phone: (515)673-1095
Frequency: 88.7. **Network Affiliation:** Independent. **Format:** Contemporary Hit Radio (CHR); Jazz; Urban Contemporary; Rhythm & Blues; Religious (Christian). **Operating Hours:** 7 a.m.-midnight; 100% local. **Key Personnel:** Don DeBoef, Engineering Dir.; John Doerge, Faculty Adviser. **Owner:** William Penn College.

★4106★
KTFC-FM
Box 102-A, Rte. 2
Sioux City, IA 51106 Phone: (712)252-4621
Frequency: 103.3. **Network Affiliation:** Satellite Radio. **Format:** Gospel. **Operating Hours:** Continuous. **Key Personnel:** Don Swanson, Owner/Gen. Mgr.

Kentucky

★4107★
WCKU-FM
651 Perimeter Dr., Ste. 102
Lexington, KY 40517 Phone: (606)269-9540
Frequency: 102.5. **Network Affiliation:** Independent. **Format:** Urban Contemporary. **Operating Hours:** Continuous. **Key Personnel:** Hozie Mack, Program Dir.; Damon Moberly, Music Dir.; Cindy Ware, Sales Mgr. **Owner:** High Communications Partnership.

★4108★
WLLV-AM
515 S. 5th St.
Louisville, KY 40202 Phone: (502)581-1240
Frequency: 1240. **Network Affiliation:** Independent. **Format:** Gospel. **Operating Hours:** Continuous. **Key Personnel:** Archie Dale, V.P./Gen. Mgr. **Owner:** Full Force, Inc.

★4109★
WLOU-AM
2549 S. 3rd St.
Louisville, KY 40208 Phone: (502)636-3535
Frequency: 1350. **Network Affiliation:** Sheridan Broadcasting. **Format:** Urban Contemporary. **Operating Hours:** Continuous; network news, remainder local. **Key Personnel:** Mildred J. Staton, Operations Manager; Ange Canessa, Music Director; Neal O'Rea, Chief Engineer. **Owner:** Johnson Communications.

★4110★
WQKS-AM
905 S. Main St.
1480 Broadcast Plaza
Hopkinsville, KY 42240-2098 Phone: (502)886-1480
Frequency: 1480. **Network Affiliation:** ABC Radio; NBC Radio. **Format:** Urban Contemporary. **Operating Hours:** Continuous; 5% network, 95% local. **Key Personnel:** John N. Hall, III, President. **Owner:** Pennyrile Broadcasting Co.

★4111★
WRLV-AM
PO Box 550
Salyersville, KY 41465 Phone: (606)349-6125
Frequency: 1140. **Network Affiliation:** KyNet; ABC Radio. **Format:** Gospel. **Operating Hours:** Sunrise-sunset; 10% network, 90% local. **Key Personnel:** Jim Bradley, Pres./Sales and Promotion Gen. Mgr. **Owner:** Licking Valley Radio Corp.

★4112★
WTCV-AM
Main & Harrison Sts., Ste. A
Greenup, KY 41144 Phone: (606)473-7377
Frequency: 1520. **Network Affiliation:** KyNet. **Format:** Southern Gospel. **Operating Hours:** Continuous; 5% network, 95% local. **Key Personnel:** Robert L. Scheibly, Exec. V.P.; Ronnie Bell, Station Mgr. **Owner:** Greenup County Broadcasting.

★4113★
WWXL-AM
Rte. 5, Box 50
Manchester, KY 40962 Phone: (606)598-5102
Frequency: 1450. **Format:** Gospel. **Operating Hours:** 5:30 a.m.-midnight. **Key Personnel:** Ermel Ison, Gen. Mgr./Gen. Sales Mgr.; Lonnie Marcum, Operations Mgr. **Owner:** Wilderness Hills Broadcasting Inc.

Louisiana

★4114★
KBCE-FM
Box 69
Boyce, LA 71409 Phone: (318)793-4003
Frequency: 102.3. **Network Affiliation:** Southern Broadcasting; Sheridan Broadcasting. **Format:** Urban Contemporary. **Operating Hours:** Continuous. **Key Personnel:** Gus E. Lewis, Pres./Gen. Mgr. **Owner:** Gus E. Lewis.

★4115★
KDKS-FM
1000 Grimmett Dr.
Shreveport, LA 71107 Phone: (318)221-5357
Frequency: 92.1. **Network Affiliation:** Independent. **Format:** Urban Contemporary. **Operating Hours:** Continuous; 100% local. **Key Personnel:** Murray Franks, Gen. Mgr.; Dawn Herring, Business Mgr.; Bill Sharp, Program Dir. **Owner:** Dawe Co., Inc.

★4116★
KFXZ-FM
3225 Ambassador Caffery Pkwy.
Lafayette, LA 70506-7214 Phone: (318)898-1112
Frequency: 106.3. **Network Affiliation:** ABC Radio. **Format:** Urban Contemporary. **Operating Hours:** Continuous; 2% network, 98% local. **Key Personnel:** Jim Thompson, V.P. Radio; Carl Dureausseau, Local Sales Mgr.; Larry Lynn, Operations Mgr.; Dave Robinson, Chief Engineer; Kim Pillette, Office Mgr.; Wynn Day, News Dir.; Chuck Harrison, Music Dir. **Owner:** Vetter Communications Co. Inc. Native American Communities; Green Gems: An Environmental Film Guide.

★4117★
KJCB-AM
413 Jefferson St.
Lafayette, LA 70501 Phone: (318)233-4262
Frequency: 770. **Network Affiliation:** ABC Radio. **Format:** Jazz; Religious; Urban Contemporary; Oldies. **Operating Hours:** Continuous. **Key Personnel:** Joshua Jackson, Sr., Pres.; Horatio Handy, Gen. Mgr. **Owner:** Joshua Jackson, Sr.

★4118★
KOKA-AM
1315 Milam St.
Shreveport, LA 71101 Phone: (318)222-3122
Frequency: 980. **Network Affiliation:** NBC Radio; Sheridan Broadcasting. **Format:** Religious (Black). **Operating Hours:** 5 a.m.-midnight. **Key Personnel:** Diane Camp, Gen. Mgr.; Eddie Giles, Program Dir. **Owner:** Cary D. Camp.

★4119★
KRUS-AM
Box 430
500 N. Monroe St.
Ruston, LA 71270 Phone: (318)255-2530
Frequency: 1490. **Network Affiliation:** AP Radio. **Format:** Urban Contemporary. **Operating Hours:** 20 hours daily; 1% network, 99% local. **Key Personnel:** Dan Hollingsworth, Pres./Gen. and Sales Mgr.; Gary McKenney, Station Mgr.; L.W. Green, Music and Sports Dir.; Gene Haynes, News Dir. **Owner:** Ruston Broadcasting Co., Inc.

★4120★
KSLU-FM
University Sta.
PO Box 783
Hammond, LA 70402 Phone: (504)549-2330
Frequency: 90.9. **Network Affiliation:** American Public Radio (APR). **Format:** Jazz. **Operating Hours:** Continuous; 35% network, 65% local. **Key Personnel:** Ron Nethercutt, Gen. Mgr.; Ken Benitez, News Dir.; Paul Burt, Chief Engineer; Craig Williams, Program Dir.; Joyce Savoie, Bus. Mgr.; John Pisiotta, Music Dir. **Owner:** Southeastern LA University.

★4121★
KXZZ-AM
311 Alamo St.
Lake Charles, LA 70601 Phone: (318)436-7277
Frequency: 1580. **Network Affiliation:** Sheridan Broadcasting. **Format:** Urban Contemporary. **Operating Hours:** Continuous; 100% local. **Key Personnel:** Albert Johnson, Pres./Owner; Dixie Johnson, Gen. Mgr./Owner; Daniel Johnson, Sales Mgr.; Rob Moore, Program Dir. **Owner:** Dixie Broadcasters, Inc.

★4122★
KYEA-FM
516 Martin St.
West Monroe, LA 71292 Phone: (318)322-1491
Frequency: 98.3. **Network Affiliation:** Sheridan Broadcasting; ABC Radio. **Format:** Urban Contemporary. **Operating Hours:** Continuous; 100% local. **Key Personnel:** John K. Wilson, Gen. Mgr. **Owner:** Frank D. Stimley.

★4123★
WABL-AM
Bankston Rd.
PO Box 787
Amite, LA 70422 Phone: (504)748-8385
Frequency: 1570. **Network Affiliation:** ABC Radio; Louisiana; Unistar. **Format:** Full Service; Urban Contemporary. **Operating Hours:** Sunrise-sunset; 30% network, 70% local. **Key Personnel:** Charles Hart, Gen. Mgr. **Owner:** Amite Broadcasting Co., Inc.

★4124★
WQUE-AM
1440 Canal St.
New Orleans, LA 70112 Phone: (504)581-1280
Frequency: 1280. **Network Affiliation:** Independent. **Format:** Urban Contemporary. **Operating Hours:** Continuous; 100%. **Key Personnel:** Derek Monette, Program Dir.; Karen Cortello, Music Dir.; Monica Pierre, News Dir.; John S. Rockweiler, Gen. Mgr. **Owner:** Clear Channel Communications.

★4125★
WQUE-FM
1440 Canal St.
New Orleans, LA 70112 Phone: (504)581-1280
Frequency: 98.3. **Network Affiliation:** Independent. **Format:** Urban Contemporary. **Operating Hours:** Continuous; 100%. **Key Personnel:** Derek Monette, Program Dir.; Karen Cortello, Music Dir.; Monic Perre, News Dir.; John S. Rockweiler, Gen. Mgr. **Owner:** Clear Channel Communications.

★4126★
WXOK-AM
Box 66475
6819 Cezanne Ave.
Baton Rouge, LA 70896 Phone: (504)927-7060
Frequency: 1460. **Network Affiliation:** Independent. **Format:** Urban Contemporary. **Operating Hours:** Continuous. **Key Personnel:** Dennis Lee, Gen. Mgr. **Owner:** Winnfield Life Broadcasting Inc.

★4127★
WYLD-AM
2228 Gravier
New Orleans, LA 70119 Phone: (504)822-1945
Frequency: 940. **Format:** Religious; Urban Contemporary. **Operating Hours:** Continuous; 5% network, 95% local. **Key Personnel:** Florence Marchand, Program Dir.; Lyle Henderson, Promotions Coord.; Darlene Sylvers, Music Dir. **Owner:** Inter Urban Broadcasting Co.

Maryland

★4128★
WANN-AM
PO Box 631
Annapolis, MD 21404 Phone: (301)269-0700
Frequency: 1190. **Network Affiliation:** Independent. **Format:** Urban Contemporary. **Operating Hours:** Sunrise-sunset. **Key Personnel:** M.H. Blum, Pres.; M.W. Pittman, Engineering V.P.; R.Z. Goldberg, Sales V.P.; H. Adams, Exec. V.P.; Jeff Blum, News Dir.; Hilda Clark Evans, Music Dir. **Owner:** Annapolis Broadcasting Corp.

★4129★
WBGR-AM
334 N. Charles St.
Baltimore, MD 21201 Phone: (301)727-1177
Frequency: 860. **Network Affiliation:** NBC Radio. **Format:** Gospel. **Operating Hours:** Continuous; 5% network, 95% local. **Key Personnel:** Pastor Durant, Program Dir.; Cal Hackett, Asst. Program Dir.; David Brown, News Dir.; Mert Hill, Traffic Mgr.; Sam Beasley, Gen. Mgr. **Owner:** Jack Mortenson. Directory of Precollege and University Minority Engineering Programs.

★4130★
WBZE-AM
PO Box 1650
Waldorf, MD 20604-1650 Phone: (301)870-8700
Frequency: 1030. **Network Affiliation:** National Black. **Format:** Gospel. **Operating Hours:** Sunrise-sunset. **Key Personnel:** Reggie Hales, Gen. Mgr. **Owner:** Peter Gurickus.

★4131★
WEAA-FM
Hillen Rd & Coldspring Ln.
Baltimore, MD 21239 Phone: (301)444-3564
Frequency: 88.9. **Network Affiliation:** National Public Radio (NPR). **Format:** Blues; Gospel; Ethnic (Caribbean). **Operating Hours:** 18 (Continuous hours on weekends); 5% network, 95% local. **Key Personnel:** Preston Blakely, Gen. Mgr.; Alphie Williams, Music and Program Dir.; Charles Fant, Chief Engineer. **Owner:** Morgan State University.

★4132★
WEBB-AM
3000 Druid Park Dr.
Baltimore, MD 21215 Phone: (301)367-9322
Frequency: 1360. **Network Affiliation:** Independent. **Format:** Adult Contemporary. **Operating Hours:** Continuous. **Key Personnel:** Dorothy Brunson, Gen.Mgr. **Owner:** Brunson Communications.

★4133★
WESM-FM
University of Maryland, Eastern Shore
Backbone Rd.
Princess Anne, MD 21853 Phone: (301)651-2816
Frequency: 91.3. **Network Affiliation:** National Black; AP Radio; Sheridan Broadcasting. **Format:** Jazz; Eclectic; Religious; Urban Contemporary; Big Band/Nostalgia; Blues. **Operating Hours:** 6 a.m.-2 a.m.; 30% network, 70% local. **Key Personnel:** Robert A. Franklin, Dir.; Milton Blackman, Program Dir.; Michael Jenkins, Music Dir. **Owner:** University of Maryland, Eastern Shore.

★4134★
WJDY-AM
1633 N. Division St.
Salisbury, MD 21801 Phone: (301)742-5191
Frequency: 1470. **Network Affiliation:** CBS Radio. **Format:** Urban Contemporary. **Operating Hours:** Sunrise-sunset. **Key Personnel:** J.P. Connor, Jr., Gen. Mgr.; Brad Connor, Sales Manager. **Owner:** Connor Broadcasting.

★4135★
WWIN-AM
6th Fl.
200 S. President St.
Baltimore, MD 21202 Phone: (301)366-1400
Frequency: 1400. **Network Affiliation:** Independent. **Format:** Urban Contemporary. Simulcast with WWIN-FM. **Operating Hours:** Continuous. **Key Personnel:** Barry Smith, Gen. Mgr. **Owner:** Regan Henry.

★4136★
WWIN-FM
200 S. President St., 6th Fl.
Baltimore, MD 21202 Phone: (301)332-8200
Frequency: 95.9. **Network Affiliation:** ABC Radio. **Format:** Urban Contemporary. Simulcast with WWIN-AM. **Operating Hours:** Continuous. **Key Personnel:** Bob Woodward, Gen. Mgr. **Owner:** Ragan Henry. Over, All I Well, My Mother's Faith in God, (all sheet music) all by James Hendrix.

Massachusetts

★4137★
WILD-AM
90 Warren St.
Boston, MA 02119 Phone: (617)427-2222
Frequency: 1090. **Network Affiliation:** National Black; ABC Radio. **Format:** Urban Contemporary. **Operating Hours:** Sunrise-sunset; 3% network, 97% local. **Key Personnel:** Kendell Nash, Pres.; Monte Bowens, Gen. Mgr.; Neal Perlstein, Gen. Sales Mgr.; Stephen Hill, Program Dir.; Va Lynda Robinson, News Dir.; Dana Hall, Music Dir. **Owner:** Nash Communications Corp.

★4138★
WJJW-FM
Campus Center
N. Adams State College
North Adams, MA 01247 Phone: (413)663-9136
Frequency: 91.1. **Network Affiliation:** Independent. **Format:** Jazz; Ethnic; Religious; Urban Contemporary; Oldies. **Operating Hours:** 7 a.m.-3 a.m. **Key Personnel:** Mike Hsu, Gen. Mgr.; Jennifer Cavalluzzi, Program Dir.; Brian McDonough, Music Dir. **Owner:** N. Adams State College.

★4139★
WLVG-AM
1972 Massachusetts Ave.
Cambridge, MA 02140 Phone: (617)576-2895
Frequency: 740. **Network Affiliation:** Independent. **Format:** Religious; Urban Contemporary. **Operating Hours:** Sunrise-sunset; 100% local.

Key Personnel: Rev. E.W. Jackson, Sr., Gen. Mgr.; Allen Redd, Assistant Gen. Mgr.; Don Long, Production Manager; Theodora Jackson, Traffic Supervisor. **Owner:** Inspiration Communications.

★4140★
WMLN-FM
1071 Blue Hill Ave.
Milton, MA 02186 Phone: (617)333-0311
Frequency: 91.5. **Network Affiliation:** Mutual Broadcasting System. **Format:** Ethnic (Diversified). **Operating Hours:** Continuous; 5% network, 95% local. **Key Personnel:** Alan Frank, Radio Dir.; Gayle McMillan, Station Mgr. **Owner:** Curry College.

★4141★
WWKX-FM
8 N. Main St.
Attleboro, MA 02703-2282 Phone: (508)222-1320
Frequency: 106.3. **Network Affiliation:** CBS Radio. **Format:** Urban Contemporary. **Operating Hours:** Continuous. **Key Personnel:** Gene Lombardi, Gen. Mgr.; Bill O'Brian, Program Dir. **Owner:** Ten Mile Communications.

Michigan

★4142★
WCHB-AM
32790 Henry Ruff Rd.
Inkster, MI 48141 Phone: (313)278-1440
Frequency: 1440. **Network Affiliation:** Independent. **Format:** Religious; Blues. **Operating Hours:** Continuous. **Key Personnel:** Mary Bell, Pres. **Owner:** Bell Broadcasting Co.

★4143★
WDZZ-FM
1830 Genesee Tower
Flint, MI 48503 Phone: (313)767-0130
Frequency: 92.7. **Network Affiliation:** Independent. **Format:** Urban Contemporary. **Operating Hours:** Continuous. **Key Personnel:** Sam Williams, Gen. Mgr.; Scott Williams, Program Dir.; Rick Pettyford, Sales Mgr. **Owner:** Erie Coast Communications.

★4144★
WFLT-AM
317 S. Averill
Flint, MI 48506 Phone: (313)239-5733
Frequency: 1420. **Network Affiliation:** Independent. **Format:** Religious (Christian); Gospel. **Operating Hours:** Continuous. **Key Personnel:** Rev. A.J. Pointer, Pres.; Rev. J.C. Curry, V.P.; Anita Thornton, Operations Mgr.; Jeff Lavalley, Asst. Operations Mgr. **Owner:** Christian Broadcasting Assoc.

★4145★
WGPR-FM
3146 E. Jefferson Ave.
Detroit, MI 48207 Phone: (313)259-8862
Frequency: 107.5. **Network Affiliation:** Independent. **Format:** Urban Contemporary. **Operating Hours:** Continuous. **Key Personnel:** George Mathews, Pres. **Owner:** Intl. Masons, Inc.

★4146★
WGVU-FM
301 W. Fulton
Grand Rapids, MI 49504-6492 Phone: (616)771-6666
Frequency: 88.5. **Network Affiliation:** National Public Radio (NPR); AP Radio. **Format:** Jazz; Information. **Operating Hours:** Continuous; 25% network, 75% local. **Key Personnel:** Michael T. Walenta, Gen. Mgr.; Sam Eiler, Station Mgr.; Scott Hanley, Program Mgr.; David Moore, News Dir.; Chris Barbee, Producer/Reporter/Sports Dir. **Owner:** Grand Valley State University.

★4147★
WILS-AM
PO Box 25008
Lansing, MI 48909-5008 Phone: (517)393-1320
Frequency: 1320. **Network Affiliation:** Independent. **Format:** Urban Contemporary. **Operating Hours:** Continuous. **Key Personnel:** Andrew MacDonald, Gen. Mgr. **Owner:** MacDonald Broadcasting. Hidden in History, Forging the Future; Hispanic America: Freeing the Free, Honoring Heroes; My Own Book; The PR (Public Relations) Handbook, all by Hammer.

★4148★
WJLB-FM
645 Griswold St., No. 633
Detroit, MI 48226-4177
Frequency: 97.9. **Network Affiliation:** Westwood One Radio. **Format:** Urban Contemporary. **Operating Hours:** Continuous; 5% network, 95% local. **Key Personnel:** Verna S. Green, V.P./Gen. Mgr.; Shel Leshner, Gen. Sales Mgr.; Steve Hegwood, Operations Mgr.; Myrna Johnson, Business Mgr.; Bernadette Banko, Mktg. Dir.; Mildred Gaddis, Public Affairs and News Dir. **Owner:** Booth American.

★4149★
WJZZ-FM
2994 E. Grand Blvd.
Detroit, MI 48202 Phone: (313)871-0590
Frequency: 105.9. **Network Affiliation:** Independent. **Format:** Jazz. **Operating Hours:** Continuous; 100% local. **Key Personnel:** Mary Bell, Pres.; Wendell Cox, V.P.; Eric B. Bass, Gen. Sales Mgr.; Robert Bass, Asst. to the Pres.; Terry Arnold, Program Dir.; Treva Bass, Chief Engineer; Deborah F. Copeland, Local Sales Mgr. **Owner:** Bell Broadcasting Co.

★4150★
WKWM-AM
PO Box 828
Kentwood, MI 49518-0828 Phone: (616)676-1237
Frequency: 1140. **Network Affiliation:** Sheridan Broadcasting. **Format:** Urban Contemporary. **Operating Hours:** Sunrise-sunset; 100% local. **Key Personnel:** Richard Culpepper, Gen. Mgr.; Frank Grant, Station Mgr./Program Dir. **Owner:** Michelle Broadcasting.

★4151★
WLLJ-AM
206 E. State
Box 393
Cassopolis, MI 49031-0393 Phone: (616)445-2543
Frequency: 910. **Network Affiliation:** AP Radio; National Black; Satellite Music. **Format:** Adult Contemporary; Urban Contemporary; Oldies. **Operating Hours:** Continuous; 90% network, 10% local. **Key Personnel:** Larry Langford, Jr., Pres.; Darlene Harris, Station Mgr. **Owner:** Larry Langford, Jr.

★4152★
WNMC-FM
1701 E. Front St.
Traverse City, MI 49684 Phone: (616)922-1091
Frequency: 90.9. **Network Affiliation:** IBS. **Format:** Jazz; Ethnic; Urban Contemporary; Alternative/New Music/Progressive; Blues. **Operating Hours:** 20 hours daily; 100% local. **Key Personnel:** John Lockard, Gen. Mgr./Program Dir.; Diane Danks, On Air Dir.; Michael Lloyd, Music Dir. **Owner:** Northwestern Michigan College.

★4153★
WQBH-AM
2050 CNB Bldg.
Detroit, MI 48226 Phone: (313)965-4500
Frequency: 1400. **Format:** Urban Contemporary; Rhythm & Blues; Jazz. **Operating Hours:** Continuous. **Owner:** TXZ, Inc. dba Detroit Broadcasting, Inc.

★4154★
WTLZ-FM
126 N. Franklin St., Ste. 514
Saginaw, MI 48607 Phone: (517)754-1071
Frequency: 107.1. **Format:** Jazz; Ethnic; Religious; Urban Contemporary. **Operating Hours:** Continuous; 10% network, 90% local. **Key Personnel:** Jack Lich, CEO and Gen. Mgr.; Don Wiggins, General Sales Mgr.; Kermit Crockett, Program Director; Steve Fox, Music and Sports Director; D'Ante Toussaint, News and Public Service Director; Jillian Rae Miley, Admin. Asst./Promotions/Community Servic; Rosa Chaffer, Traffic and Continuity Director; Chris Banks, Religious Programming Director. **Owner:** WTL, Inc.

★4155★
WXLA-AM
5920 S. Logan
Lansing, MI 48911 Phone: (517)393-6397
Frequency: 1180. **Network Affiliation:** Independent. **Format:** Urban Contemporary. **Operating Hours:** Sunrise-sunset. **Key Personnel:** Helena Dubose, Gen. Mgr. **Owner:** Diamond Broadcasters. Smith.

★4156★
WYCE-FM
2820 Clyde Park Ave. SW
Wyoming, MI 49509-2995 Phone: (616)530-7506
Frequency: 88.1. **Format:** Full Service; Hispanic; Ethnic (African, British Isles). **Operating Hours:** 5:30 a.m.-midnight; 100% local. **Key Personnel:** Lee Ferraro, Station Mgr.; Thom Bland, Operation Coord.; Peter Bus. **Owner:** Grand Rapids Cable Access, Inc.

Minnesota

★4157★
KBEM-FM
1555 James Ave.
North Minneapolis, MN 55411 Phone: (612)627-2833
Frequency: 88.5. **Network Affiliation:** American Public Radio (APR); ABC Radio. **Format:** Jazz. **Operating Hours:** Continuous; 5% network, 95% local. **Key Personnel:** Robert Montesano, Station Mgr.; J.D. Ball, Music Dir./Program Dir. **Owner:** Minneapolis Public Schools.

★4158★
KTCJ-AM
Butler Sq.
100 N. 6th St.
Minneapolis, MN 55403
Frequency: 690. **Network Affiliation:** Independent. **Format:** Jazz. **Operating Hours:** Sunrise-sunset: 100% local. **Key Personnel:** Alan Lawson, Program Dir.; Mike Boen, Gen. Mgr.; Jeff Litt, Gen. Sales Mgr. **Owner:** Parker Communications.

Mississippi

★4159★
WACR-AM
1910 14th Ave. N.
PO Box 1078
Columbus, MS 39703 Phone: (601)328-1050
Frequency: 1050. **Network Affiliation:** National Black. **Format:** Religious; Urban Contemporary. **Operating Hours:** Sunrise-sunset; 5% network, 95% local. **Key Personnel:** Danny Bard, Gen. Mgr.; R.H. Brown, Program Dir. **Owner:** T & W Communications, Inc.

★4160★
WALT-AM
3436 Hwy. 45 N.
Box 5797
Meridian, MS 39302 Phone: (601)693-2661
Frequency: 910. **Network Affiliation:** ABC Radio. **Format:** Urban Contemporary. **Operating Hours:** Continuous. **Key Personnel:** Steve Poston, Program Dir.; Sheila McLain, News Dir.; Becky Harry, Sales Mgr. **Owner:** New South Broadcasting Corp.

★4161★
WAML-AM
318 W. 5th St.
PO Box 367
Laurel, MS 39440 Phone: (601)425-4285
Frequency: 1340. **Network Affiliation:** NBC Radio; Mississippi. **Format:** Gospel. **Operating Hours:** 6 a.m.-midnight. **Key Personnel:** Gerald Williams, Gen. Mgr.; Mike Golden, Program Dir. **Owner:** Pine Belt Broadcasting.

★4162★
WBAD-FM
PO Box 4426
Greenville, MS 38704-4426 Phone: (601)335-9265
Frequency: 94.3. **Network Affiliation:** Sheridan Broadcasting. **Format:** Urban Contemporary. **Operating Hours:** 21 hrs. daily; 8% network, 92% local. **Key Personnel:** William D. Jackson, Owner/Mgr.; Stanley S. Sherman, Sec./Treas./Owner; Walter Wilson, Program Dir.; Mike Woods, Sales Mgr. **Owner:** Stanley S. Sherman and William D. Jackson.

★4163★
WESY-AM
7 Oaks Rd.
PO Box 5804
Greenville, MS 38704-5804 Phone: (601)378-9405
Frequency: 1580. **Network Affiliation:** Sheridan Broadcasting. **Format:** Religious; Urban Contemporary. **Operating Hours:** Sunrise-sunset; 8% network, 92% local. **Key Personnel:** William D. Jackson, Mgr.; Jerome Daniels, Music Dir.; Stanley S. Sherman, Sec./Treas.

★4164★
WJMG-FM
1204 Gravel Line St.
Hattiesburg, MS 39401 Phone: (601)544-1941
Frequency: 92.1. **Network Affiliation:** Sheridan Broadcasting. **Format:** Urban Contemporary; Adult Contemporary. **Owner:** Circuit Broadcasting Co.

★4165★
WKKY-FM
PO Box 1919
McComb, MS 39648-1919 Phone: (601)475-4108
Frequency: 104.9. **Network Affiliation:** ABC Radio. **Format:** Urban Contemporary. **Operating Hours:** Continuous. **Key Personnel:** Michael Redd, Gen. Mgr.; Lee Crawford, News, Music and Program Dir.; Eric Suthoff, Production Mgr. **Owner:** Wayne Dowdy.

★4166★
WKRA-AM
1400-B E. Salem Ave.
PO Box 398
Holly Springs, MS 38635 Phone: (601)252-1122
Frequency: 1110. **Network Affiliation:** Mississippi. **Format:** Country; Black Contemporary Gospel. **Operating Hours:** Sunrise-sunset. **Key Personnel:** Rick Williams, Program Dir./News Dir.; Barbara Gilliam, Office Mgr. **Owner:** Ralph H. Doxey.

★4167★
WKXG-AM
Browning Rd.
Greenwood, MS 38930 Phone: (601)453-2174
Frequency: 1540. **Network Affiliation:** Sheridan Broadcasting. **Format:** Urban Contemporary; Rhythm & Blues; Gospel. **Operating Hours:** 6 a.m.-10 p.m.; 10% network, 90% local. **Key Personnel:** James Chick,

Gen. Mgr.; Milton Glass, Station Mgr.; Herman Anderson, Program Dir.; Rea Holmes, Office Mgr. **Owner:** Telesouth Communications, Inc.

★4168★
WKXI-AM
222 Beasley Rd.
Jackson, MS 39206 Phone: (601)957-1300
Frequency: 1300. **Network Affiliation:** Sheridan Broadcasting. **Format:** Adult-Oriented Soul. **Operating Hours:** Continuous. **Key Personnel:** Herb Anderson, Program Dir.; Becky Elkin, Sales Mgr. **Owner:** Opus Media Group.

★4169★
WLTD-FM
Rte. 1, Box 288E
Lexington, MS 39095 Phone: (601)834-1114
Frequency: 106.3. **Network Affiliation:** Southern Broadcasting. **Format:** Urban Contemporary; Rhythm & Blues; Public Radio. **Operating Hours:** 6 a.m.-1 a.m.; 8% network, 92% local. **Key Personnel:** Philip Scott, Vice President/General Manager; James Williams, Sales Manager; Samual Brown, Program/Music/News Director. **Owner:** J. Scott Communications.

★4170★
WMIS-AM
20 E. Franklin
Natchez, MS 39120 Phone: (601)442-2522
Frequency: 1240. **Network Affiliation:** NBC Radio; National Black. **Format:** Urban Contemporary. **Operating Hours:** Continuous. **Key Personnel:** Diana E. Nutter, Pres.; Jim Nutter, Sec./Treas.; Jim Dulaney, Gen. Mgr./V.P.; Donnie Staford, Operations Mgr.; Lee Nichols, Music Dir.

★4171★
WMLC-AM
PO Box 949
Monticello, MS 39654 Phone: (601)587-7997
Frequency: 1270. **Network Affiliation:** USA Radio. **Format:** Gospel. **Operating Hours:** Sunrise-sunset. **Key Personnel:** Dave Nichols, II, Gen. Mgr./Owner; Donna Nichols, Program Dir.; Dave Henry, Sales Mgr. **Owner:** Monticello Broadcasting.

★4172★
WNBN-AM
1290 Hawkins Crossing Rd.
Meridian, MS 39301 Phone: (601)483-7930
Frequency: 1290. **Network Affiliation:** National Black. **Format:** Religious (Gospel); Urban Contemporary. **Operating Hours:** 5 a.m.-5:35 p.m. **Key Personnel:** Sherwin Gaddis, Sales Mgr.; Rev. Bobby Wallace, Program Dir. **Owner:** Frank Rackley.

★4173★
WOAD-AM
1850 W. Lynch St.
Jackson, MS 39203 Phone: (601)948-1515
Frequency: 1400. **Network Affiliation:** NBC TV. **Format:** Black Gospel. **Operating Hours:** Continuous. **Key Personnel:** Carl Haynes, V.P./Gen. Mgr.; Jimmy Anthony, Program and Music Dir.; Gwen Cannon, Station Mgr.; Judi Patterson, Gen. Sales Mgr.; Michelle Walker, News Dir. **Owner:** Holt Communications Corp.

★4174★
WORV-AM
1204 Graveline
Hattiesburg, MS 39401 Phone: (601)544-1941
Frequency: 1580. **Network Affiliation:** National Black; Sheridan Broadcasting. **Format:** Urban Contemporary; Gospel; Rhythm & Blues. **Operating Hours:** Sunrise-sunset. **Key Personnel:** Vernon Floyd, Gen. Mgr.

★4175★
WQIC-AM
2711 7th St.
Meridian, MS 39301 Phone: (601)693-4851
Frequency: 1450. **Format:** Urban Contemporary. **Operating Hours:** Continuous; 95% network, 5% local. **Key Personnel:** Ken Rainey, Mgr.; Larry Carr, Program Dir. **Owner:** David Majure.

★4176★
WQIS-AM
1260 Victory Rd.
PO Box 1229
Laurel, MS 39441 Phone: (601)425-1491
Frequency: 890. **Network Affiliation:** ABC Radio. **Format:** Urban Contemporary. **Operating Hours:** Sunrise-sunset. **Key Personnel:** Jay Schneider, Gen. Mgr. **Owner:** Design Media, Inc.

★4177★
WRDC-AM
114 T.M. Jones Hwy.
Boyle, MS 38730 Phone: (601)843-8225
Frequency: 1410. **Network Affiliation:** National Black. **Format:** Religious; Urban Contemporary. **Operating Hours:** Continuous; 5% network, 95% local. **Key Personnel:** Joseph Appiah, Gen. Mgr.; Louis Cotton, Music and Program Dir.; G. Brooke, Office Mgr.; Larry Scott, Sports Dir.; E. Fontaine, Promotions Dir.; E. Hemphill, News Dir. **Owner:** Joseph Appiah.

★4178★
WRJH-FM
PO Box 145
Brandon, MS 39043 Phone: (601)825-5045
Frequency: 97.7. **Network Affiliation:** Christian Broadcasting (CBN). **Format:** Gospel. Simulcasts WRKN-AM. **Operating Hours:** 6 a.m.-midnight. **Key Personnel:** June Harris, Gen. Mgr.; Vickie Ferrer, Office Mgr.; Jeff Steele, Program Dir.; Stan Carter, Chief Engineer. Insane Nigger, Student/Teacher Work Manual, both by Mack B. Morant; Guyanese Seed of Soul: How to Prepare West Indian Food by Yvonne John; Prose and Poetic Expressions of a Black Woman by Marie Ransom.

★4179★
WRKN-AM
PO Box 145
Brandon, MS 39043 Phone: (601)825-5045
Frequency: 970. **Network Affiliation:** Christian Broadcasting (CBN). **Format:** Gospel. Simulcasts WRJH-FM. **Operating Hours:** Sunrise-sunset. **Key Personnel:** June Harris, Gen. Mgr.

★4180★
WTYJ-FM
20 E. Franklin
Natchez, MS 39120 Phone: (601)442-2522
Frequency: 97.7. **Network Affiliation:** NBC Radio; National Black. **Format:** Urban Contemporary. **Operating Hours:** Continuous. **Key Personnel:** Diana E. Nutter, Pres.; Jim Nutter, Sec./Treas.; Jim Dulaney, Station and Sales Mgr.; Donnie Staford, Operations Mgr.; Lee Nichols, Music Dir.

Missouri

★4181★
KATZ-AM
1139 Olive St.
St. Louis, MO 63101 Phone: (314)241-6000
Frequency: 1600. **Network Affiliation:** Satellite Music; ABC Radio; National Black. **Format:** Urban Contemporary. **Operating Hours:** Continuous. **Key Personnel:** Tracy Lewis, Gen. Mgr.; Rod King, Operations Mgr. **Owner:** Inter Urban Broadcasting of St. Louis.

★4182★
KATZ-FM
1139 Olive St.
St. Louis, MO 63101 Phone: (314)241-6000
Frequency: 100.3. **Network Affiliation:** Independent; ABC Radio. **Format:** Jazz. **Operating Hours:** Continuous. **Key Personnel:** Tracy Lewis, Gen. Mgr. **Owner:** Inter Urban Broadcasting of St. Louis.

★4183★
KCXL-AM
810 E. 63rd St.
Liberty, MO 64110 Phone: (816)333-2583
Frequency: 1140. **Network Affiliation:** Sheridan Broadcasting. **Format:** Adult Contemporary; Urban Contemporary. **Operating Hours:** Sunrise-sunset. **Key Personnel:** Chuck Moore, Gen. Sales Mgr.; Dell Rice, Program Mgr./Music Dir.; David Boucher, News Dir. **Owner:** Kansas City Communications.

★4184★
KIRL-AM
3713 Hwy. 11 N.
St. Charles, MO 63301 Phone: (314)946-6600
Frequency: 1460. **Format:** Jazz; Gospel; Urban Contemporary. **Operating Hours:** Continuous. **Key Personnel:** William E. White, Chrmn./Gen. Mgr./Music Dir.; Bernie Hayes, News Dir.; Columbus Gregory, Program Dir.; Sharon Walters, Office Mgr. **Owner:** Bronco Broadcasting Co., Inc.

★4185★
KMJM-FM
532 De Baliviere
St. Louis, MO 63112 Phone: (314)361-1108
Frequency: 107.7. **Network Affiliation:** Independent. **Format:** Urban Contemporary. **Operating Hours:** Continuous. **Key Personnel:** Linda O'Connor, Gen. Mgr. **Owner:** Noble Broadcasting.

★4186★
KPRS-FM
3 Crown Ctr., Ste. 118
Kansas City, MO 64108 Phone: (816)471-2100
Frequency: 103.3. **Network Affiliation:** Sheridan Broadcasting; ABC Radio. **Format:** Urban Contemporary; Rhythm & Blues; News. **Operating Hours:** Continuous. **Owner:** KPRS Broadcasting Corp.

★4187★
KPRT-AM
2440 Pershing Rd.
Kansas City, MO 64108 Phone: (816)471-2100
Frequency: 1590. **Network Affiliation:** Sheridan Broadcasting. **Format:** Gospel. **Operating Hours:** Continuous. **Key Personnel:** Michael Carter, Gen. Mgr./Pres. **Owner:** Mildred Carter.

★4188★
KSTL-AM
814 N. 3rd. St.
St. Louis, MO 63102 Phone: (314)621-5785
Frequency: 690. **Network Affiliation:** Independent. **Format:** Ethnic; Religious. **Operating Hours:** Sunrise-sunset; 100% local. **Key Personnel:** William K. Haverstick, Pres.; Doris Grebas, Gen. Mgr.; David Dale, Program Dir.; Chris Davis, Sales Mgr. **Owner:** Radio St. Louis, Inc.

Nevada

★4189★
KCEP-FM
330 W. Washington St.
Las Vegas, NV 89106 Phone: (702)648-4218
Frequency: 88.1. **Network Affiliation:** Sheridan Broadcasting. **Format:** Rhythm & Blues; Urban Contemporary. **Operating Hours:** Continuous; 15% network, 85% local. **Key Personnel:** Robert Scott Adams, Gen. Mgr.; Louis Conner, Jr., Asst. Prog. Dir./Music Dir.

New Jersey

★4190★
WBJB-FM
Brookdale Community College
Lincroft, NJ 07738 Phone: (201)842-1827
Frequency: 90.5. **Network Affiliation:** Independent. **Format:** Jazz. **Operating Hours:** 6 a.m.-midnight; 100% local. **Key Personnel:** Stewart W. Edwards, Sales, Station and Promotions Mgr. **Owner:** Brookdale Community College.

★4191★
WNJR-AM
600 N. Union Ave.
Hillside, NJ 07205 Phone: (201)688-5000
Frequency: 1430. **Network Affiliation:** National Black. **Format:** Urban Contemporary. **Operating Hours:** Continuous. **Key Personnel:** Elizabeth Satchell, Gen. Mgr.

★4192★
WUSS-AM
1507 Atlantic Ave.
Atlantic City, NJ 08401 Phone: (609)345-7134
Frequency: 1490. **Network Affiliation:** National Black. **Format:** Urban Contemporary. **Operating Hours:** Continuous; 5% network, 95% local. **Key Personnel:** Dob Mehl, CEO; Maurice Singleton, III, Operations and Program Dir.; Marc Q. Thomas, Gen. Sales Mgr. **Owner:** James Cuffee. Civilization by Chancellor Williams; Black Men: Obsolete, Single, Dangerous by Haki R. Mandhubuti; Wings Will Not Be Broken by Daniel Holmes; The Bass Bed and Other Stories by Pearl Cleage.

New York

★4193★
WAER-FM
215 University Pl.
Syracuse, NY 13244-2110 Phone: (315)443-4021
Frequency: 88.3. **Network Affiliation:** National Public Radio (NPR); Mutual Broadcasting System. **Format:** Jazz; News. **Operating Hours:** 5 a.m.-1 a.m.; 30% network, 70% local. **Key Personnel:** David Anderson, Gen. Mgr.; JoAnn Urofsky, Program Dir.; Jim Johnston, News Dir.; Barbara Tepper, Devel. Dir. **Owner:** Syracuse University.

★4194★
WBLK-FM
712 Main St., Ste. 112
Buffalo, NY 14202 Phone: (716)852-5955
Frequency: 93.7. **Network Affiliation:** CBS TV. **Format:** Urban Contemporary. **Operating Hours:** Continuous. **Key Personnel:** Howard Ebo, Gen. Mgr. **Owner:** WBLK Broadcasting Corp.

★4195★
WBLS-FM
801 2nd Ave.
New York, NY 10017 Phone: (212)661-3344
Frequency: 107.5. **Network Affiliation:** Independent. **Format:** Urban Contemporary. **Operating Hours:** Continuous. **Key Personnel:** Pierre M. Sutton, Pres./Gen. Mgr. **Owner:** Percy Sutton.

★4196★
WDKX-FM
683 E. Main St.
Rochester, NY 14605 Phone: (716)262-2050
Frequency: 103.9. **Network Affiliation:** Independent. **Format:** Urban Contemporary; Jazz; News; Sports. **Operating Hours:** Continuous; 100% local. **Key Personnel:** Andrew Langston, Gen. Mgr.; Gloria M. Langston, Station Mgr.; Andre Marcel, Program Dir. **Owner:** Monroe County Broadcasting Co. Ltd.

★4197★
WGMC-FM
Box 300
North Greece, NY 14515 Phone: (716)225-5300
Frequency: 90.1. **Network Affiliation:** Mutual Broadcasting System. **Format:** Jazz; Ethnic; Bluegrass; Sports. **Operating Hours:** 19 hours daily; 1% network, 99% local. **Key Personnel:** Lee Rust, Operations Dir.; Carl Vernetti, Underwriting Dir.; Eric Gruner, Program Dir. **Owner:** Greece Central School District.

★4198★
WLKA-FM
Box 155
Canandaigua, NY 14424 Phone: (716)394-1550
Frequency: 102.3. **Network Affiliation:** ABC Radio. **Format:** Jazz. **Operating Hours:** Continuous. **Key Personnel:** Jim Heredeen, Gen. Mgr. **Owner:** Dell Broadcasting Co.

★4199★
WRKS-FM
1440 Broadway
New York, NY 10018 Phone: (212)642-4300
Frequency: 98.7. **Network Affiliation:** The Source; Unistar. **Format:** Urban Contemporary. **Operating Hours:** Continuous. **Key Personnel:** Charles M. Warfield, Jr., V.P./Gen. Mgr. **Owner:** Summit Broadcasting Corp.

★4200★
WUFO-AM
89 LaSalle Ave.
Buffalo, NY 14214 Phone: (716)834-1080
Frequency: 1080. **Network Affiliation:** Sheridan Broadcasting. **Format:** Urban Contemporary; Gospel. **Operating Hours:** 6 a.m.-9 p.m. **Key Personnel:** Lenore Williams, Operations Mgr.; David Wilson, Program Dir.; Dwayne Landers, Music Dir. **Owner:** Sheridan Broadcasting Corp.

★4201★
WWRL-AM
41-30 58th St.
Woodside, NY 11377 Phone: (718)335-1600
Frequency: 1600. **Network Affiliation:** NBC Radio; National Black; Mutual Broadcasting System. **Format:** Gospel; Talk. **Operating Hours:** Continuous. **Key Personnel:** Vince Sanders, V.P./Gen. Mgr. **Owner:** Unity Broadcasting Network New York, Inc.

North Carolina

★4202★
WAAA-AM
Box 11197
4950 Indiana Ave.
Winston-Salem, NC 27116 Phone: (919)767-0430
Frequency: 980. **Network Affiliation:** National Black. **Format:** Urban Contemporary. **Operating Hours:** Continuous. **Key Personnel:** Ms. Mutter D. Evans, Pres. & Gen. Mgr. **Owner:** Media Broadcasting Corp.

★4203★
WARR-AM
PO Box 577
Warrenton, NC 27589 Phone: (919)257-2121
Frequency: 1520. **Network Affiliation:** Sheridan Broadcasting; National Black. **Format:** Religious; Rhythm & Blues; Jazz; Urban Contemporary. **Operating Hours:** 6 a.m.-8:15 p.m. **Key Personnel:** J. L. Wright, Sales and Station Mgr.

★4204★
WBCG-FM
PO Box 38
Murfreesboro, NC 27855 Phone: (919)398-4111
Frequency: 98.3. **Network Affiliation:** North Carolina News. **Format:** Urban Contemporary. **Operating Hours:** 6 a.m.-midnight; 65% network, 35% local. **Key Personnel:** Sammy Doughtie, Gen. Mgr.; Tony Doughtie, Program Mgr.; Dana Edwards, Sales Mgr.; Nita Futrell, Music Dir.; Bob Ward, Operations Mgr. **Owner:** Dr. M. Scott Edwards.

★4205★
WBMS-AM
3945 Market St. No. B
Wilmington, NC 28403-1403 Phone: (919)763-4633
Frequency: 1340. **Network Affiliation:** Southern Broadcasting. **Format:** Urban Contemporary. **Operating Hours:** Continuous. **Key Personnel:** Dorothy Brunson, Owner; A. Gray, Gen. Mgr. **Owner:** Dorothy Brunson.

★4206★
WBTE-AM
Hwy. 175
Windsor, NC 27983 Phone: (919)794-3131
Frequency: 990. **Network Affiliation:** North Carolina News. **Format:** Religious (Contemporary Gospel). **Operating Hours:** Daylight. **Key Personnel:** Louise R. Hughes, Gen.Mgr. **Owner:** Jean M. Stevens.

★4207★
WCKB-AM
PO Box 789
Hwy. 421 S.
Dunn, NC 28334 Phone: (919)892-3133
Frequency: 780. **Network Affiliation:** North Carolina News. **Format:** Gospel. **Operating Hours:** Sunrise-sunset; 100% local. **Key Personnel:** Charles L. Fowler, Pres.; Al Myatt, News and Sports Dir.; Linda Mathews, Traffic Mgr.; Margie Raynor, Program Dir.; Ronald C. Tart, Sales and Gen. Mgr. **Owner:** North Carolina Central Broadcasters.

★4208★
WDRV-AM
212 Signal Hill Dr.
Statesville, NC 28677 Phone: (704)872-0956
Frequency: 550. **Network Affiliation:** CBS Radio. **Format:** Gospel; News & Information; Sports. **Operating Hours:** 6 a.m.-10 p.m.; 10% network, 90% local. **Key Personnel:** David Wise, Program, Music, and Sports Dir.; Angela Henley, Traffic and Office Mgr.; Dave Arnold, Gen. Sales Mgr.; Thomas Gentry, Gen. Mgr.; Wendell Echols, Pres. **Owner:** Statesville Family Radio, Inc.

★4209★
WDUR-AM
2515 Apex
Durham, NC 27713 Phone: (919)493-7461
Frequency: 1490. **Network Affiliation:** National Black. **Format:** Contemporary Gospel. **Operating Hours:** Continuous. **Key Personnel:** Del Spencer, Program Dir.; Fred Adams, Gen. Mgr. **Owner:** Pinacle Broadcasting.

★4210★
WEAL-AM
1060 Gatewood Ave.
Greensboro, NC 27405 Phone: (919)272-5121
Frequency: 1510. **Network Affiliation:** Southern Broadcasting; National Black. **Format:** Urban Contemporary. **Operating Hours:** Daylight hours. **Key Personnel:** Rees Poag, Owner and President; Nancy Cooper, Vice President and Gen. Mgr.; Don Davis, Program Director; Lisa Darnell,

General Sales Mgr.; Jamie Workman, Promotions Director. **Owner:** Rees Poag.

★4211★
WEGG-AM
Rte. 2 Hwy. U.S. 117 N.
PO Box 608
Rose Hill, NC 28458 Phone: (919)289-2031
Frequency: 710. **Network Affiliation:** ABC Radio. **Format:** Gospel and Black Gospel; Agricultural. **Operating Hours:** Sunrise-sunset; 5% network, 95% local. **Key Personnel:** Patricia Pratt, Sales and News Dir.; Kay Garriss, Office Mgr./Program Dir.; Suzanne Wilson, Farm Dir.; Scott Saueraugh, Sports Dir. **Owner:** Jeff B. Wilson.

★4212★
WFXC-FM
2515 Apex
Durham, NC 27713 Phone: (919)493-7461
Frequency: 107.1. **Network Affiliation:** Independent. **Format:** Urban Contemporary. **Operating Hours:** Continuous. **Key Personnel:** Del Spencer, Program Dir.; Fred Adams, Gen. Mgr. **Owner:** Pinnacle Broadcasting.

★4213★
WGCR-AM
PO Box 720
Pisgah Forest, NC 28768-0720 Phone: (704)884-9427
Frequency: 720. **Format:** Gospel; News; Talk. **Operating Hours:** Sunrise-sunset; 20% network, 80% local. **Key Personnel:** Randy C. Barton, Gen. Mgr.; Larry W. Spears, Program Dir.; Kristi H. Johnson, News Dir.; Suzanne M. Horton, Office Mgr. **Owner:** Anchor Baptist Broadcasting Association, Inc.

★4214★
WGIV-AM
2520 Toomey Ave.
Charlotte, NC 28203-5548 Phone: (704)342-2644
Frequency: 1600. **Network Affiliation:** National Black; Southern Broadcasting; North Carolina News. **Format:** Ethnic; Rhythm & Blues; Gospel. **Operating Hours:** Continuous; 70% network, 30% local. **Key Personnel:** Chester Williams, Gen. Mgr.; Pete Brown, Gen. Sales Mgr.; Fred Graham, Program Dir. **Owner:** Broadcasting Partners, Inc.

★4215★
WGSP-AM
4209 F. Stewart Andrew Blvd.
Charlotte, NC 28217 Phone: (704)527-9477
Frequency: 1310. **Network Affiliation:** Independent. **Format:** Gospel. **Operating Hours:** Continuous. **Key Personnel:** Laurence Means, Gen. Mgr.; Letricia Loftin, Program Dir. **Owner:** Willis Broadcasting.

★4216★
WGTM-AM
Hwy. 42 W.
Wilson, NC 27893 Phone: (919)243-2188
Frequency: 590. **Format:** Gospel. **Owner:** Campbell Hauser Corp.

★4217★
WIKS-FM
207 Glenburnie Dr.
PO Box 2684
New Bern, NC 28561 Phone: (919)633-1500
Frequency: 101.9. **Network Affiliation:** Independent. **Format:** Urban Contemporary. **Operating Hours:** Continuous; 99% local. **Key Personnel:** Steve Taylor, President; Mike Binkley, Vice President and Gen. Mgr.; B.K. Kirkland, Program Director; Jean McCormick, Promotions Director; Margie Oates, Business Manager.

★4218★
WJMH-FM
4002 E. Spring Garden
Greensboro, NC 27407 Phone: (919)855-6500
Frequency: 102.1. **Network Affiliation:** Independent. **Format:** Ethnic; Contemporary Hit Radio (CHR); Urban Contemporary. **Operating Hours:** Continuous. **Key Personnel:** Chris Bailey, Program Director; Kelly Masters, Music Director; David Patella, Sales Mgr.; Roger Stockton, Vice President and Gen. Mgr. **Owner:** Beasley Broadcast Group.

★4219★
WJOS-AM
1141 Elk Spur St.
PO Box 1038
Elkin, NC 28621 Phone: (919)835-2511
Frequency: 1540. **Network Affiliation:** ABC Radio. **Format:** Gospel. **Key Personnel:** John Wishon, News Dir.; Alan Combs, Station, Music, and Promotion Mgr.; Chris Newman, Sports Dir.; Leon Reece, Gen. Mgr. **Owner:** Tri-County Broadcasting Co. Inc.

★4220★
WLLE-AM
522 E. Martin St.
Raleigh, NC 27601 Phone: (919)833-3874
Frequency: 570. **Network Affiliation:** Southern Broadcasting; Sheridan Broadcasting. **Format:** Rhythm & Blues. **Operating Hours:** Continuous; 100% local. **Owner:** Henry & Prentice Monroe.

★4221★
WNAA-FM
North Carolina A&T State University
Price Hall, Ste. 200
Greensboro, NC 27411 Phone: (919)334-7936
Frequency: 90.1. **Network Affiliation:** Sheridan Broadcasting. **Format:** Jazz; Urban Contemporary; Eclectic; Religious. **Operating Hours:** 6 a.m.-3 a.m.; 100% local. **Key Personnel:** Tony Welborne, Gen. Mgr./Program Dir.; Yvonne Anderson, Music Dir.; Judith Malik, Public Affairs Dir.; Larry Allen, Chief Engineer. **Owner:** North Carolina A & T State University.

★4222★
WOKN-FM
PO Box 804
Goldsboro, NC 27530 Phone: (919)734-4213
Frequency: 102.3. **Network Affiliation:** USA Radio. **Format:** Urban Contemporary. **Operating Hours:** Continuous; 100% local. **Key Personnel:** Reggie Swinson, Music Director; Avetta J. Swinson. **Owner:** Robert and Jimmy Swinson.

★4223★
WOOW-AM
304 Evans St. Mall
Greenville, NC 27834 Phone: (919)757-0365
Frequency: 1340. **Network Affiliation:** National Black. **Format:** Talk; Jazz; Gospel; Rhythm & Blues. **Operating Hours:** 5 a.m.-midnight. **Key Personnel:** Jim Rouse, Pres./Gen. Mgr.; Evelyn Cohen, Office Mgr.; T.L. Davis, Music Dir. **Owner:** The Minority Voice, Inc.

★4224★
WPEG-FM
520 Hwy. 29 N.
Concord, NC 28025 Phone: (704)786-9111
Frequency: 97.9. **Network Affiliation:** Independent. **Format:** Urban Contemporary. **Operating Hours:** Continuous. **Key Personnel:** Pete Brown, Gen. Sales Mgr. **Owner:** Broadcasting Partners, Inc.

★4225★
WQOK-FM
8601 6 Forks Rd., Ste. 609
Raleigh, NC 27615 Phone: (919)848-9736
Frequency: 97.5. **Network Affiliation:** ABC Radio. **Format:** Urban Contemporary. **Operating Hours:** Continuous. **Key Personnel:** Brenda Rand-Davis, Promotions Dir.; Cy Young, Program Dir.; Tre Tailor, News Dir.; Bill Pope, Gen. Sales Mgr. **Owner:** Four Chiefs, Inc.

★4226★
WRCS-AM
Rte. 1, Box 13B
Ahoskie, NC 27910 Phone: (919)332-3101
Frequency: 970. **Format:** Black Gospel. **Operating Hours:** 6 a.m.-sunset. **Key Personnel:** Linda Futrell, Operations Mgr.; Shirley Perry, Music and Program Dir. **Owner:** Cumberland A & A Corp.

★4227★
WRRZ-AM
701 Bus. S.
Clinton, NC 28328 Phone: (919)592-2165
Frequency: 880. **Network Affiliation:** North Carolina News. **Format:** Country; Religious; Urban Contemporary. **Operating Hours:** Sunrise-sunset; 5% network, 95% local. **Key Personnel:** Dave Denton, Program, News, and Sports Dir.; Pam Blanchard, Music Dir. **Owner:** D. Patrick Dixon and David Denton.

★4228★
WRSV-FM
600 N. Grace St.
PO Box 2666
Rocky Mount, NC 27802 Phone: (919)442-9776
Frequency: 92.1. **Network Affiliation:** Southern Broadcasting. **Format:** Rhythm & Blues; Religious; Urban Contemporary. **Operating Hours:** Continuous; 2% network, 98% local. **Key Personnel:** Charles O. Johnson, General Manager; Angela Smith, Administrative Assistant. **Owner:** Northstar Broadcasting Corp.

★4229★
WRVS-FM
1001 Parkview Dr.
Elizabeth City, NC 27909 Phone: (919)335-3517
Frequency: 90.7. **Format:** Urban Contemporary. **Operating Hours:** 6 a.m.-1 a.m. **Key Personnel:** Edith J. Thorpe, Gen. Mgr./Program Dir.; Paula Sutton, Public Affairs Dir.; Andre Smith, News and Sports Dir.; Dorothy Keith, Traffic Coord. **Owner:** Elizabeth City State University Board of Trustees.

★4230★
WSMX-AM
Box 16049
500 Kinard Dr.
Winston-Salem, NC 27115
Frequency: 1500. **Network Affiliation:** Southern Broadcasting. **Format:** Adult Contemporary; Religious; Urban Contemporary. **Operating Hours:** 12 hours daily. **Key Personnel:** Curtis Dawkins, Music Director; Al Martin, Program Director. **Owner:** Bishop S.D. Johnson.

★4231★
WSMY-AM
616 Aurealian Springs Rd.
Weldon, NC 27870 Phone: (919)536-3115
Frequency: 1400. **Network Affiliation:** Sun Radio. **Format:** Talk; News; Top 40; Religious; Urban Contemporary. **Operating Hours:** 6 a.m.-midnight; 100% network. **Key Personnel:** Charles Beaver, Gen. Mgr.; Frank White, Station Mgr.; Beatrice White, Promotions. **Owner:** Faver Broadcasting.

★4232★
WSNC-FM
Winston-Salem State University
Winston-Salem, NC 27110 Phone: (919)750-2320
Frequency: 90.5. **Network Affiliation:** ABC Radio; Southern Broadcasting. **Format:** Talk; Jazz; News; Eclectic; Sports; Urban Contemporary; Oldies. **Operating Hours:** 7 a.m.-1 a.m.; 5% network, 95% local. **Key Personnel:** Sonja Williams, Gen. Mgr.; Marua Thompson, News Dir.; Derrick Whitmore, Program Dir.; Juan Isler, Music Dir.; Forrest McFetter, Production Mgr.; Joy Bridges, PSA Dir. **Owner:** Board of Trustees of Winston-Salem State University.

★4233★
WSRC-AM
3202 Guess Rd.
Durham, NC 27705 Phone: (919)477-7999
Frequency: 1410. **Network Affiliation:** Sheridan Broadcasting. **Format:** Sports; Religious; News. **Operating Hours:** Continuous. **Key Personnel:** Chester Davis, Program/Music and Sports Dir.; George Bridges, Sales Mgr.; Joann Jones, Office Mgr. **Owner:** Willis Broadcasting.

★4234★
WTNC-AM
726 Salem St.
PO Box 1920
Thomasville, NC 27360 Phone: (919)472-0790
Frequency: 790. **Network Affiliation:** Southern Broadcasting; National Black. **Format:** Religious. **Operating Hours:** Continuous. **Key Personnel:** Silvia Romaine, Gen. Mgr.; Arwyn Palmer, Program Dir. **Owner:** Alvin R. Rooks, Sr.

★4235★
WVCB-AM
Shallotte Broadcasting Co.
PO Box 314
Shallotte, NC 28459 Phone: (919)754-4512
Frequency: 1410. **Network Affiliation:** Independent. **Format:** Gospel. **Operating Hours:** Daylight. **Key Personnel:** John G. Worrell, Gen. Mgr. **Owner:** John G. Worrell.

★4236★
WWIL-AM
812-C Castle St.
Wilmington, NC 28401 Phone: (919)763-3364
Frequency: 1490. **Network Affiliation:** Christian Broadcasting (CBN). **Format:** Religious (Black Gospel, Contemporary Christian, Praise and Worship). **Operating Hours:** Continuous. **Key Personnel:** James Grey, Gen.Mgr. **Owner:** Forsam Communications.

★4237★
WYZD-AM
1311/2 Atkin St.
PO Box 797
Dobson, NC 27017 Phone: (919)386-8134
Frequency: 1560. **Format:** Gospel. **Operating Hours:** Daylight hours. **Key Personnel:** John Comer, Pres./Owner. **Owner:** Dobson Broadcasting, Inc.

★4238★
WZFX-FM
225 Green St., Ste. 900
Fayetteville, NC 28302 Phone: (919)486-4991
Frequency: 99.1. **Network Affiliation:** ABC Radio. **Format:** Urban Contemporary. **Operating Hours:** Continuous; 1% network, 99% local. **Key Personnel:** Larry Williams, V.P./Gen. Mgr.; Tony Lype, Program Dir.; Russ Boyum, Sales Mgr.; Joyce Ohajah, News Dir.; Janet Patterson, Sr. Account Exec.; Robin Gray, Office Mgr.; Gene Crim, Gen. Sales Mgr. **Owner:** Joyner Communications.

★4239★
WZOO-AM
Box 460
Asheboro, NC 27204 Phone: (919)672-0985
Frequency: 710. **Network Affiliation:** Independent. **Format:** Southern Gospel. **Operating Hours:** Sunrise-sunset. **Key Personnel:** Ann Caveness, Gen. Mgr.; D.W. Long, Pres.; Max Parrish, Chief Engineer.

Ohio

★4240★
WABQ-AM
8000 Euclid Ave.
Cleveland, OH 44103 Phone: (216)231-8005
Frequency: 1540. **Network Affiliation:** Independent. **Format:** Gospel. **Operating Hours:** Sunrise-sunset. **Key Personnel:** Denver Wilborn, Sales Mgr.; Dorothy Long, Bus. Mgr. **Owner:** Jack Linn.

★4241★
WBBY-FM
114 Dorchester Sq.
Box 14
Westerville, OH 43081 Phone: (614)891-1829
Frequency: 103.9. **Network Affiliation:** NBC Radio. **Format:** Jazz. **Operating Hours:** Continuous. **Key Personnel:** James B. Pidcock, V.P./Gen. Mgr.; Marilyn Cordial, News Dir.; Mike Perkins, Operations Mgr.

★4242★
WCKX-FM
510 E. Mound St.
Columbus, OH 43215-5539 Phone: (614)464-0020
Frequency: 106.3. **Network Affiliation:** ABC Radio; NBC Radio; Sheridan Broadcasting. **Format:** Urban Contemporary. **Operating Hours:** Continuous. **Key Personnel:** Jack Harris, Owner/Gen. Mgr.; Rick Stevens, Program Dir. **Owner:** Jack Harris.

★4243★
WCPN-FM
The Cleveland Centre. Ste. 300
3100 Chester Ave.
Cleveland, OH 44114 Phone: (216)432-3700
Frequency: 90.3. **Network Affiliation:** National Public Radio (NPR). **Format:** Jazz; News. **Operating Hours:** 5 a.m.-12:30 a.m. **Key Personnel:** Kathryn Jensen, Gen. Mgr. **Owner:** Cleveland Public Radio, Inc.

★4244★
WIZF-FM
7030 Reading Rd., No. 316
Cincinnati, OH 45237 Phone: (513)351-5900
Frequency: 100.9. **Network Affiliation:** Independent. **Format:** Urban Contemporary. **Operating Hours:** Continuous. **Key Personnel:** James Hutchinson, Gen. Mgr.; Todd Lewis, Program Dir. **Owner:** James Hutchinson and Tom Lewis.

★4245★
WJMO-AM
11821 Euclid Ave.
Cleveland, OH 44106 Phone: (216)795-1212
Frequency: 1490. **Network Affiliation:** Independent. **Format:** Urban Contemporary. **Operating Hours:** Continuous. **Key Personnel:** Curtis E. Shaw, Gen. Mgr.; Dave Urbach, Gen. Sales Mgr.; Sandra Barnett, Office Mgr. **Owner:** United Broadcasting Co.

★4246★
WJMO-FM
2156 Lee Rd.
Cleveland Heights, OH 44118 Phone: (216)371-3534
Frequency: 92.3. **Network Affiliation:** ABC Radio. **Format:** Urban Contemporary. **Operating Hours:** Continuous. **Key Personnel:** Curtis E. Shaw, V.P./Gen. Mgr.; Steve Harris, Program Dir.; George Curran, Sales Mgr.; Sandra Barnett, Office Mgr. **Owner:** United Broadcasting Co.

★4247★
WJTB-AM
105 Lake Ave.
Elyria, OH 44035-5013
Frequency: 1040. **Network Affiliation:** Independent. **Format:** Urban Contemporary. **Operating Hours:** Sunrise-sunset. **Key Personnel:** James Taylor, Gen. Mgr. **Owner:** Taylor Broadcasting Co.

★4248★
WMMX-AM
16 S. Broad St., Ste. 5
Box 1110
Fairborn, OH 45324 Phone: (513)878-9000
Frequency: 1110. **Network Affiliation:** USA Radio. **Format:** Gospel. **Operating Hours:** Sunup-sundown. **Key Personnel:** Tim Livingston, Station Mgr.; Norman Livingston, Gen. Mgr. **Owner:** L and D Broadcasters.

★4249★
WNOP-AM
1518 Dalton Ave.
Cincinnati, OH 45214 Phone: (513)241-9667
Frequency: 740. **Format:** Jazz. **Operating Hours:** 12 hours daily; 95% local. **Key Personnel:** Al Vontz, Gen. Mgr.; William Faulkner, Operations and Station Mgr.; Val Coleman, Sales Mgr.; Fred Williams, Engineer. **Owner:** Dayton Heidelberg Distributing Co.

★4250★
WNRB-AM
PO Box 625
Niles, OH 44446 Phone: (216)652-0106
Frequency: 1540. **Network Affiliation:** ABC Radio. **Format:** Urban Contemporary. **Operating Hours:** Sunrise-sunset. **Key Personnel:** Dominic Baragona, Gen. Mgr.; Robert Doane, Pres.; Gary Zocolo, V.P./Operations Mgr. **Owner:** W.N. Broadcasting.

★4251★
WVKO-AM
4401 Carriage Hill Ln.
Columbus, OH 43220 Phone: (614)451-2191
Frequency: 1580. **Network Affiliation:** Southern Broadcasting; Unistar. **Format:** Urban Contemporary. **Operating Hours:** Continuous. **Key Personnel:** Al Fetch, Gen. Mgr. **Owner:** Saga Communications.

★4252★
WVOI-AM
PO Box 5408
Toledo, OH 43613 Phone: (419)243-7052
Frequency: 1520. **Network Affiliation:** Sheridan Broadcasting. **Format:** Urban Contemporary. **Operating Hours:** Continuous. **Key Personnel:** Ken McDowell, Dr., Gen. Mgr./Owner; Casey McMichaels, Program Dir.; Pierre Price, Music Dir. **Owner:** McDowell Communications Co. of Ohio, Inc.

★4253★
WXTS-FM
2400 Collingwood
Toledo, OH 43620
Frequency: 88.3. **Network Affiliation:** Independent. **Format:** Jazz. **Operating Hours:** Continuous; 100% local. **Key Personnel:** John Kuschell, Station Mgr.

★4254★
WZAK-FM
1729 Superior Ave.
Cleveland, OH 44114 Phone: (216)621-9300
Frequency: 93.1. **Network Affiliation:** CBS Radio. **Format:** Urban Contemporary. **Operating Hours:** Continuous; 100% local. **Key Personnel:** Xenophon Zaphis, Pres./Gen. Mgr.; Michael J. Hibler, V.P.; Lee Zaphis, V.P./Operations; George Cohn, Natl. Sales Mgr.; Lynn Tolliver, Program Dir.; Bobby Rush, Music Dir.; Pam Halter, Controller; Ralph Poole, Promotions Dir.; Saulette Reed, Traffic Dir.; Renee Zapis, Office Mgr. **Owner:** Xenophon Zapis.

Oklahoma

★4255★
KPRW-AM
4045 NW 64th
Oklahoma City, OK 73116 Phone: (405)848-9870
Frequency: 1140. **Network Affiliation:** Sheridan Broadcasting. **Format:** Urban Contemporary. **Operating Hours:** 6 a.m.-11 p.m. **Key Personnel:** Larry Bastida, Gen. Mgr. **Owner:** Surrey Broadcasting.

★4256★
KTOW-FM
8886 W. 21st St.
Sand Springs, OK 74063 Phone: (918)446-1903
Frequency: 102.3. **Network Affiliation:** Independent. **Format:** Urban Contemporary. **Operating Hours:** Continuous. **Key Personnel:** Tim Barraza, Gen. Mgr.; Tony Barrow, Program Dir.; Gunnar Guinan, Operations Mgr. **Owner:** Luther Grahm.

★4257★
KXOJ-AM
Box 1250
Sapulpa, OK 74067 Phone: (918)224-2620
Frequency: 1550. **Network Affiliation:** ABC Radio; Oklahoma News. **Format:** Urban Contemporary. **Operating Hours:** Continuous. **Key Personnel:** Mike Stevens, Gen. Mgr. and Owner. **Owner:** Mike Stevens.

Oregon

★4258★
KMHD-FM
26000 SE Stark
Gresham, OR 97030 Phone: (503)661-8900
Frequency: 89.1. **Format:** Jazz. **Operating Hours:** 6 a.m.-2 a.m. **Key Personnel:** John Rice, Gen. Mgr.; Tom Costello, Station Mgr. **Owner:** Mount Hood Community College.

Pennsylvania

★4259★
WADV-AM
720 E. Kercher Ave.
PO Box 940
Lebanon, PA 17042 Phone: (717)273-2611
Frequency: 940. **Network Affiliation:** Mutual Broadcasting System. **Format:** Southern Gospel. **Operating Hours:** 5 a.m.-midnight. **Key Personnel:** Ken Meinhart, Operations Mgr.; Wilmer Borneman, Mgr.; Luke Hess, Account Exec. **Owner:** F.W.K. Inc.

★4260★
WAMO-AM
411 7th Ave., Ste. 1500
Pittsburgh, PA 15219 Phone: (412)471-2181
Frequency: 860. **Network Affiliation:** Sheridan Broadcasting. **Format:** Jazz. **Operating Hours:** Sunrise-sunset; 2% network, 98% local. **Key Personnel:** Ronald R. Davenport, Gen. Mgr.; Eric Faison, Program Dir.; Art Goewey, Music Dir.; Jerry Lopes, News Dir. **Owner:** Sheridan Broadcasting Corp.

★4261★
WAMO-FM
411 7th Ave., Ste. 1500
Pittsburgh, PA 15219 Phone: (412)471-2181
Frequency: 105.9. **Network Affiliation:** Sheridan Broadcasting. **Format:** Urban Contemporary. **Operating Hours:** Continuous; 5% network, 95% local. **Key Personnel:** Ronald R. Davenport, Gen. Mgr.; Eric Faison, Program Dir.; Art Goewey, Music Dir.; Jerry Lopes, News Dir. **Owner:** Sheridan Broadcasting Corp.

★4262★
WCXJ-AM
2001 Wylie Ave.
Pittsburgh, PA 15219 Phone: (412)391-1670
Frequency: 1550. **Network Affiliation:** National Black. **Format:** Religious; Urban Contemporary. **Operating Hours:** 18 hrs. daily. **Key Personnel:** Del King, Gen. Mgr./Program Dir.; J.V.A. Winsett, Pres. **Owner:** Unity Broadcasting, Inc.

★4263★
WDAS-AM
Belmont Ave. & Edgely Dr.
Philadelphia, PA 19131 Phone: (215)878-2000
Frequency: 1480. **Network Affiliation:** Independent. **Format:** Religious, Talk. **Operating Hours:** Continuous. **Key Personnel:** Kernie L. Anderson, Gen.Mgr. **Owner:** Unity Broadcasting Network, Inc.

★4264★
WDAS-FM
Belmont Ave. & Edgely Dr.
Philadelphia, PA 19131 Phone: (215)878-2000
Frequency: 105.3. **Network Affiliation:** Independent. **Format:** Urban Contemporary. **Operating Hours:** Continuous. **Key Personnel:** Kernie L. Anderson, Gen. Mgr.; Joseph Tamburro, Program Dir. **Owner:** Unity Broadcasting Network, Inc,.

★4265★
WIBF-FM
Benjamin Fox Pavilion, Ste. A-104
PO Box 1188
Jenkintown, PA 19046 Phone: (215)887-5400
Frequency: 103.9. **Format:** Ethnic; Religious. **Operating Hours:** Continuous; 60% network, 40% local. **Key Personnel:** Douglas Henson, General and Sales Mgr.; Don Hess, News Dir.; Larry Molinaro, Music Dir. **Owner:** Fox Broadcasting Co.

★4266★
WIMG-AM
PO Box 436
Washington, PA 18377
Frequency: 1300. **Network Affiliation:** National Black; Sheridan Broadcasting. **Format:** Gospel. **Operating Hours:** Continuous. **Key Personnel:** Walter Brickhouse, V.P./Regional Mgr. **Owner:** Willis Broadcasting Corp.

★4267★
WJSM-AM
RD 2, Box 87
Martinsburg, PA 16662 Phone: (814)793-2188
Frequency: 1110. **Network Affiliation:** Christian Broadcasting (CBN). **Format:** Southern Gospel. Simulcast WJSM-FM. **Operating Hours:** Continuous. **Key Personnel:** Larry Walters, Gen. Mgr.

★4268★
WJSM-FM
RD 2, Box 87
Martinsburg, PA 16662 Phone: (814)793-2188
Frequency: 92.7. **Network Affiliation:** Christian Broadcasting (CBN). **Format:** Southern Gospel. Simulcasts WJSM-AM. **Operating Hours:** Continuous. **Key Personnel:** Larry Walters, Pres./Gen. Mgr.; Sherwood Hawley, V.P./Program Dir.; Hap Ritchey, Music Dir. **Owner:** Martinsburg Broadcasting, Inc.

★4269★
WKDU-FM
3210 Chestnut St.
Philadelphia, PA 19104 Phone: (215)895-2580
Frequency: 91.7. **Network Affiliation:** Independent. **Format:** Jazz; Ethnic; Religious; Urban Contemporary; Alternative/New Music/Progressive. **Operating Hours:** Continuous. **Key Personnel:**

Andrea L. Welker, Gen. Mgr.; Joe Laird, Program Dir.; Chris Lairez, Program Dir. **Owner:** Drexel University.

★4270★
WLIU-FM
Office of Student Activities
Lincoln University, PA 19352 Phone: (215)932-8300
Frequency: 88.7. **Format:** Public Radio; Adult Contemporary; Jazz; Rhythm & Blues; Urban Contemporary; New Age; Religious; News. **Operating Hours:** Noon-3 a.m. **Key Personnel:** Terrence Johnson, Program Manager; David Sullivan, Station Manager; Earnest R. Smith, Program Director. **Owner:** Lincoln University.

★4271★
WPLW-AM
201 Ewing Rd.
Pittsburgh, PA 15205 Phone: (412)922-0550
Frequency: 1590. **Network Affiliation:** National Black. **Format:** Religious. **Operating Hours:** 6 a.m.-sunset. **Key Personnel:** Robert Hickling, Gen. Mgr. **Owner:** Hickling Broadcasting Corp.

★4272★
WSAJ-AM
Grove City College
Grove City, PA 16127 Phone: (412)458-3303
Frequency: 1340. **Network Affiliation:** Independent. **Format:** Jazz; Religious. **Operating Hours:** 7:15-8:45 p.m. Tues.-Thurs.; 7:30-8:30 p.m. Sun. **Key Personnel:** Everett DeVelda, Gen. Mgr.; Deena Philage, Program Dir.; David O. James, Student Program Dir. **Owner:** Grove City College.

★4273★
WTEL-AM
1349 Cheltenham Ave.
Philadelphia, PA 19126 Phone: (215)276-0500
Frequency: 860. **Network Affiliation:** Independent. **Format:** Religious; Ethnic. **Operating Hours:** Daytime. **Key Personnel:** Raul Delgada, Gen. Mgr. **Owner:** Beasly Broadcasting.

★4274★
WUSL-FM
440 Domino Ln.
Philadelphia, PA 19128 Phone: (215)483-8900
Frequency: 98.9. **Network Affiliation:** ABC Radio. **Format:** Urban Contemporary. **Operating Hours:** Continuous. 98% local, 2% other. **Key Personnel:** Bruce Holberg, Pres./Gen. Mgr.; Martin Conn, Gen. Sales Mgr.; Dave Allan, Program Dir.; Loraine Ballard Morrill, News Dir.; Angela High, Promotions Dir.; James Loftus, Sales Dir. **Owner:** Tak Communications, Inc.

Rhode Island

★4275★
WOTB-FM
140 Thames St.
Newport, RI 02840 Phone: (401)846-6900
Frequency: 100.3. **Network Affiliation:** Independent. **Format:** Jazz. **Operating Hours:** Continuous. **Key Personnel:** William Lancaster, Jr., Gen. Mgr./Sales Mgr. **Owner:** Bernard Perry.

★4276★
WRIB-AM
200 Water St.
East Providence, RI 02914 Phone: (401)434-0406
Frequency: 1220. **Network Affiliation:** Independent. **Format:** Religious; Ethnic. **Operating Hours:** 6 a.m.-10 p.m. **Key Personnel:** John Pierce, Gen. Mgr. **Owner:** Carter Broadcasting.

South Carolina

★4277★
WASC-AM
PO Box 5686
Spartanburg, SC 29304 Phone: (803)585-1530
Frequency: 1530. **Network Affiliation:** ABC Radio; National Black. **Format:** Urban Contemporary. **Operating Hours:** Daylight. **Key Personnel:** K. Joe Sessons, Gen. Mgr. **Owner:** New South Broadcasting.

★4278★
WCIG-FM
U.S. Hwy. 76
Mullins, SC 29574 Phone: (803)423-1140
Frequency: 107.1. **Network Affiliation:** South Carolina. **Format:** Urban Contemporary. **Operating Hours:** 6 a.m.-midnight; 8% network (news only), 92% local. **Key Personnel:** James F. Ramsey, Pres./Mgr.; Eugene Brantley, Operations Mgr. **Owner:** Mullins and Marion Broadcasting Co.

★4279★
WDOG-FM
Hwy. 125 NW
Allendale, SC 29810
Frequency: 93.5. **Network Affiliation:** ABC Radio; South Carolina News. **Format:** Country; Urban Contemporary. **Operating Hours:** 6 a.m.-midnight. **Key Personnel:** H. Carl Gooding, Pres. and Gen. Mgr.; Charles R. "Rick" Gooding, Program Dir., Sales Mgr., and Night Music Dir.; Lisa Gooding, Traffic Dir. **Owner:** Good Radio Broadcasting.

★4280★
WFXA-FM
104 Bennett Ln.
North Augusta, SC 29841 Phone: (803)279-2330
Frequency: 103.1. **Network Affiliation:** ABC Radio; CBS Radio. **Format:** Urban Contemporary. **Operating Hours:** Continuous; 98% local. **Key Personnel:** Betty Chesney, Accounting; Bill Lawson, Sales Mgr.; Walter Brumbeloe, Chief Engineer; Carl Conner, Program and Music Dir.; Carroll Redd, News and Program Dir.; Eleanor Hodges, Traffic and Office Mgr.; Bill Jaeger, Gen. Mgr. **Owner:** Davis Broadcasting Co., Inc.

★4281★
WHYZ-AM
PO Box 4309
Greenville, SC 29608-4309
Frequency: 1070. **Network Affiliation:** Southern Broadcasting. **Format:** Urban Contemporary. **Operating Hours:** Sunrise-sunset. **Key Personnel:** M. McClung, Station Mgr.; C. McClung, Business Mgr. **Owner:** Twenty First Century Communications, Ltd.

★4282★
WJKI-AM
Box 576
Woodruff, SC 29388 Phone: (803)476-2191
Frequency: 1510. **Network Affiliation:** ABC Radio; South Carolina News. **Format:** Gospel. **Operating Hours:** 6:30 a.m.-8:30 p.m.; 10% network, 90% local. **Key Personnel:** Norma L. Stokes, Gen. Mgr.; Leslie P. Cooper, Pres.; Manning Strickland, Program Dir.; Vince Hayes, Account Exec. **Owner:** Jackie Cooper Media, Inc.

★4283★
WLBG-AM
Box 1289
Laurens, SC 29360 Phone: (803)984-3544
Frequency: 860. **Format:** Urban Contemporary. **Operating Hours:** 6 a.m.-midnight. **Key Personnel:** Emil Finley, Pres.; Kevin St. John, Program Dir.

★4284★
WLGI-FM
Rte. 2
PO Box 69
Hemingway, SC 29554 Phone: (803)558-2977
Frequency: 90.9. **Network Affiliation:** Independent. **Format:** Talk; Ethnic; Urban Contemporary; Gospel. **Operating Hours:** 6 a.m.-9 p.m.; 100% local. **Key Personnel:** Bill Willis, Program Dir.; Gregory Kintz, Production and Technical Support Dir.; Ezekial Brown, Music Dir.; Laurie "CJ" James, Gospel Music Dir.

★4285★
WLWZ-FM
PO Box 19104
Greenville, SC 29602-9104
Frequency: 103.9. **Network Affiliation:** CBS Radio; Southern Broadcasting. **Format:** Ethnic; Urban Contemporary. **Operating Hours:** Continuous. **Key Personnel:** Valerie Whitted, Sales Mgr. **Owner:** Voyager Communications III.

★4286★
WMCJ-AM
314 Rembert Dennis Blvd.
PO Box 67
Moncks Corner, SC 29461 Phone: (803)761-6010
Frequency: 950. **Network Affiliation:** South Carolina News. **Format:** Gospel. **Operating Hours:** Continuous. **Key Personnel:** Dorothy Mitchum, Gen. Mgr.; Ken Willmott, News Dir.; Merideth McCrea, Traffic Mgr. **Owner:** Berkeley Broadcasting Corp.

★4287★
WMNY-AM
Rte. 1, Box 189
Santee, SC 29142-9718 Phone: (803)854-2671
Frequency: 1370. **Network Affiliation:** CNN Radio. **Format:** Urban Contemporary. **Operating Hours:** Continuous; 100% local. **Owner:** Clarence Jones.

★4288★
WMNY-FM
Rte. 1, Box 189
Santee, SC 29142-9718 Phone: (803)854-2671
Frequency: 100.3. **Network Affiliation:** CNN Radio. **Format:** Urban Contemporary. **Operating Hours:** Continuous; 100% local. **Owner:** Clarence Jones.

★4289★
WMTY-AM
370 Burnett
Greenwood, SC 29646 Phone: (803)223-4300
Frequency: 1090. **Network Affiliation:** Mutual Broadcasting System; South Carolina News. **Format:** Urban Contemporary. Simulcasts WMTY-FM. **Operating Hours:** 6 a.m.-two hours past sunset. **Key Personnel:** Betty L. Black, Gen. Mgr.; Stan Lewis, Operations Mgr./News Dir. **Owner:** United Community Enterprises.

★4290★
WMTY-FM
370 Burnett
Greenwood, SC 29646 Phone: (803)223-4300
Frequency: 103.5. **Network Affiliation:** Mutual Broadcasting System; South Carolina News. **Format:** Urban Contemporary. Simulcasts WMTY-AM. **Operating Hours:** 5 a.m.-12.30 a.m. **Key Personnel:** Betty L. Black, Gen. Mgr.; Stan Lewis, Operations Mgr./News Dir. **Owner:** United Community Enterprises.

★4291★
WPAL-AM
1717 Wappoo Rd.
Charleston, SC 29407 Phone: (803)763-6330
Frequency: 730. **Network Affiliation:** ABC Radio; National Black. **Format:** Rhythm & Blues. **Operating Hours:** Continuous; 5% network, 95% local. **Key Personnel:** William Sanders, Pres./Gen. Mgr.; Juanita W. LaRoche, V.P./Asst. Gen. Mgr.; Don Kendricks, Operations Mgr.; Tony Robertson, News Dir.

★4292★
WQIZ-AM
Box 903
St. George, SC 29477 Phone: (803)563-2772
Frequency: 810. **Network Affiliation:** Sheridan Broadcasting. **Format:** Gospel. **Operating Hours:** Sunrise-sunset. **Key Personnel:** Christopher M. Johnson, Gen. Mgr. **Owner:** Trident Communications.

★4293★
WQKI-AM
Riley Rd.
St. Matthews, SC 29135 Phone: (803)874-2777
Frequency: 710. **Network Affiliation:** Sheridan Broadcasting. **Format:** Urban Contemporary. **Operating Hours:** Sunrise-sunset; 10% network, 90% local. **Key Personnel:** Andy Henderson, Music Dir.; Ron Shuler, Sports; Robert Newsham, Mgr. **Owner:** Robert Newsham.

★4294★
WSSB-FM
Box 1915
Orangeburg, SC 29117 Phone: (803)536-8938
Frequency: 90.3. **Network Affiliation:** National Black. **Format:** Urban Contemporary. **Operating Hours:** 7 a.m.-12 a.m.; 15% network, 85% local. **Key Personnel:** Gil Harris, Gen. Mgr. & Sports Dir.; Carolyn Carter-Harris, Program Dir. & News Dir.; Marion White, Public Affairs & Public Service Director. **Owner:** WSSB-FM.

★4295★
WTGH-AM
1303 State St.
Cayce, SC 29033 Phone: (803)796-9533
Frequency: 620. **Network Affiliation:** Independent. **Format:** Gospel. **Operating Hours:** 18 hours daily. **Key Personnel:** Raleigh Williams, Gen. Mgr.; Josh Lorrick, Program Dir. **Owner:** Midland Communications.

★4296★
WUJM-AM
1 Carriage Ln.
Bldg. C-200
Charleston, SC 29407 Phone: (803)571-5555
Frequency: 1450. **Network Affiliation:** Mutual Broadcasting System. **Format:** Urban Contemporary. Simulcast of WUJM-FM. **Operating Hours:** Continuous. **Key Personnel:** C.J. Jones, Pres.; Bob Casey, Programming V.P.; Lyn Greene, Bus. Mgr. **Owner:** Jones-Eastern Radio.

★4297★
WUJM-FM
1 Carriage Ln.
Bldg. C-200
Charleston, SC 29407-6080 Phone: (803)556-4080
Frequency: 94.3. **Network Affiliation:** Mutual Broadcasting System. **Format:** Urban Contemporary. Simulcasts WUJM-AM. **Operating Hours:** Continuous; 98% local, 2% other. **Key Personnel:** Jim Gooden, News Dir. **Owner:** Jones-Eastern Radio, Inc.

★4298★
WVGB-AM
PO Box 1477
Beaufort, SC 29902 Phone: (803)524-4700
Frequency: 1490. **Network Affiliation:** Sheridan Broadcasting. **Format:** Religious; Oldies. **Operating Hours:** Continuous. **Key Personnel:** William A. Galloway, Pres.; Vivian M. Galloway, V.P.; Donzella Hendix, Gen. Mgr. **Owner:** William A. Galloway.

★4299★
WWDM-FM
Bradham Blvd.
Drawer 38
Sumter, SC 29150 Phone: (803)495-2558
Frequency: 103.1. **Format:** Urban Contemporary. **Operating Hours:** Continuous. **Key Personnel:** John Marshall, Owner/Gen. Mgr.; Andre Carson, Program Dir. **Owner:** John Marshall.

★4300★
WWWZ-FM
Fairfield Office Park, Ste. 304
1064 Gardner Rd.
Charleston, SC 29407 Phone: (803)556-9132
Frequency: 93.5. **Network Affiliation:** Sheridan Broadcasting. **Format:** Urban Contemporary. **Operating Hours:** Continuous; 100% local. **Key Personnel:** Clifford Fletcher, Pres.; Dean H. Mutter, Exec. V.P.; Bonnie Schwartz, Production and Traffic Dir. **Owner:** Millennium Communications.

★4301★
WYNN-AM
Box F-14
170 E. Palmetto St.
Florence, SC 29501 Phone: (803)662-6364
Frequency: 540. **Network Affiliation:** Sheridan Broadcasting. **Format:** Jazz; Black Gospel; Blues. **Operating Hours:** Continuous; 1% network, 99% local. **Key Personnel:** James N. Maurer, Pres.; Pansy Morgan, Sales Mgr.; Olie Williams, Program Dir.; Paige Smith, Office Mgr. **Owner:** Forjay Broadcasting Corp.

★4302★
WYNN-FM
170 E. Palmetto St.
PO Box F-14
Florence, SC 29501 Phone: (803)662-6364
Frequency: 106.3. **Network Affiliation:** Sheridan Broadcasting. **Format:** Urban Contemporary. **Operating Hours:** Continuous; 1% network, 99% local. **Key Personnel:** James N. Maurer, Pres.; Pansy Morgan, Sales Mgr.; Fred Brown, Program Dir.; Ernie Frierson, Public Affairs Dir.; Paige Smith, Office Mgr. **Owner:** Forjay Broadcasting Corp.

★4303★
WZJY-AM
1233 Ben Sawyer Blvd.
Mount Pleasant, SC 29464 Phone: (803)881-2482
Frequency: 1480. **Network Affiliation:** CNN Radio. **Format:** Gospel. **Operating Hours:** Continuous. **Key Personnel:** Loretta Drummond, Gen. Mgr.; Sam Dennis, Program Dir. **Owner:** Magdalene Williams.

Tennessee

★4304★
KHUL-FM
80 N. Tilman, Ste. 110
Memphis, TN 38111 Phone: (901)323-0101
Frequency: 101.1. **Network Affiliation:** CNN Radio. **Format:** Urban Contemporary. **Operating Hours:** Continuous.

★4305★
KWAM-AM
80 N. Tillman
Memphis, TN 38111 Phone: (901)323-2679
Frequency: 990. **Network Affiliation:** Independent. **Format:** Gospel. **Operating Hours:** 5 a.m.-midnight. **Key Personnel:** Bill Squartino, Gen. Mgr. **Owner:** Rivers Network.

★4306★
WABD-AM
150 Stateline Rd.
Clarksville, TN 37040 Phone: (615)431-5555
Frequency: 1370. **Network Affiliation:** Independent. **Format:** Urban Contemporary. **Operating Hours:** Continuous; 100% local. **Key Personnel:** Tom Cassetty, Gen. Mgr.; Lee Erwin, Operations Mgr. and News Dir.; Jerry Silvers, Program and Music Dir. **Owner:** Southern Broadcasting Corp.

★4307★
WBCV-AM
261/2 6th St.
PO Box 68
Bristol, TN 37621 Phone: (615)968-5221
Frequency: 1550. **Network Affiliation:** Independent. **Format:** Gospel. **Operating Hours:** Sunrise-sunset. **Key Personnel:** Jennings Dotson, Gen. Mgr. **Owner:** Sunshine Broadcasters.

★4308★
WBOL-AM
PO Box 191
Bolivar, TN 38008 Phone: (901)658-3690
Frequency: 1560. **Network Affiliation:** National Black. **Format:** Talk; News; Southern Gospel; Urban Contemporary. **Operating Hours:** Daytime. **Key Personnel:** Opal J. Shaw, Program Mgr.; Johnny W. Shaw, News Dir.; Daniel Bufford, Music Dir. **Owner:** Shaw's Broadcasting.

★4309★
WDIA-AM
112 Union Ave.
Memphis, TN 38103 Phone: (901)529-4300
Frequency: 1070. **Network Affiliation:** Independent. **Format:** Rhythm & Blues. **Operating Hours:** Continuous. **Key Personnel:** Ernie Jackson, Gen.Mgr. **Owner:** Ragan Henry National Ltd. Partnership.

★4310★
WETB-AM
PO Box 4127
Johnson City, TN 37602 Phone: (615)928-7131
Frequency: 790. **Network Affiliation:** USA Radio. **Format:** Gospel. **Operating Hours:** 6 a.m.-11 p.m. **Key Personnel:** Paul Gobble, Gen. Mgr.; Scott Onks, Program Dir.

★4311★
WFKX-FM
425 E. Chester
Jackson, TN 38301 Phone: (901)427-9616
Frequency: 95.9. **Network Affiliation:** Independent. **Format:** Urban Contemporary. **Operating Hours:** Continuous; 100% local. **Key Personnel:** James E. Wolfe, Jr., Pres./Operations and Gen. Mgr.; Tim Lambert, Sales Mgr.; Dave Shaw, Program Dir. **Owner:** Wolfe Communications, Inc.

★4312★
WHRK-FM
112 Union Ave.
Memphis, TN 38103 Phone: (901)529-4397
Frequency: 97.1. **Network Affiliation:** Independent. **Format:** Urban Contemporary. **Operating Hours:** Continuous. **Key Personnel:** Rick Coffey, Gen. Mgr. **Owner:** Ragan Henry National Ltd. Partnership.

★4313★
WJTT-FM
409 Chestnut St., Ste. A154
Chattanooga, TN 37402 Phone: (615)265-9494
Frequency: 94.3. **Network Affiliation:** CBS Radio. **Format:** Urban Contemporary. **Operating Hours:** Continuous. **Key Personnel:** James Brewer, II, Gen. Mgr.; Judi Waters, Bus. Mgr. **Owner:** Jettcom, Inc.

★4314★
WKJQ-AM
Iron Hill Rd.
PO Box 576
Parsons, TN 38363 Phone: (901)847-3011
Frequency: 1550. **Network Affiliation:** Independent. **Format:** Gospel. **Operating Hours:** Sunrise-sunset; 100% local. **Key Personnel:** Ralph D. Clenney, Owner/Mgr.; Edna Maxwell, Traffic Dir.; Dwight Lancaster, News Dir. **Owner:** Ralph D. Clenney.

★4315★
WLOK-AM
363 S. 2nd St.
Memphis, TN 38103 Phone: (901)527-9565
Frequency: 1340. **Network Affiliation:** Southern Broadcasting; National Black. **Format:** Religious. **Operating Hours:** Continuous; 2% network, 98% local. **Key Personnel:** Freddie Henderson, Gen. Mgr.; Corey Maclin, Program Dir.; Corey Maclin, News Dir. **Owner:** Gilliam Communications, Inc.

★4316★
WMOT-FM
Middle Tennessee State University
Murfreesboro, TN 37132 Phone: (615)898-2800
Frequency: 89.5. **Network Affiliation:** National Public Radio (NPR). **Format:** Jazz. **Operating Hours:** 5 a.m.-midnight Sun.-Thur., 6 a.m.-2 a.m. Fri. & Sat.; 30% network, 70% local. **Key Personnel:** John L. High, Dir. of Broadcasting; John Egly, Operations Dir.; Randy O'Brien, News Dir.; Gary Brown, Chief Engineer; Greg Lee, Program Dir.; Laura L. McComb, Development Coordinator; Shawn Jacobs, News Producer; Rhonda Wimberly, Traffic Dir. **Owner:** Middle Tennessee State University.

★4317★
WNAH-AM
44 Music Sq. E.
Nashville, TN 37203 Phone: (615)254-7611
Frequency: 1360. **Network Affiliation:** Mutual Broadcasting System; Sheridan Broadcasting. **Format:** Gospel. **Operating Hours:** Continuous. **Key Personnel:** Hoyt Carter, Jr., Gen. Mgr./Program Dir. **Owner:** Hermitage Broadcasting Co.

★4318★
WNOO-AM
1200 Mountain Creek Rd.
Chattanooga, TN 37405 Phone: (615)894-1023
Frequency: 1260. **Network Affiliation:** Sheridan Broadcasting; National Black. **Format:** Rhythm & Blues. **Operating Hours:** Sunrise-sunset. **Key Personnel:** Bill McKay, Pres./Gen. Mgr.; Diane Crane, Traffic Mgr. **Owner:** Tennessee Communications L.P.

★4319★
WRKM-AM
102 Z Country Ln.
Carthage, TN 37030 Phone: (615)735-1350
Frequency: 1350. **Network Affiliation:** Independent. **Format:** Gospel. **Operating Hours:** 5 a.m.-midnight; 5% network, 95% local. **Key Personnel:** Judith A. Wood, V.P.; Dex Jones, Sports Dir.; Anna Marie, News Dir.; Johnny Lynn, Music and Program Dir.; Teresa Schnabel, Traffic Mgr.; Brent Stone, Production Mgr. **Owner:** John and Judith A. Wood.

★4320★
WSMS-FM
Memphis State University
Memphis, TN 38152 Phone: (901)678-3176
Frequency: 91.7. **Network Affiliation:** Independent. **Format:** Jazz. **Operating Hours:** 6 a.m.-midnight; 100% local. **Key Personnel:** Robert W. McDowell, Gen. Mgr. **Owner:** Memphis State University.

★4321★
WSVT-AM
PO Box 549
Lebanon, TN 37088-0549 Phone: (615)459-7777
Frequency: 710. **Network Affiliation:** Independent. **Format:** Southern Gospel. **Operating Hours:** 6 a.m.-8 p.m. **Key Personnel:** Larry Garner, Gen. Mgr.; Chris Goodson, Program Dir. **Owner:** Jack Barsack.

★4322★
WVOL-AM
1320 Brick Church Pike
PO Box 70085
Nashville, TN 37207 Phone: (615)227-1470
Frequency: 1470. **Network Affiliation:** National Black. **Format:** Ethnic; Religious; Urban Contemporary. **Operating Hours:** Continuous. **Key Personnel:** Samuel Howard, Gen. Mgr.; Pat Smith, Local Sales Mgr.; Clarence Kilcrease, Community Affairs/Program Dir.; Karen Black, Traffic Dir.; Tonia Robinson, Continuity Dir.; Sue Dolleris, Admin. Asst.; Clinton Hooper, Chief Engineer. **Owner:** Phoenix Communications Group, Inc.

★4323★
WWGR-AM
PO Box 1530
La Follette, TN 37766-1530 Phone: (615)566-1000
Frequency: 960. **Network Affiliation:** Independent. **Format:** Gospel. **Operating Hours:** 6 a.m.-6 p.m. **Key Personnel:** Barbara Nulf, Operations Mgr.; Jack Williams, Music Dir. **Owner:** Lafollette Broadcasting, Inc.

★4324★
WXSS-AM
1188 Minna Pl., Ste. 214
Memphis, TN 38104 Phone: (901)726-5010
Frequency: 1030. **Network Affiliation:** Independent. **Format:** Jazz; Blues; Gospel. **Operating Hours:** Continuous. **Key Personnel:** Pervis Spann, Gen. Mgr.; Cynthia Andrews, Office Mgr. **Owner:** Minority Broadcasting Midwest.

Texas

★4325★
KALO-AM
7700 Gulfway
Port Arthur, TX 77642 Phone: (409)963-1276
Frequency: 1250. **Network Affiliation:** Sheridan Broadcasting. **Format:** Urban Contemporary; Gospel. **Operating Hours:** Continuous Tues.-Sun., 5 a.m.-midnight Sun. **Key Personnel:** Glenn Schiller, Gen. Mgr. **Owner:** Clear Channel Communications.

★4326★
KBUK-AM
4638 Decker Dr.
Baytown, TX 77520 Phone: (713)424-7000
Frequency: 1360. **Network Affiliation:** Sheridan Broadcasting. **Format:** Religious. **Operating Hours:** Continuous. **Key Personnel:** Dewayne Cook, Program Dir.; Donovan Howard, Promotions Dir.; Michael L. Mosley, Music Dir.; Corliss A. Rabb, Public Affairs Dir.; Darrell E. Martin, Gen. Mgr. **Owner:** Salt of the Earth Broadcasting Corp.

★4327★
KBWC-FM
711 Wiley Ave.
Marshall, TX 75670 Phone: (214)938-8341
Frequency: 91.1. **Format:** Urban Contemporary. **Operating Hours:** 16 hours daily; 25% network, 75% local. **Key Personnel:** Melvin C. Jones, Sr., Manager; Ruby Sibley, Assistant Manager; Marvette Washington, Music Director. **Owner:** Wiley College.

★4328★
KCHL-AM
Box 1067
San Antonio, TX 78294 Phone: (512)359-1067
Frequency: 1480. **Format:** Jazz; Gospel; Urban Contemporary. **Operating Hours:** 8 a.m.-10 p.m. **Key Personnel:** John Hiatt, Pres.; Chuck Wall, V.P./Gen. Mgr.; Mac McClennehan, Program Dir.; Rosenda Burns, News Dir.; Joe McCormack, Promotions Dir. **Owner:** Vision Communications, Inc.

★4329★
KCOH-AM
5011 Almeda
Houston, TX 77004 Phone: (713)522-1001
Frequency: 1430. **Network Affiliation:** Sheridan Broadcasting. **Format:** Urban Contemporary; Talk. **Operating Hours:** Continuous; 10% network, 90% local. **Key Personnel:** Mike Petrizzo, Exec. V.P./Gen. Mgr.; Travis O. Gardner, V.P./Music, Program and Promotions Dir.; Michael Harris, News Dir./Talk Show Host; Ralph Cooper, Sports Dir. **Owner:** KCOH, Inc.

★4330★
KDLF-AM
3185 Merriman Ave.
Port Neches, TX 77651 Phone: (409)727-2177
Frequency: 1150. **Network Affiliation:** USA Radio. **Format:** Gospel. **Operating Hours:** 6 a.m.-10 p.m. **Key Personnel:** Don Hebert, Gen. Mgr. **Owner:** Christian Crusade Corp.

★4331★
KHRN-FM
Hwy. 6 S., Box 1075
Hearne, TX 77859 Phone: (409)279-9211
Frequency: 94.3. **Format:** Urban Contemporary; Hispanic; Gospel. **Operating Hours:** 6 a.m.-midnight. **Key Personnel:** Pamela J. Walker, Gen. Mgr.; Joe Lee Walker, Sales Mgr.; A.J. Whiteside, Program Dir. **Owner:** Freckles Broadcasting, Inc.

★4332★
KHVN-AM
545 E. John Carpenter Fwy.
Irving, TX 75062 Phone: (214)556-8100
Frequency: 970. **Network Affiliation:** ABC Radio; Unistar. **Format:** Gospel. **Operating Hours:** Continuous. **Key Personnel:** Jim Stanton, V.P. and Gen. Mgr.; Buddy Howell, Gen. Sales Mgr.; Warren Brooks, Program Dir. **Owner:** Summit Broadcasting Corp.

★4333★
KIIZ-AM
5902 E. Business Hwy. 190
Killeen, TX 76543 Phone: (817)699-5000
Frequency: 1050. **Network Affiliation:** Independent. **Format:** Urban Contemporary. **Operating Hours:** Daytime. **Key Personnel:** Ken Williams, Owner/Gen. Mgr.; Dwayne McClayne, Program Dir. **Owner:** Mid-Texas Communications.

★4334★
KJBX-AM
6602 Quirt
Lubbock, TX 79408 Phone: (806)745-5800
Frequency: 580. **Network Affiliation:** ABC Radio. **Format:** Urban Contemporary. **Operating Hours:** Continuous; 100% local. **Key Personnel:** Chuck Heinz, Gen. Mgr.; Lynn Michael, Operations Mgr./Program Dir. **Owner:** The Dowe Co., Inc., of Texas.

★4335★
KJMZ-FM
545 E. John Carpenter Fwy., 17th Fl.
Irving, TX 75062 Phone: (214)556-8100
Frequency: 100.3. **Network Affiliation:** Unistar. **Format:** Urban Contemporary. **Key Personnel:** Jim Smith, Gen. Mgr.; Jeff Hillery, News Dir.; Buddy Howell, Gen. Sales Mgr.

★4336★
KKDA-FM
PO Box 530860
Grand Prairie, TX 75053 Phone: (214)263-9911
Frequency: 104.5. **Network Affiliation:** Independent. **Format:** Urban Contemporary. **Operating Hours:** Continuous. **Key Personnel:** Hyman Childs, Owner/Gen. Mgr.; Michael Spears, Gen. Mgr. **Owner:** Hyman Childs.

★4337★
KMHT-FM
911 Loop Dr., Ste. 110
Longview, TX 75604-5017 Phone: (214)938-6789
Frequency: 103.9. **Network Affiliation:** Satellite Music; AP Radio. **Format:** Rhythm & Blues; Urban Contemporary. **Operating Hours:** Continuous, except midnight-6 a.m. Mon. **Key Personnel:** Paul Adcock, Gen. Mgr.; Nora Adcock, Sales Mgr.; Brenda Watkins, Operations Mgr. **Owner:** Bayou Broadcasting, Inc.

★4338★
KMJQ-FM
24 Greenway Plaza
Houston, TX 77046 Phone: (713)623-0102
Frequency: 102.1. **Network Affiliation:** Independent. **Format:** Urban Contemporary. **Operating Hours:** Continuous. **Key Personnel:** Monte Lang, Sr. V.P./Gen. Mgr.; Ron Atkins, Program Dir. **Owner:** Noble Broadcasting.

★4339★
KMXO-AM
221 N. Leggett
Abilene, TX 79603 Phone: (915)672-5700
Frequency: 1500. **Format:** Talk; Hispanic; News; Eclectic; Country; Religious; Urban Contemporary; Classical. **Operating Hours:** Sunup-sundown. **Key Personnel:** Ray Silva, Owner, Pres., and Mgr.; Cecar Cano, Music Dir.; Felicha Band, Assistant Mgr. **Owner:** Ray Silva.

★4340★
KNBO-AM
PO Box 848
New Boston, TX 75570 Phone: (214)628-2561
Frequency: 1530. **Network Affiliation:** USA Radio. **Format:** Contemporary Christian; Southern Gospel; Inspirational. **Operating Hours:** Sunrise-sunset; 33% network, 67% local. **Key Personnel:** Richard E. Knox, Pres. **Owner:** Bowie County Broadcasting Co., Inc.

★4341★
KNTU-FM
University of North Texas
Box 13585
Denton, TX 76203 Phone: (817)565-3688
Frequency: 88.1. **Network Affiliation:** Texas State. **Format:** Jazz. **Operating Hours:** 6 a.m.-midnight. **Key Personnel:** Samuel J. Sauls, Station Mgr.; J. Russell Campbell, News/PA and Station Development Mgr.; Frank Bonner, Chief Engineer. **Owner:** University of North Texas.

★4342★
KPVU-FM
PO Box 156
Prairie View, TX 77446-0156 Phone: (409)857-4511
Frequency: 91.3. **Format:** Jazz; Top 40; Gospel. **Operating Hours:** 20 hours daily. **Key Personnel:** Dr. Lori Gray, Gen. Mgr.; Larry Coleman, Program Dir.; Carol Means, News Dir. **Owner:** Prairie View A&M University.

★4343★
KRBA-AM
121 Calder Sq.
PO Box 1345
Lufkin, TX 75901 Phone: (409)634-6661
Frequency: 1340. **Network Affiliation:** Texas State. **Format:** Ethnic; Country; Religious. **Operating Hours:** Continuous. **Key Personnel:** Stephen Yates, Gen. Mgr.; Melanie Quine, Office Mgr./Traffic Dir. **Owner:** Darrell E. Yates.

★4344★
KRZI-AM
1018 N. Valley Mill Dr.
Waco, TX 76710 Phone: (817)772-0930
Frequency: 1580. **Network Affiliation:** Unistar. **Format:** Oldies; Hispanic; Black Gospel. **Operating Hours:** 6 a.m.-midnight: 80% network, 20% local. **Key Personnel:** Van D. Goodall, Jr., Pres./Gen. Mgr.; Wendy Rigby, News Dir./Sports Dir. **Owner:** KRZI, Inc.

★4345★
KSAU-FM
Dept. of Communications
Box 13048
Nacogdoches, TX 75962 Phone: (409)568-4000
Frequency: 90.1. **Network Affiliation:** ABC Radio. **Format:** Jazz; Urban Contemporary; Alternative/New Music/Progressive. **Operating Hours:** 9 a.m.-1 a.m. Sat.-Sun.; 1 p.m.-1 a.m. weekdays; 2% network, 98% local. **Key Personnel:** Dr. Joe Oliver, Gen. Mgr.; Jeff Hutchinson, Station Mgr.; Paul Wicker, Program Dir. **Owner:** Stephen F. Austin State University.

★4346★
KSGB-AM
3105 Arkansas Ln., No. A-2
Arlington, TX 76016-5826 Phone: (817)469-1540
Frequency: 1540. **Network Affiliation:** Independent. **Format:** Gospel. **Operating Hours:** 6 a.m.-1 a.m. **Key Personnel:** Mary Gaines, Gen. Mgr.; Jack Stuart, Sales Mgr.; Jerome Thomas, Music Dir. **Owner:** Stuart Gaines Broadcasting.

★4347★
KSKY-AM
2727 Inwood Rd.
Dallas, TX 75235 Phone: (214)352-3975
Frequency: 660. **Network Affiliation:** Independent. **Format:** Gospel. **Operating Hours:** Continuous. **Key Personnel:** Bill Simmons, Gen. Mgr.; Freda Wells, Public Affairs and Program Dir.; Kathie Watson, Sales Mgr. **Owner:** Broadcasting Partners of Dallas, Inc.

★4348★
KTSU-FM
3100 Cleburne Ave.
Houston, TX 77004 Phone: (713)527-7905
Frequency: 90.9. **Network Affiliation:** Independent. **Format:** Jazz; Religious; Oldies. **Operating Hours:** Continuous; 100% local. **Key Personnel:** Bernard M. Walker, Gen. Mgr. and Devel. Dir.; Claude "Rick" Roberts, Operations Mgr.; Detria Ward, Traffic Mgr. **Owner:** Texas Southern University Board of Regents.

★4349★
KZEY-AM
PO Box 4248
Tyler, TX 75712 Phone: (903)593-1744
Frequency: 690. **Network Affiliation:** AP Radio. **Format:** Urban Contemporary. **Operating Hours:** Continuous. **Key Personnel:** Bud Kitchens, Gen. Mgr.; John Sims, News and Sports Dir.; Kenn Williams, Operations and Music Dir.; Bob Uzzell, Traffic Dir. **Owner:** Hawthorne Broadcasting.

Utah

★4350★
KMGR-AM
5282 South 320 West, Ste. D-272
Salt Lake City, UT 84107 Phone: (801)264-1075
Frequency: 1230. **Network Affiliation:** Satellite Music. **Format:** Urban Contemporary (Heart & Soul). **Operating Hours:** Continuous. **Key Personnel:** Ruk Adams, Gen. Mgr. **Owner:** B & B Broadcasting, L.P.

Virginia

★4351★
WANT-AM
1101 Front St.
Richmond, VA 23222 Phone: (804)321-5662
Frequency: 990. **Network Affiliation:** Independent. **Format:** Urban Contemporary. **Operating Hours:** Continuous. **Key Personnel:** Nancy Freeman, Owner; John Galloway, Gen. Mgr.; Valerie Clayton, Office Mgr.; Lorenzo Thomas, Program Dir. **Owner:** Nancy Freeman.

★4352★
WBTX-AM
PO Box 337
Broadway, VA 22891 Phone: (703)896-8933
Frequency: 1470. **Network Affiliation:** Christian Broadcasting (CBN). **Format:** Gospel. **Operating Hours:** 6 a.m.-sunset; 5% network. **Key Personnel:** David M. Eshleman, Pres./Owner; Jim Snavely, Music and News Dir. **Owner:** Massanutten Broadcasting Co., Inc.

★4353★
WCDX-FM
2809 Emerywood Pkwy., Ste. 300
Richmond, VA 23294 Phone: (804)672-9300
Frequency: 92.7. **Network Affiliation:** Independent. **Format:** Urban Contemporary; Top 40. **Operating Hours:** Continuous. **Key Personnel:** Ben Miles, Gen. Mgr.; Gary Young, Program Dir.; Larry Jones, Gen. Sales Mgr. **Owner:** Sinclair Telecable.

★4354★
WGCV-AM
3267 S. Crater Rd.
Petersburg, VA 23805 Phone: (804)733-4567
Frequency: 1240. **Network Affiliation:** Independent. **Format:** Gospel. **Operating Hours:** Continuous. **Key Personnel:** Connie Balthrop, Gen. Mgr.; Cavell Phillips, Program Dir. **Owner:** Paco-John Broadcasting Corp.

★4355★
WILA-AM
865 Industrial Ave.
PO Box 3444
Danville, VA 24543 Phone: (804)792-2133
Frequency: 1580. **Network Affiliation:** Sheridan Broadcasting. **Format:** Urban Contemporary (Heart & Soul). **Operating Hours:** Sunrise-sunset; 1% network, 99% local. **Key Personnel:** Lawrence Toller, Program Dir.; Katrina Crews, News Dir.; Frances McMillan, Pres. **Owner:** Frances R. McMillan.

★4356★
WJJS-AM
1105 Main St.
Madison Heights, VA 24551 Phone: (804)847-1266
Frequency: 1320. **Network Affiliation:** Unistar; CBS Radio; Sheridan Broadcasting. **Format:** Urban Contemporary. **Operating Hours:** Continuous; 10% network, 90% local. **Key Personnel:** Phil Showers, V.P./Gen. Mgr. **Owner:** CRS Communications, Inc.

★4357★
WKBY-AM
Rte. 2, Box 105A
Chatham, VA 24531 Phone: (804)432-8108
Frequency: 1080. **Network Affiliation:** National Black. **Format:** Religious; Urban Contemporary. **Operating Hours:** Sunrise-sunset. **Key Personnel:** Susan Neal, Station Mgr.; Vickie Prittchett, Music and News Dir.; Richard Towler, Sales Mgr. **Owner:** William L. Bonner.

★4358★
WMYK-AM
168 Business Park Dr., No. 100
Virginia Beach, VA 23462 Phone: (804)671-9400
Network Affiliation: ABC Radio. **Format:** Urban Contemporary. **Operating Hours:** Continuous. **Key Personnel:** Paul Lucci, Pres./Gen.

Mgr.; Lon Goldman, Local Sales Mgr.; Kevin Brown, Program Dir. **Owner:** Edge Broadcasting Co.

★4359★
WMYK-FM
168 Business Park Rd., Ste. 100
Virginia Beach, VA 23462 Phone: (804)473-1194
Frequency: 93.7. **Network Affiliation:** Independent. **Format:** Urban Contemporary. **Operating Hours:** Continuous. **Key Personnel:** Paul Lucci, Gen. Mgr.; Kevin Brown, Program Dir. **Owner:** Edge Broadcasting.

★4360★
WOWI-FM
645 Church St., Ste. 400
Norfolk, VA 23510-2809 Phone: (804)622-4600
Frequency: 102.9. **Network Affiliation:** Southern Broadcasting; National Black. **Format:** Urban Contemporary. **Operating Hours:** Continuous; 5% network. **Key Personnel:** Bishop L.E. Willis, Owner; Walter A. Brickhouse, V.P. and Gen. Mgr.; Steve Crumbley, National Program Dir.; Sylvia Hodges-Melvin, Promotions Dir.; Gladys Debnam, Sales Assistant. **Owner:** Willis Broadcasting Corp.

★4361★
WPLZ-FM
3267 S. Crater Rd.
Petersburg, VA 23805 Phone: (804)733-4567
Frequency: 99.3. **Network Affiliation:** Independent. **Format:** Urban Contemporary. **Operating Hours:** Continuous. **Key Personnel:** Connie Balthrop, Gen. Mgr.; Phil Daniel, Program Dir. **Owner:** Paco-John Broadcasting Corp.

★4362★
WRAP-AM
645 Church St., Ste. 201
Norfolk, VA 23510-1712
Frequency: 1350. **Network Affiliation:** ABC Radio; National Black. **Format:** Urban Contemporary. **Operating Hours:** Continuous. **Key Personnel:** David W. Palmer, President and Gen. Mgr.; Ron Madison, Sales Mgr.; Joe Wetherbee, Systems Manager and Chief Engineer; Chester Benton, Program Director; Don Roberts, News Director; H.J. Ellison, Music Director; Jackie Bowe, Sports Director. **Owner:** Target Broadcast Group, Inc.

★4363★
WTOY-AM
709 Bowman Ave.
Salem, VA 24153 Phone: (703)387-1480
Frequency: 1480. **Network Affiliation:** National Black; Sheridan Broadcasting. **Format:** Urban Contemporary. **Operating Hours:** 5:30 a.m.-10 p.m. **Key Personnel:** Theresa Davis, Gen. Mgr. **Owner:** Ward Broadcasting Corp.

★4364★
WVST-FM
Virginia State University
Box 10
Petersburg, VA 23803 Phone: (804)524-5932
Frequency: 91.3. **Network Affiliation:** Sheridan Broadcasting. **Format:** Classical; Jazz; Rhythm & Blues; News; Sports; Religious. **Operating Hours:** 6 a.m.-1 a.m.; 5% network, 95% local. **Key Personnel:** Paul Alatorre, Station Mgr.; Will Harris, Program Dir.; Denise Tyson, Traffic Dir.; Leon Brooks, Program Dir.; Rachman Hafiz, Research Dir. **Owner:** Virginia State University.

Washington

★4365★
KARI-AM
4840 Lincoln Rd.
Blaine, WA 98230 Phone: (206)734-4221
Frequency: 550. **Network Affiliation:** AP Radio; Moody Broadcasting; Satellite Music. **Format:** Gospel. **Operating Hours:** Continuous. **Key Personnel:** Gary L. Nawman, Operations Mgr.; Jan Larsen, News Dir.; Jim Scott, Chief Engineer; Don Bevilacqua, Gen. Mgr. **Owner:** Birch Bay Broadcasting Co., Inc.

★4366★
KEWU-FM
KEWU-R T.V.
Dept. MS. 105
Cheney, WA 99004 Phone: (509)359-2850
Frequency: 89.5. **Network Affiliation:** Independent. **Format:** Jazz. **Operating Hours:** 100% local. **Owner:** Eastern Washington University.

★4367★
KKFX-AM
2815 2nd Ave., No. 550
Seattle, WA 98121 Phone: (206)728-1250
Frequency: 1250. **Network Affiliation:** ABC Radio. **Format:** Urban Contemporary. **Operating Hours:** Continuous; 10% network, 90% local. **Key Personnel:** Robert L. Wikstrom, Gen. Mgr.; Deacon Baker, Program Dir.; Nikki Hill-Garrett, Promotions Mgr. **Owner:** Bingham Communications Group, Inc.

★4368★
KRIZ-AM
2600 S. Jackson
Seattle, WA 98144 Phone: (206)329-7880
Frequency: 1420. **Network Affiliation:** Independent. **Format:** Urban Contemporary. **Operating Hours:** Continuous. **Key Personnel:** Chris Bennett, CEO/Gen. Mgr.; Frank Barrow, Operations Mgr. **Owner:** Kris Broadcasting, Inc.

West Virginia

★4369★
WVKV-AM
Box 1080
Hurricane, WV 25526 Phone: (304)562-9155
Frequency: 1080. **Format:** Gospel. **Operating Hours:** Daytime. **Key Personnel:** Theresa Milliken, Station Mgr.; Jim Milliken, Gen. Mgr. **Owner:** Milliken Investment Corp.

Wisconsin

★4370★
WMVP-AM
4222 W. Capitol Dr., Ste. 1290
Milwaukee, WI 53216 Phone: (414)444-1290
Frequency: 1290. **Network Affiliation:** Satellite Radio. **Format:** Urban Contemporary. **Operating Hours:** Continuous. **Key Personnel:** Victor Singleton, Promotions Dir.; Don Rosette, Gen. Mgr.; Billy Young, Program Dir.; Roger Williams, Gen. Sales Mgr.; Ella Smith, Community Relations Dir.; Larry Bandy, News Dir. **Owner:** Suburbanaire, Inc.

★4371★
WNOV-AM
3815 N. Teutonia Ave.
Milwaukee, WI 53206 Phone: (414)449-9668
Frequency: 860. **Network Affiliation:** Independent. **Format:** Blues; Gospel. **Operating Hours:** 5:30 p.m.-8:30 p.m. **Key Personnel:** Sandra Robinson, Station Mgr. **Owner:** Gerald Jones.

★4372★
WYMS-FM
Drawer 10K
Milwaukee, WI 53069 Phone: (414)475-8389
Frequency: 88.9. **Network Affiliation:** American Public Radio (APR). **Format:** Jazz; Ethnic; Blues. **Operating Hours:** Continuous; 10% network, 90% local. **Key Personnel:** Glenda Landon, Gen. Mgr.; Roger Dolbrick, Station Mgr.; Coy Davis, Program Dir. **Owner:** Milwaukee Public Schools.

TELEVISION STATIONS

California

★4373★
KNTV-TV
645 Park Ave.
San Jose, CA 95110 Phone: (408)286-1111
Channel: 11. **Network Affiliation:** ABC. **Format:** Commercial TV. **Operating Hours:** 6 a.m. - 2 a.m. **Key Personnel:** Stewart Park, Gen. Mgr. an Prog. Dir. **Owner:** Granite Broadcasting, Inc.

District of Columbia

★4374★
WHMM-TV
2222 4th St. NW
Washington, DC 20059 Phone: (202)806-3200
Channel: 32. **Network Affiliation:** Public Broadcasting Service (PBS). **Format:** Public TV. **Operating Hours:** 8 a.m. - 12:30 a.m. **Key Personnel:** Edward Jones, Jr., Gen.Mgr. **Owner:** Howard University Board of Trustees.

Florida

★4375★
WTVT-TV
3213 W. Kennedy Blvd.
Tampa, FL 33609 Phone: (813)876-1313
Channel: 13. **Network Affiliation:** CBS. **Format:** Commercial TV. **Operating Hours:** Continuous. **Key Personnel:** David Whitaker, Gen.Mgr. **Owner:** WTVT Holdings, Inc.

Georgia

★4376★
WGXA-TV
PO Box 340
Macon, GA 31297 Phone: (912)745-2424
Channel: 24. **Network Affiliation:** ABC. **Format:** Commercial TV. **Key Personnel:** Ken Gerdes, V.Pres/Gen.Mgr. **Owner:** WGXA-TV.

Illinois

★4377★
WEEK-TV
2907 Springfield Rd.
Peoria, IL 61611 Phone: (309)698-2525
Channel: 25. **Network Affiliation:** NBC. **Format:** Commercial TV. **Operating Hours:** 5:30 a.m. - 1:30 a.m. **Key Personnel:** Dennis Upah, Gen.Mgr./Prog. Dir. **Owner:** Gramote Broadcasting Corp.

Indiana

★4378★
WPTA-TV
3401 Butler Rd.
Box 2121
Ft. Wayne, IN 46801 Phone: (219)483-0584
Channel: 21. **Network Affiliation:** ABC. **Format:** Commercial TV. 5:30 a.m. - 2 a.m. **Key Personnel:** Barbara Wigham, V.Pres./Gen.Mgr. **Owner:** Granite Broadcasting, Inc.

★4379★
WRTV-TV
1330 N. Meridian St.
Indianapolis, IN 46206 Phone: (317)635-9788
Channel: 6. **Network Affiliation:** ABC. **Format:** Commercial TV. **Operating Hours:** 5:30 a.m. - 2:30 a.m. **Key Personnel:** John B. Proffitt, V.Pres./GEM **Owner:** McGraw-Hill Broadcasting Co., Inc. **Formerly:** WFBM-TV (1972).

Louisiana

★4380★
WNOL-TV
1661 Canal St.
New Orleans, LA 70112 Phone: (504)525-3838
Madelyn Bonnot, Gen.Mgr.
Channel: 38. **Network Affiliation:** Independent; Fox. **Format:** Commercial TV. **Operating Hours:** Continuous except 1 a.m. - 6 a.m. Mon. **Owner:** Quincy Jones Broadcasting, Inc.

Maine

★4381★
WVII-TV
371 Target Industrial Circle
Bangor, ME 04401 Phone: (207)945-6457
Channel: 7. **Network Affiliation:** ABC. **Format:** Commercial TV. **Operating Hours:** Varies; 5-5:30 a.m. - 12-2:30 a.m. **Key Personnel:** Barbara Cyr, Gen.Mgr. **Owner:** Seaway Communications.

Michigan

★4382★
WGPR-TV
3146 E. Jefferson Ave.
Detroit, MI 48207 Phone: (313)259-8862
Channel: 62. **Network Affiliation:** Independent. **Format:** Commercial TV. **Operating Hours:** Continuous. **Key Personnel:** George Matthews, Pres./Gen.Mgr. **Owner:** Int'l Masons, Inc.

Minnesota

★4383★
KBJR-TV
KBJR Bldg.
Duluth, MN 55802 Phone: (218)727-8484
Robert F. Kalthoff, Pres./Gen.Mgr.
Channel: 6. **Network Affiliation:** NBC. **Format:** Commercial TV. **Operating Hours:** 5:30 a.m. - 2 a.m. **Owner:** Granite Broadcasting Corp.

Mississippi

★4384★
WLBM-TV
4608 Skyland Dr.
PO Box 5840
Meridian, MS 39302-5840 Phone: (601)485-3030
Channel: 30. **Network Affiliation:** NBC. **Format:** Commercial TV. **Owner:** Pluria Marshall, V.Pres/Gen.Mgr.

★4385★
WLBT-TV
715 S. Jefferson St.
Jackson, MS 39205 Phone: (601)948-3333
Channel: 3. **Network Affiliation:** NBC. **Format:** Commercial TV. **Operating Hours:** 5:30 a.m. - 2 a.m. **Key Personnel:** Frank Melton, Pres./Gen.Mgr. **Owner:** Civic Communications.

New York

★4386★
WHEC-TV
191 East Ave.
Rochester, NY 14604 Phone: (716)546-5670
Channel: 10. **Network Affiliation:** NBC. **Format:** Commercial TV. **Operating Hours:** Continuous Sun.-Thurs.; sign-off at 3 a.m. Fri. & 2 a.m. Sat. **Key Personnel:** Arnold Klinisky, Gen.Mgr. **Owner:** Viacom Broadcasting.

★4387★
WKBW-TV
7 Broadcast Plaza
Buffalo, NY 14202 Phone: (716)845-6100
Channel: 7. **Network Affiliation:** ABC. **Format:** Commercial TV. **Operating Hours:** Continuous. **Key Personnel:** Stephen H. Kimatian, Pres./Gen.Mgr. **Owner:** Queen City Broadcasting.

Oregon

★4388★
KBSP-TV
4923 Indian School Rd. NE
Salem, OR 97305 Phone: (503)390-2202
Channel: 22. **Network Affiliation:** Independent. **Format:** Commercial TV. **Operating Hours:** Continuous. **Key Personnel:** Judy Koenig, Gen.Mgr./Prog.Dir. **Owner:** Blackstar Communications, Inc.

Texas

★4389★
KTXS-TV
PO Box 2997
Abilene, TX 79604 Phone: (915)677-2281
Clay Milstead, Gen.Mgr.
Channel: 12. **Network Affiliation:** ABC. **Format:** Commercial TV. **Operating Hours:** 6 a.m. - 12:30 a.m. **Owner:** Lamco Communications, Inc.

Virginia

★4390★
WJCB-TV
1930 Pembroke Ave.
Hampton, VA 23669 Phone: (804)627-7500
Dwight Green, Gen.Mgr.
Channel: 49. **Network Affiliation:** Family Television Network. **Format:** Commercial TV. **Operating Hours:** 7 a.m. - midnight.

Wisconsin

★4391★
WJFW-TV
S. Oneida Ave.
PO Box 858
Rhinelander, WI 54501 Phone: (715)369-4700
Channel: 12. **Network Affiliation:** NBC. **Format:** Commercial TV. **Operating Hours:** 6 a.m. - 2 a.m. **Key Personnel:** Marie Platteter, Gen.Mgr. **Owner:** Seaway Communications.

(17) VIDEOS

Entries in this chapter are arranged alphabetically by video title. See the User's Guide at the front of this directory for additional information.

★4392★
ABA Commission on Minorities and Judicial Administration Division The
American Bar Association
Commission on Public Understanding
About the Law
750 N. Lakeshore Dr.
Chicago, IL 60611 Phone: (312)988-5000
1988. **Program Description:** Issues of prejudice in the courtroom are discussed. **Length:** 15 mins. **Format:** Beta, VHS, 3/4'' U-matic. **Acquisition:** Purchase, Rent/Lease. **Use:** School/Group/Institution, Closed Circuit Television, In-Home Viewing, Special Use Restrictions Apply.

★4393★
Abraham Lincoln and the Emancipation Proclamation
American Educational Films
3807 Dickerson Rd.
Nashville, TN 37207 Phone: 800-822-5678
1973. **Program Description:** An examination of the dilemma confronting Lincoln over the troubling issue of Negro slavery. **Length:** 25 mins. **Format:** Beta, VHS, 3/4'' U-matic. **Acquisition:** Purchase. **Use:** School/Group/Institution, Special Use Restrictions Apply.

★4394★
Adam Clayton Powell
Phoenix/BFA Films
468 Park Ave., S.
New York, NY 10016 Phone: (212)684-5910
1977. **Program Description:** The story of the controversial Black congressman and his struggle against oppression and injustice to Blacks in America. The program contains an interview with Powell, conducted shortly before his death by WABC-TV's Gil Noble. **Length:** 58 mins. **Format:** Beta, VHS, 3/4'' U-matic. **Acquisition:** Purchase. **Use:** School/Group/Institution, Special Use Restrictions Apply.

★4395★
Affirmative Action: Is It the Answer to Discrimination?
American Enterprise Institute for Public Policy Research
1150 17th St. NW
Washington, DC 20036 Phone: (202)862-5800
197?. **Program Description:** A panel of lawyers, academicians, and journalists meet to discuss the legality of granting preference to people on the basis of sex, race, and national origin. **Length:** 60 mins. **Format:** 3/4'' U-matic. **Acquisition:** Rent/Lease, Purchase. **Use:** School/Group/Institution, Broadcast television.

★4396★
Africa
Michigan Media
University of Michigan
400 4th St.
Ann Arbor, MI 48109 Phone: (313)764-8228
1977. **Program Description:** A look at the Black against Black conflicts in Africa, which are more critical than the Black/White struggle that often overshadows them. **Length:** 29 mins. **Format:** 3/4'' U-matic, Other than listed. **Acquisition:** Rent/Lease, Purchase. **Use:** School/Group/Institution, Closed Circuit Television, Cable Television, Broadcast Television.

★4397★
Africa: An Introduction
Phoenix/BFA Films
468 Park Ave., S.
New York, NY 10016 Phone: (212)684-5910
1981. **Program Description:** This show is an overview of Africa and the many different people who make up the population. **Length:** 22 mins. **Format:** Beta, VHS, 3/4'' U-matic. **Acquisition:** Purchase. **Use:** School/Group/Institution, Special Use Restrictions Apply.

★4398★
Africa Calls: Its Drums and Musical Instruments
Carousel Film & Video
260 5th Ave.
New York, NY 10016 Phone: (212)683-1660
1971. **Program Description:** An African lives, works, and communicates through his music. **Length:** 23 mins. **Format:** Beta, VHS, 3/4'' U-matic. **Acquisition:** Purchase. **Use:** School/Group/Institution, Special Use Restrictions Apply.

★4399★
Africa: Historical Heritage
Britannica Films
310 S. Michigan Ave.
Chicago, IL 60604 Phone: (312)347-7958
1971. **Program Description:** Archeologists' research reveals the development of African culture, law, and medicine. From the ''Afro-American History'' series. **Length:** 9 mins. **Format:** Beta, VHS, 3/4'' U-matic. **Acquisition:** Rent/Lease, Purchase, Trade-in. **Use:** School/Group/Institution, Special Use Restrictions Apply.

★4400★
Africa Is My Home (Revised)
Atlantis Productions
1252 La Granada Dr.
Thousand Oaks, CA 91360 Phone: (805)495-2790
197?. **Program Description:** This film provides an insight into the life of an African girl who is born at the time of Nigerian independence and who grows to maturity while Nigeria confronts the issues and conflicts of a developing nation. **Length:** 19 mins. **Format:** Beta, VHS, 3/4'' U-matic. **Acquisition:** Purchase. **Use:** School/Group/Institution, Special Use Restrictions Apply.

★4401★
Africa Today
King Features Entertainment
235 E. 45th St.
New York, NY 10017 Phone: (212)682-5600
1983. **Program Description:** This program studies all of the changes and conflicts that affect African nations today. **Length:** 14 mins. **Format:** Beta, VHS, 3/4'' U-matic. **Acquisition:** Rent/Lease; Purchase. **Use:** School/Group/Institution.

★4402★
African Art
Journal Films, Inc.
930 Pitner Ave.
Evanston, IL 60202 Phone: (312)328-6700
197?. **Program Description:** The influence of contemporary African history on today's artist is outlined. **Length:** 13 mins. **Format:** Beta, VHS, 3/4" U-matic. **Acquisition:** Rent/Lease; Purchase. **Use:** School/Group/Institution.

★4403★
African Art and Sculpture
Carousel Film & Video
260 5th Ave.
New York, NY 10016 Phone: (212)683-1660
1971. **Program Description:** Reveals the African's sense of beauty and curiosity as displayed in works of art. **Length:** 21 mins. **Format:** Beta, VHS, 3/4" U-matic. **Acquisition:** Purchase. **Use:** School/Group/Institution, Special Use Restrictions Apply.

★4404★
African National Congress of South Africa
Marilyn Perry TV Productions, Inc.
677 5th Ave., 5th Fl.
New York, NY 10022 Phone: (212)308-2250
1983. **Program Description:** This tape features a politically oriented interview with Johnny Makatini, Representative of African National Congress of South Africa to the U.N. **Length:** 28 mins. **Format:** 3/4" U-matic. **Acquisition:** Rent/Lease, Purchase. **Use:** School/Group/Institution, Closed Circuit Television, Cable Television, Broadcast television, Special Use Restrictions Apply.

★4405★
African Soul: Music, Past and Present
Carousel Film & Video
260 5th Ave.
New York, NY 10016 Phone: (212)683-1660
1971. **Program Description:** A demonstration of early African music and song, including an original African jazz performance. **Length:** 17 mins. **Format:** Beta, VHS, 3/4" U-matic. **Acquisition:** Purchase. **Use:** School/Group/Institution, Special Use Restrictions Apply.

★4406★
Africans, The
Annenberg/CPB Collection
1111 16 St. NW
Washington, DC 20036 Phone: (202)955-5100
1986. **Program Description:** This series of programs examines the history and culture of Africa, from the time of the pharaohs to the modern struggle against apartheid in South Africa. **Length:** 60 mins. **Format:** Beta, VHS, 3/4" U-matic. **Acquisition:** Rent/Lease, Purchase, Duplication, Free Loan. **Use:** School/Group/Institution, Closed Circuit Television, Cable Television, Special Use Restrictions Apply.

★4407★
Afro-American Music, Its Heritage
Communications Group West
1640 5th St., No. 202
Santa Monica, CA 90401 Phone: (213)451-2525
1972. **Program Description:** Represents 250 years of Black music, from the talking drums of West Africa to contemporary rhythm and blues, and gospel. **Length:** 16 mins. **Format:** Beta, VHS, 1/2" reel, 3/4" U-matic. **Acquisition:** Rent/Lease, Purchase. **Use:** School/Group/Institution, Closed Circuit Television, Special Use Restrictions Apply.

★4408★
Afro-American Perspectives
Maryland Center for Public Broadcasting
11767 Bonita Ave.
Owings Mills, MD 21117 Phone: (301)356-5600
1979. **Program Description:** "Afro-American Perspectives" presents a college credit course combining televised lessons, on-campus seminars, and related work assignments. Focuses on the Black American: the heritage and the struggles as one component in a complex society. **Length:** 30 mins. **Format:** Beta, VHS, 3/4" U-matic. **Acquisition:** Rent/Lease, Purchase. **Use:** School/Group/Institution, Closed Circuit Television, Cable Television, Broadcast Television.

★4409★
Afro-Caribbean Festival
New Jersey Network
1573 Parkside Ave.
Trenton, NJ 08625 Phone: (609)292-5252
1983. **Program Description:** Dance troupes from Africa, Puerto Rico, Haiti, and the Dominican Republic perform in this dance extravaganza. **Length:** 90 mins. **Format:** VHS, 3/4" U-matic. **Acquisition:** Rent/Lease; Purchase. **Use:** School/Group/Institution.

★4410★
Alberta Hunter
Sony Video Software (SVS, Inc.)
1700 Broadway, 16th Fl.
New York, NY 10019 Phone: (212)757-4990
1982. **Program Description:** The famed jazz vocalist gets righteous at the Smithsonian with "Rough and Ready Man," "Remember My Name," "Handyman," and other hits. **Length:** 58 mins. **Format:** Beta, VHS, 8mm. **Acquisition:** Purchase. **Use:** In-Home Viewing.

★4411★
American Documents
Learning Corporation of America
108 Wilmot Rd.
Deerfield, IL 60015-9990 Phone: (708)940-1260
1989. **Program Description:** A series of American history programs for people who want to review or learn. Titles include "Martin Luther King, Jr.: Letter from Birmingham Jail." **Length:** 75 mins. **Format:** Beta, VHS, 3/4" U-matic. **Acquisition:** Rent/Lease; Purchase. **Use:** School/Group/Institution, Restrictions Apply.

★4412★
America's Music
Century Home Video, Inc.
2672 S. La Cienega Blvd.
Los Angeles, CA 90034 Phone: (213)837-7000
1987. **Program Description:** A series of programs featuring vintage musical appearances by veterans of basically American styles of music–gospel, jazz, country, folk, blues and rock. **Length:** 60 mins. **Format:** VHS. **Acquisition:** Purchase. **Use:** In-Home Viewing.

★4413★
Among Brothers: Politics in New Orleans
PBS Video
1320 Braddock Pl.
Alexandria, VA 22314-1698 Phone: (703)739-5380
1987. **Program Description:** This program examines the new urban politics where Blacks often run for elected office against other Blacks. The tape also examines new coalition building. **Length:** 60 mins. **Format:** Beta, VHS, 3/4" U-matic. **Acquisition:** Rent/Lease, Purchase, Duplication, Off-Air Record. **Use:** School/Group/Institution, Closed Circuit Television, In-Home Viewing, Special Use Restrictions Apply.

★4414★
Anasa Briggs: Apartheid
San Diego State University
Learning Resource Center
San Diego, CA 92182 Phone: (714)265-5726
1983. **Program Description:** The details of apartheid in South Africa are examined–divestiture, federal constraints, public protests and more. **Length:** 30 mins. **Format:** Beta, VHS, 3/4" U-matic. **Acquisition:** Rent/Lease, Purchase. **Use:** School/Group/Institution, Special Use Restrictions Apply.

★4415★
Anasa Briggs: Blacks in Agriculture
San Diego State University
Learning Resource Center
San Diego, CA 92182 Phone: (714)265-5726
1983. **Program Description:** A look at how corporate monopolies, socioeconomic influences and racial stereotypes have all but kept

Blacks from the agriculture industry. **Length:** 30 mins. **Format:** Beta, VHS, 3/4'' U-matic. **Acquisition:** Rent/Lease, Purchase. **Use:** School/Group/Institution, Special Use Restrictions Apply.

★4416★
Anasa Briggs: Gospel Festival
San Diego State University
Learning Resource Center
San Diego, CA 92182 Phone: (714)265-5726
1984. **Program Description:** A look at gospel music, with a performance by 40 singers from various churches in the San Diego area. **Length:** 30 mins. **Format:** Beta, VHS, 3/4'' U-matic. **Acquisition:** Rent/Lease, Purchase. **Use:** School/Group/Institution, Special Use Restrictions Apply.

★4417★
Anasa Briggs: Martin Luther King Jr. Memorial Special
San Diego State University
Learning Resource Center
San Diego, CA 92182 Phone: (714)265-5726
1984. **Program Description:** Briggs interviews the administrators of San Bernadino, California, regarding their involvement in the building of a King memorial in their town, in the form of a 11-foot bronze statue. **Length:** 30 mins. **Format:** Beta, VHS, 3/4'' U-matic. **Acquisition:** Rent/Lease, Purchase. **Use:** School/Group/Institution, In-Home Viewing.

★4418★
Anasa Briggs: Water of Your Bath
San Diego State University
Learning Resource Center
San Diego, CA 92182 Phone: (714)265-5726
1984. **Program Description:** Briggs looks at the work of modern Black poets Langston Hughes, Margaret Walker, Don L. Lee, Notzake Shange, Sonia Sanchez and others. **Length:** 30 mins. **Format:** Beta, VHS, 3/4'' U-matic. **Acquisition:** Rent/Lease, Purchase. **Use:** School/Group/Institution, In-Home Viewing.

★4419★
And Justice for Some
Downtown Community TV Center
87 Lafayette St.
New York, NY 10013 Phone: (212)966-4510
1983. **Program Description:** This documentary examines the unfairness of the justice system towards minorities. **Length:** 7 mins. **Format:** 1/2'' reel, 3/4'' U-matic. **Acquisition:** Rent/Lease, Purchase. **Use:** School/Group/Institution, Closed Circuit Television, Cable Television, Broadcast television, Special Use Restrictions Apply.

★4420★
Angola: Victory of Hope
Cinema Guild
1697 Broadway, Rm. 802
New York, NY 10019 Phone: (212)246-5522
1976. **Program Description:** The history of Angola from colonization by Portugal to the Declaration of Independence in 1976. Subtitled and narrated in English. **Length:** 72 mins. **Format:** Beta, VHS, 3/4'' U-matic. **Acquisition:** Rent/Lease, Purchase, Duplication. **Use:** School/Group/Institution, Special Use Restrictions Apply.

★4421★
Any Child Is My Child
Cinema Guild
1697 Broadway, Rm. 802
New York, NY 10019 Phone: (212)246-5522
1989. **Program Description:** The oppression of children by the apartheid regime in South Africa is the focus of this film. **Length:** 54 mins. **Format:** Beta, VHS, 3/4'' U-matic. **Acquisition:** Purchase. **Use:** School/Group/Institution.

★4422★
Apartheid—Part V
PBS Video
1320 Braddock Pl.
Alexandria, VA 22314-1698 Phone: (703)739-5380
1987. **Program Description:** A documentary with rare footage of the 1987 confrontations between dissident White Africaners and Black leaders from the outlawed African National Congress (ANC) in racially torn South Africa. **Length:** 60 mins. **Format:** Beta, VHS, 3/4'' U-matic. **Acquisition:** Purchase, Rent/Lease. **Use:** School/Group/Institution, Special Use Restrictions Apply.

★4423★
Are People All the Same?
Pyramid Film & Video
Box 1048
Santa Monica, CA 90406 Phone: (213)828-7577
1977. **Program Description:** This part of the "Who We Are" series features live action and animation showing children the meaning of race and the uniqueness of each and every person. **Length:** 9 mins. **Format:** Beta, VHS, 3/4'' U-matic. **Acquisition:** Rent/Lease, Purchase, Duplication License. **Use:** School/Group/Institution, In-Home Viewing, Special Use Restrictions Apply.

★4424★
Assault On Affirmative Action
PBS Video
1320 Braddock Pl.
Alexandria, VA 22314-1698 Phone: (703)739-5380
1986. **Program Description:** The issue of reverse discrimination is explored in this video. **Length:** 60 mins. **Format:** Beta, VHS, 3/4'' U-matic. **Acquisition:** Purchase, Rent/Lease. **Use:** School/Group/Institution, Special Use Restrictions Apply.

★4425★
The Autobiography of Miss Jane Pittman
Prism Entertainment
1888 Century Park, E. Ste. 1000
Los Angeles, CA 90028 Phone: (212)277-3270
1974. **Program Description:** The history of Blacks in the South is seen through the eyes of a 110-year-old former slave. From the Civil War through the Civil Rights movement, Miss Jane Pittman relates every piece of Black history, allowing the viewer to experience the injustices. Based on the novel by Ernest J. Gaines. Moving television drama was highly acclaimed and received nine Emmy awards. **Format:** Beta, VHS. **Acquisition:** Purchase. **Use:** In-Home Viewing.

★4426★
Back Inside Herself
Women Make Movies
225 Lafayette St., Ste. 212
New York, NY 10012 Phone: (212)925-0606
1984. **Program Description:** This poetic film urges Black women to reject imposed notions and create their own identities. **Length:** 5 mins. **Format:** Beta, VHS, 3/4'' U-matic. **Acquisition:** Purchase, Rent/Lease. **Use:** School/Group/Institution, Special Use Restrictions Apply.

★4427★
Barriers, The
Michigan Media
University of Michigan
400 4th St.
Ann Arbor, MI 48109 Phone: (313)764-8228
1970. **Program Description:** An exploration of the patterns of urban development unique to the U.S., and the White attitudes that combine to create a Black ghetto. **Length:** 29 mins. **Format:** 3/4'' U-matic. **Acquisition:** Rent/Lease, Purchase. **Use:** School/Group/Institution, Closed Circuit Television, Cable Television, Broadcast television.

★4428★
Beauty Basics for the Contemporary Black Woman
Cambridge Career Products
1 Players Club Dr.
Charleston, WV 25311 Phone: (304)344-8550
1987. **Program Description:** The Broadway star Sheryl Lee Ralph tells Black women how to make themselves up so they'll look their best. **Length:** 30 mins. **Format:** VHS. **Acquisition:** Purchase. **Use:** School/Group/Institution, In-Home Viewing.

★4429★
Beauty in the Bricks
New Day Films
853 Broadway, Ste. 1210
New York, NY 10003 Phone: (212)477-4304
1981. **Program Description:** A 15-year-old Black girl lives in a low income project with dreams like most other children. This program follows the routine of Karen Morgan and her friends. At the conclusion, Karen is accepted into a Dallas high school for gifted children. **Length:** 29 mins. **Format:** Beta, VHS, 3/4'' U-matic. **Acquisition:** Rent/Lease, Purchase. **Use:** School/Group/Institution, Special Use Restrictions Apply.

★4430★
Behind the Scenes
New York State Education Department
Center for Learning Technologies
Media Distribution Network
Rm. C-7, Concourse Level
Albany, NY 12230 Phone: (518)474-1265
197?. **Program Description:** Juanita Hall introduces and sings songs made famous by Blues singers such as Bessie Smith and Billie Holliday in this program. **Length:** 30 mins. **Format:** Beta, VHS, 1/2'' reel, 3/4'' U-matic, 2'' Quad. **Acquisition:** Duplication, Free Duplication. **Use:** School/Group/Institution, Special Use Restrictions Apply.

★4431★
Benny Carter
Sony Video Software (SVS, Inc.)
1700 Broadway, 16th Fl.
New York, NY 10019 Phone: (212)757-4990
1982. **Program Description:** The archetypal jazz saxophonist, mentor to Miles Davis and Charlie Parker, performs "A Train," "Honeysuckle Rose" and "Autumn Leaves." **Length:** 57 mins. **Format:** Beta, VHS, 8mm. **Acquisition:** Purchase. **Use:** In-Home Viewing.

★4432★
Bernard's Gang
New Dimension Media, Inc.
85895 Lorane Hwy.
Eugene, OR 97405 Phone: 800-288-4456
1987. **Program Description:** A teenage boy becomes a leader of a gang in a South African shanty town. **Length:** 28 mins. **Format:** Beta, VHS. **Acquisition:** Purchase, Rent/Lease. **Use:** School/Group/Institution.

★4433★
Bessie Smith and Friends
Audiofidelity Enterprises
PO Box 86
Rahway, NJ 07065 Phone: (201)388-5000
1986. **Program Description:** Three jazz shorts are presented on this tape: "St. Louis Blues" (1929), the only film appearance of blues singer Bessie Smith; "Pie Pie Blackbird" (1932), starring Nina Mae McKinney and the dancing Nicholas Brothers with Eubie Blake and His Orchestra; and "Boogie Woogie Dream" (1941), featuring a youthful Lena Horne, boogie woogie pianists Albert Ammons and Pete Johnson and Teddy Wilson's Band. **Length:** 39 mins. **Format:** Beta, VHS. **Acquisition:** Purchase. **Use:** In-Home Viewing.

★4434★
Best of Black Journal, The
William Greaves Productions
80 8th Ave., Ste. 1701
New York, NY 10011 Phone: (212)206-1213
1970. **Program Description:** A series of programs that encompass various aspects of the Black experience from the fine arts to politics. **Length:** 25 mins. **Format:** Beta, VHS. **Acquisition:** Rent/Lease, Purchase. **Use:** School/Group/Institution, Broadcast television.

★4435★
Beyond Black and White
Motivational Media
12001 Ventura Pl., No. 202
Studio City, CA 91604 Phone: (818)508-6553
1984. **Program Description:** This program dramatizes the psychological and sociological origins of prejudice against minorities and women. **Length:** 28 mins. **Format:** Beta, VHS, 3/4'' U-matic. **Acquisition:** Purchase. **Use:** School/Group/Institution, Closed Circuit Television.

★4436★
Big Bands at Disneyland
Walt Disney Home Video
500 S. Buena Vista St.
Burbank, CA 91521 Phone: (818)840-1875
1984. **Program Description:** The swinging big band sounds of Lionel Hampton, Woody Herman, and Cab Calloway are captured in these three concerts taped at Disneyland. Available in VHS Stereo and Beta Hi-Fi. **Length:** 60 mins. **Format:** Beta, VHS. **Acquisition:** Purchase. **Use:** In-Home Viewing.

★4437★
Biko: Breaking the Silence
Filmakers Library, Inc.
133 E. 58th St.
New York, NY 10022 Phone: (212)355-6545
1988. **Program Description:** This film traces Steve Biko's role in the Black Consciousness movement in South Africa. Biko, who was murdered by the government, played a unique and powerful role in opposing apartheid. **Length:** 52 mins. **Format:** VHS, 3/4'' U-matic. **Acquisition:** Rent/Lease, Purchase, Duplication. **Use:** School/Group/Institution, In-Home Viewing, Special Use Restrictions Apply.

★4438★
Black America Series
Centre Productions, Inc.
1800 30th St., Ste. 207
Boulder, CO 80301 Phone: (303)444-1166
1990. **Program Description:** Various Black people who have made important contributions to their race are profiled. **Length:** 32 mins. **Format:** Beta, VHS, 3/4'' U-matic. **Acquisition:** Purchase, Rent/Lease. **Use:** School/Group/Institution, Special Use Restrictions Apply.

★4439★
Black Americans
Society for Visual Education, Inc. (SVE)
1345 Diversey Parkway
Chicago, IL 60614-1299 Phone: (312)525-1500
1989. **Program Description:** Black Americans who have made notable achievements in their fields are given brief biographies in these two programs. **Length:** 20 mins. **Format:** VHS, 3/4'' U-matic. **Acquisition:** Purchase, Duplication. **Use:** School/Group/Institution, Closed Circuit Television, In-Home Viewing.

★4440★
Black Americans: Part I
Dallas County Community College District
Center for Telecommunications
4343 N. Hwy. 67
Mesquite, TX 75150-2095 Phone: (214)324-7988
1980. **Program Description:** This is the first of two programs that trace the history of Black Americans from the Reconstruction period through World War II. **Length:** 28 mins. **Format:** 3/4'' U-matic. **Acquisition:** Purchase. **Use:** School/Group/Institution, Closed Circuit Television.

★4441★
Black Americans: Part II
Dallas County Community College District
Center for Telecommunications
4343 N. Hwy. 67
Mesquite, TX 75150-2095 Phone: (214)324-7988
1980. **Program Description:** In the second program the history of Black Americans from the Civil Rights Movement of the 1950's to contemporary issues is discussed. **Length:** 28 mins. **Format:** 3/4" U-matic. **Acquisition:** Purchase. **Use:** School/Group/Institution, Closed Circuit Television.

★4442★
Black and Tan/St. Louis Blues
Blackhawk Films
5959 Triumph St.
Commerce, CA 90040-1688 Phone: (213)888-2229
1929. **Program Description:** Two early jazz two-reelers are combined on this tape: "Black and Tan" is the first film appearance of Duke Ellington's Orchestra, featuring Cootie Williams and Johnny Hodges. "St. Louis Blues" is the only surviving film made by legendary blues singer Bessie Smith. She is backed by the Hall Johnson Choir, members of the Fletcher Henderson band directed by James P. Johnson and dancer Jimmy Mordecai. **Length:** 36 mins. **Format:** Beta, VHS. **Acquisition:** Purchase. **Use:** In-Home Viewing.

★4443★
Black and White: "Unless We Learn to Live Together"
American Educational Films
3807 Dickerson Rd.
Nashville, TN 37207 Phone: 800-822-5678
1973. **Program Description:** Martin Luther King's words set the tone for this examination of Black-White relations over the years. **Length:** 16 mins. **Format:** Beta, VHS, 3/4" U-matic. **Acquisition:** Purchase. **Use:** School/Group/Institution, Special Use Restrictions Apply.

★4444★
Black and White: Uptight
Phoenix/BFA Films
468 Park Ave., S.
New York, NY 10016 Phone: (212)684-5910
1969. **Program Description:** Prejudice is the issue in this probing show. The social and economic differences that exist between Blacks and Whites are examined. Narration by Robert Culp. **Length:** 35 mins. **Format:** Beta, VHS, 3/4" U-matic. **Acquisition:** Purchase. **Use:** School/Group/Institution, Special Use Restrictions Apply.

★4445★
The Black Athlete
Pyramid Film and Video
Box 1048
Santa Monica, CA 90406 Phone: (213)828-7577
1979. **Program Description:** The changing role of Blacks in sports is reviewed. Footage of early Black athletes such as Jack Johnson, Joe Louis, and Jackie Robinson is included with interviews of O.J. Simpson, Harry Edwards, Muhammed Ali, Arthur Ashe, and others. **Length:** 58 mins. **Format:** Beta, VHS, 3/4" U-matic. **Acquisition:** Rent/Lease; Purchase; Trade-In. **Use:** School/Group/Institution, Closed Circuit Television, In-Home Viewing, Special Use Restrictions.

★4446★
Black Catholics: People of Hope
Franciscan Communications
1229 S. Santee St.
Los Angeles, CA 90015 Phone: (213)746-2916
1987. **Program Description:** Black activity in the Catholic church is followed. **Length:** 28 mins. **Format:** Beta, VHS, 3/4" U-matic. **Acquisition:** Purchase, Rent/Lease. **Use:** School/Group/Institution, Special Use Restrictions Apply.

★4447★
Black Caucus
Michigan Media
University of Michigan
400 4th St.
Ann Arbor, MI 48109 Phone: (313)764-8228
1970. **Program Description:** A look at the movement of the Black man, from the outskirts of political participation to the heart of politics. Part of the "Black Experience" series. **Length:** 29 mins. **Format:** 3/4" U-matic, Other than listed. **Acquisition:** Rent/Lease, Purchase. **Use:** School/Group/Institution, Closed Circuit Television, Cable Television, Broadcast television.

★4448★
Black Delta Religion
Center for Southern Folklore
1216 Peabody Ave.
PO Box 40105
Memphis, TN 38104 Phone: (901)726-4205
1974. **Program Description:** The evolution from traditional rural to sanctified urban religious services in the Mississippi Delta is examined. **Length:** 15 mins. **Format:** Beta, VHS, 3/4" U-matic. **Acquisition:** Purchase. **Use:** School/Group/Institution, In-Home Viewing. Special Use Restrictions Apply.

★4449★
Black Dimensions in American Art
AIMS Media Inc.
6901 Woodley Ave.
Van Nuys, CA 91406-4878 Phone: (818)785-4111
1970. **Program Description:** This program examines the important creations of America's most celebrated Black artists, representing every major style in painting today. **Length:** 11 mins. **Format:** Beta, VHS, 3/4" U-matic. **Acquisition:** Purchase; Duplication License. **Use:** School/Group/Institution, Special Use Restrictions Apply.

★4450★
Black Experience and American Education
Michigan Media
University of Michigan
400 4th St.
Ann Arbor, MI 48109 Phone: (313)764-8228
1970. **Program Description:** A look at how the American education system has affected and has been affected by the Black experience. Part of the "Black Experience" series. **Length:** 29 mins. **Format:** 3/4" U-matic, Special order format. **Acquisition:** Rent/Lease; Purchase. **Use:** School/Group/Institution, Closer Circuit Television, Cable Television, Broadcast Television.

★4451★
Black Experience, The
Michigan Media
University of Michigan
400 4th St.
Ann Arbor, MI 48109 Phone: (313)764-8228
1970. **Program Description:** This program looks at the origins of Black Americans: how history has shaped their attitudes, and crucial choices Blacks have made to influence history's course. **Length:** 29 mins. **Format:** 3/4" U-matic, Other than listed. **Acquisition:** Rent/Lease, Purchase. **Use:** School/Group/Institution, Closed Circuit Television, Cable Television, Broadcast television.

★4452★
Black Genealogy
Maryland Center for Public Broadcasting
11767 Bonita Ave.
Owings Mills, MD 21117 Phone: (301)356-5600
Program Description: This series of three untitled programs examines the procedure for gathering and compiling a family history, and explains some of the problems that Blacks encounter in tracing their "roots." **Length:** 30 mins. **Format:** Beta, VHS, 3/4" U-matic. **Acquisition:** Rent/Lease; Purchase. **Use:** School/Group/Institution, Closed Circuit Television, Cable Television, Broadcast Television.

★4453★
Black Girl
University of California at Berkeley
Extension Media Center
2176 Shattuck Ave.
Berkeley, CA 94704 Phone: (415)642-0460
1982. **Program Description:** A Black girl struggles against obstacles to become a ballet dancer. **Length:** 30 mins. **Format:** VHS, 3/4'' U-matic. **Acquisition:** Purchase, Rent/Lease. **Use:** School/Group/Institution, Special Use Restrictions Apply.

★4454★
Black Has Always Been Beautiful
Indiana University Audio-Visual Center
Bloomington, IN 47405-5901 Phone: (812)335-8087
1971. **Program Description:** Presents photographs by James Van DerZee of Harlem school children, Black Yankees, Marcus Garvey, and many others. **Format:** Beta, VHS, 1/2'' reel, 3/4'' U-matic. **Acquisition:** Rent/Lease; Purchase; Duplication License. **Use:** School/Group/Institution, Closed Circuit Television, Broadcast Television, In-Home Viewing, Special Use Restrictions Apply.

★4455★
Black Heroes
Society for Visual Education, Inc. (SVE)
1345 Diversey Parkway
Chicago, IL 60614-1299 Phone: (312)525-1500
1989. **Program Description:** Harriet Tubman, Nat Turner, Martin Luther King, Jr., and others who have advanced the cause of racial equality are profiled. **Length:** 20 mins. **Format:** VHS, 3/4'' U-matic. **Acquisition:** Purchase, Duplication. **Use:** School/Group/Institution, Closed Circuit Television, In-Home Viewing.

★4456★
Black High School Girls
Martha Stuart Communications Inc.
PO Box 246
Hillsdale, NY 12529 Phone: (518)325-3900
198?. **Program Description:** Indiana students discuss their lives, families, schools, peers, and related topics. **Length:** 29 mins. **Format:** 3/4'' U-matic, 2'' Quad. **Acquisition:** Rent/Lease; Purchase. **Use:** School/Group/Institution, Closed Circuit Television, Cable Television, Broadcast Television, In-Home Viewing.

★4457★
Black History: Lost, Stolen or Strayed
Phoenix/BFA Films
468 Park Ave., S.
New York, NY 10016 Phone: (212)684-5910
1968. **Program Description:** Bill Cosby is narrator of this eye-opening show which reviews the Black contribution to the development of the United States. **Length:** 54 mins. **Format:** Beta, VHS, 3/4'' U-matic. **Acquisition:** Purchase. **Use:** School/Group/Institution, Special Use Restrictions Apply.

★4458★
Black Jazz and Blues
Video Yesteryear
Box C
Sandy Hook, CT 06482 Phone: (203)426-2574
1938. **Program Description:** Three classic jazz/blues shorts, "St. Louis Blues," "Symphony in Black," and "Caldonia." **Length:** 44 mins. **Format:** Beta, VHS. **Acquisition:** Purchase. **Use:** In-Home Viewing.

★4459★
Black Journal
WNET/Thirteen Non-Broadcast
356 W. 58th St.
New York, NY 10019 Phone: (212)560-3045
1977. **Program Description:** A series of current-interest interviews with the common theme of Black presence in a White world. **Length:** 30 mins. **Format:** Beta, VHS, 3/4'' U-matic. **Acquisition:** Rent/Lease, Purchase. **Use:** School/Group/Institution, Closed Circuit Television, In-Home Viewing.

★4460★
Black Like Me
United Home Video
4111 S. Darlington St., Ste. 600
Tulsa, OK 74135 Phone: (918)622-6460
1964. **Program Description:** Based on John Howard Griffin's successful book about how Griffin turned his skin dark brown with a drug and traveled the South to experience prejudice firsthand. **Length:** 1964. **Format:** Beta, VHS. **Acquisition:** Purchase. **Use:** In-Home Viewing.

★4461★
Black Literature
NETCHE (Nebraska ETV Council for
Higher Education)
Box 38111
Lincoln, NE 68501 Phone: (402)472-3611
1971. **Program Description:** These programs illustrate the fact that Black literature includes a dynamic and forceful body of work by writers with a wide variety of experience and styles. **Length:** 30 mins. **Format:** Beta, VHS, 1/2'' reel, 3/4'' U-matic. **Acquisition:** Rent/Lease; Purchase. **Use:** School/Group/Institution, Closed Circuit Television, Broadcast Television, Special Use Restrictions Apply.

★4462★
Black Migration
Michigan Media
University of Michigan
400 4th St.
Ann Arbor, MI 48109 Phone: (313)764-8228
1970. **Program Description:** A look at the economic, political, and social conditions in the South between 1876 and 1914. Part of the "Black Experience" series. **Length:** 29 mins. **Format:** 3/4'' U-matic, Special order format. **Acquisition:** Rent/Lease; Purchase. **Use:** School/Group/Institution, Closed Circuit Television, Cable Television, Broadcast Television.

★4463★
Black Mother Black Daughter
National Film Board of Canada
1251 Avenue of the Americas, 16th F.
New York, NY 10020-1173 Phone: (212)586-5131
1984. **Program Description:** This is an examination of the lives of Black women in a predominantly White area. **Length:** 29 mins. **Format:** Beta, VHS, 3/4'' U-matic. **Acquisition:** Purchase, Rent/Lease. **Use:** School/Group/Institution, Special Use Restrictions Apply.

★4464★
Black Music in America: From Then Till Now
Learning Corporation of America
108 Wilmot Rd.
Deerfield, IL 60015-9990 Phone: (312)940-1260
1971. **Program Description:** The history of the Black people's contribution to American music. Includes performances by Louis Armstrong, Mahalia Jackson, Duke Ellington, Count Basie, Nina Simone, and Bessie Smith. **Length:** 28 mins. **Format:** Beta, VHS, 3/4'' U-matic. **Acquisition:** Rent/Lease, Purchase. **Use:** School/Group/Institution, Special Use Restrictions Apply.

★4465★
Black Music in America: The Seventies
Learning Corporation of America
108 Wilmot Rd.
Deerfield, IL 60015-9990 Phone: (312)940-1260
1979. **Program Description:** From Diana Ross and Motown to Donna Summer and disco, this musical excursion includes clips of over 75 groups showing the growth and influence of Black music and performers in the 1970's. **Length:** 32 mins. **Format:** Beta, VHS, 3/4'' U-matic. **Acquisition:** Rent/Lease, Purchase. **Use:** School/Group/Institution, Special Use Restrictions Apply.

★4466★
Black Music Now
NETCHE (Nebraska ETV Council for Higher Education)
Box 83111
Lincoln, NE 68501 Phone: (402)472-3611
1970. **Program Description:** Professor Baker discusses jazz as an art form and the role of Black music in Black culture. **Length:** 30 mins. **Format:** 1/2" reel. **Acquisition:** Rent/Lease, Purchase, Subscription. **Use:** School/Group/Institution, Closed Circuit Television, Broadcast television, Special Use Restrictions Apply.

★4467★
Black Olympians 1904-1984: Athletics and Social Change in America
Churchill Films
12210 Nebraska Ave.
Los Angeles, CA 90025 Phone: (213)207-6600
1986. **Program Description:** A mini-history of the role of the Black athlete in the Olympic Games, including Jesse Owens, the Mexico City '68 salute and more. **Length:** 28 mins. **Format:** VHS, 3/4" U-matic. **Acquisition:** Purchase. **Use:** School/Group/Institution, In-Home Viewing, Special Use Restrictions Apply.

★4468★
Black P. Stone Nation
Martha Stuart Communications Inc.
PO Box 246
Hillsdale, NY 12529 Phone: (518)325-3900
198?. **Program Description:** "The Black Stone Rangers" is a former gang from Chicago that has redirected its energies to urban renewal for the Black community. **Length:** 29 mins. **Format:** 3/4" U-matic, 2" Quad. **Acquisition:** Rent/Lease; Purchase. **Use:** School/Group/Institution, Closed Circuit Television, Broadcast Television, In-Home Viewing.

★4469★
Black Panthers: Huey Newton/Black Panther Newsreel
International Historic Films, Inc.
Box 29035
Chicago, IL 60629 Phone: (312)436-8051
1953. **Program Description:** A film focusing on the "Free Huey Newton" rally in California; a separate video features an interview with Newton from Alameda County Jail, plus the Panther 10-point plan presented by Bobby Seale. **Length:** 53 mins. **Format:** Beta, VHS, 3/4" U-matic. **Acquisition:** Purchase. **Use:** School/Group/Institution, In-Home Viewing.

★4470★
Black Paths of Leadership
Churchill Films
12210 Nebraska Ave.
Los Angeles, CA 90025 Phone: (213)207-6600
1986. **Program Description:** Profiles of three important Black leaders in American history: Booker T. Washington, W.E.B. DuBois and Marcus Garvey. **Length:** 28 mins. **Format:** VHS, 3/4" U-matic. **Acquisition:** Purchase. **Use:** School/Group/Institution, In-Home Viewing, Special Use Restrictions Apply.

★4471★
Black People Get AIDS Too
Churchill Films
12210 Nebraska Ave.
Los Angeles, CA 90025 Phone: (213)207-6600
1988. **Program Description:** The myth that AIDS is a White male disease is explored in this video. Available in two different versions. **Length:** 20 mins. **Format:** Beta, VHS, 3/4" U-matic. **Acquisition:** Purchase, Rent/Lease, Duplication License. **Use:** School/Group/Institution, In-Home Viewing, Special Use Restrictions Apply.

★4472★
Black People in the Slave South, 1850
Britannica Films
310 S. Michigan Ave.
Chicago, IL 60604 Phone: (312)347-7958
1972. **Program Description:** The story of cotton slaves in the South, who were subjected to harsh treatment from plantation owners and politicians. From the "Afro-American History" series. **Length:** 11 mins. **Format:** Beta, VHS, 3/4" U-matic. **Acquisition:** Rent/Lease, Purchase, Trade-in. **Use:** School/Group/Institution, Special Use Restrictions Apply.

★4473★
Black Plays in White Theater
New York State Education Department
Center for Learning Technologies
Media Distribution Network
Rm. C-7, Concourse Level
Albany, NY 12230 Phone: (518)474-1265
197?. **Program Description:** The attitude of White people towards plays written by Black authors is discussed in this program. **Length:** 30 mins. **Format:** Beta, VHS, 1/2" reel, 3/4" U-matic, 2" Quad. **Acquisition:** Duplication, Free Duplication. **Use:** School/Group/Institution, Special Use Restrictions Apply.

★4474★
Black Poetry of the Midwest
NETCHE (Nebraska ETV Council for Higher Education)
Box 83111
Lincoln, NE 68501 Phone: (402)472-3611
1977. **Program Description:** Unknown to many, the Midwest played a key role in the development of Black literature. This lesson explores such literary figures as James Emanuel, Melvin B. Tolson, Malcolm X, and Oscar Micheaux. **Length:** 30 mins. **Format:** Beta, VHS, 3/4" U-matic. **Acquisition:** Rent/Lease; Purchase.

★4475★
Black Policeman: The Writing on the Wall—-Black Exemplars
American Educational Films
3807 Dickerson Rd.
Nashville, TN 37207 Phone: 800-822-5678
1973. **Program Description:** Profile of Bill Baldwin, a Washington D.C. policeman, a man who loves his job. During riots, Baldwin worked night and day to save the city, and was then the victim of prejudice. The honest way he dealt with his problem is the focus of this program. **Length:** 16 mins. **Format:** Beta, VHS, 3/4" U-matic. **Acquisition:** Purchase. **Use:** School/Group/Institution, Special Use Restrictions Apply.

★4476★
Black Presence in the Caribbean, The
NETCHE (Nebraska ETV Council for Higher Education)
Box 83111
Lincoln, NE 68501 Phone: (402)472-3611
1970. **Program Description:** The history of Blacks in the Caribbean is summarized. **Length:** 30 mins. **Format:** Beta, VHS, 3/4" U-matic. **Acquisition:** Purchase, Rent/Lease, Subscription. **Use:** School/Group/Institution, Closed Circuit Television, Broadcast television, Special Use Restrictions Apply.

★4477★
Black Roots in Africa
Atlantis Productions
1252 La Granada Dr.
Thousand Oaks, CA 91360 Phone: (805)495-2790
197?. **Program Description:** Traces the historical and cultural roots of American Blacks in Africa. **Length:** 17 mins. **Format:** Beta, VHS, 3/4" U-matic. **Acquisition:** Purchase. **Use:** School/Group/Institution, Special Use Restrictions Apply.

★4478★
Black Shadows on a Silver Screen
Lucerne Media
37 Ground Pine Rd.
Morris Plains, NJ 07950 Phone: (201)538-1401
1976. **Program Description:** A look at the segregated Black film industry making features for Black communities from 1915 through 1950. Part of the "American Documents" series. **Length:** 55 mins. **Format:** Beta, VHS, 3/4" U-matic. **Acquisition:** Purhase. **Use:** School/Group/Institution, Special Use Restrictions Apply.

★4479★
Black Soldier, The
Phoenix/BFA Films
468 Park Ave., S.
New York, NY 10016 Phone: (212)684-5910
1968. **Program Description:** Narrated by Bill Cosby, this show illustrates the history of Black American participation in America's armed forces. **Length:** 26 mins. **Format:** Beta, VHS, 3/4" U-matic. **Acquisition:** Purchase. **Use:** School/Group/Institution, Special Use Restrictions Apply.

★4480★
Black Studies
University of Arizona VideoCampus
Harvill Bldg., No. 76
Box 4
Tucson, AZ 85721 Phone: (602)621-1735
1980. **Program Description:** A series which discusses the native origins and roots of Black Americans. **Length:** 60 mins. **Format:** 1/2" reel, 3/4" U-matic. **Acquisition:** Rent/Lease; Purchase. **Use:** School/Group/Institution, Clsoed Circuit Television, In-Home Viewing.

★4481★
Black Sugar
Indiana University Audio-Visual Center
Bloomington, IN 47405-5901 Phone: (812)335-8087
1987. **Program Description:** The horrendous conditions that Haitian sugar workers suffer while in the Dominican Republic are documented. **Length:** 58 mins. **Format:** VHS, 3/4" U-matic. **Acquisition:** Purchase, Rent/Lease. **Use:** School/Group/Institution, In-Home Viewing.

★4482★
Black Thumb
Phoenix/BFA Films
468 Park Ave., S.
New York, NY 10016 Phone: (212)684-5910
1970. **Program Description:** A Black man tends the garden behind a suburban home which he owns. A White salesman assumes he is a hired handyman. **Length:** 7 mins. **Format:** Beta, VHS, 3/4" U-matic. **Acquisition:** Purchase. **Use:** School/Group/Institution, Special Use Restrictions Apply.

★4483★
The Black West
Beacon Films
930 Pinter Ave.
Evanston, IL 60202 Phone: (312)328-6700
1982. **Program Description:** Cowbody George Ellison, rodeo star Frank Greenway, and frontiersperson Eunice Norris share the experience of being Black in the Wild West in this program, part of the "Were You There?" series. **Length:** 28 mins. **Format:** Beta, VHS, 3/4" U-matic. **Acquisition:** Purchase. **Use:** School/Group/Institution, Special Use Restrictions Apply.

★4484★
Blacks and the Constitution
PBS Video
1320 Braddock Pl.
Alexandria, VA 22314-1698 Phone: (703)739-5380
1986. **Program Description:** A look at how the rights of Blacks have changed in this country from slavery times to the present, with respect to the Constitution. **Length:** 60 mins. **Format:** VHS, 3/4" U-matic. **Acquisition:** Rent/Lease, Purchase. **Use:** School/Group/Institution, Closed Circuit Television, Cable Television.

★4485★
Blacks and the Movies
NETCHE (Nebraska ETV Council for Higher Education)
Box 83111
Lincoln, NE 68501 Phone: (402)472-3611
1977. **Program Description:** Presents an interview with film critic Donad Bogle. **Length:** 30 mins. **Format:** Beta, VHS, 3/4" U-matic. **Acquisition:** Rent/Lease; Purchase. **Use:** School/Group/Institution, Closed Circuit Television, Broadcast Television, Special Use Restrictions Apply.

★4486★
Bloodlines and Bridges: The African Connection
PBS Video
1320 Braddock Pl.
Alexandria, VA 22314-1698 Phone: (703)739-5380
1986. **Program Description:** This program follows Marian Crawford, an American orphan, who traveles to Africa in search of her family's past. **Length:** 30 mins. **Format:** Beta, VHS, 3/4" U-matic. **Acquisition:** Rent/Lease, Purchase, Duplication, Off-Air Record. **Use:** School/Group/Institution, Closed Circuit Television, In-Home Viewing, Special Use Restrictions Apply.

★4487★
Bloods of 'Nam, The
PBS Video
1320 Braddock Pl.
Alexandria, VA 22314-1698 Phone: (703)739-5380
1987. **Program Description:** This documentary follows the lives of Black soldiers who fought against discrimination in the army and disillusionment when they returned home. **Length:** 58 mins. **Format:** Beta, VHS, 3/4" U-matic. **Acquisition:** Purchase, Rent/Lease. **Use:** School/Group/Institution, Special Use Restrictions Apply.

★4488★
Bloody Schemes
Cinema Guild
1697 Broadway, Rm. 802
New York, NY 10019 Phone: (212)246-5522
198?. **Program Description:** The African slave trade is chronicled in this film. From the voyage of John Hawkins to the establishment of towns and forts along Africa's coasts, to full-scale trading, the film documents the vital nature of imposed labor on European and American economies. **Length:** 18 mins. **Format:** 3/4" U-matic, Other than listed. **Acquisition:** Purchase. **Use:** School/Group/Institution.

★4489★
Blues 1
Video Gems
731 N. La Brea Ave.
PO Box 38188
Los Angeles, CA 90038 Phone: (213)938-2385
1983. **Program Description:** Brock Peters is the host of this historic journey to "the roots" of the Blues. **Length:** 58 mins. **Format:** Beta, VHS. **Acquisition:** Purchase. **Use:** In-Home Viewing.

★4490★
Bob Marley-Legend
RCA/Columbus Pictures Home Video
3500 W. Olive Ave.
Burbank, CA 91505 Phone: (818)953-7900
1984. **Program Description:** This rockumentary looks at the life and music of Bob Marley and featuers thirteen of his songs. **Length:** 55 mins. **Format:** Beta, VHS, Laser optical videodisc. **Acquisition:** Purchase. **Use:** In-Home Viewing.

★4491★
Bombing of West Philly, The
PBS Video
1320 Braddock Pl.
Alexandria, VA 22314-1698 Phone: (703)739-5380
1987. **Program Description:** The true story of the 1983 bombing of the headquarters of MOVE, a violent Black urban cult. **Length:** 58 mins. **Format:** Beta, VHS, 3/4" U-matic. **Acquisition:** Purchase, Rent/Lease. **Use:** School/Group/Institution, Special Use Restrictions Apply.

★4492★
Booker T. Washington: The Life and the Legacy
Your World Video
80 8th Ave., Ste. 1701
New York, NY 10011 Phone: (212)206-1215
1986. **Program Description:** A dramatized biography of the Negro humanist and leader. **Length:** 30 mins. **Format:** Beta, VHS. **Acquisition:** Purchase. **Use:** In-Home Viewing.

★4493★
Booker T. Washington's Tuskegee America
AIMS Media, Inc.
6901 Woodley Ave.
Van Nuys, CA 91406-4878 Phone: (818)785-4111
1981. **Program Description:** A biography of Washington–his life, career and achievements. **Length:** 25 mins. **Format:** Beta, VHS, 3/4" U-matic. **Acquisition:** Rent/Lease, Purchase, Duplication License. **Use:** School/Group/Institution, Special Use Restrictions Apply.

★4494★
Born to Swing—The Count Basie Alumni
Kino International Corporation
333 W. 39th St., Ste. 503
New York, NY 10018 Phone: (212)629-6880
1989. **Program Description:** The richness of swing music Kansas City style is explored in this film, which includes an impromptu jam session. **Length:** 50 mins. **Format:** Beta, VHS. **Acquisition:** Purchase. **Use:** In-Home Viewing.

★4495★
Botswana Wildlife Album
New York State Education Department
Center for Learning Technologies
Media Distribution Network
Rm. C-7, Concourse Level
Albany, NY 12230 Phone: (518)474-1265
197?. **Program Description:** The wildlife and people of Botswana are examined in this program. **Length:** 29 mins. **Format:** Beta, VHS, 1/2" reel, 3/4" U-matic, 2" Quad. **Acquisition:** Duplication, Free Duplication. **Use:** School/Group/Institution, Special Use Restrictions Apply.

★4496★
Boy King, The
Coronet/MTI Film & Video
108 Wilmot Rd.
Deerfield, IL 60015-9990 Phone: (312)940-1260
1988. **Program Description:** The early life of civil rights leader Martin Luther King, Jr. is examined in this drama. **Length:** 48 mins. **Format:** Beta, VHS, 3/4" U-matic. **Acquisition:** Purchase, Rent/Lease. **Use:** School/Group/Institution, Special Use Restrictions Apply.

★4497★
Boyhood of Martin Luther King, The
Film Fair Communications
10900 Ventura Blvd.
PO Box 1728
Studio City, CA 91604 Phone: (818)985-0244
1984. **Program Description:** A dramatization of events from Martin Luther King's childhood which influenced his later years. **Length:** 14 mins. **Format:** Beta, VHS, 3/4" U-matic. **Acquisition:** Purchase, Duplication License. **Use:** School/Group/Institution, Special Use Restrictions Apply.

★4498★
Brother with Perfect Timing, A
Kino International Corporation
333 W. 39th St., Ste. 503
New York, NY 10018 Phone: (212)629-6880
1988. **Program Description:** An unusual film biography of the innovative jazz musician. Ibrahim left South Africa in the 1960's and integrated many different cultures into his music: African, Arabic, Oriental, European and American. The musician talks about his childhood, the spiritual implications behind his music and demonstrates parts of his music that he doesn't show in concert. **Length:** 90 mins. **Format:** Beta, VHS. **Acquisition:** Purchase. **Use:** In-Home Viewing.

★4499★
Busing and Integration
Dallas County Community College District
Center for Telecommunications
4343 N. Hwy. 67
Mesquite, TX 75150-2095 Phone: (214)324-7988
1979. **Program Description:** This program traces the most important court cases on the subject from Brown vs. the Board of Education to the present. **Length:** 29 mins. **Format:** 3/4" U-matic. **Acquisition:** Purchase. **Use:** School/Group/Institution, Closed Circuit Television.

★4500★
Busted Dreams
New Jersey Network
1573 Parkside Ave.
Trenton, NJ 08625 Phone: (609)292-5252
1983. **Program Description:** A group of Black people talk about the tough circumstances which have destroyed their dreams. **Length:** 30 mins. **Format:** VHS, 3/4" U-matic. **Acquisition:** Rent/Lease, Purchase. **Use:** School/Group/Institution.

★4501★
Cab Calloway and His Orchestra
Audiofidelity Enterprises
PO Box 86
Rahway, NJ 07065 Phone: (201)388-5000
1986. **Program Description:** Cab Calloway, the King of Hi-De-Ho, is featured with his band in this compilation of vintage films. The tape begins with an excerpt from the 1935 short, "Jitterbug Party" and the "Mama, I Wanna Make Rhythm" number from the 1937 feature film, "Manhattan Merry-Go-Round." Next are four 1942 Soundies, "Blues In the Night," "Minnie the Moocher," "Virginia, Georgia and Caroline" and "The Skunk Song." The program concludes with several 1950 Telescriptions, "I Can't Give You Anything But Love," "Minnie the Moocher" and "St. James Infirmary." **Length:** 30 mins. **Format:** Beta, VHS. **Acquisition:** Purchase. **Use:** In-Home Viewing.

★4502★
Call of the Jitterbug, The
Filmakers Library, Inc.
133 E. 58th St.
New York, NY 10022 Phone: (212)355-6545
1988. **Program Description:** During the 1930's a new form of dance was created. It was called the Jitterbug. This program documents its development within the Black community and its influence on modern dance and race relations. **Length:** 35 mins. **Format:** VHS, 3/4" U-matic. **Acquisition:** Rent/Lease, Purchase, Duplication. **Use:** School/Group/Institution, In-Home Viewing, Special Use Restrictions Apply.

★4503★
Children of Pride
Praeses Productions
28 Greene St.
New York, NY 10013 Phone: (212)925-1599
1984. **Program Description:** A documentary about a Black Harlem man who has adopted over a dozen handicapped Black children, the family thus formed, and the tribulations he's confronted in the process. **Length:** 60 mins. **Format:** Beta, VHS, 3/4" U-matic. **Acquisition:** Purchase. **Use:** School/Group/Institution, In-Home Viewing.

★4504★
Children Were Watching, The
Direct Cinema Limited, Inc.
Box 69799
Los Angeles, CA 90069 Phone: (213)652-8000
1960. **Program Description:** A look at families facing integration as a six-year-old Black girl enters school in New Orleans. **Length:** 58 mins. **Format:** Beta, VHS, 3/4" U-matic, Other than listed. **Acquisition:** Rent/Lease, Purchase. **Use:** School/Group/Institution, In-Home Viewing, Special Use Restrictions Apply.

★4505★
Cimarrones
Cinema Guild
1697 Broadway, Rm. 802
New York, NY 10019 Phone: (212)246-5522
1982. **Program Description:** This film recreates the experience of African slaves in Peru during the early nineteenth century, by which time many slaves had rebelled against their captors and built villages in the mountains. The film portrays, in great detail, life at the villages. **Length:** 24 mins. **Format:** 3/4" U-matic, Other than listed. **Acquisition:** Purchase. **Use:** School/Group/Institution.

★4506★
Classified People
Filmakers Library, Inc.
133 E. 58th St.
New York, NY 10022 Phone: (212)355-6545
1987. **Program Description:** This documentary examines the tragedy of apartheid in South Africa and its affects on one family, where the children are classified White and the father Black. **Length:** 55 mins. **Format:** VHS, 3/4" U-matic. **Acquisition:** Rent/Lease, Purchase, Duplication. **Use:** School/Group/Institution, In-Home Viewing, Special Use Restrictions Apply.

★4507★
Clinical Cerebrovascular Disease in Hypertensive Blacks
Emory Medical Television Network
Emory University
Emory Medical Television Network-Department C
1440 Clifton Rd., NE
Atlanta, GA 30322 Phone: (404)727-5817
1986. **Program Description:** A look at stroke in Blacks and how it is caused by environmentally-caused hypertension. **Length:** 33 mins. **Format:** VHS, 3/4" U-matic. **Acquisition:** Rent/Lease, Purchase, Subscription. **Use:** School/Group/Institution, Closed Circuit Television, Cable Television, Broadcast Television, Special Use Restrictions Apply.

★4508★
Coffee Colored Children
Women Make Movies
225 Lafayette St., Ste. 212
New York, NY 10012 Phone: (212)925-0606
1988. **Program Description:** A semi-autobiographical film about the effects of racism on children. **Length:** 15 mins. **Format:** Beta, VHS, 3/4" U-matic. **Acquisition:** Purchase, Rent/Lease. **Use:** School/Group/Institution, Special Use Restrictions Apply.

★4509★
Color of Friendship, The
Learning Corporation of America
108 Wilmot Rd.
Deerfield, IL 60015-9990 Phone: (708)940-1260
1981. **Program Description:** A Black student and a White boy strike up a friendship at a recently integrated junior high which is put to the test when racial strife breaks out (shown as an ABC Afterschool Special). **Length:** 47 mins. **Format:** Beta, VHS, 3/4" U-matic. **Acquisition:** Rent/Lease, Purchase. **Use:** School/Group/Institution, Special Use Restrictions Apply.

★4510★
The Color Purple
Warner Home Video
4000 Warner Blvd.
Burbank, CA 91522 Phone: (818)954-6000
1986. **Program Description:** Celie (Whoopi Goldberg's debut) is a poor, Black girl. Separated from her sister and forced into a brutal marriage, she fights for her self-esteem by making friends with a jazz singer. Spanning 1909 to 1947 in a Georgia small town, the movie chronicles the joys, pains, and people in her life. Strong performances by Danny Glover, Oprah Winfrey (also her film debut), and Margaret Avery highlight this critically acclaimed movie. Brilliant photography by Allen Davian and musical score by Quincy Jones (who co-produced) compliment this film. Based on the Pulitzer Prize-winning novel by Alice Walker. **Length:** 154 mins. **Format:** Beta, VHS, Laser optical videodisc. **Acquisition:** Rent/Lease; Purchase. **Use:** In-Home Viewing.

★4511★
Color Schemes
Women Make Movies
225 Lafayette St., Ste. 212
New York, NY 10012 Phone: (212)925-0606
1989. **Program Description:** The misconceptions of racial assimilation is explored through the metaphor of "color wash." **Length:** 28 mins. **Format:** Beta, VHS, 3/4" U-matic. **Acquisition:** Purchase, Rent/Lease. **Use:** School/Group/Institution, Special Use Restrictions Apply.

★4512★
Color Us Black
Indiana University Audio-Visual Center
Bloomington, IN 47405-5901 Phone: (812)335-8087
1968. **Program Description:** A look at the Black man's struggle for identity over and above the White norm, as explained by a student group from Howard University. **Length:** 60 mins. **Format:** 3/4" U-matic, Other than listed. **Acquisition:** Rent/Lease, Purchase. **Use:** School/Group/Institution, Closed Circuit Television, In-Home Viewing, Special Use Restrictions Apply.

★4513★
Come Back, Africa
Mystic Fire Video
PO Box 1092
Cooper Station
New York, NY 10276 Phone: (212)941-0999
1960. **Program Description:** A classic documentary about a Zulu family surviving under apartheid in South Africa. **Length:** 83 mins. **Format:** Beta, VHS. **Acquisition:** Purchase. **Use:** In-Home Viewing.

★4514★
Count Basie and Friends
Audiofidelity Enterprises
PO Box 86
Rahway, NJ 07065 Phone: (201)388-5000
1986. **Program Description:** Count Basie, his Orchestra and Septet are featured in these four shorts: "Band Parade" (1943), "Basie's Conversation," "Basie Boogie," and "Sugar Chile Robinson, Billie Holiday and Count Basie" (all 1950). Helen Humes sings "If I Could Be With You One Hour Tonight" and Billie Holiday sings "Now, Baby, or Never" and "God Bless the Child." **Length:** 37 mins. **Format:** Beta, VHS. **Acquisition:** Purchase. **Use:** In-Home Viewing.

★4515★
Count Basie Live at the Hollywood Palladium
VCL Home Video
Glen Professional Centre
2980 Beverly Glen Circle, Ste. 302
Los Angeles, CA 90077 Phone: (213)474-4225
1984. **Program Description:** One of the Count's last concerts taped at the Hollywood Palladium. Songs performed include "Shiny Stockings," "Splanky" and "Big Stuff." **Length:** 60 mins. **Format:** Beta, VHS. **Acquisition:** Purchase. **Use:** In-Home Viewing.

★4516★
Crisis: Behind a Presidential Commitment
Direct Cinema Limited, Inc.
Box 69799
Los Angeles, CA 90069 Phone: (213)652-8000
1964. **Program Description:** The story behind the forced integration of the University of Alabama, the last college in the country to openly deny admittance to Black students. **Length:** 58 mins. **Format:** Beta, VHS, 3/4" U-matic, Other than listed. **Acquisition:** Rent/Lease, Purchase. **Use:** School/Group/Institution, In-Home Viewing, Special Use Restrictions Apply.

★4517★
Cry of Defiance, A
Michigan Media
University of Michigan
400 4th St.
Ann Arbor, MI 48109 Phone: (313)764-8228
1970. **Program Description:** A discussion of social movements created by the Black community in opposition to White bigotry. Part of the

"Black Experience" series. **Length:** 29 mins. **Format:** 3/4" U-matic, Other than listed. **Acquisition:** Rent/Lease, Purchase. **Use:** School/Group/Institution, Closed Circuit Television, Cable Television, Broadcast television.

★4518★
Cycles
Women Make Movies
225 Lafayette St., Ste. 212
New York, NY 10012 Phone: (212)925-0606
1988. **Program Description:** A lively experimental film that reflects on Black womanhood. **Length:** 15 mins. **Format:** Beta, VHS, 3/4" U-matic. **Acquisition:** Purchase, Rent/Lease. **Use:** School/Group/Institution, Special Use Restrictions Apply.

★4519★
Dancing Lion—An African Folktale, The
Film Fair Communications
10900 Ventura Blvd.
PO Box 1728
Studio City, CA 91604 Phone: (818)985-0244
1978. **Program Description:** Differentiates African Music from Western Music by its rhythms. **Length:** 11 mins. **Format:** Beta, VHS, 3/4" U-matic. **Acquisition:** Purchase, Duplication License. **Use:** School/Group/Institution, Special Use Restrictions Apply.

★4520★
Day to Remember: August 28, 1963, A
PBS Video
1320 Braddock Pl.
Alexandria, VA 22314-1698 Phone: (703)739-5380
1978. **Program Description:** Documentary about the 1963 civil rights demonstration in Washington, D.C., led by Dr. King. **Length:** 29 mins. **Format:** Beta, VHS, 3/4" U-matic. **Acquisition:** Rent/Lease, Purchase, Off-Air Record. **Use:** School/Group/Institution, Closed Circuit Television, Cable Television.

★4521★
Different Drummer: Blacks in the Military, The
Films, Inc.
5547 N. Ravenswood Ave.
Chicago, IL 60640-1199 Phone: (312)878-2600
1983. **Program Description:** This series examines the history of Black involvement in all American military conflicts from colonial times to the present day. **Length:** 58 mins. **Format:** Beta, VHS, 3/4" U-matic. **Acquisition:** Rent/Lease, Purchase. **Use:** School/Group/Institution, Special Use Restrictions Apply.

★4522★
Different Drummer: Elvin Jones
Rhapsody Films
30 Charlton St.
New York, NY 10014 Phone: (212)243-0152
1979. **Program Description:** A profile of jazz drummer Elvin Jones, undisputed as the major influence in contemporary drumming. This program features his composition "Three Card Molly," and Jones discusses how it was composed and performs the piece with his quartet in a special recording session. The program also includes a look at his family, a discussion of his roots in Black church music, and the beginnings of his career in postwar Detroit. Jones recalls his experiences working with Miles Davis, Charlie Mingus, and Bud Powell, and is seen playing with John Coltrane. **Length:** 28 mins. **Format:** Beta, VHS, 3/4" U-matic. **Acquisition:** Purchase. **Use:** School/Group/Institution, In-Home Viewing.

★4523★
Dizzy Gillespie
Flower Films
10341 San Pablo Ave.
El Cerrito, CA 94530 Phone: (415)525-0942
1965. **Program Description:** A look at the music of one of the inventors of "Bebop" Jazz in the 1940's. Gillespie discusses his beginnings and his theories of music. **Length:** 20 mins. **Format:** Beta, VHS, 3/4" U-matic. **Acquisition:** Purchase. **Use:** School/Group/Institution, In-Home Viewing.

★4524★
Dizzy Gillespie
Sony Video Software (SVS, Inc.)
1700 Broadway, 16th Fl.
New York, NY 10019 Phone: (212)757-4990
1981. **Program Description:** This program presents a jazz concert by Dizzy Gillespie featuring his compositions "Be Bop" and "Birks' Works." **Length:** 19 mins. **Format:** Beta, VHS. **Acquisition:** Purchase. **Use:** In-Home Viewing.

★4525★
Dizzy Gillespie's Dream Band
Sony Video Software (SVS, Inc.)
1700 Broadway, 16th Fl.
New York, NY 10019 Phone: (212)757-4990
1981. **Program Description:** This program presents a concert by Dizzy Gillespie featuring his songs "Groovin' High" and "Hothouse," played by an all star band of Gillespie alumni. **Length:** 16 mins. **Format:** Beta, VHS. **Acquisition:** Purchase. **Use:** In-Home Viewing.

★4526★
Do The Right Thing
MCA/Universal Home Video
70 Universal City Plaza
Universal City, CA 91608 Phone: (818)777-4300
1989. **Program Description:** An uncompromising, brutal comedy about the racial tensions surrounding a White-owned pizzeria in the Bed-Stuyvesant section of Brooklyn on the hottest day of the summer, and the violence that eventually erupts. Written and directed by Spike Lee. **Length:** 95 mins. **Format:** Beta, VHS, Laser optical videodisc. **Acquisition:** Rent/Lease; Purchase. **Use:** In-Home Viewing.

★4527★
Dr. Martin Luther King, Jr.
Society for Visual Education, Inc. (SVE)
1345 Diversey Parkway
Chicago, IL 60614-1299 Phone: (312)525-1500
1988. **Program Description:** From his childhood to his death in 1968, the life of Dr. King is revealed. **Length:** 15 mins. **Format:** VHS, 3/4" U-matic. **Acquisition:** Purchase, Duplication. **Use:** School/Group/Institution, Closed Circuit Television, In-Home Viewing.

★4528★
Dr. Martin Luther King, Jr...An Amazing Grace
CRM/McGraw-Hill Films
674 Via de la Valle
PO Box 641
Del Mar, CA 92014 Phone: (619)453-5000
1978. **Program Description:** This program takes several stirring speeches by Dr. Martin Luther King, Jr. to give a first-hand account of this man, known as the "peaceful warrior." Even though he felt violence was not the answer, his leadership caused a civil rights movement beginning in 1955 with the bus boycott to one of full-scale international importance. Available as a whole or in two parts. **Length:** 62 mins. **Format:** Beta, VHS, 3/4" U-matic. **Acquisition:** Purchase. **Use:** School/Group/Institution, Special Use Restrictions Apply.

★4529★
Dream Deferred, A
Michigan Media
University of Michigan
400 4th St.
Ann Arbor, MI 48109 Phone: (313)764-8228
1970. **Program Description:** After the American Revolution, slavery became unique to Blacks and provided for the early economic development of our nation. Part of the "Black Experience" series. **Length:** 29 mins. **Format:** 3/4" U-matic, Other than listed. **Acquisition:** Rent/Lease, Purchase. **Use:** School/Group/Institution, Closed Circuit Television, Cable Television, Broadcast television.

★4530★
Duke Ellington and His Orchestra
Audiofidelity Enterprises
PO Box 86
Rahway, NJ 07065 Phone: (201)388-5000
1986. **Program Description:** Duke Ellington and His Famous Orchestra are featured in two vintage film shorts, "Black and Tan" (1929) and "Symphony in Black" (1934). Also included are three 1952 Telescriptions: "Sophisticated Lady," "Caravan" and "The Hawk Talks." **Length:** 40 mins. **Format:** Beta, VHS. **Acquisition:** Purchase. **Use:** In-Home Viewing.

★4531★
Ease 'Em Back
Education Development Center
39 Chapel St.
Newton, MA 02160 Phone: (617)969-7100
19??. **Program Description:** This video program documents the development of the EDC "Ethnic Studies Project: African Art and Culture." It shows students of all age levels enthusiastically involved in the creation of different African arts and crafts: tie-dying, batiking cloth, weaving, and making religious masks, to name a few. **Length:** 60 mins. **Format:** 3/4" U-matic, Other than listed. **Acquisition:** Rent/Lease, Purchase. **Use:** School/Group/Institution, Closed Circuit Television, Cable Television, Broadcast television.

★4532★
Echocardiographic LVH in Blacks
Emory Medical Television Network
Emory University
Emory Medical Television Network-
Department C
1440 Clifton Rd., NE
Atlanta, GA 30322 Phone: (404)727-5817
1986. **Program Description:** A look at the effectiveness of echo-based cardiological assessment on the average Black physiology. **Length:** 35 mins. **Format:** VHS, 3/4" U-matic. **Acquisition:** Rent/Lease, Purchase, Subscription. **Use:** School/Group/Institution, Closed Circuit Television, Cable Television, Broadcast television, Special Use Restrictions Apply.

★4533★
EEOC Story
William Greaves Productions
80 8th Ave., Ste. 1701
New York, NY 10011 Phone: (212)206-1213
1972. **Program Description:** An informal look at how The Equal Employment Opportunity Commission helps out women, minorities and the business world. **Length:** 38 mins. **Format:** Beta, VHS. **Acquisition:** Rent/Lease, Purchase. **Use:** School/Group/Institution, Broadcast television.

★4534★
1861-1877: Civil War and Reconstruction
CRM/McGraw-Hill Films
674 Via de la Valle
PO Box 641
Del Mar, CA 92014 Phone: (619)453-5000
1965. **Program Description:** This program examines the political conflicts over the issue of slavery that led to the Civil War. It also illustrates how the Emancipation Proclamation and the Thirteenth, Fourteenth and Fifteenth Amendments sought to protect the Negro's newly won freedom. Part of the "History of the Negro in America" series. **Length:** 20 mins. **Format:** Beta, VHS, 3/4" U-matic. **Acquisition:** Purchase. **Use:** School/Group/Institution, Closed Circuit Television, Special Use Restrictions Apply.

★4535★
El-Hajj Malik el-Shabazz (Malcolm X)
CRM/McGraw-Hill Films
674 Via de la Valle
PO Box 641
Del Mar, CA 92014 Phone: (619)453-5000
1978. **Program Description:** This program follows the rise of Malcolm X as a leader and outstanding spokesman for the Black American movement. Several unanswered questions are raised about his violent death. Available as a whole or in two parts. **Length:** 58 mins. **Format:** Beta, VHS, 3/4" U-matic. **Acquisition:** Purchase. **Use:** School/Group/Institution, Special Use Restrictions Apply.

★4536★
Epidemiology of Hypertension in Blacks: World
Emory Medical Television Network
Emory University
Emory Medical Television Network-
Department C
1440 Clifton Rd., NE
Atlanta, GA 30322 Phone: (404)727-5817
1986. **Program Description:** A symposium-based discussion on the effects of modern living on the Negro physiology. **Length:** 30 mins. **Format:** VHS, 3/4" U-matic. **Acquisition:** Rent/Lease, Purchase, Subscription. **Use:** School/Group/Institution, Closed Circuit Television, Cable Television, Broadcast television, Special Use Restrictions Apply.

★4537★
Equal Opportunity
Barr Films
3490 E. Foothill Blvd.
PO Box 5667
Pasadena, CA 91107 Phone: (213)681-2165
1983. **Program Description:** This program explores the meaning of equal opportunity within the context of affirmative action, racial discrimination, past discrimination, union contracts, seniority, fairness and the Bill of Rights. **Length:** 22 mins. **Format:** Beta, VHS, 3/4" U-matic. **Acquisition:** Rent/Lease, Purchase. **Use:** School/Group/Institution, Special Use Restrictions Apply.

★4538★
Equal Rights
Dallas County Community College District
Center for Telecommunications
4343 N. Hwy. 67
Mesquite, TX 75150-2095 Phone: (214)324-7988
1979. **Program Description:** This program shows the struggle some minority groups have endured to gain their civil rights. **Length:** 29 mins. **Format:** 3/4" U-matic. **Acquisition:** Purchase. **Use:** School/Group/Institution, Closed Circuit Television.

★4539★
Equality
PBS Video
1320 Braddock Pl.
Alexandria, VA 22314-1698 Phone: (703)739-5380
1977. **Program Description:** Explores the meaning of equality from the vantage points of many Americans; attempts to determine if equality is a valid concept in terms of age, sex, race, and economic opportunity. **Length:** 59 mins. **Format:** Beta, VHS, 3/4" U-matic. **Acquisition:** Rent/Lease, Purchase, Off-Air Record. **Use:** School/Group/Institution, Closed Circuit Television, Cable Television.

★4540★
Equally Free
National Geographic Society
17th & M Sts., NW
Washington, DC 20036 Phone: (202)857-7378
1975. **Program Description:** A look at the Virginia Convention's first attempt to write a declaration of human rights. **Length:** 21 mins. **Format:** 3/4" U-matic, Special order format. **Acquisition:** Purchase; Trade-in, Duplication License. **Use:** School/Group/Institution, In-Home Viewing, Special Use Restrictions.

★4541★
Ernie and Rose
Filmakers Library, Inc.
133 E. 58th St.
New York, NY 10022 Phone: (212)355-6545
1984. **Program Description:** This film looks at the friendship between Ernie and Rose, one Black and one White, who watch out for each other in their old age. **Length:** 29 mins. **Format:** VHS, 3/4" U-matic. **Acquisition:** Rent/Lease, Purchase, Duplication. **Use:** School/Group/Institution, In-Home Viewing, Special Use Restrictions Apply.

★4542★
Ethics and Human Rights
American Humanist Association
7 Harwood Dr.
PO Box 146
Amherst, NY 14226-0146 Phone: (716)839-5080
1977. **Program Description:** Aryeh Neier (executive director of the American Civil Liberties Union) discusses the diversity of the ACLU's involvements, and the Union's stand on such issues as reverse discrimination and fairness compared to personal liberty. Part of "Ethics in America" series. **Length:** 30 mins. **Format:** 3/4" U-matic, Other than listed. **Acquisition:** Rent/Lease, Purchase. **Use:** School/Group/Institution, Closed Circuit Television, Cable Television.

★4543★
Eye of the Storm, The
Center for Humanities, Inc.
Communications Park
Box 1000
Mount Kisco, NY 10549 Phone: (914)666-4100
1984. **Program Description:** This program provides a valuable lesson in prejudice when a school teacher singles out blue eyed students as a minority group. **Length:** 25 mins. **Format:** Beta, VHS, 3/4" U-matic. **Acquisition:** Purchase. **Use:** School/Group/Institution, Special Use Restrictions Apply.

★4544★
Eyes On the Prize
PBS Video
1320 Braddock Pl.
Alexandria, VA 22314-1698 Phone: (703)739-5380
1986. **Program Description:** A comprehensive six-part series on the history of the American Civil Rights Movement from World War II to the present. **Length:** 60 mins. **Format:** Beta, VHS, 3/4" U-matic. **Acquisition:** Rent/Lease, Purchase, Off-Air Record. **Use:** School/Group/Institution, Closed Circuit Television, Cable Television.

★4545★
Eyes on the Prize II: America at the Racial Crossroads (1965-1985)
PBS Video
1320 Braddock Pl.
Alexandria, VA 22314-1698 Phone: (703)739-5380
1987. **Program Description:** The American civil rights movement, from the mid-sixties to mid-eighties, is traced. **Length:** 30 mins. **Format:** VHS, 3/4" U-matic. **Acquisition:** Purchase. **Use:** School/Group/Institution, Closed Circuit Television, In-Home Viewing, Special Use Restrictions Apply.

★4546★
Falasha: Agony of the Black Jews
Filmakers Library, Inc.
133 E. 58th St.
New York, NY 10022 Phone: (212)355-6545
1983. **Program Description:** This is a stirring documentary on the Falashas of Ethiopia who are persecuted by Ethiopians for being Jewish and rejected by Israel for being Black. **Length:** 28 mins. **Format:** Beta, VHS, 3/4" U-matic. **Acquisition:** Purchase. **Use:** School/Group/Institution.

★4547★
Farrakhan the Minister
WNET/Thirteen Non-Broadcast
356 W. 58th St.
New York, NY 10019 Phone: (212)560-3045
1972. **Program Description:** Black Muslim Minister Louis Farrakhan tells of his hopes and plans for the Black people of America in an interview with Ellis Haizlip. **Length:** 58 mins. **Format:** Beta, VHS, 3/4" U-matic. **Acquisition:** Rent/Lease, Purchase. **Use:** School/Group/Institution, Closed Circuit Television, In-Home Viewing.

★4548★
Fat Black Mack
Texture Films, Inc.
5547 N. Ravenswood Ave.
Chicago, IL 60640 Phone: (312)878-7300
1970. **Program Description:** A mix of animation, music and enchantment work to tell the story of Mack, a Black feline upset with his appearance. When Mack ultimately accepts himself, he realizes color is irrelevant to character. The film is designed to help develop self-identity and encourage pride in young Black children. **Length:** 5 mins. **Format:** Beta, VHS, 3/4" U-matic. **Acquisition:** Purchase. **Use:** School/Group/Institution.

★4549★
Fats Waller and Friends
Audiofidelity Enterprises
PO Box 86
Rahway, NJ 07065 Phone: (201)388-5000
1986. **Program Description:** The jovial Fats Waller appears in the only four Soundies he made, all from 1941: "Your Feet's Too Big," "Ain't Misbehavin'," "Honeysuckle Rose" and "The Joint Is Jumpin'." Also on this tape are seven other Soundies by an assortment of performers. **Length:** 29 mins. **Format:** Beta, VHS. **Acquisition:** Purchase. **Use:** In-Home Viewing.

★4550★
Fields of Endless Day
National Film Board of Canada
1251 Avenue of the Americas, 16th Fl.
New York, NY 10020-1173 Phone: (212)586-5131
1987. **Program Description:** This film takes a look at the history of the Black population in Canada. **Length:** 59 mins. **Format:** Beta, VHS, 3/4" U-matic. **Acquisition:** Purchase, Rent/Lease. **Use:** School/Group/Institution, Special Use Restrictions Apply.

★4551★
Fight Against Slavery
Time-Life Video
1271 Avenue of the Americas
New York, NY 10020 Phone: (212)484-5940
1977. **Program Description:** The history of slavery in a powerful, haunting six-part dramatization filmed on location in Africa. **Length:** 56 mins. **Format:** Beta, VHS, 3/4" U-matic, Other than listed. **Acquisition:** Rent/Lease, Purchase. **Use:** School/Group/Institution, Special Use Restrictions Apply.

★4552★
Fighter for Freedom—The Frederick Douglass Story
National AudioVisual Center
National Archives & Records Administration
Customer Services Section PZ
8700 Edgeworth Dr.
Capitol Heights, MD 20743-3701 Phone: (301)763-1896
1987. **Program Description:** This is a documentary on the life of the famous freed slave. **Length:** 17 mins. **Format:** Beta, VHS, 3/4" U-matic. **Acquisition:** Purchase. **Use:** School/Group/Institution, Special Use Restrictions Apply.

★4553★
Finally Got the News
Cinema Guild
1697 Broadway, Rm. 802
New York, NY 10019 Phone: (212)246-5522
1970. **Program Description:** A look inside the automobile factories in Detroit through the eyes of Black workers. Examines the Black Revolutionary Workers efforts to create a new union. **Length:** 55 mins. **Format:** Beta, VHS, 3/4" U-matic. **Acquisition:** Rent/Lease, Purchase, Duplication. **Use:** School/Group/Institution, Special Use Restrictions Apply.

★4554★
Flyers in Search of a Dream
PBS Video
1320 Braddock Pl.
Alexandria, VA 22314-1698 Phone: (703)739-5380
1986. **Program Description:** The intriguing story of America's pioneering Black aviators during the golden age of aviation in the 1920's and 1930's. **Length:** 60 mins. **Format:** Beta, VHS, 3/4'' U-matic. **Acquisition:** Rent/Lease, Purchase, Off-Air Record. **Use:** School/Group/Institution, Closed Circuit Television, Cable Television.

★4555★
Follow the North Star
Time-Life Video
1271 Avenue of the Americas
New York, NY 10020 Phone: (212)484-5940
1975. **Program Description:** A suspenseful adventure examining the issues of freedom, conscience and civil liberties during the time when the country was split over the slavery question. **Length:** 47 mins. **Format:** Beta, VHS, 3/4'' U-matic, Other than listed. **Acquisition:** Rent/Lease, Purchase. **Use:** School/Group/Institution, Special Use Restrictions Apply.

★4556★
Frederick Douglass
Britannica Films
310 S. Michigan Ave.
Chicago, IL 60604 Phone: (312)347-7958
1972. **Program Description:** Depicts the contributions of Frederick Douglass, who fathered the Black protest movement. From ''Afro-American History'' series. **Length:** 9 mins. **Format:** Beta, VHS, 3/4'' U-matic. **Acquisition:** Rent/Lease, Purchase, Trade-in. **Use:** School/Group/Institution, Special Use Restrictions Apply.

★4557★
Frederick Douglass: An American Life
Your World Video
80 8th Ave., Ste. 1701
New York, NY 10011 Phone: (212)206-1215
1986. **Program Description:** A dramatized biography of the Negro leader and abolitionist. **Length:** 30 mins. **Format:** Beta, VHS. **Acquisition:** Purchase. **Use:** In-Home Viewing.

★4558★
Free Paper Come
Time-Life Video
1271 Avenue of the Americas
New York, NY 10020 Phone: (212)484-5940
1977. **Program Description:** This episode of ''Fight Against Slavery'' follows one of the most important rebellions in which slaves fought for their own freedom, led by Daddy Sharp, in Jamaica in 1832. **Length:** 53 mins. **Format:** Beta, VHS, 3/4'' U-matic, Other than listed. **Acquisition:** Rent/Lease, Purchase. **Use:** School/Group/Institution, Special Use Restrictions Apply.

★4559★
Freedom Frontier
Media Project, Inc.
PO Box 4093
Portland, OR 97208 Phone: (503)223-5335
1976. **Program Description:** This program documents the history of Black people in the state of Oregon. **Length:** 55 mins. **Format:** Beta, VHS, 1/2'' reel, 3/4'' U-matic. **Acquisition:** Rent/Lease, Purchase. **Use:** School/Group/Institution, Closed Circuit Television, Special Use Restrictions Apply.

★4560★
From Dreams To Reality—A Tribute to Minority Inventors
National AudioVisual Center
National Archives & Records Administration
Customer Services Section PZ
8700 Edgeworth Dr.
Capitol Heights, MD 20743-3701 Phone: (301)763-1896
1986. **Program Description:** Ossie Davis narrates this tribute to minority inventors in an effort to motivate minority students to become scientists. **Length:** 28 mins. **Format:** Beta, VHS, 3/4'' U-matic. **Acquisition:** Purchase. **Use:** School/Group/Institution, Special Use Restrictions Apply.

★4561★
From Sunup
Maryknoll World Productions
Maryknoll, NY 10545 Phone: 800-227-8523
1988. **Program Description:** The lives of African women who have to work constantly just to squeeze out a meager living are portrayed. **Length:** 28 mins. **Format:** VHS. **Acquisition:** Purchase, Rent/Lease. **Use:** School/Group/Institution.

★4562★
From These Roots
William Greaves Productions
80 8th Ave., Ste. 1701
New York, NY 10011 Phone: (212)206-1213
1974. **Program Description:** Narrated by Brock Peters, this view of the 1920's ''Harlem Renaissance'' features the work of Cab Calloway, Paul Robeson, Ethel Waters, Duke Ellington, Langston Hughes and Claude MacKay. Music by Eubie Blake. **Length:** 28 mins. **Format:** Beta, VHS, 3/4'' U-matic. **Acquisition:** Purchase. **Use:** School/Group/Institution, In-Home Viewing.

★4563★
Fundi: The Story of Ella Baker
Icarus Films
200 Park Ave., S., Ste. 1319
New York, NY 10003 Phone: (212)674-3375
1986. **Program Description:** Ella Baker's nickname ''Fundi'' comes from the Swahili word for a person who passes skills from one generation to another. This film documents Baker's work in the civil rights movement of the 1960s, and her friendship with Dr. Martin Luther King. **Length:** 45 mins. **Format:** 3/4'' U-matic. **Acquisition:** Purchase. **Use:** School/Group/Institution, Special Use Restrictions Apply.

★4564★
Gathered Into One
UMCom Video
810 12th Ave., S.
Nashville, TN 37203 Phone: (615)256-0530
1982. **Program Description:** This tape looks at the growing needs of the Ethnic Minority Local Church. **Length:** 20 mins. **Format:** 3/4'' U-matic. **Acquisition:** Rent/Lease, Purchase. **Use:** School/Group/Institution, Cable Television, Broadcast television.

★4565★
George Washington Carver
Rainbow Educational Video, Inc.
170 Keyland Court
Bohemia, NY 11716 Phone: (516)589-6643
1988. **Program Description:** The life of the Black scientist and inventor is recalled. **Length:** 29 mins. **Format:** VHS. **Acquisition:** Purchase. **Use:** School/Group/Institution.

★4566★
Gettin' to Know Me
Great Plains National Instructional Television Library (GPN)
University of Nebraska at Lincoln
PO Box 80669
Lincoln, NE 68501-0669 Phone: (402)472-2007
1979. **Program Description:** The Jacksons, a contemporary Southern Black family, maintain their family's character by remembering and

exploring the Black folklore that is their heritage. Programs are available individually. **Length:** 30 mins. **Format:** Beta, VHS, 3/4" U-matic. **Acquisition:** Purchase. **Use:** School/Group/Institution, Closed Circuit Television, Cable Television, Broadcast Television.

★4567★
Getting to Know Barbara
Anti-Defamation League of B'nai B'rith
Audio-Visual Department
823 United Nations Plaza
New York, NY 10017 Phone: (212)490-2525
1986. **Program Description:** A profile of a determined Black woman who rose from her impoverished beginnings to become the head of a multi-million dollar advertising agency. **Length:** 12 mins. **Format:** Beta, VHS, 3/4" U-matic. **Acquisition:** Purchase. **Use:** School/Group/Institution, Closed Circuit Television, Cable Television, Broadcast Television, In-Home Viewing.

★4568★
Gift of the Black Folk
Pyramid Film and Video
Box 1048
Santa Monica, CA 90406 Phone: (213)828-7577
1978. **Program Description:** The lives and accomplishments of Denmark Vesey, Harriet Tubman, and Frederick Douglass are surveyed. **Length:** 16 mins. **Format:** Beta, VHS, 3/4" U-matic. **Acquisition:** Rent/Lease; Purchase; Trade-in. **Use:** School/Group/Institution, Closed Circuit Television, In-Home Viewing, Special Use Restrictions Apply.

★4569★
Gloria
Filmakers Library, Inc.
133 E. 58th St.
New York, NY 10022 Phone: (212)355-6545
1984. **Program Description:** The circumstances surrounding the shooting of a Black female mental patient are examined. **Length:** 27 mins. **Format:** Beta, VHS, 3/4" U-matic. **Acquisition:** Purchase. **Use:** School/Group/Institution.

★4570★
Glory
RCA/Columbia Pictures Home Video
3500 W. Olive Ave.
Burbank, CA 91505 Phone: (818)953-7900
1989. **Program Description:** A rich, historical spectacle chronicling the 54th Massachusetts, the first Black volunteer infantry unit the Civil War. The film manages to artfully focus on both the 54th and their White commander, Robert Gould Shaw. Based on Shaw's letters. Denzel Washington won Best Supporting Actor. **Format:** Beta, VHS, Laser optical videodisc. **Acquisition:** Rent/Lease; Purchase. **Use:** In-Home Viewing.

★4571★
Good Mornin' Blues
PBS Video
1320 Braddock Pl.
Alexandria, VA 22314-1698 Phone: (703)739-5380
1979. **Program Description:** B.B. King narrates this documentary about blues music from its earliest origins until World War II. **Length:** 59 mins. **Format:** Beta, VHS, 3/4" U-matic. **Acquisition:** Rent/Lease, Purchase, Off-Air Record. **Use:** School/Group/Institution, Closed Circuit Television, Cable Television.

★4572★
Goodyear Jazz Concert with Duke Ellington
Video Yesteryear
Box C
Sandy Hook, CT 06482 Phone: (203)426-2574
1962. **Program Description:** Duke Ellington and the Band start with "Take the A Train" and run through five other all-time Ellington hits. **Length:** 27 mins. **Format:** Beta, VHS, Other than listed. **Acquisition:** Purchase. **Use:** In-Home Viewing.

★4573★
Goodyear Jazz Concert with Louis Armstrong
Video Yesteryear
Box C
Sandy Hook, CT 06482 Phone: (203)426-2574
1961. **Program Description:** A studio performance by Louis Armstrong's All Stars. Tunes include "When It's Sleepy Time Down South," "C'est si Bon," "Someday You'll Be Sorry," "Jerry," "Nobody Knows de Trouble I've Seen," and "When the Saints Go Marching In." **Length:** 27 mins. **Format:** Beta, VHS, Other than listed. **Acquisition:** Purchase. **Use:** In-Home Viewing.

★4574★
Gospel at the Symphony
The Market Place
PO Box 4126
Rockford, IL 61110 Phone: (815)963-0300
1984. **Program Description:** A compilation of Black Gospel music including "O Happy Day," "Worship the Lord," and "I Need to Pray." **Length:** 48 mins. **Format:** Beta, VHS. **Acquisition:** Rent/Lease; Purchase. **Use:** School/Group/Institution, In-Home Viewing.

★4575★
Gotta Make This Journey: Sweet Honey In the Rock
American Federation of Arts
41 E. 65th St.
New York, NY 10021 Phone: (212)988-7700
1983. **Program Description:** A documentary about the radical Black women's singing group Sweet Honey in the Rock, centering on their ninth anniversary concert. Interspersed throughout the concert footage are interviews with the singers and with other Black women. **Length:** 58 mins. **Format:** Beta, VHS, 3/4" U-matic. **Acquisition:** Purchase, Rent/Lease. **Use:** School/Group/Institution, In-Home Viewing.

★4576★
Grateful Peasantry, A
Time-Life Video
1271 Avenue of the Americas
New York, NY 10020 Phone: (212)484-5940
1977. **Program Description:** This episode of "Fight Against Slavery" focuses on Parliament's great slavery debate in 1792 which concluded with the passage of an amendment to gradually abolish slavery. **Length:** 56 mins. **Format:** Beta, VHS, 3/4" U-matic, Other than listed. **Acquisition:** Rent/Lease, Purchase. **Use:** School/Group/Institution, Special Use Restrictions Apply.

★4577★
Great Americans: Martin Luther King, Jr.
Britannica Films
310 S. Michigan Ave.
Chicago, IL 60604 Phone: (312)347-7958
1982. **Program Description:** Three of Martin Luther King Jr.'s friends speak of him. Also, some remarks from his wife are included. **Length:** 24 mins. **Format:** Beta, VHS, 3/4" U-matic. **Acquisition:** Rent/Lease, Purchase, Trade-in. **Use:** School/Group/Institution, Special Use Restrictions Apply.

★4578★
Great Jazz Bands of the 30's
Discount Video Tapes, Inc.
833 "A" N. Hollywood Way
PO Box 7122
Burbank, CA 91510 Phone: (818)843-3366
1935. **Program Description:** A package of 1931-35 Vitaphone musical shorts, featuring several of the great Black jazz bands of the period. Titles are: "Pie Pie Blackbird," "Don Redman and his Orchestra," "Cab Calloway's Hi-De-Ho," "Rhapsody in Black and Blue" and "Symphony in Black." **Length:** 50 mins. **Format:** Beta, VHS. **Acquisition:** Rent/Lease, Purchase. **Use:** In-Home Viewing.

★4579★
Grover Washington, Jr. in Concert
Warner Home Video, Inc.
4000 Warner Blvd.
Burbank, CA 91522 Phone: (818)954-6000
1982. **Program Description:** The lush, soulful music of Grover Washington, Jr. is captured in one of his rare public performances along with musicians Eric Gale, Richard Tee, and Steve Gadd. Songs include "Just the Two of Us," "Winelight," and "Come Morning." In stereo. **Length:** 53 mins. **Format:** Beta, VHS. **Acquisition:** Purchase. **Use:** In-Home Viewing.

★4580★
Hairpiece: A Film For Nappy-Headed People
Women Make Movies
225 Lafayette St., Ste. 212
New York, NY 10012 Phone: (212)925-0606
1985. **Program Description:** An irreverent, animated satire on the standards of beauty imposed on Black women in our society. **Length:** 10 mins. **Format:** Beta, VHS, 3/4" U-matic. **Acquisition:** Purchase, Rent/Lease. **Use:** School/Group/Institution, Special Use Restrictions Apply.

★4581★
Hands That Picked Cotton
PBS Video
1320 Braddock Pl.
Alexandria, VA 22314-1698 Phone: (703)739-5380
1985. **Program Description:** This program allows viewers to draw their own conclusion on the politics of the south, where Blacks have gained political power but are still working for economic progress. **Length:** 60 mins. **Format:** Beta, VHS, 3/4" U-matic. **Acquisition:** Rent/Lease, Purchase, Duplication, Off-Air Record. **Use:** School/Group/Institution, Closed Circuit Television, In-Home Viewing, Special Use Restrictions Apply.

★4582★
Hard Road to Glory, A: The Black Athlete in America
Eastman Kodak Company
c/o Wood Knapp
Knapp Press
5900 Wilshire Blvd.
Los Angeles, CA 90036 Phone: (213)937-5486
1987. **Program Description:** Tennis player Arthur Ashe and actor James Earl Jones narrate this documentary, which features footage of Jackie Robinson, Jesse Owens and Joe Louis. **Length:** 90 mins. **Format:** Beta, VHS, 8mm. **Acquisition:** Purchase. **Use:** School/Group/Institution, In-Home Viewing.

★4583★
Harlem Harmonies Vol. 1
Audiofidelity Enterprises
PO Box 86
Rahway, NJ 07065 Phone: (201)388-5000
1986. **Program Description:** Nine Soundies and film shorts by popular Black jazz bands and vocalists are compiled on this tape. Selections include: "The Lonesome Road" (Tharpe/Millinder-1941), "Jungle Jig" (Dandridge-1941) and "Hot in the Groove" (Hawkins-1942). **Length:** 35 mins. **Format:** Beta, VHS. **Acquisition:** Purchase. **Use:** In-Home Viewing.

★4584★
Harlem Harmonies Vol. 2
Audiofidelity Enterprises
PO Box 86
Rahway, NJ 07065 Phone: (201)388-5000
1986. **Program Description:** Another compilation of jazz performances from film shorts and Soundies. Selections include: "Hot Chocolate" (Ellington-1941), "Calypso Blues" (Cole-1951) and "Unlucky Woman Blues" (Horne-1941). **Length:** 34 mins. **Format:** Beta, VHS. **Acquisition:** Purchase. **Use:** In-Home Viewing.

★4585★
Harlem in the Twenties
Britannica Films
310 S. Michigan Ave.
Chicago, IL 60604 Phone: (312)347-7958
1987. **Program Description:** Harlem didn't become a predominantly Black area until the twenties, and has remained so ever since. **Length:** 10 mins. **Format:** Beta, VHS, 3/4" U-matic. **Acquisition:** Purchase, Trade-in. **Use:** School/Group/Institution, Special Use Restrictions Apply.

★4586★
Harriet Tubman and the Underground Railroad
Phoenix/BFA Films
468 Park Ave., S.
New York, NY 10016 Phone: (212)684-5910
1972. **Program Description:** Harriet Tubman stands out as a woman of rare courage and abilities. The program follows one of her most dangerous trips leading a group of four slaves out of Maryland. Walter Cronkite interviews. **Length:** 21 mins. **Format:** Beta, VHS, 3/4" U-matic. **Acquisition:** Purchase. **Use:** School/Group/Institution, Special Use Restrictions Apply.

★4587★
Herbie Hancock and the Rockit Band
CBS/Fox Video
1211 Avenue of the Americas
New York, NY 10036 Phone: (212)819-3200
1984. **Program Description:** Filmed live at the Hammersmith Odeon and Camden Hall in London, England, this program takes the home viewer through a multi-media presentation of break dancing, scratch music, robots and an explosive light show. In VHS Hi-Fi and Beta Hi-Fi. **Length:** 70 mins. **Format:** Beta, VHS. **Acquisition:** Purchase. **Use:** In-Home Viewing.

★4588★
Heritage in Black
Britannica Films
310 S. Michigan Ave.
Chicago, IL 60604 Phone: (312)347-7958
1969. **Program Description:** A 200-year panorama that stretches from the first struggles of Black people to be free of chains to today's struggles to be free of invisible bonds. **Length:** 27 mins. **Format:** Beta, VHS, 3/4" U-matic. **Acquisition:** Rent/Lease, Purchase, Trade-in. **Use:** School/Group/Institution, Special Use Restrictions Apply.

★4589★
Heritage of Slavery, The
Phoenix/BFA Films
468 Park Ave., S.
New York, NY 10016 Phone: (212)684-5910
1968. **Program Description:** CBS News reporter George Foster interviews descendants of plantation owners and presentday Black activists, demonstrating the parallels between attitudes under slavery and now. **Length:** 53 mins. **Format:** Beta, VHS, 3/4" U-matic. **Acquisition:** Purchase. **Use:** School/Group/Institution, Special Use Restrictions Apply.

★4590★
Hey, Cab
Phoenix/BFA Films
468 Park Ave., S.
New York, NY 10016 Phone: (212)684-5910
1970. **Program Description:** Dramatizes a true experience of a Black journalist, Bob Teague. A cab deliberately bypasses the Black man stranded on the rain swept curb. Based on "Letters to a Black Boy." **Length:** 11 mins. **Format:** Beta, VHS, 3/4" U-matic. **Acquisition:** Purchase. **Use:** School/Group/Institution, Special Use Restrictions Apply.

★4591★
The History of the Negro in America Series
CRM/McGraw-Hill Films
674 Via de la Valle
PO Box 641
Del Mar, CA 92014 Phone: (619)453-5000
1965. **Program Description:** Through the use of graphic materials, photographers, and newsreel footage, this series traces the African-American's part in American history. All programs are available individually. Titles: 1. 1619-1860: Out of Slavery; 2. 1861-1877: Civil War and Reconstruction; 3. 1877-Today: Freedom Movement. **Length:** 20 mins. **Format:** Beta, VHS, 3/4" U-matic. **Acquisition:** Rent/Lease; Purchase. **Use:** School/Group/Institution, Clsoed Circuit Television, Special Use Restrictions Apply.

★4592★
Hollywood Shuffle
Virgin Vision
6100 Wilshire Blvd., 16th Fl.
Los Angeles, CA 90048 Phone: (213)857-5200
1987. **Program Description:** Robert Townsend's self-conscious comedy about a struggling Black actor in Hollywood trying to find work and getting nothing but stereotypical roles. **Length:** 81 mins. **Format:** Beta, VHS. **Acquisition:** Rent/Lease; Purchase. **Use:** In-Home Viewing.

★4593★
Homeland
Media Guild
11722 Sorrento Valley Rd., Ste. E
San Diego, CA 92121 Phone: (619)755-9191
1989. **Program Description:** A Black farming family struggles against all sorts of opposition in the early 1960s. **Length:** 28 mins. **Format:** Beta, VHS, 3/4" U-matic. **Acquisition:** Purchase. **Use:** School/Group/Institution, Special Use Restrictions Apply.

★4594★
How Can North Americans Assist the Education and Training of South Africans and Namibians?
Michigan State University
IMC Marketing Division
East Lansing, MI 48826-0710 Phone: (517)353-9229
1988. **Program Description:** A discussion about the educational future of people in South Africa. **Length:** 40 mins. **Format:** Beta, VHS, 3/4" U-matic. **Acquisition:** Purchase, Rent/Lease. **Use:** School/Group/Institution, Closed Circuit Television.

★4595★
Howl at the Moon
Texture Films, Inc.
5547 N. Ravenswood Ave.
Chicago, IL 60640 Phone: (312)878-7300
1982. **Program Description:** A Black domestic servant for a White family in Johannesburg, South Africa shares a dream with other people: to become legal residents of a Black township–even if they must bribe an official to achieve this dream. **Length:** 40 mins. **Format:** Beta, VHS, 3/4" U-matic. **Acquisition:** Purchase. **Use:** School/Group/Institution.

★4596★
Humanity Defiled
Michigan Media
University of Michigan
400 4th St.
Ann Arbor, MI 48109 Phone: (313)764-8228
1970. **Program Description:** The emergence of slavery in the new world colonies and the alternatives open to Whites are examined. **Length:** 29 mins. **Format:** 3/4" U-matic, Other than listed. **Acquisition:** Rent/Lease, Purchase. **Use:** School/Group/Institution, Closed Circuit Television, Cable Television, Broadcast television.

★4597★
I Am Somebody
Icarus Films
200 Park Ave. S, Ste. 1319
New York, NY 10003 Phone: (212)674-3375
1970. **Program Description:** The story of 400 poorly paid Black women hospital workers in South Carolina who went on strike in 1969 for 113 days to demand union recognition and increase in their hourly wage. **Length:** 28 mins. **Format:** 3/4" U-matic. **Acquisition:** Rent/Lease; Purchase; Duplication. **Use:** School/Group/Institution.

★4598★
"I Have a Dream": Martin Luther King, Jr.
King Features Entertainment
235 E. 45th St.
New York, NY 10017 Phone: (212)682-5600
1983. **Program Description:** This program chronicles the life of the great civil rights leader from his birth to the tragic assassination in 1968. **Length:** 14 mins. **Format:** Beta, VHS, 3/4" U-matic. **Acquisition:** Rent/Lease, Purchase. **Use:** School/Group/Institution, Special Use Restrictions Apply.

★4599★
"I Have a Dream...": The Life of Martin Luther King
Phoenix/BFA Films
468 Park Ave., S.
New York, NY 10016 Phone: (212)684-5910
1968. **Program Description:** The program brings a better understanding of the philosophies and ideals that King exemplified. Actual news footage is used. **Length:** 35 mins. **Format:** Beta, VHS, 3/4" U-matic. **Acquisition:** Purchase. **Use:** School/Group/Institution, Special Use Restrictions Apply.

★4600★
I Know Why the Caged Bird Sings
USA Home Video
c/o IVE
21800 Burbank Blvd.
PO Box 4062
Woodland Hills, CA 91316 Phone: (818)888-3040
1979. **Program Description:** A Black writer's memories of growing up in the rural South during the 1930s. A strong performance by Esther Rolle. Made for television film based on the book by Maya Angelou. **Length:** 100 mins. **Format:** VHS. **Acquisition:** Purchase. **Use:** In-Home Viewing.

★4601★
I Wonder Why
CRM/McGraw-Hill Films
674 Via de la Valle
PO Box 641
Del Mar, CA 92014 Phone: (619)453-5000
1964. **Program Description:** A young Black girl wonders in a monolog of her thoughts, "Why don't people like me?" **Length:** 6 mins. **Format:** Beta, VHS, 3/4" U-matic. **Acquisition:** Rent/Lease, Purchase. **Use:** School/Group/Institution, Special Use Restrictions Apply.

★4602★
Iawo
Cinema Guild
1697 Broadway, Rm. 802
New York, NY 10019 Phone: (212)246-5522
1978. **Program Description:** The transfer of the Yoruba cult by Black slaves to the western hemisphere is examined. The ideological, religious, and sociological meanings of the initiation of women into the cult are also depicted. English subtitles. **Length:** 40 mins. **Format:** Beta, VHS, 3/4" U-matic. **Acquisition:** Rent/Lease, Purchase, Duplication. **Use:** School/Group/Institution, Special Use Restrictions Apply.

★4603★
Illusions
Women Make Movies
225 Lafayette St., Ste. 212
New York, NY 10012 Phone: (212)925-0606
1982. **Program Description:** A challenging film about two Black women in Hollywood. One is a studio executive who "passes" for White, the

other is the singing voice for a White Hollywood star. **Length:** 34 mins. **Format:** Beta, VHS, 3/4" U-matic. **Acquisition:** Purchase, Rent/Lease. **Use:** School/Group/Institution, Special Use Restrictions Apply.

★4604★
I'm Gonna Git You Sucka
MGM/UA Home Video Inc.
10000 W. Washington Blvd.
Culver City, CA 9232-2728 Phone: (213)280-6000
1988. **Program Description:** A parody of 1970's blaxploitation films, from "Shaft" to "Blacula." Written and directed by Keenan Ivory Wayans. **Length:** 89 mins. **Format:** Beta, VHS, Laser optical videodisc. **Acquisition:** Purchase. **Use:** In-Home Viewing.

★4605★
In Black and White: Civil Rights Organizations
New Jersey Network
1573 Parkside Ave.
Trenton, NJ 08625 Phone: (609)292-5252
1988. **Program Description:** This program explores the history and current programs of the National Urban League, the National Association for the Advancement of Colored People, and the National Council of Negro Women. **Length:** 30 mins. **Format:** VHS, 3/4" U-matic. **Acquisition:** Rent/Lease, Purchase. **Use:** School/Group/Institution.

★4606★
In Remembrance of Martin
PBS Video
1320 Braddock Pl.
Alexandria, VA 22314-1698 Phone: (703)739-5380
1986. **Program Description:** This program documents the celebrations in Atlanta during the observance of the first federal holiday for Martin Luther King Day. Historical footage and interviews are combined with the festivities throughout the city. **Length:** 60 mins. **Format:** Beta, VHS, 3/4" U-matic. **Acquisition:** Rent/Lease, Purchase, Off-Air Record. **Use:** School/Group/Institution, Closed Circuit Television, Cable Television.

★4607★
In the Best of Times
Pennsylvania State University AV Services
University Division of Media & Learning Resources
Special Services Bldg.
Pennsylvania State University
University Park, PA 16802 Phone: (814)865-6314
1980. **Program Description:** This part of the "U.S. Chronicle" series examines Seattle's economic boom, benefitting everyone except the unemployed Blacks of Seattle. **Length:** 29 mins. **Format:** 3/4" U-matic, Other than listed. **Acquisition:** Rent/Lease, Purchase. **Use:** School/Group/Institution, Special Use Restrictions Apply.

★4608★
In the Company of Men
Your World Video
80 8th Ave., Ste. 1701
New York, NY 10011 Phone: (212)206-1215
1964. **Program Description:** A document of communication breakdown between foremen and minority workers, and how it can be fixed. **Length:** 28 mins. **Format:** Beta, VHS, 3/4" U-matic. **Acquisition:** Rent/Lease, Purchase. **Use:** School/Group/Institution, In-Home Viewing.

★4609★
In the Shadoe of the Capitol
PBS Video
1320 Braddock Pl.
Alexandria, VA 22314-1698 Phone: (703)739-5380
1984. **Program Description:** This program investigates how several former Black civil rights activists grapple with politics, power and hard times. **Length:** 60 mins. **Format:** Beta, VHS, 3/4" U-matic. **Acquisition:** Rent/Lease, Purchase, Off-Air Record. **Use:** School/Group/Institution, Closed Circuit Television, Cable Television.

★4610★
Integration in Public Schools
New York State Education Department
Center for Learning Technologies
Media Distribution Network
Rm. C-7, Concourse Level
Albany, NY 12230 Phone: (518)474-1265
1974. **Program Description:** The problems that educators and administrators face with racial integration in schools is examined. **Length:** 30 mins. **Format:** Beta, VHS, 1/2" reel, 3/4" U-matic, 2" Quad. **Acquisition:** Duplication License, Free Duplication. **Use:** School/Group/Institution, Special Use Restrictions Apply.

★4611★
International Sweethearts of Rhythm, The
Cinema Guild
1697 Broadway, Rm. 802
New York, NY 10019 Phone: (212)246-5522
1986. **Program Description:** A film biography of The International Sweethearts of Rhythm, a popular women's jazz band of the 1940's, remembered for its music and racially integrated membership. **Length:** 30 mins. **Format:** Beta, VHS, 3/4" U-matic. **Acquisition:** Rent/Lease, Purchase, Duplication. **Use:** School/Group/Institution, Special Use Restrictions Apply.

★4612★
Interview with Clarence Muse, An
Indiana University Audio-Visual Center
Bloomington, IN 47405-5901 Phone: (812)335-8087
1979. **Program Description:** A vital voice in the Black theatre, Clarence Muse founded the famed Lafayette Theatre Players and performed in vaudeville, legitimate stage, films, radio and TV. A few months before his death, Clarence Muse taped this conversation. **Length:** 180 mins. **Format:** 3/4" U-matic. **Acquisition:** Rent/Lease, Duplication, Duplication License. **Use:** School/Group/Institution, Closed Circuit Television, In-Home Viewing, Special Use Restrictions Apply.

★4613★
Is It OK to Be Me?
Pyramid Film & Video
Box 1048
Santa Monica, CA 90406 Phone: (213)828-7577
1977. **Program Description:** This part of the "Who We Are" series shows children how it feels to be a minority, what it means to be prejudiced, and two separate ways of treating people who are different. **Length:** 6 mins. **Format:** Beta, VHS, 3/4" U-matic. **Acquisition:** Rent/Lease, Purchase, Duplication License. **Use:** School/Group/Institution, In-Home Viewing, Special Use Restrictions Apply.

★4614★
"Isitwalandwe": The Story of the South African Freedom Charter
Cinema Guild
1697 Broadway, Rm. 802
New York, NY 10019 Phone: (212)246-5522
1980. **Program Description:** This film documents the adoption of the South African Freedom Charter, a blueprint for a future non-racial and democratic South Africa. **Length:** 51 mins. **Format:** Beta, VHS, 3/4" U-matic. **Acquisition:** Purchase. **Use:** School/Group/Institution.

★4615★
It's Not a One Person Thing
Green Mountain Post Films, Inc.
PO Box 229
Turners Falls, MA 01376 Phone: (413)863-4754
1978. **Program Description:** A look at the formation of the poverty-fighting Federation of Southern Cooperatives in the heat of the civil rights movement in 1967. **Length:** 30 mins. **Format:** Beta, VHS, 3/4" U-matic. **Acquisition:** Rent/Lease, Purchase. **Use:** School/Group/Institution, Closed Circuit Television, Broadcast television, Special Use Restrictions Apply.

★4616★
Jane Kennedy—To Be Free
PBS Video
1320 Braddock Pl.
Alexandria, VA 22314-1698 Phone: (703)739-5380
1971. **Program Description:** Jane Kennedy, a nurse turned civil rights/antiwar activist, who was jailed for erasing computer tapes used by a company manufacturing napalm, talks about her beliefs and her commitment to them. **Length:** 27 mins. **Format:** Beta, VHS, 3/4" U-matic. **Acquisition:** Rent/Lease, Purchase, Off-Air Record. **Use:** School/Group/Institution, Closed Circuit Television, Cable Television.

★4617★
Jazz and Jive
Blackhawk Films
5959 Triumph St.
Commerce, CA 90040-1688 Phone: (213)888-2229
193?. **Program Description:** Duke Ellington provides early jazz background in "Black and Tan," his first movie. Dance numbers accompany Dewey Brown in "Toot the Trumpet," followed by Major Bowes in "Radio Revels." **Length:** 60 mins. **Format:** Beta, VHS. **Acquisition:** Purchase. **Use:** In-Home Viewing.

★4618★
Jazz Concert #1: Louis Armstrong and Duke Ellington
Glenn Video Vistas, Ltd.
6924 Canby Ave., Ste. 103
Reseda, CA 91335 Phone: (818)981-5506
1961. **Program Description:** Louis and his All-Stars play their theme song and more. Featured are Jewel Brown, Trummy Young, Billy Kyle, Joe Darensbourg, Danny Barcelona, and Billy Cronk. Duke and his Band, featuring Harry Carney, Russell Procope, Ray Nance, Johnny Hodges, Jimmy Hamilton, Paul Gonzalves, Cat Anderson, Lawrence Brown, Sam Woodyard, Aaron Bell, and Shorty Baker perform "Take the "A' Train," and more. **Length:** 54 mins. **Format:** Beta, VHS. **Acquisition:** Purchase. **Use:** In-Home Viewing.

★4619★
Jazz Concert #3
Glenn Video Vistas, Ltd.
6924 Canby Ave., Ste. 103
Reseda, CA 91335 Phone: (818)981-5506
193?. **Program Description:** Five musical shorts featuring such top Black entertainers as Louis Armstrong, Duke Ellington, Cab Calloway, Eubie Blake, and Don Redman. **Length:** 60 mins. **Format:** Beta, VHS. **Acquisition:** Purchase. **Use:** In-Home Viewing.

★4620★
Jazz: Earl Hines and Coleman Hawkins
Kino International Corporation
333 W. 39th St., Ste. 503
New York, NY 10018 Phone: (212)629-6880
1965. **Program Description:** An historic musical session with Earl "Fatha" Hines (piano and vocals) and Coleman Hawkins (tenor sax). Songs include: "But Not For Me," "I'm A Little Brown Bird Looking For A Blue Bird," "Fine and Dandy," "One More Choice," and "Crazy Rhythm." **Length:** 28 mins. **Format:** Beta, VHS. **Acquisition:** Purchase. **Use:** In-Home Viewing.

★4621★
Jazz in America
Nelson Entertainment
335 N. Maple Dr., Ste. 350
Beverly Hills, CA 90210-3899 Phone: (213)285-6000
1981. **Program Description:** An historical tribute to bebop by way of two concerts performed at Lincoln Center by Dizzy Gillespie and his Dream Band. **Length:** 90 mins. **Format:** Beta, VHS. **Acquisition:** Purchase. **Use:** In-Home Viewing.

★4622★
Jazz Is a Personal Thing
Michigan Media
University of Michigan
400 4th St.
Ann Arbor, MI 48109 Phone: (313)764-8228
1974. **Program Description:** The origins of jazz and how it works. Part of the "Music Shop" series. **Length:** 29 mins. **Format:** 3/4" U-matic, Other than listed. **Acquisition:** Rent/Lease, Purchase. **Use:** School/Group/Institution, Closed Circuit Television, Cable Television, Broadcast television.

★4623★
Jazz: The Intimate Art
Direct Cinema Limited, Inc.
Box 69799
Los Angeles, CA 90069 Phone: (213)652-8000
1980. **Program Description:** A close look at four of the greatest jazz musicians representing various branches of jazz–Louis Armstrong, Dizzy Gillespie, Dave Brubeck, and Charles Lloyd. **Length:** 55 mins. **Format:** Beta, VHS, 3/4" U-matic, Other than listed. **Acquisition:** Rent/Lease, Purchase. **Use:** School/Group/Institution, In-Home Viewing, Special Use Restrictions Apply.

★4624★
Jesse Jackson and Carolyn Shelton: Pushing for Excellence
Phoenix/BFA Films
468 Park Ave., S
New York, NY 10016 Phone: (212)684-5910
1978. **Program Description:** Rev. Jesse Jackson and Carolyn Shelton, a young Black stewardess, believe that excellence in schools is a prerequisite for minority success. **Length:** 17 mins. **Format:** Beta, VHS, 3/4" U-matic. **Acquisition:** Purchase. **Use:** School/Group/Institution, Special Use Restrictions Apply.

★4625★
Jesse Jackson: We Can Dream Again
MPI Home Video
15825 Rob Roy Dr.
Oak Forest, IL 60452 Phone: (708)687-7881
1988. **Program Description:** News coverage, from beginning to triumphant conclusion, of Jackson's speech at the 1988 Democratic convention on July 19, 1988, where Michael Dukakis was eventually chosen as the nominee. The video was released 5 days after the speech. **Length:** 60 mins. **Format:** Beta, VHS. **Acquisition:** Purchase. **Use:** In-Home Viewing.

★4626★
Jivin' in Bebop
Hollywood Home Theatre
1540 N. Highland Ave.
Hollywood, CA 90028 Phone: (213)466-0121
1946. **Program Description:** A compilation of all-Black music from the 1940's, featuring singers and dancers of the period known as "jive." **Length:** 60 mins. **Format:** Beta, VHS. **Acquisition:** Purchase. **Use:** In-Home Viewing.

★4627★
John Coltrane: The Coltrane Legacy
Video Artists International, Inc.
PO Box 153
Ansonia Station
New York, NY 10023 Phone: (212)799-7798
1987. **Program Description:** A musical portrait of the legendary saxophonist, featuring rare performances from his few television appearances in the 50's and early 60's. Selections include "So What," "My Favorite Things," "Ev'ry Time We Say Goodbye," and "Afro Blue," from the collection of jazz film historian David Chertok. Some portions are in black and white; in HiFi Stereo. **Length:** 61 mins. **Format:** Beta, VHS. **Acquisition:** Purchase. **Use:** In-Home Viewing.

★4628★
John Scofield: On Improvisation
DCI Music Video
541 Avenue of the Americas
New York, NY 10011 Phone: (212)924-6624
1985. **Program Description:** The basics of music theory as applied to jazz improvisation, are demonstrated by the renowned guitarist and Miles Davis. **Length:** 60 mins. **Format:** Beta, VHS. **Acquisition:** Purchase. **Use:** In-Home Viewing.

★4629★
Just Doin' It
William Greaves Productions
80 8th Ave., Ste. 1701
New York, NY 10011 Phone: (212)206-1213
1976. **Program Description:** This is a lighthearted look at life in two Black barbershops in Atlanta, Georgia. **Length:** 28 mins. **Format:** Beta, VHS. **Acquisition:** Rent/Lease, Purchase. **Use:** School/Group/Institution, Broadcast television.

★4630★
Keeping the Faith
PBS Video
1320 Braddock Pl.
Alexandria, VA 22314-1698 Phone: (703)739-5380
1987. **Program Description:** A history of the Black church which played which played a key role in the 1960's Civil Rights Movement. **Length:** 58 mins. **Format:** Beta, VHS, 3/4" U-matic. **Acquisition:** Purchase, Rent/Lease. **Use:** School/Group/Institution, Special Use Restrictions Apply.

★4631★
Kenya
Cinema Guild
1697 Broadway, Rm. 802
New York, NY 10019 Phone: (212)246-5522
1988. **Program Description:** An analysis of Kenya's struggle against White domination from the 19th century to the Mau Mau rebellion against the British in 1952. Of particular interest is the role of the Kikuyu and Jomo Kenyatta, President of Kenya from 1964-78. **Length:** 30 mins. **Format:** Beta, VHS, 3/4" U-matic. **Acquisition:** Rent/Lease, Purchase, Duplication. **Use:** School/Group/Institution, Special Use Restrictions Apply.

★4632★
Kid Thomas and the Preservation Hall Band
Phoenix/BFA Films
468 Park Ave., S.
New York, NY 10016 Phone: (212)684-5910
198?. **Program Description:** This program pays tribute to a unique band whose music recalls the sound of the ragtime and jazz bands of the early 1920s. **Length:** 58 mins. **Format:** Beta, VHS, 3/4" U-matic. **Acquisition:** Purchase. **Use:** School/Group/Institution, Special Use Restrictions Apply.

★4633★
King
Pacific Arts Video
50 N. La Cienega Blvd., Ste. 210
Beverly Hills, CA 90211 Phone: (213)657-2233
1988. **Program Description:** A documentary about the work of civil rights leader Dr. Martin Luther King, Jr. The film traces the movement King led from the Montgomery bus boycott to the peaceful Reverend's assassination in Memphis. **Length:** 103 mins. **Format:** Beta, VHS. **Acquisition:** Purchase. **Use:** In-Home Viewing.

★4634★
King: A Filmed Record, Montgomery to Memphis
Richard Kaplan Productions, Inc.
290 W. End Ave.
New York, NY 10023 Phone: (212)787-0258
1969. **Program Description:** A documentary look at the career of Dr. Martin Luther King, Jr., from the 1955 Montgomery, Alabama bus boycotts to his murder in 1968. **Length:** 26 mins. **Format:** 3/4" U-matic, 2" Quad. **Acquisition:** Rent/Lease, Purchase. **Use:** School/Group/Institution, Closed Circuit Television, Cable Television, Broadcast television, In-Home Viewing.

★4635★
King: Montgomery to Memphis
Texture Films, Inc.
5547 N. Ravenswood Ave.
Chicago, IL 60640 Phone: (312)878-7300
1970. **Program Description:** The life of Martin Luther King is explored, from his early days as a minister in Montgomery to his assassination in 1968. (Also available in a 180-minute version which includes testimonials by outstanding Americans). **Length:** 103 mins. **Format:** Beta, VHS, 3/4" U-matic, Other than listed. **Acquisition:** Purchase. **Use:** School/Group/Institution.

★4636★
Land of Fear, Land of Courage
CC Films
National Council of Churches
475 Riverside Dr., Rm. 860
New York, NY 10115-0050 Phone: (212)870-2575
1982. **Program Description:** Anglican Bishop Desmond Tutu, leader of the battle against apartheid, discusses the timebomb of racial politics, the growing fear behind both sides of the color-bar. **Length:** 60 mins. **Format:** Beta, VHS, 3/4" U-matic. **Acquisition:** Purchase. **Use:** School/Group/Institution, Closed Circuit Television.

★4637★
Larry P. Case, The
Indiana University Audio-Visual Center
Bloomington, IN 47405-5901 Phone: (812)335-8087
1978. **Program Description:** A look at the Larry P. case, a class action brought by parents of Black children in the San Francisco School District to end the use of culturally biased I.Q. tests. **Length:** 30 mins. **Format:** 3/4" U-matic, Other than listed. **Acquisition:** Purchase. **Use:** School/Group/Institution, Closed Circuit Television, In-Home Viewing, Special Use Restrictions Apply.

★4638★
Last of the Blue Devils, The
Direct Cinema Limited, Inc.
Box 69799
Los Angeles, CA 90069 Phone: (213)652-8000
1980. **Program Description:** The story of the music that came out of 1930's Kansas City, where many jazz greats had their roots: Count Basie, Lester Young, Buster Smith, Eddie Durham, Jimmy Rushing, Walter Page, Hot Lips Page, Ernie Williams, Bennie Moten, Big Joe Turner, and Jay McShann. **Length:** 90 mins. **Format:** Beta, VHS, 3/4" U-matic. **Acquisition:** Rent/Lease, Purchase. **Use:** School/Group/Institution, In-Home Viewing, Special Use Restrictions Apply.

★4639★
Lay My Burden Down
Indiana University Audio-Visual Center
Bloomington, IN 47405-5901 Phone: (812)335-8087
1966. **Program Description:** A look at the plight of a Negro tenant farmer of the South, and the hardships faced by his family. **Length:** 60 mins. **Format:** 3/4" U-matic, Other than listed. **Acquisition:** Rent/Lease, Purchase. **Use:** School/Group/Institution, Closed Circuit Television, In-Home Viewing, Special Use Restrictions Apply.

★4640★
Legacy of a Dream
Richard Kaplan Productions, Inc.
290 W. End Ave.
New York, NY 10023 Phone: (212)787-0258
197?. **Program Description:** A moving documentary in words and images of the legacy of Dr. Martin Luther King, Jr. **Length:** 29 mins. **Format:** 3/4" U-matic, 2" Quad. **Acquisition:** Rent/Lease, Purchase. **Use:** School/Group/Institution, Closed Circuit Television, Cable Television, Broadcast Television, In-Home Viewing.

★4641★
Lionel Hampton
Sony Video Software (SVS, Inc.)
1700 Broadway, 16th Fl.
New York, NY 10019 Phone: (212)757-4990
1983. **Program Description:** This program presents the jazz music of Lionel Hampton backed up by a 20-piece band. **Length:** 24 mins. **Format:** Beta, VHS. **Acquisition:** Purchase. **Use:** In-Home Viewing.

★4642★
Lionel Hampton's One Night Stand
Independent United Distributors
430 W. 54th St.
New York, NY 10019 Phone: (212)489-8130
197?. **Program Description:** This is a jazz music extravaganza, featuring vibraphonist Lionel Hampton's Orchestra with some special guests. **Length:** 50 mins. **Format:** Beta, VHS. **Acquisition:** Purchase. **Use:** In-Home Viewing.

★4643★
Little Joke, A
Churchill Films
12210 Nebraska Ave.
Los Angeles, CA 90025 Phone: (213)207-6600
1985. **Program Description:** An animated film about two schoolgirls whose friendship is strained because one repeats a racial joke she heard from the other. For kids. **Length:** 12 mins. **Format:** VHS, 3/4'' U-matic. **Acquisition:** Purchase. **Use:** School/Group/Institution, In-Home Viewing, Special Use Restrictions Apply.

★4644★
Long Shadows
James Agee Film Project
3161/2 E. Main St.
Johnson City, TN 37601 Phone: (615)926-8637
1986. **Program Description:** An analysis of how the resonating effects of the Civil War can still be felt on society, via interviews with a number of noted writers, historians, civil rights activists and politicians. **Length:** 88 mins. **Format:** 3/4'' U-matic. **Acquisition:** Purchase. **Use:** School/Group/Institution, Special Use Restrictions Apply.

★4645★
Lorraine Hansberry: The Black Experience in the Creation of Drama
Films for Humanities
743 Alexander Rd.
Princeton, NJ 08540 Phone: (609)452-1128
1975. **Program Description:** A profile of this Black woman playwright. **Format:** Beta, VHS, 3/4'' U-matic. **Acquisition:** Rent/Lease; Purchase. **Use:** School/Group/Institution, Special Use Restrictions Apply.

★4646★
Losing Just the Same
Indiana University Audio-Visual Center
Bloomington, IN 47405-5901 Phone: (812)335-8087
1966. **Program Description:** The hope and despair of the American Black community is examined, as seen in the story of one urban family. **Length:** 60 mins. **Format:** 3/4'' U-matic, Other than listed. **Acquisition:** Rent/Lease, Purchase. **Use:** School/Group/Institution, Closed Circuit Television, In-Home Viewing, Special Use Restrictions Apply.

★4647★
Louis Armstrong
King Features Entertainment
235 E. 45th St.
New York, NY 10017 Phone: (212)682-5600
1983. **Program Description:** The words and music of Louis ''Satchmo'' Armstrong are featured in the program along with interviews with Billy Taylor, Peggy Lee, Al Hibbler and Satchmo himself. **Length:** 13 mins. **Format:** Beta, VHS, 3/4'' U-matic. **Acquisition:** Rent/Lease, Purchase. **Use:** School/Group/Institution, Special Use Restrictions Apply.

★4648★
Louis Armstrong
Direct Cinema Limited, Inc.
Box 69799
Los Angeles, CA 90069 Phone: (213)652-8000
1968. **Program Description:** A look at the virtuoso jazzman's personality as expressed through his music. **Length:** 58 mins. **Format:** Beta, VHS, 3/4'' U-matic, Other than listed. **Acquisition:** Rent/Lease, Purchase. **Use:** School/Group/Institution, In-Home Viewing, Special Use Restrictions Apply.

★4649★
Louis Armstrong and His Orchestra
Audiofidelity Enterprises
PO Box 86
Rahway, NJ 07065 Phone: (201)388-5000
1986. **Program Description:** Louis' 1942 big band is featured, with vocalist Velma Middleton, in four Soundies: ''Swingin' On Nothin','' ''Sleepy Time Down South,'' ''Shine'' and ''You Rascal You.'' Also included is a 1965 TV appearance by Louis and the All-Stars. **Length:** 33 mins. **Format:** Beta, VHS. **Acquisition:** Purchase. **Use:** In-Home Viewing.

★4650★
Louis Armstrong—Chicago Style
Worldvision Home Video, Inc.
660 Madison Ave.
New York, NY 10021 Phone: (212)832-3838
1975. **Program Description:** How Louis Armstrong managed to fight the mob in the early 1930's and become a great jazz trumpeter-vocalist is the incident portrayed in this TV-movie. **Length:** 74 mins. **Format:** Beta, VHS. **Acquisition:** Purchase. **Use:** In-Home Viewing.

★4651★
Louis Armstrong: The Gentle Giant of Jazz
AIMS Media, Inc.
6901 Woodley Ave.
Van Nuys, CA 91406-4878 Phone: (818)785-4111
1988. **Program Description:** A biography of the masterful trumpet genius, covering his life from poverty in New Orleans to worldwide acclaim. **Length:** 24 mins. **Format:** Beta, VHS, 3/4'' U-matic. **Acquisition:** Purchase, Duplication License. **Use:** School/Group/Institution, Special Use Restrictions Apply.

★4652★
Mahalia Jackson
Phoenix/BFA Films
468 Park Ave., S
New York, NY 10016 Phone: (212)684-5910
1974. **Program Description:** A portrait of the late gospel singer Mahalia Jackson. Includes footage of her performing eleven songs. **Length:** 34 mins. **Format:** Beta, VHS, 3/4'' U-matic. **Acquisition:** Purchase. **Use:** School/Group/Institution, Special Restrictions Apply.

★4653★
Mahalia Jackson and Elizabeth Cotten: Two Remarkable Ladies
Mastervision Inc.
969 Park Ave.
New York, NY 10028 Phone: (212)879-0448
1974. **Program Description:** A close-up look at a pair of successful Black women performers: ''Mahalia Jackson'' is a filmed biography of the legendary singer, and ''Freight Train,'' the courageous story of pioneer folksinger Elizabeth Cotten. **Length:** 58 mins. **Format:** Beta, VHS. **Acquisition:** Purchase. **Use:** In-Home Viewing.

★4654★
Maids and Madams: Apartheid Begins in the Home
Filmakers Library, Inc.
133 E. 58th St.
New York, NY 10022 Phone: (212)355-6545
1986. **Program Description:** The relationship between maid and madam in South Africa is a microcosm of the apartheid system. Some White employers are kind, while others are brutal. This film examines this complex relationship, where the Black women are trapped by racial

injustice and the White women by fear. **Length:** 52 mins. **Format:** VHS, 3/4" U-matic. **Acquisition:** Rent/Lease, Purchase, Duplication. **Use:** School/Group/Institution, In-Home Viewing, Special Use Restrictions Apply.

★4655★
Makhalipile: The Dauntless One
Cinema Guild
1697 Broadway, Rm. 802
New York, NY 10019 Phone: (212)246-5522
1989. **Program Description:** This film profiles the life and work of Archbishop Trevor Huddleston, who has fought relentlessly against racial tyranny in South Africa. **Length:** 54 mins. **Format:** Beta, VHS, 3/4" U-matic. **Acquisition:** Purchase. **Use:** School/Group/Institution.

★4656★
Malcolm X
Carousel Film & Video
260 5th Ave.
New York, NY 10016 Phone: (212)683-1660
1965. **Program Description:** A biography of Black activist Malcolm X beginning with his eighth grade year in school as an honor student and class president, to his assassination because of his beliefs. **Length:** 23 mins. **Format:** Beta, VHS, 3/4" U-matic. **Acquisition:** Purchase. **Use:** School/Group/Institution, Special Use Restrictions Apply.

★4657★
Mama, I'm Crying
Filmakers Library, Inc.
133 E. 58th St.
New York, NY 10022 Phone: (212)355-6545
1987. **Program Description:** A passionate and personal view of the brutality of apartheid in South Africa, as told by two childhood friends, one Black, the other White. Now middle aged, they believed change would peacefully come to their country. Today's young people no longer share their view, and will sacrifice their lives for racial justice. **Length:** 52 mins. **Format:** VHS, 3/4" U-matic. **Acquisition:** Rent/Lease, Purchase, Duplication. **Use:** School/Group/Institution, In-Home Viewing, Special Use Restrictions Apply.

★4658★
A Man Called Adam
Charter Entertainment
335 N. Maple Dr., Ste. 350
Beverly Hills, CA 90210 Phone: (213)285-6000
1966. **Program Description:** A jazz musician is tortured by prejudice and the guilt by his having accidentally killed his wife and baby years before. **Length:** 103. **Format:** Beta, VHS. **Acquisition:** Purchase. **Use:** In-Home Viewing.

★4659★
Man in Africa—Heritage and Transition
New York State Education Department
Center for Learning Technologies
Media Distribution Network
Rm. C-7, Concourse Level
Albany, NY 12230 Phone: (518)474-1265
196?. **Program Description:** This series examines the people and cultures of Africa. **Length:** 30 mins. **Format:** Beta, VHS, 1/2" reel, 3/4" U-matic, 2" Quad. **Acquisition:** Duplication, Free Duplication. **Use:** School/Group/Institution, Special Use Restrictions Apply.

★4660★
Manchild Revisited: A Commentary by Claude Brown
PBS Video
1320 Braddock Pl.
Alexandria, VA 22314-1698 Phone: (703)739-5380
1987. **Program Description:** This program graphically illustrates the problems being faced by young Black men in this country. Claude Brown takes viewers into America's urban areas where violent crime, drug abuse, unemployment, and family abandonment are everyday occurrances. **Length:** 60 mins. **Format:** Beta, VHS, 3/4" U-matic. **Acquisition:** Rent/Lease, Purchase, Duplication, Off-Air Record. **Use:** School/Group/Institution, Closed Circuit Television, In-Home Viewing, Special Use Restrictions Apply.

★4661★
Mandela—Free At Last
JCI Video
21550 Oxnard St., Ste. 920
Woodland Hills, CA 91367 Phone: (818)593-3600
1990. **Program Description:** A portrait of Nelson Mandela and his country of South Africa is painted on the occasion of his release from prison, using clandestine footage smuggled out of the country, including Mandela's complete first speech after his release, produced by the Emmy Award-winning series "South Africa Now." **Length:** 79 mins. **Format:** Beta, VHS. **Acquisition:** Purchase. **Use:** In-Home Viewing.

★4662★
Mandela: The Man and His Country
MPI Home Video
15825 Rob Roy Dr.
Oak Forest, IL 60452 Phone: (708)687-7881
1990. **Program Description:** A documentary profiling South Africa's most visible anti-apartheid activist. **Length:** 50 mins. **Format:** Beta, VHS. **Acquisition:** Purchase. **Use:** In-Home Viewing.

★4663★
Marcus Garvey: Toward Black Nationhood
Films for the Humanities
743 Alexander Rd.
Princeton, NJ 08540 Phone: (609)452-1128
198?. **Program Description:** This film exhibits how Marcus Garvey's call for an independent Black nation in the 1920's influenced modern civil rights movements throughout the world. **Length:** 42 mins. **Format:** Beta, VHS, 3/4" U-matic. **Acquisition:** Purchase. **Use:** School/Group/Institution, Special Use Restrictions Apply.

★4664★
Martin Luther King Commemorative Collection
MPI Home Video
15825 Rob Roy Dr.
Oak Forest, IL 60452 Phone: (708)687-7881
196?. **Program Description:** A compilation of two films honoring the late civil rights leader: "In Remembrance of Martin," and "The Speeches of Martin Luther King." **Length:** 115 mins. **Format:** Beta, VHS. **Acquisition:** Purchase. **Use:** In-Home Viewing.

★4665★
Martin Luther King: "I Have a Dream"
Knowledge Unlimited, Inc.
Box 52
Madison, WI 53701-0052 Phone: (608)836-6660
1990. **Program Description:** This film gives a quick background of the civil rights movement as an introduction to Dr. King's famous speech, which, in its entirety, closes out this video. **Length:** 28 mins. **Format:** VHS. **Acquisition:** Purchase, Rent/Lease. **Use:** School/Group/Institution.

★4666★
Martin Luther King, Jr.: A Man of Peace
Journal Films, Inc.
930 Pitner Ave.
Evanston, IL 60202 Phone: (312)328-6700
1968. **Program Description:** This program is an intimate look at the man, the minister, the father, and the leader of the civil rights movement. King expresses his philosophy of non-violence, the future of the civil rights movement, and his personal feelings about death. **Length:** 29 mins. **Format:** Beta, VHS, 3/4" U-matic. **Acquisition:** Purchase. **Use:** School/Group/Institution, Special Use Restrictions Apply.

★4667★
Martin Luther King, Jr.: From Montgomery to Memphis
Phoenix/BFA Films
468 Park Ave., S.
New York, NY 10016 Phone: (212)684-5910
1969. **Program Description:** Dr. Martin Luther King, Jr. first rose to national prominence as a result of a struggle against bus segregation in Montgomery. **Length:** 27 mins. **Format:** Beta, VHS, 3/4" U-matic. **Acquisition:** Purchase. **Use:** School/Group/Institution, Special Use Restrictions Apply.

★4668★
Martin Luther King Jr.—The Assassin Years
Centron Films
108 Wilmot Rd.
Deerfield, IL 60015-9990 Phone: (708)940-1260
1978. **Program Description:** A look at Dr. King's early years, which also follows his great civil rights crusade throughout the South. He won the Nobel prize in 1964 and was killed four years later. **Length:** 26 mins. **Format:** Beta, VHS, 3/4'' U-matic. **Acquisition:** Purchase. **Use:** School/Group/Institution, Special Use Restrictions Apply.

★4669★
Martin Luther King—The Legacy
Media Guild
11722 Sorrento Valley Rd., Ste. E
San Diego, CA 92121 Phone: (619)755-9191
1989. **Program Description:** The importance and impact that the famous civil rights activist had is sadly remembered on the anniversary of his death. **Length:** 79 mins. **Format:** Beta, VHS, 3/4'' U-matic. **Acquisition:** Purchase. **Use:** School/Group/Institution, Special Use Restrictions Apply.

★4670★
Matter of Insurance, A
Time-Life Video
1271 Avenue of the Americas
New York, NY 10020 Phone: (212)484-5940
1977. **Program Description:** A dramatic change in public opinion occurs in this episode of the "Fight Against Slavery" series when a slave captain who has murdered more than 130 Africans is charged on an insurance claim, not murder. **Length:** 52 mins. **Format:** Beta, VHS, 3/4'' U-matic, Other than listed. **Acquisition:** Rent/Lease, Purchase. **Use:** School/Group/Institution, Special Use Restrictions Apply.

★4671★
Mau Mau
Films, Inc.
5547 N. Ravenswood Ave.
Chicago, IL 60640-1199 Phone: (312)878-2600
1973. **Program Description:** This segment of "Black Man's Land" reveals that Mau Mau was an army set up to fight repression and aggression. Although they won their struggle against the British, the Mau Mau suffered the consequences. Also available in a 28-minute edited version. **Length:** 52 mins. **Format:** Beta, VHS, 3/4'' U-matic. **Acquisition:** Purchase. **Use:** School/Group/Institution, Special Use Restrictions Apply.

★4672★
Max Roach: In Concert/In Session
DCI Music Video
541 Avenue of the Americas
New York, NY 10011 Phone: (212)924-6624
1985. **Program Description:** Roach demonstrates his playing ability first in the studio, then in an appearance at the 1982 Kool Jazz Festival. **Length:** 60 mins. **Format:** Beta, VHS. **Acquisition:** Purchase. **Use:** In-Home Viewing.

★4673★
Maya Angelou
NETCHE (Nebraska ETV Council for Higher Education)
Box 83111
Lincoln, NE 68501 Phone: (402)472-3611
1982. **Program Description:** Robert Cromie, columnist/book reviewer, obtains some insight into the complex human spirit of the multi-talented Maya Angelou in this two-part series. **Length:** 30 mins. **Format:** Beta, VHS, 1/2'' reel, 3/4'' U-matic. **Acquisition:** Rent/Lease; Purchase. **Use:** School/Group/Institution, Closed Circuit Television, Broadcast Television, Special Use Restrictions Apply.

★4674★
Men of Bronze
Films Inc.
5547 N. Ravenswood Ave.
Chicago, IL 60640-1199 Phone: (312)878-2600
1977. **Program Description:** Valor and pride in the midst of prejudice is the theme of this film about an all-Black World War I combat regiment which spends 191 days under fire on the front lines. **Length:** 58 mins. **Format:** Beta, VHS, 3/4'' U-matic. **Acquisition:** Rent/Lease; Purchase. **Use:** School/Group/Institution.

★4675★
Mental Health Needs of Minority Children
Social Psychiatry Research Institute
150 E. 69th St.
New York, NY 10021 Phone: (212)628-4800
1981. **Program Description:** This program describes the special problems of minority groups, Blacks, Hispanics and native Americans, with an emphasis on preventive work with children in school settings so as to avoid the continued high incidence of neurosis and psychoses in this population. **Length:** 50 mins. **Format:** 1/2'' reel, 3/4'' U-matic. **Acquisition:** Rent/Lease, Purchase. **Use:** School/Group/Institution, Closed Circuit Television.

★4676★
Mike Manieri
Sony Video Software (SVS, Inc.)
1700 Broadway, 16th Fl.
New York, NY 10019 Phone: (212)757-4990
1983. **Program Description:** One of the jazz cross-over movement's leaders, Manieri riffs through his favorite tunes at NYC's 7th Avenue South: "Crossed Wires," "Bamboo" and "Bullet Train." **Length:** 60 mins. **Format:** Beta, VHS, 8mm. **Acquisition:** Purchase. **Use:** In-Home Viewing.

★4677★
Miles of Smiles, Years of Struggle
Benchmark Films, Inc.
145 Scarborough Rd.
Briarcliff Manor, NY 10510 Phone: (914)762-3838
1983. **Program Description:** The history of the Black Pullman Porters is told through a reunion of retired porters, archival films and stills, vintage Hollywood footage and a 100-year-old porter's widow. **Length:** 59 mins. **Format:** Beta, VHS, 3/4'' U-matic. **Acquisition:** Purchase. **Use:** School/Group/Institution, Closed Circuit Television.

★4678★
Mini-Films on Prejudice
Anti-Defamation League of B'nai B'rith
Audio-Visual Department
823 United Nations Plaza
New York, NY 10017 Phone: (212)490-2525
1983. **Program Description:** A series of 30 and 60-second public service spots, mostly by celebrities, that serve as a motivating device to indicate what prejudice is all about. useful for students; also distributed free of charge to TV stations. Available together or separately. **Length:** 1 mins. **Format:** Beta, VHS, 3/4'' U-matic. **Acquisition:** Purchase. **Use:** School/Group/Institution, Closed Circuit Television, Cable Television, Broadcast Television, In-Home Viewing.

★4679★
Minnie the Moocher and Many, Many More
Icarus Films
200 Park Ave., S., Ste. 1319
New York, NY 10003 Phone: (212)674-3375
1983. **Program Description:** Jazz legend Cab Calloway narrates this tour of the great Harlem jazz clubs of the 1930s. **Length:** 55 mins. **Format:** 3/4'' U-matic. **Acquisition:** Purchase. **Use:** School/Group/Institution, Special Use Restrictions Apply.

★4680★
Minor Altercation, A
Cinema Guild
1697 Broadway, Rm. 802
New York, NY 10019 Phone: (212)246-5522
1976. **Program Description:** This video explores racial tensions in American public schools. **Length:** 30 mins. **Format:** Beta, VHS, 3/4" U-matic. **Acquisition:** Rent/Lease, Purchase, Duplication. **Use:** School/Group/Institution, Special Use Restrictions Apply.

★4681★
Minorities
CRM/McGraw-Hill Films
674 Via de la Valle
PO Box 641
Del Mar, CA 92014 Phone: (619)453-5000
1977. **Program Description:** This program from the "American Condition" series examines the economic status of Black Americans today, with evidence of continued discrimination and its cost to all Americans. **Length:** 15 mins. **Format:** Beta, VHS, 3/4" U-matic. **Acquisition:** Rent/Lease, Purchase. **Use:** School/Group/Institution, Special Use Restrictions Apply.

★4682★
Minority Youth: Felicia
Phoenix/BFA Films
468 Park Ave., S.
New York, NY 10016 Phone: (212)684-5910
1971. **Program Description:** Discrimination and prejudice greatly affect young Black people's goals. Felicia hopes to go to college to help improve the attitudes of the apathetic adults. **Length:** 12 mins. **Format:** Beta, VHS, 3/4" U-matic. **Acquisition:** Purchase. **Use:** School/Group/Institution, Special Use Restrictions Apply.

★4683★
Miracle of Intervale Avenue, The
Ergo Media, Inc.
PO Box 2037
Teaneck, NJ 07666 Phone: (201)692-0404
19??. **Program Description:** An intriguing documentary about a Jewish community in a decaying South Bronx area that continues to survive and the remarkable interacting of the Jews, Blacks and Puerto Ricans who help each other. **Length:** 65 mins. **Format:** VHS. **Acquisition:** Purchase. **Use:** In-Home Viewing.

★4684★
Motown 25: Yesterday, Today, Forever
MGM/UA Home Video Inc.
100000 W. Washington Blvd.
Culver City, CA 90232-2728
1983. **Program Description:** This is the TV all-star salute to Berry Gordy that features a musical duel between the Four Tops and The Temptations and the reunion of The Jackson Five. **Length:** 130 mins. **Format:** Beta, VHS, Laser optical videodisc. **Acquisition:** Purchase. **Use:** In-Home Viewing.

★4685★
MOVE: Confrontation in Philadelphia
Temple University
Department of Radio-TV-Film
Philadelphia, PA 19122 Phone: (215)787-8483
1980. **Program Description:** A look at the events leading up to the police arrest of MOVE, a radical Black political commune. The video journalists reveal the complex relationship of media bias, police harrassment, and subtle economic motivation in the violent removal of MOVE. **Length:** 60 mins. **Format:** 3/4" U-matic. **Acquisition:** Rent/Lease, Purchase. **Use:** School/Group/Institution, Special Use Restrictions Apply.

★4686★
Mozambique: The Struggle for Survival
Cinema Guild
1697 Broadway, Rm. 802
New York, NY 10019 Phone: (212)246-5522
1988. **Program Description:** The struggle over the future of Mozambique is examined, particularily the attempt by South Africa to destablize the country through its sponsorship of the Mozambique National Resistance (RENAMO), an organzation committed to terrorism. **Length:** 57 mins. **Format:** Beta, VHS, 3/4" U-matic. **Acquisition:** Rent/Lease, Purchase, Duplication. **Use:** School/Group/Institution, Special Use Restrictions Apply.

★4687★
Mr. Charlie
JEF Films
Film House
143 Hickory Hill Circle
Osterville, MA 02655 Phone: (617)428-7198
194?. **Program Description:** Famous bandleader, Charlie Barnett, is featured in this Technicolor special, with his orchestra and various guests. **Length:** 60 mins. **Format:** Beta, VHS. **Acquisition:** Purchase. **Use:** In-Home Viewing.

★4688★
My Name Is Abbie, Orphan of America
Icarus Films
200 Park Ave., S.
Ste. 1319
New York, NY 10003 Phone: (212)674-3375
19??. **Program Description:** This is both a profile of Abbie Hoffman and a portrait of an era. Abbie recounts his involvement in the early civil rights movement, how he became a speaker at Anti-Vietnam War demonstrations, the famous "Chicago Seven" Trial, and his eventual flight and underground involvement. **Length:** 28 mins. **Format:** 3/4" U-matic. **Acquisition:** Purchase. **Use:** School/Group/Institution, Special Use Restrictions Apply.

★4689★
My Past Is My Own
Pyramid Film & Video
Box 1048
Santa Monica, CA 90406 Phone: (213)828-7577
1989. **Program Description:** Two Black teenagers go back in time to the civil rights movement of the sixties. **Length:** 47 mins. **Format:** Beta, VHS, 3/4" U-matic. **Acquisition:** Purchase, Rent/Lease. **Use:** School/Group/Institution, In-Home Viewing, Special Use Restrictions Apply.

★4690★
Mystery in Swing
Video Yesteryear
Box C
Sandy Hook, CT 06482 Phone: (203)426-2574
1940. **Program Description:** This is an all-Black mystery with music, about a trumpet player who has snake venom put on his mouthpiece. **Length:** 66 mins. **Format:** Beta, VHS. **Acquisition:** Purchase. **Use:** In-Home Viewing.

★4691★
Nat "King" Cole/The Mills Brothers/The Delta Rhythm Boys
Audiofidelity Enterprises
PO Box 86
Rahway, NJ 07065 Phone: (201)388-5000
1986. **Program Description:** Nat Cole (with and without his Trio), the Mills Brothers and the Delta Rhythm Boys are featured in this compilation of fifteen Soundies and Telescriptions. Songs include "You Call It Madness," "Home," "I'm an Errand Boy for Rhythm" (Cole), "Paper Doll," "Lazy River," "You Always Hurt the One You Love" (Mills Bros.), "Take the A Train" and "Never Underestimate the Power of a Woman" (Delta Boys). **Length:** 47 mins. **Format:** Beta, VHS. **Acquisition:** Purchase. **Use:** In-Home Viewing.

★4692★
Nationtime, Gary
Your World Video
80 8th Ave., Ste. 1701
New York, NY 10011 Phone: (212)206-1215
1972. **Program Description:** Narrated by Sidney Poitier and Harry Belafonte, this is a document of the first National Black Political Convention, held in Gary, Indiana. **Length:** 90 mins. **Format:** Beta, VHS, 3/4" U-matic. **Acquisition:** Rent/Lease, Purchase. **Use:** School/Group/Institution, In-Home Viewing.

★4693★
Native Son
Lightning Video
60 Long Ridge Rd.
PO Box 395
Stamford, CT 06907 Phone: (203)359-3637
1986. **Program Description:** The second film adaptation of the classic Richard Wright novel about a poor Black man who accidentally kills a White woman and then hides the body. **Length:** 111 mins. **Format:** Beta, VHS. **Acquisition:** Purchase. **Use:** In-Home Viewing.

★4694★
Negro Ensemble Company, The
Films for the Humanities
743 Alexander Rd.
Princeton, NJ 08540 Phone: (609)452-1128
1987. **Program Description:** The goals and remarkable achievements of this Black theater troupe are documented herein. **Length:** 58 mins. **Format:** Beta, VHS, 3/4" U-matic. **Acquisition:** Purchase. **Use:** School/Group/Institution, Special Use Restrictions Apply.

★4695★
Negro Slavery
CRM/McGraw-Hill Films
674 Via de la Valle
PO Box 641
Del Mar, CA 92014 Phone: (619)453-5000
1969. **Program Description:** The slavery issue in America is analyzed in this program, with special emphasis on the approaching Civil War. Slavery is covered from the seventeenth century, when the English first decided to use African slaves, to the election of Abraham Lincoln as president in 1861. Part of the "American History" series. **Length:** 25 mins. **Format:** Beta, VHS, 3/4" U-matic. **Acquisition:** Purchase. **Use:** School/Group/Institution, Closed Circuit Television, Special Use Restrictions Apply.

★4696★
Negro Soldier
International Historic Films Inc.
3533 S. Archer Ave.
Chicago, IL 60609 Phone: (312)927-2900
1944. **Program Description:** This wartime documentary focuses on Blacks' participation in World War II, and examines the important role played by Black Americans in U.S. history. **Length:** 40 mins. **Format:** Beta, VHS, U-matic. **Acquisition:** Purchase. **Use:** School/Group/Institution, In-Home Viewing.

★4697★
Negroes: The Social Volcano
Cornell University
Media Services Distribution Center
7-8 Research Park
Ithaca, NY 14850 Phone: (607)255-2091
1987. **Program Description:** After Marcos was ousted, little changed for Black sugar plantation workers in the Philippines. **Length:** 30 mins. **Format:** VHS. **Acquisition:** Rent/Lease. **Use:** School/Group/Institution, Closed Circuit Television, Cable Television, Broadcast television, In-Home Viewing.

★4698★
Nelson Mandela: Free At Last
JCI Video
21550 Oxnard St., Ste. 920
Woodland Hills, CA 91367 Phone: (818)593-3600
1990. **Program Description:** Documentary of the recent activity of the African National Congress, and the resulting release of Nelson Mandela after twenty-five years in prison for his work to stop South African apartheid. Includes interviews with ANC principals, and Mandela's first speech after his release. An important educational tool on the problems of apartheid. **Length:** 79 mins. **Format:** VHS. **Acquisition:** Purchase. **Use:** In-Home Viewing.

★4699★
Newport Jazz Festival
CBS/Fox Video
1211 Avenue of the Americas
New York, NY 10036 Phone: (212)819-3200
1962. **Program Description:** Jazz greats in concert at the famed jazz festival include Count Basie, Duke Ellington, Roland Kirk, Ruby Braff, Peewee Russell, Joe Williams, Oscar Peterson Trio with Ray Brown, Lambert, Hendricks and Bavan, and others. **Length:** 60 mins. **Format:** Beta, VHS. **Acquisition:** Purchase. **Use:** In-Home Viewing.

★4700★
Nice Colored Girls
Women Make Movies
225 Lafayette St., Ste. 212
New York, NY 10012 Phone: (212)925-0606
1986. **Program Description:** The relations established between Aboriginal women and White men are explored in this film. **Length:** 25 mins. **Format:** Beta, VHS, 3/4" U-matic. **Acquisition:** Purchase, Rent/Lease. **Use:** School/Group/Institution, Special Use Restrictions Apply.

★4701★
No Vietnamese Ever Called Me Nigger
Cinema Guild
1697 Broadway, Rm. 802
New York, NY 10019 Phone: (212)246-5522
1968. **Program Description:** A powerful documentary depicting through interviews with Black Vietnam veterans the racism they confronted in the armed forces and at home. **Length:** 68 mins. **Format:** Beta, VHS, 3/4" U-matic. **Acquisition:** Rent/Lease, Purchase, Duplication. **Use:** School/Group/Institution, Special Use Restrictions Apply.

★4702★
Notice to Quit (The Lion Never Sleeps)
Jem Music Video
3619 Kennedy Rd.
PO Box 708
South Plainfield, NJ 07080 Phone: (201)753-6100
1987. **Program Description:** South African music and music videos create a portrait of life, by South African artists, under apartheid. **Length:** 52 mins. **Format:** Beta, VHS. **Acquisition:** Purchase. **Use:** In-Home Viewing.

★4703★
Of Black America Series
Phoenix/BFA Films
468 Park Ave., S.
New York, NY 10016 Phone: (212)684-5910
1968. **Program Description:** The Black heritage and history are presented in this five-part series. From the early days of slavery to the influence of soul music, narrator Bill Cosby and news reporters relate an examination of the Black struggle and plight. Programs are available individually. **Length:** 37 mins. **Format:** Beta, VHS, 3/4" U-matic. **Acquisition:** Purchase. **Use:** School/Group/Institution, Special Use Restrictions Apply.

★4704★
Old African Blasphemer, The
Time-Life Video
1271 Avenue of the Americas
New York, NY 10020 Phone: (212)484-5940
1977. **Program Description:** This episode of the "Fight Against Slavery" series details the horrors of a typical slave ship's Atlantic crossing. At the helm is a captain who later became an abolitionist preacher. **Length:** 55 mins. **Format:** Beta, VHS, 3/4" U-matic, Other than listed. **Acquisition:** Rent/Lease, Purchase. **Use:** School/Group/Institution, Special Use Restrictions Apply.

★4705★
Old, Black and Alive!
New Film Company
7 Mystic St., Ste. 310
Arlington, MA 02174 Phone: (617)641-2580
1986. **Program Description:** Seven elderly Black people share their insight, faith and strength on the subject of aging. **Length:** 28 mins. **Format:** Beta, VHS, 3/4" U-matic. **Acquisition:** Rent/Lease, Purchase. **Use:** School/Group/Institution, In-Home Viewing.

★4706★
On Black America
American Humanist Association
7 Harwood Dr.
PO Box 146
Amherst, NY 14226-0146 Phone: (716)839-5080
1972. **Program Description:** The director of the Public Policy Training Institute and founder of the Congress of Racial Equality discusses the gains made in the struggle for equal rights and offers constructive guidelines for future action. Part of the "Humanist Alternative" series. **Length:** 30 mins. **Format:** 3/4" U-matic, Other than listed. **Acquisition:** Rent/Lease, Purchase. **Use:** School/Group/Institution, Closed Circuit Television, Cable Television.

★4707★
On My Own: The Traditions of Daisy Turner
Filmakers Library, Inc.
133 E. 58th St.
New York, NY 10022 Phone: (212)355-6545
1987. **Program Description:** Daisy Turner, a 102 year old Black women, provides the viewer with an oral history of her family's history in rural Vermont. **Length:** 28 mins. **Format:** VHS, 3/4" U-matic. **Acquisition:** Rent/Lease, Purchase, Duplication. **Use:** School/Group/Institution, In-Home Viewing, Special Use Restrictions Apply.

★4708★
On the Road with Duke Ellington
Direct Cinema Limited, Inc.
Box 69799
Los Angeles, CA 90069 Phone: (213)652-8000
1980. **Program Description:** A cinema-verite portrait of the great jazz performer/composer leading his band through "Satin Doll," crisscrossing the country, and working on his compositions. **Length:** 58 mins. **Format:** Beta, VHS, 3/4" U-matic, Other than listed. **Acquisition:** Rent/Lease, Purchase. **Use:** School/Group/Institution, In-Home Viewing, Special Use Restrictions Apply.

★4709★
One Man's Property
Time-Life Video
1271 Avenue of the Americas
New York, NY 10020 Phone: (212)484-5940
1977. **Program Description:** This episode of the "Fight Against Slavery" series traces the events leading up to the Somerset Case in 1772, in which the judge declared that it was unlawful for one man to be the property of another on English soil. **Length:** 56 mins. **Format:** Beta, VHS, 3/4" U-matic, Other than listed. **Acquisition:** Rent/Lease, Purchase. **Use:** School/Group/Institution, Special Use Restrictions Apply.

★4710★
One More Hurdle
Film Fair Communications
10900 Ventura Blvd.
PO Box 1728
Studio City, CA 91604 Phone: (818)985-0244
1988. **Program Description:** The true story of a Black girl who attempts to be a champion horse rider. **Length:** 47 mins. **Format:** Beta, VHS, 3/4" U-matic. **Acquisition:** Purchase, Duplication License. **Use:** School/Group/Institution, Special Use Restrictions Apply.

★4711★
Opportunities for the Disadvantaged
American Educational Films
3807 Dickerson Rd.
Nashville, TN 37207 Phone: 800-822-5678
1977. **Program Description:** A look at the development of special strategies for the minority group, or the economically deprived. **Length:** 17 mins. **Format:** Beta, VHS, 3/4" U-matic. **Acquisition:** Purchase. **Use:** School/Group/Institution, Special Use Restrictions Apply.

★4712★
Opportunities in Criminal Justice
William Greaves Productions
80 8th Ave., Ste. 1701
New York, NY 10011 Phone: (212)206-1213
1978. **Program Description:** The wide variety of career opportunities available to women and and minorities in the criminal justice system. **Length:** 25 mins. **Format:** Beta, VHS. **Acquisition:** Rent/Lease, Purchase. **Use:** School/Group/Institution, Broadcast television.

★4713★
Organization of African Unity
Marilyn Perry TV Productions, Inc.
677 5th Ave.
5th Fl.
New York, NY 10022 Phone: (212)308-2250
1981. **Program Description:** An interview with Ambassador Oumarou Youssoufou, the Organization of African Unity's Executive Secretary to the U.N. Ambassador Youssoufou discusses the organization's fundamental goal–the complete elimination of colonialism and racism from Africa. **Length:** 28 mins. **Format:** 3/4" U-matic. **Acquisition:** Rent/Lease, Purchase. **Use:** School/Group/Institution, Closed Circuit Television, Cable Television, Broadcast television, Special Use Restrictions Apply.

★4714★
Ornette Coleman Trio
Kino International Corporation
333 W. 39th St., Ste. 503
New York, NY 10018 Phone: (212)629-6880
1966. **Program Description:** A philosophical as well as musical account of Coleman's work on a project called "Who's Crazy" for the Living Theatre. **Length:** 26 mins. **Format:** Beta, VHS. **Acquisition:** Purchase. **Use:** In-Home Viewing.

★4715★
Other Faces of AIDS
PBS Video
1320 Braddock Pl.
Alexandria, VA 22314-1698 Phone: (703)739-5380
1989. **Program Description:** Jesse Jackson is interviewed about the much higher risk of AIDS in minority groups. **Length:** 60 mins. **Format:** VHS, 3/4" U-matic. **Acquisition:** Purchase. **Use:** School/Group/Institution, Closed Circuit Television, In-Home Viewing, Special Use Restrictions Apply.

★4716★
Our Friend Angela
International Historic Films, Inc.
Box 29035
Chicago, IL 60629 Phone: (312)436-8051
197?. **Program Description:** A Soviet-filmed report about Angela Davis and her friends Kondra and Franklin Alexander in the U.S.S.R. Narrated in English. **Length:** 25 mins. **Format:** Beta, VHS, 3/4" U-matic.

Acquisition: Purchase. Use: School/Group/Institution, In-Home Viewing.

★4717★
Paris Blues
Key Video
1211 Avenue of the Americas, 2nd Fl.
New York, NY 10036 Phone: (212)819-3238
1961. **Program Description:** Two jazz musicians, one White, one Black, strive for success in Paris. Score by Duke Ellington. In HiFi. **Length:** 100 mins. **Format:** Beta, VHS. **Acquisition:** Purchase. **Use:** In-Home Viewing.

★4718★
Passing the Message
Icarus Films
200 Park Ave., S.
Ste. 1319
New York, NY 10003 Phone: (212)674-3375
1983. **Program Description:** A program on the independent trade unions in South Africa. **Length:** 47 mins. **Format:** 3/4'' U-matic. **Acquisition:** Purchase. **Use:** School/Group/Institution, In-Home Viewing.

★4719★
Paul Robeson—The Tallest Tree in Our Forest
Phoenix/BFA Films
468 Park Ave., S.
New York, NY 10016 Phone: (212)684-5910
1977. **Program Description:** A program which gives the viewer a rare opportunity to see, hear, and gain some insight into the scholar, actor, singer, and humanitarian Paul Robeson, who passed away in 1976. **Length:** 90 mins. **Format:** Beta, VHS, 3/4'' U-matic. **Acquisition:** Purchase. **Use:** School/Group/Institution, Special Use Restrictions Apply.

★4720★
Picking Tribes
Women Make Movies
225 Lafayette St., Ste. 212
New York, NY 10012 Phone: (212)925-0606
1988. **Program Description:** A young woman's struggle to find an identity between her Black American and Native American heritages is examined through vintage photographs and watercolor animation. **Length:** 7 mins. **Format:** Beta, VHS, 3/4'' U-matic. **Acquisition:** Purchase, Rent/Lease. **Use:** School/Group/Institution, Special Use Restrictions Apply.

★4721★
Playboy Jazz Festival
RCA/Columbia Pictures Home Video
3500 W. Olive Ave.
Burbank, CA 91505 Phone: (818)953-7900
1984. **Program Description:** Some of the world's greatest jazz musicians from Dave Brubeck to Sarah Vaughn are gathered together in this concert taped at the Hollywood Bowl in California. In VHS Dolby Hi-Fi Stereo and Beta Hi-Fi Stereo. **Length:** 90 mins. **Format:** Beta, VHS. **Acquisition:** Purchase. **Use:** In-Home Viewing.

★4722★
Politics of Resistance, The
Michigan Media
University of Michigan
400 4th St.
Ann Arbor, MI 48109 Phone: (313)764-8228
1970. **Program Description:** An examination of Black insurrections of the 1700's and inner conflicts within the slave system. Part of the "Black Experience" series. **Length:** 29 mins. **Format:** 3/4'' U-matic, Other than listed. **Acquisition:** Rent/Lease, Purchase. **Use:** School/Group/Institution, Closed Circuit Television, Cable Television, Broadcast television.

★4723★
Power Versus the People
William Greaves Productions
80 8th Ave., Ste. 1701
New York, NY 10011 Phone: (212)206-1213
1972. **Program Description:** The Equal Employment Opportunity Commission examines the discriminatory actions of several large corporations at a series of hearings in Houston, Texas. **Length:** 36 mins. **Format:** Beta, VHS. **Acquisition:** Rent/Lease, Purchase. **Use:** School/Group/Institution, Broadcast television.

★4724★
Prejudice: A Lesson to Forget
American Educational Films
3807 Dickerson Rd.
Nashville, TN 37207 Phone: 800-822-5678
1973. **Program Description:** An interview with people who exhibit unconscious prejudices against minorities. **Length:** 17 mins. **Format:** Beta, VHS, 3/4'' U-matic. **Acquisition:** Purchase. **Use:** School/Group/Institution, Special Use Restrictions Apply.

★4725★
Prejudice: Causes, Consequences, Cures
CRM/McGraw-Hill Films
674 Via de la Valle
PO Box 641
Del Mar, CA 92014 Phone: (619)453-5000
1974. **Program Description:** This program focuses on research findings and their implications for dealing with prejudice against women and racial, national, and ethnic groups. **Length:** 24 mins. **Format:** Beta, VHS, 3/4'' U-matic. **Acquisition:** Purchase. **Use:** School/Group/Institution, Closed Circuit Television, Special Use Restrictions Apply.

★4726★
Prejudice Film, The
Motivational Media
12001 Ventura Pl., No. 202
Studio City, CA 91604 Phone: (818)508-6553
1984. **Program Description:** The historical background of contemporary forms of prejudice are examined in this program. **Length:** 28 mins. **Format:** Beta, VHS, 3/4'' U-matic. **Acquisition:** Purchase. **Use:** School/Group/Institution, Closed Circuit Television.

★4727★
Prejudice: Perceiving and Believing
MTI Teleprograms, Inc.
108 Wilmot Rd.
Deerfield, IL 60015-9990 Phone: (708)940-1260
1977. **Program Description:** How stereotyped classification by race, religion, and sex rather than by individual worth can prevent positive personal interactions. **Length:** 28 mins. **Format:** Beta, VHS, 3/4'' U-matic. **Acquisition:** Rent/Lease, Purchase. **Use:** School/Group/Institution, Closed Circuit Television, Special Use Restrictions Apply.

★4728★
Prophet of Peace: The Story of Dr. Martin Luther King, Jr.
University of California at Berkeley
Extension Media Center
2176 Shattuck Ave.
Berkeley, CA 94704 Phone: (415)642-0460
1986. **Program Description:** Drawings by Morrie Turner highlight this biography of the famous civil rights activist. **Length:** 23 mins. **Format:** VHS, 3/4'' U-matic. **Acquisition:** Purchase, Rent/Lease. **Use:** School/Group/Institution, Special Use Restrictions Apply.

★4729★
Psychosocial and Environmental Factors in Hypertension in Blacks
Emory Medical Television Network
Emory University
Emory Medical Television Network-
Department C
1440 Clifton Rd., NE
Atlanta, GA 30322 Phone: (404)727-5817
1986. **Program Description:** A look at the epidemiologic evidence to surrounding the environmental effect on Blacks' hypertension. **Length:** 24 mins. **Format:** VHS, 3/4" U-matic. **Acquisition:** Rent/Lease, Purchase, Subscription. **Use:** School/Group/Institution, Closed Circuit Television, Cable Television, Broadcast Television, Special Use Restrictions Apply.

★4730★
Race Movies: The Popular Art of the 1920's
National AudioVisual Center
National Archives & Records
Administration
Customer Services Section PZ
8700 Edgeworth Dr.
Capitol Heights, MD 20743-3701 Phone: (301)763-1896
1985. **Program Description:** This video examines the works of early Black filmmakers, from the very first movies to the heyday of the 20's. **Length:** 20 mins. **Format:** Beta, VHS, 3/4" U-matic. **Acquisition:** Purchase. **Use:** School/Group/Institution, Special Use Restrictions Apply.

★4731★
Racism 101
PBS Video
1320 Braddock Pl.
Alexandria, VA 22314-1698 Phone: (703)739-5380
1989. **Program Description:** Racism in such prestigious college campuses as Harvard, Smith and Columbia is examined in this program. **Length:** 58 mins. **Format:** Beta, VHS, 3/4" U-matic. **Acquisition:** Purchase, Rent/Lease. **Use:** School/Group/Institution, Special Use Restrictions Apply.

★4732★
Racism and Minority Groups I
University of Washington Instructional
Media Services
Kane Hall, DG-10
Seattle, WA 98195 Phone: (206)543-9909
1973. **Program Description:** Each of the major racial minorities is presented in historic and current respective and members of each group respond to the series' presentations. Programs available individually. **Length:** 30 mins. **Format:** 3/4" U-matic. **Acquisition:** Rent/Lease. **Use:** School/Group/Institution.

★4733★
Racism and Minority Groups II
University of Washington Instructional
Media Services
Kane Hall, DG-10
Seattle, WA 98195 Phone: (206)543-9909
1973. **Program Description:** These programs are a continuation of "Racism and Minority Groups I." Programs are available individually. **Length:** 30 mins. **Format:** 3/4" U-matic. **Acquisition:** Rent/Lease. **Use:** School/Group/Institution.

★4734★
A Raisin in the Sun
RCA/Columbia Pictures Home Video
3500 W. Olive Ave.
Burbank, CA 91505 Phone: (818)953-7900
1961. **Program Description:** A sensitive drama of a Black family's escape from their frustrating life in a crowded Chicago apartment. **Length:** 128 mins. **Format:** Beta, VHS, Laser optical videodisc. **Acquisition:** Purchase. **Use:** In-Home Viewing.

★4735★
Ready to be a Wise Man
Direct Cinema Limited, Inc.
Box 69799
Los Angeles, CA 90069 Phone: (213)652-8000
1987. **Program Description:** Racial prejudice is explored in this film about a Southern minister's young son in the late 1950s. **Length:** 30 mins. **Format:** Beta, VHS, 3/4" U-matic. **Acquisition:** Purchase, Rent/Lease. **Use:** School/Group/Institution, Special Use Restrictions Apply.

★4736★
Renovascular Hypertension and Diabetic Nephropathy in Blacks
Emory Medical Television Network
Emory University
Emory Medical Television Network-
Department C
1440 Clifton Rd., NE
Atlanta, GA 30322 Phone: (404)727-5817
1986. **Program Description:** A look for professionals on the clinical advantage of examining the paucity of renovascular hypertension in Blacks. **Length:** 22 mins. **Format:** VHS, 3/4" U-matic. **Acquisition:** Rent/Lease, Purchase, Subscription. **Use:** School/Group/Institution, Closed Circuit Television, Cable Television, Broadcast television, Special Use Restrictions Apply.

★4737★
Resurgence: The Movement for Equality vs. the Ku Klux Klan
Icarus Films
200 Park Ave., S., Ste. 1319
New York, NY 10003 Phone: (212)674-3375
1981. **Program Description:** A documentary about two opposing political forces: union and civil rights activists, and the ever present Ku Klux Klan and American Nazi Party. **Length:** 54 mins. **Format:** 3/4" U-matic. **Acquisition:** Purchase. **Use:** School/Group/Institution, Special Use Restrictions Apply.

★4738★
Revival
Liguori Publications
1 Liguori Dr.
Liguori, MO 63057-9999 Phone: 800-527-1153
1989. **Program Description:** Various religious people talk about the growing role that Blacks are playing in the Catholic Church. **Length:** 15 mins. **Format:** Beta, VHS. **Acquisition:** Purchase. **Use:** School/Group/Institution, In-Home Viewing.

★4739★
Revolutionaries in Theology
NETCHE (Nebraska ETV Council for
Higher Education)
Box 83111
Lincoln, NE 68501 Phone: (402)472-3611
1976. **Program Description:** The film shows that the rediscovery of the experience of the Black church and the increased involvement of women in the life and leadership of the whole church are creating a revolution in the academic life of church. **Length:** 30 mins. **Format:** 1/2" reel, 3/4" U-matic. **Acquisition:** Rent/Lease, Purchase, Subscription. **Use:** School/Group/Institution, Closed Circuit Television, Broadcast television, Special Use Restrictions Apply.

★4740★
Rhythm and Blues Review
Glenn Video Vistas, Ltd.
6924 Canby Ave., Ste. 103
Reseda, CA 91335 Phone: (818)981-5506
1955. **Program Description:** A unique gathering of great musicians and singers were brought together for this review filmed revue, selected from a series of musical shorts called Telescriptions. **Length:** 60 mins. **Format:** Beta, VHS. **Acquisition:** Purchase. **Use:** In-Home Viewing.

★4741★
Ribbon, The
Icarus Films
200 Park Ave., S., Ste. 1319
New York, NY 10003 Phone: (212)674-3375
1987. **Program Description:** A documentary about the "Peace Ribbon" which was made to protest the South African army's occupation of Black townships. While the documentary was being made, a general state of emergency was declared, and the film follows the women who helped make the ribbon through this frightening and spiritually challenging time. **Length:** 50 mins. **Format:** 3/4" U-matic. **Acquisition:** Purchase. **Use:** School/Group/Institution, Special Use Restrictions Apply.

★4742★
Rich
AIMS Media, Inc.
6901 Woodley Ave.
Van Nuys, CA 91406-4878 Phone: (818)785-4111
1988. **Program Description:** A Black teenager fights to go on to college and become a success. **Length:** 21 mins. **Format:** Beta, VHS, 3/4" U-matic. **Acquisition:** Purchase, Rent/Lease. **Use:** School/Group/Institution, Special Use Restrictions Apply.

★4743★
Road Home, The
AIMS Media, Inc.
6901 Woodley Ave.
Van Nuys, CA 91406-4878 Phone: (818)785-4111
1989. **Program Description:** Charles Ratcliff, a Black Vietnam vet, talks about war, violence, parenthood, and prejudice. **Length:** 9 mins. **Format:** Beta, VHS, 3/4" U-matic. **Acquisition:** Purchase, Rent/Lease. **Use:** School/Group/Institution, Special Use Restrictions Apply.

★4744★
Rock and Roll Review
Glenn Video Vistas, Ltd.
6924 Canby Ave., Ste. 103
Reseda, CA 91335 Phone: (818)981-5506
1955. **Program Description:** An all-star show filmed onstage at Harlem's Apollo Theater. **Length:** 60 mins. **Format:** Beta, VHS. **Acquisition:** Purchase. **Use:** In-Home Viewing.

★4745★
Roll of Thunder, Hear My Cry
Learning Corporation of America
108 Wilmot Rd.
Deerfield, IL 60015-9990 Phone: (708)940-1260
1978. **Program Description:** The struggles of a Black family to hold on to the land they have owned for three generations is seen through the eyes of a young girl. Set in the South of 1933 and based on the novels of Mildred Taylor. **Length:** 1978. **Format:** Beta, VHS, 3/4" U-matic. **Acquisition:** Rent/Lease; Purchase. **Use:** School/Group/Institution, Special Use Restrictions Apply.

★4746★
Roots
Warner Home Video
4000 Warner Blvd.
Burbank, CA 91522 Phone: (818)954-6000
1977. **Program Description:** The complete version of Alex Haley's saga following a Black man's search for his heritage, revealing an epic panorama of America's past. Available on six 90-minute tapes. **Format:** Beta, VHS, Laser optical videodisc. **Acquisition:** Rent/Lease; Purchase. **Use:** In-Home Viewing.

★4747★
Rosedale: The Way It Is
Indiana University Audio-Visual Center
Bloomington, IN 47405-5901 Phone: (812)335-8087
1976. **Program Description:** A look at racial tension in Rosedale, New York when the first Black family moved into the White neighborhood. **Length:** 57 mins. **Format:** 3/4" U-matic, Other than listed. **Acquisition:** Rent/Lease, Purchase. **Use:** School/Group/Institution, Closed Circuit Television, In-Home Viewing.

★4748★
Round Midnight
Warner Home Video, Inc.
4000 Warner Blvd.
Burbank, CA 91522 Phone: (818)954-6000
1986. **Program Description:** An aging, alcoholic, world-weary jazz saxophonist comes to Paris in the late 1950's seeking an escape from his self-destructive existence. He meets a worshipful young French fan who spurs him on to one last burst of creative brilliance. A moody, heartfelt homage to such expatriate bebop musicians as Bud Powell and Lester Young. In Digital Hi-Fi Stereo. Also available in a Spanish-subtitled version. **Length:** 132 mins. **Format:** Beta, VHS, Laser optical videodisc. **Acquisition:** Purchase. **Use:** In-Home Viewing.

★4749★
Roy Wilkins—The Right to Dignity
National AudioVisual Center
National Archives & Records Administration
Customer Services Section PZ
8700 Edgeworth Dr.
Capitol Heights, MD 20743-3701 Phone: (301)763-1896
1978. **Program Description:** The story of Roy Wilkins' long career with the National Association for the Advancement of Colored People. His important role in the 1954 Brown v. Board of Education Supreme Court decision is highlighted, along with his activity in the Civil Rights legislation of the 1960's. **Length:** 20 mins. **Format:** Beta, VHS, 3/4" U-matic, Other than listed. **Acquisition:** Purchase. **Use:** School/Group/Institution, Special Use Restrictions Apply.

★4750★
Running With Jesse
PBS Video
1320 Braddock Pl.
Alexandria, VA 22314-1698 Phone: (703)739-5380
1989. **Program Description:** A profile of the first Black American to establish himself as a serious contender for the presidency. **Length:** 60 mins. **Format:** Beta, VHS, 3/4" U-matic. **Acquisition:** Purchase, Rent/Lease. **Use:** School/Group/Institution, Special Use Restrictions Apply.

★4751★
Sacred Music of Duke Ellington, The
MGM/UA Home Video, Inc.
8670 Wilshire
Beverly Hills, CA 90211 Phone: (213)967-2296
1982. **Program Description:** A performance of Ellington's three Sacred Concerts, taped at St. Paul's Cathedral in London. In Dolby HiFi Stereo. **Length:** 90 mins. **Format:** Beta, VHS. **Acquisition:** Purchase. **Use:** In-Home Viewing.

★4752★
St. Louis Blues
Cinema Guild
1697 Broadway, Rm. 802
New York, NY 10019 Phone: (212)246-5522
1929. **Program Description:** In her only film appearance, famed blues singer Bessie Smith sings "St. Louis Blues" in a lowdown cabaret after being betrayed and abused by her boyfriend. A Vitaphone two-reel short, with music by members of the Fletcher Henderson and vocal backup by the Hall Johnson Choir. **Length:** 17 mins. **Format:** Beta, VHS, 3/4" U-matic. **Acquisition:** Rent/Lease, Purchase, Duplication. **Use:** School/Group/Institution, Special Use Restrictions Apply.

★4753★
School Daze
RCA/Columbia Pictures Home Video
3500 W. Olive Ave.
Burbank, CA 91505 Phone: (818)953-7900
1988. **Program Description:** Spike Lee's second film, a comedy about the racial, fraternity-oriented tensions, romances, conflicts and all-out battles during a Black college's homecoming weekend. Written by Lee. **Length:** 114 mins. **Format:** Beta, VHS, Laser optical videodisc. **Acquisition:** Purchase. **Use:** In-Home Viewing.

★4754★
Scott Joplin
Pyramid Film & Video
Box 1048
Santa Monica, CA 90406 Phone: (213)828-7577
1977. **Program Description:** This is a biographical look at the life and work of ragtime composer Scott Joplin. **Length:** 15 mins. **Format:** Beta, VHS, 3/4'' U-matic. **Acquisition:** Rent/Lease, Purchase, Duplication License. **Use:** School/Group/Institution, In-Home Viewing, Special Use Restrictions Apply.

★4755★
Search for a Black Christian Heritage
Liguori Publications
1 Liguori Dr.
Liguori, MO 63057-9999 Phone: 800-527-1153
1989. **Program Description:** A series that was made with the intention of increasing the awareness of what Blacks have contributed to Judeo-Christian heritage. **Length:** 120 mins. **Format:** Beta, VHS. **Acquisition:** Purchase. **Use:** School/Group/Institution, In-Home Viewing.

★4756★
Second American Revolution, The
PBS Video
1320 Braddock Pl.
Alexandria, VA 22314-1698 Phone: (703)739-5380
1982. **Program Description:** The revolution of Black America, from emancipation through Martin Luther King's historic march 100 years later. Ossie Davis and Ruby Dee join host Bill Moyers. Available on 2 tapes. **Length:** 120 mins. **Format:** Beta, VHS, 3/4'' U-matic. **Acquisition:** Rent/Lease, Purchase, Off-Air Record. **Use:** School/Group/Institution, Closed Circuit Television, Cable Television.

★4757★
"Separate But Equal"
Britannica Films
310 S. Michigan Ave.
Chicago, IL 60604 Phone: (312)347-7958
1988. **Program Description:** In the 1890s, the Supreme Court ruled that though Whites could keep Blacks segregated, both groups had to have access to equal facilities. **Length:** 8 mins. **Format:** Beta, VHS, 3/4'' U-matic. **Acquisition:** Purchase, Trade-in. **Use:** School/Group/Institution, Special Use Restrictions Apply.

★4758★
Seventeen
Icarus Films
200 Park Ave., S., Ste. 1319
New York, NY 10003 Phone: (212)674-3375
1982. **Program Description:** This documentary focuses on Lynn, a high school senior who becomes the object of neighborhood racism when she dates a Black man. Made in 1982, this film eerily foreshadows the 1989 racial murder in Bensonhurst. **Length:** 120 mins. **Format:** 3/4'' U-matic. **Acquisition:** Purchase. **Use:** School/Group/Institution, Special Use Restrictions Apply.

★4759★
She's Gotta Have It
Key Video
1211 Avenue of the Americas, 2nd Fl.
New York, NY 10036 Phone: (212)819-3238
1986. **Program Description:** Spike Lee wrote, directed, edited, produced, and starred in this light romantic comedy about an independent-minded Brooklyn girl who invites her three suitors over to her house for dinner together. Naturally, complications ensue. **Length:** 84 mins. **Format:** Beta, VHS. **Acquisition:** Purchase. **Use:** In-Home Viewing.

★4760★
Shirley Verret
Facets Multimedia Inc.
1517 W. Fullerton Ave.
Chicago, IL 60614 Phone: (312)281-9075
1978. **Program Description:** A look at a year in the life of the famous Black diva, on stage and off, including footage of her performing Iphigenie at the Paris Opera, Tosca at the Arena di Verona, Dalila at the Royal Opera House Covent Garden, and Carmen at La Scala. **Length:** 60 mins. **Format:** Beta, VHS. **Acquisition:** Purchase. **Use:** In-Home Viewing.

★4761★
Singing Stream: A Black Family Chronicle, A
Davenport Films
Route 1
Box 527
Delaplane, VA 22025 Phone: (703)592-3701
1987. **Program Description:** This film shows how the traditions of gospel music helped to promote family loyalty and purposefulness to a Southern Black family from the 1930's to the present. **Length:** 57 mins. **Format:** Beta, VHS. **Acquisition:** Purchase. **Use:** In-Home Viewing.

★4762★
Sippie
Kino International Corporation
333 W. 39th St., Ste. 503
New York, NY 10018 Phone: (212)629-6880
1989. **Program Description:** This documentary takes a look at the life and music of blues singer/songwriter Sippie Wallace, a contemporary of Bessie Smith and Ma Rainey. **Length:** 23 mins. **Format:** Beta, VHS. **Acquisition:** Purchase. **Use:** In-Home Viewing.

★4763★
1619-1860: Out of Slavery
CRM/McGraw-Hill Films
674 Via de la Valle
PO Box 641
Del Mar, CA 92014 Phone: (619)453-5000
1965. **Program Description:** This program first looks at slavery as it was practiced in Greece and Rome. It then moves to West Africa and shows civilization as it existed there before the beginning of the slave trade. Lastly, it depicts the Negro in America–as a freeman and slave, as patriot during the American Revolution, and as a participant in the abolitionist movement. Part of the "History of the Negro in America" series. **Length:** 20 mins. **Format:** Beta, VHS, 3/4'' U-matic. **Acquisition:** Purchase. **Use:** School/Group/Institution, Closed Circuit Television, Special Use Restrictions Apply.

★4764★
Slavery and Slave Resistance
Coronet/MTI Film & Video
108 Wilmot Rd.
Deerfield, IL 60015-9990 Phone: (708)940-1260
1978. **Program Description:** Story of slave oppression and resistance from the colonial period to the Civil War. **Length:** 25 mins. **Format:** Beta, VHS, 3/4'' U-matic. **Acquisition:** Purchase. **Use:** School/Group/Institution, Closed Circuit Television, Special Use Restrictions Apply.

★4765★
Slave's Story, A
Learning Corporation of America
108 Wilmot Rd.
Deerfield, IL 60015-9990 Phone: (708)940-1260
1972. **Program Description:** Dramatization of William and Ellen Craft's actual escape from slavery in 1848. **Length:** 29 mins. **Format:** Beta, VHS, 3/4'' U-matic. **Acquisition:** Rent/Lease, Purchase. **Use:** School/Group/Institution, Special Use Restrictions Apply.

★4766★
A Soldier's Story
RCA/Columbia Pictures Home Video
3500 W. Olive Ave.
Burbank, CA 91505 Phone: (818)953-7900
1984. **Program Description:** A Black army attorney is sent to a southern army base to investigate the murder of an unpopular sergeant. Features World War II, Louisiana, jazz and blues, and racism in and outside the corps. From the Pulitzer Prize-winning play by Charles Fuller, with most of the Broadway cast. Fine performances by Denzel Washington and Adolph Caesar. **Length:** 101 mins. **Format:** Beta, VHS, Laser optical videodisc. **Acquisition:** Purchase. **Use:** In-Home Viewing.

★4767★
Some Are More Equal Than Others
Carousel Film & Video
260 5th Ave.
New York, NY 10016 Phone: (212)683-1660
1971. **Program Description:** Considers the legal treatment of ethnic minorities and shows how the system works mostly against the poor. **Length:** 40 mins. **Format:** Beta, VHS, 3/4" U-matic. **Acquisition:** Purchase. **Use:** School/Group/Institution, Special Use Restrictions Apply.

★4768★
Some People
Intermedia Arts of Minnesota, Inc.
425 Ontario St. SE
Minneapolis, MN 55414 Phone: (612)627-4444
1988. **Program Description:** The stories of seven Black characters, living on the outside of society, are told through dance and vignette storytelling. **Length:** 19 mins. **Format:** 3/4" U-matic. **Acquisition:** Purchase, Rent/Lease. **Use:** School/Group/Institution, Special Use Restrictions Apply.

★4769★
Sometimes I'm Up, Sometimes I'm Down
New York State Education Department
Center for Learning Technologies
Media Distribution Network
Rm. C-7, Concourse Level
Albany, NY 12230 Phone: (518)474-1265
196?. **Program Description:** This film dramatizes what it was like to live in the slave colony of John's Island, South Carolina. **Length:** 30 mins. **Format:** Beta, VHS, 1/2" reel, 3/4" U-matic, 2" Quad. **Acquisition:** Duplication, Free Duplication. **Use:** School/Group/Institution, Special Use Restrictions Apply.

★4770★
Song of the Spear
Cinema Guild
1697 Broadway, Rm. 802
New York, NY 10019 Phone: (212)246-5522
1986. **Program Description:** The role of culture in the struggle for national liberation in South Africa is explored in this documentary. **Length:** 57 mins. **Format:** Beta, VHS, 3/4" U-matic. **Acquisition:** Purchase. **Use:** School/Group/Institution.

★4771★
Sonny Rollins Live
Rhapsody Films
30 Charlton St.
New York, NY 10014 Phone: (212)243-0152
1973. **Program Description:** A live concert with tenor saxophone player Sonny Rollins. Included in the band are Bob Cranshaw (bass), Walter Davis, Jr. (piano), Masuo (guitar), and David Lee (drums). They perform the numbers "There Is No Greater Love," "Don't Stop the Carnival," "Alfie," and "St. Thomas." **Length:** 36 mins. **Format:** Beta, VHS, 3/4" U-matic. **Acquisition:** Purchase. **Use:** School/Group/Institution, In-Home Viewing.

★4772★
Sophisticated Ladies
J2 Communications
10850 Wilshire Blvd., Ste. 1000
Los Angeles, CA 90024 Phone: (213)474-5252
1984. **Program Description:** A revival of the classic Ellington show with over 30 Duke originals performed by his original orchestra, including "Solitude," "Take the 'A' Train," "Mood Indigo," "It Don't Mean a Thing," and more. In HiFi Stereo **Length:** 90 mins. **Format:** Beta, VHS. **Acquisition:** Purchase. **Use:** In-Home Viewing.

★4773★
Soul of the Islands
Cinema Guild
1697 Broadway, Rm. 802
New York, NY 10019 Phone: (212)246-5522
1988. **Program Description:** The history and culture of Haiti is presented here through poetry and music. **Length:** 30 mins. **Format:** Beta, VHS, 3/4" U-matic. **Acquisition:** Purchase. **Use:** School/Group/Institution.

★4774★
Sounder
Paramount Home Video
5555 Melrose Ave.
Los Angeles, CA 90058 Phone: (213)468-5000
1972. **Program Description:** Adapted from the novel by William Armstrong, this chronicles the struggles of a Black family of sharecroppers in rural Louisiana during the Depression. When the father is sentenced to jail for stealing in order to feed his family, they must pull together even more, and one son finds education to be his way out of poverty. Cicley Tyson brings strength and style to her role, with fine help from Paul Winfield. **Length:** 105 mins. **Format:** Beta, VHS, Laser optical videodisc. **Acquisition:** Rent/Lease; Purchase. **Use:** In-Home Viewing.

★4775★
Soundies Vol. I and II
Festival Films
2841 Irving Ave., S.
Minneapolis, MN 55408 Phone: (612)870-4744
1942. **Program Description:** A package of eight Soundies, featuring top jazz talents of 1941-42 performing the following numbers: "Shine"–Louis Armstrong and his Orchestra; "Ain't Misbehavin'"–Fats Waller and his Rhythm; "Thanks for the Boogie Ride" and "Let Me Off Uptown"–Gene Krupa and his Orchestra with Anita O'Day and Roy Eldridge; "Lazy Bones"–Hoagy Carmichael and Dorothy Dandridge; "Minnie the Moocher," "Blues in the Night," and "Virginia, Georgia and Caroline"–Cab Calloway and his Orchestra. **Length:** 28 mins. **Format:** Beta, VHS. **Acquisition:** Purchase. **Use:** School/Group/Institution, In-Home Viewing.

★4776★
South Africa
Carousel Film & Video
260 5th Ave.
New York, NY 10016 Phone: (212)683-1660
1988. **Program Description:** A controversial look at the problems facing South Africa today, under the Apartheid policies. Alternatives to the present government are discussed. **Length:** 49 mins. **Format:** VHS, 3/4" U-matic. **Acquisition:** Purchase. **Use:** School/Group/Institution, Special Use Restrictions Apply.

★4777★
South Africa
Marilyn Perry TV Productions, Inc.
677 5th Ave., 5th Fl.
New York, NY 10022 Phone: (212)308-2250
1983. **Program Description:** This program features interviews with David Steward, Counselor of the Permanent Mission of South Africa to the U.N., Vere Stock, the honorable Consul General and Carl Frank Noffke, Information Counselor of the Embassy of South Africa to the U.S. **Length:** 28 mins. **Format:** 3/4" U-matic. **Acquisition:** Rent/Lease, Purchase. **Use:** School/Group/Institution, Closed Circuit Television, Cable Television, Broadcast television, Special Use Restrictions Apply.

★4778★
South Africa Belongs to Us
Icarus Films
200 Park Ave., S.
Ste. 1319
New York, NY 10003 Phone: (212)674-3375
1982. **Program Description:** With portraits of five ordinary women and four women leaders, the film depicts the struggle of the Black women for human dignity in the face of apartheid: from the struggle of feeding her children to the total liberation of her people. **Length:** 57 mins. **Format:** 3/4" U-matic. **Acquisition:** Purchase. **Use:** School/Group/Institution, Special Use Restrictions Apply.

★4779★
South Africa: The Solution
Journal Films, Inc.
930 Pitner Ave.
Evanston, IL 60202 Phone: (708)328-6700
1989. **Program Description:** Historical factors are given to show why South Africa is in the state it is today. A view is also given of how it might look in the future. **Length:** 38 mins. **Format:** Beta, VHS, 3/4" U-matic. **Acquisition:** Purchase, Rent/Lease. **Use:** School/Group/Institution, Special Use Restrictions Apply.

★4780★
South Africa: The White Laager
Learning Corporation of America
108 Wilmot Rd.
Deerfield, IL 60015-9990 Phone: (708)940-1260
1978. **Program Description:** A documentary about the the political and economic forces that have led to the South African racial policy of apartheid. **Length:** 58 mins. **Format:** Beta, VHS, 3/4" U-matic, Other than listed. **Acquisition:** Rent/Lease, Purchase. **Use:** School/Group/Institution, Special Use Restrictions Apply.

★4781★
South Africa Today: A Question of Power
Journal Films, Inc.
930 Pitner Ave.
Evanston, IL 60202 Phone: (708)328-6700
1988. **Program Description:** Two South African newspaper editors, one Black, one White, talk about the problems that their country has. **Length:** 55 mins. **Format:** Beta, VHS, 3/4" U-matic. **Acquisition:** Purchase, Rent/Lease. **Use:** School/Group/Institution, Special Use Restrictions Apply.

★4782★
South African Essay: Fruit of Fear
Indiana University Audio-Visual Center
Bloomington, IN 47405-5901 Phone: (812)335-8087
1965. **Program Description:** A look at the two societies existing in South Africa today–the Black majority and the ruling White minority. **Length:** 59 mins. **Format:** 3/4" U-matic, Other than listed. **Acquisition:** Rent/Lease, Purchase. **Use:** School/Group/Institution, Closed Circuit Television, In-Home Viewing, Special Use Restrictions Apply.

★4783★
South African Essay: One Nation-Two Nationalisms
Indiana University Audio-Visual Center
Bloomington, IN 47405-5901 Phone: (812)335-8087
1965. **Program Description:** A look at the country's Nationalist Party and the policy of strict separation of people according to tribal and racial origins. **Length:** 59 mins. **Format:** 3/4" U-matic, Other than listed. **Acquisition:** Rent/Lease, Purchase. **Use:** School/Group/Institution, Closed Circuit Television, In-Home Viewing, Special Use Restrictions Apply.

★4784★
South African Farm, A
Documentary Educational Resources, Inc.
101 Morse St.
Watertown, MA 02172 Phone: (617)926-0491
1985. **Program Description:** A view of apartheid seen through the daily workings of a farm worked by Blacks, but owned by a Czech emigre in South Africa. **Length:** 51 mins. **Format:** Beta, VHS, 3/4" U-matic. **Acquisition:** Rent/Lease, Purchase. **Use:** School/Group/Institution, Special Use Restrictions Apply.

★4785★
South African Universities in the Apartheid System
Michigan State University
IMC Marketing Division
East Lansing, MI 48826-0710 Phone: (517)353-9229
1988. **Program Description:** Colleges in South Africa still remain racially separate. This video expresses the country's dehumanizing education system. **Length:** 42 mins. **Format:** Beta, VHS, 3/4" U-matic. **Acquisition:** Purchase, Rent/Lease. **Use:** School/Group/Institution, Closed Circuit Television.

★4786★
South by Northwest
Great Plains National Instructional Television Library (GPN)
University of Nebraska at Lincoln
PO Box 80669
Lincoln, NE 68501-0669 Phone: (402)472-2007
1975. **Program Description:** A series of docudramas exploring the role of Black cowboys and pioneers in the development of the American Northwest from the late 1700's to the turn of the century. Programs available individually. **Length:** 29 mins. **Format:** Beta, VHS, 3/4" U-matic, Other than listed. **Acquisition:** Rent/Lease, Purchase, Duplication License, Off-Air Record. **Use:** School/Group/Institution, Closed Circuit Television, Cable Television, Broadcast Television.

★4787★
Soweto to Berkeley
Cinema Guild
1697 Broadway, Rm. 802
New York, NY 10019 Phone: (212)246-5522
1988. **Program Description:** This video traces the anti-apartheid movement at the University of California-Berkeley during the 1985-86 school year. **Length:** 50 mins. **Format:** Beta, VHS, 3/4" U-matic. **Acquisition:** Rent/Lease, Purchase, Duplication. **Use:** School/Group/Institution, Special Use Restrictions Apply.

★4788★
Spirit of St. Elmo Village, The
Carousel Film & Video
260 5th Ave.
New York, NY 10016 Phone: (212)683-1660
1989. **Program Description:** Rozzell and Roderick Sykes, two Black artists, were able to change a slum section of Los Angeles into a world of art and beauty. **Length:** 26 mins. **Format:** Beta, VHS, 3/4" U-matic. **Acquisition:** Purchase. **Use:** School/Group/Institution, Special Use Restrictions Apply.

★4789★
Spirit to Spirit: Nikki Giovanni
Direct Cinema Limited, Inc.
Box 69799
Los Angeles, CA 90069 Phone: (213)652-8000
1987. **Program Description:** A visually arresting portrait of poet Nikki Giovanni against a background of some of her themes including the Civil Rights struggle and the Women's Movement. **Length:** 30 mins. **Format:** Beta, VHS, 3/4" U-matic. **Acquisition:** Purchase, Rent/Lease. **Use:** School/Group/Institution, Special Use Restrictions Apply.

★4790★
Stars on Parade/Boogie Woogie Dream
Video Yesteryear
Box C
Sandy Hook, CT 06482 Phone: (203)426-2574
1946. **Program Description:** This is a pair of all-Black musicals which shows off a host of talent from the 1940's. **Length:** 55 mins. **Format:** Beta, VHS, Other than listed. **Acquisition:** Purchase. **Use:** In-Home Viewing.

★4791★
State of Apartheid: South Africa, The
Journal Films, Inc.
930 Pitner Ave.
Evanston, IL 60202 Phone: (708)328-6700
197?. **Program Description:** This program examines the controversy surrounding the State of apartheid in South Africa. **Length:** 13 mins. **Format:** Beta, VHS, 3/4" U-matic. **Acquisition:** Rent/Lease, Purchase, Duplication License. **Use:** School/Group/Institution, Closed Circuit Television, Special Use Restrictions Apply.

★4792★
Storm of Strangers
Films, Inc.
5547 N. Ravenswood Ave.
Chicago, IL 60640-1199 Phone: (312)878-2600
1983. **Program Description:** This series introduces America's ethnic and racial minorities to each other. **Length:** 29 mins. **Format:** Beta, VHS, 3/4" U-matic. **Acquisition:** Purchase. **Use:** School/Group/Institution, Special Use Restrictions Apply.

★4793★
Stormie: The Lady of the Jewel Box
Women Make Movies
225 Lafayette St., Ste. 212
New York, NY 10012 Phone: (212)925-0606
1987. **Program Description:** Black male impersonator Storme DeLarverie is profiled in this documentary. **Length:** 21 mins. **Format:** Beta, VHS, 3/4" U-matic. **Acquisition:** Purchase, Rent/Lease. **Use:** School/Group/Institution, Special Use Restrictions Apply.

★4794★
Struggle for Los Trabajos
William Greaves Productions
80 8th Ave., Ste. 1701
New York, NY 10011 Phone: (212)206-1213
1972. **Program Description:** When a job applicant is rejected by a company official he lodges a complaint of job discrimination with the Equal Employment Opportunity Commission. **Length:** 23 mins. **Format:** Beta, VHS. **Acquisition:** Rent/Lease, Purchase. **Use:** School/Group/Institution, Broadcast television.

★4795★
Stubborn Hope
Icarus Films
200 Park Ave., S., Ste. 1319
New York, NY 10003 Phone: (212)674-3375
1985. **Program Description:** A chronicle of a few months in the life of South African exile, and well-known poet Dennis Brutus. **Length:** 28 mins. **Format:** 3/4" U-matic. **Acquisition:** Purchase. **Use:** School/Group/Institution, Special Use Restrictions Apply.

★4796★
Sun Will Rise, The
Icarus Films
200 Park Ave., S., Ste. 1319
New York, NY 10003 Phone: (212)674-3375
1983. **Program Description:** A harrowing documentary about the members of the African National Congress who were sentenced to death for their anti-apartheid activities. **Length:** 35 mins. **Format:** 3/4" U-matic. **Acquisition:** Purchase. **Use:** School/Group/Institution, Special Use Restrictions Apply.

★4797★
Talk About Me, I Am Africa
Icarus Films
200 Park Ave., S., Ste. 1319
New York, NY 10003 Phone: (212)674-3375
1980. **Program Description:** This video was shot secretly in South Africa and contains theatre pieces which protest the government's apartheid policies. **Length:** 54 mins. **Format:** 3/4" U-matic. **Acquisition:** Purchase. **Use:** School/Group/Institution, Special Use Restrictions Apply.

★4798★
Television Linking Culture
New York State Education Department
Center for Learning Technologies
Media Distribution Network
Rm. C-7, Concourse Level
Albany, NY 12230 Phone: (518)474-1265
197?. **Program Description:** This tape shows how television programs produced under the Emergency School Aid Act can eliminate stereotyping and racial isolation. **Length:** 30 mins. **Format:** Beta, VHS, 1/2" reel, 3/4" U-matic, 2" Quad. **Acquisition:** Duplication, Free Duplication. **Use:** School/Group/Institution, Special Use Restrictions Apply.

★4799★
Texaco's Swing into Spring
Discount Video Tapes, Inc.
833 "A" N. Hollywood Way
PO Box 7122
Burbank, CA 91510 Phone: (818)843-3366
1959. **Program Description:** Benny Goodman, his orchestra and his guests present a swinging hour of jazz in this famous TV special. Originally telecast in April, 1959, the featured numbers include "Why Don't You Do Right," "Air Mail Special" and "Bountain Greenery." **Length:** 60 mins. **Format:** Beta, VHS. **Acquisition:** Rent/Lease, Purchase. **Use:** In-Home Viewing.

★4800★
Thelonious Monk: Straight, No Chaser
Warner Home Video, Inc.
4000 Warner Blvd.
Burbank, CA 91522 Phone: (818)954-6000
1989. **Program Description:** Acclaimed documentary on the famous jazz pianist, featuring remembrances from friends and colleagues, and copious performance footage, including the rarely-seen 1967-68 on-the-road sequences shot by Michael and Christian Blackwood. **Length:** 0090 mins. **Format:** Beta, VHS, Laser optical videodisc. **Acquisition:** Purchase. **Use:** In-Home Viewing.

★4801★
Thinnest Line, The
Women Make Movies
225 Lafayette St., Ste. 212
New York, NY 10012 Phone: (212)925-0606
1988. **Program Description:** An exploration of the friendship between two Black women–one a filmmaker, the other a mother. **Length:** 10 mins. **Format:** Beta, VHS, 3/4" U-matic. **Acquisition:** Purchase, Rent/Lease. **Use:** School/Group/Institution, Special Use Restrictions Apply.

★4802★
This Is the Home of Mrs. Levant Graham
Pyramid Film & Video
Box 1048
Santa Monica, CA 90406 Phone: (213)828-7577
1971. **Program Description:** A portrait of an urban Black mother. **Length:** 15 mins. **Format:** Beta, VHS, 3/4" U-matic. **Acquisition:** Rent/Lease, Purchase, Duplication License. **Use:** School/Group/Institution, In-Home Viewing, Special Use Restrictions Apply.

★4803★
Through Young People's Eyes
Cinema Guild
1697 Broadway, Rm. 802
New York, NY 10019 Phone: (212)246-5522
1983. **Program Description:** This documentary examines the effects of poverty on Black and Hispanic teenagers, especially girls. **Length:** 29 mins. **Format:** Beta, VHS, 3/4" U-matic. **Acquisition:** Rent/Lease, Purchase. **Use:** School/Group/Institution, Special Use Restrictions Apply.

★4804★
Tight Packers and Loose Packers
Time-Life Video
1271 Avenue of the Americas
New York, NY 10020 Phone: (212)484-5940
1977. **Program Description:** This episode of the "Fight Against Slavery" series examines the conflicts between the abolitionists and those with vested interests in the slave trade. **Length:** 57 mins. **Format:** Beta, VHS, 3/4" U-matic, Other than listed. **Acquisition:** Rent/Lease, Purchase. **Use:** School/Group/Institution, Special Use Restrictions Apply.

★4805★
Time and Dreams
Temple University
Department of Radio-TV-Film
Philadelphia, PA 19122 Phone: (215)787-8483
1976. **Program Description:** A look at the changes that have come to Greene County since the coming of the civil rights movement. **Length:** 52 mins. **Format:** 3/4'' U-matic. **Acquisition:** Rent/Lease, Purchase. **Use:** School/Group/Institution, Special Use Restrictions Apply.

★4806★
To Free Their Minds
William Greaves Productions
80 8th Ave., Ste. 1701
New York, NY 10011 Phone: (212)206-1213
1974. **Program Description:** A teacher learns how to deal with the demands of teaching an interracial class. **Length:** 24 mins. **Format:** Beta, VHS. **Acquisition:** Rent/Lease, Purchase. **Use:** School/Group/Institution, Broadcast television.

★4807★
To Kill a Mockingbird
MCA/Universal Home Video
70 Universal City Plaza
Universal City, CA 91608 Phone: (818)777-4300
1962. **Program Description:** A White southern lawyer defends a Black man accused of raping a White woman. **Length:** 129 mins. **Format:** Beta, VHS, Laser optical videotape. **Acquisition:** Rent/Lease; Purchase. **Use:** In-Home Viewing.

★4808★
Toni Morrison
Home Vision
5547 N. Ravenswood Ave.
Chicago, IL 60640-1199 Phone: (312)878-2600
1988. **Program Description:** In this documentary, Pulitzer Prize winning author Toni Morrison discusses her novel "Beloved." **Length:** 30 mins. **Format:** Beta, VHS. **Acquisition:** Purchase. **Use:** In-Home Viewing.

★4809★
Tribute to Billie Holiday, A
Media Home Entertainment, Inc.
5730 Buckingham Parkway
Culver City, CA 90230 Phone: (213)216-7900
1979. **Program Description:** This tribute to Billie Holiday features the talents of Nina Simone, Maxine Weldon, Morganna King, Carmen McRae, and Esther Phillips. The orchestra was arranged and conducted by Ray Ellis with additional arranging by Tommy Newsom. **Length:** 57 mins. **Format:** Beta, VHS. **Acquisition:** Purchase. **Use:** In-Home Viewing.

★4810★
Tribute to Malcolm X
Indiana University Audio-Visual Center
Bloomington, IN 47405-5901 Phone: (812)335-8087
1969. **Program Description:** A profile of Malcolm X and the influence he had on the Black liberation movement, as told by his widow, Betty Shabazz. **Length:** 15 mins. **Format:** 3/4'' U-matic, Other than listed. **Acquisition:** Rent/Lease, Purchase. **Use:** School/Group/Institution, Closed Circuit Television, In-Home Viewing, Special Use Restrictions Apply.

★4811★
Troublemakers
Cinema Guild
1697 Broadway, Rm. 802
New York, NY 10019 Phone: (212)246-5522
1966. **Program Description:** The Newark Community Union Project, founded by Tom Hayden in 1965, is examined. The project encourages Blacks to become involved in the community. **Length:** 54 mins. **Format:** Beta, VHS, 3/4'' U-matic. **Acquisition:** Rent/Lease, Purchase, Duplication. **Use:** School/Group/Institution, Special Use Restrictions Apply.

★4812★
Turnaround
New York State Education Department
Center for Learning Technologies
Media Distribution Network
Rm. C-7, Concourse Level
Albany, NY 12230 Phone: (518)474-1265
197?. **Program Description:** This series emphasizes the contributions of minorities to history. **Length:** 10 mins. **Format:** Beta, VHS, 1/2'' reel, 3/4'' U-matic, 2'' Quad. **Acquisition:** Duplication. **Use:** School/Group/Institution, Special Use Restrictions Apply.

★4813★
Tuskegee Institute
King Features Entertainment
235 E. 45th St.
New York, NY 10017 Phone: (212)682-5600
1983. **Program Description:** This program profiles the Tuskegee Institute and some of its famous alumni such as Booker T. Washington and George Washington Carver. **Length:** 15 mins. **Format:** Beta, VHS, 3/4'' U-matic. **Acquisition:** Rent/Lease, Purchase. **Use:** School/Group/Institution, Special Use Restrictions Apply.

★4814★
Two Dollars and A Dream
Filmakers Library, Inc.
133 E. 58th St.
New York, NY 10022 Phone: (212)355-6545
1988. **Program Description:** A vivid biography of Madame C.J. Walker, a child of slaves, who became America's first woman millionaire by manufacturing skin and hair care products. **Length:** 56 mins. **Format:** VHS, 3/4'' U-matic. **Acquisition:** Rent/Lease, Purchase, Duplication. **Use:** School/Group/Institution, In-Home Viewing, Special Use Restrictions Apply.

★4815★
Two Rivers, The
Icarus Films
200 Park Ave., S., Ste. 1319
New York, NY 10003 Phone: (212)674-3375
1985. **Program Description:** The political, economic and cultural background to the tensions and pain in South Africa today are focused on in this documentary. **Length:** 60 mins. **Format:** 3/4'' U-matic. **Acquisition:** Purchase. **Use:** School/Group/Institution, Special Use Restrictions Apply.

★4816★
220 Blues
Phoenix/BFA Films
468 Park Ave., S.
New York, NY 10016 Phone: (212)684-5910
1970. **Program Description:** "220 Blues" is a sensitive study of awakening racial awareness. Sonny is a star high school track man and has the widespread admiration of his peers. **Length:** 18 mins. **Format:** Beta, VHS, 3/4'' U-matic. **Acquisition:** Purchase. **Use:** School/Group/Institution, Special Use Restrictions Apply.

★4817★
Vanishing Family—Crisis in Black America, The
Carousel Film & Video
260 5th Ave.
New York, NY 10016 Phone: (212)683-1660
1988. **Program Description:** This documentary examines the disintegration of the Black family structure. The social structure erected by the state, welfare assistance, and the lack of male role models are focused on. **Length:** 64 mins. **Format:** VHS, 3/4'' U-matic. **Acquisition:** Purchase. **Use:** School/Group/Institution, Special Use Restrictions Apply.

★4818★
Vegetable Soup I
Great Plains National Instructional Television Library (GPN)
University of Nebraska at Lincoln
PO Box 80669
Lincoln, NE 68501-0669 Phone: (402)472-2007
1975. **Program Description:** By dramatizing the positive value of human diversity, this series counters the negative, destructive effects of racial prejudice and isolation. Also available in 78 15-minute programs. All programs are available individually. **Length:** 30 mins. **Format:** Beta, VHS, 3/4" U-matic. **Acquisition:** Purchase. **Use:** School/Group/Institution, Closed Circuit Television, Cable Television, Broadcast television.

★4819★
Vegetable Soup II
Great Plains National Instructional Television Library (GPN)
University of Nebraska at Lincoln
PO Box 80669
Lincoln, NE 68501-0669 Phone: (402)472-2007
1978. **Program Description:** The second season of a series that promotes racial and ethnic harmony. Also available in 60 15-minute programs. All programs are available individually. **Length:** 30 mins. **Format:** Beta, VHS, 3/4" U-matic. **Acquisition:** Purchase. **Use:** School/Group/Institution, Closed Circuit Television, Cable Television, Broadcast television.

★4820★
Vidalia McCloud—A Family Story
Carousel Film & Video
260 5th Ave.
New York, NY 10016 Phone: (212)683-1660
1988. **Program Description:** A documentary focusing on one family of Black Americans in a migrant town in Central Florida over a three year period. During this time the mother, Vidalia, worked as a fruit picker, short order cook and at times collected welfare. **Length:** 28 mins. **Format:** VHS, 3/4" U-matic. **Acquisition:** Purchase. **Use:** School/Group/Institution, Special Use Restrictions Apply.

★4821★
Visions of the Spirit: A Portrait of Alice Walker
Women Make Movies
225 Lafayette St., Ste. 212
New York, NY 10012 Phone: (212)925-0606
1989. **Program Description:** Pulitzer Prize-winning author Alice Walker is profiled in this documentary which shows the writer as mother, daughter, philosopher and activist. **Length:** 58 mins. **Format:** Beta, VHS, 3/4" U-matic. **Acquisition:** Purchase, Rent/Lease. **Use:** School/Group/Institution, Special Use Restrictions Apply.

★4822★
Voice of the Fugitive
Films, Inc.
5547 N. Ravenswood Ave.
Chicago, IL 60640-1199 Phone: (312)878-2600
1978. **Program Description:** This is the story of the "underground railroad" where many slaves went in order to get their freedom in Canada. From the "Adventures in History" series. **Length:** 28 mins. **Format:** Beta, VHS, 3/4" U-matic. **Acquisition:** Rent/Lease, Purchase. **Use:** School/Group/Institution, Special Use Restrictions Apply.

★4823★
Walk Down My Street
New York State Education Department
Center for Learning Technologies
Media Distribution Network
Rm. C-7, Concourse Level
Albany, NY 12230 Phone: (518)474-1265
196?. **Program Description:** Excerpts from a musical satire about problems faced by Black and Puerto Rican minorities in New York City are performed. **Length:** 30 mins. **Format:** Beta, VHS, 1/2" reel, 3/4" U-matic, 2" Quad. **Acquisition:** Duplication, Free Duplication. **Use:** School/Group/Institution, Special Use Restrictions Apply.

★4824★
Watermelon Man
RCA/Columbia Pictures Home Video
3500 W. Olive Ave.
Burbank, CA 91505 Phone: (818)953-7900
1970. **Program Description:** The tables are turned for a bigoted White man when he wakes up one morning only to discover has become Black. Black actor Godfrey Cambridge takes on both roles. The first film directed by Melvin Van Peebles. **Format:** Beta, VHS, Laser optical videodisc. **Acquisition:** Purchase. **Use:** In-Home Viewing.

★4825★
We Learn About the World
Video Knowledge, Inc.
29 Bramble Lane
Melville, NY 11747 Phone: (516)367-4250
1980. **Program Description:** This program portrays the adventures of a young Black boy who lives in the city. **Length:** 30 mins. **Format:** Beta, VHS, 3/4" U-matic. **Acquisition:** Purchase. **Use:** School/Group/Institution, In-Home Viewing.

★4826★
We Shall Overcome
Knowledge Unlimited, Inc.
Box 52
Madison, WI 53701-0052 Phone: (608)836-6660
1989. **Program Description:** The complete story of the struggle that Black Americans have faced in order to reach equality. **Format:** VHS. **Acquisition:** Purchase. **Use:** School/Group/Institution.

★4827★
We Still Have a Dream
Maryland Center for Public Broadcasting
11767 Bonita Ave.
Owings Mills, MD 21117 Phone: (301)356-5600
1988. **Program Description:** Six people who marched on Washington in 1963 talk about how things have changed. **Length:** 30 mins. **Format:** Beta, VHS, 3/4" U-matic. **Acquisition:** Purchase. **Use:** School/Group/Institution, Closed Circuit Television, Cable Television, Broadcast television.

★4828★
What Color Is Skin?
Pyramid Film & Video
Box 1048
Santa Monica, CA 90406 Phone: (213)828-7577
1977. **Program Description:** This part of the "Who We Are" series combines live action and animation to show that individual skin coloring is determined by the amount of melanin in the skin. **Length:** 9 mins. **Format:** Beta, VHS, 3/4" U-matic. **Acquisition:** Rent/Lease, Purchase, Duplication License. **Use:** School/Group/Institution, In-Home Viewing, Special Use Restrictions Apply.

★4829★
What Could You Do with a Nickel?
Icarus Films
200 Park Ave., S. Ste. 1319
New York, NY 10003 Phone: (212)674-3375
1982. **Program Description:** A documentary about 200 Black and hispanic women employed by the City of New York who joined together to form the first domestic workers union in the United States. **Length:** 26 mins. **Format:** 3/4" U-matic. **Acquisition:** Purchase. **Use:** School/Group/Institution, Special Use Restrictions Apply.

★4830★
What Makes Me Different?
Pyramid Film & Video
Box 1048
Santa Monica, CA 90406 Phone: (213)828-7577
1977. **Program Description:** This part of the "Who We Are" series combats prejudice by explaining and discussing some of the physical differences among people. **Length:** 9 mins. **Format:** Beta, VHS, 3/4" U-matic. **Acquisition:** Rent/Lease, Purchase, Duplication License. **Use:** School/Group/Institution, In-Home Viewing, Special Use Restrictions Apply.

★4831★
What's a Heaven For?
National AudioVisual Center
National Archives & Records Administration
Customer Services Section PZ
8700 Edgeworth Dr.
Capitol Heights, MD 20743-3701 Phone: (301)763-1896
1966. **Program Description:** A portrayal of Booker T. Washington in a collage of Cine-art to show his emerging philosophy and the impact he had as a freed slave upon his people and his country. **Length:** 17 mins. **Format:** Beta, VHS, 3/4" U-matic, Other than listed. **Acquisition:** Purchase. **Use:** School/Group/Institution, Special Use Restrictions Apply.

★4832★
Where Dreams Come True
National Aeronautics & Space Administration (NASA)
Lewis Audiovisual Library
6100 Columbus Ave.
Sandusky, OH 44870 Phone: (419)626-2594
1979. **Program Description:** This video explores and explains the career opportunities in NASA for minorities and women. Jobs range from clerks, secretaries, electricians all the way to astronauts, system analysts, and computer programmers. **Length:** 28 mins. **Format:** 3/4" U-matic, 1" Broadcast type C, 2" Quad. **Acquisition:** Free Loan. **Use:** Broadcast television, Special Use Restrictions Apply.

★4833★
White Man's Country
Films, Inc.
5547 N. Ravenswood Ave.
Chicago, IL 60640-1199 Phone: (312)878-2600
1973. **Program Description:** This segment of the "Black Man's Land" series tells how Kenya was ignored until a railroad was built. Settlers arrived and land was allocated soon afterward. Also available in 28-minute edited version. **Length:** 51 mins. **Format:** Beta, VHS, 3/4" U-matic. **Acquisition:** Purchase. **Use:** School/Group/Institution, Special Use Restrictions Apply.

★4834★
Who's Different?
Phoenix/BFA Films
468 Park Ave., S.
New York, NY 10016 Phone: (212)684-5910
1986. **Program Description:** Two high schoolers learn about the evils of prejudice. **Length:** 26 mins. **Format:** Beta, VHS, 3/4" U-matic. **Acquisition:** Purchase. **Use:** School/Group/Institution, Special Use Restrictions Apply.

★4835★
Wilma
RCA/Columbia Pictures Home Video
3500 W. Olive Ave.
Burbank, CA 91505 Phone: (818)953-7900
1977. **Program Description:** Based on the true story of Wilma Rudolph, a young Black woman who overcame polio to win three gold medals at the 1960 Olympics. **Length:** 100 mins. **Format:** Beta, VHS, Laser optical videodisc. **Acquisition:** Purchase. **Use:** In-Home Viewing.

★4836★
Winnie (Mandela)
Carousel Film & Video
260 5th Ave.
New York, NY 10016 Phone: (212)683-1660
1987. **Program Description:** This documentary concentrates on Winnie Mandela, the leading figure in South Africa's anti-apartheid struggle. Also depicted are scenes of extreme violence in this struggling country. **Length:** 15 mins. **Format:** VHS, 3/4" U-matic. **Acquisition:** Purchase. **Use:** School/Group/Institution, Special Use Restrictions Apply.

★4837★
Woman and the Blues, A
New York State Education Department
Center for Learning Technologies
Media Distribution Network
Rm. C-7, Concourse Level
Albany, NY 12230 Phone: (518)474-1265
196?. **Program Description:** Juanita Hall sings the blues songs made famous by Bessie Smith and Billie Holiday. **Length:** 30 mins. **Format:** Beta, VHS, 1/2" reel, 3/4" U-matic, 2" Quad. **Acquisition:** Duplication, Free Duplication. **Use:** School/Group/Institution, Special Use Restrictions Apply.

★4838★
World Turned Upside Down
Films, Inc.
5547 N. Ravenswood Ave.
Chicago, IL 60640-1199 Phone: (312)878-2600
1976. **Program Description:** James Armistead, a Black slave, is recruited by Lafayette to spy on Lord Cornwallis in the Revolutionary War. He learns the British strategy, warns Lafayette, and the Americans defeat Cornwallis in this segment of the "Ourstory" series. **Length:** 27 mins. **Format:** Beta, VHS, 3/4" U-matic. **Acquisition:** Purchase. **Use:** School/Group/Institution, Special Use Restrictions Apply.

★4839★
Yes, Ma'am
Filmakers Library, Inc.
133 E. 58th St.
New York, NY 10022 Phone: (212)355-6545
1981. **Program Description:** This program looks at Black household workers of New Orleans who have spent their whole working lives employed by one wealthy White family, and the strong attachments that have developed on both sides. **Length:** 48 mins. **Format:** Beta, VHS, 3/4" U-matic. **Acquisition:** Purchase. **Use:** School/Group/Institution.

★4840★
Yonder Come Day
CRM/McGraw-Hill Films
674 Via de la Valle
PO Box 641
Del Mar, CA 92014 Phone: (619)453-5000
1976. **Program Description:** Through the songs and words of Bessie Jones, this program gives an anthology of slave culture revealing its Afro-American origins. **Length:** 26 mins. **Format:** Beta, VHS, 3/4" U-matic. **Acquisition:** Purchase. **Use:** School/Group/Institution, Special Use Restrictions Apply.

★4841★
You Got to Move
Icarus Films
200 Park Ave., S., Ste. 1319
New York, NY 10003 Phone: (212)674-3375
1985. **Program Description:** A documentary about the people of Tennesee's legendary Highlander Folk School who have worked for union, civil, environmental and women's rights in the south. **Length:** 87 mins. **Format:** 3/4" U-matic. **Acquisition:** Purchase. **Use:** School/Group/Institution, Special Use Restrictions Apply.

★4842★
Your Move
University of California at Berkeley Extension Media Center
2176 Shattuck Ave.
Berkeley, CA 94704 Phone: (415)642-0460
1982. **Program Description:** A young Black couple encounters many problems after they move to a different city. **Length:** 25 mins. **Format:** VHS, 3/4" U-matic. **Acquisition:** Purchase, Rent/Lease. **Use:** School/Group/Institution, Special Use Restrictions Apply.

★4843★
Zarico
National Film Board of Canada
1251 Avenue of the Americas, 16th Fl.
New York, NY 10020-1173 Phone: (212)586-5131
1987. **Program Description:** The development of Zarico, the folk music of the French-Negro Creole culture of Southwestern Louisiana is traced in this film. **Length:** 58 mins. **Format:** Beta, VHS, 3/4'' U-matic. **Acquisition:** Purchase, Rent/Lease. **Use:** School/Group/Institution, Special Use Restrictions Apply.

★4844★
Zimbabwe
Cinema Guild
1697 Broadway, Rm. 802
New York, NY 10019 Phone: (212)246-5522
1988. **Program Description:** Iterviews with Robert Mugabe, Joshua Nkomo, Ian Smith, and others trace the history of Zimbabwe through the European search for gold and minerals to the overthrow of White minority rule in the 1970's. **Length:** 30 mins. **Format:** Beta, VHS, 3/4'' U-matic. **Acquisition:** Rent/Lease, Purchase, Duplication. **Use:** School/Group/Institution, Special Use Restrictions Apply.

MASTER NAME AND KEYWORD INDEX

The Master Name and Keyword Index is an alphabetical listing of all organizations, agencies, and publications included in BAID. Index references are to ***entry numbers****rather than to page numbers. Consult the "User's Guide" for more detailed information about the index.*

Index

Index

Index